ENCYCLOPEDIA OF MURDER & VIOLENT CRIME

ERIC HICKEY EDITOR

California State University, Fresno

ENCYCLOPEDIA OF
MURDER
&
VIOLENT
CRIME

SAGE Publications
International Educational and Professional Publisher
Thousand Oaks ▪ London ▪ New Delhi

For information:

 Sage Publications, Inc.
2455 Teller Road
Thousand Oaks, California 91320
E-mail: order@sagepub.com

Sage Publications Ltd.
6 Bonhill Street
London EC2A 4PU
United Kingdom

Sage Publications India Pvt. Ltd.
B-42, Panchsheel Enclave
Post Box 4109
New Delhi 110 017 India

Printed in the United States of America

Library of Congress Cataloging-in-Publication Data

Encyclopedia of murder and violent crime / edited by Eric Hickey.
    p. cm.
Includes bibliographical references and index.
ISBN 0-7619-2437-X (Cloth)
    1. Murder-Encyclopedias. 2. Violent crimes-Encyclopedias. I. Hickey, Eric W.
HV6515.E5323 2003
364.15´23´03—dc21

                            2003001505

Printed on acid-free paper

03   04   05   06   07   08   09   10   9   8   7   6   5   4   3   2   1

Contents

Acknowledgments

Amy Bouasy	Jami Jenkins	Mike Bardsley
Amy Bronswick	Jana Price-Sharps	Monica Myers
Brianna Satterthwaite	Katherine Ray	Nicole Mott
Byron Viets	Laura White	Phil Caporale
Carla Marquez	Linda Cepeda	Rocky Underwood
Colleen Condren	Lisa Anderson	Sarah Ferguson
Debbie Wray	Lisa Andrews	Sharon Shaffer
Denise Lowe	Lynn Gunn	Tatia Smith
Elizabeth Stanczak	Marcee Kerr	Vikki Irby
Elliott E. Lane Jr.	Marlene Deal	Yvonne Martinez
Holly Peacock-Hickey	Martha Hernandez	The staff at Sage

List of Entries

Reader's Guide

To assist readers in locating articles on related topics, this list classifies entries into these general topical categories: Aggression, Criminal Investigation, Cults, Death Penalty, Family Violence, Forensic Science, Gangs, Government-Sanctioned Violence, Homicide, Juvenile Crime, Kidnapping, Legal Response to Violent Crime, Mass Murder, Motives for Violence, Organized Crime, Police and Violence, Psychological Theories and Diagnoses for Violent Behavior, Serial Murder, Serial Murderers, Sex Crimes, Terrorism, Victimology, Vigilantism, and Violent Crime. Some article titles may appear in more than one category.

AGGRESSION

Aggression: Biological Theories
Aggression: Evolutionary and Anthropological
    Theories
Aggression, Feminist Perspective
Aggression: Sociological
    Theories
Alcohol and Aggression
Antisocial Personality Disorder
Batterers and Abusive Partners
Cycle Theory of Violence
Elder Abuse
Family Violence
Homicide
Mass Violence
Media, Violence in the
Motives for Murder
Paraphilia
Pedophilia
Police Brutality
Predicting Violent Behavior
Psychopaths
Rape
Road Rage
Robbery
Serial Murder
Sexual Offenses
Stalking
Violent Behavior: Personality Theories
Violent Behavior: Psychoanalytic
    Theories
Violent Behavior: A Psychological
    Case Study
Women and Violence

CRIMINAL INVESTIGATION

Ballistics
Criminal Justice Practitioner
Criminalistics
Cyberstings
False Confessions
False Memory Syndrome
FBI Top 10 Most Wanted List
Federal Bureau of
    Investigation (FBI)
Forensic Science
Geographic Profiling
Predicting Violent Behavior
Prevention of Crime and Violent
    Behavior
Profiling
Signature Killers
Threat Assessment
Uniform Crime Reports (UCR)
ViCLAS
Victimology

CULTS

Cults
Koresh, David
Manson, Charles/Manson Family

MOTIVES FOR VIOLENCE

Aggravating and Mitigating
  Circumstances
Aggression
Alcohol and Aggression
Batterers and Abusive Partners
Beltway Snipers
Cycle Theory of Violence
Drug Trade
Family Violence
Gender Violence
Helter-Skelter
Homicide, Motivation for Murder
Less-Dead
Medical Murders
Motives for Murder
Munchausen Syndrome by Proxy
Paraphilia
Pedophilia
Predicting Violent Behavior
Profiling
Rape
Road Rage
Robbery
Serial Murder
Sexual Offenses
Substance Abuse and Homicide
Vehicular Homicide
Vigilantism

ORGANIZED CRIME

Capone, Alphonse "Al"
Chicago Mob
Drug Cartels
Drug Trade
Falcone, Giovanni
Floyd, Charles Arthur (Pretty Boy)
Gambino Crime Family
Gangs
Genovese Crime Family
Gotti, John
Luciano, Charles "Lucky"
Murder for Hire
Organized Crime
Police Corruption
St. Valentine's Day Massacre
Union Station Massacre

POLICE AND VIOLENCE

Community Attitudes Toward
  Violent Crime
Criminal Justice Practitioners
Cyberstings
Hostage Taking
Organized Crime
Police Brutality
Police Corruption
Prevention of Crime and Violent
  Behavior
Racial Profiling
Special Weapons and Tactics Teams
Suicide by Cop
Threat Assessment
Workplace Violence and Homicide

PSYCHOLOGICAL THEORIES AND DIAGNOSES FOR VIOLENT BEHAVIOR

Aggression: Psychological Theories
Antisocial Personality Disorder
Arsonist's Portrait
Attachment Deficiency and Violence
Brawner Test
Court-Ordered Psychological
  Assessment
Diagnostic and Statistical Manual of
  Mental Disorders (DSM)
Jekyll and Hyde Syndrome
Juvenile Firesetters
Less-Dead
MacDonald Triad
Mentally Disordered Offenders
M'Naughten Rule
Motives for Murder
Paraphilia
Pedophila
Predicting Violent Behavior
Psychopathology Checklist-Revised (PCL-R)
Psychopaths
Psychosocial Risk Factors for Violent
  Behavior
Violence: Phenomenology
Violent Behavior: Personality Theories
Violent Behavior: Psychoanalytic Theories
Violent Behavior: A Psychological
  Case Study
XYY Syndrome

Contributors

Alex Alvarez, Ph.D.
Director, The Martin-Springer Institute for
  Teaching the Holocaust, Tolerance and
  Humanitarian Values
Northern Arizona University
Flagstaff, Arizona

Lisa Colleen Andersen
Master's Student, California State University, Fresno
Fresno, California

Lisa Andrews, M.S.
Doctoral Student, Sam Houston State University
Huntsville, Texas

Michael P. Arena, M.A.
University of California Extension, Santa Cruz
Santa Cruz, California

Michael Bardsley
Master's Student
LaPorte, Indiana

Curt Bartol, Ph.D.
Professor and Director, Forensic Psychology Program
Castleton State College
Castleton, Vermont

James Black, Ph.D.
Professor/Chair, Legal Studies
University of Tennessee
Knoxville, Tennessee

Amy Bouasy, M.S.
Criminology
Valencia, California

Miranda Brockett, Psy.D.
Department of Justice
Federal Correctional Institute, Marianna
Marianna, Florida

Amy Bronswick, Psy.D.
Clinical Psychologist
San Quentin State Prison
San Quentin, California

Phil Caporale
Sheriff's Sergeant
Fresno County Sheriff's Department
Fresno, California

Natalie Cardonna, M.S.
Deputy Probation Officer III, Madera County
  Probation Department
Madera, California

Joyce L. Carbonell, Ph.D.
Psychology Department and Women's Studies Program
Florida State University
Tallahassee, Florida

Linda Cepeda, M.S.
Dinuba, California

Brian Champion, M.L.S., M.A.
Doctoral Candidate
World Politics Librarian
Brigham Young University
Provo, Utah

Nileen Clark
Undergraduate Student, California State
  University, Fresno
Fresno, California

Colleen Condren
Master's Candidate
Lansing, Michigan

Carol Coppock, M.S.N., F.N.P., C.S., R.N., B.C.
Professor, California State University, Fresno
Fresno, California

Gary V. Cortner, M.S.
Assistant Laboratory Director
California Department of Justice
*   Regional Laboratory*
Fresno, California

Peter Cramer
Tvavagen 3
196 31 Kungsangen
Sweden

L. Edward Day, Ph.D.
Asst. Professor of Criminal Justice
*   and Sociology*
Pennsylvania State University, Altoona
Altoona, Pennsylvania

Marlene M. Deal, M.S., Ph.D.
Fresno, California

Deirdre M. B. D'Orazio, Ph.D.
Cayucos, California

Thomas R. Dull, Ph.D.
Professor, Department of Criminology
California State University, Fresno
Fresno, California

Kim Egger
Graduate Student
Freeport, Texas

Steven A. Egger, Ph.D.
University of Houston, Clear Lake
Houston, Texas

William L. Eller, J.D.
Deputy Prosecuting Attorney
Yakima, Washington

Sarah Ferguson
Doctoral Candidate-AIU/CSPP
Psychology Intern-Boston University
*   School of Medicine*
Boston, Massachusetts

Kenneth R. Fineman, Ph.D.
Associate Clinical Professor of Medical
*   Psychology*
Department of Psychiatry & Human Behavior
School of Medicine
University of California, Irvine
Irvine, California

James Alan Fox, Ph.D.
The Lipman Family Professor of Criminal Justice
Northeastern University
Boston, Massachusetts

Kimberly L. Freiberger
Doctoral Candidate, Virginia Commonwealth
*   University*
Richmond, Virginia

John Randolph Fuller, Ph.D.
Department of Sociology, Anthropology,
*   and Criminology*
State University of West Georgia
Carrollton, Georgia

Karen Gardner
Supervisory Special Agent
Federal Bureau of Investigation
FBI Academy
Quantico, Virginia

Lt. Milt Gauthier
Madera County Sheriff's Department
Bass Lake, California

L. Kay Gillespie, Ph.D.
Chair, Department of Criminal Justice
Weber State University
Ogden, Utah

Christian Draven Godwin, Ph.D.
Los Angeles, California

Bradford L. Gorby, M.S.
Police Officer
Los Angeles Police Department
Long Beach, California

Lynn Gunn, M.S.
Doctoral Candidate, University of New Brunswick
Fredericton, New Brunswick

Victoria Hamilton, J.D.
Fresno, California

Mark Hamm, Ph.D.
Department of Criminology
Indiana State University
Terre Haute, Indiana

Laura W. Hamon, Ph.D.
Bakersfield, California

Kathleen M. Heide, Ph.D.
Professor, Department of Criminology
University of South Florida
Tampa, Florida

Martha Hernandez
Undergraduate Student, California State
*   University, Fresno*
Fresno, California

Kevin Howells, Ph.D.
Professor, Forensic and Applied Psychology
*   Research Group*
University of South Australia,
*   North Terrace*
Adelaide, South Australia

Vikki Irby, M.S.
Madera County Probation Officer
Madera, California

Jami Jenkins, M.S.
Undergraduate Student, California State
*   University, Fresno*
Fresno, California

Bill Jones
California Secretary of State
Sacramento, California

Marcee Kerr
Seattle, Washington

Susann Kimmelman
Doctoral Candidate, City University of
*   New York*
John Jay College of Criminal Justice
New York, New York

Patricia Kirby, Ph.D.
The College of Notre Dame
Baltimore, Maryland

Lloyd Klein, Ph.D.
Asst. Professor, Department of History
*   and Social Sciences*
Louisiana State University
Shreveport, Louisiana

Vickie Krenz, Ph.D.
Department of Health Science
California State University, Fresno
Fresno, California

Linda Lou Kreuger-Long, M.S.
Serving Sangamon
Springfield, Illinois

Marc J. LaFountain, Ph.D.
Department of Sociology, Anthropology, and
*   Criminology*
University of West Georgia
Carrollton, Georgia

Jack Levin, Ph.D.
Director and Professor, Brudnick Center on
*   Violence and Conflict*
Northeastern University
Boston, Massachusetts

Robert Levine, Ph.D.
Department of Psychology
California State University, Fresno
Fresno, California

Elliott Leyton, Ph.D.
Department of Anthropology
Memorial University
St. John's, Newfoundland
Canada

Denise Lowe
Coarsegold, California

Tracey Lowey
Crime Analyst
Calgary Police Department
Calgary, Alberta, Canada

Michael D. Lyman, Ph.D.
Columbia College
Columbia, Missouri

Carla Marquez
Graduate Student
The Graduate Center, City University of New York
New York, New York

Yvonne Martinez, Psy.D.
Central California Women's Facility, Mental Health
*   Department*
Chowchilla, California

N. Jane McCandless, Ph.D.
Department of Sociology, Anthropology, and Criminology
State University of West Georgia
Carrollton, Georgia

Richard McCorkle, Ph.D.
Department of Criminal Justice
University of Nevada, Las Vegas
Las Vegas, Nevada

Robert McNamara, Ph.D.
Department of Sociology
Furman University
Greenville, South Carolina

Terance Meithe, Ph.D.
Department of Criminal Justice
University of Nevada, Las Vegas
Las Vegas, Nevada

Donna Mobley-Lutz, M.S.
Program Manager, Fresno County
  Department of Children and Family
  Services
Fresno, California

Nicole L. Mott, Ph.D.
Court Research Associate
National Center for State Courts
Williamsburg, Virginia

Monica Myers
Master's Student, California State
  University, Fresno
Fresno, California

James E. Newman, M.P.A.
Professor, Criminal Justice Program
Rio Hondo College
Whittier, California

Ian Nisbet, M.A.
Griffith Adolescent Forensic Assessment
  and Treatment Centre
Mt. Gravatt Campus, Griffith
  University
Queensland, Australia

Janna Oddie, Psy.D.
Central California Women's Facility, Mental
  Health Department
Chowchilla, California

Steven Opager
Salt Lake City, Utah

Holly Peacock-Hickey
Coarsegold, California

Thomas Petee, Ph.D.
Department of Sociology
Auburn University
Auburn, Alabama

Stefanie Petrucci-Mahaffey, M.S., J.D.
Deputy District Attorney
Sacramento County Office of the
  District Attorney
Sacramento, California

Gary W. Potter, Ph.D.
Department of Criminal Justice and
  Police Studies
Eastern Kentucky University
Richmond, Kentucky

Jana Price-Sharps, Ed.D.
Professor, Forensic Psychology Program
Alliant International University
Fresno, California

Catherine Purcell, Ph.D.
Forensic Psychologist, North Kern State Prison
California Department of Corrections
Tehachapi, California

Katherine Ray
Master's Student, California School of
  Professional Psychology
Fresno, California

Lorraine R. Reitzel, M.A.
Doctoral Candidate, Clinical Psychology
Department of Psychology
Florida State University
Tallahassee, Florida

Albert R. Roberts, Ph.D.
Professor and Director of Faculty Development
Interdisciplinary Program in Criminal Justice
Rutgers, State University of New Jersey
Livingston College Campus
Piscataway, New Jersey

D. Kim Rossmo, Ph.D.
Director of Research, Police Foundation
Washington, D.C.

Brianna Satterthwaite
Doctoral Candidate, California School of
  Professional Psychology
Fresno, California

Harald Otto Schweizer, Ph.D.
Professor, Department of Criminology
California State University, Fresno
Fresno, California

Sharon Shaffer, M.S.
Captain, Fresno Police Department
Fresno, California

Candice Skrapec, Ph.D.
Professor, Department of Criminology
California State University, Fresno
Fresno, California

Tatia Smith
Master's of Arts Program, Vermont
*   College*
Dallas, Texas

Elizabeth M. Stanczak, Ph.D.
Assistant Director, Counseling Services
University of Texas, San Antonio
San Antonio, Texas

Sandra S. Stone, Ph.D.
Associate Professor, Department of Sociology,
*   Anthropology, and Criminology*
State University of West Georgia
Carrollton, Georgia

Elizabeth Swearingen
Doctoral Candidate
University of California, Davis/California
*   State University, Fresno*
Fresno, California

Tawnya Tangel, M.Ed., J.D.
Deputy Prosecuting Attorney
Yakima, Washington

Jim Tarver
Senior Criminologist
Fresno County Sheriff's Department
Fresno, California

Marsha L. Tarver, Ph.D.
Department of Criminology
California State University, Fresno
Fresno, California

Patricia Tjaden, Ph.D.
Tjaden Research Corporation
Breckenridge, Colorado

Judith Tucker, M.S.
Senior Investigator, Fresno County District
*   Attorney's Office*
Fresno, California

Rocky C. Underwood, Ph.D.
Clinical Psychologist
California State Prison—Corcoran
Mental Health Services
Corcoran, California

Margaret Vandiver, Ph.D.
Department of Criminology and
*   Criminal Justice*
University of Memphis
Memphis, Tennessee

Byron Viets
Master's Candidate, California State
*   University, Fresno*
Fresno, California

Corey J. Vitello, M.A.
Forensic Psychology Program
School of Social and Policy Studies
Alliant International University
Fresno, California

Valeska Vitt
Doctoral Candidate
Johann Wolfgang Goethe University,
*   Frankfurt*
Frankfurt/Main, Germany

Steven D. Walker, Ph.D.
Department of Criminology
California State University, Fresno
Fresno, California

Harvey Wallace, J.D.
Chairman, Department of
*   Criminology*
California State University, Fresno
Fresno, California

Alexa Wasserman, Psy.D.
Forensic Psychologist, Central California
*   Women's Facility*
Chowchilla, California

Eidell Wasserman, Ph.D.
Victim Services Consultant
Verdi, Nevada

Haley Suzanne Whitford, Ph.D.
Forensic and Applied Psychology Research Group
University of South Australia, City East Campus
Adelaide, Australia

Christopher R. Williams, Ph.D.
Department of Sociology, Anthropology, and
*   Criminology*
State University of West Georgia
Carrollton, Georgia

Robyn L. Williams, M.A.
San Diego, California

Mindy S. Wilson, M.A.
Doctoral Candidate, Pennsylvania State University
University Park, Pennsylvania

Arthur Wint, J.D.
Department of Criminology/ Peace and
*   Conflict Studies Program*
California State University, Fresno
Fresno, California

Janice E. Clifford Wittekind, Ph.D.
Asst. Professor, Department of Sociology
Auburn University
Auburn, Alabama

Vickie L. Woosley
Supervisory Special Agent
Federal Bureau of Investigation
FBI Academy
Quantico, Virginia

Debbie Wray
McCormick, Barstow, Sheppard, Wayte &
*   Carruth LLP*
Fresno, California

Steven M. Wright
Forensic and Applied Psychology
*   Research Group*
University of South Australia,
*   North Terrace*
Adelaide, South Australia

Jane A. Younglove, M.S., J.D.
Associate Professor, Forensic Psychology Program
School of Social and Policy Studies
Alliant International University
Fresno, California

Elinor M. Zorn, M.D.
Child Advocacy Program
Children's Hospital of Central California
Madera, California

Preface

Violence is globally pervasive and represents ethnic, racial, religious, and geopolitical disparities. History is replete with mass murders, genocides, and ethnic cleansings, all holocausts in their own right. Indeed, there are universal explanations for murder that are expressed through cultural filters. In general terms, people kill others as a result of greed, alcohol consumption, ethnic and racial issues, religion, sexual property, social status, mental illness, and a need for power and control. Often, these explanations overlap and cannot be clearly separated when ascribing causality. For example, in cultures that prohibit women from partaking in civil life activities such as voting, socializing, and working, men create the laws and violently punish women for disobedience. The same men who use their culture and/or religion to subjugate women for their own good also use their religion/culture to justify killing them. In Lebanon, for example, "honor killings" are sometimes carried out against women who dishonor the family.

In rural areas of India, girls are sometimes killed for refusing to participate in arranged marriages. Endogamous societies maintain strict standards of conduct toward its members, and deviation from those expectations often elicits swift and violent community reactions. In China, another endogamous society, population is controlled by government sanctions. Families are encouraged to have but one child. Additional children mean that a family will be punished financially and limited as to where they are allowed to live. The quest to control family size in the world's most populous society directly conflicts with the cultural expectation of passing down the family name. Because males alone pass on the family name, a newborn male is welcomed with opened arms. In rural China, however, where cultural tradition remains unchallenged, female babies are often drowned. Although killing a child in China is not legally allowed, cultural norms and needs often supercede the law.

The United States has long been viewed as a violent and dangerous nation in comparison with other countries. There are, however, problems in attempting direct comparisons. Cross-national crime comparisons involve an array of methodological limitations. Crime is defined differently in many countries, as well as how agencies collect data and store and analyze and report findings. In the global scheme, the United States has far more violent crime when compared with countries similar in socioeconomic development. For example, the United States has a murder rate approximately twice that of Argentina and Romania, 5 times that of Australia and Canada, 10 times that of France, 17 times that of Japan and Ireland, and 25 times that of Iceland. In countries that are less socially and politically stable, the opposite appears to be true. Mexico has a murder rate nearly double that of the United States; El Salvador and the Russian Federation about 3 times the U.S. rate; and Colombia, 9 times that in America. American culture is not only the most murderous of Western societies, but we also export our violence to other nations in the form of entertainment.

AMERICAN MURDER AND OTHER VIOLENT BEHAVIOR

Over a 350-year period, approximately 12 million slaves were transported from Africa to nations wanting cheap labor. Although several million went to Brazil and other countries, the United States received approximately 700,000 men, women, and children. Many others died en route as a result of starvation, disease, and brutal treatment. The accepted violence against blacks, such as beatings and lynching, by parts of American society persisted until the civil rights movement and desegregation of the 1960s.

Killing and violent behavior has permeated the historical development of America. Colonial America was established at the demise of millions of Native Americans who were dehumanized and massacred at the hands of expansionists. Colonization of America was a violent and deadly process, not merely a broken treaty. Asians endured severe persecutions as they came to America looking for jobs and a future. Many died while building railroads as a result of bigotry, ethnocentrism, and racism. The American melting pot pitted Catholics against Protestants, white against color, and the haves against the have-nots. The struggle brought with it the inevitable clash of capitalism with the demands of the working class. Unions sprang up across America to champion the cause of the poor. With the labor movement, strikes were organized, and with strikes, violence often erupted. To add to the tension of our foundling nation, moral entrepreneurs fervently tried to eradicate the social ills of drinking and prostitution.

American violent culture was further molded by the advent of the Civil War, which left tens of thousands of mutilated and dead young men on cannon-scarred battlefields. Many of these Americans had just arrived from native homelands in Europe, hoping to start new lives. The enmity created from the bloodiest conflict in American history lasted for many generations. Blood feuds spawned acts of violence that kept families, towns, and states in upheaval. Ethnicity, race, and country of origin became dividing lines for newcomers to America and resulted in assaults, assassinations, and riots in several U.S. cities.

The United States is well versed in city riots that have resulted in massive damage, injury, and loss of life. Both the Watts riots of Los Angeles of 1965 and the Detroit riot in 1967 resulted in dozens of deaths. Along the way, America experienced several wars and conflicts that have helped frame our social conscience about the necessity and legality of violence. Each conflict, World War I, World War II, Korea, Vietnam, Kosovo, Desert Storm, Afghanistan, and Iraq, has created its own version of violence.

Violent conflict has been glamorized by Hollywood. Crime and its inherent violence are big business. Criminal homicide constitutes a sinister but fascinating portion of the dark side of most societal landscapes. We talk about it, watch movies depicting it, read about it in newspapers, and listen to radio, television and Internet news reports about it. Murder sells as entertainment irrespective of the fact that killing brings so much suffering to families, relatives, and friends of the victims. The pattern of gender-specific killing is constant in American society: Men kill men most commonly, followed by men killing women. Next, women kill men, and least likely, women kill women. Men talk more violence, they watch more violence, and they do more violence than women.

The taking of a human life is a homicide, but not all homicides are murders. In the United States, there are three forms of homicide: *justifiable* (occurs in the defense of property or life), *excusable* (accidental or unintentional killing), and *criminal* (illegal killings). Criminal homicides, the most common form of homicides, are further subdivided into *manslaughter* and *murder*. Manslaughter can be classified as either voluntary (a highly emotional or passionate killing) or involuntary (death resulting from recklessness or carelessness). Murder is classified into three subcategories: felony (occurs during the commission of another felony), first degree (includes premeditation and deliberation), and second degree (without premeditation or deliberation but also without concern for the safety of a victim and with intent to do serious bodily injury).

Some killings are state sanctioned, as in the application of capital punishment. In California, the cause of death listed on a death certificate of a person executed by the state is "Homicide." Indeed, murder is the illegal killing of another human being that usually carries with it severe penalties: prison time and in some cases, even death. Most people who kill do so but once. In the United States, with the exception of the 300 to 400 victims per year killed by serial murderers and gang members who kill more than once, most other killings are thought to be crimes of passion. Although many murders are crimes of passion, the variation in motivation for murder can extend from obvious to complex and multifaceted. Motivation-based homicides, all of which are illegal, have been categorized in the *Crime Classification Manual* into four groups:

1. Criminal enterprise homicide: contract (third-party killing); gang motivated; criminal competition; kidnap; drug; product tampering; insurance/inheritance-related (individual or commercial profit); and felony murder and situational felony

2. Personal cause homicide: erotomania; domestic (spontaneous or staged); argument/conflict (argument or conflict); authority; revenge; nonspecific motive; extremist (political, religious, socioeconomic); mercy/hero (mercy or hero); and hostage

3. Sexual homicide: organized; disorganized; mixed; and sadistic

4. Group cause homicide: cult; extremist (paramilitary or hostage); and group excitement.

SOURCE: John Douglas, Ann Burgess, Allen Burgess, Robert Ressler, *Crime Classification Manual: A Standard System for Investigating and Classifying Violent Crimes,* 1992, Lexington Books.

Classifying homicides can be problematic as we account for the multitude of variations for killing. Homicides are classified principally by moral and legal concepts that take into account community standards, attitudes, and specific legal standards to be adhered to in determining intent, culpability, and sentencing. Special circumstances are required in California for a murderer to receive the death penalty. Typical special circumstances include poisoning, lying in wait, and previous killings. Special circumstances may vary from state to state depending on issues that are peculiar to that state. California includes armor-piercing bullets and drive-by shootings as two special circumstances. Thus, new variations in murder classification can develop with time, technology, and social evolution. Murders and violent acts in Western societies are judged by their perceived gravity, the ability of courts to prosecute acts of murder, and a host of mitigating facts and social variables.

Historically, the killing of a stranger in the United States has generally been more likely to draw harsher penalties than killing a member of one's family, especially if the victim is a baby and the mother is the perpetrator. There are exceptions, such as in the case of Andrea Yates, a woman in Texas who drowned her five children. Her case received enormous media attention. During that same time period, a man killed his five children using carbon monoxide and received very little media response. Why do some offenders receive such enormous media coverage and others disappear quickly? Much of our assessment of killing involves contextual causality. The way we explain murder tends to be linked with how we perceive and assess the offenders and victims, and victim-offender relationships, including their histories and the circumstances under which the killings occurred. In many societies, women who kill their children or intimate partners rarely receive death sentences, whereas women who kill when involved in drug deals or gang activity are more likely to find themselves on death row. Even then, women in the United States seldom receive the death penalty for murder. California has more than 600 male inmates on death row in San Quentin State prison. By contrast, 14 women are confined to death row in California's Chowchilla State prison.

California has more people incarcerated and on death row than any other place in the entire world. As someone once said, "The level of civilization in a society can be judged by observing its prisoners." Many of those we incarcerate are doomed to become repeat offenders. The cycle of violence perpetrated on American society continues to be the purview of a limited number of habitual offenders who for myriad reasons do not rehabilitate. We remain as ambivalent about who and how to incarcerate offenders as we do about the efficacy of punishments, including the death penalty.

Murder and violent acts are part of the American landscape. The perception of violence and killing in America is that murders are increasing. The reality of homicidal acts is affected by many societal factors that include poverty, unemployment, education, social class, gender, race and ethnicity, income, geographic location, age, and other social indices. The Federal Bureau of Investigation's Uniform Crime Report (UCR) provides information on index crimes that include murder and nonnegligent manslaughter, forcible rape, robbery, aggravated assault, burglary, larceny theft, motor vehicle theft, and arson. These crimes are used to measure crime trends by state and as a nation. Murder information is contained in the Supplementary Homicide Report (SHR) of the UCR. Although efforts are made to gather accurate data, there are continuing problems, including lack of reporting by some agencies, inadequate record keeping, inconsistency in classifying crimes, overreporting, and political agendas. Despite these problems and the ever present "dark figure of crime" (unreported crime), the UCR provides a window view of criminal activity that is used to guide public policies involving crime control.

In 2001, current or former spouses or other intimate partners constituted 20% of the nonfatal violence against female victims age 12 and older. In recent years, most intimate partner violence has involved female victims. Of the 588,490 acts of violence in 2001 against women and girls by intimate partners, aggravated and simple assault were the most common. This included 502,690 threats, attempted attacks, and attacks without weapons that resulted in minor injuries. By contrast, there were 103,220 non-fatal violent offenses committed by intimates against men and boys that year. The Department of Justice also reported for 2001 that more than 44,000 robberies and nearly 42,000 rapes were committed against women and girls by domestic or intimate acquaintances. Although these numbers may be difficult to put into context, consider that the total number of such acts has fallen by nearly 50% in recent years. In 1993, for example, there were more than 1.1 million such crimes against women and almost 163,000 against men. In 2000, the most recent year available for homicide data, the Federal Bureau of Investigation reported that 1,247 women and 440 men were killed by intimate partners. Again, these figures constitute a decline beginning in 1976. In that year, about 1,600 women and nearly 1,400 men were murdered by intimate partners.

Murder in America represents less than .02% of all violent crime, and homicide rates in comparison with the past 20 years are relatively low. American perception is generally that homicide rates are high and violence is pervasive. Much of this is fueled by frequent media reports of serial and mass murder. Serial murder is a rare phenomenon but elicits community fears of strangers preying on women and children. Ted Bundy, John Wayne Gacy, and Albert DeSalvo, the Boston Strangler, have become infamous celebrities. Mass murders now occur every 6 days in America. More than half of them are intrafamilial, and the others occur in public by strangers making their final angry statements to the world. However, all the mass murders and all the serial killings combined in most years do not constitute more than 1 out of 20 homicides in the United States.

Our perceptions about violence and killing are perpetuated enormously by media portrayals of murder. The fear of criminal victimization is primarily a fear of violence, not a fear of property loss. Most Americans are more concerned for their physical safety than property protection. Nearly half of American citizens are afraid to walk alone at night and believe that crime is a major issue in our society. Although risk of violent victimization has decreased dramatically since the late 1980s, the fear of violent crime remains high. In the 2000 presidential elections, crime was the number one concern for many voters.

The school shootings at Columbine and the 7-year string of postal shootings fueled public perception that violent crime was and is out of control. The outcome is that we demand that more and more crime bills be passed by the government. Three strikes laws continue to be upheld in our courts as more get-tough-on-crime legislation is passed. It is not, however, just the fear of violent crime that makes citizens want more crime and prison reform. The victims' movement has been growing for several years. Along with civil rights advocates who champion women's and minority rights, conservative coalitions that include religious groups, American Association of Retired Persons (AARP), the National Rifle Association (NRA), and an increasingly vocal group of crime victims, the response to actual and perceived violent crime mounts steadily. California State University, Fresno, was the first academic institution to offer a 4-year bachelor's program in victimology and victim services. Several schools now offer courses in victimology and victim services, as well as summer institutes. Crime reform is expensive, but so is crime. Both need close scrutiny in order to better understand the nature, extent, and prognosis of violent crime.

As Stephanie Roper, a young Maryland college student, penned in her journal shortly before she was abducted, raped, tortured, and murdered by two violent offenders, "Every person can make a difference, and every person should try." Indeed, our focus is so often on the societal anomalies of violent crime that we ignore other more pervasive forms of violence and killing. Domestic violence, child abuse, drunken-driving crashes, and sexual assaults all have horrific costs. The toll is devastating to the social fabric of American life. Acts of violence cannot be accurately counted, they can only be estimated, but understanding and addressing violence and murder is our societal mandate.

About the Editor

Currently teaching criminal psychology at California State University, Fresno, **Dr. Eric Hickey** has had considerable field experience working with the criminally insane, psychopaths, sex offenders, and other habitual criminals. As an adjunct professor at California School of Professional Psychology, he teaches courses and supervises dissertations in criminal personalities, sex crimes, and psychopathology. Dr. Hickey is also an adjunct instructor for the American Prosecutor's Research Institute at the National Advocacy Center in Columbia, South Carolina, where he profiles cyber-stalkers, criminal personalities, and sexual predators. His research involving hundreds of victims of stalking examines the psychology and classification of stalkers, victim-offender relationships, intervention, deterrence strategies, and modes of victim assistance.

Dr. Hickey has published books and articles and lectured extensively on the etiology of violence and serial crime. His book *Serial Murderers and Their Victims,* 3rd edition (2002), is used as a teaching tool in universities and by law enforcement in studying the nature of violence, criminal personalities, and victim-offender relationships.

The media, including *NPR, Larry King Live, 20/20, A&E, Good Morning America, Court TV, Discovery,* and *TLC,* often seek Dr. Hickey's expertise. A former consultant to the FBI's UNABOM Task Force, he assists law enforcement and private agencies and testifies as an expert witness in both criminal and civil cases. He conducts training seminars for agencies involving the profiling and investigating of sex crimes, arson, homicide, stalking, workplace violence, and terrorism. Internationally recognized for his research on multiple-homicide offenders, Dr. Hickey has trained VIP protection specialists at the International Security School in Israel in profiling stalkers and counterterrorism. He is currently writing his first novel and is also involved in developing a documentary television series on predatory crime.

AERONAUTICAL MASS MURDER

Aeronautical mass murder can be defined as the deliberate destruction of civilian aircraft in an effort to cause the death of its passengers and/or those on the ground. Although the act is not necessarily novel, its study remains underdeveloped. The first proven case of aeronautical mass murder in commercial aviation took place on October 10, 1933, when a United Airlines Boeing 247 crashed en route from Cleveland to Chicago. All seven passengers and three crewmembers were killed when the twin-engine aircraft went down just west of Gary, Indiana. An investigation indicated that a blast from an explosive device, constructed of a timer and nitroglycerine, caused the aircraft's fuselage to separate from its tail assembly. It was believed that the bomb had been hidden aboard the aircraft in a brown package at a previous stop in Newark, New Jersey. The culprit and motive for the attack were never identified.

Since 1933, there have been more than 40 instances of aeronautical mass murder. The motivations for these crimes have been criminal (i.e., insurance fraud), idiosyncratic (i.e., psychological instability), and political (i.e., terrorism). The modus operandi include suicide skyjackings, surface-to-air attacks, and explosive devices. For example, in September 1949, a Douglas DC-3 operated by Quebec Airways slammed into a hill roughly 40 miles (65 km) north of Quebec, killing the 23 people onboard. The twin-engine aircraft had suffered an explosion in the forward luggage compartment. Police investigators determined that J. Albert Guay, whose wife was a passenger on the aircraft, had

masterminded the plot to kill his spouse and collect on her $10,000 insurance policy. On May 7, 1964, Pacific Airlines Flight 773 crashed in Oakland on its way from Reno to San Francisco, killing the 44 people onboard. It was believed that the pilots of the Fairchild F-27A twin-engine turboprop were shot with a .357 Magnum wielded by Francisco Gonzales. Gonzales, who had been suffering from personal problems, had purchased the weapon a day before he left for Reno. He had also told acquaintances a week earlier of his desire to kill himself.

Terrorism is also a frequent motivation for aeronautical mass murder. The preferred method of terrorists has been to sabotage aircraft with explosive devices. Between 1947 and 1995, there were 105 attempted and successful bombing attacks on airliners, 85% of which were committed by terrorists. Terrorist organizations target passenger airliners for several reasons. For example, they offer a concentration of people in an enclosed environment that is especially susceptible to sabotage. Airliners also have a significant symbolic value. National carriers such as El Al, British Airways, Air France, American, United, and Air India are associated with particular countries. The following incidents are three of the most deadly cases of aeronautical mass murder committed by terrorists in recorded history. Although the three cases have similar motives, they demonstrate an escalated level of sophistication, commitment, and casualties.

JUNE 23, 1985

At approximately 7:13 a.m., Air India Flight 182 disintegrated over the Atlantic Ocean off the southwestern coast of Cork, Ireland. The wide-bodied Boeing 747 airliner, which originated in Toronto, was carrying 307 passengers and 22 crewmembers from Montreal to London, with a final destination of India. While cruising at 31,000 feet, the aircraft suffered catastrophic structural failure, causing it to break up while in flight, killing all 329 persons aboard. Evidence from the wreckage indicated that an explosion in the airliner's forward cargo hold caused the structural damage to the aircraft. The sabotage theory was substantiated by a bomb blast that occurred that same day at Tokyo's Narita airport. The device was hidden in a piece of luggage and exploded prematurely while it was being taken to a waiting area to be loaded onto Air India Flight 301, also bound for India. The blast killed two baggage handlers and injured four.

An investigation revealed that on June 20, 1985, a male suspect purchased tickets in cash for two passengers to fly to India from a Canadian Pacific ticket office in Vancouver. The first ticket was for travel from Vancouver to Toronto, then on to Montreal. On arrival, the passenger would connect with Air India Flight 182. The second ticket was for a passenger to travel from Vancouver to Tokyo, then connect with Air India Flight 301. On the morning of June 22, 1985, a man checked his baggage at Vancouver International Airport through to Air India Flight 182. Later that morning, another man checked his luggage through to Air India Flight 301, connecting in Tokyo. Neither passenger ever boarded their respective flights.

In 1991, Inderjit Singh Reyat, a man believed to have ties to the Sikh militant movement, was convicted and imprisoned in connection with the bombing deaths at Narita airport, in Tokyo. On October 27, 2000, Canadian authorities arrested two suspects for the murders of the 329 passengers on Flight 182 and the two baggage handlers at the Tokyo airport. The two suspects were believed to have connections to a militant organization dedicated to the creation of a Sikh homeland in India's Punjab State. The attacks were suspected to have been committed in retaliation for the Indian Army's assault on a Sikh holy shrine in Amritsar, Punjab, on June 6, 1984. The trial was set to begin in November 2002.

DECEMBER 21, 1988

At 7:00 p.m., Pan American World Airways Flight 103 had reached its cruising altitude of 31,000 feet as it prepared to cross the Atlantic Ocean after leaving London's Heathrow airport. At 3 minutes past the hour of 7, air traffic controllers observed the aircraft break up on their radar screens. The flight, which had originated in Frankfurt, Germany, was on its way to New York City when an improvised explosive device, believed to have been concealed in the shell of a radio-cassette player and hidden in a suitcase, detonated in the aircraft's left forward cargo hold. Like Air India Flight 182, the explosion caused catastrophic structural failure. The cockpit and forward fuselage immediately separated from the rest of the plane. The remaining portions of the aircraft were ripped apart and descended on a wide area in Lockerbie, Scotland. Along with the 259 passengers and 16 crewmembers aboard the aircraft, 11 people were killed on the ground.

On November 14, 1991, the United States and Britain formally charged Abdelbaset Ali Mohmed Al Megrahi and Al Amin Khalifa Fhimah for carrying out the attack on Pan Am Flight 103. Officials alleged that the two suspects were Libyan intelligence officers retaliating for the United States' bombing of Tripoli, Libya, in 1986. On January 31, 2001, the three Scottish judges who presided over the special court at Camp Zeist, in Holland, sentenced Megrahi to life in prison; Fhimah was acquitted due to lack of evidence connecting him to the attack.

Speculation regarding exactly who was behind the attack has persisted. Some believe that the attack was actually masterminded and funded by the Iranian government, not by Libya as the trial implied. According to this theory, the Iranian government contracted with the Popular Front for the Liberation of Palestine (PFLP) to carry out the attack in revenge for the USS *Vincennes* accidental downing of a commercial Iranian Airbus over the Persian Gulf in July 1988, killing 290 civilians. The theory speculates that the bomb originated in Frankfurt—the origination point of Pan Am Flight 103 and home to a PFLP unit—as opposed to Malta, where Megrahi was located.

SEPTEMBER 11, 2001

At 8:45 a.m., American Airlines Flight 11 slammed into the 110-story north tower of the World Trade Center in lower Manhattan. The Boeing 767 commercial airliner was en route from Boston to Los Angeles with 92 people onboard. At 9:03 a.m., a second airliner, United Airlines Flight 175, struck the south tower. The second aircraft, which had 65 people onboard, was also a Boeing 767 traveling from Boston to Los Angeles. All 157 passengers and crew members aboard the two flights were killed. Both of the twin towers eventually collapsed as a result of the damage, killing approximately 3,000 people, including 414 officials from the New York City Fire and Police departments.

At 9:43 a.m., American Airlines Flight 77 crashed into the Pentagon, in Washington, D.C. After leaving Dulles International Airport, the Boeing 757 was diverted from its route to Los Angeles. All 64 persons onboard were killed, as well as 25 people working in the government facility. At 10:10 a.m., United Airlines Flight 93, en route from Newark to San Francisco, crashed in the woodlands of western Pennsylvania. Officials believe the aircraft may have headed for the White House or Camp David if it were not for a small group of passengers who wrestled control away from the skyjackers. All 44 people onboard the flight perished in the crash.

The airliners were commandeered by 19 assailants, who worked in four- and five-person teams. They are suspected of being members of the al-Qaeda terrorist organization, led by Osama bin Laden. Armed with makeshift knives, the skyjackers, who had received pilot training, overtook the airliners and deliberately crashed them into symbols of the United States' economic and military power, killing themselves in the process. The attacks represented several new developments in the commission of terrorist-motivated aeronautical mass murder. Rather than planting explosive devices on an aircraft, the fully fueled planes were used as the incendiary weapons. Furthermore, the attack undoubtedly required an unprecedented degree of sophisticated training, planning, and coordination. It also appears to mark the first example of a successful aeronautical mass murder-suicide motivated by terrorism. Finally, by intentionally piloting the airliners into highly populated areas, the skyjackers drastically increased the number of casualties resulting from the attacks.

As demonstrated in this case and those before it, aeronautical mass murder will continue to represent a significant threat to human life if suicide bombers and saboteurs continue to demonstrate an unyielding commitment to their aims and creativity in their methods.

—*Michael P. Arena*

See also AIR RAGE; MASS MURDER; MASS VIOLENCE; MOTIVES FOR MURDER; MURDER-SUICIDE; PROFILING; TERRORISM

Further Reading

Gero, D. (1997). *Flights of terror: Aerial hijack and sabotage since 1930.* Newbury Park, CA: Patrick Stephens.

Hoffman, B. (1997). Aviation security and terrorism: An analysis of the potential threat to air cargo integrators. In P. Wilkinson & B. Jenkins (Eds.), *Aviation terrorism and security* (pp. 54-69). Portland, OR: Frank Cass.

Jenkins, B. (1997). Aircraft sabotage. In P. Wilkinson & B. Jenkins (Eds.), *Aviation terrorism and security* (pp. 50-53). Portland, OR: Frank Cass.

Merari, A. (1997). Attacks on civil aviation: Trends and lessons. In P. Wilkinson & B. Jenkins (Eds.), *Aviation terrorism and security* (pp. 9-26). Portland, OR: Frank Cass.

Wallis, R. (2001). *Lockerbie: The story and the lessons.* Westport, CT: Praeger.

AGGRAVATING AND MITIGATING CIRCUMSTANCES

Aggravating and mitigating circumstances are important legal considerations in the sentencing of convicted offenders under modern sentencing laws in the United States. Evidence regarding the two areas is typically presented during a sentencing hearing after the offender has been convicted, and is weighed by the decision maker in deciding on the appropriate disposition. Aggravating circumstances are factors that make an offense seem worse to the evaluator. In contrast, mitigating circumstances are factors that suggest that the offense or the offender should be regarded in a less harsh way by the sentencing authority. These circumstances are relevant concerns in murder cases in which a convicted offender is facing the death sentence. They are also critical considerations in many states that have adopted determinate or presumptive sentencing.

In 1972, the United States Supreme Court, the highest court in the nation, held in *Furman v. Georgia* that the death penalty as it was being administered at the time constituted "cruel and unusual punishment," in violation of the Eighth and Fourteenth Amendments. The Court in this landmark ruling did not abolish capital punishment, but made it clear, however, that new legislation drafted with respect to the death penalty must ensure that its imposition in the future remedied the random and capricious nature of sentencing policies in the past.

Four years later, the United States Supreme Court, in recognizing that various state death penalty laws had adequately reduced the arbitrariness of previous statutes, allowed capital punishment to resume under certain conditions. In the 1976 case of *Gregg v. Georgia,* the Court approved a two-stage process whereby jurors would first determine the guilt of an offender standing trial for murder. If the accused were found guilty of capital murder, the jury would consider aggravating and mitigating factors and then make a recommendation to the judge to impose either the death sentence or imprisonment. The judge, after careful consideration of the jury's recommendation, would make findings with respect to aggravating and mitigating factors and then impose the appropriate sentence.

In an attempt to comply with the Supreme Court's directive, the typical modern death penalty statute contains separate lists of aggravating and mitigating factors. Aggravating circumstances are typically limited by statute. The prosecutor must prove that at least one aggravating circumstance exists for the defendant to be eligible for the imposition of the death penalty. In most jurisdictions, however, the prosecution may offer proof relevant only to establishing one of the previously delineated aggravating criteria; aggravating circumstances not previously set out in the statute are typically irrelevant. In contrast, the defense is not limited to the specific mitigators enumerated in the state statute. In the 1978 case of *Lockett v. Ohio,* the Court struck down the Ohio law that did not allow the sentencing judge to consider nonstatutory mitigators (which included, in this particular case, the defendant's age, character, lack of specific intent to bring about death, and relatively minor participation in the crime). As a result, during the sentencing phase, defense attorneys are typically allowed to introduce any case-related factors that may be viewed as mitigating.

Although aggravating factors vary across the states, a number of them are commonly encountered. Common aggravators pertain to the quality of the offense or the intent of the offender. For example, according to Florida statues, aggravating factors include homicides that are "especially heinous,

atrocious, and cruel" or are committed by offenders who "knowingly created a great risk of death to many persons" or who acted "in a cold, calculated, and premeditated manner without any pretense of moral or legal justification."

It is considered an aggravating circumstance when an offender commits murder when he or she has been previously convicted of another violent felony and/ or is currently under legal authority in connection with a prior felony conviction. It may be deemed an aggravating circumstance if the capital felony was committed during the commission of certain felonious crimes, for the purpose of monetary gain, to avoid a lawful arrest, or to effect an escape from custody. The killing of certain categories of victims is also considered an aggravator in many jurisdictions. Examples of special victim classes include (a) law enforcement officers and public officials engaged in the performance of their official duties and (b) those who are seen as more vulnerable, such as children under 12 years old, the elderly, or the disabled. More recent statutes have included the commission of a capital felony by a gang member as an aggravating factor.

Certain mitigating factors are also fairly common across the states. These include the age of the defendant and his or her lack of a significant prior criminal history. Circumstances in which the offender's participation was relatively minor or in which the victim participated in the defendant's criminal conduct or consented to the act are typically viewed as mitigators. Many state statutes also contain psychological mitigators. In Florida, for example, it is considered a mitigating circumstance if the offender committed the murder while he or she was "under the influence of extreme mental or emotional disturbance" or if he or she "acted under extreme duress or under the substantial domination of another person." A third psychological mitigator addresses whether the defendant's capacity "to appreciate the criminality of his or her conduct or to conform his or her conduct to the law was substantially impaired."

Nonstatutory mitigators may be introduced if they are relevant to understanding the defendant's involvement in the murder or his or her present condition. These factors might include, for example, the effects of egocentrism; child maltreatment; being raised in a dysfunctional family; peer pressure; mental retardation; the effects of extreme drug or alcohol abuse or substance addiction on a defendant's intellectual, emotional, and moral development; the presence of remorse; and the defendant's amenability to treatment.

The delineation and use of aggravating and mitigating circumstances have not been limited to death penalty statutes. By the mid-1990s, at least 20 states, as well as the federal government, had enacted legislation to restrict the range of permissible sentences. Although there are many variations, the idea behind the adoption of determinate sentencing was to narrow prosecutorial and judicial discretion by authorizing departures from the presumed sentence only under carefully prescribed guidelines. Departures upward or downward by a certain percentage were authorized only under narrow circumstances by the finding of aggravating or mitigating circumstances, respectively. Many of these factors are essentially variations of the aggravating and mitigating factors developed with respect to the death penalty.

—Kathleen M. Heide

See also COURTS; CRIMINAL JUSTICE; DEATH PENALTY

Further Reading

Fla. Statutes, § 921.141(5) 2000.
Gregg v. Georgia, 428 U.S. 153 (1976).
Lockett v. Ohio, 438 U.S. 586 (1978).

AGGRESSION: BIOLOGICAL THEORIES

Behavior is the result of the complex interactions of many variables—psychological attributes such as one's temperament or tolerance to frustration; social forces including racism, poverty, and the economy more broadly; and situational factors such as loss of a job or the death of a child—but it is ultimately how these factors act on and with various aspects of the biological substrate of the individual that determines how they will or will not manifest as specific behaviors. To a large extent, the biological makeup of the individual determines behavioral probabilities and thus behavioral patterns. Aggression is generally understood as any form of behavior intended to gain power or dominance over and/or to cause harm to another. In this regard, specific instances of aggression are generally viewed as the product of volition; the behavior is seen as a matter of choice. However, when our focus turns to patterns of aggressive behavior, including episodes of impulsive violence, a more complex picture emerges, one with decidedly biological underpinnings.

Aggression is not synonymous with violence, for people can behave aggressively without committing violent acts. A correlation between the two, however, is undeniable. The more aggressive a person is, the greater the likelihood will be for that person to be involved in, if not create, circumstances that situate him or her against others, thus increasing the possibility of a violent outcome. The word *violence* derives from the Latin root *vio,* denoting "force." The etymological origin of the term *biological* is the Greek *vios,* meaning "mode of life." In its broadest context, then, aggression is a life force: purposive as an agent of vitality.

Within species, aggressive behaviors confer reproductive advantage to males in their competition for territory and access to females. The propensity toward aggression in male members of mammalian species is well established as an adaptive strategy serving individual and species survival. In accordance with these principles, theories of evolutionary psychology begin with the premise that human behavior has archaic biologic origins and propose that mental functions undergo natural selection over time. To the extent that reproductive success is enhanced by aggressive traits, they are selected and carried over into the next generation. Examining the basic mechanisms involved in aggression through comparative animal studies better positions us to understand how more recently evolved capacities (notably language and consciousness) contribute to aggressive behavior in humans.

In human embryogenesis, a gonad appears after 6 weeks of cellular differentiation. This gonad has the potential to develop into testicular or ovarian tissue, depending on the presence of a single (SRY) gene on the Y chromosome. If this gene is present, the gonad develops into a testis. In general, in humans and other mammals, it is the presence or absence of a Y chromosome that determines the sex of offspring. During critical periods of prenatal development (in humans, this begins in the 7th week), hormonal secretions by an embryonic testis determine the sexual fate of all sexual structures by way of masculinizing the body—and the brain.

This biological disposition of human males to aggression, compounded by the differential socialization of humans according to gender, has led to significant disparity between the sexes in terms of aggressive behaviors. Crime statistics make clear the preponderance of males in the population of violent offenders. Despite this and conventional wisdom, researchers such as Björkqvist and Niemelä propose that females may be as aggressive as males, but not recognized as such because their modes of aggression tend to be less physical and less direct. For example, verbal hostility, as in shouting obscenities or rumor mongering, constitutes a prevalent mode of aggression in females. However, females can behave in individual cases as violently as males. This fact notwithstanding, males have been the main perpetrators of violence across cultures and across time and thus the focus of most studies on aggression.

Research on laboratory animals shows how aggression can be elicited by manipulating environmental conditions. For example, introducing an "intruder" rat to colonies of both laboratory and feral rats reliably elicits attack by the dominant rat in the colony. This common response by both types of rats suggests a neural basis for their aggressive responses. Studies also demonstrate the importance of prior social experience where proclivity to exhibit aggression does not conform to the usual stimulus contexts. For example, exposing otherwise docile hamsters to extended periods of physical threat by putting them in the home cage of a larger male results in the creation of the equivalent of the "playground bully": a hamster that will go on to attack smaller hamsters whenever presented with them. The social experience—in this case, prolonged threat—prompts neurochemical changes in the areas of the hamster's brain that regulate aggression (by changing levels of, for example, serotonin and vasopressin). These alterations in the neurochemistry of the hamster's brain are the proximal cause of the behavioral changes. The environment changes the biology, which, in turn, changes the behavior.

Because of the inextricable link between the mind and brain, one cannot speak of psychology (particularly mental disorder) without implying biology. Increasingly, evidence suggests a biologic, if not genetic, foundation for serious mental disorders. Studies of schizophrenics demonstrate a neurological basis for the hallucinatory experience: during auditory hallucinations, for example, the neurons are firing in the same regions of the brain known to process auditory information. Psychotic individuals cannot differentiate voices "in their head" from those originating in their external realities. It would appear that this is because

neurophysiologically, the two are indistinguishable. The violence of the psychotic who strikes out at others in response to his hallucinations thus has a biological component, if not a biological basis.

Although aggression is inherent in the human condition as an adaptive trait, there is a line beyond which aggressive behaviors become maladaptive. In criminal violence, the behaviors themselves do not distinguish their adaptability, but rather the motivations that underlie them. The criminality of an act derives from the intent of the actor to do harm to others. Some violent attacks are calculated predatory actions designed to achieve a particular outcome, and others are impulsive. In both cases, the predominant motive forces are biological. Beyond a matter of mere choice, the individual's behavior is largely driven by the complex orchestration of his or her biology.

To further compound the picture, the brain invests more energy in stopping individuals from behaving in particular ways (resisting impulses) than it does directing them to do things. Urges to act aggressively largely arise from the more primitive limbic structures of the brain and are managed by higher-order cortical brain functions of the frontal lobes, particularly the prefrontal cortex. When an individual engages in acts of predatory or impulsive violence, the issue has less do with why (the underlying urges) than with the mechanisms that inhibit the urges. In other words, what happened to the "brakes"? The braking mechanism in question resides in the frontal lobes of the brain. Recent studies of violent behavior have focused on the higher-order activities of the frontal lobes, including the formation of judgments and maintaining attention. Such functions generally moderate the impulses to act aggressively that originate from other regions of the brain, particularly the amygdala, in the limbic system.

More broadly, a number of psychophysiological measures have been found to correlate with violent and antisocial behavior. Reduced skin conductance rates (as measured by Galvanic skin response), lower heart rates, and a preponderance of slow brain wave (theta wave) activity in more serious offenders attests to a trend toward psychophysiological underarousal in these individuals.

We are, it appears, witnessing the emergence of a kind of "neuroanatomy of violence." This knowledge—coupled with research that demonstrates that our biology is changed by our life experiences—illustrates at once the hope and the frustration of coming to a comprehensive understanding of violent behavior. Science is identifying the biological and environmental determinants of aggression, but the mechanisms by which they interact are largely unknown. Even in cases in which an abusive formative environment has led to violence later in life, a biological component is undeniable. We see, as one example of our pursuit to understand violent behavior, cognitive science poised to discover how the emotional memory of such abusive childhood incidents is stored and recalled and then later acted on.

By virtue of the undisputed connection between brain activity and behavior, the brain occupies the focal point for understanding aggression. The intricate connections between the brain's billions of neurons make possible the ordinary (the beating of the heart) and the extraordinary (the ability for introspection). Certainly, many factors are involved in the expression of aggression, but the interrelationships among them contribute most to the complexity of the behavior. The hub of this activity is the brain: the primary center that processes information about the internal and external environments and from which emanates the electrochemical instructions for behavior.

Other biological factors (as well as nonbiological factors) have roles in violence to the extent that they affect brain function, for example, neurotransmitters. Actions of neurotransmitter chemicals in the brain have long been implicated in behavior. Research shows, for example, how experimentally reducing serotonin levels results in an increase in impulsive and aggressive behaviors. A variety of neurotransmitters are involved in the biochemistry of impulse control and thus the expression or suppression of aggressive behavior. Research on steroids has long linked circulating testosterone with propensity toward competitive and aggressive behavior. Androgens not only influence but are also influenced by aggressive behavior; furthermore, the form the aggression takes is largely shaped by environmental factors. Some individuals hormonally disposed to behave aggressively may not act in violent ways yet are nonetheless driven to dominate others. Their behavior may be no less antisocial, found among the perpetrators of chronic and serious white-collar offenders. In such cases, the difference appears to be attributable to a rearing environment that values success but prohibits violence. The biological proclivity toward aggression is there, but its manifestation is a function of social forces.

In addition to these biological factors, a growing literature attests to the role of nutrition in aggressive behavior. For example, some individuals are very susceptible to changes in blood glucose levels, whereby either hyper- or hypoglycemic conditions results in hostile behavior. Other ingested substances, such as alcohol, reduce the inhibitory effects of the cerebral cortex, rendering an individual more likely to behave on impulse. Research has also linked exposure to naturally occurring elements, such as lead and cadmium, as well as environmental contaminants, such as pesticides, with violent behavior due to compromised brain function.

Increasingly, clinicians and researchers are using brain-imaging techniques together with neuropsychological tests in their work with violent predatory offenders. Results tend to offer converging evidence of cognitive deficits. Although the research on the biological bases of aggression is not only inconclusive but also replete with conflicting findings, there is no question that aggression is rooted in the biological substrate of the human being.

The brain is not a blank slate at birth to be filled out by life experience nor is it a genetically predetermined repertoire of fixed ways to behave in particular situations. Although research is beginning to link specific genetic mutations to impulsive violence, making one-to-one connections between genes and violent behavior is much too simplistic. Results do permit us, however, to identify genetic risk factors that interact with other biological factors and environmental conditions and may influence behavior, for example, lowering the threshold for irritability. There are also genetically based insulating factors, such as high cognitive ability, that have been shown to mitigate impulsivity. As the field of behavioral genetics evolves, more will be learned about the heritability of aggression—be it directly through the effects of specific genes or indirectly through genetic correlates that increase the probability of agonistic behavior. A more comprehensive understanding of aggressive behavior awaits the kind of research that will elucidate the interactions between the variables involved in the etiology of violence and thus be predicated on further advances in biological technology.

Research on biological contributions to aggressive behavior has resulted in substantial, although incomplete, insights into aggressive behavior. As biology provides more answers to questions of aggression and, specifically, violence, society will be increasingly challenged to apply this knowledge in the determination of criminal culpability. To what extent is it due to biology, and to what extent free will? To complicate the issue, the boundaries between biological mechanisms and the psychological or social variables associated with violence are becoming less distinct, with each set of factors seen as affecting the other. In view of this complexity, future research may be well advised to frame the search for understanding violence in terms of biological "risk factors" and "protective factors."

The importance of the interactions between and among biological and nonbiological factors must be underscored. Violence is not a matter of one factor combining with another factor in an additive, linear manner (whereby 1 plus 1 equals 2), but is, rather, a function of one factor interacting with another, resulting in any number of permutations (so that only rarely does 1 plus 1 equal 2). It is a case in which the whole is much greater than the sum of its parts. This analogy may go far to explain the persistence of violence in society despite our efforts to eradicate it. The notion of crime control presupposes an understanding of its origins. Much remains to be learned.

—*Candice A. Skrapec*

See also AGGRESSION, PSYCHOLOGICAL AND SOCIOLOGICAL THEORIES; PSYCHOSOCIAL RISK FACTORS FOR VIOLENT BEHAVIOR; PREDICTING VIOLENT BEHAVIOR; XYY SYNDROME

Further Reading

Björkqvist, K., & Niemelä, P. (1992). New trends in the study of female aggression. In K. Björkqvist & P. Niemelä (Eds.), *Of mice and women: Aspects of female aggression.* San Diego, CA: Academic Press.

Grisolia, J. S., Sanmartin, J., Luján, J. L., & Grisolia, A. (1997). *Violence: From biology to society.* Amsterdam: Elsevier.

Moeller, F. G., Dougherty, D. M., Swann, A. C., Collins, D., Davis, C. M., & Cherek, D. R. (1996). Tryptophan depletion and aggressive responding in healthy males. *Psychopharmacology, 126,* 97-103.

Pincus, J. H. (2001). *Base instincts: What makes killers kill?* New York: Norton.

Raine, A. (1993). *The psychopathology of crime: Criminal behavior as a clinical disorder.* San Diego, CA: Academic Press.

Raine, A., Brennan, P. A., Farrington, D. P., & Mednick, S. A. (Eds.). (1997). *Biosocial bases of violence.* New York: Plenum.

AGGRESSION: EVOLUTIONARY AND ANTHROPOLOGICAL THEORIES

Anthropology has contributed a great deal to our understanding of interpersonal human aggression (a behavior in which one person uses physical or verbal abuse to attack, dominate, or humiliate another). The evidence suggests that levels of interpersonal aggression vary enormously between societies and do so according to their "stage of social and cultural evolution." This use of the word *evolution,* however, is highly misleading because it implies that there has been a simple and unilinear evolution from the primitive and violent to the civilized and nonviolent: In fact, nothing could be further from the truth.

During the thousands of years of human prehistory, most of our ancestors lived in small bands of hunters, gatherers, and fishers. In such small and mobile groups, tight controls were exercised over the potential aggression of their members and specifically stigmatized violence (because peaceful cooperation ensured the maximum collective benefit in the food quest). Later, as human beings developed social arrangements more complex than the traditional small band (such as clans, lineages, or later, small states), the larger societies were able to mobilize many more potential warriors for predatory military operations against their neighbors. Aggressivity thus took on a new political and economic desirability for the emerging elites who would be enriched and empowered by such actions. This was enhanced still further with the development of the bureaucratic modern state, which, long before the Christian Era, had become little more than a ruthless war-making machine, favoring violent persons and mercenary politics. Only in the late 19th century did modern states, especially in Western Europe and North America, began to perceive the dangers inherent in continuous aggression and to resocialize their members toward a greater docility, at least in peacetime (muting or eliminating, for example, the blood feud, the duel, and the right of an individual to defend his honor).

To achieve its ends, each culture thus transmitted coded messages that validated or negated violence as an appropriate and manly response to frustration, according to the wishes of the dominant group. Moreover, each culture "chose" how much it would socialize internalized self-control in its citizens and how much it would punish its members for failing to exercise appropriate impulse control. Thus, if we are to understand the causes of aggression, we must first examine the factors that cause it to vary so enormously around the world.

THE SIGNIFICANCE OF AGGRESSION

Why is the amount of aggression in a society of such importance? Partly, it is for purely humanitarian reasons: Aggression is one of the things that people rightly fear the most, yet understand the least. Moreover, although restitution is possible for a property crime (your purse may be stolen and then returned), no one can make proper restitution for a violent crime, especially murder. Every assault or murder has ugly reverberations that go far beyond the original terrible act. It may destroy not only the life of the victim but also cause lifelong grief and suffering for the victim's children, parents, grandparents, siblings, relatives, and partners. At the same time, the act erodes an entire community's sense of confidence and neighbors' trust in each other. Violence also tells us a great deal about the nature of the society and the stresses, strains, and conflicts that are built into any civilization in a particular time and place.

CHARACTERISTICS OF VIOLENCE IN THE "PRIMITIVE" WORLD

Many so-called primitive societies (such as the Yanomamo of South America) have very high levels of violence, so the temptation to romanticize all primitive society as a Garden of Eden should be resolutely resisted. Nevertheless, many preindustrial, small-scale and simply organized societies (often with their own distinct languages, customs, and religions) succeeded in minimizing serious violence, rendering aggression as inappropriate for most (or even all) circumstances. In such cultural contexts, well studied among peoples such as the Fore of New Guinea, the Semai of Malaysia, and the !Kung Bushmen of the Kalahari Desert, the optimum conditions for low-aggressivity cultures are as follows.

A. *The social structure* is capable of minimizing disputes by creating few opportunities for power struggles between individuals for personal power, prestige, or wealth. To make this possible, the society can have only the most rudimentary divisions of labor

(e.g., man or woman, young or old), not the infinite distinctions between human beings in modern stratified industrial societies.

Among the Semai, Fore, and !Kung peoples, for example, there is little creation of wealth (only food and essentials tools are produced), so there are no wealthy elites. Moreover, there are no hierarchies of power or prestige, and none of the elaborate ranks of nobles and commoners, holy men and profane, warriors and weaklings, and ranked officials and the powerless that structure humiliation and subordination in complex societies. Moreover, social-leveling mechanisms (cultural practices that ensure no one is allowed to dominate others) also control behavior in these societies. Thus a !Kung hunter who boasts about his skill with bow and arrow or a Semai woman who refuses to share her food or possessions according to the established rules of sharing may be subjected to a barrage of insult, ostracism, or religious penalty until they can bear it no more.

Potential or actual disputes between persons are resolved through elaborate cultural practices of community negotiation rather than a punitive system of police and courts. For example, in some traditional Inuit ("Eskimo") bands and African tribes, disputes between individuals had to be resolved not by fighting or harassment between the disputing parties, but by communitywide "song fights" in which members of each "side" sang satirical songs to demoralize the other: The community itself awarded victory to those who sang the best songs, as opposed to those who had the best objective "case" (for no such notions of case law, or even fixed rules, are found in many of these societies). Similar institutions abound in primitive society and usually involve councils of elders or village assemblies convened to settle the dispute, disperse the anger between the disputants, and repair any damage to the harmony of the social order.

B. *The culture,* the system of integrated beliefs that members of a society hold and transmit from generation to generation, must also abhor or ban aggression and teach its members that such displays are both inappropriate and inhuman. Sometimes the culture denies even the very possibility that "real people," those of us who are fully human, are capable of anger and aggressivity. In this spirit, the Semai compare themselves favorably with Europeans and Asians, who, they say, beat their children, whereas "We Semai do not get angry." That is, Semai nature is one in which anger is impossible. Such societies raise their children with minimal restraint and few arbitrary rules or regulations, allowing each child to develop naturally at his or her own pace, surrounded by a cocoon of protective warmth and love from adult villagers. Moreover, children grow up in a milieu in which they never see violent adults and are thus offered no violent role models. They tend to grow into nondominant adults who are receptive to the personalities of others and sensitive to the changing needs and moods of their fellows.

THE EVOLUTION OF DIFFERENCES AMONG MODERN SOCIETIES

Modern Western industrialized developed societies are very much the same in many ways: Their standards of living, rates of illness and death, and degrees of literacy, delinquency, divorce rates, and the like all tend to be very similar. But levels of accurately measurable aggression (i.e., homicide; rates of other violent crimes tend merely to measure reporting, not occurrences, of the offenses) differ enormously, by a factor of 10 or 20. Homicide rates in the United States, for example, have hovered near 10 per 100,000 population per year (Mexico and Russia's rates are double or triple that), whereas the per capita rates in Western Europe are a fifth of those in the United States, and rates in England or Japan are even lower. In some countries (or even regions of one country), serious violence is a rare and isolated event, one that seizes the imagination of the public and creates considerable fear and consternation, whereas in other societies, such violence is an everyday fact of life, barely warranting the attention of the public or mention in the media.

CHARACTERISTICS OF VIOLENCE AND HOMICIDE IN THE MODERN WORLD

Acts of serious aggression are most frequent in societies that have not quite stilled the last echoes of the old feudal law of the blood feud, societies that still hold deep beliefs that it is the responsibility of the individual, not the courts, to avenge the family's honor. Moreover, there is a tendency in such relatively violent societies, however unconscious it may be, for the culture to glorify and validate violent acts and violent actors. Serious aggression is least frequent in societies in which the dominant culture dispenses feelings of embarrassment, shame, and even revulsion at the mere thought of interpersonal aggressive display.

We know that violence is overwhelmingly a *male domain:* Males are the primary perpetrators (usually 9 out of 10) of homicides, and they are also usually the primary victims, although at a lesser extreme (usually 6 or 7 out of 10 victims). We know also that despite fear and stereotyping, murder is usually *intraracial;* That is, African Americans murder other African Americans, whites murder whites, and Asians murder Asians. Again, we know that murder is largely a matter of *social class:* 9 out of 10 typical killers in modern societies are from the less fortunate sector of society: the poor and the disenfranchised, the chronically underemployed or unemployed, those without professional or educational qualifications, those with limited social skills, and those with chronic drug or alcohol dependencies. The upper and middle classes rarely murder: They are far more likely to fight enemies with legal action than weapons.

Our greatest fear is that we might be attacked by evil strangers (such as serial killers), but in fact the overwhelming majority of killings are perpetrated by *family, friends, and associates* of victims. Finally, the statistical chance of being murdered varies also by the *regions* in which we live: Traditionally, the Old South had the highest rate of homicide in America, but that had begun to change by the 1960s, and for some time now the highest rates of homicide have tended to be in the major cities across the United States, such as New York, Los Angeles, Detroit, and New Orleans. States such as North Dakota and New Hampshire still have very low homicide rates.

"EXPLANATIONS"

The literature is studded with strongly argued "explanations" for aggressive behavior, but they tend to be political or ideological in origin, and inconclusive. It is a plausible argument that there is often a relationship between a widespread availability of firearms carried on the street and a chance that an encounter might explode into a homicide. But this is often confused with private ownership of firearms, and it does not appear to apply in countries such as Switzerland or Canada, where firearms are usually kept safely locked away. It is an equally plausible argument that because most violence is committed by males (and the most dangerous social situation everywhere in the world is when two males confront one another), there might be something in the male genetic, biochemical, or psychological makeup that gives them a tendency toward violence. Yet men everywhere are the same in virtually every biological, chemical, and psychological way, and if such biological or psychological factors determined violence, then their homicide rates would be the same everywhere.

Most important, it seems clear that any "innate" violence can be overridden in cultures that abhor aggressivity and in structures that minimize conflict. Curiously, and in defiance of common sense, severe penalties for homicide appear to have little effect: The countries with the least ruthless punishments (especially Western Europe) tend to have lower homicide rates, whereas the countries with the heaviest punishments (including the United States, which is unique among developed western nations in its retention and routine use of the death penalty) still have the highest offense rates.

—Elliott Leyton

See also AGGRESSION, BIOLOGICAL, PSYCHOLOGICAL, AND SOCIOLOGICAL THEORIES; MOTIVES FOR MURDER; PREDICTING VIOLENT BEHAVIOR

Further Reading

Archer, D., & Gartner, R. (1984). *Violence and crime in cross-national perspective.* New Haven, CT: Yale University Press.

Bohannan, P. (Ed). (1967). *Law and warfare: Studies in the anthropology of conflict.* New York: Natural History Press.

Chagnon, N. (1968). *The Yanomamo.* New York: Harcourt Brace Jovanovich.

Dentan, R. K. (1968). *The Semai: A nonviolent people of Malaya.* New York: Holt, Rinehart & Winston.

Leyton, E. (1986). *Compulsive killers: The story of modern multiple murder.* New York: New York University Press. Published simultaneously in Canada (and in 1989 in the United Kingdom) under the title *Hunting humans: The rise of the modern multiple murderer.* London: Penguin; Toronto: McClelland and Stewart.

Leyton, E. (1995). *Men of blood: Murder in everyday life.* Toronto: McClelland and Stewart; London: Penguin.

Leyton, E. (1999). Serial and mass murderers. In Lester Kurtz (Ed.), *Encyclopedia of violence, peace & conflict.* New York: Academic Press.

Montagu, A. (Ed.) (1978). *Learning non-aggression: The experience of non-literate societies.* Oxford: Oxford University Press.

Sahlins, M. (1961, April). The segmentary lineage: An organization of predatory expansion. *American Anthropologist 63,* 2, pp. 322-345.

AGGRESSION: FEMINIST PERSPECTIVE

Feminist theory represents divergent perspectives that are still emerging; however, there is widespread consensus that traditional academic research has failed to recognize the relationship between power and gender in violence. Feminist perspectives challenge the claim that individual pathology is the root cause of violent behavior and use gender as a starting point for analysis of violence. In this view, violence reflects issues of gendered power, oppression, and resistance in the larger society. Most research by feminists focuses on violence against women that revolves around two core concepts, situated knowledge and patriarchy. Feminists argue that gender-based power relations underscore all social institutions, including economic, political, educational, social, religious, and familial. This perspective thus asserts that the root causes of violence against women are contained within unequal relations of power between men and women.

Feminist theory grew out of an interdisciplinary approach incorporating the disciplines of psychology, sociology, anthropology, politics, economics, religion, biology, and culture. Feminist analysis of violence is informed by everyday lived experiences of women. Because situated knowledge involves the interaction of culture, gender, and power, feminists seek to understand violence from a sociocultural and gendered perspective. Studying violence as it is situated in the lives of women makes explicit the societal relations of power, gender bias, political entitlements, and male privilege that are systemic under patriarchy.

Feminist theory defines *patriarchies* as systems of male privilege and power that are embedded in societal rules, norms, beliefs, practices, and policies and therefore serve to subordinate, control, and dominate women. Violence against women thus represents one form of patriarchal control, both on an individual and societal level. Feminists assert that patriarchy preserves power in males as the dominant group through exploitation of women as the subordinated group. Patriarchal systems of power become visible in the stratification of society according to class, race, and gender. Patriarchy thus presents a challenge to individual freedom and personal autonomy because it structures social relations on the basis of male power and privilege. Systemic submission of women to social structures of male domination occur in many arenas, including the family, workplace, media, religion, law, economics, politics, and education. Women as well as men often participate below the level of self-awareness in the social reproduction of patriarchy within society.

Power within patriarchy is often expressed as aggression, violence, or coercion. More subtle expressions of male power over women serve to restrict options available to women. For example, economic power is found in sex segregation in the workplace, placing women in underpaid and devalued positions that economically disadvantage them. Welfare payment to mothers trapped in poverty is one example of patriarchal state power that systemically promotes the passivity and submission of women. High rates of poverty, in turn, exacerbate violence as women remain with abusive partners because of economic dependence. Feminists thus assert that women must gain equal access to political, social, and economic resources in order to have real freedom from aggression, violence, and coercion.

HISTORICAL PERSPECTIVE

The women's liberation movement of the 1960s and 1970s, known as "second-wave feminists," rejected the notion of separate public and private spheres and asserted that gender relations within the private sphere shaped all public interaction. This perspective was expressed in the feminist slogan "The personal is political." Feminist analysis of violence sought to bridge the private/public divide by asserting that although sexual politics may "begin in the bedroom," it reflects wider public problems. The lived experiences of violence experienced by women in the private sphere provided ample evidence that violence against women was symptomatic of widespread societal gender oppression.

Out of the women's liberation movement came the new terms for violence, including *domestic violence, wife abuse, battered-wife syndrome, rape-trauma syndrome,* and *sexual harassment.* The woman's movement pushed for legislation to secure equal rights and protection for women under the law. Feminist activism forced national recognition of how violence against women in the private sphere was actually a political act and therefore the responsibility of the state to address. The Violence Against Women Act (VAWA) passed in 1994 represented landmark legislation that criminalized personal violence against women in the private

sphere and mandated female advocacy and mandatory arrests for violent offenders.

Legal definitions of violence against women have focused on the physical acts of rape, battery, assault, incest, child abuse, stalking, and sexual harassment. The idea of individual pathology as the root cause of violence grew out of a developmental model informed by empirical research in the field of clinical psychology. Feminists argued that the psychological model based on individual pathology was flawed because it ignored pervasive, systemic, and universal social patterns of male power expressed as violence. According to Francine Pickup (2001), an international human rights activist, "Violence is not just committed by abnormal or psychologically disturbed individuals, but is a pervasive systemic, and universal phenomenon cutting across race, class, religion, age, ethnicity and geographics" (p. 11).

Pickup further argued that the prosecution of sex crimes as individual acts allowed society to give the appearance of justice being served, while at the same time accommodating perverse and disturbing systems of male control and domination. In response to narrow definitions of violence from psychodevelopment models, feminists sought to widen the definition of gender violence to any act that created fear, isolation, deprivation, or subordination in women. This expanded definition of violence included behaviors of verbal abuse, emotional abuse, surveillance, threats, coercion, force, and control by men over women.

Feminism further expanded the definition of gender-based violence to include acts associated with reproduction, such as selective female sex abortion, forced sterilization, and female infanticide. Selective-sex abortion and female infanticide represent practices of aborting female fetuses or babies because they are devalued in a particular culture. Forced sterilization, informed by theories of Eugenics or social Darwinism, was viewed as a way to restrict women considered unfit from procreating. In addition, child marriage and prostitution also reflect the violent sexual subordination of women. Although child marriage is illegal in the United States, it is widespread in developing countries.

Patriarchal power is made more explicit by widening the definition of gender-based violence. For example, isolated acts of rape serve to create a climate of fear in all women and in turn restrict their autonomy and freedom. And the common advice given to women not to go out alone at night, park in a dark place, or wear provocative clothing provides evidence for how society views public space as a male domain. Responsibility for avoiding male violence in public is therefore placed on women, which further serves to subordinate and marginalize them. Oxfam, a global human rights organization based in London, cited that over one third of women and girls in the world will be victims of rape, sexual assault, murder, slavery, mutilation, or torture. Oxfam concluded that because such widespread gender violence prevented the full participation of women in society, gender violence represented a crime against humanity. This led international feminist organizations to widen the definition of violence against women, calling it a violation of basic human rights.

COLLECTIVE SOCIAL PATHOLOGIES

Using a systems approach, feminist analysis of gender-based violence revealed that violence is not the result of isolated individual pathology, but is more representative of widespread collective pathologies. For example, feminists demonstrated how patriarchy promotes the objectification of women's bodies into body parts or sex objects, allowing sexuality to become a site for men to exercise power over women. The linkage of sex with power made rape and coerced sex a common experience for many women as their bodies became objects for men to use, violate, and then throw away. Evidence for this is seen in the ubiquitous exploitation of women as sex objects in advertising, pornography, and media violence.

Militarization is another form of patriarchy that promotes violent extremes in males and, by extension, the subordination of women and children. Feminists argue that because militarism legitimates violence as a means of conflict resolution, it promotes the abuse of power as a way to conquer or control women. Research has established that in times of war and extreme militarism, women often experience extreme forms of violence. Women's bodies become sites for territorial conquest, which is played out as violent acts of rape, mutilation, murder, and forced impregnation. Forced impregnation acts as a form of ethnic cleansing that allows the conquerors to perpetuate patriarchal lines of progeny through impregnation. Violent acts of war against women are well documented in recent war-torn countries such as Bosnia, Rwanda, Somalia, Cambodia, Uganda, and Afghanistan.

VIOLENCE IN WOMEN

The overwhelming majority of violent behavior is committed by men; therefore, the feminist perspective on women who commit violent acts is undertheorized. Contemporary feminist research seeks to address the rising incidents of violent behavior in women. Some feminists assert that female violence represents the move toward masculinization in the women's liberation movement. Other feminists argue that patriarchal systems disadvantage women as both perpetrators and victims of crime. For example, more than 44% of women incarcerated for murder have killed abusive partners.

Some feminists use battered-wife syndrome to explain how women are forced into violent behavior by previous years of abuse. Others argue that female incarceration rates reflect how poverty and the marginalization of women encourage criminal behavior for economic reasons. Contemporary feminists agree that violence in women is an area that needs to be addressed in order to understand the violent behavior of women from a sociocultural perspective.

STRATEGIES FOR SOCIAL CHANGE

There is widespread agreement among feminists on the notion that any effective strategies for change must be directed toward basic social changes in gender inequality. Feminists assert that social change must address cultural, political, and economic systems that perpetuate patriarchy and the exploitation of women. Individual intervention programs against violence such as shelters and therapy represent only the first step toward positive social change. Individual shelters have difficulty coping with widespread abuse and the high demand for services. Individual therapy is helpful in healing emotional damage but does not address societal changes.

Feminists, therefore, call for activism beyond the individual level to address violence at the systemic level. Typically, this takes the form of educational campaigns, advocacy groups, political action committees, consciousness-raising groups, and cooperative organizational alliances. According to a recent women's studies text, the basic social changes needed to address violence at the societal level mandate broad changes in patterns of gender socialization in areas such as education, politics, and economics to (a) challenge the objectification and commodification of women's bodies,

(b) change the legal definition of gender-based violence as a violation of basic human rights, (c) provide equitable economic access and development for women to promote security and independence, and (d) foster widespread collaboration and alliances to end violence against women.

—Elizabeth Swearingen

See also BATTERERS AND ABUSIVE PARTNERS; BATTERED WOMAN'S SYNDROME; CYCLE THEORY OF VIOLENCE; DOMESTIC VIOLENCE; ETHNIC CLEANSING; GENDER VIOLENCE; RAPE; VICTIMOLOGY; WOMEN AND VIOLENCE

Further Reading

Bowker, L. H. (Ed.). (1998). *Masculinities and violence.* Thousand Oaks, CA: Sage.

Chafetz, J. S. (1998). From sex gender roles to gender stratification: From victim blame to system blame. In K. A. Myers, C. D. Andersen, & B. J. Risman (Eds.), *Feminist foundations toward transforming sociology* (pp. 159-164). Thousand Oaks, CA: Sage.

Dines, G., Jensen, R., & Russo, A. (1998). *Pornography: The production and consumption of inequality.* New York: Routledge.

Emerick, N. M. (2001). *The Violence Against Women Act of 1994: An analysis of intent and perception.* Westport, CT: Praeger.

Hoffman, J. (2001). *Gender and sovereignty: Feminism, the state, and international relations.* New York: Palgrave.

Jacobs, S., Jacobson, R., & Marchbank, J. (Eds.). (2000). *States of conflict: Gender, violence, and resistance.* New York: St. Martin's.

Kirk, G., & Okazawa-Rey, M. (2001). *Women's lives: Multicultural perspectives* (2nd ed.). Mountain View, CA: Mayfield.

Martin, S. E., & Jurik, N. C. (1996). *Doing justice, doing gender.* Thousand Oaks, CA: Sage.

Pickup, F. (2001). *Ending violence against women.* London: Oxfam.

AGGRESSION: PSYCHOLOGICAL THEORIES

Aggression has been defined as the intention and the attempt to unduly control, harm, or destroy another individual by physical, social, emotional, or psychological means. This definition applies to aggression toward objects as well. Aggression can be active or passive; direct or indirect; and verbal or physical. Moreover, it can be carried out in an overt or covert manner. The words *aggression* and *violence* are often used interchangeably, but they actually have different meanings. For example, one can be aggressive and not be violent, yet a person who is violent is also being aggressive. Thus, aggression is the key ingredient in all violent actions. For the purpose of this entry, the type of aggression discussed herein is the type related to *criminal violence.*

Historically, aggression has been part of human nature and has been viewed from an evolutionary perspective as adaptive. Some argue that aggression represents a biologically or genetically programmed set of responses. However, if this were truly the explanation for aggression, the rates of violence across cultures, nations, and races would be more congruent. The view that aggression and violence are explainable by psychological factors provides a more workable foundation from which to build an understanding of its potential causes.

It is not to be discounted that aggression seems to have a relation to biological or genetic substrates, as well as more largely based sociological factors, for these likely contribute to the survival of the species. However, aggression and violence are not inevitable events in life. Thus, the psychological factors related to the aggressive and/or violent individuals reside as the mitigators of action. Aggressive and/or violent behaviors, like all other behaviors, are choices in which the perpetrator chooses to engage.

There are two types of aggression, *hostile/expressive* and *instrumental.* They are distinguished by the expected goals, or motivations, of the perpetrator of such acts. Hostile/expressive aggression is generally perpetrated in reaction to some form of anger-inducing situation, which could be in the form of a personal failure, an insult, or an actual physical assault. The use of hostile/expressive aggression has one goal: to make the victim(s) suffer. Hostile/expressive aggression is characterized by intense and individually disorganizing anger within the perpetrator.

Instrumental aggression, on the other hand, has its genesis in competition and desires on the part of the perpetrator, which may relate to objects, status, or both that are in the possession of others. Harm may be perpetrated toward the possessor, the object, and/or status themselves. However, even in cases in which harm toward the possessor of the object/status may not be intended, the perpetrator's perceived need to obtain or destroy what the victim has (and they have not) will lead them to engage in aggressive actions to accomplish their goal, regardless of the cost.

Several theories, or models, have been offered to explain aggression from a psychological perspective. Some of these have a degree of overlap with sociological or biological theories but are nonetheless predominantly psychologically driven.

PSYCHOLOGICAL THEORIES

Theory of Imitation

Gabriel Tarde (1843-1904), a forerunner of modern learning theorists, believed that people learn behaviors through imitating others. In regard to criminality, Tarde indicated three "laws of imitation": (a) persons in close and/or intimate contact will imitate each other's behaviors; (b) imitation of behavior moves from the "top down" (the youth will imitate the elder, the poor imitate the rich, etc.); and (c) the "law of insertion," which dictates that newly acquired behaviors are superimposed on previously acquired behaviors. Subsequently, these new behaviors either reinforce or discourage the prior customary behaviors of the group. Although this theory overlaps with sociological theories, it remains psychological primarily because the individual must still moderate the decision to imitate, or not, the observed behavior of others. Otherwise, people would all behave like automatons.

Psychoanalytic/Psychodynamic Theory

Psychoanalysis or psychodynamic psychotherapy was developed by Sigmund Freud during the late 1800s and early 1900s. In 1922, Freud postulated that there are three parts of the mind and that their interplay constitutes the structure of one's personality. The first part is the *id,* representing the unconscious biological drives or needs for food, sex, and other life-sustaining factors. The id is directed by the *pleasure principle,* which requires our impulses to be satisfied via instant gratification, without regard to the rights or needs of others.

The second part is the *ego.* The ego develops over the first few years of life as the child learns that impulses cannot always be instantly gratified. It is the ego that compensates, or mitigates, the demands of the id and guides the individual to maintain behavior within the boundaries of social convention. The ego is

directed by the *reality principle,* which accounts for the practical and conventional standards of society.

The third part is the *superego.* The superego also develops over time and is the representation of moral standards and values incorporated from one's parents, significant others, and the community. The superego has two elements, the *conscience* and the *ego ideal.* The conscience delineates right from wrong and forces the ego to control the id. The ego ideal represents the individual's idealized self-image. The superego is directed mostly by the conscience.

In regard to aggression and/or violence, the psychodynamic theory posits that the perpetrators of such acts have one of two deficits in their character structure of the id, ego, and superego. Some have developed a weak ego that is unable to moderate the impulsive demands of the id. Others have underdeveloped superegos, resulting in deficits in conscience. The psychoanalytic or psychodynamic theory is much more involved than this brief description, and the reader is encouraged to investigate its tenets through other sources.

Behavioral Theories

Although the psychodynamic theory implies that human beings are a compilation of conflicting drives, impulses, and controls that are largely outside our awareness, the behavioral theories see human beings differently. Behavioral theories speak more to the uniquely human characteristic of possessing the ability to exercise conscious control over our thought processes, motivations, and actions. Behavioral research has also shown little evidence that humans are innately dangerous and violent or that we are controlled by the instincts or impulses of the id. Behavioral theories maintain that behaviors are developed through our learning histories and through the processes of reinforcers and consequences. Therefore, the behavioral theories tend to view criminal aggression and violence as *learned responses* and not the representation of gross abnormalities or moral depravity.

Frustration-Aggression Hypothesis

In 1939, Dollard, Doob, Miller, Mowrer, and Sears postulated that aggression is the direct result of frustration. Although this makes intuitive sense, however, the difficulty with this notion is that frustration is difficult to define and measure. What one person finds frustrating, another may not. Moreover, a situation a person finds frustrating in one context may not seem frustrating in another context. Aggressive and/or violent behavior appears to be more complex than the frustration-aggression hypothesis suggests. In fact, research has shown that frustration does not always lead to aggression and that conversely, aggression does not always occur when one is frustrated. Nonetheless, it has been shown that higher levels of perceived frustration within the perpetrator will likely serve as a facilitator of aggression.

Berkowitz revised this model by indicating that for frustration to occur, the perpetrator must have previously expected or anticipated the attainment of a goal or desire. Berkowitz's revised frustration-aggression hypothesis offers five elements. First, the individual is prevented in some manner from attaining a goal or desire. Second, frustration is the result, which produces a negative feeling state, usually anger. Third, the negative feeling state then predisposes or readies the individual to act aggressively. Engaging in aggressive action will depend on the individual's learning history, interpretation of the circumstances, and pattern of responding to frustrating conditions and the relative presence of aggression-eliciting stimuli in the environment. The fourth element that determines if aggression will be generated is the degree to which the perpetrator perceives the situation as intentionally placed on him or her. The fifth element is the degree to which the perpetrator perceives the level of frustration as aversive.

Berkowitz's revised frustration-aggression hypothesis considers the degree of cognitive mediation within the perpetrator of aggression to be a core factor in determining whether or not the individual engages in aggressive actions. This revision is also referred to as the *cognitive-neoassociation model.*

Excitation Transfer Theory

In 1988, Zillman postulated that physiological arousal can be readily generalized from situation to situation. This is a result of the fact that regardless of its genesis, physiological arousal slowly dissipates over time. Thus, preexisting arousal that is combined with an additional negative affective state may increase the likelihood of an aggressive response. This is most likely to occur when the residual arousal has declined to the point of being outside conscious awareness. In this manner, the perpetrator is unaware of residual arousal from a previous situation, which in turn increases the level of arousal toward the new and probably unrelated situation. Moreover, the risk of overreaction and aggression increases in this new situation. Although this theory is in line with the biological and genetic theories, it has at its base the level of individual psychological awareness of internal feeling states and the ability to govern one's choices of action accordingly.

Social Learning Theory

The notion of social learning theory implies a strong social component to aggressive behavior. This is not debated from the psychological perspective. In fact, it merely underscores the individual psychological processes in choosing which acts from our repertoire to engage in.

Social learning theory is most frequently associated with Albert Bandura. This theory suggests that the individual is an active problem solver: one who perceives, encodes, interprets, and makes decisions according to the parameters of his or her environment. Thus, social learning theory considers both the external factors and the internal factors as significant elements of behavioral action. It is imperative in social learning theory that individual factors be considered, such as perception, cognitions, expectations, competencies, and values. Social learning theory considers human beings to possess individual and unique worldviews and live according to those parameters.

Social learning theory assumes that we learn from observing and listening to those around us. Criminal aggression, therefore, is considered to be initially acquired through association and observation. However, whether or not the behavior is maintained is determined by the level and type of reinforcement it generates. Likewise, the more importance, or higher status, possessed by the model of the aggressive behavior, the more likely the observed aggression will be imitated. Moreover, these aggressive behaviors are likely to be more valued and imitated if the model receives no adverse consequences and/or acquires the goal.

There are three principle sources of aggressive behavioral models: (a) prominent and respected family members who tend to use aggressive tactics, (b) environmental circumstances in which the individual frequently witnesses aggression to solve a variety of problems, and (c) situations presented by the media.

Based on the type and value of the model and the reinforcement contingencies attached to aggressive behavior, the individual may still choose to refrain from engaging in aggressive actions. Social learning theory posits four factors that may facilitate an individual's choice to act aggressively: (a) being involved in an event that heightens physiological arousal, (b) possessing an assortment of aggressive skills acquired from others or the media, (c) holding an expectation that the aggressive action will produce an individually desired outcome, and (d) maintaining a belief that the aggressive behavior is considered appropriate or valued in the current social context. Nevertheless, the psychological factors within the individual account for the integration and delineation of these influential factors before an individual chooses to engage in an aggressive action.

Cognitive Theory

The variety of cognitive theories are too numerous and broad for this discussion. Thus, only two theories will be covered here: Kohlberg's moral development and information processing.

Kohlberg's Theory of Moral Development

Kohlberg (1969) postulated that human beings tend to progress through six stages of moral development. People tend to make decisions and judgments about right and wrong for different reasons, depending on the stage of development they have achieved. Kohlberg's six stages of moral development are as follows:

1. Right is obedience to power and avoidance of punishment.
2. Right is taking responsibility for oneself, meeting one's own needs, and leaving to others the responsibility for themselves.
3. Right is being good in the sense of having good motives, having concern for others, and possessing empathy.
4. Right is maintaining the rules of a society and serving the welfare of the group or society.
5. Right is based on recognized individual rights within a society, with agreed-upon rules or a social contract.
6. Right is an assumed obligation to principles applying to all humankind: justice, equality, and respect for human life.

Kohlberg classified individuals according to the stage of this model at which their moral development stopped. Kohlberg and his colleagues applied this model to criminals. They found that criminals had significantly lower moral development (e.g., Stages 1 and 2) than their noncriminal counterparts (e.g., Stages 3 and 4) from the same social background. Recent research has shown that those at the lowest stages of moral development are deterred from criminal aggression secondary to their fear of punishment. Those individuals in the middle stages of moral development are deterred from criminal aggression secondary to their consideration of the reactions of family and friends. Those individuals at the highest stages of moral development are deterred from criminal aggression secondary to their belief in a sense of duty to others, as well as a belief in universal human rights.

Information Processing

The tenants of information-processing theories use mental perceptions within the individual to understand their thoughts, emotions, decisions, and corresponding behaviors. According to the information-processing model, when an individual makes a decision, it is preceded by a sequence of cognitive processes, including (a) encoding the stimuli into information that can be interpreted, (b) a search of memory and learning history for a proper response and potential alternate actions, (c) a final, summative review of the information acquired and processed, and (d) the decision to act or not.

According to this theory, the aggressive individual processes information incorrectly. One explanation of this is the notion of the *cognitive schema*, or mental script. These schemata are cognitive patterns learned early in childhood that govern the individual's interpretation, reaction, and expectation of outcome of any given circumstance. Aggressive individuals, therefore, have learned improper schemata. When individuals develop such cognitive patterns, they perceive others as being more hostile and aggressive to them and intending to cause them harm, though there is actually no real, objective threat. In other words, a disturbed, or negative schema renders the individual to negatively misread the cues available and increases their risk of becoming aggressive. This is referred to as the *hostile attribution model*. It may, for example, be a particular situational factor in cases of date/acquaintance rape.

OTHER ASPECTS OF AGGRESSION

Mental Illness and Aggression

Certain mental illnesses present with higher levels of aggression than others. However, it is to be noted that the majority of individuals suffering from mental illnesses are not criminally aggressive or violent. In fact, only approximately 20% of those incarcerated in the prison setting are diagnosably mentally ill on Axis I of the *DSM-IV* (*Diagnostic and Statistical Manual of Mental Disorders,* 4th ed.). Nonetheless, certain mental illnesses, such as psychotic disorders and mood disorders, may produce symptoms that lower the threshold of aggressive behavior. Most of these individuals, with proper medication and medication compliance, can significantly reduce their risk of aggressive and/or violent behavior.

The two largest risk factors related to a mentally ill individual becoming aggressive and/or violent are (a) failure to take medication and (b) abusing illicit substances and/or alcohol. The number of offenders who are found insane is very small. Nonetheless, some are found not guilty by reason of insanity and therefore not culpable for their aggression because the aggressive action was judged to be a direct result of a severe mental illness.

Personality and Aggression

Although it was noted that the majority of inmates in prison do not have a diagnosable mental illness, when one considers Axis II of the *DSM-IV,* or personality disorders, significantly more inmates are diagnosable, usually with *antisocial personality disorder. Personality* is defined as the relatively stable pattern of behavior, thoughts, and emotions that distinguish the individual. Personality also represents the characteristic manner in which one adapts to life's demands and the patterned manner in which one's interpersonal relationships evolve, maintain, or disintegrate. Some personality, or characterological, disorders and syndromes are related to aggression and/or violence. These would include antisocial personality disorder and, although not diagnosable, the syndromes of sociopathy and psychopathy. They typically involve a considerable disregard for lawful behavior; a disregard for, or the exploitation of, the rights and/or safety of others; and a history of criminal conduct. The field of personality theory is extensive

and beyond the scope of this manuscript. The reader is encouraged to explore these theories through other works.

Intelligence and Aggression

The association of low intelligence and aggression has been debated for decades. The fact remains that any correlation between these two factors is low, at best. Certainly, one could argue that the relationship exists when assessing a population of inmates. However, this does not account for the aggressive individuals who have not been incarcerated. Likewise, it does not account for gender differences and/or cultural differences. Moreover, some research indicates that IQ scores tend to decline slightly with age, yet criminal aggression also tends to decline with age, so according to the hypothesis, one would then expect higher levels of aggression.

Clearly, this is an area that has some research merit, however, for it has been shown that higher education levels tend to act as a protective factor for those who are at risk along other actuarial risk factors. This does not explain why serial killers tend to be of average to above average in intelligence. The connections between intellectual level and criminal aggression will likely be debated for some time.

Fantasy and Aggression

In his work with serial killers, Eric Hickey has indicated a significant and individual psychological factor in aggressive and/or violent behavior: fantasy. Hickey indicates that long before perpetrators enact their aggression, they engage in a pattern of fantasy development. These fantasies progress from an initial fleeting thought, through a period of increasing frequency and refinement, to approximation behaviors (i.e., trial runs), and finally, to the aggressive action. This is clearly the case with sexual offenders, as well as most other types of offenders. It is a metacognitive process in which offenders' thinking is related to their aggressive ambitions. This is a deeply individual and psychologically based phenomenon driven by the uniquely perceived internal interpretations of the aggressive individual and the world in which they believe themselves to exist.

—Marlene Deal

See also Diagnostic and Statistical Manual of Mental Disorders; Mentally Disordered Offenders; Predicting Violent Behavior; Psychopaths

Further Reading

American Psychiatric Association. (1994). *Diagnostic and statistical manual of mental disorders* (4th ed.). Washington, DC: Author.

Bandura, A. (1983). Psychological mechanisms of aggression. In R. G. Geen & E. I. Donnerstein (Eds.), *Aggression: Theoretical and empirical reviews* (Vol. 1). New York: Academic Press.

Bartol, C. (2002). *Criminal behavior: A psychosocial approach* (6th ed.). New Jersey: Prentice Hall.

Berkowitz, L. (1989). Frustration-aggression hypothesis: Examination and reformulation. *Psychological Bulletin, 106,* 59-73.

Dollard, J., Doob, L. W., Miller, N. E., Mowrer, O. H., & Sears, R. R. (1939). *Frustration and aggression.* New Haven, CT: Yale University Press.

Eysenck, H. J. (1996). Personality and crime: Where do we stand? *Psychology, Crime & Law, 2,* 143-152.

Hare, R. (1993). *Without conscience: The disturbing world of the psychopaths among us.* New York: Pocket Books.

Hickey, E. W. (2002). *Serial murderers and their victims* (3rd ed.). Belmont, CA: Wadsworth.

Katz, J. (1988). *Seductions of crime: Moral and sensual attractions to doing evil.* New York: Basic Books.

Kohlberg, L. (1969). *Stages in the development of moral thought and action.* New York: Holt, Rinehart & Winston.

Simon, R. I. (1996). *Bad men do what good men dream: A forensic psychiatrist illuminates the darker side of human behavior.* Washington, DC: American Psychiatric Press.

Toch, H. (1997). *Violent men: An inquiry into the psychology of violence.* Washington, DC: American Psychological Association.

Zillman, D. (1988). Cognitive-excitation interdependencies in aggressive behavior. *Aggressive Behavior, 14,* 51-64.

AGGRESSION: SOCIOLOGICAL THEORIES

Why do individuals commit violent acts that injure or kill other people? This is perhaps the most difficult question for society to grapple with because there are so many types and levels of violence that finding a simple answer is impossible. Nevertheless, theorists have developed a range of explanations that include biological, psychological, and sociological perspectives on the causes and control of violent behavior.

The sociological explanations may be the most problematic because they suggest that it is not the individual criminal who is solely errant but that more broadly, something about society is responsible for producing violent behavior. When cross-cultural comparisons are performed, it is clear that some societies experience far greater violence than others. Therefore, an examination of sociological theories of violence can be particularly enlightening. Some of the most prominent types of sociological theories include social disorganization theory, criminal learning theory, strain and subcultural theories, labeling theory, and critical theories. Many of these theories deal with crime in general, but also speak to the problems of violence.

SOCIOLOGICAL THEORIES

Social Disorganization Theory

One of the persistent features of violence is that much of it occurs in the same neighborhoods, generation after generation. Although a variety of cultures and nationalities may have passed through these neighborhoods, violence and crime remain consistent features. These high-crime neighborhoods are characterized by low social economic status, mobility (people moving in and out), and ethnic heterogeneity (residents of varied cultural backgrounds). Consequently, early 20th-century theorists connected with the sociology department at the University of Chicago speculated that the social disorganization of the community contributed more to the production of crime and violence than did the motivation of individuals. By strengthening the institutions of the community such as schools and recreational centers, it was believed that crime could be successfully addressed.

Criminal Learning Theory

According to sociologist Edwin Sutherland's theory of differential association, crime is learned from parents, peers, society, and especially from friends. Crime and violence are more likely to be learned from deviant peers than from law-abiding ones. When criminal behavior is learned, the education includes not only the motivation for committing the crime but also the techniques, rationalizations, and attitudes that allow one to believe that the crime is necessary or desirable. The likelihood that crime is learned is mediated by the *frequency* of criminal associations, the *intensity* of the relationships, when the relationship happens *(priority),* and how long the relationships last *(duration).* Consequently, the more contact on has with undesirable associates, the more likely one is to learn criminal behavior. Parents are constantly screening their children's friends to ensure that their children are not being exposed to values and attitudes that favor the commission of criminal or violent behaviors.

Strain Theory

Strain theory is a perspective developed by Robert Merton that suggests that individuals experience frustration or strain from their inability to realize their aspirations. Merton says that in the United States, there is a cultural goal of material wealth and that people are judged by their economic well-being. The approved cultural means to this goal of wealth demand that we work hard, delay gratification, and play by the rules. Some individuals experience strain when they find racism, class biases, or other structural barriers systematically blocking the culturally approved means to their goals.

Merton specifies several adaptations to this perceived strain: conformity, innovation, ritualism, retreatism, and rebellion. For the purposes of explaining violence, *innovation* is the most interesting of these adaptations. Rather than getting a good job and working hard to achieve the goals of financial wealth, the innovator will resort to physically taking money from others by way of, for example, mugging, bank robbery, or convenience store holdups. In many ways, society doesn't care how one obtains money, just that one has money. Strain theory is an example of the old saying "The end justifies the means." The culturally approved goal of obtaining wealth is more firmly fixed in society than the culturally approved means of getting a good education and working hard. Therefore, it is not surprising that many individuals use crime and violence as means to satisfy their desires for wealth.

Subcultural Theory

According to some theorists, individuals commit crimes and violence because they adhere to a different set of values than does the dominant society. Cultural deviance and subcultural theorists examine commitment to society from the viewpoint of the delinquent or criminal and find that these types are simply obeying a different set of rules or norms. Walter Miller suggests that there is a lower-class culture whose "focal concerns" are centered on deviant behavior rather than conformity. These focal concerns are trouble, smartness, toughness, fate, and autonomy. This set of values brings youth in constant conflict with authority figures. The emphasis on physical prowess and excitement often lead to the commission of violent crimes. From the viewpoint of a youth, these behaviors are a mark of status and a reason for self-esteem, rather than a reason to feel shame.

Another theorist, Elijah Anderson, has articulated a "code of the street" to explain how minority youths have developed a subculture of violence that governs their behavior in public places. According to Anderson, youth seek to display their status by flamboyant dress, overtly masculine behavior, and developing a reputation for "having nerve." If someone disrespects the youth, even though the affront might be inadvertent, the code of the street demands that it be met with an immediate threat or physical violence. Consequently, slight encounters such as bumping into someone, which may warrant an "Excuse me" in the dominant society, could be grounds for physical violence on the streets of the inner city.

Labeling Theory

Labeling theory does not address why individuals commit crimes or violent behaviors directly, but rather how those caught up in the criminal justice system develop self-concepts that encourage them to commit more crimes. When the tag or label of *delinquent* or *criminal* is placed on youth, it has implications for both how society will treat them and how they will react.

According to labeling theory, when such labels are successfully applied to an offender, that individual will be shunned, shamed, and denied opportunities by society. It may be difficult for the offender to find employment, maintain relationships, or escape the surveillance of law enforcement, because the label of criminal acts as a stigma that causes others to expect from the offender a higher standard of conduct than most people are held to. Consequently, even minor violations of the law may result in severe sanctions because of the offender's history. The "Three Strikes and You're Out" laws in states such as California demonstrate how the label of *repeat offender* can result in long prison sentences for minor crimes.

A second part of the labeling perspective that has more relevance in a discussion of deviance is concerned with the change in self-concept of those who are stuck with the criminal label. Secondary deviance involves the internalization of the deviant label. Offenders who are treated as dangerous and untrustworthy people start to act that way. Labeling theory argues that a self-fulfilling prophecy develops in which offenders become the criminals they are treated as. This process limits to an even greater degree the legitimate opportunities for the offender to engage in lawful employment and healthy relationships. Violent behavior becoming part of the offender's identity can lead to a vicious cycle of crime, criminal sanction, and more crime.

Some labeling theorists suggest that it would be best for the criminal justice system not to insert minor offenders into the "jaws of the justice system," because the process accelerates their criminal identities. For a great many youth, minor crime and violence are part of rites of passage that are quickly discarded. According to this theory, by arresting and punishing minor infractions of the law, the criminal justice system makes the youth into serious criminals.

One of the policy implications of labeling theory that would directly affect the rate of violence in society is the issue of decriminalization. When society has laws that are not supported by large parts of the population, widespread law breaking often results in violence. The prohibition of alcohol was ineffective but had the unintended consequence of establishing a violent and dangerous black market. Many argue that today's "war on drugs" is having the same impact by forcing many otherwise law-abiding citizens to engage in dangerous and sometimes violent behaviors to buy drugs, obtain money to buy drugs, and/or protect their illegal drug-selling activities.

Critical Theories of Violence

A number of criminological theories locate the problems of crime and violence not in the individual offender, but in the very structure of society. Conflict theory seeks to explain why crime and violence are such prominent features of lower-class neighborhoods by examining the inequities experienced by the less privileged as they are affected by the power of society's elite classes. Those with power are able to manipulate the criminal justice system and the law-making process to ensure that their interests are protected.

Although some might consider this a rather cynical way to view society, critical theorists believe that there is a concentrated and influential campaign by the powerful to maintain and enhance their position in society. One need only look at the differences in the way street crimes are punished compared with corporate or white-collar crime. According to critical theorists, the rich and powerful have many advantages over others in their contact with the criminal justice system. They make the laws, name the judges, and are able to hire high-priced, competent attorneys. Because of the disadvantages suffered by lower classes of people, they are forced to be both the perpetrators and the victims of violence. Corporations that pollute rivers, make dangerous products, or employ people in unsafe working environments greatly harm society, but their practices are not recognized as being violent in the same way that a teenager who mugs a tourist would be.

Another critical theory of violence involves the expectations of sex role behavior. Feminist criminologists point out that women are victims of spousal abuse, sexual abuse, and rape. Because of the patriarchal nature of our society, women are denied opportunities, victimized by the favoritism shown to the male role, and given second-class citizenship. Feminists see a range of ways in which women suffer from violence, from pornography to homicide. In many countries, women and children are victims of extreme forms of violence because men control the social institutions of society that provide the legitimacy for female subjugation. In some countries in the Middle East and Asia, a husband, father, or brother may kill a teenage girl who has premarital sex, because it dishonors the family. Even in the case of rape, the girl is considered a blight on the family honor and can expect severe punishment, or possibly death, from her male relatives. Feminist criminologists view this extreme example as part of a continuum of patriarchal violence against women that is found around the globe.

CONTEXT

This review of the sociological theories of violence has not been exhaustive. There are many more theories, and many of the ones presented here have fascinating variations that highlight different aspects of violence.

In addition, the biological and psychological theories of violence that are not covered here sometimes overlap with sociological theories in their focus and applicability. It is sufficient to say that the study of violence includes a wide range of explanations because violence is a complicated and multifaceted feature of society.

—*John Randolph Fuller*

See also AGGRESSION, BIOLOGICAL, FEMINIST, AND PSYCHOLOGICAL THEORIES; GANGS; JUVENILE OFFENDERS; PREDICTING VIOLENT BEHAVIOR; VIOLENT BEHAVIOR

Further Reading

Meadows, R. J. (2001). *Understanding violence & victimization*. Upper Saddle River, NJ: Prentice Hall.

Moyer, I. L. (2001). *Criminological theories: Traditional and nontraditional voice and themes*. Thousand Oaks, CA: Sage.

Riedel, M., & Welsh, W. (2002). *Criminal violence: Patterns, causes, and prevention*. Los Angeles: Roxbury.

AIR RAGE

Until 10 years ago, most people were unaware that incidents of in-flight violence and disruptive behavior had occurred aboard commercial aircraft. However, airline employees had long been aware of incidents regarding problem passengers and the inherent safety threat posed by violent behavior aboard airborne airplanes.

In 1997, the Airline Pilot's Association discussed the issue at the first International Conference on Disruptive Passengers. The conference was attended by more than 200 people from diverse organizations, and the intent of the meeting was to use directed discussions to gain a better understanding of the problem and to determine how to best deal with the issue. The participants cited the causes of incidents of disruptive behavior as follows:

- 25%, alcohol intoxication
- 16%, seat assignments
- 12%, hostile, abusive, or threatening behavior
- 10%, tobacco issues
- 9%, carry-on luggage
- 8%, passenger perception
- 5%, food complaints
- 15%, undetermined causes

Soon after this conference, the media attached the catch phrase "air rage" to these incidents of misbehavior.

It is important to emphasize that air rage is not a new phenomenon. The first recorded incident occurred in a commercial flight in 1947, when an inebriated passenger boarded a flight in Miami that was bound for Cuba. He assaulted a fellow passenger with a bottle and injured two crewmembers who tried to subdue him. At the end of the flight, he was turned over to local authorities but was released due to jurisdictional questions about international flights. This incident led to the creation of the International Civil Aviation Organization (ICAO) and international laws that awarded jurisdiction over offenses committed onboard an aircraft to the country in which the aircraft was registered. To date, more than 170 countries have signed the agreement, making it the second most successful legal instrument in modern international civil aviation.

Another early incident of misbehavior occurred in 1950, when a mentally disturbed passenger assaulted a crewmember, and required the aircraft's first officer and two passengers to subdue him. In the 1960s, passenger disruption evolved from individual assaults to airline terrorism and hijacking, increasing the potential danger. In May 1962, the first aircraft was hijacked to Cuba. Within a few months, the United States government enacted legislation that made it a crime to commit or attempt to commit air piracy. As the threat of hijacking increased, the ICAO began work on another legal instrument that addressed the legal aspects of aircraft terrorism on an international scale. As a result of wide acceptance of these laws by countries worldwide, the number of incidents of aircraft hijacking decreased steadily. These incidents have not ceased, however, as evidenced by a recent skyjacking of an Afghani Airliner and the September 11, 2001, hijackings of four domestic airplanes by al-Qaeda terrorists, with the resultant destruction of the World Trade Towers in New York City and damage to the Pentagon.

An examination of the Federal Aviation Association (FAA) records of the 1970s reveals the types of behavior that cabin crews have faced for decades. They range from minor unruliness to overt violence, violation of smoking regulations, intoxication, bomb threats, and abuse. The records also indicate the increase in the number of these incidents. In 1978 and 1979 alone, there were approximately 40 reported incidents on the FAA Incident Database Web site.

This trend continued in 1980. At least four flights made unscheduled landings because of passenger problems. Two incidents of cockpit entry attempts were reported that year. From 1981 through 1989, there were at least 10 unscheduled landings, 10 physical assaults on crewmembers, one case of attempted cockpit entry, four incidents in which physical restraint was required, and one threat to blow up an airplane. In 1988, the Aviation Safety Reporting System (ASRS) began recording voluntary crewmember reports regarding airline safety concerns and incidents. To date, over 78,519 reports have been entered. Although this information is considered "anecdotal," it provides additional insight into what is happening in the air—but does not provide any comfort to the nervous air passenger.

The information collected in the 1990s is even more disquieting. In 1998, an industry report cited a 400% increase in disruptive incidents between 1993 and 1998. These incidents included an escalation of violence in which a disgruntled employee smuggled weapons aboard and used them to seriously injure crew members. Three of the most serious incidents occurred outside the United States and resulted in fatalities. The effects of disruption on cockpit routines and pilot concentration, especially during landing and takeoff, emphasize the danger posed to passenger safety. These disruptions have resulted in runway incursions, pilots flying the improper radials, and other deviations from standard cockpit procedures.

The problems that terminal and flight crews have experienced over the past five decades have resulted in mostly positive responses from the industry. Enhanced training of personnel, improvements in communication skills, and attitudes that encourage safety have been some of the improvements. A multidisciplinary approach toward understanding and reducing incidents involving psychologists, aviators, law enforcement, government, training professionals, and the flying public appears to be the most successful approach in dealing with these problems. Continued vigilance is vital because although disruptive passenger incidents are a factor in only a small fraction of all commercial flights, a single incident by one member of this small minority of passengers can directly impact hundreds, if not thousands, of lives in a very tragic manner.

—*Marlene Deal*

See also AERONAUTICAL MASS MURDER

Further Reading

Dahlberg, A. (2001). *Air rage: The underestimated safety risk.* London: Ashgate.

Sheffer, M. P. (2001). *The problem passenger: A history of airline disruption 1947 to present.* The Skyrage Foundation.

Thomas, A. R. (2001). *Air rage: Crisis in the skies.* Amhearst, NY: Prometheus Books.

CHARLES ALBRIGHT

Charles Albright was a serial killer in Texas between 1990 and 1991. He murdered several female prostitutes, engaging in paraphilic sexual behavior or autoerotic asphyxia, and in ritualistic trophy taking, surgically removing the eyeballs of his victims.

At the time of the murders, Charles was a 57-year-old husband and father, though he'd had an earlier history of juvenile delinquency, property crimes, and prior incarcerations. As a child, he experienced mental and emotional abuse, including rejection by his parents. In this unstable home environment, Charles developed an intense hatred for women, though as an adult, he often flirted with members of the opposite sex and enjoyed impressing them with his varied artistic talents. He was a skillful painter and musician, and women seemed to adore him. A very intelligent man, he was fluent (or at least claimed proficiency) in Latin, Spanish, and French, and became a biology teacher and skilled taxidermist. Charles had a great sense of humor and was portrayed as the class clown in college. He was also athletic, enjoyed coaching football, and played slow-pitch softball. People knew him as an affable man who knew how to mingle and be accepted in groups.

Yet this seemingly faithful family man had a disturbing side seldom seen by others. In fact, he was a consummate liar and con man, a true Jekyll-and-Hyde personality. Over time, he developed masochistic attitudes and carefully concealed his history of thefts, forging his college transcripts to make it appear that he had graduated. He was often unemployed and frequented prostitutes. In fact, he once referred to his biological mother as a prostitute, although there was no proof of his accusation. When he was 51 years old, he raped a 13-year-old girl but managed to minimize the incident.

From becoming increasingly sexually aggressive with women, Charles went on to murder several female prostitutes. He derived great satisfaction in bludgeoning and shooting his victims and also developed a fascination and obsession for their eyes. (He often attempted to paint "perfect" eyes but would sometimes do portraits without them because he felt he could not do them justice.) Autopsies performed on his victims revealed that their eyeballs had been surgically removed without damaging the eyelids. This trophy taking was his "signature." The eyes were never recovered.

While incarcerated in a state prison, Charles has continued his obsession with eyes. He subscribes to a magazine devoted to iridology and has kept the first issue of *Omni* magazine (October 1978), which displays the image of an eyeball on the cover as if it were floating in the air.

—*Eric W. Hickey*

Portions of this entry are drawn from *Serial Murderers and Their Victims,* 3rd edition (2002) by E. W. Hickey, published by Wadsworth: Belmont, CA.

See also Paraphilia; Serial Murder; Signature Killers; Trophy Taking

Further Reading

Hollandsworth, S. (1993, May). See no evil. *Texas Monthly,* pp. 92-140.

Matthews, J. (1996). *The eyeball killer.* New York: Zebra Publishers.

ALCOHOL AND AGGRESSION

Aggression can be demonstrated by verbal or physical attack and may be an emotional or instrumental expression. There has been growing support for the explanation that many violent behaviors result from a self-protective response to perceived aggression. Similarly, the frustration-aggression hypothesis supports the idea that an individual who experiences frustration is more likely to react aggressively due to cognitive error. It is not entirely clear how this relates to the relationship between alcohol consumption and aggressive or violent behavior. A growing body of scientific evidence suggests that there is not a direct link between the two. It seems more likely that the interaction of neurobiochemical, psychological, situational, and cultural variables can explain the ties between alcohol and aggression.

When an individual is in an inebriated state, cognitive functioning may be mediated by both situational and cultural variables. This is in part because of the limitations imposed on rationality and decision-making skills when one is in that state. People who have consumed substantial amounts of alcohol have greater difficulty in thinking clearly, making it harder for them to exercise sound judgment and substitute more acceptable behaviors, such as calm argument, for inappropriate aggressive responses. The information a person uses to guide his or her responses is reduced by the increasing amount of alcohol consumed. The person begins to focus on details of the situation, thereby impairing his or her ability to perceive the situation as a whole. This unstable perceptual ability narrows the individual's attention, which can lead to misunderstandings, misinterpretations, and flawed reactions. However, this information does not explain why the majority of people drink alcohol without becoming aggressive or why aggression and violence occur in the absence of alcohol.

Experiments conducted under controlled conditions confirm that the determinants of aggressive behavior in different cultural groups are cultural beliefs and social norms rather than alcohol effects. In fact, it was concluded that the cultural belief that alcohol causes aggression led subjects to become aggressive when administered a placebo. There is a large amount of cross-cultural variation in drinking behaviors. In some societies, alcohol is associated with violent behavior and antisocial stance. However, South American and Mediterranean societies, for instance, tend to remain peaceful and enjoy harmony when drinking. When the immediate social context is nonaggressive and cultural beliefs and norms inhibit aggression, drinking is highly unlikely to lead to aggression.

Neuropsychology has linked aggression and low frustration tolerance to cortical reactivity. Evidence that increased or decreased reactivity of the brainstem coupled with a decreased moderating capacity of the limbic or cortical areas will increase an individual's aggressivity has pointed to chronic traumatic stress, neglect, and dysregulated serotonin or norephinephrine systems as precipitators. Deprivation of key developmental experiences will result in persisting primitive and immature behavioral reactivity, which predisposes an individual to violent behavior. In later years, a loss of solid cortical functioning due to alcohol intoxication, dementia, or stroke will also result in losses of modulation of aggressivity, which is mediated by the brainstem and midbrain.

—*Yvonne Martinez*

See also SUBSTANCE ABUSE AND HOMICIDE

Further Reading

Milgram, G. G. (1993) Adolescents, alcohol and aggression. *Journal of Studies on Alcohol, Suppl. 11,* 53-61.

Perry, B. D. (2002, April 25). *Aggression and violence: The neurobiology of experience.* Available on the World Wide Web at Scholastic Teacher Resource Center: http://teacher.scholastic.com.

ALFRED P. MURRAH FEDERAL BUILDING, *See* OKLAHOMA CITY BOMBING

ANGELO, RICHARD (LONG ISLAND'S "ANGEL OF DEATH"), *See* POISONINGS: MEDICAL SETTINGS

ANGELS OF DEATH, *See* MEDICAL MURDERS; POISONINGS: MEDICAL SETTINGS

ANGER MANAGEMENT, *See* BATTERERS AND ABUSIVE PARTNERS

ANIMAL ABUSE, *See* MACDONALD TRIAD

ANTHROPOLOGY, *See* AGGRESSION: EVOLUTIONARY AND ANTHROPOLOGICAL THEORIES

ANTISOCIAL PERSONALITY DISORDER

Antisocial personality disorder (APD) is a diagnostic category of the *Diagnostic and Statistical Manual of Mental Disorders,* 4th Edition *(DSM-IV),* which is characterized by a "pervasive pattern of disregard for, and violation of, the rights of others that begins in childhood or early adolescence and continues through adulthood." Behaviors and characteristics associated with the disorder include irresponsibility, unstable interpersonal relationships, deceitfulness, manipulations, erratic work histories, unlawful behaviors, disregard for the safety of self or others, conning others for profit or pleasure, failure to conform to societal norms, superficiality, a lack of remorse for harmful behavior, and/or an indifference to the harm caused to others. These characteristics are not uncommon in other personality disorders. Furthermore, one or more of these characteristics can be displayed in an individual who would not fit the diagnostic criteria of APD. Due to these issues and others, the diagnosis of APD must be made by a qualified clinician using the specifics of the disorder and collateral information.

By virtue of being a personality disorder, APD indicates an inflexible, maladaptive, and persistent pattern of behavior that causes significant impairments in functioning or subjective distress; this excludes criminal, aggressive, or antisocial behaviors engaged in by an individual who does not match the diagnostic criteria for APD. Not everyone who commits a crime, takes advantage of others, or harms others suffers from APD. In addition to the above criteria, APD can be diagnosed only in someone over the age of 18 and in someone with a history of being diagnosed with a conduct disorder. However, the diagnosis cannot be made if the behaviors occur during the course of schizophrenia or a manic episode. It is important to note that not everyone with a conduct disorder will develop APD.

Individuals diagnosed with APD may suffer from other disorders, such as substance abuse, mood disorders, paraphilia, or a number of psychiatric disorders. The causes of APD are not yet fully understood, although it appears that both genetic and environmental variables are involved. Individuals diagnosed with APD have in some studies been shown to have unique neurological functioning and/or physiology such as slow frontal lobe activities and low serotonin levels. There is evidence for a familiar pattern indicating a genetic base. Children and adolescents diagnosed with a conduct disorder are at greater risk for developing APD if they experience abuse or neglect, unstable parental attachments, and/or inconsistent parental discipline. Research in this area must be read with a critical eye, given that most participants are institutionalized, involved in the criminal justice system, and/or in some sort of mental health treatment. The results are not always generalizable beyond the participants of the study.

Concerns have been expressed regarding this disorder. Some believe APD is overdiagnosed in certain populations (such as in minorities), whereas others believe it is underdiagnosed in certain populations (such as in females). The *DSM-IV* provides the following warning: "[APD] appears to be associated with lower socioeconomic status and urban settings. Concerns have been raised that the diagnosis may at times be misapplied to individuals in settings in which seemingly antisocial behaviors may be part of a protective survival strategy." Although this statement appears to apply to those living in urban areas, it could also pertain to prison settings. The *DSM-IV* goes on to warn that "Neither deviant behaviors (e.g., political, religious, or sexual) nor conflicts that are primarily between the individual and society are mental disorders unless the deviance or conflict is a symptom of a dysfunction in the individual."

—*Sarah Ferguson*

See also AGGRESSION: PSYCHOLOGICAL THEORIES; DIAGNOSTIC AND STATISTICAL MANUAL OF MENTAL DISORDERS; MENTALLY DISORDERED OFFENDERS; VIOLENT BEHAVIOR

Further Reading

American Psychiatric Association. (1994). *Diagnostic and statistical manual of mental disorders* (4th ed.). Washington, DC: Author.

Black, D. W., & Larson, L. (2000). *Bad boys, bad men: Confronting antisocial personality disorder.* London: Oxford University Press.

ARMENIAN GENOCIDE, *See* GENOCIDE

ARSON

U.S. ARSON TRENDS, PATTERNS, AND BASE RATES

Arson is a crime of violence. Incendiary and suspicious causes of firesetting or arson remain the number one cause of property damage due to fire in the United States. Arson sometimes targets people and can lead to homicide. In 1999, for the 5th straight year, juvenile firesetters accounted for half or more of those arrested for arson. In 1999, the number of incendiary and suspicious structure fires was 72,000, and the death toll was 370. From 1980 to 1999, the death toll was 16,018. From 1980 to 1998, there were 45,000 incendiary and suspicious vehicle fires; 115,000 incendiary or suspicious fires set in grass, brush, and wildlands; and 61,999 civilian injuries. Property damage to structures and vehicles caused by incendiary and suspicious fires totaled $1.281 billion in 1999. Adding outdoor fires and fires of other unknown cause to that figure, losses to arson or suspected arson totaled around $2 billion.

The base rate for arson and fires of suspicious origin is about 100 per 100,000 reported fires started in the United States. An estimated 7% to 8% of the estimated incendiary or suspicious fires can be linked to illegal drug activity. Of arson arrestees, 6.9% were under the age of 10, and 35.8% of were under the age of 15. According to the FBI statistics, 17% of 1999 arson offenses were solved by arrest. Of all arson arrests, 2% lead to conviction. Most arson—80% to 85%—is never solved.

In 1998, children started 67,490 fires, 70% in grass or outdoor trash. They caused 232 civilian deaths and 1,896 civilian injuries. Direct property damage was $234.7 million. From 1980 to 1998, children accounted for 7,141 civilian deaths, and there were 47,021 civilian injuries. In recent years, 2 out of 5 of preschool deaths were related to the fireplay of children, most of them less than 6 years of age.

FIRESETTING AND ARSON

The term *firesetting* is used in addition to the term arson, because the former term more aptly encompasses both the incendiary and curiosity (pathological and nonpathological) tendencies of some juveniles. Considering that juveniles are responsible for more than 50% of arsons, some discussion of this group's contribution to the overall problem is relevant. The crime of arson generally requires an intentional act on the part of an individual to maliciously burn the property of another. Convicting a juvenile of arson is sometimes difficult because of statutes that link culpability to age, even when violence was intended by a juvenile's firestarting. To more adequately discuss the behaviors and risk factors associated with arsonists and juvenile firesetters, it might be appropriate to first discuss, in general, the characteristics thought to produce this often devastating behavior.

The Etiology of Deviant Fire Behavior

The dynamic-behavioral formulation of firesetting is a way of conceptualizing firesetting, arson, false-alarm setting and other forms of deviant fire behavior. It states that such behavior occurs as a function of the interaction between dynamic historical factors that predispose the firesetter/arsonist toward a variety of maladaptive and antisocial acts; historical environmental factors that have taught and reinforced firesetting as acceptable; and immediate environmental contingencies that encourage the continuation of fire deviant behavior. Independent variables such as personality, psychosocial conditions, and environmental factors predict the occurrence of the dependent variable, fire deviant behavior. Personality and individual characteristics consist of demographic, physical, emotional, motivational, and psychiatric variables. Social issues relate to family, peer, and other social variables. Environmental conditions concern the events, thoughts, feelings, and reinforcement that occur immediately prior to, during, and after firesetting. These variables interact in such a way as to produce deviant fire behavior or increase the risk of that behavior reoccurring.

Juvenile Risk Factors

Research suggests that there are sets of variables that describe the risk factors that produce firesetting in childhood. It is noteworthy that a reasonably high percentage of adult arsonists acknowledge having set fires when they were children. Thus, there is a connection between many of the early risk factors for juvenile firesetters and risk factors for adult arsonists. Unfortunately, comprehensive studies focused on specifying the base rate of adult arsonists who have set fires as children have not been performed.

When evaluating juvenile firesetters, especially those 10 years of age or under, one might frequently assume that the fire was either accidental or due to curiosity. When a child sets a fire, especially a young child, it is typical to infer that there is no pathological element to the firesetting and also that violence to persons or property was not intended. Many members of the justice system, as well as the mental health system, believe that children—especially those under 7 years old, but even as old as 14—lack the *mens rea* to intentionally set a fire. This view is less acceptable to those in the fire service and law enforcement professions and to others who have focused their attention on juvenile firesetting.

Of the juveniles who set fires, perhaps 60% set fires out of curiosity and thus by definition do not set fire with a malicious intent to manifest violence. The remaining 40% of juveniles who set fires do so in a violent manner, with motivations similar to those in the adult population of arsonists. (As will be seen, juvenile risk factors for firesetting parallel the risk factors for adult arsonists.)

Juveniles who set fires generally come from problematic family backgrounds and are often raised by single parents. Frequently, the father is out of the home, or if still in the home manifests a relatively distant relationship with the (usually) male firesetter. The personalities of many juvenile firesetters are affected by a lack of appropriate parenting to the extent that the juvenile often appears quite unassertive and lacking in social skills. As such, the juvenile rarely manifests appropriate peer relationships. He may be extremely passive and unable to interact appropriately with peers or may manifest a false bravado, interacting with delinquent/antisocial peers but never fully developing age-appropriate peer relationships.

Significant school problems are usually a function of poor motivation and, often, poor parental supervision. Firesetters are usually of at least average intelligence. Often, they are quite bright, setting a significant number of fires before being caught. It is believed that many firesetting juveniles suffer from attention deficit-hyperactive disorder. This hypothesis requires further research.

Firesetting during childhood or adolescence does not occur in a behavioral vacuum. These youngsters engage in a variety of other inappropriate behaviors including truancy, stealing, and other forms of aggression that are more property focused than not. A significant percentage of juvenile firesetters engage in property crimes in response to frustration rather than asserting themselves or aggressing in a more direct manner. In other words, they will attack one's property instead of one's person. Juveniles, as well as adults, who use fire against persons are significantly more disturbed than those who do not.

Many firesetting juveniles will manifest psychiatric diagnoses. Significant psychiatric disorders will put youngsters at risk for a variety of maladaptive behaviors, of which firesetting appears to be a priority response. High risk for firesetting can be attributed to the presence of the previously noted factors, a lack of appropriate early supervision relative to issues of fire safety, and inappropriate parental response to fireplay.

Adult Risk Factors

The risk factors for firesetting in an adult are quite similar to the factors identified for juveniles, and accordingly, most adult arsonists admit to having set fires or engaging in significant fireplay as children or adolescents. The typical arsonist is a white male between 25 and 32 years of age. He is unemployed or in a semiskilled job, often dissatisfied with his occupational status. He has no criminal history, but frequently has difficulties in his interpersonal relationships and passive qualities that presage his focus on property destruction. The early risk factors in juvenile arsonists, such as family dysfunction, peer problems, school issues, behavioral dysfunction, and psychiatric difficulties, appear to have their adult parallels.

VIOLENCE AND DANGEROUSNESS

Needless to say, any child or adult who is careless with fire or who intentionally sets a fire is dangerous and capable of causing significant damage to human life and property. Curious young children who have no intent to do harm or who are too young to form the intent to engage in arson can nonetheless start deadly fires. There is no correlation between psychopathology and the amount of damage caused by a fire. A 3-year-old can cause as devastating a fire as an adult pyromaniac. No matter who starts them, fires are potentially lethal.

There are at least eight types and 25 or more subtypes of firesetters/arsonists. The dynamic-behavioral formulation helps to discern the motives that form the basis for their deviant fire acts. It is equally important

to recognize the reinforcement obtained by these individuals in order to more fully understand the motives for firesetting, the need to continue firesetting, and the potential for violence.

Violence, or the propensity for violence, is perceived to operate on a continuum. The degree of a firesetter's/arsonist's damage to persons or property and/or the intensity of his intention to cause injury, death, or severe property damage defines his place on that continuum. Understanding the issues inherent in each firesetter/arsonist type, what motivates each type, and how these factors interact with relevant reinforcers for deviant fire acts helps one to predict the individual's potential for violence and his propensity for repeating these acts.

Reinforcement for Arson/Firesetting

The dynamic-behavioral formulation suggests that three primary types of reinforcement predispose the firesetter/arsonist to repeat his behavior: *sensory, cognitive,* and *concrete.* Each form of reinforcement may be observed in one or more of three situations related to firesetting/arson incidents. The first concerns the actual setting of a fire or the observance of a fire. The second concerns the object or objects burned. The third concerns the changes that occur in the aftermath of a fire (see Table 1).

It will be apparent from looking at the examples in Table 1 that more than one type of reinforcement can be relevant to a set fire. In fact, a sensory reinforcer often has a cognitive component, as in the case of an arsonist who sets a fire to feel a sense of power and control. One may find that a physiological state corresponds to the expressed feeling of elation, as well as a cognition that represents an internal state of mastery over the environment. Does the individual set the fire to attain the physiological state, or is he primarily reinforced by a fantasy of omnipotence and power? Also, some concrete reinforcers may have a strong cognitive component, as in the case of a murderer covering up a crime by burning the evidence, then manifesting anger reduction, a sense of completed revenge, or peace of mind, believing that he has "gotten away" with the crime.

Types of Firesetters/Arsonists

The first column of Table 2 reflects a way of looking at and grouping those who engage in deviant fire

Table 1   Examples of Reinforcement for Firesetting/Arson

Reinforcement for Setting and Observing the Fire, Burning Specific Objects, and Events Caused by the Fire

Sensory Reinforcement	Cognitive Reinforcement	Concrete Reinforcement
Elation	Power	Insurance money
Sexual arousal	Revenge reduction	Specific reward
Anxiety reduction	Hate reduction	Money payoff
Depression reduction	Control	Rehire for arson
Tension release	Anger reduction	Crime cover-up
Curiosity	Jealousy payback	
Sensory arousal	Revenge completion	
Power	Emotional pain reduction	
Control	Peace of mind	
Happiness	Sense of hope	
Excitation	Peer attention	
Pleasure		
Spiritual elation		

acts. Although it may appear that each of the major six pathological types (exclude *accident* and *curiosity*) reflect a homogeneous motive, this is not the case. There is a similarity of motivational issues within a given type but there is also significant variability. In any given case, there is also a tendency for more than one type of motivation to apply, and these factors can be fluid and can vary with the changing intensity and valence of reinforcement.

The 25 pathological subtypes reflect a variety of situations typical of fire deviant criminal behavior. As examples, the *interpersonal* type suggests one who was spurned and burns the house of an estranged lover. This type may reflect one who has been abused and uses fire to call attention to his plight. The antisocial qualities of the *vandalistic* arsonist are illustrated by the criminal's lack of focus on, and opportunistic choice of, what is burned. This is contrasted with the *psychotic* arsonist's focus on a target that has significant meaning and is often inexorably enmeshed with his delusional system.

Of special interest are the subtypes that are linked to homicide. They include the *interpersonal, cover-another-crime, hate, paranoid, psychotic, mass hysteria,* and *attention-to-cause* subtypes. Although it is certainly possible that other firesetter types have planned and committed homicides, compared with other arsonist subtypes, these seven subtypes appear to have a relative propensity toward that kind of crime. There may be a similarity between the *interpersonal* type and the *hate* type; the interpersonal difficulties between the arsonist and his victim may encompass

hate. However, the hate focus of an arsonist does not necessarily involve an interpersonal issue. The paranoid may act under the impression that murdering someone in an inhabited dwelling is called for by his system. The *attention-to-cause* subtype, at times motivated by delusional ideation, can plan and kill an individual or can engage in multiple acts of domestic terrorism.

Types of Firesetters/ Arsonists and Reinforcement

The literature concerning arson and firesetting was strongly influenced by the Freudians. Thus, early typologies focused on intrapsychic conflicts and other psychodynamic issues. In particular, they focused on urethro-erotic issues. Presently, theorists from other orientations as well as neo-Freudians tend to focus more on the aggressive aspects of firesetting and arson. Although typologies in general tend to be descriptive, sometimes reflecting general behavioral observations and sometimes theoretical orientations, typologies seem most beneficial when they reflect on issues that ultimately allow for more efficient risk assessment, diagnosis, and/or treatment.

The types and subtypes of firesetters/arsonists listed in Table 2 are all dangerous. Most have the potential for violence. Not all, however, commit homicide. The dynamic-behavioral formulation suggests that an analysis of the reinforcement history of a firesetter/ arsonist will provide relevant information concerning that individual's violence potential, as well as providing

Table 2   Confluence of Factors That Help Predict Levels of Violence or Homicide

	Reinforcement From Setting/Observing Fire			Reinforcement From What Is Burned			Reinforcement From Fire Aftermath		
	Sensory	*Cognitive*	*Concrete*	*Sensory*	*Cognitive*	*Concrete*	*Sensory*	*Cognitive*	*Concrete*
Types of Firesetters									
Curiosity	Lo	None							
Accidental	None	None	None	None	None	None	None	None	None
Cry for Help/Crisis									
Interpersonal	Lo-Hi & Hom	Lo-Hi & Hom			Lo-Hi & Hom	Hi & Hom		Lo-Hi & Hom	Hi & Hom
Intrapersonal	Mod-Hi & Hom	Lo-Hi			Lo-Hi			Lo-Hi	
Vicarious	Mod-Hi	Lo-Mod			Lo-Mod			Lo-Mod	Lo-Mod
Would-be hero		Lo-Mod						Lo-Mod	Lo-Mod
Firefighter setter	Lo-Hi	Lo-Mod		Lo-Hi			Lo-Hi	Lo-Mod	Lo-Mod
Delinquent/ Antisocial									
Fire for profit						Mod-Hi			Mod-Hi
Cover another crime						Hi & Hom			Hi & Hom
Vandalism	Mod-Hi	Lo-Mod		Mod-Hi & Hom			Mod-Hi	Lo-Mod	Mod-Hi
Hate	Mod-Hi & Hom	Mod-Hi & Hom			Mod-Hi	Hi & Hom	Mod-Hi & Hom	Mod-Hi	Hi & Hom
Revenge	Mod-Hi	Mod-Hi		Mod-Hi	Mod-Hi	Mod-Hi	Mod-Hi	Mod-Hi	Mod-Hi
Severely Disturbed									
Paranoid	Mod-Hi & Hom	Mod-Hi & Hom		Mod-Hi & Hom	Mod-Hi & Hom		Mod-Hi & Hom	Mod-Hi & Hom	
Psychotic	Mod-Hi & Hom	Mod-Hi & Hom		Mod-Hi & Hom	Mod-Hi & Hom		Mod-Hi & Hom	Mod-Hi & Hom	
Sensory reinforcement controlled	Lo-Hi	Lo-Hi		Lo-Hi	Lo-Hi		Lo-Hi	Lo-Hi	
Pyromania	Lo-Hi	Lo-Mod		Lo-Hi	Lo-Mod		Lo-Hi	Lo-Mod	
Self-harm		Mod-Hi Suicide			Mod-Hi Suicide			Mod-Hi Suicide	

30

Table 2 (Continued)

	Reinforcement From Setting/Observing Fire			Reinforcement From What Is Burned			Reinforcement From Fire Aftermath		
	Sensory	*Cognitive*	*Concrete*	*Sensory*	*Cognitive*	*Concrete*	*Sensory*	*Cognitive*	*Concrete*
Cognitively Impaired									
Retarded	Lo	Lo					Lo	Lo	
Cognitively impaired	Lo-Hi	Lo-Mod		Lo-Hi	Lo-Mod		Lo-Hi	Lo-Mod	
Fetal alcohol syndrome	Lo-Hi	Lo-Mod		Lo-Hi	Lo-Mod		Lo-Hi	Lo-Mod	
Fetal drug syndrome	Lo-Hi	Lo-Mod		Lo-Hi	Lo-Mod		Lo-Hi	Lo-Mod	
Learning disability	Lo-Hi	Lo-Mod		Lo-Hi	Lo-Mod		Lo-Hi	Lo-Mod	
Sociocultural									
Mass hysteria		Mod-Hi & Hom			Mod-Hi & Hom			Mod-Hi & Hom	
Attention to cause		Mod-Hi & Hom			Mod-Hi & Hom			Mod-Hi & Hom	
Community Approved									
Southern woodburner	Lo	Lo		Lo	Lo		Lo	Lo	
Religious		Lo	Lo		Lo	Lo		Lo	Lo
Satanic	Unknown	Unknown	Unknown	Unknown	Unknown	Unknown	Unknown	Unknown	Unknown
Wildland	Mod-Hi	Hi		Mod-Hi	Hi		Mod-Hi	Hi	

31

information necessary for the development of a treatment plan.

Table 2 suggests that an understanding of the interaction between motivational factors and type of reinforcement will provide important information concerning the intensity of violence that one may expect. Violence, for the sake of simplicity, is quantitatively defined as low (Lo), moderate (Mod), or high (Hi), and possibly encompassing homicide (Hom). (These rankings are based on the author's experience.) It remains for research to define each cell with an accurate description of violence intensity and rate of occurrence. It is believed that the valence as well as the intensity of a reinforcer will often be in states of flux, varying with the interactions between the dynamic historical variables, historical environmental variables, and immediate environmental contingencies discussed previously.

An analysis of the sequence of cognitive, sensory, and behavioral components of the firestarter will ideally eventuate in the identification of the most relevant variables (as noted in Tables 1 and 2). However, many additional factors may be considered when evaluating the violence potential of an arsonist. As an example, in the simplest form of an action systems approach, David Canter discusses the relevance of the firestart reflecting either an instrumental or an expressive quality. The expressive quality reflects a locus of cause within a person. Thus, the fire allows the arsonist to express an inner need or an emotion. The fire changes how the arsonist feels. The instrumental quality reflects an external locus of cause. The objective, usually some fire-related destruction, is a consequence that is (primarily) outside the arsonist's emotional state. The objective is instrumental. The instrumental or expressive qualities are then focused on a person or an object.

In its most robust form, this theory posits interactions between the psychological source of the firestart (internal or external events) and the effect of the fire (directed internally or externally). This dimension allows the evaluator to formulate additional subtypes, such as the repeat arsonist, the delinquent firesetter, the self-destructive arsonist with a psychiatric history, and the arsonist with a failed relationship.

Although the community's interest in fire, firesetters, or arsonists is as old as history, an empirical focus on this subject matter is not. The high cost in human suffering and property loss requires continued community focus on basic research, detection, and intervention programs.

—*Kenneth R. Fineman*

See also Juvenile Firesetters; Macdonald Triad; Methods of Murder

Further Reading

Canter, D., & Fritzon, K. (1998). Differentiating arsonists: A model of firesetting actions and characteristics. *Legal and Criminological Psychology, 3,* 73-96.

Fineman, K. R. (1995). A model for the qualitative analysis of child and adult fire deviant behavior. *American Journal of Forensic Psychology, 13*(1), 31-60.

Fritzon, K., Canter, D., & Wilton, Z. (2001) The application of an action systems model to destructive behaviour: The examples of arson and terrorism. *Behavioral Sciences and the Law, 19*(5-6), 657-690.

Hall, J. (2001a). *U.S. Arson trends and patterns* (pp. 1-63). Quincy, MA: National Fire Protection Association.

Hall, J. (2001b). *Children playing with fire* (pp. 1-35). Quincy, MA: National Fire Protection Association.

Kolko, D. J. (2001) Firesetters. In C. R. Hollin (Ed.), *Handbook of offender assessment and treatment* (pp. 391-413). New York: Wiley.

Schwartzman, P., Stambaugh, H., & Kimball, J. (1998). Arson and juveniles: Responding to the violence (Report 095). *Major fires investigation project* (pp. 1-20). Washington, DC: United States Fire Administration, Federal Emergency Management Agency.

ARSONIST'S PORTRAIT

Ricki A. has spent several years in prison for serial arson. The tall, thin Hispanic male, 29 years old and gay, has set hundreds of fires. He was instrumental in making Fresno the "arson capital of California" until his arrest and incarceration. The fire and the men who fight the flames sexually motivate him. He likes to visit fire stations, meet the firemen, and learn all he can about the fire equipment and fire districts. Ricki has memorized all the boundaries of each fire district in Fresno. He sometimes set two fires in a district to cause more excitement. He watched the fire, and in his fantasies, he directed the firefighters in their work. Ricki collected a box of souvenirs from his 23 major fires and buried them in Fresno. He often drives by the area and thinks about digging up the trophies.

Ricki has a long history of other crimes, including prostitution at the age of 15, theft of a police car, fraud, sexual assault, burglary, impersonation of a police officer, and assault. He set fires in Fresno over an 11-year period, beginning at age 12 with trash fires and escalating to burning down businesses at night. No one was ever killed, although several persons were forced to evacuate an apartment complex when one of his fires spread out of control.

Indeed, there are no acceptable excuses for Ricki's criminal behavior, but there are reasons. Although highly dangerous today, he was once a true victim. His father abandoned the family when Ricki was a small child. When he was 5 years old, a neighbor sexually molested him and continued to do so for several years. The man subdued the boy into compliance by threatening to harm his own dog. He also abused the boy, for example, by inserting the barrel of a gun into the boy's rectum and pulling the trigger. Then, at age 14, Ricki was raped by a 24-year-old male he met while making crank phone calls.

Today, Ricki is a friendly, talkative person but masks tremendous anger toward his mother for not protecting him from the neighbor and for not meeting his child-hood emotional needs. He had craved attention so badly that abusive attention seemed better than none at all. Having been diagnosed as a paranoid schizophrenic, Ricki is now on parole and takes medication, seeing his parole officer and psychiatrist once a month. He has great difficulty in finding work because most employ-ers will not risk having an arsonist in the building. Ironically, Ricki never sets fires to places he is person-ally affiliated with, such as school, home, and work.

Unfortunately, the prognosis for Ricki is not good. He harbors pathological attitudes and behaviors and still maintains his interest in fire, collecting fire mem-orabilia and admitting to having urges and fantasies about starting fires, especially when he becomes stressed and anxious. He frequently calls the author (E.H.) at times like this, just to talk. As a way of cop-ing with his fire fantasies, Ricki now volunteers for the American Red Cross. In this capacity, he often gets to help out at the sites of fire emergencies, where he is in close contact with the fires and the firemen fighting them. For now, this seems to appease his personal desire to act out by setting his own fires.

—*Eric W. Hickey*

Portions of this entry are drawn from *Serial Murderers and Their Victims,* 3rd edition (2002) by E. W. Hickey, published by Wadsworth: Belmont, CA.

See also ARSON; ATTACHMENT DEFICIENCY
AND VIOLENCE; JUVENILE FIRESETTERS

ARYAN BROTHERHOOD

The Aryan Brotherhood originated on the West Coast during the 1960s, specifically in 1967 in the San Quentin State Prison, California Department of Corrections. The Brotherhood, which has members in prisons throughout the United States, exhibits an intense hatred of Jews and blacks, including members of black gangs such as the Crips, Bloods, and Black Guerrilla Family (BGF). Members are recognized by identifiers and symbols such as the shamrock clover leaf, the ini-tials "AB," swastikas, double lightning bolts, and the numbers "666." Membership in the Aryan Brotherhood has traditionally come from white male inmates. A life-long allegiance is a requirement, and a significant act of violence is commonly required before membership is earned. The Brotherhood has ties to the Aryan Nations, an Idaho-based paramilitary organization that advocates racial violence and white supremacy.

See also BLOODS; BLACK GUERRILLA FAMILY;
CRIPS; GANGS: DEFINITIONS; HATE CRIMES;
WHITE ARYAN RESISTANCE; WHITE SUPREMACISTS

—*Lisa Andrews*

ASIAN ORGANIZED CRIME,
See DRUG TRADE; ORGANIZED CRIME:
TRANSNATIONAL

ASPHYXIATION,
See METHODS OF MURDER

ASSASSINS

HISTORICAL PERSPECTIVE

Assassination of a high-ranking governmental offi-cial or other well-known personality has always been considered a special type of violence. The term *assassin* comes from the Arabic word *hashshashin* and is defined as the sudden or secret attack of a politically important person for hire or for fanatical reasons. Many assassins plan their attacks, and there is an abundance of evidence that some of these individuals follow their "prey" prior to the events. Understanding this type of individual lends another perspective on the multifaceted phenomenon of stalking. Assassination is as old as recorded history and as common as the morning headlines. Franklin Ford's classic *Political Murder: From Tyrannicide to Terrorism* is the most comprehensive text on the history of assassinations.

Ford points out that some civilizations have experienced a high rate of assassinations, whereas others have been relatively free of this form of violence. The early city-state of Athens had few assassinations. The political structure was such that the council or assembly could vote to dismiss members, and the citizens of Athens could publicly ostracize their political leaders. These mechanisms provided alternatives to the more drastic remedy of poison or the knife. Contrary to the movies depicting frequent assassinations of various Roman leaders, the Roman Empire was also relatively free from this type of killing for almost 400 years. Although the citizens of Rome engaged in personal vendettas and even stoning of individuals accused of private transactions, the public officials of Rome were considered immune from this form of violence. This immunity from assassination lasted until approximately 150 years before the birth of Christ.

One of the first organized groups of assassins was formed during the Middle Ages. Established at the end of the 11th century, the Order of Assassins, or *hashshashin*, was a secret Islamic sect founded by Hasan-i Sabbah, whose mission was to attack and kill Christians and the leaders of the Sunnites (the more moderate Muslims), who ruled their land. The sect seized the mountain of Alamut, in Northern Persia, and from that stronghold waged a campaign of terror and murder against their opponents.

The candidates for admission to the order were given hashish to drink and under its influence were taken to a secret tropical garden. On recovering their senses, they were told they were in paradise. After several days of drinking, eating, and engaging in sex, they were again drugged and returned to the shrine, and were told that if they obeyed the master—or were slain carrying out his orders—they would once again be transported back to paradise.

Many assassins carried out their attacks while under the influence of hashish. Although leadership of the order was hereditary, it drew its recruits from all segments of society. They committed every conceivable crime known to man, including the murder of numerous public officials in the Persian Empire. For about 150 years, the Order of Assassins held Persia and Asia Minor in terror. In 1256, the Mongols broke their hold on these regions. To this day, the name *hashshashin* is considered by many to be synonymous with the premeditated slaying of rulers.

During the 16th and 17th centuries, assassinations seemed to be caused more by mental illness than political ideologically. Francois Ravaillac assassinated Henry IV of France, claiming that he was ordered by God to kill the king. After a decline in political killings during the 18th century, assassinations of political leaders rose sharply during the 19th century. The Russian John Bellingham shot and killed Spencer Perceval in the lobby of the House of Commons, and Luigi Luccheni shot Empress Elizabeth of the Austria-Hungry Empire.

AMERICAN ASSASSINS

Assassinations of public officials in the United States have been studied and analyzed by a number of scholars, commissions, governmental agencies, and other interested private citizens. This republic has established quite a history of slayings in its relatively short existence of 200-plus years. The attacks include attempted and actual assassinations of political leaders, including presidents, governors, senators and congressmen, mayors, state legislators, judges, and other public officials. A wide variety of weapons or killing instruments have been used for these assassinations, but the weapon of choice appears to be the handgun. The following describe some of the most well-known incidents.

Several state governors have been killed and/or wounded, both while serving and after leaving office. For example, in 1963, Governor John Connally, of Texas, was shot and wounded while riding in a procession with President Kennedy, who died during the same incident.

Only two U.S. Senators have been victims of political violence during their terms of office. In 1859, California Senator David C. Broderick was shot dead in a duel by a political opponent. Louisiana Senator Huey Long is the only senator to have been assassinated.

Lee Harvey Oswald after his arrest for assassinating President John F. Kennedy in 1963. A few days later Oswald was shot to death by Jack Ruby. Several U.S. presidents have been the targets of assassins.

Source: Copyright © CORBIS.

Long was a controversial political figure in 1935. His assassin was Carl Weiss, 29 years old, a popular physician from a wealthy family. Weiss apparently shot and killed Long because of his announced plan to gerrymander Weiss's father-in-law, a prominent judge and political opponent of Long, out of office. The public's response to the killer was particularly unusual. Thousands of citizens, including prominent business, political, and social figures from all over the South, attended Weiss's funeral and declared him a hero.

Representatives in the U.S. Congress have been relatively safe from the assassin's bullet. One of the most famous assassination attempts of a congressman occurred in 1954. Three members of the Puerto Rican National Party entered the visitors' gallery in the Capitol Building and began shooting at congressmen in session. The men claimed to have acted so as to bring attention to the fact that Puerto Rico was still not

free. Five congressmen were injured during the attempt, but none of them died.

Several mayors and former mayors have died as a result of assassinations. In 1893, the mayor of Chicago, Carter Harrison, was shot and killed by Eugene Patrick Joseph Prendergast. Prendergast claimed that Harrison had promised him that he would appoint him as corporate counsel for the city. The media publicized the similarities between Harrison's death at the hands of a disgruntled office seeker and that of President Garfield, who died in the same way.

The presidency has been the target of a number of assassinations and attempted assassinations. There does not appear to be any correlation with party affiliation, public policies, or strong leadership. Table 3 summarizes the assassin, his or her target, and the date of the violence.

EVALUATING THE BEHAVIOR

Behavior Models

There have been two basic approaches to understanding American assassins: sociological and psychological models. The sociological model focuses on a number of factors in an effort to explain the frequency of assassinations in the United States. Some authorities argue that there is a relationship between social inequity and political violence, whereas others focus on the status or primary group relationships of assassins, such as occupational stability or martial status, to explain their actions.

The psychological model emphasizes the dysfunction and pathology of assassins. A number of scholars have proposed various psychological theories regarding assassins and have analyzed their psychological characteristics. Some have concluded that such people live in a fantasy world in which they act to carry out a scared mission that usually involves an attempt to kill the target.

Assassin Typologies

In an attempt to understand the motivation, characteristics, and types of assassins, a number of researchers have established assassin typologies. There is considerable controversy surrounding these efforts. Two respected and cited researchers in this area are discussed below.

James Clarke's 1982 text, *American Assassins, the Darker Side of Politics,* is considered a classic

Table 3   Presidential Assassinations and Attempts

Assassin	Target	Date
Richard Lawrence	President Andrew Jackson	1835
John Wilkes Booth	President Abraham Lincoln	1865
Charles Guiteau	President James A. Garfield	1881
Leon Czolgosz	President William McKinley	1901
John Schrank	Presidential Candidate Theodore Roosevelt	1912
Guiseppi Zangara	President-Elect Franklin Roosevelt	1933
Oscar Collazo and Griselio Torresola	President Harry Truman	1950
Lee Harvey Oswald	President John Kennedy	1963
Sirhan Sirhan	Presidential Candidate Robert Kennedy	1968
Arthur Bremer	Presidential Candidate George Wallace	1972
Lynette Fromme	President Gerald Ford	1975
Sara Jane Moore	President Gerald Ford	1975
John W. Hinckley Jr.	President Ronald Reagan	1981

examination of this form of public violence. Clarke established four classifications of assassins: Type I assassins are political in nature, Type II assassins are concerned with their own problems and only secondarily with causes, Type III assassins are psychopaths, and Type IV assassins are irrational and suffer from delusions.

Type I: These assassins view their acts as a sacrifice of themselves for a political ideal. They understand the implications and personal consequences of their acts. Although Type I assassins may attempt to escape after the act, their beliefs and zeal suggest that capture and death are an acceptable risk. If captured, they do not recant or seek leniency. Their extremism is rational and principled.

Type II: These assassins have an overwhelming and aggressive need for acceptance, recognition, and status. However, there is no evidence of psychoses in these assassins. They fully appreciate the personal consequences of their acts. They always have "significant others" in their lives. The assassination may generate recognition that has been denied them in their personal lives and in some cases may place guilt on those who have denied them in the past. This type of assassin is primarily concerned only with himself/herself and his or her personal problems.

Type III: These assassins are psychopaths. They do not exhibit rage or hatred at a particular person; rather, they focus on targets that represent the culture or group as a whole. They have no political values or beliefs and are contemptuous of normal social convention. They accurately perceive reality but cannot respond to it emotionally.

Type IV: These assassins suffer from mental disorders characterized by hallucinations and delusions of persecution and/or grandeur. Their contact with reality is so minimal that they cannot truly understand the significance of their actions or others' reactions to their actions. They believe that their mission is mystically or divinely inspired. Many of these assassins meet the legal definition of insanity.

Park Dietz and his associates conducted another highly respected scientific survey of those who attack or approach public figures. The study, titled *Mentally Disordered Offenders in Pursuit of Celebrities and Politicians,* was one of the first of its kind in the nation. Its purpose was to develop a means of identifying persons who are likely to engage in such behavior. The information was collected from records of the U.S. Capitol Police and a prominent Los Angeles security consulting firm that specializes in a wide variety of security matters, including protecting celebrities from stalkers. The data included letters and other communications from the subjects, as well as information from police records. The subject's sex, age, martial status, education, criminal history, number of threats, psychological and emotional evaluations, and approaches toward the target were all collected and analyzed.

The purpose of the study was to develop a new behavioral science technique to help prevent assassination and other attacks on political leaders. Dietz and his colleagues analyzed their data and determined that a number of variables may be considered to be risk enhancing. The significant factors included telephoning or writing multiple letters, providing identification in the communication, repeatedly mentioning emotional attachment, or expressing a desire for a face-to-face meeting. Dietz's research is important because it presents a different perspective on threats made to public officials. However, like all studies of this type, its conclusions must be balanced against the consequences of failing to act on threatening communications. As history has illustrated, there are many who aspire to and succeed in killing public officials.

THE SECRET SERVICE

History of the Secret Service

The Secret Service began in time of national crisis in 1865. It was originally formed to combat the high rate of counterfeiting that was occurring during the Civil War. On April 14, 1865, the secretary of the treasury approached President Lincoln and asked permission to do something about the bogus bills circulating in the Union. Lincoln gave his okay. Later that evening, in an ironic turn of events, he was assassinated by John Wilkes Booth. Presidents were not yet protected from assassins—that idea and task would come later.

The Secret Service began on July 5, 1865, when Secretary McCulloch swore in its first chief, William P. Wood. From that date until 1901, the Secret Service served in a variety of investigative functions, including arresting counterfeiters and members of the Ku Klux Klan, serving as special operatives during the war with Spain, and investigating land fraud in the western United States.

After Lincoln was assassinated, there was some discussion of establishing a unit to protect the president, but no action occurred. Garfield was killed in 1881 by another assassin's bullet, yet no official action was taken to protect future presidents. During Grover Cleveland's tenure as president, the Secret Service was occasionally called on to protect him, despite any formal laws mandating such duty. In 1901, President McKinley was the third president to be killed by an assassin. His death finally galvanized Congress into discussing the issue of presidential protection. Although no federal law would be enacted for the next 6 years, from the time of McKinley's death, the Secret Service assumed the role of protecting presidents.

The role of the Secret Service has been expanded over the years. In 1917, threats against the president became a felony, and the Secret Service assumed the duty of guarding the president as well as his immediate family. In 1930, after an unknown visitor entered the White House dining room, President Herbert Hoover decided that the existing White House protective unit should be merged with the Secret Service and that it should handle all aspects of presidential protection. On May 14, 1930, Congress gave supervision of the White House police to the chief of the Secret Service. In 1951, after a failed assassination attempt on President Truman, Congress passed a law authorizing additional protection of the president-elect and the vice president. After the assassination of Robert Kennedy in 1968, the Secret Service was given authority to protect presidential candidates.

The Secret Service of today is a well-trained professional law enforcement organization. It continues to carry out its mission of protecting the president and others from the assassin's knife, bullet, or bomb. It uses technology and other methods in its never-ending quest to ensure the safety of those it guards. One of the more recent developments is a study by the Secret Service that increases knowledge about American attackers and assassins. In 1990, the organization began a long-range study, titled the "Exceptional Case Study Project," of persons known to have engaged in approaching, following, or attacking those the Secret Service protects. The Exceptional Case Study Project is an important step in developing and analyzing relevant information about individuals who attack public officials and public figures in the United States.

The Secret Service Mission Statement

The Secret Service is charged with protecting the life of the president and vice president of the United States and their immediate families; the president-elect and vice-president-elect and their immediate families; former presidents and their wives; the widows of former presidents until death or remarriage; children of a former president until they reach 16 years of age; heads of foreign states or foreign governments; and at the direction of the president, official representatives of the United States performing special missions abroad. Furthermore, the Secret Service provides security at the White House complex, the Treasury Building and Treasury Annex, buildings that house presidential offices, the vice president's residence, and various foreign diplomatic missions in the Washington, D.C., metropolitan area and in other areas as designated by the president.

CONCLUSION

Assassination of high-ranking governmental officials is a special form of violence. It has existed since biblical times, and no "cure" has been found. Some assassinations appear to be spontaneous, whereas others involve detailed planning and execution. Assassins who stalk their targets, be they presidents or celebrities, are of special interest to professionals who research stalking behavior.

In many countries, assassination is used as a political weapon to subvert or destroy existing governments. Government in the United States does not lend itself to this form of political terrorism, and therefore most American assassins are not motivated by a desire to destroy or overthrow the government. The research into American assassins has produced conflicting and contradictory results. Some scholars argue for a typology of assassins, and some claim that such classification is flawed. Other researchers continue the debate as to whether assassins are mentally ill. Despite the importance of understanding assassins' behavior, there has been no agreement on basic approaches to studying this type of violence.

—*Harvey Wallace*

See also BRADY BILL; MOTIVES FOR
MURDER; MURDER FOR HIRE; NOT GUILTY
BY REASON OF INSANITY (NGRI); STALKING

Further Reading

Clarke, J. W. (1982). *American assassins, the darker side of politics.* Princeton, NJ: Princeton University Press.

Dietz, P. E., et al. (1991, September). Threatening and otherwise inappropriate letters to members of the United States Congress. *Journal of Forensic Sciences 36*(5), p. 1446.

Dietz, P. E., & Mitchell, D. A. (1989, October 15). *Mentally disordered offenders in pursuit of celebrities and politicians.* Report submitted to the National Institute of Justice, Washington D.C.

Ford, F. (1985). *Political murder: From tyrannicide to terrorism.* Cambridge, MA: Harvard University Press.

Heaps, W. A. (1969). *A special kind of murder.* New York: Meredith.

Kirkham, J. F., Levy, S. G., & Crotty, W. J. (1969, October). *Assassination and political violence: A report to the National Commission on the Causes and Prevention of Violence.* Washington, DC: GPO.

Roberts, M. (1990). *Moments in history. 1865-1990.* Washington, DC: U.S. Secret Service.

ASSISTED SUICIDE, *See*
EUTHANASIA; KEVORKIAN, JACK; SUICIDE

ATLANTA CHILD MURDERS,
See WILLIAMS, WAYNE

ATROPINE, *See* POISONERS;
POISONING: MEDICAL SETTINGS

ATTACHMENT DEFICIENCY AND VIOLENCE

Over the past 50 years, the contemplation of a link between attachment deficit and the genesis of psychopathological patterns of behavior, such as repetitive violent acts, appears to be increasing in importance. Children who are victims of violence—due to dysfunctional interactions with parents, siblings, or peers or being forced to rely on unstable family structures with inadequate role models—suffer from various frustrations and often become violent offenders later in life. The development of a negative self-concept and low self-esteem deriving from a lack of empathic capabilities and understanding of compassionate feelings seems to make cruel and violent behavior not only possible, but likely.

THE NATURE OF ATTACHMENTS

The existence and quality of early attachments eventually serve as both risk and protective factors, reinforcing the notion that these interactions have a considerable impact on the genesis of a psychopathology. Secure attachments lower the individual's vulnerability for psychological destabilization in handling stressful or negative situations. Attachment deficits have the opposite effect, leading to disturbed attachment behavior. Therefore, attachment deficits are often interpreted as causative factors for aggressive and violent behavioral patterns.

When inadequate coping strategies are internalized due to dysfunctional socialization and attachment experiences, the basic ability to distinguish right from wrong cannot be developed. The result is the misinterpretation of violent actions as an appropriate technique for conflict solving. While attempting to repair the damaged self, the appliance of aggression and violence leads individuals to believe in a false sense of power and control over others and their own lives. This consequently supplies them with a misdirected understanding of the world, enhancing isolation and allowing the outside world to remain a hostile place.

The first attachment theorists, John Bowlby and Mary Ainsworth, discussed the connection between early child-parent interactions and later attachment behavior, as well as personality development of the child. Ainsworth, being more empirically based, focused on the psychological availability of the primary caregivers and their sensitivity toward their children's needs. In addition, she conducted a thorough investigation of distinguishable attachment qualities.

Bowlby and Ainsworth had postulated a genetic predisposition for the formation of the first attachment, but not until recently did a new interest in the influence of biochemical interactions arise. Studies investigating increased levels of cortisol in connection with stress in insecure-attached children implied an influential biological component within the complex development of behavioral patterns.

In the International Diagnostic Classification systems (ICD-10) and *Diagnostic and Statistical Manual of Mental Disorders,* 4th edition (*DSM-IV*), the attachment phenomenon receives very little recognition as it relates to the connection between attachment deficits and deviant personality development or formation of violent behavioral patterns. In fact, attachment disorders are directly mentioned in only a few categories in either manual.

In the ICD-10, "Disorders of Social Functioning With Onset Specific to Childhood or Adolescence," unifying the "Reactive Attachment Disorder of Childhood" (F94.1) and the "Disinhibited Attachment Disorder of Childhood" (F94.2), emphasizes attachment issues. The *DSM-IV* presents the "Reactive Attachment Disorder of Infancy or Early Childhood" (313.89), which recognizes the described dynamics, uniting one inhibited and one disinhibited type. In addition, the "Unsocialized Conduct Disorder" (F91.1) and the "Social Anxiety Disorder of Childhood" (F93.2) can be found in the ICD-10, and the *DSM-IV* also refers to a "Parent-Child Relational Problem" (V61.20).

FORMATION OF ATTACHMENTS THROUGHOUT THE COURSE OF LIFE

Inconsistent and inconsequent attention of caregivers leads to confusion and disorientation in children, who then do not develop effective strategies for attempting to manage life's challenges. With some kinds of behavior, the child experiences variable (and therefore unforeseeable) consequences exercised by caregivers, a deficient understanding of adequate social interactions results. Abuse is another influential factor in this context. In addition to provoking feelings of anxiety, inadequacy, and worthlessness, it leads to attachment deficits deriving from the impaired attachment capabilities and facilitates the internalization of dysfunctional coping strategies, producing a negative perception of the world and possibly contributing to violence as a familiar behavioral resort.

Children and caregivers can be understood as parts of an interdependent, continuously progressing system. Attachment can be described as an affective relationship or emotional bond with a caregiver. Its destruction following a permanent separation from the caregiver has a strong impact on the child's well-being at the time, as well as his or her further development. Healthy attachments, as interactive systems, allow the child to choose the path of autonomy, whereas symbiotic attachments (dependency) do not enable the individual to experience the necessary amount of explorative actions.

Infants first react with universal patterns toward others, then slowly start to differentiate stimuli, and their reactions become increasingly selective. Although in the beginning, the influences that determine an infant's behavior are mostly environmental, the infant's own developing perception of reality soon takes over.

The first attachment is of a fair stability and affects an individual over his or her entire life span, serving as a precondition for any further attachment. In the ideal case, it develops during the first 3 years of childhood. However, depending on the individual's path of life, the potential for forming such an attachment remains until early adolescence.

If the primary caregiver leaves a child's environment, fear and the activation of attachment behavior arises in the child, who will then try to reconnect with the caregiver as fast as possible, attempting to restabilize his or her emotional condition. Having a secure attachment as an emotional basis enables an infant to explore his or her environment fearlessly, without the experience of anxiety or emotional distress. On the other hand, the lack of a secure attachment, or attachment deficit, leads to extreme fearfulness stemming from a deep-seated sense of powerlessness.

The primary attachment to a caregiver usually progresses into a goal-corrected partnership. This partnership facilitates the contemplation of mutual objectives, enabling the child to understand the caregiver's perspective and serving as a precondition for the ability to understand advanced emotional states, such as empathy and compassion.

During adolescence, the first attachment becomes weaker, and individuals start creating their own strategies for the resolution of conflicts. The second attachment to a member of a peer group (usually of the opposite gender) eventually becomes the primary concern. The third attachment finally develops with one's own offspring.

In addition to these three deeply meaningful trusting attachments, some shallower ones usually form, which are hierarchically structured in accordance with their suspected effectiveness as a means of protection against perceived threats from the outside world. These shallow relationships do not generate pain or a sense of disorganization when they break apart and are comparable to the pseudoattachments seen in children 3 to 4 years old.

Depending on their attachment experiences, children develop cognitive and emotional inner representations that become increasingly more stable. These representations, being mainly concepts about the self, the caregiver, and the caregiver's availability, do not contain ideas about personality traits of the caregiver, but about the quality of the attachment to the caregiver.

Mary Ainsworth studied qualities of attachment using the "strange situation procedure." This procedure activated attachment behavior through short separations from the primary caregiver and resulted in her discovery of three different attachment qualities: the secure attachment, the insecure-avoidant attachment, and the insecure-ambivalent attachment.

In the secure attachment, individuals showed slight irritation as a result of separation from the caregiver, but they did not limit their explorative behavior and quickly reconnected with the caregiver on the caregiver's return.

In the insecure-avoidant attachment, individuals demonstrated hardly any irritation at all during the separation from the caregiver, but on the caregiver's return, they avoided physical contact with the caregiver and failed to display any interest toward the caregiver.

In the insecure-ambivalent attachment, individuals exhibited extreme emotional reactions during the separation from the caregiver as well as on being reunited with the caregiver, including both strong resistance and anger.

In the 1980s, a fourth attachment pattern, the disorganized attachment, was introduced. It focused more on the organization than the quality of the attachment. In this disoriented attachment, individuals demonstrated contradictive behavioral patterns, such as intensively searching for the caregiver but refusing contact from them, as well as signs of anxiety. A connection to abusal backgrounds was postulated.

ATTACHMENT QUALITY AND ATTACHMENT DISORDER

The factors having the strongest impact on attachment quality are the caregiver's responsiveness (attentiveness toward the child), ability to be affectionate, and sensitivity. Social factors, critical life events, and general dispositions also should be taken into account. The caregiver's sensitivity is defined as the ability of the caregiver to recognize, interpret, and promptly as well as adequately respond to the infant's needs.

Research into the childhood of violent delinquents has emphasized the significance of certain distinct dysfunctional constellations in their upbringing. Most of these constellations focus on unresponsive mothers, rejecting fathers, abuse, and varying caregivers, in addition to unstable social environments. Overall, the conditions of the immediate surroundings, or the family system, of a developing infant seem to have the strongest impact, relating to the culmination of frustration and genesis of violence.

Attachment disorders, deriving from a combination of insecure-avoidant, ambivalent, and disorganized features found among abused and mistreated children, must be understood as a complex pattern of interdependently connected aspects as well. The individual's disposition, mainly including self-concept and coping strategies, in addition to the social and familial influences, all must be considered equally. In individuals with attachment disorders, the primary attachment always remains incomplete, and the phase of the goal-corrected partnership is never reached.

A stable relationship with the caregiver as a protective factor appears to be a good basis for a healthy emotional development. If this stable relationship is joined with an adequately supportive environment, the chances for a desirable developmental course are even better. On the other hand, the early violation of trust by a caregiver appears to lay the foundation for later pathology in an individual.

The qualities of attachments described by Ainsworth can be understood in the child's strategies to adapt, resulting from past interactions with caregivers and socialization experiences. Disorganized attachments can then be contributed to the child's inability to form adaptive strategies. Attachment disorders in insecure-avoidant individuals are characterized by compulsivity and overadjustment. Attachment disorders in insecure-ambivalent individuals result in maladjustment and overt aggression.

After contemplating many factors of considerable importance in the development of attachments or attachment deficits, parental empathy, responsivity, and sensitivity seem to be the most important. When these factors are combined with other elements, such as abuse; deprivation; deviant or mentally disordered caregivers; impaired communicative and interactive patterns deriving from inadequate upbringing techniques (consisting mainly of repetitive degradation of the child, extreme authoritarian child-rearing practices, and inconsistent reactions); a dysfunctional environment; or racial discrimination, the child consequently must reorganize and therefore implement his or her inadequate coping strategies.

Children possessing secure attachments can rely on their internalized adequate coping strategies and will not easily feel menaced by life events. Individuals with attachment deficits lack these adequate coping strategies and might therefore quickly resort to deviant (violent) behavioral patterns, without any relation to the severity of the frustration. This can also serve as an explanation why victims of childhood violence often resort to violent behavior themselves.

Violence is legitimized by mistreated individuals as an "adequate" or at least familiar strategy in the prevention of degradation and in the process of developing or maintaining a bond with another person. This understanding then leads to a vicious circle, reinforcing detachment from others and causing further aggression.

The use of physical or verbal aggression by victims of childhood violence can be understood as an attempt to form attachments, demonstrating the wish for affection in an inadequate manner. A frustrating attachment history results in the expectation of rejection by others. In an attempt to avoid humiliation caused by rejection by others, the individual prefers to seek contact in this inappropriate way. This allows the interpretation of aggression and violence as indicators of a deep-seated desire for attachment.

The internalization of inadequate social and familial influences in addition to a negative predisposition facilitate antisocial and violent aggressive behavior in individuals. Caregiver techniques contributing to this downward spiral result in a lack of empathy and compassion in the child, causing a pessimistic view of the world. This constellation allows the genesis of aggressive violence to then become not only comprehensible, but even likely.

—*Valeska Vitt*

See also Child Abuse; Psychosocial Risk Factors for Violent Behavior; Psychopaths

Further Reading

Ainsworth, M. D. S., Blehar, M. C., Waters, E., & Wall, S. (1978). *Patterns of attachment.* Hillsdale, NJ: Lawrence Erlbaum.

American Psychiatric Association. (1994). *Diagnostic and statistical manual of mental disorders* (4th ed.). Washington, DC: Author.

Atkinson, L., & Zucker, K. J. (1997). *Attachment and psychopathology.* New York/London: Guilford.

Bowlby, J. (1969). *Attachment and loss. Vol. 1: Attachment.* New York: Basic Books.

Bowlby, J. (1973). *Attachment and loss. Vol. 2: Separation, anxiety, and anger.* New York: Basic Books.

World Health Organization (1993). *The ICD-10 classification of mental and behavioural disorders.* Geneva, Switzerland: Author.

AUTOEROTIC ASPHYXIA, *See* PARAPHILIA

AUTOMATED FINGERPRINT IDENTIFICATION SYSTEM (AFIS), *See* CRIMINALISTICS

B

BAADER–MEINHOF GANG

Andreas Baader and his girlfriend, Gudrun Ensslin, bombed a department store in Frankfurt, Germany, in April 1968. This followed many tumultuous years of leftist revolution among German citizens and students. Their motives were to overthrow the post–World War II democracy, which they deemed oppressive. After Baader and Ensslin had spent 2 years in prison for their bombing, a left-wing journalist named Ulrike Meinhof helped them to escape. The media began to call their terrorist organization the "Baader-Meinhof Gang." Supporters of this leftist terrorist faction referred to themselves as the "Red Army Faction" (RAF). By 1972, most of the leaders had been captured. The RAF followers retaliated by kidnapping and killing nearly a dozen people in hopes of securing their leaders' release.

The effort failed, and the leaders remained in custody. The Baader-Meinhof terrorists began receiving assistance from Middle Eastern terrorist organizations to aid in pressuring the German government to release their leaders. Once it was clear that the government would not concede to the faction's pressures, three of the main leaders, Andreas Baader, Gudrun Ensslin, and Jan-Carl Raspe, committed suicide in prison. By 1977, the Baader-Meinhof era was over, although remnants of the group stayed active until they completely disbanded in 1998. Overall, the Baader-Meinhof Gang and the RAF are believed to be responsible for the killing of 30 to 50 people, including German government officials and U.S. military personnel. A final letter from the terrorist group noted the strategic errors that had contributed to its demise but expressed no apparent remorse for the terrorism or murders.

—*Brianna Satterthwaite*

See also TERRORISM

BACKPACKER MURDERS, *See* MILAT, IVAN

F. LEE BAILEY

F. Lee Bailey (formerly known as Francis Lee Bailey) is a legendary and controversial defense attorney and one of the most contentious figures in the practice of law in the United States. He has been involved in many high-profile cases, representing clients such as Patricia Hearst, Dr. Sam Sheppard (whose case inspired the making of the movie *The Fugitive*), the notorious serial killer "the Boston Strangler," and most recently, O. J. Simpson. Bailey has been a keynote speaker and guest expert on television and radio shows regarding the topics of law, media, politics, current events, society, and culture.

—*Lisa Andrews*

BALLISTICS

Ballistics is the study of the motion or travel of projectiles and their flight performance. *Internal* or *initial ballistics* studies the projectile from within the weapon, including forces within the gun barrel and the velocity at which a bullet exits the chamber, also known as *muzzle velocity*. The speed at which a bullet travels through a given weapon's barrel is based on factors such as bullet composition and shape, length of the barrel, how much energy is transferred to the bullet from the expansion of burning gunpowder, and the amount of gunpowder available for efficient burning within a given cartridge. *External* ballistics studies a bullet's flight pattern, including the energy with which a bullet leaves the weapon's chamber, the mass and shape of the bullet, air resistance/drag, gravitational forces, and distance of travel.

Terminal ballistics refers to the injury pattern of a bullet on the target. A long, heavy bullet composed of an alloy of lead and antimony jacketed in copper offers the least dispersion of energy from the bullet to the target, thus allowing the bullet to travel deeper, if not through, the intended target. At the other extreme, spherical-shaped bullets offer the greatest release of energy to the target and in fact may not even make contact with the intended target. Different types of bullet shapes are designed to give up various amounts of energy to their intended targets depending on the type of weapon used, range from the weapon to the target, and purpose of use.

Terminal ballistics also encompasses the wounding potential of a bullet. Tissue damage is primarily produced in two ways: (a) laceration and crushing, as seen with low-velocity bullets and (b) cavitation, wherein a permanent cavity is caused by the path of the bullet, as seen in high-powered rifles. Shock waves, which compress the medium and travel ahead of the bullet, may cause damage to a target, but serious effects seen from cavitation are extremely rare. Bullet shape plays an important role in wounding potential. A bullet having a soft lead point or "hollow point" is designed specifically to deform on impact, allowing the bullet to impart all its energy to the target.

The examination of bullets (partial or whole) in crime laboratories occurs through the comparison of class and individual characteristics. Recovered bullets from a crime scene may be compared with bullets obtained from test-firing a suspected weapon. The bullets are then compared by juxtaposition using a comparison microscope. Class comparisons specifically refer to the type of caliber and rifling patterns on a bullet made as the bullet was fired from a weapon. Caliber and rifling marks can be readily seen in whole bullets,

whereas in partial bullets or deformed bullets, this comparison may be next to impossible. Once a positive class comparison is obtained, individual characteristics are then examined to determine whether a specific weapon was used. Individual characteristics are based on bullet striae arising from imperfections within a weapon's barrel. Weapon barrel imperfections cause a striae pattern as specific and unique as a fingerprint.

—Monica Myers

See also CRIMINALISTICS

BARROW, CLYDE, *See* PARKER, BONNIE, AND CLYDE BARROW

BARTON, MARK, *See* MASS MURDER

COUNTESS ELIZABETH BATHORY

Elizabeth Bathory, also known as the "Blood Countess," was born on August 7, 1560, to George and Anna Bathory. The Bathory family was one of the richest and most powerful Protestant families in Hungary. Elizabeth's relatives included an uncle who was a Satan worshipper, a lesbian aunt who enjoyed torturing servants, and a brother who was a drunkard and a lecher. At 15, Elizabeth was married to Ferencz Nadasdy, whom Elizabeth had been betrothed to since the age of 11. While her husband was away, Elizabeth began to experiment with witchcraft and sadistic tendencies. She beat the female servants and slaves, using knives, molten wax, razors, branding irons, and silver pincers to extract blood from the victims to satisfy her sexual urges. Many of her castles were equipped with torture and mutilation chambers. Elizabeth was never convicted of any murders but was found criminally insane and placed in detention within the castle. Countess Elizabeth Bathory killed nearly 650 female servants and slaves.

—Lisa Andrews

See also SERIAL MURDER: INTERNATIONAL INCIDENCE; TORTURE; VAMPIRES, WEREWOLVES, AND WITCHES

BATTERED CHILD SYNDROME

In 1962, Dr. C. Henry Kempe and his associates published a paper on physical abuse of children and introduced the term *battered child syndrome*. It describes injuries resulting from repetitive nonaccidental trauma to and maltreatment of children. The publicity that has developed around this term has been critical in focusing interest in child physical abuse. It has provided the basis of many laws for reporting child abuse throughout the country. Mandated reporters, including doctors, nurses, social workers, and teachers, are required by law to report suspicious injuries in children. They are protected by law from liability if these reports are made in good faith.

Child physical abuse is a serious problem in the United States today. Reports of abused children reach about 3 million each year. About a third of these are substantiated on further investigation. About 1,200 children die of abuse or neglect each year. It can take many forms. In early infancy, the most common form of severe child abuse is *shaken baby syndrome,* a term that applies to brain injuries that result when a baby is violently shaken. In older children, blunt abdominal trauma is a more typical injury in fatal abuse cases. Fractures can also be part of the battered child syndrome. When evaluating fractures as part of abuse, one must look at whether the description of the trauma fits the type and severity of the fractures. Burns, although not generally considered battering, can be part of battered child syndrome. Bruises may be the only visual evidence of trauma. Without intervention, battery often escalates to the death of the child.

SHAKEN BABY SYNDROME

Special note should be made of shaken baby syndrome, a form of battered child syndrome that occurs mainly in children under 3 years of age, with peak incidence at about 4 months of age. The primary injury is brain damage due to shaking, often combined with an impact of the head against a surface. Fractures are found in about one third of the infants with shaken baby syndrome, indicative of the extreme violence of the shaking. It is not uncommon to find additional injuries that predate those from the shaking that brings the child to the hospital.

Rotational forces that occur with shaking lead to a number of injuries, including intracranial hemorrhage

Child abuse is a pervasive problem in many societies and cultures. Children become the targets of abuse and killing when parents and guardians exercise poor parenting skills. Long after the scars have healed, abused children remember how they were made to feel, feelings that may haunt them throughout their lives and increase the likelihood of victimization as adults.

Source: Copyright © Peggy & Ronald Barnett / CORBIS.

from breaking of the bridging veins and diffuse axonal injury from shearing forces, which break the fragile axons from the nerve cells. In addition, shaking leads to injury to the blood vessels of the retinas of the eyes, with hemorrhaging and occasional dislocation of the retinas.

Sequelae of severe shaking can include death, severe brain damage, and blindness. Within a group of 31 shaken babies seen over a 20-month period, 6 (20%) died, and an additional 4 suffered severe permanent brain damage. Less data are available regarding the long-term effects of the shaking on learning.

One of the controversies in shaken baby syndrome is whether or not the shaking alone causes the severe brain injuries or whether an impact is necessary. Some studies demonstrate that impact associated with a shaking injury significantly increases the amount of damage. The high frequency of skull fractures and bruising of the head noted in shaken babies supports the conclusion that impact is often an important component of a shaking injury.

ABDOMINAL TRAUMA

Blunt force abdominal trauma is also a significant component of the battered child syndrome. Abusive abdominal trauma has a high rate of death; it is the leading cause of abuse-related death in children outside the shaken baby age range. Perhaps the main reason for the lethality of this injury is the prolonged time between the injury and the seeking of medical attention. Weeks may pass between the time of the abdominal trauma and the recognition of the nature of the injury. A factor leading to delay is the fact that the child is usually brought to the medical care system without a history of trauma, resulting in lengthy medical investigations and delay in appropriate treatment.

FRACTURES

One of the features of battered child syndrome that Dr. Kempe and his associates pointed out so clearly was the repetitive nature of the injuries. Although this pattern is not apparent in all cases, one often finds evidence of old fractures or histories of other injuries during the evaluation of an acute abusive injury. Because of this, the series of X rays performed to look for old fractures is often referred to as a *Kempe series.*

In assessing fractures for abuse, it is important to look both at the timing and pattern of injuries. One must assess the developmental stage of the infant to determine if it is reasonable that the injury could have occurred in the manner described by the caregiver. Certain fractures, such as spiral fractures in a pre-ambulatory infant, are highly suggestive of abuse. However, in an older child, a spiral fracture is a common accidental injury. Finding new fractures in combination with fractures that show signs of healing or with other types of injuries leads to increased suspicion of abuse.

LEGAL IMPLICATIONS

Another significant result of focusing on battered children is the impact it has had on the legal system. In 1991, the U.S. Supreme Court reviewed the case of *Estelle v. McGuire,* overturning the decision of the Court of Appeals. In this case, the defendant had been found guilty of second-degree murder in the death of his daughter. There was clear evidence of abusive injuries over a prolonged period of time. The justices held that evidence of prior injuries to the infant could

be admitted to demonstrate a pattern of abuse and prove battered child syndrome. More recently, in a California case (*California v. Valdez,* 2002), the Supreme Court of the State of California held up the conviction of a parent for allowing her child to be in the care of a friend whom she feared and knew to be dangerous.

—*Elinor M. Zorn*

See also CHILD ABUSE; CHILD KILLERS; FAMILY VIOLENCE

Further Reading

Estelle v. McGuire, 502 U.S. 62, 112 S.Ct. 475, 116 L.Ed.2d 385 (1991).

Jones, J. G. (Ed.). (1998). *A guide to references and resources in child abuse and neglect.* Elk Grove Village, IL: American Academy of Pediatrics.

Kempe, C. H., Silverman, F. N., Steele, F. S., Droegemiller, W., & Silver, H. K. (1962). *The battered child syndrome. JAMA, 181,* 17-24.

People v. Eva Valdez, Ct.App. 3 CO32849, Ct.App. 3 C032849, Super. Ct. No. 97F03986 (2002).

BATTERED MEN'S SYNDROME, *See* BATTERERS AND ABUSIVE PARTNERS; BATTERED WOMAN'S SYNDROME; DOMESTIC VIOLENCE

BATTERED WOMAN'S SYNDROME

The term *battered woman's syndrome* (BWS), first coined by Dr. Lenore Walker in 1979, describes a pattern of psychological and behavioral characteristics found in women living in violent relationships. It also provides a possible explanation for why abused women continue to remain in battering relationships.

Central to the concept of BWS is the theory of *learned helplessness.* Learned helplessness theory predicts that an individual's self-efficacy can be diminished through abusive interactions. The aversive experiences associated with trauma lower the victim's perception of effectiveness in being able to control what happens to him or her.

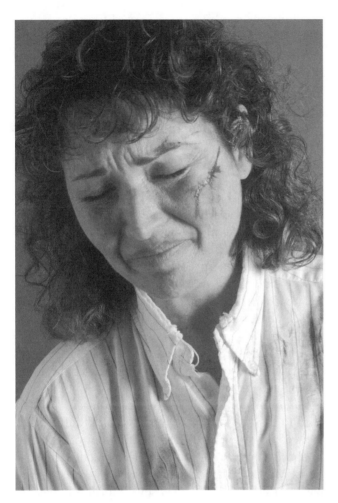

Spousal abuse is pervasive in many societies and cultures, especially where women are the victims. Every year thousands of women are injured or killed as a result of intimate violence. In the United States, there is a high correlation between spousal abuse and alcohol consumption. After an attack, the husband or partner often vows to change and is contrite. This "honeymoon" phase leads to a tension-building phase that often culminates in another violent attack.

Source: Copyright © Rick Gomez / CORBIS.

CHARACTERISTICS OF BWS

Walker specifies that a woman who has experienced two complete battering cycles can be classified as a *battered woman*. Battering cycles are characterized by a period of tension building, followed by an acute battering episode, and ending with a reconciliation or loving period. BWS has been described as a subgroup of what the American Psychological Association (APA) defines as *post-traumatic stress disorder* (PTSD). Although there is not one definitive profile of a sufferer of BWS, generally there are four main characteristics:

1. The woman accepts responsibility for her batterer's actions.
2. The woman is unable to place the responsibility for the violence elsewhere.
3. The woman fears for her life and/or the lives of her children.
4. The woman believes her abuser is omnipresent and omniscient.

Battered women also frequently suffer from low self-esteem and severe stress reactions. In addition, some argue that battered women may not be able to accurately discern the level of dangerousness in a given incident. They contend that BWS/PTSD can explain how, because of flashbacks or other experiences associated with past victimization, a victim of prior abuse can regard a current situation as dangerous when objectively it is not.

APPLICATIONS

The emergence of BWS in domestic violence research has brought wide public attention to the conditions of battered women and, combined with feminist advocacy, has prompted changes in the trials of battered women charged with killing their abusers.

BWS has been used in criminal cases since the late 1970s. Contrary to popular belief, it has not been used as a discrete defense to criminal charges. Rather, it is typically used, along with other relevant information, to support claims of self-defense. The term generally relates to expert testimony that describes the social and psychological effects of continued battering, and characterizes the history of the relationship between the defendant and the decedent.

CRITICISMS

Early criticism of BWS centered on the use of learned helplessness theory to explain why battered women remain in violent relationships. Specifically, women's advocates believed that because of the word *helplessness,* the theory could be easily misinterpreted to perpetuate the image of women as mentally weak, powerless, or incompetent. Such criticism has led researchers to distinguish learned helplessness from *being helpless.* The theory suggests that continual battering, with unsuccessful attempts to escape, diminishes a woman's motivation to respond. What results is a state of "learned" helplessness in which the battered woman loses the ability to foresee what she will do to produce a particular outcome (end the abuse, escape the relationship, etc.).

More recent criticisms of BWS focus on its medicalization of battering victims. Critics contend that it presents women as helpless and psychologically debilitated. They say that the use of pathological terminology diminishes the perception of the rationality of the victim; by characterizing the actions or thoughts of the woman as pathological because she is suffering from a *syndrome,* the woman is viewed as irrational or mentally incapacitated. In fact, they argue, although some of her psychological and social reactions to trauma may be pathological, others are fairly reasonable. Social scientists are working toward reevaluating the term. Critics of the term argue for the redefining of BWS, believing that descriptions of "battering and its effects" provide appropriate explanations while avoiding stigmatization.

—*Mindy S. Wilson*

See also AGGRESSION: FEMINIST PERSPECTIVE; BATTERERS AND ABUSIVE PARTNERS; CYCLE THEORY OF VIOLENCE; DOMESTIC VIOLENCE; FAMILY VIOLENCE; GENDER VIOLENCE; SELF-DEFENSE; VICTIMOLOGY

Further Reading

Maguigan, H. (1998). It's time to move beyond "battered woman's syndrome." *Criminal Justice Ethics, 17,* 1, 50-57.

Walker, L. E. (1979). *The battered woman.* New York: Harper & Row.

Walker, L. E. A. (1999). *The battered woman's syndrome.* New York: Springer.

BATTERERS AND ABUSIVE PARTNERS

There is much debate about the goals of batterers programs and whether or not they are effective in reducing and eliminating woman battering. In evaluating the issue, it is helpful to identify and discuss different approaches and complex tensions that exist in the field of batterer intervention. A greater understanding can be gained by examining the history of batterer intervention programs, including the impact of feminism and the battered women's movement, social work, and the criminal justice system; identifying the range of models used in batterer intervention; reviewing the research on the effectiveness of programs; and considering recommendations for enhanced policy and program developments.

DEFINITION OF TERMS

The terms *domestic violence* and *battering* warrant particular attention.

Domestic violence: For these purposes, the term refers to the pattern of behavior used to maintain power and control over another person in an intimate relationship, including physical and sexual assault, verbal abuse, and emotional abuse. Although other terms such as *family violence, spouse abuse,* and *battered women* are often used to refer to this pattern, domestic violence is frequently viewed as the more neutral and encompassing definition.

Battering: Although domestic violence is often used to imply a more encompassing, less value-laden view of the problem, different definitions of battering or abusive behavior lead to different practice implications. Most legislators, as expressed in the laws they pass, consider only the most severe forms of abuse as battering, including various forms of physical attack, some threatening behaviors, and sometimes stalking. These parameters place battering in the category of criminal behavior in most states, along with physical assaults, attempted assaults, and threatening and menacing behavior. Other definitions concentrate on physical violence and include sexual abuse only in accompaniment with physical violence. To encompass the widest range of behaviors associated with battering and domestic violence, for these purposes, the term will encompass both criminal and noncriminal behavior unless otherwise noted.

SCOPE OF THE PROBLEM

The prevalence of domestic violence among intimate partners is overwhelming in American society. Approximately 8 million women report being battered by boyfriends, spouses, or ex-spouses annually (Roberts, 2002). Approximately 2,000 battered women are killed by the batterers, and 750 battered women kill their intimate partners each year (Roberts, 2002).

However, not all domestic violence is lethal or life threatening in nature. In fact, the duration and severity of woman battering varies across the life span from pushes, shoves, and slaps briefly sustained by high school and college age women to aggravated assault, permanent scars, and serious injuries endured by chronically battered women.

A continuum of the duration, severity, and outcomes among different levels of woman battering was recently developed on the basis of 501 cases (Roberts, 2002). This study (and the continuum that was developed) has practical implications for the type of interventions that seem more likely to be effective with certain types of batterers. For example, "short-term batterers," who commit one to three low-level incidents including yelling, pushing, shoving, and throwing things, should receive different types of intervention than the chronic weekly or "weekend" batterer who abuses his partner repeatedly for many years with increasing severity (e.g., broken bones, concussions). Several different typologies and profiles of batterers have been developed over the past decade. These typologies are usually based on demographic, sociological, psychological, psychiatric, and criminal justice history characteristics and attributes. Because the criminal justice system usually classifies offenders on the basis of low- versus high-level risk of dangerousness, the batterer characteristics usually receiving the most attention are criminal history, mental illness, and substance abuse history.

Most men have been socialized to hide their innermost thoughts, emotions, and feelings. Being strong, being in control, and creating a tough exterior have historically been viewed as synonymous with being a "real man." Men who batter women have never learned how to cope successfully with their angry feelings. Batterers usually bottle everything up inside, stress and pressure builds, and like a pressure cooker, they explode.

Although batterers are represented in all races, religions, ethnic groups, and socioeconomic levels, certain personality and psychological factors seem to be characteristic of batterers and distinguish them from nonbatterers. According to research in Connecticut, Indiana, New Jersey, and New York, batterers frequently display the following characteristics:

♦ Low self-esteem and weak ego functioning
♦ Poor impulse control
♦ Believes in myths about the traditional and patriarchal marriage

♦ Adheres to old-fashioned beliefs in male supremacy and superiority
♦ Fails to take responsibility for his actions and blames his wife or girlfriend
♦ Is extremely jealous
♦ Exhibits severe stress reactions, during which he uses drinking and woman battering to cope
♦ Frequently uses sex as an act of aggression to enhance his self-esteem

Some believe that the majority of men who batter women can be helped to change their threatening, coercive, and assaultive behavior patterns. The four main types of intervention available in a growing number of jurisdictions are as follows: mandated arrests, psychoeducational groups, court-mandated 4-, 8-, 12-, or 26-week group counseling, and community-wide interagency systems of batterer intervention. The systematic communitywide collaborations between the judicial system and social service and mental health agencies seem to be the most helpful. This type of intervention model was originally developed in Quincy, Massachusetts, and Duluth, Minnesota, and it has been expanded to other states and cities in the United States.

In the field of domestic violence, a growing number of programs work with the batterer. These programs are often looked on with suspicion by victim advocates and directors of shelters for battered women. There is profound disagreement about how, or even whether, to intervene with batterers. Some researchers find that batterer intervention programs are an important part of preventing further domestic violence, and others find that batterer intervention programs do not deter future violence. Some, such as legal advocate Barbara Hart, maintain that programs for men who batter may be dangerous and hold out false hopes for women; others don't want funds that could be used for victims reallocated to "help" batterers. Given the wide range of professionals involved in the field of domestic violence, this lack of common ground has created tensions and polarization.

BATTERER INTERVENTION PROGRAMS

History of Services

In the early 1970s, the women's and battered women's movements identified "wife beating" as a social problem in the United States and vocalized the need for an expanded public role in identifying and responding to domestic violence. The movement began a nationwide shift by reframing what some men called "discipline" or "obedience" as abuse and violence. By the late 1970s, social services began to cater specifically to the needs of battered women. Prior to that time, services were uncoordinated, requiring women to locate disparate services—accepting emergency funds from the Salvation Army to flee abusers, for example, or finding themselves in shelters for the homeless with no security from abusers or specialized services for victims of domestic violence.

Some pre-1980 services were inappropriate; for example, police officers responding to a domestic incident would walk the abuser around the block to "cool off," without making an arrest. Service providers in a wide range of settings began to express the need for a range of public services to address the behavior of abusers, such as shelters, counseling centers, and support groups for victims of domestic violence, including batterer intervention programs.

Batterers' programs began as voluntary men's group responses to the message of the battered women's movement and an attempt at confronting, among men, the feminist notion that patriarchy enables men to batter and abuse their female partners. In 1976, the Victims Information Bureau of Suffolk County, New York (VIBS), began offering individual and group counseling for batterers. Organized in 1977, Emerge (a batterers' treatment program) was developed at the request of women working in Boston area shelters. In 1978, Abusive Men Exploring New Directions (AMEND) was established in Denver, with the purpose of helping men to redirect their anger, stop physical violence, and establish healthier relationships with women. Similar programs began to appear across the United States with the philosophy that male dominance and misogyny were the root of violence against women and that abusive men were willful and should be accountable for their behavior.

Role of Social Work and Other Mental Health Professionals

The profeminist program philosophies of early batterer intervention programs clearly contrasted with those of the established mental health professions, in which the focus was on keeping the family intact and domestic violence was often viewed as a relational problem. The involvement of social work in domestic violence and batterer intervention began as a face-off with feminists. As opposed to the feminist focus on putting the woman first and providing concrete services for women (i.e., physically helping to move battered women out of their homes and into safe shelters), early social work emphasized mutual support of both men and women, often from an individualistic psychotherapeutic perspective, advocating consciousness-raising groups for men in an effort to change male attitudes and behavior toward women.

Early encounters between feminists and social workers created a framework in which the two groups were diametrically opposed. Feminist-directed battered women's shelters were run by former battered women and paraprofessionals, whereas professionally operated shelters hired clinical directors with master's degrees in social work (MSW) and practice experience.

Although the social work professional theory base has expanded to include systems theory and an ecological perspective, psychological perspectives on the life span continue to dominate much of social work knowledge about human behavior. However, the push for social action and advocacy of a feminist perspective within social work practice has been growing in the field of domestic violence.

Criminal Justice System Responds to Battered Women's Advocates

As the domestic violence movement expanded, increasing attention was given to the role of the criminal justice system in responding to domestic violence. Until the 1980s, domestic violence was largely ignored as a criminal problem by the criminal justice system. Responding police officers talked to the abuser but rarely made an arrest, leaving the man at home with the woman, who was at risk for additional violence because she'd called for help. As public awareness of domestic violence increased and in response to pressure from battered women's advocates, the criminal justice system began to set up more rigid and systemic responses to domestic violence. By 1988, every state had passed acts that created civil and criminal remedies for victims of domestic violence, and by 1992, protective orders were available to abused women in all 50 states. Social workers, battered women's advocates, and mental health agencies developed batterers intervention programs in areas across the United States.

Purpose of Batterer Intervention Programs

A wide variety of interventions and expectations exist for batterer intervention programs: to punish abusers who are caught by the criminal justice system; to hold men accountable for their abusive behavior; to educate men about sexism, patriarchy, and the role that domestic violence plays in maintaining a patriarchal system; to change behavior by providing tools to control and manage anger and thus create healthy, loving relationships; and to change intrapsychic patterning by identifying and resolving childhood and other affective trauma that leads to battering as an adult.

Despite the lack of consensus regarding the purpose of batterer intervention programs, in recent years, there has been a steady increase in referrals to and growth of such programs. Increased referrals are part of the criminal justice system's growing response to domestic violence since the beginning of the battered women's movement. Referrals to programs have proliferated primarily through the courts as more and more states recognize domestic violence as a crime and develop specific programs to remedy the problem.

Models of Batterer Intervention Programs

Different theories of domestic violence offer divergent explanations of the root causes of battering and emphasize specific focal points for intervention and change. (For a comprehensive review of domestic violence theories with case study applications, see Mary Brewster's chapter in the *Handbook of Domestic Violence Intervention Strategies.*)

Individual Models

Individually focused models identify the root cause of violence as grounded in the psychology and history of the individual batterer. Psychological approaches emphasize that personality disorders or early experiences of trauma predispose some individuals to violence. Primary diagnoses for these individuals include a range of mental illness and personality disorders, such as paranoid, borderline personality, passive-aggressive, pathological, depression, narcissistic, and antisocial.

Researchers and practitioners have developed a number of typologies and overarching characteristics of men who batter. In a review of the literature on typologies of male batterers, Holtzworth-Munroe and Stuart suggested three descriptive dimensions: (a) *family-only batterers,* who are generally reported to engage in the least severe types of violence, exhibit little psychopathology, and tend to be less likely to have violence-related legal problems; (b) *dysphoric/borderline batterers,* who are often found to perpetrate moderate to extreme battering, including sexual abuse, and are more likely to evidence borderline and schizoid personality characteristics and have drug and/or alcohol problems; and (c) *generally violent/antisocial batterers,* who not only engage in moderate to severe violence against their partners but also have the most extensive history of general criminal behavior and are more likely to have substance abuse problems and antisocial personality disorders. A further study identified a fourth group, *low-level antisocial batterers,* who exhibit antisocial behavior and moderate levels of domestic and general violence.

Most recently, the literature in this area has broadened focus to the development and use of risk assessment tools to predict and assess repeat abusers. Dutton and Kropp review the history of development of risk assessment lists and recent efforts to empirically validate the proliferation of risk assessment scales. They conclude by supporting the need for more published research on the reliability and validity of these tools. If properly applied, risk assessment scales could assist in serving as the basis for determining the treatment/program for individual batterers and safety assessment for victims.

Family Models

The family systems approach views domestic violence from an interactive perspective. Using this approach, violent behavior is seen as a relationship issue and part of a chain of escalating retributive strategies used alternately by each member of the couple. Family systems theory leads to treatment that involves improving communication and conflict resolution skills between couples and among family members. Both members of the couple, as well as others in the family unit, can develop communication and conflict resolution skills through *solution-focused brief therapy,* which locates the problem in the interaction rather than in the pathology of one individual; focuses on solving the problem rather than looking for causes; and accentuates the positive, for example, examining occasions when the couple avoided violence.

Most current group treatment programs are psychoeducational, focused on teaching behavior and attitude change, with many having underlying profeminist orientations. The programs vary in length, but most are short-term, ranging from 4 to 26 weeks in length. Intervention programs include (a) a range of cognitive behavioral intervention techniques, such as anger management, problem-solving skill training, and communication training and (b) development of social skills, such as communication, assertiveness, and stress reduction.

Effectiveness of Batterer Intervention Programs

The literature is full of published program evaluations that each use quite different success criteria. At one end of the continuum, some researchers have used significant positive change or statistically significant changes in a desired direction among participants to claim success, such as reducing the number of violent incidents or lowering the lethality of violence. At the other end of the continuum, advocates have pressed for nothing short of a transformation of program participants until men are prepared to take action against a woman-battering culture. These positions illustrate the ends of the continuum along which there are many positions concerning what signals a program that "works."

For a thorough review of the research literature on batterers' programs, see Hanson's comprehensive chapter in the *Handbook of Domestic Violence Intervention Strategies*. Some research has shown programs to have some effectiveness. One review of evaluation studies found that in different programs, using varying methods of intervention, a large proportion of men stop their physically abusive behavior subsequent to involvement in batterer intervention programs, reporting successful outcomes ranging from 53% to 85% (Edleson, 1996).

One study found that men who participated in longer-term batterer intervention programs (26 weeks) showed significantly lower recidivism rates at 6 and 12 months after sentencing than those who participated in either shorter-term programs (8 weeks) or received unrelated sentencing such as community service, fines, or probation (Davis, Taylor, & Maxwell, 2000). Another study found that 2 out of 3 men randomly

assigned to receive either structured educational programs or those combining education with group processing were reported by their women partners to have stopped violent behavior during 6- and 18-month follow-up periods, and they achieved more stable outcomes than did those randomly assigned to a less structured, self-help program (Edleson & Syers, 1991).

In evaluating judicially mandated referrals, Davis and colleagues randomly assigned men convicted of misdemeanor domestic violence, in cases in which the prosecution, judge, and defense agreed to treatment, to either 39 hours of a batterer intervention group (some were assigned to complete the treatment in 26 weeks and others in 8 weeks) or a community service program irrelevant to domestic violence. The purpose of the experiment was to assess the impact of treatment on men presumed to be motivated, because it is often argued that an intervention cannot be expected to work for individuals against their will. The results showed that treatment completion rates were higher for the 8-week group than for the 26-week group. However, only defendants assigned to the 26-week group showed significantly lower recidivism at 6 and 12 months post-sentencing compared with defendants in the control group, indicating that longer programs appear to be more effective than shorter ones.

CONCLUSIONS AND RECOMMENDATIONS

Even as research continues to debate the effectiveness of batterer intervention programs, the number of these programs continues to proliferate as pro-arrest policies bring increasing numbers of batterers to court for offenses related to domestic violence. In fact, by the late 1990s, nearly every state used batterer intervention programs; administrators estimated that nearly 80% of their clients were referred by the courts (Healey, Smith, & O'Sullivan, 1998).

Because studies indicate that 31% of women will be physically or sexually assaulted by an intimate partner in their lifetimes (Commonwealth Fund, 1999), an intervention that also reduces the likelihood of future domestic violence will benefit women. In addition, because many women stay with their partners even after their arrests and convictions, it is essential to identify and use effective programs that can change abusive behavior, rather than simply delaying it during a period of incarceration.

In conclusion, we offer the following recommendations to help practitioners and policymakers:

1. Develop coordinated community responses to domestic violence: Emerging research indicates that batterer intervention programs are only as effective as the overall system, including establishment of consistent police and court action for domestic violence, accountability of batterer intervention programs to the criminal justice system, swift and decisive sanctions for batterers who drop out of programs or reoffend, and providing appropriate ongoing outreach, support, and services to victims.

2. Need for standards for batterer intervention programs: Although some states have developed standards for batterer intervention programs, including program length, philosophy and model of intervention, and rules of participation, other states have not. New York State, for example, has no approved state-sanctioned standards for such programs. In New York City, batterer intervention programs for court-mandated participants can vary in length from as few as 4 to as many as 52 sessions, and interventions can range from lecturing to cognitive-behavioral to psychodynamic "therapy." A consensus of standards, principles, and batterers program guidelines should be developed and implemented in all 50 states.

—Albert R. Roberts
and Bea Hanson

See also AGGRESSION: FEMINIST PERSPECTIVE; BATTERED WOMAN'S SYNDROME; CYCLE OF VIOLENCE THEORY; DOMESTIC VIOLENCE; FAMILY VIOLENCE; GENDER VIOLENCE; VICTIMOLOGY

Further Reading

Commonwealth Fund. (1999, May). *Health concerns across a woman's lifespan: The Commonwealth Fund 1998 survey of women's health.*

Davis, R. C., Taylor, B. G., & Maxwell, C. D. (2000, January 2). *Does batterer treatment reduce violence? A randomized experiment in Brooklyn.* New York: Victim Services.

Dutton, D. G., & Kropp, P. R. (April, 2000). A review of domestic violence risk instruments. *Trauma, Violence & Abuse, (1)*2, pp. 171-181.

Edleson, J. L. (1996). *Controversy and change in batterers' programs.* In J. L. Edleson & Z. C. Eisikovits (Eds.), *Future interventions with battered women and their families* (pp. 154-169). Thousand Oaks, CA: Sage.

Edleson, J. L., & Syers, M. (1991). The effects of group treatment for men who batter: An 18-month follow-up study. *Research in Social Work Practice, 1,* pp. 227-243.

Healey, K., Smith, C., & O'Sullivan, C. (1998). *Batterer intervention: Program approaches and criminal justice strategies.* Report of Abt Associates to the National Institute of Justice, Washington, DC.

Holtzworth-Munroe, A., & Stuart, G. L. (1994). Typologies of male batterers: Three subtypes and the differences among them. *Psychological Bulletin, 116,* pp. 476-497.

Roberts, A. R. (Ed.). (2002). *Handbook of domestic violence intervention strategies.* New York: Oxford University Press.

MARTHA BECK AND RAY FERNANDEZ

Martha Beck was born into poverty in 1920. Raped at the age of 13 by her brother, she continued to gain weight, appeared emotionally unstable, and suffered from low self-esteem. By the time she'd been married and divorced several times, she was declared an unfit mother, and authorities removed her two young children. One of the children was illegitimate. When Martha pressed for marriage, the father elected suicide rather than marrying her. She was able to complete high school and worked as a nurse at a city maternity hospital until she was fired in 1947. At some point, she began sending letters to the "Lonely Hearts Club" from an advertisement in the local newspaper, and in this way met her future murder accomplice.

Ray Fernandez was born in Spain in 1914. Considered a shy, introverted man, he was happily married until he received a head injury at age 31. His demeanor changed, as did his personality, and he began to believe that he possessed psychic powers that enabled him to make women fall in love with him. For the next few years, he was described as a "sleazy gigolo with a toupée and a gold tooth" and managed to swindle dozens of women out of their financial assets, but was caught in 1949.

When Fernandez was released from prison, Beck proposed that the two of them become partners and continue the confidence games together. She would pose as his sister. Although Fernandez found her unattractive, they became sexual partners as well, engaging in extremely "degenerate" practices. Martha eventually became jealous of the relationships Ray developed with their victims and began putting barbiturates into their food. Ray then murdered the unsuspecting victims. In one case, Martha "assisted" by drowning a dead woman's 2-year-old child in the bathtub. She initiated the killing and appeared to enjoy watching the child die. In another instance, she struck the victim repeatedly on the head. The two were linked to approximately 20 murders by the time they were apprehended and convicted, and they were executed on March 8th, 1951.

—Eric W. Hickey

Portions of this entry are drawn from *Serial Murderers and Their Victims*, 3rd edition (2002) by E. W. Hickey, published by Wadsworth: Belmont, CA.

See also TEAM KILLERS; SERIAL MURDERS

Further Reading

Seagrave, K. (1992). *Women serial and mass murderers.* North Carolina: McFarland.

THE BELTWAY SNIPERS

Early in the morning on Wednesday, October 2, 2002, the first of many shots began a reign of terror transforming Washington, D.C., and surrounding areas into a killing field. Routine activities such as pumping gas, shopping, sitting on a bench, or waiting in a bus became matters of life and death. No one in public view was safe until the suspects were apprehended on October 24, 2002.

The story, however, did not begin in the D.C. "Beltway" area. Eight months earlier, in Tacoma, Washington, Keenya Cook was home alone with her 6-month-old daughter. She rose to answer the doorbell and was shot point-blank in the face with a .45-caliber handgun. The bullet that killed Keenya was meant for her aunt, who lived in the same house. She had taken sides with Mildred, wife of John Allen Williams, during their divorce, and he had intended that she pay for that decision with her life. Instead, her niece was dead.

After the shooting, John Allen Williams, also known as John Allen Muhammad, left Tacoma with 17-year-old John Lee Malvo, his protégé and self-proclaimed stepson. On September 21, 2002, Kellie Adams was locking up the ABC Liquor Store in Montgomery, Alabama. She later recalled how she felt as if "she had been hit by lightning" when a bullet entered her head. A moment later, Claudine Lee Parker, a coworker,

was shot in the back and died almost instantly. Police, arriving at the scene, saw someone rummaging through a victim's purse. John Lee Malvo escaped, leaving nothing behind except one fingerprint.

Two days later, in Baton Rouge, Louisiana, Malvo and Muhammad were suspected of firing a single shot that killed Hong Im Ballenger as she left her job at the Beauty Depot. Malvo stole her purse and fled through the woods, evading bloodhounds and police. Ballistic examination linked the rifle used in the Louisiana shooting to the shooting in Alabama.

The South was no longer a safe haven for the two fugitives from Washington State. They began to move north and east, eventually ending up in the area surrounding the U.S. Capitol. At 5:20 p.m. on Wednesday, October 2, 2002, an unsuspecting shopper was walking in front of a craft store in Aspen Hill, Maryland. A shot rang out, but it missed the shopper's head and shattered a plate glass window, narrowly missing a clerk at the cash register. After that attack, there were no more misses. A few minutes later, in Silver Springs, Maryland, just 2 miles from the craft store, shots rang out again. James D. Martin was killed in the parking lot of a grocery store, where he had stopped to run an errand for his wife. He was a Vietnam veteran, working as an analyst for the National Oceanic and Atmospheric Administration. The killers hid for the remainder of that evening in preparation for the massacre they would commit the following day.

A lot of killing would be done on October 3, 2002, and the snipers started early. At 7:41 a.m. in Rockville, Maryland, James Buchanan Jr. was mowing a client's lawn when he was shot once in the torso. He died a few minutes later. Three miles north and 31 minutes later, Premkumar Walekar was filling his cab with gasoline in preparation for his workday. A single gunshot rang out, and he fell to the ground, dead. A few minutes later and 2 miles north of the gas station where Walekar was shot, Sara Ramos was sitting on a bench in a small shopping center enjoying the fall morning. She was shot once in the head and died at the scene. Five miles from the shopping center in Kensington, Maryland, at 9:58 a.m., Lori Ann Lewis-Rivera had stopped to vacuum out her minivan when a shot to the torso killed her. The snipers did not strike again until 9:15 p.m., when they killed an immigrant from Haiti, 72-year-old Pascal Charlot, of Washington, D.C., while he was walking his dog in his neighborhood.

Authorities were trying to identify any possible connection between the victims. With each additional victim, it became clearer that the killings were random. One witness believed that he saw the suspects flee in a burgundy-colored Chevrolet Caprice. Another witness claimed that two men in a white van sped away after one of the shootings. Despite looking at hundreds of white vans and meticulously investigating each of the victims for common links, no usable information was discovered. Other than ballistics and location, the only common feature seemed to be that the unfortunate victims were totally unrelated and happened to be at the wrong place at the wrong time. The random nature of the shootings terrified residents of the area and literally shut down all nonessential activities. Schools were placed under emergency lockdown, children were kept away from windows, people left work early or remained home all together, nonessential appointments were canceled, and customers stayed away from businesses.

The next day, October 4, at 2:30 p.m., a rifle shot struck a woman while she was loading packages into her minivan in a craft store parking lot. Despite being critically wounded, she survived after being taken to a local hospital. There were no witnesses to this shooting. By this time, ATF (Alcohol, Tobacco, and Firearms) agents had confirmed that the sniper had used a high-powered rifle using .223-caliber ammunition in at least four of the shootings. They concluded that the scarcity of witnesses meant they were shot from a considerable distance. It was known that the weapon is considered accurate up to 650 yards.

Except for funerals for victims, which began on Sunday, October 6, all was quiet in the Beltway area until the next day. A 13-year-old boy was being driven to school by his aunt. She stopped at 8:09 a.m. to let the boy out in front of his school. As she was driving away, she heard the report of a rifle and looked in her rearview mirror to see her nephew drop to the sidewalk. She backed up and opened the passenger side of the car. He told her he had been shot and then crawled into the car before slumping down. She drove him to the nearest emergency clinic, and he survived. The media had recently reported that all the victims were adults and that children did not appear to be targets. The snipers had apparently responded to the ill-fated public information. He was the youngest victim and the one who established that no one was off-limits, even children.

Law enforcement searched the woods behind the school and discovered a shell casing and an area of matted foliage that indicated someone had lain in wait, sniper style. They also discovered a Tarot card with the message "Dear Policeman, I am God" written on it. Possibly, the sniper was trying to establish a relationship with the police, similar to the unsolved Zodiac case in San Francisco and the Son of Sam Murders committed by David Berkowitz in New York.

Two days later, on Wednesday, October 9, at 8:15 p.m., Dean Harold Meyers was filling his gas tank in Manassas, Virginia, when he was killed by a single shot. He was the seventh person to die and the ninth victim in the Beltway area. Despite an immediate response by law enforcement, evidence was rare and witnesses unhelpful. The last three attacks had occurred near major highways, and witnesses had repeatedly described a white van at the scene. Police responded by stopping dozens of white vans, but nothing was found.

Two days later, at 9:30 a.m., Kenneth Bridges was fatally shot while he stood filling his car with gasoline in Fredericksburg, Virginia. The attack occurred with a Virginia State Trooper parked within 50 yards of the station. The officer heard the shot but never saw the shooter. Once again, witnesses reported a white Chevy Astro Van leaving the scene. Authorities blocked all major arterial routes within minutes but failed to catch any suspects. By then, law enforcement was swamped with as many as a 1,000 calls per hour pouring into the hotline.

There were no killings during the weekend. Residents canceled outdoor events and avoided wooded areas and shopping areas immediately adjacent to main highways and intersections. Many avoided gas stations until it was absolutely necessary. On Monday at 9:15 p.m., the killing resumed. This time, the victim was Linda Franklin, an FBI analyst from Arlington, Virginia, who was shopping with her husband at a home improvement store. As they were loading their car, she was shot in the head and died instantly. Again, roadblocks produced no suspects. One alleged witness, Matthew Dowdy, reported that he saw the shooter, the gun, and the getaway car. It was not until Friday, October 18, that police determined Mr. Dowdy had fabricated his story. He was arrested and charged with "knowingly and willfully making a materially false statement to police."

The next shooting took place, for the first time, on a weekend. On Saturday, October 19, shortly before 8:00 a.m., a man was shot in the stomach as he was leaving the Ponderosa Steak House in Ashland, Virginia.

He was critically injured but survived extensive abdominal surgery. In searching the area surrounding the restaurant, police found a note from the sniper. The killer once again claimed that he was God and blamed five of the deaths on police incompetence and for failure by police to respond to his phone calls. In addition, the sniper provided his bank account number, credit card data, and pin number so that authorities could deposit $10 million. He finished the note with the chilling statement, "Your children are not safe anywhere at any time." On Sunday, Police Chief Moose used the media to try to contact the killer. His attempts evoked a call that was traced to an area close to a Virginia gas station, where police detained a Hispanic man driving a white van. It was determined that the man was not involved in the shootings. Several other potential suspects were apprehended and released throughout the day.

On Tuesday, October 22, 2002, Conrad Johnson, a bus driver, stood in the doorway of his empty bus in Aspen Hill, Maryland. A single rifle shot struck his abdomen, and he died a few minutes later at a local hospital. Again, the shooting resulted in a massive police response, blocking traffic routes and interrogating witnesses. Although no suspects were found, a bulletin with a composite description had been prepared in Alabama that linked John Allen Muhammad and his young companion, John Lee Malvo, to the sniper killings in that state. Chief Moose, in turn, released a notice that the two were wanted for questioning in the Beltway killings and that they may have been driving a blue Chevrolet Caprice with a New Jersey license plate. At the same time, federal investigators in Washington State examined a tree trunk on the property where Muhammad had once lived. Ballistic evidence linked him to the Beltway cases. A few hours later, at 3:19 a.m. on Thursday, October 24, the two suspects were arrested while asleep in their car at a rest stop in Frederick County, Maryland. It was the end of 22 days of terror. The toll was 13 dead and 3 wounded. Now, law enforcement would try to discover what had motivated the killers.

John Allen Williams grew up in Baton Rouge, Louisiana. He was raised by his grandmother and his aunts, rather than by his biological parents. He joined the Muslim religion in 1988 and changed his name from Williams to Muhammad to honor this choice. His first marriage, in 1982, was to his high school sweetheart, with whom he had one child. They divorced in 1988, and he married for a second time that same year.

John Allen Muhammed, age 41, known as the Beltway Sniper, referred to himself as "God" and triggered one of the largest manhunts in American history. He is linked to the killing of 10 victims and the wounding of three others in the Washington, DC area, as well as shootings in other areas of the United States.

Source: Copyright © AFP / CORBIS.

The second marriage produced three children and lasted until 2000. Both divorces were characterized by acrimonious arguments over the custody of the children. His second wife claimed that he was irrational and repeatedly threatened her life. She was worried that if the family continued to live together, the children would suffer psychological damage as a result of his abuse.

Williams served in the Louisiana National Guard from 1978 to 1985; however, his service was not without incident, and he was disciplined twice. The most serious offence was for striking a noncommissioned officer in the head. He enlisted in the army in 1985 and was posted to Fort Lewis, in Washington State; Germany in 1990; Fort Ord, California, in 1992; and back to Ft. Lewis in 1993. He did not receive sniper training in the military but did earn a marksmanship badge with an expert rating in the use of the M-16 rifle. During his military career, he served as a combat engineer, a metal worker, and a water transport specialist. He was discharged in 1994 and then served in the Oregon National Guard until 1995.

Despite his tendency toward violence, his early record is remarkably free of arrests. He was suspected in a shoplifting incident and was arrested twice for driving without a license, but he never was convicted or served time for any offense. He was not a competent businessman, entering into partnerships in a karate studio and an auto repair business that both failed. In late March, 2000, he took his three children from his second marriage and fled to Antigua. He met and lived with a woman and her son, John Lee Malvo. Muhammad returned to the United States and was joined by the boy and his mother, who entered the United States illegally in 2001 in Washington State. Muhammad formed a close relationship with the boy, and they began traveling together, while the mother seemed to drop out of the picture. In August 2001, they lived in a homeless shelter north of Seattle, and John Lee attended school for a few months. They left the area in February 2002 and went to Alabama, where the shootings started, then on to Louisiana and finally to Washington, D.C.

John Lee Malvo was a child without a father. His mother brought several men into his life but none with whom he could form a close bond. John's mother was often away working on other Caribbean islands trying to earn enough money to take care of herself and her son. Consequently, as a young teen, he was left on his own to care for himself. By the time John Muhammad came into his life, the teen was ready to follow anyone who showed him kindness and attention. The young Malvo had no idea of the motives of his mentor and quickly became his protégé. Muhammad trained John to fire a rifle and eventually introduced him to friends as his "sniper." As in other cases of spree and serial murder in which more than one assailant is involved, one offender usually serves as the leader. In this case, a 41-year-old man seduced a vulnerable 17-year-old into a trail of murder.

This case drew international attention. Prior to finding the suspects, there was a media frenzy in trying to determine who the perpetrators might be. Theories ranged from a deranged killer to Taliban sleeper cells. Several criminal profilers were consulted and assisted in the investigation, but ultimately no one had it completely right. No one picked two black men, one still a teen, to be the killers. Profiling was criticized as ineffective for failing to figure out

John Lee Malvo, age 17, after his capture for his role in the Washington, DC Beltway Sniper shootings that took the lives of 10 victims and wounded three others. He is also linked to shootings in other areas of the United States.

Source: Copyright © AFP / CORBIS.

who the offenders were in time to save lives. In the end, the offenders themselves made contact with law enforcement and provided clues that eventually led to their capture. Questions were raised because the offenders did not fit the profile of someone who does such crimes. In truth, every case of serial, spree, or mass murder has established profiles that describe general characteristics of offenders who commit such crimes. What made the D.C. snipers unique was that they were black and that there were two of them. This alone made the case an anomaly even among multiple homicide offenders. In only about 20% of such cases are offenders black, and only 1 in 4 cases involves offenders working together. Even in the best of circumstances, cases sometimes fail to fit the profile.

The motivations for this case are indeed common to almost all such offenders. John Muhammad had lost his job, and his wife had divorced him and filed a restraining order against him. When he abducted his children and left the country, the FBI found him and returned the children to their mother. At 41, he was very angry at the American government for taking his children and had no money and no resources. He was happy that the World Trade Towers had been destroyed and felt it was justified. In short, he had lost his voice in a society that measures success by one's education, employment, financial resources, and family stability. John Muhammad had lost everything and wanted vengeance. Meeting John Malvo provided him with someone to assist him in that quest. If convicted, both men will face the possibility of the death penalty.

—Marlene Deal and Eric W. Hickey

See also BALLISTICS; CRIMINALISTICS; BERKOWITZ, DAVID; FORENSIC SCIENCE; PROFILING; SERIAL MURDER; SPREE MURDERS; TEAM KILLERS; ZODIAC KILLER

Further Reading

Court TV News. (2002). *From Army service to arrest, Muhammad's life follows tangled path.* Retrieved November 13, 2002, from the World Wide Web at: http://www.courttv.com/news/sniper/102402_profile_ap.html.

Court TV News. (2002). *Sniper suspects linked to murders in Louisiana, Alabama.* Retrieved November 13, 2002, from the World Wide Web at: http://www.courttv.com/news/sniper/110102_unsolved_ap.html.

Fox News. (2002). *Fact sheet: Sniper shootings.* Retrieved October 29, 2002, from the World Wide Web: http://www.foxnews.com/story/0,2933,65103,00.html.

Fox News. (2002). *Profile of those killed.* Retrieved October 23, 2002, from the World Wide Web at: http://www.foxnews.com/story/0,2933,65519,00.html.

Maier, N. (Ed.). (2002). *The untold story. 23 days of terror . . . The snipers* (AMI Specials: Vol. VI, No. 3). Boca Raton, FL: America Media.

DAVID RICHARD BERKOWITZ (SON OF SAM)

For 13 months, during 1976 to 1977, David Berkowitz, "Son of Sam" or "The .44-Caliber Killer," held the attention of millions of people in New York City and across the country. On eight "hunting" forays, he shot 13 young men and women, killing 6 of them. Seven others were severely injured after he fired on young women or couples parked in their cars at night. Investigators finally tracked him down through a parking ticket placed on his car while he was in the area looking for a victim. They expected the killer to be a monster but instead found a well-mannered, 24-year-old postal worker, who lived alone. His apartment was filthy, littered with liquor bottles, and the walls scratched with graffiti. On one area of the wall he had scrawled, "In this hole lives the wicked king."

To those few who knew him, he lived a rather uneventful life. Born out of wedlock, he had been placed for adoption. He was an exceptional student, frequently taunted by his classmates for being Jewish. He served 3 years in the U.S. Army, worked as a security guard, and once worked as an auxiliary New York police officer. His most notable character trait seemed to be that he was introverted and liked to roam the streets alone at night. On July 29, 1976, two young women, Donna Lauria, a medical technician, and Jody Valenti, sat talking in their car, when David walked out of the shadows and fired five shots through the windshield. Donna died quickly; Jody was wounded in the thigh. In October, he fired on a young couple through their rear windshield, wounding the young man. In November, David walked up to two women sitting in their car in Queens, and as he asked for directions, he pulled out his .44-caliber gun and fired at both women, paralyzing one of them.

On January 30, 1977, a young couple saying goodnight to each other had their windshield shattered with gunfire. Christine Freund died a few hours later of her injuries. On March 8, 1977, an Armenian student, Virginia Voserichian, was approaching her mother's house when David met her on the sidewalk and shot her directly in the face, killing her instantly. On April 17, 1977, in the same area as some of the other attacks, David shot to death Alexander Epaw and Valentina Swiani as they sat in their automobile. A note was found at the scene that read in part: "I love to hunt. Prowling the streets looking for fair game—tasty meat. The women of Queens are prettiest of all." The killer had identified himself as "Son of Sam" in letters he had sent to a New York columnist, James Breslin. By now, the city was beginning to panic, but David still easily found victims. In June, he shot out the windshield of another car, wounding the two occupants.

David Richard Berkowitz became known as the "Son of Sam" because he claimed that his neighbor Sam's dog instructed him to kill. During his reign of terror in New York City, Berkowitz also earned the moniker of ".44-Caliber Killer," gunning down victims while they sat in their cars.

Source: Copyright © Bettmann / CORBIS.

In July, David decided to relocate his killing to the Brooklyn area, to throw off the police. At 1:30 a.m., he fired four shots through the windshield of a car, striking a young couple. Stacy Moskowitz died a few hours later, and her friend Robert Violante was blinded for life. It was here that David's car was ticketed, and shortly thereafter he was linked to the killings. David was arrested exclaiming, "You finally got me!" In fact, he had planted several clues during the year-long ordeal by sending threatening notes to his Yonkers neighbors. Sam Carr had received such letters and made reports to police that Berkowitz was out to get him because his dog barked too much. On April 27, shortly after Carr received the letters, his dog was shot by David with his .44-caliber gun. Berkowitz's capture proved to be providential for an unknown number of young New Yorkers. He told

police that he'd been planning a raid on a Hampton discotheque that night and that authorities "would be counting bodies all summer." Indeed, police found a submachine gun and a note to authorities lying on the seat of his car.

At first, Berkowitz claimed he'd committed the killings because demonically possessed dogs commanded him to do so. Years later, he would recant those claims publicly by saying that the need to justify those shootings in his own mind had caused him to fabricate that story. He said he'd simply wanted to pay back his neighbor, Sam Carr, for all the noise his dog made, so he created the story that "Sam" was telling him to kill using the dogs as a medium. In a letter he sent to David Abrahamsen, a psychiatrist who determined Berkowitz to be competent for trial, he conceded the following:

I will always fantasize those evil things which are part of my life. I will always remain a mental pervert by thinking sexual things, etc. However, almost everyone else is like me, for we commit numerous perverted sexual acts in our minds day after day. I will always think of violence, for only a monk, perhaps, could ever succeed in eliminating these desires and thoughts. But what I hope to do is mature to such a point in which I will develop a deeper respect for human life and an increased respect and appreciation for humanity. (Abrahamsen, 1985, p. 23)

David Berkowitz received six 25-years-to-life consecutive sentences for the murders to which he confessed, with a recommendation that he never be paroled. He was sent to Sullivan Correctional Facility, in Fallsburg, New York, to serve out his time. Berkowitz converted to Christianity in 1987 after reading a Bible given to him by an inmate. In 1998, in a collaborative effort with evangelical pastors, he helped produce two Christian videos, "Son of Sam/Son of Hope" and "The Choice is Yours With David Berkowitz," in efforts to persuade others to repent. New York passed a "Son of Sam" statute prohibiting criminals from profiting financially from their crimes, which has been challenged in the courts in recent years.

—Eric W. Hickey

Portions of this entry are drawn from *Serial Murderers and Their Victims,* 3rd edition (2002) by E. W. Hickey, published by Wadsworth: Belmont, CA.

See also METHODS OF MURDER; SERIAL MURDER

PAUL BERNARDO AND KARLA HOMOLKA

Paul Bernardo, dubbed the "Scarborough Rapist," sexually assaulted at least 18 women between May 4, 1987, and April 6, 1991.

During his formative years, Bernardo had begun to display signs of scoptophilia, peeping through windows at young women to achieve sexual gratification. At the age of 16, his mother, Marilyn Bernardo, informed him that Kenneth Bernardo was not his father; the boy was the product of an illicit affair with a prominent businessperson. Following this, the distance between Bernardo and his parents increased, as did his aggressive behavior toward women. On completion of a bachelor's degree in commerce and unable to find full-time employment as an accountant, Bernardo began to smuggle cigarettes across the border.

Karla Homolka spent her formative years in a lower-middle-class suburb in St. Catharines, Ontario. Homolka was described by friends as studious and actively involved in various extracurricular activities. At the age of 17, in an act of rebellion, she quit high school and began working at a veterinary hospital. In September 1987, she met Bernardo at a pet store convention and began dating him. He was a frequent weekend guest at the Homolka residence, where Karla lived with her parents and two sisters, Lori and Tammy. During visits, Bernardo became increasingly infatuated with the youngest sister, Tammy. Described by criminologist Candice Skrapec as a malignant narcissist, Homolka was incapable of tolerating a challenge. She perceived her sister as a threat to her relationship with Bernardo, a perception that ultimately resulted in Tammy's death.

On December 24, 1990, Karla drugged her 15-year-old sister with a sleeping medication called Halcion. She then administered Halothane, a general anesthetic, and she and her fiancé Bernardo sexually assaulted Tammy. As a result of the anesthetic, a drug Karla had illegally obtained from the veterinary hospital where she was employed, her sister stopped breathing. Her death was listed as accidental, a result of choking on her own vomit.

In early 1991, Bernardo and Homolka began to cohabit, in a rented bungalow in St. Catharines. Approximately 16 months later, 14-year-old Leslie Mahaffy was taken from outside her home by Bernardo. Two days later, on June 17, 1991, the girl was killed after being tortured and raped. Ironically, on June 29, 1991, the day Mahaffy's remains were discovered, encased in concrete, Homolka and Bernardo celebrated their wedding. In April 1992, 15-year-old Kristen French was kidnapped by Homolka and Bernardo while walking home from school. Within days, the girl was dead.

Shortly thereafter, following a severe beating inflicted by her spouse, Homolka sought medical attention at a local hospital in St. Catharines, Ontario. With encouragement from family members, Homolka pressed assault charges against Bernardo. This incident acted as a catalyst that ultimately led to the arrest of Paul Bernardo as the "Scarborough Rapist" and the murderer of three women. Homolka negotiated a plea bargain in exchange for testifying against her spouse. In 1993, with a publication ban in place, team-killer Karla Homolka received two 12-year sentences, to be served concurrently, in exchange for testifying against her spouse and partner about the murders of Leslie Mahaffy and Kristen French. As part of the plea-bargain agreement, Homolka was granted immunity from prosecution in the death of her sister Tammy. (Ironically, according to Candice Skrapec, none of the victims died until Karla Homolka became involved.) She is eligible for mandatory release in July 2005.

Bernardo is serving life sentences for his role in the killings of 3 women and sexual attacks on 13 more. In addition to the life sentences, Bernardo is classified a dangerous offender as defined in section 753 (a), (i), (ii), and (iii) of the Criminal Code of Canada and thereby detained in a penitentiary for an indeterminate period. This finding is based on psychiatric evaluations in which Bernardo, according to the American Psychiatric Association *Diagnostic and Statistical Manual of Mental Disorders,* 4th edition *(DSM-IV),* fit into three broad categories: sexual disorder, alcohol abuse, and personality disorder, with a poor prognosis for treatment.

Following the arrest and conviction of Bernardo and the plea bargain granted to Homolka, an investigative review was conducted. The report, "Bernardo Investigation Review" (1996) found systematic problems specifically related to a lack of cooperation between law enforcement agencies. The lack of cooperation, in part, allowed Homolka and Bernardo to elude law enforcement officials and continue sexually assaulting and killing victims.

Serial killing is not a recent phenomenon in Canada, as demonstrated in the cases of Clifford Olson, Noel Winters, Lila and William Young, Michael McGray, and David Threinen. Yet none of the aforementioned offenders captured media attention as the case of team killers Karla Homolka and Paul Bernardo. Many unanswered questions remain about them.

—Lynn Gunn

See also SERIAL MURDER; TEAM KILLERS

Further Reading

American Psychiatric Association. (1994). *Diagnostic and Statistical Manual, 4th edition.* American Psychiatric Association, Washington, DC.

Skrapec, C. (2001). Phenomenology and serial murder. *Homicide Studies, 5*(1), 46-63.

BIANCHI, KENNETH, AND ANGELO BUONO, *See* TEAM KILLERS

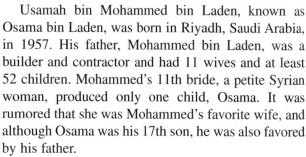

OSAMA BIN LADEN

Usamah bin Mohammed bin Laden, known as Osama bin Laden, was born in Riyadh, Saudi Arabia, in 1957. His father, Mohammed bin Laden, was a builder and contractor and had 11 wives and at least 52 children. Mohammed's 11th bride, a petite Syrian woman, produced only one child, Osama. It was rumored that she was Mohammed's favorite wife, and although Osama was his 17th son, he was also favored by his father.

Mohammed bin Laden moved his family from Yemen to Saudi Arabia to enhance business opportunities for his construction company. Mohammed had connections with the royal family in Saudi, the house of al-Saud. Ultimately, bin Laden's construction corporation became one of the largest and most profitable construction companies in Saudi Arabia. Mohammed's connection to the house of al-Saud furthered his ability to gain lucrative government contracts, including the rebuilding of mosques, the development of new airports and roads, and construction of other major facilities.

Mohammed further strengthened his ties to the Royal House of al-Saud by actually paying government employees' salaries for several months when the Saudi treasury ebbed low. In turn, Mohammed was rewarded with future government contracts in Saudi Arabia. He died in a plane crash in 1967; however, King Faisal continued to be supportive of bin Laden Construction. It has been estimated that the corporation was worth $36 billion in the 1990s. Although initially developed as a construction company, the bin Laden corporation had long ago diversified into other business interests, including telecommunications and import/export.

The development of Osama's religious beliefs were undoubtedly rooted in the teachings of his father, Mohammed, a devout Muslim. He believed in the importance of religious and community leaders working together to strengthen Muslim devotion in his country. It is reported that Mohammed spent a great deal of money financing ongoing religious meetings, called *halqas.* Later, Osama would also be involved in

BACK

Reward poster offering up to $25 million for information leading to the capture of Al Qaeda leaders Ayman al-Zawahiri and Osama bin Laden.

Source: U.S. Department of Defense.

As a young man, Osama bin Laden chose a traditional Moslem education. He majored in economics and management while attending one of the finest universities in Saudi Arabia, Saudi King Abdul Aziz University, rather than attending a university in Europe or the United States, where many of his brothers were educated. Although it is reported that Osama engaged in fairly typical activities during his college years, his views changed after the upheaval in the Middle East during the 1970s, especially the 1973 defeat of the Arab States by Israel in the Yom Kippur War. During this time, he began to question the political policies of the United States, specifically their role in backing Israel during the war.

Soon after the war ended, King Faisal was killed by a nephew who was educated in the United States. This added fuel to Osama's rage at the United States. For bin Laden, history had illustrated the need for the country's return to a more fundamental Islamic doctrine to prevent the corruption, drugs, and promiscuity that he associated with Western culture. The Soviet Union's decision to invade Afghanistan and kill that nation's president, thereby establishing its own government, represented a pivotal point in Osama's career as a militant fundamentalist. Along with other Islamic fundamentalists, he chose to join together in an Islamic fundamentalist doctrine, crossing national lines, to protect the Islamic world as they view it.

the rebuilding of the mosques in his country, as well as the rekindling of his followers' interest in a more traditional Muslim lifestyle.

Bin Laden has been the focus of much debate and speculation. Although he is most known for his tendency to strike aggressively, his followers describe him as being slow to act, rather than impulsive, and as quiet, thoughtful, wise, intelligent, and observant. There have been reports of him struggling with ill health, but he has denied experiencing any problems.

During the invasion of Afghanistan by the Soviet Union, bin Laden went to Pakistan to set up a recruitment station and training camp for Muslim fundamentalists. At this point, he organized the Islamic Salvation Front (ISF) to bolster the Afghan *mujahideen*. His goal was to provide military training and tactical instruction in strategic warfare. During this time, Osama was also recruiting physicians, bomb and munitions experts, military strategists, and engineers, as well as Muslim experts who had been trained abroad. It is estimated that over 25,000 Muslim fighters from approximately 35 countries participated in the Afghanistan struggle. During the war against the Soviet Union, bin Laden first experienced actual combat, in which he was reported to be a fearless fighter.

It was also during this time that Osama bin Laden developed the al-Qaeda organization. Since the 1990s, it appears that the primary purpose of the al-Qaeda network has been to mount numerous anti-American propaganda campaigns. The organization has reportedly been active in Sudan, Lebanon, and Afghanistan. Bin Laden took responsibility for an attack on Somalia in 1993 and an attempt to bomb U.S. military personnel in 1992. During this time, he was also awarded several construction contracts in Sudan. The United States encouraged Riyadh to press charges against bin Laden for his terrorist activities. Osama's long-term family ties to the Royal House of Saudi made this a tense situation for the Saudi government. However, due to increasing pressure to take bin Laden to task for his terrorist activities, eventually a warrant was issued for his arrest, charging him with terrorist crimes in both Algeria and Egypt.

In February 1994, the world was surprised when Saudi Arabia denied bin Laden continued citizenship. However, he continued to develop relationships with other Islamic fundamentalist leaders who were either in exile in Europe or in other Middle Eastern countries. In 1996, due to the increasing political pressure to extradite him to Saudi, bin Laden returned to Afghanistan. According to intelligence services in the United States, at this point, Osama established a drug-trafficking network between Afghanistan and Iran to reestablish his depleted funds.

Osama first came into contact with the Taliban after returning to Afghanistan. He joined forces with them to further his goal of developing governmental rule in the Middle East based on strict fundamentalist Islamic law and to continue his fight against what he saw as corrupt American and Israeli policies. To strengthen his ties to the Taliban, Osama married his oldest daughter to the Taliban's leader, Mullah Muhammad Omar, in 1998. The Taliban soldiers are Sunni Muslims, viewing themselves as students of theology and soldiers of Islam. The organization emphasizes the older interpretations of Islamic law

and moral code. Their focus has reportedly become increasingly orthodox in nature, holding a severely restrictive view of women and opposing minority sects, including Shiism, Iran's state religion. It is reported that the Taliban may have as many as 60,000 members.

On Osama's return to Afghanistan, he met with other Islamic fundamentalist leaders near an Afghan/Arab training camp to develop a plan to thwart American and Israeli power. He and his second in command, Ayman al-Zawahiri, focused their attention on building an intricate network of active fundamentalist Muslim terrorists worldwide. Ayman al-Zawahiri is reportedly the Egyptian leader of the Jihad and may even be responsible for initially converting Osama to the fundamentalist view of Islam.

In excerpts taken from a publicly circulated document signed by bin Laden, made public throughout the Muslim world and also distributed through the Internet, the basis for his beliefs were verified. He discussed the hardships and aggression that he believes the people of Islam have reportedly suffered at the hands of the Christians and the Israeli Jews. In addition, he made it clear that he felt justified in orchestrating harsh retaliatory strikes for these perceived injustices. Accordingly, he aimed these strikes specifically against the United States. Perhaps one of the most disturbing threads in bin Laden's public statements is his continued praise and apparent rejoicing at the deaths of American soldiers and innocent American citizens. Apparently feeling justified in his terrorist activities, in August 1996, Osama published and signed a declaration of Jihad against the United States.

Osama has been very adept in training the Bin Laden Brotherhood to become increasingly financially independent. Perhaps his early training in economics and management laid the foundation for this part of his program. The Bin Laden Brotherhood no longer relies solely on the financial support from their leader. However, it is clear that the bin Laden fortune was a cornerstone in the initial development of the organization. It is difficult to estimate the substantive nature of Osama's fortune. However, if estimates are correct, his personal fortune approximates $300 million, and his family's assets are around $5 billion. The Brotherhood also reportedly obtains significant contributions from Gulf States, including Saudi Arabia. Wealthy Saudi businessmen are reported to contribute substantial sums, and nonprofit organizations have also been set up to raise money for the bin Laden cause. Laundering organizations such as "Save Bosnia Now," a U.S.-based nonprofit organization, have been linked to the Bin Laden Brotherhood. Intelligence agency experts believe that these organizations serve as a funnel for large sums of money that are ultimately used to finance the terrorist activities of the Brotherhood.

The terrorist network established by Osama and the Bin Laden Brotherhood has infiltrated much of Europe. They have developed intricate networks in Great Britain, Germany, and other European countries. Recent intelligence reports indicate that Osama's network has branched out into China, Southeast Asia, and several of the former Soviet Islamic republics. Other countries that are at risk of becoming intimately associated with the Bin Laden Brotherhood include Thailand, Malaysia, Indonesia, and the Philippines.

Bin Laden is revered by many fundamentalist Muslims, symbolizing courage and protection from their perceived enemies, Israel and the United States. However, in the United States, bin Laden has become associated with violent terrorist attacks and death. His terrorist activities include the October 2000 bombing of the U.S.S. *Cole,* while the vessel was in Yemen to refuel. He has reportedly organized other unsuccessful attacks, including an explosion in Seattle on New Year's Eve 2000 and the bombing of an Australian nuclear reactor during the Olympic Games of the same year. A videotape surfaced in the summer of 2001 in which he encouraged his followers to participate in the Jihad against the United States and Israel. Osama is also thought to have been responsible for orchestrating the most serious terrorist attack ever experienced on U.S. soil, the September 11, 2001, destruction of the World Trade Center Towers and attack on the Pentagon by hijacked commercial aircraft.

It is doubtful that the destruction will end with the tragedy of September 11, 2001. Intelligence sources indicate that bin Laden has actively sought out deadly biological weapons. In addition, several alleged members of bin Laden's group have reportedly inquired about the use of crop-dusting planes, and several have illegally obtained licenses to haul hazardous materials. In addition, it is thought that he may have been responsible for the Anthrax outbreak in the United States in 2001. Many authorities and intelligence sources anticipate continued similar terrorist activities from Osama bin Laden and his organization.

—*Jana Price-Sharps*

See also Aeronautical Mass Murder; History of Violence in Religions; Motives for Murder; Terrorism

Further Reading

Hudson, R. A. (1999). *Who becomes a terrorist and why: The 1999 government report on profiling terrorists.* Guilford, CT: Lyons.

Jacquard, R. (2002). *In the name of Osama bin Laden: Global terrorism and the Bin Laden Brotherhood.* London: Duke University Press.

Landau, E. (2002). *Osama bin Laden: A war against the West.* Brookfield, CT: Twenty-first Century Books.

BIOLOGICAL FACTORS IN VIOLENT BEHAVIOR, *See* Aggression: Biological Theories; Violent Behavior

THE BLACK GUERRILLA FAMILY

The Black Guerrilla Family (BGF) was formed at San Quentin Prison, in California, in 1966, by former Black Panther member George L. Jackson. Influenced by radical political theorists, the BGF is based on a Marxist/Maoist/Leninist ideology. It is one of the most politically oriented of all prison gangs.

The original intent of George Jackson's organization was to rechannel the rebellious energies of African Americans away from crime toward political activity. A gradual shift occurred in the organization's primary function with the adoption of a revolutionary philosophy revolving around the idea of using violence to overthrow the racist, imperialist United States establishment. Many believe Jackson was murdered by prison officials because of his beliefs, whereas others believe he was killed in a thwarted prison escape involving violence against prison staff.

Today, the BGF's primary philosophical goals are the education of African American inmates about racism, and maintaining pride and dignity while incarcerated. The BGF's organizational goals are cultural unity, protection of African American inmates, and various criminal acts.

The BGF is a highly organized gang with a formal rank structure consisting of a central executive committee, field generals, captains, lieutenants, and soldiers. Membership entry occurs through sponsorship, and potential members must pass a screening committee investigation. On acceptance, a new member must take a death oath, pledging a lifelong commitment of loyalty to the BGF. It is thought that most Crips (a well-known gang originating in Los Angeles) become automatic BGF members once they enter the prison system. Members are often tattooed with antigovernment/ antiofficial symbols or identifiers specific to the BGF. Identifiers and symbols are primarily a black dragon overtaking a prison or prison tower and/or a crossed saber and shotgun with the initials B.G.F.

It is estimated that the BGF has a California inmate membership of approximately 200 individuals, 50 of whom are housed at San Quentin Prison. These members are political allies with La Nuestra Familia, Black Liberation Army, Symbionese Liberation Army, Weather Underground, and various African American street gangs. In addition to the United States political establishment, BGF enemies include the Mexican Mafia, Aryan Brotherhood, Aryan Brotherhood of Texas, and the Texas Syndicate.

Prison and law enforcement officials consider the BGF to pose a serious threat to corrections and law enforcement personnel who represent the government and the law. The BGF is the most violent and assaultive gang toward correctional staff.

—Monica Myers

See also Aryan Brotherhood; Bloods; Crips; Gangs

BLACK HAND

Black Hand was the name given to various secret criminal groups and gangs organized in Italy and operating in the United States in the late-19th and early-20th centuries. The symbol of a black hand became an instrument of terror to those victimized through blackmail, extortion, and violence. For example, potential victims received letters threatening death, marked with "the hand." At the peak of power, a significant portion of the Italian population were victims of the gang's protection racket in New York City and other cities where the Black Hand's influence was felt.

Other anarchist, militaristic, nationalistic, criminal, and terrorist organizations throughout the 19th and 20th centuries have used the name and symbol of the Black Hand.

—Monica Myers

BLACK MARKET

Black markets are illicit markets for commodities or goods developed in response to and in violation of set-price and allocation controls. Strong black markets exist particularly in countries undergoing the process of industrialization, many of which experience a shortage of consumer goods or have set the official exchange value of domestic currency too high in terms of the purchasing power of foreign money. Black markets for currency are often termed *parallel markets* and have been recognized as a major aspect in the economic survival of some countries.

—Monica Myers

BLACK PANTHER PARTY,
See Black Guerrilla Family

BLACK WIDOWS, *See*
Serial Murder; Poisoners

BLOOD FEUD, *See*
Aggression: Evolutionary and Anthropological Theories

THE BLOODS

The Bloods are a street gang based in Los Angeles, California, originally formed by Sylvester Scott and Vincent Owens for protection against the Crips gang. A shift in objectives to criminal activity for profit and other predatory activities ensued shortly after the gang's formation. The gang's leadership and organizational structure is fluid, and violent acts are a method by which respect is achieved and maintained. Gang membership initiation rituals, such as being "beat in," tend to reflect the overall violent tendencies of the gang culture. Typical Blood gang identifiers/ symbols include the color red in clothing, the use of red bandannas or rags, and specific Blood gang tattoos.

—*Monica Myers*

See also CRIPS; GANGS

BLUEBEARD, *See* HOCH, JOHANN OTTO; LANDRU, HENRI DESIRÉ

BOMBERS/BOMBING, *See* KACZYNSKI, THEODORE; MCVEIGH, TIMOTHY; METHODS OF MURDER; OKLAHOMA CITY BOMBING; OLYMPIC PARK BOMBING; TERRORISM

BONNIE AND CLYDE, *See* PARKER, BONNIE, AND CLYDE BARROW

BOOT CAMPS, *See* PREVENTION OF CRIME AND VIOLENT BEHAVIOR

BOSNIAN GENOCIDE, *See* GENOCIDE

BOSTON STRANGLER, *See* DESALVO, ALBERT HENRY; SIGNATURE KILLERS

THE BRADY BILL

Named after James Brady, presidential press secretary, who was wounded in a failed assassination attempt on President Ronald Reagan in 1981, the Brady Bill mandated a national 5-business-day waiting period and background check on all persons buying handguns through licensed dealers.

Signed into law in 1993 by President Bill Clinton, the original bill contained a "sunset provision," which took effect in 1998. This provision replaced the 5-business-day waiting period with a system allowing for an instant background check through a federal database of criminal records called the "National Instant Check System" (NICS).

Much debate continues to swirl around the Brady Bill and its actual effectiveness. Advocates claim success via figures of denial of purchases (600,000 denials within the first 6 years after the passage of the Brady Law). Critics claim that most felons buy guns on the street and therefore the law is ineffective for those it is intending to thwart, at the expense of every individual's right to keep and bear arms as stated in the Constitution's Second Amendment.

—*Monica Myers*

See also ASSASSINS; GUN CONTROL

BRANCH DAVIDIANS, *See* CULTS; KORESH, DAVID

THE BRAWNER TEST

In 1972, the federal justice system of the United States rejected the Durham rule, which advocated that the criminal act was caused by a perpetrator's mental illness; if this could be proven beyond a reasonable doubt by the prosecutor, the defendant would not be held accountable for his or her actions. In its place, the federal justice system installed the 1972 Brawner Test, which was largely based on an insanity rule found in the model penal code (MPC) of 1962. This was used by approximately one half of the states but has been held in disfavor and restricted in its use since the trial of John Hinckley, the attempted assassin of former President Reagan.

The Brawner Test originated in the case law of *United States v. Brawner*, which states,

> A person is not responsible for criminal conduct if at the time of such conduct as a result of mental disease or *defect*, he lacks substantial capacity either to appreciate the wrongfulness of his conduct or to conform his conduct to the requirements of the law. (471 F.2d 969, D.C. Dir, 1972, p. 973)

The Brawner Test requires the prosecutor to prove beyond a reasonable doubt that the defendant lacks the capacity to appreciate the wrongfulness of his or her conduct or the ability to control his or her behavior. It recognizes partial responsibility for criminal conduct including the possibility of an irresistible impulse beyond one's control. It also excludes from this definition any habitual or otherwise antisocial conduct. This is known as the *caveat paragraph* and is intended to exclude criminal psychopaths or those with antisocial personality disorder from using the insanity defense.

The test dominated federal and state practice until the Hinckley trial, but the adverse public reaction to the outcome of this trial relegated the Brawner Test to less use. Instead, a new standard resembling the original M'Naughten Rule was adopted, which once again places the burden of proof of insanity on the defendant. Some states still supplement M'Naughten with an irresistible impulse test when recognizing that the wrongfulness of the behavior is not in question but rather the power to resist the influences of uncontrollable impulses.

—*Marlene Deal*

See also HOMICIDE: IRRESISTIBLE IMPULSE RULE; M'NAUGHTEN RULE; NOT GUILTY BY REASON OF INSANITY (NGRI)

THEODORE "TED" BUNDY

One of the most prolific and elusive serial killers in history, Theodore Bundy unleashed his murderous rage on an estimated 35 women while maintaining the facade of the boy next door. He was handsome, charming, confident, and dangerous, qualities that enabled him to go undetected for years. From early 1974, the stranger called "Ted" hunted young women in Washington, Oregon, Utah, Idaho, Colorado, and Florida. Bundy, a law student and Young Republican, sometimes wore an arm cast to appear vulnerable and helpless. He had a penchant for killing attractive young females with dark shoulder-length hair, parted in the middle. Once he enticed his victims to his car, he bludgeoned, raped, and tortured them.

Theodore Robert Bundy was born, illegitimate, in 1946, in Vermont. To avoid shame, the family pretended he was his mother's little brother. He never knew his father, and his mother later married John Bundy. At age 3, Bundy was found standing over his aunt's bed holding a butcher knife. Despite his intelligence in school, he was described as volatile and unpredictable. He was a compulsive masturbator and a voyeur or "peeping Tom," also arrested on suspicion of burglary and auto theft. In 1972, Bundy graduated with a degree in psychology from the University of Washington; he developed a program for offenders and designed a rape pamphlet for the county. He became adept at blending into his environment like a social chameleon.

Bundy's brutal crimes began in Washington, with Linda Healy. She was abducted and murdered on January 31, 1974. Another victim survived after being assaulted and bludgeoned. From March 1974 on, several young women vanished. In November of 1974, Carol DeRonch was attacked and miraculously

Theodore "Ted" Bundy, sexual predator and serial killer who, during the 1970s, murdered approximately 35 young women in the states of Washington, Colorado, Utah, and Florida.

Source: Copyright © Bettmann / CORBIS.

escaped from Bundy's clutches. That same day, still driven to kill, he kidnapped Debbie Kent. The killings continued despite police efforts to establish the identity of the murderer. After Bundy moved to Colorado to attend law school, women continued to disappear. Then, on August 16, 1975, after being arrested for possession of burglary tools, he was identified by Carol DeRonch as the man who had attempted to kill her.

While awaiting trial in Colorado for murder, Bundy escaped from the courthouse and dodged police until he was recaptured, only to escape again from Garfield County Jail. In 1977, he moved on to Tallahassee, Florida; and in January 1978, he raided the Chi Omega sorority house at Florida State University. Before the massacre was over, Margaret Bowman and Lisa Levy had been viciously raped and killed. Bite marks discovered on their bodies provided key evidence at his trial.

Weeks later, he stole a VW van and killed Kimberly Leach, 12, who was taken from her school in Lake City, Florida. Her body was found 2 months later in a state park. During his trial, in which he defended himself, an extremely narcissistic Bundy showed no signs of remorse. Asked why he had committed the murders, he claimed that pornography had snatched him from his childhood. He claimed to have killed over 100 women, but estimates are closer to 35. Bundy, the consummate psychopath and sexual predator, was electrocuted on January 24, 1989, at a Florida state penitentiary.

—*Amy Lynne Bronswick*

See also Motives for Murder; Serial Murder; Signature Killers

Further Reading

Hickey, E. W. (2002). *Serial murderers and their victims* (3rd ed.). Belmont, CA: Wadsworth.

Newton, M. (2000). *The encyclopedia of serial killers.* New York: Checkmark Books.

Time Life Books. (1992). *Serial killers: Profiles of today's most terrifying criminals.* Alexandria, VA: Time Life Books.

CAMBODIAN GENOCIDE,
See GENOCIDE

CAMPUS VIOLENCE

Several high-profile cases of campus violence spurred federal legislation requiring colleges and universities to make their crime statistics public. The Awareness and Campus Security Act of 1990 (Title 20 Sec. 1092) was the first law requiring all public and private college and university campuses participating in federal student aid programs to disclose information about campus crime and security policies. Renamed the Jeanne Clery Disclosure of Campus Security Policy and Campus Crime Statistics Act (referred to as the Clery Act) in 1998, an amendment of the law occurred in response to allegations of colleges and universities using loopholes in the law to manipulate reportable crime data.

Critics claimed that colleges and universities wanted to avoid bad publicity by misreporting crime data figures, whereas the institutions claimed the federal reporting requirements were too vague. Amendments made to the Clery Act specifically addressed these purported areas of vagueness, while additionally granting the department of education the power to impose sanctions of up to $25,000 for each offense of misreporting committed.

All public and private college and university campuses participating in federal student aid programs are required to post statistics under categories of crime such as alleged homicides, rapes, assaults, arson, hate crimes, burglaries, liquor law violations, and drug arrests on the department of education's Web site, where the public can readily access and view the data.

CAPITAL PUNISHMENT, *See* COURTS; DEATH PENALTY; DEATH ROW

ALPHONSE "AL" CAPONE

Alphonse "Al" Capone was an American-born Italian gangster who held great fascination for the American public. His crime syndicate controlled Chicago's alcohol, gambling, protection, and racketeering activities during the 1920s and 1930s. At his peak, Capone was estimated to have taken in extraordinary amounts of money for the time, often in excess of $105,000 per year. The excessive wealth and lavish expenditures helped bring about a guilty verdict in Capone's tax evasion trial in 1931.

With good behavior and work credits, Capone served 6 years and 5 months of his 11-year sentence. He spent the final year being treated in the medical section of the prison after the syphilis he'd contracted as a young man moved into the tertiary stage.

Al Capone died at the age of 48, from cardiac arrest, 8 years after his release from prison.

—Monica Myers

See also CHICAGO MOB; ORGANIZED CRIME: DOMESTIC

CAUSE OF DEATH, *See* CRIMINALISTS; METHODS OF MURDER

CENTENNIAL OLYMPIC PARK BOMBING, *See* OLYMPIC PARK BOMBING

CHAMBER OF HORRORS, *See* MADAME TUSSAUD

CHAPMAN, MARK, *See* MOTIVES FOR MURDER

Andrei Chikatilo, known as the Russian Ripper and Butcher of Rostov, stalked and killed over 50 children. Within a month of his arrest and conviction, Chikatilo was executed by Russian security.

Source: Copyright © CORBIS.

THE CHICAGO MOB

During the 1920s, the Eighteenth Amendment to the Constitution prohibited the sale and production of alcohol in the United States. As a result of Prohibition bootlegging, the illegal distribution of alcohol became the trade of gangsters. One of the most notorious Chicago mobsters was Al Capone. Because bootlegging and gambling proved to be so lucrative, there were many gang rivalries. Tensions came to a head on Valentine's Day in 1929, in what later became known as the "St. Valentine's Day Massacre." During the massacre, seven gangsters were brutally murdered by rival gang members dressed as police officers. With this event and the end of Prohibition in 1933, the flourishing crime industry began to die out, although not without affecting the city of Chicago's reputation for crime and violence for years to come.

—*Jami Jenkins*

See also CAPONE, ALPHONSE; ORGANIZED
    CRIME; ST. VALENTINE'S DAY MASSACRE

ANDREI CHIKATILO: THE "RUSSIAN RIPPER"

Andrei Chikatilo killed 14 young girls, 21 boys, and 18 women between 1978 and 1990. He came to be known as the "Russian Ripper" for the brutal nature of his crimes, in which he stalked, murdered, and cannibalized his victims.

Born in the Ukraine in 1936, Chikatilo was known as a modest, intelligent man who enjoyed playing chess. His education from Rostov University included degrees in Russian language and literature, engineering, and Marxist-Leninism. During his career as a killer, Chikatilo was married, with two children, a boy and a girl about the same ages as many of his victims. He was considered a steady wage earner, never forceful or violent with his children. By the time he was arrested in 1990 for the "Forest Strip Murders" in the town of Novocherkassk, near Rostov, Chikatilo seemed to be a gray-haired grandfather living a reclusive lifestyle—but was far from it.

Life had been hard for Chikatilo. His older brother Stepan had been abducted and cannibalized during the Ukrainian famine of the 1930s. He grew up fearful and insecure, wishing for a successful career. His chances for success had been thwarted in part by his father, who, after World War II, was sent to a prison camp for allowing himself to be taken prisoner by the Germans. Everything Chikatilo did, including his military experience, he perceived as inconsequential. Indeed, his employment record was disturbing. He first worked as a dorm monitor at a local mining school. His history of peeping through keyholes and wandering into girl's toilets eventually led to his termination.

Chikatilo's forced relocation to Shakhty, in the south of Russia, meant a reduction in job status and quality of life for his family. Suffering from low self-esteem and a pronounced sense of inferiority around groups of people, he harbored a "hero fantasy" to compensate for his sense of failure. He became a master at manipulating and molesting children of all ages. His increased attraction to children gradually stifled any desire for his wife. As a manifestation of his own self-hate, he admitted his "sexual weakness" to the police but explained to them that his interest in children was something from his distant past; now that he was married, with children, he had overcome such urges. To the police, the explanation seemed plausible enough. Unfortunately for dozens of children, Chikatilo's pedophilia would not be examined closely enough to see through his deception.

By this time, he had murdered two children. His first victim in 1978 was 9-year-old Lena Zakotnova. He lured her to a dilapidated shack he used for a private retreat, stabbed her several times, and threw her in a nearby river to die. A scarf had been tied around her eyes. Considering the amount of evidence Chikatilo left behind, his capture should have been inevitable. A bungled investigation and a desire by investigators to close the case led to the confession and conviction of another man. Meanwhile, Chikatilo's progressively violent fantasies fueled his next murder of 17-year-old Larisa Tkachenk, whom he strangled and mutilated.

Chikatilo was promoted to senior engineer in a factory in Rostov-on-Don in 1981. This promotion would require that he travel within the region. He relished the opportunity to meet young people traveling alone. Chikatilo hunted his victims in and around train and bus stations on his way to and from work. He kindly offered them candy, money, and comfort as enticements to take a little walk with him over to the forest strips, where they could be alone. He became adept at targeting naive, trusting victims who perceived him as a nice man. Chikatilo's escalation in brutality was incredible. Due to his sense of inferiority, he would not allow his victims to look at him during the attacks. The victim's stare disturbed the killer's paraphilic fantasies. His third victim was a 12-year-old girl, whom he picked up at a bus stop and killed in some nearby bushes. By July, 1981, he had killed three more victims: two girls, aged 14 and 16, and a 9-year-old boy.

Still, his drive for killing increased. In December 1982, he murdered 10-year-old Olya Stalmach, stabbing her many times. Over the next 8 years, Chikatilo killed savagely on impulse. He hunted runaways, intellectually slower children, and young women who thought him to be just another man looking for a sexual encounter. His established methods of torture and killing seldom varied, and typically his victims received between 30 and 50 stab wounds—one boy had over 70. His violent acts earned him the name of "Ripper."

In 1984, he was faced with a criminal complaint for theft, dismissed from his job, and lost his membership in the Communist party. His anger and fantasies continued to drive his attacks. One of Chikatilo's later victims, 11-year-old Yaroslav Makarov, was killed shortly before his capture in 1990.

Initially, investigation of the murders was handled by local police and was rife with incompetence. With the frequency of new victims, the Russian attorney general's office took control of the investigation. Police had decided that they were looking for a dishonorably discharged police officer. Chikatilo was no police officer, though he did have a great interest in police work.

By 1984, police had arrested, detained, and interrogated dozens of men who were known pedophiles, several mentally disordered youth, and homosexuals. In 1985, Inspector Kostov joined the manhunt, and other law enforcement agencies, including the FBI, consulted with him. The persistence of Kostov ultimately lead to Chikatilo's capture and his confession to all the murders. One month after his confession, Andrei Chikatilo was executed with a bullet to the back of his head. International interest in this case led to the making of the video *Citizen X* and the writing of at least three books.

—*Eric W. Hickey*

NOTE: Portions of this profile were previously published in Eric Hickey's *Serial Murderers and Their Victims,* 2002, 3rd ed. Belmont, CA: Wadsworth Publishers.

See also Homicide; Paraphilia; Pedophilia; Rippers; Serial Murder: International Incidence

Further Reading

Cullen, R. (1993). *The killer department.* New York: Pantheon.

Lourie, R. (1993). *Hunting the devil.* London: Grafton.

CHILD ABUSE

In 2000, 1,236 children died from abuse in the United States, according to the Washington, D.C.-based Child Welfare League of America. That would average out to at least three children per day. Most children who die are younger than 6 years old. These deaths represent an alarming trend in the abuse of children in the United States. In 1994, there were over 664,000 reports of child abuse/neglect in the State of California. Of those reported, about 90,000 of the children were living in foster care (U.S. Department of Health and Human Services, Children's Bureau, 1998).

In tracking the incidence and prevalence of child abuse in the United States, the findings of the Third National Incidence Study of Child Abuse and Neglect (NIS-3) show a sharp increase in the problem. An estimated 1,553,800 children in the United States were abused or neglected in 1993 (National Clearinghouse on Child Abuse and Neglect):

♦ The estimated number of sexually abused children rose from 119,200 in 1986 to 217,700 in 1993 (an 83% increase).

♦ The number of physically neglected children increased from an estimated 167,800 at the time of the NIS-2 to an estimated 338,900 in the NIS-3 (a 102% increase).

♦ There was a 333% increase in the estimated number of emotionally neglected children, from 49,200 in the NIS-2 to 212,800 in the NIS-3.

♦ The number of physically abused children was 269,700 at the time of the NIS-2 but increased to 381,700 during the NIS-3 (a 42% increase).

Children of single parents were at higher risk of physical abuse and of all types of neglect and were overrepresented among seriously injured, moderately injured, and endangered children. Compared with their counterparts living with both parents, children in single-parent families showed the following:

♦ 77% greater risk of being harmed by physical abuse

♦ 87% greater risk of being harmed by physical neglect

♦ 74% greater risk of being harmed by emotional neglect

♦ 220% greater risk of being educationally neglected

♦ Approximately 80% greater risk of suffering serious injury or harm from abuse or neglect

♦ Approximately 90% greater risk of receiving moderate injury or harm as a result of child maltreatment

♦ 120% greater risk of being endangered by some type of child abuse or neglect

According to the National Clearinghouse on Child Abuse and Neglect, children in single-parent households and those living with only their fathers were approximately 1²/₃ times more likely to be physically abused than those living with their mothers only. Family income was significantly related to incidence rates in nearly every category of maltreatment. Compared with children whose families earned $30,000 per year or more, those in families with annual incomes below $15,000 year per showed the following tendencies:

♦ 22 to 25 times more likely to experience some form of abuse

♦ More than 44 times more likely to be neglected

♦ About 12 to 16 times more likely to be victims of physical abuse

♦ Almost 18 times more likely to be sexually abused

♦ 13 to 18 times more likely to be emotionally abused

♦ 40 to 48 times more likely to experience physical neglect

♦ 27 to 29 times more likely to be emotionally neglected

♦ Nearly 56 times more likely to be educationally neglected

♦ 22 to 60 times more likely to die from maltreatment of some type

♦ More than 22 times more likely to be seriously injured by maltreatment

♦ About 18 to 20 times more likely to be moderately injured by abuse or neglect

♦ 39 to 57 times more likely to be classified as having inferred injuries

♦ More than 31 times more likely to be considered endangered, although not yet injured, by some type of abusive or neglectful treatment

The study also found that children were more often neglected by female perpetrators (87% by females versus 43% by males). This is explained by the fact that mothers and mother-substitutes tend to be the primary caretakers and are the primary persons held accountable for any omissions or failings in care-taking. In contrast, children were more often abused by males (67% were abused by males versus 40% by females). The prevalence of male perpetrators was greatest in the category of sexual abuse, in which 89%

of the children were abused by males compared with only 12% by females.

Among all abused children, those abused by their birth parents were about equally likely to have been abused by mothers as by fathers (50% and 58%, respectively), but those abused by other parents, parent-substitutes, or other, nonparental perpetrators were much more likely to be abused by males (80% to 90% by males versus 14% to 15% by females). For sexual abuse, the child's relationship to the perpetrator made very little difference; males clearly predominated as perpetrators, whatever their relationships to the children (National Clearinghouse on Child Abuse and Neglect).

FORMS OF ABUSE

Child abuse pertains to the emotional, physical, or sexual abuse or neglect of children by their parents, caregivers, or guardians that results in significant emotional harm, serious risk of harm, or injury to the child. This maltreatment can take many forms, from failure to provide for the basic needs of the child to severe physical abuse. The majority of *nonaccidental trauma* injuries are reported to be contusions, and the primary sites of injury are reported to be to the face and buttocks. The hand is the most common instrument used to injure a child. However, children are also injured using various other methods. For example, some children suffer cigarette burns, fractures, and more serious injuries. These nonaccidental trauma include intentional injuries that are impulsive acts generated by anger and frustration or that result from harsh discipline or from inadequate supervision.

Cases of *neglect* include instances of a child being left alone, unsupervised in a car, on the street, or in a public shopping area. Neglect also includes cases in which a child is frequently involved in accidents or endangering situations, is not provided sufficient or nutritious food, or lives in unsanitary or unsafe conditions, which include fire hazards and lack of basic heating or plumbing. Neglect can also include living in a situation in which there is mental illness, substance abuse, or lack of understanding in how to care for a child.

Sexual abuse involves any sexual activity with a child in which consent is not or cannot be given, including sexual contact by force or threat of force, regardless of age of the perpetrators, and all sexual contact between adults and children, whether or not the child understands the nature of the activity. This includes incestuous activities between parents or siblings. Sexual abuse includes physical (fondling, penetration), visual (viewing pornographic material or voyeurism), or verbal sexual references and sexual degradation.

The following are a few specific types of child abuse.

Reactive Attachment Disorder of Infancy or Early Childhood. Reactive attachment disorder of infancy or early childhood is a disturbance of interpersonal interaction due to the neglect of a child's physical and emotional needs by the caregiver. It can also occur when a child has multiple caregivers, making it difficult for the child to develop appropriate bonds.

Shaken Baby Syndrome. This form of abuse involves violently shaking an infant or young child, resulting in a severe form of head injury. It usually occurs in children younger than 2 years old but can be seen in children up to the age of 5 years. The results of the severe injuries to the infant or young child can include permanent brain damage, seizures, or even death. The injuries may not be visible, and this is by far the most difficult form of abuse to identify in young children.

Munchausen's Syndrome by Proxy. Munchausen's syndrome by proxy is also known as *factitious disorder by proxy.* This syndrome involves the caregiver deliberately exaggerating or fabricating physical, psychological, or behavioral problems in another individual, typically an infant or young child, to gain some form of attention or gratification.

SOCIETAL SAFEGUARDS AGAINST CHILD ABUSE

Physicians, teachers, and mental health professionals, among others, are required by law in most states and countries to report all suspected incidents of child abuse. Suspicion is typically aroused when patterns of injuries do not match the reported cause or when a pattern of injury is reported that is not developmentally possible. For example, a 2-day-old infant is unlikely to "roll" out of bed. Children's risk of being abused increases if their caregivers were victims of abuse; the caregivers lack understanding of the child's needs; there are unrealistic expectations of the child; there are stressors within the family; the caregivers have strong beliefs regarding corporal punishment; the caregivers have poor self-images; or the caregivers

Table 1   Cost of Foster Care

Type of Care	Number of Wards Now Served	Annual Cost for One Ward
Regular foster care	7,449	$11,957
Relative foster care (children staying with relatives)	7,310	$11,231
Specialized foster care (children with severe physical or mental disabilities)	4,289	$32,536
Institutions and group homes (unlocked multibed facilities)	1,882	$90,319 (institutions) $86,271 (group homes)
Independent living (older teens who live on their own in supervised programs)	835	$46,252

Source: University of Illinois Children and Family Research Center.

are mentally disturbed. The risk increases for the child as the number of risk factors increases.

Abused children are often removed by child protective services to foster homes, group homes, or placed with other relatives. One problem in protecting children is increasing costs both to the state and victims themselves, who often are shuttled to several placements before they are no longer wards of the state. For example, in the Illinois Department of Children and Family Services, a youth often moves within the system, with an average of $16,425 being spent on each in 2002. Nationally, the child welfare system is overwhelmed with a record number of abuse claims, while caseworker salaries are lagging, and the turnover rate is high. Federal statistics show that nearly 67% of the children in the Department of Child and Family Services system for more than 2 years have lived in at least three different places—a traumatizing number considering that they were already taken from their first homes. (See Table 1.)

—*Elizabeth M. Stanczak and Eric W. Hickey*

See also ATTACHMENT DEFICIENCY AND VIOLENCE; BATTERED CHILD SYNDROME; CHILDREN AS VICTIMS OF SEX CRIMES; CHILD KILLERS; EXPLOITATION OF CHILDREN; FAMILY VIOLENCE

Further Reading

Carter, J. (1998). Addressing domestic violence: The vision of the community partnerships. *Safekeeping, 3*(1), 1-5.

Daro, D., & Cohn, A. H. (1988). Child maltreatment evaluation efforts: What have we learned? In G. T. Hotaling, D. Finkelhor, J. T. Kirkpatrick, & M. A. Straus (Eds.), *Coping with family violence: Research and policy perspectives* (pp. 275-287). Newbury Park, CA: Sage.

National Clearinghouse on Child Abuse and Neglect Information. Available on the World Wide Web at: nccanch@calib.com.

Osofsky, J. D. (1996). Island of safety: Assessing and treating young victims of violence. *Zero to Three Bulletin, 16,* 5-8.

Stark, E., & Flitcraft, A. H. (1988). Women and children at risk: A feminist perspective on child abuse. *International Journal of Health Services, 18*(1), 97-118.

Sykes, D., & Symons-Moulton, B. (1990). *A handbook for the prevention of family violence.* Hamilton, Ontario: Seldon Printing.

University of Illinois Children and Family Research Center. Available on the World Wide Web at: cfrcwww.social. uiuc.edu/centres/main.htm.

U.S. Department of Health and Human Services, Children's Bureau. (1998). *Child maltreatment 1996: Reports from the states to the national child abuse and neglect data system.* Washington, DC: U.S. Government Printing Office.

CHILD ABUSE: TREATMENT AND PREVENTION

Treating survivors of child abuse and preventing new cases is an important first step in raising healthy children and fostering a safe society. Several studies suggest that child abuse and neglect increase the risk of many different negative consequences, including involvement in serious delinquency and homicide.

Victims of abuse account for a large proportion of the clients in both the mental health and criminal justice systems. Research and clinical findings suggest that most of these clients have survived multiple victimizations extending over several years.

Children who grow up in abusive families develop a variety of coping strategies that help them survive. However, many of these strategies are maladaptive in the outside world. For example, some victims of childhood abuse fight back by becoming aggressors. Others victimized by family violence withdraw and anesthetize themselves with drugs and alcohol. Many suffer from low self-esteem, anxiety, chronic depression, symptoms of post-traumatic stress, difficulty in developing relationships, and dissociative episodes.

Abused children's poor self-esteem, distorted thinking, inability to express emotion in a healthy way, and self-defeating and often destructive and impulsive behavior are typically the products of years of neglectful, inadequate, and abusive parenting. *Integrative therapy* is a process of cognitive, emotional, and physical restructuring that has been successfully used to treat hundreds of abused individuals. Cognitive restructuring involves effecting more rational and congruent thinking and developing a positive self-image. Emotional change includes learning healthy strategies for accepting, experiencing, and releasing feelings. Physical change consists of breathing more effectively, learning stress management techniques so that the body is more relaxed, and being more in touch with bodily sensations and needs.

In integrative therapy, an eclectic approach is taken. Traditional therapeutic strategies associated with psychodynamic and humanistic approaches, cognitive therapy, and behavioral techniques are employed as they seem appropriate. The therapist assumes the role of a healthy, supportive adult for the abused youth. Slowly, these clients are shown how to provide for themselves the support and nurturing that they did not receive from their parents. Old, destructive messages are replaced with new, constructive ones.

Awareness and discharge of emotions is basic to resolving issues related to child abuse and neglect. Accordingly, an experiential approach is used by therapists with specialized training working in a safe environment to facilitate clients' confronting and resolving feelings associated with early childhood mistreatment.

At the beginning of therapy, the client's level of personality development must be assessed in order to chart realistic and effective treatment goals and objectives. In addition, obtaining as complete a psychosocial history as possible is essential to ensure that family history and dynamics can be effectively addressed. The client's psychosocial history is of paramount importance in reexamining the past, coping with the present, and projecting the future. If the child's reentering the family unit is expected or desired, family therapy, as well as individual therapy, is recommended for the child and his or her parents.

A therapeutic relationship must be developed between the therapist and the child for the youth to feel safe enough to participate fully in the therapeutic process. Although certain techniques can be used to build rapport rapidly, clients in many cases will need considerable time before they can trust the therapist. If a crisis has preceded the referral, the youth's current situation must be recognized and handled. Attention must be focused on helping the youth to understand the context, that is, the family psychopathology that led to the abuse. Take the example of a young boy who may have had to take on responsibilities and duties that children are not normally expected to fulfill. As a result, his life may have become increasingly focused on taking care of others at the expense of his own needs. He needs to understand, however, that this care-taking role has typically come at an enormous cost and may have robbed him of his childhood.

Central to this abused child's recovery is the understanding that he has certain basic rights as a human being, including the rights to feel, see, hear, and think and the right to the security of his own body. Abuse and neglect often cause the child to abrogate the self. He was probably told not to cry, not to be angry, and not to express any other "negative" emotions. He may have been assured that problems such as alcoholism did not exist in the family. He learned to deny his own experience in order to receive approval from his parents. As this incongruence developed between what he knew to be reality and the distorted perception he adopted to gain parental approval, the child abandoned his core self.

The abused child needs to take an inventory of himself and identify his personal successes as well as his failures. The youth must count his survival among his successes. By focusing on his strengths, the youth can accept that he is not a "bad person." He needs to be encouraged to take credit for what he did to help the family unit survive as long as it did.

Special attention is needed in cases in which abused youths acted out against society or struck back at the abusive parents. The youth must become aware that he made mistakes and engaged in destructive and unhealthy behavior. If he acted out in school or in the community as a result of the stress at home, this behavior must also be evaluated honestly. If he killed an abusive parent, this issue has to be faced directly. The youth must come to see that his behavior, although often understandable, is not acceptable by societal standards.

In addition to having distorted perceptions of his family situation and himself, the abused child may feel numb when he enters therapy and may suffer from post-traumatic stress disorder. During the therapeutic process, the youth may come to experience feelings typically associated with the grieving process, such as anger, sadness, and fear, particularly in cases in which the youth killed a parent.

When he is terrified or enraged, the youth may sense that his body is out of control due to his autonomic reactions. When an individual attempts to control the expression of intense emotions, his body becomes an armor of defense: The rigidity of the body defends the individual from experiencing the intensity of feeling. The therapist must help the abused child release his emotions slowly and safely. The therapeutic environment must be safe for the youth to get in touch with his feelings and discharge them.

The abused child may try to hurt himself as therapy progresses because he may believe that he ought to be punished and made to suffer for any antisocial actions that he took or the anger that he feels. This behavior may be the result of the youth's experience that it is safer to turn anger inward rather than outward. In addition, the youth may have learned to direct anger toward himself rather than toward the abuser.

The abused child generally enters therapy with a negative self-image, the result of abusive and neglectful parenting. In the early stages of therapy, internalized shame is at its peak. The youth who has killed a parent, in particular, feels as though he has betrayed his family and himself and has exposed himself and his family to public scrutiny and judgment. The therapist must give the abused child positive affirmations (e.g., "You are a good human being," "You have a right to your feelings") from the beginning and heighten his awareness of his fundamental rights as a human being.

The therapist serves as a positive adult figure throughout the treatment process. Responding with support and understanding to the youth's younger self is critical, because regression to early childhood

behavior and feelings is often part of the recovery process. The therapist sets limits and teaches problem-solving skills.

When the adolescent has regressed emotionally, he becomes aware of the depth of early needs not met by caretakers. The therapist validates the client's unmet needs and explores the effects of this neglect, teaching the youth how to begin to satisfy his needs in a healthy, adult manner. With the therapist's assistance, the youth learns to give himself more self-nurturing messages, such as "I am O.K.," "I'll be O.K., no matter what," or "I love you."

One goal of the integrative therapy model, a positive self-image, has benefits that go beyond the individual. People with positive self-images make healthier choices for themselves. Because many of these choices affect others, society benefits when individuals are guided toward greater emotional health and maturity. Abused and neglected individuals who have worked through the fear, anger, sadness, and shame associated with years of maltreatment are more likely to break the intergenerational cycle of abuse than those who remain untreated.

The undeniable realities and effects of child abuse and neglect in our society are being recognized increasingly as everyone's responsibility. Despite the increased public attention given to child mistreatment, many people are unclear about what to do when confronted with this problem. Teachers, doctors, hospital personnel, and law enforcement officers are legally mandated to report abusive incidents. Anyone who suspects that a child is being mistreated should, at a minimum, call the local or state agency that investigates child abuse and neglect cases. The caller's identity is kept confidential. Reports in many states can be made anonymously. If the agency determines that the child is in danger, he or she will be removed from the home and placed in a temporary shelter until he or she can be safely returned to the home or other suitable arrangements can be made.

Although early intervention in cases of suspected abuse is important, prevention is far better. Child maltreatment can be prevented by making classes easily available to help parents cope with the stresses of raising children, particularly special needs children. Serious consideration should be given to incorporating child development and parenting-skills classes into junior high and high school curricula for both boys and girls. Research has indicated that (a) increasing the knowledge of present and future parents about home and child management and (b) enhancing the development of good communication skills, healthy emotional ties, and parent-child bonding assist in child maltreatment prevention.

In addition to teaching adults and teenagers about child development and good parenting skills, elementary, junior high, and high schools should develop courses on child abuse and neglect. The curricula should be designed to help students recognize various types of child abuse and neglect and encourage them to take appropriate action if victimized or threatened with victimization. The programs should aim to foster the development of self-esteem and conflict resolution skills to aid youth in self-protection. The earlier these behaviors are targeted, the earlier they can be stopped and any accompanying damage or difficulties can be addressed therapeutically.

Children must also be informed about the effects of parental alcoholism and chemical dependency. Research has indicated that children who are being raised in chemically dependent families are at a higher risk of being abused or neglected. Schools are the most appropriate vehicle to educate children in this regard because they may be the only institutions to have any meaningful contact with children from chemically dependent families. Available estimates suggest that there are over 11 million children of alcoholics under the age of 18 (National Association for Children of Alcoholics).

Children and adolescents need to learn the difference between functional and dysfunctional families. They should be informed about support groups, such as Ala-teen, that help youth cope effectively with problems that arise from living in a home with an addicted parent. These groups should be allowed and encouraged to meet in the schools during lunch, free periods, and/or immediately following classes.

Abused children also need a supportive network immediately available to guide them through the process of obtaining help—without this, victimization is likely to continue. Currently, mistreated children in most states are on their own unless and until the social service agency investigates and files a petition alleging dependency. Once a dependency petition is filed, some assistance for the mistreated child is likely to be forthcoming in most jurisdictions in the United States. Typically, a *guardian ad litem,* a person acting as the child's guardian in a particular action, acts as the child's advocate in court proceedings.

Children need an advocate before the filing stage is reached, someone to stand by the decision to report the mistreatment. A child advocate program is a means to ensure that children's allegations are properly and promptly investigated and that appropriate action is taken. A program of this nature could be administered either as a separate entity or as an expanded component of guardian ad litem programs. A child advocate program relying heavily on volunteers could easily be implemented in school settings.

The rise in reported cases of child abuse in recent years underscores the need for increased awareness of the devastating nature and effects of child maltreatment and increased public involvement in prevention. Public service advertising through radio, television, and the print media have played a large role in educating the public about the problem of child maltreatment, particularly since the mid-1970s. In addition to informing viewers about what types of behavior and words are abusive, the media can publicize places where abusive parents can get help and what actions concerned citizens can take to help prevent child abuse. The media can alert viewers of the increased risk of chemically dependent parents abusing and neglecting their children and publicize the location of support groups and community facilities where they can get help. The media can also carry the message to abused children that help exists by advertising community resources available to them.

Child maltreatment is a killer. Often, significant damage comes not in human bloodshed, but in the death of the human spirit. Awareness of the problem provides the opportunity to change the conditions that give rise to child mistreatment and allow it to persist.

> Child abuse . . . is too complex a problem, too deeply engrained in the ways our communities are organized and our families are structured for any one profession or any one sector of society to be in a position to prevent abuse—all sectors need to be involved and do have a role to play. (Donnelly, 1991, p. 102)

—*Kathleen M. Heide*

See also ATTACHMENT DEFICIENCY AND VIOLENCE; BATTERED CHILD SYNDROME; CHILD KILLERS; FAMILY VIOLENCE; VIOLENT FEMALE JUVENILE OFFENDERS

Further Reading

American Psychiatric Association. (1994). *Diagnostic and statistical manual of mental disorders* (4th ed.). Washington, DC: Author.

Briere, J. N. (1992). *Child abuse trauma: Theory and treatment of the lasting effects.* Newbury Park, CA: Sage.

Cohn, A. H. (1983). *An approach to preventing child abuse.* Chicago: National Committee on the Prevention of Child Abuse.

Donnelly, A. C. (1991). What have we learned about prevention: What should we do about it. *Child Abuse and Neglect, 15,* 102.

Heide, K. M. (1994). Evidence of child maltreatment among adolescent parricide offenders. *International Journal of Offender Therapy and Comparative Criminology, 38.*

Heide, K. M. (1995). *Why kids kill parents: Child abuse and adolescent homicide.* Thousand Oaks, CA: Sage.

Heide, K. M. (1999). *Young killers: The challenge of juvenile homicide.* Thousand Oaks, CA: Sage.

Heide, K. M., & Solomon, E. P. (1992). Intervention strategies for victims of sexual abuse: A model for building self-esteem. *International Review of Victimology, 2.*

National Association for Children of Alcoholics. (2001, July 7). Available on the World Wide Web at: www.nacoa.net.

Smith, C., & Thornberry, T. P. (1995). The relationship between childhood maltreatment and adolescent involvement in delinquency. *Criminology, 3.*

Solomon, E. P., & Heide, K. M. (1999). Type III trauma: Toward a more effective conceptualization of psychological trauma. *International Journal of Offender Therapy and Comparative Criminology, 43.*

Widom, C. S. (1994). Childhood victimization and risk for adolescent problem behavior. In M. E. Lamb & R. Ketterlinus (Eds.), *Adolescent problem behaviors.* Mahwah, NJ: Lawrence Erlbaum.

CHILD KILLERS

The act of homicide is sometimes difficult to accept and comprehend. The murder of a child, however, defies the concepts of civility and justice in the world. Even homicide investigators have shown greater amounts of post-traumatic stress disorder following the investigation of the murder of a child. The murder of innocent children has occurred throughout history and has been widespread across nations and cultures. The early sacrifice of children was accepted as routine, if not required in some cases, during the biblical era. Two examples of this reside in the core doctrine of the Judeo-Christian religion. First, the Christian God is reputed to have sacrificed his son, Jesus Christ, for the so-called eternal salvation of all people. Second, the biblical prophet Abraham was commanded by God to sacrifice his son, Isaac, to prove his faith. Fortunately for Isaac, Abraham was later commanded by God to desist before the sacrifice was completed. Moreover, even the military's use of the term "infantry" relates to the sending out of the youthful members of society to fight, and likely to die, in times of war.

During the mid- to late 1800s, the economic and social pressures of the time led some to rid themselves of children who were unwanted or considered "surplus" babies. During this time, children under the age of 1 year accounted for approximately 60% to 65% of all homicides in England. France at this same time only listed two criminal acts against children; abortion and infanticide. This was in response to the eventual depopulation of the country secondary to the very high numbers of induced abortion and infanticide of the times. Abuse, sexual molestation, abandonment, and malnutrition (even to death) were previously not considered crimes. Some believed that this form of killing was an acceptable method of fertility control, irrespective of the probable negative results to the woman's body and her future reproductive capability. Since that time, many child protection reforms, albeit slowly, have been enacted.

The murder of children has historically been condoned when it has made some adaptive sense for the parents, usually the mother, or the even the child. For example, these justifiable circumstances might include the illegitimate paternity of the infant or the unlikely survival of the child due to health problems. It was also somewhat common for parents over a brief period of time to consider the potential survival and reproductive fitness of the child before deciding whether to deprive the infant of his or her life. In other words, there may have been an unspoken "waiting period." In contemporary societies, the murder of children is unacceptable in all circumstances and in all forms. Nonetheless, children in modern societies are still completely vulnerable and subject to the power of adults.

When a child is murdered within the first 24 hours after being born, the referring term is *neonaticide.* When the child is older than 24 hours and under the age of 5 years, the referring term is *infanticide.* Beyond the age of 5 years and up to the age of 18 years, the term is *early filicide.* Over the age of 18, the term is *late filicide.* There are no specific terms to delineate the gender of child murder. Because the Latin root word for a son is *filius* and the Latin root word for daughter is *filia*, filicide appropriately refers to either gender.

Children are murdered by their mothers, fathers, stepparents, siblings, grandparents, and other family members. They have also been murdered by babysitters and caregivers, friends and peers, and strangers. The reasons are probably as varied as the types of victims and methods used. However, a few trends have emerged. The murdering of a child seems to be mostly related to abuse/neglect, hatred/rage episodes, sexual assault, and denial of pregnancy.

OVERVIEW OF CHILD KILLING

Childhood victims are close in race and gender composition to the general population. They are most often killed by relatives. Most child murders occur at home during the midday hours, either at the midweek or weekend (Chew, McCleary, Lew-Marices et al., 1999). Approximately 70% of the offenders are the parents or stepparents; 60% to 70% mothers; and 30% to 40% fathers or stepfathers (Bourget & Bradford, 1990; Stroud & Pritchard, 2001; Vanamo, Kauppi, Karkola, et al., 2001.) Approximately 60% of the victims are males. Mothers tend to kill younger victims than do male parents. Approximately 50% of these victims have documented histories of previous abuse, and approximately 50% of the offenders suffered from mental illness at the time of the murder (Stroud & Pritchard, 2001). Biological fathers who kill children have higher rates of being mentally ill than do the mothers. Stepfathers who murder children tend to live with the victims' mothers and to be coassailants with the women. Adults who are not familial relatives have sexual motivation associated with murdering children. The most frequent causes of death are head injuries with intracranial hemorrhage, drowning, suffocation, strangulation, battery with intra-abdominal trauma, stabbing, and gunshot wounds.

The major motivations for these crimes relate to two forms of lethal violence: competitive violence and predatory violence. In competition-related violence, the child is seen as an obstacle to the parent's ambitions or desires. In predatory violence, the child is seen as the desired object (i.e., sexual motivation). Children who are very young (0 to 4 years) and those in adolescence (13 to 18 years) are generally murdered during competitive violence. Children between the ages of 5 and 12 years are generally victims of predatory violence or murder-suicide events involving the entire family. In regard to gender, males are more likely to be victims of competitive violence, and females are more likely to be victims of predatory violence.

Mental illness appears to be a major factor in child murder. The predominant psychological disorders implicated in these cases include major depressive disorder, schizoaffective disorder, schizophrenia, affective disorders, reactive disorders, mental retardation, and unspecified psychosis. However, only about 30% of these offenders have ever been psychiatrically hospitalized, and only about 30% of these offenders receive any psychological treatment prior to the homicide (Xie & Yamagami, 1995). Agencies are involved with about two thirds of these offenders prior to the murders. Of those seen by these agencies, about two thirds involve a history of violence toward the victims and about one third are seen explicitly for reported violence toward the victims. Actions are taken in about two thirds of these cases; female offenders are most often referred to mental health treatment, and male offenders are most often referred to child protective services and other law enforcement agencies. Interestingly, about 1 in 30 murdered children with histories of prior abuse also have siblings who die of sudden infant death syndrome (SIDS).

Most child killings are committed in states of fear, panic, depression, psychosis, or dissociation. Some are the result of the displacement of the murderer's original aggression from their own parents, spouses, or siblings. Most of these homicidal parents indicate personal feelings of intense involvement and investment in the parenting of their children. However, they also tend to indicate high levels of perceived personal stress from their unstable mental states previous to the murder. Most homicidal parents indicate having no awareness of warning signs or premeditative planning of the homicides. Overall, parental child killers tend to suffer from various forms of mental illness, social isolation, and difficulties in formulating successful interpersonal relationships.

Neonaticide

Mothers are the most likely offenders (70%) in neonaticides (Kaye, Borenstein, & Donnelly, 1990). Neonaticidal mothers are usually the youngest of child killers, most of them not far out of childhood themselves. They tend to be unmarried, and the majority are still dependent on their families of origin. These women are overrepresented among minority groups and have lower socioeconomic status, lower education levels, and fewer medically known induced abortions prior to the homicide.

Neonaticidal mothers have been characterized as being more passive and dependent in their personality styles and as having fears of abandonment relating their own mothers' emotional states during pregnancy and childbirth. Many of these women (63%) have histories of psychological and sexual abuse during their childhoods (Haapasalo & Petaja, 1999). Many are raised in negligent and incestuous homes. As a result, they are prone to engage in significant denial of their pregnancies. Sometimes this denial of pregnancy is so significant that the birth takes them by surprise. It has been hypothesized that during the birth process, the neonaticidal mother experiences significant ego-disorganization secondary to the dissolution of their denial, combined with abandonment fear, and this is the genesis of the homicidal act on her newborn, or neonate. These women tend to experience dissociative hallucinations, depersonalization, and intermittent amnesia at delivery. These abnormal experiences are likely due to being overwhelmed by pregnancy and the birth process without an external support network to assist them, as well as having low personal coping resources. These conditions have been referred to as *postpartum psychosis.*

The main motivations for neonaticide include factors such as the child being the product of extramarital paternity, the child being the product of rape or sexual abuse, and viewing the child as an obstacle to parental ambition. It appears that some form of illegitimate conception is the most common motive. These young mothers, for various motivations, refuse to accept the mother-identification process. This is likely due to their developmental and psychological immaturity and/or the dysfunctional disruptions in their own parent-child relationships.

International studies have shown that gender does not alter the level of risk for neonaticide. Neonaticidal deaths are not related to child behaviors, physical abnormalities of the child, maternal parity, or the marital status of the parents of the victim. These killings seem more related to maternal isolation and the psychological well-being of the mother during pregnancy and birth of the child. The neonaticidal event is not usually followed by the suicide of the parent. The main methods of death in neonates are strangulation, suffocation, or fatal abandonment. Some are fatally beaten, but rarely are weapons used.

Infanticide

Infanticide has been historically referred to as a rational act of survival against unbearable and unforgiving social conditions. It is not considered a mental disorder secondary to pregnancy, childbirth, or the lactation process. Other factors, such as the comorbidity of mental illness, low socioeconomic status, domestic violence, and cultural norms and mores may precipitate infanticide.

In infanticide events, as the age of the victim increases, so does the level of lethal violence. Mothers are more likely to commit more passive forms of murder (e.g., asphyxiation, drowning, abandonment) and to kill younger children. Fathers and stepfathers are more likely to use more active violence (e.g., beating, shaking) and to kill older children. Strangers who commit infanticide are likely to use the most violent means (e.g., knives and guns) to commit these murders, and their crimes usually involve sexual motivation.

Research has indicated that the typical infanticide offender is Caucasian, between the ages of 25 and 35. These offenders are usually married and not under the influence of drugs or alcohol. However, they typically have histories of psychological disturbances of an affective or psychotic nature, are altruistically motivated, and generally kill only one child. This child is usually the youngest child and is between the ages of 2 and 5 years. Male children have shown to be more at risk (54%), yet the number of female victims indicates a relatively similar (46%) level of risk (FBI, 1995-2000).

Although infanticide is often referred to as a "female crime," male and female offenders are about equal in numbers. Most of them are married and are either first-time parents or have one other child. Slightly more than half (55%) of these victims had evidence of physical trauma prior to the fatal injury (Brewster, Nelson, Hymel-Kent, et al., 1998). Less infanticide offenders (23%) than neonaticide offenders (63%) have histories of abuse in their own childhoods (Brewster et al., 1998; Haapasalo & Petaja, 1999).

Many of these parents (up to 70%) admit to explicit thoughts and fantasies of aggression toward their children during times of stress and perceived inadequacies in their ability to parent (Levitzky & Cooper, 2000). Moreover, approximately 25% admit to thoughts and fantasies of infanticide during these stressful episodes (i.e., colic, reflux, inconsolability). As a result, the bonding process is severed by parental impatience, rage, anger, and feelings of incompetence.

During these moments, the child is likely to be shaken, beaten, or struck with any readily available domestic object. The majority of infanticides, albeit previously fantasized about, are usually unintentional and are frequently the end result of abuse over time. The typical infanticide occurs during the midday hours, during the midweek or weekend, and within the victim's home.

Infanticide appears to be the result of the culmination of the predispositional factors of the parent's psychological and socialization experience, limited interpersonal and/or familial supports, and economic stress. Infanticides, like neonaticides, are not usually followed by the suicide of the offender.

Filicide

Research has suggested that filicide cases may be divided into three types, those conducted with a rational motive during a crisis situation, real or perceived; those resulting from the combination of characterological defects and low IQ levels within the offender; and those that are characteristically similar to manslaughter. Furthermore, filicide has been classified into at least 11 categories of motive, including retaliation killings; jealously of, or rejection by, the victim; the unwanted child; disciplinary style; altruism; psychosis; Munchausen syndrome by proxy; sexual or ritual abuse; self-defense; no intent to kill or injure; and some of unknown or unclear motivation. From these classifications, it has been shown that male offenders tend to predominate in retaliatory, jealousy, and disciplinary motives. Female offenders tend to predominate in motives related to unwanted children, altruism, and psychosis. It appears that parents at risk of filicide share many of the same characteristics as battering parents.

School-aged children are also at increased risk of being part of multiple filicides. These events are usually the result of altruistic motivation in which all the children are murdered to "spare them" of parentally perceived injustices of the world or as part of the murder-suicide of the family annihilator. These murder-suicides usually center on the imminent or recent dissolution of a marriage or termination from the offender's job. They are the events in which children are most likely to be murdered with a firearm by parents. Suicide is attempted in about one third (30%) of these cases, and in about two thirds (60%) of these cases, offenders also try to kill their spouses (Marleau, Poulin, Webanck, Roy, Laporte, et. al., 1999; Statistics Canada, 1997).

Children Murdered by Strangers

Between 1995 and 2000, 160 children were killed by their babysitters. Of these victims, 65% were male (FBI, 1995-2000). Three of these victims were the sons of offenders, one was the daughter of an offender, one was committed by a brother, and one by a sister. Fifteen were killed by other family members, three by friends, one by a neighbor, and two by employees of the victim's parents. However, the largest number of victims ($n = 131$) were murdered while an acquaintance of the family was babysitting. The type of weapons most frequently used (77%) in these cases were personal weapons (i.e., hands or feet) and resulted in beatings, shakings, and drownings (FBI, 1995-2000).

Juvenile gang murders are noteworthy in child killings by strangers and peers. Between 1995 and 2000, 4,648 minors were murdered in juvenile gang activities. Clearly, males were at greatest (95%) risk. These children were murdered by three main categories of offenders: acquaintances (43%), unknown offenders (34%), and strangers (23%). Overwhelmingly (96%), firearms of some sort were the weapons in these killings (FBI, 1995-2000). Between 1995 and 2000, 1,196 cases of murder involved both offenders and victims who were under 18 years of age. Even though there has been an alarming increase in children being murdered by their peers in school shooting incidents, these events account for a relatively small number of juvenile homicide victims.

Regarding children murdered by serial killers, the following information has been reported in the professional literature (Hickey, 2002). Child abductions by strangers accounted for the largest percentage (64%) of missing children found dead. Approximately one fourth (23%) of children abducted and later found dead were abducted by a parent or relative. The relative risk of a child being the victim of a serial killer is low compared with their risk of being murdered in a domestic homicide. Even though serial killers generally murder adults, young adolescent women and young school-aged children of both genders are prime targets of serial killers who murder children. About 1 in 4 (24%) serial killers indicate that they have killed at least one child. About the same percentage (26%) indicate that they target only children. The majority (74%) of serial child killers are male, and all but a few are Caucasian. Hickey (2002) indicated important gender differences among

Table 2 Percentage of Children Murdered by Age, by Gender, and by Race, 1995-2000

			Gender			Race			
	Total	% Child Murders	Male	Female	Unk.	White	Black	Other	Unk.
Total	100.0	n/a	76.3	23.5	0.2	48.4	47.8	2.7	1.1
Under 18	11.5	100.0	69.3	30.6	0.1	49.4	46.0	3.6	1.0
Under 1	1.5	13.0	55.3	44.4	0.3	58.3	36.0	2.9	2.8
1 to 4	2.2	18.9	53.5	46.4	0.1	53.5	42.5	3.1	1.0
5 to 8	0.7	5.7	50.9	49.1	0.0	56.9	37.8	5.0	0.3
9 to 12	0.6	5.0	53.5	46.5	0.0	62.5	31.5	5.4	0.6
13 to 16	3.9	33.5	77.3	22.7	0.0	46.0	49.5	3.7	0.7
17 to 18	2.8	23.9	85.9	14.1	0.0	41.7	54.2	3.3	0.8

Source: U.S. Dept. of Justice (1995–2000).

serial child killers. The female serial child killer is more likely to murder her own family members or relatives. The male serial child killer is more likely to murder children who are strangers. Female child serial killers are less likely to travel to find victims and are much more likely to use passive forms of violence (e.g., poison) in their murders. Male serial child killers, on the other hand, are much more likely to travel around in search of suitable victims, as well as far more likely to use more serious and blatant forms of violence in their murders (e.g., mutilation, strangulation, bludgeoning, or shooting).

The motives of serial child killers vary by gender as well. For males, the most likely motive is sexual gratification (68%), followed by control over the victim (42%), or a combination of motives (59%). Female serial child killers are mostly motivated by financial reasons (38%), followed by a combination of motives (33%). Overall, serial child killers seem to be mostly, and equally, motivated by sexual gratification (53%) or a combination of motives (53%). Approximately one fourth (23%) of serial child killers are willing to indicate that they found enjoyment or pleasure in murdering children (Hickey, 2002).

The rates of mental illness among serial killers is relatively low. However, as a group, they are overrepresented in psychopathy. In other words, they do not seem to be either diagnosably mentally ill or legally insane, simply psychopathic. Children are especially vulnerable to the psychopathic tendency of serial killers to lure them in and prey on their vulnerable and powerless social, psychological, emotional, and developmental position, as well as their naïveté toward the dangers of the world.

OFFICIAL STATISTICS ON CHILD MURDERS

The data reported in this section are from official reports from the U.S. Department of Justice (1995-2000). Between 1995 and 2000, there were 90,869 homicides in the United States. Of these murders, 10,468 (11.5%) were children under 18 years of age. Of the murdered children, 7,255 (69.3%) were male, 5,174 (49.4%) were Caucasian, and 4,815 (46.0%) were African American. Children are at the greatest risk of being murdered at the early and later parts of childhood. For example, as indicated in Table 2, children between the ages of 13 and 18 had the greatest risk (57.4%), followed by those under the age of 5 years (31.9%).

The risk of childhood murder in Caucasians and African Americans shifts over the course of childhood. For example, Caucasian children under 5 years of age accounted for 55.9% of these victims, and African American children of the same age accounted for 39.3% of these victims. Between the ages of 5 and 12, Caucasians accounted for 59.7%, and African Americans accounted for 34.7% of these victims. By adolescence, ages 13 through 18, Caucasians accounted for 43.9% of these victims, yet African Americans accounted for 51.9%. The average rate (per 100,000 persons) per year was 2.4 for Caucasians, 9.4 for African Americans, and 2.3 for other racial groups. About two thirds (61%) of these children were killed by parents, and about one fourth (23%) were killed by male acquaintances. Only 3% were killed by strangers. Most of the victims (69.3%) and most of the offenders (64%) were males.

According to the FBI *Uniform Crime Reports,* the murder of sons and daughters constituted 3.1% of the

Table 3   Percentage of Children Murdered by Age and by Type of Weapon, 1995-2000

	Total	*Under 18*	*Under 1*	*1 to 4*	*5 to 8*	*9 to 12*	*13 to 16*	*17 to 18*
Total	100.0	100.0	100.0	100.0	100.0	100.0	100.0	100.0
Firearms	66.8	54.2	2.9	12.9	35.8	47.1	80.3	83.9
Knives	13.1	6.8	2.0	3.4	8.3	10.8	8.0	9.2
Blunt objects	4.9	3.9	6.0	7.8	5.0	5.6	2.1	1.8
Personal weapons	6.4	19.1	53.9	49.6	17.0	9.6	2.8	1.6
Poison	0.1	0.2	0.3	0.4	0.7	0.6	0.0	0.0
Explosives	0.3	0.4	0.5	1.0	0.8	0.8	0.1	0.0
Fire	0.9	2.5	0.8	4.9	11.3	9.8	0.9	0.0
Narcotics	0.2	0.4	1.3	0.5	0.8	1.3	0.1	0.1
Strangulation	1.4	1.5	1.2	1.2	3.0	3.5	1.5	1.0
Asphyxiation	0.7	2.5	10.5	4.1	2.3	2.3	0.4	0.1
Other	5.4	8.5	20.6	14.1	15.0	8.7	3.8	2.5

SOURCE: U.S. Dept. of Justice (1995–2000).

total homicides between 1995 and 2000. Of these, the murder of sons was slightly more (55%) than the murder of daughters. If one considers that all these killings of offspring involve minor children, then this type of child murder would constitute 26.6% of the total number of children killed. However, some of these children were adults when killed, and as a result, the 26.6% would likely be an overestimate. Nonetheless, on average, 255 sons and 209 daughters are murdered each year in the United States. According to the *Uniform Crime Reports,* the most common circumstances recorded as the precipitators of these murders were *other* (73%), *other argument* (15%), and *unknown* (8%).

Over the 24-year period from 1976-1999, the overall rate (per 100,000 persons) of murder and nonnegligent manslaughter was 8.5 (1.9 for those victims under age 13, and 7.1 for those victims age 14 through 17). The overall percentage of child homicide is approximately 12% of the total annual homicides in the United States. In other words, about 1,745 children are murdered each year, which equates to approximately 5 children murdered every day in the United States.

The younger the victim, the greater the likelihood of being murdered by a family member (67.5% for children under age 5). The older the victim, the greater the likelihood of being murdered by a stranger (67.3% for children aged 15 through 17). Children between the ages of 5 and 14 have relatively equal risks for being murdered by a family member (22.6%), an acquaintance (20.6%), or a stranger (25.0%). Children under 1 year of age are most likely (61.1%) to be beaten to death (e.g., by personal weapons, blunt objects, or

strangulation), as are those between the ages of 1 and 4 years (58.6%). Children murdered between 5 and 12 years of age show a transitional increase toward death by firearms (41.9%) and knives (9.6%). Murder victims aged 13 through 18 show similar risk for being killed by a knife (8.6%) yet substantially increased risk (82.1%) of being murdered by a firearm (see Table 3).

—*Rocky Underwood*

See also BATTERED CHILD SYNDROME; CHILD ABUSE; FAMILY HOMICIDE; CHIKATILO, ANDREI; SCHOOL SHOOTINGS; DODD, WESTLEY ALLEN; MURDER-SUICIDE; SERIAL KILLERS; PSYCHOPATHS; WILLIAMS, WAYNE

Further Reading

Bourget, D., & Bradford, J. M. (1990). Homicidal parents. *Canadian Journal of Psychiatry, 35*(3), 233-238.

Brewster, A. L., Nelson, J. P., Hymel-Kent, P., et al. (1998). Victim, perpetrator, family, and incident characteristics of 32 infant maltreatment deaths in the United States Air Force. *Child Abuse & Neglect, 22*(2), 91-101.

Chew, K., McCleary, R., Lew-Marices, A., et al. (1999). The epidemiology of child homicide in California, 1981-1990. *Homicide Studies, 3*(2), 151-169.

Federal Bureau of Investigation. (1995-2000). *Crime in the United States: Uniform crime reports.* Available on the World Wide Web at: http://www.fbi.gov/publications.

Haapasalo, J., & Petaja, S. (1999). Mothers who killed or attempted to kill their child: Life circumstances, childhood abuse, and types of killing. *Violence & Victims, 14*(3), 219-239.

Hickey, E. W. (2002). *Serial murderers and their victims* (3rd ed.). Belmont, CA: Wadsworth.

Kaye, N. S., Borenstein, N. M., & Donnelly, S. M. (1990). Families, murder, and insanity: A psychiatric review of paternal neonaticide. *Journal of Forensic Sciences, 35*(1), 133-139.

Levitzky, S., & Cooper, R. (2000). Infant colic syndrome-maternal fantasies of aggression and infanticide. *Clinical Pediatrics, 39*(7), 395-400.

Marleau, J. D., Poulin, B., Webanck, T., Roy, R., Laporte, L., et al. (1999). Paternal filicide: A study of 10 men. *Canadian Journal of Psychiatry, 44*(1), 57-63.

Statistics Canada. (1997). *Juristat: Homicide in Canada, 18*(12).

Stroud, J., & Pritchard, C. (2001). Child homicide, psychiatric disorder and dangerousness: A review and an empirical approach. *British Journal of Social Work, 31*(2), 249-269.

U.S. Department of Justice. Federal Bureau of Investigation. (1995-2000). *Crime in the United States, Uniform crime reports.* Available on the World Wide Web at: http://www.fbi.gov/publications2.

Vanamo, T., Kauppi, A., Karkola, K., et. al. (2001). Intra-familial child homicide in Finland 1970-1994: Incidence, causes of death and demographic characteristics. *Forensic Science International, 117*(3) 199-204.

Xie, L., & Yamagami, A. (1995). How much of the child murder in Japan is caused by mentally disordered mothers? *International Medical Journal, 2*(4), 309-313.

CHILD MOLESTER, *See* CHILDREN AS VICTIMS OF SEX CRIMES; CYBERSTINGS; PEDOPHILIA; SEX OFFENDERS

CHILD PORNOGRAPHY, *See* CYBERSTINGS; EXPLOITATION OF CHILDREN; PEDOPHILE ORGANIZATIONS

CHILDREN AND ADOLESCENTS WHO KILL, *See* GANGS; JUVENILE KILLERS; SCHOOL SHOOTINGS; VIOLENT FEMALE JUVENILE OFFENDERS

CHILDREN AS VICTIMS OF SEX CRIMES

Statistics, crime reports, and newspaper articles reveal that for many children, childhood is anything but pleasant; it is frightening, sad, and even horrific. Parents and other adults do not necessarily guard children against harm, and abuse can be perpetrated in a variety of ways: physical neglect and physical, emotional, and sexual abuse.

Physical neglect is the failure to provide the child with the basic necessities of life: food, clothing, schooling, medical care, and a place to live. Physical abuse results from nonaccidental physical injury to a child: broken bones, abrasions, lacerations, burns, bruises, internal injuries, and head injuries. Emotional abuse is the failure to provide appropriate attention and affection, perhaps by chronic belittling and humiliation. Sexual abuse is any type of inappropriate sexual activity with a child, such as fondling, digital penetration, intercourse, sodomy, and oral copulation. Perpetration of abuse on a child may not stop at one type of abuse.

All forms of child abuse emotionally traumatize a child. In addition, children of sexual abuse go through a secondary trauma in the crisis of discovery and subsequent disclosure that they have been sexually abused. In 1983, Roland C. Summit published a paper titled "The Child Sexual Abuse Accommodation Syndrome." He explored and identified the most typical reactions of children who had been sexually abused. Dr. Summit noted that "children's attempts to reconcile their private experiences with the realities of the outer world are assaulted by the disbelief, blame and rejection they experience from adults" (p. 177). Most adults have little, if any, formal knowledge of child psychology, victimization, or sex abuse trauma. When children finally bring themselves to disclose that they have been sexually violated, they are often met with entrenched beliefs and expectations that do not lend support to their disclosure. According to Dr. Summit, "Such abandonment by the very adults most crucial to the child's protection and recovery drives the child deeper into self-blame, alienation, and revictimization" (p. 177).

Attitudes held by adults about the way children respond to being sexually violated collide with children's realities and their attempts to cope with such abuse. These adult "myths" open the door for children to be repeatedly traumatized. The following are common examples of misinformed attitudes commonly held by adults, even practitioners in the criminal justice system, that sabotage children when they attempt to disclose the occurrence of sexual molestation.

1. Children will tell someone after being molested.

Reality: For children, secrecy results largely from fear and can be a promise of safety. Children are fearful that they will be blamed for the assault, or if they tell, that they will not be believed. They are fearful of physical retaliation because perpetrators may threaten them with physical harm to themselves or their mothers, siblings, or pets. They are fearful of emotional retaliation from the abuser or other family members, having been told, for example, that everyone will turn against them if they reveal the abuse. Other forms of retaliation my be threatened, such as withholding money that allows the child to participate in after-school activities or sports. The perpetrator may even take a seemingly less ominous approach and elicit loyalty from the child with messages to the effect that "This is our little secret, something special between just you and me."

Statistics substantiate the sad truth that family members or trusted adults—not strangers—molest the majority of children. In a child's world, these trusted adults define reality. In the case of molestation, the perpetrator defines the reality of the relationship by proscribing that the victim refrain from telling anyone else about it.

2. Children will say "No" to the perpetrator.

Reality: Children do not have equal power in authoritarian relationships with any adult, particularly one directed by a perpetrator. They are helpless to say "no" when that person is a parental figure or some other "designated" trusted adult, such as a teacher, a coach, or a priest. They may feel they are required to be obedient and affectionate with this known person and that saying "No" means risking the loss of emotional support. It must be understood that this does not equate to consent.

3. Children do not return to their abusers.

Reality: The victimization of children often starts very young, before they enter preschool. It should be obvious that a child this young knows nothing outside the home and is in no position to flee the perpetrator, who is most likely a parent or another caretaker. Even after being molested, children cannot conceptualize that this person would purposely cause harm to them, and furthermore, their very survival depends on the presence of that person in their life.

Even at older ages, children's situations don't afford them a choice other than remaining where they are. They do not readily have at their disposal the means to leave a bad situation—be it home, school, or church—no access to money, transportation, or some place to run to where they wouldn't be eventually forced to return. The perpetrator may also reinforce the idea that other adults would be unwilling to help if the child were to turn to them.

In this situation of entrapment, a normal child's response to is to adapt in whatever way possible: stay at school longer so as not to have to come home, stay in his or her room at home to avoid the perpetrator, or drop out of activities in which the perpetrator is involved. Leaving the situation altogether is usually not an option the child can envision or enact.

4. Children will eventually make full disclosures.

Reality: Most ongoing sexual abuse is never disclosed, and if it does occur, disclosure may be delayed and incomplete. Disclosure may come at a time when the accommodation factors have broken down and are no longer serving the child. It may also be a time when the child is in turmoil and acting out, thus giving the child less credibility. In attempting to disclose, children may give up a little information to test the type of response they receive. If the initial reaction is nonsupportive or highly emotional, it may frighten the child, and the disclosure process may be abandoned.

5. When a child retracts his or her original claim of molestation, it means that the initial statement was a lie.

Reality: Children do recant, but this does not mean that the molestation did not occur. In disclosing, children are hoping the molestation will stop. Instead, they may face blame and emotional abandonment from their parents or caregivers. In situations in which the perpetrator is the father, stepfather, or boyfriend, mothers in denial may side with the offender, and thus the child has lost support from both parents. Even if they are believed, children face the possibility of being uprooted from their homes, separated from their families, or being placed in different schools. They suffer the burden of destroying the family and the previously established standard of living.

Thus, the cost of disclosure for children becomes even greater than that of the molestation itself. They feel responsible for the chaotic aftermath of their claims and have no control over the situation other than to take back their original statements. For many adults, the retraction carries more weight than the disclosure. Probably for the same reasons the child chose to recant, to avoid confronting a devastating situation, they chose to believe that the original disclosure was a lie.

—*Judith L. Tucker*

See also CHILD ABUSE; EXPLOITATION OF
    CHILDREN; PEDOPHILIA; SEX OFFENDERS

Further reading

Summit, R. C. (1983). The child sexual abuse accommodation syndrome. *Child Abuse & Neglect, 7,* 177-193.

COLBERT, JAMES, *See* MASS MURDER

COLUMBINE/LITTLETON SCHOOL SHOOTING

On April 20, 1999, Columbine High School in Littleton, Colorado, was the scene of the most horrific act of school violence in U.S. history. The events that occurred that day were no accident. After a lengthy and methodical planning phase, Eric Harris, age 18, and Dylan Klebold, age 17, arrived at school ready to elicit fear and bring death to students and faculty. Armed with a small cache of firearms and a significant number of homemade bombs, the two carried out their mission.

Beginning at 11:10 a.m., the two parked their cars in the southwest parking lot, entered the school with duffel bags containing two 20-pound propane bombs, and planted them in the cafeteria. They returned to the parking lot and waited for the bombs to explode as the timer reached 11:17 a.m. Only one bomb detonated, however. Additional bombs were placed in both Harris's and Klebold's vehicles, set to discharge as

they reentered the school, but they failed to go off. At approximately the same time, a bomb exploded in an open field a few miles from the school as a diversionary tactic for law enforcement.

Minutes later, Harris and Klebold were overheard by a witness saying "Go! Go!" The first shots were fired outside the school near the parking lot, killing two students and wounding eight other people. From the beginning of the episode, the two had been continually tossing explosive devices toward the school and areas adjacent to the building.

As Klebold and Harris continued to fire their weapons into the school, the first law enforcement responder arrived. Gunfire was exchanged between Harris and a deputy from the Jefferson County Sheriff's Office. The gunmen then entered the northwest side of the school and continued the shooting confrontation with police outside. The gunfire and explosions caused mass pandemonium inside the building as students and teachers scrambled for cover.

Teacher Dave Sanders, hearing the shots, came down from the second floor stairway toward the entrance of the school, where the gunfire originated. Seeing the offenders, he attempted to double back to warn students of the danger and was shot twice in the back. Sanders managed to veer into a classroom but bled to death before medical help arrived.

Harris and Klebold ascended to the second floor and continued their assault, walking through the hallway while shooting randomly. They entered the library, where Harris opened fire down the length of the counter. The offenders walked through the library toward the windows, killing one student on the way, and then proceeded to shoot outside at law enforcement and fleeing students. Next, they turned their attention back to the students, taunting their intended victims, killing 10 and wounding 12.

From there, Harris and Klebold reentered the hallway and headed toward the science wing. They were witnessed shooting into empty classrooms. The two then ventured to the empty cafeteria. Realizing that one bomb was remaining, as video footage shows, Harris unsuccessfully attempted to detonated it with gunfire. Klebold managed to partially detonate it, resulting in a fire.

Returning to the library, Klebold and Harris again initiated gunfire out the window with law enforcement. Shortly after the last shot was fired, the two offenders committed suicide with gunshots to the head. On completion of the incident, at 12:08 p.m., a total of 13 were dead, not including the offenders, and another 20 were wounded. Later, it was discovered that Harris and Klebold had intended on killing several hundred victims so they would be remembered as the greatest mass murderers of all time.

—*Thomas A. Petee and
Janice E. Clifford Wittekind*

See also JUVENILE KILLERS; MEDIA,
VIOLENCE IN THE; SCHOOL SHOOTINGS

Further Reading

Jefferson County Sheriff's Office. (2000). Columbine High School shootings, April 20, 1999. *The Jefferson County Sheriff's Office Report* [CD-Rom].

COMBINED DNA INDEX SYSTEM (CODIS), *See* CRIMINALISTICS

COMFORT ZONE KILLERS, *See* SERIAL MURDER

COMMUNITY ATTITUDES TOWARD VIOLENT CRIME

Violent crime has become an important issue in modern society. Community residents live in fear of victimization resulting from criminogenic social conditions, such as drug dependency and poverty, and uncertainty regarding adequate protection from potential harm. An examination of community perceptions of violent crime includes actual versus projected risks for victimization status; the outgrowth of community participation in sanctioned programs; the enactment of empowerment, advocacy, and social transformation resulting from emergent community attitudes; and the relationship between community attitudes and defined criminal justice responses.

COMMUNITY PERCEPTIONS: COLLECTIVE BEHAVIOR DYNAMICS

The media and missives from law enforcement officials convey the impression that violent crime is rampant in the United States. Citizens derive the perception that they are extremely vulnerable to attack by violent criminal assailants. In reality, FBI statistics show that there is approximately a 1 in 10 chance that someone will be faced with a violent criminal offender, and chances are closer to 1 in 1,000 of becoming a violent crime victim. Senior citizens report the highest fear of violent crime, but people in this age group are actually least at risk because they tend not to venture out during late afternoon and evening when violent crime is at its peak. The fear of crime among senior citizens and others is reinforced by persistent exposure to local news reports featuring violent crime as their lead stories. Just a few incidents may be generalized as a "crime wave."

The "marketing" of violence through the media and persistent public messages has had a huge effect on fundamental relationships among communities. For example, pointed racial profiling in public service messages about the prevalence and dangerousness of violent crime can generate hatred and aggressive reactions toward marginalized groups (e.g., blacks, Latinos, and Arab Americans) and target hardening on the part of law enforcement. The citizenry generally accepts messages transmitted from government or law enforcement officials, even though they may specifically target or enable the stereotyping of minorities. Such groups become a priori suspects, scapegoated in an ill-fated attempt to control the crime problem. In this way, everyday attitudes toward criminal violence reinforce a crime control ideology fueled by the presence of an uncomfortable tension. Ironically, this ideology emphasizes the pursuit of peace while framing its appeal in the representation of belligerent social attitudes.

Symbolic slogans in the media give context and validation to citizen perceptions. For example, the public service campaign "McGruff the Crime Dog," which urges citizens to "Take a Bite Out of Crime," demonstrates an acceptable community resistance to violent crime. It targets diverse populations of children (e.g., don't accept candy or rides from strangers) and adults (learn to secure homes against burglars before going out).

COMMUNITY INVOLVEMENT

Coproduction

Community attitudes toward violent crime are heightened when citizens are co-opted into working with the criminal justice system to fight crime. The issue of citizen coproduction sends the message that citizens are "deputized" to assist criminal justice officials in keeping the streets safe from violent criminals.

Citizen coproduction efforts are achieved mainly through a concern for neighborhood safety and the application of systematic public relation campaigns. Programs such as "America's Most Wanted" and "Unsolved Mysteries" have directly involved citizens in the fight against crime. Viewers are recruited as the "eyes and the ears" of the municipal law enforcement system, and they are encouraged to call in information or otherwise alert authorities to criminal acts.

In effect, responsibility for community safety is shared with community residents. The citizen as informant is particularly relevant as the 2001 Federal Patriot Act seeks to recruit individuals in an effort to participate in programs such as "Operation TIPS" (Terrorist Information and Prevention Systems). The government can choose individuals with the authority to visit citizen homes (mailmen, cable repair personnel, etc.) and require that they note and report any suspicions that individuals are aiding and abetting terrorist activity.

Citizen Mobilization

Three basic programs have evolved as recommended modes of participation for citizens concerned with violent crime: Crimestoppers, Neighborhood Watch, and Auxiliary Patrols. An overview of driving forces behind these programs points toward their integration of sanctioned surveillance and citizens' attitudes toward criminal behavior, and their ramifications for the quality of life.

All three organizations were created by a criminal justice system engaged in recruiting citizens as an "army" fighting against crime. Each is interconnected with some degree of anticrime participation and the invoking of the criminal control mode. CrimeStoppers is the most passive. Citizens need only watch their own blocks or monitor select televised crime enactments and call the local authorities. There is a reward based on funds raised by the community or the seriousness of the crime. Citizens feel they have a vested interest in fighting violent crime and need not use a gun or approach a violent perpetrator.

Neighborhood Watch is a much more organized form of community participation channeling localized efforts against crime. Citizens are trained as "block watchers" by community police representatives. Some

citizens are given walkie-talkies and urged to report any suspicious behavior. Urban housing projects have endorsed the Neighborhood Watch program through the formation of tenant patrols wherein residents monitor pedestrian traffic in the hallways.

Auxiliary Patrol is the most active of the three approaches. Community residents patrol their neighborhoods or ride around in automobiles. Any suspicious activity is reported to authorized police officers for proper investigation. Auxiliary Patrol members can impose citizen arrests in some situations. Such groups are kept under tight control by criminal justice authorities. Politicians and criminal justice representatives recognize that problems could arise from vigilante attitudes toward violent criminals or terrorists.

Sanctioned Surveillance and Paramilitarization

Citizen participation in justice-sponsored programs comprises a form of sanctioned surveillance, retaliation against crime that stresses obedience as underlying social behavior. Citizens willingly participate, with the ideology that the lives they save include their family, friends, and perhaps their own. In effect, the police may be seen as the domestic link of the standing army and citizen patrol participants represent paramilitary reserves.

Some groups of citizens form self-styled paramilitary organizations apart from the law enforcement system, most notably, the Guardian Angels, led by Curtis Sliwa. The group was endorsed by the public as an alternative to high violent crime rates in New York City during the 1970s. The New York City police department eventually negotiated some control over the group's activities during the 1980s. The Guardian Angels have faded from the public spotlight except for Sliwa's appearances on a New York City radio station and a nationally telecast cable program.

—*Lloyd Klein*

See also Homicide, Perceptions of; Media, Violence in the; Police Brutality; Prevention of Crime and Violent Behavior; Vigilantism

Further Reading

Kenney, D. J. (1987). *Crime, fear and the New York City subways: The role of citizen action.* New York: Praeger.
Mendelsohn, H., & O'Keefe, G. J. (1984). *Taking a bite out of crime: The impact of a mass media crime prevention*

campaign. Washington, DC: National Institute of Crime.

Rosenbaum, D. (Ed.). (1986). *Community crime prevention: Does it work?* Beverly Hills, CA: Sage.

Rosenbaum, D., Lurigio, A., & Lavrakas, P. (1989). Enhancing citizen participation and solving serious crime: A national evaluation of crime stoppers programs. *Crime and Delinquency 35*(3), 378-400.

COMPLIANT VICTIM, *See* GENDER VIOLENCE; TEAM KILLERS; VICTIMOLOGY

CONFESSIONS, FALSE, *See* FALSE CONFESSIONS

CONNALLY, GOVERNOR JOHN, *See* ASSASSINS

COPYCAT EFFECT, *See* MASS MURDER; MEDIA, VIOLENCE IN THE; SCHOOL SHOOTINGS; SERIAL MURDER

CORRECTIONAL PRACTITIONERS, *See* CRIMINAL JUSTICE PRACTITIONERS

CORRECTIONAL PSYCHOLOGY, *See* FORENSIC PSYCHOLOGY

CORRUPTION, *See* ORGANIZED CRIME; POLICE CORRUPTION

COSTELLO, FRANK, *See* ORGANIZED CRIME: DOMESTIC

COURT-MANDATED TREATMENT

Court-mandated treatment is also referred to as court-ordered treatment, state-ordered treatment, or compulsory treatment. It is a form of therapeutic intervention ordered by the courts or sanctioned by the state as a rehabilitative effort for criminal offenders. Mandatory treatment most often occurs in community settings, as opposed to correctional treatment in an institution (e.g., criminal mental hospital, prison, or jail). In the case of criminal offenders, courts often order the type, frequency, and/or length of mandatory treatment specific to correcting the offending behavior. Probation officers (or parole officers, when an offender has been incarcerated prior to the referral to treatment) are charged with the duty of monitoring court-ordered treatment. Mandatory treatment is often a condition of the probation or parole agreement and allows the courts to revoke probation or parole and implement incarceration for failure to comply with the terms of the agreement, such as failure to participate, make progress, or initiate treatment. Domestic violence offenders, sex offenders, and substance abusers are the most common offenders referred for mandatory treatment. Juveniles, including truant children, may also be sentenced to engage in such treatment.

State agencies have the power to order treatment and make engaging in treatment a requirement for averting arrest and/or the loss of some liberties. For example, as a means of intervention, child protective services often refer parents deemed abusive toward their children, following an investigation, to mandatory treatment.

The types of treatment that can be implemented during mandatory treatment vary and may include one (or a combination) of the following: group therapy, individual therapy, couples therapy, family therapy, and/or psychoeducation. These treatment types may be based on a number of psychological theories or modes of intervention, such as cognitive-behavioral, strict behavioral, or structural family therapy or others which may be deemed more appropriate for the offender and offending behaviors. Cognitive-behavioral interventions with psychoeducation have been found to be the most effective for mandatory treatment of criminal offenders. For example, the goals of a sex offender treatment program are likely to include having the offender (a) take full responsibility, (b) identify and change cognitive distortion, and (c) identify and change their behavioral responses to cues, among other goals. Individuals referred for child-rearing issues or juvenile delinquency often include a combination of psychoeducation and family therapy.

At one time, almost any licensed mental health professional could provide mandatory treatment. However, as the demand for such treatment increased, both state-imposed regulations and professionally developed standards emerged. Some states issue a license or registration to a provider who meets their qualifications for providing specific forms of mandatory treatment and then require referrals for the treatment. A recent example of how registered mandatory-treatment networks are developed occurred in 2000 with the passage of Proposition 36 in California. Proposition 36 diverts first-time nonviolent drug offenders to treatment rather than incarceration. Once the voters passed this measure, the state was to create a referral network based on the needs of the offender; thus, inpatient detoxification programs, outpatient providers, and residential programs needed to be identified, inspected to ensure compliance with state regulations, registered with the state, and made available to offenders.

A provider can be an individual, a clinic, or an agency that provides therapeutic treatment. Professional groups have developed standards for practice and ethics related to forensic practices. The American Psychiatric Association, the Association for the Treatment of Sexual Abusers, and the American Psychological Association have all addressed ethical issues and/or provided guidelines to their members who engage in forensic practices.

Confidentiality is a major issue for such practitioners. The nature of mandatory treatment implies that those monitoring the treatment for the courts or the state need to have access to information known to providers, such as whether the offender participated, has made progress, or is considered rehabilitated. This eliminates the sanctity of therapist-client confidentiality. Clients involved in voluntary therapeutic treatment hold the privilege to determine whom the treatment practitioner can release information to and the extent of the information. Individuals receiving mandatory treatment do not have this right. Other related issues include length of treatment, progress criteria, and termination.

—*Sarah Ferguson*

Further Reading

Kratcoski, P. (1999). *Correctional counseling and treatment* (4th ed.). Prospect Heights, IL: Waveland.

Munetz, M. (1997). Can mandatory treatment be therapeutic? *New directions for mental health services* (No. 75, 1st ed.). San Francisco: Jossey-Bass.

Sheilagh, H., & Muller-Isbern, R. (2000). *Violence, crime & mentally disordered offenders: Concepts & methods for effective treatment & prevention*. New York: John Wiley.

COURT-ORDERED PSYCHOLOGICAL ASSESSMENT

A wide variety of psychological assessments may be ordered by the court to assist in making decisions involving legal matters. A psychologist may be called on to help determine whether a defendant is competent to stand trial or was insane at the time of the offense. These evaluations usually consist of a clinical interview and psychological testing. In all forensic evaluations, the final decision is made by the court (judge or jury), not by the psychologist or expert witness. Of the different types of forensic mental health evaluations, the most frequently requested are violence risk assessments, competency to stand trial evaluations, and insanity evaluations.

VIOLENCE RISK ASSESSMENT

Frequently, criminal courts call on mental health professionals to evaluate the dangerousness of violent and sex offenders. The main goal of these evaluations is to determine the likelihood that an individual will commit violent crimes, either now or in the future. Since violent behavior is not all that common, prediction can often lead to an extremely elevated number of false positives. A false positive mistakenly identifies someone as a future risk when in fact they are not. This may result in offenders being inappropriately incarcerated or denied release from prison.

Certain characteristics, such as the nature and seriousness of the crime, arrest and conviction history, and substance abuse, have been related to predicting the probability that an offender will commit a new violent crime. The idea that mental health professionals can predict future violence is very controversial. Should an offender be released once he or she has served time? Several studies indicate that such predictions can be made, although the accuracy is debatable. Up until the early 1980s, it was believed that these predictions were accurate some of the time, whereas others argued that the prediction of dangerousness was near to impossible. However, recent literature suggests that in certain situations, clinicians can indeed accurately predict dangerousness.

Clinical and Statistical Prediction

There are two general approaches to violence risk assessment: clinical and statistical. Using the clinical method, the clinician forms an impression about the offender by focusing on clinical symptoms based on an offender's criminal history and the results of psychological test data. Clinicians are also needed to understand the personality structure of the individual, the factors that led to past violent behaviors, and how these factors might influence future violent acts. The mental health professional must be able to describe, using clinical analysis, why the offender did what he or she did and under what circumstances he or she is likely to repeat it. Of the different assessment tools available, the most subjective are clinical judgements. As a result, a clinical interview alone cannot be used to make an accurate prediction.

In contrast to clinical prediction, statistical tools are based on empirical research that establishes which individuals, because of certain factors, are at relatively higher risk. When statistics are applied to a violent population (i.e., prison inmates), better predictions can be made. Modern research suggests that predicting future violence can be improved over chance by the use of statistical methods.

Violence Prediction Methods

Mental health professionals have myriad empirically based risk assessment tools at their disposal to evaluate an offender's potential for future violence. One of the more popular tests used to assess risk for violence is the Psychopathy Checklist-Revised (PCL-R). The PCL-R was developed using both male inmates and male forensic psychiatric patients and shows high levels of accurate prediction of violence and recidivism. The Rapid Risk Assessment for Sexual Offense Recidivism (RRASOR), as developed by Hanson in 1997, is another popular risk assessment tool. The RRASOR contains four items that are scored from the offender's criminal records: prior sexual offenses, age less than 25, nonfamilial victims, and male victims. It is believed the RRASOR is useful as a sexual offender

recidivism-screening instrument. Other statistical methods include the Violent Risk Appraisal Guide (VRAG), the Sex Offender Risk Appraisal Guide (SORAG), the Minnesota Sex Offender Screening Tool-Revised, and the Spousal Assault Risk Assessment Guide (SARA).

Sexual Offenders

In the 1980s, many states passed sexual predator laws that ordered sexual offenders determined to be still dangerous to be civilly committed until they were deemed to be no longer at risk. The laws are applied to offenders, typically men, who are about to be paroled from prison. To civilly commit someone, the state must show that the offender has a history of sexual offenses, currently suffers from a mental disorder, and has a strong potential to engage in future acts of sexual violence.

Mentally Disordered Offenders

One of the more controversial issues is whether there is a link between violence and mental illness. In the last 10 years, research has found a moderate connection between violent behavior and diagnosable mental disorder. Notwithstanding this association, most mentally ill individuals are no more violent than people who are not mentally ill. Studies show that murders committed by the mentally disordered occur much less frequently than among the non–mentally ill population. Among mentally disordered violent offenders, individuals diagnosed with psychosis and substance abuse are at much higher risk than those who suffer either type of disorder.

Factors Related to Violence Risk Assessment

Recent studies on violence risk assessment indicate that specific attributes are more related to future dangerousness than others. For example, demographic factors such as race have been recognized as potential predictors; for example, African American individuals are associated with higher violence risk. Other factors include gender (males at higher risk than females) and age (youth at higher risk). Personality disorders, such as antisocial personality disorder, are also significantly related to adult criminal behavior. Background factors associated with future violence and dangerousness include arrest history, juvenile delinquency, and age of first offense (age below 13 years is a significant predictor of adult criminality). Finally, contextual factors such as availability of weapons and victim accessibility are clearly linked to the prediction of violence.

ASSESSMENT OF COMPETENCY

In criminal court, competency comes into question in several different areas of legal proceedings. First, if a confession is to be admitted at trial, a defendant must be competent to waive his or her Miranda rights. The defendant has to be competent to stand trial (the most commonly assessed competency) and if convicted must be competent to be sentenced. The defendant must also be found to have been competent at the time of the crime in order to have criminal responsibility for the offense. A defendant must also be found competent to be executed in cases in which the death penalty is likely. In the determination of competency, one determination does not necessarily lead to other findings of similar competency. For example, an individual can be competent to stand trial but not competent (or insane) at the time of the offense. Or, he or she could have been competent (or sane) at the time of the offense but be incompetent at the time of trial. If a defendant is found not competent to stand trial, the trial may be postponed until competency is restored. However, if there is no indication that the defendant will ever be found competent, the charges may be dismissed.

Competency to Stand Trial

Competency to stand trial is a legal concept allowing the delay of court proceedings for individuals who are unable to participate in their own defense due to a mental disorder. Competency issues can be raised prior to, during, and before the end of a trial. When competency is called into question, the defense attorney or prosecutor will present evidence to the court that the defendant is mentally ill, or mentally retarded, and does not have the capacity to understand the charges against him or her or assist the attorney in a defense. The court will then order that a competency evaluation be performed by a mental health professional (usually a psychologist or psychiatrist).

The U.S. standard for competency was first established in 1960 in *Dusky v. United States,* in which the U.S. Supreme Court held that rational understanding of the criminal proceedings and ability to assist an attorney are required. To be judged competent, the defendant must have a basic understanding of the charges against him or her, how the legal system functions, and the possible consequences of the trial. In addition, the defendant must be able to help his or her attorney build a proper defense. Historically, there has been a low threshold for a determination of competency, and only those individuals with severe mental illness or mental retardation have been found incompetent.

Mental illness can greatly impair a defendant's reasoning, judgement, and memory and can hinder his or her ability to comprehend and process information. These impairments make it challenging for a mentally ill defendant to understand the trial he or she is facing. Symptoms of mental illness such as paranoia, psychosis, or mania can also considerably impede a defendant's ability to help the attorney with his or her case. Incompetent defendants are typically ordered by the court for treatment to restore them to competency so that they can be tried for their alleged offenses. It is estimated that approximately 2% to 8% of all criminal defendants are referred for competency evaluations.

Psychological Reports

In the evaluation, the psychologist will perform a lengthy interview of the defendant. The psychologist is required to focus on the defendant's understanding of the nature of his or her crime, awareness of the legal system, and ability to understand and discuss potential defenses. In addition, the psychologist will likely use psychological tests or forensic assessment instruments, such as the MacArthur Competence Assessment Tool—Criminal Adjudication (MacCAT-CA) or the Competence Assessment for Standing Trial for Defendants with Mental Retardation (CAST-MR), to support clinical impressions and to screen for the possibility that the defendant is faking an illness or impairment to avoid trial.

Competency evaluations typically address the following areas: (a) laws to meet the requirements for competency to stand trial in that state; (b) the defendant's background information, including psychiatric, medical, and substance abuse history; (c) current level of mental and cognitive functioning; (d) evaluation of the defendant's ability to understand the charges against him or her, to understand the roles of the courtroom players, to distinguish between different pleas, to understand the possible verdicts, to assist in the defense, to adequately engage with the attorney, and to display acceptable courtroom behavior; and (e) whether or not the defendant's mental illness or mental retardation (if any) has influenced his or her competency to stand trial. Issues of malingering (faking symptoms of mental illness) will be addressed in cases in which the defendant is determined to be incompetent. Moreover, if the defendant is found incompetent, the psychological report will also discuss the defendant's need for treatment.

Restoration of Competency

The treatment for restoring competency typically involves the use of psychotropic medication to stabilize the mental disorder. Additionally, psychotherapy is used to increase the defendant's understanding of the legal process, including understanding of the charges and the possible consequences of these charges. Restoration of competency should not address the crime, whether the defendant is guilty, or the defendant's mental state at the time of the offense.

When and if competency is restored, the defendant is returned to court to stand trial. In certain instances, the competency of some individuals cannot be restored due to chronic mental illness or severe mental retardation. Even if an individual's competency is found to be unrestorable, the court will still evaluate the risk posed to him- or herself or to others. Based on the assessment of risk, a defendant will either be released, committed to a psychiatric hospital, committed to a forensic hospital, or transferred to a facility for the mentally retarded.

INSANITY AND CRIMINAL RESPONSIBILITY

Criminal responsibility refers to the defendant's state of mind at the time of the alleged crime. A person cannot be convicted of a crime if it can be proved that he or she lacked the ability to form criminal intent because of insanity. The law recognizes that certain mentally ill individuals who have committed criminal acts should not be considered guilty. For a wrongful act *(actus reus)* to be a crime, the offender must have a guilty mind *(mens rea)*. A defense of "not guilty by reason of insanity" (NGRI) may be introduced on the grounds that the defendant did not "know" or "appreciate" the meaning and consequences of his or her actions. The verdict of NGRI applies when the criminal act was committed with a state of mind, related to mental illness, that renders the individual blameless.

Legal Standards

The elements necessary for NGRI vary among states. The oldest test, dating back to 1843, is the *M'Naughten Rule,* which maintains that the defendant is not responsible if he or she committed the criminal behavior while acting under a defect of reason from disease of the mind so as not to know the nature and quality of the act and not to know that the act was wrong.

The second test of insanity, introduced in 1922, is termed *irresistible impulse.* Under this rule, a defendant is not responsible for an offense if he or she was unable to control an act or impulse because of mental illness. In 1954, the *Durham Rule,* the third test of insanity, held that a defendant is not criminally responsible if his or her illegal act was the product of a mental disease. This is also known as the *product rule.* In 1966, the American Law Institute (ALI) Formulation was proposed in the model penal code. Under ALI, a person is not responsible for criminal conduct if at the time of the offense, as a result of mental disease, he or she lacks substantial capacity either to appreciate the wrongfulness of the conduct or to conform his or her conduct to the requirements of law.

Burden of Proof

A defendant is usually presumed to be sane and therefore is the one who must raise the question of criminal responsibility. If the defendant can produce evidence of insanity, the burden of proof lies in the prosecutor's ability to prove that the defendant was, in fact, responsible at the time of the alleged crime. If the prosecutor fails to meet this burden of proof, a jury may, after finding that the defendant committed the act, also find him or her not guilty by reason of insanity.

Not Guilty by Reason of Insanity (NGRI)

Less than 1 in 500 defendants enter a plea of NGRI, and over 90% of these defendants are found guilty. When a defendant is found NGRI, the defendant is not released back into society. Rather, he or she is sent to a forensic hospital for a designated period of time. Depending on the offense, this can actually be longer than the sentence would have been if the person was found guilty and incarcerated. As with competency, being unable to understand the nature and consequences of the offense is not an easy threshold to reach. The defendant must be unduly impaired.

In most cases, these individuals are so out of contact with reality that they were not aware that they had committed a crime or that what they were doing was wrong. Those found NRGI, for this reason, usually have extensive histories of mental illness.

Psychological Reports

As in the case of competency, clinical interviews are conducted, and psychological testing is usually administered. This is both to determine whether an illness is present and to screen for faking mental illness. In insanity evaluations, the psychologist reviews all available records in order to reconstruct the defendant's state of mind at the time of the crime. Insanity evaluations address the following areas: (a) laws to meet the requirements for an insanity defense in that state, (b) the defendant's background information, including psychiatric, medical, and substance abuse history, (c) description of the offense by the defendant, (d) diagnostic and clinical impressions and reasons why a specific diagnosis was made, (e) description of the association between the defendant's behavior at the time of the offense and the symptoms of his or her mental illness, and (f) relationship of the defendant's mental state and behavior with insanity defense requirements in that state.

Issues of malingering are also addressed. If a defendant is found insane based on NGRI, an acquittal is usually followed by commitment to a psychiatric hospital; these are often involuntary admissions. Once hospitalized, the defendant will be evaluated for dangerousness, risk for future violence, and the need for psychiatric treatment. This involuntary commitment can be justified by the need to protect society from further harm as a consequence of the defendant's mental illness.

—*Amy Lynne Bronswick*

See also FORENSIC SCIENCE; MENTALLY DISORDERED OFFENDERS; M'NAUGHTEN RULE; NOT GUILTY BY REASON OF INSANITY (NGRI); PREDICTING VIOLENT BEHAVIOR; PSYCHOPATHY CHECKLIST-REVISED (PCL-R); PSYCHOSOCIAL RISK FACTORS FOR VIOLENT BEHAVIOR

Further Reading

Cohen, D. A. (1996). Notes on the clinical assessment of dangerousness in offender populations. *Psychiatry on-line, 1997*. Available on the World Wide Web at: www.ccspublishing.com/j_psych.htm.

Grisso, T. (1986). *Evaluating competencies: Forensic assessments and instruments.* New York: Plenum.

Melton, G. B., Petrila, J., Poythress, N. G., & Slobogin, C. (1997). *Psychological evaluations for the courts: A handbook for mental health professionals and lawyers* (2nd ed.). New York: Guilford.

Otto, R. K., & Heilbrun, K. (2002). The practice of forensic psychology: A look toward the future in light of the past. *American Psychologist, 57(1),* 5-18.

Rogers, R., & Shuman, D. W. (2000). *Conducting insanity evaluations* (2nd ed.). New York: Guilford.

Schwitzgebel, R. L., & Schwitzgebel, R. K. (1980). *Law and psychological practice.* New York: John Wiley.

Zapf, P. A., & Roesch, R. (2000, Summer). Mental competency evaluations: Guidelines for judges and attorneys. *Court Review,* pp. 28-35.

COURTS: ORGANIZATION

To understand the role of federal and state courts, it is essential to have a grasp of the principles of the American criminal justice system. There is no more confusing, frustrating, and complex environment than the criminal court system. This section will provide a brief overview of the judicial system in the United States.

THE PRINCIPLE OF FEDERALISM

The court system in the United States is based on the principle of federalism. The first Congress established a federal court system, and the individual states were permitted to continue their own judicial structures. There was general agreement among the nation's founders that individual states should retain significant autonomy from federal control. Under this concept of federalism, the United States developed as a loose confederation of semi-independent states having their own courts, with the federal court system acting in a very limited manner. In the early history of our nation, most cases were tried in state courts. Only later did the federal government and the federal judiciary began to exercise jurisdiction over crimes and civil matters. Jurisdiction in this context simply means the ability of the court to enforce laws and punish individuals who violate those laws.

As a result of this historical evolution, a dual system of state and federal courts exists today. Therefore, federal and state courts may have concurrent jurisdiction over specific crimes. For example, a person who robs a bank may be tried and convicted in state court for robbery, then tried and convicted in federal court for the federal offense of robbery of a federally chartered savings institution.

THE STATE COURT SYSTEM

Historically, each of the 13 original states had its own unique court structure. This independence continued after the American Revolution and resulted in widespread differences among the various states, some of which still exist today. Because each state adopted its own system of courts, the consequence was a poorly planned and confusing judicial structure. As a result, several reform movements have attempted to streamline and modernize this system.

Many state courts can be divided into three levels: trial courts, appellate courts, and state supreme courts. Criminal cases start and finish in trial courts. This court conducts the entire series of acts that culminate in either the defendant's release or sentencing. State trial courts can be further divided into courts of limited or special jurisdiction and courts of general jurisdiction. The nature and type of case determine which court will have jurisdiction.

Limited Jurisdiction

Courts that hear and decide only certain limited legal issues are courts of limited jurisdiction: They hear or decide certain types of minor civil or criminal cases, such as traffic tickets or setting bail for criminal defendants. There are approximately 13,000 local courts in the United States, called county, magistrate, justice, or municipal courts. Judges in these courts may be either appointed or elected. In many jurisdictions, these are part-time positions, and the incumbent may have another job or position in addition to serving as a judge. However, simply because they handle minor civil and criminal matters does not mean these courts do not perform important duties. Often, the only contact the average citizen will have with the judicial system occurs at this level.

In addition, courts of limited jurisdiction may hear certain types of specialized matters such as probate of wills and estates, divorce, child custody matters, and juvenile hearings. These types of courts may be local courts or, depending on the state, may be courts of

general jurisdiction designated by statute to hear and decide specific types of cases. For example, in California, a superior court is considered a court of general jurisdiction; however, certain superior courts are designated to hear only juvenile matters, thereby becoming a court of limited jurisdiction.

General Jurisdiction

Courts of general jurisdiction are granted authority to hear and decide all issues that are brought before them, occurring anywhere within the state. They normally hear all major civil or criminal cases and are known by a variety of names, such as superior courts, circuit courts, district courts, or courts of common pleas. Some larger jurisdictions such as Los Angeles or New York may have hundreds of courts of general jurisdiction within the city limits. Typically, these courts hear civil cases involving the same type of issues that courts of limited jurisdiction do, although the amount of damages will be higher and may reach millions. They also hear the most serious forms of criminal matters, including death penalty cases.

Courts of general jurisdiction traditionally have the power to issue injunctions that prohibit individuals from performing certain acts or require them to perform certain functions or duties. This authority is derived from the equity power that resides in courts of general jurisdiction.

Equity is the concept that justice is administrated according to fairness, as contrasted with the strict rules of law. In early English common law, such separate courts of equity were known as "Courts of Chancery." These early courts were not concerned with technical legal issues; rather, they focused on rendering decisions or orders that were fair or equitable. In modern times, the power of these courts has been merged with courts of general jurisdiction, allowing them to rule on matters that require fairness as well as the strict application of the law. The power to issue temporary restraining orders in spousal abuse cases comes from the equitable powers of the court.

Appellate Jurisdiction

Appellate jurisdiction is reserved for courts that hear appeals from both limited and general jurisdiction courts. These courts do not hold trials or hear evidence. They decide matters of law and issue formal written decisions or "opinions." There are two classes of appellate courts: *intermediate,* or courts of appeals; and *final,* or supreme courts.

Courts of Appeals

Approximately half the states have designated intermediate appellate courts, or courts of appeals. These courts may be divided into judicial districts that hear all appeals within their district. They hear and decide all issues of law that are raised on appeal in both civil and criminal cases. Because these courts deal strictly with legal or equitable issues, there is no jury to decide factual disputes; they accept the facts as determined by the trial court. Intermediate appellate courts have the authority to reverse the decisions of the lower courts and to send the matter back with instructions to retry the case in accordance with their opinions. They also may uphold the decision of the lower courts. In either situation, the party who loses the appeal at this level may file an appeal with the next-higher appellate court.

Supreme Courts

Final appellate courts are the highest state appellate courts, also known as supreme courts or courts of last resort. There may be five, seven, or nine justices sitting on these courts, depending on the state. They have jurisdiction to hear and decide issues dealing with all matters decided by lower courts, including ruling on state constitutional or statutory issues. This decision is binding on all other courts within the state. Once the appellate court has decided an issue, the only appeal left is to file in the federal court system.

THE FEDERAL COURT SYSTEM

Whereas state courts had their origins in historical accident and custom, federal courts were created by the U.S. Constitution. Section 1 of Article III established the federal court system, providing for "one Supreme Court, and . . . such inferior Courts as the Congress may from time to time ordain and establish." From this beginning, Congress has engaged in a series of acts resulting in today's federal court system. The Judiciary Act of 1789 created the U.S. Supreme Court and established district courts and circuit courts of appeals.

Federal District Courts

Federal district courts are the lowest level of the federal court system. These courts have original jurisdiction over all cases involving violation of federal statutes and handle thousands of criminal cases per year.

Federal Circuit Courts

Federal circuit courts of appeals are the intermediate appellate level courts within the federal system, called *circuit courts* because the system is divided into 11 circuits. The 12th Circuit Court of Appeals serves the Washington, D.C., area. They hear all criminal appeals from the district courts and habeas corpus appeals from state court convictions. These appeals are usually heard by panels of three of the appellate court judges, rather than by all the judges of each circuit.

U.S. Supreme Court

The United States Supreme Court is the highest court in the land. It has the capacity for judicial review of all lower court decisions, as well as state and federal statutes. By exercising this power, the Supreme Court determines which laws and lower court decisions conform to the mandates set forth in the U.S. Constitution. The concept of judicial review was first referred to by Alexander Hamilton in the *Federalist Papers,* in which he described the Supreme Court as ensuring that the will of the people is supreme over the will of the legislature. This concept was firmly and finally established in our system when the Supreme Court asserted its power of judicial review in the case of *Marbury v. Madison* (1803).

Although it is primarily an appellate court, the Supreme Court has original jurisdiction in the following cases: cases between the United States and a state; cases between states; cases involving foreign ambassadors, ministers, and consuls; and cases between a state and a citizen of another state or country.

The Court hears appeals from lower courts, including the various state supreme courts. If four justices of the U.S. Supreme Court vote to hear a case, the court will issue a *Writ of Certiorari.* This is an order to a lower court to send the records of the case to the Supreme Court for review. The court meets on the first Monday of October and usually remains in session until June. The court may review any case it deems worthy of review, but it actually hears very few of the cases filed. Of approximately 5,000 appeals each year, the court agrees to review about 200, but may not issue an opinion on each case.

—Harvey Wallace

See also JURISDICTION

Further Reading

American Bar Association. (1987). *Law and the courts: A handbook about United States law and court procedures.* Chicago: Author.

Siegal, L., & Senna, J. (1994). *Juvenile justice.* St. Paul, MN: West Publishing.

Stuckey, G., Roberson, C., & Wallace, H. (2001). *Procedures in the justice system* (6th ed.). Upper Saddle River, NJ: Prentice Hall.

Territo, L., Halsted, J., & Bromley, M. (1992). *Crime and justice in America: A human perspective.* St. Paul, MN: West Publishing.

CRIMES OF OBEDIENCE

Crimes of obedience result from the tendency of ordinary people to commit illegal, immoral, or unethical acts against others when ordered by someone in authority or having power over them. There have been many examples of such crimes in the world's history, including the My Lai Massacre, in Vietnam, and the Holocaust, in Germany. Several psychological studies have examined this type of behavior.

MILGRAM'S EXPERIMENT IN OBEDIENCE

Stanley Milgram, a psychologist at Yale University, performed an experiment to study the conflict between an individual's obedience to authority and personal conscience. He wanted to understand how someone might justify acts of genocide. In the experiment, he enlisted student volunteers to administer electric shocks of increasing intensity to the "subjects," also called "learners," on the other side of a barrier. In reality, these people were actors pretending to be shocked. As the students increased the "electric shocks," the actors pretended to express their discomfort audibly. Some students were obviously upset by this, but 60% continued to administer the shocks until a level of 450 volts was supposedly reached. No student stopped before a level of 300 volts was administered. The students did question whether they should continue administering the shocks, but once reassured by the experimenter or authority that they would not be responsible for any harm to the learners, most of them continued with the experiment.

MY LAI MASSACRE

Incidents have occurred during wartime in which members of the military are known to have harmed unarmed civilians because they were ordered to do so by superiors. A well-known example is the "My Lai Massacre," during the Vietnam War. On March 16, 1968, Charlie Company, 11th Brigade, entered the village of My Lai, a heavily mined area under Vietcong influence. Charlie Company had experienced several injuries and losses in the area in the weeks preceding this event. They were on a "search and destroy" mission that turned into a massacre of over 300 unarmed women, children, and elderly from the village. After the incident, when asked why they committed such acts, men from Charlie Company reported that they were bound to obey the orders of their superiors.

THE HOLOCAUST

In March 1938, the Nazis began systematically suppressing the freedoms of Jews in Germany and Austria, and the first concentration camp was established in Mauthausen by Adolf Eichmann. By 1939, Jewish citizens had lost nearly all their rights and most of their property. In October of that year, the Nazis begin euthanasia of sick and disabled Jews in Germany. Though a 39-nation meeting took place to address the situation, no action was taken to assist the victims.

In January 1940, the Nazis opened a new concentration camp, Auschwitz, in Poland. By February, the regime had invaded Poland, and in March, Denmark and Norway fell under their power. Jewish citizens in each of these countries faced the same losses as German Jews. Two ghettos, Krakow and Warsaw, were sealed off, confining more than 470,000 Jewish men, women, and children.

By the end of 1941, it was estimated that more than a million Jews had been murdered as German troops seized territories for Hitler. In December, Hans Frank, of Poland, told fellow cabinet members that they must rid themselves of all feelings of pity for the Jews. He announced that the Jewish population must be annihilated to maintain the structure of the Reich. Atrocities continued through 1943.

In March 1944, U.S. President Roosevelt condemned the German and Japanese for their "crimes against humanity." By November 1945, the Nuremberg International Tribunal took place, in which the war crimes of several Nazi officers and officials were examined. The officers and officials claimed they were "simply following orders." These acts may be considered the largest-scale modern day crime of obedience: Approximately 6 million European Jewish citizens were estimated to have been murdered in the Holocaust at the hands of the Nazis, leaving only 3.5 million European survivors.

—*Elizabeth M. Stanczak*

See also ETHNIC CLEANSING; GENOCIDE; MASS VIOLENCE; MEDICAL VIOLENCE; WAR ATROCITIES

Further Reading

Ermann, M. D., & Lundman, R. J. (1996). *Corporate and governmental deviance: Problems of organizational behavior in contemporary society.* New York: Oxford University Press.

Kelman, H. C., & Hamilton, V. L. (1989). *Crimes of obedience: Toward a social psychology of authority and responsibility.* New Haven and London: Yale University Press.

Mixon, D. (1989). *Obedience and civilization: The origins of authorized crime.* London: Pluto.

CRIME OF PASSION, *See* HOMICIDE, TYPES OF, AND DEGREES OF MURDER; MOTIVES FOR MURDER

CRIME SYNDICATES, *See* ORGANIZED CRIME

CRIMINAL, BORN, *See* AGGRESSION: BIOLOGICAL THEORIES; HOMICIDE, PERCEPTIONS OF

CRIMINAL ENTERPRISE MURDER, *See* MOTIVES FOR MURDER

CRIMINAL JUSTICE PRACTITIONERS

Practitioners in the criminal justice system have specific responsibilities and function within three subsystems. They work in federal, state, and local jurisdictions within the subsystems of law enforcement, courts, and corrections. The roles of practitioners differ depending on jurisdiction and subsystem assignment, which are interrelated in some instances. For example, the federal government has primary jurisdiction regarding terrorist activity, yet federal officers and prosecutors work with state and local agencies to collect information, locate suspects, and make arrests. Federal prisoners are housed in local jails while they await trial.

Although the criminal justice system is interrelated in the United States, it is also purposefully decentralized. Federal and state practitioners work together to solve and prevent crime, collect crime statistics, and provide training services, but the decentralized structure of America's government clearly divides and defines criminal justice authority. The purpose of this structure is to allow states significant authority over their own affairs and to give them the majority of policing responsibilities. For example, there are federal police agencies, but there is no national police force. This decentralized approach to government allows for state and local practices to largely shape justice. The majority of criminal justice practitioners work within these state and local governments.

LAW ENFORCEMENT PRACTITIONERS

In the United States, there are over 17,000 federal, state, and local law enforcement agencies. Federal agencies administered by various branches of the government enforce federal criminal laws, investigate federal property crimes, perform specialized functions in criminal matters, and assist other law enforcement agencies. Departments include the Justice Department (for the Federal Bureau of Investigation and Drug Enforcement Administration), the Treasury Department (for Alcohol, Tobacco, and Firearms; Secret Service; and Internal Revenue Criminal Investigations Division), and the Immigration and Naturalization Service (for the Border Patrol).

The majority of police in the United States work for state and local agencies that employ 100 or fewer officers (Reaves, 2000). They are responsible for enforcing laws, apprehending criminals, protecting the public from criminal activity, and developing crime prevention programs. Those agencies employ civilian and sworn personnel, the latter having completed police academy training and having the authority to apprehend and arrest criminals. Civilian (or nonsworn) employees of law enforcement agencies generally support those agencies as dispatchers, crime scene investigators, community service officers, and clerical personnel.

State and local agencies include municipal police departments that employ police officers in incorporated cities; county and parish sheriff's departments that employ deputies and constables in rural and unincorporated metropolitan areas; and state police agencies that employ troopers, highway patrol officers, investigators in specialized units, and forensic science personnel. These agencies receive their authority from state and local statutes, engage in crime prevention and detection activities, and are sometimes called "first responders." They are usually the first to be contacted by the public and the first to arrive at crime scenes. In this capacity, they are charged with first restoring the peace, providing aid to injured persons, apprehending criminals, and investigating crimes.

Whether they occur in federal or state jurisdictions, a basic tenet of criminal investigation involves building cases that are presented in court. This requires participation from various practitioners, especially in complicated investigations such as homicides. The following is a general example of the work groups involved in solving a homicide in most jurisdictions.

Whether they are park rangers on federal land or local police in metropolitan neighborhoods, when officers are dispatched to a call, safety is the priority, both theirs and others'. At a homicide scene, officers stabilize the incident and secure it from further hazards, provide aid and assistance, apprehend suspects, gather information, collect and preserve physical evidence, and engage in follow-up investigations using information collected at the scene. Officers in small agencies may be responsible for most aspects of the investigation, while larger agencies employ detectives and other specialty investigative units. Crime scene investigators are trained practitioners who use a variety of physical evidence collection procedures, such as fingerprints, shoe tracks, bullet trajectory, blood and hair samples, blood spatter patterns, and crime scene analysis. Any evidence that needs further chemical analysis is sent to the crime lab. The crime lab practitioners are trained to analyze biological, chemical, and DNA evidence.

Investigators and pathologists gather additional data from the coroner's office regarding the death of the victim. The reports collected from the officers, crime scene investigators, the coroner's office, and the crime lab are sent to the homicide detectives.

Detectives review the reports and begin a strategy for solving the homicide. If a suspect is identified through a fingerprint comparison, detectives can order a blood sample from the suspect to see if there is a DNA match. If there is a match, detectives will secure a warrant for the suspect's arrest. After the suspect's arrest, the detectives work with the district attorney's office to file the case in the court system.

COURT SYSTEM PRACTITIONERS

The practitioners in the criminal court system have similar roles in both federal and state courts. Federal and state courts are separated into various levels, with state courts having additional levels that handle juvenile cases.

The federal court system comprises the U.S. District Courts, U.S. Courts of Appeals, and the Supreme Court. The state court system is made up of trial courts of limited jurisdiction, trial courts of general jurisdiction, and appellate courts. In general, practitioners include judges, U.S. attorneys, or deputy attorneys general in federal matters; prosecuting, district, or state's attorneys in state matters; defense attorneys, investigators, grand juries, court-appointed advocates, and guardians *ad litem* for juveniles; and victim/witness advocates. The vast majority of criminal cases are handled at the state level, and the following is an example of a case going through a typical state system.

Suspects who are arrested for crimes are usually either booked into jail or cited and released. If booked, they are photographed and fingerprinted, and they must be taken to court within 48 hours for an initial appearance to hear their criminal charges, be advised of their rights, and be given the opportunity for bail. This process involves several practitioners, including prosecuting and defense attorneys (and their follow-up investigators) and judges. The prosecuting attorney, also called the state's attorney, district attorney, or commonwealth attorney, advocates on behalf of the people of the state. They rely on cases assembled by law enforcement officials and follow-up information gathered by investigators who work for the prosecuting attorneys. On major cases, prosecutors are actively involved with the criminal justice process from the arrest, disposition, hearing, trial, and sentencing. Defense attorneys can be public defenders or private practitioners. The court appoints a public defender when a defendant can not afford an attorney. In some cases and on approval by the judge, defendants can appear *in pro per,* acting as their own defense counsel.

Judges have the responsibility of ensuring justice and preserving the rights of all participants in the court process. They make rulings based on precedent and statutes, determine what evidence is admissible, instruct juries on procedures, and preside over the flow of the court process. Judges also set bail based on the severity of the crime and statutes and recommendations from attorneys. Bail is a sum of money that is used to ensure that defendants who are not incarcerated will return to court for trial on the appointed date. Bond companies often pay bail with a 5% to 15% deposit advanced by the defendant.

The court system practitioners also include victim/witness advocates. These advocates provide services to victims of crimes and their families. They work in a variety of areas within the criminal justice system, the majority as part of the prosecuting attorney's office. Probation departments, law enforcement agencies, social service agencies, and some private organizations employ other victim/witness advocates. Services they provide include help with understanding the criminal justice process, immediate needs of housing or medical and psychological services, transportation to and from court, victim compensation and restitution, and help with victim impact statements for the trial. These statements are read in the sentencing portion of the trial with the hope of influencing the judge to increase sentencing for the defendant on behalf of the victim.

The juvenile court process is very complex, involving many aspects of the adult system as well as the basic philosophy of "acting in the best interest of the child." The juvenile defense attorney becomes the advocate for the child as well as the courtroom representative. When the juvenile has been abused, neglected, or in need of dependant care, a guardian *ad litem* is appointed by the court. Along with these two representatives, a court-appointed special advocate (CASA) is available to advise and advocate for the child.

CORRECTIONAL PRACTITIONERS

Correctional practitioners are employed at the federal, state, and local levels. The correctional system involves probation, community service, restitution, jail, prison, and parole. The federal correctional system houses inmates for federal offenses; state and local correctional facilities house inmates for crimes against states and provide holding facilities for federal prisoners awaiting trial. More than 90% of inmates are in state and local prisons. Defendants receiving a sentence of 1 year or less reside in local jails, and sentencing over 1 year requires housing in state prison facilities. There are also specialized facilities for incarceration and observation of persons considered mentally incapacitated.

Correctional officers, sometimes called guards, are trained to work in the subculture of inmates. They attend correctional academies that teach them about custodial strategies, laws and custodial policies, inmates' attitudes, and officer safety. Prisons tend to be overcrowded, violent environments, and officers are continually exposed to the possibility of violence, medical emergencies, and gang activities. In addition to correctional officers, nonofficers include psychologists, counselors, medical staff, and a variety of support personnel.

On release from prison, inmates are assigned parole officers for a specific period of time. Parole officers review parole board requirements set forth for parolees and monitor them with the hope of keeping them from becoming involved in criminal activity again. The job of parole officers is a difficult one and requires them to enforce the law as well as become social workers for large caseloads of parolees. They help parolees find jobs, work through family reunification, and face the many difficulties of living "on the outside."

Probation officers work with defendants who are not sent to correctional facilities, but are conditionally released back to the community while under supervision. These defendants have usually committed crimes that are less serious; but due to prison overcrowding, more serious offenders are being sentenced to probation rather than prison. Probation officers are similar to parole officers in that their role involves both law enforcement and social work. The essential goal of probation officers is to keep probationers from engaging in criminal activity. This is very difficult to accomplish due to large caseloads and limited resources to help implement change in probationers' behavior. Probation officers also work with juveniles sentenced to community service programs and criminal justice boot camps. These sentencing programs provide criminal justice practitioners with alternative methods to meet the needs of juveniles and work toward prevention of future deviant acts.

—Marsha L. Tarver

See also COURTS: ORGANIZATION; CRIMINALISTICS; FORENSIC SCIENCE

Further Reading

Beck, A. J. (2000). *Prisoners in 1999* (NCJ 183476). Washington, DC: Bureau of Justice Statistics.

Camp, S. D., Saylor, W. G., & Wright, K. N. (2001). Racial diversity of correctional workers and inmates. *Justice Quarterly, 18*(2), 411-426.

Reaves, B. A. (2000). *Local police departments* (NCJ 173429). Washington, DC: Bureau of Justice Statistics.

Roberson, C., & Wallace, H. (1998). *Introduction to criminology.* Incline Village, NV: Copperhouse.

Tarver, M., Walker, S., & Wallace, H. (2002). *Multicultural issues in the criminal justice system.* Boston: Allyn & Bacon.

CRIMINAL PROFILING, *See* CRIMINALISTICS; FORENSIC SCIENCE

CRIMINAL PSYCHOLOGY, *See* AGGRESSION; FORENSIC SCIENCE; HOMICIDE, MOTIVATION FOR MURDER; MOTIVES FOR MURDER; VIOLENT BEHAVIOR

CRIMINALISTICS

Criminalistics involves the application of science to law-related matters. It is a specialty that combines many disciplines: the efforts of chemists, biologists, toxicologists, and latent-print and questioned-document examiners, among others. Different from criminologists, who address the causes, correction, and prevention of criminal behavior, criminalists analyze materials, or physical evidence, recovered from crime scenes. They work with police, lawyers, and probation officers in a combined effort to solve crimes.

Criminalists use scientific techniques and procedures in the laboratory, documented as good science practice within the scientific community, to analyze physical evidence, which is eventually used in a court of law to determine the guilt or innocence of a suspect. Possession of the evidence must be properly documented, with the dates and times the items were handled, and by whom. This is defined as the *chain of possession,* and it is imperative that this chain not be broken. If it is broken, the court will decide whether the evidence can be used or whether its integrity has been compromised. If the evidence is found to have been compromised, it cannot be used in a court of law.

FROM THE CRIME SCENE TO THE LABORATORY: COLLECTION AND ANALYSIS OF PHYSICAL EVIDENCE

Preserving the Scene

The first step in properly processing a crime scene is to take swift and sure steps to see that the area is properly secured against any kind of disturbance. The police must then obtain a search warrant before anything else is done. Nothing should be touched, and no one should be allowed to enter except crime scene personnel trained in such investigations. A record should be kept of all persons entering the crime scene. If questions arise later, this record can be used to determine who was present.

Photographs show everything that is present at the crime scene. They should be taken from as many angles as possible to correctly convey relationships of evidence at the scene to items such as a body or weapon. Sometimes, crime scenes are too cluttered to be useful in pointing out specific items. In this case, sketches are used to show the important details and physical relationships.

The search for evidence is next. A drop of blood, a paper match, a fired bullet, a piece of paper, a thread of fiber, or strand of hair can all be physical evidence. Anything that is found is photographed and sketched for later use. Evidence that is transitory in nature should be collected first, such as gasoline that could evaporate. Then, the items are collected, tagged, and placed in proper containers, all packaged separately, to prevent the loss or contamination of evidence samples. A record is kept of all items collected at the crime scene before they are transported to the crime laboratory. All items must be marked by the person collecting them so that a proper chain of evidence can be maintained.

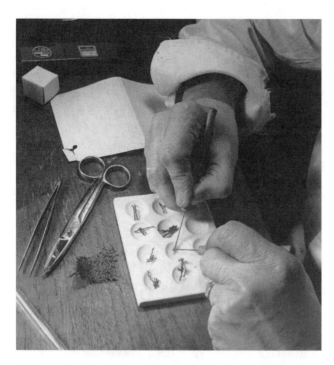

A forensic scientist or criminalist in a crime laboratory examines fragments of cloth from a car and clothing found at a scene of a hit-and-run incident. Criminalistics are increasingly more sophisticated in the use of technologies to examine physical evidence. Today, one of the cutting edges of forensic science is the examination of DNA evidence.

Source: Copyright © Hulton-Deutsch Collection / CORBIS.

Occasionally, special techniques must be used to collect the evidence samples. Techniques such as vacuuming, tape lifting, and laser searches should be done only by properly trained personnel who have specialized equipment, to avoid missing important evidence.

Forensic Photography

A camera is essential for crime scene work as well as in the laboratory. Photographs provide a permanent record of conditions and circumstances that may change as time passes. Criminalistics is a comparative science in that the criminalist is constantly comparing photographs of evidence, such as bullets, cartridge cases, and fibers, and photographs must be taken to document these comparisons. Latent fingerprints and questioned-document examiners also use photographs in their comparisons. Usually, these are side-by-side comparisons that illustrate the similarities seen in the evidence itself to the reference samples submitted by the suspect.

Photographs of the crime scene are of particular importance in any crime, but especially in cases of homicide. Photographs must be taken of the crime scene before anything is moved or removed as evidence in order to document its position relative to other items at the scene. The photographer's initials, date, case number, and item number should appear in all photographs. Rulers are placed in photographs of shoe and tire impressions so that later enlargements can be made 1-to-1 or life size for comparison purposes. 35mm, 120-format cameras and 4-by-5 cameras are especially good when photographing evidence. Negatives from photographs taken by these cameras can be enlarged to many times their original size with excellent clarity.

Digital cameras present special problems when used by criminalists in the crime laboratory. Because of the possibility of changing or manipulating digital images by computer, a mechanism must be present to demonstrate to the court that these images are a true and accurate representation of the evidence or crime scene they depict. Procedures must be in place either to clearly illustrate that these images have not been changed from their original content or to document any changes made.

Latent Fingerprints

Latent means hidden. To be seen, a latent fingerprint must be developed, or specially treated. Fingerprints are composed of water, salts, proteins, oils, and other matter secreted through the pores of the fingers, palms, or soles of the feet. Latent fingerprints can be made visible by dusting them with fingerprint powder of a contrasting color to the surface that they are on. After being photographed, the developed fingerprint can then be lifted with an adhesive such as transparent tape and placed onto a clean white 3-by-5 card. This card should be marked appropriately, because it is now evidence. Fingerprints can also be found at crime scenes in blood, oil, grease, soft putty, or other substances. These materials should never be dusted because powder could ruin the print.

Latent fingerprints can be developed on paper evidence by a variety of chemical methods, but ninhydrin currently remains the method of choice. Ninhydrin is a chemical that reacts with the proteins and amino acids secreted in perspiration. When a latent print is made visible using ninhydrin], it is typically purple in color.

Another technique, often performed in an airtight container, is cyanoacrylate ester, or superglue fuming. Superglue is often used for surfaces such as aluminum foil, rubber, vinyl, leather, and guns. If a latent fingerprint is present and it is fumed with superglue, the print will become visible as a white fingerprint and can then be photographed.

Laser techniques are also used to find and process evidence for latent fingerprints. Surfaces such as plastic bags, tape, and hard, shiny objects can be sprayed with a florescent spray, such as rhodamine 6G, and then examined for latent fingerprints with laser light or an alternate light source. A latent fingerprint will glow in such light and, as always, must be photographed for comparison purposes.

Once fingerprints are developed, lifted, and photographed, they must be compared to known fingerprints from potential suspects. The comparison process has in the past been done by hand but has now been largely taken over by computer technology. The Automated Fingerprint Identification System (AFIS) electronically compares latent prints from a crime scene with the fingerprints in its files and lists the likely matches. A latent-print analyst then confirms this match by hand. Depending on the system, AFIS can scan 500 to 1,200 prints per second. Computer systems like this have revolutionized police work and have made a very time-consuming job easier and more effective.

Questioned Documents

Questioned-document analysis answers questions such as "Who really signed the contract?" or "Did someone alter the amount of the check?" The changing of a document's amount can be done by closing in numbers; for example, by changing $131 into $989 on a contract, sales receipt, or other legal document, someone can realize a hefty profit. Sometimes, additional words or phrases are added to contracts, wills, or other legal documents. Document experts prove forgeries by enlarging both the questioned signature or amount of the check and a known (unforged) signature or sample writing and then comparing the two. They look for directionality and breaks in the pen stroke, pauses, and crossed and dotted letters. They can also see through ink using special lighting to determine whether a change has been made.

The equipment needed to perform document examinations is similar to that for other types of evidence. Microscopes, cameras, and other photographic equipment; low-power magnifiers; and an assortment of chemical reagents are necessary to do the work. In addition, special gauges are essential to the study of the writing features, widths of lines, thickness of paper, and other physical factors.

Alcohol, Controlled Substances, and Toxicology

Drinking ethyl alcohol interferes with an individual's ability to process information, as well as reaction time, vision, and hearing. Blood and breath tests for alcohol are commonly used by police to determine a person's ethyl alcohol concentration while driving. Newer, portable, hand-held breath-testing equipment is most desirable to the police, because it can be used at the scene almost immediately after the subject has been stopped. A blood alcohol level of 0.08% W/V is associated with the inability to operate a motor vehicle in a safe manner.

Controlled substances and certain drugs, such as heroin, cocaine, valium, methamphetamine, and marijuana, are mind- and mood-altering substances that are illegal almost everywhere in the world. Cases involving controlled substances cases make up a large part of the workload of crime laboratories, usually thousands of cases annually. To process such a large volume, criminalists have devised analysis schemes to help them complete procedures quickly, with analytical results that are very accurate. All analytical work includes a built-in review process, which can be used by the laboratory's management staff, as well as defense experts at a later time.

Controlled substances are broken down into classes of drugs, narcotics, depressants, stimulants, and hallucinogens. The analysis procedures usually begin with the criminalist noting and recording whether the evidence is sealed. The evidence is then opened and weighed, and a net weight is recorded for use in court at a later time. Color tests are generally used first and yield a reaction, such as purple or orange-brown, that gives the criminalist an idea of the class of drug present. Also termed *presumptive tests,* they give only preliminary nonspecific results. Specific tests such as instrumental tests and crystal tests are often used in combination with color tests to positively identify a particular controlled substance.

Toxicology is the science of poisons, and the toxicologist tries to establish the presence or absence of a particular poisonous substance or drug in a victim's body. Many poisons do not show obvious symptoms, however. A case of homicide by poisoning can very well go undetected.

Some of the more commonly encountered nondrug toxins are carbon monoxide, hydrogen cyanide, and neurotoxins, and heavy metals such as lead, mercury, arsenic, and copper. The screening test most widely used by toxicologists is thin-layer chromatography (TLC), gas chromatography (GC), and immunoassay. Gas chromatography/mass spectrometry is generally accepted as the confirmatory test of choice.

Firearms and Tool Marks

When a gun is made, a cylindrical chamber, called the *bore,* is drilled in the barrel for the bullet to travel down. In the process, spiral grooves, or *rifling,* are left in the barrel. They impart a spin to the bullet and cause it to follow a straight trajectory, thus determining the gun's accuracy.

When a gun is fired, the firing pin strikes the primer, causing the gunpowder inside the cartridge case to explode and the bullet to separate from the cartridge case and travel down the barrel. As it is traveling down the barrel, the rifling on the hard surface of the steel barrel cuts distinctive marks, or striations, into the softer surface of the lead bullet. When viewed under a comparison microscope, these marks can link a bullet to a particular weapon, as can fired cartridge cases. The cartridge case is also marked on firing and may contain firing pin marks, ejector marks, chambering marks, and ejector marks. Semiautomatic guns eject the fired cartridge case and immediately reload the next one, whereas the cartridge case remains in the chamber of the revolver cylinder after firing.

Criminalists also examine the gun for a serial number to determine if it was stolen. Occasionally, the serial number will be filed off, but can be restored by using chemical etching solutions and should then be photographed, as it will fade in time.

The victim's clothing can be tested for burned and unburned powder residues, often associated with the proximity of the gun muzzle when it was fired. Usually, this distance must be within 4 to 5 feet for any residues to be left. Chemical solutions can be applied to the clothing fabric to enhance visualization of the residues. The Greiss test is used to locate nitrite particles on a paper overlay of the garment. The sodium rhodizonate test is used to locate lead particles

by causing them to appear first as a pink color, followed by a blue-violet color.

Computerized imaging technology, called the Integrated Ballistic Identification System (IBIS), has made possible the storage of fired bullet and cartridge case characteristics in a manner similar to automated fingerprint files. IBIS is designed to provide a database of bullets and cartridge cases from many crime scenes as a way of cross-referencing specific firearms. When only fired bullets and cartridge cases are found at a crime scene without a gun, these evidence items are entered into the IBIS system. The possibility is good that they come from guns that have been previously fired in other crimes and can thus provide links to suspects.

Similarly, tool marks appear as indented impressions, cuts, gouges, or abrasions into a softer surface, for example door frames, windows, doorknobs, or locks. They are typically left in burglary cases as a result of the prying and cutting actions of screwdrivers, crowbars, and bolt cutters, and, like bullet striations, can be observed under a comparison microscope. One problem associated with tool mark comparisons is the difficulty in reproducing the mark in the laboratory. The tool must be experimented with at different angles and assorted pressures as it is tested, commonly on lead, a soft substance. If successfully reproduced, laboratory test marks may show microscopic agreement of striae to a questioned sample from a crime scene.

DNA Analysis

DNA, deoxyribonucleic acid, is a "genetic blueprint," some portion of which is passed on from one generation to the next. Every cell nucleus in an individual's body contains identical DNA. It is found in white blood cells, tissue, hair roots, dental pulp, spermatozoa, bone marrow, urine, saliva, and sweat. With the exception of identical twins, no two people have the exact same DNA, thus the term *DNA fingerprint.*

DNA is packaged in the chromosomes of the cell nucleus. A locus is a location on a chromosome referred to as a "genetic marker." By examining different loci, analysts can discriminate between individuals in a population. Approximately 99.7% of human DNA is identical, so only a small percentage shows variability.

Currently, two primary methods are used in forensic DNA analysis: RFLP (restriction fragment length polymorphism) and PCR (polymerase chain reaction). RFLP is the older method of the two and requires a larger, less degraded forensic sample compared with PCR. Because most forensic samples have been environmentally abused or are very small, PCR is the more useful method in crime laboratories, and RFLP is being used less and less. PCR technology allows the analyst to "biologically Xerox" target loci. In this way, comparisons can then be made between physical crime scene evidence and known reference samples.

STR (short tandem repeats) is the most commonly used DNA method in crime laboratories today. STR is automated, provides for high discrimination, and being a PCR method, can be used with most forensic samples. In the United States, crime laboratories use 13 core loci for STR analysis. Nationwide, participating crime laboratories can enter STR data from casework into the national computer database known as CODIS (Combined DNA Index System), which can compare these files to known convicted offenders. Casework DNA profiles can also be compared with other casework profiles nationwide to determine if a perpetrator has committed crimes in more than one state.

DNA typing has become an essential tool in crime laboratories, replacing conventional protein electrophoresis and ABO blood classification typing. DNA not only aids in solving current crimes but also helps solve old crimes with physiological evidence that may have been unsuccessfully examined in the past.

Trace Evidence

Trace evidence may be very small in size and quantity, thus hard to see and easily overlooked or lost at crime scenes. It may consist, for example, of fibers, glass, paint, flammable liquids, or fire debris samples in arson cases. Trace evidence is often sought in serial murder cases in which evidence is needed to connect many murder victims to one suspect.

Fibers. A single thread is made up of many fibers. Criminalists visualize them using portable lasers or an alternate light source, and collect them with tape lifts, vacuums, and tweezers. Fibers can be transferred when two garments come in contact with one another and thus are used to connect suspects to victims by associating their respective environments with one another. For example, substance from the suspect's environment, such as fibers from carpet, may be present on the victim's body or elsewhere at the crime scene.

Criminalists identify cotton, rayon, silk, and many other fibers simply by their appearance under the microscope. If the microscopic techniques fail to indicate to the criminalist what the fiber is, instrumental and solubility tests are used to identify the sample.

Glass. Criminalists recognize the difference between window glass, bottle glass, glass from eyeglasses, and vehicle glass by using tests that measure density, thickness, color, refractive index, and elemental composition. Analysis may further reveal, for example, that a piece of glass found on a suspect matches a fragment missing along a broken edge of a window at the crime scene, having been deposited back on that person after the firing of a gun through a window. This is called a *physical match,* in that there is a puzzle-like fit between the two samples.

Paint. Paint is usually found at crime scenes in two forms, paint smears and paint chips. Criminalists often analyze paint-smudged tools or paint chips after burglaries. Occasionally, paint may be found on the bumper of a hit-and-run vehicle. Based on their layers and sequence, paint found on a bullet that has traveled through a door can determine location from which the bullet was fired. A physical match is also possible between paint from the crime scene and a sample from the suspect's clothing. Paint samples are generally analyzed using solubility tests, microscopic observation, and instrumental analysis. Nondestructive tests are always performed on evidence samples before destructive tests to save as much of the sample as possible.

Fire Debris Analysis. One of the first things fire investigators and criminalists do at a fire scene is to search for the point of origin, often using accelerant-sniffing dogs and portable hydrocarbon detectors. Suspected debris is collected and placed in suitable containers such as sterile paint cans. Most flammable chemicals are highly volatile and can easily be lost by evaporation to the atmosphere. Instrumental analysis is currently the method of choice by criminalists to identify the sample as gasoline or other easily obtained flammable liquids.

RECONSTRUCTION OF THE CRIME SCENE

Police often use physical evidence to help them piece together what happened at the crime scene. Blood spatters can position the suspect and victim in a case and indicate the approximate number of blows and whether the person was left- or right-handed. Bullet trajectories demonstrate the angle of a bullet's flight and indicate where the weapon was fired from. Stomach contents and rigor mortis can help to establish when the victim was killed. Other indicators can indicate if the victim was moved after death. These crime scene techniques help investigators and prosecutors reconstruct a clear picture of the crime scene at the time of the crime and compare it with a suspect's testimony.

STANDARDS AND FUTURE ADVANCES IN CRIMINALISTICS

Crime laboratories may participate in voluntary accreditation programs to demonstrate that their operations, procedures, personnel, equipment, and safety programs meet established standards. One of them is the Crime Laboratory Accreditation Program of the American Society of Crime Laboratory Directors/ Laboratory Accreditation Board (ASCLD/LAB). Certification is a voluntary program in which a criminalist may show competence in an area of criminalistics by passing a written examination prepared by a professional society such as the American Academy of Forensic Sciences. Both accreditation and certification help ensure that criminalists in crime laboratories perform at an acceptable level of competence and that the quality of work is maintained.

Research and training are the key to improved criminalistics in the future, and it is clear that through advances in computerized imaging technology and DNA study, physical evidence will continue to be increasingly and more effectively used as time goes by.

—*Gary V. Cortner*

See also BALLISTICS; CRIMINAL JUSTICE PRACTITIONERS; FORENSIC SCIENCE; PROFILING

Further Reading

De Forest, P., R., Gaensslen, R. E., & Lee, H. C. (1983). *Forensic science: An introduction to criminalistics.* New York: McGraw-Hill.

Kirk, P. (1974). In J. I. Thorton (Ed.), *Crime investigation* (2nd ed.). New York: John Wiley.

Saferstein, R. (2001). *Criminalistics: An introduction to forensic science* (7th ed.). Upper Saddle River, NJ: Prentice Hall.

CRIMINALLY INSANE, *See* COURT-ORDERED PSYCHOLOGICAL ASSESSMENT; MENTALLY DISORDERED OFFENDERS; M'NAUGHTEN RULE; NOT GUILTY BY REASON OF INSANITY (NGRI)

THE CRIPS

The Crips are one of the most notorious criminal street gangs in the United States. The predominantly African American gang emerged from the social turmoil of the 1960s and came to prominence in South Central Los Angeles during the 1970s. The gang is organized into different subgangs or "sets" based on location or community, such as the Compton Crips or Los Angeles Crips. Rival gangs, particularly the Bloods, have battled with the Crips over territory, control, and "respect," resulting in hundreds of lives lost among gang members and innocents. Criminal activity includes narcotics trafficking, robbery, burglary, extortion, and murder. Since the 1990s, the Crips have become nationwide, with sets in Chicago, New York, and other large metropolitan areas.

—*Byron Viets*

See also BLOODS; DRUG TRADE; GANGS

CULTS

The term *cult* has traditionally referred to non-mainstream religious groups that practice their own eccentric rituals. In recent years, however, public focus has centered on a number of pathological groups that have come to sensational, violent endings: the mass suicides of 918 followers of the Reverend Jim Jones in Guyana in 1878; the 80 followers, including 18 children, of Branch Davidian leader David Koresh who died by fire or gunfire following the FBI siege of their compound near Waco, Texas, in

1993; and the 39 young men of the Heaven's Gate cult who followed leader Marshall Applewhite to their deaths in 1997.

Somewhere between 1,000 and 5,000 cults are currently estimated to exist in the United States alone. Surveys conducted over the past two decades indicate that between 2 and 5 million Americans have at some time been involved with cultic groups. A survey of adults in Montreal and San Francisco found that approximately 20% of respondents had participated in "new religious and parareligious movements," although more than 70% of these encounters were short-lived. Most of these groups are small, but others have tens of thousands of members (see, e.g., Langone, 1988).

Margaret Singer, in her book *Cults in Our Midst,* describes 10 categories of cults in the United States: Neo-Christian religious, Hindu and Eastern religious, occult/witchcraft/satanic, spiritualist, Zen and Sino/Japanese philosophical-mystical, racist, flying saucer and outer space, psychology and psychotherapy, political, and self-help and self-improvement.

Many cult experts have observed an increasing heterogeneity on many levels in cultic groups and their members. Marcia Rudin served for many years as director of the international cult education program for the American Family Foundation, generally considered the most important organization for dispensing information about cults and providing recovery programs for cult victims. She argues that five of the biggest changes in cults in the last 25 years are as follows:

1. Cults now market themselves through more socially mainstream goals and issues. Rather than offering spiritual salvation, they offer promises of financial success, social achievement, and personal happiness. As a result, they appeal to a wider, mainstream population.

2. The economic and racial backgrounds of cult members are now more varied. Cults used to mostly target white, middle-class to wealthy recruits, often in hopes of accessing their financial resources and those of their parents. Groups now appeal to a wider spectrum of social classes. In particular, recruitment of minorities has increased.

3. Because the cult population is broader and more heterogeneous, the problems created by these groups have become more complex. Twenty-five years ago, the modal problem Marcia Rudin dealt with involved middle-aged parents worried about their college-aged children. The problems now involve a wide variety of family situations ranging, for example, from young adults worried about their parents or grandparents to parents seeking custody of children from a spouse still in a group.

4. Over the last two decades, however, there has been increasing membership and problems in virtually every region of the world: the Far East, the Middle East, Central Asia, Africa, Australia, South America, Western Europe, and with the breakdown of the Soviet Union, extraordinary growth of groups in Eastern Europe.

5. Many cults now have political agendas that span the right and the left. As a result, the problems created by these groups are no longer limited to estrangement between families and friends. They are now seen as a threat to human rights, pluralism, and democracy throughout the world.

WHAT IS A CULT?

Distinguishing between cults and their more benevolent counterparts can sometimes be difficult. Michael Langone, the executive director of the American Family Foundation, defines a cult as follows:

A group or movement exhibiting a great or excessive devotion or dedication to some person, idea, or thing, and employing unethically manipulative techniques of persuasion and control designed to advance the goals of the group's leaders, to the actual or possible detriment of members, their families, or the community. Unethically manipulative techniques of persuasion and control include but are not limited to: isolation from former friends and family, use of special methods to heighten suggestibility and subservience, powerful group pressures, information management, suspension of individuality or critical judgment, promotion of total dependency on the group, and fear of leaving. (Langone, 1988, p. 1)

This definition certainly captures the kind of pathological groups that have come to be associated with the term cult. But what distinguishes a destructive cult from a creative new movement? Even if one limits the term to religious organizations, the distinction can be fuzzy. After all, virtually every mainstream religion organization in existence now was initially perceived as being a cult. It is easy to see after the fact that groups such as those in Jonestown and Waco were destructive.

But recognizing this early on, however, before the pathology and violence became apparent, was much more difficult. When we consider all the suspect nonreligious groups that exist today, the question becomes that much more complicated. Is the Taliban a cult? The KKK? The Marines? A football team? Each, clearly, fits some aspects of Langone's definition. The issue becomes one of degree. To help clarify the distinction, Langone and his colleagues have developed a Group Psychological Abuse Scale, which assesses several types of group abuse and may be useful in differentiating cults from innocuous groups.

Given the difficulty of objectively defining the symptoms of a cult, some scholars argue that it is more useful to focus on types of relationships that enter into cultlike thinking. Margaret Singer, for example, defines a cultic relationship as "one in which a person intentionally induces others to become totally or nearly totally dependent on him or her for almost all major life decisions, and inculcates in those followers a belief that he or she has some special talent, gift, or knowledge (Singer, 1995, p. 7). She suggests three general dimensions:

1. The origin of the group and role of the leader.

   Cult leaders are self-appointed, persuasive persons who claim to have a special mission in life or to have special knowledge.

   Cult leaders tend to be determined and domineering and are often described as charismatic.

   Cult leaders center veneration on themselves.

2. The power structure or relationship between the leader or leaders and the followers.

   Cults are authoritarian in structure.

   Cults appear to be innovative and exclusive.

   Cults tend to have a double set of ethics.

3. The use of a coordinated program of persuasion, often referred to as thought reform or brainwashing.

   Cults tend to be totalistic or all encompassing in controlling their members' behavior and also ideologically totalistic, exhibiting zealotry and extremism in their worldviews.

   Cults tend to require members to undergo major disruptions or changes in their lifestyles.

Marshall Herff Applewhite and Bonnie Lu Nettles. Petty criminal and founder of UFO groups, Applewhite formed H.I.M. (Human Individual Metamorphosis), T.O.A.(Total Overcomers Anonymous), and Heaven's Gate. In 1997, Applewhite convinced 41 people to commit mass suicide with him in order to travel to the comet Hale-Bopp and board a spaceship that was to transport them to nirvana.

Source: Copyright © Bettmann / CORBIS.

WHO JOINS CULTS?

The most notable findings from research on the type of person who joins cults are actually the non-findings. For example, there has been a notorious lack of success in trying to identify a singular "cult-prone" personality type. Different cults attract different types of individuals.

Even more surprising is the picture of relative psychological normalcy that emerges. Because cult members often engage in pathological behavior, it is often assumed they have pathological personalities to begin with. The description that emerges of the modal cult joiner is, however, one of disturbing normalcy. Virtually every study of these groups has found that the average member's personality profile falls within the "normal" range. One study, for example, concluded that about two thirds are from psychologically functional families and exhibit age-appropriate behavior before joining. Only about 5% to 6% show signs of serious psychological disturbance at the time they become members. The majority come from middle-class backgrounds and are well educated (Singer, 1995).

This relative normalcy shouldn't be surprising considering that cults usually have little to gain from recruiting deviant, unstable people. Leaders are typically looking for members who will be good fundraisers, recruiters, and effective operators of cult-owned businesses or cult-related seminars. In other words, the prototype of an ideal cult member isn't very different from the kind most organizations look to recruit: attractive, productive, intelligent, energetic people who are dedicated to their work.

Although no single cult-prone personality type has been discovered, some similarities in the momentary circumstances surround the modal joiner. First, they tend to be at an unhappy point in their lives at the time they're recruited and in many cases have experienced a recent loss or disappointment. Second, they're frequently in limbo between meaningful affiliations, for example, between high school and college or school and a job, recently fired, jilted by a romantic partner, have just moved, or perhaps are generally unsure what to do next with their lives. This is the kind of people cult leaders look for. Cults specialize at providing simple answers to complex questions. Old problems, such as food, housing, bills, and taxes, become things of the past. Daily routines are choreographed by the leader, sometimes down to specific details. "No one is to use Crest Toothpaste," Jim Jones instructed followers at one point. "The only toothpaste that will make your gums resistant to atomic radiation (a great fear of Jones's) is Phillip's toothpaste" (Levine, 2003, p. 139). Many cults extend these instructions to more significant life choices, even deciding who should marry. The Moonies have become infamous for their mass wedding ceremonies, in which Reverend Sun Myung Moon arranges and then marries tens of thousands of couples at once, most to spouses they've never met and who speak different languages. In Jonestown,

all marriages were dissolved, and Jones took control of who slept with whom.

The inner life of cult members becomes equally simplified. Once they internalize the group doctrine as truth, every thought is guided by a clear and simple map of reality. The process becomes simpler yet when the leader filters all incoming information and strictly controls how members are to think about it. In Jonestown, Jim Jones's "news" broadcasts and other rantings were piped loudly over the microphone nonstop, 24 hours a day. Any questions about right and wrong, good and bad, were unambiguously "answered."

Jeannie Mills and her husband, Al, spent 6 years as key figures in Jones's People's Temple and, eventually, in Jonestown. Before defecting, Jeannie served as head of the temple's publications office, Al served as official photographer, and both were members of the prestigious planning committee. In her book, *Six Years with God,* Jeannie Mills recalled,

I was amazed at how little disagreement there was between the members of this church. Before we joined the church, Al and I couldn't even agree on whom to vote for in the presidential election. Now that we all belonged to a group, family arguments were becoming a thing of the past. There was never a question of who was right, because Jim was always right. When our large household met to discuss family problems, we didn't ask for opinions. Instead, we put the question to the children, "What would Jim do?" It took the difficulty out of life. There was a type of "manifest destiny" which said the Cause was right and would succeed. Jim was right and those who agreed with him were right. If you disagreed with Jim, you were wrong. It was as simple as that. (Mills, 1977, p. 147)

Even language is simplified as cults create their own "loaded language" of words and expressions. Simple labels are assigned to complex situations; every ambiguity is reduced to a cult cliché. Former member Steven Hassan recalls,

In the Moonies, whenever you have difficulty relating to someone either above or below you in status, it is called a "Cain-Abel problem." It doesn't matter who's involved or what the problem is, it's simply a "Cain-Abel problem." The term itself dictates how the problem must be resolved. Cain must obey Abel and follow him, rather than kill him as was written about in the Old Testament.

Case closed. To think otherwise would be to obey Satan's wish that evil Cain should prevail over righteous Abel. A critical thought about a leader's misconduct cannot get past this roadblock in a good member's mind. (Hassan, 1988, p. 62)

NORMAL PERSUASION LEADING TO PATHOLOGICAL BEHAVIOR

Although the behavior of cultic groups may be pathological, the process can usually be explained by the same basic principles of social psychology that explain any persuasion process. The leader, like a good salesman, dangles a product that appears to fill the member's need, perhaps the promise of an extended family, a more fulfilling religion, or the seeming opportunity to do something truly positive for the world. The recruit is then drawn in deeper, in gradually escalating steps, still using essentially "normal" powers of persuasion and influence. The form of the entire process is normal. The content makes cults pathological.

Deborah Layton was a member of Jones's People's Temple. She grew up in Berkeley, California, with financially well-off, highly educated, socially conscious parents. She was a rebellious child, often in trouble, and her parents sent her to boarding school in England in hopes of "turning her around" in her teens. During this time, her brother, Larry Layton, joined the People's Temple. Larry encouraged Deborah to visit the temple, and on a vacation home when she was 17, she first met Jim Jones. Jones used his charm and charisma on Layton, complimenting her and paying her special attention. Equally important, his philosophy, a radical commitment to interracialism and social justice, fired the rebellion within her. Supersalesman Jones knew just the right buttons to push. Deborah returned to England, where she received weekly letters from Jones reminding her how much the temple needed her and what an important role she could play in their social revolution. She joined the temple at the age of 18, along with her mother.

Layton became a member of Jones's inner circle, where she was exposed to his many flaws. But by now she was in too deep. Like so many others, she secretly questioned "Father" but rationalized her doubts and remained faithful to his socialist vision. "I thought that it must be extremely painful for Father to sacrifice his own goodness for the larger cause, as he did when he committed—or ordered us to commit—reprehensible or illegal acts," Layton (1998) wrote. "I saw his moral transgressions as purely altruistic—something like the means justify the end. And who was I to criticize him?" Then in December 1977, when Layton and her mother traveled to the new headquarters in Jonestown, Guyana, they were confronted by conditions that resembled an armed labor camp more than a communal tropical paradise, ranging from quasi-starvation to psychological and physical abuse. Layton waited for an opportunity to escape. It came in May 1978, when Jones trusted her to go on a public relations trip to Georgetown, the Guyanese capital. In a breathtaking sequence of events, Layton fled to the American Embassy and was granted asylum and flown back to the United States.

Weeks after, she began speaking openly about her experiences in Jonestown, including the infamous "white nights"—Jones's mass suicide practice drills. Layton's reports were the single most important inspiration for Congressman Leo Ryan's investigative mission to Guyana, which ended with the assassination of Ryan, three newsmen, and a defector and led to mass suicide at Jonestown. Layton's brother Larry was a gunman in the attack on Ryan's party, for which he was not released from prison until 2002. Layton's mother died of cancer at Jonestown days before the suicides (without the benefit of pain medication, which Jones had impounded for himself).

In her book *Seductive Poison,* Layton describes how a relatively normal person can become caught up in such pathology. She describes how she was patiently induced, through small, step-by-step commitments, to eventually become trapped in a situation she never saw coming. Members start with just a few hours each week working for the church and eventually progress to signing over all their personal property, becoming isolated from the outside world, and tolerating a violent and abusive environment.

The problems began slowly. Little was asked from new members. They came to services voluntarily and might give a few hours of time each week working for the church. The commitments escalated slowly, in small increments. More and more participation was required of members. Services and meetings became longer, increasing to whole weekends and several evenings each week. Even children had to learn to sit through ordeals as long as 8 and 9 hours at a time. One was expected to attend out-of-town services held to recruit new members. Every other weekend when the temple was housed in Ukiah, in Northern California, the entire core family of 400 took a 10-hour bus ride to Los Angeles for recruiting work.

Members were gradually asked to hand over more of their possessions. One week, Jones introduced the "church commitment": Members in good standing were to begin giving 25% of their income to the temple. The next week he asked, "Who in this room still has a checking or savings account?" The week after that, "Who still has a life insurance policy?" Eventually, members were required to sign over all personal property, their houses, social security checks—everything. After a while they were made to live in the temple to save money and help the temple work more efficiently. Children were often cared for by other families. Contact with outsiders was strongly discouraged.

Even the abuse and violence came in gradual steps. Layton (1998) explained:

> I think what's most important for people to understand is nobody joins with somebody they think is going to hurt them or kill them. It can happen in any abusive relationship. A woman thinks a guy is good-looking, he's so nice, you go out on a few dates, he buys you a few presents. Then, one time, he hits you. But then he apologizes. And you think, he's so good to me, and he bought me that present. Then maybe you have a child together. Then he hits you and the child. It's often so far down the road that you realize, "Oh my God. There's something definitely wrong here." But by that time you're in so many ways entrapped. And that's how I think it happened at Jonestown. It was so gradual.

Layton's story demonstrates how intelligent people become caught up in a destructive cult environment mentality engineered by a manipulative, sadistic leader. The leader, Jones, didn't trap Layton with torture and brainwashing, however. He used kindness, approval, social support, shared goals, a sense of purpose, persuasive leadership, loyalty, guilt, and, more than anything, love. This is basic social psychology existent in most group dynamics, so unextraordinary and applied so gradually, it catches the members completely off-guard.

THE ILLUSION OF INVULNERABILITY

The fact that the group pathology of cults can be so different from the sum of its individual personalities demonstrates the basic lesson of social psychology: the power of the situation to override personality predispositions. People have images of the "type" of person they are and that they are not the type of person who gets seduced by manipulators like Jim Jones. This illusion of personal invulnerability is comforting. Cult leaders understand, however, that everyone is prone to act out of character when caught up in certain situations and that the greater one's illusion of personal invulnerability, the less prepared one is for defending against psychological manipulation.

A common admonition one hears from cult experts and former cult members is not to fool oneself into a false sense of immunity. Jackie Speier, who is now a California State Senator, put it well. Speier was a member of Congressman Leo Ryan's entourage during the ill-fated visit to Jonestown that set off the suicides. She survived the murders at the airstrip by playing dead. Looking back on the insanity of Jonestown, Speier offers an admonition: "No one should ever be so arrogant as to think it can't happen to them. We're all susceptible on one level or another."

—*Robert Levine*

See also Crimes of Obedience; Koresh, David; Manson, Charles

Further Reading

Chambers, W., Langone, M., & Malinoski, P. (1996). *The group psychological abuse scale.* Paper presented at the annual meeting of the American Psychological Association, Toronto, Canada.

Hassan, S. (1988). *Combating mind control.* Rochester, VT: Park St.

Langone, M. (1988). *Cults: Questions and answers.* Weston, MA: American Family Foundation.

Layton, D. (1998). *Seductive poison.* New York: Anchor Books.

Levine, R. (2003). *The power of persuasion: How we're bought and sold.* New Jersey: John Wiley.

Mills, J. (1979). *Six years with God.* New York: A & W Publishers.

Rudin, M. (2002). Twenty-five years observing cults: An American perspective. *Cultic Studies Review, 1,* 1-4.

Singer, M. (1995). *Cults in our midst.* San Francisco: Jossey-Bass.

CULTURAL FACTORS IN VIOLENT BEHAVIOR, *See* AGGRESSION, SOCIOLOGICAL THEORIES

CUNANAN, ANDREW, *See* SERIAL MURDER

CUTTING, *See* METHODS OF MURDER

CYANIDE, *See* POISONERS, PRODUCT TAMPERING

CYBERAGGRESSION

Broadly speaking, cyberaggression refers to insults, threats, harassment, and stalking perpetrated against individuals and groups on the Internet using various modes of transmission, including electronic mail (e-mail), chat rooms, news groups, mail exploders, instant messaging, and the World Wide Web. Cyberaggression is referred to by many names, including cyber crime, cyberstalking, electronic harassment, and Internet threats. Examples of specific incidents of cyberaggression include repeatedly sending harassing and threatening e-mail messages; sending racially or sexually offensive jokes through company e-mail; soliciting sex from minors through e-mail, chat rooms, or news groups; posting another person's photograph or private information on a highly accessible electronic bulletin board; sending repeated messages that cause a computer system to shut down (mail bombing); sending abusive e-mail or news group messages that attack an individual in overly harsh, often personal tones (flaming); posting unsolicited or abusive messages in a person's Web page guest book; and depicting a person as a prostitute or someone who enjoys kinky or sado-masochistic sex. Cyberaggression is inextricably linked to growth of the Internet, which in addition to facilitating advances in nearly every aspect of our society has also created new means of perpetrating aggression and intimidation. Use of the Internet has grown at a remarkable rate in the United States in the past 20 years, from an estimated 500,000 users in 1980 to an estimated 90 million users in 1999 (U.S. Department of Justice, 1999). As access to the Internet increases, so will opportunities to commit cyberaggression.

DESCRIPTIONS OF CYBERAGGRESSION INCIDENTS

♦ An honors graduate student at the University of San Diego terrorized five fellow female students for over a year by repeatedly sending them threatening e-mail messages, sometimes as many as five a day, because he thought they were laughing at him and causing others to ridicule him, when in fact they didn't even know him.

♦ A man in Texas posted a notice on the Web claiming that a 9-year-old girl was available for sex, providing her home phone number, with instructions to call 24 hours a day.

♦ A woman in Los Angeles had several men come to her residence and offer to rape her after a man had impersonated her in various Internet chat rooms and on-line bulletin boards, where he posted her telephone number, address, and messages that she fantasized about being raped.

♦ A University of Michigan student published a lurid fantasy of rape, torture, and murder in an Internet newsgroup using the name of a female student in his class and corresponded with another man via e-mail about how he would carry out the attack.

♦ A woman in Maryland who posted a warning on the Internet about a company that tried to charge an exorbitant fee to review a book she had written received more than 200 harassing e-mail messages and discovered that her name, address, and home telephone number had been posted with several Internet sex newsgroups, along with messages inviting people to call or stop by her home any time.

♦ A woman in Texas received numerous nasty e-mails and discovered that her e-mail address and a photograph of a nude woman had been posted on the Internet, after she had gotten into an argument with a man during an online discussion about advertising.

PREVALENCE OF CYBERAGGRESSION

To date, there has been no comprehensive study of cyberaggression in the United States or elsewhere.

Thus little is known about the extent and nature of cyberaggression, the circumstances under which it is likely to occur, or its consequences on both individual victims and the society at large. Nonetheless, a growing body of statistics based on anecdotal information from law enforcement agencies and Internet service providers, studies of off-line stalking victimization, and surveys of select Internet users suggests that cyberaggression is a widespread problem and is growing in both complexity and frequency.

An informal survey by the U.S. Department of Justice (2001) indicates that Internet service providers are receiving a growing number of complaints about harassing and threatening behaviors on-line, with one major Internet service provider reporting 15 complaints of cyberstalking per month. Both the Los Angeles District Attorney's Office Threat Assessment Unit and the Manhattan Sex Crimes Unit estimate that approximately 20% of their cases involve e-mail or electronic communications (U.S. Department of Justice, 1999). The Computer Investigation and Technology Unit of the New York City Police Department estimates that about 40% of their cases involve electronic harassment and/or threats (U.S. Department of Justice, 1999). Extrapolating figures from a study of off-line stalking in the United States, CyberAngels (2000), an on-line resource and advocacy group for victims of cyber-crimes, estimates there are approximately 63,000 Internet stalkers and 474,000 Internet-stalking victims worldwide. Researchers at the University of Cincinnati, who surveyed a nationally representative sample of college women about their experiences as victims of sexual assault and stalking, found that 25% of the victims had been stalked via their e-mail addresses (Fisher, Cullen, & Turner, 2000). A survey of 500 members of Systers, an electronic mailing list for women in computer science, found that 20% of respondents reported being the targets of sexual harassment via the Internet (Betts & Maglitta, 1995). And finally, researchers conducting a study of on-line victimization of youths aged 10 to 17 who regularly use the Internet found that 20% had received sexual solicitations over the Internet in the past year, about a quarter of which induced fear or distress in the victims (Finklehor, Mitchel, & Wolak, 2000).

CHALLENGES TO LAW ENFORCEMENT

Cyberaggression presents unique challenges to law enforcement. Recent informal surveys indicate the majority of law enforcement agencies nationwide have no experience investigating or prosecuting cyberaggression cases (U.S. Department of Justice, 2001). This is due in part to the fact that most police officers have not been trained to recognize the seriousness of cyberaggression incidents. According to CyberAngels, many victims who report their cyberaggression to the police say the police did not take the on-line harassment seriously until it became off-line harassment. In addition, many law enforcement agencies lack personnel with expertise in computers or Internet use.

Lack of coordination between law enforcement and Internet service providers also hampers the investigation and prosecution of cyberaggression cases. Historically, contact between Internet service providers and law enforcement has been sporadic and episodic. In addition, law enforcement agencies are typically unfamiliar with the types of on-line behaviors prohibited by Internet providers or the procedures and policies implemented to follow up user complaints. Many experts believe that better coordination is needed between law enforcement and Internet service providers before serious inroads can be made in controlling cyberaggression.

In addition, jurisdictional issues hamper law enforcement responses to cyberaggression. Perpetrators often reside in different cities or states than their victims, making it difficult for local law enforcement agencies to investigate allegations of cyberaggression without first obtaining cooperation from other law enforcement agencies. Moreover, because some instances cross national borders, consideration must be given to how nations can work together to target cases of international cyberaggression.

Many legal scholars agree that current state and federal laws do not adequately protect victims of this type of crime. For example, most states do not have laws that explicitly cover harassment and stalking via electronic communications; neither do federal laws address interstate cyberaggression. Thus, the first step in fighting cyberaggression must be the enactment of adequate laws that enable law enforcement to investigate and prosecute such crimes.

—*Pat Tjaden*

See also CYBERSTINGS; STALKING

Further Reading

Betts, M., & Maglitta, J. (1995, February 12). ISP policies target e-mail harassment. *Computerworld.*

CyberAngels. (2000). *How prevalent is cyber-stalking?* Retrieved from the World Wide Web January 2000 at: http://www.cyberangels.org/stalking/defining.html.

Finklehor, D., Mitchell, K., & Wolak, J. (2000). *Online victimization: A report on the nation's youth.* Alexandria, VA: National Center for Missing and Exploited Children.

Fisher, B. S., Cullen, F. T., & Turner, M. G. (2000). *The sexual victimization of college women* (NCJ 182369). Washington, DC: U.S. Department of Justice, Bureau of Justice Statistics.

Meloy, J. R. (1998). *The psychology of stalking: Clinical and forensic perspectives.* San Diego, CA: Academic Press.

Snow, R. L. (1998). *Stopping a stalker: A cop's guide to making the system work for you.* New York: Plenum.

U.S. Department of Justice. (1999). *Cyberstalking: A new challenge for law enforcement and industry* (Attorney General's report to the vice president). Washington, DC: Author.

U.S. Department of Justice. (2001). *Stalking and domestic violence* (NCJ 186157). Washington, DC: Violence Against Women Office.

CYBERSTALKING, *See* PEDOPHILE ORGANIZATIONS; STALKING

CYBERSTINGS

The Internet provides individuals throughout the world with the ability to easily communicate with others. Most people use the Internet as a tool to engage in legitimate tasks, but some engage in illegal behavior on-line. Because it is easy to hide one's identity on the Internet, individuals who commit crimes in "cyberspace" are often difficult to locate. Law enforcement officers have had to throw out conventional methods and find new ways to curtail Internet crime. *Cyberstings* are undercover operations conducted to apprehend individuals who victimize others through use of the Internet.

APPROPRIATE CIRCUMSTANCES FOR CYBERSTINGS

Many criminals have been investigated by use of cyberstings, including murderers, stalkers, extremists,

solicitors of fraud, gamblers, and those who deal in the black market sale of babies. Most commonly, however, law enforcement officers target sexually deviant behavior, including involvement in prostitution rings, child pornography rings, and child molestation. Individuals who operate and/or participate in prostitution and child pornography Web sites use screen names and passwords and feel confident that law enforcement will not detect them. Furthermore, the ability of the Internet to transmit data in an instant provides immediate gratification for deviant appetites of sex offenders.

Child molesters and pedophiles use the Internet as an avenue to communicate freely and anonymously with minors in sexually explicit ways. They can search for victims by accessing member profile information as it is available from various Internet companies, including America Online. Parents often do not know what their children are looking at or with whom they are communicating while they are on the Internet, and even if they are told, the perpetrators' identities are still unknown.

CYBERSTING TECHNIQUES

Depending on the type of case and situation, law enforcement officers use a variety of techniques when conducting cyberstings. Officers go on-line in an undercover capacity and conduct targeted investigations, arrange for buy/bust meetings with offenders, cruise the Internet for identification and apprehension purposes, or create their own Web sites to attract suspects.

Targeted Stings

Investigators commonly conduct targeted sting operations, which occur when a report is made to law enforcement regarding a crime that has occurred on the Internet. The investigator may acquire a user name and other information from the informant or victim of the crime and then pose as that individual while "chatting" on-line to further attract the perpetrator. In some cases, the victim actually chats with the offender under officer supervision. In this case, the officer or victim will attempt to get information necessary for a successful criminal prosecution of the offender. After the offender feels comfortable enough with the situation, a meeting is set up in which the offender is arrested. These targeted operations typically occur in cases of sex-based dialogue with children, fraud, and prostitution rings.

One example of a targeted sting occurred in 2002, when the FBI set up a cybersting called "Operation Candyman." The FBI had been investigating a child pornography Web site that consisted of a membership of individuals who traded ideas and photos regarding the sexual abuse of children. An undercover FBI agent joined the Candyman Web site and participated in the exchange of information with Candyman's members. As a result of the information collected, subpoenas were issued to Internet providers for registration and user information; at least 89 people in 26 states were arrested, including a member of the clergy, a nurse, a school bus driver, and a member of law enforcement. The Candyman Web site had an estimated 7,000 members from at least 10 countries.

Buy/Bust Operations

Buy/bust operations most commonly occur when undercover officers buy something illegal, such as narcotics, and then "bust" the seller for the illegal transaction. Similar operations are used to catch individuals selling illegal items on-line. The undercover officer buys an illegal item and uses the information received as a result of the sale to obtain leads to the source or to obtain search warrants and arrest warrants.

In 2001, Russia and the United States joined forces in "Operation Blue Orchid" to investigate a Moscow-based child pornography sales Web site. The Cybersmuggling Center in Virginia conducted an undercover buy of child pornography from the Blue Orchid site and as a result received information that led to the name of the site's operator. Law enforcement then obtained a search warrant and searched the operator's apartment. Records found in that apartment led to more searches and 15 arrests in the United States alone.

Identification and Apprehension Operations

Psychological profiling plays a role in identification and apprehension operations. An undercover officer takes on an assumed identity in chatrooms, using information involving victimology, risk assessment, and offender actions, along with the Web site at which the chat occurs, to attract certain types of potential offenders. As previously described, the officer tries to get information to determine whether a person is engaging, has engaged, or is about to engage in criminal conduct. If there is reason to believe that this is

true, a meeting is set up, and the offender is usually met by a decoy officer who arrests the offender.

An example of a cybersting using this method is directly connected with the arrest and conviction of former Disney Corporation executive Patrick Naughton. A male FBI agent posed as a 13-year-old girl on-line in a chatroom and posted lewd messages. The agent continued to chat with the user and eventually arranged a meeting on the Santa Monica Pier. A decoy officer stood waiting on the pier, and when Naughton arrived and made contact with the decoy, FBI agents arrested him.

Web Site Creation

In addition to using existing Web sites to identify and apprehend offenders, law enforcement officers have also set up their own Web sites advertising illegal items. One extreme cybersting designed to catch individuals purchasing child pornography occurred in Italy. Italian law enforcement set up a site advertising child pornography. When the site visitors made purchases, they input personal information to complete the purchase and have their items shipped. Italian authorities used this information to locate and arrest the buyers. As a result of this sting operation, Italian authorities filed charges against more than 1,700 people.

PREVALENCE OF CYBERSTINGS

Cyberstings occur on local, national, and international levels. Locally, because of limited resources, cyberstings are most often targeted stings. Local authorities usually rely on tips from victims and informants in their investigations of individuals for prostitution, child molestation, and fraud. On a national level, the FBI's Innocent Images program and the U.S. Customs' Child Pornography Program have been leading the nation in the investigation of sexual abuse and exploitation of children on the Internet.

Large-scale cyberstings tend to be international because of the expansiveness of the Internet. In 1998, 14 countries coordinated "Operation Wonderland." To qualify as a member and attain access to the Wondlerland Web site, applicants had to provide 10,000 images of child pornography. Individuals arrested for possession of child pornography in England told British authorities about the site, which used private chatrooms encrypted with secret passwords, and supplied pass codes, screen names, and cyberlinks. Through a coordinated effort, international law enforcement was able to make many arrests, shut down the Web site, and retrieve as many as 750,000 graphic images.

THE EFFECT OF CYBERSTINGS

On a local, national, and international level, law enforcement officers are making great efforts to lessen the amount of Internet crime through use of cyberstings. Internet-based sting operations have extinguished at least three major child pornography rings. The arrests made during the course of these operations have also assisted in identifying offenders who are actively engaged in one-on-one abuse. For example, law enforcement found that 36 people arrested in the Blue Orchid sting were actually sexually abusing children.

The advent of cyberstings will enable law enforcement to continue to conduct operations that protect Internet users, especially children. The Internet is never going to be free of criminal offenders, but with a little caution on the part of Internet users and a growing experience on the part of law enforcement, the "information superhighway" can become a safer, more secure environment.

—*Stefanie Petrucci-Mahaffey*

See also CYBERAGGRESSION; PEDOPHILIA;
    PEDOPHILE ORGANIZATIONS; STALKING

Further Reading

Casey, E. (2000). *Digital evidence and computer crime.* San Diego, CA: Academic Press.

Cybercrime. (August, 1999). A report from the attorney general to the vice president of the United States *1999 report on cyberstalking: A new challenge for law enforcement and industry.* Available on the World Wide Web at: http://www.cybercrime.gov/cyberstalking.htm.

THE CYCLE THEORY OF VIOLENCE

BATTERING: A 3-PHASE CYCLE

The *cycle theory of violence* is a term used in domestic violence research to describe the pattern of battering over time. Developed by Dr. Lenore Walker in 1979, this theory identifies three distinct phases associated with a recurrent cycle of battering: (a) a tension-building period, (b) an acute battering incident, and (c) a reconciliatory, loving period. Because this theory was based on Walker's observations of battered women, the language used to describe each phase is gender specific.

Phase 1: Tension Building

During this time, the battered woman feels as though the pressure is mounting and anticipates that a severely abusive incident is imminent. Although it is not unusual for physical abuse to take place, this stage is characterized by primarily verbal abuse, with minor battering incidents. The woman usually accepts some of the responsibility for her batterer's actions, not because she believes that she should be abused, but because she hopes her behavior can prevent the abuse from escalating. She may be nurturing and compliant or try to avoid her batterer so as to not provoke him.

Walker suggests that the battered woman uses denial as a psychological defense, denying her own anger at being hurt in order to help herself cope. She may identify with her batterer's faulty reasoning, blaming his abusive behavior on her own inability to please him. For example, she may reason that perhaps the meal she prepared was overcooked, or she should have kept the children quieter. Additionally, the woman may attribute her batterer's behavior to external factors, such as his alcohol use or work-related stress. These attributions provide her with a false sense of hope; she believes that if she waits it out, the situation will change and her batterer's behavior will improve. However, these minor battering incidents will merely escalate, and her behavior can only, at best, delay the second phase of the battering cycle, the acute battering incident.

Phase 2: Acute Battering Incident

Eventually, all strategies become ineffective, and the batterer ceases to respond to any controls. The second stage, the briefest of the three stages, is described by Walker as the uncontrollable release of the tensions that were built up in the earlier phase. During this phase, major battering occurs.

In Phase 2, contrary to Phase 1, the batterer assumes full responsibility for the battering, acknowledging that his rage was out of control. Often, the batterer focuses on justifying his behavior. His initial objective was to "teach her a lesson," not intending to inflict any particular injury on her. However, by the time he stops, she has usually been severely beaten.

The movement from Phase 1 to Phase 2 is typically attributed to external causes or the batterer's internal state, such as alcohol use or stress, rather than the battered woman's behavior.

If the police are called at all, it is usually during Phase 2 (although fewer than 10% of the women in Walker's study had ever notified the police). However, many battered women believe that police contact will not prevent future abuse and may escalate the violence. Consequently, battered women are often reluctant to pursue police action and may even be hostile toward responding officers.

Phase 3: Loving Contrition

The third phase usually follows immediately after the acute battering incident. Phase 3 is characterized by loving, contrite behavior as the batterer attempts to make up for his violent behavior during Phase 2. It is an unusually calm, loving period. During this phase, the batterer is usually sorry for his actions and may shower the woman with gifts or beg for her forgiveness. He typically appears to be sincere in his apology and promises never to hurt her again.

The batterer often truly believes that the battering will never occur again. The batterer may feel as though he will never allow himself to lose control in the future. He may even modify other aspects of his behavior, such as quitting drinking or finding a job, to demonstrate his commitment to change. He may act similarly to his behavior during courtship. He manages to convince everyone involved that this violent incident was the last and that this time he really means to keep his promises.

The woman also wants to believe that her batterer really can change and that the violence will end. Immediately after the acute battering incident, the woman may be confused and frightened. The batterer's courting behavior and promises during Phase 3 can act as positive reinforcement for remaining in the relationship by providing her with love and reassurance. The battered woman chooses to believe that her batterer's behavior during Phase 3 is indicative of his true self and that if he got the necessary help, he would be this way all the time.

Contact with outside assistance is most likely to occur during this phase. However, this is also the time when the man is most loving and there is the most motivation for the battered woman to remain in the relationship. Walker states that helpers of battered women may become continually frustrated as the woman usually accepts reconciliatory action from her batterer. She may move back into their home, drop any criminal charges, halt divorce or separation proceedings, or generally try to work on mending their relationship.

As Phase 3 ends, Phase 1 begins again, and the pattern of behavior continues. The length and intensity of each phase varies for the same couple over time, as well as among couples. Walker suggests that as the battering relationship continues, the tension-building phase becomes longer, and the loving period becomes shorter.

The hope of an idealized relationship promised in Phase 3 usually becomes more and more difficult for the battered woman to maintain as the relationship continues. Subsequently, the woman's self-image deteriorates as she accepts that she is holding on to a false belief; she is enduring psychological and physical abuse for brief periods of loving behavior.

BATTERED WOMAN SYNDROME

The cycle theory of violence explains why battered women are reluctant to leave their abusive partners and is the basis for battered woman syndrome. *Battered woman syndrome* is a term developed by Walker to describe the psychological, emotional, and behavioral consequences of living in a violent relationship. Walker suggests that a woman who has experienced two complete cycles can be classified as a *battered woman*.

The cycle theory of violence may be more appropriate for understanding battering patterns among some couples than others. Although the theory is widely known throughout domestic violence research, it has not been extensively tested. Some studies suggest that intimate violence patterns, experiences, and responses vary among types of couples. Therefore, though this theory accurately characterizes some battered women and their batterers' experiences, further research is needed in this area.

—*Mindy S. Wilson*

See also BATTERED WOMEN'S SYNDROME; BATTERERS AND ABUSIVE PARTNERS; FAMILY VIOLENCE; VICTIMOLOGY

Further Reading

Walker, L. E. (1979). *The battered woman.* New York: Harper & Row.

Walker, L. E. (2000). *The battered woman syndrome* (2nd ed.). New York: Springer.

D

JEFFREY DAHMER

On July 22, 1991, Jeffrey Dahmer, age 31, was arrested in Milwaukee, Wisconsin, and became one of the most notorious serial killers in American history. His crimes were so horrific and his motivations so disturbing that few persons have been able to fully grasp the depth of his psychopathology. At age 8, Jeffrey is believed to have been sexually abused by a neighbor boy. His father, oblivious to Jeffrey's inner struggles, recalled that his son was a loner and a poor student. He was unaware of his adolescent son's use of alcohol, his more than scientific interest in dissecting road kills, and his penchant for young men. In 1978, at age 18, only 3 weeks after his senior high school prom, Jeffrey killed and dismembered his first victim, a 17-year-old male, a deed kept secret from everyone. This coincided with years of family turmoil culminating in the divorce of Jeffrey's parents. His mother took the youngest son, David, to live with her, while Jeffrey remained with his father.

This perceived abandonment by his mother and the estrangement he felt with his father only added to Jeffrey's distorted thinking. He joined the military but was discharged for abuse of alcohol. He began working a night shift at the Ambrosia Chocolate Company in Milwaukee and in 1986 received a year's probation for exposing himself to young boys. He struggled with his sexual orientation and felt that being gay was wrong. His inner struggles and depression found him frequently contemplating suicide, but he was also developing increasingly aberrant sexual fantasies, which enhanced his capacity for killing. He struggled against the urge to harm other human beings but was torn by the sexual fantasies and driven by his need to control his life by controlling others. After the first homicide, Dahmer is reported to have visited graveyards in hopes of retrieving a corpse rather than kill another person, but he finally yielded to his growing fantasies, and his attempts to succeed in education and employment failed miserably.

To most of his victims, he seemed like an average person wanting to be sociable. A resident of Milwaukee's West Side, Dahmer lived alone in an apartment. He frequented bars, some of them gay, looking for contacts. Initially, he used his grandmother's basement to have sex with drugged men and act out some of his deviant fantasies. He often rented cheap rooms at bathhouses, where he gave alcohol laced with drugs such as Halcion (a sleeping pill) to his victims. Potential victims, many of them African American or Asian, were then brought to his apartment. He brought others directly to his apartment, had sex with them, and then offered them tainted alcohol. The process became routine for him. Dahmer then handcuffed his victims, who were unaware that the alcohol had been laced with drugs, and led them into the bedroom. This was his killing room, where he kept and disposed of his victims. Most of his victims were strangled to death and dismembered. While some of his victims lay unconscious, Dahmer drilled holes into their skulls in attempts to make zombies out of them. In this state, he either hoped or fantasized they would become his sex slaves and never leave him. Dahmer also cannibalized several of his victims.

The goal of all this carnage was, in fact, pitiful. Dahmer imagined that by consuming his victims, they would become part of him and make him more powerful. He fantasized having his two favorite victims, fully skeletonized, standing on either side of him. He, Dahmer, would be sitting in a large black chair like the one used by the antagonist in the movie *Star Wars*. Directly behind him, on a shelf and between the two skeletons, would rest the shrunken skulls of several of his victims. This scene was a powerful one for Dahmer. In his mind, he would achieve the ultimate. Surrounded by his victims, who now had become part of him, Dahmer fantasized a sense of power and control unlike any he had ever felt before.

The last victim Dahmer attempted to lure into the killing chamber managed to escape and alert two police officers on patrol. (Over the years, four other potential victims had also escaped and told their stories to police and friends, but still Dahmer had remained free.) He told them that Dahmer had tried to handcuff him and that his bedroom contained photographs of dead men. When the police went to the apartment, Dahmer greeted them at the door and appeared very cooperative. Stepping inside, the officers noticed a severe stench. One of the officers asked for the key to the handcuffs still attached to the arm of the intended victim. Dahmer insisted on retrieving it himself from the bedroom. Concerned for their own safety, one of the officers moved past him and entered the bedroom first. What he found would soon become international headlines.

A barrel containing human remains stood in one corner, and two skulls lay unconcealed in a box. Restraining Dahmer, the officers looked around the apartment and found additional decomposing skeletal and human remains, counting at least 11 skulls. Some of them had been carefully cleaned and prepared, to be part of the shrine fantasized by Dahmer. Three skulls had been spray painted black and silver. A complete skeleton hung from a shower spigot. There was a human head in the refrigerator. Various chemicals were also discovered, including muriatic acid, ethyl alcohol, chloroform, and formaldehyde, along with several Polaroid photographs of dismembered victims. The next day, Dahmer confessed to murdering and dismembering 15 to 17 young men and boys. He blamed no one or anything for his crimes, not his parents, society, nor pornography.

Jeffrey Dahmer was sentenced to 15 consecutive life sentences (957 years) and incarcerated at the Columbia Correctional Facility in Portage, Wisconsin. There, he was the recipient of much fan mail and letters from curiosity seekers. Several writers sent him money, some from as far off as South Africa and Europe. In contrast, the families of the victims obtained judgments against Dahmer totaling more than $80 million. Dahmer admitted that he should never be allowed freedom again because he still felt the compulsion to kill, but he did not wish to remain in prison. On November 28, 1994, Dahmer was beaten to death by Christopher J. Scarver, another inmate serving time for murder. His remains were cremated, although efforts were made by his mother to have her son's brain donated to science.

—*Eric W. Hickey*

Portions of this entry are drawn from *Serial Murderers and Their Victims*, 3rd edition (2002) by E. W. Hickey, published by Wadsworth: Belmont, CA.

See also LUST MURDER; MOTIVES FOR MURDER; PARAPHILIA; PSYCHOPATHS; SERIAL MURDER; TROPHY TAKING

Further Reading

Dahmer, L. (1994). *A father's story*. London: Little, Brown.
Purcell, C. (2000). *An investigation of paraphilias, lust murder and the case of Jeffrey Dahmer: An integrative theoretical model*. Doctoral dissertation, California School of Professional Psychology, Fresno, California.

DANN, LAURIE, *See* MASS MURDER

DAVIDIANS, *See* KORESH, DAVID

THE DEATH PENALTY

THE PURPOSE AND HISTORY OF CAPITAL PUNISHMENT

Capital punishment, or the death penalty, is the most severe form of criminal punishment: the legal and justified termination of a convicted offender's life as punishment for his or her crime(s). Historically, this has been accomplished by various forms of execution. Offenders have been stoned, bludgeoned, beaten, broken on the wheel, drawn and quartered, eviscerated while alive, buried alive, burned alive, drowned, garroted, beheaded, hanged, shot by firing squad, electrocuted, poisoned by lethal gas, and most currently, poisoned by lethal injection. Executions were carried out in public settings until the 1830s, when they also began to be carried out inside prison boundaries. The last public execution in the United States was conducted on August 14, 1936, in Kentucky. An estimated 20,000 people witnessed that execution.

The purpose and/or goals of capital punishment are threefold. The first goal is to provide *retribution,* the principle that demands that convicted offenders be made to pay for their crimes; if an individual murders another, the offender must pay for the crime with his or her own life. The second goal of capital punishment is to incapacitate the offender. *Incapacitation* is the principle that demands that convicted offenders be prevented from committing additional crimes against innocent persons in the community. Imprisonment is the most common form of incapacitation; however, many offenders continue to commit crimes within prison, for example, physical and/or sexual assault and murder of other inmates and prison staff. Some also continue to commit drug offenses and direct gang-related activities on the streets from inside prison. The death penalty is the only punishment that affords true incapacitation against additional crimes from a given offender.

The third goal of capital punishment is *deterrence.* The principle of deterrence has two levels, general and specific. Specific deterrence discourages a specific offender from committing a crime. General deterrence discourages other would-be offenders from engaging in crimes. The death penalty posits that by executing those guilty of capital offenses, other potential criminals will choose not to commit crimes because of the extreme cost of the punishment. If a law is to have a deterrent effect, it must be common knowledge that a particular offense will result in a specific punishment and that punishment must be carried out. Thus, if punishment is delivered in a swift and certain manner, potential offenders are more likely to desist from their criminal impulses, fantasies, or plans before the commission of the acts. The death penalty does not, of course, satisfy the goals of rehabilitation and restorative justice, the reasoning being that capital crimes are considered so heinous that those purposes would appear moot.

If the murder is to be considered a capital offense and eligible for the death sentence, the murder must be committed willfully, deliberately, and with pre-meditation, along with special circumstances. Special circumstances vary from state to state but usually involve criteria such as a prior murder by the offender;

murder with multiple victims; murder of a peace officer, witness, prosecutor, or judge; lying in wait; torture with the intent to kill; murders that involve mutilation and/or dismemberment of the victim or their remains; murders committed due to the race, ethnicity, nationality, or religion of the victim; murder committed during the commission of another felony; murder by poisoning; and conspiracy or solicitation to commit murder.

From the inception of the United States as a nation until the late 1960s, capital punishment was irregularly imposed and carried out as a result of variations in the sociopolitical climate. From 1968 to 1972, the U.S. Supreme Court suspended the use of capital punishment, in light of increasing debate over the constitutionality of the punishment and public opinion polls indicating relative declines in support of it. In 1972, the Court ruled in *Furman v. Georgia* that although capital punishment itself was not unconstitutional, the seemingly arbitrary and discriminatory manner of its application was, thereby violating Eighth Amendment protection against cruel and unusual punishment. Thus, the death penalty was banned until such time as the states could develop more fair and equitable methods of applying it. As a result, every death row inmate at both the state and federal levels had their sentences reduced to life in prison (including notorious criminals such as Charles Manson).

In 1976, the U.S. Supreme Court ruled in *Gregg v. Georgia* that with the revised system of death penalty administration, capital punishment no longer violated the Eight Amendment. From the *Gregg v. Georgia* case, the Court required the trier of fact (i.e., judges or juries) to account for both aggravating and mitigating factors in determining sentencing, to develop a bifurcated trial process (e.g., a guilt or innocence phase and a sentencing phase), and to perform a proportionality review to examine whether a death sentence had been imposed in similar cases. Shortly thereafter, 38 states and the federal government reenacted capital punishment statutes and began sentencing offenders of capital crimes to death. In 1977, Utah was the first of these states to carry out a death sentence when they executed Gary Gilmore by firing squad.

Presently, in the United States, more than 3,600 male and more than 50 female inmates await execution on death row. Since 1976, of the approximately 22,000 annual convictions for murder and nonnegligent manslaughter, only about 300 offenders per year have been sentenced to death for their crimes. However, the number of executions carried out has never exceeded 74 per year. In other words, even though current public opinion is 75% in favor of capital punishment, only 1.5% of the annual murder offenders are sentenced to death. Moreover, a maximum of only 2% of those already on death row have been executed in any given year. Nonetheless, the U.S. Supreme Court has ruled that the Constitution requires due process and equal protection (Fourteenth Amendment) and prohibits cruel and unusual punishments (Eighth Amendment). As a result, capital cases are thus held to the highest standards of fairness and careful implementation of procedures.

Death row inmates tend to be poorly educated men and women from low-income backgrounds. Minorities are overrepresented for their percentage of the population, yet Caucasians account for the greatest number of death row inmates and executions. The criminal histories of these inmates have reportedly shown that 66% have prior felony convictions, 9% have prior homicide convictions, and 34% were on probation/parole or in prison at the time of their offenses. The majority of murders in the United States occur in the southern states, as well as the majority of death row inmates and executions. Political issues and concerns appear to be an important factor in the number of death sentences and executions. For example, given certain community concerns (i.e., crime rates and local candidates presenting a "tough on crime" stance), campaign and electoral issues may alter a jurisdiction's rate of capital punishment. Indeed, some research has shown that many states have so-called death belts, or regions within a death penalty state that have higher frequencies of imposed death sentences.

THE CAPITAL PUNISHMENT CONTROVERSY

The death penalty has been controversial for as long as it has been practiced. Arguments are typically based either on moral or utilitarian philosophies. Moral arguments in favor of the death penalty state that murderers should not outlive their victims, at the expense of society, and that they must forfeit their lives if justice is to be served. Moral arguments against the death penalty include the notions that mistakes can and have been made that result in innocent people being executed, that capital punishment is discriminatory to the poor and ethnic minorities, and that only God has the right to take a life (and society does not).

The utilitarian arguments in favor of the death penalty indicate that the punishment deters other criminals, exacts appropriate retribution, and provides a sense of justice for the victims, their families, and society. Moreover, they claim, it places a high value on life and is less expensive than warehousing offenders in prison for life. The utilitarian arguments against the death penalty state that there is no evidence to support the effects of deterrence, especially considering that most murders are committed while under the influence of illicit substances, due to mental illness, or as a result of uncontrollable rage. For this reason, they argue, murderers are not able to control their actions and as a result never consider the threat of capital punishment before or during their crimes. In addition, utilitarians state that it is wrong for a government to participate in the intentional killing of its citizens, which may produce a "brutalization effect," that is, making the society more violent overall. They believe that executions convey a harmful message to society that life is cheap and expendable and that the appropriate response to violence is more violence.

Other opponents have been noted as saying that capital punishment as a method of expressing social vengeance unalterably impedes our moral progress; that arbitrary discretion (such as race, gender, age, and IQ) is found in every case; and that "when a nation does violence to human beings, by conducting wars or executing criminals, it incites its citizens to more criminal violence than they would otherwise commit" (Wilkes, 1987, pp. 27-28). According to another opponent,

> For there to be equivalence, the death penalty would have to punish a criminal who had warned his victim of the date at which he would inflict a horrible death on him and who, from that moment onward, had confined him at his mercy for months. Such a monster is not encountered in private life. (Gettinger, 1983)

Proponents of capital punishment have stated that punishment should be gauged according to the seriousness of the crime: The highest penalty should be reserved for the worst crimes. They hold that the death penalty is usually the last legal resort with these offenders, is the safest way of protecting society, and is more economically feasible than a sentence of life without parole.

Carrington (1978) in his book titled *Neither Cruel Nor Unusual* indicted that "it is high time the rights of the victims were recognized in our criminal justice system" and that "we need to create a better sense of legal and moral balance" (p. 14). Over the past several years, victim impact statements have been routinely considered in several death penalty states. These statements outline the devastation of physical, emotional, and financial hardships suffered by victims and their families. Along these lines, Douglas (1999) stated,

> Regardless of your ethical opinion, calling [execution] "premeditated violent homicide" (as the American Civil Liberties Union has deemed it) is an action that I find morally repugnant because it places the killer and the victim on the same level and, therefore, trivializes the critical distinction between the guilty and the innocent. We owe [the victim's] memory more than that. (p. 79)

RELATED CONSIDERATIONS CONCERNING CAPITAL PUNISHMENT

Evaluating the Death Penalty as a Deterrent

For some potential offenders, the death penalty actually is a deterrent. Others commit capital crimes despite being aware of the possible outcome. During the commission of the crimes, they fully expect to "get away with it." The effectiveness of any particular deterrent is difficult to assess because the people who are deterred do not come to our attention. There is no way of knowing what crimes are avoided because would-be perpetrators paused to consider the actions as not worth losing their lives over, although occasionally, individuals tell of murderous intentions being sidetracked by various interruptions that led them to abandon their crimes, at least temporarily.

Deterrence is a concept that must be measured over time. In other words, to truly measure the deterrent effect of the death penalty, society would need to make a long-term decision to enforce capital punishment on a regular basis. A period of 25 to 30 years of consistent and fair, as well as swift and certain, application of execution for capital murder would be required to collect enough data to begin to evaluate its effectiveness as a deterrent.

Cost Factors

The cost and time for trying capital crime in court is higher due to the extra care that must be taken when a person's life is at stake, and becomes even greater during the appeals process. Some argue that though these trials are exorbitantly expensive, defendants often do not receive adequate counsel, being that average rate of compensation for counsel in these cases is about $15 to $20 per hour. Others argue that because the hourly compensation rate is so low and the costs of the trial so high, defendants are actually receiving far more hours of legal representation than other defendants. Another point of view holds that whatever the level of representation, the length and expense of trials have a lot to do with financial concerns of attorneys.

States are mandated to provide any and all medical care, including cancer treatments, HIV treatment, and even organ transplants, as well as regular mental health care for those in need of services, education, job training, food, clothing, electricity, and so forth. When taken altogether, these costs amount to extremely high budgetary demands. In fact, with 33 correctional facilities across the state, the California Department of Corrections budget exceeds $3.5 billion per year. At one California maximum-security prison with a population of 5,500 inmates, over 800 (15%) have been diagnosed as having Hepatitis-C. The monthly medical cost to treat each inmate for just this chronic and infectious disease is approximately $1,200. In other words, for this one prison, the monthly and yearly costs to treat this one disease are $960,000 and $11,520,000, respectively. When one considers the costs of kidney dialysis, cancer, and even the obligation to perform organ transplants if necessary, the health care costs become exponential.

Moreover, the costs to house inmates for life continue to rise as the population of inmates ages in the United States. Not only are prisons the nation's largest housing projects, they are also soon to become the nation's largest nursing homes. These figures also do not account for inmates who are frequently assaultive and destructive, costing the states thousands upon thousands each year to replace destroyed property, conduct disciplinary hearings, and pay for medical costs for others (inmates and prison staff) injured by their behavior. When one adds all of these costs over a lifetime, or even 40 years, the costs are extremely high.

"Costs," however, are not only financial. Executing a person is very serious business and involves great moral and legal issues. Intangible costs include how we feel individually and as a nation about taking lives. Many oppose the death penalty on the grounds that it constitutes cruel and unusual punishment or that executions fail to serve as a general deterrence to murder. A major issue in recent years is the reality that with the application of forensic science and DNA research, several persons once on death row were found innocent and have been freed. DNA analysis has proven with little room for doubt that some persons have been erroneously placed on death row. In some cases, persons have been executed for crimes they never committed. Consequently, capital punishment stirs great debate and uneasiness about its efficacy.

The average time from sentencing to execution in capitol cases ranges from 11 to nearly 15 years, depending upon the state. In fact, most death row inmates die of natural causes, suicide, or are murdered in prison. Therefore, even if a convicted murderer is sentenced to death, the chance of them actually being executed is minimal.

Capital Punishment and Special Populations

The Eighth Amendment prohibits the execution of offenders found to be legally insane. The U.S. Supreme Court ruled in *Ford v. Wainwright* (1986) that offenders must be able to comprehend that they have been sentenced to death and understand the reasons for that sentence. It is important to note that having a mental illness does not equate with insanity. Insanity is based on the legal concept of *mens rea,* or "guilty mind," the ability to formulate a criminal intent. Individuals found to be legally insane are not capable of developing mens rea. Mental illness is a diagnosable condition, which may or may not preclude the development of mens rea. Insanity is determined in the legal arena by the trier of fact, the judge or jury, whereas mental illness is determined by either a psychologist or a psychiatrist. Although the Eighth Amendment prohibits the execution of the insane, it does not prohibit the execution of the mentally retarded (*Penry v. Lynaugh,* 1989). However, on June 20, 2002, the U.S. Supreme Court ruled that the execution of an individual with an IQ of less than 70 on a standardized intelligence test violates the Eighth Amendment's protection against cruel and unusual punishment (*Atkins v. Virginia,* 2002).

The U.S. Supreme Court has made several rulings regarding juvenile offenders being tried as adults in capital cases. In *Kent v. United States* (1966) and *In re Gault* (1967), the Court ruled that juveniles must be afforded the same due process and equal protection rights as adults when under transfer, or waiver, to adult court. In *Eddings v. Oklahoma* (1982), the Court ruled that a juvenile defendant's youthful age should be considered as a mitigating factor when determining sentencing. The Court offered three major decisions regarding juveniles in the late 1980s. In *Thompson v. Oklahoma* (1988), the Court ruled that the execution of those under the age of 16 did not fit with the "evolving standards of decency that mark the progress of a maturing society." In *Stanford v. Kentucky* (1989), the Court again ruled that the minimum age at which the death penalty should be considered is 16 years. That same year, the execution of juveniles was upheld in *Wilkins v. Missouri* (1989), but the minimum age of imposing capital punishment was left open for each individual state to delineate.

Recent Supreme Court Rulings

In addition to *Atkins v. Virginia* (2002), the U.S. Supreme Court's ruling in *Ring v. Arizona* (2002) changed the manner in which convicted killers are sentenced to death. It was decided that having a sole individual (a judge) make the determination as to whether capital punishment is warranted violates the offender's Sixth Amendment right to a jury trial. Thus, the Court's 7-2 ruling stipulates that juries only, not judges, must be the entity to decide whether a convicted killer is to be executed. As a result of this ruling, 168 death sentences in five states were overturned. The majority of these cases will need to be reheard by a jury to determine whether capital punishment is still the proper disposition in these cases. The five states directly affected by this ruling are Arizona, Idaho, Montana, Colorado, and Nebraska, and it may also be extended to Florida, Alabama, Indiana, and Delaware, which have similar sentencing systems. If *Ring v. Arizona* is extended to these additional four states, the ruling could affect nearly 800 death row inmates.

ONGOING DEBATE

The use of capital punishment will probably be debated on many grounds for as long as humans exist. Proponents believe that the more contemporary forms of execution (i.e., lethal injection) are not cruel and unusual; that the punishment is more humane than were the offenders' actions toward their victims, thus adding to the moral development of society; and that it is a structured, justified, and economical use of deadly force, which enacts retribution, permanent incapacitation, and ultimately deterrence, thus protecting communities from future crime.

Opponents believe that in carrying out the death penalty, there is cruelty in waiting for death, cruelty in the manner of death, and cruelty to the innocent persons who care about the condemned. They believe that mistaken decisions result in innocent people being executed, as has increasingly been shown through recent advances in forensic science; that capital punishment is discriminatory to the poor and ethnic minorities; that it does not deter criminal acts; that society does not have the right to take a life; and that punishment by death merely reinforces the idea that the appropriate response to violence is more violence.

—Rocky Underwood

See also COURT-ORDERED PSYCHOLOGICAL ASSESSMENT; DEATH ROW; EXECUTION PROCESS; VIOLENCE: BRUTALIZATION EFFECT

Further Reading

Atkins v. Virginia, 00-8452 260 Va. 375, 534 S. E. 2d 312 (2002).

Bedau, H. (1982). *The death penalty in America.* New York: Oxford University Press.

Black, C. (1974). *Capital punishment: The inevitability of caprice and mistake.* New York: Norton.

Carrington, F. (1978). *Neither cruel nor unusual.* Westport, CT: Arlington House.

Douglas, J., & Olshaker, M. (1999). *The anatomy of motive.* New York: Scribner.

Eddings v. Oklahoma, 455 U.S. 104 (1982).

Ford v. Wainwright, 477 U.S. 399 (1986).

Furman v. Georgia, 408 U.S. 238 (1972).

Gettinger, S. (1983, December 5). Awaiting execution. *The New York Times.*

Gregg v. Georgia, 428 U.S. 153 (1976).

In re Gault, 387 U.S. 1 (1967).

Kent v. United States, 383 U.S. 541 (1966).

Paternoster, R. (1991). *Capital punishment in America.* New York: Lexington Books.

Penry v. Lynaugh, 492 U.S. 302 (1989).

Ring v. Arizona, 01-488 200 Ariz. 267 25P. 3d 1139 (2002).

Stanford v. Kentucky, 492 U.S. 361 (1989).

Thompson v. Oklahoma, 487 U.S. 815 (1988).

Wilkes, J. (1987, June). Murder in mind. *Psychology Today,* 27-32.

Wilkins v. Missouri, 492 U.S. 361 (1989).

DEATH PENALTY: JUVENILES

Since the death penalty was reinstated in 1976, there have been 18 executions of juvenile offenders, approximately 2.4% of the total number of executions; 10 executions occurred during the 1990s. There are currently 83 inmates on death row who were sentenced as juveniles, approximately 2.24% of the total death row population (NAACP, 2002).

Currently, 38 states and the federal government authorize the death penalty. Sixteen of these states and the federal government mandate that the individual must be at least 18 years of age at the time of the crime to be eligible for the death penalty. Twenty-two states permit the execution of offenders who committed capital offenses prior to their 18th birthday. Five states have chosen 17 as the minimum age, and 17 states have chosen 16 as the minimum age (Death Penalty Information Center, 2002). Twenty-two states permit the execution of an offender who committed a capital crime as a juvenile, but the majority of juvenile defendants on death row were sentenced to death in the state of Texas (see Table 1).

On February 4, 1999, Sean Sellers, 16 years old at the time of his offense, was the first juvenile offender under 17 years of age to be executed in 40 years. Sellers was sentenced to death for the murder of his

Table 1   Juveniles and the Death Penalty

Age 18[a]	Age 17[b]	Age 16[c]
California	Florida	Alabama
Colorado	Georgia	Arizona
Connecticut	New Hampshire	Arkansas
Illinois	North Carolina	Delaware
Indiana	Texas	Idaho
Kansas		Kentucky
Maryland		Louisiana
Montana		Mississippi
Nebraska		Missouri
New Jersey		Nevada
New Mexico		Oklahoma
New York		Pennsylvania
Ohio		South Carolina
Oregon		South Dakota
Tennessee		Utah
Washington		Virginia
Federal government		Wyoming

a. Total: 16 states and federal.
b. Total: 5 states.
c. Total: 17 states.

mother and stepfather, Vonda and Paul Bellafatto, and for the death of Robert Paul Bower. The teen was executed in Oklahoma despite evidence of mental illness and protests from many international organizations. International organizations such as the United Nations Convention on the Rights of the Child as well as other international treaties and agreements have given most countries cause to abandon the death penalty for juvenile offenders. For example, since 1990, juvenile offenders have been executed in only six countries, including the United States, Iran, Pakistan, Yemen, Nigeria, and Saudi Arabia.

The Supreme Court has made decisions based on the Eighth Amendment's "cruel and unusual punishment" clause to bar the death penalty for juveniles below 16 years of age. In 1958, the Supreme Court decided in *Trop v. Dulles* that the interpretation of the Eighth Amendment contained an "evolving standard of decency that marked the progress of a maturing society." In light of that decision, the Court recognized that in determining the meaning of "cruel and unusual," it must first determine what the community's current sentiments were. When the Court later applied the "evolving standards of decency" concept to the death penalty in *Furman v. Georgia* (1972), public opinion was mentioned and discussed explicitly in five of the nine separate opinions written.

Justice Marshall in *Furman* (1972) argued that "even a punishment that served a valid legislative purpose and was not excessive could violate the Eighth Amendment if popular sentiment abhors it" (p. 332). With this in mind, Marshall concluded that the death penalty violated the Eighth Amendment because it had become morally unacceptable to the people of the United States at that time in history.

In addition, according to *Coker v. Georgia* (1977), the Court noted that "Eighth Amendment judgments should not be, or appear to be, merely the subjective views of individual justices; judgment should be informed by objective factors to the maximum possible extent" (p. 584). As a result of the Court's interpretation of previous case law, community sentiment has become a central concern in determining the constitutionality of the death penalty.

In 1988, the Supreme Court was asked to address the death penalty for a juvenile in *Thompson v. Oklahoma* (1988). Petitioner William Wayne Thompson had been convicted of first-degree murder and sentenced to death. The Court of Criminal Appeals of Oklahoma had affirmed the decision before the case was appealed to the U.S. Supreme Court. A plurality of the Court held that executing a 15-year-old defendant constituted "cruel and unusual punishment" according to the Eighth Amendment. The Court concluded that this amendment, made applicable to the States by the Fourteenth Amendment, prohibits the execution of a person below 16 years of age at the time of his or her offense.

Justice Stevens's opinion concluded that the relative lack of experience, education, and intelligence of teenagers makes them less able to evaluate the consequences of their actions and that they are more influenced by emotion and peer pressure. Stevens found that because juveniles have a lower standard of culpability and a larger capacity for growth, the death penalty would serve no deterrent effect, therefore undermining retribution served by the punishment. Justice O'Connor, the fifth vote to overturn, concurred but declined to set a minimum age.

Since *Thompson v. Oklahoma* (1988), the Eighth Amendment stands as the only constitutional protection afforded to juvenile offenders below the age of 16 against the death penalty. Because the decision was a plurality opinion, the decision carries less weight under stare decisis than does a majority opinion, leaving the issue open for future challenge.

One year later, in *Stanford v. Kentucky* (1989) and *Wilkins v. Missouri* (1989), the Court was asked to determine whether the imposition of capital punishment on offenders who were 16 and 17 years old constitutes cruel and unusual punishment. In the combined cases, the Supreme Court ruled that the Eighth Amendment does not prohibit the death penalty for 16- and 17-year-olds who have committed murder. The plurality opinion held that the proper standard to apply when determining the "evolving standards of decency that marked the progress of a maturing society" (*Trop v. Dulles,* 1958) was to examine the statutes passed by the various state legislatures.

In evaluating community sentiment to help determine their opinion in the case, the justices in *Stanford v. Kentucky* considered the fact that states are more likely to impose the death penalty on adults (18 years or older) and less likely to impose it on 17-, 16-, and 15-year-olds, with less likelihood of this exposure the lower the juvenile's age. Justice Scalia claimed, however, that the petitioners did not establish that the execution of offenders below 18 years of age is categorically unacceptable to juries and prosecutors and ruled that the juvenile death penalty is not unconstitutional for 16- and 17-year-olds. It is not apparent from this ruling whether other evidence of community sentiment, including international law, jury-sentencing behavior, and social science research, were considered.

There are various arguments to support and oppose the death penalty for juveniles. Violent juvenile crime has been the reason most often cited by legislators and politicians to justify the sentence. Arguments against the juvenile death penalty include the abhorrent childhoods suffered by most defendants; society's failure to protect children from abuse and neglect and to provide long-term solutions to societal problems that reinforce violent behavior; and the belief that children should be given the chance for rehabilitation. International human rights organizations continue to lobby against the execution of juvenile defendants, and because the death penalty for juvenile offenders is a violation of international law, some scholars predict that it is only a matter of time before the United States joins the rest of the world in abolishing this practice.

—*C. Draven Godwin*

See also EXECUTION; JUVENILE KILLERS

Further Reading

Coker v. Georgia, 433 U.S. 584 (1977).

Death Penalty Information Center. (2002, January). *Execution of juvenile offenders.* Available on the World Wide Web at: http://www.deathpenaltyinfo.org/juvchair.html.

Finkel, N. (1993). Socioscientific evidence and Supreme Court numerology: When justices attempt social science. *Behavioral Sciences and the Law, 11,* 67-77.

Finkel, N., Hughes, K., Smith, S., & Hurabiell, M. (1994). Killing kids: The juvenile death penalty and community sentiment. *Behavioral Sciences and the Law, 12,* 5-20.

Furman v. Georgia, 408 U.S. 238 (1972).

Hale, R. (1997). *A review of juvenile executions in America.* Lewiston, NY: Edwin Mellon.

Haney, C., & Logan, D. (1994). Broken promise: The Supreme Court's response to social science research on capital punishment. *Journal of Social Issues, 50,* 75-101.

NAACP Legal Defense and Educational Fund. (2001, October 1). *Death row U.S.A.* Available on the World Wide Web at: http://www.deathpenatlyinfo.org/firstpage.html.

Stanford v. Kentucky, 492 U.S. 361 (1989).

Thompson v. Oklahoma, 487 U.S. 815 (1988).

Trop v. Dulles, 356 U.S. 86 (1958).

Wilkins v. Missouri, No. 87-6026 (1989).

DEATH ROW

The cell is 8 feet long, 6 feet wide, and 10 feet high. Aside from the condemned inmate who occupies this space, there is also a bed, a toilet, and a small writing table. There is not much room for amenities, not much space for moving around, and not much privacy. This is the typical death row cell, where the condemned await death. For the most part, each inmate spends 23 out of 24 hours a day locked in this cell and is only allowed out for a brief shower and irregular recreation. Much of the schedule depends on the availability of the correctional staff who work on "the row."

Over time, the concept of isolating those about to be executed has evolved from the Tower of London and its "apartments" to the modern-day correctional facility with its population of condemned prisoners. When executions by hanging were conducted in Folsom Prison, there were five cells located on the second floor of the gallows room, numbered 1 through 5. A rope was attached to the ceiling just outside in Cell Number 1. As each condemned inmate was executed, the others moved up one cell. The men in Folsom came to know that place as "death row."

Although some prisons in which executions are conducted still have "death rows," none as extreme as old Folsom, many now have what is called "death status." Men who have been sentenced to die and are awaiting the result of their appeals are allowed to mingle with other death status inmates, and in some institutions even with other inmates serving lesser sentences. Part of the reason for this change is the reality that those sentenced to death might wait as long as 14 to 18 years. Traditionally, for the condemned, there was no programming, no activities, or work opportunities. With the lengthy appeals process and the amount of time before an execution actually takes place today, it has seemed more appropriate to allow these individuals to have some kind of productive activities. Acknowledgment of the fact that "there is life on death row" has altered correctional policy and practice.

Close to 4,000 inmates (including approximately 50 women) currently await executions on "death rows" around the United States. For each one, time is measured differently, yet there are cycles and stages experienced in common. Generally, to begin with, they feel anger and resentment. As time stretches out, this is replaced by stoicism, with cautious optimism and hope—after all, some appeals have successfully resulted in commutation or even reversal. In the latter stages, the condemned prisoner experiences resignation and introspection.

Individuals sentenced to death occupy a peculiar status in the inmate pecking order. Other inmates both respect and fear them. They are the apotheosis of the criminal world, having committed the ultimate crime and been dealt the ultimate punishment. These "dead men walking" have little to lose in the realm of further punishment, and with death hanging over their heads, they have little time or interest in the games and politics of the general prison society.

The expendable residents of death row, however, cannot escape the constraints of living in society, albeit a unique one. They still, as a group, experience the social obligations and expectations of living with others. Among these residents who have only their pending deaths in common, petty grievances sometimes become major issues—a clogged sink or missing newspaper—and personal grudges and animosities develop. Yet as one inmate explained, "Sure we have disagreements and disputes, but they don't last long. We can't afford that. All we have is each other and so it doesn't pay to stay mad at anybody. We're going to be together for a while." Cliques often develop, and some residents, especially women, form closer relationships than others.

The death row experience for women can be quite different from that of men. Historically, most prisons did not have specific facilities for women awaiting execution. These women were kept in hospitals or mental health units, and when it was time, they were transported to the execution facility. More recently, newer prisons have been designed to house women under sentence of death. In some, they are allowed to interact with each other and participate in group activities.

Despite the amenities and enhanced (though limited) programming for condemned inmates, death row/death status remains a bleak experience. "Death row is a horrible way of life," according to one woman inmate. Another was grateful for being sentenced to die rather than being given a life sentence. He said, "I was afraid I would get life. I can't do life. I can do death, but I can't do life."

The death row experience is one of boredom and repetition, day after day, the same regimen, the same faces, the same food. The increasing use of execution in the United States in general and by some states specifically has failed to have much of an impact on the warehousing of those waiting to die. The appeals process and changing opinions regarding capital punishment allow some hope for these condemned inmates. In the meantime, they wait.

—*Kay Gillespie*

See also DEATH PENALTY; EXECUTION PROCESS

Further Reading

Gillespie, L. K. (2003). *The death chamber: Exploring executions.* Boston: Allyn & Bacon.

Weinstein, B., & Bessent, J. (1996). *Death row confidential.* New York: HarperCollins.

DEATH WITH DIGNITIY, *See*
EUTHANASIA; KEVORKIAN, JACK

DELINQUENTS, *See*
JUVENILE OFFENDERS

ALBERT HENRY DESALVO

Albert DeSalvo—also known as "The Measuring Man," "The Green Man," and "The Boston Strangler"—murdered 13 women between 1962 and 1964. Born in Chelsea, Massachusetts, in 1931, DeSalvo was forced to live in extremely impoverished conditions. Often neglected, he was subjected to cruel beatings at the hands of his alcoholic father. He was forced to watch while his father abused and beat his mother. On one occasion, he watched his father break each of his mother's fingers, one after the other. On another occasion, his father sold him and his sister into slavery to a farmer for several months. In 1944, Mrs. DeSalvo divorced her husband, taking her six children with her.

His love for his mother and his hatred for his father seemed to bring out the worst in Albert. He remembered later how much he enjoyed shooting cats with his bow and arrow. His father had trained him well in stealing from stores, and Albert became proficient at the task. He gradually developed a liking for breaking and entering homes, which he began to do frequently during the next 20 years.

By the time he was 12, Albert had been arrested twice, once for larceny and once for breaking and entering. He was incarcerated at Lyman School for delinquent boys, where he learned a great deal more about burglary. After his release, he began to apply himself full-time to breaking and entering homes. Albert tried to bridge the gap between himself and those who were affluent. He was no more able to attain middle-class respectability than he was able to satisfy his enormous sex drive. He became sexually active with both girls and homosexuals in the neighborhood and gained a reputation for his remarkable sexual capacity. At 17, he joined the military and served with the occupation forces in Germany. Before returning, he won the U.S. Army middleweight boxing championship and married his wife, Irmgard. In 1955, at age 23, DeSalvo was charged with his first sex offense, involving the molestation of a 9-year-old girl. The charges were dropped when the parents of the girl refused to proceed with the case. In 1956, he was honorably discharged from the military.

In 1958, DeSalvo's first child was born, and he briefly ceased his breaking-and-entering activities. However, his wife refused to submit to his excessive sexual demands, and his financial status seemed to be worsening. In a short time, Albert received two separate suspended sentences for breaking and entering.

Before long, DeSalvo earned the nickname "The Measuring Man," conning his way into scores of apartments by explaining that he represented a modeling agency and was in search of talent. Producing a measuring tape, he would take occupants' personal measurements, touching them inappropriately whenever possible. He later would claim that most of his victims were quite willing to have their measurements taken, that few complained, and a few even removed their clothing. He never attacked or harmed any of them but promised they would soon be hearing from his agency.

Eventually, Albert was arrested once again for breaking and entering and was sentenced to 2 years' imprisonment. He earned his release in 11 months. According to police, at that time, DeSalvo was still known only as a breaking-and-entering criminal. He returned home, again rejected by his wife until such time that he could prove he had mended his ways.

Overwhelmed with frustration, Albert began changing from the harmless "Measuring Man" to an aggressive, violent personality. He began tying up some of his victims and raping them. He always wore green pants during these forays and was soon dubbed "The Green Man." Police estimate that he attacked several women. Feelings of rejection, sexual frustration, and inferiority to others became intolerable by June 1962, when he attempted his first murder of a woman in her apartment. Apparently, during the attack, he saw himself in a mirror by the bed and it jolted his sensibilities, so he stopped. A week later, he began killing in earnest.

Most of DeSalvo's victims were strangled and sexually assaulted. Over 60% were older women, although most of his last few victims were young women. He seemed to enjoy desecrating the corpse and then ransacking the apartment. He often tied a bow under the chin of his victim after he had killed her.

Although DeSalvo was unsure of his motives for killing, he was even less sure why he suddenly stopped in January 1964. Perhaps he felt he had given the supreme insult to society through the explicit humiliation of his last victims. DeSalvo continued to enter the homes of unsuspecting women as "The Green Man," tying them up and raping them, but he no longer killed his victims. Eventually, after a description had been given to the police by one of his victims, Albert was arrested as "The Green Man" and was linked to sexual assaults in Massachusetts, Connecticut, New Hampshire, and Rhode Island. He was sent to Bridgewater, a mental institution, for evaluation, but not until the spring of 1965 did he confess to being "The Boston Strangler."

DeSalvo's confession, however, was given under special circumstances that protected him from prosecution for the murders. He never came to trial for the murders but instead was sent to prison for his many sexual assaults committed as "The Green Man." In 1967, he entered Walpole State Prison to serve a life sentence. Six years later, Albert DeSalvo was stabbed to death by a fellow inmate.

—*Eric W. Hickey*

Portions of this entry are drawn from *Serial Murderers and Their Victims,* 3rd edition (2002) by E. W. Hickey, published by Wadsworth: Belmont, CA.

See also LUST MURDER; MOTIVES FOR MURDER;
    PARAPHILIA; SERIAL MURDER; SEXUAL OFFENSES;
    SIGNATURE KILLERS

Further Reading

Hickey, E. W. (2002). *Serial murderers and their victims* (3rd ed.). Belmont, CA: Wadsworth.

DIAGNOSTIC AND STATISTICAL MANUAL OF MENTAL DISORDERS (DSM)

The *Diagnostic and Statistical Manual of Mental Disorders* is a taxonomy of mental disorders published by the American Psychiatric Association and currently in its fourth edition (*DSM-IV;* 1994). The first edition was published in 1952 and was the first publication to categorize mental disorders for the purpose of clinical utility. Since that time, the *DSM* has developed into a tool that allows professionals from various fields to communicate effectively with one another for research, educational, statistical, and clinical purposes. The *DSM* is established within a medical model, a method with international recognition. It is complementary to the *International Statistical Classification of Disease and Related Health Problems* published by the World Health Organization.

The *DSM* is similar to any medical text outlining diagnoses used for categorization. Categorizing disorders or diseases has a long history as a means of organizing and communicating information for the purposes of treatment or research. The *DSM* is relatively easy to read and comprehend; however, the application of material is far more complicated. The text itself merely provides a means by which professionals with sufficient experience and training can diagnose disorders. Understanding the meaning of these diagnoses requires experience and appropriate training.

The current edition of the *DSM* was developed as the result of work groups and task forces that comprehensively reviewed published literature, analyzed data, and investigated field trails to validate diagnostic criteria induced in the text. The result of this process was the inclusion of 16 diagnostic conditions:

Each is conceptualized as a clinically significant behavioral or psychological syndrome or pattern that occurs in an individual and is associated with present distress or disability or with significant increased risk of suffering, death, pain, disability, or an important loss of freedom not expected or culturally sanctioned responses to a particular event. (American Psychiatric Association, 1994, p. xxi)

Each diagnostic category provides information regarding primary features, subtypes, specifiers, recording procedures, associated features, common course of the disorder, familiar patterns, differential diagnosis, and features specific to culture, age, and gender.

It should be noted that within the *DSM-IV* text are cautions toward its use within the forensic arena. Diagnostic information was not written for legal usage; therefore, its use within a forensic setting or for forensic purposes is at a "significant risk" for being "misused or misunderstood" (APA, 1994, p. xxiii). The fourth edition also includes cautions and guidelines about how to use diagnoses when working with someone from a cultural background that differs from the clinician. Disorders can present differently across cultures, and diagnoses can be inaccurately applied when the diagnostician is unfamiliar with the culture of the individual being evaluated.

—*Sarah Ferguson*

See also AGGRESSION; ANTISOCIAL PERSONALITY DISORDER; MENTALLY DISORDERED OFFENDERS; VIOLENT BEHAVIOR

Further Reading

American Psychiatric Association. (1994*). Diagnostic and statistical manual of mental disorders* (4th ed.). Washington, DC: Author.

American Psychiatric Association. (1994-1997). *DSM-IV sourcebook* (Vols. 1-3). Washington, DC: Author.

Hays, P. A. (2001). *Addressing cultural complexities in practice: A framework for clinicians and counselors.* Washington, DC: American Psychological Association.

DNA PROFILING, *See* CRIMINALISTICS; FORENSIC SCIENCE

WESTLEY ALLAN DODD

Westley Allan Dodd began sexually abusing children when he was 13 years old, starting with exposing himself to young girls and boys around his neighborhood. Dodd claims he was unhappy as a child because his parents fought constantly and did not provide him with any emotional support. When his parents divorced, Dodd's behaviors escalated to the molestation of children. He sought out children he knew who were close to him. At the age of 14, he molested his 8- and 6-year-old cousins. Dodd also placed himself in situations in which he would have access to children, such as babysitting for neighborhood kids and working as a camp counselor. At the age of 18, he began to seek out children that were not known to him.

Dodd eventually joined the navy and was stationed in Bangor, Washington. He preyed on children who lived on the naval base; made trips to Seattle, where he approached children in movie theater restrooms; and started using money to lure children to secluded places where he would order them to take down their pants. Dodd was eventually arrested and discharged from the navy. He was again arrested after he tried to accost a young boy and served 19 days in jail. Throughout the next few years, Dodd continued to be arrested but spent no significant time in jail.

By 1986, Dodd had sexually assaulted at least 30 children. Despite court-ordered counseling, he made no attempt to control his behavior, and in fact began to have fantasies of murdering his victims. In 1987, Dodd chose his first victim. He approached an 8-year-old boy he had met while working as a security guard and asked him for help in finding a "lost boy." The boy, sensing danger, told Dodd that he was going home and would be right back. When the boy went home, he told his mother of the incident, and she called the police. Dodd was charged but spent only 118 days in jail.

Dodd moved to Vancouver in 1989. He familiarized himself with the area and found David Douglas Park a good place to prey on new victims. On September 4, Dodd accosted two brothers, molested them, and stabbed them to death. He found more satisfaction in killing than molesting. On October 29, 1989, Dodd abducted his third murder victim. He lured the child away from a schoolyard and took him to his apartment, where he tied the boy up, molested him, and eventually strangled him while he was sleeping. Afterward, Dodd moved him to his closet and photographed him, eventually discarding of the body near Vancouver Lake.

Not long after the boy's body was found, Dodd was arrested after trying to abduct another boy from a movie theater restroom. Dodd eventually confessed to the three murders and was charged with 3 cases of first-degree murder, in addition to attempted kidnapping for the boy he'd tried to abduct from the theater. He pled guilty to all charges and was sentenced to death by hanging. Dodd was executed on January 5th, 1993.

—Colleen Condren

See also CHILD KILLERS; PEDOPHILIA; SERIAL MURDER; SEX OFFENDERS

Further Reading

Ressler, R. K., Burgess, A. W., & Douglas, J. E. (1988). *Sexual homicide: Patterns and motives.* New York: Lexington Books.

Steinhorst, L. (1994). *When the monster comes out of the closet.* Salem, Oregon: Rose Publishing.

DOMESTIC BATTERING, *See* BATTERERS AND ABUSIVE PARTNERS; BATTERED CHILD SYNDROME; BATTERED WOMAN'S SYNDROME; FAMILY VIOLENCE

DOMESTIC HOMICIDE, *See* FAMILY HOMICIDE; MOTIVES FOR MURDER

DOMESTIC VIOLENCE, *See* FAMILY VIOLENCE

DOMESTIC VIOLENCE: SAME-SEX PARTNERS

Historically, domestic violence referred to the physical, emotional, psychological, and/or verbal mistreatment of a husband or wife, usually of a wife by her husband. Over the years, society began to recognize that other types of domestic living arrangements, including same-sex couples, were equally vulnerable to in-home violence. Violence perpetrated by one partner against the other in an intimate relationship, regardless of gender or sexual orientation, is a complex phenomenon that exists in all economic, racial, ethnic, and age groups. However, there are significant differences between same-sex and opposite-sex domestic violence with respect to the source and dynamics of the violence, as well as in the legal response. Understanding these differences is necessary for effectively remedying the problem.

NATURE AND EXTENT OF SAME-SEX DOMESTIC VIOLENCE

In the United States, lesbian and gay male couples are not allowed legally to marry (although in some states, they enjoy very limited, marriage-like privileges through recent domestic partner registration laws). As a result, their relationships have been expressly or implicitly excluded from the reach of domestic violence legislation, and violence in a same-sex household has been treated instead as criminal assault or battery. Domestic violence laws, however, afford a higher level of protection against continuing violence. Among the advantages is that many laws require the perpetrator to undergo counseling. Also, a restraining order for domestic violence is more readily obtainable. Over time, same-sex relationship advocates have successfully pushed for similar protections, and presently, domestic violence laws in more than 40 states and the District of Columbia expressly provide for law enforcement response to same-sex domestic violence.

At the same time, at least nine of these states retain antisodomy laws, so that in many cases, a same-sex partner must first admit to committing a crime before seeking protection, although prosecution does not necessarily follow. Although individual definitions vary from state to state, *sodomy* as used here refers to all sexual activity other than sexual intercourse between a male and a female, and it includes sexual activity engaged in by lesbians and gay men. In *Bowers v. Hardwick,* 1986, the U.S. Supreme Court ruled that antisodomy laws do not unconstitutionally infringe on a gay person's fundamental right to privacy.

According to a 1998 National Crime Victimization Survey, an estimated 1 million incidents of violence were committed against intimate partners, and women accounted for about 85% of these incidents. A 2001 report by the Bureau of Justice Statistics revealed that in each year between 1993 and 1999, 10% of domestic violence incidents were committed by a male against a male partner. Over the same period, 2% of the total number of violent incidents were committed by a female against a female partner. An estimated 25% to 33% of same-sex couples engage in violent behavior, as is the case for opposite-sex couples.

The demographic characteristics of same-sex partners involved in domestic violence generally mirror that of the U.S. population as a whole: Most are white, followed by Hispanic, black, and Southeast Asian. Age ranges from under 18 to over 65. Females and males are equally represented (Moore, 2001).

DYNAMICS OF SAME-SEX DOMESTIC VIOLENCE

There is a wealth of literature about domestic violence existing today. However, domestic violence theories are based mostly on data from opposite-sex couples. Only recently has scientific attention been directed toward domestic violence within the lesbian and gay community. The paucity of research on the problem stems in part from the reluctance of lesbians and gay men themselves to acknowledge the existence of domestic violence in their communities. For example, women in same-sex relationships, embracing the archetype of the nurturing female as a deterrent to violence, have been hesitant to admit that the same type of violence that men perpetrate on women can affect them as well. Men in same-sex relationships are often hesitant to admit to being victimized in light of the stigma associated with vulnerability. This hesitancy has deterred researchers with an interest in the lesbian and gay community from making a critical self-examination on any significant scale. Nevertheless, based on the limited studies that have been done, a clearer picture of same-sex domestic violence is emerging.

One trend has been to acknowledge that the traditional feminist, patriarchal model of domestic violence fails to adequately describe same-sex violence. In the late 1970s, Lenore Walker proposed a "cycle of violence" model for understanding domestic violence. Her theory highlighted the physical, financial, and emotional power imbalance inherent in a male-female relationship as "allowing" a man to abuse "his property." It also helps explain why so many abused females in opposite-sex relationships, fearing the males' power, do not readily leave. The cycle-of-violence theory describes a repeated pattern of escalation of violence, a violent episode, followed by a "honeymoon" phase, in which the perpetrator solicits forgiveness and promises not to reabuse. Over time, the honeymoon phase disappears as the violent episodes increase in frequency and severity.

The foregoing gender-based, power-imbalance model does not apply to same-gender domestic violence, at least not in the same way, because any power imbalance that lies at the source of same-sex abuse must stem from sources other than socially constructed, gender-based roles. For example, most gay males and lesbian women have not adopted or have actively rejected the traditional marriage relationship roles that are grounded in gender (i.e., dominant male-husband and dependent female-wife). Others vary or alternate between these roles. Furthermore, on average, males earn more than females, regardless of sexual orientation. Thus, the economic differential that both creates and reinforces the traditional marriage roles typically does not exist in same-sex relationships. Although financial problems may contribute to the violence in a same-sex couple relationship, the violence does not flow from the privilege/disadvantage paradigm that affords males the ability to earn more money and enjoy greater social esteem.

Neither do physical size or strength differential that is intrinsic in most male-female couples, often used to a domestic abuser's advantage, reliably enhance understanding of same-sex domestic violence. Because they share gender, most same-sex partners also share inherent physical strengths and limitations.

There is a significant power that a same-sex partner holds over the other that is independent of gender or gender role: the power to "out" (disclose sexual orientation). It is known that disclosing this information can and does imperil jobs, friendships, and family ties. It also can expose the disclosed partner to physical harm in the form of "gay bashing," targeting lesbians and gay men for harm because of their actual or perceived alternative sexual orientation. In addition, revealing HIV-positive or AIDS status for some gay males in abusive relationships can cause the loss of health insurance as an added devastating feature.

Other distinctions between opposite-sex and same-sex domestic violence stem from the absence of social sanction of same-sex relationship permanency, in contrast to the expectation of permanency in heterosexual relationships. Often, an abused heterosexual woman is expected to stay with an abusive mate in the interest of preserving the marriage/relationship, often for the sake of children, and to leave only when it becomes intolerable or impermissibly jeopardizes the children. Most communities have domestic violence resources designed to assist these families. Very rarely are such resources available for same-sex couples, even when children are involved, because there is no equivalent expectancy of permanency in, or public support for, same-sex households. Psychologists, social workers, and family therapists are not routinely trained to recognize and treat same-sex domestic violence. Also, heterosexual women in domestic violence shelters often object to the presence of lesbian women in their midst, which renders these shelters a suboptimum choice.

There may be limited resources in some communities specifically for women in abusive same-sex relationships, but they are virtually nonexistent for men, regardless of sexual orientation. Therefore, because same-sex relationships are not viewed as part of the greater social institution of "family" in which society has a vested interest, the violence in same-sex relationships often goes ignored or neglected.

Another difference between opposite-sex and same-sex domestic violence with respect to males is the inability or unwillingness to define what is happening to them as abuse because it is inconsistent with the male identity. All males, gay or heterosexual, are inculcated from birth with the notion that men do not complain about suffering. They may not even see themselves as victimized unless the harm results in serious, permanent physical injury; less serious physical, verbal, and emotional abuse are seldom reported. As a result, violence is inadvertently tolerated by gay men in their relationships, making outreach and preventative efforts exceptionally difficult. This is compounded by the absence of positive role models for gay and lesbian families, which allows "internalized homophobia," or the adoption by gay men and lesbians of society's proscription against same-sex relationships, to go unchecked. Consequently, many victims of same-sex violence are particularly reluctant to report their abuse because they feel they deserve what they get.

In sum, widely accepted gender-based models useful for understanding domestic violence in opposite-sex couple relationships fail to account for all the unique features and dynamics of same-sex couples. Clearly, much more research about the nature and dynamics of same-sex domestic violence is needed. At a minimum, enhanced understanding will better serve efforts to reduce the incidence of domestic violence in all family relationships. The most commonly invoked intervention method, calling on law enforcement, would be the first to benefit.

RESPONSE TO SAME-SEX DOMESTIC VIOLENCE

When a battered spouse calls for help, typically it is the police who first respond to the call and who then necessarily determine whether he or she will find protection. One approach to intervention in domestic violence is arresting one of the parties and providing social and psychological services to the perpetrator. Traditionally, however, police have been reluctant to make arrests for domestic violence because it was viewed as a "family matter" not warranting intrusion by outsiders. Also, domestic violence calls are considered to pose the most danger to responding officers as a result of the unpredictability and extreme tension associated with the incident, which is often compounded by drugs or alcohol. However, when no one is arrested in an incident of domestic violence, perpetrators are twice as likely to reinjure the victim. Consequently, most police departments are now mandated to arrest one or both of the partners.

Society, including law enforcement, has tended to view same-sex domestic violence less as involving a perpetrator and victim and more as involving mutual combatants. Aversive stereotypes that operate to deter law enforcement response include characterizing the violence as mere "cat fights" between women or between two men perceived as effeminate or "sissy." Only in the past 10 years has same-sex violence been included in most states' domestic violence laws. However, homophobia (fear and ignorance about lesbians and gay men) may induce law enforcement officers to react impassively or even adversely to calls of same-sex domestic violence.

It is commonly assumed in the lesbian and gay community that the police cannot be relied on for protection from harm of any sort. This mistrust follows a long history of mistreatment by the police during the time when being lesbian or gay itself was illegal, culminating in a 1969 uprising that occurred outside the Stonewall Bar, frequented by gay men in New York's lower-Manhattan district. (The Stonewall incident marked the beginning of the "gay movement," which ultimately paved the way for states to modify their laws to, among other things, extend domestic violence laws to same-sex couples.) Consequently, law enforcement has acquired a reputation for being adverse to responding appropriately to same-sex domestic violence, not treating it as seriously as opposite-sex domestic violence and minimizing, or even

mocking, the danger involved. This, in turn, reinforces the gay population's fear and mistrust of the police, so that most victims of same-sex domestic violence fear further victimization at the hands of the police, being "outed," or perhaps worst, being ignored and left exposed to retaliatory violence. Thus, access to assistance for same-sex victims of domestic violence may be blocked both by law enforcement's actual history of negative response as well as the couple's own internalization of the gay cultural notion of the police as an adversary.

Other reasons for inability to rely on the police include an often overlooked dilemma faced by noncitizens living in the United States. An abused woman or man in a same-sex relationship who is not a legal resident, or whose immigration status is in question, faces the double threat after reporting the abuse of having to "come out" and risk deportation or denial of reentry. Language and cultural barriers, as well as the absence of specialized legal resources, often complicate the filing of domestic violence charges or defending against them for these individuals.

Furthermore, all gay people who report or are arrested for domestic violence place themselves in the very harsh spotlight of the criminal justice system. It is impossible to proceed without disclosing sexual orientation, which gives rise to vulnerability to further victimization not only by criminal justice system employees and participants but also by the community as a whole. It is not surprising, then, that lesbian and gay couples are much less likely to report domestic violence compared with the population as a whole. Law enforcement and the criminal justice system provide the only mechanism for initiating protection against continuing violence.

Must this Catch-22 persist? Perhaps not. The personal attitudes of police officers need not directly translate into aversive response to same-sex domestic violence, at least in states that require response. One study, in 2002, after California amended its domestic violence law to include same-sex couples, revealed that it is possible for responding officers to elevate duty over homophobia and respond as required by the law. When asked to respond to questions about a scenario of domestic violence in which the sexual orientation of the involved couple was nontraditional, no significant differences were found in how the police officers perceived the scenario. Although this runs counter to common belief, it suggests that the extension of domestic violence laws to same-sex couples can pave the way for equal reliance on law enforcement for help, regardless of the sexual orientation of the involved couple. As Jane Younglove and colleagues (2002) concluded, "Given the other difficulties that same-sex couples face, and given that the gay and lesbian community by itself has not been able to reduce domestic violence, it seems ill advised to continue to engage in combat with even a reluctant ally" (p. 16).

—*Jane A. Younglove and Corey J. Vitello*

See also Batterers and Abusive Partners

Further Reading

Bowers vs. Hardwick, 478 U.S. 186 (1986).

Letellier, P. (1994). Gay and bisexual male domestic violence victimization: Challenges to feminist theory and responses to violence. *Violence and Victims, 9*(2), 95-106.

Moore, K. (2001). *Lesbian, gay, bisexual and transgender domestic violence in 2000.* New York: National Coalition of Anti-Violence Programs.

Younglove, J. A., Kerr, M. G., & Vitello, C. J. (2002). Law enforcement officers' perceptions of same-sex domestic violence: Reason for cautious optimism. *Journal of Interpersonal Violence, 17*(7), 760-772.

DOSS, NANNIE ("GIGGLING GRANDMA"), *See* Poisoners

DRACULA, *See* Serial Murder: International Incidence; Vampires, Werewolves, and Witches

DRUG CARTELS

Drug cartels are composed of independent drug-trafficking organizations that have pooled their resources and elected to cooperate with each other. They are often incorrectly conceived of as single, organized crime groups with thousands of members, wide geographical scope, and vertical control of the drug business from the point of harvest to the point of retail sales on the streets. To the contrary, the cartels are merely associations of many smaller organized crime groups into a loose confederation of business associates. Some of the syndicates in a cartel may produce raw materials. Others may have well-established modalities for transportation. Still others may have money-laundering operations in place or important political and law enforcement connections to facilitate the creation of corrupt relations.

Drug-trafficking groups may decide to enter into a cartel relationship for any number of reasons. Most commonly, smaller, independent syndicates enter into a franchise relationship with a larger, better organized, and more stable syndicate. Another reason for the creation of a drug cartel is to bring together traffickers with differing strengths in the various aspects of the drug trade. In this arrangement, each of the independent syndicates realizes that it has a weakness that can be compensated for by other syndicates. An organization with strong connections to the growers of a particular plant may need to align with another organization possessing skilled chemists to convert that plant into a high-quality drug. Another organization may be skilled in smuggling, and another criminal network may have access to buyers in another country.

Occasionally, independent drug syndicates come together because of a need for highly specialized services. For example, opium-growing warlords in the Golden Triangle (Burma, Laos, Thailand) of Southeast Asia established working relationships with various Chinese Triads because they needed to move their product to markets worldwide and launder their profits, and an adequate financial structure was not available to them. In cases like these, drug cartels provide "references" and contacts for the establishment of contractual arrangements related to specific tasks.

Finally, a more contemporary form of drug cartel operations involves a simple exchange of goods or services exchanged between independent criminal organizations. An example of this is the relationship between Colombian cocaine syndicates and drug-trafficking organizations in Mexico. To move their cocaine into the United States, Colombian groups contract with Mexican organizations, which take half the load they are smuggling as their fee and distribute it to smaller Mexican drug-trafficking organizations in the United States for retail sale.

COLOMBIAN COCAINE CARTELS

Colombian drug-trafficking organizations handle 75% of the world's cocaine. Colombia's role as a cocaine producer is geographically determined. It shares borders with Peru and Bolivia, major coca leaf growers. In addition, Colombia is close to its major cocaine market, the United States, which is only a 2 ½-hour flight from Miami. Finally, Colombia is the only country in South America with both Caribbean and Pacific Ocean coastlines, opening up a variety of options for maritime and air-smuggling routes.

Coca leaves are transported to Colombia from Peru and Bolivia along remote mountain trails to hundreds of locations where the rudimentary process of converting them into coca paste is accomplished. The coca paste is then carried in light aircraft to cocaine-producing facilities in the Colombian interior, where it is processed into cocaine hydrochloride, the white crystalline powder. After being "cut," this is sold to cocaine users.

Colombian cocaine cartels did much of their own smuggling in the 1970s and 1980s, using maritime shipping and both private and commercial aircraft. By the 1990s, however, they had subcontracted the distribution of cocaine to Mexican drug traffickers. The cocaine was moved from Colombia to Mexico, where it was turned over to Mexican organizations for transport to the United States. By the 1990s, most cocaine entering the United States was coming through Mexico. Recently, Colombian drug cartels have made the smuggling process easier by adding chemical compounds to cocaine hydrochloride to produce "black cocaine," which is undetectable by standard chemical tests or drug-sniffing canines.

Some Colombian cartels continue to be active in the United States. These cartels establish "cells" in specific geographic areas, typically structured around familial relations or long-time friendships. This arrangement impedes infiltration attempts by investigators. Cells are structurally compartmentalized, with a well-defined division of labor. Each cell specializes in a different aspect of the cocaine trade in the geographic location in which it is found. Some cells transport drugs, some are responsible for storing cocaine for future sale, and some engage in money laundering and have no contact with the drug itself. Others are involved in the actual wholesale trading of cocaine to retail drug networks. Cells are made up of 10 employees who have no knowledge about the membership, location, or activities of other cells. Cell structure is characterized by a rigid chain of command in which the head of each cell reports to a regional director for the cartel, and only to that individual. The regional director, in turn, reports to a designated individual in Colombia.

Colombian cartels make use of the most sophisticated communications technologies. Particularly important are state-of-the-art encryption devices, which translate communications into indecipherable codes. Encryption technology not only hides information about drug transactions but also obscures financial information related to money laundering.

The Medellin Cartel

The first major Colombian cartel appeared in the mid-1970s, headquartered in Medellin and led by the Ochoa brothers, Carlos Lehder, Pablo Escobar, and Jose Rodriguez Gacha. The Medellin Cartel dominated the cocaine trade in New York and Miami. The name "Medellin Cartel" is somewhat misleading, however. The cartel was never a single drug-trafficking organization, but rather a loose organizational confederation of many drug syndicates operating out of Medellin.

Carlos Lehder introduced the idea of moving cocaine on small private aircraft from a transshipment point. In 1976, Lehder bought a sizable portion of the Bahamian island of Norman's Cay, only 225 miles southeast of Miami. He built an airstrip as a refueling spot for the aircraft that flew cocaine from Colombia and then on to the United States.

The tendency of some of the Medellin Cartel's associates to use violence as a method of dispute settlement eventually led to the cartel's downfall. Cartel members were responsible for the 1984 assassination of Rodrigo Lara Bonilla, Colombia's Minister of Justice, and a subsequent attack on the Colombian Supreme Court. The Colombian government, in response, extradited Lehder to the United States in February 1987. He was convicted of cocaine trafficking and sentenced to 135 years in a federal prison, a sentence that was reduced in return for his cooperation in the prosecution of Panamanian dictator Manuel Noriega. Medellin Cartel violence continued, however, marked by the 1989 bombing of an Avianca commercial airliner that killed 110 people, including two police informants. In addition, Pablo Escobar also placed bounties of $1,000 to $3,000 on police officers in Colombia. In June 1991, Escobar turned himself in to Colombian authorities but escaped confinement in July 1992. In December 1993, after a nationwide manhunt, Escobar was shot to death by Colombian police at a residence in Medellin.

The Cali Cartel

In the 1980s, cocaine trafficking groups based in Cali, a city 200 miles south of Medellin, gained prominence in the cocaine market. The Cali Cartel was not a single organizational entity, but a confederation of syndicates sharing resources and cooperating with each other. Cali Cartel members shunned publicity, avoided violence, and posed as legitimate businessmen. They used sophisticated business techniques to manage their operations and avoid arrest. Thousands of contract employees were used as surrogates to handle the actual cocaine trafficking. Every aspect of the business was insulated from other aspects.

The leaders of the Cali Cartel included the Rodriguez-Orejuela brothers, Jose Santacruz-Londono, "Pacho" Herrera-Buitrago, and Victor Julio Patino-Fomeque. Several Cali leaders were under indictment in the United States in the 1990s, but the Colombian constitution forbade their extradition. Under pressure from the Clinton administration, the Colombians used information developed by U.S. investigations to indict the Cali Cartel's leadership in Colombia.

Colombian Heroin Syndicates

One reason that the Colombian cartels passed off much of their wholesaling business of cocaine to Mexican drug organizations was the increasing Colombian role in the production and sale of heroin. Starting in the late 1980s and increasing in the 1990s, Colombian cartels have expanded into the growing and smuggling of high-grade heroin, supplying 65% of the U.S. heroin market. By growing their own opium, Colombian drug organizations have reduced their reliance on Peruvian and Bolivian coca leaf suppliers. The opium poppy grows exceptionally well along the eastern slopes of the Central Andean Mountains in Colombia. Opium growers in Colombia work under contract to a drug cartel. The cartel supplies the growers with seeds and agricultural supplies, and the grower agrees to sell the opium gum to the cartels. Chemists process the opium gum into morphine base and then into heroin. Because heroin is smuggled in small quantities, the methods for smuggling are virtually unlimited. Some smugglers use hollowed-out shoes or sew the drug into the lining of their clothes, some hide it in other shipments of commercial goods, and others swallow it after wrapping it in condoms. The Colombian heroin trade is dominated by a series of new, smaller drug cartels operating independently of the cocaine cartels.

Contemporary Colombian Cartels

In the new millennium, the Cali Cartel no longer dominates the cocaine market. Law enforcement efforts against the Medellin and Cali Cartels had the effect of further segmenting and decentralizing the drug trade in Colombia, making it harder than ever to control. A number of veteran drug traffickers who had operated under the aegis of the Cali Cartel have become significant powers in their own right.

As of 2002, much of the cocaine traffic in Colombia is centered in the northern Valle del Cauca region, of which Cali is the capital city. Cocaine traffickers in this region operate independently of each other and have passed some of the major responsibilities for cocaine smuggling and wholesaling on to drug-trafficking syndicates in Mexico. Among the new drug organizations in this region are the Henao-Montoya syndicate, the Montoya-Sanchez organization, and the Urdinola-Grajles network. These groups are closely allied with right-wing death squads and paramilitary units in the region under the control of Carlos Castano.

In Cali, Victor Patino-Fomeque, a Cali Cartel leader, continues to direct a drug syndicate from prison. The Cali-based Herrera-Vasquez organization moves large quantities of cocaine to the United States via Central America and Mexico. The Herrera organization also launders drug money destined for Colombia through Panama and Mexico. In Bogota, "Juvenal" Bernal-Madrigal provides transportation services for Mexican Colombian traffickers. He is responsible for multi-ton shipments of cocaine and the transportation of large amounts of drug money from Colombia to Mexico. Finally, in Medellin, the Ochoa brothers are also back in the cocaine business.

MEXICAN DRUG CARTELS

Mexican drug syndicates have been trafficking marijuana and heroin for decades. In the 1990s, they entered the cocaine market, first as surrogates for Colombian syndicates and then as partners. Mexico's 2,000-mile border with the United States, much of which is in isolated rural areas with rugged terrain, makes it an obvious transshipment site for drugs. Its extensive coastal and inland mountain systems create perfect havens for growing marijuana and opium poppies. In addition, there is an enormous flow of legitimate commerce across the U.S.-Mexican border every day. By 1999, 295 million people, 88 million automobiles, and 4.5 million trucks and railcars were entering the United States from Mexico. That volume of commerce creates many opportunities for drug smuggling. Mexico is also a haven for drug trafficking because of widespread corruption in its law enforcement and judicial systems and the lack of resources available to Mexican police.

In the 1980s, Mexican drug syndicates acted as transshipment agents for Colombian organizations. By the 1990s, Mexican traffickers were paid 50% of each shipment. This arrangement allowed them to enter the wholesale cocaine business. By 1995, Mexican cartels dominated the wholesale cocaine market in the midwestern and western United States.

Mexican cartels are compartmentalized and have a strong chain of command emanating from Mexico. The cartels have surrogates throughout the United States that manage day-to-day activities. Unlike other drug syndicates, which have insulated their home base operations by granting greater autonomy to cells in foreign countries, Mexican syndicates still retain a system whereby Mexican-based leaders provide specific instructions to their foreign-based operatives on issues such as warehousing drugs, transportation services, and money laundering.

Two thirds of the cocaine sold in the United States is transshipped from Mexico. Cocaine comes into Mexico from Colombia by air or boat and is transported by truck to repositories in Juarez or Guadalajara. From these repositories, cocaine is driven across the border, most commonly to Los Angeles, Chicago, and Phoenix. Surrogates in those cities have contractual arrangements with trucking companies to move the cocaine across the country to smaller warehousing facilities closer to the point of sale. Individuals working in these "stash houses" guard the supplies and make arrangements for their distribution by wholesalers.

Mexican cartels also play a large role in the U.S. methamphetamine market. They engage in the large-scale production of methamphetamine, operating clandestine laboratories in Mexico and California capable of producing hundreds of pounds of the drug.

Mexican heroin makes up about 29% of the U.S. heroin supply. The cartels produce 6 metric tons of heroin a year for sale in the United States. Because of crude refining methods, Mexican heroin is frequently

dark in color and sticky or gummy, resulting in its name, "black tar" heroin.

Like many criminal organizations in the early stages of establishing control of an illicit market, Mexican syndicates engage in widespread violence. Examples include the 1998 killings of 22 people in Baja California Norte carried out by rival drug traffickers; and 300 murders took place in Tijuana in 1998, 75% of which were attributable to drug-trafficking disputes (DEA, 2002).

Major Mexican cartels include the Arellano-Felix organization, based in Tijuana, which moves multi-ton quantities of cocaine and marijuana and significant amounts of heroin and methamphetamine. The Caro-Quintero syndicate is based in Sonora and specializes in trafficking in cocaine and marijuana. The Juarez Cartel is heavily involved in the trafficking of cocaine, heroin, and marijuana. The Amezcua-Contreras organization is based in Guadalajara. It is a massive methamphetamine-trafficking syndicate and a major supplier of precursor chemicals to other methamphetamine syndicates. This syndicate controls much of the legitimate trade in chemicals in Mexico as well.

DOMINICAN DRUG ORGANIZATIONS

The Dominican Republic is one of the poorest countries in the world. Dominican drug traffickers began as retail cocaine dealers in emigrant communities in the United States. The most famous of these communities was the Washington Heights area of New York City. In the mid-1970s, Dominican immigrants moved into this community and began handling Colombian-supplied cocaine. Soon, their trafficking activities had spread into New Jersey, Connecticut, and some of the affluent suburbs of New York.

In the 1990s, Dominican traffickers entered the wholesale cocaine market by offering Colombian suppliers a better deal than Mexican syndicates, a smuggling fee of only 25% of the load. Using drug distribution systems already established in emigrant communities, two major Dominican drug syndicates emerged. One, operating out of the Dominican Republic, provides "stash sites" for cocaine shipments. Cocaine is transported into the Dominican Republic in small boats or by airdrops. Dominican traffickers then smuggle the drugs into Puerto Rico in boats, repackage the drugs, and ship them to the continental United States in containerized maritime cargo ships or on routine commercial air flights. Once in New York City, the cocaine is distributed by a second syndicate of ethnic Dominicans that operates along the East Coast. Dominican syndicates rotate members in the United States. Typically, they move operatives in for a 2-year stay and then retire them to the island.

SOUTHEAST ASIAN HEROIN CARTELS

The opium-growing regions of Burma and Laos have made Southeast Asia the second-largest source region for the world's supply of heroin. Cultivating the opium poppy is still the economic mainstay of the many hill tribes living in isolated, rural, impoverished areas of Southeast Asia. Heroin is often smuggled on fishing boats down the Gulf of Thailand and then transferred to the major international maritime shipping centers of Singapore and Hong Kong. In addition to Thailand, Cambodia is being increasingly used as a transshipment route for heroin.

Massive criminal organizations, virtually immune from law enforcement interference because of widespread corruption in the governments and business communities of Southeast Asia, have been able to work in close collusion with police, the military, politicians, and businessmen to spawn a massive drug-and-sex trade empire in the region. Drug trade profits are the source for most new commercial and business investments in the region.

Heroin production is dominated by ethnic drug-trafficking armies operating mostly in Burma's remote opium-producing region. The drug-trafficking armies had begun as insurgent groups, often supported by the CIA. Over the years, however, these armies have primarily engaged in heroin trafficking and in other illicit and lucrative economic activities, including gem smuggling, illegal logging, and timber smuggling. As a result of its continuing political repression, the military regime in Burma has negotiated treaties with most of these armies, which allows the regime to fight any social or political changes in the country in return for free rein for drug traffickers.

Ethnic Chinese criminal organizations and some Thai criminal networks act as brokers, financial backers, and transporters in the Southeast Asian heroin trade. Operating out of major regional commercial centers in Bangkok, Hong Kong, Singapore, and Taiwan and using a wide array of interchangeable front companies and legitimate businesses, Chinese and Thai criminal networks also arrange financing and transportation of drugs, routing drugs through many different ports, largely by commercial shipping, to their final destinations.

—*Gary W. Potter*

See also DRUG TRADE; ORGANIZED CRIME: TRANSNATIONAL

Further Reading

Drug Enforcement Administration. (2002, July). *Mexico country brief.* Washington, DC: Author.

Eskridge, C. (1998). The Mexican cartels: A challenge for the 21st century. *Criminal Organizations, 12,* 1, 2.

Jackall, R. (1997). *Wild cowboys: Urban marauders and the forces of order.* Cambridge, MA: Harvard University Press.

Kline, H. (1995). *Colombia: Democracy under assault.* Boulder, CO: Westview.

Renard, R. (1996). *The Burmese connection: Illegal drugs and the making of the Golden Triangle.* Boulder, CO: L. Rienner Publishers.

Schaffer, E. (1996). Mexico's internal state conflict over the war on drugs. *Criminal Organizations, 10,* 3.

Zabludoff, S. (1998). Colombian narcotics organizations as business enterprises. *Transnational Organized Crime, 3,* 2.

DRUG COURTS, *See* PREVENTION OF CRIME AND VIOLENT BEHAVIOR

THE DRUG TRADE

DRUG TRAFFICKING IN THE 21ST CENTURY

Most of the cocaine, heroin, MDMA (also known as "Ecstasy"), and methamphetamine consumed in the United States is smuggled into the United States by international criminal organizations from source countries in Latin America, Asia, and Europe. Cocaine consumption in the United States, the world's most important and largest market, has declined somewhat since its peak in the late 1980s but has remained relatively stable for most of the last decade. Cocaine is produced in the South American Andean countries of Colombia, Peru, and Bolivia. Colombia is the source of an estimated 90% of the cocaine supply in the U.S. market (DEA, 2002).

Fueled by high-purity, low-cost heroin introduced into the U.S. market by Southeast Asian and Colombian traffickers, heroin use in the United States increased significantly in the early to mid-1990s. The purity of heroin currently available in the United States is higher than ever. Southwest Asia's "Golden Crescent" (Afghanistan and Pakistan) and Southeast Asia's "Golden Triangle" (Burma, Laos, and Thailand) are the world's major sources of heroin for the international market, but Colombia is the largest source for the U.S. heroin market and Mexico the second largest. Colombia and Mexico account for about 75% of the U.S. heroin market, with heroin from Southeast Asia making up most of the remainder (U.S. Department of State, 2002).

The use of synthetic drugs in the United States, many of which come from abroad, increased markedly in the last decade of the 20th century. Beginning in the 1990s, there was a dramatic surge in the worldwide production and consumption of synthetic drugs, particularly amphetamine-type stimulants, including methamphetamine and Ecstasy. The majority of methamphetamine available in the U.S. market is produced by Mexican traffickers operating in the United States or in Mexico. The Drug Enforcement Administration (DEA) estimates that Mexican trafficking groups control 70% to 90% of the U.S. methamphetamine supply. There has been a significant increase in methamphetamine production in Southeast Asia in recent years. Although little has found its way to the U.S. market from Southeast Asia, increasing quantities of "Thai Tabs" have been seized in the western United States.

Most of the Ecstasy in the U.S. market is produced in the Netherlands. Amsterdam, Brussels, Frankfurt, and Paris are major European hubs for transshipping Ecstasy to foreign markets. The Dominican Republic, Suriname, and Curacao are used as transshipment points for U.S.-bound Ecstasy from Europe, and Mexican and South American traffickers are also becoming involved in the trade.

Marijuana remains the most widely used and readily available illicit drug in the United States. Although most of the marijuana consumed in the United States comes from domestic sources, including both outdoor and indoor cannabis cultivation, a significant share of the U.S. market demand is met by marijuana grown in Mexico, with lesser amounts coming from Jamaica, Colombia, and Canada. Very little of the cannabis grown by other major producers—including Morocco,

Lebanon, Afghanistan, Thailand, and Cambodia—comes to the United States.

International drug-trafficking organizations have extensive networks of suppliers, front companies, and businesses to facilitate narcotics smuggling and laundering of illicit proceeds. As mentioned, Colombian and Mexican trafficking organizations dominate the drug trade in the Western Hemisphere. In the Asian source regions, heroin production is dominated by large trafficking organizations, but the networks smuggling heroin from Asia are more diffuse. Asian heroin shipments typically change hands among criminal organizations as the drug is smuggled to markets in the United States and elsewhere.

The evolution of the international drug trade has included greater involvement by a growing number of players and more worldwide trafficking of synthetic drugs. Criminal organizations whose principal activities focus more on traditional contraband smuggling, racketeering enterprises, and fraud schemes have become increasingly involved in international drug trafficking. Although they generally are not narcotics producers themselves, many organized crime groups—including those from Russia, China, Italy, and Albania—have cultivated and expanded ties to drug-trafficking organizations to obtain cocaine, heroin, and synthetic drugs for their own distribution markets and trafficking networks. Traffickers from many countries increasingly are eschewing traditional preferences for criminal partnerships with single ethnic groups and collaborating in the purchase, transportation, and distribution of illegal drugs.

Taking advantage of more open borders and modern telecommunications technology, international drug-trafficking organizations are sophisticated and flexible in their operations. They adapt quickly to law enforcement pressures by finding new methods for smuggling drugs, new transshipment routes, and new mechanisms to launder money. In many of the major cocaine- and heroin-producing and transit countries, drug traffickers have acquired significant power and wealth through the use of violence, intimidation, and payoffs of corrupt officials.

STRUCTURE OF DRUG OPERATIONS

The trade in illegal drugs represents the most complex organizational configuration found in organized crime. A large number of criminal organizations (probably in the tens of thousands) are engaged in the distribution of illegal drugs in the United States. In addition, the drug business is highly segmented into importing, wholesaling, and retailing operations, all handled by different syndicates moving the drugs down a long vertical chain.

In a very simple outline, the drug trade operates as follows: The drug wholesaler purchases the drug from an importer. This transaction requires that the individuals at the top of the wholesale organization have sufficient liquid capital to make discount buys. The importer and the wholesaler represent different organizations or syndicates. The arrangement between the importer and the wholesaler may require the creation of an additional position if the wholesaler, in an attempt to hold down costs, agrees to incur the risk of moving the contraband from its point of entry to his or her sales area. In this case, "mules" or "runners" are paid by the trip to physically move the drug to the distribution points. Once the drugs have arrived in the area in which they will be distributed, the wholesaler again uses mules to deliver them to the retailing organizations that have purchased them. The retailers either pay cash up front (by far the preferred method of doing business) or take the commodity on consignment, agreeing to pay after retail sales are completed. The latter arrangement is obviously far riskier and often requires that mules also serve as collectors and be appropriately compensated for the added responsibility.

Importers bring large quantities of cocaine or heroin into the United States. They are responsible for making arrangements for the purchase of the drugs at their points of origin: for heroin, probably the Golden Triangle (Laos, Burma, Thailand), the Golden Crescent (Afghanistan, Iran, Pakistan), or Mexico, and for cocaine, Bolivia, Colombia, or Peru. The importer must employ highly skilled smugglers to transport the drugs and coordinate shipments. Most importing syndicates calculate a certain amount of loss of inventory to law enforcement interdiction efforts. Once the drug arrives in the United States, the importer's role is finished, and the wholesaler takes charge of the operation.

Wholesalers receive imported drugs of high degrees of purity, and one of the first things drug wholesalers do is dilute the drugs they have purchased. This means that the drug is mixed with a variety of substances, such as mannite, lactose, or quinine, in the case of heroin, often doubling, tripling, or quadrupling the actual volume and weight of the drug mixture. In the case of heroin and cocaine, wholesalers usually dilute the drug to a level of purity of

A Colombian army soldier places cocaine packs confiscated in the jungle on April 12, 2001. The troops are part of operation "Black Cat" that aims to sever the links between leftist rebels of the Revolutionary Armed forces of Colombia (FARC) and Colombia's booming cocaine trade. The drug trade leads to the deaths of many people every year who are involved in the use, distribution, and manufacturing of illegal drugs.

Source: Copyright © Reuters NewMedia Inc. / CORBIS.

about 25% before selling it to retail trafficking organizations, which actually move the substance to customers.

Cocaine and heroin wholesalers must go to great lengths to conceal their criminal activities. The organization must be highly mobile, often without a permanent business address. Communication must be in person, through pager systems that allow messages to be exchanged from public telephones, or through expensive and highly sophisticated encryption technologies that translate messages into indecipherable codes. The organization must provide a buffer between those wholesaling large quantities of drugs and the highly visible street dealers. No evidentiary trail linking the pusher and the supplier can be tolerated. There can be no payroll checks or inventories. The wholesaler then passes the drug along to a variety of retail or "street" syndicates, usually in ounce quantities. The street syndicate once again reduces the purity level of the drug, to 10% to 15%, and repackages it in "bundles," in the case of heroin, and grams, in the case of cocaine, for sale to users.

Retail drug networks can be described in various ways. A good exemplar for how the retail trade works are street-level heroin retailers in Detroit. There are three primary roles in these syndicates. At the top level, the "crew boss" manages the street syndicate, obtains heroin from a wholesaler, supplies it to "runners," and collects money for the drug sales from the runners. Runners, at the second level, are salespersons who work a specific location in a neighborhood (a corner, a street, a particular building) and sell the heroin to users. They carry very little heroin with them, preferring to return to the crew boss frequently for additional supplies. Possessing only small amounts of the drug discourages potential robberies and minimizes product attrition in the case of police interference. "Guns," the third participant in a street syndicate, are heavily armed members who set up surveillance close to the actual points of sale and provide security for the runners. They not only watch out for police but also intervene if there is an attempted robbery and control other disorders that threaten the conduct of business. The average crew boss can earn as much as $1,500 a week, and the average runner as much as $800.

VIOLENCE AND THE DRUG TRADE

The profits realized from the sales of illegal drugs are so high that competition becomes intense and turf wars result. This is particularly true in the opening phase of a drug market. For example, considerable violence was associated with the initial street markets in crack cocaine during the mid-1980s. By the early 1990s, those markets had stabilized, and violence had receded. The same pattern is clearly noted in the history of Prohibition, in which early illicit liquor markets were marked by widespread violence, which was replaced within 3 or 4 years by relative peace and a high degree of cooperation between bootlegging syndicates. The importance of the illegal status of drugs in creating violence-prone drug markets was clearly established in studies of the crack market in New York City. The researchers found that 85% of "crack-related" crimes were the direct result of market-related issues, primarily territorial disputes among crack dealers (Salekin & Alexander, 1991).

Researchers analyzed homicides in New York in which cocaine or crack use had played a role and identified five specific types of relationships between drugs and murder:

1. *Psychopharmacological* homicides are murders in which the ingestion of a drug or withdrawal symptoms related to addiction causes individuals to become angry, aggressive, irrational, or violent, resulting in them committing murders or being the victims of killings. This relationship is the one usually thought of when the term "drug-related crime" is used.

2. *Economic-compulsive* homicide results from situations in which a drug user engages in a violent crime to obtain money with which to buy drugs. Illicit drug users, particularly those who have developed addictions to drugs such as heroin, do commit crimes such as robbery, burglary, prostitution, and drug dealing as a means of raising funds to support their drug habits. However, these crimes are rarely violent and rarely result in homicide. In fact, in 1999, only 13.3% of prison inmates reported that they had committed their crimes to raise money for drug purchases. In addition, only 11.5% of those inmates who had committed violent crimes reported that they were linked to drugs (Rasmusseen & Benson, 1994).

3. *Systemic homicides* are instances of drug dealers using violence as a competitive business strategy in the drug black market. Prime examples are competition over turf and infringement of street brand names for drugs.

4. *Multidimensional homicides* are murders that contain multiple events, making it difficult to discern what really precipitated the violent acts.

5. *Homicides with drug-related dimensions* are murders in which the perpetrator and/or the victim are using drugs but reasons other than drugs were considered the primary explanation for the murder.

The researchers concluded that the psychopharmacological model, the model typically identified with the concept of drug-related crime, and the economic-compulsive model, also identified with such crime, rarely applied in cases of murder. Rather, it was competition in the drug business, or systemic homicides, that caused most allegedly drug-related homicides.

In Los Angeles, police discovered a similar relationship, in other words, that turf wars between street gangs that were related to drive-by shootings in that city were not caused by the ingestion of drugs. Rather, they were caused by the exigencies of the illegal cocaine market and the profits to be realized in that market. Another study of New York City homicides estimated that 40% of the 414 drug-related homicides studied were the result of business competition in the drug market and, once again, not the consumption or effects of the drugs themselves (*New York Times*,

1992). In 1999, only 4.9% of violent crime victims in the United States reported that their assailants had been using drugs. Similarly, in 1999, the Uniform Crime Reporting Program of the FBI reported that only 4.5% of the 12,658 homicides in which circumstances were known were drug related.

—*Gary W. Potter*

Further Reading

Drug Enforcement Administration. (2002). *Changing dynamics of cocaine production in the Andean region.* Washington, DC: Author.

FBI says Los Angeles gang has drug cartel ties. (1992, January 10). *New York Times,* A12.

Goldstein, P., Brownstein, H., Ryan, P., & Belluci, P. (1997). Crack and homicide in New York City: A case study in the epidemiology of violence. In C. Reinarman & H. Levine (Eds.), *Crack in America: Demon drugs and social justice* (pp. 113-130). Berkeley: University of California Press.

Lyman, M., & Potter, G. (1998). *Drugs in society: Causes, concepts and control* (3rd ed.). Cincinnati, OH: Anderson.

Rasmussen, D., & Benson, B. (1994). *The economic anatomy of a drug war.* Lanham, MD: Rowman & Littlefield.

Salekin, R. T., & Alexander, B. K. (1991). Cocaine and crime. In A. S. Trebach & K. B. Zeese (Eds.), *New frontiers in drug policy* (pp. 105-111). Washington, DC: Drug Policy Foundation.

United Nations. (2000). *World drug report, 2000.* New York: Author.

U.S. Department of State. Bureau for International Narcotics and Law Enforcement Affairs. (2000). *International narcotics control strategy report, 1999.* Washington, DC: Author.

Wisotsky, S. (1986). *Breaking the impasse in the war on drugs.* New York: Greenwood.

DRUNK DRIVING, *See* ROAD RAGE; VEHICULAR HOMICIDE

DROWNING BY FORCE, *See* METHODS OF MURDER

DUPONT, JOHN; *See:* NOT GUILTY BY REASON OF INSANITY (NGRI)

DYATHANASIA, *See* EUTHANASIA; KEVORKIAN, JACK

E

ELDER ABUSE

Elder abuse is defined as an illegal act that harms an individual over the age of 65. It includes the following, separately or in combination: physical abuse, emotional or psychological abuse, sexual abuse, neglect, abandonment, and financial or material exploitation. Although this age group is one of the least victimized in our society, the injuries they suffer are severe and often life threatening. Because elder abuse is most often perpetrated by a family member, friend, care provider, or one known to the elder victim, it is much less likely to be reported. It is estimated that only one sixth of the 2.5 million cases of elder abuse annually are reported (National Center on Elder Abuse, 1998).

STATISTICAL OVERVIEW

1. There are approximately 2.5 million incidents of elder abuse each year, but only 1 in 6 incidents are reported.
2. Individuals over 80 years old are abused or neglected at a rate 2 or 3 times higher than those under 80.
3. In almost 90% of the abuse incidents with a known perpetrator (the majority of the cases), the perpetrator is a family member; 60% are adult children or spouses.
4. Almost half of all elder abuse (48.7%) is neglect; 35.4% is emotional/psychological abuse; 30.2% is financial/material exploitation; 25.6% is physical abuse; abandonment (3.6%) and sexual abuse (0.3%) are the least common types.

5. Seventy-five percent of the victims of elder abuse suffer from physical frailty and have great difficulty caring for or defending themselves.
6. The majority of the states have mandatory reporting laws for specified professionals; the most common elder abuse reporters are physicians and health care providers, family members and relatives, and other services providers (National Center on Elder Abuse, 1998).

DEFINITION OF TERMS

Physical abuse: the use of force that may result in bodily injury, physical pain, or impairment. It includes violent acts such as striking, hitting, beating, shoving, shaking, slapping, kicking, pinching, and burning.

Emotional or psychological abuse: the infliction of anguish, pain, or distress through verbal or nonverbal acts. It includes verbal assaults, insults, threats, intimidation, humiliations, harassment, social isolation, silent treatment, or treating the older person like an infant.

Sexual abuse: nonconsensual sexual contact of any kind with an elderly person. It includes unwanted touching, rape, sodomy, coerced nudity, or sexually explicit photographing.

Neglect: the refusal or failure to fulfill any part of a person's obligation or duties to an elder. It includes failure of fiduciary responsibilities to provide care or failure to provide life necessities such as food, water, clothing, shelter, personal hygiene, medicine, comfort, and/or safety.

Abandonment: the desertion of an elderly person by an individual who has assumed responsibility for providing care or who has physical custody. Desertion can take place in any private or public facility.

Financial or material exploitation: the illegal or improper use of an elder's funds, property, or assets. It includes cashing the person's check without permission, forging the person's signature, misusing or stealing the person's money or property, coercing or deceiving the person into signing any document, and the improper use of guardianship or power of attorney.

TYPES OF CRIMES

Sexual Assault

Approximately 683,000 women are raped annually in the United States; 1% of these victims are over the age of 65 (Kilpatrick, Edmunds, & Seymour, 1992). As with other crimes, even though the number victimized may be small, the consequences of rape for elderly women are drastic and often life threatening. Elderly rape victims often suffer much more physical damage due to their frailty, including damage to the vaginal lining, infections, bruising, cuts that heal very slowly, or broken or crushed hips or pelvis due to brittleness caused by the aging process.

The psychological trauma caused by rape can be overwhelming. Most rape victims have tremendous guilt and blame, but self-blaming can be even more pronounced with elderly victims. The loss of dignity at this stage of life when an individual expects to be respected and nurtured is even more devastating than with younger rape victims. Feelings of shame and embarrassment that others will find out also decrease the chances that an elderly woman will approach others for assistance and help and increase the psychological stress of the crime, which makes that individual even more vulnerable to further physical maladies. Many elderly victims of rape are also isolated from family and friends, either because they have been placed in a nursing home, the family has moved away, or friends may not be in good health.

These factors often cause elderly victims to have a much more difficult time recovering from the assault both physically and psychologically.

Domestic Violence

The elder victims of domestic violence have begun to receive much attention. Many national organizations, including the American Association of Retired Persons, have made it one of their top priorities. Studies in this area, thus far, are sparse because age has seldom been a salient research factor in domestic violence.

Despite the lack of research, several patterns (or types) of elderly domestic violence have emerged in recent years:

1. Spousal abuse that has been present and continued since early in the marriage.
2. Spousal abuse that began late in life although not present earlier in the marriage. This abuse can be exacerbated by numerous age-related conditions: retirement, increased dependency, diminished physical abilities, or diminished mental capacity.
3. Spousal abuse in a newly married elderly couple. These marriages often combine financial exploitation with physical abuse.
4. Spousal abuse of widows, previously abused by their husbands, by their adult children.

Elderly victims of domestic violence, although smaller in number than other age groups, are at greater risk due to their frailty and lack of access to adequate services. There has been a debate in the field of domestic violence as to the causes of this lack of access. One perspective places the blame on the victim: Social norms from a previous age may prevail in older women; for example, asking for help is a sign of weakness, and divorce or separation are not acceptable alternatives; she may be dependent on her spouse financially; she may feel too old to start a new life; and her adult children may not be supportive of her leaving.

Another prevalent perspective indicates a service delivery problem. There are almost no shelters for this specific age group, no specialized training in the issues of the elderly or the specific concerns of the elderly domestic violence victim, and few agencies have advocates designated specifically for this population. With the aging of the "baby boomers" and the growth of this age group, service delivery will need to be addressed in the near future. This focus would include elderly developmental issues, access issues, privacy issues, medical staffing, age-appropriate peer groups, community outreach programs, and training on age-related issues.

Physical Assault and Homicide

Elderly crime victims are the least likely to be physically injured during a crime, but when they are injured, they are more likely to suffer serious injuries than other crime victims—that is, twice as likely as others to be seriously injured and hospitalized. The murder of elderly individuals generally occurs during the commission of another crime, and they are much more likely to be murdered by strangers than are any other age group. The fact that they often are unable to resist and protect themselves contributes to the seriousness and lethal nature of the crimes perpetrated against them.

In addition to the overall serious nature of their injuries, the aftermath of an assault includes a pervasive, continuous fear in elderly individuals, compounded by the lack of an extended social support network. Often, victim advocates are not aware of the special needs of elderly individuals. Used to dealing with younger victims, they may provide their usual services and then leave, often telling the victim to call for further help—but the elderly victim, not wanting to be a burden, often does not call them back for assistance.

Burglary

As isolation increases due to many aspects of the aging process, the world of the elderly becomes their homes. Retirement often leads to diminished visits to and from friends and family, and other physical activities become more difficult. Thus, the majority of elderly victims are harmed near or in their homes.

The elderly are not necessarily burglarized at a higher rate than other age groups, nor is the monetary amount of their losses higher; however, losses through burglary often affect the elderly much more than other groups. The long-term sentimental value of the lost objects can cause continuous rumination and depression in older victims, which decreases their ability to care for themselves. The loss of even a small amount of money from their fixed income may mean they must go without food, clothing, medication, or other necessities. Even when they have insurance, large deductibles on older items may mean they simply cannot replace them.

Because of their fear of being revictimized and their inability to protect themselves, the elderly are much more likely to relocate following a burglary. This added disruption makes them even more vulnerable to various stress-related illnesses.

Fraud

Fraud occurs "when a person or business intentionally deceives another with promises of goods, services, or financial benefits that do not exist or were never intended to be provided." Fraud victims experience an extreme personal violation that causes them to distrust their own judgment, distrust others, and completely question their worldviews. Both public knowledge and lack of it can decrease the possibility that an elderly victim of fraud will ask for help. Their financial security may be tenuous for months, sometimes years. Their guilt is increased when their families' financial viability is also destroyed. For an elderly victim, in addition to the increased embarrassment of being an "older and wiser" person who was victimized, a fixed income decreases his or her options in managing the financial loss and can lead to the added trauma of the loss of independence.

A major difference between burglary and fraud and the other common violent crimes mentioned is that compensation and services are available for the victims of violent crime, but not for property crimes. Recent Victims of Crime Act (VOCA) Guidelines from the Office for Victims of Crime (OVC) do not provide compensation for losses, but do make it possible for fraud victims to receive certain services: the immediate emotional and physical needs of an elderly victim, reimbursement for counseling services and support groups, credit counseling and income management services, and the expenses of making a restitution case can be covered by VOCA funds.

—*Steven D. Walker*

See also BATTERERS AND ABUSIVE PARTNERS; FAMILY VIOLENCE; RAPE; ROBBERY

Further Reading

Jerin, R., & Moriarty, L. (1998). *Victims of crime.* Chicago: Nelson-Hall.

Kilpatrick, D. G., Edmunds, C., & Seymour, A. (1992). *Rape in America: A report to the nation.* Arlington, VA: National Center for Victims of Crime; Charleston, SC: Medical University of South Carolina, Crime Victims Research and Treatment Center.

National Center on Elder Abuse, American Public Human Services Association. (1998, September). *The national elder abuse incidence study 1996: Final report.* Washington, DC: U.S. Department of Health and Human Services, Administration for Children and Families and the Administration on Aging.

Nerenberg, L. (1996). *Older battered women: Integrating aging and domestic violence services.* Washington, DC: National Center on Elder Abuse.

Nerenberg, L. (1999). *Forgotten victims of elder financial crime and abuse.* Washington, DC: National Center on Elder Abuse.

Torres-Gil, F. (1997). The social context of aging. *Understanding and combating elder abuse in minority communities.* Washington, DC: National Center on Elder Abuse.

Wallace, H. (1998). *Victimology: Legal, psychological, and social perspectives.* Boston: Allyn & Bacon.

ENURESIS, *See* MacDonald Triad

EPINEPHRINE, *See* Poisoners; Poisoning: Medical Settings

EROTOPHONOPHILIA, *See* Lust Murder; Paraphilia

ETHNIC CLEANSING

Ethnic cleansing, as a deliberate process of murdering minority groups of people so that land and/or wealth may be wrongfully taken, is probably as old as human history. It has been perpetrated in the name of nationalism and patriotism for centuries, but according to the David Levinson, the term *ethnic cleansing* seeped into the contemporary vernacular around 1988, when it was first used in reference to a localized conflict in Azerbaijan. There, local Azeris in Ngorno-Karabakh were "cleansing" the area of Armenians. The term received international exposure in 1992 when journalists cited the phrase to describe atrocities perpetrated in the devolving state of Yugoslavia, where culturally dominate Serbs "cleansed" various areas of Serbia of Muslim minority Bosnians and Croats. According to some reports, the Serbian-controlled Yugoslavia military drove 700,000 ethnic minorities from their homes in Bosnia, forcibly relocated another 600,000 persons, killed an unknown number, perhaps in the tens of thousands, and dumped their bodies in mass and unmarked graves.

The Serbs resurrected the tactic of mass rape of women as a tool of ethnic terror. In some places, virtual concentration camps were established in which Muslim girls and women were imprisoned and systematically and routinely raped by groups of Serbian soldiers, police, and other officials as a method of breaking down minority resistance to the Serbs, and as a way of demoralizing the confined. Simultaneously, while the women were herded into camps, men and boys between the ages of 15 and 50 were dragged from homes and taken in groups of differing sizes to a variety of locations and never seen again, leading many international investigators to look for forensic remains in mass graves, some of which were detected only by satellite photographs.

The most egregious and notorious example of ethnic cleansing surfaced in the 20th century, with the Nazi practice during World War II of targeting Jews, gypsies, the mentally deficient, and physically infirm for government-sponsored and systematic extermination. The killing of more than 6 million persons, confined and executed in concentration camps, stands as an indelible indictment of man's inhumanity to man.

The Armenian genocide in World War I similarly stands as a particularly odious episode. The Turks of the Ottoman Empire, allied with the Germans and Austro-Hungarians in fighting the British and the French, killed approximately 1.5 million Armenians in 1915, as a way of securing eastern Turkey as a Muslim state at the expense of the Christian (Greek Orthodox) Armenians.

Ethnic cleansing has been responsible for the elimination of entire tribes and/or ethnic groups of people. Biblical writers recount episodes of Israelite and Philistine massacres, and Roman legions had few qualms about annihilating groups of opposing civilians. Spanish conquistadors savaged indigenous Andean tribes in their pursuit of imperial treasure, and American settlers pushing westward, backed by the technology of the U.S. Army, did not hesitate to permanently remove Native Americans from lands the settlers wished to occupy. In the 1960s, Ugandan dictator Idi Amin expelled all Ugandans of South Asian origin from Uganda and effectively "cleansed" Uganda of non-Africans.

William A. Schabas's monumental work *Genocide in International Law* cites conventions and treaties that protect minorities and endangered persons. The word *genocide* comes from the Greek word for group or tribe *(genos)* and the Latin word for killing *(cide)*. Under the 1948 United Nations Convention on Genocide, there are five definitional distinctions,

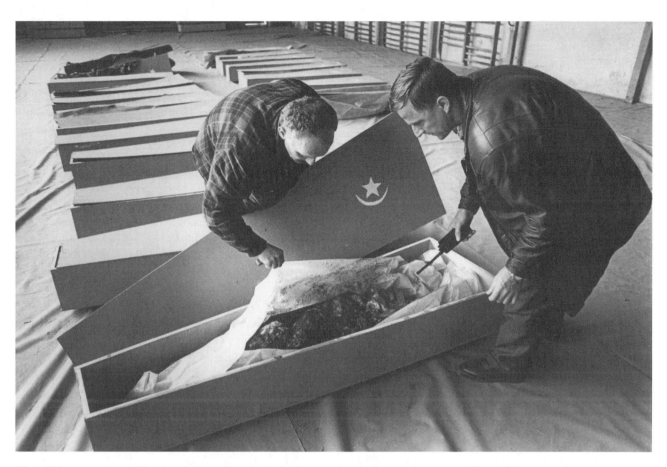

Identifying relatives killed by Serbs, a Bosnian Muslim man home from refuge in the United Kingdom views the remains of victims found in the Laniste 1 mass grave in Kljuc. Ethnic cleansing occurs in many forms throughout the world.

Source: Copyright © Howard Davies / CORBIS.

meaning that any of the following acts committed with the intent to destroy in whole or in part a national, ethic, racial, or religious group constitutes genocide, genocidal actions, or ethnic cleansing:

1. Killing members of the group
2. Causing serious bodily or mental harm to members of the group
3. Deliberately inflicting on the targeted group living conditions designed to result in physical destruction of the group in whole or in part
4. Imposing means intended to prevent births within the group
5. Forcible transferring of the group's children to any other group

Motivations for ethnic cleansing may be racism, anti-Semitism, fascism, totalitarianism, nationalism, or any other system that elevates, in practice or in theory, one group of people above another. The antidote to genocide is democratic openness, sociopolitical toleration, cultural diversity, and shared economic prosperity.

—*Brian Champion*

See also CRIMES OF OBEDIENCE; GENOCIDE; HATE CRIMES; MASS VIOLENCE; WAR ATROCITIES

EUROPEAN ORGANIZED CRIME, *See* ORGANIZED CRIME, TRANSNATIONAL

EUTHANASIA

Euthanasia derives from a compound of two Greek words meaning "good death." It involves the idea of "dying well," that is, of avoiding or shortening suffering and instead implementing a relatively painless passage into death. Most expressions of euthanasia involve the idea of the assistance of another individual, usually a physician.

Euthanasia is most often used in reference to the hastening of the death, or "mercy killing," of a severely ill individual. Various terms, however, have been developed to more clearly identify the different categories involved in the cessation of life. Among these are the following: passive euthanasia, active euthanasia, active voluntary euthanasia, and active involuntary euthanasia. There is also the use of *palliative* care, which involves the management of pain and discomfort without curative medical care; however, this may involve the use of pain management that can hasten the death of the individual. This, however, is not considered euthanasia.

More specifically, *passive euthanasia* involves allowing the cessation of life by the termination of life support medical procedures, such as use of hydration and gastronomy tubes. *Active euthanasia* refers to the deliberate cessation of life of a suffering patient, but not someone who simply does not want to live anymore due to stress, emotional fatigue, or severe life conditions that make living "unbearable." *Active voluntary euthanasia* involves the use of some lethal agent to end the life of a mentally competent suffering patient who seeks the assistance of a physician to complete the act. *Active involuntary euthanasia* refers to the intervention of a physician to terminate the life of a suffering patient without the patient's informed consent. Most forms of euthanasia involve controversy. Much debate has occurred over the "right" of individuals to die and the circumstances under which society will allow cessation of life.

The debate is ongoing and intense, whether it has to do with Dr. Jack Kevorkian ("Dr. Death") espousing the decriminalization of assisted suicide, which he views as an "honorable medical service"; the request of a patient to forgo life-sustaining treatment; or the asserted constitutionality of an individual's "right to die." Central considerations are traditional religious doctrines, philosophical attitudes toward the value and meaning of life, and the social/moral taboo against suicide, assisted suicide, or being involved in some way in causing the death of another person. The following is a brief overview of some of the main areas of controversy.

PHILOSOPHICAL ATTITUDES AND RELIGIOUS DOCTRINE

A central area of controversy concerns disparate attitudes about death and dying. Some embrace death as a deliverance from earthly bonds. Others espouse a view that values and fosters life and sees death as the enemy that must be fought and overcome. This value is a key component of modern medical practice.

The core tenets of most religions include valuing human life. Most Judeo-Christian doctrines frown on euthanasia as going against the principle that God can give life and take a life. In this view, individuals who seek the cessation of life through active euthanasia are usurping God's role. This is considered murder, a violation of the Sixth Commandment, and a violation of God's law. Most doctrinal stances of the various Jewish and Christian sects concur in their opposition to active euthanasia but would allow passive euthanasia, in which all medical options have been exhausted, to allow the patient to forgo further treatment that artificially prolongs life. A possible exception to this consensus is the position of the Unitarian Universalists, who believe that one should be protected from criminal sanction if one chooses to exercise the right to "die with dignity" in keeping with individual freedom of choice.

Followers of Islam believe that pain and suffering are a part of God's (Allah's) will, and therefore ending suffering by taking the patient's life is to interfere with the will of God. Both the Koran and the Sunna of the Prophet speak to the sanctity of life. The Koran specifically commands Muslims not to kill themselves. It therefore follows that to terminate one's life, or to ask someone else to terminate it, would in turn be forbidden.

Hindus and Buddhists believe that karma dictates the life journey one has to travel, and that dharma, or the ethical construct that holds communities together, dictates how karma will "flow." To interfere with the flow of karma by terminating the current consequences of "past-life behavior" is to relegate the individual to continue to pay the debt owed to karma in the next life. Thus, active euthanasia produces negative karma for both the patient and the physician. In both traditions, then, the matter of the "right to die" is disposed of in the realization that terminal illness is part and parcel of the repayment of the "karmic debt." Better to provide compassionate care and let the patient confront the result of past existence than to postpone it for another existence.

THE "RIGHT TO DIE"

One of the first laws to recognize the right of an individual to die without prolongation of life by medical means was the California Natural Death Act of 1976, sponsored by Assemblyman Barry Keene. He was prompted to draft the statute by his experience with a neighbor whose physicians inserted nasogastric and ventilator tubes without her consent. The Keene Act allows for the use of a "living will" to outline the patient's desire to "die with dignity."

The case of Nancy Cruzan is often touted as one in which the U.S. Supreme Court expressed support for the "right to die." In fact, however, the Court decided by a plurality in favor of a Missouri requirement that "clear and convincing" evidence be submitted to show that Ms. Cruzan would have decided to remove life-sustaining tubes had she been competent to do so. The case arose out of an accident in which Ms. Cruzan was thrown from her vehicle and stopped breathing. She was resuscitated by emergency service personnel but suffered brain damage that left her in a persistent vegetative state. After efforts to restore her health proved to no avail, her parents sought to have the tubes removed. They secured a judgment in their favor from the lower court, but it was reversed on appeal to the Missouri Supreme Court.

On appeal to the U.S. Supreme Court, the case was decided by a plurality of votes, led by Chief Justice Rehnquist, who stated in the main opinion that a patient had the right, hypothetically, to refuse artificially delivered hydration and nutrition. However, the Court's decision in *Cruzan v. Director, Missouri Department of Health* (1990) was that in this case, the evidence did not meet the standard of proof (clear and convincing) that Ms. Cruzan would have made the decision to exercise the "right to die" had she been able. The case was remanded for further deliberations in keeping with the Court's decision. Subsequently, the Cruzans secured sufficient witnesses who were able to present evidence consistent with the required standard of proof, and after 3 years of court battles, they were allowed to end her life support.

Clearly, the Court seemed to embrace the prospects that there is within the Constitution the reservation of the "right to die" as part of the liberty interest protected by that document; however, the Court did not actually establish that decision, but merely "hinted" at it as something that would have to be decided at a later date, with the appropriate case properly before it.

A few years after the Cruzan decision, in 1994, the citizens of the State of Oregon passed by initiative the controversial Death with Dignity Act of 1994. Many groups opposed the law, and legal challenges to it resulted in delaying its immediate implementation. After many court battles, the law was again submitted to the voters, this time by the opponents of the measure, but it passed by an overwhelming 60% vote.

FORGOING LIFE-SUSTAINING TREATMENT

No discussion of the right of an individual to forgo life-sustaining treatment is complete without reference to the benchmark 1976 case decided on behalf of Karen Ann Quinlan. This case, decided by the New Jersey Supreme Court, laid down the principle to be followed in determining the right of an individual to refuse treatment or of individuals acting as the individual's agent to do so on his or her behalf. Karen fell into a coma following a party with her friends. She was in a persistent vegetative state, requiring a respirator to sustain life. Her parents requested that her physicians disconnect her from the respirator, but they refused to do so on the grounds that it would be committing homicide. Her father, Joseph Quinlan, sought court relief, and in the case of *In re Quinlan* (1976), the New Jersey Supreme Court found in his favor. This set the stage for legislation throughout the United States allowing for the forgoing or withdrawal of life-sustaining treatment under certain circumstances (passive euthanasia). It also foreshadowed the revolution in the relationship between patients and physicians in patients' assertion of their right to refuse medical treatment.

A benchmark case that underscores this revolution in patients' rights is *Bouvia v. Superior Court* (1986). Elizabeth Bouvia was a quadriplegic who suffered from severe cerebral palsy, resulting in her becoming completely bedridden. With the help of friends, she managed to survive the ravages of her illness, securing a bed in a community hospital, where doctors inserted and maintained a nasogastric tube against her will and without her consent. She sought an injunction against the facility and the physicians to require the removal of the tube, even though it was their considered medical opinion that to do so would result in her death. At trial, the court denied her a preliminary injunction, and she appealed.

The California Appellate Court answered the question of whether a patient has the right to refuse medical treatment even when to do so creates a life-threatening condition in the affirmative. According to the court's opinion, an adult of sound mind has the right to exercise control over his or her own body in determining whether or not to submit to lawful medical treatment. The court further held that the state's interest in preserving life or preventing suicide, or even to protect innocent third parties, does not supersede the patient's right to self-determination. Patients have the right to say "No" to treatment, even when to do so may mean the hastening of death. This result, however, did not lay to rest the question of whether aiding in or causing the cessation of life is a constitutionally protected right.

PHYSICIAN-ASSISTED SUICIDE

The American Medical Association takes the position that it is inconsistent with a physician's Hippocratic oath for a physician to take a patient's life. The association distinguishes between passive euthanasia and the taking of life in the form of assisted suicide. Still, in addition to Dr. Kevorkian, some in the medical profession believe that there are circumstances under which a physician can and should assist a patient with the cessation of life. This issue came to a head in the case of *Washington v. Glucksberg* (1997), in which the U.S. Supreme Court held that states may properly prohibit the aiding or causing of a suicide.

Two cases, one from Washington and one from New York, were presented to the Court, appealing the prohibition of physician-assisted suicide as being a violation of the Fourteenth Amendment's Due Process Clause. A unanimous Court stated that there had been no violation of the Fourteenth Amendment, because the history of American jurisprudence evidenced an adherence to the common law practice of punishment or disapproval of both suicide and assisted suicide. The Court further held that the "right" to assistance in committing suicide is not a fundamental liberty interest that can be protected by the U.S. Constitution.

CONCLUSION

The legal, philosophical, and social implications surrounding the issue of euthanasia are such that it will remain controversial for quite some time to come. Advances in medical science will probably exacerbate the controversy rather than alleviate it. The core values

of freedom of choice and preserving human life will continue to clash. For now, it is clear that passive euthanasia has general acceptance. However, despite the support garnered in favor of the passage of the Oregon Death with Dignity Act, a clear distinction remains in the United States between forgoing life-sustaining treatment and actively taking a life. Furthermore, there still remains no constitutionally protected "right" to assisted cessation of life. Evolving societal, legal, and philosophical standards will eventually have to bring this controversy to its ultimate conclusion.

—*Arthur Wint*

See also KEVORKIAN, JACK; SUICIDE

Further Reading

Bouvia v. Superior Court, 225 Cal.Rptr. 297 Cal. App.2d District (1986).

Clark, N. (1997). *The politics of physician assisted suicide.* New York: Garland.

Cruzan v. Director, Missouri Department of Health, 110 S. Ct. 2841 (1990).

Filene, P. G. (1998). *In the arms of others.* Chicago: Ivan R. Dee.

Hillyard, D., & Dombrink, J. (2001). *Dying right: The death with dignity movement.* New York: Routledge.

In re Quinlan, 70 N.J. 10, 355 A.2d 647 (1976).

Larue, G. A. (1985). *Euthanasia and religion.* Los Angeles: The Hemlock Society.

Scherer, J. M., & Simon, R. J. (1999). *Euthanasia and the right to die: A comparative view.* New York: Rowman & Littlefield.

Uhlmann, M. M. (Ed.). (1998). *Last rights? Assisted suicide and euthanasia debated.* Grand Rapids, MI: Eerdmans.

Washington v. Glucksberg, 117 S.Ct. 2258 (1997).

Zucker, M. B. (1999). *The right to die debate.* Westport, CT: Greenwood.

THE EXECUTION PROCESS

Historically, there has been an ongoing debate about the use of death as a penalty for crimes. Execution is the process of applying this penalty. It has taken many forms and has involved extensive symbolism, ceremony, and ritual, which have been applied to humans as well as animals and inanimate objects.

Originally, the purpose of punishment was to extract confessions or to divine the guilt or innocence of the accused. Thus, boiling in oil, submerging in water, or placing burning coals in the hands of those suspected of offenses were intended to provide a "sign." The innocent were said to experience no negative effects from these actions, whereas the guilty died as a result—thus, confirming their guilt.

As the history of punishment evolved toward the actual execution of the condemned, death was protracted to the extent that it became the final result, but only after extensive suffering. The condemned individual was often hanged until almost dead, then taken down and punished with hot irons or brands, often disemboweled while still living, then drawn and quartered, with various parts of the body publicly displayed on gates or bridges at the entranceways to cities and towns.

The idea that offenders should suffer pain and torture was eventually replaced with the idea that justice required fair, swift, and humane action. Death was prescribed for specific offenses, and public executions took place to impress on society the consequences of violating the law. This justice required "a life for a life" and was not necessarily limited to humans.

It was not unusual for animals to receive the same punishment as that meted out to humans. In France, a bull involved in a highway killing was hanged from a public gallows. In Slovenia, a pig was tried and hanged for mutilating a young girl. Additionally, chickens, goats, rats, and cows were executed for offenses ranging from killing children to being involved in "unnatural acts." In 1916, in Erwin, Tennessee, an elephant was hanged for killing her trainer.

Inanimate objects were believed to deserve the same punishments. In China, wooden idols were beheaded for being present at the assassination of a high government official. In Russia, the bell used to signal an assassination attempt on the royal family was banished to Siberia. In Scotland, boats in which occupants had drowned were beached and allowed to rot so as to avoid sharing the sea with the other "innocent craft."

In some countries, executions were so common that the state appointed official executioners. The Sanson family occupied the hereditary position of state executioners in France for over 200 years. England appointed executioners after extensive interviews and apprenticeships. The last official executioner in England was Albert Pierrepoint, whose father and uncle had also held the same position. Pierrepoint resigned in 1956, shortly before England abandoned the use of capital punishment.

Although hanging has probably been the most common method of execution, there have been many others, including the guillotine, crucifixion, beheading with swords or axes, suffocation, and burning at the stake. Historically, in the United States, five methods of execution have been used: hanging, firing squad, electric chair, gas chamber, and lethal injection. Although all five are currently available, most states are either using lethal injection or have it as an option. Even the federal government, which previously relied on the states in which crimes occurred to conduct its executions, has now constructed its own execution facility at Terre Haute, Indiana, and exclusively uses lethal injection for federal executions. The execution process, while varying from state to state, in general consists of some specific stages, including the following.

Commutation Hearing. Some states have boards of pardons who hear final appeals from the condemned asking for a commutation of the sentence from death to life in prison. Also available is the final appeal to the governor of the state for clemency.

Death Watch. At some point prior to the execution, depending on the state, generally from 24 to 48 hours, the condemned inmate is removed from death row to a cell where there is constant, 24-hour surveillance. This period of time is generally referred to as the "death watch." Here, the condemned is isolated so as to avoid any suicide attempts, and visitors, mail, and all activity are monitored. A death watch log is kept to document all activity during these final 24 hours. The last meal is served in the cell, and from there, the condemned leaves to be executed. The short distance to the execution chamber is traditionally referred to as "the last mile."

Execution Chamber. A variety of roles and assignments are involved in the execution process. Those assigned to the death watch rotate so as to stay awake and be ever vigilant. When the condemned inmate is removed from the deathwatch cell, it is done by the "tie-down" team. These officers (selected from among volunteers from the prison staff) escort the inmate into the death chamber, where the execution will take place. They help position the condemned on the gurney and fasten the straps (arms, thighs, knees, waist, chest). When this is completed, they leave the chamber.

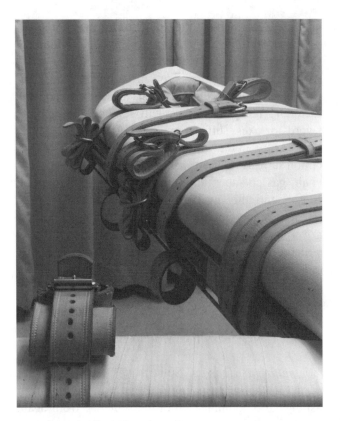

Lethal injection table.

Source: Copyright © Mark Jenkinson / CORBIS.

Execution. The execution itself is usually presided over by the warden or assistant warden. At a pre-arranged signal (removing of glasses or unbuttoning of jacket), the executioners begin administering the lethal doses: first, sodium pentothal, followed by Pavulon, a muscle relaxant to stop the lungs, and finally, potassium chloride to stop the heart. Because the medical profession considers it a violation of the Hippocratic oath to participate in taking a life, the executioners are often military or staff medical technicians. However, generally a physician will wait outside the execution chamber and be called in to attest to the death of the condemned. (Cause of death is usually recorded as "homicide.")

Witnesses. Throughout this process, several groups are allowed (some required) to be present as witnesses. Official or "government" witnesses can include prison/corrections personnel, as well as representatives of the governor's office, state attorneys, and others with specific assignment. Another group consists of media witnesses, usually chosen by lot so as to

provide fair access for news coverage. The condemned inmate is allowed to chose a small number of witnesses, which can include family members, attorneys, or others who have provided assistance, but no other inmates. More recently, members of the victim's family have been allowed to witness the execution.

When all is completed and the time of death noted, everyone leaves the execution chamber, the witnesses are escorted out, and the "tie-down" team enters the chamber to remove the body. Generally, the family claims the body and makes their own funeral arrangements. When this does not occur, the state takes charge and generally cremates the remains.

As evidenced by the Supreme Court in *Furman v. Georgia* (1972) and the subsequent moratorium on capital punishment, there continues to be a debate about the role of executions. Public opinion ebbs and swells, and the courts continue to review challenges to the existence of such a penalty. Issues regarding the execution of women and juveniles as well as the debate over "cruel and unusual" acts, race and ethnic disparities, cost, and length of appeals continue to create emotion and vociferous debate. DNA testing and the manipulation of evidence have caused some (including state governors) to doubt whether this ultimate sanction is being applied fairly and equitably. The future of executions and the execution process will continue to be an issue of great interest and discussion.

—*Kay Gillespie*

See also CRUEL AND UNUSUAL PUNISHMENT; DEATH PENALTY; DEATH ROW

Further Reading

Furman v. Georgia, 408 U.S. 238 (1972).

Gillespie, L. K. (2003). *The death chamber: Exploring executions.* Boston: Allyn & Bacon.

Johnson, R. (1998). *Deathwork: A study of the modern execution process.* Belmont, CA: Wadsworth.

EXPLOITATION OF CHILDREN

Children are sexually exploited for many reasons. Many offenders who harm children are pedophiles. The American Psychiatric Association defines a *pedophile* as a person who over at least a 6-month period of time has recurrent, intense sexually arousing fantasies, sexual urges, and/or behaviors involving sexual activity with a prepubescent child or children (ages 13 years or younger). Such fantasies, sexual urges, or behaviors cause clinically significant distress or impairment in social, occupational, or other important areas of day-to-day functioning. The person inflicting this behavior is, by definition, at least 16 years of age and at least 5 years older than the child victim. This does not include a late adolescent who is involved in an ongoing sexual relationship with a 12- or 13-year-old individual, either heterosexual or gay.

Individuals afflicted with pedophilia generally report an attraction to children of a particular age range. Some individuals prefer males, others prefer females, and some are aroused by both males and females. Pedophilia involving female victims tends to be reported more than crimes involving male victims. In today's world, children are often faced with situations that can turn volatile without warning. Children by nature are trusting and demonstrate a desire to learn new things. When a child associates with an adult pedophile who is sexually stimulated by child pornography, the offender may seem to be a very caring, gentle, and safe person.

Pedophiles tend to be adult males and often appear to be hardworking, overly religious, and well liked by both parents and children. They tend to be better educated, and a pedophile teacher is often the most popular teacher in the school. This is part of the grooming process that wins the trust of both adults and children. Pedophiles actively seek out children who are quiet, needy, or have problems at home. They will give great attention to several different children whom they do not abuse, attempting to build a sense of trust with parents and teachers in an educational setting. Music teachers and coaches are often in a position to be one-on-one with students, and they accomplish their seduction gradually, without coercion.

Parents should be aware of certain warning signs, such as the child suddenly not wanting to go to school or changes in the child's behavior or academic performance. The child may demonstrate abrupt mood changes, aggressive behavior, and withdrawal from family and friends. Sometimes, a child comes home with new toys, clothes, or money that is unexplained, or they demonstrate age-inappropriate sexual behavior.

"VIRTUAL" CHILD PORNOGRAPHY

On April 16, 2002, the U.S. Supreme Court overturned the congressional ban of child pornography. This long-standing ban was put into law many years before the creation of computer graphics. In the past, the creation of child pornography required the physical participation and exploitation of children. Photographing or filming of children in sexually oriented activities is a form of exploitation whether the child is identifiable and lives in the United States or not.

In today's high-tech world, "virtual porn" has been created that in some situations does not even involve "real" children. Sexually explicit images of children can now be created without physically photographing or filming them. The child image can be created from a "morph" to combine a child in a nonsexual situation with an adult in a sexual situation. Pictures of adults can be modified so they appear to be children. In the end, the result can be made to look exactly like a child in a sexual situation. If this image were real, it would be a felony, but if it is "virtual," it is a matter of free speech. Either way, however, children are harmed. When material is introduced showing both children and adults in sexual situations, it tends to give the impression that such behavior is normal and acceptable. Child pornography is often used to lure children into sexual acts, convincing them that such behavior is not out of the ordinary. With the Internet being flooded with virtual or real child pornography, authorities are faced with the controversial censorship of the Internet and freedom of speech.

International child pornography on the Internet is a major concern and has brought experts together from North America, Europe, and Asian countries to build a global society in which children are protected and respected from exploitation through the Internet. They are attempting to reinforce international cooperation between law enforcement and the judiciary, establish codes of conduct among Internet service providers, encourage the creation of hotlines from which to report child pornography found on the Internet, and to raise awareness and mobilize public opinion against child pornography.

In March 1998, *CyberTipline* was launched as an on-line resource for the reporting of crimes related to the sexual exploitation of children in cyberspace. Ernie Allen, president of National Center for Missing and Exploited Children, said, "The message is not that the Internet is not a safe place for kids but that prevention, education, and information coupled with the use of filtering technology like *Surfwatch* and *NetNanny* can help people feel secure that their children are not in danger while engaging in on-line activities."

RELIGION AND SEXUAL MISCONDUCT

Although the Pope has addressed the problem of sexual abuse in the Catholic Church as a "crisis affecting not only the Church but society as a whole," Catholic leaders say that the presence of some gays in the priesthood is what leads to child abuse. Local priests, monsignors, bishops, and archbishops have shuffled child molesters from parish to parish, putting children in harm's way rather than damaging the church's reputation or risking more victims coming forth to demand restitution. The church has determined that there is a moral difference between a priest who sexually abuses children and the "average" abuser of young women, indicating that the priests would be protected from prosecution.

In America, the actual number of pedophiliac priests is a matter of controversy, leading experts to estimate that approximately 6% of priests have been involved in sexual misconduct with minors. In the Roman Catholic Church, more than 800 priests have been removed from the ministry due to allegations against them. An estimated 1,400 insurance claims have been made, and the church has already paid out as estimated $1 billion in liability with an estimated $500 million pending. Carolyn Heggen has demonstrated that although the best predictor of sexual abuse of a child by his or her parents tends to be alcoholism, the second-best predictor is conservative religious belief.

CHILD EXPLOITATION LAWS

In 1987, the U.S. Department of Justice established the Child Exploitation and Obscenity Section (CEOS), which was expanded in 1994. This is a group of attorneys who have specialized in the prosecution of obscenity, child exploitation, child abuse cases, international child abduction, and victim witness issues. On request, CEOS provides litigation support, technical assistance, and training to federal investigators and prosecutors who work on child sexual exploitation cases, including child pornography, child prostitution, sexual tourism, and sexual abuse occurring on federal lands.

A number of relatively new statutes have been passed affecting federal child exploitation laws. First, the Child Online Protection Act was signed on October 21, 1998, and prohibits anyone using a commercial Web site from knowingly making a communication that is "harmful to minors" available to those less than 17 years of age for commercial purposes. The defendant must have knowledge of the character of the material, defined as

pictures, writing, or recordings, that are obscene or that the average person would find, with respect to minors, to appeal to prurient interests, to depict sexual activity in a patently offensive way, and to lack serious literary, artistic, political, or scientific value. This is a misdemeanor punishable by up to a 6-month prison sentence and a $50,000 fine for each violation. There is also a $50,000 civil penalty for each offense.

The Protection of Children From Sexual Predators Act of 1998 established new criminal offenses, amended existing statues, and provides for enhanced penalties. Three new definitions concern (a) the use of interstate facilities to transmit information about a minor, prohibiting the use of the mail or facility of interstate or foreign commerce to transmit information about a minor under 16 years of age for criminal sexual purposes; (b) the transfer of obscene material to minors; and (c) the expansion of *sexual activity* to include the production of child pornography. Amendments and clarifications address (a) attempt provisions; (b) coercion and enticement of a minor by mail or any facility of interstate or foreign commerce, increasing the maximum sentence to 15 years; (c) expansion of the jurisdictional reach of federal child pornography production statutes; (d) zero tolerance for possession of child pornography; (e) reducing phrase redundancy; and (f) pretrial detention of persons (charged with such offenses) on the grounds of dangerousness.

Maximum penalties were increased, and repeat offenders now receive additional penalties—the death penalty if a minor under 14 years of age dies as a result of making "snuff" films of minors; and forfeiture and civil remedies provide incentives for local, state, and federal investigative work. The use of administrative subpoenas allows for more efficient access to computer records and other documents, requiring electronic service providers to report evidence of child pornography offenses. As a result of these changes in the law, several cases have been prosecuted by the U.S. Attorney's Office.

—*Linda Lou Kreuger-Long*

See also CYBERSTINGS; PEDOPHILIA; PEDOPHILE
    ORGANIZATIONS; WHITE SLAVERY

Further Reading

Burkett, E., & Bruni, F. (1993). *A gospel of shame: Children, sexual abuse and the Catholic Church.* NY: Viking, Penguin.

Child Online Protection Act (COPA) H.R. 4328, P. L. 105-277 (1998).

Heggen, C. (1993). *Sexual abuse in Christian homes and churches.* Pennsylvania: Herald Press.

Magid, L. (2002, April 16). *Does virtual child porn equal child exploitation? Los Angeles Times* Syndicate International. Available on the World Wide Web at: http://www.larrysworld.com/articles/synd_virtualporn.htm.

Protection of Children From Sexual Predators Act, PL. 105-314 (1998).

School Reform News. (2000). *Profile of a pedophile.* Available on the World Wide Web at: http://www.heart-land.org/education/jan00/profile.htm.

GIOVANNI FALCONE

Born in Palermo, Italy, in 1939, Giovanni Falcone was the son of Arturo Falcone, director of a provincial chemical laboratory, and Luisa Bentivegna. He spent part of his youth in the Magione District, which suffered extensive destruction during the Allied aerial attacks of 1943. Falcone received a classical education and briefly attended Livorno's naval academy prior to studying law. In 1961, he graduated from law school and practiced law for 3 years before being appointed as a judge in 1964. By the 1970s, Falcone was hearing cases involving organized crime. During the next decade, Falcone's work in the courtroom helped dissolve the aura of mystique and myth surrounding the structure and culture of the Mafia. By the 1980s, following years of bloodshed (and the murders of police officers and judges), he was making headway in this pursuit.

Falcone was also an innovator in that he persuaded several important Mafiosi, most notably Tomasso Buscetta, to talk about the Mafia and provide useful information about its activities. Cooperation with authorities was also important, because the Mafia is an international organization. Before Falcone's efforts, little progress had been made in prosecuting Sicilian Mafiosi who moved about the United States, particularly in the New York area, without being traced by Italian authorities or identified by the American system. Later, the success of the "Pizza Connection" trial in the United States owed much to Falcone's efforts in Italy.

In 1986 and 1987, Falcone and others presided over the "Maxi Trial" of 475 alleged Mafiosi in Palermo. The case, a parallel to the Pizza Connection trial, drew international attention by bringing the Mafia out into the open—but most of the 338 criminals convicted served little more than token sentences before being released under Italy's lax penal code, with its extremely high burden of proof. Mafia kingpin Michele Greco and Salvatore Riina, Greco's successor from Corleone, were eventually convicted.

The Mafia permeates every facet of the Sicilian economy, whether in the form of the drug trade, money laundering, political corruption (payoffs and kickbacks), or the *pizzo* (protection money). Statistically, the problem is far worse in Palermo than in Catania. Giovanni Falcone knew this, and so did most Sicilians. Apart from cases of localized interest, Falcone handled important narcotics cases, which were then the Mafia's stock and trade internationally. For all the press attention he received, Falcone became a lone crusader, and community folk regarded him as a folk hero. Meanwhile, the Mafia was contemplating Falcone's murder and actually attempted it several times.

Falcone and his staff continued their work in the anti-Mafia pool headquartered in Rome. This entailed a national position for Falcone as Italy's main prosecutor for Mafia cases and extensive travel between Rome and Palermo. Along the autostrada on May 23, 1992, near the town of Capaci, Falcone's car was exploded by a mass of plastic explosive placed in a small underpass. Falcone's wife, Francesca Morvilio, also a magistrate, was killed with him along with the members of his escort, police officers Rocco Di Cillo, Vito Schifani, and Antonio Montinaro. Back in Palermo, assassins were already plotting the murder of Paolo Borsellino, the judge who worked with Falcone.

Several important Mafiosi were arrested in Sicily in the years following, and the last decade has seen a marked reduction in Mafia-related crime. Falcone may not have defeated the organization, which still thrives today, but he certainly hindered its growth.

—Linda Cepeda

See also ORGANIZED CRIME: TRANSNATIONAL

Further Reading

Salerno, V. (2002). Remembering Judge Falcone. *Best of Sicily Magazine.* Available on the World Wide Web at: http://www.bestofsicily.com/mag/art48.htm.

FALSE CONFESSIONS

A false confession is a term used within the criminal justice system to describe a situation in which an individual admits to committing an act that they actually did not commit. These confessions are problematic because innocent people are often sentenced to prison or jail as the result of their statements. There are three types of false confessions: voluntary false confessions, coerced-compliant false confessions and coerced-internalized confessions. Each can be elicited by law enforcement officials in a variety of ways.

As many as 6,000 individuals are wrongfully convicted each year on the basis of false confessions. Some have been historically notable; for example, when Charles Lindbergh's baby was kidnapped, more than 600 people admitted to the crime. In the late 1940s, Elizabeth Short, an aspiring actress, was murdered in Los Angeles, and the case became known as the "Black Dahlia." More than 30 people confessed to the crime, which remains unsolved to this day.

Studies show that people can be coerced into admitting to doing things they did not actually do. One research study asked 79 students to participate in an experiment on a computer involving time reaction. The students were told that the computer would crash if they touched a specific key. During the experiment, the computer crashed, regardless of whether the student touched the key. Half the participants were told that they had been seen touching the key by one of the researchers. The students were then asked to

sign a confession stating that they had caused the computer to crash by hitting the key. All students who were told that they had been seen hitting the key signed the confession. Overall, 69% of the students signed the confession, 28% began to believe that they had actually touched the key, and 9% created details that supported their false beliefs.

Individuals provide false confessions for a number of reasons. One explanation, which stems from a psychoanalytic approach to psychology, suggests that a false confession stems from one's unconscious compulsion to confess. The characteristics of an individual also contribute to the likelihood that he or she will offer a false confession. People with below-average intelligence are more vulnerable to suggestion, as are people who are categorized as introverts. Individuals with low self-esteem, a lack of assertiveness, or high levels of anxiety are also more easily influenced.

Such factors, combined with the procedures used by law enforcement officials in interrogation, can lead to false confessions. Law enforcement officials are trained to rely on various methods to encourage suspects to admit to being guilty without their realizing it. An investigator may place the suspect in a soundproof and minimally furnished room, blame the victim or an accomplice, use feigned sympathy and friendship, or present exaggerated claims about the evidence, all in an attempt to gain an admission of guilt from the individual. Other techniques include wearing the suspect down with a long interview process, having the investigator over- or understate the seriousness of the offense and the magnitude of the charges, and making appeals to God or religion to arouse a sense of guilt in the individual.

The first type of confession, the *voluntary false confession,* is a statement offered in the absence of pressure from law enforcement officials. A person may spontaneously admit to an offense for a variety of reasons. The individual may be attempting to protect a friend or a relative. The person may also have an unconscious need to release guilt over a past wrongdoing. The previous event can be real or imagined and does not necessarily have to be identifiable. Finally, many individuals will make a voluntary false confession to a lesser crime to avoid the penalties associated with a larger crime.

The second type of confession, *a coerced-compliant false confession,* occurs when an individual confesses to the crime despite knowledge of their innocence due to extreme techniques by investigators during the interrogation. Well-known examples of such confessions occurred in the 17th century, when torture, threats, and promises were used to elicit admissions from individuals presumed to be witches.

The third type of confession is the *coerced-internalized false confession*. This occurs when an innocent suspect is anxious, pressured, confused, or fatigued and then subjected to highly suggestive methods of interrogation in which they come to believe that they have actually committed the crime. These confessions are especially problematic because once individuals believe in their guilt, the original contents of their memory of the event are irreversibly altered or are not retrievable.

Such false confessions typically have two factors in common. First, suspects are generally vulnerable to suggestion due to their age, naïveté, lack of intelligence, or influence of drugs or alcohol. Second, false evidence, a rigged polygraph, or evidence from other forensic tests is presented to suspects to convince them they are guilty. An individual may also offer confessions of this type in an attempt to reduce or escape an aversive situation and replace it with a pleasant consequence. For example, a suspect who is held for hours without food in a cold room may ultimately confess to obtain food and warmer clothing.

—*Miranda Brockett*

See also FALSE MEMORY SYNDROME; FORENSIC PSYCHOLOGY

Further Reading

Conti, R. (1999). The psychology of false confessions. *The Journal of Credibility Assessment and Witness Psychology, 2*, 14-36.

Kassin, S., & Kiechel, K. (1996). The social psychology of false confessions: Compliance, internalization, and confabulation. *Psychological Science, 7*, 125-128.

Loftus, E., & Ketcham, K. (1994). *The myth of repressed memory.* New York: St. Martin's.

Wrightsman, L. (1998). *Psychology and the legal system* (4th ed.). Pacific Grove, CA: Brooks and Cole.

FALSE MEMORY SYNDROME

Prior to the late 1980s and early 1990s, the phrase "false memory" was not commonplace and may only have been discussed among researchers studying memory. However, during this decade, the phenomenon occurred in which both children and adults were documented in recalling memories of violent sexual abuse, with no external evidence to corroborate their memories. Many of these newly recalled memories were determined to be untrue and subsequently retracted by the alleged victims. This strange event occurred so frequently during this time period that it became known as the false memory syndrome (FMS), defined as "a condition in which a person's identity and interpersonal relationships are centered around a memory of traumatic experience which is objectively false but in which the person strongly believes" (Kihlstrom, 1998, p. 16).

RECOLLECTION SCENARIOS

Adult Victims

A common scenario that began to arise in the late 1980s and early 1990s consisted of an adult, most often female, entering therapy for assistance with a personal problem and suddenly or gradually recalling memories from her childhood of being sexually abused by one or more perpetrators. Sometimes the molester was a parent, sometimes both parents, and sometimes another family member. Some women even began to have memories of being victims of satanic rituals involving numerous people. They recalled being raped by these people or being made to witness babies killed and sacrificed or being forced to drink blood or urine. The women insisted that they'd had no recollection of these events until the memories began to surface as adults, despite their claims of now remembering being abused from toddler through teenage years. These victims would then sue or press criminal charges against the alleged molester, who often was the parent. This person may have been found guilty or culpable based only on testimony of recovered memories. One example involved a woman in her late 20s who suddenly remembered that her father had molested and then murdered her best friend in the fourth grade. After 20 years with no memory of this, she'd had a flashback and recalled witnessing the entire incident and being warned by her father not to tell anyone. The father was arrested and charged with the murder based on this recovered memory.

Children and Day Care

Another phenomenon that began to emerge during this decade was that of a day care facility being accused of ritualistic and cultic sexual abuse. It began in 1983 with the McMartin day care case in Manhattan Beach, California. A mother of a 2-year-old boy (who later was diagnosed with paranoid schizophrenia) became worried that her son had been sexually abused. She informed the police, who repeatedly questioned her son about whether such incidents had taken place. Finally, they were convinced that a teacher at the day care center had molested him. The police warned the other parents of the school, and these parents became worried and questioned their children, who were mostly 3 to 4 years old. The children at first denied any abuse, but after continuous questioning and pressure, they began to describe stories of satanic rituals by the day care staff, eventually convincing parents and authorities that they had been molested—despite a lack of any physical evidence and the bizarre nature of their stories.

In a similar case, in Wenatchee, Washington (1994-95), other preschoolers were questioned in a coercive and leading manner and began to accuse their teachers of having perpetrated bizarre sexual acts upon them. The teachers of these preschoolers were convicted of numerous counts of child sexual abuse and sent to prison, all on the basis of children's testimony that was likely created out of suggestibility and leading questions. Often, these children denied being sexually abused but would later admit to it after grueling questioning by therapists, police, and parents. They then came to believe that abuse had occurred and may now have memories of incidents that likely never happened. Other cases such as the Little Rascals day care in North Carolina, the Kelly Michaels case in New Jersey, the Dale Akiki case in San Diego, and the alleged molestation rings in Jordan, Minnesota; Niles, Michigan; and Miami, Florida and other communities across America made headlines, made careers, and destroyed lives. One by one, they crumbled in court or were overturned on appeal

Murder, Alien Abductions, Witchcraft, and Freud

Although the false-memory phenomenon is most often referenced in sexual abuse cases, it does arise in other situations. In one case, two boys confessed to murdering another boy when police interrogated them, yet evidence proved that the children did not commit the crime. There are other cases of people having false memories of being assaulted or other

alleged perpetrators admitting to crimes they did not commit and believing they committed them because they had memories of it. (Somtimes DNA evidence can be used as proof.) There are even people (and this does not include the mentally ill) who believe they have been abducted by aliens and experimented on in laboratories because they have memories of these incidents. Looking back in history, one can find similarities in the Salem witch trials, in which people were burned at the stake after being accused of witchcraft by children who later retracted their accusations.

Sigmund Freud was an early proponent of the idea of false memory. In patients he diagnosed with hysteria, he believed that they had repressed (or pushed to their unconscious minds) early traumatic events of sexual abuse that he was able to help them recall through hypnosis. However, he later changed his viewpoint and believed that these women never actually were sexually abused but had only fantasized about sexual relations with their fathers.

MANIPULATION OF MEMORY

The creation of false memories is not a passive process. Several factors can lead to the recollection of memories that are later determined to be false. First of all, a well-meaning therapist can influence the creation of false memories through suggestion and coercion in a vulnerable person. During the time this phenomenon was rampant, therapists and self-help literature reported numerous symptoms that could be signs that one was sexually abused. These symptoms included eating disorders, depression, anxiety, low self-esteem, and fear of the dark. Individuals looking for answers to their problems may hear this kind of information and start wondering if they were abused and simply did not remember.

Various techniques are used in therapy to assist the patient in recalling memories, such as hypnosis, body work, visual imagery, regression, truth drugs, journaling, and dream interpretation. These techniques can be suggestive and leading. Research has shown that hypnosis creates false memories or distorts real memories through suggestion by the therapist. When a therapist, who may be viewed as an expert and authority figure, uses "techniques that increase the demand to recover memories of abuse, that encourage constructive memory processes, and that discourage careful reality monitoring," then the likelihood for creating false memories increases (Hyman & Loftus, 1997, p. 12). Those who retract their claims of being victimized as children often concede that their therapists encouraged their memories and beliefs, and some even sue their therapists in court.

As discussed in the day care situations, memories can also be created through suggestion and coercion. One experiment demonstrated that false memories of being lost in a shopping mall could be created in a person by another family member suggesting that it really happened. The subject recalled specific details and emotions from a nonexistent incident.

False memories have an impact on many areas in society. They can devastate families and destroy the lives of innocent people, who may even serve time in prison. The legal system has been influenced as a result of these cases by changing statutes of limitations that allow charges to be brought against an individual based on when the memory surfaces and not on when the incident allegedly occurred. These trends have caused fear and doubt in individuals about their own pasts and the possibility of being falsely accused.

—*Janna L. Oddie*

See also FALSE CONFESSIONS; FORENSIC PSYCHOLOGY

Further Reading

Bjorklund, D. F. (Ed.). (2000). *False-memory creation in children and adults: Theory, research, and implications.* Mahwah, NJ: Lawrence Erlbaum.

Hyman, I. E., & Loftus, E. F. (1997). Some people recover memories of childhood trauma that never really happened. In P. S. Appelbaum et al. (Eds.), *Trauma and memory: Clinical and legal controversies* (pp. 3-24). New York: Oxford University Press.

Kaplan, R., & Manicavasagar, V. (2001). Is there a false memory syndrome? A review of three cases. *Comprehensive Psychiatry, 42,* 342-348.

Kihlstrom, J. F. (1998). Exhumed memory. In S. J. Lynn & K. M. McConkey (Eds.), *Truth in memory* (pp. 3-31). New York: Guilford.

Loftus, E. F., & Ketcham, K. (1994). *The myth of repressed memory: False memories and allegations of sexual abuse.* New York: St. Martin's Griffin.

Pendergrast, M. (1995). *Victims of memory: Incest accusations and shattered lives.* Hinesburg, VT: Upper Access.

FAMILY HOMICIDE

For an unfortunate minority of people, family life consists of a series of personal intrusions, abuses of personal rights, assaults on both body and mind, and even severe trauma—to the extent of homicide within their own homes, committed by members of their own family.

There are several forms of family murder, or *intrafamilial homicide,* the most prevalent being *sponsicide/intimaticide,* or the killing of one's spouse or intimate partner. *Neonaticide* is the murdering of a newborn within the first 24 hours of life. *Infanticide* is the murdering of a child from 1 day old up to 5 years of age. *Filicide* is the murder of one's own child over the age of 5 years: *early filicide* for a child between the ages of 5 and 18 years and *late filicide* for a child over the age of 18 years.

When children murder their parents, it is called *parricide.* Sibling abuse is the most common form of domestic violence, sometimes escalating into a homicide, or *siblicide.* When people kill individuals from their extended family (e.g., aunts, uncles, grandparents, and cousins), it is called *kinicide.*

Intrafamilial homicide can also take the form of homicide-suicide, usually committed among spouses, and family mass murder, or *familicide.* The relative risk of being a victim of intrafamilial homicide varies depending on one's status, or role, in their family. Table 1 outlines the frequency of different types of intrafamilial murder over a 7-year period, 1990 to 1996, as reported in the Supplementary Homicide Report published by the Federal Bureau of Investigation.

Table 1   Forms of Intrafamilial Homicide, 1990–1996

Type of Intrafamilial Homicide (IFH) (N = 17,783)	N	% IFH
Uxoricide (wife)	5,784	32.53
Kinicide (other family members)	2,577	14.50
Mariticide (husband)	2,311	13.00
Filicide (son)	2,164	12.17
Filicide (daughter)	1,585	8.91
Patricide (father)	1,149	6.46
Fratricide (brother)	1,124	6.32
Matricide (mother)	859	4.83
Sororicide (sister)	230	1.29

Source: Underwood (2000).

Other research has produced similar statistics; about 20% (i.e., 4,000) of annual murders and nonnegligent manslaughter in the United States involve family members as both the perpetrators and the victims (Silverman & Mukhergee, 1987). These statistics have been similarly reported in Canadian and British studies as well (Cooper, 1994; Statistics Canada, 2000). Those studies have indicated that approximately 50% of intrafamilial murders are spouses/intimate partners. Furthermore, British studies have indicated that intrafamilial murders accounted for just under 50% of all homicides (Home Office, 1986). In other words, one of the most important intervention points for the public health problem of homicide, as with most social concerns, begins in the home.

In his book titled *Fatal Families: The Dynamics of Intrafamilial Homicide,* Ewing outlined five clear risk factors that contribute to murder within the family: (a) domestic violence, (b) overwhelming social stress, (c) mental illness, (d) alcohol and drug abuse, and (e) easy access to firearms, especially handguns. In other words, murdering a family member is not just one form of domestic violence; domestic violence is frequently the cause of the murder. Sometimes the stress of care giving, loss of employment, loss of health, and so on can produce a state of anomie and psychological decompensation that results in homicidal actions. In regard to mental illness, it has been estimated that 12% of those who murder a spouse, 16% of those who murder their children, 25% of those who murder a parent, and 17% of those who murder a sibling have some form of diagnosable mental illness. The incidence of substance abuse and homicide has been debatable. This is due in large part to the lack of adequate data collection on this topic. However, most of the research data gathered indicates that alcohol consumption may have significantly contributed to approximately 50% of these family murders (Ewing, 1997; Parker & Auerhahn, 1999).

TYPES OF INTRAFAMILIAL HOMICIDE

Sponsicide/Intimaticide

Rasche (1993) identified several motives for spouse/intimate partner homicide, with male possessiveness (49%) and females using self-defense (16%) being the most prominent. The killing of a spouse/intimate partner has routinely been related to escalating and pervasive domestic violence. The research on domestic violence indicates that the majority of battered women remain in their abusive relationships throughout their lives, find some way to leave abusive relationships, or are eventually murdered by their abusers. It is rare that a violent relationship improves. In fact, once violence has occurred in a relationship, it will be repeated. Over time, if not quickly and adequately dealt with, domestic violence will become more frequent and more severe. It is estimated that in over 90% of these murders, local law enforcement agencies had between one and five contacts with the couples for domestic disturbance and domestic violence calls in the 2 years preceding the murder (Bunge, 2002; Dawson & Langan, 1994, 1995; Fedorowycz, 2001; Wilson & Daly, 1994).

Males appear to become homicidal secondary to experiencing a significant loss (e.g., loss of employment, loss of health). Women appear to become homicidal secondary to the accumulation of stress related to domestic violence. Regardless of why these individuals become homicidal, it seems evident that they are unable to cope with and/or respond adaptively to high levels of both subjective and objective stress. The overwhelming majority of these killings (90%) occur at the couples'/victims' homes. Of the remaining 10% of these murders, the majority occur at the victim's workplace or other relatives' homes; few occur elsewhere (Bunge, 2002; Dawson & Langan, 1994, 1995; Fedorowycz, 2001; Wilson & Daly, 1994). Women tend to kill their spouses/intimate partners in the living room, bedroom, or kitchen, whereas men tend to kill in various locations. Routine activities theory may be useful in explaining the choice of weapons and circumstances of these killings. The research related to racial differences in these murders has shown that African American husbands are more likely to be killed than Caucasian husbands. However, Caucasian wives were more likely to be murdered than African American wives.

For both men and women, age is the greatest risk factor. The research indicates that being under the age of 25 is the highest risk period of sponsicide/intimaticide. As in most cases of homicide, men tend to use firearms (60%) and women tend to use knives and cutting instruments more often than men. Men use physical force in their murders more than women do, 31% and 10%, respectively (Shackleford, 2000; Statistics Canada, 2000).

Women Who Kill Their Spouses/Intimate Partners

Some research has shown that some women murder their spouses/intimate partners for reasons related to comfort needs (i.e., financial gain). However, most do so in response to some form of victim-precipitated assault. Often, these homicidal women have extensive histories of abuse from the men they kill. Generally speaking, these women are in their early to mid-30s, are mothers, and are living with their families. Many are uneducated, unemployed, and are likely to have a prior arrest record. They generally murder in response to an argument or volatile confrontation with their spouses/intimate partners. Usually, these murders take place in the bedroom, living room, or kitchen between the hours of 2:00 p.m. and 2:00 a.m. These women have been portrayed as being disadvantaged and socially isolated, and tend to have relationships with men who are poorly equipped to succeed. They are reportedly denied and/or possess few social, educational, and personal strengths to improve their condition, and frequently view themselves victims in a male-dominated world.

However, Browne, using a larger and more representative subject pool, noted other characteristics of women who kill their partners. She indicated that many of these women came from abusive backgrounds during childhood, typically by their fathers. Other researchers have noted that these women possess characteristics such as (a) being sufferers of frequent and severe verbal abuse, (b) being victims of frequent and often brutal assaults, (c) having been threatened frequently with death, (d) having a histories of suicide attempts, (e) being more highly educated than their partners, and (f) living apart from their abusers at the time of the murder.

Several other predictive factors have been noted to precede fatal violence by women: (a) the severity of the woman's injuries from the abuse, (b) the abuser's drug and alcohol use and the frequency of the abuser's intoxication, (c) the frequency of abusive episodes, (d) forced or threatened sexual acts by the abuser, (e) a history of suicidal threats by the woman, and (f) repeated threats of murder made by the abuser.

Women reportedly have a tendency to blame themselves when they commit this type of homicide. It should be noted, however, that only a small percentage of women in abusive relationships ever resort to homicide to solve their perceived hopeless situations.

In fact, research has shown that women who are the victims of long-term abuse tend to develop feelings of helplessness and anomie, which makes it all the more difficult for them to fight back against their abusers. It has thus been suggested that these women are striking back only because they have exhausted all perceived methods to end their suffering. Although the battered woman syndrome has been admitted in the trial of some of these women, it is rarely successful as a defense.

The point of leaving the relationship is the most dangerous time for women and children who are attempting to escape the abuse. Leaving the abuser represents such a threat of abandonment that the abusive spouse/intimate partner would rather murder the woman than let her leave. Conversely, however, abusers who prevent their spouses/intimate partners from leaving may jeopardize their own lives in the process. The battered woman's seeming passivity may actually be her desperate attempt and last active defense against turning her resentment and rage into homicide.

Men Who Kill Their Spouses/Intimate Partners

Men who murder their spouses/intimate partners reportedly tend to be quiet, have high dependency and acceptance needs, have difficulty in their ability to relate to the world around them, have a need for external validation, and tend to exhibit higher levels of both objective and subjective stress in their daily lives. Frequently, these homicidal men have been raised in emotionally constricting homes and consequently have a great deal of difficulty expressing their emotions. According to Humphrey and Palmer, male sponsicide/intimaticide offenders are more likely to have experienced considerable losses throughout their lives (i.e., parental separation/divorce/death, abandonment, or parental institutionalization). Later in life, when they experience job-related difficulties, forced relocations, or changes in marital status, these stressful events are likely to aggregate into homicidal ideation and/or actions, usually against individuals these offenders fear losing the most.

It appears that men who feel unable to exert adequate and adaptive control in their lives outside of their families are at increased risk of inappropriately and maladaptively exerting control within the parameters of their family settings. They appear to need the validation of their spouses/intimate partners and have a compulsive need to control them. As a result, they tend to objectify their spouses/intimate partners and view them as a form of property. As mentioned, leaving an abusive relationship is the period of highest risk. Therefore, if a homicidally abusive man is placed in a situation in which his spouse/intimate partner is exercising personal autonomy (which he likely perceives to be at his great personal expense), whether within the confines of the relationship or while attempting to escape the relationship, violence and/or homicide is seen as the most effective solution. In other words, murdering his spouse/intimate partner may be simply seen as a means to effect control over her and the relationship.

Men who commit sponsicide/intimaticide, compared with nonhomicidal males, are more likely to have extensive histories as drug and alcohol abusers, to be more frequently intoxicated, and to be more frequently both verbally abusive and physically violent. These men have been shown to have higher rates of emotional, physical, and sexual abuse as children compared with nonhomicidal men. Sponsicidal/intimaticidal men are also more likely to have histories of perpetrating sexual violence against their spouses/intimate partners prior to murdering them.

Parricide

Parricide, the murder of one's parent, is usually committed by sons. When a daughter commits an act of parricide, she is likely to coerce the help of a male friend or male sibling to commit the murder. Dawson and Langan (1994) estimated that about 2% of annual homicide victims are killed by their children. British research has shown that sons will most likely murder their parents with explosive violence secondary to either prolonged provocation, parental brutality, or various forms of abuse. Heide identified three main types of parricide offenders: (a) the severely abused child, (b) the severely mentally ill child, and (c) the dangerously antisocial child.

Parracidal events involve the culmination of complex and severely dysfunctional family dynamics. This type of homicide is usually the end result in families that possess the combined effects of multiassaultive family patterns, easy access to firearms, high levels of alcohol consumption, and strong feelings, real or perceived, of helplessness by the children in coping with the multiple stresses within the home. It has been estimated that approximately two thirds of boys aged 11 to 20 who are charged with murder actually killed their fathers, stepfathers, or mothers' intimate partners while these men were actively assaulting their mothers, or shortly thereafter the abusive episode.

Filicide

Filicide refers to the murdering of one's own child at any age. There are various classifications of filicide according to the age of the child.

Neonaticide

Neonaticides, or the murder of a newborn within the first 24 hours of life, are usually committed by the mother. Most of these offenders are young teenagers without any financial or emotional support from their families. They may also deny or hide their pregnancies to avoid reprisals. As a result, they dispose of the children immediately after birth in a state of desperation and confusion. The majority of these offenders do not have the psychological or emotional development necessary to become parents. Secondary to their situations, they experience high levels of anomie, even to the point of complete dissociation during the delivery process. Nonetheless, other than factors related to pregnancy and childbirth, these mothers have very low rates of diagnosable mental illness.

Infanticide

Infanticide is the murdering of one's child who is over 24 hours old and under 5 year of age. These parents tend to be young, but still older than the neonaticide offenders. They tend to be experiencing high levels of subjective and objective stress as primary caregivers, with little to no resources to facilitate their adjustment. They are more likely than neonaticide offenders to have diagnosable psychological disorders. Recent research and case evidence has suggested a potential connection between multiple child deaths related to sudden infant death syndrome (SIDS) in a family and the possibility of infanticide. At this time, new guidelines are being considered by the American Academy of Pediatrics toward the processing of death scene evidence and autopsy findings in children suspected of perishing from SIDS.

Filicide

Filicide is the general term for the killing of one's child at any age by the parent(s), but it is also used to define murder of a child over the age of 5 years. Early filicide is the murder of a child between 5 years and 18 years of age. Late filicide is the killing of an adult child over the age of 18 years. Several patterns have been identified that describe the filicidal behavior of some parents. The first is *altruism,* in which filicidal parents hold the belief, delusional or rational, that they are doing the children a favor by sparing them from some form of future pain and/or suffering (e.g., religious delusions or secondary to terminal or chronic illness).

Second is *fatal abuse,* in which filicide occurs as the end result of a pattern of significant abuse, neglect, or abandonment or as the result of accidental fatal abuse (i.e., shaken baby syndrome, excessive and unintended force). In these cases, the parents intended to physically discipline or punish the child, but did not intend murder. Overloading of caregiver frustration may be the genesis of accidental fatal abuse.

Third, some parents have killed their children as a result of mental illness or as secondary to substance abuse. Fourth, some parents have killed their children simply because they don't want them anymore. For example, they may be seen as a financial liability or as a barrier to the parents' ambitions; they may murder them because the child is the product of an unsupported union (e.g., extramarital affair, rape, illegitimate); or they may have grown weary of the continual conflicts between themselves and their children and their failure to effect change in their children's behavior. Some parents will murder their children for the financial gains of easy-to-acquire life insurance policies. And, finally, it has been noted that on occasion, though quite rarely, one spouse/intimate partner, or estranged spouse/ intimate partner, has murdered a child as a means of revenge or of traumatizing the other individual.

Siblicide

There are two types of siblicide: *fratricide,* or the killing of one's brother, and *sororicide,* or the killing of one's sister. Siblicide has been the least studied expression of intrafamilial homicide. Sulloway hypothesized that older siblings would be more siblicidal. Yet in reviewing Canadian homicide data between 1974 and 1995, Marleau and Saucier (1998) found that only 44% of their 266 cases supported this notion, and Underwood and Patch's (1998) findings with 202 cases in the United States data coincide with those results.

One of the more recent examinations of siblicide rates is Dawson and Langan's *Special Report on Murder in Families,* published through the Bureau of Justice Statistics (1994). This report was based on homicide data for 1988. According to their findings, 85% of siblicide offenders and 73% of siblicide victims were male. Victim and offender ethnicity showed that approximately one third were Caucasian, two thirds were African American, and 2% were of other ethnic backgrounds. Approximately 10% of victims were under 12 years of age, 2% were 12 to 19 years of age, 43% were 20 to 29 years of age, 43% were 30 to 59 years of age, and 3% were 60 years or older. Alcohol was reported to play a role in approximately one half of the siblicides in Dawson and Langan's study. Approximately one fifth of incidents involved mental illness. When sisters murdered siblings, approximately half the victims were brothers. Firearms were used in approximately one third of the siblicides.

Dawson and Langan's work is limited in certain ways, however. Their sample was drawn from only 33 counties across the United States and examined data on only 123 cases of siblicide. In addition, their figures in regard to criminal history, mental health history, and substance abuse were derived from only a portion (approximately one third to two thirds) of the cases reviewed for their report. Underwood's (2000) research on 1,236 cases of siblicide provides the most comprehensive data on this subject to date.

In various studies, Underwood and Patch found that the incidents of siblicide occur throughout the life span; the rate of sibling homicide appears to be stable at around 1.0% of the total homicide rate in the nation. In other words, 1 of every 100 homicides involves one sibling killing another. They found that siblicide is more common in the South than in any other region in the United States. Juveniles accounted for only approximately 10% to 16% of the offenders and 11% to 17% of the victims (Patch & Underwood, 1998; Underwood & Patch, 1998, 1999; Underwood, 2000). Males were more likely to be both victims and offenders than were females. Yet females were far more likely to be victims than offenders.

Regarding victim-to-offender relationship, Underwood and Patch found that a distinct relationship hierarchy existed, the frequency being, highest to lowest, (a) brothers killing brothers, (b) brothers killing sisters, (c) sisters killing brothers, and (d) sisters killing sisters. Firearms and knives were overwhelmingly the weapons of choice, and some form of interpersonal argument was the precipitating circumstance to the homicidal event. African Americans were overrepresented for their population ratio yet equal in the number of incidents with Caucasians. Underwood (2000) significantly expanded the database on siblicide, and the reader is encouraged to review his extensive analysis of this form of intrafamilial homicide.

Familicide

Familicide refers to the killing of multiple members of one's family, if not the entire family. This type of homicide offender has been referred to as the "family annihilator." Dietz defined this individual as the murderer who kills an entire family at one time and may even kill the family pet. This person is generally the senior male of the family, often has a history of alcohol abuse, and exhibits great periods of depression. However, recent cases have shown that these events are also perpetrated both by younger males in the family and by mothers.

The motivations for this type of murder reside within the disturbed psyche of the offender. The available data from such cases indicate that these offenders frequently and/or pervasively feel alone in the world, experience frequent and significant periods of anomie, and typically feel helpless to effectively create positive change in their lives. When they feel they have reached their personal limits of dealing with the stresses of their lives, they enact a personal campaign of significant violence aimed against those who share their homes and sometimes others who are not family members. Their homicidal behavior is driven by the despair of their own lives. More often than not, within familicides, the family annihilator also commits suicide. The majority of homicide-suicides involve family members, usually ex-spouses or separating spouses.

Geographic mobility plays a very small role in familicide. Given that these murders are usually committed within the offender's own residence, the family annihilator tends to live in the area where the crimes are committed. Usually, the familicide offenders have resided in the same community throughout their lifetimes. Thus, their spatial mobility is stable. They choose to end the lives of their families for reasons that are sometimes unclear, not only to investigators but to the killer as well. These individuals possess an intrinsic motivation for their killings, and their anticipated gains are expressive in nature. Their victim selection is specific to family members but may extend out to those whom they feel have caused them to suffer in some way or another. Thus, their victim-offender relationship is affiliative, and consequently their victims have nonspecific traits.

CONCLUSION

The family is a complex social system consisting of many roles and demands and is both a closed system and a private social group. As such, its interactions and behaviors are withheld from the view of others as much as possible. Familial social interactions tend to be more intense, emotional, and consequential than other interactions. In addition, familial systems are multidimensional, and the direction of familial influence appears to be reciprocal, whether positive or negative. These factors, as well as many others, make the task of understanding this phenomenon extremely complicated. It is hoped that in time, researchers will be able to develop deeper levels of understanding in regard to familial relationships and lower the risk of intrafamilial homicide.

—*Rocky Underwood*

See also Battered Woman's Syndrome; Child Killers; Cycle Theory of Violence; Homicide, Types of, and Degrees of Murder; Motives for Murder; Murder-Suicide; Women and Violence; Yates, Andrea

Further Reading

Barnard, G. W., Vera, H., Vera, M. I., & Newman, G. (1982). Til death do us part: A study of spouse murder. *Bulletin of the American Academy of Psychiatry and the Law, 10,* 271-280.

Browne, A. (1987). *When battered women kill.* New York: Free Press.

Bunge, V. P. (2002). National trends in intimate partner homicide, 1974-2000. *Juristat, 22*(5), Canadian Center for Justice Statistics.

Conway, Z. (1989). Factors predicting verdicts in cases where battered women kill their husbands. *Law and Human Behavior, 13,* 253-269.

Dawson, J. M., & Langan, P. A. (1994). *Murder in families.* Washington, DC: U.S. Department of Justice, Office of Justice Programs.

Dawson, J. M., & Langan, P. A. (1995). *Spouse murder defendants in large urban counties* (NCJ 153256). Washington, DC: Department of Justice, Bureau of Justice Statistics.

Dietz, P. (1986). Mass, serial and sensational homicides. *Bulletin of the New York Academy of Medicine, 62,* 477-491.

d'Orban, P. T. (1979). Women who kill their children. *British Journal of Psychiatry, 134,* 560-571.

d'Orban, P. T., & O'Conner, A. (1989). Women who kill their parents. *British Journal of Psychiatry, 154,* 27-33.

Ewing, C. P. (1997). *Fatal families: The dynamics of intrafamilial homicide.* Thousand Oaks, CA: Sage.

Fedorowycz, O. (2001). Homicide in Canada-2000. *Juristat, 21(9).* Canadian Center for Justice Statistics.

Frieze, I. H., & Browne, A. (1989). Violence in marriage. In L. Ohlin & M. Tonry (Eds.), *Family violence* (Vol. 11). Chicago: University of Chicago Press.

Heide, K. (1993). Parents who get killed and the children who kill them. *Journal of Interpersonal Violence, 8(4),* 531-544.

Holmes, R. M., & Holmes, S. T. (1994). *Murder in America.* Thousand Oaks, CA: Sage.

Home Office. (1986). *Criminal statistics: England and Wales, 1985.* London: HMSO.

Humphrey, J. A., & Palmer, S. (1987). Stressful life events and criminal homicide. *Omega: Journal of Death and Dying, 17,* 299-308.

Korbin, J. (1986). Childhood histories of women imprisoned for fatal child maltreatment. *Child Abuse and Neglect, 10,* 331-338.

Mann, C. R. (1988). Getting even? Women who kill in domestic encounters. In S. L. Johann & F. Osanka (Eds.), *Representing battered women who kill.* Springfield, IL: Charles C Thomas.

Marleau, J. D., & Saucier, J. F. (1998). Birth order and fratricidal behavior in Canada. *Psychological Reports, 82(3),* 817-818.

Pagelow, M. D. (1989). The incidence and prevalence of criminal abuse of other family members. In L. Ohlin & M. Tonry (Eds.), *Family violence* (Vol. 11). Chicago: University of Chicago Press.

Parker, R. N., & Auerhahn, K. (1999). Drugs, alcohol, and homicide: Issues in theory and research. In M. D. Smith & M. A. Zhan (Eds.), *Homicide: A sourcebook for social research* (pp. 176-191). Thousand Oaks, CA: Sage.

Patch, P. C., & Underwood, R. C. (1998, October). *Siblicide abuse and sibling homicide among juveniles.* Unpublished paper. Presented at the YWCA Domestic Violence Institute & Family Violence & Sexual Assault Institute's 4th International Conference on Children Exposed to Family Violence, San Diego, CA.

Rasche, C. (1993). Given reason for violence in intimate relationships. In A. Wilson (Ed.), *Homicide.* Cincinnati, OH: Anderson.

Shackleford, T. K. (2000). Wife killing: Risk to women as a function of age. *Violence & Victims, 15(3),* 273-282.

Statistics Canada. (2000). *Family violence in Canada: A statistical profile, 2000.* Ottawa: Canadian Center for Justice Statistics.

Sulloway, F. J. (1996). *Born to rebel: Birth order, family dynamics, and creative lives.* New York: Pantheon Books.

Underwood, R. C. (2000, June). *My brother's keeper or my brother's killer: An in-depth investigation into the phenomenon of sibling homicide.* Dissertation Abstracts International, Section B: The Sciences and Engineering, Vol. 61(11-B) (p. 6151). University Microfilms International. (DAI# AAT 9994804).

Underwood, R. C., & Patch, P. C. (1998, March). *Siblicide: An analysis of dynamics and demographics.* Unpublished paper. Presented at the 23rd Annual Conference of the Forensic Mental Health Association of California, Pacific Grove, CA.

Underwood, R. C., & Patch, P. C. (1999). Siblicide: A descriptive analysis of sibling homicide. *Homicide Studies: An Interdisciplinary & International Journal, 3(4),* 243-247. (NCJ# 178108).

Walker, L. E. (1979). *The battered woman.* New York: Harper & Row.

Walker, L. E. (1989). *Terrifying love: Why battered women kill and how society responds.* New York: HarperCollins.

Wilson, M., & Daly, M. (1994). Spousal homicide. *Juristat, 14(8).* Ottawa: Canadian Center for Justice Statistics.

FAMILY VIOLENCE

Family violence is most broadly defined as violence by and against members of the same family or household. There is extensive evidence of the existence of violence within the family since the earliest beginnings of family life. Historically, this type of violence has not been regarded as criminal or of social concern, but rather as a family matter, neither very serious nor worthy of criminal prosecution. Prior to 1970, the leading academic journal in the area of family studies, *Journal of Marriage and Family,* did not publish a single article containing the word "violence" in its title. Only in the last few decades have academics, researchers, child and women advocates, legislators, and other concerned members of society begun to open this door and focus on what is now considered to be an extensive social problem.

Certain unique factors in family life make this form of violence distinctive from others that are common in our society and can stimulate conflict and violence: emotional intensity of involvement, time at risk, age and sex discrimination, family privacy, involuntary membership, ascribed roles, and high level of stress. There is some dispute as to what forms of violence should fall within the broad category of domestic violence. The following section includes child abuse and neglect, spousal abuse, spousal rape, elderly abuse, and family homicide.

TYPES OF FAMILY VIOLENCE

Child Abuse and Neglect

Historically, the further back in time in many societies, the less adequate the child care and the more likely abuse, abandonment, traumatization, and murder of children. Unwanted newborns (imperfect, sickly, deformed, illegitimate, twins, or females) were thrown on the dung heap to die. Children were often mutilated to improve their potential as beggars. Beatings and whippings were an expected part of childhood. As evidence of a child's station within society, the SPCA (Society for Prevention of Cruelty to Animals) was established quite some time before the SPCC (Society for Prevention of Cruelty to Children). In fact, the famous 1866 New York child abuse case of Mary Ellen Wilson actually turned to protection under the SPCA, because the SPCC wasn't created until 1874.

Modern concern with child abuse had its beginnings with the research of Dr. C. Henry Kempe and his colleagues and their discovery in 1962 of "battered child syndrome," which detailed evidence of repeated multiple bone fractures of children suspected of being abused. Throughout the 1960s, child welfare and protective services were very influential in bringing the serious problem of child abuse and neglect to the public's attention.

On an annual basis, state child protective services (CPS) agencies receive and refer for investigation an estimated 2 million reports of child abuse and neglect, which involve over 2.3 million children. The number of children reported annually has more than tripled over the past 20 years for which this data has been collected (National Child Abuse and Child Neglect Data System, 1998).

Child Abuse Categories

Physical abuse is nonaccidental bodily injury inflicted against a child under the age of 18 years. It is an act that often represents unreasonably severe or unjustifiable corporal punishment. This includes willful cruelty or deliberate assault, such as cutting, biting, burning, twisting limbs, or other forms of torture.

Symptoms indicating this form of abuse are bruises in various stages of healing; bruises on mouth, arms, back, buttocks, or thighs; frequent burns, welts, or broken bones from unlikely "accidents"; human bite marks on arm, leg, shoulder, or neck; fractures of the jaw, skull, nasal passage, or spiral breaks of arm or leg; limping or obviously slow mobility or no movement at all; wearing inappropriate clothing, such as long sleeves in hot weather or refusing to undress for gym; learning disabilities or developmental lags in cases where no indicated psychological or physical anomalies exist.

Emotional abuse is the nonphysical mistreatment of a child, including the willful causing of child to suffer, unjustifiable mental suffering including humiliation, degradation, property violence, isolation, threats, and emotional withholding.

Symptoms indicating this form of abuse are poor self-esteem; regressive behavior, such as pants-wetting and thumb-sucking; anxiety, withdrawal behavior, or overly aggressive behavior; being very disruptive and demanding attention; speech disorders and developmental lags or slowness.

Child neglect is the failure of the parent or caretaker of the child to provide adequate shelter, food, medical care, supervision, and clothing or the exposing the child to exploitation or an unwholesome or unsafe environment.

Symptoms indicating this form of abuse are evidence of malnutrition, such as being underweight, very pale, or becoming exhausted easily; uncleanliness; skin sores; always hungry, extortion of food or lunch money from other children; lack of normal strength and endurance; and need of dental care or eyeglasses.

Sexual abuse refers to the exploitation of a child for the sexual gratification of an adult or older person. Sexual activities include indecent exposure, fondling, verbal stimulation, pornography, molestation, and rape. When it occurs between family members, it is called *incest.*

Factors indicating this form of abuse are being apprehensive and fearful of physical contact or affection; bruises, bleeding, or infection in genital or anal areas; torn or stained underclothing; sexually explicit knowledge beyond the child's age; and sexually transmitted diseases or pregnancy.

Spousal Abuse

Spousal abuse is defined as assaultive or abusive behavior between adults who are married, cohabiting, or having an ongoing (or had a prior) intimate relationship. Battering can be categorized into the following four forms: (a) physical abuse, (b) psychological abuse, (c) sexual abuse, and (d) destruction of property. From the earliest historical times, there has been documentation of the battering of wives. For many centuries, the law as well as social convention have allowed the husband the authority to chastise or use violence against his wife and children. Under the English common law, the wife was regarded as man's property or chattel. The concept "rule of thumb" refers to the legal doctrine that permitted a husband to beat his wife with a stick as long as that stick was no thicker than his thumb.

Although child abuse is a very serious problem in this country, and there is strong evidence of a growing problem with elderly abuse, wives are still the most common victims of family violence. The studies estimating the magnitude (prevalence and incidence) of spousal abuse in the United States have varied dramatically. These figures are affected by reporting and definitional variations. Sociologists roughly estimate that between 3 and 6 million women are physically abused by their domestic partners on an annual basis. It is unfortunately true that woman who are slapped and shoved around, methodically beaten, raped, or killed are part of one of our most sacred institutions, the family (see Box 1).

Characteristics of Abused
Spouses and Their Abusers

Numerous factors seem to increase the likelihood of abuse or violence in an intimate relationship.

Box 1   Women You Know May be Victims

Domestic violence is a problem shared by women of every age, religion, ethnic background, income, and educational level. Battered women may be any age, 16 or 85. They are housewives, secretaries, teachers, sales clerks, and lawyers. They live in large cities, small towns, and rural areas. As different as their background may be, battered women have much in common. They are all victims of physical, verbal, or emotional abuse.

According to the Federal Bureau of Investigation, every 18 seconds, somewhere in America, a woman is beaten.

♦ 50% of American wives are beaten by their partners at least once during their married lives.

♦ 20% of hospital emergencies are cases in which women are beaten by their partners.

♦ 25% of all reported victims of spousal abuse are pregnant women.

♦ Over 40% of women who are murdered die at the hands of their husbands or lovers.

♦ 73% of abusive males came from homes in which they watched their fathers beat their mothers.

♦ 63% of boys age 11 to 20 who commit homicide murder the men who abuse their mothers.

♦ In one half of spouse-abusing families, the children are battered as well.

♦ Battering violence against women occurs more often than incidents of rape, mugging, and car accidents combined.

♦ Once a woman has been victimized by domestic violence, she faces a high risk of further victimization. Within 6 months, approximately one third will be revictimized.

Source: Statements from brochure, "Violence: Could It Strike You?" Domestic Violence Intervention Services, Inc., Tulsa, Oklahoma.

Included among these factors are dating violence, youth, premarital pregnancy, isolation, and emotional or financial dependence. A wide range of features have been associated with domestic abusers who abuse their spouses, including low self-esteem, poor impulse control, insatiable ego needs, authoritative personality, jealousy, social isolation, fear of abandonment, moodiness, limited capacity for delayed reinforcement, employment problems, alcohol and drug dependency, violence in home of orientation, becoming easily angered, traditional attitudes, and lack of emotional expression.

Why would an adult who is being victimized stay in that abusive relationship? Battered spouses are often threatened with greater violence if they take any action against their partners. Fear is one of the most common reasons that the abused victim does not report the crime. Others include economic dependence; the cyclical nature in which affectionate, loving, and contrite behavior often follows the abusive episode; privacy issues; guilty feelings of failure; isolation, ignorance, or feeling helpless.

Marital Rape

During the 1970s, the two major feminist rallying points were those of rape and spouse abuse. The intersection of these two issues, forced marital intercourse or marital rape, was brought to the nation's attention in the *State of Oregon v. Rideout* (1978), in which a man was charged with the rape of his wife and brought to criminal trial. The traditional Anglo-Saxon legal definition of rape grants the husband immunity from prosecution for forced intercourse with his wife. This lack of recourse is important in light of the fact that the person most likely to force a woman to have unwanted sexual intercourse is her spouse or significant other. Research has shown that more than 15% of women are raped by their spouses. The psychological and emotional damage of this sexual assault is more extensive and harmful than that experienced by those raped by a stranger. Factors such as loss of trust, fear, and isolation from supportive individuals increases the emotional damage caused by marital rape. Over the last few decades, there has been a trend toward altering criminal sanctions concerning spousal immunity, and today, most states have either narrowed the immunity (charged spouse with rape if legally separated) or eliminated it altogether.

Elder Abuse

Facts of Elder Abuse

The proportion of the elderly population (age 65 and older) has risen dramatically over the last few decades and will continue to rise for the foreseeable future. Approximately 15% of the American population are elderly today, and by 2030, they will represent 22% of the population, with over 66 million Americans being 65 or older. Estimates of the percentage of elderly persons who are abused range from 4% to 8%, with best estimates suggesting that at least 1 million elderly persons are abused by their caretakers each year. The elderly have commonly been victims of four general types of abuse: physical (including sexual) abuse, physical neglect, psychological/emotional abuse, and financial exploitation. Only a small percentage of these victimizations are reported to the authorities. Studies suggest that only 7% to 10% of all cases of elderly abuse are reported to the police or social service agencies.

Victims of elder abuse are of advanced age with impairments, isolated, and inexperienced with financial matters. The victims are more likely to be women, age 75 to 85 years, often frail, middle to lower class, often having assets over $50,000. They often suffer from mental or physical disabilities, frequently live alone, and are socially isolated. These victims rarely report their victimization because of fear of future retaliation, fear of being removed from their homes, or ignorance that the conduct was criminal.

Elder abuse is most often perpetrated by family members or by persons in a position of trust. The profile of perpetrators of elderly physical abuse or neglect shows that they are most often family members, usually adult children. Although male caretakers are more likely to abuse the elderly physically, female caretakers are more likely to neglect or psychologically abuse the elderly. The majority of abusers are middle-aged and are the victims' primary care providers and offspring of the abused.

The profile of offenders who perpetrate financial exploitation of the elderly includes many of the same characteristics as those listed for physical abusers. In addition, these offenders are frequently dependent on their victims (often live with victims), may be abusing drugs or alcohol, have histories of depression or mental illness, are either unemployed or have spotty work records, and have histories of financial problems.

Elder Abuse Categories

Physical abuse of the elderly is nonaccidental bodily injury inflicted against a person over the age of 65 committed by the caretaker or family member. The abuse can be either an assault, battery, sexual assault, or unreasonable physical constraint.

Factors indicating this form of abuse are bruises, cuts, broken bones, burns, signs of confinement such as rope burns or bindings, untreated injuries, frequent changes of doctors, frequent need of emergency care, mistrust of others, and regressive or overly aggressive behavior.

Neglect of the elderly is the failure of the caretaker of an elderly or dependent adult to provide food, clothing, or shelter, assist in personal hygiene, provide necessary medical care, or protect from health and safety hazards.

Factors indicating this form of abuse are malnutrition or weight loss; bed or pressure sores; unclean or soiled linen or clothing; withholding of medication; absence of glasses, hearing aids, or dentures; absence of food, water, or heat; untreated medical condition.

Financial exploitation of elderly occurs when the caretaker or financial custodian of an elder or dependent adult appropriates the elder's money or property for any use outside the lawful execution of their financial trust.

Factors indicating this form of abuse are unusual activity in bank or other financial accounts, change in the elder's property titles, suspicious activities on credit cards, forged or suspicious signatures on documents, an elder not receiving pension or government payments, lack of services or amenities the elder had in the past, disconnected utilities and other services, mail being redirected to a new address, untreated medical or mental health problems, and missing property.

THEORETICAL EXPLANATION OF FAMILY VIOLENCE

Research and theoretical development in the area of family violence has existed for only the last couple of decades. In the early years of family violence research, there was an attempt to use traditional criminological theories as the basis for this research and the resulting causal explanations. There is, however, strong evidence supporting the belief that the characteristics of family violence are fundamentally different from traditional street (generally stranger) violence. If this is in fact true, then family violence needs its own "family-based theories" to help explain this unique behavior and to guide necessary social policy, treatment, and programs. This section discusses several recently developed family-violence-based concepts and theories. The

theories include patriarchal-masculinity theory, cycle of violence-intergenerational theory, disavowal theory, and finally, the battered woman's syndrome.

Patriarchal-Masculinity Theory

The patriarchal-masculinity theory suggests that our society supports the dominance of males over females and accepts the Freudian view that males are biologically, psychologically, and socially superior to females. According to this theory, society should be dominated by the superior males, with females and children as their property or possessions placed in a subordinate position. In this view, societal customs and laws uphold the power differential between men and women and legitimize different gender roles, which leads to the use of force and violence by dominant males against women and children.

Under the patriarchal perspective, men have the historical and legal right to use violence to protect their dominant position over women. Historically, the patriarch, or "king," had the right to use or dispose of his property or possessions as he saw fit. This theory would conclude that patriarchal attitudes, social norms, and legal protections have been largely responsible for the historical pattern of violence toward women and children.

Cycle of Violence-Intergenerational Theory

The cycle of violence theory is one of the most popular and widely accepted theories of family violence. It hypothesizes that victims of family violence will themselves eventually become the abusers of their family members; for example, children who are abused will abuse their own children. They would also be more likely to victimize their younger siblings, their wives, or even, years later, their own elderly parents. Thus, individuals will grow up to be abusive because they were abused. According to this theory, a never-ending cycle of family physical violence is passed from one generation of the family to the next.

Within the field of family violence, there is much debate and controversy as to the validity of this theory. The overall consequences of family abuse have not been well researched or documented, and determining which factors are responsible (causal) for future behavior is difficult at best. As an example, a study that asks a group of batterers, within a court-ordered treatment program having no appropriate control group, about their childhood abuse is so wrought with methodological limitations as to make any research generalizations almost meaningless. Research may be able to conclude that those who are abused as children will be more likely to abuse their own children than those who are not abused. However, it is also true that many, probably the majority, of those who were abused as children will not grow up to repeat that pattern of abuse on their own children.

Disavowal Theory

It is a common belief among many laypersons and professionals within the justice system that drug and alcohol use is a major cause of family violence. This belief is supported by numerous studies that have shown a strong relationship between alcohol and drug use and various forms of family violence. The use and abuse of drugs, particularly alcohol, is often noted as a major factor in the area of spousal violence. A large majority of men who abuse their spouses are alcohol users, many of them being daily users and abusers of alcohol. Although studies show an association between alcohol use and incidents of spousal abuse, they do not show this to be a matter of cause and effect. Disavowal theory suggests that the use of alcohol is not the reason or cause for the abuse, but an excuse that allows spousal abusers to abuse and then deny responsibility. Thus, alcohol becomes a technique in which some abusers start drinking when they feel like abusing their spouse, with the notion that if they are drunk or under the influence of alcohol, society will place far less direct blame on them for the beating of their spouses.

Battered Woman's Syndrome

Battered woman's syndrome refers to a unique behavioral and psychological reaction to a series of common experiences by women who are physically abused by a dominating male over an extended period of time. It includes the psychological impact of the battering cycle, common personality traits of the battered woman, and various social and economic factors that make it difficult for the woman to leave the battering relationship.

The physical abuse of battered women tends to escalate in frequency and severity over the period of the relationship. The concept of battered woman syndrome was originally developed by Lenore E. Walker, in *The Battered Woman,* in which she noted that the relationship is not one of constant abuse, but of a battering cycle that includes tension building; violent episodes or acute explosions; and a period of contrition, love, and affection—and then the cycle of violence starts all over again. The personality traits common among battered women include low self-esteem; depression; traditional values concerning female sex roles, family, and marriage; and guilt and feelings of failure and learned helplessness.

—*R. Thomas Dull*

See also BATTERED CHILD SYNDROME; BATTERED WOMAN'S SYNDROME; BATTERERS AND ABUSIVE PARTNERS; CHILD ABUSE; DOMESTIC VIOLENCE; ELDER ABUSE; FAMILY HOMICIDE; MURDER-SUICIDE; WOMEN AND VIOLENCE; YATES, ANDREA

Further Reading

McGee, C. (2000). *Childhood exploration of domestic violence.* Philadelphia, PA: Jessica Kingsley.

Snow, R. L. (1997). *Family abuse: Tough solutions to stop the violence.* New York: Plenum Trade.

Walker, L. (1979). *The battered woman.* New York: Harper & Row.

Wallace, H. (2002). *Family violence: Legal, medical, and social perspectives* (3rd ed.). Boston: Allyn & Bacon.

THE FEDERAL BUREAU OF INVESTIGATION

HISTORY OF THE FBI

During the administration of President Theodore Roosevelt, Attorney General Charles Bonaparte created within the Department of Justice a corps of special agents that consisted of former detectives and Secret Service men. In May 1908, when it became illegal for the Department of Justice to hire or engage any Secret Service personnel, Attorney General Bonaparte appointed Chief Examiner Stanley Finch as the leader of a group of 34 agents, which later became known as the Bureau of Investigation.

The Mann Act of 1910, which prohibited the interstate transportation of women for immoral purposes, greatly increased the task of the Bureau of Investigation. Over the next few years, it expanded to more than 300 agents and 300 support personnel. Field offices existed in major cities and were directed by a Special Agent in Charge, who reported to headquarters in Washington. In 1919, William Flynn replaced Finch as the head of the Bureau of Investigation and became the first individual to call himself director.

When J. Edgar Hoover took over as director of the Bureau on May 10, 1924, there were approximately 440 special agents in 9 field offices throughout the United States. By the end of the decade, there were 30 field offices and nine divisional offices. In an ongoing effort to enhance the image of the agency, Hoover fired any agents he deemed unqualified or unsuitable. He introduced performance appraisals, regular field office inspections, and a formal training course for new agents. He further required that new agents be 25 to 35 years old and have a law or accounting background.

In 1924, Congress merged the Bureau of Criminal Identification and the collection of fingerprint cards maintained by the International Association of Chiefs of Police into one central location in Washington, D.C. This new National Division of Identification and Information became part of the Bureau of Investigation.

Under Hoover, the Bureau continued to expand. By 1939, the number of agents had increased to more than 650, support employees numbered over 1,000, and there were field offices in 42 cities. The Bureau had been renamed the United States Bureau of Investigation in 1932 and finally in 1935 was called the Federal Bureau of Investigation (FBI).

By 1940, the FBI had also established itself as a leader in evidence analysis and law enforcement training. The technical lab was expanded and had extensive specializations in identification and analysis of guns, tool marks, tire marks, and other forms of evidence. The FBI National Academy trained and taught new techniques and information to law enforcement officials from the United States and around the world.

Concerns that communist sympathizers had infiltrated the U.S. government were building in the late 1940s. Hoover focused the resources of the FBI on the threat of communism in the government and throughout the country. The investigation and arrest of alleged spies was an emphasis of the Bureau during the 1950s.

In the 1960s, Congress passed sweeping new civil rights legislation. With the added responsibility of investigating individuals and groups intent on violating these statutes, the FBI grew to over 6,700 agents and 9,300 support personnel in over 58 field offices and 12 legal attaché offices.

J. Edgar Hoover died in 1972, having served as director for almost 48 years. L. Patrick Gray became acting director and was the first to appoint women as special agents. In 1973, director Clarence Kelley, who served until 1978, established three main priorities for the Bureau: organized crime, white-collar crime, and foreign counterintelligence. He emphasized the need for more ethnic, racial, and gender diversity within the ranks of the organization. By the late 1970s, the FBI employed 8,000 agents, 11,000 support personnel, and 13 legal attachés.

Judge William Webster was appointed director in 1978. He included counterterrorism as a fourth priority for the FBI. In 1982, the FBI and DEA (Drug Enforcement Agency) were given concurrent jurisdiction over drug violations and began working on cases together.

Judge William Sessions directed the FBI from 1987 to 1993. He targeted violent crime and attempted to strengthen the Bureau's response to white-collar crime.

In September 1993, Louis J. Freeh began his term as Director of the FBI, emphasizing the globalization of crime and the need for international cooperation. He appointed the first woman, Hispanic and African American, to be named assistant director. Director Freeh began the construction of a new state-of-the-art FBI forensic lab. Freeh resigned in June 2001.

Director Robert Mueller took office on September 4, 2001, just one week before the terrorist attacks on the New York World Trade Center and the Pentagon. He has responded by reorganizing the FBI and refocusing its priority on protecting Americans by preventing future terrorist attacks. He has shifted the emphasis of the Bureau to a proactive response, as opposed to the many decades of reactive behavior. The organization hopes to hire an additional 900 agents with specializations in Middle Eastern languages, computer analysis, and engineering.

ORGANIZATIONAL STRUCTURE

The FBI consists of approximately 11,400 special agents, 16,400 support personnel, 40 legal attachés, 400 satellite offices, and 56 field offices. A special agent in charge (SAC) supervises each field office and reports directly to headquarters (FBIHQ).

The four major divisions at FBIHQ are overseen by executive assistant directors. The executive assistant director for criminal investigations supervises the cybercrime division and the criminal investigative division. The executive assistant director for counterterrorism and counterintelligence oversees the office of intelligence, the counterterrorism division, and the counterintelligence division. The executive assistant director for law enforcement services supervises the training division, the criminal justice information services division, the laboratory division, the aviation and language service, and international and law enforcement operations. The executive assistant director for administration supervises the records division, office of professional responsibility, office of economic and employment opportunities, administration services, security, finances, and information resources.

The four executive assistant directors are responsible to the deputy director of the Bureau, who reports directly to the FBI director. Throughout this organizational chart are supervisors, assistant special agents in charge (ASAC), special agents in charge (SAC), assistant unit chiefs, unit chiefs, section or division chiefs, deputy assistant directors, and assistant directors. Nearly 9,800 employees (support and special agents) are assigned to FBIHQ. The high number of personnel at FBIHQ and the recent bogging down of field information sent to headquarters has highlighted the bureaucracy of the FBI. In his reorganization attempts, Director Mueller is hoping to streamline the flow of information from the field to headquarters and to give the field office greater decision-making power.

Special Units for Homicide

The Behavioral Science Unit provides programs of training, research, and consultation in the behavioral and social sciences for the FBI and law enforcement community. The research of the unit emphasizes the solution of violent crimes through a greater understanding of offenders, their behavior, and their motives.

Supervisory special agents, forensic psychologists, research analysts, and police officers make up the unit. Oftentimes, the research is conducted in conjunction with other agencies and academic institutions. The Behavioral Sciences Unit coordinates and supports other FBI units, such as the National Center for the Analysis of Violent Crime (NCAVC) and the Critical Incident Response Group (CIRG).

NCAVC includes the Violent Criminal Apprehension Program (VICAP), which collects and analyzes data from throughout the country. The main information concerns homicides, missing persons, and unsolved crimes. The data is entered and compared with other submitted cases in hopes of analyzing similar information and assisting with solutions.

CIRG offers investigative and operational support to federal and local law enforcement agencies. The members of the unit train child abductor coordinators for the various FBI field offices. The Child Abduction Serial Murder Investigative Resources Center (CASMIRC) is part of CIRG. The unit works closely with the Center for Missing and Exploited Children.

CONCLUSION

The Federal Bureau of Investigation states that "FBI" stands for Fidelity, Bravery, and Integrity. Throughout the 20th century, the organization grew from a group of unnamed detectives to one of the most elite and certainly one of the largest law enforcement agencies of modern time. The 21st century offers great challenges for the Bureau. Time will determine if a bureaucracy as large and as enmeshed as the FBI is able to change to meet the new demands and challenges facing them.

—*Patricia L. Kirby*

See also FBI TOP 10 MOST WANTED PROGRAM; JURISDICTION; UNIFORM CRIME REPORTS

Further Reading

Kessler, R. (2002). *Bureau: The secret history of the FBI.* New York: Saint Martin's.

Vise, D. (2001). *The bureau and the mole.* Berkeley, CA: Grove/Atlantic.

THE FBI TOP 10 MOST WANTED PROGRAM

On February 7, 1949, an article titled "FBI's Most Wanted Fugitives Named" appeared in the *Washington Daily News.* It was written by a reporter from United Press International after he had contacted the FBI and asked for information on the "toughest guys" the FBI was searching for. The FBI provided the information in the hope that the publicity would help capture these dangerous offenders. Much to the delight of director J. Edgar Hoover, the list created a sensation. Because of the initial success, the FBI "10 Most Wanted Fugitives" program was developed, and a year later, on March 14, 1950, the first list was published. The 10 Most Wanted List originally appeared on bulletin boards of public buildings, but with the advent of more modern communication systems, such as the Internet, the list is currently available across the country and the rest of the world on the FBI Web site (www.fbi.gov). In addition, the list is broadcast through a weekly ABC radio network program called *FBI This Week* and through other viewer participation programs such as *America's Most Wanted: America Fights Back.*

The list is compiled from candidates submitted by the 56 FBI field offices throughout the United States. There are two main criteria to determine who should be placed on the list. First, the fugitive must be considered an extremely dangerous menace to society and/or have a long record of committing serious crimes. Second, the FBI must believe that the national publicity will assist in apprehending the fugitive. Often, individuals on the list are dangerous but not widely known by the general press and therefore not well-known to the general public.

Once a name has been submitted, it is reviewed by special agents in the Criminal Investigative Division (CID) and the Office of Public and Congressional Affairs. The selected candidates are submitted to the assistant director of the CID for his or her approval and then to the deputy director of the FBI for final approval. The name remains on the list unless the individual is captured, found dead, or surrenders; the process against them is dismissed by a court of law; or they no longer fit the Top 10 criteria. When a fugitive is removed from the list, another is selected to take the position. Occasionally, the list exceeds 10 names, which has occurred 11 times since its inception. An additional name may be added when there is a full list and another individual is sought immediately. For example, James Earl Ray, Martin Luther King's suspected killer, was added in the 1960s. On October 17, 1970, four additions were made to the list, bringing it to an all-time high of 16. It is important to note there is no ranking of names on the list, and they are all considered equal.

As of June 2002, there have been 475 individuals on the "10 Most Wanted Fugitives" list. Of these, 445 have been located, 145 of them as a direct result of citizen cooperation. Process was dismissed against 15 of the individuals on the list. Five fugitives were removed from the list because they no longer fit the list criteria. The average time a name is listed is 316 days. The longest a name has been listed is 6,800 days and counting, and the shortest time on the list was an amazing 2 hours. Austin Bryant was arrested just 2 hours after he was placed on the list on January 8, 1969. He was charged with killing two FBI agents in Washington, D.C.; bank robbery in Baltimore, Maryland; and escaping from prison, where he'd been serving time for robbery and assault.

The types of fugitives that have appeared on the list over the years of its existence have changed frequently to reflect the changes in society as a whole. The first list included three murderers, a bank robber, an armed robber, two prison escapees, a kidnapper, and an individual wanted for aggravated assault (see Table 1). Most had escaped custody and were being sought so they could be returned to prison. The most recent list includes a terrorist, a racketeer, two bank robbers, two drug dealers, one murderer/arsonist, two murderers, a child pornographer, and a bomber. Many of the newer individuals have also escaped from custody mandated by courts.

It is interesting to note that in the 1950s, the list was comprised of bank robbers, burglars, car thieves, and murderers. In the 1960s, the list reflected the revolutionaries active during this period of social revolution, dominated by individuals involved in the destruction of government property, sabotage, and kidnapping. By the 1970s, the focus had shifted to organized crime and terrorism. During the 1980s and up to the present, the emphasis on terrorism has continued, as well as an active interest in drug-related crimes and serial murder (see Table 2).

The 10 Ten Most Wanted List has been remarkably successful in alerting the general public regarding dangerous offenders who may be living among them. Informers are encouraged by the financial rewards they may receive for the successful capture of listed individuals if the information provided is relevant. These rewards may range from $50,000 to $5 million, depending on the offender. The list has also generated spin-off media vehicles that encourage audience participation in apprehending criminals through the informant mode, which also takes place through the increased, high-tech activity on the Internet. It is comforting to know that criminals "can run but they cannot hide indefinitely." There will always be willing

Table 1   The First FBI 10 Most Wanted List

Name	Date on List	Date Removed From List	Crimes Committed
Thomas James Holden	3/14/50	6/23/51	Killed his wife and her two brothers
Morley Vernon King	3/15/50	10/31/51	Killed his wife and left her in a steamer trunk
William Raymond Nesbit	3/16/50	3/18/50	Attempted murder and murder of two cohorts in crime of burglary; unlawful flight to avoid confinement
Henry Randolph Mitchell	3/17/50	7/18/58	Dropped from list when courts dropped bank robbery charge. Prosecutors felt that the memory of witnesses would be diminished after eight years, so the process was dismissed.
Omar August Pinson	3/18/50	8/28/52	Unlawful flight to avoid confinement (charge: murder); burglary
Lee Emory Downs	3/20/50	4/7/50	Unlawful flight to avoid prosecution; burglary
Orba Elmer Jackson	3/21/50	3/23/50	Unlawful flight to avoid confinement (charge: assault and burglary)
Glen Roy Wright	3/22/50	12/13/50	Former associate with Karpis-Barker Gang; unlawful flight to avoid confinement (charge: robbery)
Henry Harland Shelton	3/23/50	6/23/50	Unlawful flight to avoid confinement; (charges: kidnapping; car theft)
Morris Guralnick	3/24/50	12/15/50	Unlawful flight to avoid prosecution for aggravated assault, three counts

Table 2   Current FBI Ten Most Wanted List

Name	Date on List	Crimes Committed
Osama (Muhammed) bin Ladin	6/7/99	Bombings of U.S. embassies in Tanzania, Nairobi, and Kenya; terrorist attacks throughout the world Murder of U.S. nationals outside the U.S.; conspiracy to murder U.S. nationals outside the U.S.; attack on a federal facility resulting in death
James J. Bulger	8/19/99	Racketeering; murder, 18 counts; conspiracy to commit murder; conspiracy to commit extortion; narcotics distribution; conspiracy to commit money laundering; extortion; money laundering
Victor Manuel Gerena	5/14/84	Bank robbery; unlawful flight to avoid prosecution for armed robbery; theft from interstate shipment
Hopeton Eric Brown	1/2000	Drug-related offenses; murder in relation to drug trafficking; attempted murder of a witness
Robert William Fisher	1/2000	Unlawful flight to avoid prosecution for first-degree murder, three counts; arson of an occupied structure
Glen Stewart Godwin	12/7/96	Unlawful flight to avoid confinement; murder
Richard Steve Goldberg	1/2000	Unlawful flight to avoid prosecution for lewd act on a child, six counts; possession of child pornography, two counts
Eric Robert Rudolph	5/5/98	Maliciously damaged, by means of an explosive device, buildings and property, which resulted in death and injury
James Spencer Springette	1/2000	Conspiracy to import and distribute cocaine; conspiracy to launder monetary instruments
Donald Eugene Webb	1/2000	Unlawful flight to avoid prosecution for murder; attempted burglary

eyes to assist the FBI, and those eyes are sharper because of the FBI 10 Most Wanted List.

—Marlene Deal

See also FEDERAL BUREAU OF INVESTIGATION; COMMUNITY ATTITUDES TOWARD VIOLENT CRIME; "TOP HOODLUM" PROGRAM

Further Reading

Dove, D. J., & Maynard, J. M. (2000). *FBI's Ten Most Wanted Fugitives Program, 50th anniversary, 1950-2000.* Lisbon, MD: K & D Limited.

FBI UNIFORM CRIME REPORT (UCR), *See* UNIFORM CRIME REPORTING PROGRAM

FELONY MURDER STATUTES, *See* HOMICIDE, TYPES OF, AND DEGREES OF MURDER

FEMINISM, *See* AGGRESSION: FEMINIST PERSPECTIVES

COLIN FERGUSON

On the evening of December 7, 1993, a rush-hour train ride from New York City to Long Island erupted in violence. Without provocation or apparent motive, a black man suddenly began shooting his semiautomatic pistol at white and Asian passengers as he walked up and down the aisle on the crowded train. Three passengers subdued the man as he paused to reload his weapon. Six people were killed, and over 20 others were wounded. Colin Ferguson, a 36-year-old man, was held in the shooting. When it was over, he simply said, "I've done a bad thing."

Ferguson, a native of Kingston, Jamaica, was a single, unemployed man living in Brooklyn, New York at the time of the murders. After his arrest, police found

Colin Ferguson boarded a train in New York in December, 1993 and committed mass murder. Ferguson, 37, killed six commuters and wounded 19 during a three-minute rampage on a Long Island Rail Road train.

Source: Copyright © CORBIS.

notes in his pockets expressing his hatred of whites and Asians and the abuse of African Americans by American institutions. Police noted that the seemingly random shooting of the passengers, all either white or Asian, may not have been random after all.

Ferguson was charged with six murders and 19 attempted murders. His trial began in 1994 and became front-page news, not so much because of the legal proceedings themselves, but because of the antics of Ferguson, his attorneys, and Nation of Islam leaders. Ferguson fired one attorney, and the court appointed the well-known radical attorneys William Kunstler and Ronald Kuby. Kunstler and Kuby planned to use the notes found in Ferguson's pockets to present an insanity defense based on "black rage." Defense psychiatric experts agreed that Ferguson was delusional and had major psychiatric problems.

Ferguson fired his attorneys because they claimed that he was insane at the time of the crime, and requested that he be allowed to represent himself. After consideration by the judge, Ferguson was allowed to defend himself, with the condition that he accept an attorney to advise him during trial.

The trial became even more absurd when Ferguson cross-examined the victims of the shootings, ranting at the court and at witnesses. The trial continued to its circus-like end, and the jury found Ferguson guilty of all charges. On March 23, 1995, the judge sentenced Ferguson to 315 $^2/_3$ years in prison.

That should have been the end of the case, but the antics of Ferguson and his attorneys continued. In February 1998, attorneys argued before an appeals court that a number of errors had occurred, one of them being that Ferguson had not been allowed to ask potential jurors about their attitudes toward African Americans and how they would feel seeing crime scene photos in which only people of their own race were injured. The appellate court upheld the conviction, and Colin Ferguson is serving his sentence in a prison in upstate New York.

—*Kim Egger*

FERNANDEZ, RAY, *See*
BECK, MARTHA, AND RAY FERNANDEZ

FILICIDE, *See* CHILD KILLERS;
FAMILY HOMICIDE; HOMICIDE

FIRESETTING, *See*
ARSON; JUVENILE FIRESETTERS

CHARLES ARTHUR "PRETTY BOY" FLOYD

Raised in the Cherokee Indian Territory of Oklahoma, Charles "Pretty Boy" Floyd was probably the last of the great social bandits in America. Unlike other gangsters of the 1920s and the Depression era,

Floyd was known as a hard worker, who perhaps would never have led a life of crime had he been able to find legitimate work. In 1924, Floyd married a 16-year-old girl. Times were already tough for sharecroppers in eastern Oklahoma. A year after their marriage, Floyd's wife became pregnant, and he turned to crime. He was caught committing a $5,000 payroll robbery and received a 3-year sentence. After serving half his sentence, Floyd was released, and he continued to commit payroll robberies on his own until he joined forces with a few professionals. In 1930, while working his way east, Floyd and another criminal were arrested for the robbery of a bank in Sylvania, Ohio. Floyd was given 10 to 25 years; however, he leaped through an open train window approximately 10 miles before arriving at the Ohio State penitentiary. He successfully escaped, and his fame back in Oklahoma was now established. He would never spend another day behind bars during the rest of his life.

Floyd made his way to Toledo, Ohio, where he joined forces with Bill "the Killer" Miller, the slayer of at least five men. While working with Miller, Floyd turned from a quick-triggered gunman to a "public enemy," as he became known. Both men traveled to Michigan, where they executed several $100 to $300 jobs by holding up filling stations and lone farmers. By the time they reached Kansas City, they had enough money to retire. The pair spent some time at Mother Ash's place, a brothel of considerable standing. Some say it was the ladies at the brothel who first gave Floyd the nickname of "Pretty Boy."

Up until then, Floyd was notorious for robbing banks, either alone or with the help of his trusted associates. The first person he killed was Chief of Police Carl Galliher, who stopped him from robbing a bank in Bowling Green, Ohio, on April 16, 1931. That day, Floyd was accompanied by Bill Miller, Beulah Bird and her sister Rose, and two women from the brothel. Floyd and Miller opened fire against law enforcement officials, but Floyd was the one who killed Chief Galliher and wounded another officer. Miller was also killed, Beulah was injured, and Rose was captured. Floyd escaped in a car and returned to Oklahoma, where he joined forces with 40-year-old George Birdwell, a former church deacon who had turned outlaw. The pair worked together for only a short time period; Birdwell was killed late in 1932 while pulling a bank robbery in which Floyd had not participated.

After Birdwell's death, Floyd gravitated to Kansas City, where he hooked up with the Dillinger gang, mainly operating with his associate, Adam Richetti. On June 17, 1933, Floyd and Richetti were reported as the culprits behind the "Union Station Massacre" in Kansas City, in which four lawmen and their prisoner were gunned down in an attempt to free Frank "Gentleman" Nash, a notorious underworld figure. Floyd maintained to his death that he was never involved in this crime. During the next 17 months, every law enforcement officer in the country hunted Floyd and Richetti.

On October 22, 1934, things finally came to an end for "Pretty Boy" Floyd. He and Richetti were spotted in a wooded area near Wellsville, Ohio. The local police were called out, including Chief McDermott and patrolman Chester Smith. Firearms were issued, but Smith refused a weapon; instead, he kept his 32-20 Winchester rifle. He told everyone that if they found Floyd, he would be running. They checked the backroads in the area in which Floyd had reportedly been seen, finally coming to the Conkle farm. Floyd had knocked on the door, posing as a lost hunter, and had asked for a ride to the bus line. Ellen Conkle took pity on him and welcomed him into her home, feeding him a meal for which he paid $1, then volunteered her brother, Stewart Dyke, to drive Floyd to the bus station. He and Floyd were getting into the car when two police cars were spotted speeding along the narrow dirt road. Floyd jumped from the car to hide behind a corncrib. Police spotted him as they approached the farm, and Chester Smith recognized the face as "Public Enemy Number 1," with a $23,000 dead-or-alive reward on his head.

Floyd ran, was hit in the arm with a shot from Smith's rifle, but continued to flee, darting for cover in the wooded area nearby. Once the agents and local police all started firing, Floyd fell to the ground, his gun by his side. Smith noticed Floyd had another weapon in his belt—he'd had two Colt .45 automatics but never fired a single shot. The patrolmen carried Floyd, still alive, to the shade of an apple tree, where he died within minutes.

Floyd was never part of a gang and worked only with a few trusted accomplices. Boldly entering banks in broad daylight and never wearing a mask, he was always a gentleman in his crimes: well groomed, immaculately dressed, and courteous to his victims.

—*Linda Cepeda*

See also UNION STATION MASSACRE

Further Reading

Sifakis, C. (2001). Charles Arthur "Pretty Boy" Floyd (1901-1934): Public enemy. In *The encyclopedia of American crime, 1* (2nd ed., pp. 320-322). New York: Facts On File.

FORENSIC SCIENCE: LABORATORIES

It is difficult to describe any single model that applies to modern forensic science laboratories (also known as forensic labs and crime labs), because their sizes, sophistication, and capabilities differ widely between regions and jurisdictions. The majority function within federal, state, and local law enforcement agencies. A few exist within other public agencies such as coroner's offices and universities, and some privately owned laboratories provide services for a variety of physical evidence examinations. The following is a brief and general history of crime labs in America, with examples of services that they perform.

THE HISTORY OF AMERICAN FORENSIC LABORATORIES

The value of scientific analysis of physical evidence became widely recognized during the early decades of the 20th century. In the United States, the Los Angeles Police Department created the first forensic laboratory in 1923. It was founded by police chief August Vollmer in Berkeley, California, who also created the first academic organization for the study of criminalistics at the University of California at Berkeley in the early 1930s. The Berkeley program gained official accreditation and notoriety in the late 1940s under the direction of renowned criminalist Paul Kirk. In the early 1930s, the national laboratory of the FBI was established to offer forensic science services to law enforcement agencies throughout the country.

The number of crime labs increased significantly through the 1960s, driven by drug-related prosecutions throughout the country. In recent years, the development of forensic DNA technology has significantly contributed to the number and sophistication of modern crime laboratories.

FORENSIC LABORATORY ORGANIZATION

Although many crime laboratories operate under the jurisdiction of local governments, some state governments also provide forensic services to local agencies. An example of this is California's model of statewide laboratories operated by the Department of Justice Bureau of Forensic Sciences. These labs provide regional facilities that assist local agencies with crime scene investigations and the subsequent analysis of physical evidence.

Criminalists work for forensic laboratories and usually have college degrees in natural science (such as chemistry, microbiology, physics, or molecular biology) combined with specialized technical training. They can be generalists who process crime scenes, reconstruct events on the basis of evidence, and conduct laboratory analyses. Some specialize in different aspects of laboratory work, such as organic analysis for drugs, inorganic analysis of explosives residue, or molecular biology for DNA. Crime labs also employ technicians who are specially trained in various aspects of forensic science. Technicians often work specifically as fingerprint analysts, document examiners, crime scene investigators, or footwear and tire track impression experts.

As previously mentioned, forensic laboratories throughout the country offer a wide variety of services depending on their size, jurisdiction, and sophistication. The type of operation described here includes the full range of services that might be offered by a premier, well-funded laboratory affiliated with a large government entity. In reality, most crime labs offer some variation of the following example and supplement their efforts through assistance from other government and private labs. The following section titles and organizational information vary to a great extent between agencies.

Crime Scene Investigation Section

Because physical evidence often originates from crime scenes, it is logical to begin with the crime scene investigation section. Specially trained personnel from this unit respond to scenes at which physical evidence is present. They employ a variety of techniques and conventions to locate, record, collect, and preserve physical evidence. Some of the evidence (such as latent fingerprints, blood, bullets, or documents) will be analyzed later at the crime lab. Other

evidence (such as a suspect's red hat identified by an eyewitness) might end up in a property room to be retrieved in its original condition and directly introduced at trial.

This unit is responsible for creating photographic records, video, and diagrams of crime scenes and evidence items. Crime scene investigators usually begin the crucial record of the "life of the evidence," known as a *chain of custody*. To qualify as reliable evidence that is admissible in court, this record must clearly establish the origin of the evidence, the various persons who had control of it, and the tests to which it was subjected.

Physical Science Section

Criminalists in physical science units perform inorganic analysis of explosives residue and paint, organic analysis of controlled substances, and some of them specialize in the examination of synthetic fibers, glass, or soil minerals.

Biological Science Section

This section handles a diverse collection of biological evidence, including serology in general (body fluids) and DNA analysis in particular; hair comparisons; the examination of plant products, insects, traces of poison, and drug evidence from human tissue; evidence from postmortem examinations; and the excavation of human remains. Staffing in this section might include serologists, microbiologists, molecular biologists, forensic botanists, entomologists, toxicologists, pathologists, and specialists in physical anthropology.

Fingerprint Examination Section

Fingerprints are among the most familiar conventions of physical evidence, and the recovery, examination, and identification of latent fingerprints is vital to many investigations. Fingerprint examiners are specially trained in various recovery techniques, comparisons, and computerized searches. They analyze friction ridge patterns and minute details on fingers, palms, and sometimes the soles of the feet.

Document Examination Section

Forensic document examiners receive extensive and specialized training regarding all aspects of evidence related to documents. They examine handwriting to determine sources of authorship. They also examine typewriting, computer printing, facsimile and photocopy technology, and graphic arts processes to determine sources and authenticity of documents. Chemists with specialized training perform writing instrument and paper analysis.

Firearms and Impression Evidence Section

Criminalists sometimes specialize in firearm identification and analyze weapons, bullets, cartridge cases, shells, and gunshot residue on evidence exposed to shooting environments. They usually perform tool mark comparisons as well. Footwear and tire track comparisons can fall under this section or may be performed by lab technicians.

Other Specialty Sections

The sections outlined above provide a general summary of most aspects of the work performed in forensic laboratories. Some crime labs might include specialty services such as polygraph testing, voiceprint analysis, and computer crime analysis.

The foregoing crime lab model would be rare indeed, given the size and expense of such an operation. Most forensic science practitioners work in labs that are not so vastly inclusive of all disciplines and that provide some variations on or portions of the services described.

PROFESSIONAL ORGANIZATIONS AND LAB CERTIFICATION

There are various organizations that seek to provide peer evaluation of research, guidelines for standardization, quality control of techniques and practices, and ongoing training and education for forensic laboratory personnel. Among these are the American Academy of Forensic Science, American Society of Crime Laboratory Directors, International Association for Identification, and regional organizations such the California Association of Criminalists.

These organizations hold annual seminars that include continuing education and training. They sponsor refereed journals and general newsletters that provide opportunities for the publication of timely research, technical information, and organizational news. They constitute a network of professionals that provide support and accountability in the field.

The American Society of Crime Laboratory Directors provides formal certification for crime laboratories that meet specific scientific standards. This certification is central to the ability of criminalists to present findings and offer expert testimony in certain areas of forensic science.

—*James A. Tarver*

See also CRIME SCENE INVESTIGATION; CRIMINALISTICS; FORENSIC SCIENCE; GEOGRAPHIC PROFILING; PROFILING

Further Reading

Moenssens, A. A., Inbau, F. E., Starrs, J., & Henderson, C. (1995). *Scientific evidence in criminal and civil cases* (4th ed.). Minneola, NY: Foundation.

Saferstein, R. (2001). *Criminalistics: An introduction to forensic science.* Upper Saddle River, New Jersey: Prentice Hall.

FORENSIC SCIENCE: PSYCHOLOGY

The term *forensic* refers generally to anything pertaining to the law or the courts of justice and encompasses both criminal and civil law. Consequently, forensic science is the scientific study of issues, incidents, and evidence in relation to legal principles and cases. Examples of forensic science include forensic engineering, forensic linguistics (language), forensic medicine, forensic pathology, forensic psychiatry, and forensic psychology. Forensic laboratories are usually maintained or sponsored by governmental agencies specifically to examine physical evidence in criminal and civil matters and are expected to provide testimony on the physical evidence in a court of law. These laboratories may be asked to examine latent fingerprints, firearms and ballistics, explosives and fire debris, toxic material, and other pertinent evidence found at or near the crime scene and may then be expected to provide expert testimony to the court.

Psychology is the science of behavior and mental processes. Forensic psychology refers broadly to the production and application of psychological knowledge to the civil and criminal justice systems. It includes areas such as police psychology, the psychology of crime and delinquency (criminal psychology), correctional psychology (including institutional and community corrections), psychology and law, risk assessment for the schools, custody determinations, victim services, and the delivery and evaluation of intervention and treatment programs for juvenile and adult offenders. Forensic psychology is a rapidly emerging field of both academic study and professional application.

Forensic psychology can be divided into four major categories: legal psychology, correctional psychology, police psychology, and criminal psychology. Police psychology and correctional psychology are the major applied branches of forensic psychology, whereas criminal psychology and psychology and law are the major research arms. There is, however, considerable overlap among the four areas in both research and application.

The growth in the field is demonstrated by the recent development of several graduate programs in forensic psychology (both at the master's and doctoral level) throughout the world, particularly in Canada, the United States, the United Kingdom, and Australia. All the graduate programs specialize or focus on one of the four major areas. Most of the graduate programs in the United States concentrate either on clinical psychology as it relates to corrections or social psychology as it relates to legal psychology. Some universities offer a combined J.D. and Ph.D. as part of the academic package, although partly due to the academic rigor involved, the "package" has become less popular to students in recent years. Programs in police psychology are exceedingly rare in the United States and Canada, although in the United Kingdom, there are several programs called "investigative psychology." Canada leads the world in research in correctional psychology, and the curricula in Canadian forensic programs reflect this empirical attention. Students graduating from the any of the worldwide graduate programs are expected to be able to analyze, organize, apply, and transmit existing knowledge in the field of forensic psychology, broadly defined. Examples of some of the things that a forensic psychologist (depending on their specialty) may be asked to do include the following:

♦ Evaluate the effectiveness of preschool intervention strategies designed to prevent violent behavior during adolescence

♦ Assist police departments in determining optimal shift schedules for their employees

♦ Establish reliable and valid screening procedures for correctional officer positions at correctional facilities or for law enforcement officer positions at various police and sheriff departments

♦ Assist attorneys in jury selection through community surveys and other research methods

♦ Evaluate the effectiveness of a variety of existing programs for juvenile and adult offenders, such as victim-offender reconciliation programs, teen courts, or health education programs

♦ Consult with attorneys and the courts concerning custody decisions, conflict resolution, and the validity of assessment procedures used in the evaluation of various psychological conditions

♦ Consult with legislators and governmental agencies as research policy advisers

♦ Develop a psychological profile for a local police department of a serial burglar frequently victimizing a neighborhood

FOUR AREAS OF FORENSIC PSYCHOLOGY

Legal Psychology

Legal psychology is an umbrella term for the scientific study of a wide assortment of psychology and law topics, including competencies and criminal responsibility (insanity defense), civil commitment, the psychology of the jury, the psychology of evidence, methods of interrogation, family law, child custody determinations, eyewitness identification, forensic hypnosis, facial composites, deception, and the effects of pretrial publicity on jury decision making.

Legal psychologists are interested in things such as how false confessions are produced or whether deception and lying can be detected. Current research, for example, strongly suggests that skillful manipulation can lead to false confessions. Under these circumstances, even an innocent person may come to believe the information provided by police and may also come to believe that he or she is guilty of the crime. Extant research has also discovered that very few people, professionals or laypersons, are able to detect deception (or honesty) with much accuracy or consistency, even though many (especially professionals) firmly believe they can.

Another example of legal psychology research is the creation of facial composites from the memory of eyewitnesses. Composites are considered indispensable aids to criminal investigation by most police agencies.

Composites are reconstructions of faces through memory, and they are built either with the help of an artist's sketching skills or by using the various commercial kits available to law enforcement. In recent years, kits have been replaced by computer-based systems in which features are stored on discs and the face is put together on a video display unit. Research by forensic psychologists, however, has revealed that computer systems are no more accurate in developing accurate facial composites than kits or artists. So far, the forensic research has consistently found that facial composites developed from the memory of eyewitnesses are poor models of the "real" face of the offender.

Correctional Psychology

Correctional psychology is the fastest growing of the two applied branches of forensic psychology. The number of persons incarcerated in the United States is approaching 2 million and growing daily. Correctional psychologists are sometimes distinguished from psychologists working in correctional facilities. The correctional psychologist typically has "specific academic and/or program training in correctional philosophy, systems, offender management, forensic report writing, treatment aimed at reducing recidivism, and outcome research" (Althouse, 2000, p. 436). Many—if not most—psychologists working in corrections do not have this specific background. Nevertheless, they clearly offer valuable services to corrections. For our purposes, we will use the terms interchangeably.

Boothby and Clements (2000) conducted an extensive survey of 830 psychologists working in state and federal prisons across the United States. All of the 59% who held doctorate degrees worked in federal prisons, and state prisons employed master's and doctoral level psychologists about equally. According to the survey, correctional psychologists spend most of their time on administrative tasks (30%), followed by direct treatment of inmates (26%), and psychological testing and assessment (18%). Very little time was devoted to research (6%).

Psychologists working in correctional facilities are guided by a series of recently updated standards developed by the American Association for Correctional Psychology. These standards provide the minimum acceptable levels for psychological services offered to offenders, whether they are adults or juveniles, held in local, state, or federal facilities, as well as in the community. They cover a wide range of principles and services, including licensure, staffing requirements, confidentiality issues, duty to warn, professional development, informed consent, segregation, and a host of other topics relating to this work.

Police Psychology

Police psychology is the research and application of psychological principles and clinical skills to law enforcement and public safety. The term *police psychology* is somewhat imprecise because it appears to preclude other law enforcement agents, such as deputy sheriffs, fish and wildlife agents, airport security, marshals, constables, and the many types of federal agents. The term *law enforcement* is more encompassing. However, even that term has its critics, who argue that police enforce the law selectively and minimally. The real work of police, the critics assert, is maintaining order, keeping the peace, or being coproducers, with citizens, of public safety. For these purposes, police psychology will be considered as being broadly defined.

The relationship between psychology and law enforcement has waxed and waned over the years, with considerable forensic psychology involvement followed by periods of quiet. Overall, as law enforcement agencies have become more professional, law enforcement supervisors and directors have become better educated, and the public has become more critical and concerned, there has been a substantial increase in the need for forensic psychologists to become more involved in preemployment psychological assessment, fitness-for-duty evaluations (FFDE), special unit evaluations, hostage team negotiations, and deadly force incident evaluations. Special unit evaluations include the selection and training of special weapons and tactics teams (SWAT), tactical response teams (TRT), and hostage negotiation teams (HNT). Forensic psychologists are also increasingly asked to do investigative-type activities such as criminal profiling, psychological autopsies, handwriting analysis, and eyewitness (or earwitness) hypnosis.

Criminal Psychology

Criminal psychology is the science of the behavioral and mental processes of the criminal offender. It is primarily concerned with how criminal behavior is acquired, evoked, maintained, and modified. Recent research has focused on the offender's cognitive versions of the world, especially his or her thoughts, beliefs, and values and how they can be changed. It assumes that various criminal behaviors are acquired by daily living experiences, in accordance with the principles of learning, and are perceived, coded, processed, and stored in memory in a unique fashion for each individual. Criminal psychology examines and evaluates prevention, intervention, and treatment strategies that have been tried in reducing criminal behavior, and includes both adult and juvenile issues. The following are two areas of most interest to criminal psychologists at this point in time: profiling and psychopathy.

Criminal Profiling

Criminal profiling refers to the process of identifying personality traits, behavioral tendencies, geographical location, and demographic or biographical descriptors of an offender based on characteristics of the crime. Criminal profiling has been called many things, including psychological profiling, criminal personality profiling, or more technically, "criminal investigative analysis" or "crime scene analysis." Although psychological profiling was used by the Office of Strategic Services (OSS) during World War II, the technique became popular in law enforcement circles since first used by the FBI in the early 1970s. In more recent years, of course, profiling has become extremely popular in the public eye with the motion picture *Silence of the Lambs* and the TV series *CSI: Crime Scene Investigation,* in the United States, and *Cracker,* in the United Kingdom. However, profiling has been used in some capacity by law enforcement and novelists long before World War II. For example, the fictional detective Sherlock Holmes, first created by Sir Arthur Conan Doyle in 1887 in the story *A Study of Scarlet,* certainly employed profiling in his always masterful search for the offender.

The ultimate goal of criminal profiling is to provide a rough behavioral composite of a suspect that will aid law enforcement in reducing the pool of possible suspects to a manageable number. It is by no means a precise science, despite entertainment and news media claims to the contrary. To a very large extent, the profiling process is dictated by the quality of the research data that has been collected on previous offenders who have committed similar crimes. It

should be emphasized that criminal profiling is not restricted to the violent crimes of serial murder or serial sexual offending but can also be extended to property crimes, including arson, burglary, shoplifting, fraud, and robbery.

In a sense, criminal profiling is a form of prediction. Based on myriad crime scene data and patterns, the profiler tries to "predict" who the offender or offenders might be, and where and how the next crime will occur. It should be emphasized, however, that profiling, even in its most sophisticated form, can rarely point directly to the person who committed the crime. Instead, the process helps develop a reasonable set of hypotheses for determining who may have committed the crime. If completed correctly, a profile will provide some statistical probabilities of the demographic, geographic, and psychological features of the offender. More important, it should eliminate large sectors of the population from further investigation.

One of the more interesting features of offending patterns is that they often occur or cluster within certain geographical areas, such as a specific area of a city. There are two major ways these crime patterns may be analyzed: geographical profiling and geographical mapping. *Geographical profiling* is concerned with analyzing the spatial movements of a single serial offender, whereas *geographical mapping* is concerned with analyzing the spatial patterns of crimes committed by numerous offenders over a period of time.

The value of geographical profiling lies in the assumption that some serial offenders commit crimes within the geographical area they know and feel comfortable in, sometimes near their own residences. Everyone develops mental or cognitive maps of their familiar surroundings and residences, and offenders certainly do the same. Mental maps shape how we find our way around the environment, for example, how we find our way home or to the grocery store, and help us make decisions about what we do and where we do it.

Psychopathy

Although it is always wise to be cautious in cataloging humans into neat diagnostic packages, extensive research in recent years has revealed that the term *psychopath* does have considerable validity as a distinguishing behavioral pattern. The term refers to an individual who exhibits a discernible pattern differing from the general population in its level of sensitivity, empathy, compassion, and guilt. The typical, true psychopath (also called a *primary psychopath*) may or may not engage in antisocial or criminal behavior, although these individuals demonstrate callous and unemotional feelings toward others and a lack of concern for societal rules and regulations.

Psychopaths who have continual contact with the criminal justice system because of frequent offending are referred to as *criminal psychopaths*. Although their criminal behavior runs the gamut of petty theft and fraud to murder, criminal psychopaths are especially vicious and violent, and their motivations for the violence are sometimes difficult to identify. Robert Hare, one of the world's leading experts on psychopathy, reports that nearly half the law enforcement officers who died in the line of duty were killed by individuals who closely matched the personality profile of the criminal psychopath.

Currently, the best measuring instrument for adult criminal psychopathy is the Psychopathy Checklist series developed by Robert Hare and his associates. The series includes the 20-item Psychopathy Checklist-Revised (PCL-R), a shorter 12-item form called the Psychopathy Checklist: Screening Version (PCL:SV), and the P-Scan: Research Version. There is also the Psychopathy Checklist—Youth Version (PCL:SV), still undergoing research development. All four measures are conceptually similar and require considerable training to administer professionally. Although the checklists include many of the same psychopathic behaviors described earlier, all four focus on the affective (emotional), interpersonal, behavioral, and social deviance of criminal psychopathy.

The PCL-R is by far the most extensively researched of the four instruments and is used in about 60,000 to 80,000 evaluations each year. Overall, the research has strongly supported the reliability and validity of the PCL-R for distinguishing criminal psychopaths from criminal nonpsychopaths. Hare (1996) estimates that about 1% of the general population and 15% to 25% of incarcerated offenders meet the PCL-R criteria for psychopathy. In addition, once in prison, offenders who meet the PCL-R criteria exhibit violent and aggressive behaviors—including verbal abuse, threats, and intimidation—at a much higher rate than other inmate populations. Psychopaths appear to be especially well represented among convicted rapists, with reports as high as 35% to 43% among serial

rapists or rapists who killed their victims (Hare, 1996). Moreover, psychopathic inmates commit a much greater variety of offenses than do nonpsychopathic inmates. Female criminal psychopaths, although rare, are believed to follow similar patterns.

—Curt R. Bartol

See also CRIMINALISTICS; GEOGRAPHIC PROFILING; PROFILING; PSYCHOPATHOLOGY CHECKLIST (PCL-R); PSYCHOPATHS

Further Reading

Althouse, R. (2000). AACP standards: A historical overview (1978-1980). *Criminal Justice and Behavior, 27,* 430-432.

Bartol, C. R. (1996). Police psychology: Then, now, and beyond. *Criminal Justice and Behavior, 23,* 70-89.

Bartol, C. R. (2002). *Criminal behavior: A psychosocial approach* (6th ed.). Upper Saddle River, NJ: Prentice Hall.

Boothby, J. L., & Clements, C. B. (2000). A national survey of correctional psychologists. *Criminal Justice and Behavior, 27,* 716-732.

Hare, R. D. (1996). Psychopathy: A clinical construct whose time has come. *Criminal Justice and Behavior, 23,* 25-54.

Hare, R. D., Forth, A. E., & Strachan, K. E. (1992). Psychopathy and crime across the life span. In R. D. Peters, R. J. McMahan, & V. L. Quinsey (Eds.), *Aggression and violence throughout the life span.* Newbury Park, CA: Sage.

Hare, R. D., Hart, S. D., & Harpur, T. J. (1991). Psychopathy and the *DSM-IV* criteria for antisocial personality disorder. *Journal of Abnormal Psychology, 100,* 391-398.

Kosson, D. S., Smith, S. S., & Newman, J. P. (1990). Evaluating the construct validity of psychopathy on Black and White male inmates: Three preliminary studies. *Journal of Abnormal Psychology, 99,* 250-259.

Otto, R. K., & Heilbrun, K. (2002). The practice of forensic psychology: A look toward the future in light of the past. *American Psychologist, 57,* 5-18.

Serin, R. C. (1991). Psychopathy and violence in criminals. *Journal of Interpersonal Violence, 6,* 423-431.

Standards Committee, American Association for Correctional Psychology. (2000). Standards for psychology services in jails, prisons, correctional facilities, and agencies. *Criminal Justice and Behavior, 27,* 433-494.

GAMBINO CRIME FAMILY

Worth hundreds of millions of dollars, the Gambino family is one of the richest and most powerful criminal organizations in the United States today. The family has a criminal workforce of at least 800 men, and its empire ranges from every borough of New York City to the green felt of Atlantic City and Las Vegas to the heroin plants of Sicily and Asia to stolen-car outlets in Kuwait. The original family dates to the prenational syndicate days of Alfred Mineo and Steve Ferrigno in the 1920s, when Joe "the Boss" Masseria controlled the Mafia. They were murdered in 1930 in a bloody ambush carried out by Joe Profaci, Nick Capuzzi, Joe Valachi, and a gunman known now only as "Buster from Chicago." Vince and Phil Mangano took over the organization at this time, and they ran an outfit limited largely to rackets in Brooklyn, the waterfront, and gambling with horse betting, the numbers, and the Italian lottery. In 1951, Phil Mangano was murdered by orders of Albert Anastasia, and Vince disappeared. At this time, Anastasia took over and no one dared to object. Six years later, in 1957, Anastasia was killed, and Carlo Gambino took over the organization.

From 1957 to 1976, the organization flourished under Gambino's reign, and the family steadily expanded its influence and power. The relatively small Mangano operation became the biggest in New York and in the nation. When Gambino died from ill heath in 1976, Aniello Dellacroce managed the organization, followed by Paul Castello from 1981 to 1985. In 1985, John Gotti officially became the new boss of the richest and most powerful crime family in America. Gotti was arrested, convicted, and imprisoned in 1991 on a number of RICO–type crimes and was serving a life sentence when he died of cancer in 2002. Today, the Gambino Crime family is believed to be under the reign of John Gotti Jr.

—*Linda Cepeda*

See also Luciano, Charles "Lucky"; Genovese Crime Family; Gotti, John; Organized Crime

Further Reading

Kelley, R. J. (Ed.). (2000). *Gambino crime family.* In *The encyclopedia of organized crime in the United States: From Capone's Chicago to the new urban underworld* (pp. 129-130). Westport, CT: Greenwood.

Sifakis, C. (Ed.). (1999). *Gambino crime family.* In *The Mafia encyclopedia* (2nd ed., pp. 147-148). New York: Facts on File.

GANGS

Urban gangs have become one of the most pervasive problems confronting today's society. Across the United States, there is what might be called a preoccupation with gangs, especially their relationship to drugs and violence. Although it is true that there has been an escalation of violence among gang members and involvement in drugs in some form has been a feature of gang life for many years, gangs are now being exclusively blamed for the drug problems of the last decade. Part of the reason for this is that gangs have continued to grow in number and diversity across the nation, affecting both large cities and smaller communities. Thus, the problem has gone beyond merely the "urban jungles" to small-town America as well.

TYPES OF GANGS

It is fair to say that an understanding of gangs in the United States has been colored by sensational accounts of gang activities and of gang life. This image has led many people to believe that gang membership means that violence and involvement in the drug trade are automatic. Many people also believe that gangs are highly organized, with a specific division of labor. This is not necessarily the case. Taylor attempts to categorize the wide range of gang characteristics and contends there are essentially three different categories in which to classify gangs: corporate, territorial, and scavenger. *Corporate gangs* focus their attention on making money. There is a clearly defined division of labor, and the criminal activities members engage in are committed almost exclusively for profit. *Territorial gangs* focus on possession of turf, and members are quick to use violence to secure or protect what belongs to the gang. Although there is some level of organization in these gangs in that there is a clearly defined leader and particular objectives and goals of the group, it is less refined than what appears in corporate gangs. Finally, *scavenger gangs* have very little organizational structure, and the motives for becoming a member focus on a need to belong to a group. The crimes that members of this category perform are usually impulsive and often senseless. There are no objectives or goals for the organization, and the members tend to be low achievers who are prone to violent and erratic behavior.

Although it is impossible to describe every characteristic of every gang, and the popular conception of gangs focuses on African Americans and Hispanics, the following descriptions were chosen for their distinctive features, which run counter to the "conventional" gang. A discussion of these gangs also serves to identify the difficulty of making general statements about the violent nature of gangs and their involvement in drug trafficking.

Chinese Gangs

In perhaps one of the most thorough examinations of Chinese gangs, Chin (1990) describes their differences from other types of ethnic gangs. Chin argues that Chinese gangs are closely associated with, and are controlled by, powerful community organizations. In other words, they are an integral part of community life. These gangs are also influenced to a great extent by Chinese secret societies and the norms and values of the Triad subculture.

Second, the primary activity of Chinese gangs is making money. Members invest a considerable amount of money in legitimate businesses and spend a lot of time negotiating business deals. Chinese gangs develop in communities in which adult criminals serve as role models and mentors for gang members.

In keeping with their entrepreneurial efforts, drug use among Chinese gang members is rare. Although involved in drug trafficking, they themselves are not drug users. If a member begins using drugs, he is expelled from the gang. Thus, unlike black and Hispanic gangs, the establishment of Chinese gangs is not based on illicit drug use or fads. In addition, they do not experience the deterioration and poverty that other types of gangs' members experience. Rather, they grow and become economically prosperous by maintaining ties with the economic and political structure of their communities. In other words, there is a cultural component to the success of Chinese gangs: They have certain legitimacy within the community based on the historical experience of the Triad societies.

Vietnamese Gangs

While still part of an overall "Asian" category, Vietnamese youth gangs, especially in southern California, are quite different in their characteristics from Chinese gangs. This group of immigrants, having experienced racism and discrimination in the job market as well as in the classroom, have had a number of significant problems assimilating into mainstream American culture. Essentially, there are three themes that best characterize Vietnamese gangs: mistrust, hiding, and self-control.

A pervasive cultural theme of mistrust runs through Vietnamese communities, one that gang members exploit. Members of the community distrust American banks and as a result keep their valuables and money at home. Knowing this, robbery of these families is a primary activity for these gangs.

Drug dealing in Vietnamese gangs is perceived as too risky and is to be avoided. This is relatively easy to do, because robbery is so lucrative. Thus, very few, if any, Vietnamese gang members are involved in drug dealing. Drug use, however, is heavy. The drug of choice is cocaine, whereas heroin is avoided because it is perceived to make one unreliable and crazy.

Vietnamese gangs continue their low-profile approach to social life by avoiding conspicuous gang symbols such as tattoos or hand signs. Those that are used as indicators of gang affiliation are designed so that they can be easily concealed. In this way, they are able to blend into the social landscape and to more easily avoid the attention of the police. Finally, the structure of Vietnamese gangs tends to be unorganized and fluid. Membership changes constantly, and the rituals and practices of traditional gangs are noticeably absent.

In sum, Vietnamese gangs are loosely defined in terms of an organizational structure, disdain drug trafficking, and essentially attempt to conceal their gang affiliation to others. Vietnamese gangs do not claim turf, do not adopt similar modes of dress, and in some cases, avoid the use of gang names and "signs."

Crack Crews/Jamaican Posses

In contrast to traditional gangs, there is now some evidence that violent drug-selling organizations, also known as *crack crews,* have grown without gang connections. Although technically not gangs, these groups use violence to enforce organizational discipline or to resolve disputes with business associates. In short, violence is a means by which to conduct business. The development of this group has occurred in the void created by those individuals who avoid street level dealing due to the violent, unpredictable nature of the activity. As a result, what remains is a hardcore group willing to engage in violence.

Perhaps some of the youngest and most violent criminal organizations, the Jamaican posses have become an important variable in understanding the intersection between gangs, drugs, and violence. They originated in Jamaica and have immigrated to the United States, with members in virtually every major city. The posses are said to be heavily involved in cocaine and crack distribution, as well a variety of other criminal activities, such as money laundering, kidnapping, auto theft, and fraud. According to the U.S. Department of Justice, it is estimated that the posses control approximately 30% to 40% of the U.S. crack trade as well as approximately 20% of the marijuana trade.

A study by the U.S. General Accounting Office reveals that the posses are highly organized and possess considerable management skills in their illegal operations. What is perhaps most disturbing about this group, however, is their willingness and propensity for violence. The explanations for this vary, but two factors appear to be central in explaining their brutality, both of which are cultural in nature. The first is that the willingness to use violence is status enhancing: It is associated with both economic and social power. Second, there is a long tradition in the use of violence by this group, and it is in part based on their belief that violence is an occupational necessity.

Biker Gangs

Outlaw motorcycle gangs essentially began in the late 1940s, and it is estimated that there are somewhere between 800 and 900 motorcycle gangs in the United States. Although there is a good deal of variability in the characteristics of these groups, for the larger and more organized ones, drug trafficking is their principal source of income. As Kenney and Finckenauer state, some of these gangs have ties to, and are involved with, other organized crime groups.

The larger and more organized motorcycle gangs engage in a variety of moneymaking activities: prostitution, motorcycle theft, illegal arms dealing, counterfeiting, loan-sharking, and gambling. However, the most lucrative enterprise for these gangs is the manufacture of methamphetamines, LSD, and PCP. Because they both manufacture and sell their products, most researchers conclude that there is a significant level of sophistication in their organizational structure.

The social organization of motorcycle gangs is part of the reason the criminal activities members engage in are so lucrative. Virtually all gangs have written constitutions, bylaws, and formalized leadership structures. Dues are paid by members and regular meetings are held, sometimes referred to as "church." The religious connotations allow gangs to not only have their "ministers" visit members in jail but also provide the church with tax exemptions should the gang own its own church.

As Trethway and Katz note, motorcycle gangs have also developed an international presence. At least six gangs in the United States now have chapters outside the country. In fact, the Hell's Angels gang alone has chapters in 20 countries and is rapidly expanding to others. This growth, particularly in the 1980s, when biker gangs were recognized by the FBI as a major criminal enterprise, was part of the reason so much law enforcement attention was given to motorcycle gangs. In fact, in the 1980s and 1990s, the FBI, DEA, ATF, and other federal agencies successfully prosecuted some gang members using the Racketeer-Influenced and Corrupt Organization (RICO) statutes, legislation typically targeted for organized crime groups.

Since that time, like many other criminal groups, motorcycle gangs have developed a higher level of sophistication in their activities. Many members have earned college degrees in computer science, finance, criminal justice, and the law. In addition, these types of credentials have allowed biker gangs to infiltrate legitimate businesses as well as government positions. Finally, biker gangs, concerned about their public image, much like their white-supremacist counterparts, have used the recent popularity of urban professionals (sometimes referred to as RUBs, or "rich urban bikers") who have begun riding motorcycles as a way of blurring their violent image.

THE INTERPLAY BETWEEN GANGS, DRUGS, AND VIOLENCE

Past research on the relationship between gangs, narcotics trafficking, and violence is inconclusive. On one hand, it appears that gang-related violence is increasing. For instance, in 1993, gang members were involved, either as suspects or victims, in about one third of all homicides in Los Angeles County (Maxson, 1995). Moreover, between 1980 and 1989, the homicide rate in Los Angeles was more than double the rate for the entire state of California (Meehan, 1995). A prevalent theme in this city during the late 1980s was that a substantial proportion of the increasing incidence of homicide was attributable to the increasing involvement of gang members in both drug dealing and drug use. The theory had broad appeal and was accepted in the media as well as in official reports. Skolnick, for instance, found that street drug dealing in California is dominated by African American gangs organized specifically for the purpose of distributing cocaine.

In contrast, Meehan and O'Carroll suggest that it is possible that the violence relating to neighborhood cohesion is of a different type than the violence that exists for the purpose of dealing drugs. Despite its popularity, however, there is little evidence to support the theory that gang involvement in the drug trade is responsible for a substantial proportion of homicide.

Moreover, some scholars contend the connection between street gangs, drug sales, and violence appeared to have been overstated by media reports, especially during the mid-1980s, when gangs became involved in the crack cocaine trade. This perception of a close relationship between gangs, drug sales, and homicides has been challenged by a number of recent studies. For instance, in an elaborate study that drew from several different databases, Meehan and O'Carroll tried to assess the relationship between gangs, drug sales, and violence. They argue that the increase in homicides is predicated on an increase in gang involvement in the drug trade, of which there is evidence that this has not been the case. Meehan and O'Carroll conclude that gang-motivated homicides were less likely than other homicides to involve narcotics, and narcotics-motivated homicides were less likely to involve gang members. Finally, victims of gang-motivated homicides were no more likely to have histories of narcotics arrests than were other victims. In sum, they conclude that gang conflicts that result in a homicide are often independent of either involvement in the drug trade or the use of drugs.

Despite the recent increases in the use of violence by gang members, especially if their organizational viability or their competitive edge in the market is challenged, gang life may not be as dangerous as it appears to be. In fact, many researchers have found that much of gang activity is fairly mundane. In Cleveland and Columbus, Ohio, Huff found that gang members spend most of their time acting like typical adolescents (e.g., disobeying parents, skipping school). Similarly, Sullivan's study of Brooklyn gangs reveals that gang members derive a sense of satisfaction by engaging in relatively minor acts that are perceived as taking advantage of a system that they feel is stacked against them.

Consequently, despite the fact that there is a greater prevalence of individual gang violence, especially in gangs that can be characterized as having a horizontal organization, we must also understand that much of what passes for "gang-related" violence is not gang-related at all. This does not suggest that gang violence is random, unrestrained, or even confined to certain groups. What it does suggest, however, is that the relationship between these phenomena is complex and has yet to be completely understood.

In summary, what most gang members find attractive about violence are the things it sometimes can secure for them. Violence is understood to be the vehicle by which

Crips gang members in Los Angeles. In neighborhoods rife with poverty, high unemployment, and crime, gangs provide a sense of belonging and loyalty that is enforced by initiation and violence. Gangs such as Crips and Bloods are not only found in poor neighborhoods but are also well established in American jails and prisons.

Source: Copyright © Daniel Lainé / CORBIS.

objectives can be achieved when other alternatives are unavailable. Gang violence, like drug use, varies considerably, but one characteristic that helps to explain gang violence is the level of organization a particular gang possesses. This, in turn, is based on the money-making ventures in which the gang is involved. Those that are able to secure lucrative illegal ventures seem to be less likely to engage in violence. Thus, the type of gang that emerges or moves into a community depends in large part on the availability of legal and illegal opportunities within it. In contrast, in disorganized communities, where there are a lack of illegal opportunities, as well as the absence of criminal role models to regulate illegal behavior, "fighting" gangs may emerge, which include the aforementioned, highly competitive and violent drug-selling organizations.

Finally, in those cases in which gang members have failed to succeed in the legitimate market as well

as the illegitimate one, retreatist gangs, which rarely engage in violence, may emerge. These gangs are perhaps the least harmful to a community, because their activities pose little threat to the social order of a neighborhood.

—Bob McNamara

See also Aryan Brotherhood; Black Guerrilla Family; Bloods; Crips; Drug Trade; Gangs: Definitions; New Style Gangsters

Further Reading

Chin, K. (1990). Chinese gangs and extortion. In C. Ron Huff (Ed.), *Gangs in America* (pp. 129-145). Newbury Park, CA: Sage.

Fagan, J. (1993). The political economy of drug dealing among urban gangs. In R. C. Davis, A. Lurigio, &

D. Rosenbaum (Eds.), *Drugs and community.* Newbury Park, CA: Sage.

Kenney, D. K., & Finckenauer, J. O. (1995). *Organized crime in America.* Belmont, CA: Wadsworth.

Maxson, C. (1995). Research in brief: Street gangs and drug sales. In M. Klein, C. Maxson, & J. Miller (Eds.), *Two suburban cities in the Modern Gang Reader* (pp. 228-235). Los Angeles: Roxbury.

Maxson, C. (1989). Street gang violence. In N. A. Weiner & M. E. Wolfgang (Eds.), *Violent crime, violent criminals* (pp. 198-234). Newbury Park, CA: Sage.

Meehan, P. J., & O'Carroll, P. W. (1992). Gangs, drugs, and homicide in Los Angeles. *American Journal of Diseases of Children 146,* 683-87.

Skolnick, J. H., Correl, T., Navarro, E., & Rabb, R. (1989). *BCS Forum: The social structure of street drug dealing.* Los Angeles: University of Southern California.

Sullivan, M. (1989). *Getting Paid: Youth crime and work in the inner city.* Ithaca, NY: Cornell University Press.

Trethway, S., & Katz, T. (1998). *Motorcycle gangs or motorcycle mafia?* National Alliance of Gang Investigators Association. Available on the World Wide Web at: www. NAGIA.org.

Vigil, J. D., & Chong Yun, S. (1990). Vietnamese youth gangs in Southern California. In C. Ron Huff (Ed.), *Gangs in America* (pp. 146-162). Newbury Park, CA: Sage.

GANGS: DEFINITIONS

The term *gang* carries many meanings and evokes a number of different images for different people. For some, a gang is a small group of four or five adolescents who loiter on a street corner. For others, the term may identify graffiti artists, drug users, Nazi skinheads, or a group of highly organized youth whose purpose is to generate money from drug dealing.

This subject is a difficult one to address, and to find some type of working definition of gangs, one must include a discussion of some of their different characteristics. The diversity in perceptions of gangs, as well as how they are defined, presents particular challenges to communities as they attempt to deal with problems in their neighborhoods. Many experts believe that their success or failure in doing so likely rests in part in the way the problems are understood and diagnosed. People may also accord too much responsibility for criminal behavior to gangs instead of to the actual responsible individuals. "Gang-related" has become the ubiquitous marker to describe crime in many neighborhoods. This, like the popular understanding of gangs, is a distortion of facts. So, how does one define a gang?

DEFINING "GANGS"

It is important to recognize that the media, the public, and community agencies misuse the term *gang,* or at least use the term more loosely than the law enforcement community. People have come equate gangs with the highly organized drug distribution networks, such as crack cocaine. Although drug use and selling have been features of gang life for many years, and some gangs are indeed involved in drug trafficking, the perception has become that all gangs are heavily involved in this activity. In addition, gangs are more visible than in the past, and in part due to their involvement in drug trafficking, gang violence has increased. The image of the drive-by shooting also seems to many members of the public to be a common characteristic of gang life. In sum, the public's definition of the gang involves a group of individuals, mostly inner-city youth, who are highly organized, heavily involved in the drug trade, and very dangerous.

On the other hand, politicians and law enforcement officials tend to rely on legal parameters to define what constitutes a gang. However, these formal definitions often reflect only high-profile gangs or the ones that present the most pressing and obvious problems for police departments. Thus, from a law enforcement point of view, criminal behavior appears to be a key to the definition. For example, the Miami Police Department defines a gang as "a group of persons joined together to commit acts of violence or any other antisocial behavior." The Los Angeles Police Department's standard is "a group of juveniles and/or adults in a geographic area whose activities include the unlawful use of force, violence, or threats of force and violence to further the group's purpose." This is the most common definition, but it fails to recognize the fact that many gangs do not engage solely in criminal acts, or even highly visible ones.

"Gang-related" is often used to describe the criminal activities of an individual member rather than the coordinated activities of the gang itself. Although it is true that some of what is referred to as gang-related behavior is just that, much of that behavior does not actually qualify as such. The police often classify an incident as gang-related simply because the individual involved is a gang member. Maxson and Klein refer to this as a *member-based definition*. Other departments may use a *motive-based definition* if an individual acts on behalf of a gang.

Experts on gangs have great difficulty in reaching a consensus on an acceptable decision of what constitutes a gang. Part of the problem is that there is a qualitative difference between a "youth gang" and a "delinquent group." In the 1950s and 1960s, researchers viewed the gang and the delinquent group as one and the same. This trend continues today, especially when studying juveniles. However, when older adolescents and young adults are considered, researchers are quick to point out that distinctions must be made.

One way to distinguish between the two is to compare gang behavior with delinquent group behavior. Research has shown that gang youth engage in quite a bit more criminal behavior: They have higher rates of police contact, more arrests, and more drug-related offenses. Moreover, gang membership tends to inhibit what is known as the *maturational effect* whereby as youth mature, they become less likely to engage in further criminal behavior. According to one estimate, gang membership increases the probability of a criminal career. Thus, while researchers account for a great deal of diversity found in gangs, there is little agreement on how to arrive at a standardized definition. There is some agreement on the basic elements, however. According to Maxson and Klein, there are three criteria for a street gang. First, there is community recognition as a group or collectivity, a recognition by the group itself as a distinct group of adolescents and young adults, and enough illegal activities to get a consistent negative response from law enforcement and/or neighborhood residents.

Even this definition presents problems, however, because it implies a negative relationship between the community and the gang and ignores the possibility of them ever having positive interactions with residents. In contrast, Jankowski found that gangs often do have positive relationships with their local communities and often serve as "local police forces." The debate continues, and no attempt will be made to resolve it here. Nonetheless, it is important to note that even experts on the subject are unable to arrive at a consensus concerning the definition of gangs in this country. This calls attention to the need to clearly identify the characteristics of a particular gang in a given neighborhood and to resolve some of the issues

on an individual basis. To do this, one must have a certain level of knowledge about the diversity of gangs.

GANG DIVERSITY

In an effort to address diversity in the study of gangs, which, in turn, affects how they come to be defined, it is important to describe some of the different types. Our understanding in the United States has been colored by sensational accounts of street gang activities and gang life. These images have led many people to believe that gang membership automatically means violence and involvement in the drug trade, though this is not necessarily the case. Indeed, a number of gangs are involved in drug trafficking, presenting a host of problems for a given community, but other types of gangs may not present as serious a threat, though they still raise issues of public concern. There are several different typologies of gangs, but one of the easiest to understand is provided by Richard Cloward and Lloyd Ohlin.

The centerpiece of Cloward and Ohlin's theory is the concept of *differential opportunity*. According to this concept, people in all levels of society share the same success goals; however, those in the lower class have limited means by which to achieve them. People who see themselves as failures within conventional society will seek alternative or innovative ways to achieve success. Thus, individuals may become involved in gang life and crime simply because legitimate means of success are unavailable to them.

Cloward and Ohlin also see a differential opportunity structure for illegitimate means within society. The significance of this finding is that all opportunities for success, legal and illegal, are closed for most of the youth in inner-city environments. Because of differential opportunity, youth are likely to join one of three types of gangs: criminal gangs, conflict gangs, and retreatist gangs.

Criminal Gangs

These gangs exist in stable, low-income areas in which there is a close relationship between adolescents and adult criminals. In this type of environment, adolescents are recruited into organizations that provide training grounds for a "successful" criminal career. During this apprenticeship, more experienced members of the gang supervise the new members and limit activities that might jeopardize the gang's profits. Over time, the new members learn the techniques and attitudes of the criminal world and are introduced to the middlemen of the crime business, such as fences, pawnshops, and drug suppliers.

In perhaps one of the most thorough examinations of this type of gang, Chin describes the characteristics of Chinese gangs, arguing that gangs are closely associated with and controlled by powerful community organizations—an integral part of community life. These gangs are also influenced, to a great extent, by Chinese secret societies and the norms and values of the Triad subculture. The primary activity of Chinese gangs is making money. Members invest a considerable amount of money in legitimate businesses and develop in communities in which adult criminals serve as role models and mentors for gang members.

In keeping with their entrepreneurial efforts, drug use among Chinese gang members is rare. Although involved in drug trafficking, they themselves are not drug users. If a member begins using drugs, he is expelled from the gang. Thus, the establishment of Chinese gangs is not based on illicit drug use or fads. In addition, Chinese gangs do not experience the deterioration and poverty experienced by other types of gangs. Rather, they grow and become economically prosperous by maintaining ties with the economic and political structures of their communities. In other words, there is a cultural component to the success of these gangs: They have a certain legitimacy within the community based on the historical experience of Triad societies.

Conflict Gangs

Conflict gangs develop in communities identified by their dilapidated conditions and transient populations. There are no successful adult criminal role models from whom youth can learn. When this occurs, violence is used as a means of gaining status. The conflict gang must be ready to fight to protect their integrity and honor. By doing so, they gain the admiration from their peers, and this helps them develop a positive self-image.

Members of conflict gangs identify their memberships with certain colors of clothing. In the case of the Bloods and the Crips (originating in Los Angeles), the colors are red and blue, respectively. These gangs, composed primarily of African Americans, are also very territorial and concerned about turf. Members will write their gang names, monikers, names of dead members, or gang slogans on walls, sidewalks, trees,

and just about anything that can be seen in public. The Bloods and the Crips have recently focused on the drug trade as a means of financial success, although they, like many African American and Hispanic gangs, derive their status primarily from the use of violence and fighting. In other words, these gangs attempt to handle what James Vigil refers to as their "multiple marginality." When criminal opportunities do not exist, many have used their proclivity for violence as a status-conferring mechanism.

Retreatist Gangs

Retreatists are those who have attempted to achieve success through both legitimate and illegitimate means. Some may have tried crime or violence but have not been accepted into the conflict or violent gangs, nor do they seem to possess the skills to be included in criminal gangs. Cloward and Ohlin refer to this group as "double failures." They "retreat" into a role on the fringe of society, which usually involves withdrawing from social interaction and heavy use of drugs.

In perhaps one of the most thorough examinations of this type of gang, Chin describes the characteristics of Vietnamese youth gangs, especially in southern California. Essentially, there are three themes that best characterize Vietnamese gangs: mistrust, hiding, and self-control. Although drug dealing in Vietnamese gangs is perceived as too risky and is to be avoided, drug use, especially cocaine, is heavy. Vietnamese continue their low-profile approach to social life by avoiding conspicuous gang symbols such as tattoos or hand signs. The few that are used as indicators of gang affiliation are designed so that they can be easily concealed. In manner of dress, they attempt to blend in to the social landscape to avoid the attention of the police. Finally, the structure of Vietnamese gangs tends to be unorganized and fluid. Membership changes constantly and the rituals and practices of traditional gangs are noticeably absent.

Tagger Crews: A Different Type of Gang

As mentioned, a number of gangs do engage in serious criminal activity, but many, if not most, have few organizational or economic goals. Although they do not pose as serious a threat to a community, some of these groups remain problematic in some neighborhoods. For instance, "tagger crews" are some of the latest to be classified as gangs. They are groups whose reason for existence is creating graffiti, and each group competes with other crews to see who can put up the most graffiti in a given time period and/or area (note the distinction between this and the graffiti of traditional low-income ethnic gangs). In his book, *Renegade Kids, Suburban Outlaws,* Wayne Wooden describes the dynamics of tagging. Although it is a form of vandalism, the main motivation for it is respect from fellow artists.

Developed during the emergence of hip-hop culture in the early 1990s, tagging has taken on a much larger scope in the youth scene. Once a means for street gangs to stake out their turf, tagging has taken on a life of its own. It is now considered sport by a growing proportion of youth from all types of neighborhoods. According to police officials in 1993, there were 422 active crews in Los Angeles and approximately 30,000 taggers in 600 or more crews countywide.

Taggers move from the suburban areas along the highways toward the inner city, leaving their marks to indicate their presence and influence along the way. As Wooden states, in some ways, tagging is more of a passive/aggressive act. The members are not striking out against a particular person or group, but are protesting the lack of attention they receive from society.

Prison Gangs

Like their street counterparts, prison gangs have become a common feature of the American landscape. These groups evolve around (a) criminal activity (typically inside the prison, but not confined solely to it) and (b) the protection of turf and other members. Violence between them threatens the safety of other inmates, the correctional staff, and the community at large. This was especially true during the 1970s, when prison officials began to witness an increased level of disruptive activity by inmates who seemed to be affiliated with larger groups. The initial step for prison authorities was to learn more about how the groups formed and the nature of their activities. During this time, the term Security Threat Group (STG) was adopted by prison officials to identify these groups.

Most gangs, or STGs, organize themselves around racial, ethnic, or ideological lines. The former are most easily identified; the latter are sometimes overlooked. Some STGs are more militant and "political" in their orientations. This was more common in the 1960s, though a few still exist today. Members of these groups view themselves as liberators of oppressed people. In the 1980s, many STGs who focused on criminal

activities within the prison expanded their reach into the larger community, to maximize profits. Also during this time period, these groups found it advantageous to cross racial or ethnic lines and work cooperatively with each other within prisons. Although they remain rivals and have individual disputes on occasion, the groups' pursuit of profit ameliorates ideological differences. A good example of this can be found in the cooperative relationship between the Mexican Mafia and the Aryan Brotherhood.

Essentially, there are six major prison gangs in this country. They are Neta, Aryan Brotherhood, Black Guerilla Family, Mexican Mafia, La Nuestra Familia, and the Texas Syndicate. The distribution of members and chapters of each gang varies considerably, such that not all gangs are found in all prisons. For example, in Florida, the largest prison gangs are Neta and Aryan Brotherhood.

Neta is a Puerto Rican-American gang formed in 1970 in Rio Pedras prison, Puerto Rico, to stop the violence between inmates. Members are strongly patriotic and associate themselves with the revolutionary group Los Macheteros. The Neta philosophy focuses on the independence of the Island of Puerto Rico. Members salute each other by holding the crossed fingers of their right hands over their hearts. This signal has the meaning of the letter *N* in sign language and also means togetherness and unity.

The Aryan Brotherhood is made up of white males and originated in 1967 in the San Quentin State Prison, California. The Aryan Brotherhood has traditionally held a deep hatred toward African Americans and other minority groups. However, while in prison, members are ordinarily apolitical and focus more of their attention on "getting high and getting over," or making their stay in the prison as comfortable as possible. The main activities are drug trafficking and extortion.

La Neustra Familia is made up of Mexican Americans and originated in Soledad Prison, in California, in the mid-1960s. It was established to protect younger and less educated Mexican American inmates from other predators inside the prison and from the Mexican Mafia. Members of this gang are known to wear red rags and to have large tattoos, often across the entire back of the member. The number 14 is also important because *N* is the 14th letter of the alphabet. Also common is a sombrero tattoo with a dagger through it.

The Texas Syndicate is also a Mexican American gang and originated in Folsom Prison, in California, in the early 1970s. Like most, the gang was established as a way of protecting members from other gangs, particularly the Aryan Brotherhood and the Mexican Mafia. Since that time, this group has greatly expanded its membership, partly due to recruiting members from other Latin American countries, such as Cuba and Colombia. The main activities of the Texas Syndicate are drug trafficking, extortion, and pressure rackets.

The Black Guerilla Family consists of black males and was founded in 1966 in San Quentin State Prison, California, by former Black Panther member George L. Jackson. This gang is the most political of all the major prison gangs. Their philosophy focuses on Marxist/Leninist doctrine, and their goals are to eradicate racism and ultimately overthrow the U.S. government. Their symbols include crossed sabers and a shotgun, or a black dragon overtaking a prison or prison tower.

The Mexican Mafia was formed in the late 1950s at Duel Vocational Center, a youth facility in California, and has its roots in a street gang in Los Angeles. Its main focus is on drug trafficking and ethnic unity of members. Symbols include Mexican flag symbols such as the eagle with a snake, a single handprint, usually black, or initials "M.M." A hostile relationship exists between this group and La Nuestra Familia. They are said by the Bureau of Prisons to have a "kill on sight relationship" with each other, which means that prison officials must keep members of the two groups separated at all times.

The future of prison gangs, or STGs, is uncertain. Given the nature of their activities and of prison life in general, it is highly unlikely, despite aggressive attempts by prison officials, that the elimination of prison gangs will be seen at any time in the near future.

—*Robert McNamara*

See also ARYAN BROTHERHOOD; BLACK GUERILLA FAMILY; DRUG TRADE; GANGS; ORGANIZED CRIME

Further Reading

Bing, L. (1991). *Do or die.* New York: HarperCollins.

Chin, K. (1990). *Chinese subculture and criminality: Nontraditional crime groups in America (Contributions in criminology and penology).* Westport, CT: Greenwood.

Cloward, R., & Ohlin, R. (1960). *Delinquency and opportunity.* New York: Free Press.

Goldstein, A. (1991). *Delinquent gangs.* Champaign, IL: Research.

Jankowski, M. (1991). *Islands in the street.* Chicago: University of Chicago Press.

Klein, M., Maxson, C. L., & Miller, J. (Eds.). (1995). *The modern gang reader.* Los Angeles: Roxbury.

Maxson, C., & Klein, M. (1990). Street gang violence: Twice as great or half as great? In R. Huff (Ed.), *Gangs in America,* (pp. 71-100). Newbury Park, CA: Sage.

Wooden, W. S., & Blazak, R. (2000). *Renegade kids, suburban outlaws: From youth culture to delinquency.* Belmont, CA: Wadsworth.

Yablonsky, L. (1966). *The violent gang.* New York: Penguin.

GANSTA RAP, *See* GANGS; MEDIA, VIOLENCE IN THE; NEW STYLE GANSTERS; VIOLENT BEHAVIOR: A PSYCHOLOLOGICAL CASE STUDY

GARNIER, GILLES, *See* SERIAL MURDER: INTERNATIONAL INCIDENCE; VAMPIRES, WEREWOLVES, AND WITCHES

GAYS AND LESBIANS, VIOLENCE AGAINST, *See* HATE CRIMES; DOMESTIC VIOLENCE: SAME-SEX PARTNERS

GENDER VIOLENCE

Gender refers to behavior that "is recognized as masculine or feminine by a social world" (Mackie, 1987, p. 3). Although there has been an increase in violent behavior by women in recent years, violence continues to be associated with and committed by men. Pearson (1997) claims that "our refusal to concede female contributions to violence radically impedes our ability to recognize dimensions of power that have nothing to do with formal structures of patriarchy" (p. 243). The issue is illustrated in the following example. In July 1993, the *New York Times Magazine* headlined "A Woman in Prison is Not a Dangerous Man." In 1994, At the Prison for Women in Kingston, Ontario, six female inmates attacked four guards in a preplanned attempt to escape. The guards were punched, kicked, stabbed, and assaulted. The guards finally gained control, and the inmates were returned to their cells without being searched. In response to this, the inmates set fires, flung urine, and threatened the guards' lives. As a result, an emergency male team was called in; they strip-searched the female inmates and placed them in full body restraints. The incident was videotaped, and what resulted was a media portrayal of females as victims and correctional officers as victimizers.

Socialization can be defined as "the complex learning process through which individuals develop selfhood and acquire the knowledge, skills, and motivations required for participation in social life" (Mackie, 1987, p. 77). The norms, values, and mores of a society determine how a woman's behavior is perceived. For instance, a woman who does not follow the traditional passive and maternal role must therefore be defined as deviant. Merlo and Pollock believe that the perception of deviant versus nondeviant behavior allows a "Madonna/whore" duality to persist. For example, in the film *The Accused,* the victim, who is raped by multiple men in a bar, is portrayed as a "bad woman," versus a "good woman" who conforms to the stereotype of femininity. The Mike Tyson rape trial was another portrayal in which the female victim was placed in a good girl/bad girl dichotomy. A good woman should not go out alone, "drink with a man, or spend time alone with men; those who do deserve what happens to them" (Merlo & Pollock, 1995, p. 4).

The socialization process is a means of informal social control that determines what a female and male should or should not do. However, this process is restrictive for the female and the traditional choices she is allowed throughout her life: for instance, the toys she plays with as a child, and as an adult, the household role, her occupation, and even the crime she commits. The following sections will offer an overview of domestic violence, murder, and serial murder.

DOMESTIC VIOLENCE

The term *domestic* refers to the household. Society overwhelmingly associates domestic violence with women as victims and men as victimizers. Certainly, the case of Hedda Nussbaum and Joel Steinberg epitomizes the plight of battered women. During the prosecution of Steinberg in 1988 for the death of his 6-year-old daughter Lisa, Nussbaum testified that she and her daughter were subjected to years of physical abuse by Steinberg. Although no one disputed that Nussbaum was a battered woman, evident from her physical appearance, the judicial system appeared to lose sight that the victim was in fact the 6-year-old girl. This particular case was unusual, because only a small percentage of victims are severely injured.

According to the Statistics Canada Violence Against Women Survey (1993), half of Canadian women have survived at least one incident of physical or sexual violence. A Statistics Canada survey of Family Violence in Canada (1999) found that 29% of Canadian women have been assaulted by their spouses. A Commonwealth Fund survey (1998) found that approximately 31% of American women reported being physically or sexually abused by a partner (husband, boyfriend) at some point in their lives. According to a U.S. Department of Justice report (2000) on the National Violence Against Women Survey, each year, 1,510,455 women and 834,732 men are victims of physical violence by an intimate. This is an average of 3.5 victimizations per year per male victim and 3.4 per female victim, which total 2.9 million male victims and 4.4 million female victims. In the United States, a man is battered every 38 seconds, and a woman is battered every 21 seconds.

Pearson (1997) argues that although statistics indicate that women commit "a fair preponderance of spousal assaults . . . violence is still universally considered to be the province of the male" (p. 7). Since it began in 1993, Toronto's Easton Alliance for the Prevention of Family Violence has received between 3 and 10 phones call a day and 1,000 to 4,000 phone calls per year from men who are caught in violent relationships (including some same-sex relationships) and unable to leave. As do women, men stay in abusive relationships for several reasons: shame, low self-worth, denial, reluctance to give up the good aspects, and inertia. It is difficult to conceive that women actually do batter men in a patriarchal society in which men control both the private and public sphere. Pearson (1997) states, "Men destroy, women create" (p. 7). Yet researchers such as Reena Sommer, in her survey on alcoholism, inadvertently found that not only were women violent toward their spouses or boyfriends, they had also not struck in self-defense—rather, they had been angry, jealous, or high. Whether the motivation had to with control or impulse, they had physically assaulted their male intimates.

VIOLENT CRIME AND MURDER

Although men are disproportionately responsible for committing violent crimes, Pearson (1997) found that in Canada, young women now account for 24% of all violent offenses in their age group; in the United States, it is 18%. Murder is among these offenses. For example, in November 1997, when 14-year-old Reena Virk's body was found in Victoria, British Columbia, the public was shocked to learn that the perpetrators were primarily young women. The victim had been attacked by seven females. After several minutes, Reena Virk rose, bloody and disoriented, and stumbled toward the bus stop. Unfortunately, another girl and young male followed Virk, and 8 days later, her dead body was found. In 1983, Karla Faye Tucker and her boyfriend broke into the residence of Jerry Dean. Following the crime, Tucker shared with her sister that while stabbing Dean 11 times in the chest and throat, she'd had an orgasm. Unable to explain her behavior in terms of being battered or coerced by her boyfriend, Texas residents fell back on the stereotype of the "bad" woman who does not conform to societal standards of femininity.

When attempting to explain heinous acts of violence, issues of gender, social class, and ethnicity are considered. For members of society, these factors do not diminish the senselessness of the crime.

SERIAL MURDER

The Federal Bureau of Investigation Behavioral Science Unit in Virginia, noted for their psychological profiles of male serial killers, has but one category for female perpetrators, *compliant victim*. As in cases of male serial killers, the victims are perceived as worthless and, therefore, expendable. Serial killer Mary Beth Tinning murdered eight of her nine children over a relatively short span of time. Although the children were killed in rapid succession, the medical examiners refused to admit that something was amiss and reported the deaths due to Sudden Infant Death Syndrome (SIDS). In Sacramento, California, serial murderer Dorothy Puente murdered and mutilated eight male and female victims for monetary gain and possibly intrinsic (power) gain. Because the aforementioned women acted alone, they could not be labeled compliant victims.

It is not unusual for the judicial system to dismiss women involved in team killing as passive victims lacking the intellectual capability to dominate the team. As a result of these gender stereotypes, a number of women involved in team serial murder have deliberately portrayed themselves as compliant victims. An example of team killers can be found in the case of Judith Ann and Alvin Neelley. Following the sexual assault of a 13-year-old victim, Judith Ann Neelley repeatedly injected the young girl with drain cleaner in an attempt to kill her. The victim somehow survived the ordeal, and the Neelleys then drove to a remote area, where Judith Ann Neelley made one last attempt to inject the victim before shooting her. Following their apprehension, Judith Ann Neelley claimed she was a battered woman, an unwilling participant in the abduction and murder of several young women and men. The female member of such a team is often found to be an active participant in victim selection, sexual assault, and the ultimate demise of the victims. For example, over a 16-year period, British team killers Rosemary and Frederick West are believed to have together tortured, sexually assaulted, and murdered 18 young women.

When considering female and male criminality, contributing factors such as abuse issues, power relations, sexuality, and formal and informal social control mechanisms enable researchers to better understand the intrinsic and extrinsic motivation for those who commit violent crimes and the misconceptions that prevail regarding gender violence. Perhaps, as Pearson postulates, violent behavior is a human, rather than gendered, phenomenon.

—*Lynn Gunn*

See also AGGRESSION; BATTERERS AND ABUSIVE PARTNERS; DOMESTIC VIOLENCE; SERIAL MURDER; TEAM KILLERS; VIOLENT BEHAVIOR; VIOLENT FEMALE JUVENILE OFFENDERS; WOMEN AND VIOLENCE

Further Reading

Hoff, B. (1998). *Battered men: The hidden side of domestic violence*. Available on the World Wide Web at: http://www.vix.com/menmag/gjdvreso.htm.

Mackie, M. (1987). *Constructing women & men: Gender socialization*. Toronto: Holt, Rinehart & Winston of Canada.

Merlo, A., & Pollock, J. (1995). *Women, law, and social control*. Needham Heights, MA: Allyn & Bacon.

Pearson, P. (1997). *When she was bad: Violent women and the myth of innocence.* Toronto: Random House of Canada.

GENOCIDE

Genocide is one of the deadliest forms of collective criminal behavior. During the 20th century, this form of violence killed more individuals than all the wars, revolutions, and civil wars combined for the same time period. R. J. Rummell (1996) estimates that over 169 million human beings were killed in genocides and genocidal-like events during the last century. It is also important to point out that the frequency and severity of this crime has increased threefold in the last half of the 20th century. Clearly, genocide is a tremendously destructive type of violence, but what exactly is this lethal form of behavior?

DEFINING GENOCIDE

Although the term is relatively new, genocide is by no means a new type of behavior and, in fact, has been a constant throughout history. Since ancient times, conquering warlords and generals have wiped out entire populations in their attempts to build empires and quash rebellions. The word *genocide,* however, was first used in 1944 by the Polish jurist Raphael Lemkin, in his book *Axis Rule in Occupied Europe.* He wanted to criminalize Nazi atrocities and war crimes by bringing attention to their actions in occupied Europe, and he felt that existing terms such as *war crimes* or *mass murder* did not convey the sheer magnitude and intent of this type of criminality. Accordingly, Lemkin created the word from the Greek *genos,* which means race or tribe, and the Latin *cide,* which means to kill.

With motivation provided by the postwar Nuremberg trials and the advocacy of Raphael Lemkin, the United Nations established a legal framework on December 9th, 1948, to define genocide as a crime under international law. Known as the Convention on the Prevention and Punishment of the Crime of Genocide, it stipulates that any attempt to destroy a national, ethnic, racial, or religious population, in whole or in part, constitutes genocide and is a crime whether committed in peace or war. This definition also specifically articulates a variety of actions that can be considered genocidal and includes not only the overt killing of members of a group but also causing serious bodily or mental harm to members of a population; deliberately inflicting conditions of life calculated to bring about its physical destruction in whole or in part; imposing measures intended to prevent births within a group; and forcibly transferring children of a group to another population. Genocide, therefore, includes a wide assortment of behaviors, not all of which involve the direct physical murder of a people. Although most individuals picture mass shootings and gas chambers when they think of genocide, this crime also includes forcing groups into ghettos and reservations where disease, malnutrition, and starvation may kill the population. Forced sterilization as a policy may also rise to the level of genocide if the intent is to destroy all or part of a population. The mass rape of Rwandan Tutsi women, to cite another example, was considered to be genocide by a tribunal court in Rwanda because it violated the "serious bodily and mental harm" clause of the genocide convention.

Although the United Nations definition does not include this type of genocide, many scholars assert that the destruction of a culture should be considered a form of genocide. This category is often termed *ethnocide* or *cultural genocide.* The forced assimilation policies to which many Native American tribes were subjected would clearly fall into this category. Well into the 1930s, children were removed from their families and sent away to boarding schools, where they were forbidden to speak their own languages or practice traditional beliefs. Their hair was cut, and they were dressed in mainstream clothing. The explicit and overt goal of these policies was to destroy their culture and transform them into "productive" anglicized citizens. These policies were clearly ethnocidal, because they involved the attempted destruction of the unique heritage and way of life that are necessary components for any shared cultural identity.

One weakness of the United Nations definition is that it excludes political groups from the calculation. During the 20th century, there were a number of examples in which members of real or imagined political organizations were targeted for destruction in ways that exhibited all the hallmarks of genocide, and yet because of this omission in the definition, they are not considered genocide. The victims of Argentina's "dirty war" of the 1970s, in which the government targeted and "disappeared," in the vernacular of the times, leftists, communists, and subversives, belong to this category.

It should be stressed that genocide comprises a planned and systematic attempt to eliminate a population.

It is not accidental, nor does it spontaneously erupt as is often suggested. The Rwandan genocide, for example, was typically portrayed in the media as an eruption of age-old tribal hatreds. Similarly, the violence in Bosnia was depicted as merely the latest appearance of long-standing ethnic hostility. These are false images. Genocides don't "just happen." Rather, they must be planned, organized, and coordinated. The driving force behind the violence is invariably a government that sees genocide as a means to an end. In many ways, genocide is a rational and instrumental plan designed to achieve certain goals.

Genocides do, however, vary in their underlying motivation. They can be perpetrated for ideological reasons, such as occurred during the Holocaust. The Nazis combined scientific and medical beliefs concerning racial superiority with anti-Semitic attitudes and believed that they were protecting the genetic cleanliness of the Aryan race from "subhuman" Jews and "inferior" Slavs and Gypsies. The Cambodian genocide is also an example of an ideologically motivated genocide. The Khmer Rouge embraced a vision of returning Cambodia to a mythic time of greatness and glory that could be achieved only by removing all foreign and corrupting influences. Genocides can also be economic in orientation, such as has occurred in Central and South America, where native populations have been wiped out in order to open up the rain forest for the development of mineral and oil resources located there. Others are perpetrated for retributive reasons, such as a state striking back against perceived historic wrongs.

PERPETRATORS AND VICTIMS

As horrible and extreme as genocide is, it would be a mistake to believe that the perpetrators are all monsters or psychopaths. In truth, the evidence points to the opposite. Most genocidal killers are, in point of fact, remarkably normal. They are ordinary human beings engaged in extraordinary crimes. It does not take abnormality or mental pathology to be a perpetrator, merely a belief in the necessity and just nature of the violence. The Nazis believed they were protecting their nation and race from the depredations of the Jews and Slavic peoples; the Bosnian Serbs felt they were protecting the Serb people and Christianity from a Muslim onslaught; and the Rwandan Hutu thought their killing of the Tutsi was a kind of preemptive self-defense. Where do these ideas come from? Typically, these perceptions are fostered by state-controlled media outlets that consciously inflame hatred and antagonism to further the genocidal agenda of the state. This notion of the normality of the perpetrators is further supported by the reality that many thousands of citizens from all walks of life participate in genocides. There are far too many individual perpetrators for them all to be deranged or deviant.

The victims of the genocide are normal human beings who are victimized, not for anything that they have done, but simply because they are members of a group that has been chosen for extermination. Victims are merely inhabitants of a social category. Typically, they are dehumanized and scapegoated, which makes it easier to persecute and kill them. The Tutsi were portrayed as "insects," and the Jews were portrayed as "disease" and "vermin." Killing a "subhuman form of life" is easier than killing a fellow human being, and this process of dehumanization is a necessary prerequisite to genocide.

20TH-CENTURY EXAMPLES

Armenian Genocide

The first major example of genocide in the 20th century is generally considered to be the Armenian genocide. It began during the First World War, when the 3,000-year-old Turkish Armenian population was largely destroyed. Close to a million and a half Armenian men, women, and children were murdered between the years of 1915 and 1918 by the Turkish government. Faring poorly in the war, the weakened Ottoman government was overthrown by a group of Turkish nationalists often referred to as the "Young Turks." This new regime scapegoated the Armenian population and blamed them for many of the setbacks during the war as well as a host of other domestic problems. The Turkish Armenian intelligentsia and leadership were arrested first and sent to a variety of secret locations, where they were murdered. Next to die were young Armenian males serving in the military, who were also removed from their positions and placed in penal battalions, where most were killed. In this way, any possible source of resistance was quickly and efficiently eliminated. The remaining Armenians, mostly women, children, and the elderly, were then gathered together and marched out to locations in the interior desert. Along the way, they were attacked by bandits and soldiers, and many died from these attacks and from exposure, exhaustion, and starvation.

The Holocaust

The Holocaust is the most infamous of all examples of 20th-century genocides. The road to the Holocaust began with the implementation of a euthanasia program during the 1930s. This undertaking was known as the "T4 project" and resulted in the death of several thousand German citizens with mental or physical handicaps, as well as many who were labeled as being misfits or antisocial. The techniques perfected to kill those who were defined as *Lebensunwertes Lebens,* or "life unworthy of life," served later as a model for the Holocaust. After coming to power in the early 1930s, the Nazis enacted a series of decrees and statutes that began removing Jews in Germany from their jobs and taking away their legal and social rights. Once marginalized, the Jews were easily deported to ghettos in occupied Poland and from there, to extermination camps such as Auschwitz, Treblinka, Chelmno, Sobibor, Majdanek, and Belzec. In these camps, arrivals went through a process of selection in which some of the younger and more fit men and women were chosen for work details and temporary survival. The elderly, children, and women with young children were chosen for the gas chambers, disguised as disinfection showers, where they were made to strip and were then gassed to death. Afterward, special units of inmates disposed of the bodies in crematoria or mass graves after having searched the corpses for concealed valuables. In this manner, the Nazis murdered approximately 6 million Jews and several million gypsies, Slavs, and other victims.

The Cambodian Genocide

In the 1970s, Cambodia was destabilized by the war in neighboring Vietnam, which spilled over the borders and helped weaken the national government. The Kampuchean Khmer Rouge, a revolutionary communist group, was then able to overthrow the existing regime and take power. Ideologically, they were committed to recapturing the former greatness of the historic Khmer Empire and wanted to purify Cambodian society racially, socially, ideologically, and politically. Under the leadership of Pol Pot, they then proceeded to murder anyone perceived to be tainted with western influences, such as politicians, military leaders, business leaders, journalists, students, doctors, lawyers, and teachers, as well as ethnic Vietnamese, Chinese, and Moslem Chams. Before being stopped by a Vietnamese invasion in 1979, the Khmer Rouge killed between 1 and 2 million human beings.

The Bosnian Genocide

After the end of the Cold War, the nation of Yugoslavia began to fall apart as self-serving politicians manipulated ethnic tensions and hostilities in order to retain their control of power. After the Slovenian and Croatian declarations of independence in June 1991, Serbs began preparing to contest a similar declaration in Bosnia. When Bosnia declared independence in March of 1992, Serb forces in large parts of Bosnia immediately began a campaign of ethnic cleansing against non-Serbs, predominantly Bosnian Muslims. Essentially, the Serb forces sought to acquire new territory by wresting control away from the Bosnian Muslims and to ethnically cleanse the land under their dominance as they sought to create an ethnically pure greater Serbian state. This ethnic cleansing was characterized by arrests, internment in detention camps, forcible dispossession of goods and property, mass rapes of Muslim women, and executions and mass murder. Importantly, there was also an attempt to eradicate all traces of Muslim culture as Serb forces destroyed mosques, libraries, and other historic and cultural artifacts.

The Rwandan Genocide

In 1994, over the short span of a few months, approximately 1 million Rwandan Tutsi were murdered by their Hutu neighbors. Losing a war to the expatriate Rwandan Patriotic Front (RPF), the Hutu-dominated government was forced to the negotiating table. Assassinated after having to make concessions, Hutu president Habyarimana was most likely killed by extremist members of his own government. Widespread killing broke out within hours as soldiers, police, and militia groups began massacring Tutsi citizens. As opposed to the industrialized killing of the Holocaust, the Rwandan genocide involved much more personalized murder with many victims being killed individually with machetes. The killing was eventually halted when the Hutu government fell to the RPF.

THE FUTURE OF GENOCIDE

In recent years, there have been many international legal developments that provide hope for the future of genocide prevention. Because there is no statute of

Shoes of victims of Auschwitz-Birkenau extermination camp. Millions of Jews were exterminated in this and dozens of other camps built by the Nazi regime during World War II. Genocide attempts to exterminate a particular group of people based upon ethnicity or race. Other examples are the German massacre of Hereros in 1904, the Ottoman massacre of Armenians in 1915-1916, the Ukrainian pogrom of Jews in 1919, the Tutsi massacre of Hutu in Burundi in 1965 and 1972, the Paraguayan massacre of Ache Indians prior to 1974, the Khmer Rouge massacre in Kampuchea between 1975 and 1978, and the contemporary Iranian killings of Baha'is.

Source: Copyright © Michael St. Maur Sheil / CORBIS.

limitations on genocide or war crimes, indicted individuals have been arrested years later and brought to trial. Throughout the 1990s, trials were held in countries such as Italy and France for crimes committed during the Nazi years. In the wake of the genocides in Rwanda and Bosnia, international criminal tribunals were formed to punish those responsible for the killing and have had some success in bringing to justice individuals responsible for the genocides. Even heads of state are finding they are not immune to these new realities, as shown the indictment of Augusto Pinochet, the former Chilean dictator, and the indictment, arrest, and trial of Slobodan Milosovic. The ongoing development of a permanent criminal court designed to monitor and hopefully deter future outbreaks of human rights

violations is also a hopeful indication that genocides will be a less common feature of the 21st century.

—*Alex Alvarez*

See also CRIMES OF OBEDIENCE; ETHNIC CLEANSING; MASS VIOLENCE; WAR ATROCITIES

Further Reading

Alvarez, A. (2001). *Governments, citizens, and genocide: A comparative and interdisciplinary analysis.* Bloomington: Indiana University Press.

Chalk, F., & Jonassohn, K. (1990). *The history and sociology of genocide: Analysis and case studies.* New Haven, CT: Yale University Press.

Fein, H. (1993). *Genocide: A sociological perspective.* London: Sage.

Hirsh, H. (1995). *Genocide and the politics of memory: Studying death to preserve life.* Chapel Hill: University of North Carolina Press.

Horowitz, I. L. (1997). *Taking lives: Genocide and state power.* New Brunswick, NJ: Transaction.

Kressel, N. J. (1996). *Mass hate: The global rise of genocide and terror.* New York: Plenum.

Rummel, R. J. (1994). *Death by government.* New Brunswick, NJ: Transaction.

Staub, E. (1989). *The roots of evil: The origins of genocide and other group violence.* New York: Cambridge University Press.

Totten, S., & Parsons, W. S., et al. (Eds.). (1997). *Century of genocide: Eyewitness accounts and critical views.* New York: Garland.

THE GENOVESE CRIME FAMILY

The Genovese crime family is one of the five major organized crime families of New York, with about 300 members and associates. The first Don was Charles "Lucky" Luciano, and current leadership consists of Vincent "the Chin" Gigante (serving a 12-year sentence in Fort Worth, Texas) and Dominick "Quiet Dom" Cirillo. Major illicit activities of the organization include narcotics, loan-sharking, extortion, pornography, racketeering, restaurants, seafood distribution, and vending machines. The Genovese family is best known for the quiet and reserved manner in which they conduct business.

—Phil Caporale

See also LUCIANO, CHARLES "LUCKY";
ORGANIZED CRIME: DOMESTIC

Further Reading

Pileggi, N. (1985). *Wiseguy: Life in a Mafia family.* New York: Simon and Schuster.

KITTY GENOVESE

Catherine "Kitty" Genovese was murdered on March 13, 1964, a victim of repeated stabbing attacks near her home in Queens, New York. This case was unusual because it occurred in front of at least 38 of her neighbors, who did nothing to intervene, over a period of 35 minutes. Police arrived 2 minutes after they were finally summoned. The neighbors were too frightened or apathetic to get involved in Genovese's repeated calls for help. Consequently, Good Samaritan laws were passed that make passersby immune from liability when they stop to render assistance to those in need.

—Phil Caporale

VITO GENOVESE

Vito Genovese was born in Rosiglino, Italy, on November 2, 1897. He arrived in the United States in 1913 and by the late 1920s was a leading member of the "Lucky" Luciano crime family. Fleeing prosecution for murder, he returned to Italy in 1937, where he became a close friend of dictator Benito Mussolini. After World War II, Genovese returned to the United States and was arrested and charged with murder. The key witness, Peter La Tempa, was murdered while in protective custody. Genovese was released and went on to become the leader of the Genovese crime family of New York. In 1959, he was arrested, convicted for smuggling and distribution of drugs, and sentenced to 15 years imprisonment. Vito Genovese died in a prison hospital on February 14, 1969.

—Phil Caporale

See also LUCIANO, CHARLES "LUCKY";
ORGANIZED CRIME: DOMESTIC

GEOGRAPHIC PROFILING

Geographic profiling is an investigative methodology that analyzes crime locations to determine the most probable area of offender residence. It can also be defined as a spatially based information management tool for serial crime investigation. The process provides an optimal search strategy by making inferences from the locations and geometry of connected crime sites.

Specifically, geographic profiling uses the sites of a linked series of crimes to determine the most probable area of offender residence through the production of probability surfaces ("jeopardies"). These are integrated with street maps of crime areas to produce what are referred to as *geoprofiles*. A sophisticated computer system called *Rigel* accomplishes this through an algorithm that describes the spatial nature of the criminal hunt process. More generally, geographic profiling is a collection of criminal investigative techniques derived from the study of the geography of crime.

SERIAL CRIME AND BEHAVIORAL SCIENCE

Serial Crime Investigative Difficulties

Serial and "stranger" crimes are difficult to solve and pose significant challenges for law enforcement agencies because the investigations cannot work outward from the victim. Rather, the process must work inward by considering large populations of suspects (e.g., all registered sex offenders, known bank robbers, recent parolees, owners of certain vehicles types, public tips, etc.). This typically leads to information overload and resource problems. In efforts to address this situation, police and researchers have turned to the behavioral sciences.

Behavioral Science

Geographic profiling falls into the behavioral science repertoire of criminal investigative support techniques. Linkage analysis and criminal investigative analysis are the other main components of this toolkit. Linkage analysis attempts to connect related crimes through an examination of the offender's modus operandi and signature. Criminal investigative analysis (CIA) includes psychological profiling and similar techniques. Psychological profiling infers an offender's personality and behavioral characteristics from his or her crime scene behavior. Criminal or offender profiling can be more generally defined as the inference of offender characteristics from crime scene characteristics. Geographic profiling, because it infers an offender's residence area from the locations of his or her crime sites, can be considered part of criminal profiling.

CRIME THEORY

Crime Pattern Theory

As haphazard as crime may sometimes appear, there is a rationality influencing the geography of its occurrence and a semblance of structure underlying its spatial distribution. Using an environmental criminology perspective, Brantingham and Brantingham present a series of propositions that provide insight to the processes underlying the geometry of crime. Their model of offense site selection, called *crime pattern theory*, suggests that criminal acts are most likely to occur in areas where the "awareness space" of the offender intersects with perceived suitable targets (i.e., desirable targets with an acceptable risk level attached to them).

An individual's "activity space" is constructed from his or her residence, workplace, recreational sites, and the travel routes between these locations. A criminal's activity space, in conjunction with his or her "hunting" style, determines search patterns and hunting grounds. Crime locations are therefore a function of an offender's residence and activity space.

Routine Activity Theory

Routine activity theory asserts that for a contact predatory crime to occur, there must be an intersection in time and space between a motivated offender, a suitable target, and the absence of capable guardianship. The *routine activity approach* can be useful for understanding the circumstances surrounding a crime and the specific actions of the offender and the victim preceding their encounter.

Rational Choice Theory

The rational choice perspective views criminal choices and behavior as resulting from the rational consideration of costs, benefits, and efforts of alternative actions within a voluntaristic, utilitarian framework. This approach suggests that even the worst serial murderer with the most bizarre pathology functions on a basic level of rationality. In fact, it is likely that a criminal who behaves irrationally would soon be caught and therefore never become a serial offender.

CRIME SITES

A crime may involve more than one location, and these locations can group together in different ways. A murder will have encounter, attack, murder, and body disposal sites. A rape or sexual assault will have encounter, attack, rape/sexual assault, and victim release sites. An automobile theft may have vehicle theft and drop sites. A street robbery or arson typically has only a single site. The various locations connected to a crime have different meanings and uses to the offender.

Multiple crime locations cluster together in different ways. The four different site types associated with a murder, for example, can group together in eight different combinations, ranging from one (every site action occurring in the same location) to four (every site action occurring in a different location) different sites. Breaking an offense down into its constituent locations and their combination is called *crime site parsing*.

CRIMINAL HUNT

The *criminal hunt* can be divided into two stages: (a) the search for a target and (b) the attack. The search phase typically involves extensive prowling, observation, trespassing, and peeping. *Criminal target patterns* (the geographic patterns of crime sites) are the product of offender, victim, and environmental influences. Any pattern of locations is a function of the location-generating process and the background environment. The most important factors in the generation of crime locations are the following:

♦ Offender activity space: home, work, social activities, and travel routes in between
♦ Hunting style: criminal search and attack methods
♦ Hunting ground: range and areas of criminal search
♦ Target backcloth: distribution of potential targets within the hunting ground

The different types of locations associated with a crime (e.g., encounter, attack, crime, victim release, etc.) may be influenced to different degrees by these factors, suggesting the need to separately analyze any such relationships.

Other considerations are also important in the construction of a geographic profile. Research has shown a relationship between journey-to-crime distances and individual level characteristics, such as age, sex, race, and degree of organization. Offender information, including victim descriptions and a psychological profile, can therefore be relevant. Some sex offenders prefer specific ethnic types, and these groups may not be distributed evenly throughout the urban environment. Variation in neighborhood demography could therefore be a consideration in certain cases.

Land use and zoning are important factors, both in terms of the target backcloth and in determining offender anchor point type. If a geoprofile points toward a commercially zoned area, for example, then the offender's anchor point could be his or her worksite. People do not travel "as the crow flies"; rather, they follow the street layout. If they are in a vehicle, arterial and freeway routes are important. If they are on foot, jogging and bicycle paths, bus routes, and rapid transit lines are significant.

Barriers, both physical and mental, can impede movement. Physical barriers include rivers, lakes, ravines, and expressways. Psychological barriers result from neighborhood differences in race and socioeconomic status. Spatial displacement can affect where an offender commits his or her crimes. Displacement, of which there are five types, results from police actions designed to prevent crime and/or apprehend the offender (e.g., patrol saturation).

INVESTIGATIVE STRATEGIES

Suspect Prioritization

The geographic profile can focus an investigation suffering from information overload. Profiling can help prioritize hundreds or thousands of suspects, leads, and tips. Investigative leads may be obtained from information contained in various computerized police dispatch and record systems. Task force operations formed to investigate a specific series of crimes often collect and collate their information in some form of computerized major case management system. Geographic profiling can rank entries that contain street addresses, zip/postal codes, or telephone numbers.

Databases and Registries

Sexual offender registries are a useful information source for geographic profiling in cases of serial sex crimes. The addresses of known sex criminals in such registries can be prioritized from the geoprofile.

Data banks are often geographically based, and information from parole and probation offices, mental health outpatient clinics, social services offices, schools, and other agencies located in prioritized areas can also prove to be of value. It has been estimated that approximately 85% of records contain address information.

A geographic profile can be integrated with suspect vehicle and offender descriptions to search registered motor vehicle and driver's license files contained in state or provincial record systems. The description and geographic parameters act as a linear program to produce a limited set of records containing the appropriate data.

Patrol and Surveillance

The geoprofile can be used as the basis for directing saturation patrol and police stakeouts. This strategy is particularly effective if the crimes occur during specific time periods. Many criminals spend a significant amount of time searching for targets, whereas others wait in particular areas for suitable victims and the right circumstances. Police have a better chance of observing an offender prowling or loitering than in an assault, simply because considerably more time is spent hunting than attacking.

Additional police responses in the event of a new crime may be developed with a geographic profile. Many criminals return home after committing a crime, and patrol units can be directed to the area of probable offender residence in addition to responding to the crime scene. Particular attention should be paid to the most logical routes from the crime site to the high-profile area and to relevant major arterial streets, freeways, and off-ramps. Depending on the size of the hunting area, the offender's probable escape routine might also suggest possibilities for locating witnesses or closed circuit television (CCTV) and commercial video cameras.

Community Information

Known information on the offender can be mailed or delivered to those households and businesses located within the peak area of the geoprofile. People are more likely to respond to an individualized request stating that the offender resides in their neighborhood than they are to generalized television broadcasts or newspaper stories. This method generates high-quality information because it comes from individuals in a better position to know the offender from either home or work.

A thorough police canvass in the area in which a victim was abducted, attacked, or disposed of is a useful and proven investigative approach. Such efforts may also be directed within the neighborhood of probable offender residence and can use door-to-door canvassing, interviews, grid searches, information sign posting, and community cooperation and media campaigns. Investigative media strategies may use a geographic profile in attempts to generate new tips.

Summary results or full profiles can be released, depending on the details of the specific case and the status of the investigation.

Intelligence-Led DNA Screens

Investigators sometimes conduct large-scale DNA testing of males in the area of the crime scene during a sexual murder or rape investigation. Because considerable police resources and laboratory costs are involved in such "bloodings," detectives prefer to conduct intelligence-led DNA screens in which individuals are prioritized on the basis of proximity to scene, criminal record, age, and other relevant criteria. Geographic profiling can further refine this selection process and is part of the recommended Interpol protocol for DNA screening.

Other

In cases in which the identity but not the whereabouts of a criminal fugitive is known, geographic profiling may be able to assist in determining probable hiding places. Sightings, purchases, credit or bankcard transactions, telephone calls, cellular telephone switch sites, crimes, and other locational information can be used as input for the profile. This process is also applicable to extortion and kidnapping investigations. In certain missing person cases that are suspected homicides, geographic profiling can also help determine probable body disposal site areas.

Although geographic profiling is primarily an investigative tool, it also has a role in the courtroom. In addition to analyzing the geographic patterns of unsolved crimes for investigative insights, the spatial relationship between the locations of a crime series and an accused offender's activity sites can be assessed in terms of the probability of their congruence. When combined with other forensic identification findings (e.g., a DNA profile), such information increases evidential strength and likelihood of guilt. Geographic profiles can also be used as supporting grounds for search warrant affidavits.

SOFTWARE AND TRAINING

Rigel

The primary tool used in geographic profiling is a software program called *Rigel*. This Java-based system performs up to a million calculations of the CGT (criminal geographic targeting) algorithm for a given case. The software has four components, including a three-dimensional visualization capability, the analytic engine, a geographic information system (GIS), and database connectivity. Its performance is measured by the *hit score percentage,* defined as the ratio of the area searched before the offender is located to the total area covered by the crimes. Analysis of data from the initial research project at Simon Fraser University and results from police operational files show a mean hit score percentage of approximately 4.7% and a median of 3.0% (standard deviation = 4.4%).

Understudy Training Program

In 1990, the Vancouver Police Department began providing geographic-profiling services, first locally, then to the Canadian and international police communities. After the development of a training model based on the one devised for psychological profiling by the International Criminal Investigative Analysis Fellowship (ICIAF), a geographic-profiling understudy program was implemented in 1997. The first participant organizations were the Royal Canadian Mounted Police (RCMP) and the Ontario Provincial Police, followed by the United Kingdom National Crime Faculty. The Bureau of Alcohol, Tobacco and Firearms (ATF) and the *Bundeskriminalamt* (BKA), the German federal police, also plan to implement a geographic-profiling capability. The National Law Enforcement and Corrections Technology Center-Southeast Region, a component of the National Institute of Justice (NIJ), recently began training for crime analysts in the geographic profiling of property crimes.

CASE EXAMPLE

In "Project Loch Ness," which was a series of 11 sexual assaults, including one rape, in Mississauga, a suburb of Toronto, Peel Regional Police investigators developed 312 suspects. The crimes were linked through offender description, behavior, and speech; the proximity of the attacks; and the timing of the offense dates. A DNA scene sample was available, but testing all suspects was too expensive to be feasible. The detectives therefore created a prioritization scheme involving several factors, including an uncorroborated alibi, results of an initial interview, similarity to the composite sketch, the psychological profile, and the geographic profile.

Of the 312 suspects, 144 were eliminated, and the remaining 168 were categorized into three levels of priority. In the initial batch of four forensic samples, one was identified as top priority, and a match was reported in 8 days. Lee Marvin Payne was arrested in September 1998. He subsequently confessed and then pled guilty in February 2000. Payne was sixth in the prioritization from the geographic profile (a hit score of 1.9% measured by suspects and 2.2% measured by area). The case was solved through DNA and a confession, but the use of prioritization and profiling resulted in a faster investigation, substantial cost savings, and potentially fewer victims.

—*D. Kim Rossmo*

See also CRIMINALISTICS; FORENSIC SCIENCE; PROFILING; SERIAL MURDER; SEX OFFENDER REGISTRIES; ViCLAS

Further Reading

Brantingham, P. J., & Brantingham, P. L. (Eds.). (1981). *Environmental criminology.* Beverly Hills: Sage.

Brantingham, P. J., & Brantingham, P. L. (1984). *Patterns in crime.* New York: Macmillan.

Brantingham, P. L., & Brantingham, P. J. (1993). Environment, routine and situation: Toward a pattern theory of crime. In R. V. Clarke & M. Felson (Eds.), *Routine activity and rational choice* (pp. 259-294). New Brunswick, NJ: Transaction.

Cornish, D. B., & Clarke, R. V. (Eds.). (1986). *The reasoning criminal: Rational choice perspectives on offending.* New York: Springer-Verlag.

Felson, M. (1998). *Crime and everyday life* (2nd ed.). Thousand Oaks, CA: Pine Forge.

MacKay, R. E. (1999, December). Geographic profiling: A new tool for law enforcement. *The Police Chief,* pp. 51-59.

Rossmo, D. K. (1995). Place, space, and police investigations: Hunting serial violent criminals. In J. E. Eck & D. A. Weisburd (Eds.), *Crime and place: Crime prevention studies* (Vol. 4, pp. 217-235). Monsey, NY: Criminal Justice Press.

Rossmo, D. K. (1997). Geographic profiling. In J. L. Jackson & D. A. Bekerian (Eds.), *Offender profiling: Theory, research and practice* (pp. 159-175). Chichester, UK: John Wiley.

Rossmo, D. K. (2000). *Geographic profiling.* Boca Raton, FL: CRC Press.

GILLES DE RAIS, *See* SERIAL MURDER: INTERNATIONAL INCIDENCE

JOHN GOTTI

John Gotti was the New York City Gambino family crime boss in the 1980s. He took control of the organization after shooting rival crime boss Paul Castellano on December 16th, 1985, in Manhattan, New York. Gotti's consistent well-groomed, well-dressed facade led to his nickname, the "Dapper Don." He was also known as the "Teflon Don" because of his history with law enforcement: He had been charged five times but had never been convicted. He was finally arrested in 1990 when former underboss Gravano became a government informant. Gotti was convicted on charges of racketeering and conspiracy to murder and was sent to a maximum-security federal prison to serve a life sentence without the possibility of parole. He died of cancer in 2002 and was given an elaborate funeral by his family.

—*Brianna Satterthwaite*

See also GAMBINO CRIME FAMILY;
    ORGANIZED CRIME: DOMESTIC

GOVERNMENT-SANCTIONED VIOLENCE, *See* CRIMES OF OBEDIENCE; DEATH PENALTY; ETHNIC CLEANSING; EXECUTION; GENOCIDE; HISTORY OF VIOLENCE IN RELIGIONS; WAR ATROCITIES

GRAHAM, GWENDOLYN, AND CATHERINE WOOD, *See* SIGNATURE KILLERS; TEAM KILLERS

GRAHAM, JACK GILBERT, *See* AERONAUTICAL MASS MURDER

DANA SUE GRAY

In mid-February 1994, a call came in to the Riverside County Sheriff's Department reporting a body found. The deceased was Norma Davis, 86, a resident of a gated community for elderly residents. The victim had been killed in her own home by manual strangulation with a phone cord and had also been stabbed multiple times and almost decapitated. Investigators looking at the scene were amazed by the excessiveness of the attack: Much more force than necessary was used to subdue the elderly victim. The house had not been robbed, which was also surprising. Expensive jewelry had been left behind, and the only items that were missing were a Medicare check and credit cards belonging to the victim.

The investigation of Mrs. Davis's murder was stalled when the sheriff's department received another call 10 days later reporting a similar attack. The victim was 66-year-old June Roberts, who lived in the same gated community as Mrs. Davis. She was also strangled with a phone cord, and bludgeoned repeatedly with a heavy wine decanter. Mrs. Roberts was younger, in good health, physically strong from exercise, and had obviously put up significant resistance to her attacker. Once again, expensive possessions were left in place, and all that was missing were the victim's credit cards. Immediate action was taken to follow activity on these cards, and investigators were able to determine that a youngish, well-built young woman with light-colored hair accompanied by a small male child had dined in a local restaurant and bought toys and clothes at local retail stores. Even with this information, they still had no idea of who the perpetrator was.

Ten days later, Dorinda Williams was attacked in her antique store by a young woman with light-colored hair. The attacker strangled the victim with her hands and a yellow nylon rope but stopped just short of killing her. She escaped from the business with the contents of the cash register. The victim called the sheriff and was able to describe the attacker, which led investigators to Dana Sue Gray. The sheriff arranged for the alleged offender to be watched until a warrant could be obtained to examine the contents of her home, but Gray slipped away from the surveillance. While she was gone, the sheriff executed a search warrant and found much of the merchandise charged after June Roberts's death.

Five days after the attack on Mrs. Williams, while the search warrant was being executed at Gray's home, an officer in an adjoining county received a call regarding the finding of a dead body. Dora Beebe, 87 years old, had been killed in her home, strangled with a phone cord, and massively beaten with an iron.

Her checkbook and savings book were missing and investigators later learned that someone had successfully withdrawn $2,000 from Beebe's savings account only minutes after her death. Fortunately, the bank videotaped all transactions: The customer was a young woman with light-colored hair.

Investigators from both jurisdictions cooperated and were able to pinpoint Dana Sue Gray as the attacker of all four elderly victims. During the course of interrogation, Gray denied all charges, but eventually, just before her trial was to begin, she admitted to committing the murders and attack in order to remove the possibility of the death sentence from consideration. She stated that her reason for committing the crimes was lack of money. She had recently lost her position as a nurse in a local hospital because of mishandling controlled substances, and she and her live-in boyfriend had accumulated excessive debt.

At first glance, the case of Dana Sue Gray appears to be fairly straightforward, but it is stands apart for several reasons. First, Gray can be classified as a female serial murderer by the number of victims and the separation of the crimes by time. However, she differs from other female serial killers in several respects, because most of them kill partners, children, or other people under their care. Gray killed two elderly women with distant family ties and one elderly female stranger, and attacked another elderly female stranger. Traditionally, women kill at a distance with poison or guns, but Dana used an "in your face" style, strangling manually then stabbing or bludgeoning the victim. Hers is the only known series of murders committed by a woman to use this kind of direct physical contact and excessive force far beyond what was necessary to immobilize her victims. Furthermore, most women kill for profit, such as killing their husbands or children for insurance. Gray, on the other hand, killed for lethal excitement, similar to daredevil activities she frequently participated in. She took credit cards and money but only used them to "celebrate" by buying lunch, beauty shop services, and merchandise.

Dana Sue Gray's background was fairly benign. She was raised in a middle-class family; her parents divorced and remarried. Her mother died of breast cancer when Dana was 14 years old. As a child and adolescent, she did not get along well with other people and participated in many daredevil activities such as skydiving, windsurfing, hang gliding, and scuba diving. She was bright but did not do well at school, and she was constantly creating disturbances within the family. In fact, her stepbrother left home as a teenager to obtain some relief from her. Although her life was not ideal in some respects, she had always had supportive adults in her life, and they provided the necessities and some luxuries for her. Clearly, she hardly seemed a candidate for this kind of crime.

Psychological examination revealed several interesting aspects regarding Gray's rampage. It is apparent from the selection of multiple means to kill her victims that Gray was in control of her thoughts and activities. The murders show deliberation and malice exceeding that of crimes in which only one weapon is used. She killed in response to three psychological triggers: the need for money, the need for power and domination, and misplaced family anger. Money and anger at her mother for leaving her may have stimulated the choice of victim, but Dana's real satisfaction came from domination, power, and control over her victims, as evidenced by the multiple modes of death and the prolonged face-to-face struggles with her victims. She is a classic power killer who enjoyed watching her victims suffer as she murdered them.

Dana Sue Gray is an anomaly, a female serial killer who interacted physically with her victims. She is the first woman to kill multiple victims in this way, but it is not unreasonable to extrapolate that as young women become more and more physically fit and adopt traditional male behavior modes, more young women will follow her lead.

—Marlene Deal

See also GENDER VIOLENCE; SERIAL MURDER; WOMEN AND VIOLENCE

Further Reading

Braidhill, K. (2000). *To die for.* New York: St. Martin's.

GREEN RIVER KILLINGS, *See* SERIAL MURDER

GUILTY BUT MENTALLY ILL (GBMI), *See* NOT GUILTY BY REASON OF INSANITY (NGRI)

GUN CONTROL

Groups like the National Rifle Association believe in the absolute right of Americans to bear firearms—whereas Handgun Control Inc. lobbies for restrictions on the right of private citizens to possess handguns. The Second Amendment of the U.S. Constitution provides, "A well regulated Militia, being necessary to the security of a free State, the right of the people to keep and bear Arms, shall not be infringed." The controversy continues over this amendment, particularly as it relates to handguns. After the attempted assassination of President Reagan and wounding of Press Secretary Brady in 1982, the Brady Law was subsequently enacted in 1994, which requires background checks of handgun purchasers.

—*Phil Caporale*

See also ASSASSINS; BRADY BILL

H

HATE CRIMES

There is no consensus on the definition of hate crimes. However, all definitions share a common theme: At their core is the symbolic status of the hate crime victim. A crime is perpetrated because the victim represents a symbolic status that the perpetrator finds offensive. These symbolic statuses are extremely diverse in nature and may include racial or ethnic considerations (e.g., African Americans), religions (e.g., Muslims), sexual orientations (e.g., homosexuals), political affiliations (e.g., liberal), nationalities (e.g., Israeli), or even physical abnormalities (e.g., the handicapped). The killing of an African American by neo-Nazi skinheads in urban America is one example. Gay bashing in England and religious riots in India are other examples. Gang rapes in Afghanistan are still another. Hate crimes are part of the human condition. They have been a fact of life throughout recorded history and in every part of the world. The most cataclysmic event in recent United States history—the massacre of some 3,000 American citizens by Islamic extremists on September 11th, 2001, during the attacks on the World Trade Center and the Pentagon—could be considered a hate crime. The victims were chosen because of their symbolic status as Americans. Anyone at any time can suddenly become the victim of hate crime.

Historically, hate crimes in the United States have been committed by organized groups of white men with racist beliefs, and African Americans have been their most frequent victims. These crimes were not caused by individual pathologies of offenders. Rather, they emerged from a long-standing right-wing paramilitary tendency in American society. These "hate groups" have arisen in four specific historical waves. Each wave has been influenced by various social and political forces.

THE FIRST WAVE

White supremacists have existed in the United States since Reconstruction days, when the infamous Ku Klux Klan was born. Klan violence grew out of white rage over the defeat of the South in the Civil

War. From 1867 until its "official" disbandment in 1869, the original Klan thundered across the war-torn South, sabotaging Reconstruction governments and imposing a reign of terror that included an untold number of murders, lynchings, shootings, whippings, rapes, tar-and-featherings, acid brandings, castrations, and other forms of mutilation. Blacks were the Klan's primary enemy because they posed a threat to southern white male hegemony. Freedom for slaves led to recession in the southern economy; thus, class concerns became intertwined with race and masculinity issues. For the Klan, white males were in a class above all nonwhites, women, and homosexuals. This established a trend that would last for generations: The purpose of the white supremacist movement was to maintain not merely white power, but white male power. The Klan's most violent and masculine members, the notorious "Night Riders," remained anonymous, however, shrouded in secrecy and hidden behind their sheets, ghoulish masks, and tall, pointed hats.

The Ku Klux Klan was America's original hate group. Its hate crimes grew out of a dedication to the lost cause of southern white supremacy; in short, Klansmen attempted to win through terrorism what they had been unable to win on the battlefield. But the hate group was also anchored in an even deeper social force. The Klan was composed of white men who had come of age on the frontier, where successive generations of Americans had learned hard lessons about survival. Those lessons included a fierce individualism and the freedom to be whatever a person wanted to be. This led to the emergence of what became known as "frontier justice," an instant, private, and often deadly method of settling disputes without benefit of the legal system.

THE SECOND WAVE

The Ku Klux Klan reemerged in the early 20th-century as a result of two developments: massive immigration and America's entry into World War I. For many Americans, these events led to widespread fear of foreigners. Though no less violent than its predecessor, the new Klan, which at its peak in 1925 boasted some 5 million members extending from the South to the North and Midwest, stressed its role as a "benevolent brotherhood" and set out to convince nonbelievers that it was dedicated to defending the American way of life. Targets of Klan hatred now extended beyond blacks to include Asians, immigrants, and bootleggers, as well as nightclubs, roadhouses, and all manner of scandalous

behavior. With its newfound mission of social vigilance, the Klan identified its newest enemy: the Jew. Spurred on by a series of anti-Semitic articles published in the early 1920s by automobile tycoon Henry Ford, the Klan began to forge an argument that all of America's problems could be traced to an international Jewish conspiracy. Although women were allowed to join Klan auxiliaries, the heavy political lifting was still left to men, who were expected to be the propagators and protectors of the Anglo-Saxon race.

Klan membership plummeted in the 1930s and 1940s. Negative sentiment toward the Klan reached an all-time high following World War II, due to two major factors. First, with the emergence of the civil rights movement, the Klan became involved in a series of bombings and assassinations throughout the South. Second, some Klan factions in the North become more strident in their outlook and began to forge ties with the American Nazi Party. These two factors would, however, eventually lure many rural radicals back into the white supremacy underground movement during the recession-prone 1970s and 1980s.

THE THIRD WAVE

Like the early Klan, white power activists of the early 1980s were highly influenced by a militarized version of masculinity. Many of them had come of age during the Vietnam War: Their participation in that lost cause, or their failure to make a personal appearance on the battlefield, was a turning point in their lives. As adults, these men saw that the white man's world they had taken to be permanent was gone; dark forces of chaos crept upon the American landscape. That chaos took many forms—immigration, drugs, crime, the economy—all of which entered into morality debates and policy directives of the federal government. Because these hot-button issues were seeded with race and gender considerations, white supremacists exploited them to their advantage in the 1980s, much as the Klan had done in the 1920s. It therefore became not only permissible, but also morally imperative for some powerless white men to transform their personal rage into a political cause.

Masculinity and whiteness became entwined as never before: To be a "real" white man was to be hypermasculine. Paramilitary mythology came to be seen as the path to redemption. In secret paramilitary camps across rural America, white extremists of all descriptions began training in the use of assault weapons, grenades, rocker launchers, and explosives, all in preparation for a coming war against what they viewed as Jewish-inspired, race-mixing policies designed to mongrelize, and thus weaken, the Aryan race. Many extremists traded in their robes for combat boots and were reborn as Aryan warriors.

The criminal behavior of this racist underground accounted for extraordinary levels of brutality. Between 1980 and 1986, nearly 3,000 violent racist incidents took place across America, including 138 attempted or successful bombings carried out by small Klan and neo-Nazi factions. The most important paramilitary cell to emerge from this crucible of history was a gang known as The Order, the most organized and violent hate group the radical right had ever seen. Founded by Robert Jay Mathews in rural Washington state in 1983, the gang hit on a formulation of how Aryan warriors could achieve a sacred order. They armed themselves, studied guerrilla warfare, conducted assassinations, bombings, armored-truck robberies, and planned large-scale sabotage of public utilities, all as part of what they believed to be a struggle for white survival.

THE FOURTH WAVE

The Order became the revolutionary role model for the white supremacy movement. Robert Mathews—who was killed by the FBI in a dramatic shootout on Widbey Island, Washington, on December 8, 1984—had an especially deep effect on racist skinheads throughout the world. He became their martyr, a fallen hero immortalized in countless underground publications and white power rock anthems. The date of his killing by the FBI became an international memorial day for the white power world. Thus, December 8 took its place alongside April 19 (known as the "date of doom") and April 20 (Adolph Hitler's birthday) in the pantheon of Aryan mythology. Wherever white power activists gathered in the years after Mathews's death, The Order was held up as the supreme example of racial integrity. That others would attempt to emulate their terrorism was inevitable.

A fourth wave of hate groups was born of that clarion call; their primary goal was to complete The Order's unfinished business. In the United States, this offered the white supremacy movement an unprecedented point of unity. Skinhead, traditional Klan, and neo-Nazi groups all absorbed the revolutionary beliefs popularized by The Order and kept the force of their rage turned toward the federal government, especially the paramilitary arm of the Justice Department responsible for unleashing lethal

force against the Branch Davidians in Waco, Texas, on April 19, 1993. Their enemy list also included those whom they saw as receiving special treatment by the government: nonwhites and homosexuals.

From 1987 through the late 1990s, the United States experienced a remarkable surge of hate crime violence against minorities and gays, due in large part to the criminal activity of skinheads. Armed with clubs, knives, brass knuckles, and assault weapons, skinheads became a cross between neo-Nazi shock troops and modern-day night riders. Once older white supremacists saw that the new generation was willing to carry out their own violent ideals, they rushed to enlist the loyalty of skinheads everywhere.

This coalition produced an unintended consequence for the white supremacist movement. Because the skinheads are part of an international youth movement, skinheads in the United States became more inclusive of women than were contemporary Klan and neo-Nazi groups. After alliances were forged between skinheads and traditional white extremists, women began to play a role in constructing the white power agenda. Men still made up the bulk of the movement's membership, but by the mid-1990s, women comprised nearly half of the new recruits in many Klan, neo-Nazi, and skinhead organizations. This participation by women allowed them to selectively disregard aspects of the white supremacist ideology that varied from their personal beliefs and experiences. Accordingly, white power groups began to support legal abortion, interracial relationships, and homosexuality.

The fourth wave of hate groups will nevertheless be most remembered for spawning a violent generation of activists dedicated to carrying on The Order's unfinished business. Among these criminals were Timothy McVeigh and an incandescent paramilitary gang called the Aryan Republican Army, a six-member cell led by a transvestite named Peter Kevin Langan. During the mid-1990s, the gang executed a string of professionally executed bank robberies, the purpose of which was to support a series of terrorist attacks that included armored-truck heists, sabotaging public utilities, derailing trains, assassinations, bombings, and direct support for the bombing in Oklahoma City.

—*Mark S. Hamm*

See also Helter-Skelter; History of Violence in Religions; McVeigh, Timothy; Metzger, Tom; Neo-Nazi Skinheads; Vigilantism; White Aryan Resistance; White Supremacists

BRUNO HAUPTMANN

Bruno Hauptmann, a German immigrant carpenter, was convicted and executed in 1935 for the kidnapping and murder of Charles Lindbergh's 20-month-old son on March 1, 1932. Charles Jr. was missing from his crib inside the Lindbergh home and was found in the woods nearby, 10 weeks later. Hauptmann contended that he had been framed, and various conspiracy theories emerged that proposed that Lindbergh had murdered his own child in an effort to gain publicity; most of these have been refuted or withdrawn. At the time, this saga was considered the "crime of the century."

—*Brianna Satterthwaite*

Further Reading

Hubbard, K., & Duffy, T. (2001, February 26). The hero's wife. *People Weekly, 55*(8), pp. 103-105.
Tanenhaus, S. (1999, January). First in flight [Review of *Lindbergh* by Scott A. Berg]. *Books in Review,* pp. 61-63.

HAYMARKET MASSACRE

On May 4, 1886, at about 8:30 p.m., a rally of striking assembly workers met in the Haymarket area of Chicago. After 10 p.m., as the rally drew to a close, 176 policemen moved into the group, demanding dispersal of the remaining 200 workers. Without warning, a bomb exploded, and in the ensuing chaos, shots were fired by policemen and possibly workers. One officer was killed by the bomb, six officers died later, and 60 others were injured. Eight indicted men were convicted for inciting the actions of the mob. Subsequently, four were hanged, one committed suicide, two were given commuted sentences of life in prison, and another remained in prison, even though there was no case against him. On June 26, 1893, Governor John Altgeld granted full pardons to the eight, and a memorial was erected to commemorate the Haymarket Riot.

—*Phil Caporale*

HEARST, PATRICIA, *See*
KIDNAPPING; STOCKHOLM SYNDROME

HELL'S ANGELS
MOTORCYCLE CLUB, *See* GANGS

HELTER-SKELTER

The dictionary definition of *helter-skelter* is a "disorderly hurry, a confused and hasty action, or showing haste or confusion in a wild, disorderly way." Charles Manson harbored the idea of "Helter-Skelter" as a motive and catalyst for his apocalyptic vision of social disintegration, which would end with a final war. He viewed the so-called Judgment Day, Armageddon, and Helter-Skelter as one and the same and looked on African Americans as the source of evil and destruction. Charles Manson believed that if wealthy Caucasians were murdered in larger numbers, this would precipitate a racial war initiated by outraged Caucasians and perpetuated by an angry, retaliatory African American population, with the final result being Helter-Skelter.

Charles Manson has been quoted as saying, "Blackie doesn't know how to do it unless Whitey shows him how first." To ensure that the conflict would progress, he decided to mobilize his "family" to jump-start the process. Thus, Charles Manson and the members of the "Manson family" decided to set their plan in motion via the Tate/LaBianca murders in the summer of 1969.

The apocalyptic vision that Charles Manson entertained involved the ideation that once the African American population started Helter-Skelter, they would slaughter all Caucasians except himself and his family. They would be hiding out in a safe and secret location, deep in the earth in Death Valley, California. After a period of time, during which the African Americans ruled the Earth, he and his family would emerge from their hiding place. He would then "show Blackie that he has it all wrong, like he always has, and Blackie will see we're right and give it back over to us. Blackie will then take his place where he belongs, serving Whitey."

Thus, Charles Manson had a grandiose delusion of world domination, like many other cult leaders and religious fanatics. He conceived this plan by distorting the lyrics of a Beatles song, "Helter-Skelter," on their "White Album." Manson was particularly fixated on that album and believed that the Beatles were sending him personal messages and directives for the future. Apparently, that particular song tied together some of the loose ends in Manson's mind. It provided the term he was looking for to describe his apocalyptic vision of Armageddon, his envisioned major race war, and the development of future society. Unlike many other cults and their leaders, Charles Manson and "family" did not commit suicide or force their homicides by law enforcement officers; they simply wound up in prison.

It is of interest to note that the idea of Helter-Skelter has been adopted by other offenders. For example, James Clayton Vaughan Jr. (a.k.a. Joseph Paul Franklin), another white supremacist, borrowed the notion from Charles Manson. However, Franklin viewed it differently. He believed that if he killed enough African Americans, other Caucasians would follow his example and take up the fight themselves. Through their notion of "Helter-Skelter," both Charles Manson and Joseph Paul Franklin distorted reality, entertained bizarre fantasies, and were inspired by rhetoric of nihilistic chaos and neo-Nazism.

At a deeper level, Helter-Skelter was a facade for chaos. Manson, a man desperate to control everyone with whom he came in contact, was attracted to the idea of complete chaos from which he would emerge as the leader, the savior. This fantasy permeated his interactions with others. His drive to achieve his goal of Armageddon and ultimate chaos was rooted in a mind damaged by childhood trauma and crisis that left him with dark feelings of rejection, low self-esteem, and anger. Typical of people who feel impotent and have delusions of power and control, Manson found a raison d'être in pursuing his apocalyptic fantasy.

—*Marlene M. Deal and Eric W. Hickey*

See also HATE CRIMES; KACZYNSKI, THEODORE; MANSON, CHARLES/THE MANSON FAMILY;WHITE SUPREMACY

Further Reading

Bugliosi, V., & Gentry, C. (1994). *Helter-skelter: The true story of the Manson murders.* New York: Norton.

HENNARD, GEORGE,
See MASS MURDER

HERO MURDER, *See*
MOTIVES FOR MURDER

HILLSIDE STRANGLERS,
See TEAM KILLERS

HINCKLEY, JOHN JR., *See*
ASSASSINS; BRAWNER TEST; MOTIVES FOR MURDER; NOT GUILTY BY REASON OF INSANITY (NGRI)

A HISTORY OF VIOLENCE IN RELIGIONS

Throughout their histories, religions have shared a common process, enduring long periods of persecution, seeing the coming of heroic religious martyrs and missionary leaders, fighting long wars of expansion and conquest, surviving times of internal factional struggles for doctrinal purity or supremacy, resisting the temptation to blend in with other religions and philosophies of neighbors, and adjusting to times of dramatic growth and increasing popular acceptance. Between the major religions lie wide gulfs of mutual distrust and antagonism, historical disagreements, territorial encroachments, wars, and feuds. These struggles highlight the violent nature of the conflict that continues to the present between radically differing worldviews, clashing cultural values, and rival political ideologies that date back to the beginnings of their common recorded history.

The history of religious violence in the West is as long as the historical record of its three major religions, Judaism, Christianity, and Islam, with their involved mutual antagonisms and struggles to adapt and survive the secular forces that threaten their continued existence. With belief systems developed over thousands of years, religions attract adherents of every possible political persuasion. The rise of religious fundamentalism has helped define how followers relate to their world, how they see their place in the world, and the moral structures that will help them live in harmony with their religious teachings.

The historical record is replete with the histories of religious conflicts, wars caused by religious expansion, the clash of religious cultures, and factional infighting. Religions that define themselves as peace-loving communities and transmitters of a body of religious truths still tend to demonize and denigrate the religions of their opponents. They proclaim to the world that their mission to mankind is to establish peace and harmony, yet they maintain the purity of their cause by oppressing members of their own religions and those of others. They believe that peace will arrive after a hostile world accepts and embraces their message. What the historical record shows is a near constant state of violent conflict between and within these philosophical systems.

Violence of all kinds, religious, ethnic, or political, is accepted as a fact of life. The major religions of the West do share a common monotheism; they honor many of the same historical religious figures and share some overlapping areas of doctrinal beliefs. For thousands of years, a broad variety of religious philosophies of all kinds have entered the long struggle for survival and dominance in the culture wars of Western history. In the 20th century, all three major religions witnessed a rebirth of fundamentalist religious movements, with radical groups appearing at their fringes that accept violence and terrorism as the means of bringing about their vision of a new order. They see acts of violence and terrorism as sacramental acts performed as divine imperatives.

MAJOR RELIGIONS EMBRACING VIOLENCE

Christianity

Christianity was seen in its infancy as little more than another troublesome radical Jewish sect. Jesus warned his followers that they would need to sell their cloaks to purchase swords. As Christianity spread throughout the Mediterranean area, it was strengthened and changed by a successful missionary movement that gained new converts from what the Jews felt were pagans and longtime enemies. The religion struggled to survive persecution from the Jewish and Roman authorities. Along with a belief in its infancy in the efficacy of Jewish ritual and dietary regulation from its parent religion (Judaism), Christianity became a religion with a group of its own historical writings that are accepted as the "word of God," combined with portions of the Jewish canon of scripture and the Old Testament. It also retained a tendency to passionate factionalism; coped with persistent problems with schism and doctrinal orthodoxy; and maintained a belief in nonviolence tempered with a provisional acceptance of war and other forms of officially sanctioned violence as acceptable under certain specific exemptions—the concept of a "just war."

In the early church, after Christianity began to spread into Europe, fathers such as Tertullian, Origen, and Cyrian described internal dissent and schisms that constantly threatened to destroy the young religion. Riots, mass mutual excommunications, and wars between members of opposing factions marked the bitter factional infighting during Christianity's early years. Christian orthodoxy is said by scholars to be a product of the 4th century. War remains a consistently and frequently used method to ensure the religion's survival and to resolve heretical challenges from rival religions. The desire for doctrinal purity was impossible according to what were considered to be core tenets of the Christian faith and its attendant rituals.

Christianity and its missionaries continued to move the Christian message through Europe and battle with the indigenous religions and nature cults. Altars and sacred sites were destroyed, their priests killed, and their records destroyed by the representatives of the new religion. The major Christian heresies, the forces of unrest and change, unleashed the Reformation that challenged the establishment of the new religious movement.

Christianity began with what the Romans may have seen as yet another Jerusalem-headquartered, militantly disobedient, subversive, radical Palestinian Jewish splinter group. After the destruction of Jerusalem by the Romans during the Jewish revolt in 70 C.E., Christianity spread throughout the Roman Empire, from India to Britain. Followers were persecuted when they refused to swear loyalty to the pagan gods of the Romans, and Christians were excommunicated from Jewish synagogues. The first 300 years of early Christianity involved schism, heresy, and violent struggles for doctrinal supremacy between warring Christian factions, which filled the writings of the early church history. Ireaneus, the Bishop of Lyons (178-200 C.E.), recorded the violent battles between the Christians of various cities, the betrayal and assassinations of religious leaders, and the confusion over the basic doctrines of Christianity. Various issues of this new religion were all left to be resolved by early church councils: Agreement on an accepted canon of scripture; articulation and acceptance of a doctrinal consistency; and establishment of an organizational structure that would provide leadership and direction for rapid growth of the church.

The early years saw the martyrdom of thousands of Christians by the Roman authorities and divisions of the church by Montanist and Donatist heresies. As the church moved out into the world, it came in contact with the influences of the pagan religions and practices, and they began to mix with Christian beliefs and practice. The birth of Islam in the 7th Century was the beginning of the end for Christianity in the Middle East. By 1054 C.E., mutual anathemas were exchanged in Constantinople between Cardinal Humbert, representing the papacy, and Patriarch Michael Celarius, and the shaky unity of Greek and Latin Christianity was ended. Neither revoked the mutual anathemas until December of 1965.

When Martin Luther began his critical examination of the medieval Catholic Church, the time came for the medieval Christian church to examine itself and address the corruption of the church, which became a force for change that sparked the Reformation. As the church felt the pressures for change, it began looking for traitors in its midst, and thus the Inquisition was initiated.

Judaism

The history of Israel and Judaism in Palestine is told in the Hebrew Bible and the Old Testament. Recorded there are the laws, the religious rituals, and the distinctive outline of a religious and philosophical system. The Jews had been in constant conflict with their neighbors, including the Hittites, the Babylonians, Egyptians, Greeks, Assyrians, the Phoenician traders, the Syrians, and the Roman armies and traders.

Judaism survives cycles of military success and defeat, and exile and dispersion. In the process, its followers have developed enduring religious and cultural structures, a temple, a canon of accepted scripture, and religious tradition. All the while, the religion has weathered periodic internal storms of dissent and change, the emergence and disappearance of its early tribal culture, hereditary kings and royal families, prophets and prophetesses and their struggles to maintain doctrinal consistency, and a monotheistic religion in the midst of hostile polytheistic neighbor cultures. Internal unrest resulted in the division of the tribes into two kingdoms: Judah, a southern kingdom with its capital in Jerusalem, and Israel, a northern kingdom with its capital in Sechem. After Israel was defeated militarily, both kingdoms were destroyed and its people dispersed into exile. By 587 B.C., Palestine became a part of the Persian Empire. Their return from exile was followed by the development of a canon of scripture with laws, prescribed rituals, the establishment of a priestly caste, and a return to their geographical homeland.

The earliest historical record of Judaism is located in the Bible's Old Testament. It contains stories of the origins of the Jewish people, their creation stories, the origins of their distinctive rituals and cultural norms, and the shaping of their monotheistic traditions into a codified philosophical system that has lasted 4,000 years. The main body of Jews resided in Palestine for only the first third of their history. Then came their defeat by the Babylonians and their exile in 586 B.C.E. Titus, in 70 C.E., restored them to their homeland during the reign of Cyrus, where they remained up until the destruction of the Jewish State.

Judaism evolved from simpler nomadic clan or tribal patriarchal structures to a nation of distinctive organizational structures reflecting its monotheistic doctrinal system, with rituals and cultural norms that were perceived as heretical, radical, and destabilizing to the smooth operation of its host and conqueror cultures. This reaction brought Jews into protracted wars with their neighbors. Israel, as the nation of the Jews came to be called, believed that their God, Yahweh, had chosen them as his people and that their prophets and champions would protect them from abundant enemies and traitors in their midst. Their revealed mission was to fight to bring the light of their monotheistic message to the rest of the world. The history of Israel is also, in large part, the history of a small, weaker nation periodically defeated and conquered by its larger, more powerful neighbors. The list of enemies and conquerors includes the Mesopotamians, the Assyrians, the Egyptians, Persians, Greeks, and Romans.

The Jews in defeat were periodically dispersed throughout the area of the Middle East, exiled among alien cultures and religions. Their conquerors attempted to extinguish the local religions and replace them with their own. When allowed to return from exile, the Jews codified their rituals, created their scripture, established a line of hereditary kings and noble families, and developed a desire for freedom that brought about internal faction fighting. As they reestablished themselves in their former territory, they were besieged by external and internal enemies and were convulsed again by unrest caused by forces of dissent and assimilation. Surrounding cultures and competing religious systems introduced unacceptable concepts and ideas, which caused more internal pressure for doctrinal and organization changes.

The Jews became targets of persecution by successive invasions and occupations by Syrian, Samarian, and Roman armies and collaborationist governments throughout history up until the present time. The rise of Zionism and the desire of the Western allies at the end of the World War II to establish a Jewish homeland in Palestine resulted in the displacement of a native Palestinian population into refugee camps, where they have waited more than 50 years for resolution.

Israel has seen the birth of a number of right-wing religious movements within Judaism that look forward to the end of the current secular governments and to the establishment of a new government. This would be founded on the principles of Jewish law and tradition and would stop any attempt at accommodations that would permit Palestinians to stay within the biblical boundaries of Israel proper. That government would expel or relocate all Arabs from within its territorial boundaries. These groups see the current peace process as a sign of an unacceptable betrayal of a historical and religious vision of the future of Judaism.

In 1995, after a peace rally, an angry young right-wing student, Yigel Amir, claimed to be acting under orders from God when he assassinated Israeli Prime Minister Yitzhak Rabin. It was an attempt to stop any movement toward a peace treaty with the Palestinians. The treaty would likely have established a Palestinian state on what Amir considers to be land given by God by eternal covenant to the people of Israel in Old Testament times. In the assassination's aftermath, Shimon Peres watched as a 20-point lead in the preelection polls evaporated and his conservative opponent, Benjamin Netanyahu, was elected.

Amir is now portrayed by the ultra-right-wing messianic Zionists as a hero. Messianic Zionism believes in the establishment of a government strictly based on Jewish religious principles and the contemporary rebuilding of a Jewish Temple as part of the preparations for the expected arrival of the Messiah. In his appeal of his murder conviction, Amir used the justification of what is called a "pursuer's decree" in Jewish law. This law obligates any Jew to stop someone who presents a mortal danger to another Jew. He claims that Rabin's government threatened the continued peace and safety of his fellow Jews and that it was an illegitimate government because it had been elected by a religiously unacceptable coalition of Arabs and Jews.

Fundamental disagreements between the secular Israeli political parties and the clash of their radically different expectations and worldviews make sustained progress in the resolution of these differences problematic.

Islam

Islam appeared in the 7th century with the Prophet Muhammad as the instrument of Allah. In the tradition of Adam, Abraham, Moses, and Jesus, the prophet established a new noncompromising monotheistic religion that required strict adherence to a body of ritual observances. Jews, Christians, and Muslims all believe that God speaks through the scriptural record. Islam's basic scripture, the Koran, is accepted by Muslims as having been given to Muhammad, God's greatest prophet, through the agency of the angel Gabriel.

The Middle East witnessed a 20th-century revival of Arab nationalism and Islamic fundamentalism. Terrorist organizations appeared following the long, slow collapse of the Ottoman Empire, the retreat and expulsion of the Western colonialist powers from the region, the 1948 birth of the state of Israel, and the subsequent defeats and domestic disappointments of the secular Arab governments in their wars with Israel. Political organizations emerged in the region during the 1970s that fused the intense appeal of Arab nationalism with programs working for the rebirth of truly Islamic governments, the return or the reimposition of Islamic law, and the establishment of a Palestinian state in the territories occupied by Israel since 1967. The neighboring Arab governments invaded Israel in 1948 immediately after its founding, and were defeated. The expulsion of thousands of Palestinian Arabs forced their resettlement into refugee camps located in surrounding countries, where they still exist. Israel and its neighbors have been in an almost constant state of war ever since.

Unable to prevail or to accomplish their political or religious objectives through conventional warfare,

Islamic fundamentalists have turned to terrorism as their chosen method to publicize their plight and their cause. In Egypt, the Muslim Brotherhood, an Islamic fundamentalist group seeking the replacement of secular Muslim governments with theocratic governments, assassinated Egyptian Prime Minister Mahmoud Fahmy el-Nokrashy in 1948. The Palestine Liberation Organization (PLO) was formed as a nonviolent organization in 1964. After the defeat of the Arab countries in the War of 1967, Yasir Arafat has led the organization through a transformation, promoting violent action as the means of ending Israeli occupation of the West Bank and Gaza. The Islamic fundamentalist group Hamas, an offshoot of the Palestinian branch of the Muslim Brotherhood, and Hezbollah, the radical Shiite organization founded in 1978 to establish Islamic fundamentalist governments in Lebanon and the Middle East, have engaged in terrorist attacks against Israel, Egypt, the United States, and Israel's other European allies. Suicide bombers are seen as Islamic martyrs to the cause of Palestinian statehood and the rebirth of Islamic theocracies.

Islamic teachings condemn suicide but accept martyrdom for those who protect the faith and its holy places from the presence or attacks of infidels. The attacks on American Embassies in Nairobi, Kenya, and Dar es Salaam, Tanzania, in 1998 brought indictments against members of the al-Qaeda group and their leader, Osama bin Laden. Their 1998 declaration of *jihad* against the United States provided clerical sanction for the struggle against the perceived leader of the threat against the Muslim world, the United States. It provides a group willing to accept martyrdom in defense of the Islamic world.

All three of the Western world's major religions, Judaism, Christianity, and Islam, have in common a shared monotheism; they claim parts of a common historical process, honor many of the same historical figures as prophets and holy men, and even share a number of doctrinal beliefs. These religions preach tolerance and promote forms of religious nonviolence and interfaith cooperation. Under certain circumstances, however, all embrace violence, even terrorism, as a way to defend the faith from serious threats, stop the spreading of influence of other religions or other threats, and to fight, from within, the disruptions caused by internal dissent. The rebirth of radically fundamentalist religious movements poses an extremely serious threat to the world's political and economic order and stability. The 20th-century wars between Muslims and Christians, Christians and Jews, and Jews and Muslims have origins that extend back in time hundreds of years. The danger of such groups has increased as they have gained access to the technologies of mass destruction. They have become more inclined to violence, with more lethal modalities, and more mobility.

INCIDENTS OF RELIGIOUS TERRORISM

Ireland

The troubles in Northern Ireland date back to the 16th century when Henry VIII established the Protestant Church of England as the official state church and began the persecution of Catholics unwilling to become Protestants. Queen Elizabeth I, a Protestant queen, encouraged Protestant settlers, mostly Scots and English, to resettle in Northern Ireland. These settlers differed ethnically from the Irish. It started a centuries-long conflict based on both religious and ethnic differences.

During defeat of the Irish revolt of the 17th century by Oliver Cromwell's Protestant forces, thousands of Irish Catholics were massacred, and Protestants maintained their hold on power. During the 18th century, Irish nationalism was reborn after the potato famine of 1845 to 1848, and in the face of the deaths and outmigration of Irish Catholics, the Protestant Unionists consolidated their power. By the late 19th century, Irish Catholic Republicans were engaging in a campaign of bombings and assassinations against the British and their political rivals in a struggle to establish an Irish republic.

The Irish Republican Army emerged from the disastrous defeat of its 1916 uprising to resume with the Protestants a mutual war of terrorism, assassinations, and bombings that continued up until the closing years of the 20th century. The IRA orchestrated a campaign of car bombings, assassinations, shootings, and an attempt to kill British Prime Minister Margaret Thatcher in 1984. Unionist forces engaged in a war of recrimination against their Catholic enemies as well. The current negotiations between Unionists, Protestants, and the British have resulted in a current cease-fire that has greatly reduced, at least for the time being, the level of violence.

United States

On April 19, 1995, Timothy McVeigh and Terry Nichols, ideological adherents to the fundamentalist

Christian Identity Movement, followed the example of the 1993 fundamentalist Islamic bombers of the World Trade Center. They rented a Ryder rental truck and used it to deliver a crude bomb made from ammonium nitrate fertilizer and diesel fuel, which destroyed the Alfred P. Murrah Federal Building in Oklahoma City. The Christian Identity Movement is one of a number of what are categorized as American Christian White Supremacist groups. These groups are anti-Semitic, right wing, fundamentalist Christian, racist, antiabortion, homophobic, and apocalyptic in their political and religious configurations. What many have in common with other extremist ideologies is the carefully considered decision to accept violence and acts of political terrorism as acceptable means to gain public attention for their causes, to maintain a radical Christian ideology, to eliminate internal and external enemies, and to speed the achievement of their religious and political goals.

SUMMARY

Throughout their histories, Judaism, Christianity, and Islam have all embodied doctrinally sanctioned pacificism as well as outlining acceptable and sanctioned reasons for violence, wars, and martyrdom in the face of intolerable circumstances. Contemporary religious acts of terrorism are heavily symbolic. They strike at locations that are seen as secure and safe and that will make a powerfully disruptive statement, public government buildings, buses, restaurants, and busy streets. For the religious terrorist, the attack is a sacramental act completed in response to a religious imperative.

To achieve their radical political and religious objectives, modern terrorists harness modern technologies, which have become easier to use, more sophisticated, more readily accessible, and more deadly. Financial backing, logistical support, and components needed for the construction and delivery of weapons of mass destruction are believed to be available from "rogue states," or countries seen as enemies to Western democracies: Cuba, Syria, China, North Korea, Libya, Iraq, and Iran. This technology can be adapted and used for cyberterrorism, which documents the manufacture and delivery of poison gas, explosives, and biological agents; the construction and deployment of a "dirty bomb" using radioactive materials; as well as traditional war materiel, firearms, missiles, and explosives.

That the major religions of the world have done much to improve the individual lots of their respective members is beyond argument. But the inability of religious groups to coexist with one another leaves the postmodern world struggling to repair the damage they will continue to do.

—Steven Opager

See also BIN LADEN, OSAMA; TERRORISM

Further Reading

Armstrong, K. (2000). *The battle for God.* New York: Knopf.

Arquilla, J., Ronfeldt, D., & Michele, Z. (1999). *Countering the new terrorism. Prepared form United States Air Force.* Santa Monica, CA: Rand.

Hoffman, B. (1998). *Inside terror.* New York: Columbia University Press.

Lewis, B. (Ed.). (1977). *Cambridge history of Islam.* Cambridge University Press.

McManners, J. (1990). *Oxford illustrated history of Christianity.* Oxford University Press.

Sterling, C. (1981). *Terror network: The secret war of international terrorism.* New York: Holt, Rinehart & Winston.

JOHANN OTTO HOCH (BLUEBEARD)

Known as "Bluebeard" for the many women he murdered, Johann Otto Hoch frequently relocated and remarried. He is believed to have murdered 15 or more wives and collected on their life insurance policies. Hoch was finally arrested and convicted for poisoning one of them with arsenic and was hung in 1906.

—Brianna Satterthwaite

JIMMY HOFFA

James "Jimmy" Riddle Hoffa was the leader of the Teamsters Union from 1957 to 1971. Hoffa was believed to have had ties to organized crime. He was convicted of jury tampering and fraud in 1964, served 4 years in prison, and had his sentence commuted by President Nixon. While trying to regain control of the Teamsters Union, Hoffa disappeared on July 30, 1975, from a restaurant in Bloomfield Hills, Michigan. He had an appointment with Anthony Provenzano, a Teamster leader, and Anthony Giacalone, a Detroit mob leader. Both Provenzano and Giacalone denied having seen Hoffa on that day. Hoffa was declared legally dead in 1983, although his body has never been recovered.

—*Phil Caporale*

HOG TRAIL KILLINGS

Daniel Owen Conahan Jr. was a serial killer in the Punta Gorda area on Florida's Gulf Coast in the mid-1990s. He lured his victims into secluded, densely wooded areas to take nude photographs of them and then tied them to trees in mock bondage positions. Once the victims were restrained, Conahan strangled them with rope, stabbed and mutilated their bodies, and cut their genitalia. At least six deaths were attributed to Conahan, although he was convicted of the slaying of only one. He was sentenced to death in Florida's electric chair, but his case is currently on appeal. The news media dubbed the killings "The Hog Trail Killings" because the murders occurred in remote areas inhabited by wild boars.

—*Phil Caporale*

Further Reading

LaFave, W. R., & Scott, A. W. Jr. (1986). *Substantive criminal law, criminal practice series.* St. Paul, MN: West Publishing.
40 Am. Jur. 2d, §§ 104-176.

HOLOCAUST, *See* ETHNIC CLEANSING; GENOCIDE; MASS VIOLENCE; MEDICAL VIOLENCE; WAR ATROCITIES

HOMICIDE

Homicide is the taking of a person's life. This includes justifiable homicide and state-sanctioned executions as well as murder. In cases of self-defense or when states hold executions, these are viewed as homicides but are not considered illegal killings. (The cause of death on the death certificate of a person executed in California is listed as "homicide.")

A *murder*, which is a form of homicide, requires an illegal taking of another's life. Each state within the United States has very specific criteria for defining murder. From a judicial point of view, the most serious murders are *capital* cases. Such cases may qualify a person, if convicted, for a death sentence. However, most persons convicted of *first-degree* murder find their way into lengthy prison terms. First-degree murder usually includes *felony murder*, or murder committed while in the course of committing another felony, such as killing someone while robbing a bank. Other forms of first-degree murder include poisoning, lying in wait, torture, use of explosives, and in some states, such as California, using armor-piercing bullets, or "drive-by" killings.

To receive a death sentence in California, an offender must be "death eligible," which means that the person must have committed a murder. Usually, for a sentence of death, the offender must have willfully, deliberately, and with premeditation murdered another with *special circumstances*. These special or aggravating circumstances in first-degree murder include a prior murder by the offender; multiple murder; killing of a peace officer, witness, prosecutor, or judge; lying in wait; torture with intent to kill; murder due to race, ethnicity, religion, or nationality; felony murder; and use of poison. Even when an offender does receive a death sentence, the likelihood of actually being executed is minimal. In California, the average length of time for an appeals process to be completed is 14 years and 9 months. Most of the condemned in California die of illness, old age, or suicide.

VICTIMIZATION

Most people who murder kill only once, because the murders are crimes of passion. In the past several years, more victims have been killed by strangers, which has caused criminologists to create new profiles of both offenders and victims. What makes offenders select certain types of victims, especially when the murder victims are strangers? Victimization research now examines the concept of *facilitation*, or the degree to which victims make themselves accessible or vulnerable to attack. Wolfgang, in his noted Philadelphia study, examined the notion of "victim-precipitated" homicide. He observed that some victims are catalysts in fatal attacks by rendering either the first blow or a threatening gesture. Among Wolfgang's several conclusions, he found that the victim was often the husband of the offender, had been drinking, and had a history of assaultive behavior. He concluded that the victim may be one of the critical precipitating causes of his or her own death.

Reiss also studied victim-prone individuals and found they were more likely to experience the same form of victimization than to be subject to two different criminal acts. McDonald observed that victim-prone people have acquired particular attitudes and lifestyles that increase their vulnerability. According to Doerner and Lab, victim precipitation is a "major contributing factor" in serious violence. Wolfgang noted that in many instances, the characteristics of homicide victims in general resembled those of their assailants. Who became the offender and who became the victim often was determined more by chance than any other factor. He noted that few women committed murder and that most women who did commit murder were responding to the violent behavior of males. The Philadelphia study also revealed that most murders were intraracial: blacks killing blacks and whites killing whites.

FORMS OF MURDER

Mass Murder and Insanity

One form of murder that has rapidly emerged in American society is *mass murder.* Most people's immediate response on learning that someone has murdered several persons is that he or she "must be crazy." This is especially common when an individual enters a schoolyard, a shopping mall, or a restaurant and begins shooting randomly. Many such killers are found to have histories of mental problems, drug usage, and encounters with the law. For example, in Stockton, California, in January 1989, an intruder entered the Cleveland Elementary School yard and began firing rounds from a Russian-made AK-47 assault rifle. Five children were killed, and at least 30 other children wounded, many seriously, from the 110 expended rounds. The attacker then fired a bullet into his own head, killing himself instantly. Police and psychologists who investigated the case believed that something had "snapped" in him and he reacted violently.

The man's history indicated a life of drug abuse, arrests, and isolation and appeared unable to cope any longer with an intolerable existence. He could not accept the fact that others around him were becoming successful. The feelings of inadequacy, loss of self-esteem, perceived rejection by others, and failure to achieve can become too much for some individuals to bear. They finally respond by lashing back at society. In this case, the offender may have been exacting the greatest possible revenge by killing children.

Confronted with such cases, we sometimes employ terms that may blur the distinction between legal and medical definitions of mental disorders. Once an offender is charged with multiple murders, the "not guilty by reason of insanity" defense (NGRI) may be used as the defense strategy. However, as far as the criminal courts are concerned, *insanity* is a legal term, not a psychiatric distinction. The courts usually determine the state of mind of the accused before a trial commences. During the trial, the courts must then determine if the offender was insane at the time of the crime and to what extent he or she is responsible for the crime. Thus, the legal system uses the term insanity to define the state of mind of an offender *at the time of the offense;* offenders may be deemed insane at the moment of the crime and *only* for that period of time.

Insanity pleas have been commonly used by offenders charged with serious crimes such as homicide, especially when the defense team sees little hope of acquitting their client by any other means. Most legal jurisdictions ensure that NGRI offenders are automatically placed in psychiatric facilities, regardless of their present state of mind. In *Jones v. United States* (1983), the Supreme Court ruled that insanity may continue after the criminal act, and therefore the offender could be placed in a psychiatric facility until such time as he or she is determined to have recovered from his or her afflictions. For some offenders, confinement in a mental institution is tantamount to a life sentence because they must be clinically evaluated and deemed to be no longer a threat to society before they can be released.

Sexual Homicides

Some researchers differentiate *sex murderers* from *lust murderers.* The sex murderer often kills out of fear and a desire to silence the victim, whereas the lust murderer appears to harbor deep-seated fantasies. This certainly does not exclude the possibility that some rapists may also premeditate their killings and experience fantasies. For killers such as Albert DeSalvo, "the Boston Strangler," rapes are merely a continuation of progressive sexual fantasies and behaviors that finally lead to murder. Revitch and Schlesinger noted that women, although in fewer numbers than men, also are capable of developing homicidal fantasies and becoming involved in sadistic murders and mass killings.

Researchers have continued to note differences between rape murders and lust killings. Special agents from the FBI examined a sample of 36 sexual murderers, 29 of whom were convicted of killing several victims. Specifically, they were interested in the general characteristics of sexual murderers across the United States. They explored the dynamics of offenders' sexual fantasies, sadistic behaviors, and rape and mutilation murders. These investigators noted several deviant sexual behaviors practiced before, during, or after the victims had been killed. The act of rape, whether it was the actual physical act or a symbolic rape during which an object was inserted into the vagina, was found to be common among serial killers in this study. For some offenders, the act of rape served as only one form of sexual assault; they engaged in a variety of mutilations, sexual perversions, and desecration of victims' corpses.

Paraphilia and Other Sexual Misconduct

Sexual degradations have influenced our perceptions and definitions of those who kill. "Sex maniac" becomes the layperson's term for anyone capable of performing acts of sexual perversion on his or her victims. In some cases, the offenders as children were subjected to one or more of these sexual abuses themselves. In each case, the experience was deeply traumatizing. According to the *Diagnostic and Statistical Manual of Mental Disorders,* 4th edition *(DSM-IV),* published by the American Psychiatric Association (1994), many deviant behaviors are forms of *paraphilia.* Common almost exclusively to males, paraphilia involves sexual arousal through deviant or bizarre images or activities. The *DSM-IV* identifies such repetitive sexual activities as paraphilia once a pattern has been established linked to a time frame of at least 6 months. Multiple paraphilias are also commonly found in one person, but usually one paraphilia becomes dominant until replaced by another. For example, a pedophile, a person who is sexually attracted to children, may also succumb to fetishes, such as being aroused by a child's hair, rubber gloves, or self-administered enemas.

Most psychosexual disorders are a result of an aberrant fantasy system fueled by traumatic childhood and adolescent experiences. Some offenders are found in the extreme end of the paraphilic continuum when they engage in *erotophonophilia,* or lust/sexual murder. This involves the acting out of sadistic behaviors in the course of brutally torturing and murdering their victims.

PROFILING OFFENDERS

Much of the information about criminal offenders is based on taxonomies, or classification systems. Megargee and Bohn noted that researchers usually created typologies based on the criminal offense. This invariably became problematic, because often the offense comprised one or more subgroups. Researchers then examined repetitive crime patterns, which in turn created new complexities and problems. Megargee and Bohn further noted that depending on the authority one chooses to read, one will find between 2 and 11 different types of murderers. Some typologies of murder are descriptions of causation, whereas others are diagnostic in nature.

Researchers have been attempting to create profiles of the "typical" murderers as well as serial killers from statistics on offenders and victims in the United States. The most sensational of all murderers are those who are in some way involved sexually with their victims. This type of killer generates much public interest and alarm. Stories of young women being abducted, raped, tortured, and strangled appear more and more frequently in the newspapers.

The FBI, through extensive application of profiling techniques, has identified the characteristics of "organized" and "disorganized" murders. Using information gathered at the scene of the crime and examining the nature of the crime itself, agents constructed profiles of the offenders, which in turn were categorized as "organized" or "disorganized." For example, an organized murderer is often profiled as having good intelligence and being socially competent, whereas the disorganized offender is viewed as being of average intelligence and socially immature. Similarly, some crime investigators often find that organized offenders plan their murders, target strangers, and demand victims to be submissive, whereas disorganized killers may know their victims, inflict sudden violence on them, and spontaneously carry out their killings.

More specifically, organized killers profiled as lust murderers (an offender sexually involved with his victim) by the FBI possess many of the following personal characteristics:

1. Highly intelligent
2. High birth order status
3. Masculine image
4. Charismatic
5. Socially capable
6. Sexually capable
7. Occupationally mobile
8. Lives with partner
9. Geographically mobile
10. Experienced harsh discipline
11. Controlled emotions during crime
12. High interest in media response to crime
13. Model inmate

The organized lust killer also exhibits fairly predictable behaviors after the crime, including returning to the crime scene, needing to volunteer information, enjoying being friendly with police, expecting to be interrogated by investigators, and sometimes moving the victim's body to a new location or exposing the body to draw attention to the crime. The disorganized offender is characterized as follows:

1. Below-average intelligence
2. Low birth order status
3. Socially immature
4. Seldom dates
5. High school dropout
6. Father often under- or unemployed
7. Lives alone
8. Has secret hiding places
9. Nocturnal
10. Lives/works near crime scene
11. Engages in unskilled work
12. Significant behavioral changes
13. Low interest in media attention
14. Limited alcohol consumption
15. High anxiety during crime

According to the FBI, the disorganized lust killer also exhibits a variety of predictable behaviors following a murder, including returning to the crime scene, possibly attending the funeral or burial of the victim, keeping a diary, changing employment, becoming religious, experiencing changes in personality, and submitting personal advertisements in newspapers regarding his victims. Although such profiles have proven helpful in understanding offender behavior and many of the behaviors listed give researchers and law enforcement clues about the psychological

mind-sets of offenders, we have only begun to delve inside the minds of those who murder.

—*Eric W. Hickey*

Portions of this entry are drawn from *Serial Murderers and Their Victims,* 3rd edition (2002) by E. W. Hickey, published by Wadsworth: Belmont, CA.

See also FORENSIC SCIENCE; MASS MURDER; MOTIVES FOR MURDER; NOT GUILTY BY REASON OF INSANITY (NGRI); PARAPHILIA; PROFILING; VICTIMOLOGY; VIOLENT BEHAVIOR

Further Reading

American Psychiatric Association. (1994). *Diagnostic and statistical manual of mental disorders* (4th ed.). Washington, DC: Author.

Doerner, W. G., & Lab, S. (1995). *Victimology.* Cincinnati, OH: Anderson.

Jones v. United States, 103 S. Ct. 3043 (1983).

McDonald, W. (1970). *The victim: A social psychological study of criminal victimization.* Unpublished doctoral dissertation. Ann Arbor, MI: University Microfilms.

Megargee, E. I., & Bohn, M. J. Jr. (1979). *Classifying criminal offenders.* Newbury Park, CA: Sage.

Prentky, R. W., Burgess, A. W., & Carter, D. L. (1986). Victim responses by rapist type: An empirical and clinical analysis. *Journal of Interpersonal Violence, 1,* 73-98.

Reiss, A. Jr. (1980). *Victim proneness in repeat victimization by type of crime.* In S. Fineberg & A. Reiss Jr. (Eds.), *Indicators of crime and criminal justice: Quantitative studies* (pp. 41-54). Washington, DC: U.S. Department of Justice.

Ressler, R. K., Burgess, A. W., & Douglas, J. E. (1988). *Sexual homicide.* Lexington, MA: Lexington Books.

Revitch, E., & Schlesinger, L. B. (1981). *Psychopathology of homicide.* Springfield, IL: Charles C Thomas.

Scully, D., & Marolla, J. (1985). Riding the bull at Gilley's: Convicted rapists describe the rewards of rape. *Social Problems, 32,* 251-263.

Wolfgang, M. E. (1958). *Patterns in criminal homicide.* Philadelphia: University of Pennsylvania Press.

HOMICIDE: MOTIVATION FOR MURDER

Why does one person decide to murder another? Certainly, murder varies according to the motivations (e.g., the reasons for), the strategies (e.g., how the murder is carried out), and the situational context of the crime (e.g., where, when, against whom, and under what circumstances). The main factor that must occur in the killer's mind prior to the murder, if even momentarily, is that the victim(s) is/are objectified and dehumanized. This pattern of thought allows murderers to rationalize, minimize, deny, or otherwise internally justify their homicidal actions. Still, what is the motivation underlying such an extreme act?

Motive is an inner drive that causes, or compels, one to act. It is that which incites us to behave in the manner we do. Motive can be related either to internal psychological processes or to an external object of desire that produces an impelling force in the individual. When investigating a murder, one of the most important elements to determine is the killer's *modus operandi,* or *MO,* which refers to the offenders' actions and procedures used to successfully commit their murder(s). The killer's MO represents a learned behavior pattern developed through a series of successive approximations. These may range from minor thought distortions that allow for the thought of homicide during impulsive moments, to episodic fantasies of homicide, to daily homicidal fantasy and overt practicing of the homicidal plan via animal cruelty or other human victims. Thus, serial killers may change their MOs until they discover those methods that are most successful in effecting the death of their victims and that produce the desired results for the internal needs of the murderer. Serial killers may also change their MOs to avoid capture. Moreover, murder is usually committed under a combination of motives. Clearly homicide of any number of victims is a complex phenomenon with various motives and dynamics. Sometimes killers may even be unaware or unsure of their motivations to murder.

Indeed, the motivations of the single-victim (e.g., the typical murderer) and multiple-victim murderers (e.g., spree, mass, and serial murderers) are different. In most homicides, the killing is a single circumstantial event and produces one murderer (sometimes more than one) and one murdered victim. Mass murder events are also a single circumstantial event yet produce one murderer (rarely more than one) and many murdered victims. Spree murders are a series of separate homicidal events that are very close in time, days, or weeks, and produce one or more murderers and several victims in different settings. Serial murder, on the other hand, represents a process of killing and usually produces one murderer, or sometimes a team of murderers, and three or more

murdered victims over the span of several months or years.

Skrapec has indicated the need for researchers and investigators to understand the personal constructions of meaning in murderers' lives in order to gain a better understanding of their homicidal motivations. For example, in some cases, the murderer is tried, convicted, and sentenced to prison under a motive that was obvious and clear to the court (e.g., jealousy, domestic violence, etc.), only later to be discovered in the killer's treatment that the true motivation was to cover up a paraphilic sexual motivation for killing the victim. Thus, one must be careful in examining a murderer's motivations, for the apparent motive and the true motive may be distinctly different.

Many researchers have examined the motivational aspects of various types of homicide and homicide offenders and have found varying results in what motivates someone to kill. Murderers are not a homogeneous group. They present with individually derived motivations, behaviors, and cognitive organization. These unique characteristics likely account for the mixed research findings. To understand homicide, the researcher or investigator must consider both the psychological life courses of offenders and the interpersonal context between victims and their killers.

The analysis of motive has led to the development of typologies of murderers. For example, Holmes and DeBurger have indicated four types of serial killers: (a) the visionary type, (b) the mission-oriented type, (c) the hedonistic type, and (d) the power/control-oriented type.

The *visionary type* are generally responding to the commands of auditory hallucinations or psychological visions that emanate from the notions of good and evil, in other words, as part of the psychotic and/or delusional thought processes of the killer's mind. *Mission-oriented killers* believe that it is their purpose, or mission, in life to rid society of certain types of people (i.e., prostitutes, the elderly, children, homosexuals, abortion doctors, a certain racial/ethnic group, etc.). The *hedonistic type* are seen as thrill seekers who derive a sense of pleasure from killing. There are two subtypes of hedonistic murderers; those who kill for creature comforts and lust murderers, who kill for sexual gratification, often sexually mutilating their victims. The *power/control type* may use some sexual elements in their killings, yet the primary source of pleasure is not sexual, but rather derived from the killer's ability to exercise control over and exert power

Table 1   Circumstances of Murder, 1991–2000

	N	%
Total	182,733	100.0
Felony type total	34,659	19.0
Rape	846	0.5
Robbery	17,204	9.4
Burglary	1,338	0.7
Larceny-theft	251	0.1
Motor vehicle theft	374	0.2
Arson	1,108	0.6
Prostitution or other commercialized vice	136	0.1
Other sex offenses	279	0.2
Narcotic drug law violations	9,679	5.3
Gambling	168	0.1
Other, not specified	3,276	1.8
Suspected felony type total	1,341	0.7
Other than felony type total	94,028	51.5
Romantic triangle	2,550	1.4
Child killed by babysitter	287	0.2
Brawl due to the influence of alcohol	2,974	1.6
Brawl due to the influence of narcotics	1,806	1.0
Argument over money or property	3,448	1.9
Other argument	49,741	27.2
Gangland killings	1,109	0.6
Juvenile gang killings	8,611	4.7
Institutional killings	166	0.1
Sniper attack	112	0.1
Other, not specified	23,224	12.7
Unknown	52,705	28.8

Source: FBI (1992–2001).

on the victim(s). These offenders enjoy inflicting great pain on their victims and derive pleasure from watching their victim(s) cower, cringe, and beg for mercy.

Domingo has also indicated two primary types of homicide offenders, predatory and affective. The predatory killer usually targets strangers as victims, whereas the affective killer murders victims who are familiar. Therefore, the motivations of the predatory and the affective murderer would be qualitatively different.

Hickey, with his work on serial murderers, indicates that gender factors produce different motivations for murder. For example, male serial killers are motivated more by sex, control, money, and enjoyment, yet mostly by a combination of motives. Female serial killers are motivated more by money, control, and enjoyment, or a combination of motives. When serial killers murder in teams, the motivations are generally related to sex, money, control, enjoyment, yet mostly to a combination of motives.

These classifications and typologies help to organize data and facilitate professional communication.

Each of these motives for murder is useful in generating taxonomies. Motivational taxonomies help explain why murderers decide to relieve their victims of their lives. However, Hickey (2002) warns, "we erroneously assume that if we stare long and intently enough at a perceived motivation we will be able to comprehend the dynamics of its etiology" (p. 32). In other words, he means that focusing solely on motives obscures other important variables that may explain why the murder(s) occurred.

One of the largest sources of homicide data is the Uniform Crime Reports (UCR), compiled yearly by the Federal Bureau of Investigation. The UCR tabulates some of the major circumstances of murder offenses. Table 1 summarizes these murder circumstances over a 10-year time period, 1991-2000 (FBI, 1992-2001).

MOST COMMON HOMICIDAL MOTIVATIONS

The following is an outline of the global, or most common, motives employed in murder. Learning more about how individuals develop their motivations and working toward treating, eliminating, or making those motivators less enticing before homicidal actions occur could help reduce the frequency of such violent acts.

Abandonment/Rejection

Some killers find the notion of being separated from their spouses/intimate partners so destabilizing and threatening to their sense of personal identity that when the significant other decides to end the relationship, usually secondary to the killer's neurotic tendencies, the killer decides to end his or her life instead. These murders are sometimes justified by the offender's cognition that says, "If I can't have her, no one can." The killer with this type of motivation is essentially trying to desperately maintain that which has provided his or her source of personal validation as a human being: the victim. These murders typically occur when a woman has recently left or is in the process of leaving an abusive relationship, immediately following the finalization of a divorce, or when the killer discovers a significant other is either involved or fantasizing about someone else.

The homicidal motivation in a majority of school shootings are related to either abandonment and/or rejection issues. There have also been cases in which killers have murdered their victims, making it look like an accident, and then have them cremated so that they may keep the victims with them throughout the remainder of their lives. This has been seen in both elderly sponsicide and in filicide of a child with a chronic illness.

Altruism

Many acts of filicide are committed with altruistic motivation. The notion of altruistic motivation involves the killer's belief that by murdering victims, they are actually setting them free or sparing them from some future pain or suffering. Prostitute killings may involve offenders with altruistic motivations. Mercy killers also tend to present with altruistic motivation.

Cover-Up: Destruction of Evidence or Motive

Many murders are committed to silence witnesses, victims, attorneys, or investigators in order to avoid prosecution. This is seen in murders committed as part of gangland violence and organized crime. It has also been seen in cases of sexual homicide.

Alcohol and Drugs

Murders are committed as a result of being under the influence of illicit chemicals or during the sale, distribution, and theft of illegal drugs, as seen in organized crime and gangland violence.

Escape

Some people kill other human beings during situations in which they feel an intense need to escape, including fleeing from capture, fires, hostage situations, stampeding crowds, and situations involving extreme domestic violence.

Fame/Celebrity

Several murderers have planned their killings in a shocking or grandiose manner to gain tremendous media attention and thereby become infamous and immortalized in the history books. These killers may also target high-profile victims, such as movie stars and politicians.

Fatal Abuse

Fatal abuse can be the result of a chronic pattern of maltreatment or a onetime abusive episode. Some of these killings are unintended, and others are quite intentional. Some cases occur as a result of Munchausen syndrome by proxy. Fatal abuse is common among sponsicide, intimaticide, and filicide.

Protection of Self or Others

One might murder another individual to stop that person from abusing himself or herself, or murder to stop an attack toward a stranger or in self-defense.

Frustration/Anger

Some people become violent or homicidal when angry or frustrated. These killings can be the result of chronic frustration and anger such that the killer decides he or she has "had enough" and acts out; or they may be the result of extremely volatile impulses. These types of murders are seen in lovers' triangles and other sexually frustrating circumstances; unsatisfactory business dealings; doctoral dissertation committee slayings; workplace murders secondary to the loss of the killer's job, status, or health; and in cases of caregiver frustration with children, the chronically and/or terminally ill, and the elderly.

Greed

Murders committed with a motive of greed are usually seeking insurance settlements, inheritance and estate holdings, property deeds, or financial gains of a business transaction.

Hate/Resentment

Hate is an extreme emotion that finds its foundation in cognitive distortion. Hate as a motivator for homicide can be found in cases of murder secondary to homophobia, racial/ethnic prejudice, and cultural homicide (e.g., genocide). Hate is also one of the motivations of the terrorist and the homicide-suicide bomber. Resentment as a motivator is like a volcano. Rarely does a person experience feelings of resentment and leap into homicidal action. Those who murder because of resentment have generally been subjected to long histories of maltreatment, either real or perceived, by the victims. Resentful killers decide to commit murder only when they subjectively feel that they can't bear their circumstances any longer. Murders that are committed secondary to the motivation of hate and/or resentment are laden with affective elements and frequently involve overkill.

Honor

Honor killings are seen in situations such as the Japanese kamikaze pilots, wartime situations, terrorism plots, cultural and/or religious status, and retaliation to preserve one's honor (frequent in gangland violence and organized crime) and may also be seen in mercy killings committed to preserve the honor of suffering loved ones.

Indirect Killing

Indirect killings are situations in which someone dies as a result of someone else's criminal behavior but was not the intended target, or in which a person is killed by other situational factors. Examples are individuals who die of heart attacks while being held hostage or as customers in bank robberies; innocent bystanders in drive-by shootings or police actions; victims of felony evasion in high-speed police pursuits; victims of terrorism and suicide-homicide bombers; and victims killed by mistaken identity in organized crime and gangland hits. Some murderers also kill their victims in such a way as to make them appear to have been indirectly killed.

Insanity/Mental Illness

Some murders are the result of the offender's mental illness, such as schizophrenia, bipolar disorder, depression, and delusions of a religious, paranoid, or grandiose nature. Some of these murders are the result of cult involvement or Munchausen syndrome by proxy. Most murders committed involving psychological diagnoses, however, are related to personality disorders and psychopathy. It should also be noted that those suffering from mental illness are no more violent or homicidal per capita than those who are not mentally ill. Also, having a mental illness does not mean the offender is insane. Insanity is a legal concept based on the offender's ability to formulate criminal intent and is not a psychological diagnosis.

Judicial Reasons

Some examples of killings for judicial reasons are state and federal executions (e.g., as part of espionage or treason convictions); killing felons in the commission of crimes or fleeing from crimes, to protect the general public; and those who push criminal situations into "suicide-by-cop" scenarios.

Lover's Triangle

When a couple's romantic relationship becomes a source of emotional or psychological threat as a result of the inclusion of another person and the subsequently perceived exclusion of the one who once held a higher place with the spouse/intimate partner, the feelings of rejection can become so intense for some that they resort to homicide to win back their status in the relationships and their partners/spouses in general. Some killings happen by impulse, or in the heat of passion, when individuals discover that their spouses/intimate partners are unfaithful. Some are accidental and some are planned, and may also have additional financial motivations. Given the various circumstances in which these murders occur, it is difficult to predict who will become the perpetrators and who will become the victims.

Media Influence

In the United States, children are vicariously exposed to 1 million acts of violence and vicariously exposed to over 250,000 murders by the age of 18. Children watch television and movies and read comic books and stories in which the predominant manner in which the characters solve their problems is by force, violence, and firearms. Frequently in America, a toy gun is one of the first toys a young boy is given. Children listen to music that promotes violence and antisocial behavior and attitudes. The clothing frequently marketed to youth reflects a "gang-banger" style. This type of exposure has been linked to high rates of violence and murder; the level of media coverage of crime and criminals has been implicated in engendering copycat crimes and the general contagion effect of criminal behavior.

Murder-Suicide

Murders followed by or committed in conjunction with suicide are seen in cases of familicide, Japanese kamikaze pilots, homicide-suicide bombers in terrorist organizations, disciple killers, sponsicides, mercy killings, lover's triangles, and among criminals fleeing to avoid capture. In some cases, the killer's suicide may be the primary motivation. They may simply want others to "go out with them" secondary to emotional connections or altruistic ideation or for purely sociopathic reasons. Usually, the individual who commits murder-suicide is experiencing a mixture of heightened emotions related to guilt, shame, anger, and altruism.

Obedience/Acceptance

Some people deprive others of their lives because they are told to, as soldiers who are commanded to kill during wartime. Mercenaries and terrorists also kill with the motive of obedience. Disciple killers, gangland soldiers, and prison inmates may act to show obedience but may also be motivated by wanting acceptance of those they respect and are trying to emulate. Contract killers, or hit men, may kill for these reasons, though their primary motive is financial gain.

Physiological Anomalies

Some murders have been directly linked to hormonal imbalances: postpartum depression and menstruation, blood glucose level changes, seizures, traumatic brain injury, mental retardation and other developmental disorders, and somnambulism.

Pleasure/Recreation/Sport

Some murderers derive pleasure from the experience. They have made the notion of "hunting humans" a recreational activity, turning the method of murder into a type of sport. This type of killer is sometimes referred to as a "thrill killer," a motivation more often found in serial, spree, and mass murderers. Some have indicated that they find killing another human to be sexually exciting and "sensuously pleasurable."

Political Ideals

Murders committed with political motivation are seen in acts of terrorism and assassinations, in acts of war and revolution, in environmental and antiabortion activism, in the political underpinnings of organized crime, and in governments seeking to expand their land holdings and increase their level of power.

Possessiveness

Murders can result from the obsessive love of a current or former spouse or intimate partner. In these cases, killers believe that they simply can't part with the victims and would rather see them dead than to live without them.

Power/Control

Probably the most common motivation for murder is the offenders' need to resolve feelings of inferiority by exercising control and exerting power over their victim(s). Killers with this motivation are striving to gain power and control over themselves, over others, and over their life circumstances. Power and control motivation may also be seen in mercy killing, in which the act to relieve suffering in someone afflicted with a chronic/terminal illness is under the killer's own direction; in the decision to die together in cases of sponsicide, intimaticide, and familicide; and in the choice of who dies first in cases of murder-suicide.

Rage

Rage stems from a state of internally disorganizing anger. Murders that occur with a motive of rage are typically seen in lover's triangles, road rage situations, spree or mass murders, school shootings, and when a killer metes out punishment by killing someone close to the individual to whom the rage is directed.

Religion

More people have been murdered "in the name of God" or other deities than for any other motive; few, in comparison, have killed as part of satanic rituals. Countless wars, acts of terrorism, mass cult suicides, and murders based on unrighteous dominion in individual homes have been committed secondary to the religious ideation of killers throughout history. This type of killer has a tendency to convince others to commit murder as well (e.g., Charles Manson, Adolph Hitler, Osama bin Laden, Yasir Arafat). However, the majority commit murders by themselves.

Revenge

These killings involve a high degree of rage as the killers seek retaliation for being wronged or to avenge the deaths of people close to them. Examples are frequently seen in gangland violence, road rage, unsatisfactory business dealings, organized crime, lover's triangles, and in situations in which murderers seek to punish others by killing someone close to them.

Rivalry/Jealousy

Rivalry and jealousy are frequently the motives in cases of siblicide, the killing of business partners or competitors, lover's triangles, and with spouses and intimate partners who are more successful in their social or financial circles.

Sexual Property

Spouses, intimate partners, and children may be murdered by individuals who consider them as their personal sexual property. This can be seen in cases involving sponsicide, intimaticide, filicide, and lover's triangles, and those in which the victim is kept alive for several weeks, months, or longer to fulfill the sexual fantasies of the killer before being disposed of. Some murderers have also killed their spouses or intimate partners to ensure free and unencumbered access to their children for the purpose of molestation.

Sexual Sadism

Sexual sadism is usually seen as the motive in murders committed by rapists, serial killers, mysopeds, homicidal pedophiles, and other paraphilic killings, or in lust murders, such as necrophilia, hypoxophilia, sadism and masochism rituals, bondage rituals, and the making of snuff films.

Unwanted Children

Killers murder unwanted children in cases of neonaticide, infanticide, and filicide.

—*Rocky Underwood*

See also CHILD KILLERS; CRIMES OF OBEDIENCE; FAMILY HOMICIDE; HISTORY OF VIOLENCE IN RELIGIONS; JUVENILE KILLERS; LUST MURDER; MEDIA, VIOLENCE IN THE; MASS MURDER; MOTIVES FOR MURDER; MURDER-SUICIDE; PARAPHILIA; SCHOOL SHOOTINGS; SERIAL MURDER; SPREE MURDERS; TEAM KILLERS; TERRORISM; UNIFIED CRIME REPORTS; VIOLENT BEHAVIOR

Further Reading

Arrigo, B. A., & Purcell, C. E. (2001). Explaining paraphilias and lust murder: Toward an integrated model. *International Journal of Offender Therapy and Comparative Criminology, Special Issue: Sex Offenders, 45*(1), 6-31.

Bartol, C. R. (2002). *Criminal behavior: A psychosocial approach.* Upper Saddle River, NJ: Prentice Hall.

Cantor, C. H., Mullen, P. E., & Alpers, P. A. (2000). Mass homicide: The civil massacre. *Journal of the American Academy of Psychiatry and the Law, 28*(1), 55-63.

Domingo, L. S. (2001). MMPI-2 assessments of incarcerated males convicted of murder: Differentiating between affective and predatory violence. *Dissertation Abstracts International, Section B: The Sciences and Engineering, 61*(10-B), 5558.

Federal Bureau of Investigation. (1992-2001). *Crime in the United States: Uniform crime reports.* Washington, DC: Government Printing Office.

Hickey, E. W. (2002). *Serial murderers and their victims* (3rd ed.). Belmont, CA: Wadsworth.

Holmes, R. M., & DeBurger, J. (1988). *Serial murder.* Newbury Park, CA: Sage.

Holmes, R. M., & Holmes, S. T. (1994). *Murder in America.* Thousand Oaks, CA: Sage.

Myers, W. C. (2002). *Juvenile sexual homicide.* San Diego, CA: Academic Press.

Purcell, C. E. (2001). An investigation of paraphilias, lust murder, and the case of Jeffrey Dahmer: An integrative theoretical model. *Dissertation Abstracts International, Section B: The Sciences and Engineering, 62*(3-B), 1594.

Schlesinger, L. B. (2000). Profiles of homicide offenders: Motives, dynamics and prognostic indicators in youth murder. In R. S. Moser & C. E. Frantz (Eds.), *Shocking violence: Youth perpetrators and victims—A multidisciplinary perspective.* Springfield, IL: Charles C Thomas.

Skrapec, C. A. (2001). Phenomenology and serial murder: Asking different questions. *Homicide Studies: An Interdisciplinary and International Journal, 5*(1), 46-63.

Smith, M. D., & Zahn, M. A. (1999). *Homicide: A sourcebook of social research.* Thousand Oaks, CA: Sage.

Witte, G. E. (2001). A comparative analysis of serial homicide and single homicide event characteristics. *Dissertation Abstracts International, Section B: The Sciences and Engineering, 61*(8-B), 4437.

Wolfgang, M. E. (1958). *Patterns in criminal homicide.* Philadelphia: University of Philadelphia Press.

PERCEPTIONS OF HOMICIDE

Homicidal crimes of passion, though reprehensible, can at least be understood and dealt with rationally. Thus, given the cultural context of this society, most adults can "understand" that volatile interpersonal relations sometimes end in a homicidal act. Even in felony homicides and "classical murder," it is possible in a grim sort of fashion to make sense of the homicide in terms of patterns of relations, between the killer and the victim. But this cannot be said of serial killings, where an innocent person is slain, sometimes after inhuman torture and degradation by a stranger. The killers motives are unknown, and the unknown is feared most of all. (Holmes & DeBurger; 1988, pp. 24-25)

As is inherent in the preceding quotation, crimes of serious violence, especially when they appear as seemingly random and motiveless events, have the ability to incite fears within individuals from a wide spectrum of society. These offenses are sometimes conceptualized as episodes of "random violence," an evocative term that conjures fear-provoking images of patternless chaos and of victims selected at random by seemingly indiscriminate perpetrators.

To this extent, the contemplation of indiscriminate violence in society engenders great fear, and concern about motiveless, senseless violence has become a pervasive theme in contemporary culture and the crimes it plays spectacle to. Underlying these fears are schemata and prototypes of offenders, offenses, and categories of crime: crimes such as serial murder, terrorism, sexual predation, stalking, and other seemingly unpredictable threats. Often, these are crimes with a seemingly intrinsic locus of motives that may make sense to the perpetrator but not to others. This pervasive fear is also representative of a worldview in which no one is considered safe: the prospect of what Egger (1997) deems the unknown "killers among us" striking at random, proving an omnipotent and cogent threat to one's continued existence.

It is likely that the general public, when exposed to such crimes, also searches for rational explanations. Crimes of violence are thus likely to elicit attributional search. This is not surprising, as it has been evidenced that the search for causal understanding (the perceived reasons as to why an event/act has occurred) is most commonly provoked by three factors: the extent to which acts or actions are perceived as negative or aversive, whether or not they are unexpected, and whether they have symbolic importance or tap cultural concerns. Crimes involving serious violence clearly contain such underlying properties.

People thus seek to comprehend why these offenders act as they do and what it is about these types of criminals that enables them to engage in such activities. As such, these crimes are particularly conducive to attributional analyses. Surprisingly though, little empirical research has been conducted into causal explanations held by the public concerning crimes of serious violence. These explanations are of utmost importance, considering that to a large extent how we think about social problems likely shapes the manner in which we seek to address them.

CONTEMPLATING ATTRIBUTION

Attributional Theory

It has been argued by a number of expert academics that individuals seek at an elementary level to understand why events, states, or outcomes have occurred. To this extent, we live in an "attributing society," in which we seek to account for and to explain both our own behavior and the behavior of others. This provides the basis for the foundation of *attribution theory*, which is concerned with phenomenal causality, or the perceived reasons why a behavior, event, or outcome has occurred. As a consequence, questions such as "Why was I accepted or rejected for a date?" and "What makes an individual commit a heinous crime?" all are attribution-relevant concerns.

Although the specific causes of events that confront the individual are almost inexhaustible, it has been argued that all attributions share a limited number of underlying characteristics, or causal dimensions. These include locus (i.e., whether the cause lies inside or outside of the individual), stability (i.e., whether the cause is constant or varying over time), and controllability (i.e., whether the cause is or is not subject to volitional change). Attributions also often have strong emotional implications, and Weiner developed a theory that endeavored to demonstrate the interrelationship between attributions and emotions.

Attributions Concerning Crime in General

Academic researchers have long been concerned with the causes of crime, with it considered that offenders can be best rehabilitated when criminogenic factors within the offender have been ameliorated. As a result, numerous and often contradictory theories have been proposed to account for why and how some people commit crimes and others do not. Although such theories have abounded, there has been considerably less attention paid to "naive" or lay attributions concerning crime, which often differ considerably from the explicit theories put forward within academic spheres.

Reviewing the literature concerned with causal attributions for crime offered by lay people, numerous surveys and qualitative data polls have been conducted to determine public attributions concerning crime generally. More explicit research has examined "lay" implicit theories for the causes of specific forms of criminal conduct, including delinquency and rape. The resultant findings are suggestive of much variation in the explanations given, with lay theories of crime being generally both complex and multidimensional.

In studies dealing with lay attributions relevant to offense-specific crimes, Furnham and Henderson conducted a widely cited study in the United Kingdom, in which they asked participants to rate differing causal explanations in terms of how important they considered each to be in explaining the general category of "juvenile delinquency." Subsequent analysis of participants' responses revealed six distinct dimensions, which the authors labeled *defective education, mental instability, temptation, excitement, alienation,* and *parents.* Although all factors were perceived as important, the more sociologically oriented explanation of defective education was regarded as the most compelling causal factor in the commission of juvenile crime. Correspondingly, these researchers found that an absence of parental guidance and neighborhood problems were seen as the most important causes of juvenile delinquency and mental instability and genetic defects as the least important.

The picture of public attributions concerning crime causation is complicated, though, by the finding that the public does not apply the same theory to all offenses; and subsequently, lay explanations of crime are offense specific rather than global in nature. To this extent, the nature of the offense affects the kind of causal explanations favored by the public.

This was demonstrated in a study by Hollin and Howells that asked participants to offer explanations for three specific crimes: burglary, robbery, and sexual assault. Mental instability and defective education were regarded by participants as important in explaining sexual assault, whereas the crimes of burglary and robbery were more strongly attributed to factors encompassing "socialization," including defective education, deficient child-rearing patterns, and parental influence. The crime of sexual assault was clearly differentiated from those of robbery and burglary by the importance placed on the mental instability of the perpetrator. Females rated factors concerning the alienation of the offender as more important than did males when considering causes of crime.

Other studies investigating lay opinions concerning the causation of specific criminal behaviors have yielded similar results, with the public demonstrating offense-specific and multidimensional responses.

Although there has been some research into lay attributions concerning the causes of crime in general, as well as a few select studies that have looked at public perceptions of specific offenses, there has been little empirical research conducted into lay attributions concerning violent crimes, including homicide and multicide. This is despite an acknowledged public interest in such crimes and an almost macabre fascination with the offenders who commit them: individuals who arrogate themselves to the ultimate power of life and death over other human beings.

Attributions for Crimes of Serious Violence

Homicide generally refers to the unlawful killing of another human being. It may be more specifically defined as "those interpersonal assaults and other acts directed against another person that occur outside of the context of warfare and that prove fatal" (Daly & Wilson, 1988, p. 14). Analogously, *multicide* is associated with the murder of more than one individual (i.e., multiple victims), the two most recognized forms of which include serial and mass homicide.

Various academic theories have been espoused to attempt to explain the crimes of homicide and multicide. Depending on the theoretical orientation imposed, these have emphasized a diverse range of factors, including neurological abnormalities, personality disorders, psychopathology, developmental "disturbances," and sociocultural causative factors. Although these theories add some insight into understanding the theoretical bases underlying explanations for the respective crimes, they add little to comprehending lay attributions regarding them.

To gain insight into this, it is necessary to consult the few empirical studies that are available—qualitative accounts usually in the form of interviews with members of the public regarding the causes of such crimes—as well as to observe and analyze accounts derived from the conduit through which public opinion is expressed and absorbed, such as literary depictions and the popular press. Analyzing media sources is particularly useful, as it has been argued that because lay persons rarely have direct contact with offenders themselves, they likely rely on information gathered from sources such as the latter to form impressions about offenses and criminals.

Evil Acts and Actors

Based on research into the effect of the crime of serial murder on communities, it has been suggested that attributions of "evilness" and "wickedness" may be prominent in individual's causal explanations for serial and mass homicide. Baumeister adds some insight into how "evil" attributions may come to be formed, inferring that the concept of evil involves (a) the intentional infliction of harm on people; (b) the wish to inflict harm merely for the pleasure of doing so and gratuitously; (c) sadism, with evil people enjoying the suffering they cause and inflicting harm to achieve this; (d) evil acts against innocent and good victims; (e) evil acts deriving from the other, the enemy, the outsider, or the out-group; and (f) evil as representing the antithesis of order, peace, and stability.

Using this schema as a basis to examine attributions for serious crime, it is quite plausible to infer that causal explanations relating to evil may be used by lay people to describe the actions of serial and mass murderers, with the offense behaviors displayed by the former types of offenders all equating with Baumeister's conceptualization. This includes the often seemingly inhumane actions of the aforementioned offenders, involving excessively cruel torture (what experts often refer to as *overkill*) and seeking to divorce the crime from normal behavior and even routine homicide. Furthermore, the killer is perceived to clearly gain something from the offense process other than just the end result, the death of the victim.

Notions of "evil" as related to offending behavior have further been evidenced in the language of professionals including psychologists, psychiatrists, and other mental-health-associated workers. To this extent, regardless of what level of society one is from, it seems

evident that individuals do appropriate "evil" as a basis for some human actions or at least use "evil" to describe serious crimes and the offenders who commit them.

Sexual Motivations and Overtones

It has been implied that a common perception by the public is that all serial murderers are motivated by sexual desires and sadism. Popular beliefs that serial murder is the causal product of an offender's sexual deviation are further strengthened by another of the popular "myths" of serial homicide: that all serial killers are inspired by pornography.

The Role of Psychopathology, Aggression, and Frustration

The argument that lay attributions for serial homicide may emphasize factors related to the psychopathology of the perpetrator is a contention supported by the press, popular literature, and anecdotal narratives, which assign labels to the serial murderer, such as *psychopath*. It has also been argued that if someone kills simply because he or she enjoys killing for its "recreational value," this raises serious questions about the offender's rationality.

RECENT ATTRIBUTIONAL RESEARCH

Experimental research supports the contention that the former explanations feature predominantly in lay attributions concerning crimes of serious violence. In a recent study by Wright and Howells, participants were asked to provide explanations for the three distinctive offense categories of serial homicide, mass homicide, and homicide. Subjects were asked to think in general about the causes of the offender's behavior and indicate (amongst other options) what they considered such causes to be and whether they perceived these to be likely internal or external to the offender, controllable or uncontrollable, and stable or unstable over time.

Inspection of the outcome data indicated that eight main causal explanations were evident. These consisted of attributions related to the aggression and frustration, psychopathology, drug and alcohol abuse, sexual deviation, and inherent "evil" or "wickedness" of the perpetrator. Further explanations included sociologically based causes, attributions concerning the role of defective parental guidance and upbringing, and biologically based explanations for crime.

Analyses conducted to investigate differences between explanations for the differing crime types indicated that factors that were considered important in explaining the crime of serial homicide were sexual deviation, evil and supernatural forces, and psychopathology. Focal attributions for the crime of mass homicide included psychopathology, evil and supernatural forces, and drug and alcohol abuse. The crime of homicide was associated with causal attributions related to aggression and frustration, psychopathology, and drug and alcohol abuse.

Factors relating to the influence of evil/supernatural forces, sociological variables, and parental upbringing were rated as significantly more important in explaining the crimes of serial and mass homicide as compared with homicide. Drug and alcohol abuse, aggression and frustration, psychopathology- and biologically based explanations were seen as significantly more important for the crime of mass homicide as compared with serial homicide and homicide, whereas sexual deviation was rated as more important in explaining serial homicide when compared with the other two crime types.

There was one significant gender difference when discussing causal attributions for the crimes presented, with females regarding sociologically oriented explanations as significantly more important as causative factors in the commission of the presented crimes as compared with their male counterparts.

With regard to more specific attributional judgments, across all three crime types, the causes of the offender's behavior were generally perceived as internal and stable. Differences among explanations for the crime types indicated that the crime of mass homicide was considered less controllable than serial homicide and homicide. The crime of serial homicide was regarded as more controllable as compared with the crimes of mass homicide and homicide.

The aforementioned study by Wright and Howells demonstrated that generally there was a distinct preference by respondents to attribute the causes of all crimes concerned to internal factors within the offender as compared with sociologically based or other external causes. This may be explained in terms of the tendency of observers to attribute causes of behavior to the personal characteristics of the actor rather than acknowledging the influence of situational and environmental factors. It may also be argued that

observers may have a particular need to see negative behaviors as resulting from "bad" character. To see "bad" behavior as caused by situational forces means that anyone (including the respondents) may commit such offenses when external forces are strong enough. Attributing unacceptable human conduct to "possession" by evil forces and regarding the offender as so inherently different from the "normal" and decent citizen likely increases the potential for distancing oneself from the contemplation of serious violence residing within the human potential.

Reasons for attributing "evil" to the offenders of serious crimes may also be evident in the personal accounts of those personally familiar with violent offenders prior to their murderous episodes. Often, these narratives stress the seeming "normality" of the person they knew as the "quiet guy next door," an individual who had previously evidenced no obvious signs of biological abnormality or clinical symptoms associated with psychological disturbance. Consequently, when these offenders commit crimes of violence, it could be asserted that a level of dissonance is experienced by those who know them. The impression they had formed of the "normal guy next door" is contradicted by the heinous nature of the acts committed. To overcome this dissonance, attributions of evil can be suitably adopted, fitting well with the notion that those who show no outward signs of illness can commit serious crimes yet remain inherently evil.

Implications of Research

The significance of recent research has functional relevance to a wide variety of fields, including social and criminal justice policy formation and correctional treatment. It has been argued that what is done about a social problem depends in part on how it is defined. If the causes of offending are defined in internal, individual terms, then one would assume that intervention strategies and treatment programs aimed at changing the inherent qualities of the individual would be employed, as opposed to more sociologically oriented methods that would alternatively seek to rectify problematic environmental conditions.

As an extension of this, the apportioning of funds for approaches to managing offenders may well be influenced by the beliefs of those in positions to allocate them. Thus, if one believes that the primary cause of violent offending is due to the psychopathology of serious violent offenders, then attempts to prevent these crimes from occurring would likely involve measures such as greater government expenditure on mental health services for such individuals.

Attributions for crime may also have an effect on preferences for different criminal justice policies and sanctions. It has been demonstrated that individuals who attribute the causes of crime to the environment (i.e., socioeconomic factors) are less supportive of punishment and more supportive of rehabilitation as the primary objective of sentencing, whereas individuals who attribute crimes to causes "within" the individual are more likely to be punitive or retributive in their treatment philosophies.

Research concerning attributions for crimes of violence may also have functional relevance to those who come into contact with offenders of serious crimes, with the explanatory theories of groups such as probation, police, and prison officers likely exerting an effect on their behaviors toward offenders. Thus, attributions for crimes may have a significant influence on how offenders are treated on a daily basis by correctional staff.

This research also has relevance for legal professionals who are faced with cases involving serious violence. It is difficult to know what factors will influence jurors' decisions in such cases, with the latter often having to make sense of a set of events that led an offender to commit the acts for which he or she has been charged. In constructing an interpretation of such events and the behavior of the persons involved, it is considered likely that jurors would draw on their knowledge of the world and how it works. Presumably, jurors have a set of beliefs about violent offenders such as serial and mass murderers that may or may not be altered by information presented in court. Attributional research may help to elucidate these beliefs.

Other Associated Implications

It may be argued that examining lay attributions for offending behavior may add some insight into how the public perceives those associated with violent perpetrators, such as the offender's parents and family. It can be logically inferred that if the public believes that the causes of an individual's violent offending are primarily due to a defective parental upbringing, such attributions may in turn effect reactions and behaviors toward the offender's family. This was evidenced in public reactions toward the father of serial offender

Jeffrey Dahmer and the public apportioning of blame the former received for his son's misdeeds.

Further implications of the research evolve from explanations emphasizing individualistic tendencies toward criminal intent evidenced by respondents. These tendencies may be equated with Baumeister's myth of pure evil depicting aberrant forces intruding on the world of unsuspecting citizens, bringing chaos and destruction. Applying this conception, society is left blameless, freed from any responsibility for the offending behavior. A direct consequence of these images is that they restrict public empathy toward offenders and in turn favor a social climate in which more repressive policies directed toward criminals are sanctioned, as opposed to rehabilitation programs.

The research may also be considered to have implications for those working in therapeutic contexts with serious violent offenders. In such cases, it is likely that therapists are continually faced with having to make inferences about the offender's motivations, thoughts, feelings, and behaviors, all of which are all too often obscure to the offender. The manner in which most would attempt such a task is to base a fundamental comprehension on an understanding of one's own processes. Thus, it is perhaps imperative that one considers the offending individual to be like oneself, at least in terms of the processes that govern deleterious behavior. Considering offenders as more like the normative population than different from it provides a "window into their world" that would otherwise remain closed.

It follows that those who work with offenders should also accept responsibility for educating the public toward a greater understanding of the causal mechanisms underlying offending behavior—not tolerance toward offending behavior, but acceptance of the behavior as a part of the human repertoire and as potentially responsive to rehabilitative efforts. So long as one seeks to demonize offenders, it seems logical to infer that the struggle to understand them will continue, with the potential for generating insights that would help such individuals understand and change their behaviors being likely diminished.

CONCLUSION

Research has demonstrated the tendency of laypeople to apply atavistic explanations when attempting to discern the causes of serious violent offending. To this extent, although science has illuminated many of the unknowns of the modern world, attributions favoring the "supernatural" causation of behavior are seemingly still popular.

It seems evident that the layperson seeks to demarcate the boundary between the serious violent criminal and the "normal" majority by means of some qualitative difference, such as evilness, wickedness, or psychopathology. Consequently, it is revealed that in the early 21st century, serious violent offenders are regarded as subhuman. They are perceived as "monsters" who cannot change and live outside the bounds of "normal" existence. This perception of criminals as "bad" and "evil" and as lacking human sentiments may be seen as an attempt to dehumanize those who commit acts perceived as residing outside the human potential.

To this extent, it seems that although the notion of the "born criminal" has now been subsumed, there is still a need to extrude the violent offender as being intrinsically different from the rest of "normal" society. Although this should be noted, at the same time it should be emphasized that nothing is achieved toward illuminating the causes of violent offending behavior by blindly applying morally laden value labels such as "evil" when seeking explanatory mechanisms concerning crimes of serious violence. By doing so, professionals decrease their potential understanding of any likely underlying causal processes that take place within and around the offender during the criminal act, with the possibly crucial impact of social forces on creating violent individuals subsequently diminished. Indeed, to continue to locate the causes of serious violent offending solely within the individual is to disregard the influence of society in creating the problems it plays spectacle to. It is also to perpetuate the notion of the "other": the violent offender as asocial, not from the world "we know," and not from the world we also created. It may be comforting to subscribe to such notions, dismissing the murderer of strangers as freak events or aberrations, yet these behaviors are part of the human repertoire and thus have potentially profound social meaning.

—*Steven Michael Wright and Kevin Howells*

See also AGGRESSION; MOTIVES FOR MURDER; VIOLENCE: PHENOMENOLOGY; VIOLENT BEHAVIOR

Further Reading

Baumeister, R. (1998). *Evil: Inside human violence and cruelty.* New York: W. H. Freeman.

Best, J. (1999). *Random violence: How we talk about new crimes and new victims.* Berkeley: University of California Press.

Daly, M., & Wilson, M. (1988). *Homicide.* New York: Aldine de Gruyter.

Egger, S. (1997). *The killers among us: An examination of serial murder and its investigation.* Englewood Cliffs, NJ: Prentice Hall.

Fisher, J. (1997). *Killer among us: Public reactions to serial murder.* Connecticut: Praeger.

Furnham, A., & Henderson, M. (1983). Lay theories of delinquency. *European Journal of Social Psychology, 13*(2), 107-120.

Hollin, C. R., & Howells, K. (1987). Lay explanations of delinquency: Global or offense specific? *British Journal of Social Psychology, 26*(3), 203-210.

Holmes, R. M., & DeBurger, J. (1988). *Serial murder.* Newbury Park, CA: Sage.

Leyton, E. (Ed.). (2000). *Serial murder: Modern scientific perspectives.* Aldershot, UK: Ashgate.

Marshall, W. L., Anderson, D., & Fernandez, Y. M. (1999). *Cognitive behavioral treatment of sexual offenders.* Chichester, UK: Wiley.

Polk, K. (1994). *When men kill: Scenarios of masculine violence.* Melbourne, Australia: Cambridge University Press.

Weiner, B. (1986). *An attributional theory of motivation and emotion.* New York: Springer-Verlag.

Wright, S. M., & Howells, K. (2000, 21-24 September). *The killers among us: Lay attributions concerning crimes of serious violence.* Paper presented to the 36th Australian Psychological Society Annual Conference, Adelaide, Australia.

TYPES OF HOMICIDE AND DEGREES OF MURDER

Under American law, many crimes, such as theft and homicide, are divided into degrees. For example, states often divide theft into two degrees, grand and petty theft, the dividing line being a predesignated dollar value.

Determining the degree of a homicide under American law, on the other hand, is highly complicated. The federal government and each American state have developed their own unique degree schemes, creating a patchwork grading system that can confuse even the most stout-hearted legal scholar.

There are no magical numerical cutoffs in homicide law. Jurors must consider the unique circumstances of each death and juggle ethereal concepts such as blameworthiness in light of universal human frailty. Before rendering a decision, jurors must weigh the manner of the killing—was it committed with quick and painless dispatch or brutal torture?—the intent behind the killing—was it done on purpose or by accident?—and sometimes the motive for the killing—was it a calculated murder for money or an instantaneous unleashing of passionate fury?

The rules of homicide vary so dramatically from state to state that it is impossible to assess the degree of a particular homicide without reference to the laws of the state having jurisdiction over the crime. Perhaps the most dramatic demonstration of the huge variation in American approaches to homicide law is seen in *felony murder statutes*. Let us say, for example, that while robbing a liquor store, Todd was shocked to see his partner, Jonah, grab a flashlight from a shelf and beat the storeowner to death with it. In some states, Todd could be convicted of first-degree murder and sentenced to death, even if he tried to stop his partner from killing the storeowner. In other jurisdictions, Todd could not be charged with any degree of murder because he himself struck no blows. Despite this wide variation, a pattern can be seen among the various state approaches to homicide law. As long as the reader understands that statutes vary, the following general outline should aid in understanding the American approach to homicides.

Typically, homicides are classified from most blameworthy to least, as follows:

1. First-degree murder
2. Second-degree murder
3. Voluntary manslaughter
4. Involuntary manslaughter
5. Noncriminal homicides

Criminal homicide is the proper term for any homicide that is punishable by law, including murder, voluntary manslaughter, and involuntary manslaughter. Murder and manslaughter are distinct offenses, not degrees of murder. Murder is divided into two degrees in most states, though some provide a third degree of murder for killings that were not murder at common law. Manslaughter is divided into two subcategories as well, voluntary and involuntary.

I. First-Degree Murder

The most heinous of the homicide crimes fall within the category of first-degree murder, in which punishment is most severe, even death in some states. First-degree murder is often unofficially referred to as "Murder One."

Though the laws vary from state to state, several types of homicides are likely to be classified as first-degree murders, most commonly, premeditated, deliberate murder, cruel and brutal murder, and felony murder.

A. Premeditated, Deliberate Murder

Those who coldly carry out a plan to kill another can find themselves charged with first-degree murder. It is one thing to lash out in rage and strike a blow that brings about death. It is quite another to coldly weigh all options and decide on murder as the best solution.

Premeditated- and deliberate-murder statutes generally state that one is guilty of first-degree murder if he or she kills another person with both premeditation—on purpose and pursuant to a plan—and deliberation—in cold blood, not in a sudden burst of rage. The period of cool reflection that constitutes premeditation and deliberation can be extremely short; it is not how long one considers one's options, but the fact that one considered and coolly made the evil choice.

Premeditation and deliberation can be inferred from facts. For example, lying in wait to ambush a victim or slipping poison into a spouse's food and sitting by while he eats imply cool deliberation and premeditation. Jurors need not always have direct evidence such as a confession saying, "I decided to kill her so I made a plan and then carried it out," to find a defendant guilty of first-degree murder.

All jurisdictions consider deliberate and premeditated murders to be murder in the first degree. Only the punishment varies from state to state, some providing the death penalty.

B. Especially Heinous Murder

In addition to premeditation and deliberations statutes focusing on the murderers' intent, some states have also passed first-degree murder statutes that focus on the manner in which murderers commit the killing. The statutory words used to describe this concept of especially heinous murders vary from state to state. Whether called "cruel," "brutal," "atrocious," or "torturous," the idea remains constant: It is worse to physically or mentally torture someone before killing them than it is "merely" to kill them.

Thus, in some states, a murderer who brutally beat his victim before killing him might be charged with first-degree murder, whereas another who killed his victim with one shot to the head would not. Some jurisdictions would also provide for a charge of Murder One if the killer first mentally tortured the victim with vivid descriptions of impending death, even if he committed the actually killing with quick and painless dispatch.

C. Felony Murder

Recognized by the majority of American jurisdictions, the felony murder rule allows for the harshest of penalties, in some states, death, when the defendant was not the killer and never wished or planned for anyone to die at all. Under the rule, if a death occurs during the commission of certain prescribed felonies—most often burglary, sexual assault, kidnapping, and other dangerous felonies—any participant in the underlying felony can be found guilty of first-degree murder, not just the "trigger man." A common example is the bank robbery gone wrong. Two men carry out a robbery during which one of the robbers ends up shooting the bank guard. Both robbers can be convicted of first-degree murder.

The reasoning behind the felony murder rule is that anyone who carries out a potentially dangerous crime should be responsible for deaths arising from it. The rule is said to punish wrongdoers while deterring others from committing similar dangerous felonies, thereby reducing violence. Because research hasn't supported this hypothesis, some states have abandoned felony murder, but the rule is still alive in most jurisdictions.

Those who commit dangerous felonies can also be charged with first-degree murder in some states for killings actually precipitated by the victim or by law enforcement. For example, if the victim of a rape shoots at her rapist and kills a bystander instead, the rapist might, in many states, be charged with first-degree murder. And if a bank robber were to rob a bank and the security guard's shot went wide and killed the teller instead of the felon, that felon might still be destined to die in the electric chair.

Even accidental deaths can result in capital punishment under some states' first-degree murder statutes. For example, an unarmed burglar enters into a home at night; the resident hears him, hurries down the stairs, trips, and falls to her death. This is felony murder in many states, because although the burglar did not intend the woman's death, she would not have died but for his presence. Her death is said to be a direct consequence of the dangerous felony of burglary, so many states punish the burglar with the harshest sentence of all. Other states restrict application of their felony murder rule to more obviously foreseeable violent deaths.

II. Second-Degree Murder

A. Unpremeditated Intentional Murder, Second-Degree Murder by Default

If a killing is intentional but is committed without deliberation, premeditation, or heinous cruelty, and it occurs neither during the commission of another felony nor in the heat of passion, that killing is likely to fall within the category of second-degree murder. In other words, if a murder that is both intentional and criminal does not fall within any of the categories described under first-degree murder or voluntary manslaughter, it will usually fit within the default catch-all category of unpremeditated intentional murder or murder in the second degree.

For example, a husband insults his wife, the undercover officer, while she is taking off her holster, and in a rage, she shoots him dead. The jury acquits her of first-degree murder, finding no premeditation because the decision to shoot was so instantaneous. But the jurors cannot justify a finding of the lesser charge of heat-of-passion voluntary manslaughter, either, because his words were not sufficient provocation under the law. The jury will likely find the woman guilty of second-degree murder.

B. Killings While Intending to Inflict Serious Bodily Harm

Even perpetrators who meant only to injure may find themselves convicted of murder in the second degree if their victims die. The crucial question for a jury in such cases becomes "How severe an injury did the perpetrators intend to inflict?" If serious bodily injury was the aim, second-degree murder may be the appropriate charge.

For example, John becomes angry and strikes his employer in the face with a paperweight. The employer drops dead. John exclaims that he did not mean to kill him, but just wanted to break his nose. Unfortunately for John, it still counts as murder—in many states, second-degree murder because he intended to inflict serious bodily injury.

C. Killings While Resisting Arrest

Although resisting arrest is a misdemeanor under most circumstances, not the sort of dangerous crime contemplated within first-degree felony murder statutes, some jurisdictions do allow second-degree murder charges for deaths occurring while a suspect resists arrest. In resisting-arrest second-degree murder, as with felony murder, the defendant need not intend for anyone die, and the death need not have been by the defendant's own hand. It is enough that the death was a result of the arrestee's resistance.

For example, if an officer accidentally shoots and kills an innocent bystander while trying to subdue an arrestee, in some states, the arrestee would be guilty of second-degree murder because if he had not resisted arrest, the officer would not have discharged the weapon and the innocent bystander would still be alive.

D. Other Murders

The above list of second-degree murder categories is by no means exhaustive. For example, states with felony murder laws often have a catchall second-degree murder category for homicides occurring during the commission of a felony that does not fall within the specific list of underlying felony-murder crimes. To determine the degree of any homicide, reference should always be made to the laws of the state having jurisdiction over a given crime.

III. Voluntary Manslaughter

Intentional killings generally outrage society and warrant harsh sentences. Sometimes, though, the extenuating circumstances surrounding an intentional killing give rise to the conclusion that though the killing was wrongful, it was to some degree understandable in light of human frailties. Such less blameworthy killings call for mercy with a finding of voluntary manslaughter and its incumbent lesser punishment.

Black's Law Dictionary briefly defines voluntary manslaughter as "the unlawful killing of a human being without malice aforethought," meaning that the perpetrator purposely killed but without "preconceived malice" or "evil intent." Statutory specifics vary from state to state, but two situations are universally covered in some form: (a) provoked killings committed while in the heat of passion, and (b) killings committed in "imperfect" self-defense.

A. Heat-of-Passion Homicide

The most common form of voluntary manslaughter is the "heat-of-passion" homicide, in which the emotions provoked in an individual are so strong that he or she is momentarily unable to gain control of them and acts out by killing. Though such homicides are not excused, society as a whole finds them less repugnant than coldly calculated murders for personal gain or pleasure and allows for less severe punishment with a finding of voluntary manslaughter rather than murder.

Generally, a killing qualifies as heat-of-passion voluntary manslaughter if the following conditions were present:

1. The killing occurred during the "heat of passion."
2. The killing occurred before there was time to cool off.
3. The provocation actually caused the "passion."
4. The provocation was legally adequate.

Determining adequacy of provocation is difficult. Society deems it inherently unreasonable to kill another human being out of anger or passion, which is why heat-of-passion killings do not go entirely unpunished. The question for juries, then, cannot be whether the provocation would have provoked a reasonable person to kill the provoker. Rather, the question must be whether the provocation might cause reasonable people to lose their self-control such that, though unreasonable, a homicidal response was at least understandable.

Statutes and juror decisions vary, but adequate provocation is often found when a killer is unlawfully arrested, finds a spouse in the arms of another, or is painfully injured during mutual combat. Words alone, however, are virtually never adequate provocation. The provoked emotion need not be fury. Resentment, hatred, or terror may qualify, as may any other emotion sufficient to render the reasonable mind incapable of cool reflection.

B. "Imperfect" Self-Defense Killings

Those who kill in justifiable self-defense are guilty of no crime at all. But what of those who kill because they honestly but unreasonably believe their lives are in danger? Complete exoneration would be inappropriate, but on the other hand, a murder conviction would be too harsh. In such cases, where killing "in self-defense" does not actually qualify under stringent self-defense statutes, "imperfect self-defense voluntary manslaughter" statutes allow jurors to show compassion while still holding killers responsible for their poor judgment.

For example, one night while walking his dog in an alley, a man sees the silhouette of someone lurking in the shadows. Suddenly, he sees the reflection of something shiny, and jumps to the conclusion that the stranger holds a knife. He shoots the poor stranger dead. In fact, the man's keyholder had made the reflection, not a knife; and furthermore, the jury concludes that the stranger was too far away to be an immediate danger even if he had had a knife, especially since the man could easily have turned and run to the safety of a nearby lighted thoroughfare. The jury finds that although the man truly believed he was in immediate mortal danger, his belief was unreasonable under the law, so he was guilty of voluntary manslaughter.

IV. Involuntary Manslaughter

Stated briefly, involuntary manslaughter statutes generally cover homicides that are committed without intention to kill or cause serious bodily injury but are still blameworthy because they were committed with criminal negligence or recklessness, or during the commission of crimes covered elsewhere in the homicide statutory scheme. Again, statutes vary from state to state.

A. Negligent or Reckless Involuntary Manslaughter

A few states say that a finding of ordinary civil law tort negligence arising in death is sufficient to convict an individual for involuntary manslaughter. Most jurisdictions, however, require a higher degree of negligence, typically, that the defendant was actually aware that his or her conduct risked death or serious bodily injury. Some states define the requisite degree of risk as "unreasonable," others as "high." Still other states require that the risk was both unreasonable and high, which comes closer to the definition of recklessness than negligence; and the modern trend is to require actual "recklessness." To the other extreme, some jurisdictions place reckless homicides in their murder category, calling them "depraved-heart" murders.

Automobile and firearm accidents are the most common source of involuntary manslaughter convictions. Other incidences include failure to provide care when under a duty to do so; for example, the parent who allows a child's severe illness to go untreated, as well as deaths resulting from unsafe working environments and the like. The classic example is the "sweatshop homicide": Management chains the factory doors to keep seamstresses inside and working. Fire breaks out, and the trapped women are killed in the blaze. Though the managers did not intend for anyone to die, their conduct was an outrageous crime deserving punishment. They are guilty of involuntary manslaughter.

B. Unlawful-Act Involuntary Manslaughter

The modern trend is toward abolishment of unlawful-act involuntary manslaughter, but enough jurisdictions still recognize the crime for it to warrant discussion. Even in those jurisdictions still having unlawful-act involuntary manslaughter statutes on their books, not all crimes that result in unintentional deaths give rise to manslaughter charges. Typically, unlawful-act involuntary-manslaughter statutes provide for charges only when the crime underlying the death was *malum in se,* that is, inherently bad or immoral rather than legislatively prohibited, morally-neutral conduct.

Stated simply, the question becomes whether the average ordinary person would know by gut instinct that the underlying act was wrong. Interestingly, some jurisdictions interpret the term *unlawful act* so broadly that it includes even noncriminal conduct, such as tortuous trespass or other civil wrongs, as long as the conduct is inherently bad or immoral. For example, if trapped workers died in a factory fire, the managers who locked them in could be found guilty of unlawful-act involuntary manslaughter even if locking workers in was not illegal in the given state, because such conduct is civilly negligent. Other examples of involuntary manslaughter circumstances include accidental deaths from unlawful discharge of firearms, reckless driving, and possession of vicious dogs.

V. Noncriminal Homicides

Finally, some homicides are deemed noncriminal, such as killings committed in lawful self-defense or in furtherance of war. Although our society places high value on human life, there are times when one life's forfeiture is justifiable in protection of another life or of society as a whole.

—*Victoria Hamilton*

See also Courts; Death Penalty; Self-Defense, Actions Taken in

Further Reading

Champion, D. (2001). *The American dictionary of criminal justice.* Los Angeles: Roxbury.

Malmquist, C. (1996). *Homicide: A psychiatric perspective.* Washington, DC: American Psychiatric Press.

Smith, D., & Zahn M. (Eds.). (1999). *Homicide: A sourcebook of social research.* Thousand Oaks, CA: Sage.

HOMICIDE RATES,
see Homicide: Motivation for Murder; Uniform Crime Reports; Victimology: Crime Rates

HOMOLKA, KARLA,
see Bernardo, Paul, and Karla Homolka; Team Killers

HOOVER, J. EDGAR, *See*
Federal Bureau of Investigation (FBI)

HOSTAGE TAKING

A hostage is a person held prisoner to force fulfillment of demands by an individual or group. The taking of hostages is considered illegal under both international law and individual nations. The actual act is a crime, and the mistreatment of hostages is another, independent crime.

HOSTAGE-TAKING SITUATIONS

Most hostage-taking situations occur in connection with other crimes or as a result of political struggles. They may result from the intentional act of taking a specific person or group of persons because of who they represent, or as a result of a spontaneous decision. Many domestic criminals take hostages because they believe it gives them something to bargain with in exchange for their freedom.

Hijackers and other terrorists usually take hostages to demand a certain action by a government. It is most common to see revolutionaries or terrorist groups in third-world countries using this method of negotiating with human life. For example, in 1979, Iranian revolutionaries overtook the U.S. Embassy in Tehran and held a group of Americans hostage. The revolutionaries demanded that the Shah of Iran be returned to the country for trial in exchange for the hostages. The Shah died before this matter could be resolved, and the hostages were eventually released by their captors.

Not only do individuals and groups resort to hostage taking, but entire countries do so as well. History is full of instances in which civilians have been taken as hostages during times of war. During World War II (1939-1945), for example, Germany sought to control underground resistance forces by taking hostages in France, Poland, and other occupied countries. Taking civilians as hostages in times of war is different from the unlawful act of taking enemy soldiers as prisoners of war. Capturing soldiers is not considered hostage taking, and laws govern the safe return of soldiers.

Hostage taking is different from kidnapping in that *kidnapping* is defined as the act of seizing and holding a person against his or her will. Although to take a person hostage consists of same, in kidnapping, there is no intent to return the individual or group after the demands have been met. The word *kidnap* comes from two words: *kid,* or "child," and *nab,* which means "to steal." At one time, kidnapping did refer to the act of stealing children, but it has also come to be used for the seizure and holding of adults.

Hostage taking is a form of *terrorism,* which is defined as the use or threat of violence to create fear and alarm. The goals of terrorists differ from those of ordinary criminals. Most criminals want money or some other form of personal gain, whereas most terrorists commit crimes to support political causes.

Some individuals and groups use hostage taking to support a particular political philosophy or ideology.

Others, especially third-world countries, use civilian hostages to seek liberation from governments in power. Dictators and totalitarian governments also take revolutionaries as hostages to frighten or eliminate their opponents. Generally, those that employ the use of hostages attack people or groups who oppose their cause or objects that symbolize such opposition. Common victims of hostage situations include diplomats, business executives, political leaders, police, and judges. At other times, terrorists choose any target that is certain to attract media coverage.

LAW ENFORCEMENT DURING HOSTAGE SITUATIONS

The U.S. Federal Bureau of Investigation maintains a specially trained unit that is called the Hostage Rescue Team (HRT). HRT is deployed when domestic or foreign terrorists or other kinds of perpetrators take hostages in the United States. In addition to domestic cases, the United States assists in worldwide hostage negotiations with other countries, such as Great Britain, France, and Germany. U.S. allies have also developed special teams trained to handle hostage situations. In other countries, these teams have been developed along military lines.

These special teams are equipped to handle well-armed and determined opponents, with a very good chance of minimizing the loss of hostage lives. The methods of these teams in resolving hostage-taking situations are designed to discourage further acts of hostage taking by any other group of people who may contemplate such acts in the future. The catalyst for the development of these teams is acknowledged to be the Israelis and their successful 1976 rescue of hostages from Entebbe, Uganda.

Most domestic police forces in the United States have hostage-negotiating teams. Some teams are simply called the "hostage-negotiating team" or the "SWAT" team. They are made up of highly skilled officers who are specially trained to handle highly intensive and stressful situations, using special firearms and negotiations with irrational individuals.

PROFILE OF A POTENTIAL HOSTAGE TAKER

Gavin de Becker, a world-renowned expert in violence profiling, developed an evaluation process called "JACA" (Justification, Alternatives, Consequences, and Ability), which aids in identifying individuals who may be most likely to resort to hostage taking to solve their issues.

Justification: Does the person or group feel justified in using violence to resolve their problem? According to De Becker, justifications may be as simple as the old saying "an eye for an eye." Sometimes, the person or group feels that their anger is justified by past unfairness. Such people are often said to have a "chip on their shoulder." At any time, they may become excessively angry for past perceived injustices they have suffered and take it out on others.

Alternatives: Does the person perceive any viable alternatives other than violence that could achieve the desired outcome? If not, violence may be inevitable in a hostage situation. Still, in the end, a skilled negotiating team may be able to offer the hostage taker alternatives other than the death of the victims.

Consequences: De Becker argues that most people consciously or unconsciously weigh the consequences of their actions before making drastic choices. When the consequences are perceived as favorable, these individuals will act. For example, when placed in the position of having nothing to lose and everything to gain, revolutionaries will often take hostages to draw the world's attention for their plight, and the means will seem to justify the ends.

Ability: De Becker states that those with histories of successfully using violence to get what they want are more likely to use violence again. The ability to go to extremes to resolve issues is a process of building up to the violent acts.

Individuals who participate in hostage taking to resolve their issues believe that they are justified in their missions, they have no other alternatives to solve their problems, they have weighed all the consequences and ultimately decided that hostage taking is the best choice, and finally, that they have the ability to follow through with their intended plans.

—Natalie Cardonne

See also KIDNAPPING, SPECIAL WEAPONS AND TACTICS TEAMS; TERRORISM

Further Reading

De Becker, G. (1997). *The gift of fear.* New York: Little, Brown.

Garrison, W. B. (2000). *Civil War hostages: Hostage taking in the Civil War.* Shippensburg, PA: White Mane Publishing.

MacWillson, A. C. (1992). *Hostage-taking terrorism: Incident-response strategy.* New York: St. Martin's.

JAMES OLIVER HUBERTY: THE "MCDONALD'S MASSACRE"

James Huberty was raised in a strict Christian family. According to reports, he was a socially isolated child and was convinced that the world would come to an end. In preparation for this eventuality, Huberty began collecting weapons and saving supplies. Although others report that he often spoke of violence, he had never acted on his thoughts. In fact, James was considered a hardworking family man. With a wife and two daughters to provide for, he worked hard to receive training to support his family financially. He obtained a degree in sociology from a small Christian college, owned his own home, and received a license for embalming from the Pittsburgh Institute of Mortuary Science. James Huberty appeared to be a successful man living an average life.

Huberty decided not to pursue a career in the mortuary business and instead became employed as a welder. He was able to provide well for his family for more than 10 years, until the company for which he worked closed in 1982. Huberty became resentful about losing his job and increasingly discouraged over the next year about his inability to find suitable work to support his family. In 1984, he and his family relocated from Canton, Ohio, to the small Mexican town of Tijuana, where he hoped they would find a better life. Once there, he began to feel especially isolated and frustrated. He was unable to speak the language and, according to his wife, felt rejected and felt hatred and resentment toward Hispanics. Thereafter, Huberty and his family relocated to San Ysidro, a town just outside the Mexican border, where he was able to find work as a security guard for an apartment complex. However, he was fired from that job in early July of 1984.

On July 18, 1984, Huberty took his wife and children to the San Diego Zoo. After leaving the zoo, he dropped them off at home, went upstairs to change clothing, loaded the car with ammunition, and indicated to his wife that he was going out to "hunt humans." His wife, not taking him seriously, asked him to stay home with her, but Huberty left his home and drove to a nearby McDonald's restaurant, wearing camouflage pants and armed with weaponry.

Mass murderer James Huberty calmly informed his wife that he was going "hunting humans." A few minutes later, he shot and killed 21 people at a McDonald's restaurant in San Yisidro, California. He also died in the attack.

Source: Copyright © Bettmann / CORBIS.

It was 4:00 p.m., and there were many young children in the restaurant, most of them Hispanic. After entering, Huberty ordered everyone to get down on the ground. He then began shooting everyone in his path. His rampage, referred to as the "McDonald's Massacre," lasted for 90 minutes. In an attempt to save their lives, patrons were throwing themselves through the glass windows of the restaurant, but few survived. Twenty-one people were killed and 19 were injured before Huberty was finally shot and killed by a sharpshooter on the SWAT team.

Several days after the shootings, James Huberty's wife attempted to explain her husband's behavior. She described a man who had been tormented by auditory hallucinations and had been unable to obtain mental health treatment—several days prior to the massacre, he had attempted to get an appointment at a mental health clinic but was unable to obtain one. As his wife described him, the man responsible for the "McDonald's Massacre" was much more troubled than he outwardly appeared.

—*Laura Hamon*

See also MASS MURDER

Further Reading

Kelleher, M. D. (1997). *Flashpoint: The American mass murderer.* Westport, CT: Praeger.

Leyton, E. (1986). *Hunting humans: The rise of the modern multiple murder.* Toronto, Canada: McClelland and Stewart.

I

IN COLD BLOOD

The classic 1965 nonfiction novel *In Cold Blood*, by New York reporter Truman Capote, describes the grisly story of the shotgun murder of a family of four in rural Kansas in 1959.

While in prison, Dick Hickock had heard his cellmate, Floyd Wells, speak of his former employment by the wealthy Clutter family. Wells remembered seeing something that resembled a safe in Mr. Clutter's office. Immediately after his release, Hickock teamed up with a friend, Perry Smith, and made plans to rob the Clutter house. The two carefully planned their crime and entered the Clutter home—only to discover that the "safe" was actually a filing cabinet with no valuables in it. During the robbery, Hickock decided to murder the terrified family because they were eyewitnesses.

The story intensifies as each one of the Clutter family is executed, followed by the capture of Hickock and Smith, and their life on death row. Readers get a close look into the dark side of those who kill. The book was later made into a dramatic movie directed by Richard Brooks. One of the two main characters, Perry Smith, was played by actor Robert Blake. Ironically, nearly 40 years later, Blake himself was charged with the murder of his wife, Bonnie. Capote's book was a masterful description of the murder, its aftermath, and the people involved. Today, the term "in cold blood" is used colloquially to describe any brutal, grisly killing.

—*Phil Caporale*

Further Reading

Capote, T. (1965). *In cold blood*. New York: Random House.

INFANTICIDE,
See CHILD KILLERS; FAMILY HOMICIDE

INSANITY DEFENSE, *See* COURT-ORDERED PSYCHOLOGICAL ASSESSMENT; MENTALLY DISORDERED OFFENDERS; M'NAUGHTEN RULE

INTEGRATED BALLISTIC IDENTIFICATION SYSTEM (IBIS), *See* BALLISTICS; CRIMINALISTICS

INTERNATIONAL ORGANIZED CRIME, *See* DRUG CARTELS; ORGANIZED CRIME: TRANSNATIONAL

INTERNET-RELATED CRIME, *See* CYBERAGGRESSION; CYBERSTINGS; EXPLOITATION OF CHILDREN; STALKING

INVESTIGATION OF VIOLENT CRIMES, *See* CRIMINALISTICS; FORENSIC SCIENCE; GEOGRAPHIC PROFILING; PROFILING

IRRESISTIBLE IMPULSE RULE, *See* HOMICIDE DEFENSES; HOMICIDE, TYPES OF, AND DEGREES OF MURDER; COURT-ORDERED PSYCHOLOGICAL ASSESSMENT

ITALIAN MAFIA, *See* FALCONE, GIOVANNI; ORGANIZED CRIME: TRANSNATIONAL

J

JACK THE RIPPER

Compared with other serial killers, "Jack the Ripper" of Britain was not the most prolific murderer; yet, like Ted Bundy in the United States, he has become a criminal icon and a standard by which to measure other killers. In 1888, the Ripper killed at least five London prostitutes, and more likely the death toll was closer to 10 to 15—no one knows for sure, but he promised through missives to the British media that he would not stop until he had killed 20 victims.

The killer's interest in mutilation of the corpses set him apart from others who also preyed on prostitutes at the time. The Ripper was very adept at eviscerating his victims and removing their organs. His first victim was murdered on Easter Monday in London's Whitechapel, and he clearly derived sexual gratification from her dismemberment. Once the victim was killed according to his sexual fantasy, the Ripper proceeded to examine her body parts. He was not pressed for time in the case of Jeanette Kelly and had at least 2 hours to thoroughly complete his task. Her throat was cut to the spinal column, nearly severing the head. Her ears and nose had been removed and placed on a severed breast in an effort to create a face. The other severed breast lay on the nightstand covered with her kidneys and heart. Close by was the right thigh, on which rested the liver. Her sexual organs were never recovered. This practice was common with most of his victims.

"Jack" enjoyed taunting police and newspapers and sent letters written in victims' blood vowing death to all prostitutes. He even sent a victim's kidney to a citizen's vigilante committee formed to catch him.

Jack the Ripper was never caught, and many theories currently abound as to the actual identity of the killer.

—Eric W. Hickey

Portions of this entry are drawn from *Serial Murderers and Their Victims,* 3rd edition (2002) by E. W. Hickey, published by Wadsworth: Belmont, CA.

See also Rippers; Serial Murder; Signature Killers

Further Reading

Sudgen, P. (2002). *The complete history of Jack the Ripper.* New York: Carroll and Graf.

Begg, P., Martin, F., & Skinner, K. (1994). *Jack the Ripper, A to Z.* London: Trafalgar Square Publishers.

JACKSON, GEORGE L., *See* Black Guerrilla Family

THE JEKYLL AND HYDE SYNDROME

One of the most distinct examples of an individual with a split, or double, personality is embodied in Robert Louis Stevenson's novel *Dr. Jekyll and Mr. Hyde.* The duality of an individual personality can be examined in a variety of ways, good versus evil, moral versus immoral, or the conscious self versus the unconscious desires. Stevenson, before Sigmund Freud or Gordon Allport, examined what it meant to have two competing identities. The character of Dr. Jekyll and Mr. Hyde reflects the division of personality that can plague an individual. In this case, Dr. Jekyll desperately tried to maintain self-control and resilience in order to keep the appearance of a well-respected and privileged doctor within his society. Mr. Hyde, on the other hand, was not concerned with his reputation; he was eager to act out his inner desires, vile cravings, and repressed urges.

One can look at the duality of the "Jekyll and Hyde" personality as being ruled by inner impulses or basic instincts. Such individuals repress what they believe to be morally wrong thoughts, sexual desires, and inner wants that if set free could erupt in acts of violence and threaten their place in society. These two personalities severely divide one's "self," and when inner cravings are released, it gives a momentary sense of gratification by releasing the tension between the "moral" and "pleasure" sides. However, the impulse to gratify the primitive, pleasure self becomes stronger, and both sides begin to compete for dominance once again. This struggle becomes a never-ending battle for balance and stability.

One example of a Jekyll-and-Hyde personality is the life of William Deacon Brodie, who lived in the late 18th century. Brodie was supposedly as an upstanding and honorable man during the day, but by night he participated in a scandalous crime spree in Edinburgh, Scotland. Brodie was finally apprehended and sentenced to die on the gallows. In the United States, serial killer Theodore (Ted) Bundy was another individual who displayed a Jekyll-and-Hyde personality. He was described as charming, intelligent, and friendly; and as a college graduate and law school student, he was well educated. There was, however, another side to Bundy. He was arrested, charged, and later executed, having killed at least 30 women between 1973 and 1978.

—*Katherine Ray*

See also Bundy, Theodore "Ted"; Serial Murder; Violent Behavior

Further Reading

MacNally, R. T., & Florescu, R. R. (2000). *In search of Dr. Jekyll and Mr. Hyde.* Los Angeles: Renaissance Books.

Stevenson, R. L. (1978). *Dr. Jekyll and Mr. Hyde.* New York: Penguin Books.

GENENE JONES

In 1982, Genene Jones left Bexar County Medical Center Hospital, in Texas, in the wake of investigations into numerous, inexplicable infants' and young children's deaths. She then took a licensed vocational nursing position at Kerr County clinic. Shortly thereafter, the clinic was plagued by similar deaths at an alarming rate. The children were dying of lethal injections of digoxin or succinylcholine, which affect the heart rate and respiration. These injections were supposedly an attempt by Jones to demonstrate her worth as a nurse. Her plan was to save her child victims and appear as their heroine; unfortunately, most of the children did not survive. In 1984, Jones was convicted of two deaths and was sentenced to 99 years in prison with a possibility of parole in 20 years. Over her 5-year period of poisoning children, Jones was linked to approximately 40 to 50 deaths.

—*Brianna Satterthwaite*

See also Medical Murders; Serial Murder; Poisoning: Medical Settings

Further Reading

Kelleher, M. D., & Kelleher, C. L. (1998). *Murder most rare: The female serial killer.* Westport, CT: Praeger.

JONESBORO, ARKANSAS, SCHOOL SHOOTING

On March 24, 1998, at approximately 12:30 p.m., 11-year-old Andrew Golden pulled the fire alarm inside Westside Middle School in Jonesboro, Arkansas. Golden and 13-year-old Mitchell Johnson, both dressed in camouflage clothing, then took a position in a wooded area overlooking a classroom building of the school. As students filed out of the building in response to the fire alarm, Johnson and Golden opened fire.

Using three rifles and seven handguns stolen from the homes of Golden's parents and grandparents, the boys managed to get off 22 shots in under 4 minutes at the people coming out of the classroom building. They purposely aimed high at their targets, with the intention of doing more serious damage. The students and faculty were pinned down by the gunfire, their only avenue for escape closed off because the doors to the classroom building automatically locked as a consequence of the fire drill. During the ambush, Johnson and Golden killed four students and one teacher, and wounded 10 others.

Within 10 minutes after the incident had started, police arrived on the scene. Workers on the roof of a nearby construction project directed police to the area in the woods where the gunfire had originated. As Golden and Johnson attempted to retreat to a getaway van that Johnson had taken from his stepfather, they were apprehended by the police, with minimal resistance.

Speculation immediately afterward focused on whether or not Johnson and Golden had targeted their victims on the basis of gender. All five of those killed and 9 of the 10 wounded were female. There were even rumors that the whole incident was motivated by a classmate spurning Johnson's affection. However, it should be pointed out that the first group to file out of the classroom building was from an all-girls music class.

There was also a good deal of conjecture about the "gun culture" that might have influenced the shootings. Several photographs emerged of a young Golden with a variety of firearms, including one of him at 6 years of age taking careful aim with a pistol. Likewise, Johnson had grown up around firearms. Questions were raised about the rural Southern tradition of hunting and exposure to firearms at a relatively young age. However, it is unclear whether such activities can be directly linked to the shootings.

Like other school shooting incidents, the backgrounds of the offenders were closely scrutinized. Johnson, who is widely viewed as the primary catalyst for the shooting, was an "outsider" who had recently moved to Jonesboro and had trouble fitting in at the school. He had been in trouble for getting into fights, especially after his parents divorced, and aspired to be in a gang. Golden had been described by neighbors as "rowdy," "mean spirited," and "evil."

Less than 5 months after the shooting incident, both Golden and Johnson were found guilty of the slayings and remanded to the custody of Arkansas Youth Services for an undetermined period of time. Both boys will likely be held until they are 21 years of age.

—*Thomas A. Petee and Janice E. Wittekind*

See also COLUMBINE/LITTLETON SCHOOL SHOOTING; KINKEL, KIPLAND (KIP); MASS MURDER; MEDIA VIOLENCE; SCHOOL SHOOTINGS

Further Reading

Diane, M. (2002). *Too high a price for harmony: A perspective on school shootings.* Bloomington, IN: 1st Books Library Publishers.

Fein, A. H. (2003). *There and back again: School shootings as experienced by school leaders.* Lanman, MD: Scarecrow Press.

JONESTOWN MASSACRE, *See* CULTS; MASS MURDER

JURISDICTION

Why is it that some cases of homicide are considered federal offenses and others are handled in state or tribal courts? The answer involves the concept of jurisdiction. In its most basic definition, jurisdiction has to do with which court has the ability to hear and decide issues of law and fact. In homicide cases, three jurisdictions may have the ability to hear the case: state, tribal, and federal.

Most people are familiar with the idea of "double jeopardy": A person cannot be tried twice for the same crime. Double jeopardy comes into play once a person has been either acquitted or convicted of a crime. Yet some defendants are tried twice for what appears to be the same crime. Usually, these cases involve a trial in criminal court and a trial in civil court. However, there are cases in which a person is tried in two criminal courts. How is this possible? Isn't that a violation of double jeopardy? The answer is no, as long as the person is tried in two separate sovereigns. A *sovereign* is defined as an entity that is independent and in which supreme authority is vested.

DETERMINING JURISDICTION

In the United States, there are three sovereign entities: the states, federally recognized Indian Nations, and the federal government. The laws of each sovereign establish the types of crimes over which each sovereign government has jurisdiction. A person can be tried by both the state and the federal government for what appears to be the same crime if both the state and the federal government have laws that apply to the activity. For example, the police officers who were accused of beating Rodney King, in Los Angeles, were found not guilty by a state court. Subsequently, they faced charges of violating King's civil rights, a federal offense, in a federal court.

Many factors come into play in determining which court has jurisdiction over a case. One of the most important is the location of the crime. In many cases, jurisdiction is a simple matter of whether the crime was committed on federal land (e.g., national parks, military installations, Indian reservations, etc). If it happened on federal land, the federal government usually has exclusive jurisdiction over the crime. This explains why Cary Stayner faced federal charges in the death of Joie Ruth Armstrong but faces state murder charges in the February 1999 deaths of Carol Sund, Julie Sund, and Silvina Pelossa. Armstrong was murdered inside Yosemite National Park, California, on federal land, whereas the other three women were killed outside the park, on state land.

JURISDICTION IN INDIAN COUNTRY

The issue of jurisdiction becomes much more complicated when handling crimes committed in Indian country. The legal definition of *Indian country* for federal jurisdiction purposes usually means "(a) all land within the limits of any reservation under the jurisdiction of the United States government, (b) all dependent Indian communities within the borders of the United States, and (c) all Indian allotments, the Indian titles to which have not been extinguished" (BigFoot & Braden, 1998).

Tribal governments are considered sovereign nations. They have certain rights, including the right of self-governance. Tribes can exercise legislative, judicial, and regulatory powers, including enacting laws, establishing courts, and punishing tribal members for infractions of those laws. Indian nations, however, are considered to be sovereign dependent nations, and the U.S. Congress has limited the powers of tribal governments. These limitations are found in the Indian Civil Rights Act of 1968. Limitations on the length of jail sentences may be imposed on convicted offenders and also on tribal court jurisdiction. Tribal courts, for example, do not have criminal jurisdiction over non-Indians; however, they do have civil jurisdiction over non-Indians.

In the case of crimes committed in Indian country, jurisdiction depends on the type of offense, the location of the crime, the offender's race, and the victim's race. Jurisdiction also depends on whether the state or federal government has criminal jurisdiction over Indian country.

In 1953, Congress passed Public Law 280. This law, commonly known as "P.L. 280," gave six states mandatory and substantial criminal and civil jurisdiction over Indian country: Alaska (except the Metlakatla Reservation), California, Minnesota (except Red Lake Reservation), Nebraska, and Oregon (except Warm Springs Reservation). Ten other states accepted some degree of P.L. 280 jurisdiction.

Crimes committed in Indian country in non–P.L.280 states are subject to the Major Crimes Act (18 USC, Section 1153, 1998), which states in part,

> Any Indian who commits against the person or property of another Indian or other person any of the following offenses, namely murder, manslaughter . . . within the Indian Country, shall be subject to the same law and penalties as all other persons committing any of the above offenses, within the exclusive jurisdiction of the United States.

Thus, the federal government retains jurisdiction over 14 specific offenses, including murder and manslaughter, committed by Native Americans against other Native Americans in Indian country.

The tribal government also has jurisdiction over these crimes. The tribal and federal government share concurrent (running together) jurisdiction over murder and manslaughter committed in Indian country when both the victim and the offender are Native American. A defendant can be tried and convicted in both tribal and federal court for the same crime.

In the case of a felony committed in Indian country (in a non–P.L. 280 state), (a) when the defendant is Indian and the victim is non-Indian, the federal government has exclusive jurisdiction over the defendant; (b) when the defendant is a non–Native American and the victim is Native American, the federal government also has exclusive jurisdiction; and (c) when both the defendant and the victim are non-Indian, only the state has jurisdiction. There is no tribal jurisdiction. Although the federal government could prosecute these cases because they took place on federal land, they are usually tried in state court.

Establishing Jurisdiction

The issue of jurisdiction is a major concern for those handling crimes in Indian country. Public safety dispatchers (in non–P.L. 280 states) must determine which law enforcement agency should initially respond to crime. Three questions can be asked in an attempt to determine jurisdiction: (a) Did the crime occur on state land or Indian country land? (b) is the offender or victim a Native American? and (c) is the crime a felony or misdemeanor?

Although these questions may appear straightforward, jurisdiction can often be confusing. In many areas, Indian country is interspersed with non-Indian lands, often referred to as "checkerboard" areas. Jurisdiction can change from one block to another. When crimes clearly occur on state land, there is no jurisdictional confusion. When the crime occurs close to Indian country, however, massive confusion can ensue. The most confusing situation may come about when a person who is on Indian land is murdered by a person who is not in Indian land. For example, a Native American may shoot another Native American who is standing across the street. If the perpetrator is on state land but the victim is on Indian land, who has jurisdiction? Or a crime may initially seem to be misdemeanor but may end up being a felony. It is important that the correct law enforcement agency responds to the call.

Jurisdictional issues influence not only which court may hear a case but also which law enforcement agency has the responsibility to investigate the case. Law enforcement officers are limited in their jurisdiction. A state law enforcement officer, for example, may not have jurisdiction to arrest a Native American suspect in Indian country.

Federal law enforcement officers such as the Bureau of Indian Affairs (BIA) police officers may not be recognized as having jurisdiction outside Indian country. BIA law enforcement officers may not be able to arrest a suspect who has traveled into state land. The officers have no jurisdiction on state lands. Similarly, a local, non-Indian law enforcement agency may not be able to pursue a suspect who enters the "foreign" jurisdiction of Indian country.

Some communities have attempted to address this problem through cross-deputization. This process deputizes law enforcement officers within neighboring jurisdictions, granting them the authority to pursue and arrest suspects even when they are outside the boundaries of their normal duty stations. In other communities, such agreements do not exist, complicating the investigation and prosecution of perpetrators.

If a state or local officer pursues a perpetrator onto Indian land, they may continue the pursuit while notifying the tribal jurisdiction. If these officers then stop the suspect, they can detain the suspect but may not remove that person until tribal or BIA officers arrive. Nor can the state or local officers simply remove a suspect from Indian country. The defendant may need to be extradited from the tribal jurisdiction to the state.

If the wrong law enforcement agency is involved in the investigation of the case, evidence gathered illegally may not be allowed into evidence. For example, to make a legal arrest in Indian country, any existing state warrant needs to be endorsed by tribal or federal court.

Crimes committed in Indian country may involve three different law enforcement agencies: tribal, BIA, and FBI. The initial response to a crime scene is usually made by tribal law enforcement; then, the investigation is often turned over to a criminal investigator who is employed either by the tribe or the BIA. Once the crime is considered for federal prosecution, an FBI agent will usually be assigned to further investigate the case.

Public Law 280 States

In states with P.L. 280 jurisdiction, the state has criminal jurisdiction over crimes occurring in reservation areas. Someone who commits a crime on Indian land in a P.L. 280 state is treated the same way as someone who commits the crime on non-Indian land. The location of the crime is not important. The races of the victim and offender are not relevant. There is no special federal criminal jurisdiction over reservation areas in P.L. 280 states. If tribal courts exist, however, they have concurrent jurisdiction over homicides committed by Native Americans against Native American victims that take place on Indian land.

The states with P.L. 280 jurisdiction assumed criminal jurisdiction over crimes occurring in Indian country, and thus the federal government did not provide financial or technical assistance to tribal courts, nor did state governments provide such assistance. In many P.L. 280 states, tribal court development has been severely limited due to the lack of funding. Tribal communities are only now starting the process of developing tribal courts in these states. Criminal cases are primarily heard only in state court. However, as more tribal communities develop their own courts, more homicide cases may be tried both in tribal and state court.

A Comparison of Tribal and Federal Courts

When both tribal and federal courts have jurisdiction over a case, such as a homicide, there are many considerations in deciding which court will handle the case. First, each jurisdiction must have laws that cover the offense. When the U.S. Congress passed the Indian Civil Rights Act (1968), they were careful to limit tribal criminal jurisdiction to Native Americans; thus, non-Indians cannot be tried in tribal court for criminal offenses. It appears that Congress intended tribal courts to be severely limited in scope. Sentencing limitations in the Indian Civil Rights Act initially directed tribal courts to impose maximum jail sentences of 6 months for each offense, and amendments to the act increased this maximum, though only to 1 year. Such short sentences may be appropriate for misdemeanors, but they are woefully inadequate for felonies.

Congress did not plan for tribal courts to hear felony cases. The assumption was that either the federal or state (in P.L. 280 states) government would prosecute felony cases that occurred in Indian country. However, federal and state prosecutors often declined to prosecute cases in Indian country. Tribes began to believe that these cases were being ignored by the non-Indian criminal justice system and began asserting tribal court jurisdiction over felony cases involving Native American victims and perpetrators.

A tribal court may elect to hear only misdemeanor and civil cases. If a tribe does not have a code or ordinance covering felony crimes, there is no violation of tribal law and they are able to hear such cases in tribal court. In most cases, tribes do have laws pertaining to homicide, and the tribal prosecutors base their decision on whether to prosecute the crime on the usual factors in such cases: How strong is the evidence? Does prosecution serve the public interest? Are there any problems with evidence or witnesses? How strong is the overall case?

A perpetrator, knowing that the sentence in tribal court will not be very long, may decide to take responsibility for his or her crime and plead guilty. On the other hand, the defendant may know that a jury of his or her peers would be unwilling to convict members of their community for any crime, and therefore, all the defendant needs to do is ask for a jury trial and they will be found not guilty.

The decision of whether to try a case in state or federal court often takes a long time. It is not unusual for the U.S. Attorney's Office to take several months to determine whether or not to prosecute a case. This delay can be due to the difficulties of investigating cases in Indian country and the large number of cases that are referred to the U.S. Attorney's Office for prosecution. A tribal court may decide to prosecute an offender while awaiting a prosecutorial determination from the state or federal prosecutor. In some cases, the tribe may prosecute a case and incarcerate an offender after the offender is found guilty. Subsequently, he or she can be turned over to the other jurisdiction for prosecution if the federal or state government decides to prosecute the offender.

A case that is going to be tried in federal court may involve witnesses having to travel long distances to the federal courthouse. Tribal members may not be able to travel to the federal court, or they may feel uncomfortable in the strange surroundings of the federal courthouse. The court proceedings in tribal court may take place in the tribal language, whereas state and federal court proceedings take place in English. Some victims and witnesses willing to testify in their local tribal courts may not be as cooperative when they are involved in the federal system. In such a case, there may be a higher chance of a successful prosecution in tribal court than in federal court.

Tribal and federal or state prosecutors may meet together to ascertain the best way to proceed in a case. Tribal courts may have different rules of evidence, which may contribute to a higher probability of a conviction in tribal court. The murder committed may be so heinous that the limitations on sentencing available in tribal court could be considered much too lenient. The decision regarding which court should try a particular case or whether the case should be prosecuted in two different jurisdictions is made by assessing a number of considerations.

Tribal Courts

Most non-Indians are unfamiliar with the existence of tribal courts. In 1992, there were approximately 170 tribal courts, with jurisdiction over 1 million Americans (BigFoot & Braden, 1998). Although it may appear that the limitations placed on tribal courts make them ineffective, this appearance is deceiving.

Tribal courts are not only an expression of sovereignty, they are an expression of tribal beliefs and values. Most tribal courts are modeled on the American judicial system; however, tribes have the ability to incorporate their own ideals and principles into their court rules and operation. Traditional tribal ideas of justice may seem out of place in modern American society, but they have hundreds of years of history in tribal communities.

Today, the mainstream American criminal justice system is discovering the idea of *restorative justice,* an idea that is central to tribal justice systems. New programs are being developed across the nation to implement restorative-justice approaches in the prevailing American system, which in many ways has not seemed to be functioning adequately. The unique approach of tribal justice in the United States is an iportant component of the larger justice system.

—*Eidell Wasserman*

See also COURTS

Further Reading

BigFoot, D. S., & Braden, J. (1998). *Upon the back of a turtle: A cross-cultural curriculum for federal criminal justice personnel.* Oklahoma City: University of Oklahoma.

Black, H. C. (1990). *Black's law dictionary.* Chicago: American Law Institute.

JUSTIFIABLE HOMICIDE, *See* HOMICIDE, TYPES OF, AND DEGREES OF MURDER

JUVENILE FIRESETTERS

Firesetting is a serious, destructive, life-threatening problem. The National Fire Protection Association estimates that every year, children start 100,000 fires that result in billions of dollars worth of property damage, injury, and death. During the last decade, juveniles accounted for an estimated 40% of all intentionally set fire arrests.

Curiosity about fire is a normal part of a child's development, and fireplay, in and of itself, is not necessarily indicative of abnormal behavior. The majority of children who play with fire out of curiosity simply outgrow the behavior. However, when children who play with fire experience stress as a result of emotional trauma or an ongoing crisis in their lives, they are more likely to continue setting fires.

Fireplay and *firesetting* are two terms that denote completely different behavior. Fireplay refers to children who experiment with matches or other firestarting materials in an unsupervised setting. Fireplay is largely motivated by curiosity, and though it may be intentional, it is not malicious. Conversely, firesetting refers to children who actively seek out firestarting materials and ignite materials or property belonging to themselves or others. The behavior may be driven by a number of different reasons, including psychological pain and conflict, anger and revenge, and the need for attention or for excitement. Firesetting is intentional and can be malicious. Behavioral factors that distinguish fireplay from firesetting include (a) history of firestarting, (b) method of firestart, (c) ignition source, (d) target of firestart, (e) intention, and (f) antecedent behaviors.

TYPOLOGY

Children who exhibit fireplay or firesetting behavior can generally be categorized into one of two groups: nonpathological and pathological.

Nonpathological Fireplay

The majority of children who play with fire do so simply out of curiosity or by accident. These children generally come from intact families, set only one fire, and are likely to feel remorse or guilt following the incident. They typically do not intend to cause harm, do not receive satisfaction from setting a fire, and usually do not understand the consequences or destructive power of fire. They are often afraid of fire and will often attempt to call for help or to extinguish the fire themselves. Children in this category are usually male, between the ages of 5 and 10 years, and respond favorably to educational programs designed to eliminate fireplay behavior.

Pathological Firesetting

Pathological firesetters are reported to use fire more deliberately as a means of expressing anger or revenge.

These children are usually male, reside in dysfunctional families, and display other maladaptive behaviors in addition to firesetting. Pathological firesetters often exhibit significant emotional and learning disabilities, have poor peer relationships, poor school performance, and disturbing peer relationships.

Pathological firesetters can be placed into any of three subgroups: cry-for-help, delinquent, and severely disturbed. *Cry-for-help* firesetters use the firesetting behavior to draw attention to themselves in an effort to satisfy unmet emotional needs. *Delinquent* firesetters tend to be in their teens and have histories of starting fires. These teens are typically involved in other delinquent behaviors as well as firesetting. They set fires as acts of vandalism or for creating excitement and destroying property, and are usually strongly influenced by their peers. *Severely disturbed* firesetters represent the smallest percentage of pathological firesetters, although they are viewed as the most dangerous. Juveniles in this category have been noted to set fires due to lack of impulse control, desire for sexual satisfaction, or hallucinations.

Pathological firesetting is a symptom, often one of the first outward signs of a more deeply rooted problem. A cluster of personality variables predisposes a child toward firesetting, and specific circumstances set the stage for and reinforce the behavior.

FACTORS IN FIRESETTING BEHAVIOR

Psychological

Some clinical evidence suggesting that juvenile firesetters' inability to identify or express emotions is linked to recurrent firesetting. Many pathological firesetters have anger and aggression issues that manifest themselves in the behavior. There is a definite relationship between pathological firesetting and a diagnosis of conduct disorder. The *Diagnostic and Statistical Manual of Mental Disorders,* 4th edition *(DSMV-IV),* lists firesetting as one descriptive behavior used to assess the presence of conduct disorder. In addition, firesetting has been closely related to antisocial behavior in juveniles, with the most common covariates including property destruction, stealing, lying, running away, and truancy.

Demographics

Male juveniles have a higher incidence of fireplay and firesetting behavior. These behaviors have been documented in children as young as 2 years old. The average age of fireplay behavior is under 7 years old, and the average age of firesetting behavior is between 8 and 12 years. Race does not appear to be a factor in fireplay or firesetting behavior, nor does socioeconomic status.

Physical

Pathological firesetters generally have a higher incidence of physical illness, with allergies and respiratory problems most represented. A higher incidence of hyperactivity has been noted in juvenile firesetters. Sexual motivation for the act is rare in juveniles. Intelligence does not appear to be an important factor, and children who exhibit firesetting behavior range from low to superior intelligence. There is, however, a correlation between learning disabilities and firesetting.

Social Circumstances

There is a strong correlation between parental and family dysfunction and the development of juvenile firesetters. These individuals often come from unhealthy home environments, in which they are likely to experience parental separation, poor supervision, violence, parental drug and alcohol abuse, or some form of physical or sexual abuse. Juvenile firesetters have difficulty establishing and maintaining significant relationships with peers and are likely to exhibit poor behavior at school, often resulting in suspensions or expulsions.

PROGRAMS FOR JUVENILES

Recognizing the magnitude of child-set fires, many fire departments have developed intervention programs designed to educate children on fire safety and the dangers of fire, as well as identifying juveniles in need of further professional intervention.

—Lisa Andersen

See also ARSON; ATTACHMENT DEFICIENCY
    AND VIOLENCE; CONDUCT DISORDER; JUVENILE
    KILLERS; JUVENILE OFFENDERS; MACDONALD TRIAD

Further Reading

Fineman, K. R. (1995). A model for the qualitative analysis of child and adult fire deviant behavior. *American Journal of Forensic Psychology, 13,* 31-60.

Gaynor, J. (2000, June). *Juvenile firesetter intervention handbook.* Federal Emergency Management Agency, United States Fire Administration.

Gaynor, J., & Hatcher, C. (1987). *The psychology of child firesetting: Detection and intervention.* New York: Brunner Mazel.

Kolko, D. J., & Kazdin, A. E. (1986). A conceptualization of firesetting in children and adolescents. *Journal of Abnormal Child Psychology, 14*(1), 49-61.

JUVENILE KILLERS

In the early 1990s, murders committed by youth under 18 years of age were at near epidemic proportions. The numbers of juveniles arrested for murder and their percentage representation among homicide arrestees continuously increased from 1984 through 1993. Leading experts forecasted in the mid-1990s that if the escalation in homicides by juveniles continued, the United States would see an unprecedented level of human destruction by America's young during the new millennium. Contrary to predictions, arrests of juveniles for murder decreased during the next 7 years. At the beginning of the 21st century, juveniles comprised 9.3% of those arrested for murder. In 1993, they had represented 16.2% of all homicide arrestees (Snyder, 2001).

HOMICIDAL INCIDENTS

A recently published report by Howard Snyder used data submitted to the FBI from 1980 through 1999 to analyze juvenile involvement in murders in the United States over a 20-year period. The exact number of killings committed by youth every year is unknown because the FBI has no information on the killers in a large percentage of cases. For example, such data was not available in about 36% of the murders committed in 1999.

About 1,040 juveniles are known to have been involved in the murders of 15,530 people in 1999. In 59% of these cases, the youth appeared to act alone; in the remaining 41% of murders, 9% involved another juvenile, and 32% involved an adult. The proportion of homicides by juveniles that involved adult offenders increased significantly over the 20-year period of analysis.

Available data suggests that in 1999, murders by juveniles fell to their lowest level since the mid-1980s.

The decrease in murders by juveniles was largely attributed to a decline in the number of murders of acquaintances and to a lesser extent, strangers; the annual number of family members slain by youth under 18 years old stayed fairly constant over the 20-year period. In 70% of murders by juveniles, victims were killed with a firearm; in 25% of cases, another type of weapon was used, such as a knife or blunt object; in the remaining 5%, the juveniles' hands or feet were used.

Victims of Juvenile Murderers

During the 20-year time frame, those killed by juveniles were overwhelmingly male (83%) and slightly more likely to be white (51%) than black (47%). In 27% of the killings, the victims were juveniles, 1 out of 4 being between the ages of 16 through 19. More than half (52%) of the victims slain by juveniles were between the ages of 14 and 25; only 9% were more than 50 years old.

Of the victims killed by juveniles, 86% were either acquaintances (55%) or strangers (31%); the remaining 14% were parents (2%) or other family members (12%). In 82% of homicides known to be committed by juveniles over the 20-year period, the victims were most likely to be from the same racial group. Among juvenile murderers, killings of same-race victims were most common for whites (90%), followed by blacks (77%), Asian/Pacific Islanders (59%), and American Indians (45%).

Juvenile Murderers

Juvenile homicide arrestees between 1980 through 1999 were almost exclusively male (93%), disproportionately black (56%), and likely to be age 15 and older (88%). Of known juvenile killers, 17% were age 15; 29%, age 16; and 42%, age 17. During the 20-year period, on the average per year, about 35 youth 12 years of age and under were arrested for murder.

Preteen killers were slightly less likely to be male (83%) and black (51%) than their older counterparts. Relative to all juvenile murderers, they were more likely to kill family members (37%) and less likely to kill acquaintances (46%) or strangers (17%). These very young murderers used firearms in 53% of their killings.

Older juvenile killers were more likely than preteen killers to kill with other juveniles during the 20-year period. About half of 14-, 15-, 16-, and 17-year-old murderers killed alone. In contrast, 79% of killers under age 12; 69% of 12-year-old murderers; and 57% of 13-year-old killers acted alone.

Gender differences among juvenile murderers with respect to the victims they killed over the 20-year period are discernible. More than 90% of the victims slain by boys were acquaintances (55%) or strangers (37%); less than 9% were family members. In contrast, girls were more likely than their male counterparts to kill family members (39%) and less likely to kill acquaintances (46%) or strangers (15%). Between 1980 and 1999, female juvenile murderers were more likely to kill children under age 5 (21%) than were the males (2%).

Gender differences were also apparent in the racial group membership of the victims killed by black juveniles. Among black young killers, females were more likely to kill members of their own race than were males (90% vs. 76%). Black female offenders were more similar in victim selection in this respect to white male and female juvenile killers (90% and 91%, respectively) than to their male racial counterparts.

Among juvenile killers, boys were more likely to use firearms than were girls. Between 1980 and 1999, 72% of boys used firearms, compared with 38% of girls. Girls were more likely to use knives (29%) than boys (13%).

Racial differences among juvenile killers are apparent in weapon usage and victim-offender relationship. Black youth were most likely to use firearms (76%), followed by Asian/Pacific Islanders (71%), whites (62%), and Native Americans (48%). Analysis of victim-offender relationships revealed that 16% of white and 16% of Native Americans killed family members, compared with 7% of black and Asian/Pacific Islander youth.

Trends in Juvenile Homicide

Analysis of data from 1980 through 1999 indicated that the trends in juvenile homicide were largely driven by two factors: males and firearms. Throughout the period, females never comprised more than 13% of homicides, a peak that was reached in 1983 before the escalation in juvenile homicide began.

The overall trend in juvenile murder can be explained by firearm usage. In 1983, the number of young killers who used firearms was nearly equal to the number who used all other instruments. In 1994, when juvenile homicide peaked, 81% of juvenile murderers used guns. In 1999, 67% of juvenile homicide

offenders used firearms. During the period of escalation in juvenile homicide, the use of firearms as murder weapons increased among both black and white murderers. Juvenile male killers were more likely than their female counterparts to use guns, a disparity that increased in the 1990s.

PROSECUTION OF JUVENILE MURDERERS

The prosecutor's office almost always seeks to bring charges against youth who have been involved in the killing of others. The legal response to youth who kill, both historically and currently, varies widely. Prosecution may occur in either a juvenile or adult forum, depending on the law and practice in the jurisdiction. Some young killers are processed in the juvenile justice system, in which their sentences may be calculated in months. Other adolescent murderers are tried in the adult criminal justice system, in which they can legally be sentenced to life imprisonment or death. The focus in the juvenile system is more oriented toward the treatment of offenders than is the case in the adult system, in which attention is typically directed to the punishment and incapacitation of lawbreakers.

Rehabilitation in the 20th and 21st Centuries

Decrying rehabilitation for violent teens has been a popular stance in the United States for close to three decades. A study of intervention programs by Robert Martinson that concluded in 1974 that "nothing works" when it comes to the rehabilitation of juvenile delinquents has been embraced by many criminal justice agents and politicians for more than two decades, despite evidence to the contrary. Public support in the United States for rehabilitation per se has also decreased significantly, particularly for violent offenders, since the early 1970s.

More rigorous analyses of intervention strategies conducted in the late 1970s and 1980s have clearly established that rehabilitation can be effective and that many treatment programs do work. Ted Palmer's synthesis of these "meta-analyses," published in 1992, indicated that behavioral, cognitive-behavioral, skill-oriented or life skills, multimodal, and family interventions were the most successful treatment strategies for lowering recidivism among juvenile offenders. A recently published meta-analysis of 200 programs by Mark Lipsey and his colleagues (2002) specifically examined whether intervention programs could reduce recidivism among serious delinquents and explored which programs were most successful with this population. This study found an overall 12% decrease in recidivism among treated delinquents when compared with their control groups.

The treatment programs that were most effective in reducing recidivism varied to some extent among noninstitutionalized and institutionalized serious delinquents. The most effective treatment programs for noninstitutionalized serious juvenile offenders included individual counseling, interpersonal skills, behavioral programs, and multiple services. For their institutionalized counterparts, effective treatment programs included interpersonal skills, teaching families in their homes, behavioral programs, community residential programs, and multiple services. Reduction in recidivism was dramatic for both types of serious juvenile offenders. The researchers estimated that the most effective treatment programs would reduce recidivism for the noninstitutionalized offenders by 40% and for the institutionalized group, by 30% to 35%. The results of this study provided compelling data that serious juvenile offenders can be helped and that intervention can reduce recidivism. The research team maintained that new and better programs could be developed by studying the characteristics of effective programs, implementing them, and evaluating them.

Transfer to Adult Criminal Justice System

Empirical findings demonstrating that serious juvenile offenders can be successfully treated has had limited impact on public policy and sentencing practices. The 1990s were characterized by unprecedented change in the juvenile justice system as states across the United States cracked down on serious, violent juvenile crime. Increasingly, given the current mood in the United States, more juveniles are being prosecuted as adults. All 50 states and the District of Columbia have provisions to try juveniles in adult courts. Some states specifically mention murder when discussing transfer procedures in their juvenile codes. In these states, the minimum age for exercise of criminal court jurisdiction in homicide cases is often lower than in other felony cases.

There are seven types of transfer provisions, several of which can exist in one state. A survey of state practices in 1997 revealed that three types of judicial waiver provisions were evident across the United States: 46 states have provisions allowing for discretionary waiver; 14 states have mandatory provisions in which judges must waive offenders who are charged with certain offenses to adult court; and 15 states have presumptive waiver provisions whereby the burden of proof regarding the transfer decision shifts from the state to the juvenile for certain offenses. In addition to judicial waiver, 15 states have direct file provisions by which prosecutors decide in which forum to prosecute youth when both the adult and juvenile justice systems have concurrent jurisdiction. In 28 states, statutory exclusion provisions provide for automatic transfer of certain juvenile offenders to adult court. Reverse-waiver decisions in 23 states allow criminal court judges to transfer cases of juveniles from adult court to juvenile court for adjudication. Legislation enacted in 31 states stipulates that "once an adult, always an adult," meaning that once a juvenile is convicted in adult court, any subsequent cases involving that youth must also be handled in adult court.

No national data exist on the transfer of juvenile murderers to adult court. In fact, the exact number of juvenile transfers to criminal court is presently unknown. Available data provide unequivocal evidence, however, that the number has increased with the availability of easier transfer mechanisms largely enacted since the mid-1980s.

Statistics also indicate that the juvenile population at midyear in U.S. jails has risen significantly since the mid-1980s. The average daily population of juveniles in adult jail, for example, increased dramatically from 1,629 in 1985 to 7,613 in 2001. Recent advancements in reporting practices reveal that the number of juveniles in jail who were tried as adults or were awaiting trial as adults rose from 5,900 in 1995 to 6,757 in 2001.

The number of juveniles in state and federal prisons at midyear increased significantly from the mid-1980s through the mid-1990s. Since the late 1990s, the number of inmates under 18 years of age has shown a decreasing trend, which is consistent with the decreasing numbers of juveniles arrested for violent crime during this period. The number of juveniles in state prison was 5,309 in 1995; 4,863 in 1998; and 3,147 in 2001. Overall, less than 1% of state inmates were under age 18 at midyear 2001. No juveniles were held in federal prisons in 1995, 1998, and 2001.

Juveniles and the Death Penalty

The United States stands alone among other Western industrialized nations in permitting the execution of individuals for murders they committed as juveniles.

Although some evidence exists that Americans may be less approving of condemning juvenile murderers to death than adult killers, executions of youth under the age of 18 have been deemed constitutional. Three U.S. Supreme Court decisions speak authoritatively on this issue. In 1982, the Court held in *Eddings v. Oklahoma* that a defendant's youth, troubled past, and mental and emotional difficulties are relevant factors to consider in mitigation with respect to imposition of the death penalty. The Court reasoned that any mitigating factors, whether statutorily based or not, should be weighed against any statutory aggravating factors by the decision maker in arriving at a death determination.

The 1988 case of *Thompson v. Oklahoma* has been interpreted to prohibit the execution of a youth under 16 years old only in states where the minimum age of execution is not legislated. However, the Court specifically held in *Stanford v. Kentucky* (1989), decided a year after *Thompson,* that the execution of offenders for crimes they committed at ages 16 and 17 did not violate the Eighth Amendment's provisions against cruel and unusual punishment.

Victor Streib, Dean and Professor of Law at Ohio Northern University and leading authority on capital punishment, has tracked legislation and court cases with respect to juveniles sentenced to death since 1973, when the death penalty was restored in many states to conform with the Supreme Court's guidelines in *Furman v. Georgia* (1972). Streib reported that of the 40 jurisdictions that authorized capital punishment (38 states, federal military, and federal civilian), 23 states authorize executions for individuals who committed crimes under age 18. Five of these states have chosen age 17 as their minimum age. The remaining 18 states have set age 16 as their minimum, either by legislation or by court ruling. Fifteen states and the federal government restrict the death sentence to age 18 or older for young offenders who kill.

Streib estimated that over the 29-year period from January 1, 1973, to December 31, 2001, 213 of the murderers sentenced to death were juveniles at the time of crime commission. Although death sentences imposed on those under 18 years old have a high reversal rate, 18 executions of juvenile offenders have occurred since the U.S. Supreme Court held in the 1976 case of *Gregg v. Georgia* that current death penalty statutes were constitutional. These 18 cases represented 2.4% of the 749 murderers executed from 1973 to 2001. In the 1970s, no individuals were executed for murders they committed as minors; in the

1980s, there were 3; in the 1990s, 10. Five executions have occurred in the first 2 years of the 21st century: four in 2000 and one in 2001.

CONCLUDING REMARKS

There is no question that more adolescent murderers today are being transferred to stand trial in adult court than in the past. It is important to note, however, that very few youth who are found guilty of homicide in the adult criminal justice system are sentenced to life in prison without parole and even fewer are sentenced to death. The reality is that whether juvenile or adult sanctions are imposed, many adolescent murderers will be eligible for release back into society. Will these individuals be better equipped to handle life stressors and to resolve conflicts peacefully when they return to the community months or years later? Or will they pose an even greater risk to the public after reentry?

Telling information may be found in follow-up data collected on 59 juveniles who were committed to the adult Department of Corrections in Florida for murder or attempted murder, or in a few cases for manslaughter, during the period January 1982 through January 1984. Although many of these adolescents received lengthy prison sentences, 43 (73%) had been released from prison at the time of the 15- to 17-year follow-up. Results indicated that 58% of the sample subjects released from prison had returned to prison, and most of those who failed did so within the first 3 years of release.

In recent years, governmental leaders and policymakers have displayed a heightened awareness of the need for effective treatment for violent youth. The Office of Juvenile Justice and Delinquency Prevention (OJJDP) maintains that effective programs for rehabilitating violent juvenile offenders must be developed. OJJDP's "Comprehensive Strategy for Serious, Violent, and Chronic Offenders" incorporates both prevention and intervention components in an effort to reduce juvenile delinquency and to manage juvenile crime more effectively. The experts who devised this initiative conceptualized an effective model for treating juvenile offenders as one combining accountability and sanctions with increasingly intensive treatment and rehabilitation.

—Kathleen M. Heide

See also GANGS; JUVENILE FIRESETTERS; JUVENILE KILLERS; PREVENTION OF CRIME AND VIOLENT BEHAVIOR; SCHOOL SHOOTINGS; VIOLENT FEMALE JUVENILE OFFENDERS

Further Reading

Coordinating Council on Juvenile Justice and Delinquency Prevention. (1996, March). *Combating violence and delinquency: The National Juvenile Justice Action Plan.* Washington, DC: U.S. Department of Justice, Office of Juvenile Justice and Delinquency Prevention.

Eddings v. Oklahoma, 102 S.Ct. 869 (1982).

Furman v. Georgia, 408 U.S. 238 (1972).

Gregg v. Georgia, 428 U.S. 153 (1976).

Heide, K. M. (1999). *Young killers: The challenge of juvenile homicide.* Thousand Oaks, CA: Sage.

Heide, K. M., & Solomon, E. P. (In press). Intervention issues and strategies with juvenile homicide offenders. In A. Roberts (Ed.), *Critical issues in criminal justice.* Thousand Oaks, CA: Sage.

Heide, K. M., Spencer, E., Thompson, A., & Solomon, E. P. (2001). Who's in, who's out, and who's back: Follow-up data on 59 juveniles incarcerated for murder or attempted murder in the early 1980s. *Behavioral Sciences and the Law, 19,* 97-108.

Lipsey, M. W., Wilson, D. B., & Cothern, L. (2002). *Effective intervention for serious juvenile offenders.* Washington, DC: U.S. Department of Justice, Office of Juvenile and Delinquency Prevention.

Martinson, R. (1974). What works—questions and answers about prison reform. *The Public Interest, 35,* 22-54.

Palmer, T. (1992). *The re-emergence of correctional interventions.* Newbury Park, CA: Sage.

Snyder, H. N. (2001). *Law enforcement and juvenile crime.* Washington, DC: U.S. Department of Justice, Office of Juvenile Justice and Delinquency Prevention.

Snyder, H. N., & Sickmund. (1999). *Juvenile offenders and victims: 1999 national report.* Washington, DC: U.S. Department of Justice, Office of Juvenile Justice and Delinquency Prevention.

Stanford v. Kentucky, 492 U.S. 361 (1989).

Streib, V. L. (2002). *The juvenile death penalty today: Death sentences and executions for juvenile crimes, January 1, 1973-December 31, 2001.* Retrieved June 3, 2002, from the World Wide Web at: www.law.onu.edu/faculty/streib/juvdeath.htm.

Thompson v. Oklahoma, 487 U.S. 815 (1988).

JUVENILE OFFENDERS

On April 20, 1999, 17-year-old Dylan Klebold and 18-year-old Eric Harris captured worldwide attention. The two boys, both white and from privileged socioeconomic backgrounds, went on a killing spree in their Littleton, Colorado, high school. Before they turned their guns on themselves and ended their lives, 13 people lay dead, and more than 20 others were wounded. They were not the first young killers to murder their classmates senselessly in recent years and, tragically, these boys were not the last ones to participate in acts of mass destruction.

Youth violence continues to dominate the daily newspapers and evening news in the 21st century. Mass shootings characterized by multiple victims, often randomly targeted, by unhappy, angry, and alienated children and adolescents using high-powered weaponry clearly represent the most extreme form of youth violence. Although there is some evidence that incidents of this nature are increasing, fortunately, they remain rare events involving little more than a dozen youth over the last 10 years. In contrast, the number of arrestees who are known to be under 18 years of age for one of the four types of violent crimes has increased since the mid-1980s, averaging almost 100,000 per year from 1991 to 2000. More specifically, across this 10-year period, on the average, 2,150 juveniles (defined as children under 18 years of age) were arrested for murder and nonnegligent manslaughter; 4,230 more for forcible rape; another 33,454 for robbery; and 56,863 others for aggravated assault.

PUTTING YOUTH VIOLENCE IN PERSPECTIVE

In November 1993, U.S. Attorney General Janet Reno characterized youth violence as the greatest crime problem facing the United States. Her assessment was based on an examination of all arrests reported to the FBI by police agencies across the United States for violent crimes since the mid-1980s. The former prosecutor's depiction shocked many, because arrest data had indicated that violent crime in the United States had been declining for several years. Reno wanted the American public to know that juvenile involvement in violent crime was increasing at an unprecedented pace during a time when the violent crime rate among adults had been decreasing.

The number of arrests of minors for violent crimes in the United States continued to soar through 1994, a year when juveniles accounted for close to 20% of the 645,000 people arrested for violent crime for whom age was known. During the next 6 years, the number of juveniles arrested for one of the violent crimes decreased each year. Many were quick to suggest that the tide of youth violence had subsided, after noting that the percentage of violent crime arrestees who were juveniles had decreased continuously from 19.4% in 1994 to 15.9% in 2000.

Examination of juvenile arrest data over a generation, however, clearly reveals that violent crime by those under 18 years of age remains a very serious problem in the United States. Over the 30-year period from 1967 to 1996, juvenile involvement in violent crime increased substantially. The increase is particularly apparent when juvenile arrests for violent crime are compared over the 30-year period in rates, which control for any changes in the population over the time frame.

The rise in violent crime by juveniles was seen among both boys and girls of varying ages. The number of boys per 100,000 arrested for violent crimes from 1967 to 1996 increased from 24 to 36 for boys under age 13; from 291 to 640 for ages 13 and 14; from 504 to 1,175 for 15-year-olds; from 689 to 1501 for 16-year-olds; and from 783 to 1721 for 17-year-olds. The rate for girls during this 30-year period increased from 3 to 7 for girls under age 13; from 43 to 159 for ages 13 and 14; from 52 to 249 for 15-year-olds; from 44 to 255 for 16-year-olds; and from 39 to 255 for 17-year-olds.

JUVENILE INVOLVEMENT IN FOUR TYPES OF VIOLENT CRIME

Information pertaining to juvenile involvement in each of the violent crime categories is encapsulated below. Special attention is focused on juvenile homicide because of the widespread fear experienced by the public due to reports of an escalation in killings by young people beginning in the mid-1980s. Data reported on the number of violent crime incidents are restricted to cases in which law enforcement provided data to the FBI on the offenders arrested for these offenses. Characteristics of those arrested (gender, race, and location of arrest) are typically based on the average figures computed by the author using data published by the FBI over the most recently available 10-year period, from 1991 to 2000. Mean (average) data are provided rather than statistics for 1 year, because 1-year data may be unstable and not truly representative of the phenomena under investigation. References are made occasionally to crime statistics in the mid-1980s, to call attention to trends or differences that become apparent when the analysis is extended to include the years when juvenile violence began to increase.

Juvenile Involvement in Homicide

Murder and nonnegligent manslaughter are defined by the FBI in the Uniform Crime Reporting System as "the willful (nonnegligent) killing of one human being by another." Although it is difficult to assess the exact number of murders committed by juveniles because the age of the killer is not known or specified by the arresting authority in as many as a third of the cases, there is no question from available data that murders by young people have risen over the last two decades.

Analysis of crime patterns clearly indicates that youth involvement in homicide remains a serious problem in the United States in the 21st century. Homicide arrests of juveniles rose every year from 1984 through 1993. The increase in killings by young people during these 10 years was felt across the 50 states. The dramatic escalation in murders by juveniles during this time frame put the United States in the grips of fear. In 1993, the number of juveniles arrested for murder, 3,284, was 3 times higher than the number arrested in 1984 and had reached an all-time high. The rate at which juveniles were arrested for murder also increased substantially during this time frame. The juvenile murder rate peaked in 1993, at 14 per 100,000, and was more than twice the level of the early 1980s (6 per 100,000). The significant rise in murders committed by those under 18 years of age during this time frame cannot be attributed to an increase in the juvenile population during this period. In fact, the percentage of young Americans during this time frame had generally been declining.

Although the number of minors arrested for murder decreased over the period 1994 through 2000, it would be wrong to conclude that the crisis in lethal violence by youth is over. The percentage of all homicide arrests involving juveniles in 2000, after 7 years of decline, is still higher than it was in 1984 when juvenile homicide was just beginning to increase. In 1984, 7.3% of all homicide arrestees were juveniles; in 2000, 9.3% of those arrested for murder were less than 18 years of age. The mean percentage of homicide arrestees who were juveniles during the 10-year period of escalation (1984-1993) was 11.6%; the comparable mean percentage during the 7-year period of decline (1994-2000) was 13.0%. Across the most recent 10-year period (1991-2000) of all homicide arrestees, approximately 1 of 7 (13.6%) were under the age of 18.

Two recently released government reports concluded that despite the decreasing trends, the storm of youth homicide and youth violence has not abated. The U.S. Surgeon General made the following observations in a January 2001 report on youth violence (Satcher, 2001):

Since 1993, when the epidemic peaked, youth violence has declined significantly nationwide, as signaled by downward trends in arrest records, victimization data, and hospital emergency room records. But the problem has not been resolved. Another key indicator of youth violence—youths' confidential reports about their violence behavior—reveals no change since 1993 in the proportion of young people who have committed physically injurious and potentially lethal acts.

In a March 2000 report, the Bureau of Justice Statistics (Snyder, 2001) noted that "Despite the encouraging improvement since 1993, the levels of gun homicide by juveniles and young adults are well above those of the mid-1980's" and "the levels of youth homicide remain well above those of the early and mid-1980's" (p. 1). The report of the U.S. Surgeon General ended with the following warning (Satcher, 2001):

This is no time for complacency. The epidemic of lethal violence that swept the United States from 1983 to 1993 was funneled in large part by easy access to weapons, notably firearms. If the sizable numbers of youth still involved in violence today begin carrying and using weapons as they did a decade ago, this country may see a resurgence of the lethal violence that characterized the violence epidemic.

Increases in juveniles committing murder have been seen across cities, suburban, and rural areas. In U.S. cities during the last 10 years, however, juvenile involvement in homicide has remained an especially serious problem. Over the period 1991 to 2000, on the average, about 1 of every 7 homicide arrests in cities involved a juvenile. The figures for suburban and rural areas were about 1 out of 10 and 1 out of 13, respectively.

Perusal of arrest data since the mid-1980s reveals that juvenile homicide is still very much a male phenomenon. On the average, boys have accounted for 93% of juveniles arrested for murder, whether examined over the period 1991 to 2000 or 1984 to 2000. Some gender patterns are discernible since the mid-1980s and need to be watched over the next few years. The percentage of girls among juveniles arrested for

homicide showed a generally decreasing trend from 1984 through 1991. In 1984, females composed 10% of all juvenile homicide arrests; in 1991, they comprised less than 5%. Since 1992, the representation of girls among juvenile homicide arrestees has shown a generally increasing trend and reached a high of 11.3% in 2000.

The involvement of African Americans in juvenile homicide is disproportionately high, regardless of which time frame is under consideration. From 1991 to 2000, the average percentages of Caucasian and African American juvenile homicide arrestees were 41.6% and 55.7%, respectively (the remaining mean percentage, 2.8%, consisted of Asians, Pacific Islanders, Native Americans, and Native Alaskans). These statistics are quite alarming when one considers that African Americans comprised about 14% of the U.S. juvenile population during this period. Perusal of the data since 1984 reveals some interesting patterns. From 1984 through 1993, the involvement of blacks in juvenile homicide showed an increasing trend, from 45.2 to 62.3%. From 1994 to 2000, in contrast, the proportionate involvement of black youth decreased to 49.8% of all juvenile homicide arrests.

Juvenile Involvement in Forcible Rape

The Uniform Crime Reporting System defines forcible rape as "the carnal knowledge of a female forcibly and against her will. Assaults or attempts to commit rape by force or threat of force are also included." Increases in juvenile involvement in forcible rape, although not as dramatic as homicide, have been discernible since the mid-1980s. Over the period 1991 to 2000, juveniles comprised an average of 16.5% of those arrested for forcible rape. This figure was slightly higher than the percentage of juveniles arrested for rape in 1984 (15.5%), when the escalation in violent crimes by juveniles was beginning. Over the 17-year period, the proportion of rape arrests that involved juveniles ranged from a low of 14.5% in 1988 to a high of 17.2 in 1998.

Arrests of juveniles for rape were most common in the cities, followed by suburban and rural areas. Over the period 1991 to 2000, approximately 1 out of 6 rape arrestees in the cities was a juvenile. Juveniles comprised about 1 out of 7 arrests for forcible rape in suburban areas and 1 out of 8 in rural areas. The proportionate involvement of juveniles in rape arrests since 1984 has shown a noticeably increasing trend in rural areas, but not in city and suburban areas. Juvenile involvement in arrests for forcible rapes in rural areas rose from 8.5% in 1984 to 14.5% in 2000. Juvenile arrests in suburban and urban areas fluctuated over the 17-year period, differing very little from the beginning to the end of the period. Juveniles comprised 13.4% of total arrests for forcible rape in suburban areas in 1984 and 13.0% in 2000. In the cities, youth under 18 years of age made up 16.8% of forcible rape arrests in 1984 and 17.4% in 2000.

Not surprisingly, given the definition of forcible rape, arrests of juveniles for rape were almost exclusively male. The proportion of girls among juvenile rape arrestees ranged from a low of 1.2% in 2000 to a high of 2.3% in 1989. On the average, 1.8% of juvenile rape arrestees from 1991 through 2000 were females. During this 10-year period, the number of juveniles arrested for forcible rape averaged 4,230 per year; on the average, 77 of these arrestees each year were girls.

As in the case of homicide, African American youth were overrepresented in arrests for forcible rape. Of juveniles arrested for rape from 1991 to 2000, 56.8% were Caucasian, 41.4% were African American, and 1.7% were other races. Close inspection of the data indicate, however, that the percentage involvement of African American youth in rape arrests has shown a decreasing trend since the mid- to late 1980s. In 1984, for example, African Americans represented 53.8% of juveniles arrested for forcible rape; in 2000, the comparable percentage was 35.4.

Juvenile Involvement in Robbery

The FBI defines robbery as "the taking or attempting to take anything of value from the care, custody, or control of a person or persons by force or threat of force or violence and/or by putting the victim in fear." From 1991 to 2000, juveniles comprised 28.4% of robbery arrestees. Close inspection of the data reveals that juvenile arrests for robbery showed a decreasing trend from the mid- to the late 1980s and an increasing trend from the late 1980s through the mid-1990s. By 1995, nearly 1 out of 3 arrests for robbery involved a juvenile. Since 1996, the proportionate involvement of juveniles among robbery arrestees has decreased from 32.1%, to 25.3% in 2000. In 2000, approximately one fourth of robbery arrests involved juveniles, the same pattern observed in 1984 and 1985.

Like homicide and rape, the proportion of all arrests for robbery involving juveniles was highest in the cities, followed by suburban and rural areas. On the average, from 1991 to 2000, juveniles comprised 29.1% of those arrested for robbery in the cities. They constituted 24.7% of those arrested in the suburbs and 16.8 of arrestees in rural areas. Close observation of the data reveals that although the percentage of juvenile involvement in robbery arrests has decreased since the mid-1990s, the proportionate involvement of juveniles in arrests in suburban and rural areas remains noticeably higher than it was in 1984. In 1984, juveniles comprised 9% of all robbery arrests in rural areas; in 2000, they comprised 15.0%. Arrests of minors for robbery in suburban areas rose from 16.7% in 1984 to 21.9% in 2000. In contrast, little change is apparent in the cities, where youth under 18 years of age comprised 27.3% of robbery arrests in 1984 and 26% in 2000.

More than 90% of juveniles arrested during the period from 1984 through 2000 for robbery were boys. The data indicate, however, that girls have become more involved in robbery since the mid-1980s. In 1984, for example, female juveniles comprised 6.4% of all juvenile robbery arrests. Over the period 1991 to 2000, 9.0% of juvenile homicide arrestees were girls.

Juveniles arrested for robbery were disproportionately African American. From 1991 to 2000, black youth comprised 58.2% of juveniles arrested for robbery. Caucasians comprised 39.6%, and other races comprised the remaining 2.2%. Interestingly, close inspection of juvenile arrests for robbery, similar to those for rape, indicates that the proportion of black youth arrested for robbery has shown a decreasing trend since the mid-1980s. The percentage of juveniles arrested for robbery who were African American was highest at 68.5% in 1984 and lowest in 1998 and 1999, at 54.4%.

Juvenile Involvement in Aggravated Assault

Aggravated assault is defined as "an unlawful attack by one person upon another for the purpose of inflicting severe or aggravated bodily injury." Weapons and other means likely to cause death or serious bodily harm are typically associated with this type of assault. Attempts are included regardless of whether physical injury actually occurred. From 1991 to 2000, juveniles comprised 14.6% of aggravated assault arrestees. Although there are fluctuations in the data, it is interesting to note that the proportionate involvement of juveniles among aggravated assault arrestees was not much different in 2000 than in 1984. In 1984, juveniles comprised 13.4% of those arrested for aggravated assault; in 2000, they comprised 13.9%.

Juvenile arrests for aggravated assault, as for the other violent crimes, were highest in the cities, followed by suburban and rural areas. From 1991 to 2000, juveniles comprised 1 out of 7 arrests in the city, 1 of 8 arrests in suburbia, and 1 of 10 arrests in rural areas. Perusal of the data reveals an increasing trend in the proportionate involvement of youth in aggravated assaults in rural areas over time. Juvenile arrests rose from 6.6% in 1984 to 10.4% of all aggravated assault arrests in rural areas in 2000. In contrast, the proportionate involvement of juveniles in aggravated assaults from 1984 to 2000 remained fairly stable in the cities (14.4% vs. 14.5%) and suburban areas (12.7% vs. 12.3%).

The percentage involvement of girls among aggravated assault arrestees over the 10-year period was higher than those for any of the other three violent crimes. On the average, girls comprised 19.7% of juveniles arrested for aggravated assault from 1991 to 2000. An increasing trend in the proportionate involvement of girls in aggravated assault is clearly apparent in arrest data throughout the 1990s. In 1989, the arrests of girls for aggravated assault were at their lowest, at 14.8%. After 11 years of increasing involvement, the percentages of girls arrested in 2000 reached a high of 23.4% of all juvenile arrests for aggravated assault. Since the mid- to late 1990s, more than one fifth of all juveniles arrested for aggravated assault have been girls.

Among juveniles arrested for aggravated assault from 1991 to 2000, African American youth were disproportionately represented at approximately 39.7%. Caucasians comprised 58.1%, and other races comprised the remaining 2.3%. Interestingly, close inspection of juvenile arrests for aggravated assaults indicates that the proportion of black youth arrested for aggravated assault has shown a generally decreasing trend since the late 1980s. This decreasing trend in the proportionate involvement of black youth in aggravated assaults occurred in approximately the same time frame as their reduced involvement in arrests for rape and robbery. The percentage of African American juveniles arrested for aggravated assault was highest (45.6%) in 1988 and lowest in 1999 (35.2%).

CONCLUDING REMARKS

This analysis has shown that despite overall decreases in juvenile involvement in violent crimes in recent years, violent juvenile offending remains a serious concern. Four pressing issues stand out in the 21st century. First, although the percentage involvement of African American youth in violent crimes has decreased in all four violent crimes, it remains disproportionately high. Second, the increasing involvement of girls among aggravated assault arrestees suggests that more girls are choosing maladaptive coping strategies than in past generations. It is apparent that teaching healthier ways of dealing with conflict and stress must be directed to girls, as well as to boys. Third, the consistently higher involvement of youth among all four types of violent crime arrestees in cities indicates that society needs to do more in building a sense of community for these children, helping them grow up to be good citizens and moral members of society. Fourth, the noticeably increasing involvement of youth in rural areas in rape, robbery, and aggravated assault is indicative of a further breakdown in the transmission of values in the American culture.

Professionals, politicians, and the public must accept that reducing youth violence in the United States is a difficult task. Realistically speaking, neutralizing or eliminating the factors that contribute to young people becoming involved in violent incidents may take a generation or more to achieve. No single entity or segment of society can stem the tide of youth destructiveness alone. Parents, the educational system, the community, government leaders, the nation, and the media must join together to raise a healthier next generation and to build a more peaceful society.

—Kathleen M. Heide

See also Juvenile Firesetters; Juvenile Killers; Prevention of Crime and Violent Behavior; School Shootings; Violent Female Juvenile Offenders

Further Reading

Federal Bureau of Investigation. (1985-2001). *Crime in the United States (1984-2000)*. Washington, DC: U.S. Government Printing Office.

Fox, J. A. (1996). *Trends in juvenile violence*. Washington, DC: U.S. Department of Justice, Bureau of Justice Statistics.

Fox, J. A., & Zawitz, M. W. (2000). *Homicide trends in the United States: 1998.* Washington, DC: U.S. Department of Justice, Bureau of Justice Statistics.

Heide, K. M. (1999). *Young killers.* Thousand Oaks, CA: Sage.

Satcher, D. (2001). *Youth violence: A report of the surgeon general.* Washington, DC: Government Printing Office. Available on the World Wide Web at: www.surgeon-general.gov/library/youthviolence/report.html.

Sickmund, M., Snyder, H. N., & Poe-Yamagata, E. (1997). *Juvenile offenders and victims: 1997 update on violence.* Washington, DC: U.S. Department of Justice, Office of Juvenile Justice and Delinquency Prevention.

Snyder, H. N. (2001). *Law enforcement and juvenile crime.* Washington, DC: U.S. Department of Justice, Office of Juvenile Justice and Delinquency Prevention.

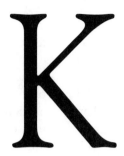

THEODORE KACZYNSKI

Starting out as an apparent terrorist bombing, the Unabomber case became the longest (nearly 18 years), largest, and most expensive manhunt in American history. Between 1978 and 1996, the Unabomber attracted worldwide attention, becoming the subject of radio talk shows, television documentaries, and hundreds of newspaper articles. A $1 million reward was offered for information leading to the arrest of the elusive killer. Code-named "UNABOMBER" because of the universities and airlines he targeted in his earlier bombings, the elusive offender rose from relatively obscure criminal status to national recognition. In all, the Unabomber killed three persons (two in California and one in New Jersey) and injured 23 others, his attacks spanning nine states. Several victims were university professors or people directly related to technology.

By 1996, more than 100 agents from the FBI, the U.S. Postal Service, and the Bureau of Alcohol, Tobacco, and Firearms were working together as the Unabomber Task Force, with the assistance of local and state law enforcement. This was the third and largest such task force to be assembled in history. After staging his first attack in Chicago in 1978, the Unabomber appeared to relocate and was thought to be living in northern California, possibly near Sacramento or San Francisco. Eight of the 16 bombings occurred either in northern California or from bombs mailed from that area. Starting in 1993, all his letters and bombs had been mailed from the San Francisco Bay area. The following list chronicles the Unabomber attacks.

Location	Date	No. of Victims
University of Illinois at Chicago, IL	5/25/78	1 injured
Northwestern University, Evanston, IL	5/9/79	1 injured
American Airlines Flight 444, Chicago, IL	11/15/79	12 injured
President, United Airlines, Chicago, IL	6/10/80	1 injured
University of Utah, Salt Lake City, UT	10/8/81	0
Vanderbilt University, Nashville, TN	5/5/82	1 injured
University of California, Berkeley, CA	7/2/82	1 injured
Boeing Aircraft, Auburn, WA	5/8/85	0
University of California, Berkeley, CA	5/15/85	1 injured
University of Michigan, Ann Arbor, MI	11/15/85	2 injured
Rentech Company, Sacramento, CA	12/11/85	1 death
CAAM's Inc., Salt Lake City, UT	2/20/87	1 injured
Physician/researcher, Tiburon, CA	6/22/93	1 injured
Yale University, New Haven, CT	6/24/93	1 injured
Advertising executive, North Caldwell, NJ	12/9/94	1 death
Timber lobbyist, Sacramento, CA	4/24/95	1 death

Several physical and psychological profiles were constructed around the Unabomber. The task force believed, for example, that he was a white male, probably in his early to mid- to late forties. He was seen once in 1987 by a secretary as he hand-delivered a bomb. Only in the latter years of his criminal career did the Unabomber begin to communicate with the public. He increasingly expressed his disdain for law enforcement, while at the same time appearing to enjoy taunting and challenging them. Although such occurrences are rare, some serial killers, such as the Unabomber and the "Zodiac Killer," from San Francisco, have enjoyed matching wits with law enforcement.

The Unabomber had a history of sending bombs and then remaining silent for periods of time. One hiatus lasted 6 years. His bomb-making skills improved markedly in sophistication. The devices were pipe bombs with antimovement or antiopening firing switches. He evolved from using smokeless powders to a mixture of ammonium nitrate and aluminum powder and took time to handcraft his devices, using wood and metal components.

The bomber claimed to be part of a clandestine organization called the "Freedom Club." He signed his letters with the initials "FC" and also carefully inscribed "FC" on his bombs. In 1995, he mailed a 35,000-word "manifesto" to the *Washington Post* and *New York Times,* threatening that if his work wasn't published, the bombings would continue. The manifesto was a redundant diatribe of denunciations against technology, advocating the dismantling of industrial technology and the redistribution of human society. The author stated that the evils of technology would eventually destroy our society and he felt it was his role to bring public attention to the pending doom. He believed that killing a few people to get the public's attention was completely justifiable. The task force, along with the media, faced a difficult dilemma: Should they choose not to be held hostage by this killer and run the risk of another attack, or submit to his demands in order to perhaps save lives and avoid another bombing? To spare another attack and in hopes that someone in the community might recognize the writing, the *Washington Post* published the manifesto. The manifesto was also made available on the Internet.

Investigations focused on several individuals, including a sailor, a handyman, and a career criminal, but they all were eliminated as suspects. Some investigators speculated that James William Kilgore, a fugitive with ties to the Symbionese Liberation Army who had gone underground after a bombing incident in 1976, could have been the Unabomber. Other investigators dismissed Kilgore as a viable suspect and looked for new leads in the investigation. For example, they looked into possible religious connections and the Unabomber's frequent usage of biblical names. Investigators also examined commonalties between the bombings and specific people involved in the technology of developing prosthetic devices.

The final suspect in this profile was Theodore Kaczynski. Federal agents near Lincoln, Montana, arrested him in 1996. His brother had read the manifesto and noticed striking similarities between some letters written by his brother and the manuscript. Kaczynski was living a hermit's life in a 10- by 12-feet shack without electricity or plumbing. Inside, investigators found letters and diaries connected to the bombings and various materials used in bomb construction. There were several detailed blueprints for bomb making, a partially completed bomb, and a completed bomb that had been packaged and partially addressed. Also found were a list of potential victims; typewriters, one of which appeared to be the one used to type the manifesto; clothing similar to that worn when the Unabomber was seen delivering a bomb in Salt Lake City; and possibly the original manifesto manuscript.

Born in 1942, Ted Kaczynski proved to be very intelligent, graduating 2 years early from high school. At age 16, he started his university studies at Harvard on a scholarship. Throughout his formal education, Ted was perceived by others to be a loner who shunned potential friends. In 1967, he earned a doctorate in math from the University of Michigan and began teaching that same year as an assistant professor at the University of California, Berkeley. Three semesters later, he suddenly resigned from his position and began living a transient lifestyle. He relocated to Montana and also spent time working odd jobs in Utah. In 1978, shortly after the first attack by the Unabomber, his brother David hired him to work in a foam rubber manufacturing company. He tried dating a female coworker, but after two dates she ended the relationship. In response, Ted retaliated by posting limericks about her around the office. When confronted by his brother about the harassment incidents, Ted became angry and was fired as a result. After that, he returned used the evils of technology as a justification for his personal agenda, promoting his own self-interests, frustrations, sense of rejection, and anger. His desire to return to a pristine lifestyle appeared to cover a more systemic motivation. He rewrote history to rationalize his behavior, wanting people to see him not as a terrorist, but as one who cared for the welfare of society. In fact, the Unabomber appeared to care for no one but himself. Though he was an intelligent man, he often engaged in jobs requiring little of his intellect. He was more of a thinker than a doer—the only things he ever completed were his bombs, an entirely self-centered task. It became apparent that Ted Kaczynski, a man of rationalization and unconscious pretense, appeared to "fit" the Unabomber profile.

Kaczynski's need to validate his life may have driven him to seek the limelight. He did not appreciate being "upstaged" by other criminals. For example, at the time of the World Trade Center explosion in February 1993, he had been inactive for over 6 years. Just over 4 months after the blast, Kaczynski struck again, twice. His message was very clear: "You may be able to catch those amateurs, but I am still here, after all these years." Then, on April 19, 1995, terrorists struck the Federal Building in Oklahoma City, killing nearly 170 people. A few days later, a timber lobbyist in Sacramento, California, became the third murder victim of the Unabomber.

Ted Kaczynski's self-pity drove him to envy. In addition to his drive for recognition, he also found pleasure in depriving others of their talents, skills, and livelihoods, sending devices that would blow off their fingers, hands, faces, or destroy their eyesight. Unable to achieve the successes and attention earned by real scientists and scholars, he did not want them to have the rewards, either. He rejected technology because he perceived that technology had rejected him. In truth, Kaczynski appears to be a man of many contradictions, frustrations, and self-deceptions. Ultimately, though, he is nothing more than an innovative serial killer.

The trial was relatively brief. Kaczynski was found to be guilty, but a paranoid schizophrenic, and was sent to federal prison with no possibility of parole. There, he continues his reclusiveness in the confines of his small prison cell and vehemently insists that he is neither schizophrenic nor insane in any way. His notoriety influenced a few living on the fringes of society to emulate him. Regardless of the eccentric

Ted Kaczynski, a serial bomber known as the "Unabomber" and author of the *Manifesto,* was hunted by state and federal law enforcement for 18 years. His obsessive need for attention drove him to create increasingly powerful bombs that killed 3 and seriously injured 26 others. He now resides in a federal prison in Colorado.

Source: Copyright © Reuters NewMedia Inc. / CORBIS.

to Montana and became more reclusive. In 1990, his father, dying of cancer, committed suicide. Ted did not attend the funeral.

Kaczynski appeared to have harbored much resentment against his family and society in general. He sent a letter to his mother referring to her as a "dog" because of his inability to form lasting relationships. His brother David, with whom he had been close in younger years, married and began a career. In many respects, Ted appeared to perceive himself as having being rejected or abandoned by those supposedly closest to him. His reclusive lifestyle may well have exacerbated a growing sense of paranoia about people and society.

According to a profile developed during the investigation, The Unabomber was a man of low self-esteem who thrived on the notoriety he achieved. He nature of the messenger, the message that Kaczynski was sending appeals to many who feel they cannot compete or be comfortable in a society that is so dominated by fast-paced technology.

—*Eric W. Hickey*

NOTE: Portions of this profile were previously published in Eric Hickey's *Serial Murderers and Their Victims*, 2002, 3rd ed. Belmont, CA: Wadsworth Publishers.

See also McVeigh, Timothy; Not Guilty by Reason of Insanity (NGRI); Oklahoma City Bombing; Terrorism; Zodiac Killer

KENNEDY, PRESIDENT JOHN, *See* Assassins

JACK KEVORKIAN

In the summer of 1989, an unknown and disenfranchised doctor created a machine that would assist ill patients in ending their lives. The machine began by intravenous delivery of a saline solution into the patient's body. Then, when the patient pushed a button, the saline stopped, and thiopental, which put the patient into a coma, was delivered for 60 seconds. When the thiopental ran out, a lethal dose of potassium chloride was delivered. The machine was called "Thanatron" by the doctor, which is Greek for "death machine." Although the doctor, Jack Kevorkian, continually ran ads in the paper to solicit "customers," his death machine went unused until the following summer.

On November 13, 1989, Ronald Adkins of Portland, Oregon, who read an article about Jack Kevorkian, called the doctor for a consultation. Mr. Adkins's wife, Janet, was only 54 years of age and was suffering from Alzheimer's disease. On June 4, 1990, Mrs. Adkins was the first person to die with the assistance of Dr. Kevorkian. Using the "suicide machine" designed by Kevorkian, Janet Adkins died from lethal injection. Over the next 9 years, Jack Kevorkian assisted many other patients in ending their lives.

Thomas Youk of Waterford, Michigan, was 52 years of age and suffered from amyotrophic lateral sclerosis, a condition in which the person experiences severe muscle spasms and atrophy. In 1998, Mr. Youk had a consultation with Dr. Kevorkian, and on September 17, 1998, with the assistance of the doctor, he died from lethal injection. This was Kevorkian's 105th assisted suicide, and the 10th since he reported that he would ignore state laws banning assisted suicide. Days after the death of Thomas Youk, Kevorkian was accused of first-degree murder and assisted suicide. On November 11, 1998, *60 Minutes* aired a video recording on national television of Kevorkian assisting in Youk's death. The doctor, acting as his own attorney, was found guilty of second-degree murder and delivery of a controlled substance on March 26, 1999, and in April was sentenced to 10 to 25 years in prison with the possibility of parole after serving 6 years.

Kevorkian, whose medical training was in pathology, had always been interested in death and dying. He received the nickname "Dr. Death" during his residency at Detroit Receiving Hospital. Although his interest in death resulted in rejection from the medical community, he spent many years of his life writing research proposals on research with corpses. Kevorkian had developed the belief early in his training as a doctor that doctor-assisted euthanasia is always ethical and acceptable. His strong belief in the ethics of doctor-assisted euthanasia became evident much later in his life.

On June 4, 1990, Dr. Kevorkian performed his first assisted suicide. Even once incarcerated, he continued to be passionate about his belief in the practice and fasted for nearly 4 weeks after his conviction. Despite Kevorkian's belief that he was assisting the ill and acting both ethically and compassionately, his beliefs were not accepted by the general medical community or the general public. After he was sentenced to prison, members of an organization named "Not Dead Yet" were pleased with the jury's verdict, indicating that they believed that Dr. Kevorkian was a serial murderer.

—*Laura Hamon*

See also Euthanasia; Motives for Murder; Suicide

Further Reading

Belluck, P. (1999). Kevorkian stumbles in his self-defense. Available on the World Wide Web at: http://query. nytimes.com/search/abstract?

Dr. Jack Kevorkian (shown here on the right), also known as "Dr. Death" and the "Suicide Doctor," is a Michigan physician whose "suicide machine" was used by several patients to end their lives. Highly controversial, Dr. Kevorkian assisted not only those who were dying but also some patients who felt they no longer wanted to live.

Source: Copyright © CORBIS.

Chronology of Events Involving Dr. Jack Kevorkian. (1996). *The Detroit News.* Available on the World Wide Web at: http://www.detnews.com/TDNHOME/ kevork. htm.

Clark, N. (1997). *The politics of physician assisted suicide.* New York: Garland.

McLean, S., & Britton, A. (1997). *The case for physician assisted suicide.* San Francisco: HarperCollins.

KIDNAPPING

Kidnapping is broadly defined as the taking and holding of another person against their will. The term *kidnap* comes from the slang terms *kid,* for "child," and *nab,* which means "to steal." Kidnapping used to apply only to child abductions but is now used to describe abductions of both children and adults. The legal definition of kidnapping differs depending on state statutes, federal law, or a foreign jurisdiction's legal code. Kidnapping may involve a demand for ransom (holding a person against his or her will until financial, political, social, or ideological demands are met), the use of force or fraud, or relatives or nonfamily members. From the present day to the past, the crime affects everyone equally, from slaves to kings, infants to adults, and the politically oppressed to the politically powerful. Anyone can be a victim of kidnapping.

Researchers and educators commonly categorize kidnapping into two groups: parental kidnapping and nonparental kidnapping. *Parental kidnapping* is the removal or retention of a child by a parent without regard for the parental rights of the other parent. Typically, these cases involve one parent taking the child when the other has lawful custody or primary visitation of the child. *Nonparental kidnapping* may involve strangers, but generally the victim and offender know each other. Victims of nonparental kidnapping often face increased danger, such as homicide and sexual assault. Although nonparental kidnapping cases receive the most media attention, they are much less frequent than parental kidnapping cases.

EARLY FORMS OF KIDNAPPING

Slavery is an early form of kidnapping. Free peoples were often kidnapped and sold into the slave trade. In Roman times, conquered nations were required to supply the Roman army with soldiers, and that was accomplished through kidnapping and enslavement. During the Middle Ages, kings and other nobility were frequently ransomed after losing battles and wars. Hostage taking is a modern form of mass kidnapping. During the 1500 to 1800s, sailors from one country were often kidnapped and forced to be sailors for other countries. This practice was called being *shanghaied* or *impressed into service* for other governments.

KIDNAPPING IN AMERICA

Early in the 20th century, kidnapping for ransom gained notoriety in America. In 1932, the son of Charles Lindbergh was kidnapped and held for ransom. This event led to the passing of the "Lindbergh Law," which focused on kidnapping across state lines and made it a federal offense punishable by death. The law was later amended in 1956 to allow the FBI to investigate any kidnapping after 24 hours, even within state lines.

Another widely publicized kidnapping occurred on February 4, 1974, with the kidnapping of Patty Hearst, heir to the Hearst fortune, by the Symbionese Liberation Army (SLA). This kidnapping marked the first time in modern American history that someone had been kidnapped for political purposes. The SLA wanted the release of two of its members from prison, as well as money from Hearst's parents. She became the victim of *Stockholm syndrome,* which occurs when the kidnapped victim becomes sympathetic to or begins to identify with his or her kidnappers or their ideology. Hearst was later convicted of bank robbery and served a short time in prison before having her sentence commuted by President Carter.

In America, the primary federal law that addresses kidnapping is 18 USC 55, Sections 1201 (Kidnapping), 1202 (Ransom Money), 1203 (Hostage Taking), and 1204 (International Parental Kidnapping). Life in prison or death is the sentence for a conviction, depending on aggravating circumstances set out in Title 18. The FBI is the agency that has jurisdiction for violations of 18 USC 55.

Historically, kidnapping has not been included in the federal database that tracks statistics for violent crimes. In 1988, a new system was created that included kidnapping. However, as of June of 2000, only 17 states have been reporting kidnapping statistics. Because of this lack of record keeping, there is not a clear picture of the number of kidnapping cases. Even under the new system, kidnapping is tracked only by two categories: family kidnapping and non-family kidnapping. These categories severely limit and disguise the true number of kidnapping cases. Many cases of kidnapping are misclassified as other crimes, such as sexual assault, fraud, homicide, and robbery.

KIDNAPPING AROUND THE WORLD

One of the most recent notable kidnappings did not take place in America, but happened to an American citizen in Pakistan. During America's war on terrorism after the September 11, 2001, attacks on the World Trade Center and the Pentagon, the kidnapping of journalist Daniel Pearl in Pakistan marked the first time in modern history that a kidnapping occurred solely for terrorist purposes. Daniel Pearl was not held for ransom or to make a political statement—he was brutally slaughtered by his barbarous, inhumane captors who called themselves the "National Movement for the Restoration of Pakistani Sovereignty."

Other hotspots of international kidnapping activity include the Philippines and Colombia. In the Philippines, the Abu Sayyaf and Moro Islamic Liberation Front (MILF) are active terrorist organizations responsible for widespread kidnappings and terrorist activities. By the mid-1990s, there were more than 100 kidnappings per year, and the numbers continue to grow. These organizations seek to ransom their captives to further support their terrorist activities and to put political pressure on nations to release members and supporters from imprisonment.

In Colombia, the Revolutionary Armed Forces of Colombia (FARC) have been supporting their leftist ideology by pursing a program of systematic kidnapping of Colombian citizens and law enforcement personnel. As a result, Colombia has the highest rate of kidnappings in the world with up to 5,000 incidents a year. Most involve foreign nationals in Colombia, in which company employees are sold back to their companies for profit by terrorist groups.

INTERNATIONAL PARENTAL KIDNAPPING

International parental kidnapping involves the unlawful taking of a child or retaining a child in a foreign country and is a growing problem. An increasing number of countries have attempted to address this concern by signing the Hague Convention. The Hague Convention on the Civil Aspects of International Child Abduction creates a uniform civil litigation process for the return of a child to those countries that have joined the organization. The United States and at least 50 other countries have ratified the Hague Convention. If the child was taken to a country that has not joined the Convention, the civil law of that county will determine the remedy for returning the child. Parents whose children have been taken to a foreign country that hasn't signed the Convention are likely to face many more legal complexities and substantial financial burden in trying to get them back.

In 1998, the American government reported 1,100 active "outgoing" cases of international parental kidnapping, with 503 new cases added in 1998 alone. Outgoing cases involve the kidnapping of children from the United States to foreign countries. Half of those 1,100 cases involve the kidnapping of children to countries that are parties to the Hague Convention. There were 241 "incoming" Hague Convention cases in 1998, in which children were taken into the United States from their home countries. These figures do not included unreported cases (U.S. Department of Justice, 1999).

—Tawnya Tangel Eller and Bill Eller

See also DEATH PENALTY; HOSTAGE TAKING; TERRORISM; STOCKHOLM SYNDROME; WHITE SLAVERY

Further Reading

Auerbach, A. H. (1998). *Ransom: The untold story of international kidnapping* (1st ed.). New York: Henry Hold.

Chiancone, J., Girdner, L., & Hoff, P. (2001). *Issues in resolving cases of international child abduction by parents.* Washington, DC: U.S. Department of Justice, OJJDP Bulletin (NCJ 190105).

Finkelhor, D., & Ormrod, R. (2000). *Kidnapping of juveniles: Patterns from NIBRS.* Washington, DC: U.S. Department of Justice, OJJDP Bulletin (NCJ 181161).

U.S. Department of Justice. (1999). *A report to the attorney general on international parental kidnapping.* Washington, DC: Author, OJJDP Report (NCJ 189382).

KING, RODNEY, *See* POLICE BRUTALITY

KIPLAND (KIP) KINKEL

On May 21, 1998, Faith and Bill Kinkel were found dead. Both bodies were covered in sheets. Faith had five bullet wounds in the head and one in the chest, and Bill had one bullet wound in his head. That same day, the perpetrator was discovered after the couple's son, Kip, age 15, entered the cafeteria in Thurston High School, Springfield, Oregon, with 50 rounds of ammunition and opened fire. Twenty-five students were wounded and two were killed. On his way to the cafeteria, Kip saw his best friend and warned him to stay away from the area.

At the crime scene in the Kinkels' home, an investigator found a letter written by Kip just after he'd committed the murders of his parents. In the letter, he wrote, "I am a horrible son. I wish I had been aborted. I destroy everything I touch . . . my head just doesn't work right. God damn these voices inside my head." The investigator also found a recently used cereal bowl, a newspaper that appeared to have been read by Kip, and a journal Kip had kept. Although Kip reported auditory hallucinations that instructed him to kill, there was evidence that he had attempted to clean the crime scene, sat down and had a bowl of cereal, and read the paper, all unusual acts for someone who had killed in a psychotic frenzy.

To the general public, Kip's family appeared to be loving and stable. His father and mother had both been high school Spanish teachers and were respected in the community. Kip's older sister, Kristen, who was attending the University of Hawaii when the murders were committed, reported an average childhood in which she and Kip were involved in various activities and had regular family dinners. However, she also indicated that Kip had a strained relationship with his father and that he had always struggled academically.

As researchers continued to search for what would cause a good child to commit murder, they discovered that Kip had been troubled since childhood. Friends reported that they had quit playing with Kip after elementary school because he continually talked about violence and torture. He had even acted on some of his violent thoughts by torturing animals. The boy had attended counseling for his anger and according to his psychologist had admitted to setting off explosives to calm himself. Kip was also taking an antidepressant, which appeared to help with his depression. Other reports indicate that even the family's housekeeper was frightened by the boy, and 8 months before the murders, she had stopped working for the Kinkels for that reason. However, despite Kip's apparent anger and constant talk of destruction, his father had bought him a 9mm Glock semiautomatic pistol. There were other signs of emotional disturbance as well, such as the explosives he had hidden under the front porch. In an interview with a psychologist after the murders, Kip said that he had hidden them out of fear that the Chinese were going to invade America.

Although Kip Kinkel reported hearing voices the day of his rampage, he did not pursue his initial insanity plea. Instead, to avoid a jury trial, he pleaded guilty to the attempted murders of 25 people and to the murders of two students and his parents. Kip's attorneys believed that a judge would be less swayed by emotions in the case and more likely to be fair and lenient than a jury. In November 1999, Kip Kinkel was sentenced to over 111 years in prison without possibility of parole.

—*Laura Hamon*

See also Columbine/Littleton School Shooting; Jonesboro, Arkansas, School Shooting; Juvenile Killers; Mass Murder; School Shootings

Further Reading

Diane, M. (2002). *Too high a price for harmony: A perspective on school shootings.* Bloomington, IN: 1st Books Library Publishers.

Fein, A. H. (2003). *There and back again: School shootings as experienced by school leaders.* Lanman, MD: Scarecrow Press.

Lefevre, G. (1998). *Profile of high school shooting suspect.* Available on the World Wide Web at: http://www.cnnsf.com/newsvault/output/spring.html.

PBS Online and WGBH Frontline. (2000). *Frontline: The killer at Thurston High.* Available on the World Wide Web at: http://www.pbs.org/wgbh/pages/frontline/shows/kinkel/trial/.

Terry, D. (1998). Shootings in a schoolhouse: The suspect: Lethal fantasies of a 15-year-old became a reality. *The New York Times.* Available on the World Wide Web at: http://query.nytimes.com/search/abstract?

KLEBOLD, DYLAN, *See* COLUMBINE/LITTLETON SCHOOL SHOOTING; MASS MURDER; MEDIA, VIOLENCE IN THE; SCHOOL SHOOTINGS

DAVID KORESH

David Koresh was an influential man who gained the loyalty of many followers. He and his cult, the Davidians, lived in peace in a compound in Waco,

Texas, until February 28, 1993. There was a warrant out for his arrest, and on that day, approximately 76 agents from the Bureau of Alcohol, Tobacco, and Firearms (ATF) went to the Davidian complex to arrest Koresh on illegal weapons charges. Unfortunately, Koresh did not cooperate, and the result was tragic. Gunfire was exchanged between the Davidians and the government agents. That day, 4 federal agents were killed, and 16 were wounded. Six Davidians were also killed, and Koresh was wounded.

February 28 was the beginning of an ongoing battle between the federal government and the Davidians. The government began to negotiate with

David Koresh, born Vernon Wayne Howell, became in 1990 the leader of the Branch Davidians, a religious sect in Waco, Texas. This doomsday cult broke away from the Seventh Day Adventists and eventually ended in a stand-off with Federal agents. Nearly 90 cult members were killed as well as four Alcohol, Tobbaco, & Firearms agents.

the Davidians, and 46 people, including 21 children, came out of the complex peacefully. However, there were still nearly 100 people remaining in the complex, and after March 23, 1993, no one else came out voluntarily. According to reports, the government became concerned about the health and safety of the children inside, and on the morning of April 19, 1993, Federal FBI agents warned the Davidians that tear gas would be used if they did not come out of the complex. The group did not come out, and that afternoon, federal agents drove tanks into buildings of the complex to spray tear gas and create exits for those inside—but the complex became engulfed in flames. At least 80 Davidians died in the fire, and David Koresh died from a gunshot wound. Only nine cult members survived.

There was speculation that the federal government was responsible for the fire and caused the deaths of the cult members. Many investigations would follow. In October 1993, an investigation on the confrontation exonerated the FBI and the Department of Justice. However, other private investigations still indicated that the government was responsible for the deaths. One of them revealed that the fire began as three separate fires, each set approximately 2 minutes apart. This finding suggested that the government agents, who had fired three pyrotechnic shells of tear gas into the compound, were responsible for the fire. Yet another investigation indicated that the fires had been set by the Davidians themselves.

In April 1995, family members of the Davidians and survivors of the confrontation filed a civil lawsuit against the government. The case was heard, and many investigations of the April 19 incident commenced. Although some investigations found that the government acted inappropriately and was ultimately responsible for the deaths, many found that the Davidians were responsible. For example, one reports that on April 19, nine Davidians fled from the complex, but none of them rescued children. In addition, the investigation described how the Davidians themselves set the fire without giving any of the sect members, including the children, the opportunity to escape. As a result of the findings against the Davidians, Judge Walter Smith dismissed the $675 million lawsuit brought by survivors and family members.

—*Laura Hamon*

See also Cults; Mass Murder

Further Reading

Judge clears government in Branch Davidian case. (2000). Available on the World Wide Web at: www.cnn.com/ 2000/LAW/scotus/09/21/waco.judgment.01/index.html.

Levine, R. (2003). *The power of persuasion: How we're bought and sold.* New York: John Wiley.

Layton, D. (1998). *Seductive poison.* New York: Anchor Books.

Mittelstadt, M. (1999). *A glance at the Waco controversy.* Available on the World Wide Web at: www.rickross. com/reference/waco/wac053.html.

Rudin, M. (2002). Twenty-five years observing cults: An American perspective. *Cultic Studies Review, 1,* 1-4.

Verhovek, S. (1998). Five years after Waco standoff, the spirit of Koresh lingers. *The New York Times.* Available on the World Wide Web at: http://query.nytimes.com/ search/abstract?res.

KU KLUX KLAN, *See* Hate Crimes; Mass Violence; Vigilantism; White Aryan Resistance; White Knights; White Supremacists

L

LA COSA NOSTRA,
See ORGANIZED CRIME

LA NUESTRA FAMILIA,
See GANGS: DEFINITIONS

LEONARD LAKE AND CHARLES NG

On July 6, 1985, Charles Ng was arrested for shoplifting at the Hudson Bay Company Department Store in Calgary, Alberta, Canada. During the arrest, Ng shot and wounded the arresting security officer. Subsequently, the Calgary police department charged Ng with robbery, attempted murder, and possession of a firearm. His partner, Leonard Lake (a.k.a. Robin Stapley) was arrested on June 2, 1985, in San Francisco for possession of a firearm and a silencer. The arrest was the direct result of the actions of his partner, Ng, who had shoplifted from a lumberyard and then placed the stolen vice in the trunk of Lake's vehicle. While detained at the San Francisco police department, Lake swallowed a cyanide pill and collapsed. He was transported to a local hospital, where he remained in a coma for 4 days until pronounced dead on June 6, 1985.

Leonard Thomas Lake was born on October 29, 1945, in San Francisco, California. Approximately 3 years later, Lake's father abandoned his mother, leaving her with three children to support. When Lake entered preschool, his mother decided to reconcile with his father and left Lake with her grandparents. The separation from his brother, Donald, and his mother resulted in a strained relationship between them. Yet following his mother's second marriage, Lake developed a cordial relationship with two half sisters. He had begun to obsess over women, particularly the idea of holding a young woman captive to fulfil his sexual fantasies. This obsession was based on a novel titled *The Collector,* in which a butterfly collector carries out a fantasy of capturing and enslaving young women.

In 1964, following the completion of high school, Lake decided to join the Marine Corps. During his service, he married in 1969 and shortly thereafter was diagnosed with a mental and psychological disorder. In 1970, he returned to California and within a year received a medical discharge from the Marine Corps. In 1972, he was divorced from his first spouse and eventually remarried, to Claralyn "Cricket" Balazs, in 1981.

Charles Chitat Ng was born in Hong Kong on December 24, 1960. Ng's parents, particularly his father, stressed the importance of education. After several applications by his father, Ng was admitted to a private Catholic school. In turn, his father expected his son to excel in school, and when Ng failed to do so, he was severely punished. Ng was eventually sent to England to live with relatives and attend school. Unfortunately, it appeared that he continued to experience problems at school and eventually was sent to California to reside with an aunt and attend Notre Dame College in San Francisco.

In October 1979, Ng enlisted in the Marine Corps and was sent to Hawaii. While stationed in Hawaii, Ng, along with two marines, stole military weapons from Marine quartermasters. While in custody for the theft, he escaped and fled to California. Ng stayed with Lake and his spouse for 6 months until law enforcement officers arrested the two men. Ng was incarcerated at Fort Leavenworth until 1984, where he reunited with Lake. He jumped bail and lived the remainder of his life as a fugitive.

In November 1982, Lake and Balazs divorced; however, they continued to date. Balazs assisted Lake and Ng (as a fugitive) and allowed them to reside in a cabin she and her father owned in Wilseyville, California. In 1984, Lake continued excavation to build a bunker that would serve a dual purpose: to survive an imminent holocaust and to fulfil his fantasies of capturing and enslaving young women. To subsist, Lake continued to commit burglaries as well as collect his deceased brother's social assistance checks. In 1984, Lake and Ng executed "Project Miranda," which involved kidnapping and holding young women in the bunker. In addition, Lake and Ng murdered several men and continued to perform thefts, or "Ops," as Lake described in his diary.

When Lake was arrested in the lumberyard parking lot, on June 2, 1985, law enforcement officials discovered the plates were registered to one of his victims. While Lake lay comatose in a hospital after taking the cyanide capsule, Balazs removed incriminating evidence from the cabin before law enforcement officials could execute a search warrant of the premises. While searching the property, law enforcement officers found the bunker, which contained a cell with a list of rules posted for the victims. In addition, officials found several tapes that contained conversations between Lake and Balazs discussing Project Miranda, young women in various stages of undress, and the torture of several victims by both Ng and Lake. Law enforcement officers searched the property, and Balazs appeared to know the location of two bodies.

When Ng was arrested in Calgary, Canada refused to extradite him; rather, he was found guilty of assault and robbery and in 1988 was sentenced to 4 ½ years in a correctional facility. In 1991, Prime Minister Kim Campbell signed a warrant for extradition. On September 26, 1991, Ng was extradited to California, where, following several years' delay, he stood trial for 12 counts of murder. On February 23, 1999, Ng was found guilty on 11 counts of murder. He remains on death row.

—*Lynn Gunn*

See also PARAPHILIA; SERIAL MURDER; TEAM KILLERS

Further Reading

Lasseter, D. (2000). *Die for me: The terrifying true story of the Charles Ng and Leonard Lake torture murders.* New York: Pinnacle.

HENRI DESIRÉ LANDRU

Serial killer Henri Desiré Landru, often called the "20th-Century Bluebeard," is considered by many to be the male version of the proverbial "Black Widow Killer." During the early 1900s, Landru romanced and swindled more than 300 women out of their life savings; 10 of them also paid with their lives.

Landru worked as a secondhand furniture dealer and automobile mechanic/garage owner. His victims were most often vulnerable middle-aged widows whom he would meet through the furniture business or through matrimonial advertisements he placed in newspapers.

In and out of prison seven times with his swindling schemes and connected to more than 30 murders, Landru eventually met his end at the guillotine on February 25, 1922.

—*Monica Myers*

LAW ENFORCEMENT, *See* COMMUNITY ATTITUDES TOWARD VIOLENT CRIME; CRIMINAL JUSTICE PRACTITIONERS; POLICE BRUTALITY; POLICE CORRUPTION; PREVENTION OF CRIME AND VIOLENT BEHAVIOR; SPECIAL WEAPONS AND TACTICS TEAMS; THREAT ASSESSMENT; WORKPLACE VIOLENCE AND HOMICIDE

LEGAL PSYCHOLOGY, *See* FORENSIC SCIENCE

LENNON, JOHN, *See* MOTIVES FOR MURDER

THE LESS-DEAD

The *less-dead* is a term coined to refer to the majority of serial murder victims, who belong to marginalized groups of society. They lack prestige or power and generally come from lower socioeconomic groups. They are considered less-dead because before their deaths, they virtually "never were," according to prevailing social attitudes. In other words, they are essentially ignored and devalued by their own communities or members of their neighborhoods and generally not missed when they are gone. Examples are prostitutes, the homeless, vagrants, migrant farm workers, homosexuals, the poor, elderly women, and runaways. They are often vulnerable in locations they frequent, and easy to lure and dominate.

A great deal less pressure is felt by the police when victims of crime come from the marginal elements of a community. The public is much less incensed, for example, over a serial murderer operating in their area when they feel little or no identification with the victims. The victims seem far from real, little attention is paid to their demise, and as a result, the general public does not feel at risk. The deaths of prostitutes, homosexuals, or the homeless fail to capture the attention of the police or the media until the number of victims becomes too large to ignore. They are considered "throwaways," perhaps even somewhat deserving of their ends. In contrast, when victims are people perceived as "blameless," such as college students or young children, public outrage often begins with the first murder and continues to build until pressure is applied to law enforcement and the perpetrator is arrested. Some journalists and writers have taken the public, law enforcement, and politicians to task for this, but their efforts have had little effect.

A good example of what happens to the this type of victim may be seen in the arrest of Joel Rifkin in New York, on June 28, 1993. When police chased and stopped him for not displaying a license plate, they found a decaying female corpse in the back of his pickup truck. After a lengthy interrogation, Rifkin confessed to having killed 17 prostitutes during the past 3 years. On the basis of this confession, the police investigation then concentrated on finding and identifying Rifkin's victims—but this proved difficult because there were few records of the victims being reported missing. In instances in which bodies of these victims had been found, they were yet to be identified when Rifkin was arrested. Until Rifkin stumbled into the hands of a New York State trooper, no one had missed his unfortunate victims.

—*Steven Egger*

See also COMMUNITY ATTITUDES TOWARD VIOLENT CRIME; MOTIVES FOR MURDER; VICTIMOLOGY

Further Reading

Egger, S. A. (1992, March). *Serial killing of the lambs of our dreams.* Essay presented at the annual meeting of the Academy of Criminal Justice Sciences, Pittsburgh, PA.

Egger, S. A. (2002). The *killers among us: An examination of serial murder and its investigation.* Englewood Cliffs, NJ: Prentice Hall.

LETHAL CHAMBER, *See* DEATH ROW; EXECUTION

LETHAL DRUG INJECTION, *See* METHODS OF MURDER

LINDBERGH KIDNAPPING, *See* FALSE CONFESSIONS; HAUPTMANN, BRUNO; KIDNAPPING

LINKAGE BLINDNESS

Law enforcement investigators sometimes do not see or are prevented from seeing beyond their own jurisdictional responsibilities. The officer's responsibility usually stops at the boundary of the jurisdiction except when hot pursuit is necessary. A police department's accountability and responsiveness to its jurisdictional clients can create a sense of isolation from the outside world. The term *linkage blindness* was coined in 1984 to denote an underlying problem with law enforcement serial murder investigations and some other crimes as well.

Intergovernmental conflict between law enforcement agencies is unfortunately a common occurrence.

The basis of these conflicts is a real or perceived violation of an agency's boundaries or geographical jurisdiction, or of the specific responsibilities of an agency to enforce specific laws. Agencies large and small continually practice boundary maintenance to protect their jurisdictions from intruder agencies moving onto their turf. The problem with boundary maintenance is that a serial killer can take advantage of these situations and, as has occurred in many instances, continue to kill until a pattern has been identified or cooperative agreements are made between agencies.

The National Crime Information Center (NCIC) provides officers indirect access to other agencies to obtain information on wanted persons and stolen property. However, the sharing of information on unsolved crimes and investigative leads is not specifically a function of this extensive nationwide information system. Reciprocal relationships between homicide investigators are at best informal and are usually within relatively limited geographical areas. The United States has the most decentralized policing system in the world, and the exchange of investigative information among police departments in this country is sometimes lacking. As a result, linkages between similar crime patterns, modus operandi, or crime signatures can be missed. Such a condition can inhibit early warning or detection of the serial murderer preying on multiple victims. The exception is when crimes are being committed within a relatively small geographic area and can more readily be seen. Law enforcement agencies operate on information, yet agencies sometimes fail to seek out, use, or process it from colleagues or other agencies.

The lack of interagency collaboration or sharing of information on unsolved homicides occurs for a number of reasons: Individual investigators may see any form of cooperation with another agency as a threat to career enhancement, a reduction of their roles in cases, or a challenge to their professional expertise. Agency rivalry creates a sense of vulnerability and fundamental distrust of "outsiders." Budgetary considerations can be a core concern for a police administrator when contemplating interagency collaboration, including which facilities will be used and how will agency costs be apportioned. The loss of policy direction may also be of concern to a police administrator because any form of collaboration will mean some loss of control and compromise.

The issue of accountability is another stumbling block to effective interagency collaboration. Anxiety over accountability means that the affected agencies may hold one another responsible for the outcome of an investigation. Interagency collaboration also means that there will be a requirement to build and maintain a consensus regarding the specific strategies and tactics. This becomes especially difficult when agencies are dominated by professionals with different ideas and theories about how such a collaboration should work. In addition, the individual officer may derive a sense of self-worth from the turf prerogatives accorded the institution, and an attack on the institution's turf, real or imagined, is taken as an attack on the employees' self-worth.

Existence of linkage blindness has been documented in retrospective analyses of serial murder cases such as John Wayne Gacy, Theodore Bundy, the Hillside Stranglers, and Richard Ramirez (the "Night Stalker"). The traveling criminal who repeats criminal acts in different law enforcement jurisdictions is indeed exploiting a systemic weakness, which frequently contributes to continued "immunity" from detection or apprehension. In a stranger-to-stranger murder case lacking in physical evidence or witnesses, criminal investigators may face a very large group of suspects, with small probability of including the offender. A review of serial murders reveals that many serial murderers are caught by chance or coincidence. In effect, the high mobility of some serial killers can result in an immunity from quick and swift apprehension. This can occur within as well as across jurisdictions; killers also manage to roam about large urban police jurisdictions with numerous precincts or district stations.

In conclusion, it may be said that law enforcement investigators sometimes do not see beyond their own jurisdictions in time to recognize the serial nature of crimes before they have escalated to alarming proportions.

—Steven Egger

See also FORENSIC SCIENCE; LAW ENFORCEMENT; SERIAL MURDER; SIGNATURE KILLERS; VICLAS

Further Reading

Egger, S. A. (1984). A working definition of serial murder and the reduction of linkage blindness. *Journal of Police Science and Administration, 12*(3), 348-357.

LITTLETON SCHOOL SHOOTING, *See*
COLUMBINE/LITTLETON SCHOOL SHOOTING

LONELY HEART'S CLUB KILLERS,
See BECK, MARTHA, AND RAY FERNANDEZ

LONG GUNS, *See*
METHODS OF MURDER

LONG, SENATOR HUEY,
See ASSASSINS

LOUKAITIS, BARRY,
See MASS MURDER

CHARLES "LUCKY" LUCIANO

Charles "Lucky" Luciano was the American Mafia's most powerful boss in the early 1930s. Born as Salvatore Lucania on November 11, 1896, in Sicily, Italy, he immigrated to New York City with his family in 1906. At the age of 10, he was involved in shoplifting and extortion. In his teens, Luciano teamed up with other young gangsters, including Meyer Lansky. By 1925, Luciano was a lieutenant for Joe Masseria, New York's leading crime boss.

Luciano recognized that even greater profits could be made if rival Mafia gangs and other organized crime groups formed cooperative relationships. When war broke out between rival New York City gangs in 1930 and 1931, Luciano saw an opportunity to realize his vision and, with the help of Meyer Lansky, arranged the murders of Masseria and rival boss Sal Maranzano. By 1934, Luciano headed a national crime syndicate.

In 1936, Luciano was sentenced to 30 to 50 years on prostitution-related charges but continued to run his empire from his cell at Clinton Prison, in Dannemora, New York. During World War II, while still in prison, the government successfully solicited Luciano's help in improving New York waterfront security. In 1946, his sentence was commuted, and he was deported to Italy, but he continued to be involved in criminal activity in the United States. Luciano died on January 26, 1962, in Naples, Italy, and was buried in Queens, New York.

—*Debbie Wray*

See also GAMBINO CRIME FAMILY; FALCONE, GIOVANNI; ORGANIZED CRIME: DOMESTIC

LUST MURDER

Lust murder is a subcategory of sexual homicide in which perpetrators sadistically and brutally murders their victims to achieve ultimate sexual satisfaction. They typically repeat their killings, thus constituting serial murder. Despite the serial aspect of these killings, lust murder still remains a distinct subcategory of both sexual and serial murder. It is also referred to as *erotophonophilia*, one of the most extreme forms of paraphilia. *Paraphilia* is defined as a sexual deviation in which the paraphilic individual seeks unusual sexual objects, rituals, or specific situations to achieve full sexual satisfaction. There are a number of essential elements to paraphilic behaviors, including fantasy, compulsive masturbation, and facilitating agents such as alcohol, drugs, and pornography. The fantasy system of the individual is a vital component in facilitating paraphilic behaviors and becomes increasingly violent over time. Lust murderers associate sex with aggression, and common themes to their fantasies often include power, domination, molestation, revenge, rape, torture, and the humiliation and suffering of others.

CHARACTERISTICS OF LUST MURDER

Lust murder or erotophonophilia is a specific form of homicide, with unique underpinnings and a specific motive. With this type of murderer, there is a vital connection between violence and sexual arousal. The motivating factor in lust murder is the sexual catalyst, as well as the paraphilic behavior. Moreover, erotophonophilia itself is a paraphilia yet also comprises several other types of the disorder. Commonly associated forms include *necrophilia* and *necrosadism* (sexual arousal and gratification with a dead body), *sadism* (sexual arousal and gratification received from the punishment and suffering of others), *anthropophagy* (an intense desire to consume the flesh of another), *picquerism* (intense desire to stab, wound, or cut the flesh of another), *vampirism* (intense desire to drink the blood of another), and *flagellation* (intense desire to beat, whip, or club another).

In addition to the sadistic dimension of erotophonophilia is the role of lust or eroticism, resulting in a strong need to not only kill but also ravage the victim. The lust murderer is motivated by the need for ultimate sexual satisfaction, which is exemplified in the torture of the victim, either pre- or postmortem. The perpetrator tortures the victim for the sole purpose of achieving an orgasm.

Lust murderers exhibit a progression of brutality with their offenses, with each subsequent murder becoming more vicious and sadistic. These offenders experience exhilarating feelings of sexual arousal and satisfaction from their actions. They are impulsive in their actions and experience the inability to escape their own fantasy worlds. In their internal thought processes, they yearn for victims with whom they can act out the themes of their fantasies. In this way, they establish "relationships" with their potential victims and often rehearse their crimes in the fantasy mode. The victims ultimately become mere props the murderers use to play out their sexually violent fantasies. Victims can be male or female and are primarily heterosexual and interracial in nature.

PROFILES OF LUST MURDERERS

Efforts have been made to determine the likelihood of persons capable of committing lust murder. Special agents within the Behavioral Science Unit of the FBI have been successful in profiling potential perpetrators of such crimes. According to their classification, there are two types of individuals who commit lust murder, the *organized nonsocial* and the *disorganized asocial* personalities. The common denominator of both types of lust murderers is the vital role of fantasy, the motivating factor. It is for this reason that both types of these murders are considered premeditated offenses, for within these fantasies lie the blueprints of the crimes likely to be committed.

It is common for the murderer to engage in a variety of fetishes. *Fetishism* is a paraphilic focus involving the use of nonliving objects (fetish). More specifically, the offender may engage in souvenir fetishes, taking either an object of clothing from the victim or a specific body part, such as a finger, lock of hair, or part of the body with a sexual association. The primary function of a souvenir fetish is for the offender to be able to relive the actual event within the context of the fantasy, usually while masturbating to achieve sexual arousal and sexual satisfaction.

Organized Nonsocial Type

The organized nonsocial lust murderer is self-centered and egocentric. These offenders have difficulty respecting the rights of others and disregard social order. In addition, this type of perpetrator harbors resentment for people yet makes no attempt to avoid being put in social situations. Instead, they manipulate others for their own personal gain and ultimate sexual satisfaction. They revel in the satisfaction received from the impact of the crime within the society in which they live, and they are capable of distinguishing what is right from what is wrong.

Crimes of the Organized Nonsocial Type

The organized nonsocial lust murderer is cunning and methodical, which is reflected in the perpetration of the crime. Victim selection is usually arbitrary relative to both types of lust murderers. The perpetrator usually lives some distance from the actual crime scene and pursues "cruising" time to seek out a victim. The organized nonsocial type is more likely to commit the crime in an isolated area and then transport the body to a location where it is then likely to be discovered. The offender is excited at the discovery of the body, as well as the reaction of society.

The most frequent method of killing for both the organized nonsocial and the disorganized asocial lust murderer is strangulation, blunt force, or the use of a pointed, sharp instrument. It is uncommon for the lust murderer to use a firearm to kill, for there is too little psychosexual gratification with such an impersonal weapon. The nonsocial types typically carry their weapons of choice on their persons and usually take them along when departing from crime scenes.

One of the most distinguishing characteristics of the lust murderer is extreme mutilation and sometimes dismembering of the victim. It is common for the offender to bite on or bite off the breasts, buttocks, neck, abdomen, thighs, or genitals, because of the strong sexual association of these body parts. It is also common for the offender to amputate limbs or breasts or to completely dissect and eviscerate the victim. This particular display of behavior is considered paraphilic and is known as *anthropophagy*. The nonsocial type may dissect the victim's body in an attempt to hinder identification. Sexual penetration of the victim is a common characteristic of this type of lust murderer and penetration can reach the point of necrophilia (postmortem sexual intercourse).

In terms of physical evidence found at the crime scene, it is uncommon for the nonsocial organized type of offender to leave evidence behind. This is primarily because they are more organized, cunning, and methodical in their actions, ultimately decreasing likelihood of arrest. Both nonsocial and asocial lust murderers are inclined to revisit the scenes of their crimes. The nonsocial type does this as a way to assess the progress of the investigation as well as to verify whether the body has been discovered. It is also common for this type of offender to obsess over the police investigation even to the point of frequenting police hangouts to gain insight on unsolved crimes or to insert themselves into the investigations.

Disorganized Asocial Type

This type of lust murderer is regarded as a loner or a social introvert. They prefer their own company and have difficulty in interpersonal relationships with others. They typically feel rejected by others and foster a sense of loneliness and helplessness. In terms of the manner in which they commit their offense, they are usually done in a very unorganized fashion, unlike the crime of the organized nonsocial lust murderer.

Crimes of the Disorganized Asocial Type

Compared with organized nonsocial offenders, disorganized killers commit their crimes in a more frenzied and less methodical manner. They are more likely to use weapons of opportunity that are typically left behind at the scene of the crime, hence the "disorganized" type. Crimes by the disorganized type are usually committed close to either their homes or places of employment, primarily because these locations provide them with a sense of security and they ultimately feel more at ease with the situation. Typically, the asocial type of offender leaves the body of the victim at the scene of the original crime and usually makes no effort to conceal it.

It has been noted that asocial types are likely to smear the victim's blood on themselves, the victim, or the surface on which the body is resting, exemplifying the uncontrollable frenzy of the attack. This lust murderer is motivated by a curious need to acclimate himself with the sexually significant parts of the victim's body and does so by exploring various parts of the sexual anatomy to determine how they function and appear beneath the surface. This strange curiosity often compels this killer to insert foreign objects into various body orifices. This offender may also ejaculate on or near the victim. It is also common for this offender to revisit the scene of the crime either to engage in more mutilation or to relive the exhilarating experience in his mind.

—*Catherine Purcell*

See also Motives for Murder; Paraphilia; Serial Murder

Further Reading

Hazelwood, R. R., & Douglas, J. D. (1980, April). The lust murderer. *FBI Law Enforcement Bulletin,* 18-22.

Hickey, E. W. (2002). *Serial murderers and their victims.* (3rd. ed.). Belmont, CA: Wadsworth.

Purcell, C. E., & Arrigo, B. A. (2001). Explaining paraphilias and lust murder: An integrated model. *International Journal of Offender Therapy and Comparative Criminology, 45,* 6-31.

Simon, R. I. (1996). Bad men do what good men dream: A forensic psychiatrist illuminates the darker side of human behavior. In R. I. Simon (Ed.), *Serial sexual killers, your life for their orgasm* (pp. 279-312). Washington, DC: American Psychiatric Press.

LYCANTHROPY, *See* JACK THE RIPPER: LYCANTHROPY; VAMPIRES, WEREWOLVES, AND WITCHES

LYNCHING

Lynching by mobs in the United States spanned roughly five decades (1880s-1930s). The mob typically acted (a) to maintain the societal hierarchy between races through terrorism, (b) to contain and eliminate any possibility of African American economic or political advance, and (c) to preserve the

Caucasian class structure. An African American might be lynched for almost any reason, from "acting suspiciously" or "being offensive" to more serious crimes, real or imagined, such as rape or assault.

Lynching originated with Col. Charles Lynch, who instated lynch laws during the Revolutionary period. At the time, the swift nature of the punishment appealed to the nation as a way to head off crime. Lynching wiped away restrictions on what one man could do to harm another man's "property," that is, slaves, and allowed interracial violence to go unchallenged. Not all lynching was racially charged; individuals of all races and ethnic origins were hung for murder, cattle rustling, and other socially unacceptable behaviors.

An anti-lynching campaign began in the 1920s, founded primarily by women, which sought to fight lynching through education, legal action, or federal legislation. By the 1930s, a growing number of Caucasian women had joined the movement, and this became the turning point in the protest against racism and segregation that would grow in the coming decades.

M

JEFFREY MACDONALD

In Fort Bragg, North Carolina, during the early hours of February 17th, 1970, military police responded to a distress call made at 544 Castle Drive. On arrival, military police checked the front door, and when there was no response, they went to the back door. Inside the house, they found a gruesome scene: the bloody body of 5-month pregnant Colette MacDonald, age 26, lying on the floor in the master bedroom. She had been stabbed numerous times in the neck and chest. Colette's husband, Green Beret Captain Jeffrey MacDonald, age 26, lay by her, with his head on her shoulder. Jeffrey was conscious and asked the police to check on their children. In the other bedrooms, the police first discovered the body of the oldest daughter, Kimberly, age 5, lying in bed. She had been stabbed in the neck and face, and her skull was fractured. Next, they found the body of Kristen, age 2, also lying in bed. Kristen had been stabbed many times in the chest and back. Colette, Kimberly, and Kristen were already dead when the police arrived. Jeffrey was taken to the hospital. His wounds included a small wound to the right side of his chest, a bruise on the left side of his forehead, and a stab wound to the abdomen and upper left arm. His chest wound collapsed part of his right lung.

MacDonald claimed that a band of Manson-like intruders had burst into the apartment and killed his wife and two daughters. He described the intruders as wearing hippie-style clothes: one female wearing a big floppy hat, one African American man, and two Caucasian men. Despite this claim, however, MacDonald was considered the prime suspect in the vicious murders.

Jeffrey and Colette had been childhood sweethearts, married in September 1963. Their first daughter, Kimberly, was born shortly thereafter, in 1964. MacDonald had been the all-American boy, very bright, energetic, and charming. He attended Princeton University and then Northwestern University medical school. He completed his internship at the Columbia Presbyterian Medical Center in New York City in June 1969 and was inducted in the Army in July 1969. In September 1969, Jeffrey was assigned duty as a medical officer at the Green Beret headquarters, Fort Bragg, North Carolina. He was considered a dedicated doctor and good solider.

In 1979, 9 years after the brutal murders, a federal court found Jeffrey MacDonald guilty of the crimes and sentenced him to three consecutive life terms. The Fourth Circuit Court of Appeals later overturned the verdict, after MacDonald had spent a year in prison, because they ruled that he had been denied a speedy trial. In March 1982, however, the United States Supreme Court voted to reverse the lower court's decision, and MacDonald returned to prison, where he remains to this day.

—*Katherine Ray*

See also FAMILY HOMICIDE

Further Reading

McGinniss, J. (1983). *Fatal vision.* New York: Signet Books.
Potter, J. A., & Bost, F. (1997). *Fatal justice: Reinvestigating the MacDonald murders.* New York: Norton.

THE MACDONALD TRIAD

The MacDonald Triad comprises three behavioral problems frequently associated with children at high risk for violence: enuresis (involuntary urination, or chronic bed-wetting), firesetting, and cruelty to animals. The childhoods of violent offenders vary in complexity. Some are much more sociopathic than others; they are more aggressive, more manipulative, express less remorse, and experience fewer feelings of guilt. Yet similar characteristics can be observed in children who do not grow up to become violent offenders. In truth, each child processes experiences differently. Children also react differently to stress, which may well be the generic predisposer to many maladaptive behaviors in childhood. Because children do not possess the same coping skills for life's stressors, some children are at greater risk of developing inappropriate behaviors.

Psychopathology during childhood can be manifested in a variety of behaviors, some of which are more noticeable or detectable than others. The three behaviors in the MacDonald Triad have been linked to having childhood maladaptive behaviors. Any one of these behaviors is not necessarily a good predictor of later adult violent behavior, and even a youth displaying all three is not guaranteed a life of violence during adulthood. However, such behaviors appear more often among the adult violent offender population than among nonoffenders.

A plethora of research on adult violence and aggression suggests that the roots can be found in childhood. Psychological profiles of those who commit homicide reveal portraits of frustration and intrapersonal conflict, and early detection and intervention of such interpersonal development is paramount. Though the triad is far from an infallible diagnostic tool, it does signal abnormal childhood development. Hellman and Blackman (1966) suggest,

> The triad is proposed as a pathognomonic sign, as an alert to both the parents and the community that the child is seriously troubled; that if this readiness to project and elicit fear or pain, to be violent and destructive, is not alleviated nor remedies found for it, this pattern of hostile behavior may well lead to adult aggressive antisocial behavior. (p. 1434)

The authors also suggest that a relationship exists between parental loss or rejection and the development of mental illness or personality disorders. Specifically, bouts of rage by persons who murder often reflect histories of maternal or paternal deprivation. The child who suffers consistently under these circumstances develops defense mechanisms, including withdrawal and denial of stress. If, however, the child chooses to revolt, he or she begins to act out feelings of rejection and resentment in acts of aggression and violence.

Kathleen Heide (1995), in her study on why children kill parents, noted that emotional neglect is damaging to a child's healthy development.

> Parents who do not give their children clear messages that they are loved, whether by words or appropriate displays of affection, such as being held, cuddled, hugged, kissed, having hands shaken, and being patted on the back, are not meeting their sons' and daughters' emotional needs. (p. 30)

Early childhood neglect impairs bonding, cognition, play, and social and emotional development. Children who continue to suffer deprivation act out in vengeance and sometimes kill the parent responsible. For example, by the age of 14, Ed Kemper had suffered much cruelty and rejection by his caustic mother. She berated and belittled him for not living up to her social expectations. Being sent away to live with his grandparents was further evidence of her contempt for him. After Kemper had killed several times (at 14, he killed his grandparents), he found he could no longer repress the hatred he felt for his mother. He eventually stabbed her to death, decapitated her, and cut out her larynx.

From a young age, children raised in dysfunctional and abusive homes develop coping skills to deal with the inherent stress. Heide (1995) writes,

> Persons in dysfunctional families characteristically do not *feel* because they learned from a young age that not feeling is necessary for psychic survival. Family members generally learn it is too painful to feel the hurt or to experience the fear that comes from feelings of rage, abandonment, moments of terror, and memories of horror. (p. 48)

Some parents cannot distinguish between punishment and discipline, and they end up acting out of frustration that has turned to anger, for example, by spanking a child. If parents did not spank when they were angry, they might seldom spank at all. Although some children do not connect this punishment with rejection, some most certainly do, and it can have serious consequences. As one 11-year-old insightfully penned in his journal after being spanked by his father for not cleaning his room, "Yesterday Dad spanked me again. Why is it that Dad's pain is always my pain too?"

The pathology and psychological disturbance that can develop in children who have suffered the trauma of severely poor parenting is indicated by behaviors outlined in the MacDonald Triad and the *Diagnostic Statistical Manual (DSM),* published by the American Psychological Association. Conduct disorders can develop in the child's preschool years but are not fully apparent until later childhood. These individuals often display low impulse control and failure to observe social norms through rebelliousness against authority. Emotionally truncated, they lack empathy and aggress arbitrarily, with little apparent provocation. The psychopathology of animal cruelty, enuresis, and firesetting can surface in some children concomitantly. Parents and authorities are often quick to punish without recognizing these behaviors as "red flags" that the child is suffering and needs help.

ANIMAL CRUELTY

> The custom of children tormenting and killing beasts, will, by degrees, harden their minds even towards men, and they who delight in the suffering and destruction of inferior creatures, will not be apt to be very compassionate, or benign to those of their own kind. (Locke, 1705/1968)

How to categorize the torturing of animals is not clear-cut. For example, some violent offenders may derive pleasure in harming animals while they are alive, but others appear to enjoy the vivisection and exploration of deceased animals. The morbid curiosity of cutting into them may facilitate the development of deviant sexual fantasies. Many violent offenders report incidents of childhood cruelty toward animals. According to the American Humane Society, animal cruelty covers a wide range of behaviors harmful to animals, including intentionally depriving an animal of food, water, shelter, socialization, or veterinary care or maliciously torturing, maiming, mutilating, or killing an animal. Felthous and Kellert, in their study of 102 men serving time in federal penitentiaries,

found that cruelty to animals during childhood occurred much more often among the aggressive criminals than among the nonaggressive criminals or noncriminals. They identified nine motivations for the childhood maltreatment of animals:

- ◆ To control the animal
- ◆ To retaliate against the animal
- ◆ To satisfy a prejudice against a specific species or breed
- ◆ To express aggression through an animal
- ◆ To enhance one's own aggressiveness
- ◆ To shock people for amusement
- ◆ To retaliate against another person
- ◆ Displacement of hostility from a person to an animal
- ◆ Nonspecific sadism

Family therapist Elana Gill notes how children who are physically or sexually abused seem to mimic their mistreatment on their companion animals. Gill notes that children learn the lessons of abuse: that people who love them hurt them and that power and dominance are preferable to the victim's plight of helplessness. In some cases, Gill observed that animal cruelty may signify preoccupation with death and that a child may be rehearsing his or her own suicide. In the case of a severely abused child named Miriam, Gill (1994) writes,

> I learned this from Miriam, a six-year-old who had been abused sexually. When I asked her to make a picture of herself, she drew a bleeding dog and herself in heaven. Miriam's drawing revealed the depth of her despair. Her mother later informed me that Miriam had recently begun slapping and choking her dog and had injured him with scissors.

According to Patterson, there are two approaches to understanding risk factors that signal development of aggression and antisocial behavior in children: *coercive family interaction patterns* and *children's attributional biases.* The first factor is found in modeling theory, in which children emulate the parents' behaviors. Some research indicates that poor parenting styles relying heavily on punitive or aversive control present children with models of force. Parent and child use aversive techniques to terminate each other's behavior. The implications of this approach suggest that a cycle of violence develops in which children subject to harsh and abusive treatment will view their abuse as normal and emulate this behavior in their interpersonal relationships.

The second approach, according to Price and Dodge, suggests that boys who show atypical aggression have deficits in *intention-cue detection.* These boys display attributional bias, in which they interpret ambiguous or neutral peer actions (e.g., being accidentally bumped in a lunch line) as being hostile and aggressive. This bias leads them to act aggressively, often causing strong peer retaliation. The parallel to animal abuse is apparent. If a peer's intention cues can be ambiguous to a rejected child, intention cues by an animal, both companion and noncompanion, may also be misinterpreted. In one case, a young boy brutalized, sexually assaulted, and eventually killed a stray dog. The boy stated that when he heard the dog barking at him, he interpreted the dog's demeanor as personally directed aggression, something he was not going to allow.

Lockwood, in *The Tangled Web of Animal Abuse: The Links Between Cruelty to Animals and Human Violence,* notes the importance of preventing animal cruelty by disciplining all such acts, even minor ones. Without proper intervention, children may graduate to more serious abuses, including violence against people. The author notes an episode relayed by one concerned mother. Her son, while playing in a room at a friend's house, decided to also play with the friend's kitten. Repeatedly throwing the kitten up to the ceiling and watching him fall amused the boy. When the mother came to retrieve her son, the kitten was found in a catatonic state. When asked what he did, the boy replied that he was just playing with it. Being a very diligent and concerned parent, the mother was distraught, wondering how her son could have been so cruel. Though an isolated incident, she did not allow this aberrant behavior to go unchallenged. She spent much time with her son expressing sorrow for the kitten and suggesting to him how he could have been more sensitive to the animal and played with him more carefully. Such parenting techniques can be critical in deterrence of animal cruelty. The behavior may be part of a constellation of other symptomatic behaviors that can point toward a child's potential for severe, maladaptive, antisocial behavior.

Animal abuse has been included in the *DSM* diagnoses of conduct disorder since 1987. Twenty states now have felony level provisions within their animal cruelty codes. Children who harm animals often are trying in maladaptive ways to express their suffering. Such violence must never be ignored.

ENURESIS

The frequent trauma some children experience as the result of physical, sexual, or emotional abuse can trigger chronic bed-wetting. Like those who practice animal torture or experimentation, chronic bed-wetters appear to cease the maladaptive behavior as they approach adulthood. Defined as unintentional bed-wetting during sleep that is persistent after the age of 5, enuresis evokes emotional and social distress for the child sufferer. It is embarrassing as well as frustrating for the child, and parents find it annoying as it means persistent interrupted sleep. For approximately 80% of children who suffer enuresis, the causes have biological roots, and heredity is a major contributing factor. Research supports the belief that enuresis is most often caused by a failure of muscular responses that inhibit urination or by a hormonal imbalance that permits too much urine to accumulate during the night. The prescription of antidepressant drugs that reduce the amount of urine produced usually eliminates the problem. In some cases, children simply outgrow the problem. However, in about 20% of children with enuresis it is an indicator, a "red flag" of something more serious.

In some cases, enuresis is considered to be an overt manifestation of internal turmoil, usually caused by disturbance in the home. Some enuretic children appear to have great difficulty in controlling their expressions of love and aggression. Some children harbor intense hostility toward their mothers and feel that they have lost them as a love object. Unconscious loss of bladder control becomes a method of retaliation. Other studies have shown a relationship between persistent enuresis, juvenile delinquency, and psychopathic personality. In one study conducted by Hellman and Blackman, it was found that enuresis was tied to aggression and fantasies of destruction. Of the 84 prisoners who served as subjects, 31 were charged with aggressive crimes against a person, and 53 were charged with misdemeanors and minor felonies; 36 were found to have enuresis. Of the 36, 33 had enuresis past the age of 8 years, and in 70%, this trait persisted into their teens.

Though relatively insignificant by itself and not as visible as other traits in the triad, it is no less important as a red flag in identifying maladaptive development in a child. Enuresis is an unconscious, involuntary, and nonviolent act, and therefore linking it to violent crime is more difficult than with animal cruelty or firesetting.

FIRESETTING

The term *firesetting* is generally used to describe the actions of juveniles, whereas *arson* describes adult behavior. Frequently, the distinction is not clearly understood, and the terms are used interchangeably. Some children display an abnormal fascination with or interest in fire. They engage in excessive fire watching, fireplay, or compulsive collecting of fire paraphernalia. They are also more prone to trigger false fire alarms. California has experienced a significantly large number of fires set by juveniles. In the United States, juveniles set about 50% to 60% of arson fires. Males are responsible for more than 90% of these fires. In 1994 and 1995, in Fresno, California, more than 70% of fires were set by juveniles, the highest per capita rates of arson fires in the country (Hickey, 2002).

Firesetting is best understood as part of a process, and not merely an act. Research of 1,200 juvenile firesetters in Fresno found a disturbing pattern of psychopathology within their families. Family dysfunction included low marital satisfaction, little or no display of affection, ineffectual role modeling, and excessive physical force in disciplining children. Children frequently report deep feelings of maternal or paternal rejection or neglect. The absence of a father is thought to contribute to aggressiveness and firesetting in boys. Indeed, among chronic firesetters, the absence of a father in the home is a salient factor. Felthous notes that attention deprivation by the father due to problems such as alcoholism frequently results in rejection. Factors such as separation from the father due to incarceration and divorce also contribute to boys' firesetting behavior.

Juvenile firesetters commonly report anxiety, depression, and resentment when feelings of abandonment surface about their relationships with parents or significant others. In turn, the perceived rejection affects self-esteem and fosters feelings of anger, and hatred and revenge fantasies. Similar to profiles in psychopathy, firesetters have less capacity for internalization, are less able to tolerate anxiety, and are less empathetic and able to form attachments to others. They are often diagnosed as having conduct disorders and display antisocial personality characteristics. Incapable of feeling adequate remorse or guilt, juvenile firesetters are more prone to be in conflict with authority figures. According to Hickey, the following are the most common psychological and behavioral problems observed in the Fresno group of juvenile firesetters:

1. Learning problems
2. Poor school behavior
3. Poor concentration
4. Lying
5. Excessive anger
6. Fights with siblings
7. Disobedience
8. Heavy influence by peers
9. Attention seeking
10. Impulsiveness
11. Impatience
12. Preoccupation with fire
13. Unhappiness in dysfunctional family
14. Pronounced need for security and affection

These 14 characteristics parallel many of the ones noted in Fineman's profile of firesetters. Children like this display distinct personality pathology, and fireplay is but one of many maladaptive behaviors. Sometimes offenders have hero fantasies: They "discover" a fire, which they have set, and may even help extinguish the flames. Even adult firefighters have been caught setting fires to draw attention to themselves and be recognized for their heroics. Delinquent or antisocial firesetters generally display little empathy or remorse for their crimes or victims. Much of their psychopathology has roots within family dynamics.

In the Fresno study, in which about half the offending children were 8 years old or younger, parental absenteeism was high. Parents consistently claimed being "present" about 80% of the time, but children's perceptions were considerably less. Here, perception is the key factor. What parents say they are doing does not really matter as much as what children perceive their parents are doing, or not doing. In addition, firesetters in the study were more frequently spanked or isolated from others on a weekly or sometimes daily basis over periods of time. These children reported having "bad" experiences, in homes often facing financial problems, family restructuring, or relocation.

Firesetting appears to be a transitory method of pathological self-expression. Fineman points out that adult firesetters usually have histories of setting fires as children but that most child firesetters do not set fires as adults. Does this mean that children who are chronic firesetters resolve their personal conflicts or mature out of the maladaptive behaviors? In all probability, many children do resolve the conflicts or mature out of the behavior. For other children, adolescence is a transitory period in which they to begin to find more personal, more deviant methods to express themselves.

The MacDonald Triad relates to a pattern of creating hurt because of hurt: The victim becomes the victimizer. Some experts feel the triad is not a sufficient diagnostic tool and that other behaviors may indicate pathology in children, including temper tantrums, excessive fighting, and truancy. When correlated with the triad, these behaviors become even more useful as childhood predictors of violence. Nonetheless, the predictive value of the three traits found in the triad when persistent in childhood is purported in many studies of adults who have committed violent crimes against society.

—Holly Peacock
and Eric W. Hickey

NOTE: Portions of this profile were previously published in Eric Hickey's *Serial Murderers and Their Victims,* 2002, 3rd ed. Belmont, CA: Wadsworth Publishers.

See also ATTACHMENT DEFICIENCY AND VIOLENCE; CONDUCT DISORDER; JUVENILE FIRESETTERS; PREDICTING VIOLENT BEHAVIOR; PREVENTION OF CRIME AND VIOLENT BEHAVIOR; VIOLENT BEHAVIOR

Further Reading

Felthous, A., & Kellert, S. (1992, Fall/Winter). In America's abuse problem. *ASPCA Animal Watch,* p. 10.

Fineman, K. R. (1995). A model for the qualitative analysis of child and adult fire deviant behavior. *American Journal of Forensic Psychology, 13*(1).

Gill, E. (1994, March/April 20-21). Children and animals: A clinician's view. *The Animal's Agenda.*

Heide, K. (1995). *Why kids kill parents: Child abuse and adolescent homicide.* Thousand Oaks, CA: Sage.

Hellman, D. S., & Blackman, N. (1966). Enuresis, firesetting and cruelty to animals: A triad predictive of adult crime. *The American Journal of Psychiatry, 122,* 1431-1435.

Hickey, E. W. (2002). *Serial murderers and their victims* (3rd ed.). Belmont, CA: Wadsworth.

Locke, J. (1968). Some thoughts concerning education. In *The works of John Locke in nine volumes* (12th ed., pp. 112-114). London: C & J Rivington. (Original work published 1705)

Lockwood, R., & Hodge, G. R. (1986, Summer). The tangled web of animal abuse: The links between cruelty to animals and human violence. *The Humane Society News.*

Patterson, G. R., DeBaryshe, B. D., & Ramsey, E. A. Developmental perspective on antisocial behavior. *American Psychologist, 44,* 329-335.

Price, J. M., & Dodge, K. A. (1989). Peers' contributions to children's social maladjustment. In T. J. Berndt & G. W. Ladd (Eds.), *Peer relationships in child development* (pp. 341-370). New York: Wiley.

MADAME TUSSAUD,
See TUSSAUD, MADAME

MAFIA, *See* FALCONE, GIOVANNI; ORGANIZED CRIME; "TOP HOODLUM" PROGRAM

MAJORS, ORVILLE LYNN,
See POISONING: MEDICAL SETTINGS

THE MANN ACT

In 1910, James Mann, a former Chicago lawyer and Republican member of the U.S. House of Representatives, authored the Mann Act (officially titled the White Slave Traffic Act) in an effort to control prostitution and immoral acts at the federal level. Between 1910 and 1916, the FBI made over 2,400 arrests under the Mann Act. The act provides severe penalties to any person who transports an individual via interstate or foreign commerce or in any territory within the United States with the intent of engaging in prostitution, debauchery, or any other sexual act for which one could be charged with a criminal offense. The act carries with it a punishment of imprisonment for up to 10 years, a fine, or both.

—Carla Marquez

Further Reading

Mann Act (White Slave Traffic Act). (1997, October). *United States attorney's manual.* Available on the World Wide Web at: www.usdoj.gov/usao/foia_reading_room/ usam/title 9/crm02027.htm.

MANSLAUGHTER, *See* HOMICIDE, TYPES OF, AND DEGREES OF MURDER

CHARLES MANSON

Charles Milles Manson was born on November 12, 1934, in Ashland, Kentucky. His final arrest took place in Los Angeles County, California, on October 12, 1970, on the charges of murder and conspiracy to commit murder. He was originally sentenced to death, but his sentence was commuted to life in prison in 1976. Since March 15, 1989, Charles Manson has been housed at the California State Prison in Corcoran, California.

Charles Manson possesses a kind of charisma that enabled him to attract many (approximately 55) wayward, itinerant, desperate, and directionless people to form a cult. He referred to these individuals as his "family," and they would later be responsible for one of the most infamous murder sprees in U.S. history. Manson was fixated on his belief that to create the social changes promoted during the 1960s, the oppressive social order needed to be dissolved into chaos. He believed that because of the intense fear and confusion generated by this state of chaos, people would run "helter-skel-ter" in the streets—and he convinced his followers to do just that. The homicidal acts in which they engaged sparked national unrest regarding our views on personal safety. No other cult group has captured the imagination of contemporary society quite like the Manson Family.

Some sociologists have argued that the sociopolitical climate was just right for someone like Charles Manson to emerge. At the time, he seemed to have developed as the product of all that was wrong in 1960s American society. He was an illegitimate child who was frequently

handed over from relative to relative and occasionally cared for by his mother, Kathy Maddox. At the time she gave birth to Charles, Maddox was living with a man named Bill Manson, though he was not the boy's real father. Some documents indicate that his biological father was a man named Colonel Scott, an African American cook from Ashland, Kentucky. The perception that his father was a black man has important implications regarding Charles's twisted philosophies, theologies, and his worldview in general.

The parent-child bond between Manson and his mother was tenuous at best. She took Charles with her to the bars and street corners where she hustled. Thus, his developing sense of self-worth was significantly affected even before his subsequent involvement with the juvenile justice system. He grew up as an outcast

The Manson Family

It was the late 1960s and the "Age of Aquarius." Young people left their homes and their schools to live on the streets, in vans, and in communes. They were following the message of the times: peace, love, drugs, and flower power. The United States was involved in the Vietnam conflict, and the future looked bleak. A generation of young people were growing up full of anger, hate, and confusion, searching for answers.

Charismatic, intelligent, and manipulative, Charles Manson was paroled from federal prison in San Francisco in 1967 and began attracting young, white, mostly female "searchers" into his "family." The use of LSD, amphetamines, and uninhibited sex, accompanied by Manson's bizarre preaching, held them together. Estimated at 50 or more members, the Manson Family traveled up and down the state of California before settling in southern California. They are believed to have been responsible for the deaths of at least 11 people in the state in a 1-year period and the attempted murders of several others. In all, the group is suspected of 35 or more murders.

The Tate-LaBianca killings were part of the acts that brought the Manson Family to worldwide attention. In July and August 1969, the Family was responsible for the gruesome mutilation and killing of 9 people: Gary Hinman, slashed to death by three of Manson's group after Charles Manson cut off Hinman's ear with a sword and then ordered his death; the particularly grisly Tate-LaBianca murders, with 7 victims, directed by Manson and performed by four group members; and Donald "Shorty" Shea, who was murdered and dismembered by two group members in the presence of Charles Manson and at his direction. None of the Family considered disobeying Manson.

(Continued, next page)

Family members have stated that they believed Manson to be the "fifth angel" in the Bible's *Book of Revelations,* often referring to him as "Jesus Christ." Manson's mind control over the family extended into the courtroom when the group was brought to trial for the Tate-LaBianca murders. Whatever Manson did or said, his followers mimicked. He refused to face the judge, shaved his head, and drew a swastika on his forehead, and the others did the same. At one point in the trial, the three female codefendants attempted to accept all responsibility for the atrocities committed, to allow for the release of Manson. All defendants in this case were found guilty and sentenced to death. With the 1976 repeal of the death penalty in California, their sentences were commuted to life in prison with the possibility of parole. To date, parole has been consistently denied for Charles Manson, Lynette Fromme, Leslie Van Houghton, and several other members of the Manson Family.

The Manson Family did not disintegrate with the imprisonment of their leader. To date, at least eight additional group members have been sentenced to prison for various crimes, ranging from grand theft to attempted murder. At a conservative count, five known Manson Family members and/or associates have been murdered, and four additional people have been murdered by Family members or associates.

Behind prison bars, 30 years later, the charisma of Charles Manson continues to draw followers and intrigue the general public. He currently resides in Corcoran State Prison, California and has been denied parole more than a dozen times.

—*Vikki A. Irby*

during the later part of the Great Depression, without a stable family to ease the stresses of poverty and emotional isolation.

Manson was taken from his mother and placed with her relatives when he was still very young. In 1940, Kathy Maddox was arrested and convicted of armed robbery and sentenced to Moundsville State Prison in West Virginia. Charles, then 6 years old, was sent to his maternal grandmother's house to live, the same home that his mother had run away from at the age of 15. His life was characterized by an environment of strict religious discipline, thanking the Lord at mealtimes, long prayer sessions before bedtime, and turning the other cheek to every aggressive act from another child. His grandparents were fanatical in their religious practices, fulfilling their Christian duty by taking care of Charles. His grandmother dominated the household, apparently stern and unwavering in her interpretation of "God's plan," demanding that those under her roof abide by her practices. Drinking and smoking were forbidden in the house. Any display of emotion toward the opposite sex was considered sinful. Facial makeup was evil and only used by the women of the streets. Anyone cursing or using the Lord's name in vain in her presence brought instant righteous condemnation. Charles never witnessed any display of affection between his grandparents. His grandfather was apparently chastised as being a sinner every time he tried to express any warmth or comforting emotions to his wife, and he maintained the harmony of the home through acquiescence and letting his wife rule the house as she saw necessary. He became psychotic and died in an asylum from kidney failure secondary to alcoholism.

After being taught to be meek at his grandparents' house, Charles was sent to his aunt and uncle in Maychem, Virginia. There, his uncle chastised him for being a sissy instead of standing his ground like any good southern man. He promised that Charles would either learn to be a man or be treated like a girl, and punished the boy for crying about being displaced from his grandmother's house or for missing his mother. Finally, to solidify his point to Charles, his uncle sent him to his first day of school dressed as a girl. Charles was teased by the other children until he was pushed into a rage. He fought a series of violent battles with the other boys in the schoolyard. He has stated that his uncle's motive for dressing him like a girl didn't help teach him how to become a man, it only taught him how to fight hard and never give up.

Two years later, Charles Manson was back with his mother again. She was released from Moundsville at age 23, and the two of them were reunited in an erratic relationship that took them around the southeastern part of the United States. His mother had become a bisexual after her experiences in prison and engaged in a variety of sexual relationships with both men and women. Young Charles witnessed each of these sexual encounters firsthand. He has stated that he was routinely jealous of his mother's male lovers and felt he was always in competition with them for her love. He apparently preferred it when his mother had sexual encounters with other women because it made him feel less emotionally and sexually threatened. Years later, Charles Manson's feeling of security among lesbians would express itself through his support and encouragement of sexual relationships among his own female "family" members in California.

Kathy Maddox soon found that she did not have the resources to raise a child. In desperation, his mother placed her son with the Order of Catholic Brothers in Terre Haute, Indiana. This was a stern and highly disciplined monastic institution, known as the Gibault Home for Boys. His mother never told Charles that he was to have a new home. Not until the second day he spent there did the 8-year-old Charlie Manson realize that his mother was not coming back and that this was, indeed, his new home.

Infractions of the rules at Gibault were punished by severe beatings with a leather strap or wooden paddle. The few privileges the Christian brothers allowed were quickly suspended when a child violated any disciplinary rule. In Manson's case, given that he was reportedly enuretic, he was often whipped, while being promised that he was being taught how to control himself by the punishment. He escaped twice in efforts to reunite with his mother. However, once he was with her again, she turned him over to the police, who promptly returned him to Gibault. Given the nature of such a setting, each time he returned, his punishments became progressively harsher. Finally, Manson escaped Gibault again for the last time.

By the time he was 12 years old, Manson was living alone in a single-room-occupancy boardinghouse in Indianapolis, stealing money to live on and scraping food out of garbage cans. He hustled money wherever he could, until the police caught him and discovered he was a minor. Consequently, young Manson was made a ward of the state and placed in the custody of Father Flanagan's Boys Town. He experienced this as an environment, like Gibault, that brought swift punishment for disciplinary infraction. Charles again escaped to avoid the incessant punishment he reportedly faced. During this escape, he stole a car, was convicted as a juvenile, and sentenced to a city juvenile institution. He proved too difficult for the city to manage and was transferred to a state institution, the Indiana School for Boys at Plainsfield. Charles was 15 years old.

The inmates at the Indiana School were not wards of the state. These were real inmates who had been convicted of violent crimes. Again, Manson claims that the guards at the Indiana School maintained a level of brutality associated with many of the institutions that were outlawed in the 1960s. However, this was 1949, and Charles Manson was a 15-year-old inmate at the mercy of the guards. He was often beaten and learned to never trust anyone.

At age 16, Manson escaped again. This time he made it all the way to California. There he stole cars, robbed grocery stores, and terrorized victims. He was arrested again and sentenced to the National Training School for Boys located in Washington, D.C. There, he believes, he became institutionally hardened for good. Manson reported that even the worst criminals had at least some family who visited them on a regular basis, but he had no one. He was surrounded by older, tougher inmates who were fully developed sociopaths.

At the National Training School, Manson finally accepted what it meant to be a lifetime criminal. The other inmates knew no other way to live except through criminal behavior. They depended on the institution for a sense of identity and a sense of being. Charles Manson grew to develop that dependence on an institutional identity as well. He grew to accept the brutality of the guards and the demeaning and dehumanizing nature of the prison system in general. He came to understand that in the perspective of the institution, human life meant very little. Manson spent 3 years in federal penal institutions, where he learned to emulate the mobsters and criminals of the times. At 19, Charles Manson was set free, legitimately, for the first time in 7 years. He was paroled on May 8, 1954.

In the very short time that Manson tasted freedom, he married a woman by the name of Rosalie Jean Willis, and they had a son, Charles Manson Jr. Manson was arrested for passing a bad check and sent back to prison for a short time. Upon his release, he became a pimp, which led to another 7 years in federal prison for running an interstate vice ring. Manson was released from the reformatory at Terminal Island, California, in 1967, even though he reportedly begged the authorities to let him stay because he felt he required the structure of the institution in order to live.

On March 21, 1967, Manson had $35 release money and his parole officer's phone number; his ex-wife had taken his son and run away with a truck driver. He had absolutely no vocational training that would have allowed him to survive on the outside for any appreciable period of time. He was 32 years old and had been in and out of prison or reform schools, continually, for the past 20 years.

Twenty-four hours after his release from Terminal Island, Charles Manson found himself in the Haight-Ashbury district of San Francisco, observing the "free sex" scene for the first time and experimenting with a wide variety of drugs. He desperately wanted to be part of the scene, and he quickly made use of his charisma to integrate with others. These were itinerant individuals whom Manson had discovered during his mingling, hippies, drug dealers, musicians, college students who episodically attended courses, high-school-age runaways, and draft dodgers who had gone underground. There were also war protesters and student activists among the groups in the Haight-Ashbury district who were traveling to keep one step ahead of the police or the FBI. Manson quickly became a fixture in these groups. He had the ability to understand such people, because many of them were social outcasts just like himself. They were lawbreakers, fugitives, young people with neither homes nor families, and artists determined to live on the fringe of society. He was constantly on the move, from the parks, to apartments, to sleeping on the floor in strange rooms. He traveled among the cities of San Francisco, Reno, Los Angeles, and Sacramento, but always wound up back at the Haight-Ashbury district in San Francisco.

Manson was not the typical resident of the Haight-Ashbury district. He was over 30 and was skilled at interpreting the key elements of other people's personalities and determining what responses would put them at ease and make them allies, friends, or sexual partners. Manson's chameleon-like skills found easy targets, and he was able to manipulate and control many of the people he met, especially the young girls. He was like a father figure to many of the girls who had run away from home, but he was also a sexual figure who seemed to know exactly what they wanted.

Manson earned money by playing music in tawdry bars in San Francisco's Tenderloin district and on the street corners for donations. He also made some money by panhandling for loose change, hustling some of the young girls he met, and through dealing drugs. In addition, he was engaged in outright burglary and in running con schemes on unsuspecting people who visited the Haight-Ashbury district to see the "local color."

By early 1969, Manson was considered a savvy, strange figure among the dropout street people in both San Francisco and Los Angeles. During the next year, he lived with hundreds of different people and had sex with both young girls and boys, making them "family" members by becoming the reflection of their respective individual needs. He also became involved with occult and Satanic groups and formed his own subgroups within them by seeking out new relationships and sexual partners. In addition, he kept pursuing his dream of a musical career and sought out relationships that would help him achieve his dream of becoming a rock-and-roll superstar.

His many faces, along with his frequently shifting moods, quickly refined his evolving chameleon-like demeanor. He could quickly blend into any group so as not to appear the odd man out. He could become the significant other of any person he met by ferreting out those personality attributes the other person was seeking. Although he was involved with at least three different occult groups during this period, his contacts with movie personalities, rock musicians, and groupies at the studios gained him entrance to a world of money, sex, power, and drugs. It was as if he had suddenly found himself in a position of power over all those he felt had been his abusers for the previous 20 years, and he used this to his advantage by exploiting his celebrity connections to circulate his music among movie studios. Ironically, he was one of the religious consultants for a movie about Jesus Christ that was produced at Universal Studios and extracted a promise from the director to use his music in the motion picture's soundtrack. He became friends with Dennis Wilson of the Beach Boys and tried unsuccessfully to get the group to play his music.

By the middle of 1969, Charles Manson and his growing Family occupied the Spahn Movie Ranch. There, they began to act out their leader's apocalyptic vision of "Helter-Skelter" that would culminate in a devastating race war. The former movie set, with its ramshackle buildings reminiscent of a frontier town in the 1880s, was owned by 81-year-old George Spahn. Spahn was unaware of most of the activities conducted by Manson and his group at the ranch. He was also unaware of any of the murders they had committed. Each Family member paid homage to Manson, who was purported to be the "fifth angel" from the Bible, and willingly carried out his ritualistic death sentences. The members of the Manson Family are classified as disciple killers. As such, they could never be alone what they could aspire to collectively. Inhibitions and fears were dissipated by the interaction of the members

Charles "Charlie" Manson became a household name for his orchestration of the Tate-LaBianca murders in Southern California during the 1960s. He claimed that his goal was to start a race war. Members of the cult that followed him, the "Family," obeyed his every word. Manson currently resides in Corcoran State Prison, California.

Source: Copyright © Bettmann / CORBIS.

in a process that is referred to as a *follie aux famille,* or group delusion. Manson psychologically maintained control over Family members by using various forms of coercion, intimidation, and other persuasive techniques, and even further by exerting a seemingly mystical force over his followers.

One of the disturbing activities that Manson had members of his Family engage in was referred to as "creepy crawling." During these exercises, they would enter families' homes and rearrange their furniture and personal belongings while the inhabitants slept. They did not harm these people, nor did they steal any property from them. The activities were designed to

increase Family member's sense of omnipotence, grandiosity, and predatory skill. Charles Manson needed only to provide a sense of direction for his eager band of disciples. In the meantime, he was also a daily polysubstance abuser, experiencing hallucinations and participating in ceremonial rituals simulating human sacrifice and torture. His Satanic visions made it increasingly more difficult for him to control his rage and to separate fantasy and reality. His obsession with Helter-Skelter drove Manson and his Family to the sensational acts that would set "the plan" in motion in the summer of 1969.

The Tate-LaBianca murders committed by Manson and his Family became one of the most infamous crimes in U.S. history. Just after midnight on August 9, 1969, five people were brutally murdered in a prominent Los Angeles neighborhood. The victims were Sharon Marie Tate, wife of movie director Roman Polanski; Abigail Folger, heiress to the A. J. Folger Coffee Company fortune; Wojiciech (Voytek) Frykowski, Abigail Folger's boyfriend and playboy; Jay Sebring, internationally renowned hairstylist and former boyfriend of Sharon Tate; and Steven Parent, a friend of the caretaker of the property. Sharon Tate was a stunningly beautiful movie actress with a reputation of being one of the nicest people to know in Hollywood. She was 8 months pregnant at the time of her murder. She was stabbed, strangled, and subjected to both physical and psychological torture before she was murdered.

Abigail Folger was stabbed 28 times. Her boyfriend, Voytek Frykowski, was beaten over the head 13 times with a hard object, shot twice, and stabbed 51 times. Jay Sebring was stabbed 7 times and shot once. Steven Parent, an 18-year-old visitor to the house that night, was shot 4 times while sitting in his car. The victims' bodies were found in various locations both inside and outside of the residence. On the front door, written in Sharon Tate's blood, was the word "PIG."

Less than 48 hours later, Leno and Rosemary LaBianca were found murdered in their home. Leno LaBianca was stabbed 12 times with a 14-inch carving fork, which was left sticking out of his stomach. He had the word "WAR" carved into his abdomen. It was later discovered that he had also been strangled and a small knife had been stuck in his throat. His wife, Rosemary, was stabbed 41 times, six being fatal wounds. Around the LaBianca house were words written in the victims' blood: "DEATH TO PIGS," "RISE," and "HEALTER SKELTER" [*sic*].

These murders were shocking in many ways: the brutal manner in which they were committed, the number of victims, the social prominence of the victims, the absence of robbery or any other clear or recognizable motive, the evidence of multiple offenders, the lack of evidence to produce suspects, the blood-written words on the walls with obscure meaning, the lack of connections between the two sets of victims, the geographic distance between the two crime scenes, the close temporal proximity, and the high degree of randomness in victim selection. The subsequent investigation and trial of Charles Manson and his Family members brought to public knowledge that they were responsible for, or suspected in, other homicides—an estimated 35 or more total.

On August 16, 1969, one week after the Tate-LaBianca murders, Manson and 25 members of the Family were arrested at Spahn Ranch as suspects in an auto theft ring. They were released a few days later due to a technicality of a misdated warrant. The group then relocated to Barker Ranch, in Death Valley, California. In early October 1969, in a 3-day police raid of the ranch, Los Angeles County Sheriff's Officers arrested Charles Manson and 23 members of the group on a variety of charges, from grand theft to arson. Two young girls in the Family implicated the group in several murders, including the Tate-LaBianca killings.

Throughout the ensuing trial of Charles Manson, Tex Watson, Bruce Davis, Leslie Van Houton, Patricia Krenwinkle, Susan Atkins, and the rest of the Manson Family, the media referred to Manson as "the most dangerous man in America." He was also, and still is, one of the most charismatic figures of the 1960s, a complex cult leader at once paranoid, grandiose, nihilistic, antisocial, manipulative, sadistic, sociopathic, predatory, revolutionary, and homicidal.

—*Marlene Deal and Eric W. Hickey*

See also CRIMES OF OBEDIENCE; CULTS; HELTER-SKELTER; MASS MURDER; MOTIVES FOR MURDER

Further Reading

Bugliosi, V., & Gentry, C. (1994). *Helter-skelter: The true story of the Manson murders.* New York: Norton.

Gilmore, J., & Kenner, R. (1996). *The garbage people: The trip to helter-skelter and beyond with Charlie Manson and the family.* Los Angeles: Amok Books.

Hickey, E. W. (2002). *Serial murderers and their victims* (3rd ed.). Belmont, CA: Wadsworth.

Holmes, R. M., & Holmes, S. T. (1994). *Murder in America.* Thousand Oaks, CA: Sage.

Norris, J. (1989). *Serial killers.* New York: Anchor Books, Doubleday.

MASS MURDER

Mass murder is a form of multiple homicide in which four or more victims are slain during a single episode. In December 2000, for example, Michael McDermott, a 42-year-old employee of Edgewater Technology in Wakefield, Massachusetts, opened fire on his coworkers, killing seven of them. In June 2001, Andrea Yates drowned her five children in Houston, Texas.

We can derive some sense of the prevalence of mass killing from the FBI Supplementary Homicide Reports (see Fox, 2000), an incident level database of more than 92% of the murders committed in the United States each year. For the years 1976 through 1999, an estimated 497,030 people were murdered in the United States. Of these, 3,956 were slain in incidents claiming four or more victims. Still, many of these mass killings involve circumstances in which the homicide may not have been intentional, most notably arson resulting in the deaths of large numbers of people. Although occasionally mass killers specifically use fire as their weapon of choice, most of these cases entail unplanned fatalities and should arguably be eliminated from consideration. After this exclusion, the 24-year period yields 599 mass killings, involving 2,800 victims and 826 killers.

On average, then, two incidents of mass murder occur per month in the United States, claiming more than 100 victims annually. Most incidents, of course, are not as widely publicized as the horrific slaughters of 14 postal workers in an Oklahoma post office in 1986 or of 23 customers in a Texas restaurant in 1991. Still, the phenomenon of the massacre or mass murder, although hardly of epidemic proportions, is not the rare occurrence that it is sometimes assumed to be.

Also based on these FBI homicide data, we have determined that the popular image of mass murder differs in significant ways from the reality of it. Although the most heavily publicized type of mass murder involves the indiscriminate shooting of strangers in a public place by a lone gunman, other kinds of mass killing are actually far more common.

Included within this scope are, for example, the disgruntled employee who kills his boss and coworkers after being fired, the estranged husband/father who massacres his entire family and then kills himself, the band of armed robbers who slaughter a roomful of witnesses to their crime, and the racist hatemonger who sprays a schoolyard of immigrant children with gunfire. Thus, the motivations for mass murder can range from revenge to hatred and from loyalty to greed; the victims can be selected individually, as members of a particular category or group or, least often, on a purely random basis.

The location of mass murder differs sharply from that of homicides in which a single victim is slain. First, mass murders do not tend to cluster in large cities as do single-victim crimes, but are more likely to occur in small-town or rural settings. Moreover, while the South (the Deep South in particular) is known for high rates of murder, this does not hold for mass murder. In comparison to single-victim murder, which is highly concentrated in urban areas populated by poor blacks, and in the Deep South, where arguments are often settled through gunfire, mass murder more or less reflects the geographic distribution of the general population.

Not surprisingly, the firearm is the weapon of choice in mass murder incidents, even more than in single-victim crimes. Clearly, a handgun or rifle is the most effective means of mass destruction. By contrast, it is difficult to kill large numbers of people simultaneously with physical force or even a knife or blunt object. Furthermore, although an explosive device can potentially cause the death of a large number of people (as in the 1995 bombing of the Oklahoma City Federal Building), its unpredictability would be unacceptable for most mass killers, who target their victims selectively.

The findings regarding victim-offender relationship are perhaps as counterintuitive as the weapon use results may be obvious. Contrary to popular belief, mass murderers infrequently attack strangers who just happen to be in the "wrong place at the wrong time." In fact, almost 40% of these crimes are committed against family members, and almost as many involve other victims acquainted with the perpetrator (e.g., coworkers). It is well-known that murder often involves family members, but this is especially pronounced among massacres.

The differences in circumstance underlying these crimes are also quite dramatic. Although more than half of all single-victim homicides occur during an argument between the victim and offender, it is relatively rare for a heated dispute to escalate into mass murder.

Some of the most notable differences between homicide types emerge in the area of offender characteristics. Compared with assailants who kill but one victim, mass murderers are overwhelmingly likely to be male, are far more likely to be white, and are somewhat older. Typically, the single-victim offender is a young male, slightly more often black than white, whereas the massacrer is typically a middle-aged white male (this profile comes into sharpest focus for mass killers who are motivated by something other than robbery).

Victim characteristics are, of course, largely a function of the offender patterns noted above, indicating that mass killers generally do not select their victims on a random basis. For example, the victims of mass murder are usually white simply because the perpetrators to whom they are related or with whom they associate are white. Similarly, the youthfulness and greater representation of females among the victims of mass murder, compared with single-victim homicide, stem from the fact that a typical mass killing involves the breadwinner of the household who annihilates the entire family, his wife and his children.

Media accounts of mass murderers tend to focus on killers who suddenly "go berserk" or "run amok"—the likes of George Hennard Jr., who in 1991 opened fire in a crowded Killeen, Texas restaurant, killing 23 victims at random. Another example is that of ex-marine Charles Whitman, who killed 14 and wounded 30 others while perched atop a tower at the University of Texas in 1966.

These sudden, seemingly episodic and random incidents of violence are as atypical as they are extreme. A majority of mass killers have clear-cut motives, especially revenge, and their victims are chosen because of what they have done or what they represent. Even cases that would seem indiscriminate to the casual observer often involve a process of selection. In August 1999, for example, Mark Barton killed nine people and wounded a dozen more during an afternoon shooting spree at two Atlanta day-trading offices. Hardly random, these were the very locations where Barton had lost nearly a half-million dollars in stock trades. Moreover, his not-so-sudden and not-so-random assault had begun days earlier, when he murdered his wife and two children. Despite the popular image, therefore, the indiscriminate slaughter of strangers by a "crazed" killer is the exception to the rule.

Finally, the more specific and focused the element of revenge, the more likely the outburst is planned and methodical rather than spontaneous and random. Also, the more specific the targets of revenge, the less likely it is that the killer's rage stems from psychosis.

Why then do they kill? Why would a 31-year-old former postal worker, Thomas McIlvane, go on a rampage in Royal Oak, Michigan, killing four fellow postal workers before shooting himself in the head? And what would cause a 28-year-old graduate student, Gang Lu, to execute five others at the University of Iowa before taking his own life? Finally, why would a 55-year-old Missourian, Neil Schatz, fatally shoot his wife, two children, and two grandchildren before committing suicide? An analysis of numerous case studies suggests that the following factors contribute to mass murder.

Frustration. In his early book, *The Psychology of Murder,* Stuart Palmer studied 51 convicted killers, most of whom had experienced severely frustrating childhood illnesses, accidents, child abuse, physical defects, isolation, and poverty. The mass murderer similarly suffers from a long history of frustration, humiliation, and failure concomitant with a diminishing ability to cope and increasingly negative self-image, which begin early in life and continue well into adulthood. As a result, this type of person may also develop a condition of profound and unrelenting depression, although not necessarily at the level of psychosis. This may explain why so many mass killers are middle-aged, having suffered for years under the accumulation of childhood and adulthood disappointments that culminate in this deep sense of frustration. For example, 41-year-old James Ruppert, who slaughtered his 11 relatives in Hamilton, Ohio, on Easter Sunday, 1975, had been extremely incompetent in school, friendships, and sports throughout his youth, lost his father at an early age, suffered from debilitating asthma and spinal meningitis, was so uncomfortable around women that he never experienced a sexual relationship, and was unable to hold a steady job as an adult. By focusing on frustration, we do not rule out the possibility in a few cases that the depression may have a biological or organic foundation. For example, Joseph Wesbecker, who murdered eight coworkers in a Louisville, Kentucky, printing plant, was being treated for depression,

which itself could have been linked to his own history of failure.

Externalization of Responsibility. Many people who suffer from frustration and depression over an extended period of time may commit suicide without physically harming anyone else. Part of the problem is that they perceive themselves as worthless and as responsible for their failures in life. Their aggression is intropunitive. Thus, a critical condition for frustration to result in extrapunitive aggression is that these individuals perceive that others are to blame for their personal problems and failures. As a response style acquired through learning, mass killers come to see themselves never as the culprit, but always as the victim behind their disappointments. More specifically, the mass murderer externalizes blame: It is invariably "someone else's fault."

A Catastrophic Loss. Given both long-term frustration and an angry, blameful mind-set, certain situations or events can precipitate or trigger violent rage. In most instances, killers experience a sudden loss or the threat of a loss that from their point of view is catastrophic. The loss typically involves an unwanted separation from loved ones or termination from employment. In 1991, for example, 39-year-old James Colbert of Concord, New Hampshire, killed his estranged wife and three daughters. Learning that his wife had started a new relationship, Colbert reasoned, "If I can't have her and the kids, then no one can." James Ruppert, by contrast, was facing eviction by his mother from the only house in which he had ever lived. Either he stopped his drinking and paid his debts or he would have to leave.

Employment problems are even more frequently found to precipitate mass killing. In 1991, for example, postal worker Thomas McIlvane had been fired from his job and lost his appeal for reinstatement just prior to his rampage in Royal Oak, Michigan. Patrick Sherrill's supervisor had threatened to fire him just 2 days before the 1986 post office massacre in Edmond, Oklahoma.

The overabundance of men among mass killers, even more than among murderers generally, may stem in part from the fact that men are more likely to suffer the kind of catastrophic losses often associated with mass murder. Following a separation or divorce, it is generally the husband/father who is ejected from the family home. Furthermore, despite advances in the status of women in America, males more than females continue to define themselves in terms of their occupational roles ("what they do" defines "who they are") and therefore tend more to suffer psychologically from unemployment.

Contagion. Although not as common as the loss of a relationship or employment, certain external cues or models have also served as catalysts or inspiration for mass murder. Although the "copycat" phenomenon is difficult to document scientifically, the anecdotal evidence is at least highly suggestive. For example, the rash of schoolyard slayings—beginning with Laurie Dann's May 1988 shooting at a Winnetka, Illinois, elementary school and ending with Patrick Purdy's January 1989 attack in Stockton, California—suggests the possibility of a "fad" element in which mass killers inspire one another. Most striking was the case of James Wilson of Greenwood, South Carolina, a "fan" of Laurie Dann. Much like his hero, in September 1988, he sprayed a local elementary school with gunfire, killing two children. When police searched Wilson's apartment, they found the *People Magazine* cover photo of Laurie Dann taped to his wall. They also learned in subsequent interviews with those who knew James Wilson that he talked about Dann incessantly.

The more recent string of teenaged school massacres also illustrates the power of imitation to inspire mass murder. On February 2, 1996, in the first of series of school shootings, 14-year-old Barry Loukaitis burst into his math class at the Frontier High School in Moses Lake, Washington, removed a high-powered rifle from beneath his long overcoat, and started firing. After killing the teacher and two classmates, he remarked, "This sure beats Algebra," a line drawn from his favorite Stephen King novella about a school shooting.

The Moses Lake school tragedy was then followed by schoolyard multiple killings in Pearl, Mississippi; West Paducah, Kentucky; Jonesboro, Arkansas; Springfield, Oregon; and Littleton, Colorado. Unlike the series of school attacks in 1988 and 1989, the newest breed of avengers are teenagers and pre-teenagers—one as young as 11 years old. Apparently, copycat effects can be so strong as to mitigate the necessity of a long-term frustration factor.

Social Isolation. Mass murderers are often characterized in the popular press as "loners." It is indeed true that many of them are cut off from sources of comfort and guidance from the very people who could have supported them when times got tough. Some live alone for extended periods of time. Others relocate great distances away from home, experiencing a sense of anomie or normlessness. They lose their sources of emotional support. It is no coincidence that mass murders tend to concentrate in areas of the nation where there are large numbers of drifters, transients, newcomers, and migrants—individuals who lack family, friends, and fraternal organizations to get them through bad times. Many Americans have for the sake of a new beginning or a last resort, migrated to states such as California, Texas, Florida, Alaska, New York, and Illinois. These states have had more than their share of mass murders.

A Weapon of Mass Destruction. Not all people who feel intensely angry, hopeless, and isolated necessarily commit mass murder. In many cases, they simply don't have the means; for example, it is almost impossible to commit a massacre with a knife or a hammer. Such weapons are potentially destructive but are not mass destructive. Killers such as James Ruppert and James Huberty were well trained in the use of firearms and owned quite a few of them. Ruppert often went target shooting on the banks of the Great Miami River; Huberty practiced at the firing range in his own basement. Moreover, both of them were armed with loaded firearms at the very time they felt angry enough to kill.

Explosives are potentially another effective means of mass destruction, as was tragically shown in Timothy McVeigh's April 1995 bombing of the Federal Building in Oklahoma City, in which 168 innocent people lost their lives. In reality, however, the lack of knowledge of the construction of powerful bombs has limited their role in mass murder in the United States. In contrast, in agricultural societies in which dynamite is readily available and firearms are not (e.g., rural China), massacres are usually committed by means of explosives, not semiautomatic rifles. Moreover, the September 11, 2001, attack on the World Trade Center and the Pentagon illustrated in a particularly tragic way that terrorists who are willing to take their own lives in order to maximize their body count can make even jet aircrafts into powerful weapons of mass destruction.

—James Alan Fox and Jack Levin

Further Reading

Campbell, A. (1991). *Men, women, and aggression.*
New York: Basic Books.

Dietz, P. E. (1986). Mass, serial and sensational homicides.
Bulletin of the New York Academy of Medicine, 62,
477-491.

Doerner, W. G. (1975). A regional analysis of homicide
rates in the United States. *Criminology, 13,* 90-101.

Dollard, J., Doob, L., Miller, N., Mowrer, O. H., & Sears,
R. R. (1939). *Frustration and aggression.* New Haven:
Yale University Press.

Fox, J. A. (2000). *The supplementary homicide reports,
1976-1999.* Ann Arbor, MI: Criminal Justice Archive, Inter-
University Consortium of Political and Social Research.

Fox, J. A., & Levin, J. (1994a). *Overkill: Mass murder and
serial killing exposed.* New York: Plenum.

Fox, J. A., & Levin, J. (1994b). "Firing back: The growing
threat of workplace homicide." *The Annals of the American
Academy of Political and Social Science, 536,* 15-30.

Fox, J. A., & Levin, J. (2001). *The will to kill: Making sense
of senseless murder.* Boston: Allyn & Bacon.

Goldberg, C. (1996). *Speaking with the devil.* New York:
Viking.

Hale, R. (1994). The role of humiliation and embarrassment in serial murder. *Psychology: A Journal of Human
Behavior, 31,* 17-22.

Henry, A., & Short, J. F. (1954). *Suicide and homicide.*
Glencoe, IL: Free Press.

Holmes, R. M., & Holmes, S. (2001). *Mass murder in the
United States.* Upper Saddle River, NJ: Prentice Hall.

Kinney, J. A., & Johnson, D. L. (1993). *Breaking point: The
workplace violence epidemic and what to do about it.*
Chicago: National Safe Workplace Institute.

Levin, J., & Fox, J. A. (1985). *Mass murder: America's
growing menace.* New York: Plenum.

Levin, J., & Fox, J. A. (2001). *Dead lines: Essays in murder
and mayhem.* Boston: Allyn & Bacon.

Palmer, S. (1960). *The psychology of murder.* New York:
Crowell.

Phillips, D. P. (1983). The impact of mass media violence
on U.S. homicides. *American Sociological Review, 48,*
560-568.

MASS VIOLENCE

Historically, mass violence became part of our
global landscape as numbers and diversities among
people began to separate and distinguish groups and
individuals. Its perpetrators may act alone, or they
may be affiliated with government or military institutions. They target men, women, and children in atrocities committed in the home or as acts of war.

Mass violence does not only consist of murder, but
can take many forms, such as rape, beatings, arsons,
and slavery. Rummel (1995) estimates that, excluding
war deaths, over 170 million violent deaths have
occurred between 1900 and 1987. An even more ominous number would include "residual deaths" or deaths
resulting from emotional and long-term physical
damage, as seen in the genocide of the Armenians in
Turkey and the "ethnic cleansing" in Bosnia, Rwanda,
Burundi, the Timorese in Indonesia, and Native
Americans. Mass violence has no boundaries in places
such as the Cambodian killing fields perpetrated by the
Khmer Rouge, the death squads in El Salvador, the
government-sanctioned killings in Argentina and Chile,
the well-documented Stalin purges, and Holocaust
murders of millions in Europe.

COMFORT WOMEN

During World War II, the Japanese Imperial Army,
as part of their colonial expansion, committed sexual
war crimes against nearly 200,000 Korean women.
The victims were forced to serve as sex slaves to the
Japanese soldiers and were referred to as *jugun ianfu,*
or "military comfort women." The Japanese government collectively conspired with the Japanese military
to institutionalize the systematic rape of Korean and
other non-Japanese women, including hundreds of
Dutch, Filipino, Thai, and other women captured
during the war. The dehumanization was so severe
that soldiers often referred to the women as "female
ammunition" and "sanitary public toilets."

Systematic rape, institutionalized prostitution, and
sexual slavery are common forms of war crimes. The
trafficking of women by the Japanese military was
institutionalized by 1910, when the Japanese colonized
Korea. Later, in 1918, the Japanese invaded Siberia
and brought with them Japanese prostitutes known as
karayukisan, or foreign-bound/China-bound women.
Under the guise of protecting Asian countries, Japan

maintained its plan of expansionism and with it, the enrollment of Korean women to keep the Imperial Army content. By the end of World War II, Japan had sent 70,000 to 80,000 Korean females between the ages of 14 and 30, both single and married, to the front lines in Asia to serve as comfort women. Most Korean women came from the lower social classes and were therefore offered to the regular Japanese troops, and European and other Asian women were reserved for the officers. Reports by comfort women reveal that they were forced to service between 30 and 40 soldiers per day or risk being beaten and tortured. The institutionalization of Korean women as sex slaves was justified by noting that without them, Japanese soldiers might be given to raping and plundering, as demonstrated in Nanjing in 1937.

THE NAZI HOLOCAUST

The Holocaust, like other genocides, is difficult to capture in words alone. Mass violence was orchestrated not only by a political/military establishment but also by a nation that supported the Third Reich and Adolph Hitler, an expansionist and a hatemonger, with a racial purity agenda that included the extermination of all Jews, gypsies, homosexuals, mentally or physically challenged, and social misfits. Hitler was an incredible mastermind at organizing mass violence at many levels, from his attempt to conquer Europe with plans of world domination and his "Final Solution" to the extermination of European Jews and others deemed unfit by Third Reich standards.

The process of extermination afforded the Nazis opportunities to engage in innovative forms of mass violence, including sterilization experiments, the Dachau hypothermia and high-altitude experiments, Joseph Mengele's studies of twins, Buchenwald biological warfare experiments, and the Nazi euthanasia project. Under the guise of Nazi medicine, doctors systematically experimented on, tortured, and exterminated victims. Nazi doctors justified their medical research as being important and useful. How quickly can a man be castrated? How long can a person survive when injected with poisons or chemicals?

The Nazis also victimized their own people by asking them to turn over any German children with mental or physical limitations, and several thousand were systematically exterminated. The first to die were those with physical deformities, followed by children who were noncompliant. Babies were placed outside in the winter months to see how long they lasted before pneumonia set in. Dr. H. Gross, also known as "Dr. Death" and "Dr. Vomit" (he administered poisons to children), was responsible for selecting and euthanizing hundreds of babies and children. Mass violence, although differentially planned and administered, affected everyone at some level.

THE MIDDLE EAST

Mass violence is systemic to competing ethnic and religious groups. The Middle East, for example, continues to be plagued by violence between Palestinians and Jews. The animosity is not only rooted in geopolitical confrontations over self-rule, but is shrouded in cultural and religious differences. Such diversities are perpetual catalysts for deadly violence. More than 1.5 million Arabs live in Israel, where as practicing Muslims, they worship at their third most sacred shrine in all of Islam, the Dome of the Rock. The nearly 5 million Jews in Israel represent extreme diversity in religiosity, from ultraorthodox to nonpracticing individuals. Their existence, however, is overshadowed by the need for survival. In addition to having to address the needs of Arabs and Jews cohabiting in the country, Israel must also balance their détente with the bordering countries of Lebanon, Syria, and Jordan. Conflict is cumulative, and with extremists on both sides agitating for the ouster of their sworn enemies from lands they both claim, escalating conflict is inevitable. The West Bank and the Gaza Strip are flashpoints for violence between Islamic militants and Jewish settlers and Israeli military forces.

Many powerful nations that have competing economic and political interests in accessing the vast oil reserves in the Middle East region anxiously monitor acts of violence in that region. Such escalations of violent acts are the harbingers of mass violence.

MANIFESTATION OF MASS VIOLENCE

Other examples of mass violence include the randomized killing of children, as in Brazil's vigilantism against homeless children or China's cultural killings of female babies to ensure that the family name is passed on through male posterity. Over time, mass violence has developed both macro- and microlevel dynamics. Some of the more salient factors in mass violence can be found in greed, sexual property, racial/ethnic hatred, colonialism, ethnocentrism, and religious intolerance. Our world, albeit relatively small, has produced an incredible amount of mass violence perpetuated by offenders as well as those who benefit from it.

The manifestation of mass violence is found in both individual and societal entities and is portrayed through instrumental and expressive aggression. *Instrumental violence* refers to those who seek material gain or destruction without manifest emotional attachments to their acts. For example, robbing a bank for the sole purpose of acquiring money is instrumental. There is no agenda or motivation other than to acquire money. The act of bank robbery is *expressive* when the crime is committed out of anger, hate, revenge, or other emotionally charged agendas. Within societies, there are individuals who engage in mass violence by either inciting others to act out or by perpetrating acts of violence themselves. The United States has seen throughout its youthful history groups of individuals led by those capable of *micro–mass violence*. The Ku Klux Klan, a fractionated, white supremacist organization, has periodically been responsible for acts of terrorism. Most of their acts of mass violence are considered to be expressive.

It is important to remember that everyone has the capability to commit a violent criminal act, but not everyone has the capacity for homicide, especially mass murder. Still, there are endless instances of people who are equipped in this manner, from institutionalized violence to the individual who inflicts harm on specific targets, as in the bombing of the Federal Building in Oklahoma City or the September 11, 2001, attacks on the World Trade Center and the Pentagon.

—*Eric W. Hickey*

See also CRIMES OF OBEDIENCE; ETHNIC CLEANSING; GENOCIDE; HISTORY OF VIOLENCE IN RELIGIONS; MASS MURDER; MEDICAL MURDERS; MOTIVES FOR MURDER; OKLAHOMA CITY BOMBING; TERRORISM; WAR ATROCITIES; WHITE SUPREMACISTS

Further Reading

Executive Committee, International Public Hearing Concerning Post War Compensation by Japan (Ed.). (1993). *War victimization and Japan: International public hearing report*. Tokyo: Toho Shuppan.

Kazuko, W. (1994, October-December). Militarism, colonialism, and the trafficking of women: "Comfort women" forced into sexual labor for Japanese soldiers. *Bulletin of Concerned Asian Scholars, 26,* 4.

National Christian Council (Ed.). (1994). *Report: The Asian solidarity forum on militarism and sexual slavery*. Nishi-Waseda, Tokyo: Author.

Staub, E. (1992). *The roots of evil: The psychological and cultural origins of genocide*. Cambridge University Press.

Totten, S., Parsons, W. S., & Charny, I. W. (1997*). Century of genocide: Eyewitness accounts and critical views*. New York: Garland.

MASSACRE, *See* ETHNIC CLEANSING; GENOCIDE; HUBERTY, JAMES OLIVER; MASS VIOLENCE; OKLAHOMA CITY BOMBING; SCHOOL SHOOTINGS; ST. VALENTINE'S DAY MASSACRE; TERRORISM

MCDERMOT, MICHAEL, *See* MASS MURDER

MCDONALD'S MASSACRE, *See* HUBERTY, JAMES OLIVER; MASS MURDER

MCILVANE, THOMAS, *See* MASS MURDER

MCMARTIN DAY CARE CASE, *See* FALSE MEMORY SYNDROME

TIMOTHY MCVEIGH

Timothy McVeigh masterminded the worst terrorist act ever perpetrated by an American citizen, the bombing of the Alfred P. Murrah Federal Building in Oklahoma City in 1995. He was raised in a rural community in upstate New York after his parents separated in 1978. A loner in high school, McVeigh enlisted in the army in 1988 and rose through the ranks to platoon leader. In 1991, after winning a Bronze Star in the Persian Gulf War, he failed to complete Green Beret school, increasing his dissatisfaction with the government.

In 1993, McVeigh began a nomadic life, selling guns at shows throughout the United States. He traveled to Waco, Texas, during the standoff between federal agents and the Branch Davidian cult and was incensed at the outcome, blaming the government when the cult resorted to suicide.

Although never linked to militant antigovernment groups, McVeigh soon began planning revenge for the Waco deaths. He enlisted the help of army buddy Terry Nichols, and they took steps to build and place a bomb at the Alfred P. Murrah Federal Building in Oklahoma City, from which McVeigh mistakenly believed the government order for the Waco assault had originated.

On April 19, 1995, McVeigh parked a rented Ryder trunk at the north side of the Federal Building, and minutes later, a fertilizer and fuel oil bomb exploded, immediately collapsing about a third of the building and killing 168 people. In 1998, he was convicted and on June 11, 2001, was executed by lethal injection.

—*Denise Nola-Faye Lowe*

See also MASS VIOLENCE; METHODS OF MURDER; NICHOLS, TERRY; OKLAHOMA CITY BOMBING; TERRORISM

Further Reading

Michel, L., & Herbeck, D. (2002). *American terrorist: Timothy McVeigh and the tragedy at Oklahoma City.* Regan Books.

Jones, S. (2001). Others unknown: Timothy McVeigh and the Oklahoma City bombing conspiracy. Public Affairs Publishers.

VIOLENCE IN THE MEDIA

The relationship between exposure to violence through media and violent behavior has been demonstrated empirically and is a topic of controversy and concern around the world as technological advances and violent crime reach unprecedented heights. For present purposes, *violence* is defined as any act or threat of action resulting in real or potential physical harm to self or other living things. Consistent with many U.S. states' laws, any sexual act with a child (an individual under the age of 18) is also considered violent. Violence in the media refers to real (e.g., televised footage of the September 11, 2001, terrorist attacks on the U.S. World Trade Center and the Pentagon) or fictitious (e.g., horror films such as *Nightmare on Elm Street*) violence as it occurs in all forms of media, including television, film, video games, the Internet, music, radio, newspapers, magazines, and books. Exposure to violence through the media has been implicated in numerous incidents of violent criminal behavior, for example, the Columbine High School massacre, in Colorado, in 1999, and several copycat murders and suicides related to rock music. Critics of violence in the media contend that it increases violent behavior and fear of victimization, creates a norm of violence, repeatedly traumatizes victims of violence, facilitates sexual abuse, and perpetuates gender role and racial stereotypes.

Since the debut of the television in the majority of American homes in the 1950s, vicarious exposure to violence through media has been a topic of heated concern. Currently, 98 out of 100 American homes have at least one television, and there is no country in which a television signal is not available either by air broadcast, cable, or satellite. With the proliferation of the music video, video game, pornography, and Internet industries, recent generations have been exposed to a wider variety and more graphic modes of violence than were earlier generations. In the United States, Canada, Great Britain, Australia, and other countries, government and private task forces have investigated the effects of media violence on consumers.

Pervasive exposure to media violence has three broad effects on people: a direct effect, a desensitizing effect, and a generalizing effect. Akin to social learning theory, the *direct effect* of witnessing violence is the imitation of aggressive behavior through observational learning and increased fantasy about violent means of conflict resolution. Aggressive behavior is further reinforced by the fact that although real-life violence typically has adverse consequences, negative consequences to the perpetrators of violence are often not depicted in media clippings.

Second, the *desensitizing effect* refers to the decreased sensitivity to the pain and suffering of others that occurs over time with exposure to violence. One's initial experiences of violence typically have a startling effect, but repeated flooding of the senses with violent stimuli engages the defenses to protect the self from the aversive effects of chronic trauma. As the individual learns to expect violence, their visceral reactions become desensitized to violent acts.

Finally, exposure to violence through media facilitates the *generalized* perception that the entire world is a hostile and dangerous place. This third effect, often referred to as the "mean world syndrome," not only leads to increased anxiety and fear of victimization but also contributes to violence by producing a perceived normative standard that violent behavior is a typical and permissible means of conflict resolution.

Although exposure to violence through media affects all ages, children are considered the most vulnerable because of their immature levels of cognitive and emotional development. Children spend 28 hours per week watching television; they are educated about violence primarily through media sources. Because children have difficulty distinguishing reality from fantasy, they are susceptible to trauma by fictitious violence and engage in a high degree of fantasy about heroism and violent problem solving. Despite the fact that more than 1,000 studies have found short- and long-term negative effects of childhood exposure to violence through media, more than two dozen violent acts are depicted in every hour of Saturday morning children's television programming, which is 5 times more violence than in evening prime-time programming.

Study results indicate that not only do children who experience violence in the media (e.g., superhero cartoons) display more aggression, they are also more likely than children who have not had such exposure to engage in violent criminal behavior as adults. Children's advocates cite that exposing children to violence in the media has similar effects as military training that employs the technique of flooding trainees with violence to reduce their inhibition against killing. They therefore allege that exposing children to media violence is a form of child abuse.

Television in the United States, unlike other countries, did not begin as a government-sponsored industry; it began as a commercial enterprise with the sole purpose of making money. Although public broadcasting has since been implemented, educational programs are still ancillary to commercial programming. Children are most negatively affected by the lack of government regulation and quality learning material available on television. On May 1, 1998,

children's programming on two Los Angeles, California, stations was interrupted by live footage of Daniel Jones committing suicide by setting himself on fire and then shooting himself in the head on a freeway. Enraged parents lobbied that if governments were more involved, younger audiences would be protected from secondary trauma from such media violence.

Interactive video games are the most recent addition to the list of violence- and sexually laden media empirically linked to violence. Increases in violent behavior, anxiety, physiological arousal, and aggressive thoughts have been empirically associated with violent video game participation. Children who have video games play them about 90 minutes a day, with males being 4 times more likely than females to play them. Fantasy violence is the most popular game category, and educational games are the least preferred by youth. Video games of the 21st century are graphically far superior than the first games of the 1970s. Social learning theorists warn that the current trend toward realism and more explicit violence may encourage increased identification with and imitation of the characters. Because of the interactive component, video games may instigate youth aggression more than violent media involving passive participation.

COLUMBINE HIGH SCHOOL MASSACRE, LITTLETON, COLORADO

On April 20, 1999, Eric Harris and Dylan Klebold went on a shooting rampage at their high school in Littleton, Colorado. They killed 12 students and one teacher before taking their own lives. Harris was known to have used the Internet for violent purposes, for example, posting violent messages on a World Wide Web site that included descriptions on how to make pipe bombs. Most Americans polled blamed the Internet at least moderately for the shootings. Both teen killers were known for frequently playing violent video games, specifically *Doom* and *Duke Nuke Em*. Such games let players take on and practice the role of killer. Victims' families claimed the massacre would not have occurred had the killers not been addicted to the super-violent video games, and they sought billions of dollars in lawsuits against the video game manufacturers and distributors.

The Columbine massacre was not the only act of school violence influenced by media. In 1997 and

1998, there were numerous armed attacks in public schools, including attacks in Pearl, Mississippi; West Paducah, Kentucky; Jonesboro, Arkansas; and Springfield, Oregon, which resulted in 12 deaths and 45 wounded. A noted similarity in all incidents was that the killers were tremendously fascinated with media violence and may have believed that killing was their personal route to fame.

With the widespread media coverage of victims in the immediate aftermath of the Columbine massacre and the terrorist attack on the U.S. World Trade Center and the Pentagon on September 11, 2001, came a surge of criticism that the media has become exclusively focused on crime coverage to the detriment of victims of violence. Critics contend that because of the vulnerability of victims during the period after a trauma, intrusive questions geared toward increasing ratings rather than ameliorating victims' pain coerce victims into reliving trauma and can facilitate a post-traumatic stress disorder (PTSD) syndrome. Victims may be further traumatized each time they watch footage relating to the violent acts.

COPYCAT MURDERS

The direct effect of media violence is demonstrated most literally in the imitation of violent incidents. In Louisiana, 1995, Sarah Edmondson and Benjamin Darras repeatedly watched *Natural Born Killers,* a film about two young lovers who go on a violent crime spree, before similarly embarking on their own crime spree, which included one killing. Several other murders were also allegedly influenced by the 1994 film. In New York, in 1992, 32-year-old Nathaniel White killed six females during a 1-year murder spree. He claimed that he was inspired by the film *Robocop* and mutilated one victim in the same manner as was depicted in the film.

Numerous deaths, many accidental, have also occurred from individuals imitating acts depicted in television programs. Examples are the 7-year-old Texas boy who killed his 3-year-old brother in 1999 by imitating a wrestling move; the accidental death of a 17-year-old male in France, in 1993, who was attempting to make a bomb in the manner depicted in the show *MacGyver;* and several violent incidents in Japan in 1998 that occurred after a Fuji television series aired in which the real-life perpetrators used butterfly knives, similar to the television character.

ROCK MUSIC SUICIDE CASES

Rock music, particularly "heavy-metal rock" (e.g., Metallica, Judas Priest, Ozzy Osbourne) and more recently "gangsta-rap," has been linked to numerous cases of teen suicide. For example, in 1984, the suicide of a 19-year-old California male was linked to the British song, "Suicide Solution," by Ozzy Osbourne. Two teen suicides in England were reportedly related to the music of singer Eminem: In January 2000, 17-year-old David Harcombe quoted lyrics from the song "Rock Bottom" in a suicide note before jumping in front of a train. In March 2001, a 13-year-old female in Hampshire, England, who was infatuated with the singer, hung herself after being sent home from school for drinking alcohol.

Although suicide is the most extreme of the ill influences of rock music media, increases in general delinquency have also been linked to the industry. Reference to sex, drugs, alcohol, and violence in rock music lyrics and videos have become increasingly more explicit. Critics of the potentially harmful messages in song lyrics emphasize that adolescence is a time of identity formation and extreme sensitivity to peer influence. They attest that lyrics with themes of alienation; violence; substance abuse; sexual behavior and other risk-taking behaviors; and sexual and racial stereotyping leave more of an imprint on the developing youth than was previously believed.

Parents, teachers, psychologists, criminologists, and other social scientists around the world who advocate prosocial child development have been pressuring governments to intervene and treat the issue of violence in the media as a public health concern, similar to the campaign against cigarette smoking. Many believe that access to violence in the media should be controlled by the government. Sexually explicit content found in daytime soap operas, films, and television and radio talk shows is often labeled as media violence on the basis of its potential negative effects on children. Likewise, the definition of violence in the media has evolved to also include vulgar, sexist, racist, and other discriminatory language. Although the government has been slow to intervene, other tactics aimed at reducing the problem of violence exposure through media have included media literacy education in schools; increased parental involvement; industry self-regulation; time restraints for violent/sexually explicit television programming (e.g., after 9 p.m.); individualized technological solutions that block out programs (e.g., the V-chip); and rating systems for music, films, television, and video games.

Myriad consumer and civil liberties associations oppose advocates against violence in the media. Such organizations strive to preserve individual freedoms such as freedom of speech and freedom of self-expression, and they admonish government attempts at regulation and intervention.

Previously unimaginable technological advances such as World Wide Web Internet accessibility and video game graphics that feature almost perfect human representations bring new concerns to the study and discussion of violence in the media. It may be that technology is advancing beyond society's ability to measure and monitor the effects of such dramatic change.

—Deirdre M. B. D'Orazio

See also Columbine/Littleton School Shooting; Community Attitudes Toward Violent Crime; Cyberaggression; Cyberstings; Juvenile Killers; School Shootings

Further Reading

Andreasen, M. S. (1990). Evolution in the family's use of television: Normative data from industry and academe. In J. Bryant (Ed.), *Television and the American family*. Hillsdale, NJ: Lawrence Erlbaum.

Smith, S. L., & Donnerstein, E. (1998). Harmful effects of exposure to media violence: Learning of aggression, emotional desensitization, and fear. In R. G. Geen & E. Donnerstein (Eds.), *Human aggression: Theories, research, and implications for social policy* (pp. 167-202). San Diego, CA: Academic Press.

MEDICAL MURDERS

Medical murders are criminal homicides committed by physicians, nurses, or other members of the medical profession. A single murder carried out by a medical professional may be categorized as a medical murder; the serial murderer who kills within the confines of a hospital, nursing home, or private practice is an even larger menace to both patients and society. Although any act of murder is abhorrent, those perpetrated by individuals who profess to care for the sick and infirm are even more horrific, capturing the imagination by the seemingly impossible dichotomy of the caregiver turned murderer. How is it that a person who trains many long, difficult years to be a physician ultimately uses that training to kill? Why does a nurse, therapist, or orderly decide to start murdering patients in their care? Why are some medical serial murderers able to kill many patients without being detected?

THE KILLING ENVIRONMENT

In trying to understand the unique nature of medical murderers, one must consider the general working environment in which most of these murders occur. Hospitals, nursing homes, and other venues of health care are places of both healing and death. Indeed, the beginning of life, care in illness, and end of life are all daily occurrences in many medical facilities. Consequently, this environment treats death as normal, the ultimate outcome of cases in which medical care could not overcome illness or age. In this milieu, death is no surprise.

Along with this overarching condition, a number of problems arise in trying to detect and capture medical serial murderers. First, as mentioned, death is not unusual in hospitals, therefore suspicions are normally not aroused by it. Second, the health care professional does not fit the image of a violent, malevolent killer. Caregivers who are serial murderers normally perform their acts quietly in the course of their daily routines, in a relatively nonviolent manner. Furthermore, people commonly think of physicians as upper-middle-class elites who are highly educated and financially successful. Because societal stratification encourages elitist deference, the natural tendency for individuals is to not suspect doctors of illegal or harmful activity. In the case of nursing, which is still heavily dominated by women, the patriarchal nature of Western society views women as caring nurturers and is reticent to accept the idea of women as murderers.

Third, hospitals and nursing homes are rife with vulnerable victims who have little means of protecting themselves, especially if they are in severe states. Fourth, the instruments used in killing patients are readily available. Drugs such as succinylcholine, Pavulon, postassium chloride, and digoxin are plentiful and are difficult to detect, or are not tested for routinely. Syringes, intravenous apparatuses, and other medical paraphernalia are disposed of easily. Finally, health care institutions have been slow to investigate suspicious activity for fear of litigation or the effects that negative publicity may have on patient admissions.

MOTIVATIONS FOR KILLING

Discerning the motivation of any serial killer is difficult, and a number of theories and profiles of medical murderers have attempted to explain the behavior. In general, these motivational theories can be placed in one of two groups. The first group comprises behaviors that are linked directly to medical practitioners and their patient population. For instance, some medical killers have stated that the feeling of having the power of life or death, the "God complex," is a crucial factor in their behavior. Others are motivated by becoming heros, saving those who are on the brink of death and thereby becoming recipients of praise and attention; unfortunately, many of these patients die from the induced illnesses. Still others are motivated by mercy killing, or euthanasia, stopping patients' suffering by ending their lives.

The second group of motivational theories stresses the internal, psychological makeup of the individual medical practitioner. As in all walks of life and in every occupation, there are psychopathic individuals who are capable of killing and show no signs of true guilt, remorse, or regret. The medical profession is not immune to these individuals, which begs the question of whether murderous psychopathic doctors and nurses calculatingly choose their occupations or whether their deadly form of psychopathy manifests itself after they begin practicing. Others have been known to derive great excitement over the procedures associated with patients who are placed in life-threatening conditions and the possibility or reality of a resultant death. Some are even excited by the opportunity of telling family members of their tragic losses. Financial gain cannot be dismissed, although in many cases, this aspect is tangential to a deeper root cause.

The state- or government-sponsored killer is another kind of medical murderer and does not strictly fit in one of the above typologies. Classic examples of such individuals were the Nazi doctors of the Third Reich, who experimented with, tortured, and authorized the deaths of tens of thousands of Jews, the mentality handicapped, and the physically disabled. Of the 23 doctors who were tried during the Nuremberg Trials in 1948, 16 were found to have committed war crimes and crimes against humanity.

Seven were eventually executed. Dr. Josef Mengele and Dr. Heinrich Gross were two of the more infamous doctors of the Nazi regime. Mengele, who controlled human experimentation and death selection at the Auschwitz concentration camp, was obsessed with developing a superior race. Dr. Gross experimented with and signed the death warrants of children at the Stienhof psychiatric hospital in Austria. Both escaped punishment.

NOTABLE EXAMPLES

Genene Jones (1978–1982)

A Texas pediatric nurse, Genene Jones, was convicted of causing the death of a 15-month-old infant using the muscle relaxant succinylcholine. She was also convicted of endangering two other infants. However, it is estimated that nurse Jones may have killed more than 40 infants and children while serving in Texas hospitals. She has been described as a having a hero complex, in which she put infants in peril so she could save them from the brink; many times, she caused their deaths instead.

Dr. Michael Swango (1983–2000)

Poisoning coworkers, killing patients, and eluding the Federal Bureau of Investigation by fleeing to Africa was all part of Michael Swango's bizarre criminal path. He is currently serving a life sentence without the possibility of parole for murdering three patients in a New York veterans' hospital. It is believed that Swango may have been responsible for the deaths of more than 200 people. Described as a charming, affable doctor, Swango was able to move within the medical establishment without suspicion by guile, forgery, and lying. A classic psychopath, he was indifferent to the murders and poisoning experiments he committed and relished the "excitement" of death.

—Byron Viets

See also EUTHANASIA; KEVORKIAN, JACK; POISONING: MEDICAL SETTINGS; PSYCHOPATHS; SERIAL MURDER

Further Reading

Hickey, E. W. (2002). *Serial murderers and their victims.* Belmont, CA: Wadsworth.

Schlesinger, L. (Ed.). (2000). *Serial offenders: Current thought, recent findings.* Boca Raton, FL: CRC Press.
Stewart, J. (1999). *Blind eye.* New York: Simon & Schuster.

MEGAN'S LAW

On July 29, 1994, a 7-year-old New Jersey girl, Megan Kanka, was violently sexually assaulted and murdered by a twice-convicted sex offender who had moved in across the street from her family. The suspect, Jesse Timmendequas, lived with two other sex offenders in Hamilton Township, a small middle-class New Jersey town. He had been released from a prison/treatment center for compulsive, repetitive sex offenders. Timmendequas had constantly refused treatment during his incarceration. He had originally been sentenced to 7½ years; however; he was released after only 6 years because he had earned good-time credits. This case generated public outrage.

During the trial, Megan's mother related how on a Friday evening in mid-July 1994, every parent's nightmare became a reality. Her husband and son were out shopping, and Megan and her sister were on a couch watching television when their mother lay down in her bedroom for a few moments to rest. When she got up, her oldest daughter told her that Megan had left the house to visit a friend. Megan was never again seen alive. Her body was recovered in a nearby park. She had been raped, sodomized, and strangled. The detective who worked on the case testified that Timmendequas talked about how he had watched Megan for some time before the murder and of his attraction to young girls. Timmendequas claimed he lured Megan into his house by offering to show her his new puppy. The girl screamed and tried to run away when he fondled her. Timmendequas put a belt around her neck and a plastic bag over her head and suffocated her. He dumped her body in a nearby park.

At the time of Megan's murder, Timmendequas was not on parole. He had been released from prison after completing his sentence. Neither his therapist, the prison treatment staff, the institution superintendent, nor the State Board of Prison Parole believed he was ready to return to society. However, they had no authority to prevent his release. Timmendequas had received a sentence of 7½ years for his second sex offense, the result of a plea bargain entered into by the prosecuting attorney and agreed to by a judge. Plea bargaining is a common occurrence in cases of child molestation and sexual assault and is primarily entered into to keep the victim from experiencing undue trauma during the trial process. If Timmendequas had been tried and convicted for his offenses, he could have been incarcerated for 30 years.

Megan's parents had no idea that the new neighbor living across the street from them posed such a dangerous threat to their young children. At the time, there were no provisions for notifying local law enforcement or the public concerning a sex offender's criminal history and presence in a neighborhood. Megan's parents channeled their grief into a nation-wide movement to require notification of communities when sex offenders move in. In New Jersey, more than 1,000 people showed up for a vigil in a local park, and more than 1,500 petitions to the governor were collected insisting on legislation that would avert recurrence of a similar tragedy. Within 2 months, the New Jersey legislature responded to public pressure by enacting a package of nine sex offender statutes that have been collectively termed "Megan's Law."

New Jersey's Megan's Law consists of three distinct components:

♦ Registration regulations for convicted sex offenders
♦ Public notification regarding sex offenders living in the community
♦ Indeterminate civil commitments for sex offenders found to be an extreme threat if released into the community

By November 1995, 47 states had enacted sex offender registration statutes. Many of these states already had laws on the books regarding the registration and tracking of released sex offenders, but they lacked provisions for notifying the public of convicted sex offenders living in their communities. Such was the case in California law, which had a provision that required persons convicted of certain specified sex offenses to register their new addresses. Megan's Law added a new dimension to the numerous existing laws regarding sex offenders who are released from incarceration.

On October 1, 1996, California's version of Megan's Law went into effect, allowing law enforcement agencies to disseminate certain information to the public regarding registered sex offenders. This is accomplished in two distinct processes. First, the public can access information by using computer terminals at their local law enforcement agencies to obtain information regarding the identity of sex offenders within a specified zip code. Secondly, law enforcement agencies may release information to the public on sex offenders, including name, race, aliases, physical description, photograph, birth date, residence address, vehicle registration information, type of victim targeted by the offender, and conditions of probation or parole. Law enforcement agencies have used various means to notify the public of high-risk sex offenders, such as billboards, flyers, newspaper ads, radio announcements, and the Internet.

The California Sexual Assault Investigators Association claims that Megan's Law has been very successful in protecting the community from convicted sex offenders and that it has allowed parents to take steps to protect their children after learning that a sex offender is living in their neighborhood. However, critics of Megan's Law claim that the majority of sex offenders never come to the attention of law enforcement and therefore are not subject to the requirements of Megan's Law. They argue that to believe that all, or even the majority, of sex offenders are registered is farcical and merely serves to provide a false sense of security for the public. They further argue that when released from custody, sex offenders have paid their debt to society and are only further stigmatized by Megan's law.

Creation of Megan's Law was a reaction to a hideous crime. Careful study of rates of recidivism, statistics surrounding new offenses committed, and application of the law will determine its effectiveness.

—*Sharon Shaffer*

See also Cyberstings; Exploitation of Children; Pedophilia; Sex Offender Registries; Sex Offenders

Further Reading

Walsh, E. R. (1998). *Sex offender registration and community notification: A "Megan's Law" sourcebook.* Civic Research Institute Publishers.

Ahearn, L. A. (2001). *Megan's Law nationwide and The Apple of My Eye Childhood Sexual Abuse Prevention Program.* Prevention Press USA Publishers.

MENGELE, DR. JOSEF,
See Mass Violence; Medical Murders; War Atrocities

MENS REA, *See* Court-Ordered Psychological Assessment; Death Penalty; Homicide; Mentally Disordered Offenders; M'Naughten Rule; Not Guilty by Reason of Insanity (NGRI)

MENTALLY DISORDERED OFFENDERS

Mentally disordered offenders (MDO) is a term most applicable in a correctional setting, because it implies someone who has been convicted of a crime and has also been diagnosed as having a mental illness (i.e., insane). Some individuals diagnosed with a mental illness may commit a crime but are not legally considered incompetent or insane. It must be noted that legal standards of psychological impairment differ from psychiatric standards. MDOs are likely to be processed through the criminal justice system and, if appropriate, spend time incarcerated in prisons or jails. MDOs also include those who did not suffer from a mental illness when they committed their crime but later developed one during their incarceration.

MDOs receive mental health services during their incarceration when services are available, for example, psychotropic medication, individual or group psychotherapy, medication monitoring, psychological assessments, substance abuse treatment, and/or self help groups such as a 12-Step program. These services are provided within the correctional facilities, and inmates who participate remain within these facilities until their release or transfer.

MDO also refers to individuals convicted of a crime but sentenced to a correctional psychiatric facility—a hospital within a prison or a prison within a hospital. These facilities are numerous throughout America and are reserved for the most disturbed: offenders suffering from severe forms of mental illness, such as psychotic disorders, or an illness that is unresponsive to treatment.

Thus, an MDO receives treatment in a therapeutic milieu, although it is likely to evidence adaptations that are not evident in psychiatric in-patient units. These mental health facilities remain correctional institutions and despite their specialized ability to treat mental illness are designed with appropriate security measures.

In addition to providing mental health treatment, facilities are equipped to provide forensic evaluations that pertain to legal questions regarding competency and insanity. Each state establishes its own policies and procedures for admitting offenders into the facilities. The federal government also maintains mental health treatment services for federal offenders diagnosed with mental illness. Admissions include transfers from prisons or jails, court-ordered individuals not yet convicted but judged insane or incompetent, and individuals whose competency is in question.

—*Sarah Ferguson*

See also COURT-MANDATED TREATMENT; COURT-ORDERED PSYCHOLOGICAL ASSESSMENT; FORENSIC SCIENCE; M'NAUGHTEN RULE; NOT GUILTY BY REASON OF INSANITY (NGRI)

Further Reading

American Psychiatric Association. (2000). *Psychiatric services in jails and prisons* (2nd ed.). Washington, DC: Author.

Wettstein, R. M. (Ed.). (2000). *Treatment of offenders with mental disorders.* New York: Guilford.

MERCY KILLING, *See*
EUTHANASIA; KEVORKIAN, JACK; MOTIVES FOR MURDER; MURDER-SUICIDE; SUICIDE

METHODS OF MURDER

In the year 2000, there were 15,517 murders and nonnegligent manslaughters in the United States. In numerous cases, it has been possible to determine the method by which these murders were carried out, but in other cases, the method was either less clear or went unreported. There are countless ways for an individual to kill another individual, but the major categories can be broken down as follows:

- Use of one's body as a weapon
- Cutting and sharp, pointed instruments
- Handguns
- Long guns
- Poisoning
- Striking instruments
- Asphyxiation by airborne chemicals or particles
- Asphyxiation by ligature
- Drowning by force
- Arson
- Injection of a lethal drug
- Bombing

Use of One's Body as a Weapon. Some killers use their hands to crush the victim's trachea and block oxygen to the mouth, nose, and brain, thereby resulting in death by strangulation. In some cases, the killer may wish the victim to suffer and cause the victim to come in and out of consciousness by applying differing amounts of pressure to the neck. In cases in which the killing is done in the heat of passion, the victim may die in a short period of time. A person's hands can also be used to physically beat the victim to death. The feet may also become deadly weapons, delivering blunt force trauma by repeated kicking. The human body becomes even more deadly when the killer has martial arts training and can kill with ease.

Cutting and Sharp, Pointed Instruments. These weapons usually take the form of knives, ice picks, machetes, or axes with which killers attempt to stab, cut, or impale their victims. Knives are the most common of these instruments and range from 3- to 4-inch blades, to hunting knives with larger-sized blades, to switchblades knives, illegal in most places, that are spring-loaded from the handle. In the inner city, switchblades are common among juveniles and are sometimes used in gangland slayings.

Handguns. Homicides are most often committed with guns, especially handguns. According to the FBI (2001), there were 15,517 murders and nonnegligent manslaughters in the year 2000. Of these, 6,686 murders were committed by handguns, or a little more than 435% of the total. Handguns basically come in two forms: the revolver and the semiautomatic pistol. Calibers on handguns (the size of the barrel) range from .22 caliber to .45 caliber. For instance, serial killer David Berkowitz was called the "44-Caliber Killer" because of the size the weapon he used to kill and wound his victims. Handguns range in size and caliber from a very small .22-caliber, one-shot derringer or .22-caliber semiautomatic pistol, to a large-caliber .357-magnum revolver or .45-caliber semiautomatic pistol. Automatic handguns are illegal, as are homemade "zip guns" sometimes found in inner-city urban areas.

Long Guns. These are rifles and shotguns. Rifles are either bolt action, lever action, pump action, or semi-automatic. They range in rifle bore size from .17 caliber to .50 caliber, with the .22 caliber and the .30-06 being the most commonly used. Shotguns range in size from the smaller .410 gauge to the larger .10 gauge. They are usually either break-open (single- or double-barreled) or pump action. The long gun is used much less often than the handgun. In the year 2000, the FBI identified only 864 homicides in which rifles or shotguns were used.

Poisoning. Killers typically place poisons in victims' food or tamper with over-the-counter drugs. The ingestion of liquid poisons is sometimes detectable from outward signs on the victim's body. Vomiting may occur once the caustic lyes or acids reach the digestive tract, causing damage to the lips, tongue, and mouth as well as the esophagus and stomach. Many liquid poisons are slow reacting and cause prolonged agony in the victim. There are numerous types of poisons, some well-known and some very rare. They take the form of liquid, gas, and powder, and some of the better-known poisonous substances are lye, carbon monoxide, various types of acids, copper sulfate, cyanide, and arsenic.

Poisoning has become a less frequent method of killing because laboratory techniques can now more readily detect most poisons due to advances in toxicology. However, the poisoner is not always caught or not caught in a timely manner. For instance, a professional hit man who operated on the East Coast for a number of years, referred to as the "Ice Man," was arrested for murders but never for poisoning some of his victims. In some instances, he was suspected of sprinkling small granules of cyanide on the victims' food while they were out of the room, and death came quickly. Vickie Dawn Jackson has recently been indicted for capital murder in four deaths that occurred while she worked as a nurse at the Nacona General Hospital, in Texas. These indictments occurred 18 months after hospital officials noticed

that patients were dying at an unusually high rate during Jackson's shifts. She is believed to have administered mivacurium chloride to her victims, a drug used to temporarily stop a patient's breathing to insert a breathing tube. Toxicology reports are still pending, but it appears that Jackson may have killed at least 24 of her patients.

Striking Instruments. Almost anything can be used to strike victims, including tire irons, pieces of wood, bats or batons, and golf clubs. Bodily injury and death may be caused by the initial and/or repeated strikes. These instruments are frequently used by a killer in the heat of passion or rage, when he or she picks up the handiest item available.

Asphyxiation by Airborne Chemicals or Particles. Victims may be asphyxiated by causing them to inhale airborne chemicals, deadly gas, or airborne pathogens. The use of carbon monoxide gas (which is technically a poison) is also a common way to disguise a murder as a suicide.

Asphyxiation by Ligature. One form of this method is the use of rope to forcibly hang someone. Another is the use of some type of elongated material wrapped around the neck to strangle the victim. The latter is the much more common method of killing, using wire, rope, or a piece of clothing, such as the victim's underclothes, which are often used as ligatures in sexual serial murders.

Drowning by Force. Drowning by force can be any situation in which the victim is involuntarily or forcibly put in a physical position so that drowning occurs. This can occur by binding someone so he or she cannot swim and throwing that person into the water; forcing a person off a boat or ship in a body of water in a location that is far enough from shore to prevent the victim from swimming to the safety of the shore or to any object that he or she can cling to; or forcibly holding a person's head under water. Such was the case with Andrea Yates, who in June of 2001, in Houston, Texas, drowned her five children (four boys and a girl) aged 6 months to 7 years. Her defense claimed that she had been suffering from postpartum depression since the birth of her 6-month-old daughter. The Texas jury thought otherwise, found her to be of sane mind, and sentenced her to life imprisonment.

Arson. The crime of arson has increased dramatically in recent years. It is estimated that more than 1,000 lives are lost each year as a result of this method of killing. Arsonists use a variety of means to start fires, such as incendiary devices, gasoline, and kerosene. Firesetting is frequently used to conceal homicide, an attempt to obliterate the fact that a murder has taken place, destroy physical evidence of the crime, and possibly conceal the victim's identity. In these cases, liquid accelerant is commonly used to start fires on or near the victims. In other cases, arson is the direct cause of a person's death, the victim having been subdued and then burned alive.

Arsonists may also be considered terrorists with extremist motivations. In these cases, the targets can be property such as research laboratories, slaughterhouses, abortion clinics, religious institutions, and racial organizations. Though they may not target specific individuals, these fires nevertheless have the potential to destroy many lives. Arsonists start fires for a variety of reasons, but when people die as a result of their actions, it is still murder.

Injection of a Lethal Drug. Some killers inject lethal substances directly into the bloodstream of their victims. Many of these instances occur in medical establishments where the killers work as nurses or doctors. For instance, Dr. Harold Shipman, of Manchester, England, was recently found guilty and given a life sentence on January 31, 2000, for killing 15 of his patients with lethal doses of morphine and diamorphine—though he is believed to have murdered at least 136 in all.

Bombing. There are two types of explosions, mechanical and chemical. A mechanical explosion occurs when high-pressure gas is produced by purely physical reactions. A common example is when a steam boiler bursts from the pressure of steam created by heating and vaporizing water. Premeditation in installing faulty valves or the manipulating of valves to cause death is indeed murder, although rare in occurrence. Chemical explosion is the more frequently used method; the generation of high-pressure gas results in reactions that change the fundamental chemical nature of the fuel. The most common of these explosions are caused by the burning of combustible fuels such as natural gas, liquefied petroleum gas, gasoline, kerosene, and lubricating oils.

A chemical explosion destroyed the Alfred P. Murrah Federal Building in Oklahoma City in 1995.

Timothy McVeigh loaded a van with 4,000 pounds of ammonium nitrate (commonly used as fertilizer) that had been soaked in fuel oil, and detonated it with high explosives. The destructive force of this device killed 167 people in the building. McVeigh was executed for this mass murder.

Devices intentionally exploded to kill people take many forms. On September 11, 2001, thousands of people died when airplanes were used as "bombs" by terrorists, who flew them into the World Trade Center, in New York City, and the Pentagon, in Washington, D.C.

—*Steven Egger*

See also ARSON; HOMICIDE; JUVENILE FIRESETTERS; MEDICAL MURDERS; POISONERS; POISONING: MEDICAL SETTINGS; TERRORISM

Further Reading

Federal Bureau of Investigation. (2001). *Crime in the United States 2000.* Washington, DC: U.S. Author.

Douglas, J. E., Burgess, A. W., Burgess, A. G., & Ressler, R. K. (1992). *Crime classification manual.* New York: Lexington Books.

Swanson, C. R., Chamelin, N. C., & Territo, L. (2000). *Criminal investigation* (7th ed.). Boston: McGraw Hill.

TOM METZGER

Tom Metzger is a notorious leader for white supremacy and hate groups in America. He has been involved with racial defamation and racial violence for 25 years. His participation has included the John Birch Society, Ku Klux Klan, Christian Identity Minister, Aryan Nation, The Order, and World Church of the Creator. Metzger reaches out to his followers and initiates recruitment through his monthly newspaper, *WAR (White Aryan Resistance)*. His strategies include outreach to convicts and youth, and he is notably a prime leader in the neo-Nazi "skinheads" movement. Metzger endorses the lone-wolf approach, which promotes individual or small-cell underground activity.

See also HATE CRIMES; NEO-NAZI SKINHEADS; WHITE ARYAN RESISTANCE; WHITE SUPREMACISTS

Further Reading

Anti-Defamation League. (2001). *Tom Metzger/White Aryan Resistance.* Available on the World Wide Web at: http://www.adl.org/learn/ext_us/Metzger.asp.

Levin, J., & McDevitt, J. (2002). *Hate crimes revisited: America's war on those who are different.* Boulder, CO: Westview.

White Aryan Resistance (WAR): Tom Metzger. Available on the World Wide Web at: http://www.gospelcome.net/apologeticsindex/w15.html.

MEXICAN MAFIA, *See* DRUG CARTELS; DRUG TRADE; GANGS: DEFINITIONS; ORGANIZED CRIME

MIDDLE EASTERN TERRORISTS, *See* BIN LADEN, OSAMA; HISTORY OF VIOLENCE IN RELIGIONS; TERRORISM

IVAN MILAT

In 1996, road worker Ivan Robert Marko Milat was convicted of murdering seven tourists between 1989 and 1992 in the Australian State of New South Wales. Known as the "Backpacker Murders," the torture and execution-style killing of the young hitchhikers is still considered Australia's largest homicide investigation.

Born in 1944 to Croatian immigrant, Steven, and his much younger wife, Margaret, Ivan was the fourth of 14 children raised on the outskirts of Sydney, Australia, in working-class Liverpool. Ivan mirrored his father's strong work ethic and obsession for order, starting his working life as a heavy manual laborer at the age of 15. All the Milat boys were infamous for their love of guns, knives, and criminal exploits. Ivan, like his brothers, began his ongoing battle with the law at age 17, including charges of breaking and entering, stealing, car theft, and robbery.

In 1971, Ivan was charged with raping one of two female hitchhikers he picked up near the area from which backpackers would start disappearing 20 years

later. After jumping bail and leaving the country, he was rearrested in 1974 and found not guilty when one of the women changed her story. In September 1992, the first of the seven murdered backpackers were discovered in Belanglo State Forest, situated off the Hume Highway, 150 kilometers southwest of Sydney. They were British tourists Joanne Walters, age 22, and her friend Caroline Clarke, age 21. In October 1993, the bodies of 19-year-old Australian tourists Deborah Everist and James Gibson were found close by. Special Task Force Air, under the command of Superintendent Clive Small, was established at this time to begin the meticulous search for more bodies and the killer(s).

In November 1993, the remains of German backpacker Simone Schmidl, age 21, were found. Three days later, the bodies of German tourists Anja Habschied, age 20, and Gabor Neugebauer, age 21, were discovered. All the victims were bound and stabbed multiple times, some suffering violent blows to the spine that probably resulted in paralysis before death. Some victims suffered sexual assault, strangulation, and multiple shots to the head. Anja Habschied was decapitated with what forensic experts believed to be a sword or machete while still alive, kneeling, her head bowed. Her head was never recovered.

Milat was initially arrested for the armed robbery of Paul Onions, a British hitchhiker who identified Ivan as the man who attacked him in January 1990 while he was traveling in Australia. Police were able to further charge Ivan with the seven murders following the discovery of a plethora of evidence at his home and other Milat family dwellings. Sentenced to jail for the term of his natural life, experts still presume that Milat did not act entirely alone. Other cases of missing persons who disappeared under similar circumstances are still being investigated.

—*Hayley Whitford*

See also SERIAL MURDER

Further Reading

Maynard, R. (1996). *Milat: The true horror of the backpacker murders.* New South Wales, Australia: Margaret Gee & Price Publishing.

Whittaker, M., & Kennedy, L. (1998). *Sins of the brother: The definitive story of Ivan Milat and the backpacker murders.* Sydney, Australia: Pan Macmillan Australia.

THE MINUTEMEN

Flourishing in the 1960s, the Minutemen was a paramilitary group established by a member of the John Birch Society, Robert de Pugh, of Independence, Missouri. Convinced that Soviet Communists were planning to invade the United States, de Pugh and his followers actively sought to create an armed militia that would both resist the Communist invaders and then help establish a more democratic America. Former *Kansas City Star* newspaper reporter J. Harry Jones, in his biography of the group, titled *The Minutemen,* details how the organization was fascinated by weapons and created weapons caches in many places east of the Mississippi, which led to consistent friction with federal law enforcement officials. Though the Minutemen are not believed to have actually executed any of their violent or gun-rich plans, they were arrested by federal officials on a number of illegal weapons possession offenses, and a few Minutemen served federal time upon conviction.

Robert Bolivar de Pugh, founder and leader of the group, was born in April 1923, in a sparsely populated area of Independence, Missouri. He served in the U.S. Army during World War II but was discharged prior to the war's end on recommendations from an army psychiatrist. During one of his trials for gun running in 1967, the prosecution entered as evidence the army's official medical report that compelled his release. According to the army, de Pugh suffered from "psychoneurosis, mixed type, severe, manifested by anxiety and depressive features and schizoid personality [making this] solider unable to perform duty due to anxiety, nervousness and mental depression." The report went on to state that "This condition is chronic and for 3 years has been attended with vague auditory hallucinations and mild ideas of reference," meaning that de Pugh admitted to hearing someone call his name but never discovered who it was.

After the war, de Pugh held a succession of low-paying jobs, mostly in sales. He attended Kansas State University for a semester and a half and a few years later enrolled at Washburn University of Topeka, again not completing a degree. In 1953, he created the Biolab Corporation, whose sole product was a dog food vitamin supplement called "Fidomin." Biolab floated between peaks and valleys of irregular cash flow, but when the company did well, de Pugh used its Independence, Missouri, offices as a mailing address from which he sent archconservative literature to anyone who responded to handbills or flyers.

A key issue with de Pugh was gun control legislation that he felt curtailed Americans' rights to own weapons. Curiously, de Pugh was never a hunter and only rarely engaged in target shooting, but he was seized of the gun issue. By 1964, he had joined the John Birch Society, a group of ardent anti-Communists who feared the American government was full of treasonist Russian sympathizers. Though he boasted in 1961 that the Minutemen membership exceeded 20,000, in 1964, he admitted that the total was slightly more than 600; by 1968, Federal Bureau of Investigation director J. Edgar Hoover estimated the number to be less than 500.

De Pugh and some of his followers were arrested in 1964 and 1966 by agents of the federal Alcohol and Tobacco Tax Unit (ATTU) of the U.S. Department of the Treasury (today known as the Bureau of Alcohol, Tobacco, and Firearms, or ATF) for illegally selling guns and the nonpayment of federal gun sales tax. In addition, the Minutemen had advocated the widespread use of ammonium nitrate bombs (similar to the one used by Timothy McVeigh and Terry Nichols to destroy the Murrah Federal Building in Oklahoma City in 1995) as a method of denying "enemy" access to bridges or structures. Some followers were arrested in New York State on suspicion of burying a number of automatic weapons and ammunition for an unspecified cause. De Pugh consistently denounced these actions, terming them "harassment," but derived pleasure from being in the public eye. His politics attracted few followers, but his public persona endeared him to single-issue Americans.

Robert Welch, the superpatriotic founder of the John Birch Society, took umbrage with de Pugh's propensity to reduce the contest with Communism to a mere gunfight, and in 1962 revoked or expelled de Pugh from the Birchers. In Gerald Schomp's autobiography, *Birchism Was My Business,* he claimed, "Welch has roundly condemned the Minutemen and the Ku Klux Klan. Members of these groups are not allowed in the Birch Society. The rule is strictly enforced by chapter leaders—with paramilitary threats if necessary." Yet the B'Nai B'rith Anti-Defamation League study by Benjamin Epstein and Arnold Forster, *Report on the John Birch Society, 1966,* indicates that de Pugh addressed a "conservative" group in September 1965 and was introduced to the audience "by James Kernodle, a Kansas City section leader of the Birch Society." De Pugh's armed anti-Communism irked Birch founder Welch, but de Pugh and the Minutemen may also have run afoul of the Birchers by refusing to limit their political readings to the "list of approved books" included in Richard Vahan's *The Truth About the John Birch Society.*

The beginning of the end for de Pugh and the Minutemen was evident in 1967. Their newsletter, called *On Target,* with rifle cross hairs in the letter *O,* became more strident, perhaps indicating grave internal weakening and divisiveness. In August 1967, four men identified with the Minutemen and other rightist groups were arrested for plotting the assassination of Herbert Aptheker, a highly visible Communist sympathizer, and were found to have stored at a number of secret locations an armory consisting of 250,000 rounds of ammunition, an antitank gun, automatic weapons, seven shotguns, 45 rifles, three hand grenades, 18 sticks of dynamite, cans of gun powder, and plastic explosive. In October 1967, New Orleans District Attorney James Garrison stated publicly, in an issue of *Playboy* magazine, that he had evidence that the Minutemen were behind the assassination of John F. Kennedy.

In January 1968, seven right-wing supporters were arrested in Redmond, Washington, after planning to rob a bank. During interrogation, one of the accused provided de Pugh's name, and federal prosecutors ultimately had enough evidence to indict de Pugh on federal conspiracy charges, even though de Pugh was in Missouri at the time of the robbery attempt. On hearing that he was wanted, de Pugh and Minutemen associate Walter Patrick Peyson disappeared, surviving on the kindness of strangers in the right-wing underground. Now, in addition to the conspiracy warrant, de Pugh was wanted on federal flight to avoid prosecution charges. On the run for 17 months, he was finally arrested in Truth or Consequences, New Mexico, and convicted on firearms, flight, and carrying arms while fleeing federal charges. He was sentenced to 11 years in federal prison but was released in May 1973. Subsequently, he tried to revive his career as a political activist and began an association with anti-Semitic and racist groups, including the Ku Klux Klan.

According to the Anti-defamation League's publication of right-wing extremists, in 1991, de Pugh was convicted on charges of a felon possessing firearms, and Iowa charged him with possession of child pornography after he was charged with sexually assaulting a 13-year-old girl. As of 2002, his whereabouts remain unknown.

—*Brian Champion*

See also GUN CONTROL; VIGILANTISM

Further Reading

Gross, R. A., & Taylor, A. (2001). *The Minutemen and their world.* Hill and Wang Publishers.
Wood, G. S. (1993). *Radicalism of the American Revolution.* New York: Random House.

THE M'NAUGHTEN RULE

The M'Naughten Rule is a legal standard used to judge whether an offender is insane (and could thus base a defense on "not guilty by reason of insanity"). The rule states that individuals are not guilty of crimes if they lack awareness of their actions. Part of this awareness concerns knowledge of the wrongfulness of the act. An individual who is deemed not responsible for his or her actions cannot be held accountable for criminal conduct.

The origination of this rule can be traced back to 1843. Daniel McNaughten created controversy when he was tried and acquitted for the murder of the British Prime Minister's secretary, Edward Drummond. Upon investigation, it became apparent that Daniel had committed the murder due to a belief that the government was persecuting him. During the hearing, medical experts provided a substantial history of mental illness in the offender, which was irrefutable by the prosecutor as grounds for the insanity defense. As a result, McNaughten was acquitted and sent to a mental hospital for treatment until his death 20 years later.

For an insanity defense to be an appropriate plea, it must meet several conditions. While committing the crime, the accused must have (a) acted under a defect of reason (b) from disease of the mind so as (c) not to have had knowledge of the wrongfulness of the act.

Since the initiation of the M'Naughten Rule in 1843, there have been few amendments to the aforementioned standards. Today, the insanity defense is still an option for defense in a court of law.

—*Amy Bouasy*

See also BRAWNER TEST; COURT-ORDERED PSYCHOLOGICAL ASSESSMENT; MENTALLY DISORDERED OFFENDERS; NOT GUILTY BY REASON OF INSANITY (NGRI)

Further Reading

Beane, B. (2002). *The new mental asylums.* Available on the World Wide Web at: http://www.christianity.com.

Grisso, T., Borum, R., Eden, J. F., Moye, J., & Otto, R. K. (2002). *Evaluating competencies: Forensic assessments and instruments (Perspectives in Law & Psychology, 16).* New York: Plenum.

Hart, H. L. A. (1968). *Changing conceptions of responsibility. Punishment and responsibility.* 189-192. Available on the World Wide Web at: http://www.lawrence.edu/fac/boardmaw/mcntn_rules.html.

Lawyers, Attorneys, and Legal Resources. (2002). The Lawyer Pages.com: [On-Line]. Available: http://www.thelawyerpages.com/legalterms/M.

Lewis, D. O. (1999). *Guilty by reason of insanity: A psychiatrist explores the minds of killers.* Ivy Books.

Walker, D. (1980). Excerpt from David Walker. *The Oxford companion to law.* Available on the World Wide Web at: http://www.lawrence.edu/fac/boardmaw/mcntn_rules.html.

MOB, THE, *See* CHICAGO MOB; GAMBINO CRIME FAMILY; GENOVESE CRIME FAMILY; MURDER FOR HIRE; NEW STYLE GANGSTERS; ORGANIZED CRIME: DOMESTIC; POLICE CORRUPTION; "TOP HOODLUM" PROGRAM

MODUS OPERANDI, *See* HOMICIDE: MOTIVATION FOR MURDER; METHODS OF MURDER; SERIAL MURDER; SIGNATURE KILLERS

THE MOLLY MAGUIRES

The Molly Maguires were a group of 20 Irish coal miners suspected of murdering 16 people in the 1870s, in Pennsylvania. Coal miners in this region worked in harsh conditions with unsafe environments, inadequate wages, and extremely long hours. A group of angry miners organized a secret terrorist association to protest. The organization was accused of murdering their superiors and other members of the Reading Railroad. On June 21, 1877, known as "Black Thursday," 10 of the accused men were hung for their involvement in the killings, and eventually the other 10 individuals were executed as well.

—*Amy Bouasy*

See also VIGILANTISM

Further Reading

Affigne, T. (1998). The Molly Maguires. *The politics of the American labor movement.* Available on the World Wide Web at: http://www.providence.edu.

Kenny, K. (1998). *Making sense of the Molly Maguires.* Oxford University Press.

Zola, E. (1954). *Germinal.* New York: Viking.

THE MOORS MURDERS

Myra Hindley and her lover, Ian Brady, were convicted of killing three children and adolescents (three of five missing children were identified) and burying them on the moors near Manchester, England, between 1963 and 1965. The location of the bodies was discovered through pictures of the couple standing on the shallow gravesites on the moors. Nude pictures were recovered of the 10-year-old female victim as well as audio tapes of the victim's screams. Both Hindley and Brady were sentenced to life in prison. In prison, Brady attempted to starve himself to death but was force-fed until he gave up the hunger strike.

—*Brianna Satterthwaite*

See also TEAM KILLERS

Further Reading

Schone, J. M. (2000, December). The hardest case of all: Myra Hindley, life sentences and the rule of the law. *International Journal of the Sociology of Law, 28*(4), pp. 273-289.

MORPHINE, *See* MEDICAL
MURDERS; POISONERS; POISONING:
MEDICAL SETTINGS

MOTHERS AGAINST
DRUNK DRIVING (MADD), *See*
ROAD RAGE; VEHICULAR HOMICIDE

MOTHERS WHO KILL,
See CHILD KILLERS; FAMILY
HOMICIDE; MURDER–SUICIDE; WOMEN
AND VIOLENCE; YATES, ANDREA

MOTIVES FOR MURDER

A murder victim lies dead, and law enforcement searches for clues to apprehend a suspect. The friends and family react in horror, and they only have one question: *Why?* English mystery author P. D. James succinctly described the motives for murder as the "4 Ls": love, lust, lucre, and loathing. To begin to understand the motives for murder, one must understand the types of murder.

CATEGORIES OF MURDER

The *FBI Crime Classification Manual* lists four major categories of homicide, with as many as 24 subtypes. The classification system is based on the underlying motives for the murder:

1. Criminal enterprise murder
2. Personal cause murder
3. Sexual homicide
4. Group cause homicide

This categorization of homicide streamlines all types of murder, which aids investigators in following through during the investigative process and can also be used to help the friends and relatives understand the reasons for the crimes.

Criminal Enterprise Murders

Criminal enterprise murders are committed for material gain, goods, territory, or favors. Mafia activity or murders committed by hit men belong to this category, as do kidnapping, product tampering, and murders carried out for insurance benefits and inheritance or monetary gain. Felony murder, a homicide that is committed during a violent crime, also falls into this classification. This kind of murder is usually unplanned, for example, a person killed during a convenience store robbery. Drug deals that have "gone bad" and gang violence over "turf" may also result in felony murder.

Personal Cause Murder

Personal cause murder is one of the most frightening and most common kinds of murder and is committed worldwide. It is committed as the result of an emotional conflict. For example, *erotomania homicide* occurs when the killer has unfounded fantasies about a public figure and stalks and murders that person. On December 8th, 1980, Mark Chapman shot former Beatle John Lennon in front of his apartment building in New York City. It was later discovered that Chapman had built a rich fantasy life around John Lennon. He imitated the musician and came to believe that he actually was Lennon. Chapman was compelled to kill Lennon because his existence threatened Chapman's fantasy life. The stalking of celebrities has come to be taken far more seriously, and the number of actors and actresses who hire bodyguards for personal protection has skyrocketed. Celebrities are not the only ones who must worry about stalking. Ex-husbands and -wives, former lovers, and strangers are all capable of stalking and murdering ordinary people. It somehow happens that the victim has come to the attention of the killer, who builds a fantasy life around the victim and is willing to kill for it.

Domestic Homicide

Domestic homicide happens when the victim and offender are members of a family or extended family. The all-too-common occurrence of the battered wife who is murdered by her husband or boyfriend is an example of this type of homicide. The death can result from an ongoing situation coming to a climax, not performing an activity to the partner's satisfaction, or the attempt to leave an abusive partner. The current domestic violence laws in the United States came about as a result of the recognition in the 1970s of the number of women who had died when they attempted to leave their abusive partners.

The death of a child as a result of child abuse is also an example of this kind of murder. Every year, the media report the deaths of children by beating, drowning, or starvation. Poverty, the loss of a job, marital problems, and mental illness can and do contribute to the death of thousands of children each year. According to health sources, child abuse is one of the leading causes of death for small children, with around 2,000 children dying annually in the United States. The death of an elderly family member also is included in this category.

Researchers are still trying to compile accurate statistics on this type of homicide. Abuse in domestic settings that escalates to homicidal rage is not uncommon in the United States but has only been recognized and condemned in the past three decades or so.

The role that alcohol and drugs play in domestic homicide is enormous. Alcohol and the presence of handguns in the home are invariably a lethal combination. Alcohol and weapons also play an enormous role in the *argument/conflict* type of homicide, which occurs between friends, family, and strangers alike. A simple argument can quickly become an event that changes lives forever when drugs and alcohol are combined with handguns.

In the year 2000, more than 3,000 deaths in the United States—more than one fourth of all homicides—were the result of arguments. Road rage incidents, bar fights, neighborhood disagreements, or arguments over money or property that end in death exemplify this category of homicide.

Authority Homicide

Authority homicide is described as the murder of an individual who represents or holds a position of authority over the killer. Many times, innocent bystanders are killed in the execution of such crimes, which then become mass murders. Former employees who murder their former bosses fall into this category of homicide, as well as homicidal threats that are carried out against political and religious figures. The assassination of Afghan Northern Alliance leader Ahmad Shah Masood in September 2001 by the followers of Osama bin Laden is representative of this type of murder. Masood was a uniting force for the people against bin Laden and the Taliban and was killed because he posed a real threat to their goals. His murder, and the loss of his knowledge and perspective, was an attempt to make retaliation of the United States against Afghanistan and the Taliban more difficult.

Revenge Homicide

Revenge homicide is the killing of a person in retaliation for the real, imagined, or perceived wrongs that the victim has committed against the killer or a person important to the killer. The victim may be unaware of the offense they committed to enrage the killer. Usually, police are able to link the killer to the victim by discovering the event that triggered the violent act. An example is that of a convict who fixates on one particular witness, vows revenge, and later, upon release, carries out the threat.

Nonspecific Homicide

Nonspecific homicide is difficult to understand. The victim's death seems senseless, and there seems to be no motive for the murder. The victim may simply be in the "wrong place at the wrong time." The killer will often commit suicide or be killed by the police, leaving all questions unanswered.

Extremist Homicide

Extremist homicide is committed by an individual for ideological reasons, which can be political, religious, or socioeconomic, though not necessarily sanctioned by the larger group representative of his or her position. For example, in the late 1970s, an unknown gunman targeted mixed-race couples across the United States. The victims were usually African American males. Finally, in September 1980, the gunman was identified as Joseph Paul Franklin. Franklin had a history of association with groups such as the American Nazi party and the Ku Klux Klan. The Franklin case is an example of social extremist murder. An example of religious extremist murder is the attack by a Roman Catholic antiabortion activist on the facilities and/or persons performing abortions. The Roman Catholic Church is opposed to abortion but does not advocate the bombing or murder of those who perform it.

Mercy/Hero Murder

Mercy/hero murders are committed with the intention of either placing victims in a life-threatening situation and "rescuing" them or rescuing the victim from a terminal condition that is painful or degrading.

The media frequently cover stories of health care workers who are responsible for the deaths of their patients. Usually, the offender health care worker has a history of being responsible for heroic actions when a patient suddenly goes into respiratory or cardiac arrest. But eventually, it is noticed that too many patients are dying and that the pattern of deaths centers around a particular shift and a particular person. The killings can go on for years before they are discovered. The victims are frequently the elderly, critically ill, and the very young, the most vulnerable patients in any medical facility. The health care worker, when finally discovered, becomes known as a serial killer or an "angel of death." This kind of murder is committed because of the need for recognition and/or the need for excitement by the killer. Nurses Genene Jones and Lynn Majors began killing their patients in attempts to be heroes.

In the case of mercy killing, the victim is usually a terminally ill family member, relative, or intimate friend of the killer. The unbearable suffering of the victim or fear of the late-stage disease process is the catalyst for the act. Doctor Jack Kevorkian is responsible for assisting many patients in their deaths. Kevorkian's patients died as a result of medication administered to relieve the suffering of the patient, not to murder them per se. Many desperate patients sought him out to end their own suffering or that of a loved one. Physician-assisted suicide is still a topic of much debate in the United States. Meanwhile, families are still faced with difficult and sometimes illegal choices when a loved one is suffering and in pain.

Hostage Homicide

Hostage homicide is described by the FBI as "a homicide that takes place within the context of a hostage situation." An example is that of hostages taken during a robbery who die over the course of the crime. It is a form of nonspecific homicide, in which the victim is chosen only because of their random presence in a particular place at a particular time.

Sexual Homicide

Sexual homicide is defined as a homicide that has a sexual component in the sequence of events that lead to a murder. The sexual meaning and elements are unique to the individual offender, may occur before, during, or after the murder, and may consist of actual sexual or symbolic sexual activity, such as the insertion of objects into the victim's body. Many serial killers fall into this category of homicide.

Children who fall prey to pedophilic killers, women who are murdered during rapes, and individuals who die during crimes in which there is evidence of sexual components are all considered victims of sexual homicide. The tragic deaths in 2002 of 7-year-old Danielle Van Dam in San Diego, California, and 5-year-old Samantha Runnion in Los Angeles, California, are both tragic examples of children who died at the hands of pedophiles.

Serial Murder

When there is more than one victim, this type of homicide is categorized as serial murder. Sexual predators such as Ted Bundy, Jeffrey Dahmer, and Brazilian Francisco de Assis Pereira were frequently charming and convincing in their relationships with others. Victims of serial murders are targeted only because they happen to be in a certain area and fit the killer's preferred victim "type." Sexual gratification is the primary motive, but the sheer brutality of the attack on the victim is often horrific. The victims of sexually motivated serial killers are not in any way responsible for their victimization; their deaths are the result of fantasy-driven homicidal desires of the offenders.

Sadistic Homicide

Sadistic homicide is a particularly gruesome form of sexual homicide. Sadistic killers uses bondage, torture, humiliation, and murder to fulfill their sexual desires, relying on the victim's response for sexual stimuli and gratification.

Individuals who enjoy mild forms of sexual bondage as a part of their sexual activities are not uncommon, but sadistic killers' appetite for bondage as part of the sex act escalates and can no longer be contained, until their fantasy-driven needs result in death. The sadistic killer is typically a white male who methodically targets and stalks his victim and finally approaches and abducts him or her. He attempts to prolong the torture for as long as possible before murdering and dumping the victim's body. This type of killer is usually intelligent and has elaborate fantasies.

Sadistic killers are not always "roaming strangers." Dr. Michael Swango liked to poison his patients and watch their suffering. He was finally stopped in the year 2000 and is imprisoned in New York. Dr. Harold Shipman, of Manchester, England, was found guilty and given a life sentence in January 2000, for killing 15 of his patients with lethal doses of morphine and diamorphine—though the actual number could be in the hundreds. Both these men likely killed out of psychological sadism, enjoying the power of life and death.

In all types of sexual homicide, the victims are not responsible for their victimization. They merely fall prey to horrible and voracious killers when their paths unfortunately cross.

Group Cause Homicide

Group cause homicide is committed by two or more individuals who share common ideologies or belief systems. Cultist, extremist, paramilitary, and hostage murder are examples of this category. *Cultist group homicide* is exemplified by the Manson murders in 1969. *Hostage extremist homicide* is best represented by the death of *Wall Street Journal* reporter Daniel Pearl, who was kidnapped in Pakistan in 2001 and murdered by a group of Islamic extremists. *Paramilitary group murder* is represented by the work of Oklahoma City bomber Timothy McVeigh and his conspirators in 1995.

Extremist group cause homicides are exemplified by the September 11, 2001, attacks on the World Trade Center in New York City; the U.S. Pentagon; and an unknown destination never reached because passengers on the airliner fought back and brought the plane down in a field in Pennsylvania. In this case, the group with which the killers were associated, the al-Qaeda, based in Afghanistan, sanctioned their actions. Militant political and religious extremist terrorist acts have killed thousands of victims worldwide.

FINAL ANSWERS

Murder always has a reason, but it is sometimes difficult or impossible to discover. How various factors contribute to violent crime is a matter of much debate. Socioeconomic pressure seems to have an effect on the homicide rate. The prevalence of violence in movies, on the television, and in music may also contribute to higher levels of similar acts in society. Some believe that the availability of handguns is a significant factor in the number of violent deaths in the United States.

Many of the victims of homicide meet their deaths at the hands of someone they know. The use of alcohol or drugs greatly increases the chance of a disagreement becoming a fatal encounter among family, friends, and strangers. In "stranger" murders, the most vulnerable victims are people on the periphery of society, referred to by Steve Egger as the "less-dead," because they are less likely to be missed when they disappear, and their deaths are less vigorously investigated. The homeless, drug addicts, prostitutes, homosexuals, the elderly, runaways, and hitchhikers are especially at risk for victimization by serial killers.

Why a murder occurs is usually discovered in the killer's own words, though the explanation sounds hollow to family and friends of the victim and fails to change the brutal facts of the crime.

—*Kim Egger*

See also CHILD KILLERS; EUTHANASIA; FAMILY HOMICIDE; HOMICIDE; HOSTAGE TAKING; JUVENILE KILLERS; KIDNAPPING; LESS-DEAD; MASS MURDER; MEDICAL MURDERS; MURDER-SUICIDE; PARAPHILIA; PEDOPHILIA; ROAD RAGE; SERIAL MURDER; SPREE MURDERS; STALKING; TERRORISM; VIGILANTISM

Further Reading

Douglas, J., Burgess, A., Burgess, A., & Ressler, R. (1992). *Crime classification manual*. New York: Lexington Books.

Egger, S. (2002). *The killers among us: An examination of serial murder and its investigation* (2nd ed.). Upper Saddle River, NJ: Prentice Hall.

Federal Bureau of Investigation. (2000). *Uniform crime report 2000*. Washington, DC: U.S. Government Printing Office.

Goldstein, P., et al. (1995). *The drugs violence nexus: A tripartite conceptual framework*. In J. A. Inciardi & K. McElrath (Eds.), *The American drug scene*. Los Angeles: Roxbury.

MOTORCYCLIST OUTLAW STREET GANGS, *See* G<small>ANGS</small>

MUDGETT, HERMAN, *See* S<small>ERIAL</small> M<small>URDER</small>: I<small>NTERNATIONAL</small> I<small>NCIDENCE</small>

MUNCHAUSEN SYNDROME BY PROXY

Munchausen syndrome by proxy is a form of child abuse instigated by the primary care giver. The abuser creates deliberate illness and/or injury to a child that may result in severe permanent damage or death. The caregiver's motive in harming the child is to gain attention for the care and/or rescue of the child from medical workers, family, and friends.

There are several commonalities among individuals that participate in this type of child abuse. The abuser is most likely to be female and is usually the child's mother. However, there have been cases that involved nurses, babysitters, and fathers. The perpetrator is likely to have a medical background and seems to enjoy the medical environment. In addition, the abuser tends to have low self-esteem and in many cases a previous history of a psychiatric disorder.

The abuser may inflict harm to the victim in a variety of ways. They may smother the child with their hands or by lying on them in hopes that the abuser can then rescue the child. It is also common for children to be over-medicated or not receive the appropriate medication.

The types of illnesses incurred by the victims are usually difficult for doctors to diagnose. As a result, the child may suffer from unnecessary and excessive lab tests and treatments. One victim of Munchausen syndrome by proxy incurred more than 200 hospitalizations and 40 surgeries as a child. A key to diagnosing this disorder is that the child's symptoms are not present in the absence of the perpetrator.

—*Amy Bouasy*

Further Reading

Artingstall, K. A. (2002). *Munchausen syndrome by proxy.* Available on the World Wide Web at: http://www. lectlaw.com.

Dowdell, E. B., & Foster, K. L. (2002). *Munchausen syndrome by proxy: Recognizing a form of child abuse.* Available on the World Wide Web at: http://www.nsweb. nursingspectrum.com/ce/ce209.htm.

MURDER FOR HIRE

Although definitions vary in terms of emphasizing the degree of sophistication involved, murder for hire is a unique type of multiple-offender homicide in which one person solicits another to kill a third person for monetary or other gain. Murder for hire can be broadly distinguished on the basis of sophistication and/or professionalism and the categorization of interpersonal attachments of solicitors and hit men as "professional/independent" and "personalized." Legally, if they are not completed, murder-for-hire schemes are handled as inchoate, or unfinished, crimes of solicitation, conspiracy, and attempt. If completed, solicitors and hired killers can be charged with murder.

At present, there is no central repository of data about murder-for-hire offending, and no reliable statistical documentation exists of the incidence and prevalence of this type of lethal violence. Only a few exploratory studies have been conducted on the topic. From these sources, information on homicide generally, and various types of anecdotal evidence (e.g., books on specific cases, newspaper stories, fiction novels, films), it seems fair to assume that murder for hire has been engaged in since at least Shakespeare's time. Yet it remains a crime that occurs infrequently when compared with the occurrence of other types of homicides and one that can easily go undetected because it is so often dealt with as a typical homicide.

HISTORICAL STAGES

Given the paucity of factual data about murder for hire, whether it is on the increase is open to speculation. It has gone through roughly a three-stage metamorphosis in America. First, in *entrepreneurial murder for hire*, those who solicited the services of a hired killer did so primarily for a mixture of racial and economic reasons. Even when hired by those motivated by personal reasons, "hired guns" tended to work independently of any organizational representation.

As the American economy stabilized around industrial activities, employment became more legitimized, and the racial violence following slavery subsided, the need for independently contracted hired guns dissipated. Spurred by the rising tide of immigration, urbanization, and the emergence of underworld criminal organizations, by the early part of the 20th century, murder for hire had become equated with the business of the underworld. This second stage assumed more of a *professional/independent* quality.

The reliance on violence as a means of internal organizational control, as well as protection from outside interference by "Mob" bosses, called for Mob-based hit men to carry out contract killings to maintain control within and between mobster organizations and to extract revenge as part of the ongoing and more highly organized nature of crime as a business enterprise. The professional hit man of the underworld came to overshadow the independent hired guns of previous eras. Gradually, as underworld business dealings assumed global proportions, there was an increased demand for assassins and terrorists. Images of hired guns or hit men as unknown assassins continue to shape conventional wisdom about murder for hire in contemporary America and other countries around the world.

There is no clear evidence to determine whether this stage of murder for hire is on the wane; however, there are signs that a new stage in murder for hire is emerging that is embedded in interpersonal and domestic relationships existing outside the realm of organized and professional crime activities. The ascendancy of a more *personalized murder for hire* resembles its predecessors in only a few core ways. The professional/independent hit man contracted to kill by a Mob boss is being supplanted by a "backdoor man," who is more friendly, casual, and amateurish. Solicitors, too, are changing. Propelled by demands for solving personal problems arising out of more intimate and informal interpersonal relationships, solicitors are prodded by expressive motives more reflective of excessive self-centeredness and self-preservation than by large-scale economic and ideological concerns or protection of Mob-based criminal enterprises.

SEQUENTIAL STAGES

Viewing the conversations and contacts that occur between solicitors and hit men as scripted behavior is a useful way to understand the sequential pattern of interaction that occurs in murder-for-hire schemes.

Contracts to kill almost invariably begin in the minds of solicitors, who have what they perceive as some type of insurmountable problem that can best be resolved by having someone else kill the originator of the problem. The time taken to cognitively develop these scripts can take from a few weeks to several months, even years. What influences the motives typically attributed to solicitors (e.g., greed, revenge, jealousy, sex, etc.) actually have on the ultimate decision to hire a killer is far more complex than research has been able to uncover. To date, researchers have had to be content with picking up the actions of solicitors at the point of approaching others to kill for them once they have already made the decision to have someone killed as a way of resolving their problems.

Once that decision has been made, solicitors elicit the complicity of a hit man, which occurs along several "tracks." The *intimate track* involves solicitors seeking hit men who are trusted friends, relatives, or acquaintances. A *staged track* involves using these and other contacts to seek the help of experienced strangers, who turn out to be undercover law enforcement agents posing as hit men. Others are the *independent track*, involving independently hired assassins, and the *organizational track*. Tracks are important in providing an underlying structure for the interactions that take place between solicitors and hit men. They shape the nature of *priming scripts* used by solicitors. In the intimate track, for example, with the absence of any a priori circumstances or conditions about killing to draw on, priming scripts initiated by solicitors do not always work. Hence, several individuals must be contacted before one of them agrees to participate, as a consequence of strategies involving varying degrees of coercion and persuasion.

In the staged track, solicitors rely on someone they believe to be more knowledgeable than they are to help them locate a hit man. Most of the interaction revolves around strategies for carrying out the killing and negotiating a fee. Undercover agents posing as hit men usually engage in more priming than the solicitor does. Priming in this track centers on more legally relevant considerations: making sure the solicitor wants the killing done, providing a way for the solicitor to back out of the lethal plot, and arranging for an exchange of money or material possessions. The independent and organizational tracks also have priming scripts unique to their structural contexts.

From the point at which the solicitor and the hit man are working within the same script, concern shifts to *contracting,* that is, determining what the hit man is to gain from the killing and *plotting* how the killing is to be accomplished. There is no discernible order to these script elements in the intimate and staged tracks beyond determining the method of payment (money, continued intimacy, payoff of bills, etc.) and the schedule of payments (e.g., how much before and after the killing), although contracting and plotting tend to occur in a far more protracted time frame in the staged track because they are bogus actions. No evidence exists to indicate how the costs of having someone killed are calculated. The same looseness holds for the plotting of how killings are to be carried out, although guns tend to be the preferred weapon of choice. Given the nature of the structural contexts and circumstances in which contract killings occur, there are usually rather explicit action rules governing these matters in the independent assassin and organizational tracks.

The outcome of a murder for hire in the intimate, independent assassin, and organizational tracks are highly lethal. Only in the staged track, because of the bogus nature of the interactions by undercover agents in the script, is the potentially lethal outcome interrupted by the apprehension of the solicitor.

CHARACTERISTICS AND CIRCUMSTANCES

Given the different tracks or types of murder for hire, different definitions used by agencies that record this unique form of homicide, and the difficulties of investigating them and uncovering evidence, reliable information on offender characteristics and offense circumstances is highly speculative. There is evidence, nonetheless, that it differs from other forms of homicide in these regards. Among its more interesting features are the participation of females in almost equal proportion to males in soliciting for murder, the distribution of murder for hire in small towns as well as highly urbanized areas, the middle-class backgrounds of participants, and the fact that participants, both solicitors and hit men, are largely white. Findings from one exploratory study showed solicitors to be almost equally divided between males and females, white, between the ages of 19 and 41, with prior arrest records. Hit men were most frequently male, white, and between the ages of 16 and 30, with arrest records. Victims were most frequently male, white, and between the ages of 26 and 49.

Not only do the number of persons contacted about participating in a murder for hire vary, the actual number of participants and methods of killing tend to vary from society to society as well, according to cultural differences. In Britain, for example, it is common to have one participant who is responsible solely for obtaining firearms, a feature missing from murder-for-hire schemes in the United States, where hit men have far easier access to guns. Knives, drowning, fires, and automobile accidents are additional methods used by hit men.

Motivations of solicitors and hit men can include domestic disputes, economic difficulties, wanting witnesses killed, lovers' quarrels, business partner conflicts, drug- or gang-related issues, and protection of business interests. Motivations among participants in murder-for-hire schemes are also much more complex than is suggested by conventional distinctions between *instrumental* (i.e., planned) and *expressive* (i.e., based on immediate situational circumstances) dimensions of homicide.

SOCIETAL RESPONSES

Public reaction to hired killings has shifted markedly over time. Early in American history, the murder of Joshua Spooner by three "hard-hearted men" hired by his wife, Bathsheba, in 1778, was considered one of the most horrible and cold-blooded crimes ever committed, but in today's world, murder-for-hire offending is portrayed with much more ambivalence in popular culture. Characterizations of solicitors and hit men in film and fiction novels range from satire and dark comedy to disturbing and repugnant. Newspaper stories are often matter-of-fact presentations.

Law enforcement actions vary depending on the particular murder-for-hire track being investigated and can involve handling these offenses as routine murders or attempts, using undercover agents, or establishing special units. In the same vein, investigative approaches can be either proactive or reactive. National law enforcement agencies are generally concerned with sophisticated, organized-crime-based contract killings. Local law enforcement agencies often engage undercover agents posing as hit men to arrest solicitors.

—James A. Black

See also ASSASSINS; ORGANIZED CRIME

Further Reading

Black, J. A. (2000). Murder for hire: An exploratory study of participant relationships. In P. H. Blackman, V. L. Leggett, B. Olson, & J. P. Jarvis (Eds.), *The varieties of homicide and its research: Proceedings of the 1999 annual meeting of the homicide research working group.* Washington, DC: Federal Bureau of Investigation.

Black, J. A., & Cravens, N. M. (2001). Contracts to kill as scripted behavior. In P. H. Blackman, V. L. Leggett, B. Olson, & J. P. Jarvis (Eds.), *The diversity of homicide: Proceedings of the 2000 annual meeting of the homicide research working group.* Washington, DC: Federal Bureau of Investigation.

Halttunen, K. (1998). *Murder most foul: The killer and the American Gothic imagination.* Cambridge, MA: Harvard University Press.

Levi, K. (1981). Becoming a hit man: Neutralization in a very deviant career. *Urban Life, 10,* 47-63.

Time, V. (1999). *Shakespeare's criminals, criminology, fiction, and drama.* Westport, CT: Greenwood.

MURDER IN FAMILIES, *See*
Battered Child Syndrome; Child Killers; Family Homicide; Homicide; Motives for Murder; Poisoners; Women and Violence; Yates, Andrea

MURDER ONE, *See* Homicide, Types of, and Degrees of Murder

MURDER-SUICIDE

Murder-suicides are tragic and unpredictable events in which the perpetrators are usually male and murder one or more individuals within a very short time, and then commit suicide. Most of the thousands of murder-suicides that take place each year occur in families, and usually the victims are wives, ex-wives, or girlfriends, and children under 10 years of age.

SCOPE OF THE PROBLEM

Homicide followed by the perpetrator committing suicide constitutes a relatively small percentage of the homicides in the United States and other countries. According to the Federal Bureau of Investigation Uniform Crime Reports, the annual number of homicides in the United States ranges from 18,000 and 23,000 per year, and official estimates of murder-suicide range from 1,000 to 1,500, or 5% to 7.5% of all reported homicides. In Australia, according to the 7-year Homicide Monitoring Program, the proportionate percentage of murder-suicides was similar to the U.S. data. Specifically, 144, or 6.5%, of the 2,226 homicide incidents reported in Australia were murder-suicides. In a British study, similar proportions of murder-suicide to murder rates were reported; 142, or 6%, of the 2,274 reported homicides were identified as murder-suicides. In the United States, Australia, and England, death by shooting is the most common method of the male perpetrators, followed by stabbing, strangulation, and/or poisoning.

A 2002 study by Karen Brock of the Violence Policy Center indicated that over 1,300 murder-suicides took place in the United States during 2001. According to this recent study, approximately three fourths of murder-suicides involved intimate couples, and 93% of these victims were female and murdered by their partners. During the first 6 months of 2001, seven populated states reported more than 10 murder-suicides, as follows: Florida (35), California (29), Texas (29), Pennsylvania (17), New York (14), Virginia (12), and Ohio (11).

PROFILE, CHARACTERISTICS, AND MOTIVES

Between 1,000 and 1,500 deaths by murder-suicide are reported each year in the United States. With regard to the relationship between the perpetrator and victim, 50% to 75% of the American murder-suicides have involved male murderers who killed their spouses or girlfriends before killing themselves. The second most frequent type of relationship between the perpetrator and victim are elderly married couples in which one partner is socially isolated or soon to be moved to a hospice or nursing home due to terminal illness such as advanced stages of cancer, Alzheimer's disease, multiple strokes, or untreated depressive disorders. This may explain the large numbers of murder-suicides in Florida, with its large elderly population.

The most common motives and mental disorders of the killers in murder-suicides seem to be jealous rage, major depression, paranoia, psychotic episodes, bipolar disorder, or antisocial personality disorder.

The typical profile of the perpetrator is a white male family member between the ages of 30 and 45 years of age, and the typical victim is a white female around 30 years of age, who is usually the intimate partner or ex-partner of the murderer. The usual weapon is a firearm, particularly a handgun. The overwhelming majority of domestic violence murder-suicides take place on the weekends. The majority of the murderers live in trailer parks, housing projects, or low-income apartments.

TYPOLOGIES AND CLASSIFICATORY METHODS

Three centuries ago, a useful typology was developed by the Swedish botanist Linnaeus. He created a scientific method of classifying plants and animals. In recent decades, typologies have been developed by criminologists, economists, geologists, psychologists, and victimologists. When studying deviant or criminal behavior, criminologists develop "types" or "categories" to systematically classify different attributes of observed phenomena.

Classification by types or levels of phenomena leads to theory construction. There are different types of levels of domestic violence, which Albert Roberts developed along a six-level continuum of the duration and severity of domestic violence. This continuum is based on 501 cases and ranges from short-term to intermediate to chronic to homicidal types. The chronic and homicidal battering cases in the Roberts study reveal several precipitants to domestic-violence-related homicide, such as specific terrorist death threats, major medical injuries, and/or violating a restraining order. However, the current review of the available research indicates a dearth of data on the criminal and histories of domestic violence severity of the couples involved in murder-suicides.

There are four types of murder-suicide, based on prevalence data from the United States. (Mass murder-suicides and suicide bombings by cults or terrorist organizations are not included here, being considered as ideologically or religiously oriented hate crimes, not murder-suicide dyads.) The most frequent type is domestic violence murder-suicide, followed by elderly murder-suicides, perpetrators with psychiatric disorders, and infanticide murder-suicides.

Domestic Violence Murder-Suicides. The male perpetrator is usually a chronic batterer who has demonstrated a long-term pattern of being dependent and controlling his intimate partner. He has become estranged from his wife or girlfriend by the threat of or actual separation or divorce from his intimate partner.

Elderly Murder-Suicides. Because the victim is usually suffering from a terminal or debilitating illness, these murder-suicides may be viewed as altruistic mercy killings or suicide pacts, or acts of hopelessness, despair, and depression. The average age of the elderly murder-suicide perpetrator is 79 years of age. Common factors affecting the older male perpetrator are marital conflict, sharply deteriorating health, and domestic violence. The most likely triggering event is an imminent threat to a couple's living arrangements, such as pending hospice care, hospitalization, or move to a nursing home.

Psychiatric Disorders. Between 10% and 30% of murder-suicides involve perpetrators suffering from serious mental illness, such as paranoid schizophrenia, psychosis, major depression, borderline personality disorder, bipolar disorder, or antisocial personality disorder. In addition to severe mental illness, these perpetrators have histories of abusing drugs and/or domestic violence.

Infanticide Murder-Suicides. This type of murder-suicide seems to be prevalent in Japan, where several hundred cases occur annually, compared with a small number of high-profile cases in the United States. The act involves children, usually less than 5 years of age, who are dependent on the mother for caretaking functions. Children and adults in Japanese culture with physical or mental handicaps are rejected by mainstream society, and murder-suicide is viewed as a just way to escape perceived shame and suffering in life. Thus, if a child seems unfit, mentally or physically disabled, the mother as primary caretaker may kill the child and herself, rather than be ostracized by the community.

PREVENTION STRATEGIES

Criminologists, victimologists, and policymakers seem to agree that one of the best methods of reducing and eliminating murder-suicide dyads is detailed legislation limiting access to firearms, and promoting gun safety. Another promising prevention strategy is to increase research collaborations between university scholars and newly developed statewide domestic violence fatality review teams that have been established in the past few years.

Most primary care physicians have little training in psychiatric assessment or domestic violence lethality risk assessment. As a result, clues and warning signs of domestic violence and suicidal ideation often go unnoticed by health care professionals. Under managed care, only a small percentage of families in need of forensic psychiatric risk assessment and treatment receive such attention. Therefore, nationwide development and implementation of workshops, training modules, and certificate programs for all health care and criminal justice professionals are critical.

—*Albert R. Roberts*

See also BATTERERS AND ABUSIVE PARTNERS; ELDER ABUSE; EUTHANASIA; FAMILY HOMICIDE; PREDICTING VIOLENT BEHAVIOR; VICTIMOLOGY; SUICIDE

Further Reading

Coid, J. (1983). The epidemiology of abnormal homicide and murder followed by suicide. *Psychological Medicine 13*, 855-860.

Murray, A. (2000). *Suicide in the Middle Ages: The curse on self-murder.* Oxford University Press.

West, D. J. (1966). *Murder followed by suicide.* Cambridge, MA: Harvard University Press.

MURRAH BUILDING, *See*
OKLAHOMA CITY BOMBING

MYSOPED, *See* CHILD KILLERS:
MYSOPED KILLERS; PARAPHILIA; PEDOPHILIA

N

NAMBLA, *See* Pedophile Organizations; Stalking

NATIONAL CRIME VICTIMIZATION SURVEY (NCVS), *See* Robbery; School Shootings

NATIONAL INCIDENT-BASED REPORTING SYSTEM (NIBRS), *See* Unified Crime Reports (UCR)

NATIONAL VIOLENCE AGAINST WOMEN SURVEY (NVAWS), *See* Women and Violence

NAZI WAR CRIMINALS, *See* Crimes of Obedience; Ethnic Cleansing; Genocide; Mass Violence; Medical Violence; War Atrocities

NEONATICIDE, *See* Child Killers; Family Homicide

NEO-NAZI SKINHEADS

Neo-Nazi skinheads are a subgroup of the skinhead culture with a propensity for committing acts of vandalism, violence, and murder against targeted groups, including blacks, Jews, Asians, Hispanics, homosexuals, and other minorities.

The "skinhead" movement first appeared in the early 1970s, when groups of dangerous-looking teens dressed in combat boots and sporting shaved heads and tattoos began to roam the streets of England. Their original purpose was to represent the working-class attitudes of toughness, patriotism, and anti-immigration—an antithesis to the "hippies" of the same period. As time went on, however, racist and neo-Nazi beliefs became popular within skinhead groups, leading to the formation of the neo-Nazi skinhead subculture.

Over the next few years, the neo-Nazi skinhead phenomenon spread from England to the rest of Europe and the United States. Today, neo-Nazi Skinheads are active in more than 30 countries around the world, with an especially strong presence in places with high rates of immigration and unemployment.

Skinheads are typically white youth between the ages of 13 and 25, and gangs range in size from just a few members to several dozen. The "skinhead look" is very recognizable: shaved head or very short hair; jeans; suspenders; combat or "Doc Marten" boots; bomber jackets, sometimes covered with Nazi symbols; and tattoos of various Nazi emblems. Beyond their physical image, the hallmark of neo-Nazi Skinheads is the glorification of Adolph Hitler and his dreams of a world dominated by the Aryan (white) race. Their ideology gives them feelings of power and superiority over others. The skinhead gang mentality and lifestyle provide a sense of belonging—a "surrogate family" to youth who often come from broken homes or single-parent families.

The self-esteem of the neo-Nazi skinhead is elevated through the degradation of others, and violence is considered the norm in this world. Their violent hatred of blacks, Jews, gays, and other minority groups is expressed through physical attacks and murder. These assaults and killings are not, however, limited to racial minorities and homosexuals. Neo-Nazi skinheads have also attacked and murdered their nonracist skinhead counterparts. The easy accessibility of firearms in the United States has been a factor in making American skinheads among the most violent in the world, and at least 45 murders are linked to this group. Skinhead groups also participate in general mayhem and vandalism, desecrating Jewish synagogues, cemeteries, and Holocaust memorials by scrawling graffiti, overturning tombstones, and shooting out windows.

Skinheads have moved beyond their own gangs to link up with other organized racist hate groups, including the Ku Klux Klan, Aryan Nations, and the White Aryan Resistance (WAR). WAR founder Tom Metzger has actively recruited skinheads into his organization, and his call for violence against minorities has been heeded by a large number of individuals. Notably, on November 12, 1988, three members of a Portland, Oregon, skinhead gang beat to death 27-year-old Ethiopian immigrant Mulugeta Seraw. In a civil lawsuit filed by the Anti-Defamation League and the Southern Poverty Law Center on behalf of Seraw's family, a jury found that Metzger and his son, John, were responsible for inciting the skinheads to commit the murder, and a judgment of $12.5 million was awarded to the victim's family in 1990.

The inflammatory hate-based beliefs of neo-Nazi skinheads, coupled with their penchant for violence, make them a dangerous force in the organized hate movement in the world today.

—*Debbie Wray*

See also HATE CRIMES; METZGER, TOM; VIGILANTISM; WHITE ARYAN RESISTANCE; WHITE SUPREMACISTS

Further Reading

Anti-Defamation League (2001). *Neo-Nazi skinheads.* Available on the World Wide Web at: http://www.adl.org/hate-patrol/neonazi.html.

The Nizkor Project (n.d.). *The skinhead international: United States.* Available on the World Wide Web at: http://www.nizkor.org/hweb/orgs/american/adl/skinhead-international/skins-united-states.html.

NETA, *See* GANGS: DEFINITIONS

NEUROLOGICAL FACTORS IN BEHAVIOR, *See* AGGRESSION: BIOLOGICAL THEORIES; ALCOHOL AND AGGRESSION; ANTISOCIAL PERSONALITY DISORDER; VIOLENT BEHAVIOR: A PSYCHOLOGICAL CASE STUDY

NEW STYLE GANGSTERS

New York City was the place of origin for organized crime in the United States in the early 1900s; now, Mob-like gangs can be found in major cities across the country. The early Mob's image was "high class," wearing tailored double-breasted suits and exuding confidence. "New style gangsters" are now exemplified by young thugs wearing baggy pants, flashy designer labels, and expensive jewelry. The method of new style gangsters is shoot to kill, and rob and steal, to support their lifestyles; they seem to have no work ethic.

Gangsters of yesteryear participated in a variety of illegal activities to gain power and money; today, the new gangsters wreak havoc and kill innocent people for no apparent reason. Movies such as *Scarface,* with Al Pacino, and *New Jack City* have glamorized the image of the modern gangster, bringing organized crime to a heightened popularity.

The popularity of rap music, particularly "gangsta rap," has given new style gangsters celebrity status. It is not uncommon for people such as slain rapper Tupac Shakur to be immortalized and glamorized for the hard lives they lived. The rap music world has made the idea of gangster life seem appealing, epitomized by song lyrics, designer clothes, jewelry, or "ice," and expensive cars. Top fashion designers and marketers have taken advantage of the gangster lifestyle by promoting the products they create.

—Tatia Smith

See also GANGS; ORGANIZED CRIME: DOMESTIC

NG, CHARLES, *See* LAKE, LEONARD, AND CHARLES NG; TEAM KILLERS

TERRY NICHOLS

Terry Nichols was an accomplice in the worst terrorist act ever perpetrated by American citizens: He helped army buddy Timothy McVeigh plan the bombing of the Alfred P. Murrah Federal Building in Oklahoma City, which killed 168 people on April 19, 1995.

Raised in rural areas of Michigan, Nichols joined the army in 1988 at 33 years of age. There, he met McVeigh during basic training. They shared a right-wing mentality and the belief that society was on the verge of self-destruction. After Nichols left the army, he had a series of menial jobs and blamed the government for all his shortcomings. When McVeigh moved onto the Nichols family farm in 1993, McVeigh, Nichols, and Nichols's brother formed their own cell of a paramilitary group called the "Patriots."

Nichols moved to Kansas in 1994 and worked on a farm until McVeigh appeared late that year, and they left together. On that same day, a person using the name "Mike Havens" bought 40 50-pound bags of ammonium nitrate fertilizer from a farm co-op. The receipt would be found in Nichols's house after the bombing.

Over the next few months, the two men stockpiled dynamite, blasting caps, and fertilizer. Two days after the bombing, Nichols turned himself in to authorities. He was tried and sentenced to life in prison with no possibility of parole.

—Denise Nola-Faye Lowe

See also MCVEIGH, TIMOTHY; MASS MURDER; METHODS OF MURDER; OKLAHOMA CITY BOMBING

NIGHT STALKER, *See* RAMIREZ, RICHARD; SERIAL MURDER

NIMBY ("NOT IN MY BACKYARD"), *See* PREVENTION OF CRIME AND VIOLENT BEHAVIOR

NOT GUILTY BY REASON OF INSANITY (NGRI)

Not guilty by reason of insanity (NGRI) is a verdict issued in criminal cases whereby the defendant, determined to be legally insane, is held not responsible for his or her criminal actions. NGRI is a possible verdict following trials in which the defendant employs the "insanity defense," arguing that the criminal behavior in question was caused by a mental disorder that existed at the time of the offense. Unlike a plea of "Not guilty," a defendant entering a plea of insanity is admitting to the acts and harms alleged by the prosecution but claiming that he or she should not be held criminally responsible for such acts and harms. Also unlike a "Not guilty" verdict, a finding of NGRI is not an acquittal. Rather, defendants judged to have been legally insane at the time of the offense and subsequently found NGRI are in almost all cases indefinitely committed to psychiatric hospitals for treatment.

Although the insanity defense became popularized in light of media attention to and public fascination with its use in high-profile cases (e.g., John Hinckley Jr., Jeffrey Dahmer, Ted Kaczynski), it is rarely employed and even more rarely successful in cases involving homicide or other violent crime. Nevertheless, questions concerning a defendant's mental state at the time of the offense are occasionally raised in criminal trials or prior to criminal trials during the course of the plea-bargaining process. Because NGRI remains a possible verdict and insanity a possible criminal defense in almost all states, it is important to understand the rationale and relevant legal issues, and clarify several common misconceptions.

LEGAL RATIONALE

Criminal law requires that to be held criminally responsible for most legal violations, a defendant must be sufficiently proven to have committed the act in question *(actus reus)* and furthermore, to have had the necessary state of mind or intent when committing that act *(mens rea)*. A plea of insanity is not intended to challenge the prosecution's claim that the defendant committed the illegal act, but to challenge the prosecution's claim that the defendant possessed the legally required state of mind during commission of that act to be found guilty.

Generally speaking, mens rea, or criminal intent, requires that the accused knowingly or purposely committed the crime with which he or she is being charged. The insanity defense, then, is a claim that the defendant did not, as a result of an existing mental disorder, have sufficient understanding of her or his actions and/or the consequences of those actions during the time they were committed. As a legal concern, an "insane" defendant who lacked sufficient mens rea at the time of the offense should not be held legally responsible for that offense. The latter represents a moral claim that has long been a tradition in Western legal thought. In much the same way that children, the mentally retarded, and the involuntarily intoxicated should not to be blamed and punished for their actions, the mentally ill also should not be held criminally responsible if, because of their mental states, they did not know that their actions were wrong or did not understand the consequences of those actions.

MENTAL DISORDER AND INSANITY

Insanity is not to be equated with mental illness alone. A defendant may have been suffering from any number of medically defined psychological disorders at the time of the offense but still not be "insane" for legal purposes. Insanity, then, must be understood as a legal standard, not a medical or psychological standard. Though the presence of mental illness is a necessary prerequisite for legal determinations of insanity, it does not in and of itself constitute insanity. Jeffrey Dahmer, for example, having killed, dismembered, and in some cases cannibalized at least 17 young men was not found to be legally insane by the jury. Although Dahmer employed the insanity defense, the jury found sufficient evidence that although some degree of mental illness may have existed at the time of his acts, he did not meet the criteria for legal insanity. One of the deciding factors in Dahmer's case seems to have been the presentation of evidence that he was, in fact, aware that his actions were wrong. Among other factors, the intricate

methods Dahmer employed to dispose of or hide the bodies were seen as evidence of his sanity.

Similarly, in the recent case of Andrea Yates, who drowned her five children in June of 2001, in Houston, Texas, substantial evidence was presented attesting to the seriousness of her mental state at the time she murdered her children. Notwithstanding this evidence, the jury found her to be criminally responsible for her actions.

In short, then, although mental disorders of varying degrees may be present in many criminal cases, their presence alone is not sufficient for a finding of legal insanity. To understand this reasoning, it is necessary to consider legal formulations of insanity.

LEGAL FORMULATIONS

The notion of mental disorder as a mitigating factor in criminal circumstances dates as far back as ancient Greece, but the contemporary legal definition of insanity can be traced to the case of Daniel McNaughton, who, in 1843, attempted to assassinate British Prime Minister Sir Robert Peel. Having mistakenly killed Peel's secretary in the attempt, McNaughten was judged to have been acting under the paranoid delusion that Peel was part of a conspiracy to kill him. Consequently, McNaughten was found not guilty by reason of insanity.

In light of public controversy surrounding the acquittal, the House of Lords formulated the first official test for determining whether a defendant was insane at the time of the offense. In short, it was established that a person is to be judged insane if (a) at the time of the offense, he or she was suffering from a mental defect and did not know, as a result of the defect, the nature and quality of the act and (b) a determination has been made that the defendant did not know that his or her actions were wrong. The M'Naughten Rule, as it came to be known, defined legal insanity as a product of mental disorder, not merely the presence of one.

The M'Naughten Rule was subsequently adopted in England and the United States as a means of defining and determining insanity, and the basic principles are still in effect in nearly half the U.S. states. Over the past 150 years, however, several revised definitions and standards have been proposed to account for some of the shortcomings of the M'Naughten Rule. Several states now recognize the "irresistible impulse standard," whereby a person may know right from wrong yet be overcome by such a mental state that he or she loses the ability to control his or her actions.

In addition, in 1972, the American Law Institute (ALI) proposed in its *Model Penal Code* that a person be judged legally insane when he or she "lacks substantial capacity to appreciate the wrongfulness of his [or her] conduct or to conform his [or her] conduct to the requirements of the law." The ALI standard, or "substantial capacity test," is now used in all federal courts and nearly half of U.S. states.

Significant differences exist between legal formulations, but in all cases, insanity is defined as a mental state at the time of the offense that was produced by an existing mental disorder and inhibited a defendant from fully recognizing what he or she was doing.

MYTHS, MISCONCEPTIONS, AND THE GBMI VERDICT

The NGRI verdict and insanity more generally have been plagued by several problems and concerns, many of which have had a significant impact on law and policy developments. Perhaps the most significant is the prevalence of misunderstandings surrounding the defense. Several myths in particular figure prominently in popular discourse. The insanity defense is often regarded as a commonly employed and often successful means for dangerous criminals to get away with violent crimes—but in reality, the insanity defense is rarely employed. Approximately 10% of criminal cases go to trial, and of these, only about 2% involve the use of the insanity defense. Furthermore, of the few cases in which insanity is employed as a criminal defense, only about 1% to 5% result in NGRI verdicts. As a gross approximation, then, for every 10,000 criminal cases, only 20 involve use of the insanity defense, with only 1 consequent verdict of "not guilty by reason of insanity."

Furthermore, contrary to popular opinion, in those few instances in which defendants are found NGRI, they are rarely released back into the community. Rather, findings of NGRI almost always prompt judges to confine such persons to mental hospitals for variable amounts of time (depending on state law and individual circumstances). Because many states place no limit on the length of commitment, many offenders end up spending an equal, if not greater, period of time incarcerated in hospitals than had they been found guilty and sentenced to prison terms. This common misconception has played a significant role in legal developments with regard to the insanity defense, perhaps most notably in the abolition of the

insanity defense in several states and the establishment of the "guilty but mentally ill" (GBMI) verdict.

In 1982, John Hinckley Jr. attempted to assassinate President Ronald Reagan. Public outcry ensued when Hinckley was found NGRI, because it was commonly believed that he had used the insanity defense as a means of avoiding responsibility and punishment for his actions. In fact, Hinckley remains incarcerated in a psychiatric hospital to this day. Nevertheless, several states eliminated the insanity defense altogether, and a number of other states adopted a verdict that allows for a defendant to be *mentally ill but also guilty* of his or her criminal acts.

A subtle shift in language, then, allows for mental illness to remain a consideration, but now the verdict includes the word "guilty," as opposed to "not guilty." A recent example of the GBMI verdict is the case of John duPont, the heir to a family chemical fortune, convicted in 1997 as a mentally ill murderer. DuPont was found to be responsible for the 1996 shooting death of Olympic gold-medal-winning wrestler David Schultz but was also recognized as suffering from paranoid schizophrenia. As a result, duPont was found GBMI. DuPont is serving a prison sentence of 13 to 30 years for the killing. Unlike NGRI, GBMI is not a criminal defense, but rather, an alternative verdict in cases in which the insanity defense is employed.

—*Christopher R. Williams*

See also Brawner Test; Court-Ordered Psychological Assessment; Dahmer, Jeffrey; Mentally Disordered Offenders; M'Naughten Rule; Motives for Murder

Further Reading

Robinson, D. (1998). *Wild beasts and idle humours: The insanity defense from antiquity to the present.* Cambridge: Harvard University Press.

Simon, R., & Aaronson, D. (1988). *The insanity defense: A critical assessment of law and policy in the post-Hinckley era.* Westport, CT: Praeger.

Slovenko, R. (1995). *Psychiatry and criminal responsibility.* New York: Wiley.

NUREMBERG TRIALS,
See Crimes of Obedience; Ethnic Cleansing; Mass Violence; Medical Violence; War Atrocities

OFFENDER PROFILING,
See FORENSIC SCIENCE; PROFILING

OKLAHOMA CITY BOMBING

In Oklahoma City, at 9:02 a.m. on April 19, 1995, a Ryder truck full of fertilizer and fuel oil parked in front of the Alfred P. Murrah Federal Building exploded, blasting a crater 30 feet wide and 8 feet deep. The front third of the nine-floor building disintegrated in a blast that was heard 15 miles away. The final death count would be 149 men and women and 19 children, with more than 500 people wounded.

The government and the American people initially suspected outside terrorist responsibility, but in reality the plan was devised by two American antigovernment survivalists in response to the Branch Davidian fire that had resulted in 84 deaths in Waco, Texas in 1993. They targeted the Murrah Building because they erroneously believed that the Waco assault order had originated from offices in that building.

Within 90 minutes after the explosion, Timothy McVeigh, one of the two eventual suspects, was arrested on an unrelated firearms charge in Billings, Oklahoma. When authorities determined that he had been involved in the bombing, he was transferred into federal custody. His coconspirator, Terry Nichols, surrendered to authorities in Kansas and was officially charged on May 10, 1995.

After a lengthy legal process involving change of venue and appeals, Terry Nichols was sentenced to life in prison without the possibility of parole, and Timothy McVeigh was sentenced to death by lethal injection. That sentence was carried out in Terre Haute, Indiana, on June 11, 2001, 3 years after the end of the trial. It was the first federal execution in 37 years.

The Murrah Building was completely demolished on May 23, 1995, after a lengthy rescue effort, and the government decided not to rebuild on the site. Instead, a 3.3-acre memorial was built to honor those who died. There are two arched entryways, one marked with "9:01," the time when everything was normal, and one with "9:03," when nothing would ever be the same. The inscription reads, "We come here to remember those who were killed, those who survived, and those changed forever. . . . May all who leave here know the impact of violence. . . . May this memorial offer comfort, strength, peace, hope and serenity."

Between the two entryways is a shallow reflecting pool watched over by 168 chairs (19 are smaller, children's chairs), arranged by floor, inscribed with the names of the victims. On the south wall of a nearby building that became the memorial museum are the words written by one of the rescue workers of Team 5, dated "4-19-95": "We search for the truth. . . . We seek justice. The courts require it. The victims cry for it. And GOD demands it!"

Until the September 11, 2001, attacks on the World Trade Center and the Pentagon, the Oklahoma bombing was the worst terrorist attack ever to take place on American soil.

—*Denise Nola-Faye Lowe*

See also HATE CRIMES; HISTORY OF VIOLENCE IN RELIGIONS; MCVEIGH, TIMOTHY; MASS MURDER; METHODS OF MURDER; NICHOLS, TERRY; TERRORISM

OLYMPIC PARK BOMBING

In the early morning hours of July 27, 1996, a pipe bomb exploded in Atlanta's Centennial Olympic Park. It was the ninth day of the summer Olympics. Between 40,000 and 50,000 people had gathered to enjoy musical entertainment when the bomb exploded. Alice Hawthorne, a 44-year-old wife and mother of two was killed instantly, and 111 others were injured. A Turkish television cameraman also died when he had a heart attack while rushing to cover the explosion.

Before the bomb exploded, a man called "911" from a pay phone near the park and reported that a bomb in Olympic Park would detonate in 30 minutes. The bomb exploded 22 minutes later. Experts immediately assumed that the bombing was the work of a domestic terrorist acting alone. Three days later, the *Atlanta Journal Constitution* printed an extra edition of the newspaper and named Richard Jewell as the FBI's prime suspect, based on information provided by unidentified law enforcement sources. Jewell, an ex–deputy sheriff, was working as a security guard for the Olympics. He was originally lauded as a hero after notifying police of a suspicious bag and had helped to clear crowds from the area where the bomb detonated just minutes later.

In the weeks that followed, the media depicted Jewell as a frustrated former police officer who fit the profile of a *lone bomber*, a term used by the FBI in investigations. Jewell was never arrested, detained, or formally charged with the crime. On October 26, the U.S. Attorney issued a press release announcing that Jewell was not a target of the investigation, based on the evidence developed to that date. The FBI was later criticized for the interrogation tactics used with Jewell, and a resulting investigation led to disciplinary action against three agents.

In October 1998, FBI officials charged Eric Robert Rudolph with the Olympic Park bombing. He was also charged with the 1997 double bombing of an Atlanta area women's health care clinic and an Atlanta nightclub. A double bombing occurs when one bomb explodes, drawing rescue workers and law enforcement to the scene. A second bomb then explodes, resulting in injuries to the workers who have arrived to assist with the first bomb. Although charged with five counts of malicious use of an explosive in violation of a federal law, Rudolph has never been captured by law enforcement officials. Various agencies have been unsuccessful in their search for Rudolph in the North Carolina mountains near his home, and the last reported sighting of him was on July 7, 1998. There is speculation that Rudolph is dead, but the search for justice has not stopped. He is currently on the FBI's most wanted list, and there is a $1 million reward for information leading to his arrest.

—Miranda Brockett

See also PROFILING

ORDER, THE: *See* HATE CRIMES

ORGANIZED CRIME: DOMESTIC

Few aspects of criminal activity inspire such fearful stereotypes as the public's overall perception of organized crime. Organized crime and its accompanying violence are nothing new in American history. Even before the nation declared its independence, outlaw groups with names like "The Sons of Liberty" formed in several colonial towns to express their opposition to British rule. A century later, ethnic gangs had become well entrenched in the urban areas of large American cities, such as New York, Boston, and Chicago. Today, organized crime plays a significant role in the nation's crime picture, with an ever-changing character.

ORIGINS OF ORGANIZED CRIME

Organized crime in America, as we know it today, had its origin in the great wave of immigrants from southern Ireland and Italy at the turn of the century. These immigrants came from environments that historically had been hostile to them. Suppressed by foreign rulers over an 800-year period, Sicilians learned to survive by relying on the strength of their own families.

Upon their immigration to the United States, Sicilian families discovered that the social environment in America was as hostile as that of their homeland. Although aspirations were encouraged, legitimate avenues to achieve them were often unavailable. At the local level, Sicilian immigrants found themselves involved in a system of politics in which patronage and protection were dispensed by corrupt politicians and small-time gangsters from earlier immigrant groups such as the Irish, German, and Jewish. However, with the passing of the Eighteenth Amendment on January 1, 1920, when the manufacture, transportation, and sale of alcoholic beverages were outlawed, Sicilian criminals became highly mobilized in an unprecedented manner. Some of the most notorious gangsters emerged during the Prohibition years, including Dutch Schultz, Owney Madden, Frank Costello, Vito Genovese, and Joe Adonis, to name only a few.

Sicilian families were every bit as ruthless in establishing their crime empires as the immigrant groups before them. They were so successful in their domination that *organized crime* soon became synonymous with the "Sicilian Mafia." Only in recent years has the term been expended to include a wide array of other criminal groups along with the Mafia. Some originated domestically, and others originated in foreign lands but practice their criminal enterprises here in the United States.

ORGANIZED CRIME TODAY

Today, organized crime provides a wide array of illegal goods and services to millions of customers on a daily basis. Although this seems like an obvious fact, its implications are important for an understanding of the inner workings of the business of organized crime.

First, the scope of organized crime activities and the volume of business engaged in by organized crime require a massive and pervasive series of networks covering the globe. Second, organized crime groups must be prepared to deliver illegal goods and services on a regular and continual basis. Thus, crime syndicates must achieve a highly efficient and effective level of organization. This is vital to understanding that organizations dealing in different goods and services are likely to have different forms of organization and are inevitably going to specialize in specific goods or services. For example, the efficient organization of a numbers gambling syndicate would most likely preclude that syndicate from engaging in the hauling of toxic wastes. The most effective type of organization in loan-sharking would be disastrously inefficient and ineffective in drug trafficking.

The infiltration of organized crime into legitimate business poses a particularly significant threat to the emerging economic order of transitional economies.

John Gotti, Gambino crime family boss in New York City, April 24, 1990 during the trial that sent him to prison for the rest of his life. Once known as the number one gangster in America, he was a fastidious dresser and often referred to as "Dapper Don." As the "Teflon Don," he often evaded criminal convictions and fancied himself as a modern day Al Capone. In 2002, he died in prison of complications of head and neck cancer.

Source: Copyright © AFP / CORBIS.

Both politically and economically, the Mafia is becoming part of the business culture in certain markets. In some cases, rather than becoming a threat to legal order, the Mafia is viewed as a rival. Whenever the state fails to provide the basic needs of its people, this creates a vacuum that organized crime can exploit.

The cooperative nature of organized crime has altered the efforts of law enforcement across the nation. Policing organized crime is no longer a regional or local endeavor. To combat organized crime, law enforcement has been forced to become more transnational itself.

Americans have felt the impact of organized crime through media coverage of Mob wars and their victims. However, little was known about the structure of organized crime until a series of commissions began to unravel its mysteries. The findings of these commissions established the magnitude of organized crime in the United States. Policymakers and politicians were shocked to learn that it had become an empire almost beyond the reach of government, with vast resources realized from a virtual monopoly on gambling, loan-sharking, drug trafficking, labor and business racketeering, murder for hire, and control of many local crime activities such as theft and fencing operations. More important, it was learned that organized crime has infiltrated an enormous number of legitimate businesses, such as stevedoring (the loading and unloading of vessels), the fish and meat industries, the wholesale and retail liquor industry (including bars and taverns), the vending-machine business, the securities and investment business, the waste disposal business, and the construction industry.

Corruption

To achieve the greatest possible return, members of many of the nation's organized crime groups have found it expedient to invest some of its capital in government. Essentially, there are two areas in which corrupt relationships between organized crime and public officials occur. The first is on the law enforcement level, and the second is between criminals who have infiltrated legitimate businesses and public officials in charge of regulating those businesses. The function of many organized crime groups, such as the American Costa Nostra, or the Colombian cartels on the international scale, is that of an illegal invisible government, and their political objective is a negative one: nullification of legitimate government. Such organizations have corrupted law enforcement figures and politicians. This does not mean to suggest that all corrupt public officials are under the control of organized crime, but those who have demonstrated a propensity for corrupt practices in general may be ideal candidates for organized crime's corrupters.

Once the importance of corruption in organized crime enterprises is recognized, one must consider how prevalent it really is. Assumably, out of tens of thousands of law enforcement officers and public officials, most possess high ethical and moral standards and are not subject to corruption. But all it takes is one carefully placed government source working on behalf of organized crime, and criminal rackets may go undetected.

Some experts have suggested that the public does not really want the laws regarding organized crime enforced as long as they do not see themselves as being victimized. Because organized crime provides the public with "services," the public does not give law enforcement much incentive to prosecute these criminals. This concept tends to ignore the effects of corruption on the government in its responsibility to the governed. Where there are dishonest public servants, a dichotomy exists. On one hand, officials are paid to uphold the common good, and on the other, some are pursuing personal gain and selfish ends; as a result, the loyalty of the public servant is transferred from the public agency to the private interest group making the bribe or payment. This results in a reduction of the efficiency and effectiveness of government, a raising of taxes, and possibly the generation of even more crime and less enforcement.

Crime Laws

Although difficult to control, specially designed legislation and law enforcement programs have enabled government agencies to assert some degree of control over organized crime. A large number of cases have been prosecuted under the Racketeer Influenced and Corrupt Organizations Act (1970). This statute addresses racketeering activities by prohibiting the investment of any funds derived from racketeering in any enterprise that is engaged in interstate commerce. Also developed in 1970, under the Organized Crime Control Act, was the Federal Witness Security Program, also know as the Witness Protection Program. This program has made it easier for witnesses to testify in court by guaranteeing them a new identity, thus protecting them from revenge. Currently, 14,000 witnesses are in the program, and it boasts a 93% success rate.

Recent Organizations

In recent years, organized crime has included groups other than the Mafia, a number of them operating in the United States. Among them are the Colombian drug cartels, whose brutality is unrivaled by any other organized crime group, as well as Russian, Jamaican, Asian, and Cuban groups. Other domestic organized crime groups include motorcycle gangs such as the Hell's Angels, the Pagans, and the Outlaws. They are organized along military lines, devoted to violence, and involved in the production and distribution of illicit drugs. Other activities include extortion, prostitution, theft and fencing operations, fraud, and gun running.

Perpetuation of Organized Crime

Organized crime exploits societies' weaknesses while making use of criminal cooperation rather than legitimate competition and is able to bend rather than break under the pressure of the criminal justice system. These are a few of the characteristics that allow the perpetuation of organized crime. Furthermore, organized crime does not produce the desire for vice or force people to use illegal drugs, gamble, or read pornography. Some see it as merely filling the void between what the government prohibits and what many people want—that is, the law contributes to the proliferation of organized crime because it denies people legal avenues to obtain desired goods and services.

If by some miracle, police could jail all 1,700 suspected Mafioso in the United States today, along with their associates (whose numbers, no doubt, range into the tens of thousands), other crime syndicates would most likely move in and take their places. Whether organized crime will ever be completely purged from society is debatable but highly doubtful.

THE FUTURE OF ORGANIZED CRIME

Although organized crime groups may be highly unpredictable in some ways, fluid and ever changing, they continue to predictably provide goods and services in demand that may not be obtained otherwise. Their infiltration in legitimate business also remains somewhat of a constant and fills two essential needs: to give organized crime groups the appearance of legitimacy and a means with which to hide enormous amounts of illegally earned revenue.

The following are some issues that may affect the future of organized crime, though it is difficult to say how they may play out.

- *New criminal groups:* Despite depictions by filmmakers and the media, Italian American groups are not dominant in modern organized crime. Recent trends suggest that groups originating in places such as Colombia, Russia, Jamaica, Vietnam, and Hong Kong pose a much greater concern than does the Mafia.
- *Language barriers:* Officials are now hampered by a lack of understanding of the language and cultures of some emerging foreign organized crime groups, for example, Asian, Jamaican, and Caribbean groups.
- *Public demand:* Illegal markets for drugs, gambling, and prostitution are driven by the demand of the public. Police agencies will address the problem of demand in the future through improved education programs and more effective competition for these services through legitimate channels.
- *Treatment:* Many experts have suggested that by paying greater attention to treating those afflicted with gambling and drug addictions, the market for purchasing such goods and services would be drastically reduced.

Rethinking strategies to control organized crime must begin with conceptualizing it as a business, not merely an alien conspiracy. Doing so will lead to an improved understanding of the causes of organized criminal behavior and the means used to organize illicit enterprises. Tighter restrictions on campaign financing, corporate registration, better monitoring of conflicts of interest, more comprehensive financial disclosure, and tighter reporting requirements for businesses would be among the minimal steps necessary to interrupt organized crime's relationships with the worlds of politics and commerce. Clearly, better control of corporate and political deviance would narrow the window of opportunity for organized crime and therefore make it more amenable to control.

The way organized crime is conceptualized and understood prescribes the means selected to control it. Although detailed policy alternatives are beyond the scope of this discussion, several thematic departures from present policy are dictated by what is known about organized crime. Specific policies can be suggested that would be directed at corruption, money laundering, improved intelligence and strategic selection of law enforcement targets, and policies directed at market demand. On the other hand, there is little reason to believe that powerful political and economic interests, which can profit handsomely from organized crime, are likely to suddenly adopt effective measures to curtail what is a major source of wealth in America.

—*Michael D. Lyman*

See also Chicago Mob; Drug Cartels; Drug Trade; Gambino Crime Family; Genovese Crime Family; Murder for Hire; Organized Crime: Transnational; Police Corruption

Further Reading

Lyman, M. D., & Potter, G. W. (2000). *Organized crime.* Upper Saddle River, NJ: Prentice Hall.

ORGANIZED CRIME: TRANSNATIONAL

The ongoing trend toward transnational organized-crime groups is a compelling development in the 21st century, with the implication that these groups are beginning to collaborate in a systematic manner to further their organizational goals on an international scale.

Organized crime is dynamic, and its inner workings undergo constant change. For example, beginning in the 1980s, Colombian and Cuban drug trafficking groups emerged in the United States, fiercely competing for cocaine and heroin markets previously dominated by traditional organized crime. More recently, with the September 2001 attacks on the World Trade Center and the Pentagon, the word *terrorism* has now entered the lexicon of international organized crime and is challenging traditional organizational models. Whether discussing "traditional" organized crime groups such as the Italian Mafia, emerging nontraditional groups from South Africa and Russia, or terrorist organizations such as Afghanistan's al-Qaeda or Colombia's FARC (Armed Revolutionary Forces of Colombia), our ability to understand the changing nature of organized crime must be tempered with the realities of a complex and changing world.

TRENDS IN THE 21ST CENTURY

Despite the internationalization of crime, little has changed in organization of syndicates. They are still rather informal, loosely structured, flexible organizations that are highly reactive to changes in the political and economic environments. The internationalization of organized crime has not resulted from some master plan by archcriminals. It is simply a reflection of the adaptability of crime syndicates, which has allowed them to respond to (a) technological advancements in communications and transportation; (b) market fluctuations resulting from the internationalization of investment capital, financial services, and banking; (c) the internationalization of manufacturing and increased segmentation and fragmentation of production across international borders; and (d) the increased emphasis on international and unrestricted trade across borders.

Organized crime syndicates continue to be rooted in local conditions, shielded by local politics (or state politics in some cases), and limited by the need to control personnel at the local level. The European Union weakens borders and encourages the free flow of people and goods. Russian, Italian, Romanian, British, and Corsican syndicates simply respond to the new reality.

Contrary to popular perceptions, "the Mafia" did not create these opportunities; rather, state and multinational corporations may be the catalyst. For example, Nigerian drug traffickers are not responsible for the enormous recent increase in international trade or heightened flow of people across borders. They merely take advantage of the situation. When they collaborate with Asian heroin producers, it does not signify the birth of a new international criminal order; it merely reflects the same types of arrangements that are occurring in the business community at large.

Poppy growers can now market their products over a wider area. Nigerian smugglers have a mechanism in place to efficiently take advantage of new technologies and opportunities. Collaboration is as natural as partnerships between U.S. car manufacturers and parts producers in Brazil or Mexico. But the fact remains that the Nigerian syndicates are firmly rooted in economic inequality and pervasive patterns of corruption that are distinctly Nigerian.

The major issue is not collaboration between and among organized crime groups, but increased political corruption brought on by greater rewards from international commerce and weakened central governments, whose powers have been surpassed and often usurped by multinational corporations. National sovereignty is not threatened by Colombian cartels, Southeast Asian warlords, Russian criminal entrepreneurs, or Zambian cattle poachers. It is threatened by pervasive and growing corruption and the increasing irrelevance of individual states in an international economy.

Global Changes

Organized crime has not changed very much from the system of patron-client relations that operates within the context of illicit entrepreneurship and is facilitated by businessmen, law enforcement officials, politicians, and traditional crime networks. Organized crime syndicates are still localized, fragmented, and highly ephemeral entities. The only difference is that the world has changed, and organized crime has adapted.

As a complex social phenomenon, organized crime has always been highly sensitive to developments in the economy, the political environment, and the social world. Dramatic recent changes in global politics and economics have affected both the opportunities and constraints confronting organized crime and as a result have initiated a series of organic changes in the way criminal organizations do business. At the beginning of the 21st century, the contexts within which criminal organizations operate are undergoing fundamental change: The emergence and development of the "global village" has fundamentally changed the context in which both legitimate and illegitimate businesses operate. Increased interdependence between nations, the ease of international travel and communications, the permeability of national boundaries, and the globalization of international financial networks have facilitated the emergence of what is, in effect, a single global market for both licit and illicit commodities.

Transnational Opportunities

Certainly, recent years have seen a vast increase in transnational commerce, as information, money, physical goods, people, and other tangible commodities move freely across state boundaries. This globalization of trade and a growing international consumer demand for leisure products have created a natural impetus for a fundamental change in the character of many criminal organizations, from essentially localized vice networks to transnational organized crime groups.

These opportunities have manifested themselves in five areas, which are outside the domain of organized crime groups but profoundly affect criminal organizations: (a) ease of international transport, (b) growth of international trade, (c) new computer and communications technology, (d) rapacious growth of global financial networks, and (e) creation and opening of new markets.

In the 21st century, the ability of people to easily move across large distances has increased dramatically, as has the ability of people to move materials across large distances. The movement of vast numbers of people across international frontiers significantly increases the recruitment base for criminal organizations around the world.

The growth of free trade and the gradual elimination of tariffs, restrictive covenants, and international barriers to commerce have resulted in explosive growth in import and export markets. The same global trade network that facilitates legitimate import-export operations also serves criminal organizations well. Global trade networks enhance the mobility of criminal organizations and create new markets for services provided by criminal organizations. The shift of some cocaine cartels to heroin as a product line and the entry of other cocaine cartels into the European market are prime examples of market mobility enhanced by international trade.

Recent innovations in computer and communications technology also have important implications for criminal organizations, particularly with regard to their overall flexibility and adaptability in hostile environments. Electronic fund transfer systems move billions of dollars around the world in a blink of an eye, making money laundering and the concealment of financial assets much easier than in the past.

Encryption technologies for faxes and cellular telephones have rendered electronic monitoring and tracing problematic at best. Signal interceptors, now readily available on aircraft, make it much easier for drug couriers to plot radar and avoid monitoring. Conducting business across state borders enhances the ability of criminal organizations to keep law enforcement at bay. Problems of coordination, security, and corruption often become insurmountable for state agencies. In addition, diversifying illicit operation and locales greatly enhance the ability of criminal organizations to recover from losses resulting from social control activity or even the acts of competitors.

Money is the most fungible of all commodities; it can be transmitted instantaneously and at low cost. It is chameleon in character, changing its identity easily. In the newly expanded global financial networks, money can be traced only with the greatest of difficulty, if at all. Governments were already at extreme disadvantages in areas of taxation, regulation, and the control of economic activities. Now, the present-day global financial network makes the transfer of profits from illegal transactions easy, fast, and virtually immune from discovery. Money laundering, already an art form, is now an art form conducted at warp speed. The internationalization of finance has rendered state law and state economic policy impotent.

Strategic Alliances

As a result of their increasingly transnational character and following the lead of transnational corporations, criminal organizations have increasingly sought out strategic alliances with other criminal organizations. For multinational corporations, strategic alliances facilitate production in which costs are low and allow corporations to take advantage of local knowledge and experience in marketing and distribution.

Criminal organizations pursue strategic alliances for many of the same reasons. First of all, strategic alliances are simply rational responses to the emergence of global markets and in particular to what are called the "global-local nexus." This may sound complex, but in fact, a global market is simply a composite of local markets that have become increasingly homogenized. For any corporation, legal or illegal, there are two ways to increase profits in the marketplace: to gain entrance to new markets and to expand market share in existing markets.

Rather than trying to insert themselves as competitors in unfamiliar territory, multinational corporations and criminal organizations often find it easier to enter local markets that have been outside their purview or area of activity when they cooperate with organizations that are already entrenched in these markets, which have greater knowledge of local conditions and are more attuned to local problems. Linking with host criminal groups to facilitate access to new markets is the major impetus behind transnational strategic alliances between criminal organizations.

Strategic alliances are also quite useful as mechanisms to neutralize and/or co-opt potential competitors in a market. Cooperative strategies often offer a rational and effective response to a highly competitive situation. Cooperation with a strong competitor already enjoying high profitability in a market can lead to local market dominance. A strong local competitor can be offered various incentives for entering into a strategic alliance. For example, the local organization's market share could be increased through the introduction of more diverse products. The promise of an entirely new market might be contingent on a strategic alliance or the exchange of some other valuable goods or services (i.e., political contacts, ancillary services, specialized support). Whatever the reasons, the promise of mutual benefit is the foundation of transnational strategic alliances between criminal organizations.

Strategic alliances are also very effective as a means of circumventing restrictions, regulations, and barriers to markets. When state regulations make it difficult to enter a market, the formation of an alliance with an organization that already has access to the market is an attractive means of overcoming obstacles.

Finally, the formation of a strategic alliance can be an indispensable means of minimizing or spreading risk. Multinational corporations know that expanding their activities and entering new markets require new investments and capital cost outlays. Being able to reduce or spread risks enables corporations and criminal organizations to take advantage of opportunities that might otherwise have appeared to be too risky. The synergy inherent in a strategic alliance means that the participants are able to do things that neither one could do alone, at least not with the same effectiveness or confidence.

Effects on Local Economies

There is considerable evidence that large transnational criminal organizations can have a profound impact on local economies. In the Andes, for example, the diversion of labor into illegal activities, the destruction of land and its use for the cultivation of coca, and the generation of inflationary pressures work together to undermine the viability of local economies, which, in countries like Peru, Bolivia, and Colombia, were already none too strong.

Further affecting local economies is the penetration of financial markets and the international banking system by organized crime. Corruption of basic financial institutions is now a major and growing concern as transnational criminal organizations use international financial networks to launder money and in some cases to provide cover for ancillary illicit activities. Even financial institutions in major developed countries are not immune.

Undermining State Legitimacy

In the long run, more dangerous than direct confrontations with state authority and threats to financial systems is the fact that defiance of established authority and corruption of state officials and institutions are undermining the legitimacy of and public support for the state itself. In countries in which governments have been chronically unable to deliver needed and expected social services, the economy is deteriorating, and the government is often perceived of as a central problem, the appeal of powerful, capable, and strong criminal organizations can overwhelm the respect for law.

Criminal organizations operating on or looking to operate on a transnational basis know that they can flourish in states with weak structures and dubious legitimacy. Nations with severe problems of economic inequalities, the dominance of traditional oligarchies, and serious political, religious, or ethnic divisions are rife with potential for organized criminal activity. In these states, the development of parallel political and economic structures is almost inevitable. In countries such as Peru, Bolivia, Laos, Myanmar, and many others, entire geographical areas are outside the control of the central government. In other states, such as Mexico, Colombia, Nigeria, and Thailand, governmental institutions may be so corrupt that they no longer have either the incentive or the capacity to reassert control.

States Within States

In circumstances in which government authority is weak or absent, powerful criminal organizations may see themselves as legitimate political authorities. As criminal organizations begin to understand the extent of their influence and power, it is not too large a leap to assume that these organizations will realize that they may be able to do more than neutralize governments: They may be able to replace them.

This, however, seems in general unlikely. Criminal organizations do not wish to be sovereignty bound. They are sovereignty free and use this freedom and flexibility to engage in activities that are difficult for states to regulate. The issue is control versus autonomy: States want control, and transnational actors want autonomy.

Transnational criminal organizations challenge aspects of state sovereignty and security that have traditionally been taken for granted. They prove the permeability of borders nominally under the control of states. Governments retain sovereignty, but if they are unable to control the importation of guns, drugs, and people into their territories, then sovereignty loses much of its significance. Sovereignty may retain its utility as a basis for diplomacy in the international society of states, but it no longer reflects real control over territory.

Criminal organizations obtain access to a state's territory through clandestine methods, minimize the opportunities for state control over their activities, and prevent real sovereignty from being exercised. Although the main purpose of their activities is to make a profit, an inevitable by-product is an implicit challenge to authority and sovereignty. The threat to state sovereignty is insidious rather than direct: It is not a threat to the military strength of the state, but it is a challenge to the prerogatives that are an integral part of statehood.

None of this should be taken to mean that all states oppose the activities of transnational criminal organizations. Alliances of convenience between states and criminal organization could pose serious security threats, especially from those trafficking in nuclear material. As soon as a trafficking network is functioning effectively, product diversification is easy. Organizations that deal in drugs can also traffic in technology and components for weapons of mass destruction. Whether the recipients of such transfers are terrorist groups or states, the link between criminal activities and security is obvious.

FUTURE TRENDS AFFECTING CRIMINAL ORGANIZATIONS

The character changes in organized crime initiated by rapidly expanding international travel and trade, developing communications technology, and globalization of finance may well be accelerated in the coming years. A number of factors point to this acceleration.

Economics of Production

For poor farmers in many nations around the world, choosing to grow drug-related crops makes the greatest economic sense. Markets for other commodities such as coffee and rice are far less profitable and very unstable. In most places, even when the necessary marketing infrastructure and expertise exist, government controls make entry into those legitimate markets almost impossible for peasants. At the same time, drug entrepreneurs are expanding into markets in which drugs have not been a major consumer item in the past. Without dramatic and unlikely changes, raw materials for drug production will continue to be readily available.

International Ungovernability

There is a global trend toward ungovernability, that is, the declining ability of governments to govern, manage a modern state, and provide adequate or effective services. In some cases, criminal organizations have been able to capitalize on the fact that large areas, such as the Andes and Amazon regions in South America or much of the Golden Triangle in Southeast Asia, have never been under effective government control.

Criminal organizations have moved into these remote regions and provided the major sources of authority and social control. In other cases, criminal organizations have begun to contest local control of areas with the government. This situation provides favorable conditions for criminal groups to establish bases of operations and safe havens, particularly in areas key to drug trafficking and alien smuggling. Political geographers predict further continuing global fragmentation. Criminal organizations thrive where governments are weak.

Immigration Streams

Local criminal organizations often expand following immigration patterns. In the next century, economic pressures and widespread ethnic turmoil are likely to generate refugees and immigrants from regions in which international criminal groups are based. Criminal organizations tend to exploit immigrant communities in a variety of ways. Those communities provide cover and concealment. Immigrant pools also provide recruits. In addition, new immigrants are usually fearful of law enforcement. Recent experiences in their countries of origin make them reluctant to cooperate with police in their new countries. It is highly likely that increased organized criminal activity will accompany the immigration of Russians, East Europeans, Asians, Middle Easterners, Kurds, and others in coming years.

Border Porosity

The long, open borders between the United States and Mexico and Canada provide ready access for criminals and illegal goods. Tens of thousands of miles of U.S. coastline are virtually uncontrollable. The opening of free trade areas, such as the American Free Trade Agreements, will lower many existing controls and reduce customs inspections as well. Certainly, similar effects can be anticipated in Europe as the European Union continues to open borders to free trade.

Continued advances in technology and international transportation will facilitate growth in transnational criminal operations. The ease of modern communications makes contact among criminal organizations easy, fast, and more secure. New digital technologies make it more difficult for law enforcement agencies to intercept communications. The movement of trillions of dollars in wire transfers each day makes it possible for most participants to evade state monitoring.

Preventing, disrupting, and prosecuting organized crime is difficult even under the best of conditions. The growth of transnational markets and the accompanying criminal organizations ready and willing to operate in those markets will make the task even more complex and immensely more difficult.

—*Michael D. Lyman*

See also Drug Cartels; Drug Trade; Falcone, Giovanni; Organized Crime: Domestic

Further Reading

Edwards, A., & Gill, P. (Eds.). (2003). *Transnational organised crime: The policy and politics of global crime.* Boston: Routledge.

Lyman, M., & Potter, G. (2000). *Organized crime.* Upper Saddle River, NJ: Prentice Hall.

Varese, F. (2001). *The Russian Mafia: Private protection in a new market economy.* Oxford University Press.

JOHN ORR

John Leonard Orr is the most prolific serial arsonist in California's history. Incredibly, he was a captain with the Glendale Fire Department's arson unit at the time of his arrest. Married five times, Orr secretly craved the attention of others. He often set a fire, only to return later and assist in the investigation—and became legendary in his ability to enter a fire scene and within an hour discover its point of origin.

Between December 1990 and March 1991, 18 fires resulted in the loss of four lives and property loss that totaled in the millions. After Orr's arrest, a search of his home revealed videos of the fires, which he had taken, and a manuscript, titled *Points of Origin,* about an arsonist who was also a firefighter. The manuscript revealed details about the fires under investigation and gave investigators insight into the mind of a serial arsonist. Orr not only basked in the attention of others but was also sexually stimulated by the process of setting fires.

In July 1992, Orr was convicted on three counts of arson and was sentenced to serve 30 years. He was later convicted in the deaths of the four victims who died in the fires and was sentenced to life without parole.

—*Denise Nola-Faye Lowe*

See also ARSON; JUVENILE FIRESETTING; MACDONALD TRIAD; METHODS OF MURDER

Further Reading

Wambaugh, J. (2002). *Fire lover: A true story.* New York: William Morrow.

OSAMA BIN LADEN, *See* BIN LADEN, OSAMA

P

PARAPHILIA

DEFINITION OF TERMS

Sexually aberrant behaviors, otherwise known as *paraphilias,* are commonly associated with crimes that are sexual and violent in nature. There are hundreds of paraphilia or sexual deviations, and some are more common than are others.

Paraphilia literally means "abnormal love." *Para* is a Greek terms for "beyond," or outside the usual, and *philia* is a Greek term for "love." Common exclusively in males, paraphilia is a group of persistent sexual behavior patterns in which unusual objects, fetishes, rituals, or situations are required for sexual arousal and ultimate sexual satisfaction. From a clinical perspective, paraphilia is defined as sexual arousal through objects or situations that are not part of normative arousal. The essential feature of all paraphilia is recurrent, intense, sexually arousing fantasies—sexual urges or behaviors that involve either nonhuman objects, such as fetishes, or the suffering of oneself or partner, children, or other nonconsenting persons. Multiple forms are often found in one person, usually with one dominant paraphilia.

Deviant sexual behaviors exist on a continuum of behaviors and vary in severity. Some forms of paraphilia can be classified as criminal in nature, such as pedophilia or rape, whereas others are regarded as seemingly harmless or nuisance behaviors, such as fetishism or "peeping Toms." At the extreme end of the continuum lies the paraphilic killer *(erotophonophilia),* also known as the "lust murderer," or sexual murderer. There are a number of essential elements to paraphilic behaviors, including fantasy, compulsive masturbation, and facilitators such as alcohol, drugs, and pornography. The role of fantasy is a key component in facilitating the paraphilic behavior, and the use of visual imagery underscores deviant behavior in predators and the offenses they commit.

Paraphilics lack sexual socialization and self-esteem and are socially unable to approach women in a sexually appropriate manner. As a result, fantasy becomes the substitute for human relationships. The individual becomes so wrapped up in his imaginary scenarios that he eventually loses all contact with reality, only to find himself impelled to actualize the fantasy. The fantasy of the paraphilic is erotically charged with themes of dominance and power control, and violent imagery such as sadism, necrosadism, rape, mutilation, cutting, stabbing, and burning of the victim. Masturbation is critical to the paraphilic fantasy system. The paraphilic typically masturbates while imagining the desired paraphilia. Compulsive masturbation essentially reinforces the paraphilic behavior, and the orgasm ultimately becomes conditioned to the paraphilia and the fantasy.

The aforementioned behaviors are conceptualized in an integrated theoretical model proposed by Purcell, which comprises other existing models on sexual murder and serial murder. Within the integrated model is a typology by which one would further understand the complex nature of sexually deviant behavior and which helps establish the role of paraphilia as a motive in sexual offenses, particularly that of the paraphilic, or lust murderer.

The first four components of the integrative model explain the systemic development of paraphilic behavior. Formative development consisting of predispostitional factors and traumatic events, low self-esteem, and early fantasy development are all factors investigated as etiological agents. Paraphilic development, paraphilic stimuli, facilitating behaviors, and an orgasmic conditioning process are interacting elements that comprise the paraphilic process. A stressor, either internal or external, functions as a trigger to past, unresolved trauma. The stressor then causes a momentary lack of control for the paraphilic individual. A response to that stressor is a behavioral manifestation. The individual, unable to cope with the trigger, retreats back into the paraphilic process, where he ultimately finds comfort and relief.

A feedback loop helps illustrate how the behavioral manifestation of parpahilia can escalate if the paraphilic chooses to execute his sexually sadistic fantasy. In vivo tryouts of the paraphilic fantasy and stimuli are done in an attempt to preserve, satisfy, and reify the internal thought processes of the paraphilic. As a result, the individual experiences an exhilarating sense of sexual satisfaction, as well as an increased need from more stimulation. Masturbation, as well as the behavioral manifestation, criminal or not, essentially acts as a reinforcer, which is then sequenced back into the fantasy system.

As stated earlier, paraphilia exists on a continuum and does have the potential to become more violent with time. Research indicates that the severity of paraphilia can be diagnosed as mild, moderate, or severe. "Normal" paraphilics can function sexually without paraphilic stimuli and fantasy. The behavior is considered abnormal only when the individual ultimately depends on the stimuli and fantasy for sexual arousal and gratification. In the absence of stimuli and fantasy, paraphilics lose the ability to function in a normal sexual manner. Moreover, they eventually become so contingent upon the paraphilia that it ultimately causes a significant distress or impairment in social, occupational, or other important areas of functioning.

CRIMINAL PARAPHILIA

Paraphilic behavior is typically against the law. The majority of research is taken from the criminal population. It is difficult to ascertain the frequency of arrests for various paraphilic behaviors. Arrests for illegal sexual activities are tabulated regularly by the criminal justice system, but unfortunately, these sexual crimes are reported under two categories, either forcible rape or other sexual offenses. This directly indicates that there is no specific category by which to classify paraphilic sexual offenses.

Paraphilias commonly found in the clinical as well as criminal arena include the following: exhibitionism, fetishism, frotteurism, pedophilia, sexual sadism, and voyeurism. Some of the following definitions can be found in the *Diagnostic and Statistical Manual of Mental Disorders (DSM-IV)*.

Exhibitionism is the exposure of one's genitals to a stranger. It is common for the individual to masturbate while exposing himself or while fantasizing about exposing himself; yet more often than not, the offender is unable to obtain an erection. With the exhibitionist, the exposure of the genitalia is followed by masturbation, which serves to reinforce the behavior and results in the repetition of the behavior. As with all paraphilia, fantasy is an essential element in facilitating the behavior, and masturbation acts as a reinforcer. The individual conditions his orgasm to the paraphilic stimuli and fantasy and eventually loses all sense of normalcy.

Fetishism is a paraphilic focus involving the use of nonliving objects (fetish). The fetish is required or strongly preferred for sexual excitement, and the absence may cause erectile dysfunction with the individual. Masturbation is common while holding, rubbing, or smelling the fetish.

Frotteurism involves touching and rubbing against a nonconsenting person, usually in a crowded place, so the offender can easily escape the encounter or blend into the background. While the offender is engaging in his paraphilic behavior, he is usually fantasizing about an exclusive caring relationship with the victim.

Pedophilia is a sexual attraction and relation with a prepubescent child (generally age 13 or younger) of either both sexes or exclusively male or female. The range in aggressiveness of these offenses can fall anywhere from very passive to extremely violent depending on the fantasy of the perpetrator.

A *voyeur* or "peeping Tom" receives sexual pleasure by looking at unsuspecting strangers, usually in the context of an intimate encounter or private moment. It is not the offender's intention to have direct contact with the victim, but to masturbate while observing the victim.

Sadism involves an act in which the individual derives sexual excitement from the psychological or physical suffering, including humiliation, of the victim. The fantasies of the individual typically involve complete control over the victim, who is terrified in anticipation of the sadistic act. The use of torture is clearly evident with the sadistic paraphilic and usually increases in severity over time. Erotophonophilia, or lust murder, is the acting out of sadistic behavior by brutally and sadistically murdering the victim.

CASE EXAMPLE: JEROME BRUDOS

Jerome Brudos was a serial lust murderer with a paraphilic interest in women's high-heeled shoes. He horrified the Oregon community during the 1960s with the grisly and bizarre paraphilic murders of four young women.

When Brudos was 5 years old, he developed a strong interest in women's high-heeled shoes after discovering a pair in the local dump. As he matured, his shoe fetish increasingly provided him with sexual arousal. Murder was not Brudos's first crime. He also engaged in fetishistic burglaries, stealing women's shoes and lingerie for his private use, fondling and wearing the garments. At the age of 13, he was arrested for the sexual assault of a 17-year-old neighbor girl. Using a knife, Brudos forced his young victim to undress and photographed her naked body. Eight months after this initial incident, Brudos assaulted another young women, breaking her nose and forcing her to disrobe.

Brudos's sexually explicit fantasies carried over into his marriage. His wife later reported that he made her walk around the house in high-heeled shoes and nothing else, and then took pictures of her. He also dressed in undergarments he had collected during his fetishistic burglaries. Brudos's first murder was that of 19-year-old Linda Slawson. She was selling encyclopedias in Brudos's neighborhood and came to his door. He lured her into his house, killed her in the garage, severed her foot, and placed it in his freezer as a souvenir fetish. He would later dress the severed foot in high-heeled spiked shoes. As the murders continued, so did the amount of violence and torture inflicted upon his victims. His garage became a torture chamber in which he constructed mirrors to help facilitate his sexually violent fantasy system.

Apprehended in June 1969, he was charged with the murders of four young women and found guilty of all. He was then sentenced to four consecutive life terms, for each life he had taken. Brudos currently resides in the Oregon State Prison.

—*Catherine Purcell*

See also CHIKATILO, ANDREI; DAHMER, JEFFREY; DESALVO, ALBERT HENRY; JACK THE RIPPER; LUST MURDER; MOTIVES FOR MURDER; PEDOPHILIA; SERIAL MURDER; SEX OFFENDERS; SEXUAL OFFENSES; STALKING; TROPHY TAKING

Further Reading

Abel, G. G., & Osborne, C. (1992). The paraphilias. The extent and nature of sexually deviant criminal behavior. *Psychiatric Clinics of North America, 15,* 675-687.

American Psychiatric Association. (1994). *The diagnostic and statistical manual of mental disorders* (4th ed.). Washington, DC: Author.

Burgess, A. W., Hartman, C. R., Ressler, R. K., Douglas, J. E., & McCormack, A. (1986). Sexual homicide: A motivational model. *Journal of Interpersonal Violence, 13,* 251-272.

Hickey, E. W. (2002). *Serial murderers and their victims* (3rd ed.). Belmont, CA: Wadsworth.

MacCulloch, M. J., Snowden, P. R., Wood, P. J. W., & Mills, H. E. (1983). Sadistic fantasy, sadistic behavior, and offending. *British Journal of Psychiatry, 143,* 20-29.

Money, J. (1990). Forensic sexology: Paraphilic serial rape (biastophilia) and lust murder (erotophonophilia). *American Journal of Psychotherapy, 64,* 26-36.

Purcell, C. E. (2000). *An investigation of paraphilias, lust murder, and the case of Jeffrey Dahmer: An integrative theoretical model.* Dissertation, Alliant University, California School of Professional Psychology, Fresno.

PARAPHILIAS ASSOCIATED WITH VIOLENT BEHAVIOR

Defined as sexual gratification through unusual sexual acts and/or fantasies, many paraphilias are not illegal. Some of the following are sexually violent and illegal. Other listed paraphilias often are a constellation of acts engaged in by persons seeking sexual stimulation, which may lead to violent and/or criminal behavior.

Agonophilia: arousal by a partner pretending to struggle

Altocalciphilia: high-heel shoe fetish

Alvinolagnia: stomach fetish

Amokoscisia: arousal or sexual frenzy with the desire to slash or mutilate women

Anililagnia: arousal from older female sex partners

Anophelorastia: arousal from defiling or ravaging a partner

Anthropophagolagnia: rape with cannibalsim

Autonecrophilia: imagining oneself as a corpse or becoming sexually aroused by simulated corpses

Biastophilia: arousal through violent rape of the victim; also called *raptophilia*

Bondage: physical or mental restriction of partners

Coprolalia: arousal from using obscene language or writing

Dacryphilia: arousal by seeing partners cry

Dippoldism: sexual arousal from abusing children

Erotomania: unreasonable love of a stranger or uninterested person

Exhibitionism: arousal through exposing one's body to inappropriate and nonconsenting people

Frottage: arousal by rubbing one's body against a partner or object

Gerontophilia: attraction to elderly partners

Hebephilia: men aroused by teenage boys

Hyphephilia: arousal from touching skin, hair, leather, fur, or fabric

Kleptolagnia: arousal from stealing

Mastofact: breast fetish

Mixoscopia: orgasm dependent on watching others having sex

Necrophilia: sex with deceased individuals

Pyromania: arousal from deliberate and purposeful firesetting

Retifism: shoe fetish

Sadism: empowerment and arousal from injuring others

Scatophilia: arousal through phone calls, using vulgar language, or trying to elicit a reaction from another party

Somnophilia: fondling strangers in their sleep

Voyeurism: arousal by watching others without their consent

PARENTS WHO KILL, *See*
CHILD KILLERS; FAMILY HOMICIDE; HOMICIDE; MOTIVES FOR MURDER; WOMEN AND VIOLENCE; YATES, ANDREA

BONNIE PARKER AND CLYDE BARROW

Clyde Barrow was born on March 24, 1909, in Telice, Texas, and was one of eight children. He was known to be sadistic and without remorse for his acts of cruelty. He had a criminal history of burglaries and auto thefts. After spending nearly 2 years in prison in

Eastham, Texas, for an earlier prison escape, Clyde persuaded another inmate to cut off two of his toes in an effort to gain an early release.

After his release, he joined up with Bonnie Parker, and they became legendary in their criminal pursuits. Bonnie was born on October 1, 1910, in Rowena, Texas. Her father, a bricklayer, died only 4 years later. Bonnie was an honor student in school and at 16, married her high school sweetheart, Roy Thornton. After Roy was sent to prison on a murder charge, Bonnie soon met Clyde, in 1930.

Bonnie Parker and Clyde Barrow terrorized small banks and storeowners in five states in a crime spree lasting 4 years during the Great Depression of the 1930s. Bonnie was caught and jailed in 1932 after one failed bank robbery but was soon released when the grand jury delivered a no-bill. Their hit-and-run heists cost the lives of 13 victims, almost all law enforcement. Clyde, who liked to drive, was known for crashing into lampposts, ditches, and off-road forays while fleeing crime scenes. They enjoyed taking photographs of one another with their Kodak Brownie, and taunting law enforcement. Six rolls of film were recovered after a shoot-out in Missouri at the home of Barrow's brother and sister-in-law, Buck and Blanche, in which two policemen where killed. The film showed Bonnie and Clyde posing with their machine guns and the rest of their gang. The legend grew as Clyde was dubbed the "Texas Rattlesnake," and Bonnie circulated poems to the newspapers about their crime forays. They were joined by others such as Ray Hamilton and William Daniel Jones, a 16-year-old whom they kidnapped from a service station. Jones was so enthralled by Clyde that he stayed with the gang and served as their driver.

Admired by many citizens for their adventurous and rebellious gangster image, "Bonnie and Clyde" were a symbol of many Americans' disenfranchised attitude toward the government and big business. Law enforcement and government officials were incensed, fearful, and embarrassed over the numerous crimes and murders committed in the course of their spree. Eventually, law enforcement caught up to the gang, and Buck was the first to die in a shoot-out. Hamilton had left the gang over disputes, and Blanche was captured. Ironically, Bonnie and Clyde would be betrayed by one of their own kind. An old prison friend of Hamilton's, Henry Methvin, himself on the run from the law, disclosed the whereabouts of the gang in order to earn his own freedom.

On May 23, 1934, Bonnie and Clyde met their end when Texas Ranger Frank Hamer and the government caught up with them in an ambush outside of the town of Sailes, Louisiana. Both were killed when the stolen beige 1934 Ford V-8 sedan they were driving was riddled with more than 160 bullets.

—Monica Myers

PAROLE OFFICERS, *See*
CRIMINAL JUSTICE PRACTITIONERS

PARTNER HOMICIDE, *See*
BATTERERS AND ABUSIVE PARTNERS; CYCLE THEORY OF VIOLENCE; DOMESTIC VIOLENCE; FAMILY HOMICIDE; HOMICIDE; MOTIVES FOR MURDER; VICTIMOLOGY

PATRICIDE, *See* FAMILY HOMICIDE

PAVULON, *See* POISONERS;
POISONING: MEDICAL SETTINGS

PCL-R, *See* PSYCHOPATHOLOGY
CHECKLIST–REVISED

PEARL, DANIEL, *See*
HOSTAGE TAKING; KIDNAPPING; MOTIVES FOR MURDER; TERRORISM

PEDOPHILE ORGANIZATIONS

Pedophilia, a form of paraphilia, can best be defined by the American Psychiatric Association's 1994 *Diagnostic and Statistical Manuel of Mental Disorders (DSM-IV).* According to the *DSM-IV,* a pedophile is as an individual who has recurrent, intense, sexually arousing fantasies about or engages in sexual behaviors involving prepubescent children 13 years old or younger. Within research on child sexual offenders, the terms *pedophile* and *child molester* are used interchangeably; however, the former is used within the psychiatric arena of assessment, diagnostics, and treatment of the sexual offender.

TYPES OF PEDOPHILE ORGANIZATIONS

Pedophiles exist within our diverse society and embody certain characteristics. Regardless of the typology or paradigm used to make clinical sense of these child sexual offenders, one thing remains constant, and that is societal disdain for such behavior. Perhaps even more alarming than the actual behavior is the fact that these offenders form groups that promote and accept their deviance toward children. Such groups include, but are not limited to, the following: NAMBLA (North American Man-Boy Love Association), Free Spirits, Renee Guyon Society, The Pedophile Liberation Front, and the Childhood Sensuality Circle (CSC).

NAMBLA is perhaps the most notorious group. It is a well-organized association comprising primarily homosexuals who have a preference for sexual relations with young boys. NAMBLA has offices in several major cities, with their headquarters in New York City. According to their Web site information, their purpose is to support the rights of all people to engage in consensual relations. They oppose laws that destroy loving relationships merely on the basis of the age of the participants.

NAMBLA unequivocally condemns all coercive or nonconsensual acts, sexual or otherwise, between people of any age. They believe, however, that a consenting child as young as 6 years old can understand sexual relations and should be allowed to engage in such activities. In addition to pedophilia, NAMBLA also endorses other sexually aberrant behavior, such as infantilism, cross-dressing, bestiality, erotic asphyxiation, and exhibitionism. They feature an "Entrapment of the Month" column on their Web site, alerting members on how to avoid covert government child pornography sting operations.

The Rene Guyon Society is also a national organization. This organization's purpose is based on Guyon's writings of *The Ethics of Sexual Acts,* written in 1934. The organization's motto is "Sex before eight or else it's too late."

Perhaps one of the more outspoken of the organizations promoting sexual relationships with children is the Pedophile Liberation Front. Their Web site features excerpts for children regarding the cause and purpose of their organization, which attempt to manipulate the reader into thinking that pedophiles are not dangerous people and that they can be trusted despite what their parents may have otherwise indicated.

Regardless of the organization, the groups have one common denominator: They all claim to have a genuine concern for the welfare of children and adolescents. They refuse see the harm in adults having sexual intercourse with minors. Moreover, they feel that sexual relationships between adults and children are healthy. These organizations are highly organized and powerful. They work with one another to escape detection. In addition, they promote the decriminalization of child molestation and pedophilia, as well as lowering the age of consent.

USE OF THE INTERNET

Highly organized pedophile organizations are a threat in many ways. With the use of the Internet, they advertise in an attempt to legitimize their beliefs and values, lure vulnerable children, and share information on how to avoid detection and prosecution. There is also a high probability that these individuals may become involved in Internet "cyberstalking," in which an individual can use the freedom and anonymity of the Internet to lure unsuspecting victims. In the chat room format, offenders can discuss their sexually violent fantasies with other perpetrators, share methods of successfully luring victims, and establish relationships with potential victims.

To combat the infiltration of pedophile organizations on the Internet, several "antipedophile" Web sites act as censors and provide information on deviant groups.

—*Catherine Purcell*

See also EXPLOITATION OF CHILDREN; PARAPHILIA; PEDOPHILIA; CYBERSTINGS; STALKING; WHITE SLAVERY

Further Reading

American Psychiatric Association. (1994). *The diagnostic and statistical manual of mental disorders* (4th ed.). Washington, DC: Author.

Hislop, J. (2001). *Female sex offenders: What therapists, law enforcement and child protective services need to know.* Idyll Arbor Publishers.

Jenkins, P. (2001). *Pedophiles and priests: Anatomy of a contemporary crisis.* Oxford University Press.

Van Dam, C. (2002). *Identifying child molesters: Preventing child sexual abuse by recognizing the patterns of the offenders.* New York: Haworth Publishers.

PEDOPHILIA

Within the large body of research regarding sexual offenses toward children, the terms *child molestation* and *pedophilia* are used interchangeably, though there are some distinctions between the two. Child molestation is a layman's term, whereas pedophilia is a diagnostic term used within the medical arena to assess and diagnose offenders with a sexual proclivity toward children. A child molester may or may not meet the scientific criteria necessary to be considered a pedophile. What follows is a description of the criteria established by the American Psychiatric Association.

Pedophilia, which is also a paraphilia, may be defined as recurrent, intense, sexually arousing fantasies about or engages in sexual behavior involving a prepubescent child or children, generally the age of 13 years or younger. The *Diagnostic and Statistical Manuel of Mental Disorders (DSM-IV)* further distinguishes two subtypes of pedophilia, which include the *exclusive* type, or sexual attraction to children only, and the *nonexclusive* type, sexual attraction to both children and adults. The behaviors described above must last over a period of at least 6 months to be considered paraphilic. The fantasies, sexual urges, or behaviors cause clinically significant distress or impairment in the social, occupational, or other important areas of functioning for the pedophile.

CHARACTERISTICS OF PEDOPHILES

There are several elements characteristic of a pedophile. The most common type of offender is the heterosexual pedophile, usually a male offender and a female child victim. Homosexual pedophilic relations involving a male offender and a male child victim occur in 20% to 23% of the cases (Bartol, 2002). A small percentage of offenders chose victims from both sexes. The sexual contact between the pedophile and the victim can range from caressing the body, fondling the genitals of the victim, or forcing the victim to manipulate the genitals of the offender, to actual penile penetration and oral copulation. In extreme cases, the sexual contact becomes violent in nature, resulting in sexual homicide of the victim. Pedophiles range in aggressiveness from passive to extremely violent, based on their fantasy development.

As with any paraphilia, the role of fantasy is a fundamental aspect of the sexually deviant behavior, perhaps the most critical catalytic force. In addition to fantasy, compulsive masturbation and facilitating agents such as pornography, drugs, and alcohol are also vital in sustaining the behavior. The sexual offender is typically a social introvert. Because of a lack of social and sexual socialization, offenders become reliant on their own internal thought processing. The fantasy world becomes a coping mechanism in which offenders can create a reality of their own, a reality of dominance and control over any situation and any person. The fantasy contains a desired paraphilia, as well as a circumstance or situation the offender has rehearsed in his mind. The pedophile's behavior can range in aggressiveness, a continuum of behavior, depending on the development and content of the fantasy system. A pedophile who is attracted to children and watches them only from afar may have a fantasy system reflecting a socially appropriate, caring relationship with the child, whereas a pedophile who is a *mysoped* (a sadistic offender), may fantasize the rape, torture, mutilation, and murder of the child.

In extensive research on pedophiles, Hickey has found that they prefer the company of children both socially and emotionally, are typically unmarried, live alone or with a relative, and have fantasies of emotional attachment and physical involvement with children.

TYPOLOGIES

Several influential theorists have devised classification typologies regarding the offending behaviors of pedophiles. Many salient variables must be considered, including personal characteristics, life experience, criminal history, and various motivational factors. Although there are other known typologies and classification paradigms, these factors are well represented in the research conducted by the National Center for Missing and Exploited Children, as well as Holmes, and Simon.

According to this research, *regressed offenders* have normal social and sexual relationships with others yet are both socially and sexually inadequate.

The individual harbors no malice toward the child, and the offense is a result of a recent stressor or experience. The incident involves sexual penetration, and the victim is usually unknown to the offender. The *fixated offender* and the *preferential child molester-seduction* and *preferential child molester-introverted* have no significant sexual or social relationships with adults and socially relate better with children. They are typically single and live "childlike" lifestyles. They relate more easily to children and perceive them as appropriate sexual objects. Their relationships with children are based on feelings of love and intimacy. This offender uses grooming and seduction techniques to lure the child victim. For example, an offender may befriend a child and slowly offer enticements to attain his or her trust, for ultimate sexual victimization, which takes the form of sexual gratification from caressing and fondling the victim. It is rare for these offenders to use physical force or to have sexual intercourse with victims.

Mysopeds, aggressive pedophiles or preferential sadistic child molesters, are more cruel in their offenses and more likely to engage in repetitive acts of sexual violence. This offender has antisocial tendencies, has no genuine love for the child, and typically obtains his victim by stalking, force, and abduction. There is a strong association between sexual arousal and sexual violence, typically ending in the fatality of the victim. The victim is usually tortured pre- and/or postmortem. The perpetrator engages in mutilation of the genitals or parts of the body with a strong sexual association.

TREATMENT IMPLICATIONS

Child sexual offenders are a heterogeneous group, and treatment must be as diversified as the individuals involved. It can range from cognitive behavioral, which focuses on restructuring the attitudes of these offenders, to psychoanalytic therapy, which addresses past issues of trauma and humiliation. The role of fantasy is critical in the etiology and perpetuation of this type of deviant behavior, so that adverse fantasy development must also be considered in the treatment of these offenders.

—*Catherine Purcell*

See also CYBERSTINGS; EXPLOITATION OF CHILDREN; MEGAN'S LAW; PARAPHILIA; PEDOPHILE ORGANIZATIONS; SEX OFFENDER REGISTRIES; SEX OFFENDERS; STALKING

Further Reading

American Psychiatric Association. (1994). *The diagnostic and statistical manual of mental disorders* (4th ed.). Washington, DC: Author.

Bartol, C. R. (2002). *Criminal behavior: A psychological approach* (6th ed.). Upper Saddle River, NJ: Pearson Education.

Handevidt, K. M. (2002). *How to pick a pedophile: Protecting kids from sexual predators and recognizing the webs they build around our families virtually unnoticed in the process of grooming our child.* Writers Club Press.

Hickey, E. W. (2002). *Serial murderers and their victims* (3rd ed.). Belmont, CA: Wadsworth.

Holmes, R. M. (1991). *Sex crimes.* Newbury Park, CA: Sage.

National Center for Missing and Exploited Children. (1987). *Child molesters: A behavioral analysis for law enforcement officers investigating cases of child sexual exploitation* (Cooperative Aggreement #86-MC-CX-K003). Washington, DC: U.S. Department of Justice.

Salter, A. (2003). *Predators: Pedophiles, rapists, and other sex offenders: Who they are, how they operate, and how we can protect ourselves and our children.* New York: Basic Books.

PERSONAL CAUSE MURDER, *See*
MOTIVES FOR MURDER

PHYSICAL ABUSE, *See*
BATTERED CHILD SYNDROME; BATTERED WOMAN'S SYNDROME; BATTERERS AND ABUSIVE PARTNERS; CHILD ABUSE; DOMESTIC VIOLENCE; ELDER ABUSE; VICTIMOLOGY

PHYSICIAN-ASSISTED SUICIDE, *See*
EUTHANASIA; KEVORKIAN, JACK; MOTIVES FOR MURDER; MURDER-SUICIDE; SUICIDE

POISONERS

People have been poisoning each other for as long as written history has existed, and probably before that. In the past, it was one of the preferred methods of eliminating people in high places silently, unobtrusively, and swiftly. With the advent of life insurance in the mid-19th century, when the victim gained monetary value, death by poisoning became somewhat of a commercial transaction.

Poisonings have evolved along with the scientific knowledge and literacy of the population, the availability of accounts in newspapers and other published material, and the fascination with all things lethal by authors grinding out fictional accounts of "the perfect murder." Some of the more common poisons include arsenic, cyanide, and strychnine; however, acids, aniline compounds, atropine, scopolamine, insulin, lye, carbon monoxide, metallic compounds, nicotine, opiates, phosphorous, sodium fluoride, and succinylcholine have also been used to kill unsuspecting victims.

The dividing line between medicines and poisons is a fine one. A compound at one dose may be therapeutic but at an increased dose may be lethal. Poisoners with access to medically used pharmaceuticals are at a distinct advantage. They are usually trusted by the victims and frequently have knowledge about what kills and what does not. Also, a patient may be legitimately taking some pharmaceuticals, making toxicological examinations less definitive.

In the 19th century, the apprehended poisoner was more likely to be a male. Examples are Dr. William Palmer, in 1856, who was thought to have poisoned as many as a dozen family members and friends for insurance and other financial gain. George Chapman, from 1897 to 1902, killed three women, all of whom were pretending to be his wives. His poison of choice was antimony. Thomas Griffiths Wainewright, in the late 1700s, killed three female relatives for the inheritance and insurance money. Not all poisoners in that era were men, however. For example, from 1852 to 1872, Mary Ann Cotton killed more than 20 victims, including husbands and children, by putting arsenic in their tea. She stood to benefit financially from the deaths of many of her victims.

In modern times, most poisoners are women. The few notable exceptions are health care workers who kill in their workplaces. This type of serial murderer is very successful and is frequently able to avoid apprehension for much longer than the more notorious male serial killers. She chooses her poison and her victims very carefully, plans the crime methodically, and is aided by society's bias that denies the existence of female serial murderers. She exhibits a preference for victims who are children, the elderly, or spouses and is often the last to be suspected of harming them. The women who kill in this manner are frequently dubbed "Black Widows" or "Angels of Death." They kill for revenge or financial gain, or both. Occasionally, a woman kills without an obvious reason for doing so, though this situation is fairly rare.

BLACK WIDOWS

"Black Widows" are extremely organized and successful female serial murderers. They typically start killing after the age of 25, and it is not unusual for them to continue to kill for 10 years or more until they are caught or quit killing for another reason. Poisoning is overwhelmingly their method of murder. Most often, Black Widows kill family members, but that is not always the case. It is not unheard of for them to kill others with whom they have close personal relationships, especially if they stand to benefit financially.

The typical Black Widow in the United States claims 6 to 10 victims throughout her active period. Outside the United States, this number increases: 13 to 21. She is trusted by her victims, she has access to their food, and she has the patience to poison them, often over an extended period of time. Usually, when the victim dies, the Black Widow is accorded sympathy and support rather than suspicion. She almost always kills for profit and does not kill indiscriminately. When she needs more money, she kills again. Because she chooses victims who trust her, her crimes seem particularly heinous. They violate society's basic assumptions about love, loyalty, guardianship, and friendship.

There have been a number of notorious Black Widows, including Belle Gunness, Judith Buenoano, Marie Besnard, Margie Velma Barfield, Blance Taylor Moore, and others, but one of the more interesting is Nannie Doss, otherwise known as "the Giggling Grandma." She was given her moniker by the press because of her tendency to giggle as she confessed one murder after another to the police. Nannie Doss was active between 1925 and 1954. During that time, she killed four of her five husbands, two of her own children, a nephew, a grandchild, two sisters, and her mother. She claimed she killed her husbands for "romance." When the current husband started to slip in her affections, she fed him rat poison (arsenic) in his food or drink and started looking for the next one. Indeed, she gained relatively little in the way of financial compensation, so that

would not appear to have been her strongest motivator. She died in prison of leukemia.

REVENGE KILLERS

Female poisoners may also kill because of revenge, but the profile of this type of killer is quite different from the organized, methodical Black Widow. This type of murderer works alone and kills individuals that she perceives have wronged her in some way or individuals who are very close to someone that she feels has harmed her. For example, if she is angry with her spouse, she may kill her children to "get back at him."

Whereas the Black Widow is patient, precise, and cunning, the revenge killer is consumed by the heat of passion, which she is unable to control. As a result, she may fail to plan her crimes carefully. Although she may be organized enough to commit several crimes, the motive will often lead authorities to her before the body count rises very high. The average revenge murderer claims three or four victims over a 2-year period. There are exceptions to this, but they are rare. In general, the Revenge Murderer kills her victims in response to some triggering response that fans the flames of her resentment. She kills in an attempt to regain some control in her life after an incident that emphasizes her feeling of rejection or abandonment. An example of this type of killer is Martha Hazel Wise. The press dubbed her "Borgia of America."

Martha's trouble began when she announced her plans to marry Walter Johns. Her family was vehemently against the marriage and demanded that she break her engagement. She refused and began hatching the plan that would eliminate the opposition to her marriage. Her first victim was her aging mother. She killed her with arsenic, but given the age and health of the victim, the death was determined to be natural. Next, Martha successfully killed her aunt and uncle in the same manner. She continued to attempt to kill other members of her family but was unsuccessful. The family members took their suspicions to the authorities, and Martha was questioned. She confessed to the three murders but denied trying to kill the others. She was convicted and sentenced to life in prison, where she died of natural causes.

PROFIT KILLERS

A third type of poisoner is a woman who kills for profit. On the surface, it would appear that this is just another Black Widow, and although there are some striking similarities in their methods and practices, there are also some significant differences. The Black Widow focuses her activities preferentially on family members, whereas the Profit Killer usually seeks victims outside her family sphere. Both the Black Widow and the Profit Killer are organized, intelligent, resourceful, and very careful in planning and executing their crimes. However, the Profit Killer tends to consider her activities as a business and therefore strives to be more covert.

The Profit Killer is usually over 25 years of age when she begins killing. Normally, she considers two types of victims: someone with whom she has developed a close relationship, such as a caretaker or trusted friend, and someone who can be easily manipulated and who represents an opportunity for profit—for example, spouses murdered at the request of their wives or husbands. Typically, the this kind of killer claims between 5 and 10 victims over a 5- to 10-year period. Whereas the crimes of the Black Widow leave us wondering about the sanctity of love and family, the crimes of the Profit Killer reduce the meaning of life to an arbitrary monetary value. They prefer poison as the weapon because it is easily introduced to food and is silently lethal.

Dorothea Montalvo Puente was a prolific Profit Killer. She leased a large Victorian home in Sacramento, California, in 1986, and set about convincing the authorities that she could effectively care for her borders despite an existing record of victimizing elderly men she had met in bars in 1982.

By 1988, social workers were becoming concerned about the high incidence of "sudden disappearances" of many of the men who had been sent to Mrs. Puente's boarding house. This concern was echoed by neighbors, who reported a persistent stench emanating from the property. When police visited Mrs. Puente to ask about one resident who had been reported missing, she reported that he had returned to Mexico, and the matter was dropped. Finally, a missing person report was filed about another one of her boarders, and the coincidence of two such reports and the persistent stench aroused more suspicion. When the property was examined more closely, a buried corpse was disinterred, and soon two more bodies were found. When they returned to arrest her, they found she had fled, but further examination of the property revealed seven more buried men.

Dorothea Puente was apprehended in Los Angeles, returned to Sacramento, and charged with nine counts of murder. At trial, she was convicted of three counts of murder and sentenced to life imprisonment without the possibility of parole. Evidence revealed that she had killed her victims for their social security checks, which she continued to receive after their deaths, as well as other assets. Though she was accused of nine killings, it is suspected that she may have been responsible for as many as 25 deaths over the course of her active period.

The Federal Bureau of Investigation Uniform Crime Reports indicate that approximately 6% of all murder is accomplished with "other" means, which include arson, bombs, and poison. In the case of serial murder, "other" weapons rise to 10%. Serial murderers selecting poison as the weapon of choice are overwhelmingly female and predominantly of the "Black Widow" type, who enhance home-cooked meals for their families with poisons ranging from arsenic to strychnine. Because these slayers do not use more traditional weapons such as guns, knives, or hammers, they are dubbed "the gentle killers," though this epithet does not recognize the havoc they wreak in their close companions or family members.

—Marlene Deal

See also METHODS OF MURDER; POISONING: MEDICAL SETTINGS; PRODUCT TAMPERING; WOMEN AND VIOLENCE

Further Reading

Bodo, B. (2002). *Tiszazug: A social history of a murder epidemic.* East European Monographs.

Hickey, E. W. (2002). *Serial murderers and their victims* (3rd ed.). Belmont, CA: Wadsworth.

Kelleher, M. E., & Kelleher, C. L. (1998). *Murder most rare: The female serial killer.* New York: Dell.

Nash, J. R. (1986). *Look for the woman: A narrative encyclopedia of female poisoners, kidnappers, thieves, extortionists, terrorists, swindlers and spies.* Evans & Company.

POISONING IN MEDICAL SETTINGS

Poisoning is the intentional or unintentional introduction of a substance that causes physiological injury to the body by its chemical action. The route of entry into the body can be ingestion, inhalation, injection, or absorption. Because any substance introduced in sufficient quantities can be poisonous, poisoning more often implies the inappropriate usage of a substance in an appropriate or excessive degree of dosage.

The commitment of the medical profession is to preserve, restore, and promote optimal physiological and emotional functioning in their individual clients; however, serial murderers are well-known in the medical profession. "Arguably, medicine has thrown up more serial killers than all other professions put together" (Kinnel, 2000). Consider the health care provider who intentionally administers a substance with the intended outcome being homicide.

POISONING BY NARCOTICS

Dr. Harold Shipman, a 51-year-old general practitioner and serial killer, is known as England's "Doctor Death." He was sentenced to life in prison after his conviction of murdering 15 elderly patients by administering lethal doses of morphine. Morphine is a narcotic, and physiologic changes that normally occur in the elderly make it imperative that these drugs be administered with caution. Absorption and metabolism of drugs are altered in the elderly because of decreased liver, renal, and gastrointestinal function. As a result, drugs are not metabolized as quickly, and blood levels of the drug remain higher for a longer period, thus increasing susceptibility to depression of the nervous and respiratory system.

Morphine can be administered orally (tablets and syrup), intravenously (IV), subcutaneously (in the fatty tissue), and rectally (suppositories). When administered by IV, it should be given in small incremental doses (1-3 mg over 1-5 minutes) until the desired effect is achieved. If morphine is administered quickly in a single large dose, as with other narcotics, respiratory depression will occur. The recipient's normal drive to breathe is inhibited, and he or she soon dies from lack of oxygen. Because morphine causes peripheral dilation of the blood vessels, hypotension (low blood pressure) is a possible side effect. Long periods of hypotension decrease blood flow to the brain and other vital organs, causing permanent damage and possible death.

As a poison, morphine is a convenient drug because it is a common drug of choice for the treatment of pain and anxiety within the outpatient (Hospice) and clinical (hospital) settings. It is used preoperatively to provide a synergistic effect to that of the general anesthetics and postoperatively to provide pain relief. Pain relief is obtained by the inhibition of impulses that would be experienced as painful and by blocking their transmission in the brain and spinal cord. Morphine is also commonly used in cardiac units to relieve the pain of a myocardial infarction (heart attack) and for the sudden onset of pulmonary edema (fluid build-up in the lungs). In these instances, morphine temporarily relieves chest pain by dilating peripheral blood vessels. This dilation shunts blood and workload away from the dying, overworked heart muscle.

In June 2001, a public inquiry opened to examine more than 400 cases in which Dr. Shipman was suspected of murder. Depending on the outcome of this inquiry, "Dr. Shipman might prove to be Britain's—and the world's—most prolific serial killer" (McDowell, 2001).

POISONING BY NEUROMUSCULAR BLOCKING AGENTS

Efren Saldivar called himself the "Angel of Death." He was a 32-year-old respiratory therapist at Glendale Adventist Medical Center in California from 1996 to 1997. In 2001, he pleaded guilty to murder by lethal injection of six elderly patients ranging in age from 75 to 87 years old. Authorities exhumed 20 bodies and found the presence of Pavulon, a potent muscle relaxer, in the remains of six. He was sentenced to seven consecutive life sentences. Saldivar confessed to police that he may have contributed to the deaths of 100 to 200 patients and killed up to 50 by lethal injection.

Genene Ann Jones, LVN (licensed vocational nurse), chose a particularly vulnerable group of patients to poison: children. Jones was working in the pediatric unit at Bexar County Medical Center Hospital, in Texas. In 1981, she requested to be put in charge of the sickest patients. When the hospital became aware of the increased mortality of children from medical conditions that should not have been fatal, the hospital administration decided to replace all the nurses in the pediatric unit. Jones resigned and became employed at a pediatric clinic. In February 1983, a grand jury was convened to investigate 47 suspicious deaths of children at Bexar County Medical Hospital. A second grand jury held hearings on seven children that had experienced seizures at the pediatric clinic. Jones's presence was the common variable in both locations. She is suspected of injecting her victims with succinylcholine, a potent muscle relaxer. A statistical report presented at the trial stated that children were 25% more likely to have had cardiac arrest and 10% more likely to die when Jones was in charge. Although Jones is suspected in many more deaths of children, staff at the hospital shredded numerous records, destroying potentially valuable evidence. Genene Ann Jones was tried and convicted of murdering 2 children. She was sentenced to 159 years but is eligible for parole in 20 years.

In the summer of 1975, up to 40 patients died of inexplicable respiratory failure at the V.A. Hospital in Ann Arbor, Michigan. Investigation by the FBI confirmed that eight men had died of poisoning by the injection of Pavulon. Two registered nurses, Sister Filipina Narcissco and Leonora Perez, were charged with eight murders, conspiracy, and attempt to poison. However, the evidence was circumstantial, and after the nurses' arrest, the hospital supervisor wrote a confession to the murders before committing suicide. With no witnesses and only circumstantial evidence, trials for the nurses were held, but the convictions were either vacated, set aside on appeal, or dismissed at the second trial. These murders remain unsolved.

In 1987, 26-year-old Richard Angelo, a medical technician and charge nurse at Good Samaritan Hospital on Long Island, New York, was soon nicknamed Long Island's "Angel of Death." As the charge nurse, he was able to freely circulate among the other nurses' assigned patients without suspicion. It is estimated that Angelo managed to kill 10 people by injecting the paralyzing drugs Pavulon and succinylcholine. He was discovered after one patient, Gerolamo Kucich, caught him putting something into his IV and managed to reach his call light before he succumbed to the effects of the drug. Kucich's assigned nurse immediately took a urine sample from Mr. Kucich and had it analyzed. The urinalysis came back positive for the presence of Pavulon and succinylcholine, neither of which had been prescribed for this patient. Angelo was convicted of two counts of second-degree murder, one count of second-degree manslaughter, one count of criminally negligent homicide, and six counts of assault. He was sentenced to 61 years to life in prison.

Pavulon and succinylcholine are neuromuscular blocking agents. These drugs act to relax the skeletal muscles by disrupting the transmission of nerve impulses. There are two main classes of blocking agents, and although their mechanisms of action differ,

their therapeutic effects are similar. The three major clinical indications for using these drugs are (a) to relax skeletal muscles as an adjunct to anesthesia before surgery to facilitate intubation (placement of a breathing tube), (b) to reduce the intensity of muscle spasm in drug-induced or electrically induced convulsions (electroshock therapy), and (c) to manage patients who are fighting mechanical ventilation (life support measures). The initial muscle weakness produced by the drugs quickly changes to a flaccid paralysis (complete loss of muscle tone). This paralysis occurs in a specific sequence, starting with the cranial nerves and small, rapidly moving muscles in the eyes, face, and neck. Next, the limbs, abdomen, and trunk muscles become flaccid, and finally, the muscles of the diaphragm are paralyzed. This all occurs within 30 seconds after injection of the drug. Recovery from the paralysis usually occurs in the reverse order. A significant factor about these drugs is that they do not cross the blood brain barrier; therefore, there is no alteration in consciousness or pain perception. Patients victimized by the inappropriate use of these drugs are not sedated and are aware of what is happening to them and experience extreme panic and anxiety, but they cannot communicate or respond as they slowly suffocate.

Until recently, poisoning by succinylcholine was difficult to detect during autopsy, especially after the victim had been embalmed. New advances in forensic science now make it possible to identify the presence of this powerful muscle relaxer. In 1992, 41 patients mysteriously died at Truman Memorial Veterans Hospital in Columbia, Missouri. In 2002, Richard A. Williams, a 36-year-old nurse, was charged with the murder of 10 of those patients. New tests identified the presence of succinylcholine in the victims.

POISONING BY SYNTHETIC ADRENALINE

On March 14, 2002, Kristen H. Gilbert, a 33-year-old registered nurse, was convicted in a U.S. District Court of three counts of first-degree murder, one count of second-degree murder, and two counts of assault to commit murder. Ms. Gilbert murdered her victims in a V.A. hospital in Northampton, Massachusetts, by administering unnecessary doses of epinephrine. It was noted that too many patients were dying of cardiac arrest and others had mysteriously succumbed to near-fatal heart failure while she was there. Exhumed bodies tested positive for epinephrine, a drug that the prosecutor Ariane Vuono called the "perfect murder weapon."

Epinephrine (a synthetic adrenalin) is a catecholamine that naturally occurs in the body. It causes some of the physiological symptoms that are experienced with fear and anxiety, most notably in the cardiovascular system. In medical settings, it is used therapeutically as a vasoconstrictor (used to control hemorrhage), and to prolong the action of local anesthetics by constricting blood vessels to prevent rapid absorption. Epinephrine can also produce some profound cardiovascular and respiratory responses and is therefore the first drug used during a cardiac arrest. It is a cardiac stimulant and a bronchial dilator. When used appropriately, epinephrine produces favorable redistribution of blood flow from the peripheral circulation to the central circulation (brain, heart, lungs) during CPR (cardiopulmonary resuscitation). Inappropriate use of epinephrine, even at low doses, can precipitate or exacerbate myocardial ischemia (decreased oxygen to the heart muscle). When given in high doses (20 mcg per minute or 0.3 mcg/kg per minute), hypertension will result in patients who are not in cardiac arrest, and it may induce or exacerbate lethal heart rhythm problems (arrhythmia), especially in patients who are receiving digitalis (a commonly prescribed heart medication). If epinephrine is given intravenously to a normal beating heart, it creates heart rhythm problems, making the heart race and progressing to malfunction, failure, and death.

Epinephrine can be administered orally (tablets and capsules), intramuscularly (in the muscle), subcutaneously (in the fatty tissue), intravenously, or through inhalation (a tube, metered aerosol, or nebulae). Epinephrine has been referred as the "perfect poison" because it occurs naturally in the body as adrenalin and breaks down rapidly, so that detection is virtually impossible after death, and also because it is used to help resuscitate people whose hearts have stopped, making unauthorized injections difficult to detect. Each of Kristen H. Gilbert's four victims was vulnerable to poisoning due to existing physical or mental illness. Witnesses for the prosecution testified that the only explanation for the sudden deaths of Gilbert's patients was poisoning by epinephrine, not existing pathology.

POISONING BY POTASSIUM CHLORIDE

Orville Lynn Majors, an LPN (licensed practical nurse), worked at Vermillion County Hospital, in Clinton, Indiana, from May 1993 to February 1995. During that time, the patient death rate rose from 26 to 101 per year. In only 22 months of Majors's employment, 147 people died, most of them during his shifts. An investigation revealed that Majors sometimes took his own initiative in "treating" patients and was observed administering IV medications, something that is not within the scope of licensure for an LPN. Investigators exhumed 15 bodies to examine tissues and found that at least six deaths were consistent with the administration of epinephrine and potassium chloride. Patient documentation noted a sudden rise in blood pressure before their hearts stopped (cardiac arrest due to hypokalemia; see below). On October 17, 1999, Majors was convicted of six counts of murder, for which he received a life sentence.

Potassium is the major cation (an ion with a positive charge) within our cells. In conjunction with sodium and chloride, it aids in regulation of osmotic pressure and the body's acid-base balance. It is one of the essential ions for normal excitability of muscle tissue, especially the heart muscle. Potassium chloride is widely used as a source of potassium when other drugs such as diuretics are used. It can be given orally (tablets, liquid, powder) or intravenously. If too much potassium chloride is administered, weakness, paralysis, impaired electrical heart conduction, and eventually cardiac arrest and death will occur. Potassium chloride is never recommended or given intravenously undiluted, and when given diluted, the solution is administered slowly (not to exceed 20 mEq per hour). Infusing it too rapidly or when not needed can cause fatal hyperkalemia (high potassium blood levels). The heart will immediately stop, and attempts to restart the heart will fail until the high potassium levels are corrected.

POISONING BY A PARASYMPATHOLYTIC

Dr. Paul Agutter used his medical knowledge in an attempt to poison his wife, rather than his patients. Agutter laced his wife's tonic water with atropine. To cover his crime, he had also introduced atropine into several bottles of tonic water at a local store for others to purchase. Dr. Geoffrey Sharwood-Smith, a consultant anesthetist, purchased the atropine-laced bottles of tonic water, and when his son and wife became ill, he recognized the symptoms of atropine poisoning and sought treatment at a hospital. Therefore, when Agutter's wife later presented at the hospital, staff were already aware of the signs and symptoms of atropine poisoning, and she was successfully treated. An investigation determined that the levels of atropine in Mrs. Agutter's gin-and-tonic were higher than the atropine-laced bottles sold in the store. Detectives concluded from the evidence that Agutter was responsible for the poisoning.

Atropine is an ancient poison derived from the nightshade plant. The Roman Emperors Augustus and Claudius were murdered by their wives with atropine. Livia, the wife of Augustus, injected figs on Augustus's fig tree with the substance, and he soon succumbed to the effects.

Because atropine is a parasympatholytic drug, it reverses the effect of the parasympathetic nervous system by inhibiting the neurotransmitter acetylcholine. Atropine binds to the receptor sites of the peripheral nervous system, blocking them from being stimulated. The drug causes a reduction in salivary, bronchial, and sweat gland secretion, which makes it useful as an anesthetic. It is widely used in ophthalmology to block normal pupil reflex to constrict with light stimulation, therefore facilitating examination of the interior of the eye. Atropine is also used in inhalers as a bronchodilator and as a way to relax the smooth muscles in the gastrointestinal tract, urinary tract, and biliary tree (gallbladder ducts).

Atropine blocks the parasympathetic nervous system that innervates the heart and blood vessels. Normal physiologic response of the parasympathetic system is to decrease heart rate and lower blood pressure. Therefore, atropine is one drug used as initial therapy for patients with symptomatic low heart rates or in patients with heart rates in the "normal range" but with a need to raise the heart rate in an attempt to achieve a more optimum blood pressure. By increasing the heart rate, atropine also increases the heart's demand for more oxygen. When it is administered to someone with decreased blood flow to the heart (myocardial ischemia), excessive increases in heart rate may worsen the ischemia and even precipitate a heart attack (myocardial infarction).

This drug can be administered orally, intravenously, intraocularly (into the eyes), endotracheally (through a tube placed into the trachea to assist patient to breathe), and topically (applied to skin, it deactivates sensory nerve endings). When used appropriately, it is relatively safe; however, it is an extremely toxic poison when used inappropriately. Toxic physiologic effects include increased blood pressure, changes in heart rate, amnesia, flushed and hot skin, poor balance (ataxia), blurred vision, confusion, and excitation.

POISONING BY MULTIPLE AGENTS

Almost immediately after graduating from medical school in 1993, Dr. Michael Swango began a criminal career of murder and assault by poisoning. Estimates range from 35 to 60 murders and 17 or more nonfatal poisonings between the years 1983 to 1997. Even after a conviction for the nonfatal poisoning of six of Swango's paramedic coworkers in 1985, he managed to continue his medical and criminal career. Swango falsified his resumé and lied about his criminal conviction and was able to convince other medical institutions to hire him.

Swango practiced medicine in the United States and Zimbabwe. After each termination for falsification of his medical resumé or suspicious deaths, he was always able to secure employment as a physician in another hospital. Swango was en route from being terminated in Zimbabwe to a new position as a physician at the Royal Hospital in Dhahran, Saudi Arabia, when he was apprehended by federal authorities at Chicago's O'Hare Airport. He was arrested on making false statements and controlled substance charges. Indicted on federal charges for three murders in July 2000, Swango pleaded guilty in a plea-bargaining agreement that the United States would not seek the death penalty or extradite him to Zimbabwe. Zimbabwe was seeking extradition on a warrant for five murders and three assault charges on patients Swango treated in 1995.

Swango is the subject of a book, numerous news accounts, and federal documents that contain an extensive history of his criminal behavior. This individual demonstrates how difficult it is to prove intentional poisoning by a health care provider. He used his medical training to select drugs that he knew would cause death but not necessarily implicate him as a suspect. Autopsy and forensic evidence concluded that he murdered and poisoned his victims using potassium chloride, succinylcholine, epinephrine, and other unidentifiable substances through intravenous and intramuscular injections. All his victims succumbed to respiratory failure, respiratory and neuromuscular paralysis, or cardiac arrest. To further his chances of success, Swango also falsely placed "Do Not Resuscitate" (DNR) orders in his victims' charts, thus preventing other hospital staff from intervening and saving his victims. Swango was sentenced to life imprisonment without the possibility of parole. He has never expressed remorse for his crimes.

DETECTION IN THE HEALTH CARE ENVIRONMENT

It is very difficult to prove that medical practitioners have committed murder by poisoning their patients, because there are rarely witnesses to poisonings. The health care milieu provides easy access to narcotics and other substances that can be used as poisons but are also commonly used in the normal treatment of a patient's illness. It must also be remembered that most patients who die in the health care environment do so of natural causes. One cannot suspect that every death of an ill patient has a suspicious origin. Health care providers can also be highly mobile and often do not remain in any one health care setting for a long period of time. Many times, staff members have moved to other locations by the time statistical analysis raises suspicion. The literature has documented some cases of medical practitioners who murder by poisoning, but many cases of suspicious deaths continue to go unsolved due to the nature of the health care environment.

—*Carol Coppock*

See also JONES, GENENE; MEDICAL MURDERS; METHODS OF MURDER; MOTIVES FOR MURDER; POISONERS

Further Reading

Kinnel, H. G. (2000, December 23). Serial homicide by doctor: Shipman in perspective. *British Medical Journal, 321,* p. 1594.

Lehne, R. A. (2001). *Pharmacology for nursing care* (4th ed.). Philadelphia: W. B. Saunders.

McDowell, J. L. (2001, November). Trust me, I'm your doctor. *The Timeline, 4*(11), pp. 51, 53-54.

PDR: Physicians' desk reference (56th ed.). (2002). Oradell, NJ: Medical Economics.

Stewart, J. B. (2000). *Blind eye: The terrifying story of a doctor who got away with murder.* New York: Simon & Schuster.

POLICE BRUTALITY

Police brutality is generally considered to be unlawful, excessive, or unreasonable use of physical force against a private citizen by a law enforcement officer in the performance of that officer's duties. Although its existence is not debated, there is disagreement about when the use of force becomes unreasonable or excessive and how frequently this occurs. The causes of police brutality are generally thought to be part of the "War on Crime" mentality, police insularity, and an elitist attitude among special police units.

EVALUATION OF POLICE BRUTALITY

The extent and frequency of police brutality in the United States is impossible to assess with any accuracy. Brutality victims fail to file complaints for a variety of reasons, and there is no central or national repository for brutality and misconduct complaints against law enforcement officers. Prosecutorial data also fails to yield much useful information, and an unknown number of cases are disposed of by individual law enforcement agencies through administrative sanctions such as terminations, forced retirements, and other disciplinary measures.

Causes of Police Brutality

For the most part, police brutality is ascribed to systemic and operational issues within law enforcement, such as the insularity of officers; the "War on Crime" mentality that has gripped most of law enforcement; the use of elite police units; and an absence of accountability by field supervisors for their subordinates. Law enforcement officers furthermore learn after the academy and during the first few years of service that excessive force is an acceptable or even desirable response in certain cases, especially when confronted with blatant disrespect.

Responses to Police Brutality

Law Enforcement Agency Policies and Procedures

Policy and procedural responses to police brutality include reviews of and changes in the selection and hiring process for entry level police officers. An increase in accountability for police supervisors and management, more stringent reporting requirements for officers involved in any use of force, and a rigorous review of their actions are also used to address the problem. Additional controls include drug testing of officers after any serious incident involving the use of force and the use of computerized tracking systems to maintain and analyze information on the use of force by officers and citizen complaint data. In California, all nonfederal agencies employing law enforcement officers are legally required to make information about the complaint (for misconduct) process readily available to the public, to facilitate the reporting of such incidents.

Federal Response to Problems With Police Brutality

In Section 210402 of the Violent Crime Control and Law Enforcement Act of 1994, also known as the "Crime Bill," the U.S. Congress required the Department of Justice to gather information on the excessive use of force by police. To accomplish this task, additional questions in the form of a self-report survey were added to the 1999 National Crime Victimization Surveys, to gather data on the prevalence of problems during traffic- and nontraffic-related contact between the public and police. Projecting the results of this survey to the entire U.S. population, less than 1% of the estimated 44 million people reporting personal face-to-face contact with police were subjected to some kind of force or threat of force. Of those, however, the majority felt that the police had acted improperly.

External or Citizen Review Boards (Civilian Oversight)

External or citizen review boards usually consist of political appointees, with a staff of nonpolice officers who investigate allegations of all types of police misconduct, including the excessive use of force, or who review the results of such investigations conducted by police themselves. They generally report directly to the chief law enforcement officer of the agency employing the officers under scrutiny. They then recommend a particular course of action based on their own investigations or review of a law enforcement agency's investigation into the allegations. Citizen or civilian review boards have no prosecutorial powers, and the chief law enforcement officer may accept or ignore their recommendations. Although the existence of such a board may be a good public relations tool for a particular law enforcement agency, such boards usually find in favor of the officer under investigation, and their existence does not appear to have a significant impact on the number of police brutality cases reported by the public.

Critics of citizen or civilian review boards point out that such boards are generally underfunded, lack the power and ability to conduct and evaluate investigations, and lack a necessary understanding of the nature of police work. In addition, there are other alternatives for persons desiring to file brutality complaints:

- Depending on the seriousness of the police conduct, the U.S. Justice Department (FBI) may accept and follow up on a complaint, in place of or in addition to an investigation by the local prosecutor, commonly known as the district attorney.
- State investigative agencies also may play a role in investigating police brutality at the local agency level.

Public Advocacy Groups and the Media

Government figures on police brutality tend to be conservative. There are private organizations, however, such as the American Civil Liberties Union (ACLU) and the Human Rights Watch, which describe the problem as a nationwide crisis. Such organizations gather their own data, particularly in the form of anecdotal and secondhand information that is difficult to verify with any degree of accuracy. These organizations focus media attention on the problem and act as catalysts for needed government responses.

—*Harald Otto Schweizer*

See also COMMUNITY ATTITUDES TOWARD VIOLENT CRIME; POLICE CORRUPTION; PREVENTION OF CRIME AND VIOLENT BEHAVIOR

Further Reading

Contacts between police and the public. (2001, February). Washington, DC: U.S. Department of Justice.

How reasonable is the reasonable man? Police and excessive force. *The Journal of Criminal Law and Criminology, 85*(2), 481-501.

Human Rights Watch. (1998). *Shielded from justice: Police brutality in the U.S.* Available on the World Wide Web at: http://www.hrw.org/reports98/police/index.htm.

Palmiotto, M. J. (Ed.) (2001). *Police misconduct: A reader for the 21st century.* Englewood Cliffs, NJ: Prentice Hall.

Skolnick, J. H., & Fyfe, J. J. (1993). *Above the law.* New York: Free Press.

Toch, H., & Geller, W. A. (Eds.). (1996). *Police violence.* Cambridge, MA: Yale University Press.

POLICE CORRUPTION

Police corruption is incompatible with the rule of law, and the degree to which it exists can seriously undermine the quality of life of citizens affected by it. A successful response to eliminate it, however, is contingent on the ability to properly define it, provide reliable data on its prevalence, and develop effective prevention and detection efforts.

Although there is no universal definition of corruption, the Office of the United Nations High Commissioner for Human Rights defines police corruption as encompassing "the commission or omission of an act in the performance of or in connection with one's duties, in response to gifts, promises or incentives demanded or accepted, or the wrongful receipt of these once the act has been committed or omitted."

EVALUATION OF POLICE CORRUPTION

Police corruption is also part of the larger problem of government corruption, and those who benefit from it are not likely to report its existence. Although this makes it impossible to accurately assess the prevalence of corruption, the perceptions of business people and members of the public in general regarding corruption in their respective countries serve as an indirect but useful mechanism.

Government corruption as a whole is generally perceived to be more common and extensive in underdeveloped and poor countries. Looking at the problem of corruption globally, the Global Coalition Against Corruption, a joint initiative between Transparency International and Goettingen University (Germany), developed a corruption perception index for 124 countries, based on surveys of businesspeople, risk analysts, and members of the public in those countries.

With a value of 10 representing "highly clean" and zero representing "highly corrupt," the United States is in 16th place alongside Israel with a 7.6 corruption rating. Finland is perceived to be the "most clean," with a corruption perception rating of 9.9, followed by Denmark, New Zealand, Iceland, and Singapore.

Publicity regarding police corruption can seriously harm the image of a police agency, impede its ability to gain cooperation from the public, and negatively affect the careers of commanders responsible for corrupt officers. As a result, some police officials may see

a greater benefit in suppressing information regarding such corrupt officers than in rigorously combating it.

Causes of Police Corruption

There is some speculation that police corruption is closely connected to police brutality and that where one occurs, the other is also prevalent. The thrill of having power over others and disenchantment with the justice process have been identified as possible motivators for acts of corruption and brutality. Greed cannot not be discounted as another or additional factor in the police corruption equation. In most serious cases of police corruption in the United States, organized crime and the illegal narcotics trade play major roles and lay the groundwork for corruption to thrive.

Response to Police Corruption

Police corruption, or the potential for it, must be addressed as early as the officer recruitment process. New officers are, or should be, screened for honesty, integrity, mental stability, past drug use, and general suitability for police work on the basis of a thorough background investigation and a variety of written and oral evaluations, which may also include a polygraph exam. This process can identify many unsuitable applicants. Others, however, may appear qualified at the point of entry, but once exposed to opportunities to benefit from corrupt acts may be unable to resist such opportunities without additional preventive steps taken by the law enforcement agency.

Additional corruption controls may include the following:

♦ Holding police supervisors accountable for the action of their subordinates.
♦ Ethics training.
♦ Sensitization to the issue of corruption while in the basic training academy.
♦ Recurrent integrity tests. One example would be the surreptitious surveillance of police officers during dispatched calls providing them with opportunities to engage in corrupt acts. The Singapore Police Force routinely conducts integrity tests of their officers, and with a corruption perception index of 9.2, Singapore and Iceland are in fourth place of countries perceived to be the least corrupt.
♦ Submission and review of personal financial statements of top police commanders.

♦ Changing a police subculture that tolerates misconduct among its ranks and stigmatizes officers who speak out about abuses committed by other officers.

♦ Limited time in assignments with significant opportunities for corruption.

♦ Providing adequate pay and benefits for police officers.

♦ Public education on the role the general public can play in the fight against corruption, particularly that it is facilitated by the public's willingness to offer or agree to corrupt arrangements with individual police officers.

♦ Creating special units external to the regular police department that are responsible for the investigation of all government corruption.

Most police agencies also have special sections or individuals responsible for internal investigations involving department personnel suspected of misconduct, including acts of corruption. Investigations by police agencies of their own personnel, however, may not be fully trusted by those concerned with police corruption. In the United States, the FBI and various state investigative agencies may in addition become involved in corruption investigations of state and local government agencies.

The Chinese Special Administrative Region of Hong Kong pioneered a unique approach with its Independent Commission Against Corruption (ICAC). The commission is an organization separate from the police department that is responsible for both investigation and prosecution of all cases of government corruption, whether on the part of a police officer or any other government official. The commission is staffed by trained investigators who follow up on corruption complaints, conduct surveillance, and gather evidence useful for prosecution in the courts.

The success of the ICAC has resulted in the creation of similar commissions in Australia and has caught the attention of officials from the Council of Europe in their own search for a response to government corruption in Europe.

—*Harald Otto Schweizer*

See also ORGANIZED CRIME; POLICE BRUTALITY

Further Reading

Independent Commission Against Corruption. *Code of conduct for law.* Available on the World Wide Web at: http://202.76.3.30/. Office of the United Nations High Commissioner for Human Rights.

Internet Center for Corruption Research. Available on the World Wide Web at: http://www.gwdg.de/~uwvw/icr.htm.

Nathanson Centre for the Study of Organized Crime and Corruption. Available on the World Wide Web at: http://www.yorku.ca/nathanson/default.htm.

Palmiotto, M. J. (2000). (Ed.). *Police misconduct: A reader for the 21st century.* Englewood Cliffs, NJ: Prentice Hall.

Roleff, T. L. (2002). *Police corruption.* Greenhaven Press.

POLICE PSYCHOLOGY,
See FORENSIC SCIENCE

POLITICAL CORRUPTION,
See ORGANIZED CRIME

POST OFFICE VIOLENCE,
See MASS MURDER; WORKPLACE VIOLENCE AND HOMICIDE

POTASSIUM CHLORIDE,
See MEDICAL MURDERS; POISONERS; POISONING: MEDICAL SETTINGS

PREDICTING VIOLENT BEHAVIOR

The desire to better understand human behavior has existed for centuries. More recently, there has been an interest in predicting human behavior, especially violent behavior, part of an inherent desire to protect society from individuals who may be a danger to others. Identifying individuals who are at a higher risk for violent behavior allows for preventative measures to better protect society. Laws exist that allow such individuals to be involuntarily committed. This has placed a burden on clinicians and researchers to determine the criteria necessary for making such predictions.

Considering the fact that every individual is unique, there is no way to definitively predict a person's behavior or propensity for violence. Although it is not an exact science, research has allowed for the identification of some key elements that help to distinguish violent from nonviolent individuals.

PREDICTIVE CRITERIA

Certain criteria for determining future violence weigh more heavily than others. For example, it is well-known that the best predictor of future violence is a history of past violence. Based on this, it is important for the clinician conducting a risk assessment to obtain a detailed history of the client's criminal past, focusing on type of crime, degree of harm, and type of weapon used, if any. Such information should be corroborated by police reports when feasible.

Substance abuse is another strong correlate with violent behavior. A vast majority of violent crimes are committed while the perpetrator is under the influence of a substance. Van Hasselt and Hersen discussed three types of situations that link substances with violence. The first category is systemic, in which violence is related to activities associated with drugs (i.e., drug "territories"). The second category is economically driven, whereupon the individual engages in violent activities to support his or her addiction. Last, the psychopharmacological factor relates to the effect that the drug has on the individual. This final category has been well documented in the literature as a serious risk factor for violence.

The effect of alcohol appears to be one of the most lethal in that it is shown to commonly increase aggression as well as lower inhibitions. Approximately 60% of violent offenders are estimated to have consumed alcohol at the time of their offenses (Van Hasselt & Hersen, 2000). Other substances such as amphetamines, cocaine, LSD, and PCP can result in feelings of disinhibition and paranoia. Interestingly, men who use cocaine are "more likely to perpetrate violent crimes whereas women who regularly use cocaine are more likely to be victims of violence" (Scott & Resnick, 2002, p. 4).

Other demographic information that has been found valuable in predicting violence is age, gender, socioeconomic status, work history, military history, and intelligence. Violence tends to increase in the late teens and early 20s. The younger individuals are when they commit their first violent act, the more likely they are to continue that pattern during their 20s. Research

has also found that men are 10 times more likely than women are to be the perpetrators of violence.

Individuals in lower socioeconomic areas are 3 times more likely to engage in violent behavior than people in moderate to high socioeconomic brackets. An individual's ability to maintain a job and the reasons for frequency in job change could provide valuable information into a person's tendency for violence. This helps identify whether the individual associates well with others and can follow job rules. People who are laid off from work are more likely to commit violent acts in comparison with their employed peers. In addition, an individual's military history, with attention placed on disciplinary measures and discharge classification, helps to give a greater picture of his or her propensity for possible violence and ability to follow rules.

The risk of violence is elevated for people of lower intelligence and/or mildly mentally retarded. Those with intellectual deficiencies often display poor coping skills and tools necessary to resolve conflict in a more appropriate manner. Oftentimes, the combination of the above demographics coupled with substance abuse drastically increases the propensity for violence.

PSYCHOLOGICAL AND EMOTIONAL FACTORS

Mental Illness

The public has maintained a perception that the mentally ill are dangerous and have a high propensity for violence. This assumption especially rings true for those diagnosed with schizophrenia. The MacArthur Research Network conducted an extensive study, one of the purposes of which was to determine whether mentally ill patients discharged from community hospitals were any more violent than other members of the community. The study found that patients without a diagnosis of substance abuse discharged from mental hospitals had comparable levels of violence with community members without a diagnosis of substance abuse. The prevalence for violence increased for patients with substance abuse problems discharged from hospitals compared with other members of the community with substance abuse problems. Much of the research confirmed that regardless of the diagnosis, a codiagnosis of substance abuse substantially increases the propensity for violence.

Aside from the clarity of knowing that substance abuse does increase the likelihood of violence in the mentally ill and nonmentally ill, there are mixed results in relation to what forms of mental illness are more dangerous than others. Some studies support the assumption that schizophrenia is the most dangerous mental illness in terms of violence prevalence. Others argue that schizophrenia is less lethal than diagnoses such as bipolar disorder and depression. Instead of pigeonholing dangerousness with a particular diagnosis, it may be more valuable to understand the specific symptoms that can increase a person's propensity for violence.

Anger is a relatively obvious symptom of many mental illnesses that has a strong link with violence. When an individual displays anger and has a history of previous acting-out behaviors, precautions should be taken. Individuals with mania tend to have an increased prevalence for assaultive behavior, but more serious violence is not common. Depressed individuals tend to have lower frustration tolerances that, when they obtain enough energy, can result in acting-out behaviors such as violence. In most of these types of incidents, the final result is murder-suicide.

Psychosis has raised several questions regarding its relationship to violence, but there do not appear to be any clear answers. Whereas one study finds that patients with delusions pertaining to outside forces controlling their thoughts are more likely to engage in assaultive behavior, the MacArthur study found just the opposite. The majority of information does appear to demonstrate that delusions of a persecutory or paranoid nature tend to lead to more assaultive and/or violent behaviors than other types of delusions. Therefore, not all forms of schizophrenia are as dangerous as others. Violence perpetrated by paranoid psychotics is usually well calculated and aimed at specific persons related to the psychosis, often relatives or friends.

Similar to delusions, certain types of hallucinations increase the risk for violence. Although the relationship was not found to be very strong, "command" hallucinations with a violent theme do increase the potential for violence. This relationship has not been found with general hallucinations.

Personality Disorders

Certain personality traits increase the risk for violence. Whether the individual has the actual personality disorder or simply traits does not significantly alter their risk for violent behavior, although a person with an actual disorder would have more symptoms. The most common personality disorder/trait affiliated with violence is antisocial behavior. These individuals are often motivated by revenge and have a lack of remorse and emotionality. The combination of antisocial personality and low IQ happens to be a lethal mix for future violence. In addition, individuals identified as psychopaths are 3 times more likely to reoffend within the first year following their release from custody.

Other personality traits that have been associated with violence are impulsivity, low frustration tolerance, difficulty handling criticism, sense of entitlement, and superficiality. Most of the time, these individuals also exhibit poor insight and blame others for their problems. Any combination of the above personality traits with substance abuse drastically increases the likelihood for violence.

RISK ASSESSMENT INSTRUMENTS

Aside from the use of clinical judgment in determining the potential for violence, many clinicians are turning to standardized risk assessment measures to determine this propensity. Many of these measures ensure that a complete history is obtained. One of the most widely used and validated tools is the Hare Psychopathy Checklist-Revised (PCL-R). The PCL-R consists of a semistructured interview along with obtaining case history information that is subsequently scored. Clinicians using the PCL-R must be trained in its usage. A screening version of the PCL-R, the PCL-SV, has also been found useful in assessing for institutional and community violence.

The Violence Risk Appraisal Guide (VRAG) incorporates the PCL-R as well as childhood history, adult criminal history, demographic variables, and psychiatric diagnoses. The VRAG is a very thorough assessment tool and has been found to be a better predictor than other tools of violence recidivism in mentally disordered offenders.

The Iterative Classification Tree (ICT) is an actuarial tool used to predict violence in mentally ill individuals recently released from psychiatric facilities. Based on the sequence of questions determined by responses to previous questions, the individual is classified into a high- or low-risk category for future violence.

These are just a few of the many assessment tools that can be used for the prediction of violence.

Although their means for gathering the information may be different, they all focus on gathering virtually the same type of data.

CONCLUSION

Violence prediction continues to be a difficult task and likely will never be an exact science, but recent research in the area has made drastic strides in helping to understand the most common factors associated with violence. Past behavior continues to reign as the leading factor in predicting violence. Substance abuse, command/paranoid hallucinations and delusions, personality disorders, and several other factors mentioned above help to identify the risk for violence. The predictive value is even stronger when these factors are combined. Continued research may help to identify other factors leading to violence or may simply help to strengthen the statistics regarding current factors.

—*Alexa Wasserman*

See also ALCOHOL AND AGGRESSION; PSYCHOPATHS: PSYCHOPATHOLOGY CHECKLIST (PCL-R); PSYCHOSOCIAL RISK FACTORS FOR VIOLENT BEHAVIOR; SUBSTANCE ABUSE AND HOMICIDE; THREAT ASSESSMENT; VIOLENT BEHAVIOR

Further Reading

MacArthur Foundation. (2001, February). *MacArthur Research Network on mental health and the law: The MacArthur community violence study.* Available on the World Wide Web at: http://macarthur.virginia.edu/violence.html.

MacArthur Foundation (2001, April). *MacArthur Research Network on mental health and the law: The MacArthur violence risk assessment study.* Available on the World Wide Web at: http://macarthur.virginia.edu/violence.html.

Monahan, J., & Steadman, H. J. (2001). *Rethinking risk assessment: The MacArthur study of mental disorder and violence.* Oxford University Press.

Scott, C. L., & Resnick, P. J. (2002). Assessing risk of violence in psychiatric patients. *Psychiatric Times, 19,* 1-16.

Van Hasselt, V. B., & Hersen, M. (2000). *Aggression and violence: An introductory text.* Boston: Allyn & Bacon.

PRESIDENTIAL ASSASSINATIONS AND ATTEMPTS, *See* ASSASSINS

PREVENTION OF CRIME AND VIOLENT BEHAVIOR

Most criminal justice experts and citizens would agree that criminal violence is the most pressing concern among law enforcement officials and the general public. The criminal justice system is charged with a clear mandate calling for a comprehensive program focused on violence prevention and protection of the public. The mandate is expressed through political officials and news media representatives reacting toward crime as one of the overwhelming social issues facing contemporary society.

To understand the nature of criminal violence and the prevention of victimization, we need to understand specific programs focused on violence prevention and the impetus for the formation of those initiatives. Thus, a discussion of violent crime and crime prevention will incorporate some background on boot camps, drugs courts, halfway houses, and shock incarceration programs as embodying a response to citizen concerns.

IDEOLOGY OF VIOLENCE PREVENTION

Violence prevention is a vital issue in the minds of most citizens and political leaders. Traditional responses to violence include application of capital punishment or the implementation of lengthy prison sentences. Politicians react to a citizen call for justice and harsh criminal punishment. An illustration of violence prevention was reflected in the 1992 Bush (George Sr.) campaign use of a political advertisement against Michael Dukakis, which depicted a revolving door built into a maximum-security prison wall. The conveyed perception was that Dukakis was "soft on crime."

The emphasis on determinate sentencing is an outgrowth of these concerns. The public came to believe that their interests were best served through placing violent offenders in prison for longer prison sentences. Citizens seemingly believed that individual incarceration was the second most effective deterrent to recidivism (the first being capital punishment).

There is, however, a contradiction in public sentiment. The public rightfully abhors violent crimes and wishes to protect itself from criminal predators. Nowhere is this more apparent than the concern for kidnapped and murdered children. There is an immediate call for swift justice and the death penalty. On the other hand, citizens are often reluctant to vote for new taxes supporting the construction of prison facilities and are even more unlikely to acknowledge that the death penalty or life imprisonment is a panacea for the cyclical rise and fall of criminal activity.

Some solutions exist for the control of recidivism and violent crime. These solutions include community-based programs geared toward handling offenders in a less costly and more efficient one-to-one manner. Corrections research indicates that approximately 90% of all violent offenders are inevitably released from prison. This factor still applies despite the reluctance of the few existent parole boards to consider favorable early release of many offenders. Those offenders not serving a life sentence inevitably "max out" their sentence (or serve the entire length).

INSTITUTIONALIZED SOLUTIONS FOR ACHIEVING VIOLENCE PREVENTION

Our question shifts to some of the applied criminal justice programs concentrating on violence prevention. Boot camps, drug courts, halfway houses, and shock incarceration are often used with select juvenile and adult criminal populations.

Boot Camps

One proposed mechanism for preventing future violence among juveniles is the establishment of boot camps, which incorporate a regime of tightly structured daily routines and unremitting discipline. In a structure designed after Marine basic training, juveniles are taught to channel their violent, self-reinforcing behavior into a prosocial programmatic direction. Strict disciplinarians stress self-responsibility and the need to depend on each other rather than perceive oneself as autonomous.

Boot camps are instrumental in the building of self-confidence and demonstrating a wide range of behavioral choices as an alternative to implicitly accepted violence. The expectation is that boot camps will reshape juvenile proclivity to violence and create a safer social environment. However, researchers dispute the long-term impact of boot camps and claim that social environment is more instrumental in producing inevitable juvenile violent behavior.

Drug Court Programs

Drug court programs with intensive supervision are another proposed solution for preventing violent behavior. Under normal situations, judicial authorities are faced with a glut of cases involving drug offenders and violent criminal behavior. Traditional criminal court sentencing focused on prescribed retribution through prison and mandated treatment programs following release from incarceration. The problems with sentencing became evident over time. The drug epidemic and rising prison populations produced added criminal justice expenditures and relatively limited deterrence through recidivist activity.

Out of this conundrum came the establishment of drug courts and concomitant intensive supervision. Drug courts specifically target substance abusers and many violent juvenile offenders. Drug users and violent offenders are treated by a team of professionals comprising a magistrate, highly trained probation or parole officers, and supporting treatment personnel. They are afforded a self-reinforcing intensive program focused on day-to-day maintenance. Drug screens, milieu therapy aimed at preventing violent recidivism, and a concern for the social well-being of offenders combine together in striving for ongoing violence prevention. Most research indicates that there is lessened recidivism and decreased costs on the criminal justice system when drug courts are used in community settings.

Halfway Houses

Halfway houses are another measure used in addition to or in lieu of traditional criminal justice punitive measures and are an important device for treating violent or nonviolent felons either on probation or parole. In essence, halfway houses are community settings wherein ex-felons requiring intensive supervision can be monitored and counseled within a milieu setting. The residence includes counselors for the ex-felons, along with supervision by support staff. Job placement, preventing individuals from straying back to their own violent ways through monitoring community behavior, and regular counseling sessions are provided in this setting.

Once again, the contradiction between crime prevention and citizen fear of crime comes into play. Much has been said about concerns surrounding prison overcrowding and the costs of prison construction. However, community residents often invoke an attitude known as NIMBY: "Not in My Backyard." Citizens want to prevent violent behavior but not at a risk to their families or themselves. An infamous case involving a released inmate named Lawrence Singleton illustrates the issue of community reluctance to situated ex-felon placements. Singleton was a celebrated felon associated with physically and sexually assaulting a 6-year-old girl while ripping the limbs from her body. He was released after spending 7½ years in prison. Under an arrangement by the state, Singleton had to serve a mandated 1-year period under intensive supervision. Unfortunately, at least a dozen communities in Northern California were reluctant to accept his presence in the community. In the end, Singleton served the 1-year period in a residential setting behind the walls of San Quentin.

Shock Incarceration

Shock incarceration is another device that serves as a community-supported technique toward preventing recidivism among violent criminals. It entails placing a juvenile or violent offender in prison for a brief period and continuing the punishment through community placement. Shock incarceration was viewed as a viable form of deterrence and probable panacea during the 1970s and 1980s.

One form of shock incarceration was attempted at Rahway State Penitentiary, in New Jersey. The 1970s experiment consisted of "lifers" (violent felons doing life sentences without the possibility of parole) hosting juvenile offenders. The selected juveniles had basically committed minor-status offenses or minor felony crimes. The inmates screamed, taunted, threatened, and physically attacked the juveniles sent into the program. Evaluation research several years later raised questions about the program's effectiveness based on the preselected nature of the sample and significance of the recidivist effect. The initial recidivist rates were low for teens entering the program; however, the long-term potential was still unknown.

Despite these shortcomings, shock incarceration became a staple of numerous talk show episodes during the late 1990s and early 2000s. Maury Povich, Jenny Jones, Sally Jesse Raphael, and others sent promiscuous or violent teens into encounter therapy groups with delinquent teens or individuals with criminal records. Some programs combined a shock incarceration technique (brief time in jail) with some time in a boot camp. One of Povich's highest-rated shows in 2000 featured the theme "Send my child to boot camp and prison."

LONG-RANGE OUTCOME

In essence, boot camps, drug courts, halfway houses, and shock incarceration have been proposed as techniques with the potential for achieving deterrence impact among violent criminals. However, the promise of community-based corrections and community violence prevention has not fully emerged in panaceas invoked by local criminal justice authorities. Programs such as drug courts are underfunded or opposed by political leaders. There is a shortage of revenue for hiring new judges and courtroom space for the actual process. Boot camps have proved ineffective because violent or potentially violent offenders have little commitment to a 6- to 18-month program bearing any real consequences for their long-term behavior. Halfway houses are often opposed by community leaders and are the first places to be targeted when recidivist criminal activity is committed by one of the assigned residents. Shock incarceration tends to produce little or no impact on criminal behavior because the sentences are relatively brief.

In conclusion, crime and violence prevention remains an ongoing concern in community settings and throughout the criminal justice system. The proposed solutions provide limited relief as the problem takes on a life of its own. Perhaps violent crime can best be controlled through a combination of these and other programs. In addition, outside social factors associated with violent behavior must be evaluated. The search for solutions will inevitably lead in different directions as this issue remains at the forefront of community concerns.

—*Lloyd Klein*

See also DEATH PENALTY; COMMUNITY ATTITUDES TOWARD VIOLENT CRIME; FORENSIC SCIENCE: PSYCHOLOGY; GANGS; JUVENILE OFFENDERS; PREDICTING VIOLENT BEHAVIOR; VIOLENT BEHAVIOR

Further Reading

Belenko, Steven. (1998). Research on drug courts: A critical review. *National Drug Court Institute, 1*(1), 1.

Cullen, F. T., & Gilbert, K. (1982). *Reaffirming rehabilitation.* Cincinnati, OH: Anderson.

Latessa, E., & Allen, H. E. (1982). Halfway houses and parole: A national assessment. *Journal of Criminal Justice, 10*(2), 153-163.

McKenzie, D. L., & Sourya, C. (1994). *Multisite evaluation of shock incarceration.* Final summary report submitted to the National Institute of Justice. Washington, DC: National Institute of Justice.

PRISON GANGS,
See GANGS: DEFINITIONS

PROBATION OFFICERS, *See*
CRIMINAL JUSTICE PRACTITIONERS

PRODUCT TAMPERING

Incidents of individuals using food and drink to deliver lethal doses of poisons to unsuspecting victims are fairly common in recorded history. However, product tampering as a means of murder wasn't much heard of until 1982, when the first and most notorious case occurred in Chicago.

All kinds of materials have been used to adulterate food and medicine. They include insecticides, pesticides, strychnine, arsenic, hydrochloric acid, mercury, mercuric chloride, fecal matter, and foreign objects such as straight pins, razor blades, staples, and glass. Cyanide is particularly popular with poisoners, because the lethal dose of 200 to 300 mg is just the amount that will fit into a typical gelatin capsule. In addition, it is readily available because it is used in a number of products found in industry (electroplating and chemical synthesis), educational chemistry laboratories, and domestic products, such as jewelry cleaners and rodent control. Another advantage of cyanide is that it is not

Store clerk removing Tylenol. In 1982, seven people in the Chicago area died after taking Tylenol capsules that had been tainted with cyanide. These victims, five females and two males, became the first ever to die from what came to be known as product tampering. The poisoned capsules had been placed on shelves in six different stores by a person(s) intent on the random killing of innocent people. Several other copycat product tamperings have occurred since the Chicago killings. The case has not been solved, and the $100,000 reward offered by Tylenol's maker, Johnson & Johnson, remains unclaimed.

Table 1   Incidents of Product Tampering Resulting in Death or Injury in the United States

Date	Incident/Location	Number of Deaths/Injuries	Perpetrator Caught?	Motive
1982	Tylenol/Chicago	7 deaths	No	Unknown
1986	Tylenol/New York	1 death	No	Unknown
1986	Contac, Teledrin, and Dietac/Texas and Florida		Yes	Financial benefit from stock trading
1986	Anacin	1 death	No	Unknown
1986	Excedrin/Washington	2 deaths	No	Unknown
1986	Dry soup/Massachusetts	1 death	No	Unknown
1987	Excedrin/Washington	2 deaths	Yes	Insurance fraud
1991	Sudafed/Washington	2 deaths/1 injury	Yes	Insurance fraud

routinely tested for in routine toxicological screens. Therefore, unless a physician or investigator specifically suspects cyanide poisoning and orders the appropriate tests, the poisoning is likely to go unnoticed.

In the first case of product tampering, known as the "Tylenol Murders," seven people in the Chicago area collapsed suddenly and died after taking Tylenol capsules that had been laced with potassium cyanide. These seven victims, five females and two males, became the first victims ever to die from what came to be known as product tampering. The investigation of this crime was intense, and it was learned that the poisoned capsules were placed on shelves in six different stores by an individual intent on killing innocent people at random. Despite examining the route the killer must have taken, the residential neighborhoods where the victims died, the poison, the method of tampering with the capsules, and potential motives of the killer, the search for the perpetrator for this crime has not been successful in two decades and is unlikely to be in the future. Authorities used the information they gathered to develop a profile of the "Tylenol Killer," some of which might be useful in other cases of random poisoning, should they occur. The characteristics include the following:

♦ White male in his 20s
♦ Lived in the Chicago area
♦ Owned a car or truck
♦ Devious but not particularly intelligent
♦ Skilled shoplifter
♦ Had few friends, no long-term friends
♦ Misanthropic, cowardly
♦ Limited income, working in a low-paying job
♦ May have a degree but is a failure in his field
♦ Objective: unknown

No evidence was ever found that anyone profited from these murders. No unusual stock trading occurred, and none of the victims were wealthy or seemed to be likely targets. Most of the victims were young and were not covered by large insurance policies. The motive may have been sheer hatred for humanity or perhaps the attempt to gain publicity or fame for another venture. Whatever the motive for the killer may have been, it appears that he did not receive the gratification he expected. What did happen as a result of this initial product-tampering case was a wave of copycat crimes. Lipton "Cup-A-Soup" was tampered with in 1986, Excedrin in 1986, Tylenol in 1986, Sudafed in 1991, and headache powder in 1992.

The government responded by establishing regulations for tamper-evident packaging for over-the-counter drugs and food items and by passing legislation that created legal punishments for criminals who tampered with food and drug products.

Although most of the incidents of product tampering have occurred in the United States, the rest of the world is not immune to this problem. In 1985, eight people died in Japan after drinking fruit juice that was contaminated with weedkiller, and during the same period of time, multiple incidents of candy contamination were reported. Table 1 lists the incidents of product tampering in the United States resulting in death or injury.

In addition to the cases that resulted in death or injury, many recorded incidents involving medications and foodstuffs failed to hurt anyone except the company manufacturing the product. These firms suffer serious financial losses when they are forced to recall products, test for contaminants, and develop new and better ways to tamper-proof their products.

The investigation of product-tampering crimes can be very difficult because there is often no discernable link between the tamperer and the victims. The situation is also complicated when authorities fail to suspect and test for poison. Constructing a profile of a tamperer is essential in conducting an effective investigation in these cases. To develop a profile, the investigator must look carefully for the motive in each case. The motives for known cases include a pretext to cause a diversion from a single homicide; corporate terrorism to influence corporate or national policy or influence corporate stock value; apparently random sociopathic acts; malicious mischief; and revenge of a disgruntled employee, former employee, or job applicant. A rare motive has involved a political terrorist threat. Most tamperers can be identified through intensive investigation of the crime if they have a tangible motive, but the random sociopathic tamperer is usually not caught unless he or she surrenders.

It is important to note that there are many more threats of tampering than actual tampering incidents. These threats are frequently made by mentally ill individuals or by people who are angry, seeking thrills, or harboring feelings of injustice toward a corporation.

By examining the number and types of tampering incidents, it is not difficult to understand how vulnerable the food, drink, and drug supply is to this kind of criminal. One must also consider the economic and social consequences, and they may be considerable. To control this kind of crime, it is essential that the media report incidents responsibly and in such a way as to avoid panic in the public. Manufacturers must be aware of how their marketing and packaging protocols protect the integrity of their products. The public must be educated to examine each product that they use to determine if the tamper-resistant barriers have been compromised. Finally, the penalties for product tampering should be publicized to discourage casual tamperers.

—*Marlene Deal*

See also METHODS OF MURDER; POISONERS; PROFILING

Further Reading

Logan, B. (1993). Product tampering crime: A review. *Journal of Forensic Sciences, 38,* 918-927.

Mitroff, I. I., & Kilmann, R. H. (1984). *Corporate tragedies: Product tampering, sabotage, and other catastrophes.* New York: Praeger.

The Tylenol murders. Retrieved from the World Wide Web on May 15, 2002, at: http://www.personal.psu.edu/users/w/x/xk116/tylenol/.

PROFILING

The term *profiling* refers to many areas of forensic science. For example, female inmate profiles have been developed by examining the lives and crimes of incarcerated women at Central California Women's Facility, in Chowchilla. Others have explored the world of credit card fraud and the types of people who repeatedly engage in such crimes. Victimologists profile the types of criminals who target the elderly and develop typologies of victim-offender relationships. Today, profiling has also become a tool used widely in criminal investigations. Profiling is developing as a science but continues to receive mixed reviews. Some professionals have been skeptical of the utility of profiling, particularly the psychologically based approach. Psychological profiling has yet to function as a "magic wand" to solve serial crimes, but it is still too early in its development to be considered a failure. Programs such as those developed around profiling often require several years of testing and refinement before they can be evaluated. For profiling to fulfill its potential, law enforcement personnel must be willing to collaborate with those in the academic and medical professions. For example, psychiatrists can be of particular value in profiling, provided law enforcement people are willing to accept and use their profiles.

Wilson and Soothill state that profiling needs a framework that has some flexibility. They note that profiling can be useful in the following ways:

- As an investigative tool where leads are limited
- Providing direction to a lagging investigation
- Giving psychological insights in conducting interviews
- Offering psychological advice for witnesses or juries
- Developing systematic computer tracking of unsolved serial murder cases
- Facilitating communication among jurisdictions dealing with serial offences
- Offering critiques of investigative procedures, forensic evidence collection, and sampling
- Providing insights for the application of theories used to explain crime and criminal behavior
- Evidence corroboration

TYPES OF PROFILING

The term *typology* has lent itself to the development of various forms of profiling that are now used as criminal investigative techniques from white-collar crimes to serial murder. The following forms of profiling will help to illustrate the emerging issues involved in criminal investigations. Geographical profiling and the scientific, empirically based offender profiling by David Canter and colleagues are both becoming leading approaches in criminal investigations. They can offer tremendous assistance to investigators in making profiling a more scientific and precise science. Investigative profiling today can be viewed from several perspectives.

Offender Profiling

Law enforcement agencies collect data, often using case studies or anecdotal information, which then is transformed into general descriptions of the types of persons most commonly associated with a certain type of criminal activity. This stereotyping is common in seeking out drug couriers and terrorists and can often be invasive and legally tenuous. Civil rights advocates quickly point out the flaws in using physical characteristics to profile criminals. Such profiling could be very misleading. For example, one might consider that people involved in fraudulent insurance claims usually are in need of money, but the opposite is actually true according to some research. Some experts are critical of American profiling, stating that profiling was originally the purview of psychologists, not the FBI. They reject the detective deductions of profiling as being anecdotal, deductive, or fictional-hero approaches to solving crimes through "gut feeling" investigations.

Clinical observations alone are insufficient in making decisions about criminal behavior. Indeed, criminologists, psychologists, and psychiatrists have been ineffectual in accurately predicting criminal behavior. Our predictive capabilities are replete with *false positives,* or incorrectly predicting that someone will behave in a certain criminal manner. Some profilers today operate under the guise of informed speculation. Like psychic detectives and astrologers, they are shrouded in ambiguity and therefore can shift their explanations to fit the situation. We are also reminded that psychology is useful in explaining a variety of crimes and that there are many differences between offenders and nonoffenders.

Canter promotes his *radex model* as a powerful tool in differentiating criminals. Using his circle theory approach, he explains that mathematically, using a computer, criminal behavior can be examined and measured from a very general level (center of the circle) to more specific "styles of offending" as one moves conceptually away from the circle center and sees more differentiation between offenders. The power of the radex model is that it identifies the salient aspects of a crime. Approaching criminal profiling from a scientific, actuarial model is having a very impressive influence on proactive investigators. American law enforcement will benefit greatly by integrating their profiling techniques with the computer modeling espoused by the Canter school.

Victim Profiling

Profilers identify the personality and behavioral characteristics of crime victims who tend to fall prey to certain types of offenders. Information can be gathered through personal records; interviews with witnesses, victims, family, and friends; crime scene examination; and autopsies. Investigators will enhance their effectiveness in murder investigations as victim/offender relationships are more closely scrutinized. Victims, even in death, are often storybooks about the offender and the circumstances of the crime.

Equivocal Death Profiling

Also sometimes referred to as *psychological autopsy,* investigators apply nonscientific information to explain the motivations of a person or group engaged in suicide pacts or difficult-to-explain deaths.

DNA Profiling

In recent years, cases of murder have been solved as a result of the advent of DNA profiling or genetic science. This includes gathering DNA from crime scenes, victims, and offenders in efforts to match up perpetrators to specific crimes. Between 1979 and 1986, a serial killer stalked, raped, and murdered at least six victims in southern California. Newly found DNA evidence from rape kits found in archived cases conclusively linked these murders. Investigators then used other profiling techniques by examining the predator's stalking and killing habits to link the killer to four more murders.

Crime Scene Profiling

Also referred to as *criminal investigation analysis,* this form of profiling is based on the FBI model developed by their Behavioral Science unit. Investigators focus on crime scene descriptions, photographs, offender behavior pre- and postcriminal act(s), traffic patterns, physical evidence, and victim information; they place less credence on psychological data. Psychosocial data are compared with other similar cases, and investigators engage in an experiential/informational guessing technique to reconstruct the offenders' personality. From the 1988 FBI study of 36 serial sexual murderers, a dichotomy of offender characteristics was developed. The "organized" offender is methodical, premeditated, mature, resourceful, and usually sexually perverted. The "disorganized" type of killer acts much more randomly and opportunistically, and often has some form of mental disorder. Their dichotomous profiles include the following characteristics:

Organized	Disorganized
Good intelligence	Average or low intelligence
Socially/sexually competent	Socially/sexually incompetent
Stable work history	Lack of stable work history
Controlled during crime	Anxious during crime
Living with someone	Living alone
Very mobile	Lives near crime scene
Follows investigation in media	Little interest in media
May leave town/change job	Little change in lifestyle
Uses alcohol prior to crime	Little alcohol use
Premeditated offense	Spontaneous offense
Victim a stranger	Victim or location unknown
Conversation with victim	Little conversation with victim
Demands submission	Sudden violence to victim
Uses restraints	Little use of restraints
Violent acts prior to death	Postmortem sexual acts
Body hidden	Body left in view
Weapon/evidence absent	Weapon/evidence often present
Transports body	Body left at scene

The problem with this dichotomous model is the lack of rigorous reliability and validity testing. Although the model has been used extensively by investigators, it may not have the utility previously assumed. Researchers in Australia found that although there is some merit to the dichotomy, a more useful evaluation of criminal behaviors is necessary. Kocsis, Cooksey, and Irwin (1999) noted,

This conceptual failing of the organized/disorganized dichotomy is more apparent when it is recognized that it makes no distinction between behaviors that commonly occur in all offenses and those that discriminate aspects of a specific offender. For example if an offender uses a knife in a sexual murder, this may not actually be a behavioral clue about the specific offender, but rather, simply a common behavior pattern observed in most sexual murders. . . . Some incorrect offender characteristics could be concluded from the use of a knife when it truly just represents a common behavior amongst most sexual murders. This failing to empirically distinguish between common behaviors and those which are discriminatory of a specific individual is a flaw that prevails throughout much of the literature on profiling in general. (p. 5)

Psychological Profiling

Tracking the serial killer and the multitude of problems posed by such a task has led, in the past few years, to the development of *psychological profiling,* a tool used to prioritize a variety of homicides and other serious crimes. Psychological profiling, also known as *criminal personality assessment,* is applied to criminal behavior profiling, offender profiling, victim profiling, and crime scene profiling. It is used by law enforcement agencies in the United States, Canada, and Britain. Swanson, Chamelin, and Territo (1984) define the intent and purpose of this type of profiling:

The purpose of the psychological assessment of a crime scene is to produce a profile, that is, to identify and interpret certain items of evidence at the crime scene that would be indicative of the personality type of the individual or individuals committing the crime. The goal of the profiler is to provide enough information to investigators to enable them to limit or better direct their investigations. (pp. 70-71)

Profilers match the personality characteristics of a certain type of offender with those of a suspect. Investigators use batteries of interviews and testing to establish their base of information. Experts are frequently called on to predict future behavior of offenders, including pedophiles, child molesters, rapists, and other sexual deviants.

Geographical Profiling

While investigators have been working to improve both crime scene profiling and psychological profiling, other researchers and investigators have been actively developing a geographical approach to criminal investigations. Also referred to as *spatial mapping,* this technique combines geography and environmental criminology to connect crime scenes to offender habitats and hunting grounds. Such profiling is empirically based and has not placed much value on motivation or personality. It does help law enforcement in deciding where to begin knocking on doors and setting up stakeouts. In the case of the "Railroad Killer," the offender had stayed near trains and therefore was likely a drifter/transient. The geographic similarities linked him to many killings, and he was eventually identified, arrested, and sent to prison.

A geographical profile includes the elements of *distance, mobility, mental maps,* and *locality demographics.* Offenders are profiled by the amount of distance covered by a serial offender. Some may travel because they have access to transportation, whereas others are limited in their access. For example, Ted Kaczynski, the Unabomber, used buses or the mail system to transport his bombs. Mental maps refer to an offender's cognitive images of his or her surroundings. As offenders become more comfortable with their tools and surroundings, they will be more likely to expand their boundaries. Offender travel routes can be critical to a serial murder investigation. Kim Rossmo, one of the noted pioneers of geographic profiling, identifies four offender styles in hunting for victims:

1. *Hunter:* Identifies a specific victim in home area.
2. *Poacher:* Prefers to travel away from home area for hunting victims.
3. *Troller:* An opportunistic killer; attacks victims while carrying out routine activities.
4. *Trapper:* A "spider and fly" scenario; enjoys laying a trap for the victim.

A geographical profile includes a study of area maps, examination of crime scenes, interviews of witnesses and investigators, and knowledge of abduction and body dumpsites in the case of serial murder. Rossmo's "Criminal Geographic Targeting," a computerized program, produces a topographical map based on crime scene information. The more crime scenes, the greater the predictability of the program. Using the 11 crime scenes of serial killer Clifford R. Olson, who raped, sodomized, and hammered boys and girls to death, Rossmo was able to pinpoint the killer's area of residence to within a four-block radius. In another case of serial rape, Rossmo used 79 crime scenes to pinpoint the actual basement of the offender's home as the location of the attacks. Scotland Yard, Dutch police, the FBI Behavioral Science Unit, and many other law enforcement agencies in need of better science to solve their cases frequently use Rossmo. Indeed, some profilers prefer geographic profiling to the methods employed by the FBI because they feel that there is greater predictive value.

M. Godwin, author of the computer program "Predator," used for geographic profiling, believes that locating body dumpsites and locations of victim abductions, or where they were last seen, will provide the best results in locating offenders. Godwin refers to "landscape layouts," which include bars, nightclubs, red-light districts, depressed, poverty-ridden areas of communities, parking lots, jogging paths, rest stops, and college campuses as preying grounds for serial killers. Killers tend to hunt in relation to where they work, live, and carry out their routine daily activities. This "geographic comfort zone" becomes the hunting grounds for serial offenders. Geography is fast becoming a tool in offender profiling that law enforcement can use with increasing accuracy.

PROBLEMS IN PROFILING

Profiling can be very useful, but caution must be exercised to avoid constructing hasty or poorly grounded profiles that may lead investigators in the wrong direction. This inevitably places a strain on resources, and most important, additional lives may be lost. Errors in the information transmitted to NCAVC (National Center for the Analysis of Violent Crime), mistaken assessments by the evaluation team, and other potential glitches mean profiles can and do go wrong. In one case, for example, a profile on a criminal suspect told investigators the man they were looking for came from a broken home, was a high school dropout, held a marginal job, hung out in "honky-tonk" bars, and lived far from the scene of the crime. When the attacker was finally caught, it was learned that the psychological assessment was 100% in error. He had not come from a broken home, had a college degree, held an executive position with a respected financial institution, did not use alcohol, and lived near the scene of the crime. With this possibility for error, the FBI warns investigators not to become so dependent on the evaluation that they neglect other leads or become biased to the point where they blindly follow only the clues that match the scenario described in the profile report.

In 1996, Richard Jewell, a security guard at the Olympic Games in Atlanta, Georgia, noticed an unattended knapsack. Concerned that it might contain a bomb, he immediately reported his findings to his superiors. While Olympic visitors were being evacuated, the sack exploded, killing one woman and injuring over 100 other people. Jewell quickly became a suspect because he "fit" the profile of someone who would set a bomb and then become a hero for saving others. He seemed to be enjoying the sudden notoriety of the event and being recognized as a public hero. Investigators also noted that he had mentioned to the media how he hoped to land a permanent job with law enforcement after the Olympics. Jewell became a prime suspect and quickly became subject to an intensive investigation. The media harassed him for several months before investigators were forced to admit that they had the wrong man. Not until November 2000 was Eric Robert Rudolph indicted, in absentia, for several bombings of abortion clinics and three Atlanta bombings, including the explosion at the Olympics.

Sometimes investigators ignore or fail to understand offender profiles and are quick to rush to conclusions based on a piece of physical evidence. In the case of the "Yosemite Park Killer" who abducted and murdered a woman, her daughter, and her teenage friend, four suspects were arrested at first. The suspects had some physical evidence that linked them to the murders. The FBI was adamant that the killers were behind bars, despite the fact that the profile, given the manner in which the victims were killed, strongly suggested that the murders were the work of a lone predator. Also, the suspects were petty criminals and drug dealers, not likely to be the types of offenders who suddenly carry out such sadistic sexual murders.

Months passed, and then there was the brutal murder (and decapitation) of a Yosemite Park worker, Jolie Armstrong. Some investigators still maintained that the men in custody were the killers of the three park tourists. Much of that line of thinking was discarded when Carey Stayner not only confessed to the Armstrong murder but also to the other three killings. The manner in which the victims were killed linked the cases. These were sexual killings in which decapitation became part of the sexual experience. They fit the psychological profile of a lone sexual predator. Stayner was sentenced to life in prison, with no possibility of parole, for the Jolie Armstrong case. At the time of this writing, he is being tried in the murders of the three other victims.

One area that geographic profiling is not designed to address is murder that occurs repeatedly in a single location or in private residences, hospitals, and nursing homes. These are the stay-at-home or at-work killers who have no dumpsites for bodies, whose victims die in their homes, and who fit no particular geographic pattern. Unfortunately, even psychological profiling often fails to identify these types of serial killers until the body counts have escalated. The profile can be a useful tool, but like any tool, it can be misused. When properly used, profiling can complement crime scene investigations and strengthen interagency and interdisciplinary cooperation.

—*Eric W. Hickey*

NOTE: Portions of this profile were previously published in Eric Hickey's *Serial Murderers and Their Victims,* 2002, 3rd ed. Belmont, CA: Wadsworth Publishers.

See also Forensic Science; Geographic Profiling; Linkage Blindness; Serial Murder; Signature Killers; ViCLAS; Victimology

Further Reading

Canter, D. V., & Alison, L. J. (2000). Profiling rape and murder. In *Offender profiling series* (Vol. 5). Aldershot, UK: Dartmouth.

Godwin, G. M. (1999). *Hunting serial predators.* CRC Press.

Goodroe, C. (1987, July). Tracking the serial offender. *Law and Order,* pp. 29-33.

Ressler, R. K., Burgess, A. W., & Douglas, J. E. (1988). *Sexual homicide.* Lexington, MA: Lexington Books.

Rossmo, D. K. (1999). Geographic profiling. In J. Jackson & D. Bekerian (Eds.), *Offender profiling: Theory, practice and research.* New York: Wiley.

Swanson, C. R., Chamelin, N. C., & Territo, L. (1984). *Criminal investigation.* New York: Random House.

Wilson, P., & Soothill, K. (1996, January). Psychological profiling: Red, green or amber? *The Police Journal,* pp. 12-20.

PROHIBITION, *See*

PROSTITUTION, *See* WHITE SLAVERY

PSYCHOLOGICAL FACTORS IN BEHAVIOR, *See* AGGRESSION:

PSYCHOLOGICAL PROFILING, *See*

PSYCHOPATHOLOGY CHECKLIST-REVISED (PCL-R)

The Hare Psychopathology Checklist-Revised (PCL-R) is an assessment instrument that is widely accepted as a reliable and valid method for assessing psychopathy. It includes a clinical interview and collateral information by which to score the 20 items that measure characteristics of a psychopath. These characteristics include interpersonal, affective, and social lifestyle aspects of psychopathy. Furthermore, the instrument has been used as an aid in determining sentencing options, treatment suitability, and institutional placement options. The instrument, due to the nature of its development and the seriousness of the implications regarding the scores, can be used only by qualified professionals trained to administer, score, and interpret the results.

CLINICAL INTERVIEW

Dr. Robert Hare developed an interview and information schedule to assist the qualified professional in conducting an effective and efficient interview. The interview begins by obtaining demographic information on the subject. Then, it moves into obtaining a chronological life history of the subject. Specific information about the documented charges and/or convictions of the subject after the age of 18 is important. The interview schedule addresses each of the 20 areas that will be scored on the instrument. There may be some items that cannot be scored, and Hare has provisions for such an event.

COLLATERAL INFORMATION

Adequate collateral information is essential to the PCL-R administration and scoring. An interview alone will never be sufficient. In fact, prior to the interview, the collateral information, in the form of records, should be reviewed so that the interview can be conducted in a more effective manner.

Qualifications for using the instrument include the following:

1. Possess an advanced degree in the social, medical, or behavioral sciences, such as a Ph.D., D.Ed., or M.D.
2. Be registered or licensed with the local state or provincial registration board that regulates the assessment and diagnosis of mental disorders.
3. Have experience with forensic populations or at least 2 years of relevant work-related experience.
4. Limit the use of the PCL-R to populations in which it has been fully validated.
5. Insure adequate training and experience in the use of the PCL-R.

Workshops are offered that will allow qualified professionals to obtain the training necessary to use the instrument. These workshops include training in interviewing and gathering collateral information. The instrument itself is scored using the information obtained. The information obtained is key to the accuracy of the instrument.

Hare's PCL-R measures the following characteristics:

1. Glibness/superficial charm
2. Grandiose sense of self-worth
3. Need for stimulation/proneness to boredom
4. Pathological lying
5. Conning/manipulative
6. Lack of remorse or guilt

7. Shallow affect
8. Callous/lack of empathy
9. Parasitic lifestyle
10. Poor behavioral controls
11. Promiscuous sexual behavior
12. Early behavioral problems
13. Lack of realistic long-term goals
14. Impulsivity
15. Irresponsibility
16. Failure to accept responsibility for own actions
17. Many short-term marital relationships
18. Juvenile delinquency
19. Revocation of conditional release
20. Criminal versatility

—*Elizabeth M. Stanczak*

See also PREDICTING VIOLENT BEHAVIOR; PSYCHOPATHS

Further Reading

Hare, R. D. (1991). *The Hare Psychopathy Checklist-Revised.* Toronto, Canada: Multi-Health Systems.

Hare, R. D. (1993). *Without conscience: The disturbing world of the psychopaths among us.* New York: Simon & Schuster (Pocket Books). Paperback published in 1995. Reissued in 1998 by Guilford Press.

PSYCHOPATHOLOGY DURING CHILDHOOD, *See* ATTACHMENT DEFICIENCY AND VIOLENCE; CONDUCT DISORDER; MACDONALD TRIAD; PREDICTING VIOLENT BEHAVIOR; PSYCHOSOCIAL RISK FACTORS FOR VIOLENT BEHAVIOR

PSYCHOPATHS

The term *psychopath* was introduced by J.L.A. Koch in his 1891 monograph, *Die Psychopathischen Minderwertigkeiten,* in his description of "psychopathic inferiorities." In 1939, Henderson described psychopaths in his book *Psychopathic States* as those afflicted with an illness:

The term psychopathic state is the name we apply to those individuals who conform to a certain intellectual standard, sometimes high, sometimes approaching the realm of defect but yet not amounting to it, who throughout their lives, or from a comparatively early age, have exhibited disorders of conduct of an antisocial or asocial nature, usually of a recurrent or episodic type, who, in many instances, have proved difficult to influence by methods of social, penal, and medical care and treatment and for whom we have no adequate provision of a preventive or curative nature. The inadequacy or deviation or failure to adjust to ordinary social life is not a mere willfulness or badness which can be threatened or thrashed out of the individual so involved, but constitutes a true illness for which we have no specific explanation. (p. 19)

CHARACTERISTICS OF PSYCHOPATHS

Thompson, in *The Psychopathic Delinquent and Criminal,* viewed psychopathic persons as those who seek momentary gratification, lack discretion, and fail to profit from experience, which leads to repeated failures. Today, psychopathy is defined as a constellation of emotional, social, and behavioral characteristics, including egocentricity, impulsivity, irresponsibility, shallow emotions, lack of empathy, lack of guilt, lack of remorse, pathological lying, and manipulativeness, coupled with the violation of social norms and expectations. Cleckley, in *The Mask of Sanity,* outlined 16 characteristics of psychopaths:

1. Intelligent
2. Rational
3. Calm
4. Unreliable
5. Insincere
6. Without shame or remorse
7. Having poor judgment
8. Without capacity for love
9. Unemotional
10. Poor insight
11. Indifferent to the trust or kindness of others
12. Overreactive to alcohol
13. Suicidal
14. Impersonal sex life
15. Lacking long-term goals
16. Inadequately motivated antisocial behavior

The term psychopath operates as a label to describe a potpourri of individuals determined by societal and medical standards to possess antisocial qualities or characteristics. Often used interchangeably with the label of *sociopath*, the psychopath often has turned out to be exactly what we want him or her to be. Psychopaths are generally viewed as aggressive, insensitive, charismatic, irresponsible, intelligent, dangerous, hedonistic, narcissistic, and antisocial. These are persons who can masterfully explain another person's problems and what must be done to overcome them but who appear to have little or no insight into their own lives or how to correct their own problems. Psychopaths who can articulate solutions for their own personal problems usually fail to follow them through. They are perceived as exceptional manipulators, capable of feigning emotions in order to carry out their personal agendas. Without remorse for the plight of their victims, they are adept at rationalization, projection, and other psychological defense mechanisms.

The veneer of stability, friendliness, and normality belies a deeply disturbed personality. Outwardly, there appears to be nothing abnormal about their personalities, even their behavior. Of course, under closer scrutiny, maladaptive behaviors are manifested. They are careful to maintain social distance and share intimacy only with those they can psychologically control. They are noted for their inability to maintain long-term commitments to people or programs. They are predators in need of others to control. Many psychopaths are not criminals and are found at all socioeconomic levels.

A hallmark of psychopathy is the belief that most psychopaths are antisocial. The etiology of psychopathy is grounded in the development of antisocial characteristics. Some psychopaths develop antisocial personality disorder (APD). The diagnosis of APD can be made only if a person had or could have had the diagnosis of conduct disorder as a child. Mainly, it is characterized as the disregard for the rights of others and the rules of society.

Criminal behavior is frequently a part of the diagnosis of APD, which is often seen as the adult version of conduct disorder. Some individuals with APDs seldom show anxiety and do not typically experience guilt over what they have done. Though cognitive behavioral therapy (CBT) has been somewhat successful in the treatment of APD, there does not appear to be any effective treatment other than incarceration, with its rigid rules and structured environment. Some people with APD will also be considered to be psychopaths. However, not all psychopaths will qualify as having APD. Furthermore, it is believed that average individuals with APD will experience "burnout" as they age, which results in a mellowing of behavior and increased conformity with societal norms.

SOCIOPATHS, PSYCHOPATHS, AND PRIMARY PSYCHOPATHS

Dr. Robert Hare has made tremendous contributions with his examination of psychopathy and the distinctions made among these terms. To further illustrate some of these distinctions, first consider these three typologies in terms of intelligence and social skill levels.

Sociopaths

The sociopath is antisocial. He possesses the demeanor of one familiar with the insides of jails and correctional facilities. He has a history of criminal behavior. He has acquired certain attributes that facilitate criminal activity: callousness, anger, indifference, and revenge fantasies. Of average to below-average intelligence, the sociopath is commonly found throughout our state prison systems. Sociopaths are seen as thrill-seeking people. They tend to be very impulsive, demonstrate violent streaks, act out tensions, and take what they want. The average sociopath will lie and can easily manipulate friendships. Sociopaths are typically seen as having something defective or deficient with their conscience. They tend to focus on their own needs or desires and are viewed as selfish or egocentric to someone who knows them. Their perceptions of the world, authority, justice, and fairness are skewed in comparison with the average person. They become adept at rationalization and convince themselves that what they want to do has social value. They seldom see their actions as inappropriate or bad.

The sociopath does not learn the social norms and cultural belief systems as others do during their childhoods. Thus, the problem is often linked to poor parenting or some form of childhood trauma rather than a feature of temperament. This describes the "common" sociopath. There are four types of sociopaths found in the literature: common, alienated, aggressive, and dyssocial.

1. The *common* sociopath is characterized by the lack of social consciousness.
2. The *alienated* sociopath is characterized by the inability to love or be loved by others.

3. The *aggressive* sociopath is characterized by an ever-present sadistic tendency.
4. The *dyssocial* sociopath is characterized by an ability to follow gang-related rules but not social norms.

Psychopaths

Compared with sociopaths, the psychopath does not have the lengthy history of criminal behavior. That is not to say that he is never arrested, but is more careful in avoiding arrest. Psychopaths learn to control impulses. They actually experience stress in the same manner as an average person, but in finding themselves in painful situations, they fail to grasp the significance of things. They are narcissistic and develop their craft of manipulation. They are likely to have expressed their psychopathy early in life by demonstrating daring and playing by their own sets of rules. They are adventurous and in constant need of cortical stimulation. Their impulsiveness leads them into temptations.

The psychopath possesses all the attributes as described by Dr. Robert Hare in the Psychopathy Checklist-Revised (PCL-R). It has become one of the most widely used methods in measuring criminal psychopathy. This instrument is used for the assessment of offenders incarcerated in prisons and psychiatric institutions. Other instruments used in the diagnosis of psychopathy are the Minnesota Multiphasic Personality Inventory (MMPI) and the Personality Assessment Inventory (PAI).

Psychopathy Checklist-Revised (PCL-R)

Factor 1: Measures a selfish, callous, and remorseless use of others and contains most of the personality characteristics considered central to the traditional clinical conception of the disorder. These traits are inferred, as opposed to explicit:

Glibness/superficial charm

Grandiose sense of self-worth/narcissism

Pathological lying

Conning, manipulative behavior

Lack of remorse or guilt

Shallow affect

Callousness/lack of empathy

Failure to accept responsibility for actions

Factor 2: Measures social deviance, as manifested in a chronically unstable and antisocial lifestyle. These traits are more explicit than those in the Factor 1 group:

Need for stimulation/proneness to boredom

Parasitic lifestyle

Poor behavioral controls

Early behavioral problems

Lack of realistic, long-term goals

Impulsivity

Irresponsibility

Juvenile delinquency

Revocation of conditional release

Other Factors:

Promiscuous sexual behavior

Many short-term marital relationships

Criminal versatility

These factors appear to vary with the age, social class, cognitive abilities, alcohol and drug abuse or dependence, violent behavior, and recidivism of the psychopath. These individuals tend to have average to above-average intelligence and are less obvious to investigators and therapists because they are less prone to show their antisocial attitudes. Psychopaths differentiate themselves from sociopaths in that they tend to display a higher level of skill in their criminal trade. Thus, they tend not to be arrested as often as sociopaths. Better adapted to their own deeply seated issues than are sociopaths, the psychopath is less obvious as a predator. He often does not physically harm a victim. The core of psychopathy is power and control over the victim through whatever means necessary to maintain or improve his status.

Primary Psychopaths

The *primary psychopath* also is antisocial, but the untrained eye will never see the true nature of the offender. These are the Ted Bundys, Edmund Kempers, and John Wayne Gacys of American society. They range between average and extremely high intelligence, perfecting the craft of manipulating others and living a life of unconscious pretense. Unlike the sociopath, who knowingly pretends to be something he is not, the primary psychopath lives his lies as his reality. Some of the "nicest" people in our communities are primary psychopaths. Friends and associates are quick to defend them: Never underestimate the power of denial.

The primary psychopath is a social chameleon, one who can blend into any environment. They often develop a psychological state of *semantic aphasia,* in which words do not carry the same meaning for them as they do for average people. In brief, they know the words but not the music. Furthermore, they seem incapable of experiencing genuine emotion, which renders them incapable of having honest relationships with other people. The primary psychopath becomes the consummate control predator. He can lie so well that his words carry complete credibility. He personifies the PCL-R and can outmaneuver law enforcement for lengthy time periods. Emotionally healthy people do not need to control others because they are already in control of themselves.

SEXUAL PSYCHOPATHS

Sex offenders use sex as a vehicle to gain control over their victims by inflicting pain and suffering. It is believed that the sexual involvement of many serial killers is a result of childhood experiences. According to Gebhard (1965), "It appears that fewer sexual psychopaths than other offenders were able to make good adjustments with their parents and their peers throughout their childhood" (p. 856). De Young (1982) notes that "the sadist sees the child victim as a representation of everything he hates about himself as well as the dreaded memories of his own childhood" (p. 125). Karpman (1954) notes similar characteristics of masochists:

Aggressive sexual crime symbolizes the inferiority feelings of the masochist and expresses his hostility toward the objects of his lust; these tendencies are integrated in the personality of the sexual psychopath as a result of long-standing emotional conflicts and stresses. (p. 72)

The offender, through violent acts, attempts to gain the control he or she has sought since childhood. As Stoller (1975) observes, "Many childhood defeats and frustrations feed into the dynamics of risk, revenge, and triumph" (p. 128).

The sexual psychopath who murders is often referred to as a "lust killer" or one who practices *erotophonophilia.* The notion of lust suggests one who possesses a particular urge not only to kill but also to ravage the victim. Methods of killing vary widely among lust killers, as do the types of mutilations that may occur before or after the victim has died. In one case, an offender described his feelings about killing, focusing on the urge to mutilate and destroy his victims before he could find relief.

MEASURING CRIMINAL PSYCHOPATHY

Psychopaths are all dangerous because that is their nature. Every psychopath wants some degree of control over his or her surroundings and the others in it. It is this quest for control that makes them psychologically, if not physically, dangerous. If this is so, then what happens when they are unable to maintain that control? Meloy (1992), in his impressive text *Violent Attachments,* states,

The nature of the psychopath's violent behavior is also consistent with his callous, remorseless, and unempathetic attitude toward his victims. I theorize that the psychopath was psycho-biologically predisposed to predatory violence, a mode of aggression which is planned, purposeful, and emotionless. (pp. 72-73)

Hare and Jutai (1959) note that psychopaths do not "peak" in their careers as do other criminals, but instead are able to maintain a consistency in their criminal behavior. Psychopaths are commonly found in institutions and constitute approximately 20% to 30% of prison populations. As mentioned, a common trait of psychopaths is their constant need to be in control of their social and physical environments. When this control is challenged, the psychopath can be moved to violent behavior.

Take the case of David, an intelligent man who was charming and engaging and possessed tremendous skills for deceiving others. Transient, he moved from one locale to another, seeking out those whom he could use. He had married several times, often before the divorce from his previous spouse had been finalized. He carefully and systematically siphoned off, diverted, and used the financial resources of each new spouse. He embezzled money from his stepchildren by forging their names on government bonds. He constantly borrowed money from others with no plans for repayment. Fastidious in his dress, versed in etiquette, and articulate in speech, he impressed everyone who had never been victimized by him as a responsible, gentle, and kind person. The man also had a passion for organization. He constantly reviewed everything about his life, his daily plans, and his goals. He always knew where he had been and what he did on any given day, week, month, or year. Indeed, he spent so much time planning and creating checklists, he never really accomplished anything. When confronted, he deftly sidestepped the issues, carefully staying out of the focus.

He rarely allowed himself to be in situations in which he might not have control. On occasion, however, he would engage in an athletic contest, such as basketball. A personality transformation inevitably occurred if his team was losing or if he did not give a stellar performance. Seething with anger and frustration, he would resort to vulgar language, extreme physical aggressiveness, and shouting at other players. The moment he was confronted about his behavior, he switched back to his former, kind self, until he returned to the game. He was a true Jekyll and Hyde. He had never been in prison, but it was only because of his manipulative abilities that he remained free.

Meloy (1992, pp. 78-80) notes that psychopaths live a "pre-socialized emotional world" in which feelings are experienced only in relation to self and never to others. They are more narcissistic and self-absorbed than nonpsychopaths and express themselves through self-aggrandizement and omnipotent control of others. This control is possible to achieve because psychopaths are significantly detached individuals possessing little capacity to form emotional bonds with others.

The continuum of psychopathic personalities includes representatives of many groups, including adolescents, sexual deviants, intellectual types, hard-core criminals, recluses, and extroverts, to name but a few. Many people may at one time or another play "mind games" with others to gain the upper hand in relationships. This does not make one a psychopath. Psychopaths become adept at this psychological game playing and ultimately become proficient at controlling their environments, a constant learning and adaptation process.

—*Elizabeth M. Stanczak and Eric W. Hickey*

NOTE: Portions of this essay were adapted from Eric Hickey's *Serial Murderers and Their Victims,* 2002, 3rd ed. Belmont, CA: Wadsworth.

See also ANTISOCIAL PERSONALITY DISORDER; BUNDY, THEODORE "TED"; CONDUCT DISORDER; PREDICTING VIOLENT BEHAVIOR; PSYCHOPATHOLOGY CHECKLIST-REVISED (PCL-R); SERIAL MURDER; VIOLENT BEHAVIOR

Further Reading

Cleckley, H. (1976). *The mask of sanity* (5th ed.). St. Louis, MO: Mosby.

Doren, D. M. (1987). *Understanding and treating the psychopath.* New York: John Wiley.

Hare, R. D. (1991). *The Hare Psychopathy Checklist-Revised.* Toronto, Canada: Multi-Health Systems.

Hare, R. D. (1993). *Without conscience: The disturbing world of the psychopaths among us.* New York: Simon & Schuster (Pocket Books). Paperback published in 1995. Reissued in 1998 by Guilford Press.

Hickey, E. W. (2002). *Serial murderers and their victims.* (3rd ed.). Belmont, CA: Wadsworth.

Peters, R., McMahon, R. J., & Quinsey, V. L. (Eds.). (1992). *Aggression and violence throughout the life span.* Newbury Park, CA: Sage.

PSYCHOSOCIAL RISK FACTORS FOR VIOLENT BEHAVIOR

Research has shown that numerous stress and compensatory protective factors have an impact on the psychic health and the personality development of individuals and therefore also influence the formation of certain behavioral patterns, such as repetitive violence. The challenges facing children and adolescents have changed over the years, going hand in hand with alterations in lifestyles as the result of and increase in urbanization, changing family forms, and political situations.

There are various theories about the essential interdependent factors at work in the genesis of psychopathology, and manifold models have been presented, meant to offer a better understanding of several developmental pathways. However, in addition to continuous changes concerning the factors of importance and the increase in existing theories and models about their interrelatedness, knowledge about their different effects on the development, and the course and the severity of any psychopathology, the concrete pathological behavior or personality pattern under investigation must also be delineated.

FORMATION OF
PSYCHOPATHOLOGICAL BEHAVIOR

The genesis of psychopathology must be recognized as a dynamic process, combining a variety of interactive factors that are not only diverse in their course but also miscellaneous as far as the particular resulting deviance is concerned.

When focusing on the psychosocial factors of importance in the formation of violent behavioral patterns and the development of deviant personality structures, research has repeatedly demonstrated that they predominantly seem to be connected to dysfunctional family systems. In addition to overly strict, authoritative, and punitive parenting, the social environment can be considered as another influential aspect. Consistent attachments to caregivers outside the family, mediating the effects of the negative relationship with the biological parents, can help give children from highly dysfunctional backgrounds the opportunity to develop along social norms. When dysfunctional family systems are joined with unstable social structures, not offering enough support during the upbringing but instead interfering with the internalizing of coping strategies, the genesis of violent behavior seems most likely.

To comprehend the complexity of these dynamics, the individual's disposition (and eventual attachment deficits), the family background (and its level of disorganization or the existence of inadequate role models), environmental influences, and concrete traumatizing life events must be recognized as interdependent factors. The progression into psychopathology unites the totality of psychosocial, biological, and sociocultural factors, but deviant behavioral patterns, such as repetitive violence, appear to mainly be the result of inadequate social and familial interactions (apart from the existence of a general predisposition). As a release mechanism for deviant behavioral patterns, the socialization through environmental influences seems to outweigh the impact of parental education and child-rearing practices. For the maintenance of the psychopathology, the opposite appears to be the case.

The formation of psychopathological behavior can be understood as an interdependent process that combines a genetically predisposed action probability and disadvantageous, unfavorable developmental conditions supplementary to the experience of traumatizing events and conflicts. Within this working diagram, the psychosocial factors take on a special position.

Psychopathological behavior and deviant personality structures, as individual patterns of maladjustment developing in the process of adapting to life's challenges, often result from conflicts arising from the attempts to master adjustment difficulties appearing throughout the course of life. Symptoms should be considered signals pointing at an existing conflict and requiring interpretation. Instead of considering the symptoms a failure of adaption to life, they must be viewed as an adaption on another (deviant) level, depending on the cognitive and affective maturity of individuals, in addition to the individual's inner representations.

To comprehend psychopathology (apart from formative processes concerning the personality development and the actual triggers generating the symptoms), the aspects of life supporting the course of the deviance must also be recognized. Most disorders foster a large variety of additional deviant behaviors reciprocating with them. Only when the constellation of the individual's cognitive, biological, and emotional disposition; personal background; the present triggering event; and actual living conditions are considered, respectively, can this possibly embrace the complete picture of any distinct psychopathology.

The combination of risk factors and disposition eventually leads to deviant (violent) actions stemming from the appliance of inadequate coping strategies. Intrapsychic structures are formed through an interactive process between the genetically predisposed developability and influences of the socialization process. Essential in the development of these structures are traumatic experiences, present conflicts, the level of self-integration, and the internalized defense mechanisms.

A causal analysis can investigate the connection between the past course of life and the psychological decompensation, whereas a situational analysis contemplates which concrete purpose the symptoms serve for the individual. The long-term effects of this pseudo-coping behavior on further development also deserve recognition.

Having learned that psychopathological symptoms etiologically are not very specific (and the same symptoms, such as violent behavior, as a consequence, possibly occur due to significantly different mental states) emphasizes once more why the attempt to understand deviance can be successful only on a multidimensional level, considering both the environmental aspects and the individual's disposition.

THE CONCEPT OF VULNERABILITY

The concept of vulnerability as one of the most widely used developmental models for mental disorders integrates psychosocial, biological, and cultural factors. It contradicts a direct causal linkage between the existence of risk factors during childhood and the manifestation of a specific disorder or deviance later in life. Instead, it proposes that each person has a certain vulnerability, consisting of inborn and required components, that mainly depends on the discrepancy between demands impinging on the individual and his or her perception of the potential fulfillment of these demands. This eventually results in decompensation, and the genesis of symptoms follows, such as demonstrations of violent actions. Social interactions as well as emotions deriving from the individual's mind-set can sometimes directly affect behavioral patterns. At other times, they only sensitize an already highly vulnerable disposition, leading to psychological decompensation.

It has been explained that the vulnerability of human beings basically describes their individual proneness to take a negative developmental course, depending on the circumstances. Furthermore, for the understanding of an unfolding deviance, the complete life history of individuals must be considered, including their family and social backgrounds, effective risk and protective factors, biological aspects, and certain concrete traumatizing events in relation to the suspected ability to cope with them. This specific constellation of factors, called *adaptive potential,* describes the extent of adequacy to which a person is able to respond to life's demands.

An individual's vulnerability determines how much stress can be managed before developing symptoms on the path towards decompensation. In a highly vulnerable person, little stressors can induce deviant behavior, whereas a person with a low degree of vulnerability can tolerate extreme situations without ensuing pathology. Stressors are considered anything requiring adjustment or reorganization of a person's situation. Whenever stressors do not exceed the threshold of vulnerability, there will be no psychopathology developing.

Protective factors, such as self-esteem, intelligence, bonding capabilities, and experienced social support resulting from adequate socialization can reduce the impact of apparent risk factors, altering or even avoiding negative chain reactions. The altering or avoidance of chain reactions then results in stronger self-confidence, the strengthening of social competence, and a sense of acceptance. Whenever the vulnerability rises due to life stressors, protective factors attempt to overcompensate this course of negativity, aiming at the avoidance of symptoms.

It must be noted that symptoms usually do not unfold as a result of single events. They are consequences of chronically unfavorable developmental processes, during which traumatizing experiences repetitively did not get intercepted. This results in a growing fragility of the individual, whose vulnerable personality then becomes increasingly likely to develop psychopathological symptoms or demonstrate deviant behavioral patterns, such as violence. Several elements are considered risk factors in this context. They can be broadly defined as biological, psychosocial, and sociocultural, but present living conditions and situational factors must also be taken into account.

Biological factors arise from pre-, peri-, and postnatal defects in addition to genetically, constitutionally, or somatically predisposed aspects. Cultural factors are comprised of social class affiliations that influence the hygiene and health standards but possibly also go hand in hand with lower educational levels and comparably inadequate parental capabilities. Sociographic factors, such as the location of the home environment, seem of equal importance, considering the aspects of anonymity and criminality as well as city or suburban life styles.

School can also have a positive or negative effect. As much as encouragement and praise appear reinforcing, pressure due to scholastic performance and the urge to disobey existing rules, which arises from a deep-seated sense of inadequacy, can be viewed as negative influences. Acceptance problems, arising from a migrational background, should also be given consideration. Traumatizing events, such as the loss of caregivers, the end of relationships, substance abuse, criminal activities, disease, accidents, or wartime experiences can be categorized as situational factors.

It appears that the social environment, in determining and mediating parental actions in joined efforts with the family structures and the individual's disposition, all play equally important roles in the complex upbringing process. The personality development and therefore also the genesis of deviant behavior depends on the vulnerability of individuals who face demands arising from everyday living. Family background, comprising parent-child interactions, communicational dynamics, attachment or bonding deriving from parents' efficiency as role models, methods of sanctioning, levels of social support, and experienced acceptance through the formation of friendships, can equally sensitize or desensitize an individual's disposition.

PSYCHOSOCIAL RISK FACTORS

Research has shown manifold pathways into diverse psychopathological patterns. The specific constellations of psychosocial risk factors relevant for violent behavioral patterns, as often found among those suffering from conduct disorder or antisocial personality disorder, can be pointed out as follows.

First, the individual's disposition and temperamental factors should receive recognition, because they lead to difficulties of adjustment and unstable emotions. Impulsivity, attention deficits, and hyperactivity also hold strong risk potential in the creation of deviant violent behavior. If breaking social rules early in life becomes instrumental in reaching personal goals and these goals are considered and legitimized by an individual as superior to the aims of others, it seems likely that a deviance of the described violent kind will unfold. The more widespread this rule-breaking pattern emerges, and the more urgently approval is becoming the prerequisite for the maintenance of self-esteem, the higher at risk the individual appears to be.

Unstable social backgrounds fostering emotional deprivation in children and allowing them to witness parental arguments, as well as family violence and antisocial tendencies of the role models, are still considered to be the main factors in the development of violence. Research has shown that violent adults and adolescents often come from abusive backgrounds themselves, never having internalized appropriate coping strategies.

The constellation outlined above consists mainly of unsatisfactory stimulation or promotion of children's abilities, abuse, maltreatment, and deprivation and represents a classical "broken home" scenario. This might also include the temporary or continuous absence of one or both parental figures, strong dissatisfaction with their roles resulting in a dysfunctional formation of self and self-worth in the child, and pessimistic feelings about the upcoming future, all having an negative impact on life choices.

A negative perception of the world and self results in the use of defense mechanisms that lead to failure in the adaption to life's challenges, thus continuing to distort reality. Without the possibility of resorting to effective coping strategies, and having a view of the outside world as a threat, violence will be a likely attempt of adaption. The missing emotional integration and family support and ensuing lack of ability to differentiate leads to avoidance, shyness, and the quest for attention and affection that stems from feelings of not being loved.

Due to restrictive socialization and aggressive methods of upbringing, empathic capabilities cannot evolve, and the understanding of social engagements, in addition to the ability to delay gratification, are missing. Persisting inadequate concepts of the world result in disorientation, a negative perception of life, a fixation on the present, and a constant expectation of failure.

Disturbances in the interpersonal relations stemming from insufficient social interactions, mainly within the family system, result in a powerful desire for constant confirmation and approval from others, as well as a pathological longing for attention, in an attempt to overcompensate for the eminent feelings of a deep-seated inadequacy. Aggressive patterns of violence soon become instrumental in this process.

—*Valeska Vitt*

See also AGGRESSION; ATTACHMENT DEFICIENCY AND VIOLENCE; CONDUCT DISORDER; COURT-ORDERED PSYCHOLOGICAL ASSESSMENT; MACDONALD TRIAD; PREDICTING VIOLENT BEHAVIOR; PSYCHOPATHS; VIOLENT BEHAVIOR

Further Reading

Cicchetti, D., & Cohen, D. (1995). *Developmental psychopathology.* New York: John Wiley.

Cohen, P., & Brook, J. (1987). Family factors related to the persistence of psychopathology in childhood and adolescence. *Psychiatry, 50,* 332-346.

Kutash, I., Kutash, S. B., Schlesinger, L. B., & Associates. (1978). *Violence-perspectives on murder and aggression.* San Francisco: Jossey-Bass.

Millon, T., Simonsen, E., Birket-Smith, M., & Davis, R. D. (1998). *Psychopathy-antisocial, criminal, and violent behavior.* New York: Guilford.

PYROMANIA, *See*
ARSON; JUVENILE FIRESETTERS

R

RACIAL PROFILING

The practice of racial profiling can be defined as any police action initiated because of an individual's race, ethnicity, or national origin without reasonable suspicion or probable cause. The practice of focusing on "people of color" in traffic enforcement as a pretext to further investigate or search is an example. When an individual's race, rather than behavior, is the reason for a police action, racial profiling is occurring. This practice is illegal and serves to alienate the police from the communities they serve.

Many law enforcement agencies have come under scrutiny for racial profiling. During the late 1990s, allegations of racial profiling became so common that communities of color coined the phrases "driving while black," "driving while brown," and "DWB" to express their frustration. Reports cite many accounts of disparate treatment of minorities by police. Many minorities have expressed concern that police have stopped them because they do not appear to "match," in other words, have the means to afford the type of vehicles they are driving. Or they are stopped while driving through predominately white neighborhoods because police believe they do not belong there and that they are involved in illegal activities. The most common complaint is that officers stop minorities for petty traffic violations, not for the purposes of issuing a citation, but as a pretext to conduct unwarranted searches or further investigation.

Nationwide surveys have confirmed that most Americans believe that racial profiling is a significant social problem that should be addressed. A Gallup Poll released in December of 1999 found that a majority of people surveyed believed that police actively engage in racial profiling, and a resounding 81% disapproved of the practice. This survey also indicated a strong correlation between perceptions of race-biased stops by police and animosity toward law enforcement.

To combat the practice of racial profiling, most law enforcement agencies have adopted a three-tiered approach, consisting of policy development, training, and demographic data collection. Policy formation is necessary to establish a new direction and emphasis, the object of which must be to protect the rights of all citizens. New policies must include guidelines regarding when a citizen can be contacted or stopped while operating motor vehicles. There must be an affirmation of required professional conduct and a prohibition of discriminatory practices. All personnel must support the policies, and they should be shared with the public to provide assurance that law enforcement agencies will not tolerate racial profiling.

It is not enough, however, to have policies prohibiting racial profiling. Departments must have training to ensure that proper guidelines are understood and followed. Training in racial profiling may be incorporated into existing training in cultural diversity and professionalism. Many states already have mandates for such training.

Many law enforcement agencies are involved in a process of data collection to both explore and refute the practice of racial profiling. Statistics comparing demographics of drivers stopped by police on traffic stops with population demographics can show whether a disproportionate number of minorities are being stopped. To accomplish this, many law enforcement agencies collect data from traffic citations, which include the reason for the stop; race, ethnicity, age, and sex of the person stopped; type of search conducted, if any; rationale for the search; contraband recovered; and enforcement action taken. Such data still may not be adequate in identifying incidents of racial profiling, because officers have discretion in whether they issue a citation, and if no citation is issued, then no data are collected. Useful data collection must include all stops conducted by officers, including those in which citations are not issued. Careful review of comprehensive data can assist law enforcement agencies in identifying incidents of racial profiling so that corrective measures can be taken to end it.

The practice of racial profiling is illegal and damages law enforcement's ability to work with the community. Developing strategies to eliminate the practice is necessary to strengthen the bond of trust between law enforcement agencies and the public they serve.

—*Sharon Shaffer*

See also COMMUNITY ATTITUDES TOWARD VIOLENT CRIME; POLICE BRUTALITY

Further Reading

Federal Bureau of Investigation. (2000, November). *Professional police traffic stops.* FBI Law Enforcement Bulletin. Washington, DC: U.S. Department of Justice.

U.S. Department of Justice. (2000, November). *Resource guide on racial profiling data collection systems.* Washington, DC: Author.

RICHARD RAMIREZ

Sitting on California's death row is Richard Ramirez, a.k.a the "Night Stalker." Ramirez stands out among other serial killers in that his savage rampage took place in such a short period of time. From June 1984 to August 1985, in addition to rapes, kidnappings, sodomy, and burglaries, he killed at least 14 victims.

Ramirez, the youngest of seven, was born in 1960, in El Paso, Texas. He moved to Los Angeles at the age of 2 and began his criminal career at the age of 9. By the time he was in eighth grade, he was smoking marijuana, sniffing glue, and was obsessed with satanism and black magic. He was a high school dropout and a loner, and on the streets of Los Angeles, he robbed, stole cars, and injected cocaine.

In 1984, a 79-year-old woman was stabbed to death in Los Angeles. Next, a 6-year-old girl was abducted and raped, but left alive. Later, a 9-year-old girl was taken from her bedroom, raped, and dumped. By the time Ramirez started to kill, he quickly ascended to a spree of violence and mayhem. His varied methods of killing (shooting, stabbing, bludgeoning) and apparent motiveless crimes made him unlike any other serial killer—and made him difficult to capture. The "Night Stalker" arbitrarily raped and murdered men and women, young and old. During the night, he slipped into darkened homes, where he shot, stabbed, and mutilated his victims. As the killings became more sadistic, he slashed a 44-year-old woman's body and cut out her eyeballs to keep as souvenirs.

The victims who lived described their attacker as a tall, gaunt Hispanic man with horrible breath and rotten teeth. From witness identifications, the identity of the Night Stalker was ultimately solved. Extensive media coverage made him a household name. Everyone knew what he looked like, and everyone wanted him apprehended. Finally, while attempting to steal a car, he was beaten down with a pipe. Ironically, the police had to protect Ramirez from the mob of people who wanted him dead.

Much would be made of his satanism, which dated back to his days of listening to rock groups such as "AC/DC" and "Black Sabbath." Sometimes, he etched satanic pentagrams on the bodies before fleeing or scrawled pentagrams in lipstick on bedroom walls. At trial, Ramirez enjoyed "playing Satan," carving a pentagram on his left palm and flashing it to photographers. It was said that Ramirez claimed that Satan would protect him; it was also said that Ramirez did not have a true devotion to the devil, but was instead a violent antisocial individual who killed for pleasure.

Seven years after being sentenced to prison, Ramirez married 41-year-old Doreen Lioy, a devoted "fan." The nonreligious ceremony was held in the

Richard Ramirez, the Night Stalker, tied to 14 murders and more than 30 assaults in California, proclaimed his loyalty to Satanism by displaying a pentagram tattooed on his left palm. He often shouted, "Hail Satan!" when leaving court and listened incessantly to his favorite AC/DC *Highway to Hell* album. His attacks included inscribing Satanic symbols in the homes of victims.

Source: Copyright © Bettmann / CORBIS.

prison's main visiting room. After reciting their vows and exchanging rings, they kissed. Richard Ramirez, housed at San Quentin State Prison, California, continues to await execution.

—*Amy Lynne Bronswick*

Further Reading

Hickey, E. W. (2002). *Serial murderers and their victims* (3rd ed.). Belmont, CA: Wadsworth.

Newton, M. (2000). *The encyclopedia of serial killers.* New York: Checkmark Books.

Schecter, H., & Everitt, D. (1996). *The A to Z encyclopedia of serial killers.* New York: Pocket Books.

JONBENET RAMSEY

On December 26, 1996, 6-year-old child beauty queen JonBenet Ramsey was found dead in the basement wine cellar of her parents' home, 8 hours after being discovered missing.

Patsy Ramsey discovered that her youngest child was missing after finding a three-page ransom note inside the family residence. Despite instructions of no police contact, she telephoned local police, who conducted a cursory search of the residence and found no obvious signs of a break-in or forced entry. The note suggested that the ransom collection would be monitored and JonBenet would be returned as soon as the ransom money was obtained. John Ramsey, the father, made arrangements for the availability of the ransom; however, no preparation was made to obtain the money.

In the early afternoon, a police detective requested that John Ramsey and two of his friends check the residence for any sign of JonBenet. The three men, led by John, went directly to the basement. Within a few moments, John found the blanket-covered body of his daughter in the wine cellar of the basement. He carried the body up the stairs, placing her on the floor of the foyer. The arrival of the coroner in the late evening authorized removal of the body by issue of a search warrant. Typically, removal of the body would be performed under consent of the parents. The resulting autopsy revealed that JonBenet had died of strangulation and an 8.5-inch skull fracture.

Case speculation by experts, the parents, and the media have provided differing theories. One theory depicts the mother as having accidentally killed JonBenet in a fit of rage after the girl had wet her bed. Several handwriting samples were taken from possible suspects who might have written the ransom note. After forensic analysis, all were cleared except for Patsy Ramsey, whose writing style bore some resemblance to the ransom note. Another theory speculates that John Ramsey killed his daughter because he had been sexually abusing her. However,

JonBenet Ramsey, 6-year-old entertainer and child beauty queen, daughter of John and Patsy Ramsey, an affluent Colorado couple, was murdered in her home on December 26, 1996. The case drew national attention when no suspect was charged and suspicions turned to possible family involvement. The case remains unsolved.

Source: Copyright © CORBIS.

the parents have adamantly held that the murder was committed by an intruder. John Douglas, former head of the FBI's Behavioral Science Unit, was hired by the Ramseys to examine the case. He concluded that the Ramseys were not involved in the murder and that it was unlikely that the case would be resolved.

A grand jury failed to indict Patsy and John Ramsey or anyone else in the death of JonBenet. Within a matter of months, the parents moved to another home, in Atlanta. Two lead investigators in the case resigned, and there have been accusations of a cover-up in the district attorney's office. The case remains unsolved.

—Vikki A. Irby

RAPE

Although the specific legal definition of *rape* varies from state to state, it generally constitutes vaginal, oral, or anal intercourse committed against a person without that person's consent. More often than not, the use of physical force, the threat of force, or intimidation is involved in an act of rape. Any sexual intercourse with a child, defined in most states as a male or female under the age of 14, qualifies as rape. *Statutory rape* is defined as sexual intercourse with a female over the age of 14 but under the legal age of consent, which in most states is 18 years of age. It is important to remember that statutory rape charges can be made even if the teenaged female gave her consent and freely participated in the sexual activity. *Date rape* is defined as rape that occurs during a pre-arranged social engagement. Outside the legal arena, rape is defined as an act of violence and control in which sex is used as a weapon. In these arguments, the statement that "rape has nothing to do with sex" is often heard.

Rape is a serious problem on a worldwide basis. Information compiled from existing studies and corresponding samples from the World Health Organization's Violence Against Women database revealed that within the past 12 months, an intimate male partner had sexually victimized 15% of adult women sampled in Guadalajara, Mexico; 37.6% in the West Bank and Gaza Strip, in Israel; 6% of the adult women in Northern London; and 48.5% in Lima, Peru. However, the rate of rape within the United States remains among the highest in the world: 4 times higher than that of Germany, 13 times higher than that of England, and 20 times higher than that of Japan. In response to such statistics, it was not surprising to find that the Fourth World Conference on Women in Beijing, in 1995, considered violence against women to be one of the 12 critical areas of concern.

Regardless of how shocking these statistics are, one of the most serious issues surrounding the crime of rape is that the actual number of rapes committed is significantly higher than the number of rapes reported. Some researchers have suggested that in the United States, fewer than 30% of all rapes are reported to law enforcement. Assuming that the 92,000 rapes reported in the United States in the year 2000 represent only 30% of all rapes committed, then the actual number of rapes committed in the United States during that year would be closer to 306,667. To further complicate matters, many have argued that the rape of men is even more underreported than the rape of women. In 1999, 1 in every 10 rape victims was male. However, it is argued that about 3% of American men have experienced an attempted or completed rape in their lifetimes.

In an effort to explain why so few rapes are reported to law enforcement, it is helpful to consider relevant issues within the United States. First, it has long been argued that someone known to the victim, often a friend, an acquaintance, an intimate partner, or a relative, commits 80% of all rapes reported. It has further been argued that knowing the rapist makes it difficult to report the crime. One might argue that ideally, all rapes should be reported. Realistically, however, it is often difficult for a victim to label a friend, a partner, or a family member as a rapist. Perhaps another part of the explanation for this widespread underreporting in the United States is found in the general public's attitudes toward the crime of rape. There remains a collection of myths about rape that too often interfere with the reporting of the crime and ultimately leave the rapists unaccountable for their actions.

Often mentioned in the category of "blaming the victim" is that the victim in some way provoked or did something to cause the rape. Comments are commonly made about a woman's clothing, specifically statements about what she was or was not wearing at the time of the crime. Sometimes people comment on what the woman may have had to drink. Men are also blamed for their victimization, for example, "It is his fault for not being able to defend himself" or "He deserved what he got because he's gay." Some victims come to believe that they actually were responsible for their own victimization. Conversely, women who have not been victimized may assume that if they always dress appropriately, never drink alcoholic beverages, or stay in their homes after dark, they will be protected from rape.

Other myths suggest that "No" really means "Yes" and that women falsely accuse men of rape just to "get back at them." Not one of these claims is valid, of course. For example, less than 5% of rape cases are based on false accusations, a percentage similar to the number of false accusations associated with other crimes.

Although the pattern of underreporting is found in all societies, the explanations that account for it vary. Rhona MacDonald, writing in the *British Medical Journal,* reported that in Peru, some women who report rapes have to deliver police summonses to their attackers; in Pakistan, police often refuse to register rape complaints; and in Jordan, there are reports of women being placed in prison after filing rape complaints, arguably for their own protection. The World Health Organization also reported that in countries where a woman's virginity is associated with family honor, unmarried women who report a rape may be forced to marry the rapist, others may be prosecuted and imprisoned for committing the crime of sex outside the legalized union of marriage, and still others may be murdered by family members, such as fathers or brothers. Some authors have suggested that as many as 5,000 women are murdered each year when their rapes are defined as events that bring shame on the family. Ironically, family members are often the ones who raped these women in the first place. Nevertheless, such responses deter women from reporting rapes and result in inaccurate statistics about a crime that could affect as many as 1 in 5 women on a worldwide basis.

Regardless of whether the victim chooses to report the crime, the consequences that victims suffer as a result of this crime are often severe. Most obvious are the physical injuries sustained by the victim during a violent attack, ranging from bruises to lifelong disabilities. In the United States, as many as 32,000 rape-related pregnancies occur annually. The World Health Organization reported that a significant percentage of adolescents seeking abortions in Bombay, India, were pregnant due to forced sex, rape, or incest. Pregnancy from rape is particularly problematic in countries where abortion remains illegal. Victims of rape are also vulnerable for contracting AIDS and other sexually transmitted diseases (STD). It has been reported that 1 in 10 rape victims in Thailand contract an STD because of a rape. And in the United States, it is estimated that as many as 30% of rape victims contract STDs as a result of the crime.

Victims of rape suffer psychological consequences, often developing and enduring feelings of shame, humiliation, and depression. In extreme cases, depression can lead to suicide. Victims also suffer opportunity costs. For example, the crime creates a climate of fear that affects lives of women by making it difficult for them to leave their homes in the evening, to travel alone on business, to develop intimate relationships, or simply to live a life free of fear.

As the crime of rape takes a tremendous toll on the lives of its victims, it also affects the larger society.

The World Health Organization reported that studies in the United States, Zimbabwe, and Nicaragua found that women who had been physically or sexually abused required more health care services. Specifically, it was reported that in the United States, the medical care costs for rape and assault victims were twice as high as the medical costs for persons who had not been victimized. There are also costs associated with the reporting, investigation, and prosecution of rape cases. It is understandable why it has been argued that rape has the highest annual victim cost of any other reported crime.

Although the crime of rape wreaks havoc in the lives of many women and men around the world, the overall treatment of rape victims has improved considerably. Activists continue to work to initiate and strengthen existing rape laws, to provide victim-assistance services, and to educate the public. War Against Rape (WAR) is a Pakistani women's organization dedicated to serving victims of rape. Forum Against Oppression of Women (FWOP) is a group based in Bombay, India, that focuses upon networking, lobbying, and helping women confront sexual assault issues. Perhaps one of the most important worldwide events occurred when a United Nations tribunal indicted eight Bosnian Serb military and police officers in connection with the rapes of Muslim women during the Bosnian war. Though rape had occurred in wars throughout history prior to the 1996 tribunal, it was always considered secondary to other crimes of war.

Much change has also occurred within the major social institutions in the United States. At one time, laws involving rape were *sex specific,* meaning that only women could be victims of rape and only men could be perpetrators. In recent years, however, state legislatures have reconsidered the sex-specific nature of these laws and have rewritten them. Prior to the 1970s, there was no such thing as rape between a man and a woman who were legally married. Since the 1970s, states have eliminated the spousal immunity clause, making it possible for a husband to be convicted of raping his wife. Today, it is estimated that 14% of married women are victims of rape committed by their husbands. In years past, it was also common for the victim's sexual history to become an issue of concern during the prosecution of the rapist. Now the institution of rape shield laws (each state has its own version) makes a victim's past sexual history irrelevant, and the Drug Induced Rape Prevention and Punishment Act of 1996 makes it a felony to give a controlled substance to anyone with the intent of committing a sexual assault.

Colleges and universities have established sexual assault response teams (SART), and medical institutions have appointed sexual assault nurse examiners (SANE). Law enforcement agencies employ specially trained officers to handle rape cases and to keep informed of the newest techniques used in the commission of the crime. In fact, the use of "date rape" drugs was discovered by law enforcement. Though not manufactured or sold legally in the United States, Rohypnol is a low-cost sleeping pill used by some rapists to incapacitate their "dates." A particularly dangerous drug, Rohypnol not only impairs judgment and motor skills but can also induce memory loss, making the investigation of a rape case even more difficult.

In the past two decades, rape crisis centers and 24-hour crisis hotlines in large cities and small towns across America have been available for the needs of victims. In some organizations, men work as allies with women toward rape prevention. For example, the group "Men Can Stop Rape" recently launched an educational effort to prevent rape among youth.

There was both applause and skepticism when the Justice Department reported a 34% reduction in the number of rapes in the year 2000. Those who applauded the decrease referred to the diligent work of thousands. Skeptics questioned the dramatic decrease and the accuracy of the survey and were further confused by the Federal Bureau of Investigation report that showed a slight increase in violent crimes during the same year.

Much progress has occurred, but important issues remain unresolved. Often, the focus is on defining rape as a "woman's issue," a perspective that exempts or minimizes the roles that men play in the prevention and elimination of rape. The rapist has been largely viewed as a single acting unit in need of attention, whether it be medical, psychological, or retaliatory in nature. For example, California mandated chemical castration for some sex offenders in 1996, and there has always been debate over whether such action is an appropriate punishment or preventative measure.

Today, the momentum of the rape-prevention movement is beginning to focus on the larger cultural and structural conditions in society that allow rape to flourish. Consider Peggy Sanday's cross-cultural study of rape wherein she identified societies in which rape appeared to be absent or rare. Within societies characterized as "rape-free," egalitarianism, economic equality, equitable resource allocation, and nonaggressive actions were all highly valued and rewarded. Within societies that were defined as "rape-prone," however, interpersonal violence, male dominance, and sexual separation were prevalent.

—*N. Jane McCandless*

See also AGGRESSION: FEMINIST PERSPECTIVE; BATTERERS AND ABUSIVE PARTNERS; SEXUAL OFFENSES; VICTIMOLOGY

Further Reading

Brownmiller, S. (1975). *Against our will: Men, women and rape.* New York: Bantam Books.

Ledray, L. (1994). *Recovering from rape.* New York: Owlet.

MacDonald, R. (2000). Time to talk about rape. *British Medical Journal, 321,* 1034-1035.

Men can stop rape. Available on the World Wide Web at: http://www.mencanstoprape.org.

Russell, D. E. H. (1990). *Rape in marriage.* Bloomington, IN: Indiana University Press

Sanday, P. (1996). Rape-prone versus rape-free campus cultures. *Violence Against Women, 2,* 191-208.

Warshaw, R. (1994). *I never called it rape: The MS. report on recognizing, fighting, and surviving date and acquaintance rape.* New York: Harper.

World Health Organization. *Violence against women.* Available on the World Wide Web at: http://www.who.int/violence_injury_prevention/vaw/prevalence.htm.

RAPE—DEFINITIONS

In common usage, we define rape as unlawful sexual intercourse by force or without mutual consent. Long perceived as primarily a sexual crime, recent interpretations align rape more closely with violence than with sex. Many types of rape exist, including those detailed here.

Acquaintance Rape

Acquaintance rape is a sexual attack perpetrated by a person who is known to the victim (for example, socially, through work, or through school) but who is not in any sort of close relationship with the victim. Specifically, an acquaintance rape is the carnal knowledge of a person by a perpetrator known to the victim, forcibly and against the victim's will or where the victim is incapable of giving consent because of his or her temporary or permanent mental or physical incapacity. Acquaintance rape can include coerced or forced oral, anal, or vaginal penetration. Research suggests that 80% of all rapes on college campuses are classified as acquaintance rapes. Females aged 16 to 24 report the highest rates of this type of victimization.

Date Rape

Date rape is rape committed by someone known to the victim or even being dated by the victim. Date rape is sometimes facilitated by the victim's inhibitions being lowered by alcoholic beverages or by the so-called date rape drug, Rohypnol, which is a tasteless, illegal sedative.

Forcible Rape

Rape without consent and against a person's will by use of force or threat of force is known as forcible rape. The perpetrator may be either known to the victim or a stranger. Historically, under common law, a man could not be convicted of raping his wife, but this interpretation of marital priviledge has changed. In most state statutes, marital status is now irrelevant, as is the victim's gender. In some statutes, forcible rape is also referred to as unlawful sexual intercourse, sexual assault, sexual battery, or sexual abuse.

Marital Rape

Marital rape is intercourse or penetration (vaginal, anal, or oral) of a spouse that is unwanted and done by force, threat of force, implied harm based on prior attacks, or when the victim is unable to consent. According to the law, a wife does not have to physically fight back against unwanted sex with her husband for it to be deemed rape. Consent is not implied simply because a woman has had sex with her husband at a previous time. Rape statutes require that consent be an act of free will.

Between 10% and 14% of married women are raped in marriage, and 25% of all rapes fall under the category of marital rape. Despite these facts that show marital rape to be a prevailing form of sexual violence, it has not received much attention from either the criminal justice system or society as a whole. Traditionally, societies have tolerated men forcing their wives to have sex against their will within the scope of marriage. Older legal definitions of rape excluded wives as victims of such a crime. These factors allowed husbands to be exempt from prosecution in cases of rape against their wives.

The basis of the marital rape exemption can be traced back to the 17th century, when Sir Matthew Hale, Chief Justice of England, wrote, "The husband cannot be guilty of a rape committed by himself upon his lawful wife, for their mutual matrimonial consent and contract, the wife hath given herself in kind unto the husband which she cannot retract" (Russell, 1990, p. 17). This position remained basically undisputed until the 1970s, when reformers urged the riddance of the spousal exemption because it did not provide equal protection from rape to all women under all circumstances.

Not until 1993 did marital rape became a crime in all 50 states in the United States, although a majority still provide some exemptions from rape prosecution for husbands. The fact that these exemptions still widely exist shows that marital rape continues to be viewed as a less serious crime than other types of rape and perpetuates the outdated belief that wives are the property of their husbands through the contract of marriage and, as such, must have sex at the husbands' will.

Rape in marriage crosses all boundaries of age, social standing, race, and ethnicity. It is most likely to occur in marriages in which other forms of domestic violence exist, although this is not always the case. As in other types of rape, marital rape is an act of violence, wherein the perpetrator attempts to establish power, control, and dominance over the victim.

Statutory Rape

Simply defined, statutory rape occurs when someone of or over the age of consent has sex with someone under the age of consent. Although the age of consent varies from state to state, currently, all states have laws that prohibit sexual intercourse with persons under a certain age. Several states have either a minimum age for the defendant or define the age difference between the minor and the defendant.

Statutory rape laws maintain that a person under the age of consent has *no legal right to give informed consent*. They also facilitate prosecution of pedophiles and those involved in child pornography and prostitution rings.

RECIDIVISM, *See* Prevention of Crime and Violent Behavior

RIPPERS

Several common themes run through the acts of murderers known as "rippers." Most salient is that they violently mutilate or literally rip their victims open and often dismember them. Most, but not all, ripper murderers select prostitutes as their victims. Jack the Ripper, in late 19th-century London, was particularly proficient at mutilating and disemboweling his victims. Often, these types of murders are committed in an uncontrollable rage leading to exceptionally violent acts. For example, in the 1970s, Peter Sutcliffe, the "Yorkshire Ripper," mutilated his victims and left bite marks, later used to link him to the crime. Rippers may also engage in cannibalism.

Ripper murderers take advantage of their victims' accessibility as well as their lifestyles, which often make them difficult to track. For instance, prostitutes may go missing, unnoticed, for long periods of time. The Yorkshire Ripper explained to his younger brother that his motive for his violent murders was to clean up the streets and rid them of prostitutes; his savage mutilation of his victims demonstrates the rage and anger he felt toward women. The opinion that prostitutes were somehow to blame for their victimization was likely shared by the some members of the public.

CASE STUDIES

Jack the Ripper

The most notorious ripper murderer was Jack the Ripper. Aside from being the first known murderer of this kind, he was also one of the earliest known serial killers. The case was notorious and has never been solved.

In 1888, London experienced a series of extremely brutal and vicious murders of prostitutes. Then, as quickly as they began, the murders stopped. The investigation was difficult because the police and local media received many letters with misleading and conflicting information. Investigators of the crimes doubted the authenticity of most of the letters. Today, scholars still debate the legitimacy of two that were evidently written by the same individual. In one, the author writes, "I am down on whores and I shant quit *ripping* them till I do get buckled." He proclaims his identity in his signature: "Yours Truly, Jack the Ripper."

The Yorkshire Ripper

Nearly a century later, another serial murderer terrorized England. Peter Sutcliffe, "The Yorkshire Ripper," killed 13 women in a 5-year period beginning in 1975 and ending in 1981. Sutcliffe began by selecting prostitutes as his victims, yet later targeted middle-class women in neighborhoods previously believed to be safe. The shift in types of victims demonstrated the vulnerability of all women, not just those leading risky lives in the red-light districts. Most often, Sutcliffe struck his victims in the head with a hammer, and once they collapsed, he stabbed and mutilated their bodies. Quite unusual for a serial killer, Sutcliffe was interrupted during some of his attacks, and seven of his intended victims survived.

Other Cases

Daniel Rolling, the "Gainesville Ripper," murdered five young students in Gainesville, Florida, over a weekend in 1990. Before sexually assaulting his victims, torturing and mutilating them, he sadistically told them everything he planned to do to them.

Richard Cottingham was known simply as "The Ripper." He began killing in 1977 and was subsequently arrested in 1980. Like the others, Cottingham targeted prostitutes as his victims. His victims, in the New Jersey and New York area, were badly mutilated; one had been stabbed to death and her body set on fire.

The ripper image has also applied to group killers, such as "The Chicago Rippers," in Illinois, during 1981 and 1982. The four men in this gang began their killings by gang-raping and stabbing a woman to death. Their other victims endured similarly sickening mutilations. After several of the gang members were arrested, they confessed to their crimes, admitting to ritualistic mutilation and to cannibalism.

—*Nicole L. Mott*

See also CHIKATILO, ANDREI (RUSSIAN RIPPER); JACK THE RIPPER; METHODS OF MURDER; MOTIVES FOR MURDER; SERIAL MURDERS; SIGNATURE KILLERS; TROPHY TAKING

Further reading

Begg, P. (1988). *Jack the Ripper*. London: Robson Books.

Rumbelow, D. (1975). *The complete Jack the Ripper*. London: W. H. Allen.

Ryzuk, M. (1994). *The Gainesville Ripper*. New York: St. Martin's.

Yallop, D. A. (1980). *Deliver us from evil*. London: Macdonald.

RISK ASSESSMENT, *See* PREDICTING VIOLENT BEHAVIOR; THREAT MANAGEMENT

ROAD RAGE

In its broadest sense, the term *road rage* can refer to any display of aggression by a driver. However, it is often used to refer to the more extreme acts of aggression such as physical assault or homicide that occur as a direct result of a disagreement between drivers. This type of behavior has become common in the United States and the rest of the industrially developed world. An individual may be a victim one day and a perpetrator the next.

Road rage is characterized by driver recklessness and "automobile anarchy," which include such mundane actions as unsignaled or unsafe lane changes, tailgating, slow starts, abrupt braking, and crowding when lanes reduce in number. These actions may be accented by obscene gestures, shouting, or blasting the horn. They have become so pervasive and routine that one elderly gentlemen commented that if he had "not received 'the bird' at least once," he had not gone anywhere that day. In the 1990s, incidents of road rage were up 51% in the first half of the decade, involving millions of victims—and few confessed perpetrators.

Aggressive driving is not new, but it has been on the increase as a result of the rise in the number of automobiles on the road in recent years. Since 1998, there has been an increase of 17% in the number of cars on the road and a 10% increase in the number of drivers. Furthermore, the number of miles driven has increased 35% since 1987, but the number of miles of road has increased only 1%. These statistics mean a lot more vehicles on the existing miles of roads. This

Road rage was coined about 1988 to make the public aware that frustrated, angry people sometimes use their vehicles to vent emotions. These emotions often seem triggered when a driver deliberately or inadvertently behaves inappropriately toward another driver. In some cases, venting emotions includes aggressive behaviors that have resulted in serious injury or death.

Source: Copyright © Anthony Redpath / CORBIS.

chronic congestion of the roadways has made habitual road rage a constant feature of modern life.

Leon James, a professor of psychology at the University of Hawaii, found that an astounding 80% of drivers are angry most or all the time while driving. Some reasons given for this state include traffic congestion, impatience at stoplights, waiting for parking spaces or for passengers to get into their cars, and the narrowing of multilane highways. These hardly seem worthy of the kind of anger generated by many hostile drivers. To understand this phenomenon, one must examine the psychology of driving.

Driving is a combination of public and private acts. Cars provide isolation and protection for drivers while propelling them through the world. Cars also provide a sense of personal power that seems to be proportional to the size and engine capability of the vehicle. In comfort, safety, anonymity, and in control of their environment, drivers feel free to behave in ways they probably never would if they were face to face with another person.

No longer are drivers satisfied with the compact or mid-sized grocery-getters or go-cart sized sports cars. If they can afford it, "road warriors" want cars they can "take control" in. Sports utility vehicles (SUVs) fit the bill for many. The average SUV is equipped with a four-wheel-drive transmission and a large engine, and even requires a ladder to enter because it is so high off the ground. These huge vehicles certainly exceed what is necessary to move a family from one place to another, but they do seem to play a vital role in feeding owners' fantasies (women as well as men) of power and importance.

The automobile can be considered a living space that the driver personally owns, and the space that it resides in is part of the driver's territory. In most parts of the world, different standards of behavior are observed within one's home and outside it. Generally, extreme displays of emotion, including aggression, are more accepted within the confines of the home. As an extension of one's living space, the automobile is also a place where higher levels of aggression are "allowable"; there, only the driver sets the standards for behavior. When another motorist invades a driver's territory by coming too close, drivers often respond with extreme displays of anger, from gestures or swearing to assault and homicide.

What are the results of this constantly increasing aggression on the highways? In 1996, the American Automobile Association (AAA) commissioned a study on the causes and effects of road rage. Louis Mizell reported that "an average of at least 1,500 men, women, and children are injured or killed each year in the United States as a result of aggressive driving." He reviewed 10,037 incidents from newspapers, police reports, and insurance reports to gather his data. He concluded that the most aggressive drivers were between the ages of 18 and 26, more likely to be males, less educated, with criminal histories or histories of violence, and drug or alcohol problems. He did not establish a definitive profile, however; almost any type of person can become aggressive on the road.

Each one of the following reasons for aggressive driving resulted in at least 25 incidents of death or injury in Mizell's study:

♦ "It was an argument over a parking space."
♦ "He cut me off."
♦ "She would not let me pass."
♦ A driver was shot to death because "He hit my car."
♦ "He was playing his radio too loud."
♦ "The bastard kept honking and honking his horn."
♦ "He/she was driving too slowly."
♦ "He would not turn off his high beams."
♦ "They kept tailgating me."
♦ "She kept crossing lanes without signaling—maybe I overreacted, but it taught her a lesson."

- "I never would have shot him if he had not rear-ended me."
- "Every time the light turned green, he just sat there."

It is important to note that these are all merely triggers for behavior. The behavior that initiates the event may be trivial but may nonetheless cause the violent release of an accumulation of anger or hostility. The deeper source of these emotions varies. Often, aggressive drivers who cause injury or death have had a recent emotional or professional setback. There also appears to be some relationship between domestic violence and aggressive driving. When a driver is angry with a spouse, he or she frequently will vent that anger while on the road. Racism and aggressive driving incidents have also been linked. Approximately 38 violent traffic accidents per year start out as simple disagreements but end up in death or injury when a traffic dispute takes on racist overtones.

Weapons play a large role in incidents of road rage. The overwhelming weapons of choice include guns and the vehicle itself, but aggressive drivers have been reported to use their fists and feet; tire irons and jack handles; baseball bats; knives; ice picks; razor blades; swords; defensive sprays; clubs such as crowbars, lead pipes, 4 × 4 timbers, and wrenches; and other miscellaneous hurled projectiles, such as beer or liquor bottles, eggs, rocks, and snowballs. Enraged motorists frequently plow into crowds or attack law enforcement personnel with their vehicles.

Is there a solution to this growing problem? Mainly, for motorists to become more aware and responsible. Remember that at least 1,500 serious injuries and/or deaths occur each year as a result of traffic disputes. Think carefully about the threat to one's safety and others. Consider the thousands of drivers on the road at any one time, some mentally or emotionally disturbed, each one potentially upset or angry or impaired by substance abuse, and primed for violence. They may be armed with weapons, and at the very least are always armed with their vehicles.

Drivers can also help reduce the risk of vehicular violence to themselves and their families by being aware of their own personal responses to occurrences while driving and trying not to become part of the problem by overreacting themselves. Remain calm in traffic, be patient and courteous to other drivers, and work to correct unsafe and possibly irritating driving habits.

—Marlene Deal

See also Vehicular Homicide

Further Reading

Berry, B. (1999). *Social rage: Emotion and cultural conflict.* New York: Garland.

Curry, R. R., & Allen, T. (Eds.). (1996). *States of rage: Emotional eruption, violence and social change.* New York: New York University Press.

Goleman, D. (1996). *Emotional intelligence.* London: Bloomsbery.

James, L. (2000). *Road rage and aggressive driving: Steering clear of highway warfare.* Amherst, NY: Prometheus Books.

McKay, G. E., & Hersey, D. (Eds.). (2000). *Road rage: Commuter combat in America.* Silvertip Books.

Mizell, L. (1998). *Aggressive driving.* Retrieved March 26, 2002, from the World Wide Web at: http.//www, aaafoundation.org/resources/index.cfm?button=agdr-text.

U.S. Government Staff. (1997). *Road rage: Causes and dangers of aggressive driving.* Hearing before the subcommittee on Surface Transportation of the Committee on Transportation. Washington, DC: U.S. Government Printing Office.

ROBBERY

Robbery is the taking or attempted taking of anything of value from the care, custody, or control of a person by force or threat of force. In addition to the element of larceny (taking the property of another with the intent to permanently deprive the person of ownership), robbery includes two other elements: The property must be taken from the person or in the person's presence, and force or the threat of immediate force must be used in the taking. Though robbery is a crime motivated by the desire to obtain money or goods, because it involves the use of force, it is generally classified as a violent offense. It is the element of force that distinguishes robbery from property crimes such as shoplifting, pickpocketing, and motor vehicle theft. Based on national data, robbers took more than $477 million dollars from their targets in the United State in 2000, with an average dollar loss of $1,170. More important, more than 1,000 murders occurred during the commission of robberies in 2000.

ROBBERY TRENDS

Two major sources of national crime data provide information on the incidence, nature, and rate of robberies, as well as other major criminal offenses that occur annually in the United States. The best known and most widely cited is the Uniform Crime Report (UCR). Compiled and published by the FBI since 1930, the UCR is based on monthly reports of known crimes submitted by state and local law enforcement agencies. The report is limited to crimes that have come to the attention of law enforcement through citizen complaints or police patrols. The second source of crime statistics is the National Crime Victimization Survey (NCVS). Information in the NCVS comes from a survey of households in the United States conducted annually since 1973 by the Bureau of Justice Statistics in conjunction with the U.S. Census Bureau. Based on interviews with household members aged 12 years and older, the NCVS is able to provide information on unreported as well as reported criminal incidents.

According to the UCR, in 2000, there were 407,842 robberies reported to or observed by police, representing a rate of 145 robberies per 100,000 inhabitants. The NCVS reports that 732,000 robberies occurred that year, constituting a rate of 320 per 100,000 persons. The discrepancy between the two reports is due primarily to the inclusion of unreported robberies in the NCVS. Indeed, according to the

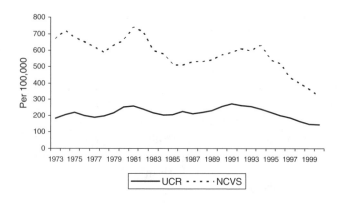

Figure 1   Trends in Robbery Rates

NCVS, less than half of all robbery victims reported their victimization to police in 2000.

Figure 1 presents trends in robbery rates from 1973 to 2000 as reported by the UCR and NCVS. Despite differences in their methodology, there is a striking similarity in robbery trends provided by the two sources. Both show that robbery rates declined in the mid-1970s and then increased sharply later that decade, peaking in 1981 with robbery rates for the UCR and NCVS at 258.7 and 740.0, respectively. Robbery rates declined during the early 1980s, but then both sources show steep increases during the late 1980s that continued through the early 1990s. UCR robbery rates were the highest in 1991, at 272.7 robberies per 100,000. According to both the UCR and NCVS, robbery rates have dramatically declined since the early 1990s.

Robbery rates vary by region of the United States and the size as well as sociodemographic composition of metropolitan areas. The highest rate of robbery in 2000 was recorded in the Northeast (156 per 100,000), followed by the South (152.3 per 100,000), the West (142.3 per 100,000), and the Midwest (126.8 per 100,000). Urban areas have higher robbery rates than suburban and rural areas. In 2000, the rate of robbery in the nation's eight cities with populations of 1 million or more was more than 3 times the national rate. In addition to size, robbery rates are also greater in areas with high racial and ethnic heterogeneity, rapid population turnover, and high unemployment.

Robbery is completed or attempted theft of property or cash directly from a person by force or threat of force, with or without a weapon, and with or without injury. According to the Bureau of Justice Statistics (2002), since 1994, robbery rates have declined, reaching the lowest levels recorded in 2001.

Source: Copyright © Roy Morsch / CORBIS.

ROBBERY SITUATIONS

Robberies can be broadly classified into two categories: institutional and personal. Institutional robbery includes the robbery of banks, convenience stores, liquor stores, pawnshops, and other commercial establishments and accounts for roughly one fourth of the total number of robberies reported to police. Personal robbery is forced theft from persons in non-commercial settings, such as street muggings, home invasions, and carjackings. Nearly two thirds of all robberies are committed against individuals on public streets, highways, and personal residences. Robberies not classified as personal or institutional are officially categorized as "other."

Bank Robbery

More than other robbery scenarios, bank robberies are more likely to capture media attention. Bank robberies, however, are relatively infrequent, comprising no more than 2% of the total number of robberies in a given year. The average dollar loss for a bank robbery in 2000 was $4,437. The physical security of banks requires more planning on the part of robbers, who consider a range of factors to determine the timing and selection of targets. These factors include (a) the number of customers or witnesses, (b) the physical presence and placement of security guards, (c) the location of teller booths, (d) the accessibility of exits and escape routes, and (e) the use and possession of a getaway car. Some bank robbers carefully scope out a number of potential targets and select the one with the highest expected yield and lowest risks; others, however, simply walk in, with little preparation, and commit the holdup.

Convenience Store Robbery

The proliferation of one-stop convenience stores over the past decade has created additional robbery targets. In 2000, approximately 6% of all robberies involved convenience stores as targets, and the average loss was $544. The location and layout of convenience stores makes them particularly attractive to robbers. Often located on major transportation arteries, the convenience store robber can quickly and easily appear, steal, and then disappear into the urban landscape. These stores are also small, easily entered and exited, and have few employees or customers to mount resistance or provide identification, particularly during the late evening or early morning hours. Though many convenience stores, as well as other commercial establishments, are equipped with security cameras, studies have found that robbers do not reject an otherwise desirable target simply because it has a camera.

Street Mugging

Street mugging refers generally to personal robbery committed on streets, in supermarket parking lots, near check-cashing establishments or ATMs (automatic teller machines), or around sporting or entertainment venues. These are places where people typically carry large sums of cash, and robbers rely partly on outward signs, clothing and jewelry, for example, to select their targets. However, interviews of robbers reveal that regardless of how much cash a potential target is believed to carry, the robber is unlikely to confront a person they believe might resist. Most robbers want to use only the level of threat or force necessary to complete the transaction; overcoming victim resistance is dangerous and time-consuming, increasing the risk to the robber of being injured, killed, or caught in the act. Whites, females, and the elderly are generally viewed by robbers as less likely to offer resistance.

Home Invasion Robbery

In a home invasion robbery, the perpetrator forcibly enters an inhabited residence, subdues the residents (sometimes by binding and gagging), and commits theft. Sometimes, home invasion robberies are botched burglaries in which the residents unexpectedly return. Strangers commit most of these robberies, but a substantial proportion, much higher than in other robbery types, are committed by ex-lovers, roommates, and co-offenders in previous criminal activities. Home invasion robberies generally account for 12% of the total number of robberies committed each year in the United States.

Carjacking

Theft of a motor vehicle by force or threat of force is known as carjacking. Victims may be threatened or forced to vacate their cars. Sometimes, the victim is forced to remain in the automobile and later dumped. The method in carjacking varies. Some carjackers surprise drivers at stop signs, others use a vehicle to force a driver off the road, still others pose as hitchhikers and forcibly take control of the vehicle after the unsuspecting driver has stopped to offer them a ride. Approximately two thirds of all carjackings occur within 5 miles of the victim's home. Males, the elderly, blacks, and urban residents are more likely to be victims of carjacking than females, the young, whites and Hispanics, and suburban and rural residents. In the vast majority of carjackings, the offenders use firearms, and victims offer no resistance or only nonconfrontational resistance, such as running away or calling for help. The lack of resistance perhaps accounts for the general absence of injury to victims. Only 16% of victims in carjackings between 1992 and 1996 were injured (an average of about 49,000 completed or attempted carjackings each year).

ROBBER TYPOLOGIES

Studies show that robbers vary according to demographic characteristics, extent of criminal activity, motivations, level of offense specialization, and degree of planning. Using these distinctions, criminologists have developed various classification systems for robbers. One of the most recognized typologies distinguishes four types of robbers.

Professional Robbers

Professional robbers have a long-term commitment to crime given it is their major source of income. They commit their first armed robberies in their mid-teens and continue their "careers" for more than a decade. A high degree of planning and organization is involved in their crimes. Some specialize in robbery to the exclusion of other offenses, and others engage in a variety of crimes. Professional robbers steal because it is direct, fast, and can be extremely profitable. They often have no legitimate source of income but rely instead on three or four "big scores" a year to support their hedonistic lifestyles. Armed and dangerous, they target commercial establishments, especially banks, and operate in groups that have clearly defined roles and duties designed to reduce the risk of apprehension and increase profitability. The average "take" in a professional robbery is $1,000 to $5,000 higher than other types of robbery.

Opportunist Robbers

The most common type of robber is the opportunist robber. Often young and from lower-class environments, opportunists prey in bands on less lucrative, more vulnerable targets, such as cab drivers, drunks, and the elderly. They do not specialize in robbery but instead engage in a variety of criminal activities and rob only when the opportunity presents itself.

Consequently, there is little planning or organization in robberies committed by this type of criminal.

Addict Robbers

Addict robbers steal to support their drug habits. They have a low commitment to robbery because of the danger involved and are generally more likely to commit nonviolent crimes to obtain money, such as burglary or larceny. Like the opportunist, their robberies are not well planned and tend to target victims that present a minimum of risk. They are less likely than professionals to use weapons and rarely commit robberies in groups. Consequently, the addict robber is more likely to resort to physical force as a means of intimidating the victim into submission.

Alcoholic Robbers

Like opportunists and addicts, alcoholic robbers have little commitment to robbery or a criminal lifestyle, nor do they carefully plan out their crimes. Often, their alcoholism has rendered them unemployable and without the few dollars needed to support their alcohol addiction. As they attempt to get money to buy more liquor, the alcoholic robber, unlike the addict robber, is frequently intoxicated at the time of the offense. For that reason, alcoholic robbers are more likely to be apprehended than the other types.

OFFENDER PROFILE

Developing an offender profile in robberies is problematic for two reasons. First, a large number of robberies committed each year go unreported to police. According to the NCVS, in 2000, only 56% of robbery victims reported their victimization to law enforcement. Second, a majority of robberies that are reported do not result in an arrest; the national clearance rate for robbery in 2000 (the proportion of all reported robberies that resulted in someone being arrested, charged, and turned over for prosecution) was 26%. On the other hand, arrest reports do provide information about the characteristics of those arrested for robbery.

The sociodemographic profile of robbers provided by arrest reports is similar to that of violent offenders in general. Males are far more likely than females to be arrested for robbery, representing approximately

90% of all arrests for the offense. Gender differences in robbery have remained relatively stable over the past several decades. More than half of those arrested for robbery were African American, and this proportion has also remained stable over the last three decades. As in crime generally, robbery is committed disproportionately by young people; nearly two thirds of those arrested for robbery were less than 25 years old. Juveniles (under age 18) accounted for 6% of all robbery arrests in 2000. Although social class is not reported in arrest reports included in the UCR, the vast majority of those arrested for robbery are from the lower economic classes in urban areas. Court records compiled in large urban jurisdictions show that almost two thirds of robbery defendants have prior felony arrests. Moreover, robbery defendants are more likely than those charged with murder, rape, or aggravated assault to have prior criminal histories.

VICTIM PROFILE

The NCVS provides information concerning the characteristics of robbery victims and reveals a profile similar to that of robbery offenders. Like perpetrators, the victims of robbery are more likely to be young, poor, urban males. According to 2000 statistics, males were robbed at rates 125% greater than females, and individuals aged 20 to 24 were more than 3 times as likely to be robbery victims than persons aged 50 to 64. Robbery rates for African Americans were more than 250% higher than those for whites and 150% higher than for Hispanics. Persons in households with annual incomes of less than $7,500 had a rate of robbery victimization nearly 4 times that of individuals in households with annual incomes of $75,000 or more. Finally, urban residents in 2000 had a robbery victimization rate more than 3 times that of residents in the suburbs and nearly 5 times that of rural residents.

NCVS data from 2000 further show that more than two thirds of all robbery victims had no prior relationships with the robbers. In fact, compared with other violent crimes, robbery was the least likely to be committed by an acquaintance or family member. Robberies in which the victim was also engaging in crime activity (e.g., the robbery of a prostitute or a drug dealer) are least likely to be reported, so rates of robbery among nonstrangers are probably higher than police arrest data indicate.

SITUATIONAL DYNAMICS IN ROBBERY

Temporal and Geographical Correlates

Robberies are more common at certain times of the day and year. The majority of personal robberies occur during the daylight hours; however, those involving firearms or knives occur more frequently at night. According to the 2000 UCR, the highest robbery rates for the year were recorded in October and December.

Weapons

Reported robberies in 2000 almost equally involved firearms (40.9%) and strong-armed tactics (40.4%). Knives or other cutting instruments were used in approximately 8% of robberies. In 10% of robberies, some other weapon was used, such as a screwdriver, lug wrench, shovel, or pool cue. Rather than being carried specifically for the purpose of committing a robbery, these weapons were simply handy when the opportunity for the robbery presented itself. Since 1980, the proportion of robberies involving firearms has remained relatively stable.

Victim Death and Injury

There were 1,048 robbery-related homicides in 2000. Though this is a disturbing statistic, the number of robbery-homicides has consistently and dramatically declined since the early 1990s. In 1993, for example, 2,305 murders occurred during robberies. The vast majority (86%) of robbery-homicides in 2000 involved a firearm, usually a handgun. Victims sustain physical injuries in roughly 1 out of every 4 robberies. These injuries include sexual assault, knife or gunshot wounds, and broken bones and bruises; nearly 10% of robbery victims require hospital care. Injury appears to be more likely in robberies in which victims resist the offenders.

Co-Offending Patterns

Robberies are more likely than other violent crimes to involve multiple offenders. According to the NCVS, about 1 in 5 violent victimizations in 1999 involved more than one offender. However, multiple offenders were involved in more than 40% of robberies that year. In robberies involving multiple offenders, victims generally identified offenders as black males between the ages of 12 and 20.

Alcohol and Drug Use

National data indicate that more than half of those arrested for robbery report being under the influence of drugs and/or alcohol at the time of the offense. More than one quarter of those convicted and sentenced to prison for robbery report having committed their crimes to buy drugs, a rate similar to that reported by inmates convicted of property offenses.

CONCLUSION

Robbery is a crime that has elements of both violent crime and property crime. Though it takes a variety of forms, robbery offenders are disproportionately poor, minority, urban males who typically prey on the innocent, the vulnerable, and those least likely to offer resistance. Though the rate of robbery has declined over the past decade, robbery continues to be a major source of public fear, a contributor to urban decay, and an intractable problem for the criminal justice system.

—*Richard C. McCorkle*
and Terance D. Miethe

See also Uniform Crime Reports; Victimology

Further Reading

Conklin, J. (1972). *Robbery and the criminal justice system.* Philadelphia: Lippincott.

Feeney, F. (1986). Robbers as decision-makers. In D. B. Cornish & R. V. Clarke (Eds.), *The reasoning criminal: Rational choice perspectives on offending* (pp. 53-71). New York: Springer-Verlag.

Gabor, T., Baril, M., Cusson, M., Elie, D., Lablanc, M., & Normandeau, A. (1987). *Armed robbery: Cops, robbers, and victims.* Springfield, IL: Charles C Thomas.

Katz, J. (1988). *Seductions of crime: Moral and sensual attractions in doing evil.* New York: Basic Books.

Miethe, T. D., & McCorkle, R. C. (2001). *Crime profiles: The anatomy of dangerous persons, places, and situations* (2nd ed.). Los Angeles: Roxbury.

Wright, R. T., & Decker, S. H. (1997). *Armed robbers in action: Stickups and street culture.* Boston: Northeastern University Press.

RUDOLPH, ERIC ROBERT, *See* FBI Top 10 Most Wanted Program; Olympic Park Bombing; Profiling

RUPPERT, JAMES, *See* Mass Murder

RUSSIAN RIPPER, *See* Chikatilo, Andrei; Serial Murder

RWANDAN GENOCIDE, *See* Genocide

S

SACRIFICIAL KILLING

The study of sacrificial killing can be traced back to the hunting rituals of early *homo sapiens*. The actor feels as though it is necessary to kill, although he nevertheless feels guilty for his actions. The slaughter is believed to provide sustenance, which brings pleasure, and thus the killing is celebrated as a renewed affirmation of life. The basic structure of the sacrificial killing is triadic: (a) sacralization in preparation for the act, (b) the "unspeakable act" itself, and (c) joyous reaffirmation of life, which often involves a sacred feast and symbolic reconstitution of the victim through "trophies," commonly displayed on the sanctuary. The concept of sacrificial killing is often spoken of with regard to ritualistic abuse and satanic practices. Since the 1984 McMartin preschool case in Manhattan Beach, California, discussions regarding ritual abuse and sacrificial killing have become more commonplace, although such allegations are often unfounded, and statistics suggest that this type of behavior is much more private than collective.

See also CULTS

SADISM, *See* PARAPHILIA

SALDIVAR, EFREN ("ANGEL OF DEATH"), *See* POISONING: MEDICAL SETTINGS

SANITY, TEST FOR, *See* BRAWNER TEST; COURT-ORDERED PSYCHOLOGICAL ASSESSMENT; M'NAUGHTEN RULE; MENTALLY DISORDERED OFFENDERS; NOT GUILTY BY REASON OF INSANITY (NGRI)

SATANIC GROUPS

Satanism and satanic cults are not new phenomena. For centuries, individuals and groups have professed allegiance to and belief in the entity described in the Bible as Satan. This entity is generally acknowledged as a being or metaphysical force that can be called on by ritual or is an innate part of every human. In early times, bad luck or inappropriate behavior was often blamed on "Satan worship," by which the unfortunate individual had been cursed or possessed. The charge of "Devil worshipper" was also used as a convenient means to do away with enemies or rivals.

Satanism has persevered as an alternative belief system. Those professing to be "satanists" do not have a standardized belief system. Some believe that all that exists is the "here and now" and that people must get all their enjoyment from the moment; others believe that by the proper practices they can receive favors; and still others use their belief in Satan as an excuse for violence and antisocial behavior.

Research has indicated that the largest concentration of satanists exists within the United States. The increased use of the Internet has allowed many groups to put their messages before a larger audience than ever before. In addition, media attention has brought recognition to some cults, such as the largest organized group, the Church of Satan.

Anton Szandor LaVey, who wrote two of the most important texts of the modern satanic movement, established this sect in the United States in 1966. His first book, *The Satanic Bible* (1969), postulates that Satan favors indulgence over abstinence and revenge over forbearance, and claims that man is no better than any other animal. He later wrote *The Satanic Rituals* (1972), which outlined rites created to attack or blaspheme Christian beliefs, while exalting the "self" and rejecting accepted social and ethical norms. According to LaVey (1969), members worship the trinity of the devil, Lucifer, Satan, and the Devil, according to the nine pronouncements:

1. Satan represents indulgence, instead of abstinence!
2. Satan represents vital existence, instead of spiritual pipe dreams!
3. Satan represents undefiled wisdom instead of hypocritical self-deceit!
4. Satan represents kindness to those who deserve it, instead of love wasted on ingrates!
5. Satan represents vengeance, instead of turning the other cheek!
6. Satan represents responsibility, instead of concern for the psychic vampires!
7. Satan represents man as just another animal, sometimes better, more often worse, than those who walk on all fours, who because of his divine and intellectual development has become the most vicious of all!
8. Satan represents all of the so-called sins, as they lead to physical, mental or emotional gratification.
9. Satan has been the best friend the church has ever had, as he has kept it in business all these years! (p. 25)

The notion of "satanic rites" has always captured the imagination of the public. Some say these are merely gestures and words adapted to the needs of every practitioner, but others claim that there are indeed standardized ceremonial rites. These practices have been rumored to include ritual sacrifice of animals or humans, torture, communing with supernatural beings, violent "Black Sabbaths," and ritualized sexual abuse. Some authorities have estimated that as many as 10,000 murders each year might be attributed to satanic rituals, and ritualized sexual abuse has garnered much interest in recent years.

Throughout the 1980s, individuals who claimed to have suffered at the hands of satanists wrote descriptions of their experiences, including lurid practices such as women being forced to be breeders of babies that were later sacrificed. Despite, or because of, their gruesome tales, most of these books became best sellers. The truth, however, is that if such groups do exist and carry out tortures and murders, they are unknown to law enforcement. The results of a 1994 national study conducted by the National Center on Child Abuse and Neglect in the United States examined 11,000 psychiatric and police workers and found over 12,000 accusations of group cult sexual abuse using satanic rituals. They found that not one of those cases involved satanic groups in which children were abused or killed. There were a few cases of individual self-styled satanic activities but most of the reports were simply false.

A few serial killers who were self-styled satanists and dabbled in satanic rituals include Donald Harvey, who murdered 58 victims in hospitals. Harvey was found with books on Satan worship. Richard Ramirez, the Night Stalker in California, liked to shout "Hail Satan!" when exiting court and displayed a pentagram tattooed on his left palm. He often inscribed satanic symbols in the homes of victims. Henry Lee Lucas alleged his involvement with Satan worship by kidnapping children to be used for human sacrifices. No proof of this was ever found. Robin Gecht and his three followers mutilated and killed young women in the Chicago area in the 1980s. They claimed to have cut up human body parts for sacrifice on an altar and cannibalized some of the remains. Robert Berdella of Kansas City admitted in 1989 to the ritual tortures and homosexual murders of several young men but denied Satan worship even though there was evidence to the contrary.

—*Denise Nola-Faye Lowe*

See also CULTS; RAMIREZ, RICHARD; VAMPIRES, WEREWOLVES, AND WITCHES

Further Reading

Hickey, E. W. (2002). *Serial murderers and their victims* (3rd ed.). Thousand Oaks, CA: Wadsworth.

LaVey, A. (1969). *The satanic bible.* New York: Avon Publishers.

Mmasi, A. S. (1998). *Satanic tortures.* Dar es Salaam University Press.

The New York Times. (1994, October 31). Study belies reports of satanic network.

Victor, J. S. (1993). *Satanic panic: The creation of a contemporary legend.* Open Court Publisher.

SCHOOL SHOOTINGS

School shootings have become a major social issue in the United States over the past decade. High-profile events such as the shootings that occurred in Jonesboro, Arkansas, and Littleton, Colorado, have resulted in extensive media coverage and intense public scrutiny, and one of the largest policy crises ever faced. This phenomenon has not been limited to the United States. Shooting incidents in Dublane, Scotland, where 16 students and one teacher were killed, and more recently Erfurt, Germany, with the killing of 14 teachers and two students, are examples of the expansion of this problem around the world.

PREVALENCE OF SCHOOL VIOLENCE

In American schools over the past few decades, the education of youth has in some sense become secondary. With the increasing frequency of violent behavior in school settings, a larger concern among administrators, parents, and students is the question of safety, even if time and resources given to violence prevention does divert focus from the educational process itself. A survey of more than 15,000 teenagers in 2000 concludes that 39% of middle schoolers and 36% of high schoolers, or more than 1 in 3 students, report not feeling safe at school (Josephson Institute on Ethics, 2001).

Victimization "at school" includes crimes occurring inside the school building, on school property, or on the way to or from school. *Nonfatal crimes* include theft and simple assault and serious violent crimes such as rape, sexual assault, robbery, and aggravated assault. *Fatal crime* refers to homicide.

In 1992, a total of 3,409,230 nonfatal crimes against students aged 12 to 18 occurred at school, or 144 per 1,000; but in 1998, that number dropped to a total of 2,715,600, or 101 per 1,000. Looking solely at the total number of crimes, it might appear that schools were actually becoming safer places. However, it is important to examine the various crime categories separately. Theft alone decreased from 2,260,500 in 1992

to 1,562,300 in 1998, but comparing the data for violent crimes across the same period, the reverse trend emerges: 1,148,600 and 1,153,000 incidents, respectively. Similarly, serious violent crime over the years continued to increase from 245,400 in 1992 to 252,700 in 1998 (Kaufman et al., 2000; Small & Tetrick, 2001).

School violence was once believed to be a problem plaguing the urban areas, but the reality is that these types of behavior have infiltrated schools located in many settings. For instance, in 1998, the rate of victimization for nonfatal crimes per 1,000 students aged 12 to 18 in urban schools was 117 per 1,000; for suburban schools, 97; and for rural schools, 93 (Kaufman et al., 2000).

All forms of school violence are serious, but shooting incidents have captured the attention of the media and society. Although the majority of school violence does not result in fatalities, the use of firearms increases the probability that an incident will result in lethality. Between the school years 1992 to 1993 and the first half of the 2001 to 2002 school year (August through December), there were 283 events resulting in 326 school-related violent deaths, which included homicides, suicides, or weapons-related deaths. These events occurred on the property of private, public, parochial, elementary, secondary, and alternative schools, on the way to or from school, while attending or on the way to or from school-sponsored events, or as direct results of school incidents, functions, or activities on or off school property. Offenders used varying methods in these lethal acts. Shootings accounted for 75% of all the deaths; stab/slashing, 14%; beating/kicking, 5%; and 2% each for hanging, strangling/asphyxiation, and unknown methods (National School Safety Center, 2002).

In homicides, firearm usage was the single most frequently used weapon. For example, from 1992 to 2001, 60% of intentional deaths involved the use of a firearm. In many ways, violent deaths occurring in schools mirror the general trends in youth violence. According to the Supplemental Homicide Report, up until 1988, the proportion of juvenile homicide victimizations involving firearms was less than 50%. Beginning in 1988, that proportion started moving upward, reaching a high of 65.3% in 1993. Similarly, by the 1990s, the number of juvenile offenders using firearms in the commission of homicides was more than triple that of those offenders using some other weapon.

Males were 77% of those victimized. The most common identifiable motive was interpersonal disputes (25%); suicides accounted for 18%; 11% were gang-related; and the motive was unknown in 29%. Other motives such as hate crimes, robbery, sexually motivated, and bullying accounted for a combined total of 12%. Accidental deaths accounted for only 5%. This data shows that two thirds of violent school deaths were intentional (National School Safety Center, 2002).

SCHOOL VIOLENCE AS MULTIPLE HOMICIDES

Prior to the 1990s, school shootings were mainly concentrated in the urban settings and frequently centered around gang activity. In fact, rates of violent victimization are substantially higher in large, inner-city high schools. However, by 1993, that trend appeared to change dramatically with a series of shootings occurring on the grounds of non-inner-city schools. Beginning with a hostage-taking incident in Grayson, Kentucky, in 1993, and culminating in the Columbine High School massacre in Littleton, Colorado, in 1999, these shootings increased in notoriety as they progressed.

The heightened attention around these events was primarily due to the fact that several shootings resulted in multiple victimizations, and in some cases, multiple homicide. From 1992 to 2001, 25 of the 283 school-related violent deaths mentioned above involved multiple-homicide victims. In general, school-associated violent deaths are rare events and even less commonly end in multiple homicides. However, from 1992 to 1999, while the total number of school-associated violent deaths declined, there was a 42% increase in shootings that resulted in multiple homicides (Anderson et al., 2001).

A brief overview of some of these events will illustrate the significance of this trend. On January 18, 1993 in Grayson, Kentucky, 19-year-old Scott Pennington held a custodian and teacher hostage and then shot and killed them both. On February 2, 1996, at Frontier Junior High School, in Moses Lake, Washington, 16-year-old Barry Loukaitis shot and fatally killed two students and one teacher with a rifle. The incident that really brought school shootings to the forefront of American society occurred the following fall in Pearl, Mississippi, when Luke Woodham, age 16, shot and killed his former girlfriend and two other

students and wounded seven at Pearl High School on October 1, 1997. Woodham was allegedly upset about the break-up of his relationship, and this was an extension of a murderous plot that began at home with the stabbing death of his mother.

A few months later, Michael Carneal, age 14, shot and killed three students and wounded five other persons on December 1, 1997, at Health High School, in West Paducah, Kentucky. One of the most startling incidents was that of the mass ambush at West Side Middle School on March 24, 1998, in Jonesboro, Arkansas. Andrew Golden, 11 years old, and his 13-year-old cousin, Mitchell Johnson, pulled a fire alarm at the school and waited outside behind a fence. As students and administrators exited the building, the two boys began firing. At the end of the rampage, four students and one teacher were dead, and 10 others wounded. During this same school year, Kipland Kinkel, age 15, entered Thurston High School, in Springfield, Oregon, killing two students and wounding another 21. This incident began at the Kinkel residence, where Kip first carried out his homicidal tendency by killing both his parents before going to school.

The worst school shooting ever in United States history took place on April 20, 1999. On that date, Columbine High School, in Littleton, Colorado, was the scene of the murderous rampage carried out by Eric Harris, age 18, and Dylan Klebold, age 17, which resulted in 13 people dead and another 20 wounded. (See Table 1.)

SCHOOL SHOOTINGS AS IMITATIVE ACTS

Although shootings in school are rare and multiple homicides even more so, they attract a great deal of public attention. The media is drawn to these high-profile cases and gives them considerable coverage, in which the public learns not only the basic information but also details as to how such crimes are carried out. This attention, notoriety, and dissemination of information may well incite others to consider engaging in similar violent acts. From such depictions, some may see the offenders as heroes, fighting back for what they felt was mistreatment or injustice. Viewers may be able to relate to the offender's situation and draw some parallels to their own lives. The ability to identify with the offenders makes it more likely that other individuals may consider committing identical or similar acts. Most of the incidents of school shootings

Table 1   Selected School Shooting Incidents

Date	Offender(s)	Age	Location	Number Killed	Number Wounded
January 18, 1993	Scott Pennington	17	Grayson, KY	2	0
February 1, 1993	Shem McCoy	17	Amityville, NY	1	1
October 12, 1995	Toby Sincino	16	Blackville, SC	1	1
November 15, 1995	Jamie Rouse	17	Lynnville, TN	2	1
February 2, 1996	Barry Loukaitis	16	Moses Lake, WA	3	1
February 19, 1997	Evan Ramsey	16	Bethel, AK	2	2
October 1, 1997	Luke Woodham	16	Pearl, MS	2*	7
December 1, 1997	Michael Carneal	14	West Paducah, KY	3	5
December 15, 1997	Joseph Todd	14	Stamps, AR	2	0
March 24, 1998	Mitchell Johnson & Andrew Golden	13 & 11	Jonesboro, AR	5	10
May 21, 1998	Kip Kinkel	15	Springfield, OR	2*	21
April 20, 1999	Eric Harris & Dylan Klebold	18 & 17	Littleton, CO	13	20

involved offenders who were socially marginal students who either retaliated after being bullied in some way or were seeking vengeance for other interpersonal disputes.

The exposure and subsequent imitation of acts has been described as the "copycat effect." Over the past several years, criminologists have revisited this in relation to crimes occurring in public places (especially schools). The origin of "copycat crime" has roots dating back to the 1800s. A modern view of this phenomenon is as follows:

> For a crime to be defined as a copycat crime there must be a generating impetus from an earlier publicized crime—a media-linked pair of crimes must exist. The perpetrators of copycat crimes must have been exposed to the publicity of an original initial crime and have incorporated major elements into their crimes. The nature, choice of victim, motivation, or technique of a copycat crime must be lifted from earlier media-portrayed crime. (Surette, 1990, p. 88)

Copycat crime has been attributed to a process of simple and direct imitation generated by observation-based social learning. Taking into consideration that all persons are not exposed directly to violence in their daily lives, observation of violence in the media is one way to "learn" both methods and techniques. Thus, imitating these horrific acts does not merely depend on a degree of emotional association by the offender but also the knowledge of how to carry out the act. Individuals are also more inclined to mimic behavior if they perceive that there are no negative consequences imposed for the actions.

PROBLEMS WITH DATA SOURCES

There may well be connections between various school shooting incidents and many commonalities among offenders, but the lack of a comprehensive data source means that these relationships cannot be empirically tested. The context and extent of school shootings and school violence in general is a difficult topic to study. Most of the information available is derived from media sources, newspaper accounts in particular. These sources of data are limited by the method of collection and lack reliability and validity checks. At present, there is no comprehensive source containing information on all types of school violence incidents.

What we do know as to the specific offense is derived from the Federal Bureau of Investigation's Uniform Crime Report (UCR), yet details are lacking. The Supplemental Homicide Reports lack any indication on the location of homicide events. The National Incident-Based Reporting System (NIBRS) will eventually remedy the shortcoming, but it is years away from full implementation. Other annual reports such as Indicators of School Crime and Safety provide accounts of different victimizations yet lack details on relationships between victims and offenders. School-Associated Violent Deaths reports provide us with useful information on incidents resulting in fatalities but not on nonlethal acts. The National Crime Victimization Survey (NCVS; an annual survey conducted by the Bureau of Justice Statistics in conjunction with the U.S. Census Bureau) begins to identify the nature and extent of the problem, but this, too, has its limitations. For example, because it is based on a sample of the U.S. population and relies on self-reports of victimization experiences, the overall incident level still goes undetermined.

These measures provide us with both offender and victimization data, but they still do not adequately capture the nature and extent of the problem. What is needed is a method of recording and reporting that conveys information about context, nature, and traits of both victims and offenders.

—*Janice E. Clifford Wittekind
and Thomas A. Petee*

See also COLUMBINE/LITTLETON SCHOOL SHOOTING; JONESBORO, ARKANSAS, SCHOOL SHOOTING; MASS MURDER; MEDIA, VIOLENCE IN THE

Further Reading

Anderson, M., Kaufmann, J., Sims, T., Barrios, L., Paulozzi, L., Ryan, G., Hammond, R., Modzeleski, W., Feucht, T., & Potter, L. (2001). School-associated violent deaths in the United States, 1994-1999. *Journal of the American Medical Association, 286,* 2698-2706.

Federal Bureau of Investigation. (2000). *Crime in the United States: Uniform crime report, 1999.* Available on the World Wide Web at: http://www.fbi.gov/ucr/99cius.htm.

Kaufman, P., Chen, X., Choy, S., Ruddy, S., Miller, A., Fleruy, J., Chandler, K., Klaus, P., & Planty, M. (2000). *Indicators of school crime and safety, 2000* (NCES2001-017NCJ-184176). Washington, DC: GPO.

National School Safety Center. (2002). *School associated violent deaths.* Available on the World Wide Web at: http://www.nssc1.org.

Small, M., & Tetrick. K. (2001). School violence: An overview. *Juvenile Justice,* 8(1). Washington, DC: GPO.

Surette, R. (1990). *The media and criminal justice policy.* Springfield, IL: Charles C Thomas.

SCOTTSBORO CASE

In 1939, nine African American teenagers were accused of gang-raping two white women while riding on a Southern Railroad freight train. The case, which was tried in Alabama and spanned nearly two decades, produced more trials, convictions, appeals, reversals, and retrials than any other case in American history. The teens, largely unacquainted with one another, came to be collectively known as the "Scottsboro Boys." Through the course of the legal proceedings, it became evident that the women alleging the rape were lying, but despite evidence supporting this notion, many of the teens were convicted. It has been suggested that the women made the accusations in an attempt to deflect attention away from their promiscuous lifestyles; they engaged in adultery and often resorted to prostitution for extra money.

The case had become a financial burden on the State of Alabama, and as a result, charges were dropped against four of the defendants. By this time, they had already served 6 years awaiting trial. The other five defendants were found guilty but over the course of time made their way out of Alabama, either through paroles or escapes. The case had many social and political ramifications and exemplified the extent of racism during the Depression Era. All nine men have since died, the last one in 1989.

—*Robyn L. Williams*

See also RACIAL PROFILING

Further Reading

Carter, D. T. (1979). *Scottsboro: A tragedy of the American South.* Baton Rouge: Louisiana State University Press.

Goodman, J. E. (1995). *Stories of Scottsboro.* New York: Vintage Books.

Linder, D. O. (2002, July). *The trials of "The Scottsboro Boys."* Available on the World Wide Web at: http://www.devrycols.edu/Bus/scottsboro.htm.

SELF-DEFENSE, ACTIONS TAKEN IN

Modern societies prohibit private citizens from resolving conflicts with violence, expecting them to call on the law enforcement branch of government for protection. However, the police cannot be within reach 24 hours a day, and when in the midst of true and immediate peril, individuals may sometimes be justified in meeting force with force. This rightful use of protective violence is called *self-defense* and is recognized by all 50 U.S. states and the federal government. The term is not limited to its obvious meaning, "defense of self." The legal community also uses self-defense to describe the defense of others and even property, though the rules defining acceptable defense of others and property vary somewhat from the rules for defense of self, as will be explained.

A successful plea of self-defense usually results in acquittal of all charges, because our society deems that citizens who are forced into violent defense have done no wrong. Thus, self-defense is said to be a "complete" or "perfect" defense. Conversely, "imperfect" defenses, such as "the heat of passion" defense to murder, result in lesser charges or sentences in recognition that although the perpetrator's act was wrongful, circumstances reduce blameworthiness and call for leniency. A citizen's decision to deflect danger with violence is usually made instantaneously, but society's subsequent inquiry into the merits of that decision is time-consuming and difficult. Law enforcement personnel and juries must manipulate a number of complicated and varying rules, while envisioning the confrontation from the perspective of the average man on the street as well as the defender's perspective. The exact rules vary from state to state, but the majority of U.S. jurisdictions require law enforcement to consider the following.

ELEMENTS OF SELF-DEFENSE

1. Honest Belief: Did the alleged defender honestly believe she/he was in danger?

When threatened, citizens must not respond with force unless they honestly believe the threats will otherwise be carried out. Anyone claiming self-defense must prove that they truly and honestly believed they were in danger. This requires jurors to evaluate the veracity of alleged defenders' assertions that they believed force was necessary for protection, a subjective inquiry.

Imagine a hypothetical world in which a heavyweight boxing champion knocked out his girlfriend (for this purposes, "Rose"), then claimed that he'd had to do so to keep her from beating him up. At his trial for battery, the jury would weigh the champion's assertion that he honestly believed Rose was about to seriously injure him against the facts that Rose, a petite Size 2, had no weapons or training in self-defense and no prior history of violence, whereas the Champ was a hugely muscled boxer with a reputation of criminal violence toward women and a prior conviction for rape. Under such circumstances, the jury would most likely conclude that the Champ's claim was a lie, an instance of blaming the victim for his own explosive temper.

2. Reasonable Belief: Did the alleged defender reasonably believe the danger was real?

The law of self-defense evinces society's expectation that citizens will exercise a certain degree of wisdom and common sense. To excuse a violent response, the belief that one is in danger must not only be honest, it must also be reasonable. This requires the jury to assess not just whether the alleged defender actually believed he was in danger, a subjective test, but also whether a reasonable person under similar circumstances would have believed the danger was real, an objective test.

Thus, in the earlier hypothetical, even if the jury believed the Champ's claim that he honestly feared for his life when he hit his girlfriend, the jury might still disregard his claim of self-defense if under the circumstances, no reasonable person would have believed the danger was real. If at the Champ's battery trial, witnesses testified that Rose's punches were actually weak flailings born of frustration with no real intent to injure, the jury would be free to convict the Champ, concluding that his fears, though honest, would not have been shared by reasonable people.

3. Dangerous Attack: Was the attack serious enough to warrant violence in response?

Jurisdictions vary as to which threatened crimes warrant lethal defense, but all agree that a victim may meet threats of death or serious bodily injury, often defined as injury requiring hospitalization, with responsive violence and even deadly force. Threat of sexual assault, armed robbery, kidnapping, and other dangerous felonies are also considered sufficient cause to resist with violence by most, if not all, jurisdictions, though some states would require the victim to stop short of lethal force.

4. Imminent Harm: Was the danger immediate?

Use of force to thwart threats of future attack is generally not justified self-defense. If there is time and opportunity, citizens are expected to seek help from the authorities. Thus, to escape punishment, people who defend with force must prove imminent danger, that is, that they were forced to use violence because they were under attack or a threat was on the verge of being carried out. Absent such imminence, U.S. jurisdictions universally disallow virtually all claims of self-defense, with the possible exception of the "battered-woman defense" discussed below.

If a woman ran after a man with a knife, screaming, "When I catch you, you're dead meat," the man might well be justified in defending himself to the death because the threat of danger is imminent. On the other hand, if for example, an Olympic gymnast said to her panel of judges, "I'll kill each and every one of you tomorrow if you don't give me perfect scores," and the judges immediately beat her, their violence would not be excused. Her threat was of future, not imminent, harm, so the judges had plenty of time obtain police protection, as required by law.

5. Reasonable Force in Response: Did the alleged defender use a reasonable amount of force in response to the threat?

Assuming that violence is justified in self-defense, there are still limits as to the amount of force one may use. The degree of response must reasonably address the degree of threat, and one whose responsive force unreasonably upped the ante as to degree of resultant injury may find himself or herself in prison.

For example, if a supervisor started slapping at an employee, the employee might be allowed to defend himself in some manner, but certainly not by using undue force, however much he might wish to. Anything more than a blocking action or perhaps a few minor defensive slaps would vitiate the self-defense claim and result in criminal conviction. In other words, it is not reasonable to kill or maim someone to stop them from inflicting a minor hurt. The degree of force allowed by law is not formulaic; evaluation is done on a case-by-case basis in light of all the attendant facts. However, one rule is fairly well etched in stone: Deadly force to defend against a nondeadly attack is generally disallowed. (See "Deadly Force" discussion below.)

6. Nonaggressor: Was the alleged defender a nonaggressor?

As a general rule, a self-defense claim is invalid if the alleged defender started the fight. Two exceptions to this rule are worth noting: First, if the initial aggressor completely withdraws from the fight and is then attacked by the "victim," self-defense may be

warranted. For example, a man gets angry and punches his son-in-law in the nose and then says, "Oops, sorry, I lost my head," and walks away. If the son-in-law chases the man and knocks him down, the father-in-law might be justified in fighting back even though he had initiated the incident.

Second, an initial aggressor's claim of self-defense might be accepted if his "victim" so escalated the fight that the aggressor had no choice but to defend with increased force. For example, if Rudy pinches Margaret and Margaret responds by mercilessly striking at Rudy's chest with a knife, Rudy would probably be justified in pulling out a gun.

OTHER SELF-DEFENSE ISSUES

Deadly Force

Though our laws recognize a limited right to meet violence with violence, in most instances, the responsive violence must stop short of deadly force. However, all jurisdictions recognize an exception when the defender reasonably believes that the attacker is about to inflict unlawful death or serious bodily harm, and many jurisdictions also allow the use of deadly force to belay kidnapping, rape, and other extreme intrusions on one's freedom and sense of inviolability. But may a victim use deadly force to defend against such crimes if he or she could safely run instead? Most jurisdictions say yes. A minority of states say no, however, citing the strong national policy against the unnecessary taking of human life. This minority rule, known as the *retreat doctrine*, holds that if we safely can, we must run from our attacker and obtain police protection rather than use deadly force.

Note that retreat is required only in a minority of jurisdictions and only in lieu of deadly force; all jurisdictions allow use of non–deadly force in self-defense despite full and safe avenues of escape. And even jurisdictions requiring retreat in lieu of deadly force make an exception when people are attacked in their own homes or places of business. This is known as the *castle exception* to the retreat doctrine.

The Self-Defense Ruse

Sometimes parties claim self-defense when in fact they orchestrated the confrontation so that they could use violence while appearing blameless. Obviously, this is not lawful self-defense. For example, Ezekiel, the schoolyard bully, snatched Jacob's basketball right in front of all their friends. When Jacob protested, Ezekiel got in his face and said, "What're ya gonna do about it? Huh? Huh? What's the matter? You chicken?" Ezekiel kept up these taunts until Jacob finally punched him. Now Ezekiel is happy because he has his excuse to pummel Jacob. Or so he thinks. The law would not protect Ezekiel, because his behavior and taunting words were an obvious ruse. His claim of self-defense would be disregarded. It should be noted, however, that poor Jacob would be in trouble, too, because the law recognizes no right to use violence in defense of one's dignity. He should have walked away.

The Battered-Woman Defense

Despite commentary to the contrary, the law of self-defense has not been modified to allow battered women to get away with murder. The fact that the decedent spouse battered the defendant in the past does not automatically give rise to a valid claim of battered-woman self-defense. In fact, each of the statutory self-defense requirements must be met before the victim of abuse will be exonerated for the homicide of her abuser.

What distinguishes the battered-woman defense from other claims of self-defense is the manner of proving the reasonableness of the defendant's belief that death or serious bodily injury was imminent. Usually, the imminence requirement of self-defense means proving that death or serious bodily injury was actually being threatened by word or deed at the very moment self-defense was used. But in the case of the battered-woman defense, even if the decedent, typically a man, was not actively threatening the defendant, typically a woman, just before she slew him, she may be exonerated in states that recognize the defense if she can prove that her spouse's pattern of abuse gave rise to a reasonable belief that she had no safe avenue of long-term escape—in other words, that to leave him was to die. In a sense, the threat is imminent because it is a never-ending constant.

At trial, psychological experts are often called to testify regarding *battered-woman syndrome,* the result of a pattern of behavior typical of abusers. The abuser cyclically abuses his spouse both physically and psychologically, then begs, cajoles, and romances until he is forgiven, then beats and abuses again, repeating the violence/contrition over and over, meanwhile cutting the woman off from support of her friends and family and threatening to injure or kill her, her children, or her loved ones if she seeks help. Usually, before such a woman "takes the law into her own hands," she has sought the protection of law enforcement to no avail and been severely beaten for her efforts. Ultimately, she comes to feel completely isolated, unprotected, worthless, and hopeless, until in a desperate bid to escape his ever-threatening presence, she finally kills the man.

Not all jurisdictions recognize the battered-woman defense, contending that to exonerate anyone under such circumstances encourages lawlessness. The trend, however, is toward recognition of the defense, due largely to political pressure from women's advocacy groups and the media.

Resisting Unlawful Arrest

Interestingly, early American law adopted the English common law rule bestowing the right of citizens to violently resist arrest if that arrest was unlawful. For example, if the sheriff was mad at Eugene for flirting with his wife and decided to arrest Eugene on trumped-up charges, Eugene would be excused for fighting off the arrest. But the turbulent 1960s in the United States brought about the virtual demise of this unlawful arrest defense. Partially in response to nationwide protesters who resisted arrest during demonstrations on the grounds that the arrests were unlawful restraints of their right of free speech and expression, many states have now limited the right to resist unlawful arrest, pointing out that nonviolent remedies, such as writs of habeas corpus or private lawsuits, are available to right the wrong of illegal arrest.

Defense of Property and Other People

The term self-defense is used by the legal community to refer not only to the defense of oneself but also to the defense of others and of property as well, and the laws are in large part the same, regardless of whom or what the defender seeks to protect. Certain unique rules have been carved out for addressing defense of others or property, however.

Defense of Others

The modern majority view holds that when one person defends another, there need be no special relationship between the defender and the person he or she defends. However, a small minority of American jurisdictions hold to the long-discarded British rule allowing forceful defense of others only if the defender and the defended are relatives, employer/employee, or the like. Regardless, just as with self-defense, force in defense of others is not justified unless the defender reasonably believes that the one he or she is protecting is in imminent danger of unlawful bodily harm and that the force is necessary to prevent the harm. But what of the situation where the defender reasonably believes force is necessary when in fact it is not? For example, suppose a person inadvertently stumbles on a rape scene being filmed in the streets of Los Angeles? Will he be imprisoned if he rushes to save the "endangered" star and kills her costar "rapist" in the process?

The vast majority of jurisdictions would exonerate the defender in this situation as long as he reasonably believed the danger to the "victim" was real. A small number of states use the *alter ego rule*, holding that the defender has no more right to use force than the "victim" would; thus if the "victim" had no right to use force to defend herself, her defender would be criminally liable for forcefully defending her.

Defense of Property

Our legal system is less sympathetic toward those who use force to protect their property than to those who use force to protect themselves or others. Reasonable use of nonlethal force to protect property is acceptable under certain circumstances, but most, if not all, jurisdictions now hold that deadly force is never reasonable for the protection of mere property. Our society values human life above property. Some jurists would note that we sometimes do allow the use deadly force in defending against home invasions such as burglaries. However, this is not a defense-of-property issue. Deadly force to protect against home invasions is not justified unless the defender reasonably believes the force is necessary to protect the people within the home, not the home or property itself.

Mutual Combat

Sports such as boxing and ice hockey provide fodder for self-defense arguments. Though many sports are violent by their very nature, the violence is expected to be proportional and directed toward the aims of the sport. When a player's aggression outstrips the sport, his opponent may be excused for matching or escalating the violence in self-defense, assuming the usual elements of a self-defense claim are met. Consider the infamous boxing match in which Mike Tyson bit Evander Holyfield's ear. Was Tyson guilty of criminal assault and mayhem? Certainly, this behavior violates boxing etiquette. Suppose that in response, Holyfield had decimated Tyson with a powerful combination of below-the-belt blows? Would Holyfield have been legally excused? Maybe. Punching below the belt is disallowed under the rules of boxing, so Holyfield's hypothetical punches would result in criminal battery charges unless law enforcement officials believed he acted to protect himself, not in vengeful retaliation.

Injury to Third Parties

If, while defending ourselves from attack, we accidentally injure an innocent bystander, the law generally will not hold us criminally responsible. For example, when Bruno attacked Felix with a tire iron, Felix pulled out his .22 and shot at Bruno, but he missed and accidentally killed Mary Jane. Felix would probably be successful in claiming self-defense. If, however, the injury to innocent bystanders was caused not by a simple accident or mere negligence, but rather by a reckless disregard for the safety of others, the best result one could hope for would be a reduction of charges, not full acquittal. For example, when Hugo attacked Rocky with a butcher knife at a busy county fair, Rocky pulled out a machine gun and laid out an arc of fire, killing Hugo and 13 others. Rocky's response recklessly risked injury to people other than his attacker; he is guilty of involuntary manslaughter in the deaths of the innocent bystanders, though his slaying of his attacker was justified.

Finally, if defenders purposely kill innocent people to save themselves, they cannot successfully avail themselves of a self-defense claim at all. We cannot sacrifice others to save ourselves.

—*Victoria Hamilton*

See also BATTERED WOMAN'S SYNDROME; HOMICIDE, TYPES OF, AND DEGREES OF MURDER; SPORTS AND VIOLENCE

Further Reading

LaFave, W. R., & Scott, A. W. Jr. (1986). *Substantive criminal law, criminal practice series.* St. Paul, MN: West Publishing.

TOMMY LYNN SELLS

Tommy Lynn Sells killed several people before authorities finally caught up with him. Eventually, he would confess to killing 13 people in numerous states across the country, over an extended period of time.

Authorities label Sells as an unconventional murderer who doesn't fit the mold of a typical serial killer because his crimes fit no particular modus operandi. He has admitted to killing men, women, and children. Because he had no modus operandi, Sells was able to elude authorities for a long period of time. He appears to have been a killer of opportunity who drifted between different cities and states, using a variety of weapons to kill his victims.

Sells is reluctant to discuss information regarding his childhood. It is known that he was born on June 28, 1964, in Oakland, California. As a child, the family moved around frequently, and Sells was bounced from relative to relative, receiving an 8th-grade education. An admitted heavy drug and alcohol abuser, Sells often found work as a carnival worker, handyman, and day laborer.

Among the most horrific of his crimes was the 1987 slaying of an Illinois family. For 13 years, authorities had no leads or suspects. Sells admitted to befriending the husband, whom he met at a truck stop and invited home. The man's wife, who was 8 months pregnant at the time, and 3-year-old son were beaten to death with a baseball bat; in the process, the woman gave birth to a daughter, who was also killed. The husband was later found in a nearby field, having been shot in the head and sexually mutilated.

Prior to December 1999, Sells was careful to leave no evidence and no witnesses. However, he now sits on death row in Texas, charged with capital murder and attempted capital murder of two young girls in Del Rio, Texas. Once again, Sells had befriended the parents of one of the victims, whom he'd met at church. He knew from the father that there would not be a male at home on the night of the crime. One girl died almost instantly after he slashed her throat, and the other girl, who was also slashed but survived the ordeal, watched in horror as her friend was killed. She pretended to be dead until Sells left and she was able to run to a neighbor's house for help. Although her vocal cords had been severed with 12-inch boning knife, it didn't stop her from helping police to create a composite sketch of the suspect, which led authorities to Sells's capture. Within a few days, he was arrested at the home he shared with his wife and her four children. Once arrested, he quickly confessed to authorities about everyone he had killed.

Authorities from across the country want to question Sells concerning many unsolved homicide cases he has confessed to. It is also possible that he will stand trial and face capital murder charges for the 1999 sexual assault and murder of a 9-year-old San Antonio, Texas, girl, who disappeared during a local celebration, and whose body was discovered about a week later.

Sells admits that he can't resist the urge to kill.

—*Tatia J. Smith*

SEPTEMBER 11, 2001, ATTACKS ON THE UNITED STATES, *See* AERONAUTICAL MASS MURDER; BIN LADEN, OSAMA; MASS VIOLENCE; MEDIA, VIOLENCE IN THE; TERRORISM

SERIAL ARSON, *See* ORR, JOHN

SERIAL KILLERS, *See* SERIAL MURDER

SERIAL MURDER

Serial murder involves the killing of three or more victims over a period of days, weeks, months, or even years. The media focus attention on these crimes because they often appear to be so bizarre and extraordinary. They engender the kind of headlines that sell newspapers: "The Atlanta Child Killer," "The Stocking Strangler," "The Hillside Strangler," "The Sunday Morning Slasher," and "The Boston Strangler." The media focus not only on how many victims were killed but also on how they died. Thus, they feed morbid curiosity and at the same time create a stereotype of the typical serial killer: Ted Bundy, Ed Kemper, Albert DeSalvo, and a host of other young white males, attacking unsuspecting women powerless to defend themselves from the savage sexual attacks and degradations by these monsters.

Serial murder is undoubtedly one of the most terrifying and fascinating phenomena of modern-day violent crime. It is also one of the most sensationalized areas of research within the fields of criminology, psychology, and sociology. Philip Jenkins (1994), in his book *Using Murder: The Social Construction of Serial Murder,* provides a scholarly examination of how serial killing has been handled by the media, law enforcement, and the public. His findings are consistent with other writers: Much of what we "know" about serial murder is based on misinformation and myth construction. As a result of the sensational nature of this form of murder, the aura surrounding it has assumed a life of its own as it filters throughout both the public and private sectors of society.

In the summer of 1981, Wayne Williams, a young African American male believed to be one of the nation's more prolific serial killers, was arrested in the Atlanta area. This case brought to the forefront the fact that not all serial killers are white, nor are the victims. Technology, specifically hair and fiber evidence, became a critical factor in convicting Williams, and forensic science became prominent in explaining why such evidence ultimately played a key role in linking Williams to the crimes. More than 20 homicides were attributed to Williams, most of them children, although he was actually convicted of murdering just 2 victims. The horror and fascination of this case focused media attention on Atlanta both during the homicides and after Williams's capture.

Within the next 3 years, several more accounts of similar cases appeared in newspapers around the country. The American public had been invaded by a new criminal type: the serial murderer. Lurking in our communities and preying on hapless victims, serial murderers had suddenly emerged from the criminal underground, possibly a by-product of technology and the moral decay of our society. Most citizens simply assumed that serial killers must be insane, but no one knew for sure. The cases of serial murder increased, as did the body counts. Eventually, the growing reality of multiple murders began to obtrude on public awareness: Something had to be done to stem the tide of homicides with no apparent motive.

By the mid-1980s, no one knew how many serial killers actually existed at any one time, but certainly the number of victims killed by such offenders did not even begin to approach 5,000, a number promoted by the media. Where that inflated figure originated is a mystery. Perhaps a piece of information exchanged during an interview between the media and law enforcement had been misinterpreted. In any event, the number appeared and immediately sparked attention. As a result, some researchers began questioning the actual extent of serial murder.

The sensationalism of serial murder spawned a plethora of novels. Because of the wide publicity given to serial murderers, a stereotype of this type of killer has formed in the mind of American society: The offender is a ruthless, blood-thirsty sex monster who lives a Jekyll-and-Hyde existence—probably next door to you! Increasingly, crime novels and movies have focused on multiple-homicide offenders. Consider the steady proliferation of multiple-homicide films noted by Main (1997) in which serial killing is the primary agenda:

Decade	Number of Serial Murder Theme Films
1920s	2
1930s	3
1940s	3
1950s	4
1960s	12
1970s	20
1980s	23
1990s	117

Although this list is not exhaustive, it is representative of each decade. It does not include films involving mass murder (the killing of a number of people all at one time) or horror films depicting vampires and murderous zombies, but only films portraying real people murdering other people. Notice the explosion of serial murder themes during the 1990s. At least half of those never made it to theaters, but went straight to videos. In the privacy of one's home, viewers are bombarded with images of graphic killings, mutilations, and sexual torture. Clearly, this cinematic emphasis has added credibility to the notion of high body counts at the hands of ubiquitous serial killer monsters.

In his 1987 book, *The Red Dragon,* Harris gave a fictional account of a serial killer who took great pleasure in annihilating entire families. Later, his work was made into the movie *Manhunter,* an engrossing drama of psychopathology, blood, and carnage.

Harris's success eventually led, in 2002, to the remake of *Manhunter* in the new version, *The Red Dragon*. Between those movies, Harris's book *Silence of the Lambs* became a box office hit. Hollywood has only begun to realize the huge market for multiple-murder movies. By 2000, movies such as *Copycat, Kiss the Girls,* and the *Scream* trilogy continued to exploit the public's fascination with serial murder, without yielding much insight about offenders. Other films, such as *Seven,* a dark, disturbing movie, attempted to offer some understanding of the murdering mind but confused viewers with the concepts of psychopathy, psychosis, and murder.

Novelists such as Bret Easton Ellis, with his exploration of psychopathy, narcissism, sadism, and murder in *American Psycho* (later made into a movie by the same name) and Caleb Carr's acclaimed serial murder thriller, *The Alienist,* clearly indicate that writers are familiarizing themselves with the topic of serial murder and have begun to inject some insightful and historical perspectives into their narratives. The fictional accounts of serial killing, however, often fail to surpass the horror described in nonfictional accounts of serial murder by writers such as Ann Rule, a former acquaintance of the serial killer Ted Bundy, who was executed in January 1989. In addition to her work on Bundy (*The Stranger Beside Me,* 1980), she has written about Randy Woodfield (*The I-5 Killer,* 1984), Jerry Brudos (*Lust Killer,* 1983), and Harvey Carnigan (*The Want-Ad Killer,* 1988).

Amid this proliferation of murder movies, female serial killers have begun to attract attention in true-crime accounts of "Black Widows" (women who, for various reasons, kill their husbands, then remarry, only to carry out the cycle of homicide again and again); nurses who kill their elderly, young, or otherwise helpless patients; mothers who murder their children; females who assist men in serial killing; and a few women who have stalked and murdered men.

As a result of the case of Jeffrey Dahmer, serial murder began to be explored not merely as an act, but as a *process*. In 1996, several books examining serial murder, including *Serial Murderers and Their Victims,* were placed on the compact disk entitled *Mind of a Killer.* This "serial murder library" allows researchers, students, and law enforcement to access a vast amount of information, including biographies, photographs, and the investigative tools used to track serial killers. In 2002, Court TV aired a documentary examining the emergence of criminal profilers: *The Elite, the New Profilers.*

Increasingly, both academicians and law enforcement are becoming involved in the study and exploration of violent serial crime and have contributed to the body of knowledge on the subject. For instance, data has been collected on transnational serial killers, that is, killers worldwide whose victims are from different countries. Others have explored the social environments of serial murderers, the biological basis for multiple homicide, dissociative states, and other forces that may affect the mind of a serial killer. Research now emphasizes the use of forensic science as a tool in examining the geographic profiling of crimes and offenders.

Law enforcement officials have been handling serial murders for many years. Computer technology, especially the development of the Internet, has expedited data collection and analysis. During the mid-1980s, the FBI established, at their Behavioral Science Unit in Quantico, Virginia (now referred to as the Critical Response Unit), the Violent Criminal Apprehension Program (VICAP). The VICAP program was designed to collect detailed information on homicides throughout the United States. Investigators like former FBI agents Robert Ressler and John Douglas, who interviewed several serial killers in the United States, have made considerable progress in understanding certain types of serial offenders. Ressler and colleagues published their findings in *Sexual Homicide* (1988). In addition, the U.S. government continues to develop programs such as the National Center for the Analysis of Violent Crime (NCAVC) to focus specifically on repetitive offenders, including serial murderers.

By 2000, a U.S. trend of increasing numbers of stranger homicides was clearly established even as homicides in general had been decreasing. Because of this increase in stranger-to-stranger homicides, in some cities, such as Los Angeles, as many as 60% of all murders occur each year without being prosecuted. The increasing number of serial murders is believed by some experts to account for some of these unsolved cases (Holmes & DeBurger, 1988).

SOME COMPARISONS BETWEEN SERIAL KILLERS AND SPREE MURDERERS

Serial killers usually make special efforts to elude detection. Indeed, they may continue to kill for weeks, months, and often years before they are found and stopped, if they are found at all. In the case of the California "Zodiac Killer" (1966-1981), the homicides appeared to have stopped, but an offender was never apprehended for those crimes. Perhaps the offender was incarcerated for only one murder and never linked to the others, or perhaps he or she was imprisoned for other crimes. Or the killer may have just decided to stop killing or to move to a new location and kill under a new modus operandi, or method of committing the crime. (There is speculation that the Zodiac Killer has stalked victims in the New York City area.) The killer may even have become immobilized because of an accident or an illness or have died without his or her story ever being told. The Zodiac case is only one example of unsolved serial murders, many of which will never be solved.

Researchers have distinguished *spree murders* from serial murder as being three or more victims killed by a single perpetrator within a period of hours or days in different locations. They often act in frenzy, make little effort to avoid detection, and kill in several sequences. Offenders may kill more than one victim in one location and travel to another location. There appears to be no "cooling-off" period even though the murders occur at different places. These murders, sometimes called *cluster killings,* tend to last a few days, or weeks. In 1997, Andrew Cunanan, a 27-year-old from San Diego, went on a four-state killing spree that culminated in the murder of fashion designer Gianni Versace in Florida. Cunanan feared that he might be infected with the AIDS virus and had vowed "revenge." Some of the five men he killed were gay, and some were not. Upon killing them with guns, knives, and blunt objects, Cunanan then stole cars and money from his victims. He continued to kill as he journeyed southeastward toward his final murder, and suicide. White (2000) thoroughly examined the differences between serial and spree murders and summarized the differences:

		Serial	Spree
1.	Murder is means of control over life	**	**
2.	Usually arrested or killed at crime scene		**
3.	Often commit suicide after the crime		**
4.	Elude arrest and detection		**
5.	Likely to travel and seek out victims	**	**
6.	Evokes long-term media/public attention	**	
7.	Kills individuals	**	
8.	Kills several in short period of time		**
9.	Murders viewed as single incident		**
10.	Minimum number of victims agreed on by researchers	4	4
11.	Murderer is usually white male	**	**
12.	Motivated primarily by material gain or revenge		**
13.	Victims usually female	**	
14.	Firearms common choice of weapon		**
15.	Kill in spontaneous rage		**

Perhaps the single most critical stumbling block that stands in the way of understanding serial murder today is the disagreement among researchers and law enforcement about how to define the phenomenon. Steve Egger's (2002) global definition of serial murder attempts to create parameters for the behavior that include the number of victims, their relationships to the offender, the apparent lack of connection between murders, geographical location, motive, role of victims, and types of victims.

For many in law enforcement, serial killing generally means the sexual attack and murder of young women, men, and children by a male who follows a pattern, physical or psychological. However, this definition fails to include many offenders and victims. For example, in 1988, in Sacramento, California, several bodies of older or handicapped adults were exhumed from the backyard of a house where they were supposed to have been living. Investigators discovered the victims had been killed for their Social Security checks. It was apparent that the killer had premeditated the murders, had selected the victims, and had killed at least six over a period of several months. Most law enforcement agencies would naturally classify this case as a serial killing—except for the fact that the killer was female. Because of rather narrow definitions of serial killing, females are often not classified as such even though they meet the requirements for the label. One explanation may simply be that we rarely, if ever, hear of a female "Jack the Ripper." Women who kill serially generally use poisons to dispose of their victims and are not associated with the sexual attacks, tortures, and violence of their male counterparts.

Many offenders actually fall into the serial killer classification but fail to meet law enforcement definitions or media-generated stereotypes of brutal, bloodthirsty monsters. The "Angels of Death" who work in hospitals and kill patients, nursing-home staff who kill the elderly, or "Black Widows" who kill their families and relatives also meet the general criteria for serial killing except for the stereotypic element of violence. These men and women do not slash and torture their victims, nor do they sexually attack them; they are the quiet killers. They are also the kinds of people who could be married, hold steady jobs, or simply be the nice man or woman who lives next door. They are rare among serial killers, just as serial murders are rare compared with other types of homicide.

To include all types of serial killers, the definition of serial murder must clearly be as broad as possible. For instance, by simply including all offenders who through premeditation killed three or more victims over a period of days, weeks, months, or years, Hickey was able to identify several women as serial killers. To suggest, for example, that all victims of serial murder are strangers, that the killers operate primarily in pairs, or that they do not kill for financial gain is derived more from speculation than verifiable evidence, given the current state of serial murder research.

In essence, serial murderers should include any offenders, male or female, who kill over time. Most researchers agree that serial killers have a minimum of 3 to 4 victims. Usually, a pattern in their killing can be associated with the types of victims selected or the method or motives for the killing. This includes murderers who on a repeated basis kill within the confines of their own homes, such as a woman who poisons several husbands, children, or elderly people in order to collect insurance. In addition, serial murderers include men and women who operate within the confines of a city or a state or even travel through several states as they seek out victims. Consequently, some victims have personal relationships with their killers, and others do not; and some victims are killed for pleasure, and some merely for gain. Of greatest importance from a research perspective is the linkage of common factors among the victims, for example, as Egger (1985) observed, the "victims' place or status within their immediate surroundings" (p. 3).

SERIAL MURDER CLASSIFICATIONS

In some serial killings, the sexual attack is an integral part of the murder both psychologically and physiologically for the offender. For other offenders, sexual attacks may represent the best way to degrade, subjugate, and ultimately destroy their victims but have little connection to the actual motive(s) for the killings.

Holmes and DeBurger have characterized four types of serial murderers and examined the motives reported to have influenced the offenders. The formation of these typologies is based on specific assumptions about the phenomenon of serial killers. These assumptions include the belief that such crimes are nearly always psychogenic, meaning that such behavior is usually stimulated not by insanity or economic circumstances, but by "behavioral rewards and penalties." The "patterns of learning" are in some way related to "significant others" who in some way reinforce homicidal behavior. A second assumption involves an "intrinsic locus of motives," whereby motives are explained as something only the offender can appreciate because they exist entirely in his or her own mind. Most "normal" people have great difficulty in fathoming why someone would want to kill other people. However, in the mind of the killer, the motivations are often very meaningful. In a final assumption, Holmes and DeBurger explain that the reward for killing is generally psychological even though some killers may benefit materially from their crimes. According to these "core characteristics" Holmes and DeBurger identify the following four types of serial killers:

1. *Visionary type:* Such murderers kill in response to the commands of voices or visions usually emanating from the forces of good or evil. These offenders are often believed to be suffering from some form of psychosis.

2. *Mission-oriented type:* These offenders believe it is their mission in life to rid the community or society of certain groups of people. Some killers may target the elderly, whereas others may seek out prostitutes, children, or a particular racial/ethnic group.

3. *Hedonistic type:* Offenders in this category are usually stereotyped as "thrill seekers" who derive some form of satisfaction from the murders. Holmes and DeBurger also identified subcategories in this typology, including those who kill for "creature comforts" or "pleasure of life." This would include individuals such as Dorothea Montalvo Puente of Sacramento, California, who was arrested in 1988 for allegedly poisoning to death at least seven destitute elderly victims in order to cash their Social Security checks. Another subcategory Holmes and DeBurger refer to is "lust murderers," which includes offenders

who become sexually involved with the victims and often perform postmortem mutilations.

4. *Power/control-oriented type:* In this typology, Holmes contends that "the fundamental source of pleasure is not sexual, it is the killer's ability to control and exert power over his helpless victim" (1985, p. 32). Some offenders enjoy watching their victims cower, cringe, and beg for mercy. In one case, an offender killed his young victims only after he had been able to break their will to survive. Once the victims had acquiesced, the offender completed his task and slaughtered them.

These general classifications of serial killers are useful in organizing existing data. Such motivational taxonomies help us to understand why certain offenders take the lives of their victims. Levin and Fox have also constructed types of serial murders, including sexual or sadistic killings that appear similar to Holmes and DeBurger's subcategory of "lust murders." Another typology similar to Holmes and DeBurger's hedonistic subtypes is described by Levin and Fox as murders of expediency or for profit. Their third typology identifies "family slayings" as a major category of murder. This "type" does not appear to be particularly consistent with their other two categories, which are constructed from motivational dynamics. Although family killers could be motivated by sadism or expediency, with few exceptions they are generally blood relatives of their victims and kill them all in a relatively short period of time.

The FBI, through extensive application of profiling techniques, has identified the characteristics of "organized" and "disorganized" murders. Using information gathered at the scene of the crime and examining the nature of the crime itself, agents constructed profiles of the offenders, which in turn were categorized as organized or disorganized. For example, an organized murderer is often profiled as having good intelligence and being socially competent, whereas the disorganized offender is viewed as being of average intelligence and socially immature. Similarly, some crime investigators often find that organized offenders plan their murders, target strangers, and demand victims to be submissive, whereas disorganized killers may know their victims, inflict sudden violence on them, and spontaneously carry out their killings.

More specifically, organized killers profiled as lust murderers (an offender sexually involved with his victim) by the FBI possess many of the following personal characteristics:

1. Highly intelligent
2. High birth-order status
3. Masculine image
4. Charismatic
5. Socially capable
6. Sexually capable
7. Occupationally mobile
8. Lives with partner
9. Geographically mobile
10. Experienced harsh discipline
11. Controlled emotions during crime
12. High interest in media response to crime
13. Model inmate

The organized lust killer also exhibits fairly predictable behaviors after the crime, including a return to the crime scene, a need to volunteer information, enjoying being friendly with police, expecting to be interrogated by investigators, or sometimes moving the victim's body to a new location or exposing the body to draw attention to the crime. The disorganized offender is characterized as follows:

1. Below-average intelligence
2. Low birth-order status
3. Socially immature
4. Seldom dates
5. High school dropout
6. Father often under- or unemployed
7. Lives alone
8. Has secret hiding places
9. Nocturnal
10. Lives/works near crime scene
11. Engages in unskilled work
12. Significant behavioral changes
13. Low interest in media attention
14. Limited alcohol consumption
15. High anxiety during crime

According to the FBI, the disorganized lust killer also exhibits a variety of predictable behaviors following a murder, including returning to the crime scene, possibly attending the funeral or burial of the victim, keeping a diary, changing employment, becoming religious, experiencing changes in personality, or submitting personal advertisements in newspapers regarding his victims. Although such profiles have proven helpful in understanding offender behavior, the minds of serial murderers have only begun to be explored.

Matching variables may be found to generate new ways of conceptualizing offenders' behavior or victimization patterns. Theodore Bundy, for example, sought out young, attractive females whom he bludgeoned and tortured to death. He was particularly specific in both victim selection and method of killing. David Bullock of New York was suspected in 1982 of killing at least 6 victims, including a prostitute, his roommate, and several strangers, by shooting each one. In this case, the killer sought out a variety of victims but used a specific method to kill them. In the case of Richard Cottingham, also known as "the Ripper," the killer hunted prostitutes in New Jersey and New York. Although he went after specific targets, he varied his methods of killing. Finally, Herbert Mullin, of California, is believed to have killed 13 victims, including campers, hitchhikers, friends, and people in their homes, using a variety of methods.

Some serial killers such as Ted Bundy always hunt for their victims and once they find a suitable person, kill and dispose of the body in remote areas. Conversely, some serial killers wait at home for their victims to walk into their traps, like the spider awaiting the fly. In some cases, the victims are killed and buried on the offender's property. In 2003, investigators in Vancouver, British Columbia, Canada, continue to sift through a pig farm in search of the remains of more than 60 prostitutes. John Wayne Gacy is believed to have killed 33 young males, most of whom became buried trophies under the offender's home. H. H. Holmes built a gas chamber in the basement of his home and advertised for housekeepers during the 1896 Chicago World's Fair. Offenders sometimes advertise in newspapers for offers of employment or marriage, waiting for unsuspecting victims to ring their doorbells. Each modus operandi may be useful in generating particular typologies of serial killers.

In noting specific variations in the degree of mobility exercised by offenders, Hickey has delineated three distinct groups of offenders: (a) traveling serial killers, who often cover many thousands of miles each year, murdering victims in several states as they go; (b) local serial killers, who never leave the state in which they start killing to find additional victims (Wayne Williams, for example, operated in several different law enforcement jurisdictions in and around Atlanta, Georgia, but never had a need to move elsewhere); and (c) serial killers who never leave their homes or places of employment, whose victims already reside in the same physical structure or are lured each time to the same location. These "place-specific" killers include nurses (male and female), housewives, the self-employed, and other individuals or accomplices who prefer to stay at home rather than go out hunting for victims.

Serial killers have often been portrayed as antisocial personality types manifesting aggressive, hostile behavior and a tendency to avoid developing close relationships. However, some serial murderers appear to be well-adjusted persons leading rather normal lives; their closest friends and family members have been surprised and shocked by their confessions of multiple homicides. The point is that offenders do not always come from the same mold. Each killer has evolved through different life events and has responded to those experiences differently. Although it may be argued that serial killers possess "fatal flaws," it remains indefensible to say that such flaws are overtly manifested or easily detected. In short, some offenders may never reveal enough of themselves in daily life to allow the identification of particular personality disorders. Understanding the psychopathology of these Jekyll-and-Hyde personalities appears increasingly complex as we explore the minds of serial murderers.

The term *psychopath* seems to "fit" the serial killer. The underlying pathology of serial killers typically is frustration, anger, hostility, feelings of inadequacy, and low self-esteem. These feelings may be manifested in many ways, but the source or underlying pathology appears as a common denominator. The *sexual psychopath* is often referred to in serial murder cases as a "lust killer" or one who practices *erotophonophilia*. The notion of lust suggests one who possesses a particular urge not only to kill but also to ravage the victim. Even among lust killers, methods of killing vary widely, as do the types of mutilations that may occur before or after the victim has died. In one case, an offender described his feelings about killing, focusing on the urge to mutilate and destroy his victims before he could find temporary relief.

The childhoods of serial killers are varied and complex. Some are much more sociopathic than other children because they are more aggressive, more manipulative, express less remorse, and experience fewer feelings of guilt. Yet similar characteristics can be observed in children who never grow up to become violent offenders. In truth, each child processes experiences differentially. Children also react differentially to stress. It may be that stress is the generic predisposer to many maladaptive behaviors in childhood. Because children do not possess the same coping skills to handle life's stressors, some children are at greater risk of developing inappropriate behaviors.

Psychopathology during childhood can be manifested in a variety of behaviors, some of which are more noticeable or detectable than others. Serial killers have been linked to childhood maladaptive behaviors such as torturing animals; enuresis, or chronic bedwetting; and firesetting. Any of these three behaviors is not a proven predictor of later adult violent behavior. Even a youth displaying all three behaviors is not guaranteed a life of violence during adulthood. However, such behaviors appear more often among the serial killer population than among nonoffenders.

Childhood trauma for serial murderers may serve as a triggering mechanism resulting in an individual's inability to cope with the stress of certain events, be they physical, psychological, or a combination of traumatizations. For serial murderers, the most common effect of childhood traumatization manifested is rejection, including rejection by relatives and parent(s). It must be emphasized that an unstable, abusive home has been reported as one of the major forms of rejection. The child or teen feels a deep sense of anxiety, mistrust, and confusion when psychologically or physically abused by an adult.

The most critical factor common to serial killers is violent fantasy. Prentky and colleagues, who studied repetitive sexual homicides, found that daydreams of causing bodily harm through sadism and other methods of sexual violence were common among offenders. The researchers concluded that the offender attempts to replicate his fantasies. Because the offender can actually never be in total control of his or her victim's responses, the outcome of the fantasy will never measure up to his or her expectations. In any case, each new murder provides new fantasies that can fuel future homicides. Ressler and his colleagues (1988) concluded that "sexual murder is based on fantasy" (p. 33).

Although fantasies are generally associated with sexual homicides, they are likely to be found in the minds of most, if not all, serial killers. The control fantasy becomes the highlight of the attack, and the sexual assault is one vehicle by which the offender can attempt to gain total control of a victim. Sexual torture becomes a tool to degrade, humiliate, and subjugate the victim. It is a method to take away from the victim all that is perceived to be personal, private, or sacred. The offender physically and mentally dominates his or her victim to a point where he or she has fantasized achieving ultimate control over another human being. Once that sense of control has been reached, the victim loses his or her purpose to the offender and is then killed. One serial killer noted in a personal interview that he had developed a ritual for torturing his victims and that he seldom varied from those methods.

—Eric W. Hickey

NOTE: Portions of this profile were previously published in Eric Hickey's *Serial Murderers and Their Victims,* 2002, 3rd ed. Belmont, CA: Wadsworth Publishers.

See also BUNDY, THEODORE "TED"; DAHMER, JEFFREY; CHIKATILO, ANDREI; DESALVO, ALBERT HENRY; HOMICIDE; KACZYNSKI, THEODORE; MANSON, CHARLES/THE MANSON FAMILY; MOTIVATION FOR MURDER; MOTIVES FOR MURDER; PARAPHILIA; PSYCHOPATHS; RAMIREZ, RICHARD; RIPPERS; SPREE MURDERS; TEAM KILLERS; ZODIAC MURDERS

Further Reading

Egger, S. A. (2002). *The killers among us: An examination of serial murder and its investigation.* Upper Saddle River, NJ: Prentice Hall.

Greswell, D. M., & Hollin, C. (1994, Winter). Multiple murder: A review. *The British Journal of Criminology 34*(1), 1-14.

Holmes, R. M., & DeBurger, J. (1988). *Serial murder.* Newbury Park, CA: Sage.

Jenkins, P. (1994). *Using murder: The social construction of serial homicide.* New York: Aldine de Gruyter.

Leyton, E. (1986a). *Hunting humans.* Toronto: McClelland and Stewart.

Main, V. (1997). *The changing image of serial killers in film: A reflection of attitudes toward crime from 1929-1995.* Master's thesis, California State University, Fresno.

Prentky, R. W., Burgess, A. W., & Carter, D. L. (1986). Victim responses by rapist type: An empirical and clinical analysis. *Journal of Interpersonal Violence, 1,* 73-98.

Ressler, R. K., Burgess, A. W., & Douglas, J. E. (1988). *Sexual homicide.* Lexington, MA: Lexington Books.

White, L. (2000). *Mass murder and attempted mass murder: An examination of the perpetrator and an empirical analysis of typologies.* Doctoral dissertation, California School of Professional Psychology, Fresno.

SERIAL MURDER: INTERNATIONAL INCIDENCE

Serial murder is commonly perceived as a distinctively and predominantly American phenomenon. Following the trend in America, foreign reporting of serial murder cases appears to be increasing, as does concern on the part of foreign law enforcement and researchers. Recognition of the existence of this phenomenon as a global, not just American, problem is necessary to detect and prevent such cases. In addition, the existence of serial murder in different parts of the world and throughout different periods of history has important implications for both investigative techniques and theoretical explanations used to understand these atrocious crimes.

HISTORY AND EXTENT OF SERIAL MURDER

Not only is serial murder found outside the United States, it existed long before America was known as such. During the late Middle Ages and Renaissance period, Europe spawned a number of notorious serial murderers. One of the most infamous was onetime French hero Gilles de Rais, who is thought to have sexually tortured and murdered hundreds of children over 8 years in the early 1400s. Around the same time, Walchian prince Vlad Tepes III (also known as "Vlad Dracul" or "Vlad the Impaler") was torturing and killing thousands of people in Transylvania. Vlad and his horrendous acts are thought to have been the inspiration for Bram Stoker's 1897 novel, *Dracula.*

Many early cases of serial murder are thought to have provided the basis for folk tales of vampires and werewolves. In 1572, citizens of a small village in France believed a werewolf was killing and eating their young children. Gilles Garnier was later tracked down and identified as the killer. Garnier was convinced that he was a werewolf and confessed to killing and eating four young children in the area. A similar 16th-century case is found in Germany, where for 25 years, Peter Stubb raped, killed, and ate citizens of Cologne. Stubb also believed he was a werewolf. In fact, several offenders were prosecuted for similar crimes in France and Germany in the 16th century.

The belief in the ability of an individual to turn into a wild beast is referred to as *therianthropy.* Therianthropy has been given as an explanation for deviant behavior throughout history and throughout the world. Such belief systems may still distort the reality of serial murderers today. For example, in 1998, a tribal chief in the Congo confessed to killing and eating five people. Villagers and the police believed the tribal chief had the ability to transform himself into a crocodile.

Another serial murderer thought to have influenced vampire lore is Hungarian Countess Elizabeth Bathory (1560-1614). She claimed to have sadistically killed more than 600 victims and bathed in their blood during the late 16th and early 17th centuries. Bathory's case is also an early illustration that serial murder is not confined to males. Other female serial murderers of the 17th century included Elizabeth Ridgway in England, Marie de Brinvillier and Catherine Deshayes in France, and Hieronyma Spara in Italy. In 1719, a female offender named La Tofania was executed for poisoning hundreds of victims in Italy.

Curiously, the literature offers few examples of serial murder in the 18th century, male or female. Documentation of serial murders appears to have grown in the 1800s, however. Early cases of serial murder in the 19th century include those of the "Bavarian Ripper," Andreas Bichel, the English "Resurrection Men," William Burke and William Hare, and German poisoner Gessinna Godfried. Toward the latter end of the 19th century, cases included those of Helena Jegado, in England, Pierre Voirbo, in France, and Vincent Verzeni, in Italy.

Some authors contend that the modern era of serial murder has its origins in the late 19th century. The case of "Jack the Ripper," the mysterious killer of five London prostitutes in 1888, has held the public's attention to this day. This is largely due to the evolving role of the popular press, which not only focused attention on the Whitechapel killings, but has maintained a keen focus on the phenomenon of serial murder ever since. Only a few years after England's Ripper case, newspapers in America likewise followed and intrigued readers with the sensational case of "The Torture Doctor," Herman Mudgett, in Chicago. Mudgett, who moved to Chicago the same year of the Ripper killings in England, confessed and was hanged for the murder of 27 victims.

Cases of serial murder in both Great Britain and the United States throughout the 19th and 20th centuries are relatively abundant and easily identified. In fact, beginning in the mid-1970s and lasting to this day, serial murder cases became so alarmingly frequent in the United States that it warranted Congressional hearings, prompted the creation of new federal and local law enforcement programs, and instigated a focus of academic research on the problem. Of course, the media also seized on the apparent "epidemic" of American serial killers, and the phenomenon quickly became sensationalized and contaminated with misinformation, one myth being that this crime was unique to the United States. The fact is that other nations have numerous cases of serial murder and Americans generally are simply not aware of them.

This lack of awareness is likely due in part to language barriers and geographical distance. Fluctuations of press freedom and media attention also play an important role in the reporting of serial murder in some countries. Such cases are now being made public in countries that formerly concealed or even denied their existence. For example, in 1997, citizens of Iran were shocked to learn that a man, referred to as the "Tehran Vampire," had raped and murdered nine women in the region. Such reports were previously forbidden in the interest of favorable public opinion about life under Islamic rule.

Similarly, the former Communist-controlled press of the Soviet Union also denied the existence of such crimes there, labeling this depraved behavior as being a result of the influence of Western culture. This ideology allowed Andrei Chikatilo (the "Russian Ripper") to murder 52 people in Rostov-on-Don between 1982 and 1990. Today, increased press freedom in Russia reveals that serial murder may be extensive there.

INVESTIGATIVE
DIFFICULTIES AND RESPONSES

Investigative difficulties may also contribute to a lack of recognition regarding foreign cases. As in the United States, serial murder cases can cause distinct problems for foreign investigators. Among the numerous factors are a lack of identifiable motive, seemingly random victims, high geographic mobility of offenders, and linkage blindness. The two most basic issues in such investigations are offender identification and crime linkage. Three specific approaches show promise in dealing with these problems: forensic DNA analysis; case linkage systems; and profiling.

DNA databases are a recent development in American and European law enforcement. In 1998, the FBI made public the National DNA Indexing System (NDIS), allowing federal, state, and local crime laboratories to store and compare DNA records from across the United States. The United Kingdom established a comparable database in 1995, and similar databases may be of great assistance to other foreign and international agencies involved in criminal investigations as well.

Centralized information networks are also relatively new and can be used to collect case-related information and help link crimes. The first computer case linkage system used in the United States for violent crime was the FBI's Violent Criminal Apprehension Program (VICAP), which became operational in 1985. Such information systems are now being used internationally. Based on VICAP, Canada's Royal Canadian Mounted Police also developed a national case linkage system, called ViCLAS (Violent Criminal Linkage Analysis System). Among the advantages of ViCLAS is its ability to collect data in any language. Partly for this reason, ViCLAS is now used in several other countries as well, including Australia, Austria, Belgium, Germany, Holland, Japan, and the United Kingdom. With the opening of national borders in many parts of the world, the next step may be to implement an international case linkage system.

An investigative approach that has gained increased attention in recent years and holds great promise for understanding and investigating serial violence is the analysis of behavioral evidence and research, often referred to as *profiling*. The FBI developed the clinical approach of profiling into a specific law enforcement tool in the 1970s. Today, profiling has grown to involve the analysis of several types of data that target specific aspects of the investigation. Examples of such criminal investigation analysis include psychological profiling, geographic profiling, and crime scene profiling.

CROSS-NATIONAL TRAINING
AND CULTURAL ISSUES

Several countries have implemented special measures such as case linkage systems and profiling techniques to deal with serial murder. Australia, Canada, Great Britain, Hong Kong, the Netherlands, Russia, South Africa, and Slovenia are among some of the nations that now have their own investigators or units specially trained in profiling and/or serial murder investigations.

Many countries have used training and procedures developed in the United States, often by way of the FBI. The problem is that this method assumes that the techniques of one country will suit another.

However, such procedures may not take into account cross-cultural or cross-national differences and therefore may not be generalizable or appropriate for other countries or cultures.

As an example, in South Africa, ritual killings referred to as "muti" killings are sometimes carried out to obtain body parts for ailments that are thought to cure witch curses. In 1995, South African police found a woman's vagina in the refrigerator of a hostel near Johannesburg. Although the outcome of the case is unknown, the discovery itself demonstrates the significance of cross-cultural awareness, training, and research. Such a crime scene would have different connotations if found in the United States versus South Africa. In muti killings, specific body parts are obtained for their particular abilities. For example, female genitalia are thought to help infertility. In the United States, the possession of a vagina would most likely be viewed as evidence of severe sexual perversion and psychopathology. This conjecture would lead investigators to a totally different set of conclusions and investigative approaches than if they considered the discovery to be at least partially related to cultural or subcultural belief systems and activities.

THE GORBY STUDY OF FOREIGN OFFENDERS AND CASES

An extensive empirical study of serial murder on an international scale was conducted by Gorby (2000). He reviewed the literature and analyzed archival data regarding 300 foreign, non-American serial murderers responsible for 241 cases between the years 1800 to 1995. The Gorby study found that serial murderers have killed in no less than 43 different countries, a figure that likely underrepresents the problem due to methodological restraints.

As in the United States, the number of identified foreign cases indicates that although serial murder is still a relatively rare phenomenon, the prevalence of cases has rapidly increased since the 1970s. Three quarters of serial murders took place since 1925, and approximately 42% began since 1975 (Hickey, 2002). Of special interest is the proliferation of this phenomenon in non-European nations over the past 20 years.

Almost half the cases in Gorby's study were identified in just four nations: the United Kingdom (47); Germany (35); South Africa (19); and Australia (17). European countries accounted for more than half the cases (137). When examined across time, serial murder

Table 2   Number of Serial Murder Cases in Foreign Countries 1800–1995 (241 cases total)

Country	Number of Cases	Percentage of Total
United Kingdom	47	19.5%
Germany	36	14.9%
South Africa	19	7.9%
Australia	17	7.1%
France	15	6.2%
Canada	13	5.4%
Russia	12	5.0%
Austria	6	2.5%
Hungary	5	2.1%
India	5	2.1%
Japan	5	2.1%
Mexico	5	2.1%
Belgium	4	1.7%
China	4	1.7%
Greece	4	1.7%
Poland	4	1.7%
Columbia	3	1.2%
Italy	3	1.2%
Brazil	2	.8%
Indonesia	2	.8%
Norway	2	.8%
New Zealand	2	.8%
Romania	2	.8%
Singapore	2	.8%
Spain	2	.8%
Switzerland	2	.8%
Yugoslavia	2	.8%
Central Africa	1	.4%
Bahamas	1	.4%
Bermuda	1	.4%
Bolivia	1	.4%
Czechoslovakia	1	.4%
Ecuador	1	.4%
Egypt	1	.4%
Iran	1	.4%
Netherlands	1	.4%
Pakistan	1	.4%
Sweden	1	.4%
Syria	1	.4%
Thailand	1	.4%
Trinidad	1	.4%
Ukraine	1	.4%
Yemen	1	.4%

cases were found in only five countries during the 75 years between 1800 to 1874, all of them European nations (United Kingdom, Germany, France, Italy, Switzerland). However, the percentage of European cases diminished in each of the 25-year periods since 1900, while non-European countries saw a steady increase. Table 2 lists the countries in which serial murder cases were identified.

The majority of foreign serial offenders in Gorby's study were male, and approximately a quarter of them were female. Serial murderers were an average of 30 years old when they started their killing and 35 when they stopped. Most (201) offenders killed alone; however, one third committed their murders with at least one accomplice. Male foreign offenders tended to kill alone, whereas females worked as part of teams.

Foreign serial murderers in the Gorby study killed a minimum of 2,917 victims, an average of 12 victims per case. Despite exceptional cases such as Andrei Chikatilo, most offenders killed 10 or fewer victims before being caught. Much like domestic offenders, foreign offenders tended to target victims outside their families, although foreign female offenders targeted at least some family members in more than half the cases. Adults, and to a lesser extent children, of both sexes were likely to be targeted by foreign offenders. Foreign offenders tended to commit their murders within a local area (85%), although a number of females were place specific.

Approximately half the male offender cases in the Gorby study contained evidence of at least some sexual behavior; only 1 of the 43 female offenders exhibited such behavior. More than one third of male serial murderers and over half of female serial murderers took material gains away from at least some of their murders. More than one third of male offenders in the study mutilated or tortured at least some of their victims; only 2 female offenders mutilated or tortured any of their victims.

A number of different killing methods were identified in Gorby's study. Male offenders tended to use a combination of methods over the length of their series, the most common being strangulation/asphyxiation and stabbing/cutting. Firearms were used in only 40 cases, far less than the 41% of American serial killers in Hickey's (2002) study. Female offenders most often used poison or withheld medical assistance from their victims. Only one female beat or bludgeoned victims to death, and only one used a firearm. No females used knives or stabbed their victims to death.

SUMMARY

Serial murder is a problem in many parts of the world. Ignorance or denial of the problem provides an opportune environment for serial predators. Considering the expansive temporal and geographic

characteristics of serial murder, along with the diverse characteristics of the offenders and their crimes, it seems apparent that multiple factors play a role in this phenomenon. An attempt to gain insight into the behavior will require a multidisciplinary approach. Researchers must examine and be willing to integrate multiple paradigms including sociological, cultural, psychological, and biological perspectives.

—*Bradford L. Gorby*

See also BATHORY, COUNTESS ELIZABETH; CHIKATILO, ANDREI (THE "RUSSIAN RIPPER"); CRIMINALISTICS; FEDERAL BUREAU OF INVESTIGATION; GEOGRAPHIC PROFILING; FORENSIC SCIENCE; LINKAGE BLINDNESS; MOTIVES FOR MURDER; PROFILING; PSYCHOPATHS; VAMPIRES, WEREWOLVES AND WITCHES; VICLAS

Further Reading

Egger, S. A. (1998). *The killers among us.* Upper Saddle River, NJ: Prentice Hall.

Gorby, B. L. (2000). *Serial murder: A cross-national descriptive study.* Master's thesis, California State University, Fresno.

Hickey, E. W. (2002). *Serial murderers and their victims* (3rd ed.). Belmont, CA: Wadsworth.

Jenkins, P. (1994). *Using murder: The social construction of serial homicide.* New York: Aldine de Gruyter.

Lester, D. (1995). *Serial killers: The insatiable passion.* Philadelphia: Charles Press.

Rossmo, D. K. (2000). *Geographic profiling.* Washington, DC: CRC Press.

SEX OFFENDER REGISTRIES

Sex offender registries are used by law enforcement agencies to identify and track sex offenders who have been convicted of specific sex offenses and/or crimes against children. These types of offenders must register in person with the local law enforcement agency having jurisdiction over the area in which they live after being released from incarceration.

The purpose of sex offender registries is twofold: First, to track sex offenders, and second, to allow law enforcement to be aware of which sex offenders are living in their jurisdictions. Beginning in 1996, law enforcement agencies began using public notification programs to advise the public when a sex offender was residing in the community. Due to changes in federal law, previously restricted information regarding sex offenders can now be shared with the public. The purpose of notification programs is to curtail registered sex offenders' ability to contact the next victim and commit another crime. Community notification programs are used to heighten public awareness of the presence of sex offenders in the community.

HISTORY

In 1947, California enacted a sex offender registration program, the first in the nation to require convicted sex offenders to notify local law enforcement agencies of their whereabouts. A few states followed California's lead; then, in 1994, federal statutes mandated sex offender registries in each state.

Beginning in 1994, in response to public safety concerns focusing on child sexual offenders and individuals who commit sexual offenses in general, the United States Congress passed the first of three laws that would radically change sex offender registries: the Jacob Wetterling Crimes Against Children and Sexually Violent Offender Registration Act (1994). The act was named after Jacob Wetterling, an 11-year-old boy who, in 1989, was kidnapped in front of his 10-year-old brother and 11-year-old friend by a masked gunman. Jacob is still missing. The Wetterling Act required states that previously did not have established sex offender registries to establish them in an effort to alert law enforcement to the presence of sex offenders in communities. To continue to receive certain federal funds, states were required to comply with the guidelines for the registration programs. States had 3 years from the original enactment date of September 13, 1994, to bring their registration programs into compliance with federal standards.

The Wetterling Act originally restricted release and dissemination of registration information but was modified on May 17, 1996, by way of "Megan's Law." With the enactment of Megan's Law, Congress required states to implement programs to notify members of the public when convicted sex offenders were released into communities. Megan's Law amended the Wetterling Act to provide for release of registration information in accordance with state laws. States were given until September 1997 to pass state versions of Megan's Law, or lose federal aid.

This law was named after Megan Kanka, a 7-year-old girl who was sexually assaulted and murdered in 1994 by a convicted repeat sex offender. Jesse Timmendequas, the man convicted of murdering Megan, had been living across the street from her residence. The girl's death led to a nationwide movement to protect children from sexual predators by notifying communities when such predators are released from incarceration.

Also in 1996, Congress enacted the Pam Lychner Sexual Offender Tracking and Identification Act, the third major piece of legislation aimed at protecting individuals and communities from sex offenders. The Lychner Act required the U.S. Attorney General to establish a national database at the FBI to track the whereabouts and movements of certain convicted sex offenders. The FBI accomplishes this mandate via the National Sex Offender Registry. In addition, the FBI was to register and verify the addresses of sex offenders who reside in states that do not have a minimally sufficient sex offender registry program. The Lychner Act also created a new federal statute making it a criminal offense for a registered sex offender to move to another state and knowingly fail to notify FBI authorities in the new state of residence. This act was named in honor of the late Pam Lychner, who was the driving force behind the organization Justice for All, founded in the summer of 1993 in Houston, Texas. Ms. Lychner was herself a victim of an attempted sexual assault and narrowly escaped her attacker.

PURPOSE

Sex offenders constitute a large and increasing population of prison inmates. Most convicted sex offenders are eventually released to the community under probation or parole supervision. The concern exists that these predators will engage in sex offenses and crimes against children after being released from incarceration. Through the passage of various sex offender laws and acts, state and federal legislatures have declared that protection of the public from these predators is of paramount governmental interest. Sexual offender registries and notification procedures allow local law enforcement officers additional avenues to protect their communities, conduct investigations, and quickly apprehend offenders who commit sex offenses and crimes against children. Notification procedures have added the components of community involvement and awareness to the protection of communities.

In a democracy, there is an ongoing struggle to strike a balance between maintaining public order and protecting individual freedoms. Notification procedures under Megan's Law are predicated on the legal premise that persons found to have committed sex offenses have a reduced expectation of privacy due to the issue of public safety. In balancing an offender's due process and other rights with the interests of public safety and security, the releasing of information about criminal sex offenders to law enforcement agencies and to the general public has taken precedence over individual freedoms. It has been determined that there is a compelling and necessary public interest that the public have information concerning persons convicted of sexual offenses in order to allow members of the public to adequately protect themselves and their children.

Furnishing the public with information regarding convicted sex offenders is a critical step toward encouraging the public to protect themselves from potential future acts by offenders and building community cooperation with law enforcement. Law enforcement has learned that it takes a collective participation involving both the community and law enforcement to safeguard neighborhoods.

VARIANCE FROM STATE TO STATE

Sex offender registries and notification procedures are not universally implemented in each state. Communities and law enforcement agencies vary greatly from state to state and within each state. The federal legislation requiring notification programs and sex registries in states that did not already have them recognized this fact and afforded states discretion in defining and implementing their programs.

Each state has a central sex offender file, which is maintained by a state agency such as the state attorney general's office, state police, or state department of corrections. Local law enforcement agencies serve as local registration sites and maintain local sex offenders' records. Copies of these records are forwarded to designated state agencies, which enter their central sex offender file information into the national sex offender registration file maintained by the FBI.

Conviction of certain sex offenses and offenses against children can result in having to register as a sex offender. Each state statutorily defines what constitutes a registerable sex offense. Although these statutes may vary between states, all states address crimes such as assault with intent to commit rape, oral copulation, or sodomy; rape; sodomy with a minor;

child molestation; penetration with a foreign object; and kidnapping with intent to commit specified sex offenses. All states have sex offender registries for adult offenders. However, juveniles are not required to register in some states, even if they have been convicted of one of the specified sex offenses or crimes against children that would mandate an adult to register. The number of years a sex offender has to register also varies from state to state.

Depending on the state, the minimum time requirement to register can be 10 years, 25 years, or for life. This mandatory registration starts from the time an offender is released from incarceration. In states that have minimum registration requirements of 10 or 25 years, the time requirement for registration is increased if the offender reoffends. Sex offenders in all states must at least register annually and every time they relocate. Some states have designated certain sex offenders as extremely high-risk offenders, also referred to as *sexually violent predators,* and require them to register every 90 days. All states require sex offenders to register in the current state of residency even if their conviction occurred in another state or in federal, military, tribal, or foreign courts. All states impose registration mandates on nonresident sex offenders who travel from their states of residency. These registration requirements impose mandates on the nonresident sex offender to register regardless of whether the offender is working, a student, or visiting. The time frame in which the nonresident sex offender must meet these registration requirements varies from state to state.

Failure to comply with sex offender registry laws is a punishable offense in every state. Punishment can range from revocation of probation or parole and/or conviction of a new offense of failing to register. Depending on the state, the offense of failing to register can either be a misdemeanor or a felony. In all states, misdemeanors are seen as less severe types of crimes than felonies.

Restrictions placed on sex offenders as to where they can live once released from incarceration vary from state to state. Some states feel they have no legal authority to direct where a sex offender may or may not live. In these states, no restrictions are placed on where a sex offender may live unless such restrictions have been ordered by the court. Other states automatically set limitations on the sex offender's residence and acceptance of employment. These restrictions address the issue of placing sex offenders near schools, child care facilities, former victims, or victims' immediate family members.

Notification programs that inform the public that a sex offender is residing in the community also vary from state to state. Most notification programs allow access to certain information regarding specific groups of sex offenders but not necessarily to all groups of sex offenders. Notification guidelines provide for levels of notification based on the risk that a particular sex offender poses to the community. In determining the risk level of a sex offender's propensity to reoffend, multiple violent offenses and the type of sexual offense are considered.

Variance can be found from state to state in how and what information is disseminated to the public. A variety of methods are used to provide public information regarding specific categories of sex offenders, including public notification bulletins, community meetings, press releases, print and broadcast media notification, CD-ROMs, and the Internet. What information is provided to the public is often based on the risk category in which the sex offender has been placed.

Great strides have been made in tracking sex offenders and releasing information to the public in an attempt to safeguard communities, but these efforts are no guarantee of safety. Sex offender registries do not list every person ever convicted of a sexual offense, and notification programs do not necessarily allow the public to know about all the registered sex offenders living in communities. This is an ever-evolving area of the law that continually tries to increase the safety of communities, particularly their children.

—*Judith L. Tucker*

See also CHILDREN AS VICTIMS OF SEX CRIMES; CYBERSTINGS; EXPLOITATION OF CHILDREN; MEGAN'S LAW; PEDOPHILE ORGANIZATIONS; PEDOPHILES

Further Reading

Ahearn, L. A. (2001). *Megan's Law nationwide and The Apple of My Eye Childhood Sexual Abuse Prevention Program.* Prevention Press USA Publishers.

Lychner Act, Pub. L. 104-236, 110 Stat. 3093 (1996).

Megan's Law, Pub.L. 104-145 (1996).

Walsh, E. R. (1998). *Sex offender registration and community notification: A "Megan's Law" sourcebook.* Civic Research Institute Publishers.

Wetterling Act 42 USC § 14071(f) (1994).

SEX OFFENDERS

Throughout time, societies have been plagued with sexually aberrant individuals who prey on helpless victims in order to pursue their own sexually violent fantasies and behaviors. At the end of the 19th century, Jack the Ripper terrified a helpless community with the sexual murders of several prostitutes within the Whitechapel District of England. In today's modern world, sexually violent criminals, child molesters, and rapists continue to harm innocent women and children. In the event of these awful tragedies, society must rely on law enforcement and the psychiatric community to provide protection, as well as an explanation for such radical behavior.

Traditionally, it has been law enforcement's responsibility to apprehend and prosecute sexual offenders, and the psychiatric community to prevent and treat them. However, the reality is that the prevention, apprehension, prosecution, and potential treatment are multifaceted. Moreover, the sole responsibility of sexual offenders doesn't lie only with the criminal justice and mental health constituents, but with society as a whole.

Sexual offenders are a relatively homogeneous class of individuals. Factors in which these offenders vary may include the frequency and type of sexual offenses they commit and differences in personal attributes such as age, ethnicity, socioeconomic status, cognitions, and beliefs. One thing does remain constant, and that is society's disdain for sexual offenders and their acts.

ETIOLOGY: NATURE VERSUS NURTURE

Within the large body of research on the various causes of sexual offending, a dichotomy exists between the "nature versus nurture" theories. Some theorists believe that sexual offenders are "born" not made, and some feel that sexual offenders are products of their environments. Theorists who contend that sexual criminals are born with a proclivity for sexual offending focus on certain biological factors. A biological example would be the *XYY chromosome theory,* examining the relationship between violent behavior and the abnormal, extra Y chromosome. Another biological explanation for the causation of sexual offending lies in the theory that sexual offenders may have inherited personality traits, predisposing them to commit acts of sexual violence.

Some theorists examine environmental factors that may shape and influence sexually aberrant behaviors. Such environmental factors may be the interpersonal relationship between the offender and his primary care provider. Research indicates that those who commit sexual violence are more likely to have been victims of abuse, which was typically sexually violent in nature.

Despite the long-standing debate over nature versus nurture, the causes of sexual offending are multidimensional. The reality is that there are many interactive factors to consider in an attempt to fully understand the dynamics of the underlying causes of sexual offenders.

ELEMENTS OF THE SEXUAL OFFENDER

Fantasy

In addition to the formative development discussed above, there are several elements inherent to this type of deviant behavior. The role of fantasy is vital. Sexually violent criminals harbor sexually violent fantasies. This fantasy system is developed early in an attempt for the offenders to maintain control over their own lives, which are typically dysfunctional as a result of severe trauma sustained in childhood. Moreover, fantasy is a means by which offenders can create scenarios in their minds involving the control, manipulation, and dominance over helpless victims. Fantasies of sexual offenders involve themes of revenge, dominance, power, control, humiliation, physical and sexual violence, and sometimes death.

Sexually violent fantasy becomes a catalyst by which offenders act out their sexual behavior. Essentially, offenders will reenact their sexual imagery in an attempt to regain some aspect of control over their own lives. Each time the fantasy is reenacted via a sexual offense, the elements and images of the fantasy will intensify in terms of intensity and level of violence. More specifically, the fantasy system becomes part of a larger cycle of behaviors in which the offender becomes addicted. The entire system of behavior becomes a self-sustaining cycle of negative behavior, similar to that of an addiction.

Other aspects of the self-sustaining cycle include *masturbation, facilitating agents* such as pornography and alcohol, as well as a *paraphilic factor,* accounting for the sexual imagery and stimuli.

Facilitating Agents

Such agents may include pornography, alcohol, or drugs. Alcohol and drugs inhibit an individual, and pornography acts as a desensitizer. These facilitators also function as stress relief for the individual when there may be either an internal or external struggle. Both pornography and mind-altering substances facilitate the fantasy process, which then facilitates the sexual behavior. These facilitators manifest into an addiction for the individual.

Masturbation

Masturbation essentially acts as reinforcement to the sexual behavior described above. Moreover, masturbation, typically compulsive in nature, in tandem with daydream and fantasy enable the individual to experience a sexually satisfying encounter by fantasizing and rehearsing the sexual stimuli to the point of orgasm. An orgasmic conditioning process becomes an integral aspect of the entire cycle of behavior described above.

These behaviors are all interactive components, which are part of an overall cycle of negative behavior that ultimately becomes self-sustaining. This systemic self-sustaining process is explored further in research on paraphilia. More specifically, Purcell examines this paraphilic cycle of behavior as a motivating element in sexual crimes, namely that of *erotophonophilia,* also called *lust murder* and *sexual homicide.* This notion of a paraphilic cycle is depicted in an integrated theoretical model of paraphilia.

WHAT IS NORMAL SEX?

In an attempt to understand the complex underpinnings of sexual offenders, as well as myriad sexual offenses they commit, it is important to have a conceptual understanding of "normal sex." What is considered normal sexual behavior? To some, this may appear to be a loaded question. Sex and sexuality are inherent to mankind; however, societies' regulations and different cultural standards can adversely affect the way in which sex and sexuality are perceived. A society determines what is considered normal sexual ideation and conduct. As individuals, people have the right to choose their own personal preference relative to the sexual behaviors in which they engage. The norms of society also determine the sexual behaviors that are considered normal versus abnormal sexuality.

As a heterogeneous society with so many individual differences, it is inevitable that individual sexuality will be diverse and variant. What one person considers normal may be regarded as abnormal by another. Because of varying perspectives on what is considered sexually appropriate, sexual behavior in general should be conceptualized as a continuum of behavior, ranging from normal to abnormal. It is inevitable that some people will need more sexual stimulation than others and may engage in more perverse behaviors in order to be sexually aroused and satisfied; however, perverse behavior may be regarded as deviant and even criminal by the society in which one lives.

Determining Normal Sexual Behavior

According to research by Holmes, there are at least four standards used to determine normalcy; however, it is difficult to ascertain the applicability of each to individual circumstances as well as which standard is regarded as the most important. Both circumstance and individual differences must be considered when making a decision to cite a standard. The following is a list of standards of sexual behavior:

- *Statistical:* what most people do
- *Religious:* what one's religion permits or prohibits
- *Cultural:* what one's culture encourages or discourages
- *Subjective:* person's judgment of their own behavior (Holmes, 1991, p. 2)

Statistical Standards

Statistical standards of behavior are determined when more than half the people within a sample either commit or perform a specific act of behavior. Essentially, this percentage validates normalcy for that given group of individuals.

Religious Standards

Historically, the role of religion has played a critical role in the development of the value system as it pertains to both individuals and societies. As a result, religious standards influence the way people perceive what is considered to be right and wrong, which consequently plays a vital role in determining what is sexually acceptable.

Cultural Standards

Culture is a normative structure within society consisting of rules, sets of words, ideas, customs, and beliefs governing that given society. Many attempts are made through societies' norms, rules, and sanctions to control and regulate sexual behavior.

Subjective Standards

According to Holmes, one of the most important standards of determining normal sexual behavior is the subjective standard. This standard legitimates behavior in the same fashion as statistical, cultural, and religious standards, but in a personal subjective manner. Holmes further contended that when an act of deviance is committed, sexual or not, attempts are made to legitimize that behavior via subjective rationalization.

Elements of Sexual Behavior: Normal and Abnormal

In addition to providing a baseline of normal sexual standards, Holmes also made an important distinction within his research in examining elements inherent to both normal and abnormal sexual behaviors. Fantasy, symbolism, ritualism, and compulsion are all factors he has identified in trying to develop a distinction between normal and abnormal sexual behaviors.

To be sexual, one must have a sexual fantasy, and without one, it is impossible to be sexual. Other theorists have also implicated the essential role of fantasy and contend that sexual fantasies are a component of normal sexual activities of most males and females. Sexual fantasy has been hypothesized to be an important aspect of sexual functioning in some of the earliest theorists in psychology.

For those engaging in variant sexual behavior, fantasy is a fundamental aspect accounting for the extreme deviation from what is typically considered normal sexual activity. A distinguishing factor between normal and abnormal fantasy is the nature and content of the fantasy. Most abnormal fantasies contain aggressive and sadistic elements, which are ultimately depicted in the dynamics of the sexual offense. According to Holmes, most people's fantasies center on willing partners in consensual, "normal" sexual acts.

Symbolism pertains to the visual aspect of sex and sexuality. A common example of sexual symbolism is illustrated in the content of advertisements marketing alcohol or cigarettes, for example, in which attractive, scantily clad women are featured to sell the products. Sex is visual, and sex sells. Holmes (1991) associated sexual symbolism with fetishism and partialism, and stated that "these philia have a sexual association attached to them" (p. 6). A wide array of female articles of clothing—bras, garter belts, and negligees— are all common fetish items.

With ritualism, the sexual act is performed in the same fashion and often in the same sequence. This can be true for sexual offenders as well as for married couples. However, with the sexual offender, the practice of ritualism essentially becomes a form of addictive behavior.

Sexual compulsion is an urge, often uncontrollable, to engage in some form of sexual behavior. This behavior can be present in normal relationships in which there is a natural impulse and need to engage in sexual activities with a consenting partner, yet it becomes abnormal when compulsivity is so overwhelmingly potent that emotions and caring for the partner are missing. Within serial sexual offenders, compulsive feelings well up inside and launch them into action. Such was the case with serial killer Ted Bundy. He stated during an interrogation in Pensacola, Florida, in the late 1970s, "There is something deep inside of me, something I can't control, it's so strong" (Holmes, 1991, p. 8).

CONCLUSION

Throughout the course of time, society has been besieged with individuals who sexually deviate from what is considered normal sexual behavior. Sex offenders are encountered within various contexts, including the criminal justice arena, correctional system, and clinical milieu. As stated earlier, the causes of sexual offending are multifaceted. Therefore, for prevention, identification, apprehension, prosecution, and possible treatment to be effective, a multidimensional approach must be taken.

—*Catherine Purcell*

See also Bundy, Theodore "Ted"; Lust Murder; Motives for Murder; Rape; Paraphilia; Pedophilia; Sexual Offenses; XYY Syndrome

Further Reading

Holmes, R. M. (1991). *Sex crimes.* Newbury Park, CA: Sage.

O'Donohue, W. O., Letourneau, E. J., & Dowling, H. (1997). Development and preliminary validation of a papaphilic sexual fantasy questionnaire. *Sexual Abuse: A Journal of Research, 9,* 167-178.

Purcell, C. E. (2000). *An investigation of paraphilias, lust murder, and the case of Jeffrey Dahmer: An integrative theoretical model.* Dissertation, Alliant University, California School of Professional Psychology, Fresno.

Purcell, C. E., & Arrigo, B. A. (2001). Explaining paraphilias and lust murder: An integrated model. *International Journal of Offender Therapy and Comparative Criminology, 45,* 6-31.

SEX OFFENDERS: ADOLESCENT

Adolescent sexual offenders are the subset of the adolescent population who have had sexual interaction with others without their consent or who have threatened sexual interaction without consent. This includes using coercion or force against same-age or older victims and using bribes or tricks against younger children who are unable by virtue of their age to consent to the sexual activity.

It is widely acknowledged that most sexual offenses are not reported to authorities. What is known about adolescent sex offenders is therefore based on the minority of cases that have been reported and may have resulted in criminal charges. The age of criminal responsibility in most English-speaking countries is 10 years, but the modal age for adolescent sex offenders is 14. The term *juvenile sex offender* also relates to this group. This term is often used in legal settings and usually distinguishes those in the juvenile jurisdiction (typically 10 to 17 years old) from the adult jurisdiction (18 years old and above).

Adolescent sex offenders engage in a range of offenses, including "hands-off" offenses such as voyeurism ("peeping Tom") and exhibitionism, minimal-contact offenses such as fondling, and violent rape and sexual homicide. Adolescents are also known to engage in illegal paraphilic behaviors such as *zoophilia* (sex with animals) and *frotteurism* (rubbing one's genitals against strangers in crowded public places).

CHARACTERISTICS OF ADOLESCENT SEX OFFENDERS

Adolescent sex offenders are a heterogeneous population. They are found among all social, racial, and religious groups. The vast majority of adolescent sex offenders (upwards of 90%) are male. They come from a diverse array of backgrounds, but many studies have shown that a large proportion, particularly those involved in the criminal justice system, have come from backgrounds of social marginalization. Many of these offenders also commit nonsexual offenses, including property offenses as well as crimes against persons.

Females have been reported to make up from 1% to 2.6% of participants in treatment programs specifically catering to adolescent sex offenders and 7% to 8% of youth referred to children's courts for sexual offenses or known to rehabilitation or corrective services in the United States (National Center for Juvenile Justice, NCJJ, 2000).

Many adolescent sex offenders have themselves been victims of physical and sexual abuse as children. The proportion is unclear, but clinical reports put the figure between 40% to 80% (NCJJ, 2000). There is some evidence that female adolescent sex offenders have experienced even more extensive and severe maltreatment than their male counterparts. Female adolescent sex offenders have typically been victims of sexual abuse at an earlier age and have a greater likelihood than males of having multiple perpetrators. Many female offenders also demonstrate repetitive patterns of sexual offending with multiple victims. In general, sexual abuse victimization among adolescent sex offenders is associated with a chaotic family background and a preference for choosing male child victims, whereas physical abuse victimization is more typically associated with sexual offending against female peers or adults.

Typologies

Attempts to understand adolescent sex offenders have typically relied on methods used to understand and treat adult sex offenders. The most common way of categorizing sex offenders has been according to whom they victimize. The two most common categories are rapists and child molesters.

Rapists

A number of studies in the United States, Canada, Britain, and Australia have shown that adolescents are responsible for approximately 20% of all reported rapes on adult women (NCJJ, 2000). Adolescents who rape peers or adults appear to differ in a number of ways from those who molest children. Peer/adult rapists tend to be older, usually 16 or 17, and are more likely than child molesters to use force or weapons in the commission of their offenses. They are also more likely to offend in company with others, to have records of previous nonsexual juvenile offenses, and to be considered generally antisocial and violent. This category of offenders is also more likely to have come from homes with harsh parental discipline and may have been witness to, or victims of, domestic violence. Adolescent rapists are more likely to assault females, although some adolescents (particularly in custodial settings) rape peer-aged males.

Some adolescent rapists victimize elderly women, leading some law enforcement agencies to adopt the rule of thumb: "The older the victim, the younger the offender," especially in the case of sexual homicide involving overkill. Although scientific support for this maxim has yet to be established, adolescent rapes of elderly women are not uncommon, and it has been theorized that elderly victims may present an easier target for sexually inexperienced and aggressive adolescents.

Child Molesters

Adolescents are responsible for between 30% and 50% of all reported sexual assaults of children (NCJJ, 2000). Adolescents who sexually assault children are generally younger than adolescent rapists and are more likely to use games or tricks, rather than threats or weapons, to gain the compliance of their victims. These offenders are likely to be socially isolated, with few peer-aged friends, and often have histories of sexual victimization themselves. They are more likely than rapists to victimize males and are more likely than rapists to victimize both males and females.

Many adolescent child molesters victimize younger siblings. Relatively little is known about adolescent (incest) sexual sibling abuse. Some studies have shown that compared with adolescents who abuse children from outside the home, adolescent sibling offenders report significantly more marital discord, parental rejection, physical discipline, negative family atmosphere, and general dissatisfaction with family relationships. They are also more likely to have been victims of child sexual assault themselves. It has been postulated that for some adolescent males who were sexually abused as children, the resulting sexually aggressive behaviors are directed toward younger siblings because they are readily accessible in the home.

Sexually Deviant Versus Adolescent Limited Offenders

Traditional approaches to understanding adolescent sex offenders have applied constructs of sexual deviancy based on research on adult sex offenders and have simply applied them to a younger population. Adolescents who sexually molest children have therefore often been considered to be "pedophilic" and received treatment in programs designed for adult pedophiles. The *DSM (Diagnostic and Statistical Manual of Mental Disorders)* criteria for pedophilia, however, require the individual to be 16 years of age and at least 5 years older than the victim. Many adolescents who molest children do not meet these criteria.

Paraphilias, including pedophilia, are also considered to have an adolescent onset and be life course persistent, yet it appears that many adolescent sex offenders desist from sexual offending once they reach adulthood.

A number of studies over the last 10 years in the United States, Canada, and Australia have shown that relatively few adolescents charged with sexual offenses come to the attention of the police for sexual offenses as adults. Such studies typically report recidivism rates of less than 15% for sexual offenses, but from 30% to 60% for nonsexual offenses (NCJJ, 2000). Although these studies are limited by the fact, already mentioned, that the majority of sexual offenses are not reported to the police, it still lends support to the contention that the majority of adolescent sex offenders actually "grow out of" rather than "grow into" their sexually abusive behavior.

More recent efforts to develop typologies for adolescent sex offenders have therefore put more emphasis on the fact that they are *adolescent* offenders rather than *sex* offenders and have been informed by the more general criminological literature on adolescent offending. Current research on adolescent sex offender typologies is seeking to better distinguish between adolescents who begin sexual offending in adolescence and develop paraphilias that continue into adulthood from those adolescents whose sexual offending is nonparaphilic and is limited to adolescence.

TREATMENT PROGRAMS

Treatment programs for adolescent sex offenders range from those delivered in the community by private therapists as part of juvenile court orders, to those delivered in residential settings in private hospitals, to those delivered by staff in secure juvenile correctional facilities. Group therapy is considered the treatment of choice but is frequently supported by individual and family therapy.

Treatment for adolescent sex offenders has evolved during the last 15 years from interventions based on adult programs primarily targeting sexual deviancy to more developmentally appropriate psychoeducational programs, which include intervention for the individual as well as "social-ecological" interventions within the various social systems in which the adolescent operates.

Some early treatment programs for adolescent sex offenders in the United States employed behavioral techniques such as "masturbatory satiation," in which the young person repetitively masturbated to deviant sexual fantasies, with the aim of making these fantasies boring and thus stripping them of their reinforcing qualities. Treatment progress was monitored by phallometric assessment, in which penile tumescence following exposure to deviant sexual stimuli was measured.

Other treatment methods have included the pairing of aversive stimuli, such as electric shock or ammonia, with deviant sexual stimuli, thus creating an aversion and avoidance to deviant sexual stimuli. Treatment programs using aversive stimuli and phallometric assessment for adolescent sex offenders were rarely implemented outside of the United States and are now considered a controversial area of practice.

Relapse Prevention

In recent years, a consensus has been reached among treatment providers in the United States, Canada, Britain, Australia, and New Zealand regarding the efficacy of a raft of cognitive-behavioral treatment elements that fall under the umbrella heading of "relapse prevention."

Relapse prevention involves having young people identify situations or practices that may put them at risk of committing further offenses and developing plans to either manage or avoid these high-risk situations. Relapse prevention plans (RPPs) may include modifications to the offender's intrapsychic processes, for example, challenging attitudes or beliefs that support offending, and may also include modifications of their lifestyles, for example changing their peer groups or refraining from substance abuse.

The development of an RPP is aided by the young person understanding his or her *offense cycle,* which is a description of thoughts and behaviors that precede and follow an offense. With minor personal variations, it is thought to be largely applicable to all adolescents who commit sexual offenses. By recognizing the signs that they are proceeding with the cycle, the young person has the choice of activating an RPP and employing alternate strategies for managing risk and avoiding reoffending.

The RPP can also be applied to nonsexual offending or other forms of abusive behavior (including self-abusive). It is increasingly being recognized by clinicians and researchers that the thoughts and behaviors that support sexual offending among adolescents also support a range of other problem behaviors that warrant intervention.

Although treatment for adolescent sex offenders has traditionally focused on the individual, the importance of including other people in the RPP is increasingly being recognized. These people may include the young person's probation officer or teachers from school. The young person's family, especially the parents, also plays a crucial role. Some treatment programs for adolescent sex offenders provide a comprehensive service that provides individual and family therapy, parent training, substance abuse therapy for other family members (if needed), and consultation with teachers in the young person's school. This focus on the developmental needs of the young people, the therapeutic significance of their wider social system, and the broader focus away from sexual deviancy sets more recent treatment approaches for adolescent sex offenders apart from programs designed for adult sex offenders.

Psychopharmacological Treatments

Some psychopharmacological interventions with adult sex offenders, including sex-drive-reducing medications, have been shown to be effective in reducing sexual offending. Such medications typically have undesirable side effects and may inhibit normal physical growth and development in adolescents. Consequently, a number of ethical concerns are associated with the use of these interventions with adolescents.

Other medications, such as the various selective serotonin reuptake inhibitors (SSRIs), are sometimes used as part of a comprehensive treatment plan, particularly when the young person has comorbid diagnoses, such as depression, anxiety, or post-traumatic stress disorder.

RISK ASSESSMENT AND PROGNOSIS

Recent research has suggested that although the rate of subsequent adult sexual recidivism from adolescent sex offenders is low, the risk of sexual recidivism is significantly reduced by the successful completion of a treatment program. Research into sexual recidivism among adolescent sexual offenders is still in its infancy; however, some tentative risk factors are starting to emerge.

Principles of Risk Assessment

Risk factors for sexual recidivism are generally categorized as either static or dynamic. *Static risk factors* have emerged from actuarial research and include historical variables such as the age at which the young person was charged with a sexual offense, the sex, type, and number of victims, and the presence or absence of other violent nonsexual offenses. These historical factors will not change over time or as the result of intervention.

Dynamic factors, on the other hand, relate to changeable factors, such as acceptance of responsibility for the offense, understanding of the offense cycle, ability to apply an RPP, and level of community support and integration.

More research has been conducted on static risk factors than on dynamic risk factors. Risk factors associated with sexual recidivism among male adult sex offenders include committing prior sex offenses, having "stranger" and/or male victims, having a sexual interest in young children, and not completing treatment. There are fewer consistent risk factors for sexual recidivism among adolescent males, although a self-reported sexual interest in children appears to be one of them. Adolescents who have histories of impulsive and antisocial behavior appear to be more likely to be charged with violent (sexual and nonsexual) offenses as adults.

The Juvenile Sex Offender Assessment Protocol (J-SOAP) is one of the few risk assessment tools developed for use with adolescent sex offenders. It has two static factor scales, one that aims to measure sexual deviancy and one that aims to measure impulsive and antisocial behavior. It also has two dynamic factor scales: one that aims to measure treatment progress and one that aims to measure community adjustment. The instrument is still in its infancy, and its predictive validity is yet to be established; however, initial research using the instrument is encouraging.

Prognosis

The link between adolescent sexual offending and adult sexual offending is unclear. Although some studies have shown that approximately 50% of adult sex offenders in prisons began their offending as adolescents, other studies have shown that only about 15% of adolescents charged with sexual offenses come to the attention of police for sexual offenses within the first 10 years of adulthood (NCJJ, 2000). More longitudinal studies will be required before the link between adolescent and adult sexual offending can be more clearly understood.

It is clear, however, that many adolescent and adult sex offenders also commit large numbers of nonsexual offenses. As a group, adolescent sex offenders are much more likely to come to the attention of the police as adults for nonsexual offenses than for sexual offenses.

It appears, therefore, that a number of complex interactions between various factors determine the pathway between adolescent and adult sexual offending. Although there seems to be a core group for whom sexual deviancy is a primary factor that best describes, motivates, predicts, and restricts their behavior, these individuals also seem to be in the minority. Other offenders, greater in number, appear to be more generally antisocial, and their sexual offenses are opportunistic and just one example of their more general delinquency or criminality. Still others appear to be both sexually deviant and antisocial and predatory. Although statistically rare, these individuals create fear out of proportion to their relatively low numbers.

—Ian Nisbet

See also Juvenile Offenders; MacDonald Triad; Rape; Paraphilia; Predicting Violent Behavior; Psychosocial Risk Factors for Violent Behavior; Sexual Offenses

Further Reading

Gray, A. S., & Pithers, W. D. (1993). Relapse prevention with sexually aggressive adolescents and children: Expanding treatment and supervision. In H. E. Barbaree, W. L. Marshall, & S. M. Hudson (Eds.), *The juvenile sex offender* (pp. 289-319). New York: Guilford.

Hunter, J. A. (2001). The sexual crimes of juveniles. In R. R. Hazelwood & A. W. Burgess (Eds.), *Practical aspects of rape investigation: A multidisciplinary approach* (3rd ed., pp. 401-419). Boca Raton, FL: CRC Press.

National Center for Juvenile Justice. (2000). *Juvenile offenders and victims: 2000 national report.* Washington, DC: Office of Juvenile Justice and Delinquency Prevention.

Prentky, R., & Righthand, S. (2001). *Juvenile sex offender assessment protocol: Manual.* Bridgewater, MA.

Ryan, G. D., & Lane, S. L. (Eds.). (1997). *Juvenile sexual offending: Causes, consequences and correction.* San Francisco, CA: Jossey-Bass.

U.S. Department of Health and Human Services, Children's Bureau. (2001). *Child maltreatment 2001: Reports from the states to the national child abuse and neglect data system.* Washington, DC: GPO.

Worling, J. R. (1995). Adolescent sibling-incest offenders: Differences in family and individual functioning when compared to adolescent nonsibling sex offenders. *Child Abuse and Neglect, 19*(5), 633-643.

Worling, J. R., & Curwen, T. (2000). Adolescent sexual offender recidivism: Success of specialized treatment and implications for risk prediction. *Child Abuse and Neglect, 24,* 965-982.

SEXUAL CHILD ABUSE, *See* Child Abuse; Children as Victims of Sex Crimes; Exploitation of Children; Pedophilia; Pedophile Organizations; Sex Offenders

SEXUAL HOMICIDE, *See* Lust Murder; Motives for Murder; Paraphilia

SEXUAL OFFENSES

Sexual offenses vary in terms of victim selection, intensity, frequency, duration, type of offense, and severity. Rape, paraphilia, incest, and sexual homicide are types of sexual offenses. There is a substantial body of research on each of these areas of sexual offending that further examines the etiology, typology, treatment, and criminal profiling of these offenders. In addition to the academic arena that provides research on the above-mentioned dimensions of sexual offenders and their subsequent behaviors, the criminal justice arena is a dimension that is typically responsible for the detection, apprehension, and prosecution of these offenders. The legal aspect of sexual offending is also responsible for creating laws that govern sexual behavior, as well as laws that punish such behaviors and ultimately protect society from such offenders. Notwithstanding, legal definitions of sexual offending, such as rape, vary from state to state.

CLASSIFICATION OF RAPE

Classification paradigms have been developed by social scientists in an attempt to advance their understanding of sexually deviant behavior. When examining behavior patterns of rapists, several typologies exist. The classic work of Nicolas Groth and colleagues has provided a solid foundation by which experts can further understand the underlying dynamics of rape, as well as the motivating factors.

According to Groth, rape from a clinical perspective is defined as any type of unwanted sexual activity imposed on a person against his or her will and without consent. Groth's typology consists of three categories; anger rapist, power rapist, and sadistic rapist. The following attributes are typical characteristics of these classifications (Groth & Hobson, 1997, chap. 8):

Anger Rapist

- Aggression: use of physical force on victim.
- Impulsive, spontaneous assault.
- Offender's mood is depressed and angry.
- Episodic offenses, short in duration.
- Use of offensive language, humiliation, and obscene language.
- No weapon, typically; if used, it is out of convenience and to hurt, not threaten, victim.
- Victim selection based on availability as well as age preference, typically the same age as offender or older.
- Psychological cognitions of offender are retaliatory aggression, retribution for perceived wrong, injustices, or rejections experienced.

Power Rapist

- Aggression: use of threat or force to gain control.
- Premeditated assault preceded by sexually violent fantasy.
- Offender's mood is anxious.
- Offenses are repetitive, with a likelihood of an increase of aggression and violence over time.
- Language is intrusive and/or instructional: asking victim personal questions.
- Victim may be held captive for a number of hours; attack may happen in a short period of time.
- Use of personal weapon to threaten or intimidate victim.
- Victim selection based on offender's perception of vulnerability.
- Psychological dynamics are deep-seated feelings of insecurity and inadequacy, compensatory aggression to feel powerful and adequate.
- Criminal history involving crimes of exploitation and of sexual offense.

Sadistic Rapist

- Aggression: eroticized physical violence, force, and power.
- Victim subjected to ritualistic behavior, torture, and abuse.
- Calculated assault, preplanned.
- Offender's mood is excitement.
- Offenses are compulsive, structured and ritualistic; torture, sexual paraphilia.
- Language is commanding, degrading.
- Assault takes place over an extended period of time; victim abducted, held hostage, tortured, possibly killed and disposed of.
- Weapon used to capture victim; use of restraints for bondage and torture.
- Victim selection determined by specific characteristics, or symbolic representation, typically a complete stranger.
- Psychological dynamics, eroticized aggression, and symbolism
- Criminal history: none, or bizarre ritualistic or violent behavior.

PARAPHILIA

From a clinical perspective, *paraphilia* is defined as recurrent, intense sexually arousing fantasies, sexual urges, or behaviors generally involving nonhuman objects, the suffering or humiliation or oneself or one's partner, or children or other nonconsenting persons, that occur over a period of at least 6 months (see the *Diagnostic and Statistical Manual of Mental Disorders, DSM-IV*). Paraphilias are common almost exclusively to males, who typically have multiple paraphilias, with one dominating. There are literally hundreds of paraphilias. Paraphilic behavior can be conceptualized as a continuum of behavior. A paraphilic can be classified as "mild," "moderate," or "severe." A person functioning in the "mild" end of the spectrum may have some elements of behavior described in the *DSM-IV* yet may be able to function socially and sexually. Moreover, a person in the "mild" and "moderate" ends of the continuum may employ paraphilic practices in their sexual behavior occasionally yet can still function sexually without the paraphilic stimuli. When the person is unable to obtain sexual arousal and satisfaction without the paraphilic stimuli and fantasy, this behavior is considered pathological.

Paraphilias typically found in the criminal and clinical arena include the following:

- Exhibitionism: (indecent exposure) intentional exposure of one's genitals to an unsuspecting person
- Frotteurism: touching or rubbing of the genitals against a nonconsenting person
- Voyeurism ("peeping Tom"): sexual pleasure by observing or watching an unsuspecting person, typically associated with intimate scenes, such as a woman undressing or a couple engaged in sexual contact
- Pedophilia (child molester): sexual attraction and relation with a prepubescent child, typically age 13 or younger
- Hebophile: sexual attraction and relation with a pubescent adolescent
- Sadism: physical and psychological suffering of a nonconsenting victim, typically using humiliation, aggression, sexual violence, and torture
- Necrophilia: sexual relations with a dead body
- Erotophonophilia (lust murder, sexual homicide): eroticized sexual violence, acting out of sadistic behavior by brutally and sadistically murdering the victim

Inherent to all paraphilia is the vital role of fantasy, masturbation, and facilitating agents such as drugs and alcohol. These behaviors become self-sustaining. In addition, various factors in early childhood development are also evident. Environmental, sociological, biological, and psychological elements have all been examined in an attempt to explain the etiology of sexual paraphilia. An integrative theoretical model of behavior proposed by Purcell demonstrates how paraphilia is a motivating factor in sexual offending. In addition to examining formative events and the self-sustaining paraphilic process, the progression of such behavior has also been explored.

The integrative paraphilic model proposes that when a stressor is present either internally or externally, the offender is unable to effectively handle and resolve the conflict and may experience momentary loss of control. This stressor functions as a trigger, having the potential to bring back negative feelings from the offender's past. This triggering effect essentially feeds back into the paraphilic cycle of behavior by way of a feedback loop, so that the behavior is sustained by masturbation, facilitators, and fantasy, finally manifesting into paraphilic behavior (see Figure 1).

The feedback loop demonstrates the potential escalation of the sexual behavior, depending on whether the offender chooses to reenact his fantasy. By acting out the paraphilic fantasy and stimuli, the offender is attempting to satisfy and complete his illusion. Each time the behavior in inaugurated, the offender experiences an exhilarating feeling of sexual satisfaction as well as an increased need for stimulation. The act, criminal or not, serves as a reinforcer and feeds back into the fantasy system and the paraphilic process of behavior.

As the fantasies become more violent in content, the nature of the paraphilic stimuli also progresses in intensity and frequency. Each time the offender reenacts his paraphilic fantasy, the need for increased stimulation becomes more critical, and the individual engages in the paraphilic cycle of behavior.

CONCLUSIONS

Rape, pedophilia, and other sexual crimes are unfortunate and disturbing aspects of human behavior. Fortunately, laws have been created in an attempt to protect society from those who choose to engage in them. In addition to the laws that govern and sanction

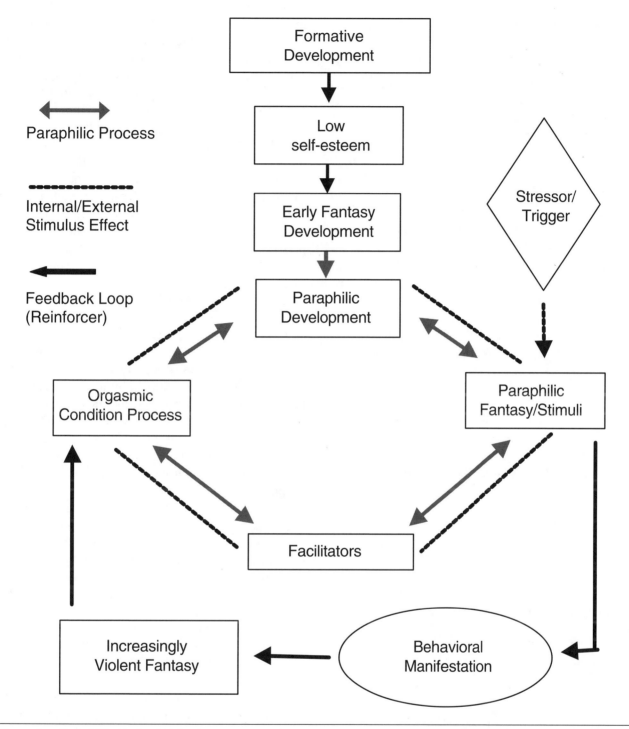

Figure 1   Paraphilic Cycle of Behavior

illegal sexual behaviors, professionals have been conducting research in an attempt to further an understanding of them. Various typologies and paradigms have been created as a way of classifying various sexual assaults.

Future studies within the area of sexual offenders would do well to continue to assess the explanatory and predictive capabilities of such models of behaviors and help advance our understanding of the clinical aspects of prevention and treatment. The legal process can have a significant effect by creating legislation to prosecute offenders, as well as aiding in the profiling, detection, and apprehension of offenders.

—*Catherine Purcell*

See also PEDOPHILIA; PARAPHILIA; PARAPHILIAS ASSOCIATED WITH VIOLENT BEHAVIOR; RAPE; SEX OFFENDERS; VICTIMOLOGY; WHITE SLAVERY

Further Reading

Abel, G. G., & Osborne, C. (1992). The paraphilias: The extent and nature of sexually deviant criminal behavior. *Psychiatric Clinics of North America, 15,* 675-687.

American Psychiatric Association. (1994). *The diagnostic and statistical manual of mental disorders* (4th ed.). Washington, DC: Author.

Groth, A. N., & Birnbaum, H. (1979). *Men who rape: The psychology of the offender.* New York: Plenum.

Groth, A. N., & Hobson, W. F. (1997). *The dynamics of sexual assault.* In L. B. Schlesinger & E. Revitch (Eds.), *Sexual dynamics of antisocial behavior.* Springfield, IL: Charles C Thomas.

Purcell, C. E. (2000). *An investigation of paraphilias, lust murder, and the case of Jeffrey Dahmer: An integrative theoretical model.* Dissertation, Alliant University, California School of Professional Psychology, Fresno.

SHAKEN BABY SYNDROME, *See* BATTERED CHILD SYNDROME; CHILD ABUSE

SHIPMAN, HAROLD, *See* METHODS OF MURDER; MOTIVES FOR MURDER; POISONING: MEDICAL SETTINGS

SIGNATURE KILLERS

CRIME SCENE CALLING CARDS

A *signature* is defined as the name of a person as written by himself or herself: a distinctive mark or characteristic indicating identity. Signatures are not solely the purview of murderers but are also often used by serial rapists and stalkers. The signature provides the offender with a greater sense of power, control, and fantasy fulfillment. Signature killers leave evidence at the scene of the crime that indicates identifying personality traits and behavioral patterns. Most signature killers are serial murderers. Some signature behaviors are postmortem activities, for example, mutilation, dismemberment, and sexual activity with a dead victim; but often, the distinctive pattern occurs prior to or during the actual act of murder. The information derived from such evidence becomes one of the most important aspects in the analysis of a violent crime scene and development of a criminal personality profile of a murderer. As handwriting experts determine personality traits from one's penmanship, so do law enforcement officers, detectives, and criminologists read into these signature elements.

The entire concept of serial murder rests on the premise that individuals are unable to cease their continuous murderous actions because of particular psychological needs and fantasies. The crime scene becomes the arena in which killers can perform, perfect, and relive their fantasies by acting out in ways that are unique to their psychological needs. Thus, crime scene behavior is an absolute, constant reflection of the violent and sadistic desires of each killer. Any brutal and destructive action at the crime scene beyond that which is necessary to complete the act of killing is considered signature behavior. Indeed, there are exceptions. Theodore Kaczynski, the infamous Unabomber, was known to have meticulously carved the initials "FC" into the homemade bombs he mailed or personally delivered to his chosen victims. The "FC" is believed to have stood for "Freedom Club," which was supposed to represent his raison d'être: He was a socially minded Robin Hood whose time it was to warn society of the pervasive ills of technology. This personalization not only made his bombs unique but also made Kaczynski an anomaly even among serial killers.

Murderers can change their modus operandi (MO) but usually not their signatures. The MO consists of methods and techniques often deemed necessary to complete the criminal act. A change in MO may be the substitution of a weapon, for instance, switching to a knife instead of a blunt instrument. This may be an intentional act to confuse law enforcement, or it may be a simple response to the circumstantial factors of the particular murder; for example, in an unexpected struggle, the murderer attempts to quickly control the victim by reaching for a nearby object such as a rock.

Signature behavior remains constant and consistent with each violent act because internal factors and influences, not external circumstances, direct the murderous interaction of the offender. The goal of serial killers is to continue to murder without being caught. If serialists believe that their killing techniques are a liability or are ineffective, they are intelligent and cunning enough to change those methods, but their distinctive behavior tends to remain constant.

TYPES OF SIGNATURES

A murderer may leave his or her personal imprint at the crime scene in various ways: high incidence of overkill, the displaying and positioning of the body, the disposal of the body, use of other instruments or foreign objects, postmortem mutilation, bondage or tying the victim, overcontrols (handcuffs, restraints), sexual activity prior to or after death, evisceration, the taking of body parts, signs of torture, imprisonment of the victim for a period of time prior to murder, and the collection of tokens and souvenirs from the victim.

"Jack the Ripper" is one of the most famous and celebrated examples of a signature killer. His savage killings occurred from August to November 1888 yet remain unsolved and of immense interest to the contemporary public and law enforcement community. Five women, all prostitutes, were murdered by the vicious slashing of their throats from ear to ear. Their bodies were mutilated and dissected. Certain organs were removed and taken from the scene. Jack the Ripper taunted the police and the news media by sending part of the kidney of one of his victims to a London newspaper. Many theories and profiles have been developed regarding the true identity of the Ripper. Suspects range from petty criminals to members of the medical profession and the royal family.

The "Boston Strangler" is a famous 20th-century signature killer. He horrified the city of Boston from June 1962 to January 1964. During that time, 13 women were sexually assaulted and strangled with pieces of their own clothing. Oftentimes, a stocking was used and tied in a bow around the victim's neck. At some of the crime scenes, victims were also bitten, cut, or bludgeoned. The victims ranged from 19 to 85 years of age. The first psychological profile described the strangler as a "mother hater" because his first 6 victims were older women. Shortly after the profile was made public, the strangler killed a 20-year-old girl and followed that murder by killing a 23-year-old. In 1965,

while serving time in prison for a series of rapes unrelated to the case, Albert De Salvo confessed to being the Boston Strangler. He described each case in such significant detail that the police became convinced of his guilt. Andrei Chikatilo, the Russian Ripper, lured children and teenagers from train stations and then gouged out their eyes so they could not watch him while he eviscerated them.

Some signature killers carefully select the locations for the disposal of the bodies of their victims, which is important because it determines who will find the body, and when. Ted Bundy, the constant seeker of notoriety and attention, is believed to have killed anywhere from 30 to 100 young women. He preselected dumpsites for the disposal of his victims. These sites were remote areas that provided him privacy while he tortured and killed his victims. Oftentimes, the heads, feet, and hands were cut off to prohibit any identification of the bodies, if and when they were found before they were scattered by wild animals. Bundy was intelligent, well educated, and good-looking. His killing started with stalking and voyeurism and progressed to rape and murder. He acted out his violent murderous fantasies between 1973 and 1978, in at least five different states. His charm and personality enabled him to use ruses to lure victims to his car. He struck them with blunt objects, rendering them unconscious, and then kept them for days. Many of his victims were sodomized and raped before being strangled. Bundy would insert foreign objects into their vaginas and apply makeup prior to disposing of the bodies in remote areas.

Females also engage in signature and serial murder, though much more infrequently. Gwendolyn Graham and Catherine Wood were employees at a nursing home in Walker, Michigan, in the late 1980s. Through their jobs, they had access to innumerable vulnerable and elderly victims. They selected women suffering from Alzheimer's disease. Gwendolyn smothered the victims with a cloth, while Catherine kept watch against witnesses or intruders. After each of their six murders, they stole personal articles and items from the victims. These souvenirs were found displayed throughout their home.

Catherine Wood confessed to her ex-husband soon after Gwendolyn Graham rejected her for a new lover. As part of her later plea bargain with authorities, Catherine testified against Gwendolyn. She stated that they felt an emotional release after killing their victims and were filled with excitement whenever they talked or fantasized about the murders.

SUMMARY

The physical evidence collected at a crime scene provides clues that are imperative for the solution of the case, but the psychological clues are of equal value to the investigator. Signs of the murderer's personality left at the crime scene are of profound importance, suggesting identifiable patterns of behavior based on deep-seated psychological needs.

Many theories exist concerning how individuals become serial and signature killers. Their childhoods are riddled with instability, trauma, abuse, and many other destructive events. Whatever the cause, the effect is devastating. The solution of the crimes committed by these individuals requires the complete integration and analysis of physical and psychological evidence of their destructive and violent behavior.

—Patricia L. Kirby

Further Reading

Hickey, E. W. (2002). *Serial murderers and their victims* (3rd ed.). Belmont, CA: Wadsworth.

Holmes, R., & Holmes, S. (1996). *Profiling violent crimes: An investigative tool* (2nd ed.). Thousand Oaks, CA: Sage.

Kelleher, M. D., & Kelleher, C. L. (1998). *Murder most rare: The female serial killer.* Westport, CT: Praeger.

Keppel, R. D., & Birnes, W. J. (1997). *Signature killers.* New York: Pocket Books.

ORENTHAL JAMES "O. J." SIMPSON

Former football star O. J. Simpson during a television interview in New York City, July, 2002. O. J. gained more notoriety when he was tried for the brutal murder of his ex-wife, Nicole Brown Simpson and her friend, Ron Goldman in what was termed the "Trial of the Century." Although Simpson was found not guilty, in a civil trial, he was later held liable for $30 million.

Source: Copyright © Reuters NewMedia Inc. / CORBIS.

On June 13, 1994, Nicole Simpson, the ex-wife of football star Orenthal James "O. J." Simpson, was found lying outside her residence with her throat cut from ear to ear. Nearby was the body of a male friend, Ronald Goldman, who had been stabbed multiple times. The children, asleep in their bedrooms, had no idea of the night's occurrences. They were awakened by police and removed from the scene.

With the intention of notifying O. J. of the night's events and the location of his children, police arrived at his residence and learned he had left the state. O. J.'s older daughter allowed the officers into his residence, where they placed a telephone call to O. J. in Chicago. One officer remained outside to check on a noise complaint, and behind one of the bungalows on the property, he found a bloody glove. Police then suspected the area might be related to the crime scene and began to secure the property. The possible relationship to the crime was established when blood evidence was found in O. J.'s vehicle, on his property, and in his residence.

The glove found at the residence matched another glove found at the homicide scene. Bloody shoe prints at the crime scene matched O. J.'s shoe size, and blood was found in and around his Ford Bronco, which resembled the eye witness reports of a white jeep leaving the area of the murders.

Upon immediate return to California, O. J. voluntarily complied with investigators, providing fingerprints, blood samples, and photographs of cuts on his hand. Within a matter of days, a warrant was issued for his arrest. Witnessed by the world via television was the resulting 60-mile, low-speed vehicle pursuit in which O. J. threatened suicide by holding a handgun to his head while his best friend drove. He eventually surrendered at his home.

The resulting criminal trial, deemed the "Trial of the Century" by the media, introduced O. J.'s "Dream Team," a group of well-known lawyers, each with a criminal justice specialization. The team immediately challenged the handling of the blood evidence by both the Los Angeles Police Department and the crime lab in an attempt to effectively convince the jury that police tampering and inept handling of the evidence made the evidence invalid.

The team also contended that a "racist cop" had planted the glove at O. J.'s residence. It was widely speculated that coming on the heels of the 1992 Rodney King trial and subsequent riot, the jury makeup (nine African Americans, two whites, and one Hispanic) made it especially beneficial to present this case as racially influenced. Throughout the trial, the media reported that public opinion regarding O. J.'s guilt was divided along racial lines.

With considerable forensic evidence against him, Orenthal James Simpson was found not guilty in October 1995, acquitted in criminal court of double homicide. Four years later, a civil jury voted unanimously to find O. J. liable for the deaths of Ronald Goldman and Nicole Brown Simpson and awarded a $33 million judgment against O. J. Four years later, Mr. Simpson began legal efforts to have the verdict thrown out, claiming that the jury had been prejudiced. Since the murders, O. J. has led a colorful life that has included assault claims by both intimates and people in his community. In one instance, his daughter made a "911" call regarding O. J. and noted that her father was a "loser."

—*Vikki A. Irby*

Further Reading

Bugliosi, V. (1997). *Outrage: 5 reasons why O. J. Simpson got away with murder.* New York: Dell.

Schmalleger, F. M. (1996). *Trial of the century: People of the State of California vs. Orenthal James Simpson.* Upper Saddle River, NJ: Prentice Hall.

SINGLETON, LAWRENCE,
See PREVENTION OF CRIME AND VIOLENT BEHAVIOR

SKINHEADS, *See*
HATE GROUPS; NEO-NAZI SKINHEADS; WHITE SUPREMACISTS

SNIPERS, *See* BELTWAY SNIPERS

SOCIOLOGY, *See* AGGRESSION:
SOCIOLOGICAL THEORIES; PSYCHOSOCIAL RISK FACTORS FOR VIOLENT BEHAVIOR

SOCIOPATH, *See* AGGRESSION:
PSYCHOLOGICAL THEORIES; ANTISOCIAL PERSONALITY DISORDER; PSYCHOPATHS

SOLICITATION TO COMMIT MURDER, *See* MURDER FOR HIRE

SON OF SAM, *See*
BERKOWITZ, DAVID RICHARD

SPECIAL WEAPONS AND TACTICS TEAMS

In the late 1960s, local law enforcement across the nation experienced situations they had never encountered before. There were incidents of massive civil unrest and riots associated with the civil rights movement. There were large-scale disturbances and mass demonstrations against the Vietnam War. There were also incidents involving snipers that killed both civilians and officers alike. Most of these incidents occurred in large urban environments. The

Swat Team members, armed with advanced weaponry, search for a possible sniper near an elementary school in Maryland, the site of several shootings by the "Beltway Snipers." One response to violent crime is the development of weapons that can deal more effectively with offenders.

Source: Copyright © AFP / CORBIS.

traditional police officers working in patrol assignments were neither trained nor equipped to respond to such incidents.

Law enforcement agencies carefully critiqued these incidents and determined that they needed a new approach to address the turmoil. As a result, many large agencies formed special elite units, equipped with special weapons and trained in a variety of tactics. These Special Weapons and Tactics teams (SWAT) were first used by local law enforcement agencies in southern California. When most of these teams were first formed, it was a voluntary assignment, and the units were generally comprised of officers who had prior military experience. SWAT was not a full-time position, but an assignment in addition to an officer's regular assignment. In these early years, many officers supplied their own weapons and

ammunition. Many of the weapons used in these units were rifles that had been confiscated from those involved in illegal activity. Often, their mission was not clearly defined beyond responding to situations that regular patrol officers were unable to handle.

The goal of SWAT is to handle emergency situations or planned tactical operations without the loss of life to citizens, suspects, or officers. Today, most large urban local law enforcement agencies have a SWAT team or access to one. Some agencies, such as the Los Angeles Police Department, have officers assigned full-time to a SWAT team. However, budget constraints, training needs, and personnel requirements do not allow all agencies to do that. Many agencies have officers assigned to a SWAT team as a corollary duty in addition to their primary assignment. Others do not have a SWAT team, but instead have agreements with larger agencies to provide the service if needed.

SWAT teams comprise highly dedicated officers who are well trained in tactics and equipped with a wide array of weaponry. Teams usually train together 2 days per month. The training covers tactics such as rappelling, team movements, and the use of chemical agents. They train extensively in the use of firearms, including handguns, shotguns, sniper rifles, and full and semiautomatic rifles. Physical conditioning and weaponless defense tactics are also stressed in the training. Members maintain top physical conditioning to meet rigorous standards. The teams that engage in quality training on a regular basis have proven to be highly effective in responding to emergency situations as well as planned tactical operations.

SWAT teams respond to situations that involve snipers, barricaded armed subjects, hostage situations, high-risk search warrants, VIP security, and protection of police and fire department personnel involved in riots or mobs. These teams may also respond to other situations that require a specialized tactical response. Oftentimes a "crisis negotiation team," made up of specially trained personnel, respond to emergency situations with the SWAT team. They report to the SWAT operations commander and are employed in the hope of bringing a positive resolution to the situation. Crisis negotiators are well versed in SWAT maneuvers but are not involved in the tactical operation.

The National Tactical Officers Association has worked to improve the professionalism and proficiency of SWAT teams. They have recently published a list of suggested guidelines to raise standards of performance expectations nationwide. SWAT teams fill a vital role for law enforcement. As law enforcement continues to evolve and become more professional, SWAT teams will do the same.

—*Sharon Shaffer*

See also HOSTAGE TAKING

Further Reading

Jones, T. L. (1996). *SWAT leadership and tactical planning.* Boulder, CO: Paladin.

Kolman, J. A. (1982). A *guide to the development of special weapons and tactics teams.* Springfield, IL: Charles C Thomas.

SPORTS AND VIOLENCE

INTRODUCTION

Sport is a form of play. Almost all higher forms of animals engage in play, but only humans have the ability to organize play into sport. Like play, sport develops and refines mental and physical skills that humans need in life. Kittens stalking and wrestling each other are instinctively developing hunting and killing skills they will need as cats. Children, whether engaging in physically active play or sport, are strengthening their bodies, honing motor skills, and becoming socialized. Regardless of the type of sport or play, violence usually figures into it in some manner.

The primary definition of *violence* is physical force that injures, damages, or causes destruction. Whereas this definition of violence carries a negative connotation, sport violence is not always negative in intent or result. Most often, sport violence is simply part of a game that all players enjoy. Some sports, such as rugby, can be casually described as organized person-on-person brawling, whereas other sports, such as tennis, are spoiled by that type of violence. However, because all sport requires some measure of aggression, competition, or intense physical activity from participants, violence is naturally part of the equation. Tennis players are not allowed to throw their rackets at their opponents in anger, but they may certainly feel like doing so and probably imagine themselves doing it. A linebacker in American football may crush his opponent's ribs with a block, but he may not grab his face mask and wrench his neck. These examples also illustrate the issue of acceptable violence versus unacceptable violence. Sports that depend on violence for their play disallow certain types of violence. For example, rugby players may stop opponents by tackling them, but not by blocking or ramming them. Tennis players use physical force to damage the tennis ball somewhat, but that is all they are allowed to damage.

Sport has always endured criticism for the amount of violence it involves—and some say, inspires. There are two major theories of violence in sport. One is that sport acts as a release for the violence that players and spectators already feel. The other is that people learn to be violent from sport.

Sports violence can also be seen as a reflection of the type and amount of violence that is already present

Mike Tyson (right), known for both his boxing skills and his violent life outside the ring. Violence in sports in the United States is common among athletes and fans.

Source: Copyright © CORBIS.

in a given culture. For example, the play in American football greatly resembles that of a well-organized army, with each of the players having a specialized duty and strategic decisions being made by an off-field staff who are in constant communication with the "field marshal," or quarterback. Another example of a sport reflecting cultural violence would be the Afghan team sport of *Buzkashi,* in which the players ride horses and pursue possession of a dead goat. Buzkashi reflects the importance of equestrian skills, communication, and teamwork, all of which are critical to tribal warfare in that country. Both sports are highly popular within their cultures and require aggression and violence to play, yet endure some intercultural and/or extracultural criticism for that aspect. This illustrates the contradictory nature of violence in sport: It is often required yet frequently criticized by the very people watching the sport or participating in it.

HISTORY OF SPORTS

Sports have always had violent elements, and in fact it can be argued that sports in the past were more violent than they are now. Changing cultural mores and ideas about human rights have actually made these "old-style" sports safer to play. When American football first made its appearance as the "Boston Game" in 1873 to 1874, players wore little protection. Due to the style of play, many men died from their injuries until rule changes were instituted in the early 20th century, and additional padding and helmets began to be required in the 1930s.

Early England saw the development of the modern form of English football (soccer), and rugby appeared in the 19th century. Both of these sports originated from the mob play of townsfolk. Legend has it that soccer was invented when some people began kicking around the severed head of a vanquished foe.

Even further back in time were the Medieval jousting sports, the bloody gladiator competitions of ancient Rome, and *tlachtli,* the Aztec ball game in which the losers are said to have been sacrificed. Many track-and-field sports evolved from ancient competitions that developed hunting and fighting skills. Even games not conceived as violent sports or even as contact sports, such as basketball, invented by James Naismith in 1891, have developed some violent attributes. If violence is natural to the human race, as some scholars say, it follows that violence appears naturally in sports that humans play.

MODERN SPORTS

Violence in current sport is far more controlled. In professional sports, referees, coaches, and professional organizations ensure that appropriate violence is applied accordingly and that inappropriate violence is punished. Recreational, amateur, and children's sports are usually refereed and controlled even at the most basic, local levels. Still, some are concerned about the level of violence even in these monitored, organized activities and feel that this type of physical competition encourages societal violence. Some truly "rough" sports have come on the scene in recent years. One, called "ultimate fighting," in which the combatants may use any fighting style, has incited debate along the lines of age-old concerns about brutality in boxing and martial arts. These matches are typically restricted to live audiences and pay-per-view cable television.

Some "out-of-play" aspects of violence in sports create controversy as well, fights that inevitably break out in team sports or tantrums thrown by participants in single-player sports. Sometimes even violence committed by players in their private lives is blamed on the violence in the sports they play, that is, that they are carrying over violence appropriate to competition into areas in which it is not appropriate.

Full Contact, Semicontact, and Noncontact

Sport can be violent regardless of the contact level, though full-contact sports are obviously the most violent. These include American football, rugby, Australian-rules football, boxing, hockey, and wrestling. The players strike each other; players are injured and sometimes killed; bodies are carried off the field; fights break out. Both spectators and players expect this level of violence, and these sports are the ones that incite the most outright criticism. Noncontact sports are not considered violent, although violence occurs nonetheless. These include tennis, golf, track and field, volleyball, and swimming/diving. Although the players do not inflict violence on each other, they impose force on objects or use intense physical force during play. The players may be injured during play. The only time criticism about violence arises is when players fight, which rarely happens, or when an individual acts out in an inappropriate manner, such as a tennis player flinging a racket.

Semicontact sports arouse the most surprising amount of controversy about violence. These sports may be defined by the rule books as "noncontact," but contact is inevitable. They include soccer, basketball, baseball, and softball. In semicontact sports, some contact is sanctioned, and some is not, and it is often up to the referee to decide. This creates stress and confusion among players. Players who initiate what they believe to be legal contact may be challenged to fights by players who suffer the contact and believe it is not legal. The situation also divides fans into two camps: those who say the contact is fine and would like to see more and those who say the game is ruined by intentional contact and would like to see the rules tightened to stamp it out.

Death and Severe Injury

In professional sports, it is legal to kill. That is, it is legally acceptable if a player's action within the rules of play results in the accidental death of another player. The most often cited incidents occur in boxing, in which one boxer may issue a "death blow" and not only be blameless for the opponent's death but also win the bout as a result. Death is not as common in other full-contact sports, but severe injury is. Scores of American football players and rugby players have suffered various levels of paralysis as a result of playing their games.

Death or injury during the commission of unacceptable violence is another matter. A player who injures another as the result of a foul or rule breakage can be penalized, fined, and/or ejected from the game.

A player who injures another during a fight can be kicked out of the sport or even sent to jail.

Acceptable Violence Versus Unacceptable Violence

The line between acceptable and unacceptable violence in sports may be very fine, and rules may be instituted to adjust the level and style of violence as needed. Generally, new rules decrease violence simply to save the players. Recently, a rule was instituted in American football asserting that the head of the quarterback may not be struck in any manner by another player. An excessive number of quarterbacks were suffering concussions and severe brain injuries, thus ending their careers early as well as affecting their day-to-day today functioning.

Women in Sports

Only in recent decades have large numbers of women participated in contact and team sports at the professional level. In the early to mid-20th century, women who became famous for playing sports did so in noncontact sports such as tennis, gymnastics, swimming, and track and field. As noted previously, some measure of violence and aggression is required for noncontact sports, but these sports are not personally violent. However, with the advent of women's contact sports, such as soccer, hockey, rugby, boxing, and American football, the issue of women and violence in sport is causing concern. Some critics say that women are neither aggressive enough nor strong enough to participate effectively in these sports, that is, to "play them as they should be played." Others worry that the nature of the sports themselves will make women and young girls more aggressive and violent. However, many women, especially those who play, say that it's about time that women become more competitive and aggressive.

Children in Sports

Most children involved in contact sports at a young age are boys. As parents' expectations of their children shift, these statistics will certainly change, but currently, boys experience the most sport violence at a young age.

The traditional sports that boys play include American football, hockey, Little League baseball, soccer, basketball, and, to a lesser extent, boxing and wrestling. Boys who do not participate in such contact sports may be teased by their peers for being "wimps" or "geeks." Therefore, many boys receive a lot of pressure from their parents and other boys to participate in these sports whether they want to or not. On the other hand, a girl who wants to participate in a contact sport may be prevented from doing so by the cultural expectations of her sex. Because many adults do not wish girls to participate in contact sports because of the inherent personal violence of the activities, they have not traditionally organized contact sports teams for girls. Girls' basketball, hockey, and soccer leagues have only recently become common, and there are practically no girls' leagues for American football, baseball, boxing, and wrestling.

The most controversial issue concerning violence and children's sports these days focuses not on the young players, but on parents' involvement. Rarely does one hear about a serious brawl breaking out spontaneously among a bunch of 10-year-olds playing baseball. It is far more common to hear about a brawl breaking out among those 10-year-olds' parents. In 2002, Thomas Junta went to jail because he beat to death boys' hockey referee Michael Costin during a dispute. Ironically, Junta was upset because he thought Costin was allowing the boys to play too rough.

A common reason given for such violent parental meddling is that some parents live vicariously through their children's athletic achievements. Some parents may expect their children to perform athletically in ways they could not and win the trophies they never won. Others may have been excellent athletes as children and expect their own children to "carry on the tradition." These pressures can push parents to bring unacceptable violence to a children's game that has been marred by none from the children themselves.

Spectators

Professional and college level contact sports are inextricably linked to their spectators, so it is during those sports that spectator violence is the most visible and often the most frightening. Professional and college level contact sports require spectators in order to make money, and they provide some of the highest levels of sport entertainment and achievement because they have the money to do so. This means that these sports require very large crowds of people to operate. Many of these fans are passionately devoted to their teams, may live vicariously through their team's achievements, and may take their team's wins and losses very personally. Also, professional and college level teams are associated with politically designated geographic areas, such as a cities, states, or countries. In essence, two teams playing a game may be considered by many fans to be a form of tribal warfare. The alcohol sold at many of these events can make the mix very dangerous. Thousands of people have been crushed to death by rampaging crowds at soccer games around the world, and in Europe, many "football hooligans"—people who tend to act out violently during matches—are considered to be so destructive that they are banned from some matches. In American college towns, it has almost become de rigeur for students to riot whether their team wins or loses an important game. Hooliganism, rioting, and violence most often occurs in connection with contact sports. Critics might point to this phenomenon as a sign that the violence in these sports has a direct effect on the violence levels among fans, especially those gathered in large crowds in which individual perpetrators are less likely to be caught.

—*John Randolph Fuller*

Further Reading

Coakley, J. (2001). *Sport in society: Issues & controversies.* New York: McGraw Hill.

Eitzen, D. S. (1996). *Sport in contemporary society: An anthology.* New York: St. Martin's.

Messner, M. A., & Sabo, D. F. (1990). *Sport, men, and the gender order: Critical feminist perspectives.* Champaign, IL: Human Kinetics Books.

SPOUSAL ABUSE, *See* BATTERED WOMAN'S SYNDROME; BATTERERS AND ABUSIVE PARTNERS; DOMESTIC VIOLENCE; FAMILY VIOLENCE; VICTIMOLOGY; WOMEN AND VIOLENCE

SPREE MURDERS

Defining spree murder is most clearly done in relation to other types of multiple murders. *Mass murderers* kill many in one incident (usually in minutes or hours), whereas *serial killers* kill numerous victims, with a "cooling off" period between each victim (often over several years). Spree murder combines characteristics of the two, generally commencing as the result of a stressor in the offender's life, whose frustration and anger are manifested in an almost continuous deadly rampage for hours or sometimes days. A spree murder is one event yet covers more than one location. Essentially, there is no cooling-off period as is found with serial murders, but unlike mass murders, there is more than one crime scene. A spree murderer is sometimes confused with a *shooting spree*. School shootings by students are examples of shooting sprees, but are not necessarily spree murders.

Spree murderers often prepare for the deadly incident by packing an arsenal of weapons for use along the way. This indicates premeditation for a high victim count. Yet uncharacteristic of an organized and planned murder, spree murderers select both intimate victims as well as unsuspecting strangers. Stranger victims are typically in the killer's path during the rampage, what are known as *convenience* killings.

Feelings of inadequacy or vulnerability drive murderers to seek power through their crimes. During their crimes, however, the killers carelessly leave traces, and the police eventually chase or corner the offenders. Spree murderers recognize that their options are limited, and typically the spree ends in suicide. Some embark on their sprees as suicide missions, recognizing that they will eventually be stopped.

CASE STUDIES

Martin Bryant

One such murder spree lasted two days in Port Arthur, Australia. Martin Bryant had packed a sports bag loaded with several rifles, a hunting knife, two sets of handcuffs, a rope, a large amount of ammunition, a video camera, and a container of gasoline. He had lunch at a café, and after he finished set the video camera on a nearby table and began shooting other patrons of the café with his semiautomatic rifle. He killed 20 people and injured several others, then left the café and murdered 4 more people, again wounding many others passing by. Bryant drove toward the nearby tollbooth and killed a woman and her two children walking beside the road. He drove a few hundred yards closer to the tollbooth and killed three men in a

car. He approached another car with a couple inside, forced the man into the trunk of his car, and shot the woman.

Continuing his rampage, Bryant drove to the Seascape Cottage, where he fired at several cars within his sight. He then removed his guns from the car and took a male hostage inside the house and handcuffed the man to a stair rail. Bryant returned outside and poured gasoline over his car and set it on fire. He then reentered the cottage, which was owned by Mr. and Mrs. Martin, against whom he held a grudge. When police arrived to find Bryant barricaded inside the cottage, they believed he could have as many as three people hostage (the man abducted from the tollbooth and the Martins). Thus, they were cautious as to how to approach the situation. The next morning, after several telephone negotiations between the police and Bryant throughout the night, Bryant set the cottage on fire. As he ran out of the cottage with his clothes ablaze, the police captured him. In all, he had killed 35 people and injured another 18 in over 19 hours' time.

Michael Ryan

Another incident was the worst killing spree in Britain, later dubbed the "Hungerford Massacre." Michael Ryan, 27 years old, began his spree in Hungerford, Berkshire, on August 19, 1987. His first victim, Susan Godfrey, was out picnicking in the morning when Ryan forced her into the forest and shot her 13 times. He then drove to a filling station and shot at the clerk but missed him. Ryan proceeded to a crowded marketplace and shot at people who were in their yards, in their cars, out jogging—anyone who moved. He continued on to his mother's house, shot her, set her house on fire, and then drove down the road and killed several people in their cars or in their homes. Eventually, Ryan made his way to a school and barricaded himself inside. He spoke with the police who tried to negotiate with him, saying, "It's funny, I have killed all those people, but I haven't the guts to blow my own brains out." Approximately 7 hours after his first victim, Ryan did turn the gun on himself, ending the violent spree, which left 16 people dead and another 14 injured.

Charles Whitman

At midnight on July 31, 1966, Charles Whitman drove to his mother's house, stabbed her in the chest, and shot her in the back of the head. He then went back home and stabbed his wife as she slept. At 11:48 the next morning, he packed a survival kit, seven various guns, three knives, and approximately 1,000 rounds of ammunition. At the Texas Tower, at the University of Texas, in Austin, Whitman killed two and wounded several others. He barricaded himself in the tower and from there, shooting like a sniper for 96 minutes, killed 11 people on the campus grounds, wounding almost 30 others.

—*Nicole L. Mott*

See also BELTWAY SNIPERS; MOTIVES FOR
    MURDER; SUICIDE BY COP; SERIAL MURDER

Further Reading

Greswell, D. M., & Hollin, C. R. (1994, Winter). Multiple murder: A review. *The British Journal of Criminology, 34,* pp. 1-14.

Hickey, E. W. (2002). *Serial killers and their victims* (3rd. ed.). Belmont, CA: Wadsworth.

Josephs, J. (1993). *Hungerford: One man's massacre.* London: Smith Gryphon.

Levin, J., & Fox, J. A. (1986). *Mass murder.* New York: Plenum.

Steiger, B. (1967). *The mass murderer.* New York: Award Books.

ST. VALENTINE'S DAY MASSACRE

February 14, 1929, will forever be remembered in history as the "Saint Valentine's Day Massacre." In an attempt to thwart his enemy's control in the bootleg liquor industry, Al Capone took revenge by staging a massacre in which several of his enemies were killed.

During the early morning raid in Chicago, the Capone gang simulated a raid against seven unarmed members of the George "Bugs" Moran gang. Shortly after a bootlegger lured Moran's men to a garage to make a buy on some liquor at a low price, several of Capone's men appeared disguised as policemen in stolen uniforms, as if to conduct a raid. After gunning down the Moran gang with machine guns, two of the alleged policemen perpetuated the ruse further by appearing to arrest the "bootleggers" and fleeing in a stolen police car.

The plan was cunning, except for one crucial detail: Bugs Moran, the target of the plan, was not among those gunned down. Late to the prospective buy and sensing trouble as he neared the garage, Moran fled when he spotted a police car. One of the dying men, in an effort to maintain his *omerta,* or code of honor and silence, refused to implicate the person responsible for the mass execution, answering that he didn't know who it was. The event received national attention and expanded Capone's celebrity image, demonstrating the lengths to which the Mob would go to control the bootlegging industry during Prohibition.

—*Tatia J. Smith*

See also CAPONE, ALPHONSE "AL";
    CHICAGO MOB; ORGANIZED CRIME: DOMESTIC

STALKING

The role of stalking in murder and other violent crimes merits exploration because it can help to explain both cognitive and behavioral aspects of victim selection and the process of criminal behavior. The act of stalking did not become a crime in the United States until 1990, when the State of California passed anti-stalking statutes to protect individuals or groups from harassment, intimidation, or violence. Since then, every state has implemented some form of antistalking legislation. The behavior generally requires three elements: a pattern of harassment over a period of time, implied or explicit threats, and intent to harm, intimidate, or create great emotional stress. The media often publicize high-profile stalking of celebrities, such as tennis star Monica Seles, who in 1993 was stabbed during a tennis match. Stalking is actually more likely to occur in cases of domestic problems in which the offender relentlessly pursues a former spouse, lover, or friend.

The Threat Management Unit of the Los Angeles Police Department has classified stalkers into four categories: *simple obsessional,* in which the offender (primarily males) knows his victim and stalks as a result of perceived mistreatment or separation; *love obsessional,* which involves stranger-to-stranger stalking, in which the offender harasses the victim to draw attention to himself; *erotomania,* which typically involves a celebrity whom the offender believes is in love with her (most offenders are female); and the rare *false-victimization syndrome,* in which the offender falsely accuses another person, real or imaginary, of stalking him or her in order to assume in the role of the victim. Most of these forms of stalking seldom end in actual violence to the victim. Prediction of violence in stalking cases is a most difficult process, however.

In their study of 210 victims of stalking, Hickey and Margulies revised the prevailing view of the process of stalking, the offenders, and the victims. Hickey identified two general categories of *offender-initiated stalking: domestic* and *stranger,* each with its own types of stalkers. A third category involves *victim-initiated stalking,* or *factitious* reporting. An important distinction made is that some stalking is noncriminal and the fact that someone may be demonstrating stalking behaviors does not prove intent. Indeed, in American society, given the many ways that humans can interact with one another, attempting to repeatedly make contact with someone does not always imply criminal intent. A person wanting an autograph, a person wanting to meet another person and feeling awkward about initiating contact, or people sending e-mails all may or may not be construed as stalking, depending on the contextual cutting point of the relationship; the duration, intensity, and frequency of the contact; past behavior of the initiator; and the level of dangerousness created by the initiator. Some part of everyday social interaction may involve low levels of noncriminal stalking, or *nuisance stalking.* Nuisance stalking can, and often does, quickly develop into various forms of criminal stalking, however.

TYPES OF STALKING

The following classification system is designed to assist potential victims of stalking in identifying, understanding, and handling offenders. Critical to this discussion is the linkage of violent offenders to stalking behaviors. Each of the following categories of stalking has different types of stalkers:

1. Domestic	2. Stranger	3. Factitious
Power/Anger	Power/Anger	False Victimization
Obsessional	Obsessional	Hero Fantasy
Nuisance	Nuisance	
	Sexual predator	
	Erotomania	

Domestic Stalking

This form of stalking commonly involves persons who are related to the victim, friends, or acquaintances and usually can be associated with one of three types of stalkers. *Domestic-power/anger* stalkers harbor feelings of hatred, revenge, and domination over their victims. Sometimes offenders are so consumed by their anger that they are inappropriately designated as being obsessed. These offenders may exhibit antisocial characteristics, low self-esteem, lack of self-confidence, insecurity, and fear, but they are not obsessed in a clinical sense. Their inability to manage their personal or public lives creates a state of perpetual frustration and anxiety. In turn, their frustrations and emotions lead them into increasingly violent acts. This is the most common type of domestic stalker and most likely to do physical harm to the victim. The victims are usually women caught up in dysfunctional relationships who leave their husbands, lovers, boyfriends, or acquaintances because they fear for their own personal safety and/or the safety of their children. Enraged, the offender often begins a campaign of relentless pursuit by harassing, threatening, and assaulting and in some cases, killing the victim.

In California, 25% of women who flee their spouses as a result of being physically assaulted and believing that the offender will kill them are ultimately stalked and killed by those angry men. In a case in Indiana, an inmate who was serving time for spousal abuse was given a home furlough to spend time with his mother. Mr. Matheny had been an exemplary prisoner, and authorities believed that he would be a very good risk for such a visit. His ex-wife knew better and feared that he would kill her if he was ever released. She was never notified of his visitation with his mother, and it cost the woman her life. Matheny made his mother sit in the passenger seat and then proceeded to drive directly to the victim's residence, where he broke into her home, grabbed her by the hair, and dragged her outside onto the driveway. Then, in front of her children and neighbors, he beat her to death with the butt end of a rife she'd had in her home for protection.

Also important in many cases, the stalking actually begins prior to the departure of the victim from the home. She may be followed, repeatedly threatened, and spied on while at work. This escalation of domestic violence begins with verbal abuse and threats to batter the victim and threats using weapons. In some cases, offenders engage in death rituals that include showing the victim the manner in which she is going to be killed if she does not stop trying to leave him or fails to meet other demands. For example, the offender may initially have an unloaded gun present in the room when he argues and fights with his significant other. Eventually, he may load the gun in her presence before or during an argument. As his frustrations increase, his sense of control decreases, forcing him to use increasingly violent forms of intimidation. Finally, the victim reports having the loaded gun pointed at her, placed against her head, or forced into her mouth.

Each stage of escalating violence brings the victim closer to death. Frequently at this point, the victim will flee her abuser, take out a restraining order, and seek refuge in a shelter for women or move in with other family, friends, or relatives. For some abusers, the departure represents abandonment and even more frustration and less control. The offender seeks retribution and vindication by stalking his victim in order to make good his threats of killing her. There are many tragic stories of women in the United States who have had such experiences.

Domestic-obsessional stalkers usually have motivations less obvious than the power/anger stalkers. Their victims are former friends or lovers, coworkers, acquaintances, and relatives. Often plagued by psychological disorders, including schizophrenia, paranoia, and personality disorders, the offenders become fixated on their victims and relentlessly pursue them. What separates obsessional from other types of stalkers is their often irrational and illogical behavior caused by psychological dysfunctioning. These offenders are sometimes persons who are gainfully employed and may appear to most others as quite normal. For the victim, however, contact with the obsessional offender becomes a series of frequent telephone calls, house calls, letters, gifts, followings, and harassment. When caught in obsessive actions, the offenders often make claims that the victims want to be with them and that they are meant to be together.

An adult male victim named Terry had been stalked for 3 years by a female neighbor. On the first day Terry had moved into his upscale house, Barbara, an attractive, divorced woman living across the street, came over to welcome Terry into the neighborhood. Their contact was brief and cordial. He made no effort to contact her nor did he ever express any romantic interest in the woman. She began calling him and asking him out. He declined, and she persisted. Phone calls

increased to dozens every day and night. She called and left voice messages informing Terry that she was pregnant with his child, that they were meant for one another, and that they needed to be together. Sometimes, her calls were laced with sexually explicit enticements and others with vindictive diatribes. Angry phone calls were augmented by home visits in which she would tap on his windows and pound on his doors at odd hours of the night. Restraining orders were useless as her obsessional fantasies escalated. Although the harassment was continual, police explained that because she was not trying to harm the victim, there was little they could do. Barbara assured law enforcement that she was just being neighborly. The harassment was relentless and lasted approximately 3 years before the offender found another object for her desires. During this entire time, the offender maintained professionalism in her career, cared for her own home, and lived an otherwise respectable life.

In other instances, the offender believes the victim to be an enemy who is plotting to do harm and must be stopped. The obsessional attachment is based in delusional beliefs that the victim is an enemy to the offender and community in which he or she resides. The offender believes that no one else is truly capable of stopping this threat and feels he or she is on a mission to save everyone. Cyberstalking is often one of several tools employed by domestic-obsessionals in connecting with their victims.

The *domestic-nuisance* stalker is an offender who uses various forms of harassment as his or her primary tools. The victims are coworkers, acquaintances, relatives, and former friends. The offender does not attempt to harm or threaten the victim. In many cases, the offender is trying to establish a friendly relationship with the victim, but through unconventional means. The offender is either misguided and lacking in adequate social skills or derives pleasure through fantasy and the behavioral process of harassment. He or she may think that the victim actually finds the harassment a bit thrilling and looks forward to hearing from the offender. Such harassment may even begin in a joking manner and escalate into stalking.

Stranger Stalking

Stranger-power/anger stalkers are primarily men who have no known prior relationships with their victims and look for random victims to control, intimidate, and harm. The Internet is becoming a popular tool for such offenders. These men exhibit antisocial characteristics, and as a result of their lack of self-confidence and self-esteem, they hunt for proxy victims on which to vent their anger. In times of economic hardship, such men turn to others on which to place blame. Neo-Nazis, skinheads, right-wing extremists, men marginalized by society, and sexists all want to vent their rage and frustrations. The Internet is proving to be an excellent tool for harassing others and spreading messages of hate toward minorities and women. Much of what appears in e-mail as threats tends to be cathartic and goes no further in stalking escalation. However, these offenders are not passive and are known for their boldness in striking out at random victims. For those wanting to affiliate, the Internet is another way to band together. Other power-anger stalkers prefer anonymity and will send repeated messages of hate to public officials, minorities, and women. In most cases, the messages tend to be cathartic and end quickly. Those who pursue sending threatening e-mails should be considered extremely dangerous.

Stranger-obsessional stalkers are individuals who suffer from a variety of psychological disorders, including paranoid schizophrenia, bipolar, and dissociative disorders. They generally should be considered dangerous because of their level of unpredictability. The objects of their attachments are strangers. Obsessionals attach because they have come to learn or believe something about other persons or organizations that may be completely false but acts as a catalyst for the attachment. The Internet is attractive to obsessionals because it allows them unlimited access to their victims. Often, obsessionals will use additional means to reach their victims.

Stranger-nuisance stalkers tend to be loners looking for opportunities to connect with others in some medium. They range from teens to middle-aged men who frequently use the Internet to meet and harass victims. They enjoy the sense of freedom they have in hacking into victims' e-mails, tampering with Web pages, and sending obscene messages. They are offenders who derive satisfaction from honing their computer skills and demonstrating their prowess. The stalking usually is short in duration and low in intensity.

Stranger-sexual predator stalkers are some of the most dangerous offenders known to our criminal justice system. They include rapists, pedophiles, child molesters, and paraphilics. They are dangerous because the outcome is frequently the actual sexual assault of a victim or psychological sexual violence of a victim. The Internet is a perfect medium for sexual predators to solicit potential victims and do it with relative impunity. Offenders frequently have criminal histories, display various psychopathic characteristics, act alone, and become very adept at using tools such as the Internet to find victims.

Stranger-erotomaniac stalkers attach themselves to other persons because they believe those persons want them and are in love with them. The victims are usually persons of public prominence. The offenders are often irrational and obsessive in their stalking behaviors. Women are more likely to become involved in such stalking cases. In several cases in which offenders are schizophrenic, psychotic, or suffering from delusional states, the stalking has turned physically violent. In such instances, the offenders are more likely to be males than females.

Factitious Stalking

In some cases, those reporting being stalked actually have fabricated the story in order to receive attention. This deception may be manifested by the person (almost always a woman) reporting the crime as someone who is following her and always watching her every move. She may report being attacked or assaulted physically or even tell investigators that she will soon be murdered. Although extensive efforts are made by law enforcement to substantiate the claims, no acceptable evidence materializes. The LAPD refers to such cases as *false victimization.* The payoff for the "victim" is repeated visits by police and other officials that provide her with the desired attention. Often, these women have experienced severe trauma or long-term issues involving feelings of abandonment, neglect, and rejection by significant others through death, divorce, and familial dysfunction. This form of Munchausen's Syndrome may also be transferred to a child, known as Munchausen's Syndrome by Proxy, in which case the illness, or in this case, stalking, involves her child. The mother or guardian makes every effort to protect her child. This entails repeated calls to police. Other factitious reporters exhibit a *hero fantasy* and want to be recognized for their efforts in tracking down their ever-elusive stalkers. Again, these factitious reporters will be extremely vigilant in assisting investigators.

METHODS OF STALKING

Site and Nonsite Stalking

The level of personal physical dangerousness to a victim can usually be measured by whether the offender is participating in *nonsite* or *site stalking*. Nonsite stalking refers to offenders who do not make personal, direct contact with the victim, but instead engage in one or more of the following behaviors:

- Telephone calls
- E-mails
- Fax messages
- Letters
- Gifts
- Voice mail
- Other forms of recorded messages

These offenders, although they often create tremendous psychological stress for their victims, do not pose physical danger. For the offenders, nonsite stalking can be cathartic and provide a sense of control and power over their victims without actually having physical contact. Indeed, some types of nonsite stalkers would not feel comfortable nor in control were they to come face-to-face with their victims. Offenders who are married or have careers and reputations they do not want placed in jeopardy will employ nonsite tactics to harass, intimidate, and control their victims. In domestic cases, nonsite-stalking offenders are careful to avoid any acknowledgment of their stalking behaviors to their victims, who may also be their coworkers, acquaintances, or relatives. Cyberstalking is a common method, among other tools, used by domestic, nonsite stalkers.

Other nonsite stalkers escalate their activities into site stalking and make direct contact with victims. Site stalking is preferred by some stalkers over nonsite stalking because they feel a greater sense of control and the direct contact fulfils physical and sexual fantasies. Site stalkers engage in one or more of the following behaviors:

- Following
- Workplace visits
- Home visits
- Signatures
- Vandalism
- Sending or leaving dangerous "gifts"
- Displaying weapons

Some stalkers will only use nonsite stalking, whereas others will exclusively use site stalking, and some will engage in both. A critical factor for law enforcement and victims is understanding that site stalking opens a Pandora's box of both physical and psychologically dangerous behaviors.

Cyberstalking

Cyberstalking is best viewed as a method of stalking employed by either domestic or stranger stalkers. Typically, most cyberstalking appears to be committed by strangers, as shown by the vast number of sexual predators, celebrity, and nuisance stalkers currently using the Internet. The stalking landscape will continue to fluctuate as more persons from all socioeconomic statuses, ethnic/racial backgrounds, political persuasions, and religious belief systems embrace the ether world. For example, the fastest-growing group of persons now gaining access to the Internet are those earning wages of less than $25,000 per year.

Cyberstalkers are often sexual predators, especially pedophiles and child molesters. Differentiating between pedophiles and child molesters is not an easy task because they are not mutually exclusive in their fantasies and behaviors. Pedophiles prefer the company of children both socially and emotionally. Although many pedophiles work in adult settings, they always prefer the company of children. They usually are not married and live alone or with a relative. Their fantasies involve being emotionally attached and, if possible, physically involved with a child. They appear on a continuum from the reclusive and self-gratified (where the pedophile does not actually seek out children, but instead uses movies, props, photographs, etc., to fulfill fantasies and sexual desires) to the aggressive pedophile who seeks out children for sexual purposes, including murder.

The child molester also prefers children but is more likely to be married and have a family. The key distinguishing factor is sexual contact with children. Once the pedophile begins to approach children, he is no longer in a benign status engaged only in sexual fantasies involving children. He is now regarded as a child molester. Pedophiles and child molesters are affiliated with NAMBLA (North American Man-Boy Love Association), the Renee Guyon Society, and other organizations of similar ilk.

The Internet has become a labyrinth in which such predators lurk. Internet chat rooms, especially those designed for younger persons, have become virtual playgrounds for sexual predators. Pedophiles who may have kept their fantasies to themselves now have a forum to discuss their thoughts with other pedophiles as well as daily opportunities to visit chat rooms and begin relationships with unsuspecting victims. In California, a 60-year-old opthamologist contacted a 13-year-old girl and after a few e-mail exchanges began sending her sexually explicit photographs. Eventually, the doctor asked to meet the girl, and she agreed. The "girl" turned out to be a police officer working Internet sex crime cases. The doctor felt that law enforcement was overreacting because there was no proof of intent to harm the child. In his words, "I only sent her a couple of photos and asked to meet her."

Internet investigators are usually aware that pedophiles derive immense psychological control and emotional satisfaction from communicating with children on-line. The pedophile/molester can remain undetected until he feels it is safe and has properly "groomed" his intended victim. His sense of safety can also be his Achilles heel, however, because as he draws his intended victim into his comfort zone, he too is becoming involved in the relationship. This involvement can cause the offender to make judgment errors when attempting to determine with whom he is really communicating, a child or an adult. Active pedophiles/molesters on the Internet often keep files on each of their victims and may have several victims at any given time.

The Internet now provides the predator with a plethora of tools and options to use in the process of stalking children, including photographs, drawings, e-mail, on-line chats, chat rooms, videos, and music. Potential rapists hunting victims can use the same tools. From a criminal's perspective, barrooms have been places of gathering for men seeking women to rape. The advent of the Internet now provides another forum in which would-be rapists can stalk women. People find themselves more willing on the Internet to talk openly about personal topics than if they were face-to-face with strangers. The computer provides a false sense of anonymity and security that leads potential victims into sharing too much information. Some victims become emotionally involved through Internet contact and after a brief meeting with their pursuers, marry quickly. One victim had married twice in one year to men she had met while looking for Mr. Right on the Internet. Both marriages had to be annulled when the victim discovered that her spouses had lied to her regarding their financial status, their employment records, and the fact that one of them was still married to another person.

Cyberstalkers who search the Internet for victims to rape sometimes keep files on their victims and build the victim profiles until the offenders feel they are ready to make their first site visit. They become adept in the art of persuasion and manipulation. In some cases, the offender will use the Internet to lure victims to his home with promises of work, courtship, sex, or money.

One of the hallmarks of sexual predators who use the Internet is their involvement with *paraphilia*. Persons involved with paraphilia derive their primary sexual gratification through bizarre imagery and/or acts, including necrophilia, voyeurism, frotteurism, and exhibitionism, to name but a few of the more than 100 forms of paraphilia. Men who engage in paraphilia usually have 4 or 5 at one time, with one dominating, for example, collecting child pornography. Sexual predators who are cyberstalkers are like wolves in sheep's clothing. The average person who has had little or no exposure to such predators is at great risk once they are drawn into e-mail exchanges. In addition, sexual predators often exhibit a variety of psychopathic characteristics, such as lack of conscience, indifference to victims' suffering, and habitual lying (see Hare's Psychopathy Checklist-Revised). In one case, the predator used his computer to lure victims to his home for sexual activities or promises of employment. Thus far, the bodies of eight of these women have been located, after the predator had raped, tortured, and murdered them.

STALKING FANTASY

Stalkers have been psychologically categorized as having antisocial, borderline, or narcissistic personalities but also have been diagnosed with impulse control, intermittent explosive, and substance abuse disorders. Some of the most noted celebrity stalkers have been found to be psychotic or paranoid schizophrenics, including Ralph Nau, the Hollywood stalker who sent thousands of letters to more than 40 celebrities, and Michael Perry, who escaped from a mental institution and managed to murder five people, including his parents, while stalking Olivia Newton-John.

For most violent offenders, particularly sex offenders, such as rapists, pedophiles, voyeurs, and exhibitionists, *stalking fantasies* are critical in the process of offending. Consider the voyeur who goes about looking for opportunities to watch people undressing or engaging in sexual activities. Voyeurs derive a sense of personal control as they secretly watch unsuspecting victims. Thinking and completing the act of voyeurism provides the offender with reinforced fantasies that will once again need to be satisfied. Like many acts of sex offending, voyeurism causes the offender's fantasies to escalate and increases the risk of victim contact.

In a case in California, a woman had separated from her husband as a result of his continuous lying, manipulation, and intimidation. He then began stalking her. On one occasion, she arrived home from work to find a pair of her underwear lying on the driveway. Another time, she looked out of the classroom where she taught school and noticed her nightgown hanging on the school fence. She had changed the locks on her home, but he was still gaining entrance. Fearing for her safety, she filed for a restraining order. A few days later, the estranged husband violated the order and was arrested as he was driving his car. Police found two boxes of photographs chronologically organized. During the 2 years the couple had been married, the husband had taken many photographs of his wife. In the beginning, the pictures were snapshots of her face, walking alone, or lying down. Eventually, he had insisted she pose in attire, such as leather and chains, which made her uncomfortable and nervous, but she had complied to humor him.

Her husband had special plans for those pictures. He had purchased some horror magazines depicting various monsters. Cutting out pictures of his wife, he taped them onto scenes of monsters lurking in dark corners of rooms or parking lots while she stood innocently looking in the scene. He had taken other photographs of her and penned in red cut marks on her neck and drops of blood on her dress. Other scenes depicted monsters killing her while she lay bound in chains and leather. Police were concerned that he was about to kill her. Although that was certainly possible, it was also possible that the offender was stalking other women (by voyeurism) in his neighborhood. His wife was a successful woman who had self-confidence and high self-esteem. He did not feel in control around her and felt she could see through his facade. Consequently, he could have been searching for victims he could control, at least in his own fantasies.

Indeed, violent offenders often engage in psychological stalking prior to physically stalking their victims. This form of "psychological foreplay" is an essential component for many murderers. Stalking fantasies prepare an offender for opportunities to physically stalk selected victims. In other cases, stalking is accomplished in fantasy only. Eventually, when the "right" victim appears, the offender is prepared to move quickly in isolating that person. Indeed, the more focused the fantasies, the greater the danger to potential victims.

—*Eric W. Hickey*

NOTE: Portions of this profile were previously published in Eric Hickey's *Serial Murderers and Their Victims,* 2002, 3rd ed. Belmont, CA: Wadsworth Publishers.

See also BATTERERS AND ABUSIVE PARTNERS; CYBERAGGRESSION; CYBERSTINGS; PARAPHILIA; PEDOPHILES; PEDOPHILE ORGANIZATIONS

Further Reading

Hickey, E., Margulies, D., & Oddie, J. (1999, February). *Victim profiling in cases of stalking and obsessional harassment.* Paper presented at the American Academy of Forensic Sciences Annual Meeting, Orlando, FL.

Meloy, R. (Ed). (1998). *The psychology of stalking.* New York: Academic Press,

Oddie, J. (2000). *The prediction of violence in stalkers.* Doctoral dissertation, California School of Professional Psychology, Fresno.

Spence-Diehl, E. (1999). *Stalking: A handbook for victims.* Learning Publications.

STAYNER, CAREY, *See* PROFILING

STOCKHOLM SYNDROME

Stockholm Syndrome is a psychological and emotional reaction that captives experience when subjected to life-threatening situations over an extended period of time. Individuals activate this survival mechanism when exposed to traumatic situations that involve a direct threat on their lives while being held against their will. The term originated following an attempted bank robbery and subsequent hostage situation in Sweden, in 1973, in which the hostages began to sympathize with their captors and resisted rescue attempts by law enforcement agencies. As a result of the media sensationalism surrounding the Swedish hostages' unusual behavior and the well-publicized kidnapping and trial of Patricia Campbell Hearst, in 1974, many social scientists and psychologists began studying the phenomenon of emotional bonding between hostages and their captors to determine whether this type of reaction was rare or more commonplace.

Victims who develop Stockholm Syndrome create emotional bonds with their captors characterized by fear of them, as well as feelings of loyalty, understanding, and sympathy to their captors' situations. In some instances, victims replace their beliefs with those of the people threatening their lives. In the bank robbery incident that gave the syndrome its name, the four hostages actively resisted rescue and actually solicited funds for their captors' legal defense.

Although Stockholm Syndrome is primarily experienced by captives in hostage or terrorist situations, it has also been identified in cult members, victims of hijackings, prisoners of war, incest victims, domestic violence victims, and in a modified form in correctional officers, but anyone can develop it when exposed to the following conditions:

♦ A direct threat to one's survival and the perception that the person making the threat is capable of acting on it.
♦ The person making threats is also perceived as being kind, because of small acts of compassion and kindness.
♦ Isolation from the outside world such that the other person's beliefs and perspectives are the only ones available.
♦ The belief that there is no escape and one's life is in the hands of the individual making the threats.

THE STOCKHOLM CASE

On August 23, 1973, Birgitta Lundbladh, Sven Safstrom, Elisabeth Oldgren, and Kristin Ehnemark, four employees of Sveriges Kreditbank in Stockholm, Sweden, were taken hostage by Jan-Erik Olsson during a bank robbery attempt. Olsson demanded that the authorities deliver his friend, Clark Olofsson, to the bank with 3 million Swedish crowns, some guns, and a car. The authorities produced Olofsson and sent him into the bank as a communication link between Olsson, the hostages, and law enforcement. Even though Olofsson did not enter the bank with Olsson and physically take the bank employees hostage, he was still considered an accomplice of Olsson's by the authorities.

The four bank employees were held hostage, had their lives threatened, and were physically abused over the course of 6 days. Despite the psychological and physical trauma they endured, they resisted rescue attempts, raised money for the legal defense of Olsson and Olofsson, and refused to testify against them at the trial. The hostages stated that they feared the authorities more than they feared the hostage takers.

PATRICIA CAMPBELL HEARST

On February 4, 1974, Patricia Campbell Hearst, granddaughter of newspaper publisher William Randolph Hearst, was kidnapped from her apartment in Berkeley, California, by two black men and a white woman claiming to be members of the Symbionese Liberation Army (SLA). More than 2 months later, on April 15, 1974, she participated in a bank robbery in San Francisco that left two people wounded. After her arrest in September 1975, Ms. Hearst claims that during the 2 months she was held captive by the SLA, she was isolated from others and kept locked in a closet, repeatedly physically and sexually abused, told she would die, and forced to make tape recordings denouncing her family and people she loved. During her trial in 1976, her defense attorney, F. Lee Bailey, hired numerous psychologists and psychiatrists to interview Hearst. The defense witnesses all provided expert testimony that as the result of her kidnapping and subsequent treatment in captivity, she was brainwashed by the SLA into adopting their ideologies and participating in criminal activity to support their cause.

The controversial trial lasted 39 days, and after 12 hours of deliberation, the jury was not swayed by Ms. Hearst's defense. Patricia Hearst was found guilty of bank robbery and a firearms charge. She received the maximum sentence, 25 years for the bank robbery and 10 years for the firearms charge. Her sentence was later reduced to 7 years, which she served at the Federal Correctional Institute in Pleasanton, California.

—*Marcee Kerr*

See also CULTS; HOSTAGE TAKING; KIDNAPPING

Further Reading

Fuselier, G. D. (1999). Putting the Stockholm Syndrome in perspective. *FBI Law Enforcement Bulletin, 68*(7), 22-25.

Graham, D. L. R., Rawlings, E., & Rimini, N. (1988). Survivors of terror: Battered women, hostages, and the Stockholm Syndrome. In K. Ylloe & M. Bograd (Eds.), *Feminist perspectives on wife abuse* (pp. 217-233). Thousand Oaks, CA: Sage.

STRANGER VIOLENCE

Theorist Marvin Wolfgang's (1958) early research on crime divided murder into two categories:

- Primary homicide: incidents of homicide involving nonstrangers and/or acquaintances known by the victim
- Secondary homicide: incidents of homicide involving attackers or assailants not known by the victim

Secondary homicide eventually became known as "stranger crime," which subsequently developed into what is now known today as "stranger violence," or attempted assault or assault resulting in injury or death in which the victim did not know the offender. This type of violent behavior is widespread and prevalent in every society and can emerge in many different forms. It has no boundaries and can take place anywhere, whether in public (streets, shopping malls, ATM machines, parks, and public transportation) or private locations (household, vehicle). It happens to people from all walks of life, and predicting its occurrence is difficult. Because of this, stranger violence continues to attract attention, adding to the overall fear of crime nationally and internationally. Although increasing criminal justice resources are being allocated to its prevention, stranger violence still remains one of the most difficult types of violence to prevent.

INCIDENTS OF STRANGER VIOLENCE

The most common incidents of stranger violence are assaults and robberies. Approximately 7 out of 10 robberies are committed by strangers. Robbery is distinguished from larceny in that robbery involves the unlawful taking of another's property by use or attempted use of force, whereas larceny does not involve force.

Other incidents of stranger violence include carjacking, gang-related activities, "being at the wrong place at the wrong time" (e.g., caught in the cross fire of a random shooting), and murder. Stalking and cyberstalking are forms of stranger violence gaining attention in incidents escalating to the occurrence of stranger-on-stranger violence.

Victims

Statistics show that males are at higher risk of being victims of stranger violence than are females. When considering gender and race, statistics indicate that the risk for being a victim is approximately the same regardless of race (white or black). However, separated out by gender, statistics show that the risk for being a victim of stranger violence is higher for black males than for white males and higher for white females than for black females. Related to race, the highest percentage of victims are blacks. Related to age, the highest percentage of victims are 16 to 24 years old. Socioeconomically, the highest percentage of victims are individuals who have never been married and whose family income is less than $7,500 (Bureau of Justice Statistics, 2001).

Offenders

Not much is known about offenders of stranger violence. The British Crime Survey (2001) reported that the vast majority (86%) of stranger violence incidents were carried out by male offenders; the incidents usually took place in the evening or at night; and alcohol and/or drugs were involved in over half (53%) of the incidents. What is known is that offenders are unpredictable, and their actions can take place in public, among other individuals, or in the privacy of a household or residence.

—*Kimberly L. Freiberger*

Further Reading

Bureau of Justice Statistics. (2001). *Criminal victimization in the United States: 1999 statistical tables* (NCJ-184938). Washington, DC: U.S. Department of Justice.

Hall, H. (Ed.). (1999). *Lethal violence: A sourcebook on fatal domestic, acquaintance and stranger violence.* Boca Raton, FL: CRC Press.

Mattinson, J. (2001). Stranger and acquaintance violence: Practice messages from the British Crime Survey. *Briefing note, 7/01.*

Meadows, R. J. (2001). *Understanding violence & victimization.* Upper Saddle River, NJ: Prentice Hall.

Reidel, M. (1993). *Stranger violence: A theoretical inquiry.* New York: Garland.

Wolfgang, M. (1958). *Patterns of criminal homicide.* Philadelphia: University of Pennsylvania Press.

STREET GANGS, *See* GANGS

STRIKING INSTRUMENTS, *See* METHODS OF MURDER

STUBB, PETER, *See* SERIAL MURDER: INTERNATIONAL INCIDENCE; VAMPIRES, WEREWOLVES, AND WITCHES

SUBSTANCE ABUSE AND HOMICIDE

According to the American Psychiatric Association (1994), substance abuse is described as follows:

A maladaptive pattern of substance use leading to impairment or distress, with one or more of the following within the last year: 1) recurrent substance use leading to a failure to fulfill role obligations at work, school, or home; 2) recurrent use in physically hazardous situations (drinking and driving, for example); 3) recurrent use-related legal problems, such as arrest for disorderly conduct; and/or 4) continued use despite social or interpersonal problems recurrently being accused or made worse by the substance. (pp. 182-183)

Although most often associated with addiction, substance abuse involves behavior that can cause significant problems without causing dependence.

CONCEPTUAL FRAMEWORK

It is clear that substance abuse has a significant relationship with criminal activity. Goldstein and colleagues proposed tripartite framework to explain the relationship between drugs and crime. This framework postulated that crimes involving drugs could be classified into three categories: psychopharmacological, economic-compulsive, or systemic factors. A *psychopharmacological* relationship involves intoxication states after taking the drug. Similarly, an increase in impulsivity may result from a substance. An *economic-compulsive* relationship may result when criminal acts are needed to stave off the symptoms of withdrawal states that appear once the drug use has stopped. Finally, a *systemic* relationship results when the drug user enters or lives within a social context in which extraordinary drug use is just one factor in a set of intercorrelated criminal behaviors.

Empirical data for this model were supported by research in which drugs and alcohol were found to be important causes of a large share of all homicides (53% of 414 homicides) in samples from New York (Goldstein, Brownstein, & Ryan, 1992). Using this framework, Anthony and Forman succinctly summarized that there is no single drugs-crime relationship. On the contrary, most drugs-crime relationships are complex rather than simple. Furthermore, MacCoun and Kilmer have suggested that further refinements are needed to understand the complex relationship of drugs and crime.

HOMICIDE AND VIOLENT BEHAVIOR

Homicide is an accurate and reliable indicator of all violent crime. In 1997, 32,436 individuals died from injuries resulting from firearms. Of these deaths, 42% were homicide victims (U.S. Department of Health and Human Services, 2000). Trends in homicide and murder rates have demonstrated a decline over the past two decades. Homicide rates increased steadily during the late 1960s and 1970s, peaking at 10.2 homicides per 100,000 persons in 1980. Following a decrease to 7.9 homicides per 100,000 persons in 1985, the rate rose again to a peak of 9.8 homicides per 100,000 persons in 1991. In 2000, the homicide rate declined to 5.8 age-adjusted homicides per 100,000 persons (Minino & Smith, 2001).

According to the Centers for Disease Control and Prevention, homicide was the 15th leading cause of death in the United States in 2000. Data from the National Center for Health Statistics (1997) showed that homicides accounted for 15% of all injury deaths, with rates highest among the 20- to 24-year-old age group. Firearms were responsible for 29% of injury deaths among persons aged 15 to 64 years and highest among persons 20 to 24 years of age (29.9 per 100,000). Furthermore, 48% of firearm deaths were homicides among the 15- to 64-year-old age group. Firearm death rates were about 8 times higher for males compared with females at ages 15 to 19 years and 20 to 24 years.

Homicide is the third leading cause of death among children aged 5 to 14 years and has become an increasing trend in childhood violent deaths. In 1996, more than 80% of fatal child abuse was attributed to infant homicides (U.S. Department of Health and Human Services, 2000).

SUBSTANCE ABUSE AND HOMICIDE

Data from the U.S. Department of Justice (2000) draws attention to the close relationship between substance abuse and homicide. According to the Office of Justice Programs, 36% of inmates who pled guilty or had been convicted of an offense reported that they were under the influence of drugs at the time of their offenses. Furthermore, 16% of interviewed convicted inmates reported that they committed their offenses to get money for drugs, and two thirds were actively involved with drugs prior to their admission to jail.

Similarly, data from the Bureau of Justice Statistics (1994) further supports the relationship between substance abuse and homicide. In 1993, 5.5% of the 23,271 homicides in which circumstances were known involved narcotics. These homicides included only a narcotics felony such as drug trafficking or manufacturing. Narcotics felony and more serious felony (i.e., armed robbery) were not calculated as drug related. Data further showed that circumstances involving illegal drugs (i.e., drug scam or dispute) accounted for 18% of the defendants and 16% of the victims. That victims and their killers were both at the murder scene because of drugs occurred in 7% of the cases. Furthermore, 12% of the victims were involved with the killer in a drug relationship.

According to the Bureau of Justice Statistics (1994), 6% of state prison inmates reported that they had belonged to gangs prior to their incarceration. Of these inmates, 81% reported past drug use, and 92% reported that their gangs fought other groups.

Data on the substance abuse among arrestees has demonstrated a trend in choice of drugs used. Cocaine has remained the drug of choice among many arrestees. In addition, a higher proportion of male adult arrestees tested positive for marijuana compared with females. The most commonly used drug among juvenile detainees was marijuana, more than 6 times higher than cocaine use by both males and females. Although opiate use remained relatively low in 1999, female adult arrestees were more likely to test positive for opiates compared with males. Geographical trends indicated that methamphetamine use was more prominent in the western part of the United States, including Portland, Sacramento, Salt Lake City, San Diego, San Jose, and Spokane. In addition, methamphetamine use was similar among juvenile and adult arrestees and more common among females (Office of Justice Programs, 2000).

Furthermore, substance abuse among arrestees tended to be geographically isolated. Research revealed that methamphetamine use is a phenomenon mainly in the western part of the United States. More than 20% of both male and female arrestee populations tested positive in Portland, Sacramento, Salt Lake City, San Diego, San Jose, and Spokane. This pattern was also consistent among juvenile arrestees and more common among females (Bureau of Justice Statistics, 2000).

Alcohol abuse has also been shown to play a significant role in vehicular homicides. Alcohol intoxication is associated with 40% to 50% of traffic fatalities, as well as nearly 50% of homicides, victim or perpetrator (Vargas & Kolts, 1986).

Males are at greater risk of homicide, both as victims and perpetrators. In 1999, 65% of the homicides involved a male perpetrator and a male victim. In comparison, 22.4% of homicides involved a male perpetrator and a female victim. Although females can be perpetrators of homicide, only 10.1% of the victims were male, and 2.4% were female (Bureau of Justice Statistics, 1999).

Homicide victimization rates have declined to their lowest point in more than two decades. In 1999, males were 3.2 times more likely than females to be murdered. In addition, African Americans are more than 5 times more likely as whites to be murdered. Although the homicide rate for young black males 15 to 24 years of age has decreased to an annual rate of 11%, to 132.0 deaths per 100,000 population between 1993 and 1994, there remain significant racial disparities in homicide rates. Young black males were 8 times more likely to be murdered compared with young white males (National Center for Health Statistics, 1997).

The factors that contribute to homicide and murder are also closely related with violent and abusive behavior. These factors include low income, discrimination, lack of education, and lack of employment opportunities (U.S. Department of Health and Human Services, 2000). Based on data from the National Center for Health Statistics (1997), homicide rates are highest among 20- to 24-year-olds, with rates higher among the black population than in any other group. Urbanization is associated with increased homicide rates, with large, core metropolitan counties 2 to 3 times higher than in other types of counties.

Drug-related circumstances for homicide are a significant risk factor among both male offenders and victims. From 1976 to 1999, drug-related circumstances accounted for 90.1% of homicides among male victims compared with only 9.9% among females. Similarly, drug-related circumstances represented 95.8% of the homicides among male offenders and only 4.1% among females. Furthermore, homicides were more likely to be gang related among both male offenders (94.4%) and victims (98.5%). Gun homicide was more likely among male victims (82.4%) and offenders (90.3%) compared with female victims (17.5%) and offenders (9.7%) (Bureau of Justice Statistics, 1994).

—*Vicki Krenz*

See also ALCOHOL AND AGGRESSION; DRUG TRADE; GANGS; HOMICIDE; PREDICTING VIOLENT BEHAVIOR

Further Reading

American Psychiatric Association. (1994). *Diagnostic and statistical manual of mental disorders* (4th ed.). Washington, DC: American Psychiatric Association.

Anthony, J. D., & Forman, V. (2002). At the intersection of public health and criminal justice. Research on Drugs and Crime Linkages (draft). *Toward a drugs and crime research agenda for the 21st century* (NCJ 194161). Washington, DC: Bureau of Justice Statistics.

Bureau of Justice Statistics. (1994). *Drugs and crime facts, 1994* (NCJ-154043). Washington, DC: Department of Justice.

Bureau of Justice Statistics. (1999). *Homicide trends in the U.S.: 1998 update* (NCJ-173956). Washington, DC: Dept. of Justice.

MacCoun, R., Kilmer, B., & Reuter, P. (2002). Research on drugs-crime linkages: The next generation. *Toward a drugs and crime research agenda for the 21st Century* (NCJ-194161). Washington, DC: Bureau of Justice Statistics.

Minino, A. M., & Smith, B. C. (2001). Deaths: Preliminary data for 2000. *National Vital Statistics Reports, 49*(12). Hyattsville, Maryland: National Center for Health Statistics.

National Center for Health Statistics (1997). *Health, United States, 1996-97 and injury chartbook.* Hyattsville, Maryland.

U.S. Department of Health and Human Services. (2000, November). *Healthy people 2010: Understanding and improving health* (2nd ed.). Washington, DC: GPO.

U.S. Department of Justice. (2000). *Office of Justice Programs Annual Report: Fiscal year 2000.* Washington, DC: GPO.

SUCCINYLCHOLINE, *See* MEDICAL MURDERS; POISONERS; POISONING: MEDICAL SETTINGS

SUICIDE

Suicide is defined as "the act or an instance of taking one's own life voluntarily and intentionally." Although it is not traditionally considered a crime against a person, it does consist of violent behavior against oneself. Some may consider a more accurate definition as "self-murder."

Several factors may play a part in an individual attempting to commit suicide. Some of these risk factors include a family history of depression, suicide, or mental illness, family violence, changes within the family dynamic (i.e., job loss, divorce, death), and substance abuse. Demographic risk factors also identify peak age ranges, and a higher percentage of males commit suicide than do females.

Cultural issues also play a part in suicide. Suicide is viewed differently in different societies. Whereas some condemn the act, other cultures praise it, depending on the circumstances in which the individual acted.

HISTORICAL AND CULTURAL ISSUES

The history of suicide goes back for centuries. Many stories in the Old Testament tell of men killing themselves for honor, and literature from the Middle Ages also depicts individuals committing suicide for a just and honorable cause. George Minois (1999) addresses suicide in the Middle Ages and states that it was divided in two social categories. In the first category, a peasant or craftsman may have taken his own life to "escape poverty and suffering." In the second category, a knight may have taken his own life to "escape humiliation and to deprive the infidel of a victory." One type of suicide was considered a noble act, whereas the other was seen as cowardice.

In later years, with the spread of Chrisitanity, suicide was condemned and considered an affront to God. It is considered immoral by Judaism and Islam, and attempts are punishable by law in many countries. In ancient Greece, suicide was tolerated for criminals; and in India, where it is now against the law, it was praised at one time.

DEMOGRAPHIC INFORMATION

The National Institute of Mental Health reports that in 1997, suicide was the eighth leading cause of death in the U.S. Specifically, 10.6 out of every 100,000 persons died by suicide. Research has shown that more than 90% of people who kill themselves suffer from depression or another diagnosable mental or substance abuse disorder.

According to the National Center for Health Statistics, over 4 times more men than women die by suicide; however, women report attempting suicide about 2 to 3 times as often as men do. In 1997, 72% of all suicides were committed by white men, and 79% of all firearm suicides were committed by white men. The highest suicide rate was for white men over 85 years of age. Adolescents also seem to fall into a higher risk category for suicide. Peak ages are determined to be ages 14 to 24.

The reasons for committing suicide can range from mental illness to substance abuse to fear. People who commit suicide can be children, adults, and the elderly. Suicide crosses all socioeconomic, age, gender, and racial boundaries.

ASSISTED SUICIDE

Although suicide may not be considered a crime, assisted suicide can be. Assisted suicide is the act of an individual who assists another in committing suicide. This can be done by providing the means (i.e., poison, medication) for the person or actually physically assisting them in the process of killing themselves. Another term that may be used for assisted suicide is *euthanasia*. Robert N. Wennberg (1989) states,

A basic distinction is made between two kinds of euthanasia, passive and active. Active euthanasia is identical with mercy killing and, roughly speaking, involves taking direct action to end a life. . . . Passive euthanasia . . . is allowing a patient to die when he or she could be kept alive by the appropriate medical procedures. (pp. 7-8)

Although assisted suicide may traditionally be identified as a case in which an individual helps another person with a terminal illness to die, in other cases of assisted suicide, the individual helps a healthy person commit suicide. An example of this would be a recent case in Michigan in which a young couple allegedly participated in the sexual assault of a 14-year-old girl. When the girl went to the authorities, the couple knew that they were most likely going to be charged with the assault. The couple went to the man's mother and told her of their situation. All three of them decided that it would be best if the couple committed suicide. The mother obtained lethal doses of medication and provided it to the couple. The mother is charged with 2 counts of assisted suicide and is awaiting trial.

—*Colleen Condren*

See also EUTHANASIA; KEVORKIAN, JACK

Further Reading

Betzold, M. (1993). *Appointment with Doctor Death.* Troy, MI: Momentum Books.

Hoyert, D. L., Kochanik, K. D., & Murphy, S. L. (1999). Deaths: Final data for 1997. *National Vital Statistics Report, 47*(19) (DHHS Publication No. 99-1120). Hyattsville, MD: National Center For Health Statistics.

Minois, G. (1999). *History of suicide: Voluntary death in Western culture.* Baltimore, MD: Johns Hopkins University Press.

Varma, P. (1976). *Suicide in India and abroad.* India: Sahitya Bhawan.

Weissman, M. M., Bland, R. C., Canino, G. J., et al. (1999). Prevalence of suicide ideation and suicide attempts in nine countries. *Psychological Medicine, 29*(1), 9-17.

SUICIDE BY COP

"Suicide by cop" is a phrase used to describe a situation in which a person wants to commit suicide but chooses to have police do the killing. The number of such incidents appears to have doubled during the last 10 years; however; it is not known whether there was an actual increase or merely improved recognition and reporting methods. There may be more incidents than are actually known, because many are disguised so that the suicidal intent of the person is never revealed.

Police officers are often involved in situations with suicidal persons. They are generally the first responders to situations with desperate persons who threaten to kill themselves. In addition, many other calls to the police turn into situations in which suicide is threatened. The majority of the calls involving barricaded suspects involve subjects who have threatened suicide, and perpetrators of crimes will often threaten suicide as a means to distract police officers and avoid arrest.

Any time an officer has contact with someone who is threatening suicide, the officer's safety is at risk. Once individuals have reached a point that they believe their life has no value, they may no longer value any life, including the life of the police officer attempting to help them. Suicidal individuals are not only a danger to themselves but also to family, friends, innocent hostages, and police officers. A suicidal person can easily become capable of committing homicide. This is one explanation for the numerous cases of murder/suicide across the nation. It is no longer unusual to hear about people killing their children or spouses and then killing themselves.

A suicide-by-cop incident can result whenever an officer has contact with a suicidal person. The situation can quickly change from the person threatening to kill himself to instead committing an act to provoke a police officer to kill.

A suicide plan can be either elaborate or impulsive. Suicide-by-cop incidents are usually impulsive, and individuals who commit suicide this way are oftentimes impulsive by nature. Record checks on such individuals may reveal arrests for assaultive behavior, multiple speeding citations, involvement in disturbances, excessive numbers of parking tickets on file, and other indicators of impulsive behavior.

Some people consider suicide to be an act of cowardice. The person intent on committing suicide may consider suicide by cop to be more acceptable. Also, a person might want to "go out big," and certainly being involved in a violent altercation with police would draw attention. Many times, suicidal individuals escalate situations so that police have little option but to kill them. Escalating behaviors may include killing an officer, firing a weapon, or making threatening movements toward the police, bystanders, or hostages. A suicidal person who refuses to follow orders, makes attempts to escalate the situation, and makes no attempt to escape, surrender, or retreat suggests a person intent on suicide by cop.

There are many documented cases of this behavior. In one case, a woman called police to her home for assistance. When the two officers arrived, she pointed a shotgun at them. They shot and killed her. Later, it was determined that the shotgun was not loaded, and a suicide letter was found in her residence. It was obvious that her intent was to provoke the officers into killing her. In another case, officers responded to a call of a domestic disturbance. When officers arrived, a male subject who had been involved in the disturbance pointed a gun at the officers. He was shot and killed by the officers. Later, neighbors stated that the man had talked about how he intended to force officers to kill him.

Suicide-by-cop situations generally evolve rapidly and provide little or no opportunity to bring in the assistance of a trained negotiator or deploy special equipment. Often, the officer is trapped into using deadly force, and the outcome is unavoidable.

—*Sharon Shaffer*

See also MURDER-SUICIDE; SPECIAL WEAPONS AND TACTICS TEAMS; THREAT ASSESSMENT

Further Reading

Parent, R. (1998). *Victim-precipitated homicide: Suicide by cop.* Canadian Police Work, Griffiths, Whitelaw and Parent. Nelson Publishers.
Suicide by cop. (1999, Summer). *The Negotiator, 10*(4).

SWANGO, DR. MICHAEL, *See* MEDICAL MURDERS; POISONING: MEDICAL SETTINGS

SYMBIONESE LIBERATION ARMY, *See* BLACK GUERRILLA FAMILY; KIDNAPPING

SYNDICATES, CRIME, *See* CHICAGO MOB; DRUG CARTELS; DRUG TRADE; GAMBINO CRIME FAMILY; GENOVESE CRIME FAMILY; FALCONE, GIOVANNI; LUCIANO, CHARLES "LUCKY"; ORGANIZED CRIME; WHITE SLAVERY

TAGGER CREWS,
See GANGS: DEFINITIONS

THE TARASOFF DECISION

Tarasoff v. the Board of Regents at the University of California (California Supreme Court 551 P.2d 334, 1976) revolved around the activities of Prasenjit Podder, a male student studying engineering and naval architecture at the University of California, Berkeley. Podder was a bright student who had overcome severe poverty and hardships in his native India. Tanya Tarasoff was young woman who befriended him at school. Podder appears to have become obsessed with the student, taping their conversations, replaying them to assess whether Tarasoff was romantically interested in him, and following her. In time, Podder's thought process became increasingly disturbed. He began to believe that people were laughing at him. He made threatening statements toward Tarasoff to a friend of his. Although he followed the advice of this friend to seek mental health treatment at the university counseling center, he mistrusted his therapist/psychologist. Podder made threatening statements during therapy while concealing his intended victim's identity and terminated treatment at the center.

Later, when Podder reported to his friend that he wanted to obtain a gun, the friend called the psychologist who had previously treated Podder. The psychologist contacted campus security and consulted with his supervisors. Campus security detained Podder,

questioned him, and then released him, with the warning to stay away from Tarasoff. The psychologist attempted to take further action but was prevented by his superiors. Podder eventually confronted Tarasoff at her home, and when she ran from him, he shot and then stabbed her repeatedly. Tarasoff's family sued the Board of Regents of the University of California for failing to protect their daughter. The Tarasoff family won the first court case but lost on appeal. The Supreme Court of California reversed the lower court's decision and awarded Taraosff's family with compensation, ruling that the university should have taken steps to ensure the young woman's safety.

Today, every mental health professional is aware of the *Tarasoff* decision. All states have similar legal statutes protecting potential victims. In general, mental health professionals are required to take steps to protect potential victims if they become aware of threats. Some interpret the *Tarasoff* decision as an erosion of the patient-therapist confidentiality; however, there are safeguards in place to ensure that confidentiality is not erroneously violated. In determining the legitimacy of a threat and whether it should be reported, a professional must assess whether it contains a serious intent, whether there is a formulated plan, and who the potential target is. When a threat is assessed as containing a focused intent, a formulated plan, and an identified victim, the professional can do one or a combination of the following to ensure the safety of the potential victim: (a) arrange for the person making the threat to be hospitalized voluntarily or involuntarily, (b) notify the identified victim of the threat, and (c) notify law enforcement. The exact responsibility of the mental health professional who becomes aware of a threat is outlined in legal statutes and varies between states.

—*Sarah Ferguson*

See also PREVENTION OF CRIME AND VIOLENT BEHAVIOR; STALKING; THREAT ASSESSMENT

Further Reading

Vandecreek, L., & Knapp, S. (2001). *Tarasoff and beyond: Legal and clinical considerations in the treatment of life-endangering patients* (Practitioner's Resource Series). Professional Resource Publishers.

TEAM KILLERS

Contrary to popular belief, serial murder is not a recent phenomenon. There are recorded incidences of serial murder during the 15th century, when Gilles de Rais was charged with the murders of 140 women. Similarly, during the 17th century, in Scotland, the Beane family is believed to have been responsible for the deaths of 1,500 victims. However, it was not until the 19th century that serial murder came to the attention of the public when "Jack the Ripper" murdered five females in London's Whitechapel district, noted for its prostitutes. Since then, acts of serial murder appear to have increased (Hickey, 2002).

TEAM SERIAL KILLERS

A *serial murderer* can be defined as an individual who kills three or more victims, strangers, relatives, and/or acquaintances over a period of time exceeding 30 days, during which the perpetrator overwhelmingly attempts to avoid capture (in contrast with mass and/or spree murderers); the motivation may be intrinsic (e.g., power motivated) or extrinsic (e.g., monetary gain). *Team serial killers* often work in pairs of two men, two women, or a man and a woman. However, in cases of killers such as the Beane family, a team consists of three or more individuals, related (termed *family killers*) or otherwise.

Despite a dearth of literature pertaining to team serial killers, it is known that offenders share some commonalities: He or she is generally Caucasian; mid-20s; completed or partially completed high school; employed as a blue-collar worker; targets strangers (male and/or female) choosing a personal approach (strangulation, suffocation), unlike mass killers, who select an impersonal method (firearm); retains trophies or souvenirs from the victims (video recording, personal items); and appears to display extreme cruelty toward victims (torture, dismemberment).

In contrast to serial killers acting alone, team killers are unique in that they share a sense of solidarity and social cohesion. On the other hand, research has demonstrated that one team member generally turns on the other, often resulting in their arrest and conviction. The following sections offer an overview of male team, female team, and male and female team killers, and family killers and victim selection.

Male Team Killers

Male team killers consist of two or more males who are generally not related, although Kenneth Bianchi and Angelo Buono, the "Hillside Stranglers," were cousins who targeted females employed as prostitutes in Los Angeles, California, between 1977 and 1978. They eventually dissolved their partnership, and Bianchi relocated in Seattle, Washington. While in Washington, Bianchi committed two murders, which led to his arrest and, ultimately, his testimony against his cousin Buono in the killing of nine Los Angeles women. Following Bianchi's arrest, he claimed that he had an alter-ego personality and therefore was not responsible for his actions. This defense was not accepted, and Bianchi was found competent to stand trial for his role in the murders.

Very few team killer offenders are diagnosed with mental disorders but, rather, are diagnosed with personality disorders such as psychopathy. Psychopathy is defined by distinctive behaviors and personality traits, including a lack of conscience. Although a personality disorder might explain in part why team killers commit serial murder, researchers have investigated other possibilities in an attempt to explain their development and motivation.

Serial killers acting alone or as teams appear to spend an exorbitant amount of their time fantasizing about the preparation of their crimes. Many offenders keep homemade videotapes, photos, or personal items of their victims to continue to relive their fantasies. For instance, following the arrest of male team killers Leonard Lake and Charles Ng, law enforcement officers located homemade videos of the torture of their victims. When team killers Bittaker and Norris were

Cousins Angelo Buono and Kenneth Bianchi, known as the "Hillside Stranglers," tortured and murdered at least 10 females, some as young as 12, and left the bodies on the hillsides of Los Angeles and Glendale, California between 1977 and 1978. The case became even more outrageous when Bianchi pretended to be suffering from dissociative identity disorder or multiple personality. Both were convicted. Buono died in prison, and Bianchi awaits an unlikely parole.

Source: Copyright © Bettmann / CORBIS.

arrested for the killing of five women in California, law enforcement officers located photographs of their victims in various stages of torture, as well as recorded pleas for mercy from one of their victims, used for their later enjoyment. It appears that the act of serial killing as a social activity bonds team killers together, establishing a sense of identity and self-expression.

With few exceptions, team offenders have suffered some degree of physical, sexual, and/or emotional abuse during their formative years. As an example, team killer Henry Lee Lucas was exposed to severe physical and emotional abuse as a child. Lucas was raised by an alcoholic mother who worked as a prostitute. She entertained clients at home, forcing Lucas, his siblings, and paraplegic father to observe. During the first years of grade school, Lucas's mother sent him to school in dresses with his hair adorned in ringlets, without food or money. On several occasions, Lucas was severely beaten by his mother. Similarly, Lucas's partner, Otis Toole, is believed to have been sexually abused by his mother.

Another possible explanation, as discussed by psychologist Candice Skrapec, is the "right of entitlement," which means that males are socialized to externalize their feelings of anger and/or rage through acts of aggression. Perhaps this might explain why approximately 85% of serial killers are male.

Female Team Killers

There are few recorded cases of female team killers. They appear to be geographically stable; that is, they remain in the same general area. Similar to serial killers (male or female) acting alone, female team killers employed in the medical profession or related profession are called *custodial killers*. As an example, Gwendolyn Graham and Catherine Wood were employed as nursing home aides in Walker, Michigan, in the late 1980s. Their victims were elderly clients, often diagnosed with Alzheimer's disease. While one of the women acted as a "lookout," the other smothered the victim. Although a few trinkets were taken from each victim, the motivation appeared to be intrinsic. Graham and Wood alleged that they murdered their clients to alleviate stress.

Similar to male teams and male and female team killers, there appears to be a dominant team member who is often instrumental in the motivation and development of the murders. (The dominant member can be male or female, depending on the dynamics of the relationship.) In the aforementioned case of Graham and Wood, Graham appeared to be the dominant partner, both in their personal and professional lives.

Unlike their male counterparts, female serial killers acting alone or as a team are often engaged in traditional occupations such as custodial work. This is in part a result of occupational sex-typing, in which an occupation is thought to be better suited to individuals of one sex than the other. Ironically, as a result of gender bias, women who commit serial murder are often able to avoid detection: Society is unwilling to believe that women are capable of committing serial murder, a belief that is reinforced by the mass media. When a female is teamed with a male, she is often dismissed by the judicial system as a "victim." In reality, the female often displays characteristics that are attributed to male serial killers, including methods of murder.

Female and Male Team Killers

In male and female team killers, consistent with the "mating gradient," the female is often younger than the male member. According to Kelleher and Kelleher (1998), one third of the women who commit serial murder have partners in their crimes, though the female serial killer acting alone is able to avoid detection for a longer period of time than a female partnered with another individual. These pairs of offenders may be geographically stable or transient, either selecting victims from their regions or traveling through various states to search for victims. Overwhelmingly, both male and female offenders have been subjected to abuse during their formative years. When comparing married and unmarried male and female teams, the female of the married team is more often directly involved in the sexual assault of the victims. The victims are generally young Caucasian women. With few exceptions, the female member testifies against the male, thereby receiving a lighter sentence for her role in the murders.

When attempting to explain female criminality, social scientists often apply theories specifically developed for males. A few theoretical frameworks are masculinity thesis, opportunity thesis, and economic marginalization thesis. *Masculinity thesis* argues a correlation between "liberated women" and increased female criminality, particularly violent criminal acts. To date, this thesis is unfounded. *Opportunity thesis* purports that as women become better educated and acquire higher positions, increased opportunities to

commit white-collar crimes will become available. The primary criticism of this argument is found in *economic marginalization thesis,* which espouses that it is the absence rather than the availability of opportunity that results in increases in female criminality. However, the aforementioned thesis does not adequately explain women (or men) who commit serial murder.

It is not unusual for the judicial system to dismiss women involved in team serial murder as passive victims lacking the intellectual capability to dominate the team. As a result of these gender stereotypes, a number of women involved in team serial murders have deliberately portrayed themselves as compliant victims. As an example, team serial killer Carol Bundy explained to her partner Douglas Clark, "If it happens we have to go against each other . . . remember, I look innocent. Impression is worth as much as facts" (Pearson, 1997, p. 47). She then "sauntered into his trial and primly announced: 'Mr. Clark had virtual control over my personality and behavior, my wants, my desires, my dreams'" (p. 47).

In a similar way, Canadian team killer Karla Homolka claimed that she was a battered woman and that her husband and partner, Paul Bernardo, had total control over her actions. To the contrary, the literature illustrates that Homolka was not only actively involved in the physical and sexual assaults of the victims but that she was instrumental in the abductions and ultimate demise of the victims. Often, when the female counterpart admits sexual involvement with the victims, the judicial system and media willingly accept her explanation of coerced participation.

Although some research has demonstrated that in cases of male and female team killers, the female is not the primary decision maker, in several instances, this belief has been unsupported. An example can be found in the case of married team killers, Judith Ann and Alvin Neelley. Following the sexual assault of a 13-year-old victim, Judith Ann Neelley repeatedly injected the young girl with drain cleaner in an attempt to killer her. The victim somehow survived this ordeal, and the Neelleys then drove to a remote area where Judith Ann made one last attempt to inject the victim before shooting her. Charlene Gallego, along with her partner and spouse, Gerald Gallego, was an enthusiastic participant in the sexual assault of nine female victims. Charlene concocted the plan to kidnap young women and keep them as "love slaves" to service her spouse and herself.

In Nova Scotia, Canada, team serial killers Lila and William Young opened a maternity home for both wed and unwed mothers. Lila, rather than William Young, appeared to be the dominant partner, selecting which infants would survive and eventually be sold to clients, and which would die, typically infants of mixed race or with a physical defect(s). The alleged method of killing included starvation of the infant. Finally, following the arrest and conviction of team killers Ian Brady and Myra Hindley, Brady was diagnosed as paranoid schizophrenic and found insane and therefore not responsible for his crimes. His partner, Hindley, on the other hand, is sane.

Perhaps, as Pearson has demonstrated when explaining females who commit single and multiple homicide, violent behavior can be viewed as a human, rather than gendered, phenomenon.

Family Killers

Historically, family killers can be traced back to 17th-century Scotland, when to subsist, Sawney Beane and his family allegedly committed robbery, murder, and ritual acts of cannibalism. Following several decades and hundreds of victims, Beane and his family were eventually arrested and executed. The motivation in the case of family killers appears to be extrinsic, that is, monetary gain. For example, "Ma Barker" encouraged her sons to commit robbery and murder during the 1930s, until the gang was shot to death in 1939. Contrary to other team killers, family killers select their victims on the basis of material reward. (See Table 1.)

Victim Selection

When examining victim selection of team serial killers, neither males nor females are race or gender specific, though they often select females as victims. Many of the victims belong to lower socioeconomic groups, in which females and males work as prostitutes, transients, migrant workers, and so on. A number of relevant factors might explain why individuals from less fortunate groups are selected as victims; they are more visible, more accessible, and are personally and geographically vulnerable. As a result, particular marginalized groups in society become potential targets for serial murderers. The sense of powerlessness of the victim is based on his or her perceived status in society.

Table 1   A Historical Sample of International Team Serial Killers, 1700–1995

Year	Country	Offenders
1600	Scotland	Sawney Beane Family
1901–02	England	Amelia Sach & Annie Walters
1928–46	Canada	Lila & William Young
1933–34	United States	Bonnie Parker & Clyde Barrow
1947–49	United States	Martha Beck & Raymond Fernandez
1953–63	Mexico	Delfina & Maria Gonzales
1958–60	United States	Gwyn & Kenneth Dudley
1963–65	England	Myra Hindley & Ian Brady
1970–73	United States	Dean Corll, David Brooks, & Elmer Henley
1971–87	England	Rosemary & Frederick West
1976–82	United States	Henry Lee Lucas & Otis Toole
1977–78	United States	Angelo Buono & Kenneth Bianci
1978–80	United States	Charlene & Gerald Gallego
1979	United States	Lawrence Bittaker & Roy Norris
1980	United States	Carol Bundy & Douglas Clark
1981–83	United States	Susan & James Carson
1982	United States	Judith Ann & Alvin Neelley
1983–85	United States	Charles Ng & Leonard Lake
1983–89	Austria	Waltraud Wagner, Maria Gruber, Irene Leidolf, & Stephanija Mayer
1984	United States	Debra Brown & Alton Coleman
1984–94	United States	Tene Bimbo Clan
1986–89	United States	Faye & Ray Copeland
1987	United States	Gwendolyn Graham & Catherine Wood
1990–92	Canada	Karla Homolka & Paul Bernardo
1995	South Africa	David Selepe & Moses Sithole

In addition, media portrayal of increased normalcy of violence toward females and increased marginalization of groups such as male and female prostitutes, transients, and others has served to reinforce their powerlessness in society. Researchers contend that many offenders are incapable of empathy, thereby reinforcing their objectivity in victim selection such that they often perceive the victims as worthless and, therefore, expendable. Additional research is required to better understand the intrinsic and extrinsic motivations for those (women and men) who together commit serial homicide.

—Lynn Gunn

See also BECK, MARTHA, AND RAYMOND FERNANDEZ; BELTWAY SNIPERS; BERNARDO, PAUL, AND KARLA HOMOLKA; COLUMBINE/LITTLETON SCHOOL SHOOTING;

In Cold Blood; Lake, Leonard, and Charles Ng;
Less-Dead; Manson, Charles/Manson Family;
Parker, Bonnie, and Clyde Barrow;
Serial Murder

Further Reading

Hare, R. (1993). *Without conscience: The disturbing world of the psychopaths among us.* New York: Guilford.

Hickey, E. W. (2002). *Serial murderers and their victims* (3rd ed.). Belmont, CA: Wadsworth.

Kelleher, M., & Kelleher, C. (1998). *Murder most rare: The female serial killer.* New York: Dell.

Pearson, P. (1997). *When she was bad: Violent women and the myth of innocence.* Toronto: Random House of Canada.

Weis J., & Keppel, R. (1999). Are serial killers special? *Murder: A multidisciplinary anthology of readings* (2nd ed.). Orlando, FL: Harcourt Brace.

TEHRAN VAMPIRE, *See* Serial Murder: International Incidence; Vampires, Werewolves, and Witches

TERRORISM

The popular concept of terrorism in the earliest years of the 21st century is often confined to acts of suicide bombings or other attacks on civilians perpetrated by enraged religious or political fanatics in the Middle East or in other locales in which these attacks receive extraordinary media coverage. However, terrorism as a political phenomenon is much older and much more diverse than the lead stories on the nightly television news might indicate.

Anarchists demonstrate on May Day, 1887.

Source: Library of Congress, Prints and Photographs Division (LC-USZ62-69545).

The functional origins of terrorism have been lost to history, but it is known that terrorism was used to achieve either military or political ends as early as the Roman Empire. *Terrorism* by definition is the use of lethal martial force against civilians in the expectation of tactical or strategic victory. In its tactical use, terrorism achieves a specific short-term objective but in its strategic aspects also functions as a tool of psychological warfare that lingers at the fringes of human memory (especially for the victims) such that others choose not to become victims themselves.

Caleb Carr, in his book *The Lessons of Terror*, clearly illustrates how Roman soldiers frequently resorted to terrorist tactics in their battle philosophy of "relentless but disciplined ferocity." When the Romans finally occupied the African city of Carthage, they laid it to waste, eliminated men, women, children, corps, livestock, and places of commerce and habitation, and on these ruins built their own city. In 9 A.D., Roman legions confronted Arminius in the Rhineland province (now Germany) and mercilessly repressed the "barbarian" invaders using terroristic total war wherein no person "despite age, gender or ability" was spared. The Germanic tribes responded in kind but ultimately lost to the numerically superior Romans. But the lesson was learned, the news of the viciousness of this battle spread throughout the empire, and the Romans never again waged any military campaign in northern Europe.

Centuries later, the Vikings used similar tactics in their pillage of Britain and the northern European sea coast. The brutality with which the Vikings pillaged struck resonant fear into nearly every coastal village, and the mere appearance of an approaching Viking ship terrorized many villagers into complete and abject submission. The Christian Crusades of the 11th to 14th centuries, while substantial military campaigns against the Muslims holding Palestine and Christian holy sites, were not above terrorizing civilians to achieve their putatively righteous objectives.

Carr notes that tracing terrorism back to, for example, an obscure source is misleading, in that it suggests that terrorism is outside mainstream political tactics. One such marginal group was the Muslin sect called *hashshashin*. This group of Shiites smoked hashish and worked themselves into drug-induced frenzies, after which they killed specifically targeted persons. The English word *assassin* comes from this term. Carr's point is that it distracts from accountability if we consider terrorism as lunatic acts of unstable persons or fanatical groups.

Suicide bomber Imad Kamel al-Zbaidi holds the Islamic Holy book, Koran, April, 2001. In the process of blowing himself up, Imad killed one Israeli and injured 40 others. The terrorist group Hamas claimed responsibility for the attack. Suicide bombing has become a common occurrence in the Middle East.

Source: Copyright © Reuters NewMedia Inc. / CORBIS.

The modern use of the term terrorist seems to come from actions of the radicalized mob in the French Revolution of the late 18th century, whose use of violent excesses in separating those loyal to the French crown from those loyal to the French state invoked mass panic. George Washington was part of a terror campaign against Native Americans as a commander in the French and Indian Wars. General William Sherman's complete devastation of Georgia in the American Civil War could also be considered part of an organized terror campaign. Genocidal actions in the 20th century perpetrated by the aggressors in World War II contributed to vengeful terrorism by Jews against Arabs in Palestine in the 1940s, as they sought

Firefighters, rescue workers, and engineers work at the Pentagon crash site on September 14, 2001.

Source: U.S. Department of Defense photograph by Tech. Sgt. Cedric H. Rudisill.

to establish a Jewish state that would ever protect Jews from racially motivated attacks and mass murders. In the process, however, Jewish nationalists resorted to the same tactics as their earlier tormentors in trying to alter the psychological environment such that it would further their political agenda.

The contemporary notion of terrorism stems from two particular actions in the 1960s. The first was the reaction of Arab states, specifically the nationalist Palestine Liberation Organization (PLO), to the success of Israel in the Six-Day War of 1967. The Arab reaction to such humiliation was to mount a terrorist campaign against Israel that initially relied on airplane highjackings and kidnappings. Later developments included airport massacres of passengers at several terminals from which the Israeli national airline departed, resulting in the mass murder of hundreds of innocent civilians. The second development was the use of automobiles as bombs, a technique first used by Irish nationalists against the British. The strategy

of a car bomb was that movement around cities was essentially undetected, and when the car was parked in the right spot and the bomb detonated at the right time, casualties and the resultant media coverage made the attack a significant event.

Thus, the combination of more elaborate devices meant to increase mass casualties and media coverage gave terrorists the platform they needed to promote their ideas and causes. Some would argue that the inclusion of the media meant that terrorists were less politically motivated than they were celebrity motivated, but the end result was essentially the same: Terrorists could garner for their cause a certain degree of notoriety when the media covered their attacks.

The content of the attacks also changed. In the late 1960s, structures or property were more often the targets. In 1970, Palestinian terrorists simultaneously hijacked three European airliners and had them rendezvous in the Libyan desert, whereupon all three jets were blown up. Since then, attacks against persons

An overhead view of Ground Zero, what was the World Trade Center in New York City.

Source: U.S. Customs Service, Department of the Treasury.

have increased, for example, the 1983 mass killing of U.S. peacekeepers in Lebanon by a truck bomb, or the bombing of the U.S. Embassy in eastern African, in which 300 people died.

The most frequent place for terrorist attacks is Israel, where Palestinian nationalists under the guise of the PLO, Hamas, or Hizbollah seek to kill Israeli citizens. The most common form of attack is the car bomb, but since the Intifadah in 1998, scores of young Palestinian men have used themselves as suicide bombers, thus bringing terrorism into shops and pedestrian areas (such as markets or malls) where automobiles are prohibited. The use of suicide bombers has also been a tool of Tamil nationalists fighting for a Tamil homeland in northern Sri Lanka. In at least a few instances, Tamil women have been suicide bombers; in one instance, the head of a female bomber was found on the roof of a nearby building after a suicide bomber assassination attempt on the Sri Lankan prime minister.

Terrorism can also be the tool of those seeking to overthrow a domestic government, as in the case of the 1995 Oklahoma City bombing of the Murrah Federal Building. Convicted and executed for his role in the attack, former U.S. Army soldier Timothy McVeigh was part of a militia movement in the United States that believed the U.S. government had deviated from a constitutional path and needed to be "realigned." His capture and trial effectively put an end to the militia movement in the United States and severely limited the activities of other domestic terrorists.

Occasionally, the word terrorism is applied to any act of violence whether the intended target is a government entity or not. "Eco-terrorism" is not terrorism per se, because it consists of criminal acts (arson, assault, battery, or even in extreme cases, murder) perpetrated by ecological fanatics against some corporate entity or a representation of the same. Attacks by such "terrorists," for example, against corporate research and development labs in which experimental mice or rats are released; the setting free of mink or other fur-bearing animals from pelt farms; or the burning of seafood wholesalers, are criminal acts but not necessarily terrorist attacks. Although their intent is to alter people's ways of life by interjecting notions of fear and apprehension, such attacks have proven to have far less significance and effect than politically motivated nationalist movements.

—*Brian Champion*

See also AERONAUTICAL MASS MURDER; ASSASSINS; BIN LADEN, OSAMA; HISTORY OF VIOLENCE IN RELIGIONS; OKLAHOMA CITY BOMBING; OLYMPIC PARK BOMBING

Further Reading

Carr, C. (2003). *The lessons of terror: A history of warfare against civilians.* New York: Random House.

Hanson, V. D. (2002). *An autumn of war: What America learned from September 11 and the war on terrorism.* New York: Anchor Books.

Lewis, B. (2003). *The crisis of Islam: Holy war and unholy terror.* Modern Library Publishers.

TEXAS SYNDICATE,
See GANGS: DEFINITIONS

THERIANTHROPY, *See* SERIAL MURDER: INTERNATIONAL INCIDENCE; VAMPIRES, WEREWOLVES, AND WITCHES

THREAT ASSESSMENT

What factors do law enforcement professionals consider when assessing the threat of any situation with the potential for violence? Early in their law enforcement careers, these professionals move through threat analysis in a conscious, step-by-step progression. As their experience levels progress, however, their abilities move from the deliberate consideration of a novice to the practiced, facile skill of an expert.

Threat assessment is the process of gathering and assessing information about persons who may have the interest, motive, intention, and capability of committing violent crimes. Law enforcement professionals use these factors when assessing the threat of violent behavior. Not all factors are present in every situation, and certain factors carry more weight than others. Recognizing the difference between thinking or making a threat and actually posing or carrying out a threat is important for investigators.

The primary responsibility of law enforcement is to determine whether a crime has been committed and to gather evidence leading to the identification, apprehension, and prosecution of those responsible. Less clear but equally important is the responsibility of law enforcement to prevent violent crimes and acts before they occur. Violent acts are prevented only when law enforcement accurately assesses threats. The four key elements of threat assessment are the potential subject, the event, the situation, and the victim. Studying these four elements provides critical information for preventing violent acts before they occur.

GENERAL FACTORS

History of Violent Behavior

For the law enforcement professional, a history of violent behavior is probably the most heavily weighted factor. People who commit violent crimes often have documented histories of problems, disputes, conflicts, and failures. Indicators such as prior arrests and convictions, earlier law enforcement calls/responses to the residence, work-related violent incidents, and training in what could be considered violent professions (e.g., butcher, professional boxer) would all draw the attention of a law enforcement professional.

One trend is of particular interest. Experienced law enforcement officers look for and interpret as significant an escalation of offenses, during which a subject progresses from petty to serious offenses. Experience also dictates that people usually gravitate to that with which they are familiar, using comfortable methods and techniques.

Environmental Scan/Immediately Observable Factors

An officer arriving at a home for a domestic disturbance call immediately scans the environment, looking for factors that could escalate or deescalate the threat of violence. Running in the mind of the officer is a litany of questions: who, what, when, where, how, and why. The list starts with "Who," because often who is present will dictate the potential for violence in a situation. The mere presence of parents, children, innocent bystanders, or victims can skew the situation quickly in one direction or another. Likewise, the presence of drugs or weapons can present an immediate and accessible threat. Violence is the product of an individual action in a setting that permits and does not hinder the action.

Nature of the Crime

Another major factor is the nature of the crime being investigated. Obviously, some crimes are inherently more violent than others. This is particularly true for law enforcement investigators working for agencies with a very broad jurisdiction (including the FBI). But probably the most dangerous of assignments is that of the everyday police officer on the street, who encounters extremely unpredictable crimes that fall under the broadest category of "people behaving badly." These officers respond to situations about which they know very little and must quickly make on-the-spot judgments about how inherently dangerous the crime under investigation is. Investigating a bounced check is generally less dangerous than a domestic violence situation. A bank robbery involving a demand note and a robber escaping on a bicycle would pose a less threatening situation than a takeover-style robbery with multiple subjects and shots fired. Officers develop this "sliding scale" of assessing immediate threats, usually based on internalized experiences from prior investigations. The study of human nature tells us that desperate people do desperate things.

Regardless of the crime, experienced law enforcement professionals make generalizations about the dangerousness of the situation, usually on the basis of factors external to the crime itself. Two factors are most important, regardless of the officer's perception of danger: the threat of suicide and whether the subject or perpetrator is armed. An armed check writer is therefore considered far more dangerous than an unarmed bank robber; and arresting an armed, fellow police officer on corruption charges poses far more risks than arresting many other types of armed persons.

In addition to the threat of suicide and whether someone is armed, officers also immediately consider whether the crime under investigation is a onetime event or is part of serial behavior. A onetime bank robber is probably less of a threat than an individual suspected in a string of 20 robberies.

Subject's Role in the Crime

Although the subject's role is not crystal clear at the outset of an investigation, most investigators have an indication from the start about a person's involvement in a crime. Officers typically can sort subjects from witnesses and then hone in on the subject's part. Was the individual acting alone, or did the subject initiate a complicated plan or strategy, acting as the kingpin? Did the subject act on impulse or passion, or is there an initial indication of premeditation and planning? Is the crime one of opportunity or one demonstrating complex predisposition? An officer assesses these factors, which provide key clues about the subject's propensity for violence. Law enforcement must also be able to understand quickly how the subject perceives reality.

Psychological Considerations

Sometimes referred to as "street corner psychologists," law enforcement investigators take a complex array of psychological factors into consideration when assessing the inherent dangerousness of subjects. Again, these factors often comprise an internal list the officer builds from personal experience, which translates into a psychological profile in action when assessing a situation. These factors include the following:

- Age
- Gender
- Ethnicity
- Socioeconomic status
- Prior victimization resulting in vigilantism or revenge
- Unique training (such as bomb building, chemistry, or military experience)
- Education level
- Marital status
- Medical history (previous treatments, including psychotropic medications and diagnosis)
- Addictions
- Race
- Family relations

♦ Occupational functioning
♦ Loss of significant relationships

The origin of this list is not scientific. It came out of discussions and conversations with in-service students at the FBI Academy (most of whom were experienced FBI investigators) in answer to the question "What psychological factors would you consider when assessing a subject's level of threat or dangerousness?" It is interesting how closely this list parallels intake factors a mental health professional would consider in performing an assessment of an individual's mental state.

Other Relevant History

Related to the indicators discussed under "History of Violent Behavior," there are other factors that an experienced law enforcement professional would consider relevant. Does the subject have a history of head injuries? Are there legal problems pending (other than the matter under investigation)? Are there significant social issues? Is there relevant medical and sexual history? Officers specifically note social issues and relevant medical history. A family history of suicide certainly elevates an interpretative threat to the officer. A subject's history of being socially isolated or a loner should also caution an experienced investigator.

In the early 1990s, the FBI began to more aggressively investigate threatening fan mail received by Hollywood celebrities. There was an overnight explosion in these types of cases, in which the FBI has jurisdiction if a threatening communication is mailed interstate. The high numbers were due to media coverage of several cases, including the murder of actress Rebecca Shafer and the malicious wounding and near murder of another actress, Theresa Saldano. The prevailing "old school" of thought in the FBI was that letter writers weren't dangerous; having penned their letters, the subjects had therapeutically "vented" and the threat actually decreased.

This way of thinking flew in the face of research results being published by forensic psychologist Dr. Park Dietz and some of the other "experts" the FBI itself consulted. The "new school" of thought asked, "How do we know?" How do we know whether an individual poses a threat when the letters are signed with a moniker and no investigative effort is spent identifying the writer and addressing the factors an investigator would consider in other types of investigations?

One particular case involved an actress who received literally hundreds of letters, signed, "Your Secret Admirer." The sender was particularly aggressive in reaching the actress, sending letters to her talent agent, family, and to other actors and actresses coappearing in productions. The letters were dismissed early on as not being a threat, but as they continued over a lengthy period of time, increased in numbers of recipients, and adopted an increasingly threatening tone, a new approach to understanding the dangerousness of the situation (generally perceived to be a nonviolent crime) was undertaken. The investigation focused on learning more about the sender and led to identifying the writer.

One of the key factors constituting relevant history was the profile, or background, of the letter sender. He was a white male in his mid-40s, with no friends, no employment, living at home with his mother, becoming increasingly focused and unable to differentiate between fantasy and reality. The threat was tangible to investigators and was confirmed by a psycholinguistic analysis of the most recent letters. A forensic psychiatrist concurred, and the subject was taken into custody, blocks from the actress's Los Angeles home. A search of his hotel room revealed a Marlin rifle with a high-powered scope.

FACTORS SPECIFIC TO HOMICIDE INVESTIGATIONS AND VIOLENT ENCOUNTERS

There are factors specific to homicide investigations and violent encounters. Generally speaking, these factors hinge on relationships: the relationship between the subject and the victim; physical relationships, including the proximity of subject and victim; access to weapons by the subject, victim, or both; and the psychological states of both the subject and the victim. A thorough investigation not only provides information about past behaviors and related conduct but also documents how the elements of threat assessment interacted. In most situations, there is something in the past that if discovered and correctly interpreted will point to the future. Identifying and correctly understanding events in the past are critical to preventing violent acts in the future.

*—Karen E. Gardner
and Vickie L. Woosley*

See also PREDICTING VIOLENT BEHAVIOR; PREVENTION OF
CRIME AND VIOLENT BEHAVIOR; PROFILING;
FORENSIC SCIENCE

Further Reading

Fein, R., & Vossekuil, B. (2000). *Protective intelligence
and threat assessment investigations: A guide for state
and local law enforcement officials* (NCJ 179981).
[Electronic version]. Washington, DC: U.S. Department
of Justice.

Fein, R., Vossekuil, B., & Holden, G. (1995). *Threat assess-
ment: An approach to preventing targeted violence.*
Research Report NCJ 155000 [Electronic version].
Washington, DC: U.S. Department of Justice.

Pinizzotto, A., Davis, E., & Miller, C. (2002, March).
Escape from the killing zone. *FBI Law Enforcement
Bulletin, 71*(3).

THREE STRIKES AND YOU'RE OUT!

Mike Reynolds is the father of Kimber Reynolds, 18,
who was gunned down in 1992 by two muggers as she
exited a restaurant in Fresno, California. Mr. Reynolds
became part of the victims' movement when his daughter became a crime statistic. In recent years, more and
more Americans are demanding harsher sentences for
violent habitual criminals.

Kimber's death, along with several other murder
victims who died at the hands of predators, prompted
Mr. Reynolds to crusade on their behalf. He is responsible for initiating two prominent California crime
laws that have been adopted in many states: "Three
Strikes and You're Out!" and "Ten, Twenty, Life."
These tough laws have affected how we classify and
punish violent habitual offenders.

In 1994, California voters approved the ballot initiative known as "Three Strikes and You're Out." It
means that people who are convicted of three felonies
could end up spending life in prison. The actual "law"
has five components: The *ballot initiative* (i.e.,
Proposition 184), the *actual statute* that was passed
(California Penal Code Section 667 b through i), and
three other code sections that identify the types of
violations that count as "strikes" against an offender.
The controversy that continues to surround the law,
now nearly 10 years old, is determining just how serious a third strike has to be before sentencing an

offender to 25 years to life. Proponents of the law
argue that the strikes are meant for serious crimes and
that judges have discretion whether or not to attach a
strike to an offender. Critics contend that some offenders are being discriminated against and sent to life
terms for relatively minor offenses determined to be
their third strikes. In April 2002, the U.S. Supreme
Court agreed to review California's three strikes law to
decide whether sentences of 25 years to life in prison
are unconstitutionally cruel when the third strike is relatively minor. In 2003, the decision of the Court
upheld the constitutionality of the California law.

The following is a statement given to the media
by California Secretary Bill Jones, titled "Three Strikes
and You're Out: A Focused, Flexible and Highly
Effective Approach to Combat Career Criminals." In
1993, as a member of the California State Assembly,
Mr. Jones wrote the initiative that would eventually
become the three strikes law.

Anytime a public official predicts that a new law will
reduce crime more than expected, cost less than
expected and prompt parolees and career criminals to
head for the state border as soon as possible, be skeptical. But in the case of California's Three Strikes and
You're Out law, it is not a prediction, it is a factual
history of what we have experienced since the adoption
of the nation's toughest repeat offender statute in 1994.

When crime goes up in a city or a state, citizens
expect action and lawmakers usually respond.

Responses in California have run the gamut from
self-esteem courses and midnight basketball to increased
police activity and sentence enhancements with varying
degrees of success, failure and taxpayer expense.

In 1993, the people of California were confronted
with a murder every 2 hours, a rape every 41 minutes, a
robbery every four minutes, an aggravated assault every
3 minutes and a car theft every 18 seconds (FBI
Uniform Crime Reports, 1992).

For every 100 FBI Index crimes reported to the police
in our state, only two people were sent to prison (FBI
Uniform Crime Reports 1991, Bureau of Justice Statistics
Correctional Populations in the United States, 1991).

The average time served in California was only
21 months, or 41 percent of the average sentence given
in court (CJI Corrections Yearbook-Adult Corrections,
1993).

The actual time an average criminal could expect to
spend in prison after taking into account the chances
of being caught, convicted and sent to prison, was only

12 days. Before we passed Three Strikes, 58 percent of those released from California's prisons committed another crime within 2 years of their release. (FBI Crime Reports, 1991, CJI Corrections Yearbook-Adult Corrections, 1993, and Bureau of Justice Statistics Correctional Populations in the United States, 1992).

After a number of high-profile child abductions and murders by career criminals with a long record of repeated arrests, incarceration, parole and re-arrest, we passed a measure to close the prison system's revolving door.

As a member of the State Assembly in 1993 I wrote, and in 1994 the state adopted, the nation's toughest and most successful Three Strikes and You're Out law. After the legislature adopted the law, California voters subsequently placed an identical measure on the ballot which was approved by 72 percent of the electorate.

When we drafted the measure we relied on several important presumptions: 1) that a significant portion of crimes in our society are committed by an extremely active, but relatively small percentage of the criminal population, 2) most criminals can be deterred from committing future crimes by a real and substantial threat of long-term incarceration, 3) criminals who cannot be deterred from repeatedly committing serious and violent felonies can and should be rendered incapable of committing additional crime through incarceration, and 4) for the law to work, it must be easy enough for the criminal element to clearly understand and recognize how it applies to them individually.

The structure of the law is intentionally simple.

♦ A criminal who is found guilty of a felony and who has previously been convicted of a serious or violent felony shall have his or her sentence doubled for the current offense.

♦ A criminal who is found guilty of a felony and who has previously been convicted of at least two serious or violent felonies shall have his or her sentence tripled or will face a sentence of 25 years to life in prison, whichever is greater.

♦ Three Strikes also required repeat offenders to serve at least 80 percent of their terms, eliminating the 50 percent good time credits that were allowed under prior law.

The simplicity of the law and the severity of the punishment have served as significant and unprecedented deterrents to crime.

The list of serious and violent crimes is composed of particularly heinous offenses such as murder, rape,

mayhem and other crimes that indisputably warrant extensive time in prison.

Once an individual has demonstrated the propensity to commit multiple serious and violent felonies, we felt it was our duty as lawmakers to protect the people of California from becoming the third fourth or fifth victim of these dangerous and devastating crimes. The very real threat of long-term incarceration for career criminals created a deterrent effect that we believe has been the predominant factor in our state's successful reduction in crime since 1994.

In just the first 6 years after California adopted Three Strikes, the crime rate in California declined 41%: more than any other state and more than twice the 19% drop experienced during that same period in the other 49 states and the District of Columbia.

Predictions that the law would instantaneously clog our civil and criminal courts, require the construction of 20 new prisons and break the budget without substantially affecting the crime were completely incorrect.

Since the adoption of Three Strikes, California's inmate population hit a plateau and has begun to decline. Predictions that the prison population would increase 84% from 125,000 inmates in 1994 to 230,000 inmates by the year 2001, were off by nearly 72,000.

The year that Three Strikes passed marked the first time in 15 years that more parolees moved out of California than came into the state from other jurisdictions.

Those who wonder if the threat of punishment can actually deter crime need look no further than the statistics showing that soon after Three Strikes passed, California immediately changed from a net importer of parolees from other states to a net exporter of parolees.

If you step onto any prison yard in the state, the inmates will tell you, with certainty, exactly how many strikes they have and what they plan to do with their lives when they are released. Clearly, the message sent by California to career criminals has been received and it has deterred repeat offenders from continuing their life of crime.

Prisoners know they have three choices when they are released: clean up their act, go to jail, or leave the state. They have been doing all three and our crime rates have plummeted.

Clearly, the law has been effective, but is it fair?

Since it was first passed, opponents have argued that the Three Strikes law is unfair because the third strike can be a felony of any grade and not necessarily a violent or serious felony.

Under the law, the commission of a crime that would otherwise trigger a relatively minor sentence can place a repeat serious and violent felon behind bars for life. We intentionally drafted the law to target the most incorrigible serious and violent repeat offenders and prevent them from turning any more innocent Californians into victims of serious and violent crime.

The rallying cry in 1994 was "No More Victims," but proposed changes to the law at the time, and virtually every year since it was passed, would require the third crime to be an additional serious or violent felony. The problem with this approach is that it would require another woman to be raped, another child to be molested or another father to be killed before removing these predators from our neighborhoods.

DISCRETION

To guarantee that each and every individual sentenced to 25 years to life in prison is treated fairly, both the judge and the District Attorney have the discretion to ignore prior convictions when it is in the furtherance of justice to do so.

That means that if a criminal with two serious or violent felonies decades ago who has lived a clean arrest-free life since is convicted of a new low-grade felony, he or she has two opportunities to have his prior strikes dismissed, thus preventing him from facing the Three Strikes penalty enhancements.

A recent case explains the policy rationale behind the decision to impose the law's toughest penalty for any felony, while also permitting both judges and district attorneys to apply their discretion to determine when an individual is dangerous or not.

A Santa Clara County defendant named Louis Marshall was convicted of stealing a couple bottles of cognac.

Given that set of facts, one would have no reason to suspect that society needs long-term protection from this man.

However, because the petty theft was preceded by prior petty theft convictions, this case was elevated from a misdemeanor to a felony. Violation of property rights is a serious concern, but would society benefit by sentencing this man to life in prison?

Most people argue that is excessive, until they hear the rest of the story.

Louis Clifford Marshall was previously arrested and convicted of multiple counts of abducting and sexually assaulting teenage girls.

Since nearly half of all child molesters are returned to prison within 3 years of their release, we believe there is a very real and substantial public policy rationale behind removing sex offenders like Mr. Marshall from the streets for any additional felony conviction, but preferably one that will not scar another innocent child for life.

With California's stringent Three Strikes law, Californians are protected from ticking time bombs like Louis Marshall. But, because the law permits prosecutors and judges to review the full criminal history of each defendant, less violent and dangerous thieves who could face life in prison under the Three Strikes law do not.

In fact most counties and judges in California routinely dismiss prior convictions in the furtherance of justice on a regular basis.

Further proof that the law is reaching its intended targets is found in a recent analysis of Three Strikes cases conducted by the *San Jose Mercury News* in December, 2001.

It hasn't overwhelmed California's prisons with vast numbers of petty criminals doing life sentences, as critics predicted. Instead, California's 7-year-old "three strikes, you're out" law appears to have accomplished the goal its supporters touted: It has targeted the state's worst repeat offenders and taken them off the streets.

After an initial flurry of convictions, three-strikes prosecutions have declined steadily. The number of these offenders now doing the 25-years-to-life sentences authorized by the law accounts for just 4 percent of inmates.

Critics continue to charge that the law is being used improperly against petty offenders, a claim that is difficult to evaluate across the state. But a *Mercury News* analysis found little evidence of such overzealousness in a review of three-strikes cases in Santa Clara County. *Of the 181 cases in which a 25-years-to-life sentence was handed down for a non-violent crime, the paper found, 95 percent of the convicts had previously committed multiple violent acts.* Prosecutors say that their success in putting away these sorts of felons—the most dangerous of California's career criminals—means there are fewer hard-core lawbreakers on the street and fewer three-strikes cases.

—San Jose Mercury News
December 28, 2001
(Emphasis Added)

Despite years of sensationalized news accounts of great injustice that focus on the severity of the final offense rather than the full criminal portfolio long-term habitual felons, the facts demonstrate a clarity of focus, the fair application of the law and an unequaled reduction in crime.

Although the law has withstood a variety of legal challenges already, we anticipate that opponents of the Three Strikes will continue to urge the courts to water down the measure. Unfortunately, those legal attacks and the extensive news coverage that accompanies even minor judicial curbing of the law will gradually diminish the important deterrent effect that the law has had on career criminals.

The best way to maintain the declining crime rates we have experienced under Three Strikes is to (1) ensure the law remains firmly intact and (2) conduct extensive public education campaigns targeted at the criminal element of this state to remind them of the penalties they face the next time they commit a felony in California.

Sadly, it will be innocent law abiding citizens who will become victims if career criminals start to believe that they can get around the Three Strikes law the same way they have evaded other sentencing statutes during their life of crime. The severity of our Three Strikes law combined with ample awareness of the measure should prevent additional Californians from becoming victims for years to come.

—*Eric W. Hickey and Bill Jones*

"TOP HOODLUM" PROGRAM

In November 1957, a New York state trooper uncovered a meeting of crime bosses from across the country at the Appalachian estate of mobster Joseph Barbara. The discovery of the meeting had a dramatic effect on FBI Director J. Edgar Hoover, who for years had denied that the Mafia still existed. In response to the revelation of a nationwide criminal network, Hoover implemented the "Top Hoodlum Program" in every major city to collect information about Mob bosses and their activities. The discovery also provided enough insight to prove that the Mafia was in actuality bigger and stronger than ever, which prompted the FBI to begin extensive use of undercover surveillance.

—*Tatia Smith*

See also FEDERAL BUREAU OF INVESTIGATION; MOB, THE

TRIBAL COURTS, *See* JURISDICTION

TROPHY TAKING

A *trophy* is in essence a souvenir. In the context of violent behavior or murder, keeping a part of the victim as a trophy represents power over that individual. When the offender keeps this kind of souvenir, it serves as a way to preserve the memory of the victim and the experience of his or her death.

The most common trophies for violent offenders are body parts but also include photographs of the crime scene and jewelry or clothing from the victim. Offenders use the trophies as memorabilia, but also to reenact their fantasies. They often masturbate or use the trophies as props in sexual acts. Their exaggerated fear of rejection is quelled in front of inanimate trophies.

Ritualistic trophy taking, as is found with serial offenders, acts as a *signature*. A signature is similar to a modus operandi (a similar act ritualistically performed in virtually all crimes of one offender), yet it is an act that is not necessary to complete the crime. For example, a modus operandi would be strangulation using a rope (specific method to kill an individual), but a signature may be postmortem mutilation of the victim's face (not necessary in the commission of the crime, but occurs at the same time as the crime). Trophy taking is one type of signature. Some of the most shocking have been seen in the cases of serial killers Jeffrey Dahmer, Ed Gein, and Jerome Brudos.

—*Nicole L. Mott*

See also DAHMER, JEFFERY; JACK THE RIPPER; HOMICIDE: MOTIVATION FOR MURDER; MOTIVES FOR MURDER; PARAPHILIA; SERIAL MURDER; SIGNATURE KILLINGS

Further Reading

Davis, D. (1995). *Milwaukee murders, nightmare in apartment 213: The true story.* New York: St. Martin's.

Schechter, H. (1989). *Deviant: The shocking true story of the original "psycho."* New York: Pocket Books.

TUCKER, KARLA FAYE,
See GENDER VIOLENCE

MADAME TUSSAUD

Marie Tussaud was born in late 1761 and died in 1850. Tussaud's widowed mother moved her children to Switzerland, where they lived with Phillipe Curtuis, a talented sculptor of wax heads. While living in the home, Marie learned the trade of wax modeling and later took her talents to the aristocrats. Some of Tussaud's more famous works were the likes of Marie Antionette and other prominent French figures; she also made casts of victims of the guillotine. In 1802, Madame Tussaud left France and took her collection of death masks to England, where they were put on display in what later became known as the "Chamber of Horrors." To this day, the museum attracts thousands of visitors annually.

—*Jami Jenkins*

TYLENOL MURDERS,
See PRODUCT TAMPERING

TYPOLOGY, USE OF, *See* HOMICIDE

U

UNABOMBER,
See KACZYNSKI, THEODORE

UNIFORM CRIME REPORTS (UCR)

The Uniform Crime Report (UCR) is the primary information source for offenses reported to state and local law enforcement in the United States. The UCR is the result of an initiative by the International Association of Chiefs of Police (IACP) in the 1920s to develop a standardized system for gathering statistics on crimes reported to police. In 1930, the Attorney General of the United States was authorized by Congress to coordinate a national crime-reporting effort under the auspices of the FBI. The UCR is published on a yearly basis and provides information on murder or nonnegligent manslaughter, forcible rape, robbery, aggravated assault, burglary, auto theft, arson, and larceny/theft offenses reported to state and local law enforcement. These eight offenses are thought to provide a fair representation of the crime picture as a whole, and their total number make up what is called a "crime index." Another part of the UCR is arrest information for a variety of offenses, including misdemeanors and felonies, and statistical information for reporting law enforcement agencies.

The number of law enforcement agencies participating in the UCR system has grown from 400 agencies in 43 states in 1930 to more than 17,000 state and local law enforcement agencies in 2001. The submission of crime data to the FBI is voluntary, but most states also have their own uniform crime-reporting requirements. Those states forward much of the data received from individual agencies within the state, as part of a state-based crime reporting effort, to the FBI for inclusion in the UCR. The UCR, however, does not contain information on the number of federal offenses reported to specific federal law enforcement agencies.

THE IMPACT OF UCR DATA

Crime statistics are the lifeblood of law enforcement agencies and are viewed as the best measure of how well the criminal justice system is doing. A rise in reported crime triggers political debates at all levels and can result in significant changes in criminal justice operations and policy:

♦ Law enforcement agencies point to a rise in reported crimes as a justification to increase their resources. Conversely, however, a decrease in crime does not usually prompt a request for a reduction of resources.

♦ With significant increases in reported crime, legislators feel the need to pass new legislation raising the penalties for particular crimes, assuming that this would deter more people from committing them.

♦ Additional funding for police due to an increase in reported crimes results in more arrests, more convictions, and a greater strain on prosecutors, the courts, and existing inmate bed space in correctional or detention facilities.

CRITICISM OF THE UCR

Above all, the UCR is a political document. Police agencies and various superordinate political entities view UCR data as a quantitative and qualitative measure of their activities. The use of the UCR as a measure of success or failure has in the past resulted in manipulation of data by some law enforcement agencies, to show success through lower numbers of reported crimes. Another problem is the faulty or incorrect classification of reported offenses due to individual differences in criminal codes and the nonreporting of some Part I crime categories. In an attempt to detect possible accidental or even intentional inaccuracies in reported crime information, the FBI carefully reviews and analyzes the data for correctness.

The main criticism of the UCR is that the data shows only crimes reported to police and as such is not an accurate measure of how much crime is actually occurring. For a variety of reasons, many victims do not report their victimization to police, and in many cases, police have considerable discretion in deciding how the report should be classified. It is also questionable that the eight offenses that make up the UCR crime index should include larceny/theft, which by itself makes up more than half of all reported index crimes and most often involves a misdemeanor, whereas the other seven offenses are felonies.

THE NATIONAL INCIDENT-BASED REPORTING SYSTEM

Recognizing that the eight index offenses that are part of the UCR are no longer useful in evaluating the complex crime picture in the United States, the FBI and the Bureau of Justice Statistics began an overhaul of the UCR in 1985. The new version of the UCR is called the National Incident-Based Reporting System (NIBRS), and it provides information on 21 different offenses reported to police; gathers additional information on victims, offenders, and arrestees; and promises improved quality control.

The change to the new reporting system is not complete, and many agencies still submit crime report information under the old UCR format. The new reporting format requires changes in data-processing software, additional training for personnel affected by the changeover, and more resources due to the increased complexity of submitting data to the UCR. As a result, law enforcement agencies experiencing funding problems have not enthusiastically embraced this new reporting format absent any tangible incentives.

—*Harald Otto Schweizer*

See also FEDERAL BUREAU OF INVESTIGATION; ROBBERY; SCHOOL SHOOTINGS; VICTIMOLOGY

Further Reading

Federal Bureau of Investigation. *Unified crime reports.* Available on the World Wide Web at: http://www.fbi.gov/ucr/ucr.htm.

U.S. Department of Justice, Office of Justice Programs. (1999, October). *Bridging gaps in police crime data* (NCJ 176365). Available on the World Wide Web at: http://www.ojp.usdoj.gov/bjs/pub/pdf/bgpcd.pdf.

U.S. Department of Justice, Office of Justice Programs. *About incident-based statistics and the National Incident-Based Reporting System (NIBRS).* Available on the World Wide Web at: http://www.ojp.usdoj.gov/bjs/ibrs.htm.

U.S. Department of Justice, Office of Justice Programs. *The nation's two crime measures.* Available on the World Wide Web at: http://www.ojp.usdoj.gov/bjs/pub/pdf/ntmc.pdf.

UNION STATION MASSACRE

On the morning of June 17, 1933, in Kansas City, Missouri, four policemen and FBI agents were escorting convicted killer Frank Nash from the Union Railway Station back to Leavenworth State Penitentiary, from which he had escaped in October 1930.

There was some concern ahead of time that an attempt might be made to either rescue Nash or kill him before he was returned to prison. Although police and agents were armed with revolvers, shotguns, and machine guns, they were no match for what was awaiting them. When agents reached the parking lot, Nash was placed in the front seat, and while they were securing themselves and their weapons in the car, several men stepped from various hiding places, surrounding them, and began a barrage of rapid gunfire.

Nash, riddled with bullets, died immediately. Four others were also killed, and two FBI agents were wounded. This incident prompted FBI Director J. Edgar Hoover to seek more power for the Bureau. As a result, the FBI received more funding, and agents were finally given full police powers and allowed to carry weapons at all times.

It was assumed, but never proven, that the alleged gunmen were Charles "Pretty Boy" Floyd, Adam Richetti, and Verne Miller. There was speculation that Nash was killed on purpose to silence him because of close Mob ties. Other theories suggest that his death was unintentional. At this point, it seems, the truth will never be learned.

—Tatia Smith

See also FLOYD, CHARLES ARTHUR "PRETTY BOY"

V

VAMPIRES, WEREWOLVES, AND WITCHES

Vampire lore has been the subject of discussion in many countries during the past few centuries. Bram Stoker's *Dracula* (1897) was modeled on the 15th-century Wallachian nobleman Vlad Tepes, also known as "Vlad the Impaler" and "Drakul" (Dragon). He was particularly known to be a "vicious and depraved sadist" who enjoyed torturing and murdering peasants who lived within his jurisdiction. Stories circulated about the secret horror chambers in the depths of his castle and how he was believed to be the devil or at least one of his emissaries. Tales evolved suggesting that some vampires could also transform themselves into werewolves. However, vampires usually had but one goal—to drink human blood—whereas werewolves mutilated and cannibalized. Vampires were also believed to be sexually involved with their victims, albeit discreetly, because of the erotic nature of sucking human blood. In his book *Man Into Wolf* (1951), Robert Eisler described a British "vampire" that in 1949 murdered nine victims and drank blood from each of them. By 1995, any erotic subtleties in vampirism had been replaced with direct expressions of sexual arousal, gratification, and their fusion with violence and death. In the film *Interview with a Vampire: The Vampire Chronicles,* vampires dine on the blood of female victims, who experience orgasmic arousal and, immediately following, terror and death.

Some people believe that evil spirits can inhabit the bodies of animals, causing them to act wildly. Just as many cultures have long entertained the notion that criminals can be possessed by demons, they have identified particular animals that are most likely to be possessed. In legends and folklore, wolves are often said to have dealings with the devil. The natural enmity between wolf and man has existed for centuries, and wolves have been hunted relentlessly. Given the belief that humans and animals can be demonically possessed, it is not surprising that the belief also exists that a possessed human could become a wolf. A person able to command such a metamorphosis became known as a werewolf (*were* was an Old English term for *man*). The belief in *lycanthropy,* or the transformation of persons into wolves, can be traced back to at least 600 B.C., when King Nebuchadnezzar believed he suffered from such an affliction. Jean Fernal (1497-1558) of France, a physician, believed lycanthropy to be a valid medical phenomenon. Many societies around the world have a term for werewolf: France, *loup-garou;* Germany, *Werwolf;* Portugal, *lob omen;* and Italy, *lupo mannaro.* In Africa, stories abound of "were-leopards" and "were-jackals," and "were-tigers" tales are common in India.

Lycanthropy was also viewed as a form of madness in which a person believed himself or herself to be an animal, usually a wolf, and expressed a desire to eat raw meat, experienced a change in voice, and had a desire to run on all fours. To ensure the perpetuation of werewolf lore, stories of those possessed usually included reminders of how difficult it was to destroy such monsters. The werewolves were believed to be extraordinarily powerful creatures who could change back to human form at will or at the break of day. Belief in these terrifying creatures was often fueled by the occasional discovery of a mutilated corpse along a highway or brought in with the tide.

To those living in the 16th and 17th centuries, witches were similar to werewolves in their transformation upon making a pact with the Prince of Darkness, or Satan. In the 16th century, Paracelsus wrote that violent, wicked men may have the opportunity to return after death as an animal, usually a wolf. The purpose of this human-to-wolf transformation was the inevitable killing of humans, particularly children, to eat their flesh. Recurrent throughout werewolf literature is the theme of *anthropophagy,* or the enjoyment of eating human flesh. Jean Grenier, a young 17th-century Frenchman, claimed to be a werewolf and confessed that he had devoured the flesh of many young girls. Another notorious werewolf was Germany's Peter Stubb, or Stump, of the 16th century. After completing a "pact" with the devil, he simply donned a wolfskin belt and was able to transform himself whenever he had the urge to kill. Naturally, he murdered those who offended him, along with several women and girls, whom he raped and sexually tortured before cannibalizing. Stubbs, who fathered a child by his daughter and then ate his own son, managed to murder 13 young children and two expectant mothers by some of the most perverse and cruel methods imaginable.

Werewolves and vampires are joined by other sinister creatures, including witches, all bent on terrorizing humankind, especially women and children. A function of the early European church was to find ways to eradicate the problems attributed to witchcraft and sorcery. Under guidance from Pope Innocent VIII, two Dominicans, Heinrich Institor (Kramer) and Jakob Sprenger, produced the first encyclopedia of demonology, the *Malleus Maleficarum* (*Witch's Hammer*), in 1486. This compendium of mythology was used for centuries to identify and destroy witches, wizards, and sorcerers. Thousands of people were "identified" through torturous means and then promptly burned at the stake. Countess Elizabeth Bathory of 15th-century Hungary became heavily involved in sorcery, witchcraft, and devil worship. Although she married and bore children, she maintained a predilection for young girls. With her husband off to the wars, she began to indulge herself in the torture and slaying of young girls and women. Stimulated by sado-eroticism, the countess bathed in the blood of her victims in order to maintain her fair complexion. She was believed to have been responsible for the deaths of more than 100 victims. The latent

or unintended outcome of the "great witch hunt," or the Grand Inquisition of the Middle Ages, was the creation of a witch "craze" that cost many innocent people their lives. Sanctioned by government, the witch-hunt took on new meaning, and practically overnight, witches were to be found everywhere. The efforts of the church and state probably did more to perpetuate the belief in sorcerers, werewolves, vampires, and witches than any other single force in society.

—*Eric W. Hickey*

NOTE: Portions of this profile were previously published in Eric Hickey's *Serial Murderers and Their Victims,* 2002, 3rd ed. Belmont, CA: Wadsworth Publishers.

See also BATHORY, COUNTESS ELIZABETH; SERIAL MURDER: INTERNATIONAL INCIDENCE

Further Reading

Bunson, M. (2000). *The vampire encyclopedia.* Gramercy.
Eisler, R. (1951). *Man into wolf.* Westport, CT: Greenwood.
Hill, D., & Williams, P. (1967). *The supernatural.* New York: Signet.
Konstantinos. (1996). *Vampires: The occult truth.* Llewellyn Publications.
Marwick, M. (1970). *Witchcraft and sorcery.* New York: Penguin.

VAN DAM, DANIELLE, *See* MOTIVES FOR MURDER

VEHICULAR HOMICIDE

There are various explanations for vehicular homicide, such as road rage, alcohol use, and revenge. The only difference between vehicular homicide and other types of homicide is that the weapon used is the vehicle. The same elements must be proven as in any homicide, and the person can be tried for murder. In Canada, the majority of the charges in vehicular homicide cases are "Dangerous Operation of Motor Vehicle Causing Death." Each of the explanations, road rage and impaired driving, will be discussed at length, including a profile of the perpetrators, factors related to each, and approaches to dealing with the incidents.

ROAD RAGE

In Canada, *road rage* has been defined as "random acts of violence or aggressive behavior carried out by frustrated or over-stressed drivers." Although road rage is not limited to Western societies, there are more frequent occurrences of road rage in Canada, the United States, and Britain than in other countries. Road rage appears to be a form of interpersonal violence that is random and potentially deadly. There are many reasons why determining the cause and a possible resolution to road rage are difficult. There is no universal definition of what constitutes road rage, it involves an aggressive act between two complete strangers, and to date, there is insufficient quantifiable data to document its existence. These are some of the reasons why road rage is difficult to understand and why proposed theories about its cause lead to a number of probabilities.

Profile of Road Rage Perpetrators

An interesting point was noted by Dr. Leon James, an expert on road rage, in which he declared that almost everyone, sometime in their lives, has thoughts of retaliation and feeling of rage while driving a vehicle. This shows that defining who is more likely to be an offender of road rage is a very difficult task. Research has indicated that both men and women are equally likely to be the perpetrators of aggressive acts while driving. It was determined that men are more likely to be involved in shootings and women are more likely to ram another vehicle. The type of vehicle, whether a car, sport utility vehicle, minivan, or truck, does not make a difference, and although a majority or offenders are under the age of 25, middle-aged drivers are also well represented. The Cincinnati police department issued an article identifying the "road rage warrior" as male, 18 to 26 years old, and poorly educated; with a criminal record, history of violence, and drug and alcohol abuse; and possibly suffering from emotional or professional setbacks. A specific profile of a road rage perpetrator is difficult to determine, however.

Factors in Road Rage

Numerous factors are related to road rage. As cities continue to grow, increased congestion on the roads and increased commuting distances contribute to the problem. Keith Brooks, traffic analyst with the Calgary Police Service (2002), indicates that in Calgary, a definite pattern shows a substantial increase in the number of registered vehicles. In March 2002, there were 666,434 registered vehicles, compared with 641,583 in March 2001. This is an increase of 20,851 registered vehicles, which does not include those vehicles not registered or registered in another province. There is almost a one-to-one ratio of registered vehicles to registered owners (.95). This, together with poor driving skills and impatience and inattentiveness behind the wheel, leads to many more incidents of road rage.

In North America, there is a cultural propensity to promote competitive and aggressive behaviors, resulting in a power struggle between drivers. People are also doing many other things while driving their cars, such as talking on cell phones, adjusting the radio, or using mapping systems, which impairs their ability to operate the vehicle. These factors, coupled with stress and drivers losing control of their emotions, are a few of the reasons for increased incidents of road rage.

Many aggressive drivers are under the influence of "impaired emotions." Impatience or inattentive acts such as driving through red lights, cutting corners, not yielding, following too close, blocking lanes, braking suddenly, and threatening by insult or gestures are all illustrations of the emotional power struggle that can lead to serious road rage incidents. More potentially deadly examples include pointing a firearm, assaulting the vehicle, and driving at excessively high speeds. If a person is standing in line in a store, the norms of society state that you should keep your emotions to yourself and not act like a "bully." For some reason, in a vehicle, it has become common, if not acceptable, to express hostility by acting out emotions.

There have been many well-publicized incidents of this type of behavior. A California man killed a small dog by throwing it into oncoming traffic in a fit of road rage. The offender had lost his temper after colliding with another vehicle, snatched the dog from the car, threw the dog into traffic, and left the scene. In Calgary, in January 2001, a BMW was traveling southbound at the same time a Jeep Grand Cherokee was also southbound, but driving slowly as if to look for an address. The Jeep approached the vehicle at a high rate of speed and struck the rear of the BMW, and both vehicles shot across the intersection toward a traffic control pole. The BMW exploded on impact as it wrapped around the pole, and burst into flames. The driver of the Jeep was charged with "Criminal Negligence Causing Death." Both examples indicate how impaired emotions lead to violent acts on the road.

Road Rage Prevention

To eliminate many of these problems, drivers must be educated on the rules of the road and more effective methods of responding to other drivers. Many people could also benefit from anger management and stress-reduction seminars. These courses can provide tools needed to control anger and reduce the likelihood of incidents. Increased police presence may also be needed to enforce speed limits and severely penalize those who drive aggressively.

The most frequently given explanation for aggressive driving is "I'm late"; thus, drivers should allow themselves more traveling time to cut down on impatience and frustration. Other suggestions to avoid road rage incidents are as follows: Don't tailgate, don't cut someone off, don't block passing lanes, don't gesture in anger, don't try to "win," don't make eye contact, and don't hesitate to call "911." Drivers must adopt a cooperative driving approach and learn not to take actions of other drivers personally, as well as being aware of the effects of their own driving habits.

IMPAIRED DRIVERS

The compelling statement by John Bates, "Road rage may be just the sober version of drunk driving," was made by the founder of Mothers Against Drunk Driving (MADD) (*Toronto Star*, 1998). Bates believes that the same person is most likely to kill you, sober or drunk.

The number of alcohol-related traffic accidents has not decreased with the amount of attention the issue has received over recent years. On average, drunk driving costs Canadians $9 billion a year and results in 4.5 deaths and 125 injuries every day. Alcohol increases the risk and the severity of a collision. It is estimated that drunk driving kills 2 times the number of Canadians as are murdered each year. Between 1999 and 2000, nearly half of the fatal motor vehicle collisions in Calgary involved alcohol, and it should be noted that the majority of persons killed in impaired-driving accidents are not the ones who cause the accidents (Calgary Police Service, 2000).

Profile of the Typical Drunk Driver

The type of person who drives drunk is typically male, between 25 and 34, and is regularly a heavy drinker or a "social drinker" who occasionally drinks heavily. People of all races, ages, and genders have been charged with drunk driving, and determining a specific profile is difficult.

Legislation and Policies

In 1999, the Government of Alberta chose to target drunk drivers by instituting a "zero tolerance" administrative license suspension (ALS). The law states that those charged with impaired-driving offenses, including failure or refusal to provide a breath sample, will have their licenses suspended for a minimum of 3 months. If the offense results in injury or death, the ALS will be a minimum of 6 months.

Drunk-Driving Prevention

Many approaches have been used to attempt to stop drunk drivers, and MADD is one of the primary organizations for this purpose. The group has outlined initiatives for the government to eliminate drunk driving:

1. *Blood alcohol limits:* Lower blood alcohol limit from .08% to .05%.
2. *Enhanced enforcement powers:* This includes the officer's legal right to stop drivers to determine whether they have valid driver's licenses and whether they are under the influence of alcohol, and to demand a blood sample if an accident occurred or in other circumstances in which drivers are unable to provide breath samples.
3. *Clarifying and redefining offenses:* Amend the Canadian Criminal Code to include a definition of impairment that is clear to both judges and police and a definition of cause of death or injury by impaired or dangerous driving.
4. *Rationalizing sentencing:* Make changes to sentencing practices that would act as deterrents to drunk drivers, including tiered sentencing to take into account mitigating factors, such as the offender's blood alcohol level concentration, prior offenses, and the occurrence of a crash, injury, or death.
5. *Addressing administrative issues:* Develop a strategy to address the issue of impaired driving and review legislation every 5 years.

90-Day License Suspension

In Calgary, Alberta, drunk drivers can be hit with a 90-day suspension even if their impaired driving charges are dropped. This anti-drunk-driving law does not violate the Charter of Rights and Freedoms because driving is a privilege, not a right. This law is independent of criminal charges because it ensures safety by deterring drunk drivers.

Graduated Licensing Program

Graduated licensing program (GLS) is aimed at ensuring that all new drivers have the necessary experience to become safe and responsible drivers. In Ontario, the young person must be 16 years of age or older and pass a vision test and a general road knowledge test. Once the young person is in the GLS, they go through two stages. The first stage lasts 12 months, and they must pass the Ministry road test to move to the second stage. The second stage lasts 12 months, and they must pass a comprehensive Ministry road test to receive the full license. There are restrictions at each level, such as who must be with you and where and when you can drive. The purpose of the program is to gradually increase the driving privileges of a new driver during the first 2 years on the road. The program has proven to be successful throughout Canada.

Alcohol Ignition Interlock Device

Alcohol ignition interlock devices are used for prevention and as a rehabilitation tool in the fight against drunk driving. The ignition interlock is a device that analyzes a breath sample for blood alcohol concentration. The device is wired into the ignition and requires the driver to provide a breath sample for the vehicle to be operational. The device randomly requests samples as the vehicle is being driven. This is to ensure that the offender will be able to drive only when his or her blood alcohol concentration level is below the legal limit. The experience in Alberta has been positive and shows that "keeping an offender under the control of the licensed driving system with an interlock device is an effective fight against impaired driving" (Department of Justice Canada, 2001).

CONCLUSION

Road rage and impaired driving are prevalent issues facing law enforcement. The public can assist the police by being aware of conditions in which aggressive behavior is more prevalent, such as during Friday afternoon peak hours, moderate traffic congestion, and

fair weather. Drivers can be alert to the possibility of encountering acts of road rage and can adjust their schedules accordingly. As for alcohol-impaired drivers, legislation appears to be the most successful intervention. The combination of enforcement, education, and legislation appears to be the most effective way to manage road safety.

—*Tracey Lowey*

See also ROAD RAGE

Further Reading

Alberta Transportation. (2000). *Ignition interlock program.* Edmonton, Alberta, Canada. Available on the World Wide Web at: http://www.saferoads.com/drivers/impaired/ignition.html.

Calgary Police Service. (1999). *Calgary Police Service Annual Report.* Calgary, Alberta, Canada. Available on the World Wide Web at: http://www.gov.calgary.ab.ca/police/facts/ar-1999/pdf.

Scott, K. M. (2000, Fall). The phenomenon of road rage: Complexities, discrepancies and opportunities for CR analysis. *The Online Journal of Peace and Conflict Resolution.*

The Toronto Star. (1998, May 31). *Drunk drivers still killing us: MADD.* Available on the World Wide Web at: http://www.flora.org/afo/forum/1480.

VICLAS

ViCLAS, or Violent Crime Linkage Analysis System, is the name of a computer database in which information about serious violent crimes is gathered. A search function has been installed, and trained ViCLAS analysts can search for crimes that may have been committed by the same offender.

HISTORY OF VICLAS

Canada

ViCLAS was developed in the mid-1980s by the Royal Canadian Mounted Police (RCMP), due to a series of serial murders. A need was evident for identifying and tracing crimes/criminals, with emphasis on violent crimes such as homicides and sexual assaults. Two of the best automated case linkage systems in the United States were merged, the FBI's ViCAP (Violent Criminal Apprehension Program) and MINN/SCAP (Minnesota State Sex Crime Analysis System). The focus was to develop a system that included both homicides and sex crimes. In 1995, ViCLAS was implemented in Canada.

Sweden

In 1993, criminal investigator Bo Wickström was assigned to a rape investigation that involved the Canadian ViCLAS program. In 1998, Wickström was asked to start a similar project in Sweden to see whether ViCLAS could be useful to Swedish law enforcement. The project was successful, and in July 2000, ViCLAS was permanently established in Sweden. Sweden has approximately 9 million inhabitants and averages 120 homicides and 1,800 rapes annually. In Stockholm, the capitol, a city of about 1 million inhabitants, approximately 200 stranger rape assaults were committed in 1998. An important issue is determining how many, if any, of these rapes were committed by the same offender.

Like many other countries, Sweden has had problems with linking together serious violent crimes such as homicide and sexual assault. The traditional methods of linkage allow investigators to link crimes by examining names, offender or crime scene descriptions, vehicles, modus operandi, weapons, DNA, and fingerprints. All these components are covered by ViCLAS. In addition, ViCLAS emphasizes the sexual, physical, and verbal behavior of the offender. Much of this concerns a new working methodology: to use linkage to determine whether or not the offender has committed crimes previously and/or will commit new crimes. Research suggests that serial criminals have been motivated to commit crimes by their insatiable fantasies. Offenders can certainly change their methods of acting out or where they find their victims, but their fantasies remain influential on how they think. Ron MacKay, the first qualified psychological profiler in Canada, explains that the fantasy ritual will continue over time and space and that the offender who rapes out of anger when he is 25 will still rape out of anger when he is 35.

INTERNATIONAL USE OF VICLAS

The ViCLAS concept has experienced considerable success, and in addition to Canada and Sweden, several other countries have adopted ViCLAS as their major case linkage system, including Denmark, England, Germany, Holland, Belgium, Austria, the Czech Republic, Australia, and some states in America. Other countries will eventually adopt this innovative system of tracking predators.

The advantage of the ViCLAS system is that the questions are the same in all countries. For this reason, it is possible to exchange information between countries. It is also possible to opt in the database for other languages besides English, including French, German, and Dutch. The data available address the following types of crimes:

- All solved or unsolved homicides and attempted homicides
- Solved or unsolved sexual assaults
- Missing persons, where the circumstances indicate a strong possibility of foul play and the victim is still missing
- Unidentified bodies, where the manner of death is known or suspected to be homicide
- All nonparental abductions and attempted abductions

The ViCLAS Analyst/Specialist

Although the system is relatively easy to operate, ViCLAS experts are needed to ask the correct questions and to interpret the responses. In Sweden and Canada, it is required that the ViCLAS analysts have worked as investigators of serious violent crimes, including sex crimes and homicides, for at least 5 years. In addition to this, they are expected to have a university education based in behavioral research, including computer skills. Analysts are expected to regularly participate in training courses and seminars to increase their knowledge and understanding of offender behavior. Since 2000, the RCMP has been training behavioral analysts in ViCLAS specialist courses.

Handling Investigations

When a violent crime related to ViCLAS is committed, the investigator fills out a form consisting of 168 questions. Each police authority in Sweden has a ViCLAS coordinator who trains investigators and controls all investigations related to ViCLAS. The coordinator makes quality checks and sends the forms together with interrogations and medical reports to the

ViCLAS unit. From the collected data, the analyst constructs a strategy for the search of similar crimes. The search includes data about victimology, the offender, modus operandi, and technical findings from the crime scene.

Behavioral Analysis

To link crimes via behavior is an interpretive and explanatory process. Nothing is definite, and linkage is made more through themes than through individual similarities. Many of the questions are developed to reveal behavioral themes, which may concern issues of rape typology, paraphilia, mental disorders, and fantasies.

Modus Operandi Versus Ritual

For the offender, modus operandi (MO) has three purposes: to ensure success, to conceal his or her identity, and to make escape possible. MO is a conditioned behavior that can be said to serve a practical purpose. MO changes over time as the offender learns new methods, through books, films, and other offenders or through failed assaults. A typical MO could be the choice of geographical area, theft of valuables, bindings, choice of weapon, and different precautionary measures.

The ritualistic pattern of behavior has a purpose: psychosexual satisfaction. It is based on fantasies and exists over time. Unlike MO, the ritualistic pattern of behavior is something that is not necessary to commit the crime. Typical ritual elements consist of the age of the victim, how the victim's clothes are taken off, reactions to resistance, theft of personal objects, the way the offender contacts the victim, and bondage. Bondage means sexual bindings, or unnecessary bindings, contrary to bindings of control that belong to the MO.

It may sometimes be difficult distinguish between MO and ritual. In general, it can be said that ritualistic patterns of behavior are most clearly seen when offenders have their victims under their control and can give full expression to their fantasies.

SUMMARY

ViCLAS must not be considered an isolated system. It is a working method that includes investigators, coordinators, analysts, and other computer systems. ViCLAS does not solve any crimes by itself, but is a tool for investigators that increases the possibilities of solving serious violent crimes locally, nationally, and internationally and leads to the incarceration of dangerous criminals.

—*Peter Cramer*

See also FORENSIC SCIENCE; HOMICIDE: MOTIVATION FOR MURDER; LINKAGE BLINDNESS; METHODS OF MURDER; MOTIVES FOR MURDER; PROFILING; SERIAL MURDER: INTERNATIONAL INCIDENCE

Further Reading

Holmes, R. M., & Holmes, S. T. (2002). *Profiling violent crimes: An investigative tool.* Thousand Oaks, CA: Sage.

Royal Canadian Mounted Police ViCLAS Unit. Available on the World Wide Web at: http://www.rcmp-grc.gc.ca/html/viclas-e.htm.

VICTIM COMPENSATION FOR VIOLENT CRIMES

Victim compensation is a direct reimbursement from the state to, or on behalf of, a crime victim for losses sustained at the hands of a criminal. The crime victim may be reimbursed for crime-related expenses, including medical costs, funeral and burial costs, mental health counseling, lost wages, or loss of support. Other compensable expenses may include the replacement or repair of eyeglasses or other corrective lenses, dental services and devices, prosthetic devices, and crime scene clean-up.

Victim compensation by government is a concept that can be traced back as far as 1775 B.C., to the Babylonian Code of Hammurabi wherein territorial governors were instructed to replace a robbery victim's lost property if the criminal was not captured. In the case of murder, the governor was to compensate the heirs from the treasury. During the Middle Ages, this practice ceased, and victims had to recover losses by suing the offender in civil court.

Margery Fry, an English magistrate, is credited with renewing interest in victim compensation in the late 1950s. Her advocacy resulted in the first victim compensation laws in New Zealand and Great Britain. Shortly thereafter in the United States,

California was the first state to initiate compensation to crime victims, followed by New York and Hawaii. Currently, all 50 states and several U.S. territories operate compensation programs. Worldwide, a number of European countries, Canada, Australia, New Zealand, and Japan have victim compensation programs fairly similar to those in the United States. The federal government became involved in victim compensation in the 1960s and in 1984 passed the Victims of Crime Act (VOCA), which mandates that the federal government provide victim compensation for federal offenses and federal funds for state compensation programs.

Victim compensation is generally available to three categories of victims. The first group consists of victims who suffer physical injury as the result of a violent criminal act, and family survivors and the estates of victims who suffer death. Few states provide compensation to victims of property crimes. The second group includes persons who are hurt or killed during an attempt to prevent a crime from taking place or while attempting to capture a suspected criminal. Finally, the third group includes any person who is injured while coming to the aid of a law enforcement officer.

To be eligible for compensation, a victim must meet certain requirements. Eligibility requirements vary somewhat from state to state, but all programs have the same basic criteria. The victim generally must (a) report the crime promptly to a law enforcement agency, (b) cooperate with police and prosecutors in the investigation and prosecution of the case, (c) submit an application to the compensation program, (d) have a cost or loss not covered by insurance or some other source, and (e) be innocent of criminal activity or significant misconduct that caused or contributed to the victim's injury or death.

—*Lisa Andersen*

See also VICTIMS OF CRIME ACT, 1984 (VOCA); VICTIM AND WITNESS PROTECTION ACT OF 1982

Further Reading

Doerner, W. G., & Lab, S. P. (1998). *Victimology.* Cincinnati, OH: Andersen.

Karmen, A. (1990). *Crime victims: An introduction to victimology.* Monterey, CA: Brooks/Cole.

Sebba, L. (1996). *Third parties: Victims and the criminal justice system.* Columbus: Ohio State University Press.

Victims of Crime Act, 42 USC § 10601 [**Sec.** 1402] (1984).

VICTIM AND WITNESS PROTECTION ACT OF 1982

Prior to the Victim Witness Protection Act of 1982 (VWPA), crime victims and witnesses were largely ignored or used as a means to identify and punish offenders in criminal proceedings. Often, victims of serious crimes were forced to suffer physical, psychological, or financial hardship with no help from the criminal justice system. In 1982, recognizing the vital importance of victims and witnesses in prosecuting and punishing criminal offenders, President Ronald Reagan enacted VWPA, the first federal victim's rights legislation in the United States. As noted in the legislation, the VWPA was enacted "to enhance and protect the necessary role of crime victims and witnesses in the criminal justice process, to ensure that the federal government does all that is possible within limitations of available resources, to assist victims and witnesses of crimes without infringing on the constitutional rights of defendants, and to provide a model legislation for state and local governments."

The VWPA provides for witness protection, restitution, and fair treatment for federal victims and witnesses of violent crimes; sets forth procedures to be followed when responding to the needs of crime victims and witnesses; and mandates that all law enforcement agencies ensure that victims and witnesses are advised of significant procedural developments in their respective cases. In addition, the VWPA makes it a federal offense to intimidate or retaliate against victims or witnesses of federal crime.

—*Lisa Andersen*

See also VICTIM COMPENSATION FOR VIOLENT CRIMES; VICTIMS OF CRIME ACT, 1984 (VOCA)

Further Reading

Adair, D. N. Jr. (1991). Recent amendments to the Victim and Witness Protection Act. *Federal Probation, 55*(1), 78.

Kahn, L. A. (1985). Victim and Witness Protection Act. *Federal Probation, 49*(1), 78-79.

Victim Witness Protection Act, P.L. 97-291, § 6, 96 Stat (1982).

VICTIMOLOGY

Although victimology as an academic discipline is a relatively new concept in the United States, the victim's movement continues to gain strength and momentum across the country. States and the federal government continue to enact laws giving victims of crime more opportunities to participate in the criminal justice system.

Currently, there are very few academic institutions offering courses of study in this discipline. Some universities do offer courses, typically found in the departments of sociology, social work, criminology, and psychology, that examine various aspects of the victim-offender relationship. Victimology is a discipline that combines theoretical research with practical experience. Although there is some interaction between these two groups or approaches, there is still a great deal they can learn from each other.

Criminology is the science on which victimology is founded. *Victimology* is the study of the victim, the offender, and society. This definition can encompass the research or scientific aspects of the discipline as well as the practical aspects of providing services to victims of crime. This combination allows for a wide-ranging examination of various issues that affect victims of crime.

A complete and accurate understanding of the concepts inherent in victimology can be attained only by a review of the development of law, its history, and its philosophy. Modern criminal law is the result of an evolutionary process in the development of law that has attempted to deal with deviant behavior in society.

THE CODE OF HAMMURABI

The Code of Hammurabi is considered one of the first known attempts to establish a written code of conduct. King Hammurabi ruled Babylon in approximately 2000 B.C. He was the sixth king of the First Dynasty of Babylonia and ruled for nearly 55 years. Babylon during that period of time was a commercial center for most of the known and civilized world. Because its fortune lay in trade and other business ventures, the Code of Hammurabi provided a basis for order and certainty. It established rules regarding theft, sexual relationships, and interpersonal violence, and it was intended to replace blood feuds with a system sanctioned by the state. The code established certain obligations and objectives for the citizens of Babylon to follow. These included the following:

1. An assertion of the power of the state. This was the beginning of state-administered punishment. Under the code, the blood feuds that had occurred previously between private citizens were barred.
2. Protection of the weaker from the stronger. Widows were to be protected from those who might exploit them, elder parents from sons who would disown them, and lesser officials from higher ones.
3. Restoration of equity between the offender and the victim. The victim was to be made as whole as possible and in turn, he or she forgave vengeance against the offender.

Of noteworthy importance in the code was its concern for the rights of victims. In reality, this code may have been the first "victim's rights statute" in history. However, it was relatively short-lived. Victims were neglected in society's rush to punish the offender, with the result that victims' rights would not resurface again until the present century.

As with any new profession, many of victimology's early thinkers proposed theories or concepts that upon further study were revealed as incorrect. However, by examining these early efforts, we can better understand the growth and present status of victimology. From its inception in the 1940s to the present day, victimology, like the study of family violence, has been an interdisciplinary approach to violence and its effect on victims.

MENDELSOHN'S THEORY OF VICTIMIZATION

Benjamin Mendelsohn was a practicing attorney. In the course of preparing a case for trial, he conducted in-depth interviews of victims, witnesses, and bystanders. He used a questionnaire that was couched in simple language and contained more than 300 questions concerning the branches of criminology and associated sciences. The questionnaire was given to the accused and all others who had knowledge of the crime. Based on these studies, Mendelsohn came to the conclusion that there was usually a strong interpersonal relationship between the offender and the victim. In an effort to further clarify these relationships, he developed a typology of victims and their contributions to criminal acts. This classification ranged from the completely innocent victim to the imaginary victim.

Many scholars credit Mendelsohn with coining the term victimology, and some consider him the "father of victimology." His typology was one of the first attempts to focus on victims of crimes rather than simply examine the perpetrator. Mendelsohn was one of two early scholars who explored the relationship between victims and offenders. The other noted early researcher in victimology was Hans von Hentig.

VON HENTIG'S THEORY OF VICTIMIZATION

In an early classical text, *The Criminal and His Victim,* von Hentig explored the relationship between the "doer," or criminal, and the "sufferer," or victim. Von Hentig also established a typology of victims. This classification was based on psychological, social, and biological factors. Von Hentig established three general classes of victims: the general classes of victims, the psychological types of victims, and the activating sufferer victim. His classification identifies victims by examining various risk factors.

Von Hentig theorized that because of their acts or behavior, a large percentage of victims were responsible for their victimization. This concept has since been repudiated by modern studies, which have more closely examined and defined the relationship between the victim and the offender.

KARMEN'S THEORY OF VICTIMOLOGY

Scholars have continued to expand their scope of inquiry and explore other aspects of the victim's role in society. Karmen discusses the development of victimology and points out that those who study this relatively new discipline have three main areas of concentration:

1. Victimologists study the reasons (if any) why or how the victim placed himself or herself in a dangerous situation. This approach does not attempt to fix blame on the victim; rather, it examines the dynamics that resulted in the victim being in the risky situation.

2. Victimology evaluates how police, prosecutors, courts, and related agencies interact with the victim. How was the victim treated at each stage in the criminal justice system?

3. Victimologists evaluate the effectiveness of efforts to reimburse victims for their losses and meet victims' personal and emotional needs.

Karmen correctly points out that victimologists view the dynamics of the victim's role in society from a multidisciplinary perspective. There is still debate among scholars, however, regarding the correct or predominate role for the victimologist.

OVERVIEW OF VICTIMOLOGY

The history of victimology is, in many ways, the history of our world. As long as there has been crime, there have been victims who have suffered. Early law viewed crime as a personal act that required response by the victim or his family. The Code of Hammurabi, though harsh and violent, recognized victims as injured parties and may have been the first victim's rights law. Other codes and laws evolved throughout history to shape our modern-day concept of justice.

A number of social forces have affected the development of victimology. The feminist movement has raised public awareness of the plight of women. The civil rights movement has resulted in a number of laws being passed that afford individuals certain rights. As crime increased, our society has become increasingly conservative and more aware of the trauma suffered by victims of crime.

The victims' rights movement began as a small group of volunteers who themselves were crime victims and who had been victimized a second time as a result of their involvement with the criminal justice system. This small group of volunteers has grown and become a powerful force in America that continues to expand and change the way victimology is viewed.

—*Harvey Wallace*

See also AGGRESSION: FEMINIST
PERSPECTIVE; LESS-DEAD; RAPE; ROBBERY

Further Reading

Drapkin I., & Viano, E. (Eds.). (1974). *Victimology: A new focus* (Vol. 2). Lexington, MA: Heath.

Karmen, A. (1995). *Crime victims: An introduction to victimology* (2nd ed.). Belmont CA: Wadsworth.

Viano, E. C. (1979). *Victim/witness services: A Review of the Model.* Washington DC: GPO.

Wallace, H. (1998). *Victimology: Legal, psychological, and social perspectives.* Boston: Allyn & Bacon.

VICTIMOLOGY: VICTIM PRECIPITATION

At its inception, criminological research focused on criminal offenders and criminal acts. In the early 1940s, criminologists began to look at victims of crime, resulting in the emergence of *victimology,* a subfield of criminology. Victimologists initially devoted much energy to the study of how victims contribute, knowingly or unknowingly, to their own victimization and potential ways they may share responsibility with offenders for specific crimes.

Early pioneers of victimology Hans von Hentig and Benjamin Mendelsohn studied behaviors, characteristics, and vulnerabilities of victims. Von Hentig studied crime victims and determined that in many violent crimes, victims contribute to their own victimization. Mendelsohn viewed crime victims as one of many factors in a criminal case, and he developed a typology of victims in terms of their degree of guilt in the perpetration of crime. Mendelsohn classified victims into six categories: (a) the completely innocent victim, who exhibits no provocative or facilitating behavior prior to the criminal attack; (b) the victim with minor guilt, who unintentionally puts himself or herself in a compromising position prior to the victimization episode; (c) the victim who is as guilty as the offender, as in cases of assisted suicide or euthanasia; (d) the victim who is more guilty than the offender and provokes the offender to commit the crime; (e) the victim who is most guilty, such as an aggressive victim who is killed in self-defense; and (f) the simulating or imaginary victim, or people who pretend that they have been victimized.

From these early studies emerged the concepts of *victim precipitation* and *victim facilitation.* Victim precipitation, generally applicable to violent crimes against a person, refers to the degree to which the victim of a crime is responsible for his or her own victimization. The victim's involvement, whether passive or active, is viewed as a causative factor in the commission of crime. *Passive precipitation* occurs when the victim unknowingly provides confrontation with another, for example, a person who is victimized because of his or her physical, social, or psychological disadvantages (i.e., women, elderly, minorities). *Active precipitation* refers to situations in which the victim knowingly or intentionally provokes a violent encounter, through actions or words, which ultimately results in a physical confrontation with another person. Active precipitation could be applied in cases in which the person who was killed or hurt was the first to use force.

Victim facilitation generally applies to theft or property crimes wherein the victim unknowingly, carelessly, and negligently makes it easier for a criminal to commit and consummate a crime. A person who leaves car keys in an unattended car, which is then stolen, is one example of a victim-facilitated crime.

—Lisa Andersen

See also LESS-DEAD; RAPE; ROBBERY; SELF-DEFENSE

Further Reading

Doerner, W. G., & Lab, S. P. (1998). *Victimology.* Cincinnati, OH: Andersen.

Karmen, A. (1990). *Crime victims: An introduction to victimology.* Monterey, CA: Brooks.

Sebba, L. (1996). Third parties: *Victims and the criminal justice system.* Columbus: Ohio State University Press.

Sgarzi, J., & McDevitt, J. (2003*). Victimology: A study of victims and their roles.* Upper Saddle River, NJ: Prentice Hall.

VICTIMS OF CRIME ACT, 1984

The Victims of Crime Act of 1984 (VOCA) provides funding for victim assistance, victim compensation, and training and technical assistance for victim service providers across the nation, with priority consideration to victims of domestic violence, sexual assault, and child abuse and underserved victims. Victims of drunk driving, surviving family members of homicide victims, and victims of physical assault, elder abuse, robbery, hate crime, arson, and financial fraud are generally considered underserved.

VOCA is funded by fines, penalties, bond forfeitures, and special assessments collected from offenders convicted of federal crimes by U.S. Attorneys' Offices, federal U.S. courts, and the Federal Bureau of Prisons. Congress established the Office for Victims of Crime (OVC) to distribute funding to states and U.S. territories. The majority of VOCA funding is distributed through formula grants, although a small portion of the fund is available for federal crime victims and for training and technical assistance in federal programs.

To be eligible for a federal grant, state programs must meet certain conditions. Programs must cover medical expenses, mental health counseling, and lost wages for victims, as well as funeral expenses and lost support for families of homicide victims. Drunk driving and domestic violence must be considered compensable crimes, and victims of domestic violence cannot be categorically excluded on the basis of their being related to or living with the offender. Programs must agree to consider all U.S. citizens who are victims of crimes within their states, regardless of the residency of the victim, as eligible for compensation. Programs also must cover their own residents who are victims of terrorism in foreign countries. Finally, programs must cover crimes falling under federal jurisdiction within the states, such as crimes occurring on Indian reservations, National Park lands, or military bases.

—*Lisa Andersen*

See also Victim Compensation for Violent Crimes; Victim and Witness Protection Act of 1982 (VWPA)

Further Reading

Doerner, W. G., & Lab, S. P. (1998). *Victimology.* Cincinnati, OH: Anderson.

U.S. Department of Justice. (2002, January). *OVC fact sheet: Victims of crime act crime victims fund.* Washington, DC: Author.

Victims of Crime Act, 42 USC § 10601 [**Sec.** 1402] (1984).

VICTIM'S RIGHTS, *See*
Victim Compensation for Violent Crimes; Victims of Crime Act, 1984; Victim and Witness Protection Act of 1982; Victimology

VIGILANTISM

Vigilante and *vigilantism* are terms most commonly associated with the American West. The term vigilante was coined from the "Committees of Vigilance" that were active in the western United States in the days following the California Gold Rush. The story is that vigilantism began in California in 1851, when the discovery of gold attracted a large population of miners eager to make their fortunes and many outlaws that were just as eager to steal theirs. The law in the area was unable to handle the crime so the citizens began taking the law into their own hands. However, while it is romantic to believe that vigilantism was a moral man's way of maintaining order in society, the truth is that vigilantism has existed for as along as there have been groups of people.

Vigilantism, as defined, is distinctly different from the action of a mob responding to a single highly emotional event, frequently fueled by alcohol. The "Vigilance Committees" held meetings, elected officers, and determined what action they deemed appropriate to punish a specific individual. This action might be flogging, banishment, or, in extreme cases, hanging. "Posting" was a common practice. The committee printed and posted handbills throughout a settlement naming criminals and warning them to leave the area by a specified date. These "postings" normally included some colorfully worded suggestions about the consequences to the malefactor if they failed to comply, for example, becoming a "guest of honor at a necktie party" (a colloquialism for lynching). Examples of posting bills from Las Vegas, New Mexico, and San Francisco survive today. In most areas of the American West, the membership of vigilance committees was kept secret. The isolation that most communities experienced led to depredations by outlaw bands and the very justified fear of reprisals, making it essential that individual citizens not be identifiable to these predators.

San Francisco and the surrounding areas produced perhaps the best known examples of vigilance committees in the American West, which operated there for a longer period that in most other areas. These committees should not be confused with "miner's courts," which were somewhat spontaneous courts of selected citizens organized in communities when a crime occurred, for example, in mining towns, in the absence of any formal court or law enforcement service. The court consisted of a judge, jury, and two or more individuals representing the concerned parties, all elected by whatever local residents were present at the time. It heard evidence, usually without the benefit of cross-examination or formal evidence procedures, and then pronounced judgment on the offender. Punishments could be anything up to and including a death sentence. This impromptu organization differed from a vigilance committee action in that a trial by jury determined the resulting punishment, and the organization was disbanded after resolving the immediate crisis.

Newspaper articles written throughout the West in the period from 1850 to 1870 show an attitude of considerable tolerance for the impromptu administration of justice. The articles are written in a style that suggests a casual acceptance of the practice. The phrase "jerked to Jesus" is not uncommon in referring to a hanging by a vigilance committee.

In its most acceptable form, vigilantism is the banding together of a group of citizens in the face of a large criminal element that the constituted authorities have been unable, or unwilling, to control. Rapid economic development in the western United States during the middle of the 19th century in widely isolated areas frequently outstripped the ability of constituted law enforcement to provide services. In more modern times, this phenomenon is particularly apparent in the postapartheid Republic of South Africa. Crime and violent behavior are rampant in the society and are not handled effectively by the judicial system of the country. This has created the opportunity for groups of individuals to take the law into their own hands. These groups claim to be restoring hope to communities, but in fact they are killing and injuring perceived perpetrators without the assistance of due process, police, or the justice system. In the process, they are committing brutal acts that eliminate the possibility of justice.

Vigilante movements that have had significant followings include the "Know-Nothings" in the 1850s, the post–Civil War Ku Klux Klan, Molly Maguires (who killed mine superintendents in Pennsylvania), the enforcement of the "lynch law" in the South following the Civil War, and antigovernment groups. They are characterized by a small core of leaders who are able to mobilize a large number of individuals who feel disenfranchised for some particular reason, which becomes the focus of the group activity. For example, following the Civil War, leaders were able to mobilize a large number of lower-middle-class Caucasians to terrorize and lynch black men. The leaders were able to capitalize on the insecurities of this group and encourage activity reflecting the contempt that southern men had for black citizens. In the name of "protecting white women's innocence" from the "raging black" man, they assaulted, tarred and feathered, and killed them. From 1882 to 1968, 4,743 people died of lynching, and which black men and women comprised

3,446 of these (Zangrado, 1991). Less credible examples of vigilantism were organizations founded by groups to protect the particular interests of one socioeconomic or racial group against "outsiders."

The American South after the Civil War produced a number of groups commonly referred to as "Night Riders," which primarily attacked officials appointed by the Federal Government of Washington, D.C., many of whom were black Americans. The southern white population vehemently resented the northern intrusion into their culture, including the appointment of black people to positions of authority, a policy perceived by the southern states as being hostile to their socioeconomic interests. This resentment often resulted in "Night Riders" burning homes and assaulting anyone they perceived to be supportive of racial equality. Assaults became so frequent and drew such attention that President U. S. Grant ordered United States Army troops into the area in force to apprehend the leaders of these groups.

As recently as 1980, a group of citizens of the small town of Skidmore, Missouri, felt compelled to take the law in their own hands. Ken Rex McElroy had been terrorizing them for years and was known for his bullying, harassment, and thievery. Each time he was charged with a crime, he managed to thwart justice. The inability of state officials to protect the citizens of Skidmore left them vulnerable and frustrated. When McElroy began spreading rumors that he was going to kill a shopkeeper, the community had had enough. McElroy arrived in his truck in front of the shopkeeper's business, and a group of men carrying hunting rifles shot and killed him. Despite an intense investigation by local, state, and federal authorities, no one was ever charged with his death.

The United States is not alone in having its citizens engage in acts of vigilantism. During the 4 years of French occupation by Germany in World War II, approximately 10,000 French citizens were known to have willingly provided assistance to the enemy; most were women who had sexual contact with them. When France was liberated, these women were rounded up, taken to public locations, and had their heads shaven, swastikas painted on their faces, and were spat on. In some cases, citizens were so outraged that offenders were beaten and hanged. There were no tribunals, courts, judges, or lawyers, just the venting of angry citizens demanding retribution for acts of treason.

Modern societies continue to experience acts of vigilantism. Such acts are often methods for espousing racial, religious, political, philosophical, or social class phenomena. Even in the most civilized environments, there will always be fringe elements that embrace violence and times when citizens take the law into their own hands.

—Lt. Milt Gauthier
and Marlene Deal

See also COMMUNITY ATTITUDES ABOUT CRIME; HATE CRIMES; MINUTEMEN; MOLLY MAGUIRES; NEO-NAZI SKINHEADS; RACIAL PROFILING; WHITE KNIGHTS

Further Reading

Anderson, W. L. (April, 2000). *Vigilante justice: A proper response to government failure.* Available on the World Wide Web at: http://www.lewrockwell.com/anderson/anderson6.html.

Burghart, T. (December, 2002). *Armies of repression: The FBI, COINTELPRO and far-right vigilante networks.* Available on the World Wide Web at: http://www.spunk.org/library/pubs/lr/sp001714/bacorr.html.

Maclean, H. N. (1988). *In broad daylight.* New York: Dell.

Moses, N. H. (Ed.). (1997). *Lynching and vigilantism in the United States: An annotated bibliography.* Westport, CT: Greenwood.

Zangrado, R. L. (1991). Excerpted from Foner & J. Garraty (Eds.), *The reader's companion to American history.* Available on the World Wide Web at: http://www.english.uius.edu/maps/poetsg l/lynching/lynching.htm.

VIOLENCE: PHENOMENOLOGY

Phenomenological studies of violence, like psychological, criminological, or sociological studies, can focus on the violator as well as the violated. The focus of phenomenology applied to studies of violence is understanding the meaning of the lived experiences, or the "lifeworlds," of the individuals.

Phenomenological studies are not concerned with determining cause-effect relations, testing hypotheses, measuring experience, or developing theoretical explanations of behavior. Rather, they rigorously follow a methodology aimed at exploring in minute detail how violators experience being violent or how victims experience being violated. Phenomenological concepts are used to interpret narratives provided by violators or victims. The purpose of this approach is to gain rich insight into a level of experience that is assumed, but not explored, in traditional human science inquiries. Although we might scientifically determine what causes a person to act, we cannot necessarily assume that we understand the meanings of those acts for the person who experienced them. Phenomenological studies are thus important for understanding criminals and deviants, but they are also important for understanding violence in a variety of everyday contexts, such as employment, families, gender, race, aging, disability, and the like. Violence is possible in any social interaction.

Because violence is possible in any social relationship, phenomenological studies begin with an understanding of how consciousness "intends," or puts together, the meanings of its lived experience. Phenomenological studies provide an understanding of consciousness, which includes felt, bodily experience (embodied experience) that is typically taken for granted by the human sciences. Without a rigorous and rich understanding of experience as it is constituted by the actions of embodied consciousness in moment-to-moment, everyday life situations, it is difficult to understand the origin of concepts like "motives" or "causes." If criminological analyses of victimizers or victims are considered the structure of a building, then phenomenological studies provide the solid foundations that that structure relies on.

Phenomenological studies do not necessarily focus on unconscious factors, but rather on factors that are simply assumed but not investigated. Without understanding how experience is lived; how it unfolds in the space and time of successive moments of "here and now"; what the features of embodied consciousness are; and how embodied consciousness uniquely perceives and interprets a particular situated event, it is difficult to claim that one understands or can explain someone's experience.

Phenomenology was originally developed in philosophy, primarily by Edmund Husserl, in the early 1900s. Whereas Husserl was a pure philosopher, his students (including Maurice Merleau-Ponty and Alfred Schutz) and other notable figures (such as Sartre and de Beauvoir) applied phenomenology to everyday life experiences. Analyses of everyday existence focus on both subjective and intersubjective aspects of experience. Subjective experiences typically refer to the individual's perception of his or her lived experience (or lifeworld) and include that individual's lived experience of another's subjective reality as part of his or her own. Intersubjective experiences refer to the reciprocal understandings individuals have of each other (which occur in the subjective experience of each individual). It is crucial to note that subjective experiences are permeated by intersubjective relations and intersubjective realities are interpreted within the unique perspective of each individual's consciousness. Phenomenological studies of violence thus could focus on the violator's or the victim's experience of himself or herself alone or on himself or herself as a subject inextricably involved with another. Because the lived experience of violence itself includes both subjective and intersubjective experiences, ideally both would be analyzed together, but that is not necessary or even always possible.

If violence is possible in any social interaction, what would the features of this experience be? Violence (whether legitimate or not) is an extension of certain fundamental activities necessary to the way consciousness operates in the practical, everyday social world. Alfred Schutz suggested that each individual's consciousness finds itself as the center of its own lived world and for that consciousness to accomplish its projects, it must "dominate" its world as part of how it "works" in and on that world. That is, it must arrange things and others around itself in zones of relevance, which vary situationally, in order to move from one "here and now" (space and time) to another in a way that provides a coherent flow to one's lived experience (i.e., one's sense of self and the world). Transcendence is the capacity of consciousness to move from one here and now to the next, and when it is blocked, incomplete, or problematic, individuals experience discomfort and/or *dis-ease,* depending on the situation and the meanings at stake in that situation. Transcendence refers to transitions between here and nows that involve not only physical movements but also cognitive, emotional, and spiritual movements of meaning over time. Thus, violence done by one to another has profound effects on one's immediate experience of one's ability to order one's own world. These effects, when not transcended smoothly, can lock individuals into a here and now that might have passed chronologically, but remains present in the lived time of everyday experiences of self, others, and the world. Thus, many criminal trials now include a statement from victims or their families, prior to sentencing, to provide details not considered relevant during the trial. Likewise, during the trial, lawyers seek to determine causes and motives without necessarily

attempting to understand the experiences of the violator as lived by the violator (versus the lawyer's construction of the violator's experience).

Whereas Schutz's approach focused primarily on the cognitive aspects of how individuals experience the presence of others, Merleau-Ponty examined the ways cognitive aspects of consciousness are located in a lived body. The *lived body* includes the physical body but refers more to one's felt or sensed experience of others and the world. Here, the lived body's capacity to sense, to move, and to feel are taken as the fundamental feature of consciousness. Merleau-Ponty thus referred to subjectivity as the "body-subject" to highlight the significance of one's "sense" of self or the other as something more profoundly meaningful, and even prior to, cognitive interpretations. Here, transcendence also includes the capacity of embodied consciousness to experience itself and its moment-to-moment relations with others as a unified field.

Though terribly abbreviated, the preceding overview permits us to consider how such an approach is used to study violence. Because the fundamental feature of consciousness is to experience its world as a unified field in which it dominates in order to complete its projects (by which it projects itself into and moves in the world), there is always the possibility of domination going awry. Because embodied subjectivity arranges the world around itself, others are often taken merely as objects to be manipulated rather than as other embodied subjects. At the core of rape, domestic violence, pedophilia, cyberviolence, and other interactions, one discovers precisely a way of being that is grounded in domination and reduces others simply to objects. Such ways of being distort the essential reciprocity necessary for the "we-relationship" (Schutz) to develop. Victims, for instance, experience the other as an alien and hostile source of suffering that warps both their experiences of their own being and that of others.

In such cases, the dominant one experiences the concentration of power and control as necessary to working on the world. The other person becomes part of the dominator's project, and in effect becomes invisible to the dominator. Here, the reciprocity of intersubjectivity is reduced to a single perspective. Victims experience themselves as instrumentally valuable to the dominator, but their invisibility denies their presence and renders their own ability to work on their projects impossible, often forcing them into codependence, terror, or flight. Victims experience the violator as an alienating presence external to them yet are strangely intimate with them in their intense awareness of their demands and actions. Their ability to transcend is inhibited and their sense of unity with their surrounding world is disrupted. In the same way the victim's flow of experience is disturbed, the project of the dominator likewise impedes yet is necessary to his or her sense of transcendence. Everyday, commonsense experience is typically uncertain, but this everyday contingency is taken for granted and is thus accounted for. The relations of violator/victim only magnify and aggravate their need to "dominate" their worlds so that even the most mundane things can be just that: mundane.

For phenomenology to be useful, it must be understood first as an attempt to describe and understand how embodied consciousness experiences its world; this lived experience is the foundation that all the human sciences build their studies on. Criminology typically assumes an understanding of how this happens. Unless the intricate details of these foundational experiences and workings of embodied consciousness are studied, scientific explanations are inattentive to the meanings of the immediately lived experiences that give birth to their studies. Criminological studies of violence thus employ concepts and theories that address power, control, lack, desire, and the like. These very concepts, however, refer to fundamental activities that embodied consciousness performs moment-to-moment to simply accomplish its projects as part of its flow of lived experiences. Without a detailed examination of these activities of embodied consciousness, violence cannot be fully understood. As criminal investigations have shown, many times the most meaningful understandings we can have arise from attention to the most minute and commonsense details. This does not mean that everyday efforts to dominate one's world, complete one's projects, and experience transcendence are necessarily violent. Rather, it means that violence and victimization themselves arise from these simple yet profoundly important concerns. More phenomenological studies of violence are needed.

—*Marc J. LaFountain*

See also AGGRESSION; HOMICIDE, PERCEPTIONS OF; VICTIMOLOGY; VIOLENT BEHAVIOR

Further Reading

Denzin, N. (1984). Towards a phenomenology of domestic violence. *American Journal of Sociology, 90,* 483-500.

Lengermann, P. M., & Niebrugge, J. (1995). Intersubjectivity and domination: A feminist investigation of the sociology of Alfred Schutz. *Sociological Theory, 13,* 25-36.

Merleau-Ponty, M. (1962). *Phenomenology of perception* (C. Smith, Trans.). London: Routledge & Kegan Paul.

Ostrow, J. (1990). *Social sensitivity: A study of habit and experience.* Albany: State University of New York Press.

Schutz, A., & Luckmann, T. (1973). *The structures of the life-world* (M. Zaner & T. Englehardt Jr. Trans.). Evanston, IL: Northwestern University Press.

VIOLENT BEHAVIOR: PERSONALITY THEORIES

When individuals commit crimes, particularly violent ones, lawyers and judges as well as the public at large are interested in determining why. An assessment of the offender's personality or ego development can be very helpful in this regard, because it is designed to reveal how a particular person makes sense of the world. In addition to helping interpret behavior, knowing an individual's personality level can be useful in evaluating the credibility of his or her statements. This is often invaluable in assessing issues related to the prognosis and likelihood of continued criminal behavior, as well as in charting appropriate treatment strategies.

Several frameworks for measuring personality or ego development currently exist. The four that have been used most extensively in classifying offenders in numerous correctional agencies across the United States and Canada are interpersonal level of maturity theory, Hunt's conceptual level, Megargee's MMPI-based typology, and Quay's adult internal management system (AIMS). Interpersonal level of maturity theory and conceptual level are theoretically derived systems; in contrast, Megargee's and Quay's classification systems are empirically derived.

These four systems can be further distinguished in terms of whether they classify offenders according to personality traits, developmental criteria, or both. Personality-based typologies distinguish people on the basis of traits, whereas classification systems based on stages or levels diagnose individuals according to developmental criteria. Megargee's MMPI and Quay's AIMS systems are personality based, conceptual level is a developmental system, and interpersonal level of maturity theory is both a developmental and personality classification system.

Megargee's MMPI-based typology was constructed for youthful and adult offenders from results obtained from the Minnesota Multiphasic Personality Inventory (MMPI), the most widely used psychological test. Ten categories were developed through a process of separating MMPI profiles on the basis of common profile configurations. Megargee gave the 10 personality types nondescript names to ensure that an empirical process sorted out the behavioral characteristics associated with each type. Classification using this system requires that an individual complete the MMPI. Research has indicated that most agencies can classify two thirds of the profiles by computer. The remaining third, consisting of tied diagnoses or unclassified cases, must be classified clinically.

Quay's AIMS system generates scores for adult offenders on five dimensions (asocial aggressive, immature dependent, manipulative, neurotic anxious, and situational) on the basis of two objective instruments. A correctional employee who is knowledgeable of the inmate's behavior completes one; a staff member who has examined the inmate's background reports and who has conducted a general intake or presentence interview completes the second. Similar administration procedures are used with juvenile delinquents, yielding type descriptions that are similar but not identical.

Hunt's conceptual level (CL) is a cognitive-developmental model initially designed for educational purposes and subsequently used with juvenile correctional populations. CL builds on conceptual systems theory, a general theory of personality development. Individuals are classified on a developmental hierarchy in terms of increasing social maturity, conceptual complexity, independence, and self-responsibility. Conceptual development proceeds through a maximum of four conceptual levels. In juvenile delinquent settings, CL has been typically used in conjunction with the conceptual level matching model to determine the level of environmental structure needed by a particular client. The paragraph completion method is used to determine CL by averaging responses to the sentence stems. Although CL is considered a continuum, applications of the system require that types be formulated. Four types have been proposed for use with delinquents.

Interpersonal level of maturity theory (I-Level) serves as one of the best frameworks of personality development theories when discussing offender populations. For more than 40 years, I-Level has been widely researched and used for treatment and management purposes with both juvenile delinquents and adult criminals. I-Level will be used here to illustrate a classification system that has a theoretically derived developmental framework that includes empirically derived personality subtypes.

I-Level originated with a group of psychology students at the University of California at Berkeley in the early 1950s. It has its underpinnings in child development, psychoanalytic theory, Lewinian theory, phenomenological theory, and social perception. Studies have indicated that I-Level has very good construct validity; that is, diagnostic categories identified by I-Level correlate well with the same or similar categories identified by other theories of personality development. The construct validity of I-Level has been demonstrated using several theoretical constructs, including the California Personality Inventory, Loevinger's ego development system, Eysenck's Personality Inventory, and four other psychological classification systems (Hunt's CL, Megargee's MMPI-Based Typology, Quay's Adult Internal Management System, and the Jesness Inventory Classification System). Although I-Level is related to some extent to both age and intelligence, research has also shown that I-Level clearly measures more than these two variables and is related to many ego development dimensions, such as need for status, internalization of values, tolerance, independence, and flexibility. In addition, several studies have established that I-Level has good predictive validity, meaning that classification by I-Level has been found to be related to the subsequent behavior of juveniles and adult offender populations in various settings.

Research has indicated that the semistructured clinical interview method is a more valid and reliable way of measuring I-Level than the use of a structured instrument, such as the Jesness Inventory. Studies have reported that agreement on I-Level ratings among experienced raters (interrater reliability) using the interview method typically exceeded 80%, even when based on the most difficult cases (e.g., Harris, 1983, 1988; Van Voorhis, 1994). Test-retest measures of I-Level using the interview method after 8 to 12 months also exceeded 80% (Harris, 1988).

I-Level classifies people into one of seven categories according to the complexity with which they perceive themselves, others, and their environments.

The theory postulates that individuals progress from Level 1 to higher levels as they resolve problems encountered at the respective levels. If the developing child has a very stressful or threatening experience, he or she may resist change and make desperate attempts to remain at his or her present level of development because it seems safer than advancing to the next higher level.

The maturity levels that have been empirically identified in the offender population range from Level 2 to Level 5. The empirically derived subtypes have been associated with these four levels. I-Level's seven stages are highlighted below, with special emphasis given to Levels 3 and 4, which comprise the majority of both juvenile and adult offenders. In one study of more than 1,000 delinquents ranging in age from 11 to 19 years of age, for example, 95% were classified as perceiving at Level 3 (31%) or level 4 (64%) (Warren, 1983).

When babies are born, they perceive at Level 1. Infants initially do not see themselves as separate from the world. As they try to satisfy basic needs, they learn to discriminate between self and nonself. For example, they come to realize in time that a thumb is part of them, but a pacifier is not.

Most infants who recognize differences between self and nonself will move on to the next integration level, in which they come to recognize that there are differences between persons and things. This level is common among very young children. An individual who perceives at Level 2 views others in terms of whether or not they give him or her what he or she wants. A person at Level 2 does not know how to predict or influence the behavior of others in any sophisticated way. He or she is capable, however, of making some very basic differentiations. For example, a baby at Level 1 has a sense that a mother and a bottle both provide sustenance. However, an infant who perceives at Level 2 knows that when he or she screams, mother might come across the room to hold him or her; a bottle on the kitchen counter will not respond by itself to his or her crying.

Two personality subtypes have been identified in offender populations at Level 2. When personal needs are not met, the *asocial passive* responds by whining, complaining, or withdrawing. The *asocial aggressive,* in contrast, responds in similar situations with open aggression.

Most children will advance to Level 3, which is considered normal development for toddlers and prepubescent children. Research has indicated that by age 14, 66% to 75% of youth will have moved beyond this level. Adolescents past age 14 who perceive at Level 3 are more likely to get into legal trouble than higher-maturity adolescents in the same age range (Harris, 1983).

Individuals classified at Level 3 know that their behavior affects the responses they get from others. Accordingly, they are primarily concerned with identifying who the powerful people are in any given situation. They try to get their needs met by figuring out what formulas to use to manipulate others into giving them what they want. Their formulas consist of conforming to the demands of the person in power at the moment or controlling others through attack or intimidation. Their behavior tends to be impulsive and their planning, short-term. Those whose perceptions are classified at Level 3 do not feel guilty or perceive a need to make amends for their misbehavior because they do not see that they have done anything wrong.

A 15-year-old boy who perceived at Level 3, for example, was riding his bicycle through the park one day, when he saw a man in his late 20s jogging. The man was wearing a large gold chain around his neck. The youth rode the bike up to the man, stopped in front of him, and pointed a handgun at him. The boy reportedly said, "Give me your rope." When the man did not comply, the youth cocked the trigger of the gun and repeated, "Give me the rope." As the man turned away from the 15-year-old and started running, the youth fired four shots into his back. When the youth was asked whether there was any way "this whole thing" could have been prevented, he nodded affirmatively and replied, "He should have given me the rope. After all, I asked him twice."

Youth at this level of perceptual development tend to view others in stereotypic ways. They do not yet appreciate that other people have needs and feelings different from their own and tend to be very concrete in their thinking. When one juvenile murderer who perceived at Level 3 was asked how he was different from his mother, he replied, "She's a lady; I'm a man. I rob people; my momma don't."

Individuals at this socioperceptual level frequently deny that they have strong feelings or deep emotional involvements, and are incapable of feeling remorse. A 16-year-old who was convicted of attempted first-degree murder related that he had shot his best friend and crippled him for life. The youth explained that when he fired the bullets into his best friend, he had mistakenly believed that his best friend had stolen money from him. When asked in light of the circumstances, how he would have felt had his friend died, the youth replied, "Better." He explained that "I would not be here today [in prison]. There wouldn't have been any witnesses."

Research has identified three personality subtypes among those who perceive at Level 3. The *immature conformist* is passive, has low self-esteem, and conforms to the demands of whomever he or she perceives as having the power at the moment. The *cultural conformist* follows the dictates of a specific group of peers. The *manipulator* does not trust others, tends to be oppositional to adults and peers, and may attack others.

Individuals who move on to Level 4 incorporate the values of "the big people," typically their parents and teachers, and strive to be like them. This perceptual level is typically reached by youth by the time they enter their teenage years. Unlike individuals at earlier stages, those who perceive at Level 4 are able to evaluate their behavior and that of others against an internalized set of standards. They are aware that behavioral choices are available to them and feel accountable for their actions. One 17-year-old boy killed a member of a rival gang after being repeatedly urged to do so by another boy. Although the young killer related that he would not have killed the other youth had it not been for the goading of his friend, this adolescent clearly saw himself as responsible for the murder. "It's my fault," the boy said. "He [his friend] played a role, but he's not the one behind the gun."

Those who perceive at Level 4 tend to be rigid about codes of correct behavior. They may experience guilt when they fail to behave in accordance with their values and are capable of feeling genuine remorse. The youth who killed the rival gang member, for example, related that he did not know that he himself could be "that savage." Although the state had decided not to seek the death penalty, the youth was facing spending the rest of his life in prison. When asked what would be the right sentence, the adolescent related that he had struggled with that issue, with part of him thinking that he deserved death, and another part hoping that he would be forgiven. He stated with anguish, "Honestly, for the crime I did and the pain I caused, I deserve prison . . . it hurts me to say that."

Those who perceive at Level 4 have some perception of the role that needs and motives play in the behavior of themselves and others. In the case above,

the youth was able to relate what led him to decide to kill the rival gang member. He explained what he was thinking before, during, and after the homicide and how his thoughts had affected his behavioral choices. He recognized that he had killed a youth about his age because he wanted to be accepted, a theme that he recognized had been a common one for him in his adolescent years.

Those who perceive at this level typically want to make something of themselves and to be recognized for their ideals and interests, and potentialities and accomplishments, by those they admire. They have the ability to make long-range plans and to delay their response to immediate stimuli. They are often concerned with their own uniqueness; however, they are capable of entering into a reciprocal relationship with other persons whose needs, feelings, ideals, or standards of behavior are similar to their own.

Four personality subtypes have been found in juvenile and adult offenders who perceive at Level 4. Two of these are classified as neurotic because their responses to situations are self-defeating and are based on unresolved events stemming from childhood. *Neurotic acting-out* (Na) offenders present as strong and in control, despite having a poor self-image and being internally conflicted. They often stay very busy as a way to distract themselves from longstanding pain, anxiety, and anger. Those who adopt an Na response pattern often challenge others verbally or behaviorally and tend to keep others at a distance, preferring not to get close. *Neurotic-anxious* (Nx) offenders respond to a poor self-image and internal conflict with guilt, depression, or anxiety. They tend to ruminate excessively about internal matters without making genuine efforts to resolve their conflicts. *Cultural identifiers* have internalized a delinquent value system that allows them to commit delinquent or antisocial acts from the standpoint of acting congruently with their beliefs. *Situational-emotional reactors* commit a crime as a maladaptive response to a current crisis or a recent emotional change.

Persons who perceive at Level 5 are rarely encountered in offender populations. These individuals continue to see themselves as accountable for their behavior. They are less rigid in their lives and less judgmental toward others than those who perceive at Level 4. Individuals classified at Level 5 are able to appreciate people who are different from them and to understand what they do and how they feel. They are capable of putting themselves in others' roles, because they can compare their impressions of events and activities with those of others. Individuals at Level 5 are increasingly aware of different ways of coping with events. They begin to distinguish roles appropriate for themselves (e.g., son, boyfriend, friend, worker, athlete) and others for different occasions. Although individuals at this level may sometimes wonder which of the roles is "the real me," they are aware of continuity in their own and others' lives. The four personality subtypes that have been found at Level 5 are the same ones that have been identified at Level 4.

Very little is known about the last two levels of personality development, Levels 6 and 7, because they are rarely encountered and have not been systematically studied. Those who perceive at Level 6 are able to perceive differences between themselves and the social roles they play. They can recognize and accept role inconsistencies in themselves and others because they are able to see continuity and stability. It is believed that very few individuals, if any, reach the ideal of social maturity associated with the highest Level, 7. Individuals at the highest stage of socioperceptual development are able to see the integrating processes in themselves and others and would be regarded as self-actualized.

The criminal justice system is premised on the legal concept that offenders are responsible for their behavior. In holding defendants who are of sound mind accountable for their behavior, the legal system is implicitly assuming that defendants perceive at I-Level 4 or higher. Increasingly, given the mood in the United States, more juveniles are being prosecuted as adults. The transferring of juveniles to the adult system is particularly problematic in light of the research findings highlighted above, indicating that many juveniles have not reached this level of personality development. Youth in the adult criminal justice system, similar to their adult counterparts, typically face long prison sentences, including life in prison, and very limited opportunities for treatment. In the absence of therapeutic programs, it is likely that many low-maturity youth in prison will remain at Level 3, being punished for years, and maybe for a lifetime, for crimes that they committed while functioning with the perception characteristics of a young child.

—*Kathleen M. Heide*

See also AGGRESSION: PSYCHOLOGICAL THEORIES; ANTISOCIAL PERSONALITY DISORDER; JUVENILE KILLERS; MENTALLY DISORDERED OFFENDERS; VIOLENT BEHAVIOR: PSYCHOANALYTIC THEORY; VIOLENT BEHAVIOR: A PSYCHOLOGICAL CASE STUDY

Further Reading

Harris, P. W. (1988). The interpersonal maturity level classification system: I-Level. *Criminal Justice and Behavior, 15*.

Heide, K. M. (1983). An empirical assessment of the value of using personality data in restitution outcome prediction. In W. S. Laufer & J. M. Day (Eds.), *Personality theory, moral development and criminal behavior.* Lexington, MA: Lexington Books.

Heide, K. M. (1999). *Young killers: The challenge of juvenile homicide.* Thousand Oaks, CA: Sage.

Jesness, C. (1988). Jesness Inventory Classification System. *Criminal Justice and Behavior, 15*.

Palmer, T. (1978). *Correctional intervention and research: Current issues and future prospects.* Lexington, MA: Lexington Books.

Quay, H. (1984). *Managing adult inmates: Classification for housing and program assignments.* College Park, MD: American Correctional Association.

Van Voorhis, P. (1994). *Psychological classification of the adult prison male.* Albany: State University of New York Press.

Warren, M. Q. (1983). Applications of interpersonal maturity level theory to offender populations. In W. S. Laufer & J. M. Day (Eds.), *Personality theory, moral development and criminal behavior.* Lexington, MA: Lexington Books.

VIOLENT BEHAVIOR: PSYCHOANALYTIC THEORIES

"Tommy Lee," a good-looking man in his 30s, was charged with multiple counts of murder for which he was facing death in the electric chair. His 10 victims, many of whom were reportedly prostitutes, were all young women who had voluntarily gotten into his car and driven off with him to wooded areas. The women were raped and ritually bound prior to being killed. Their bodies were dumped and displayed in signature ways designed to alert legal authorities that these killings were the products of one killer.

The community was outraged at the viciousness of the killer, who apparently tortured his prey prior to disposing of them. When asked why he had abducted and killed these women, the killer, a man of above-normal intelligence, had no answer. He did recall a groundswell of anger erupting inside him prior to killing his victims. Beyond that uncontrollable rage, he had no immediate explanation for his murderous behavior. Had these women done something to offend him in some way? The killer thought for a moment and replied "No." Had these women possibly humiliated him by their words or behavior? The killer responded in the negative. After some reflection, the man acknowledged that these women had done nothing to warrant the death and destruction he visited upon them.

The motivation for these killings became evident during the forensic evaluation. The springboard for this homicidal rage dated back to the man's childhood. The killer had been physically, sexually, verbally, and psychologically abused by his mother, a woman reputed by family members to be a prostitute. Although it is unknown whether his mother actually was a prostitute, this characterization does not seem unreasonable. The woman had a collection of photos of herself as a younger woman going to work at a bar, wearing a skimpy blouse, short shorts, and "go-go boots." Tommy Lee had memories of being removed from her bed, where he routinely slept until he was about 13 years of age, and placed on the living room sofa by strange men in the middle of the night when his mother returned home.

In-depth interviews with Tommy Lee's parents revealed that his parents had been divorced from one another twice and married to each other on three occasions. The mother recounted several incidents of being abducted from the street by her ex-husband when Tommy Lee was a young child. On each of these occasions, Tommy Lee's father took the boy's mother to the woods and raped her.

Tommy Lee's apparently senseless killings become understandable when viewed from a psychoanalytic perspective. Psychoanalytic theory emerged from the seminal works of Sigmund Freud (1856-1939). Freud's writings had a profound effect on the development of psychiatry and psychology in the 20th century. The broader term *psychodynamic theory* includes Freud's theory as well as the revisions of his followers. Psychoanalytic theory posits that abnormal behavior, including criminal and antisocial behavior, is caused by unconscious conflicts rooted in early childhood experiences. Psychoanalysis can be conceptualized as a complex framework addressing three interrelated theories of personality: theory of the structure of personality, of personality dynamics, and of psychosexual development.

Psychoanalysis views personality as a three-part structure made up of the id, ego, and superego. The *id* is composed of biologically based motives and instinctual drives that strive for immediate satisfaction. Two types of motives are primary: those involving "life instincts," which seek sexual gratification, and "death instincts," which are aggressive in nature and seek to unleash destructive urges. The id is present and all encompassing when an infant is born. The id is driven by "the pleasure principle," and its aim is to reduce tension and to restore physiological balance at whatever cost.

The *ego* begins to emerge during the first year of life and continues to develop during the school years. The young child learns that fulfillment of his or her instinctual demands often collides with the larger demands of society. The ego is guided by the "reality principle" in its attempts to mediate between id impulses and the real world. The ego's aim is to protect the individual, while at the same time allowing some satisfaction of instinctual needs under appropriate circumstances.

The *superego* is best conceptualized as having a conscience. Children in their preschool years begin to get a sense of the values and ideals of their parents and society, and the standards for moral behavior. The aim of the superego is to ensure that the individual keeps sexual and aggressive impulses under control and conforms to the moral dictates of society. The influence of the superego, much of which is unconscious, is responsible for a person feeling guilty when he or she fails to behave in accordance with a notion of one's "ideal self" and instead allows expression of instinctual and biologically based needs.

The three components work in concert with one another, with the ego having a critically important role. The id can be best be conceived as a "spoiled child" and the superego, as an "overdemanding parent." In this schema, the ego comes in as an effective "manager" whose mission is to allow some expression of basic needs within the legal and moral constraints of society. In this process, given reality considerations, the "libido," or energy, of the id is often blocked from expression. As a result, this energy must be displaced, and a great deal of anxiety is aroused. To diffuse this anxiety, the individual learns to use defense mechanisms, which protect the individual from conscious awareness of overwhelming anxiety. This anxiety then becomes buried in the person's unconscious.

Psychoanalysis is also a theory of personality dynamics, which conceptualizes consciousness into three levels: conscious, preconscious, and unconscious. *Conscious* refers to what is in a person's immediate awareness. The reader of this entry, for example, is thinking at this moment about the meaning of consciousness. *Preconscious* refers to content that is not in the person's consciousness at a particular time, but is immediately accessible. For example, the reader can recall, if asked, his or her birthdate, zip code, and phone number. However, up to a few seconds ago, the reader was not focused on this information and not consciously thinking about it.

In contrast, *unconscious* content is "repressed," meaning blocked out of awareness and not easily accessible. The unconscious is composed in part of painful experiences and memories, which "go underground" as a result of conflict between conscious portions of the ego and superego and the unconscious id. Expression of id influences under these conditions results in overwhelming anxiety and discomfort for the individual. Freud postulated that when these unconscious motives are disguised, they can be expressed in a way that safeguards the individual while reducing tension. The ego uses unconscious self-deceptions referred to as *defense mechanisms* to decrease conscious anxiety by distorting anxiety-producing impulses, memories, and emotions.

Defense mechanisms are often discernible when individuals are involved in criminal incidents as either victims or offenders. *Repression* refers to a process whereby people push anxiety-provoking thoughts down into unconsciousness because they are unable to process them. An adolescent who killed his father reported that at the moment he had his rifle trained on his father because he was terrified that the man would kill him, he was flooded with "forgotten" past images of his mother being repeatedly beaten by his father when he was a very young boy. *Reaction formation* occurs when individuals profess feelings or beliefs that are the opposite of what they feel on a deep and hidden level. Poor children, for example, may vandalize a high-priced sports car driven by an affluent classmate, claiming that they would not be "caught dead in it," when deep down inside, they would love to own one.

Projection is used when people transfer unacceptable motives they are experiencing onto others. A woman who is tempted to have an extramarital affair accuses her husband of cheating on her. *Rationalization* involves making excuses for one's behavior and shifting responsibility to another source. An employee who embezzles from his boss maintains that his employer does not pay him what he is worth and that she cheats customers, taking more than her fair share of profits. *Sublimation* is apparent when individuals divert id impulses into constructive and acceptable outlets. A young man with murderous impulses joins a group of foreign mercenaries where he is encouraged and expected to kill "the enemy."

Displacement, which involves transferring one's feelings onto a safer object, is recognizable in the case of Tommy Lee. In-depth interviews with Tommy Lee revealed that he hated his mother, whom he believed had been a prostitute, and harbored a great deal of rage towards her. When he abducted his victims and took them to the woods to rape them, Tommy Lee was emulating the same behavior that he had witnessed his father engage in when he was a boy. When he killed these women, Tommy Lee was filled with rage and hatred that was unconsciously displaced from its true source, his mother, onto what he perceived on an unconscious level to be a more appropriate source, that is, prostitutes. Had he killed the real object of his wrath, his mother, 10 innocent women might still be alive today. However, it was too threatening to Tommy Lee's superego to kill his mother, the person who gave him life. Tommy Lee's ego tried to achieve some balance between the id and the superego demands by allowing him to dispose of "expendable" people who, in his eyes, "contributed nothing of value to society." Although a poor solution, Tommy Lee's ego did dissipate some of the enormous physiological and psychological tension that the man was experiencing.

In addition to addressing structural components of personality and personality dynamics, psychoanalytic theory focuses on the stages of psychosexual development. Freud emphasized biological motives, and sexual motivation in particular, in his theory of human development. He stressed the importance of early childhood in the formation of personality and conceptualized personality development as proceeding in three broad stages: pregenital, latency, and genital.

The *pregenital* stage consists of three substages: the oral, anal, and phallic. These three substages are characterized by certain overriding concerns in the individual. Freud maintained that each substage has certain erogenous zones that provide satisfaction. In the *oral stage,* which is thought to take place from birth to about 2 years, babies gain pleasure from their mouth or lips by sucking at mother's breasts and having their needs met. The id is predominant during this stage. Freud maintained that if this stage is not successfully resolved, personality problems will result. For example, if the baby is overindulged in eating, he or she may become an adult who talks too much, is passive and dependent, and constantly puts things in his mouth (e.g., food, fingernails, cigarettes, drinks). If the baby is deprived, on the other hand, he or she may become an adult who is bitter, caustic, and biting.

In the *anal stage,* which is predominant during the second and third years of life, the child derives pleasure from acts of elimination, that is, urinating and defecating. During this stage, the ego begins to develop. The focus in this stage is on toilet training. Freud posited if the parents are too harsh during this period, the child may become an adult who is compulsive and excessively neat and hoards things. If the parents, in contrast, are too lax, the foundation is laid for an adult who may be messy and disorganized.

In the *phallic stage,* which typically is present in the fourth and fifth years of life, children display interest in their sexual organs. The superego starts emerging during this stage. Freud believed that children have fantasies of becoming the love object of the opposite-sex parent and doing away with the same-sex parent in the process. Freud hypothesized that if this stage is not successfully resolved by the child identifying with the same-sex parent, the child as an adult may become homosexual or seek sexual partners who are considerably older.

In the *latency stage,* which starts about age 6 and goes to adolescence, sexual interest is dormant while the individual focuses attention on learning and school. During this period, the ego and superego expand, and defense mechanisms are strengthened. In the final stage, the *genital stage,* which begins during adolescence and extends through adulthood, sexual interest resurfaces, and mature sexual relationships become possible.

Psychoanalysis is a therapeutic method as well as a theory of personality. From a psychoanalytic perspective, anxiety is the real problem and results from a collision of id impulses with ego and superego demands. Expression of aggressive and sexual urges sets off a cycle whereby the superego demands punishment. At the same time, the ego uses defense mechanisms to allow some expression of id demands and to dissipate some of the anxiety that comes from the breakthrough of unconscious impulses. In this model, anxiety and abnormal, even criminal, behavior and exaggerated defense mechanisms are merely symptoms of the problem: The real problem is the blocking of sexual and aggressive tendencies. The objective of psychoanalytic treatment is to help clients achieve insight into their repressed urges. The underlying assumption, although not empirically established, is that insight into the causes of one's behavior and inner turmoil leads to more rational problem solving and to constructive change. The psychoanalytic methods used to facilitate insight include free association, dream analysis, transference, and working through resistance to interpretation.

Psychodynamic theories that emerged during Freud's life and that have developed since his death have accepted basic Freudian tenets on the role of the unconscious, the importance of anxiety as a symptom, and the progression of personality development through invariant stages. Contemporaries of Freud, such as Karl Jung and Alfred Adler, and those who built on his work in more recent times, including Harry Stack Sullivan, Erik Erikson, Karen Horney, John Bowlby, Otto Kernberg, and Heinz Kohut, rejected biological and sexual motivation as the primary causes of anxiety. In addition, they differed from Freud in placing an exclusive emphasis on childhood. Their approach and their explanations for behavior were broader than those used by Freud. Psychodynamic theorists today focus on people's past and present interpersonal relationships, psychosocial development from birth through old age, and attachment to others as the means to understand the source of their anxiety, their maladaptive coping strategies, and their aberrant and criminal behavior.

The picture that emerges from psychodynamic theories is consistent with the portrait painted using a strictly psychoanalytic framework. From psychodynamic perspectives, Tommy Lee would be seen as a man who had difficulties relating to people from childhood through adulthood. He would be viewed as a man who failed to master ego development tasks associated with childhood, adolescence, young adulthood, and adulthood, such as learning to cope with interpersonal conflict in a healthy and mature way by dissipating his anger safely. He would be characterized as a person who failed to develop sufficiently to be capable of empathizing with other human beings, who, although they differed from him, had every right to live.

—Kathleen M. Heide

See also AGGRESSION: PSYCHOLOGICAL THEORIES; MOTIVES FOR MURDER; VIOLENT BEHAVIOR: PERSONALITY THEORIES; VIOLENT BEHAVIOR: A PSYCHOLOGICAL CASE STUDY

Further Reading

Adler, A. (1958). *What life should mean to you.* New York: Capricorn.

Bowlby, J. (1969). *Attachment.* New York: Basic Books.

Freud, S. (1949). *An outline of psychoanalysis.* New York: Norton.

Erikson, E. H. (1963). *Childhood and society* (2nd ed.). New York: Norton.

Jung, C. G. (1975). *Critique of psychoanalysis.* Princeton, NJ: Princeton University Press.

Kernberg, O. F. (1976). *Object-relations theory and clinical psychoanalysis.* New York: Aronson.

Kohut, H. (1971). *The analysis of the self.* New York: International Universities Press.

Sullivan, H. S. (1968). *The interpersonal theory of psychiatry.* New York: Norton.

VIOLENT BEHAVIOR: A PSYCHOLOGICAL CASE STUDY

Tyrone, a handsome 17-year-old African American youth, was charged with killing two convenience store clerks in two separate robberies. The adolescent, acting alone, fired directly at the lone clerk in each of the stores, instantly killing both of them. Videotapes from store cameras revealed that neither clerk resisted the robberies. In fact, in the second incident, Tyrone shot the clerk immediately upon entering the store.

The state indicted the adolescent as an adult with multiple charges, including two counts of first-degree murder, and announced its intention to seek the death penalty. Prior to trial, a plea agreement was reached, wherein Tyrone avoided a possible death sentence by agreeing to plead guilty to two counts of second-degree murder, and one count of armed robbery associated with a third armed robbery in which no one was killed.

Tyrone's arrest stunned the community in which he had lived for years. The boy had been raised for most of his life in a religious home by his grandparents, who were known to be stable people with traditional values. His grandfather was a hardworking man and provided well for his family. Tyrone had his own room

at his grandparents' home and was essentially raised as an only child by grandparents who loved and doted on him. He lived a middle- to upper-middle-class life. The family lived in a beautiful home on about 5 acres of land, with a pool, tennis court, and basketball court. A boy who had a college fund set up for him and a lucrative family business to go into was robbing and killing people. The obvious question was "Why?"

Thorough assessment revealed a confluence of psychological factors that contributed to Tyrone's violent behavior. These explanations have their underpinnings in personality development theory, psychodynamic theory, learning theory, cognitive theory, and existential theory. In addition, Tyrone's case provides an excellent illustration of continuing areas of psychological investigation in the forensic area. These include theories suggesting that individuals with low intelligence, neurological impairment, and mental illness are more likely to engage in criminal behavior than are individuals without these risk factors.

Tyrone's personality development was low. *Personality development theories* posit that ego development proceeds in a hierarchical and invariant sequence of stages through which individuals progress as they master crucial interpersonal problems associated with each level. Tyrone had progressed through the early stages associated with infancy and early childhood development. He learned that people, unlike inanimate objects, could respond to him and that he could influence the behavior of others by applying certain formulas or strategies, such as saying "Please" when he asked for something. However, Tyrone had not reached the level of personality development in which he realized that he was accountable for his behavior and that he had choices, and he had not internalized a set of values by which he judged his behavior. Rather, he thought and acted like a much younger child. He behaved impulsively without regard for the welfare of others. In his worldview, people were objects to be manipulated. Wielding a handgun gave him power to get what he wanted. Consistent with his low personality development, he was incapable of feeling genuine remorse for his murderous actions and felt no empathy for his victims or their survivors.

Tyrone's restricted personality development was partly due to the chaotic nature of his first few years of life. *Psychodynamic theories* focus on the importance of early childhood in shaping personality. Tyrone experienced early abandonment by both his biological parents and repeated breaks in the bonding process. It is questionable whether he ever bonded to anyone, including the grandparents who loved him dearly. Evidence suggested that during the short time he lived with his mother, Tyrone was neglected and abused, factors also correlated with breaks in the bonding process. In addition to lacking empathy and a connection with others, unattached children are filled with rage, which, in psychoanalytic terms, can be *displaced* onto others. From a psychoanalytic perspective, it is too anxiety provoking and painful for the child to face his aggressive and sexual urges and dependency needs. As a result, these primitive urges become buried deep in the unconscious. If the individual's defense mechanisms fail him, these *id impulses* (instinctual demands) can overwhelm the *ego* (component of the personality in touch with reality) and *superego* (conscience), bringing destruction in their wake.

From the perspective of *behavioral theory,* Tyrone's development was further compromised by poor parental role models and inconsistent discipline. Behavioral theory focuses on how individuals learn. The operant conditioning paradigm, for example, posits that behavior is influenced and shaped by its consequences. Behaviors that are rewarded will increase; those that are punished will decrease; and those that are ignored will eventually cease. As a young adolescent, Tyrone lived in several households with different ways of relating and standards for behavior, and he did not learn responsible behavior. During the 2 to 3 years preceding his arrest for the robbery/homicides, Tyrone had been living with his father, who was abusing cocaine and unavailable to guide him.

While staying with his father, Tyrone rarely went to school. He associated increasingly with delinquent youth who lived in low-income neighborhoods known for violence. The youth observed criminal acts and was exposed to antisocial attitudes. Tyrone related that he liked kids who were involved in robbing, selling drugs, and getting high. He was arrested for delinquent behavior on a few occasions. Although it was clear to the family, to the school, and to the juvenile justice system that Tyrone needed help, no meaningful intervention occurred. His irresponsible and antisocial behavior went unpunished by conventional society and was rewarded by his delinquent peers.

During his middle adolescence, Tyrone also became heavily involved in listening to "gangsta rap" music. According to *cognitive theory,* thoughts, particularly those that are frequent and rehearsed, can affect feelings and behaviors. The image of the world as a violent place is particularly extolled in "gangsta rap." Rappers sing about robbing, killing, and raping, which they maintain is part of everyday life in "the hood" for low-income members of society, particularly African Americans. The messages in the songs to which Tyrone repeatedly listened clearly influenced him. When asked specific questions during the clinical assessment, the youth responded several times with lyrics from the songs. For example, when Tyrone was asked why he shot the clerk immediately upon entering the store, he replied that he had gotten "trigga happy," one of the recordings titled as such and sung by a well-known rapper.

As he grew into his late teens, Tyrone's search for a sense of purpose led him to identify with a criminal element. *Existential theory* posits that people look for meaning in their lives and struggle with identity issues. Tyrone felt more comfortable committing crimes in the projects than working in his grandparents' business and residing in their affluent neighborhood. The youth had a history of school failure. He had been suspended repeatedly for disruptive behavior, unsuccessfully placed in more than a dozen schools, and expelled from at least three schools. The persona of being a gangster appealed to him and gave his life some organizational framework. When asked what he enjoyed doing for fun prior to being arrested, Tyrone replied that he liked to have sex with different girls, get high, and get drunk. He also indicated that he had fun making money by "selling dope and robbing."

In addition to low personality development and unfavorable influences in his early childhood and adolescence, psychological testing revealed that Tyrone was of *dull-normal intelligence.* The relationship between IQ and crime has been debated since 1913, when Charles Goring's findings that criminals were abnormally low in intelligence was published in *The English Convict.* Although there is consensus across many studies that most offenders are not mentally retarded, there is disagreement regarding the intelligence of the majority of criminals. Some studies have found that the average IQ scores of offenders were in the below-average range, whereas others have found that they were in the average to above-average range. The literature on both juvenile and adult offenders indicates, however, that, regardless of intelligence potential, many have struggled in educational settings and experience difficulties reading and performing academically.

Tyrone also had brain damage that appeared to have been present from birth. Significant disagreement exists with respect to the prevalence of *neurological impairment* in criminals, which may be partly due to differences in assessment and reporting practices used by various clinicians. Neurological assessment is most likely to be done in cases of violent offenders. Although no neurophysiological variable has yet been found, several types of indirect data suggest that brain functioning abnormalities increase the likelihood of violent behavior. Many studies have found that neurophysiological deficits in attention, memory, and language/verbal skills are common in individuals who demonstrate violent or aggressive behavior. This correlation could indicate a direct relationship between limbic system damage and violent behavior. However, some experts believe that these neurological deficits result in psychological complications, putting these individuals at higher risk for behaving violently than those who do not have these biological influences. These deficits may result in impaired communication skills that, for example, lead to distorted social interactions with peers. Alternatively, individuals with these deficits may become frustrated over their inability to compete successfully with peers in cognitive tasks and respond violently.

In apparently senseless crimes, particularly those involving extreme violence, the possibility that the offender suffers from *serious mental illness* is typically given careful consideration by defense counsel. If an offender is seriously mentally ill, he or she may be found not guilty by reason of insanity by the jury or the presiding judge at trial. In such cases, the defendant is not viewed as responsible for the violent rampage and is remanded for evaluation and treatment, rather than convicted and punished for what would otherwise be criminal behavior.

The relationship between mental illness and crime has been investigated since the 1920s. Although studies report different findings, most studies report no significant relationship between mental illness and criminality. The available literature indicates that some mentally ill individuals do commit violent crimes. However, more mentally ill individuals appear to commit nonviolent, nonserious crimes than violent and serious crimes. Most important, the majority of mentally disturbed individuals do not commit crimes at all. In fact, the bulk of serious violent and property crimes are committed by offenders with no diagnosis of mental disorder.

Tyrone was not suffering from a major mental illness when evaluated months after the killings. He did not meet the criteria for major depression, often a factor in random and senseless killings. In addition, there was no evidence of psychosis or of a history of significant alcohol or drug dependence or abuse, psychiatric disorders that on occasion do contribute to violent behavior.

Tyrone did meet the criteria for having a conduct disorder (CD) as described in the *Diagnostic and Statistical Manual of Mental Disorders,* 4th edition *(DSM-IV).* This diagnosis, applicable to children and adolescents under 18 years of age, is characterized by a long-standing pattern of violating the rights of others or disregarding major societal norms. Diagnostic criteria include specific behavioral indicators of aggression to animals and people, theft or deceitfulness, destruction of property, and other serious rule violations (e.g., truancy, running away). Conduct disorder is often the precursor to a diagnosis reserved for adults who engage in a similar response pattern, antisocial personality disorder. Data provided by Tyrone and his family indicated that as Tyrone entered his middle to late adolescent years, he persistently violated the rights of others, broke societal rules, and defied major age-appropriate societal norms. Remarks made by Tyrone suggested that he often threatened or intimidated others, had stolen while confronting a victim, had been physically cruel to animals, had lied to obtain what he wanted, and was truant from school beginning before age 13. Tyrone also manifested some sadistic and destructive traits, including a fascination with death, which suggested a need for intense psychotherapeutic intervention.

Tyrone was unquestionably sane under the M'Naughten standard of insanity, the law in his state and one of the most widely used tests of insanity today and in the past. Conduct disorder, like antisocial personality disorder, is not viewed as a serious mental disorder that significantly impairs cognitive ability, perception, and judgment. Tyrone's account of the homicidal incidents left no doubt that at the time of the two robbery/homicides, the youth was aware that he was robbing the stores. When he fired the shots that killed the two victims, he was aware that death could result from his actions. He reported that he was mentally alert when he went into the convenience stores. He was certain that on these two occasions he was not high on either alcohol or other drugs, because he liked "to be in control" when he went robbing. His change of clothes, his concern about where the car was parked, and his flight indicated that he was aware that his actions were against the law, although he did not experience them as morally wrong.

The American Law Institute's (ALI) proposed Model Penal Code test was among the mitigating factors enumerated in the state statute under which Tyrone was evaluated. This test is a broader test than the M'Naughten standard and allows mental health professionals as well as the judge and jury to consider emotional factors operating in the defendant, rather than simply cognitive considerations. The ALI test was the standard in the federal courts until 1985 and is law in close to half the states in the United States. Had it been the test for insanity, it is possible that if the case had gone to trial, Tyrone could have been found to have been insane, particularly when the other factors highlighted above were taken into account. In-depth assessment of Tyrone indicated that his capacity "to appreciate the criminality of his conduct" was "substantially impaired." At the time of the offense, the youth knew what he was doing (M'Naughten test), but it is clear from Tyrone's remarks that he had no emotional appreciation of the consequences of his behavior regarding the victims who died, those who witnessed the crime, his family, and the community at large. Tyrone's inability to appreciate the effect of his actions was due to his restricted personality development. The mental health professionals who examined Tyrone saw the defendant as nonevaluative and his actions as impulsive. The youth did not appear capable of deliberating, but rather immediately reacted to stimuli, raising the question of whether his capacity "to conform his conduct to the requirements of the law was substantially impaired" at the time of the killings.

Sentencing guidelines suggested that Tyrone be incarcerated for a period of 22 to 39 years. The judge sentenced the adolescent to 39 years in prison. Although defense counsel had hoped that the judge would impose a sentence on the lower end, Tyrone's attorneys were somewhat relieved that given the aggravating factors in the case, the judge did not exceed the recommended sentence. Tyrone's grandfather offered to use monies from the boy's trust fund to pay for psychotherapy while his grandson is incarcerated.

Psychological theories have direct relevance for treatment. Personality development theories would suggest that intervention strategies need to be designed to help offenders like Tyrone develop sufficiently to

acknowledge responsibility for their behavior; to identify and process feelings associated with the crimes and the course of their lives (e.g., remorse, pain, sadness, fear, and anger); and to rebuild their egos through education in life skills and social skills training. Psychodynamic theories would stress the importance of working through unresolved issues dating back to childhood that unconsciously undermine healthy adaptations. Behavioral theories would focus on increasing structure in the lives of youth, rewarding constructive behavior, punishing antisocial behavior, using good role models, and teaching appropriate life skills. Cognitive approaches would challenge distorted thinking of youth and guide them in choosing prosocial thinking associated with positive feelings and adaptive behaviors. Existential perspectives would challenge wayward youth to solve identity crises based on moral reflection and value-laden choices designed to contribute to making the world a better place for themselves and for generations to come.

—Kathleen M. Heide

See also AGGRESSION: PSYCHOLOGICAL THEORIES; ANTISOCIAL PERSONALITY DISORDER; CONDUCT DISORDER; HOMICIDE, TYPES OF, AND DEGREES OF MURDER; JUVENILE KILLERS; M'NAUGHTEN RULE; PREDICTING VIOLENT BEHAVIOR; VIOLENT BEHAVIOR: PERSONALITY THEORIES; VIOLENT BEHAVIOR: PSYCHOANALYTIC THEORY

Further Reading

American Psychiatric Association. (1994). *Diagnostic and statistical manual of mental disorders* (4th ed.). Washington, DC: Author.

Ellis, A. (1999). Early theories and practices of rational-emotive behavior therapy and how they have been augmented and revised during the last three decades. *Journal of Rational-Emotive and Cognitive Behavior Therapy, 17.*

Freud, S. (1949). *An outline of psychoanalysis.* New York: Norton.

Fromm, E. (1973). *The anatomy of human destructiveness.* Greenwich, CT: Fawcett.

Goring, C. (1913). *The English convict: A statistical study.* London: Her Majesty's Stationery Office.

Heide, K. M. (1999). *Young killers: The challenge of juvenile homicide.* Thousand Oaks, CA: Sage.

Magid, K., & McKelvey, C. A. (1987). *High risk: Children without a conscience.* New York: Bantam.

Monahan, J. (1996). *Mental illness and violent crime.* Washington, DC: National Institute of Justice.

Reiss, A. J., & Jeffrey, A. R. (Eds.). (1993). *Understanding and preventing violence.* Washington, DC: National Academy Press.

Skinner, B. F. (1953). *Science and human behavior.* New York: Macmillan.

VIOLENT CRIMINAL APPREHENSION PROGRAM (VICAP),
See FEDERAL BUREAU OF INVESTIGATON;
SERIAL MURDER: INTERNATIONAL
INCIDENCE; VICLAS

VIOLENT FEMALE JUVENILE OFFENDERS

Historically, in the United States, females have accounted for a small portion of serious juvenile offenses and an even smaller portion of violent offenses. Although males continue to be the majority of offenders in serious juvenile crimes, the rate of female juvenile arrests for serious violent crimes increased about twice as much as the rate for males in the latter part of the 20th century. According to data from the Federal Bureau Of Investigation's Uniform Crime Report (UCR), in 1970, the female juvenile arrest rate for violent index crimes (murder/nonnegligent manslaughter, forcible rape, robbery, and aggravated assault) was 19 per 100,000 versus 179 per 100,000 for males; in 1980, the rate had increased to 38 per 100,000 for females and 314 per 100,000 for males; and by 1995, the rate for females was 70 per 100,000 compared with 407 per 100,000 for males. Thus, the arrest rate for female juveniles for violent index crimes increased 268% from 1970 to 1995, versus 127% for males. Put another way, in 1988, girls comprised 11% of all juvenile arrests for violent index crimes, and 11 years later, in 1999, girls represented 17% of such arrests. Although female juvenile arrests increased in every offense category, the largest increase was for aggravated assault. In 1999, the last year for which complete data are available, of juveniles arrested for violent index crimes, females were responsible for 22% of arrests for aggravated assaults, 9% of robbery arrests, 8% of arrests for murder and nonnegligent manslaughter, and 2% of arrests for forcible rape.

Although official data show that females are engaging in more violent offending than ever before, it is important to note that the actual number of females arrested for violent crimes continues to be very small. For example, of the 2,468,800 juveniles arrested in 1999, females comprised 17% of the 103,900 arrested for violent index crimes, or 17,663. The estimated juvenile population at risk for arrest (youth aged 10-17) in 1999 was approximately 37,600,000. Assuming that females were about half of the 10- to 17-year-old population, then the number of female adolescents arrested for a violent crime was about .13%, or just over one tenth of 1% of the target population. Thus, although the percentage increases in arrests for female violence over the past few decades are large, they continue to represent a very small fraction of adolescent girls.

Self-report studies are another way to measure juvenile offending and have been used by criminologists for decades. These studies consistently show as well that although some females do engage in violent acts, they do so far less than their male counterparts, and as the offenses become more serious, males are the predominant offenders. For example, a self-report study of adolescents by Cernkovich and Giordano in 1979 showed that 25% of females and 48% of males admitted attacking someone with their fists, whereas 7% of females and 12% of males said they had used a weapon to attack someone. Furthermore, less than 1% of females had committed robberies, compared with 5% of males. Similarly, in the annual survey of high school seniors conducted by the University of Michigan in 1993, 13% of females and 22% of males said they had gotten into a serious fight in school or at work, but only 5% of females versus 21% of males said they had hurt someone badly enough to need bandages or a doctor. Furthermore, 1% of females and 8% of males reported that they had used a gun or knife or other weapon to get something from another person, and less than 1% of females versus 6% of males had set someone's property on fire on purpose.

In addition to the fact that female juvenile violence tends to be concentrated in less serious offenses, other factors associated with violent female behavior differ somewhat from those associated with males as well. For example, in regard to homicide, whereas male adolescents are more likely to kill an acquaintance or a stranger, females are about as likely to kill a family member as a friend/acquaintance. Females are particularly more likely to kill young children. In addition, whereas male adolescents are more likely to kill with firearms, females are more likely to use knives and other means, such as hands/feet, strangulation, and drowning, requiring them to be in close physical contact with their victims. Female violence in general is much more likely to occur within an ongoing relationship and result from some type of interpersonal conflict. Thus, some theorists have suggested that the very nature of female violence may help explain how it differs from violence committed by males.

Through traditional female socialization, girls are taught to be nurturing caretakers who assume a more passive role in social life and take primary responsibility for maintaining harmony in relationships. Thus, females have traditionally been expected to uphold stricter moral standards, thereby experiencing a stronger sense of guilt, shame, and social disapproval when their behavior violates socially accepted gender norms. Because their lives tend to be more focused on relationships with others, it would reasonably follow that their primary stresses and conflicts would occur within those relationships. If other, nonviolent means for resolving interpersonal conflicts have been exhausted or do not seem feasible, then it is likely that girls would resort to violence as a last resort.

Research on girls' violence supports that it often occurs within a context in which the girl perceives such violence to be justified, such as in response to threats or actual harm, and she may engage in violence in self-defense. That may particularly be true in situations in which female adolescents are being physically, sexually, and emotionally victimized, as research has shown is the case for the majority of girls in the juvenile justice system. Similarly, girls who are being victimized and choose to leave the situation may then resort to violence on the street as a means of self-protection.

Some early feminist theorists predicted that as females began to enjoy more equality with males and be exposed to the same opportunities, it would be expected that their behavior would begin to become more like males as well, including their involvement in crime. Although that may be true to some degree, girls still account for only about one fourth of adolescent violence; their violent offending consists predominantly of aggravated assault; and their violence tends to be of a much more personal nature than the

violence of males. So, despite the fact that more girls may be committing violent crimes, they are still small in number, and for the most part, the dynamics of female violence continue to differ from that of males. This also begs the questions as to just how much equality and opportunity girls have actually gained.

Earlier biological explanations for female criminality, typically associating girls' delinquency with their sexuality, would not account for an increase in violent behavior, because their biological makeup has not essentially changed. What has changed, though, is the fact that females are reaching puberty at increasingly earlier ages, without a corresponding shift in social and emotional maturation. Precocious sexuality places girls at higher risk for sexual abuse and exploitation at earlier ages as well, and as discussed earlier, sexual victimization may lead to female violence as self-protection or even retaliation.

Traditional psychological theories have addressed dysfunctional home lives of delinquent girls and their social maladjustment, as well as their tendency to internalize anger, leading to depression and other mental and emotional disorders. It may be that at least some degree of the increasing violence by girls is associated with increasing deterioration of their family relationships, and consequently, more internal distress. Slightly more than 30% of children in the United States currently live with only one parent, up from slightly over 20% in 1980. In addition to the stresses of parenting alone, approximately 42% of single-parent homes with children lived in poverty, compounding the stress for both parent and child. In addition, in the wake of the drug epidemic of the late 1980s and early 1990s, many young women who are mothers of children now coming into the juvenile justice system have serious substance abuse problems that have resulted in child abuse/neglect, termination of parental rights, incarceration, and/or impaired parenting abilities, often leaving their children in unstable living situations. Some research suggests severely dysfunctional family situations may have a more detrimental effect on girls than boys, resulting in attachment disorders and/or other psychosocial disturbances, such as alcohol and drug abuse, which could increase the likelihood of violent behavior.

The three leading sociological theories of delinquency—strain, social learning, and social control—do not specifically address differences in offending between males and females. Nevertheless, some aspects of these theories could offer possible explanations for the increase in girls' violence. For example, it might be reasonable to assert that as girls have gained more freedom and equality and are consequently less protected, they have also begun to experience more stress and *strain,* which could in turn lead to violence if resources were not available to help them cope in a more positive way. Or, although girls in lower-income families may be experiencing more freedom, they may find that they do not necessarily have more opportunities to improve their lives, especially economically, as recent economic shifts have resulted in increasingly limited options for less skilled workers.

A girl may find her options even more limited if she drops out of high school and has no marketable skills. Most girls in the juvenile justice system have had some type of difficulty with school, either academically, behaviorally, or both. Having increased expectations but decreased opportunities, then, may result in anger, frustration, a sense of hopelessness, alienation from mainstream society, and perhaps even violence. The strain may also result from childhood victimization or problematic family situations from which the girl perceives that there is no escape other than through violence and/or alcohol and drugs.

In terms of *social learning* theory, the argument might be made that as girls have gained more freedom, they have begun to be exposed to more people who could serve as delinquent role models and provide positive reinforcement for their delinquent behavior, including violence. That may be the case with girls' increased involvement in gangs, where they see violence modeled, have violence redefined for them as a means of protection and a way of gaining status and respect, and receive positive reinforcement from their own participation in violent activities.

Although official statistics about the extent of girls' involvement in gangs vary, the 1997 National Longitudinal Survey of Youth, conducted by the Bureau of Labor Statistics, found that 3% of adolescent females reported gang involvement. Some researchers have argued, however, that even when girls are involved with gangs, they tend to maintain more traditional female roles and do not enjoy equal status with males, and they tend to be victimized both sexually and physically by male gang members in their own and rival gangs. Others, though, have shown that at least some girls fully participate in gang activities, with a few even attaining leadership positions. However, even though those girls do engage in acts of violence, they still do

not generally reach the same level of violent offending as their male counterparts, preferring when they do fight to do so with fists and knives rather than guns, and, more often, fighting with other girls rather than with boys.

Social control theorists might argue that as both formal and informal social controls on youth have weakened, especially those controls traditionally found in the family and other major social institutions, boys and girls alike have become more likely to engage in all forms of delinquency. According to that theory, however, girls still would not be as likely to resort to violence as boys, because girls tend to maintain more positive relationships with parents, teachers, and other adults during adolescence. Studies of girls in the juvenile justice system do show, however, that compared with their nondelinquent counterparts, they tend to have weaker bonds to parents and school, have more delinquent friends, and participate in fewer mainstream activities.

None of these theories, however, fully explains the shift in female adolescent offending, leading still other criminologists to suggest that perhaps there has not been as much actual change in girls' behavior as there has been in how that behavior is defined and managed by the larger society. For example, in response to the dramatic increase in primarily male adolescent violence in the mid-1980s through the early 1990s, states began passing a rash of legislation designed to impose harsher penalties for violent juvenile offenders, and public sentiment shifted to demand more punitive treatment for juveniles who engaged in violent acts. Much of this legislation mandated sanctions for youth charged with certain offenses, so that police officers and judges, who may have been more likely to treat females more leniently in the past, no longer had the discretion to do so. Thus, more females began to be formally charged and processed through the juvenile justice system. Furthermore, as states were forced to funnel more dollars into locked facilities, fewer resources were available to provide prevention/early intervention services to less serious offenders (i.e., girls), which might have kept them from penetrating further into the system.

Other laws affecting the treatment of girls were also passed during the 1980s and 1990s. Most, if not all, states passed new family violence laws either mandating or promoting arrest if there was evidence a felony had occurred when the officer arrived at the scene. As stated earlier, a large portion of girls' violence involves family members, so more girls were subject to arrest, whereas previously the family would more likely have been referred for counseling or some other social service intervention. Similarly, with the increase in incidents of school violence in the early 1990s, many, if not most, states passed some form of "zero tolerance" policy, resulting in referrals to juvenile court for any outward display of conflict. Another large portion of girls' violence involves threats and/or fights with friends/acquaintances at school; thus, more girls were brought into the juvenile justice system for those offenses as well. Inadequate resources for public agencies such as child protective services, schools, and mental health, which were likely to have been involved earlier in the lives of delinquent girls, may also have contributed to their subsequent violent behavior by not identifying problems soon enough, or if they were identified, not providing the necessary level of intervention.

In conclusion, although the arrest rate for female adolescents for serious violent crimes has increased dramatically over the past few decades, the actual number of females that increase represents is slightly over one tenth of 1% of the 10- to 17-year-old female population. The largest category of arrests for female juveniles is aggravated assault, which can define a broad range of behaviors, including some threats and minor acts of violence, such as slapping, pushing, scratching, and pulling hair. Self-report studies consistently show a higher level of female involvement in violent acts than what is shown in arrest data, but as the violence becomes more severe, the offenders become increasingly male.

Like males, females may be more prone to violence if they have high levels of stress, blocked opportunities, dysfunctional families, delinquent friends and family members, and low levels of social control. Unlike males, females are as likely to victimize family members as friends/acquaintances, particularly young children. If they use a weapon, they are more likely to use fists, knives, or some other method that requires close physical contact rather than a gun. They are more likely to engage in violence within the context of

an interpersonal conflict occurring within an ongoing relationship and more likely to engage in violence for self-protection or because they feel the violence is justified. Violent girls tend to come from dysfunctional families, have had problems in school, may have substance abuse and/or other mental health problems, and possess few, if any, marketable skills.

At this time, the exact extent of female juvenile violent offending is unclear, as are the exact reasons behind it. What is clear, however, is that the policies and practices currently in place to respond to violent female offenders are inadequate at best and could potentially result in further harm to a population of girls who are already troubled.

—*Sandra S. Stone*

See also Aggression: Feminist Perspective; Juvenile Killers; Juvenile Offenders; Women and Violence

Further Reading

Chesney-Lind, M., & Shelden, R. G. (1998). *Girls, delinquency, and juvenile justice.* Belmont, CA: West/Wadsworth.

Federal Interagency Forum on Child and Family Statistics. (2001). *America's children: Key national indicators of well-being 2001.* Washington, DC: U.S. Government Printing Office.

Miller, J. (2001). *One of the guys: Girls, gangs, and gender.* New York: Oxford University Press.

Snyder, H. N. (2000, December). Juvenile arrests 1999. *Juvenile Justice Bulletin.* Washington, DC: U.S. Department of Justice.

Snyder, H. N., & Sickmund, M. (1999, September). *Juvenile offenders and victims: 1999 national report.* Pittsburgh, PA: National Center for Juvenile Justice.

VLAD THE IMPALER, *see* Serial Murder: International Incidence; Vampires, Werewolves, and Witches

WACO, TEXAS, *See* CULTS; KORESH, DAVID; MCVEIGH, TIMOTHY

WAR ATROCITIES

War itself can be considered an atrocity, but even in the extreme violence of war, people make distinctions between acts that are necessary to achieve a nation's war aims and those that are gratuitously cruel. Targeting civilians, killing the wounded, rape, torture, and genocide are among the acts that both offend our conscience and violate international law.

War atrocities involve three overlapping types of crime: war crimes, crimes against humanity, and violations of human rights. *War crimes,* in international law, occur only during armed combat between nations and involve acts committed against combatants and noncombatants of the opposing side. An example of a war crime is the execution of wounded soldiers. *Crimes against humanity* is a broader concept in which the victims can be nationals or nonnationals and the acts can occur in times of peace as well as war. To be defined as crimes against humanity, the acts must be intentionally directed against an identifiable group, and they must be widespread and systematic. The forced impregnation of members of a minority ethnic group by the majority as a means of destroying the minority group's ethnic identification is an example. Like crimes against humanity, legal definitions of human rights are not restricted by the nationality of the victim nor the existence of hostilities. Unlike crimes against humanity, *human rights violations* can be committed against a single person and do not have to be part of a broader plan of persecution. The torture of someone believed to have collaborated with a rebel group is an example of a human rights violation.

LEGAL RESPONSES TO WAR ATROCITIES

Sources of Law

The Ancient Greeks seem to have been the first civilization to have tribunals for sanctioning misconduct in war. The first modern trial for war crimes is generally believed to be that of Peter van Hagenbach, a knight acting for the Duke of Burgundy in 1474 who led a brutal siege of the town of Breisach, Germany. Although he claimed he was only following orders, judges of the Holy Roman Empire stripped him of his knighthood and sentenced him to death for violating the "laws of God and man."

Current international law on war atrocities is composed of two types of law, customary and codified, and two branches of law, international humanitarian law and international human rights law.

Customary law is composed of norms established through the general and consistent practice of nations and the belief that such norms are legally binding. It is in essence the set of unwritten but mutually understood behavioral rules that are followed by most nations at most times. Its chief advantage is that all countries are bound by its rules, regardless of their formal ratification or acceptance of international treaties. Its chief disadvantage is that by its very nature, its principles are not clearly defined. For this reason, some nations, especially the United States, often oppose the use of customary law because it is not positive law. Its use as the legal basis for determining war crimes is well established, however. The war crimes tribunals at Nuremberg and Tokyo following World War II as well as the recently established ad hoc tribunals for Rwanda and the former Yugoslavia are in large part dependent on customary law for their legal standing.

Codified law is written law. Much of codified law restates principles developed first in customary law. Codified law also often explicitly includes customary law as a way of extending a stronger moral status to the unwritten codes. The principal sources of written international humanitarian law, which define war crimes and some crimes against humanity, are the four Geneva Conventions of 1949 and the 1977 Additional Protocols that extend the Geneva Conventions. Other sources of restraints on the means and methods of combat can be found in the Hague Conventions of 1899 and 1907. The principal sources of international human rights law are the United Nations (UN) Charter, the 1948 Universal Declaration of Human Rights, the 1976 International Covenant on Civil and Political Rights, and the 1976 International Covenant on Economic, Social, and Cultural Rights.

Enforcing the Law

The International Committee of the Red Cross, under the 1949 Geneva Conventions and the 1977 additional protocols, is granted a mandate to train and monitor armed forces in international humanitarian law. It also is mandated by these treaties to, among other tasks, deliver packages to, visit, and register prisoners of war; to render emergency humanitarian aid to civilians in war zones; to act as intermediaries in prisoner exchanges; and to track persons displaced by war and its aftermath. The Swiss founders of the organization originally chose the red cross on a white background because it is the Swiss flag with the colors reversed. The Geneva Conventions also recognize other protected symbols such as the red crescent. Although not officially recognized by the conventions, the red Shield of David is also a respected symbol.

The educational and humanitarian responsibilities of the Red Cross stop short of law enforcement. International agreements generally expect nations to act as police and courts themselves. By both custom and treaty, grave breaches of international humanitarian law are subject to universal jurisdiction. This means that any country may detain and try anyone accused of war

crimes or crimes against humanity. In fact, nations have a legal obligation under international humanitarian law to pursue these cases. This obligation helps explain why the United States and other Western powers attempted to avoid labeling the events in Rwanda in 1994 as genocide; the admission that such a crime was occurring also created a legal obligation to intervene.

Several times in recent history, special tribunals have been set up to try individuals responsible for war atrocities. Following World War II, tribunals in Nuremberg and Tokyo tried the most culpable senior officials of the war governments of Germany and Japan. Lesser tribunals in both Europe and Asia tried other accused criminals. As alluded to above, the United Nations also established ad hoc tribunals to try those guilty of war crimes and crimes against humanity committed in the wars in the former Yugoslavia and during the genocide in Rwanda.

A statute to establish a permanent International Criminal Court (ICC) was adopted in Rome in 1998, over the opposition of the United States and six other countries (China, Iraq, Israel, Libya, Qatar, and Yemen). On April 11, 2002, the ICC treaty was ratified by enough countries to enter the statute into force beginning in July 2002. The creation of a permanent international court is a new and highly significant development in the history of international law.

The development of international law regarding war atrocities continues, and in many ways legal responses must "hit a moving target." The end of the 20th century saw increasing numbers of atrocities committed outside traditional concepts of war. Paramilitary organizations with tenuous connections to governments, rebel forces or militias with no governmental structure at all, and terrorist organizations that are multinational and lack even quasi-state backing have all been implicated in mass homicides that cry out for a response based on justice.

CASE STUDIES

Examples of atrocities can be found in any period in which people have gone to war and someone was present to record the events, even if the written record was not intended as a chronicle of war crimes. Biblical accounts, for example, repeatedly tell how the men, women, and children of conquered cities were put to the sword or sold into slavery.

One of the most famous, and bloodiest, cases from antiquity was the Roman siege of Carthage in the

Third Punic War. Both sides committed their share of atrocities. The Carthaginian general Hasdrubal, for example, took Roman prisoners to the top of the city's fortifications, mutilated and tortured them in view of the Romans camped below, then hurled them from the walls. At the end of the war, the Romans demonstrated their dedication to the complete elimination of their enemy. According to the conventional account, Carthaginians who surrendered were sold into slavery and scattered throughout the empire. Those who did not were slaughtered or burned to death in the sacking of the city. The Romans razed all remaining buildings to the ground, and legend has it that they plowed and sowed the ground with salt to emphasize that even the land itself was to remain barren.

The Medieval crusades of European Christians to take the lands of biblical history from their Muslim inhabitants produced a series of atrocities so abhorrent that they are still painfully recalled by the descendants of the victims. For example, eyewitness accounts of the fall of Jerusalem during the first crusade in July 1099 relate how men, women, and children alike were killed on the spot, some beheaded, some stabbed, some thrown into the fires. They tell of piles of heads, hands, and feet in the streets and of knights at the Temple of Solomon riding through blood up to their knees and bridle reins who fell to those bloody knees in prayer for the victory.

Complete elimination of the enemy was also the tactic of Shaka, who united the Zulu kingdom in the early 19th century. Shaka used tactics that inverted the idea of limiting violence to combatants. Several accounts, particularly from the latter part of his reign, claim that after taking the most desirable women and cattle, he ordered his armies to kill the remaining old men, women, children, and animals to ensure that the enemy tribe could never again rise to oppose him. The surviving defeated warriors, however, would be spared if they agreed to join his forces.

The origin of the total war concept is usually placed a few decades later, during the American Civil War. The march of William Tecumseh Sherman's soldiers through the South is often described as the first attempt to wage war by attacking an enemy's civilian living centers and economic bases. It is also an early modern example of reprisals against citizens. In the eyes of the Union soldiers, South Carolina, as the first state to secede, was largely responsible for the war. Union and Confederate sources alike suggest that as brutal as other portions of Sherman's campaign through the southern states may have been, none reached the level of destruction seen in South Carolina.

Among the Confederacy's contributions to the horrors of the war was the Andersonville prison camp, which foreshadowed the concentration camps of World War II. Built to hold a maximum of 13,000 prisoners of war, it reached a population peak of 32,000 prisoners 6 months after opening. With inadequate food, water, and health care, disease and starvation decimated the Union prisoners. In 15 months of operation, nearly 13,000 prisoners died. Camp commander Major Henry Wirz was tried for war crimes and hanged at the end of the war, though he claimed he had only followed orders.

The 20th century's first apparent case of genocide was the killing of between 600,000 and 2 million Armenians by Turkish forces during World War I. The event was largely ignored by Western powers both during and after the war. The methods, justifications, and relative impunity of the Armenian genocide are believed to have directly influenced Hitler's attempts at genocide.

World War II produced a catalog of atrocities that ultimately drove the creation of much of the codified international law discussed above. The Holocaust, which claimed the lives of approximately 6 million Jews, is the most thoroughly documented and analyzed genocide in human history. The clear intent, careful planning, and bureaucratic organization of the slaughter have made it the case against which all other genocides are compared. The Nazis also targeted Roma and Sinti (Gypsies), Slavs, homosexuals, and others categorized as inferior by the Nazis' racist beliefs. The Japanese armed forces, though not as committed to premeditated genocide, committed mass murder of civilians throughout China, Korea, and other conquered territories and uprooted uncounted thousands of other civilians to participate in forced labor. It has been estimated that 100,000 Asian women were forced into Japanese military brothels to serve the army as "comfort women." The Allies, for their part, turned weapons of mass destruction against civilian population centers. The fire bombings of Dresden and Tokyo and nuclear attacks against Hiroshima and Nagasaki, for example, each killed tens of thousands of noncombatants in a single day.

Questionable conduct by American forces in Vietnam received international attention after the events at the Vietnamese village of My Lai. American soldiers entered My Lai on March 16, 1968. Angered by recent casualties, the soldiers resorted to the indiscriminate slaughter of all the men, women, and children present in the village. Eyewitness accounts reported the gang rape of girls before they were murdered. Although military investigators later identified fewer than 10 armed Viet Cong among the dead, hundreds of villagers lost their lives. The approximately 20 villagers who survived were spared, according to the testimony of Lt. William Calley, so they could be used as human mine detectors. Although the event involved several grave breaches of the Geneva Conventions, Lt. Calley was the only person convicted of crimes. As with so many war criminals before him, his defense that he had simply followed orders was disallowed.

The 20th century closed with two events that refocused international attention on large-scale, state-sponsored violence. Wars in the former Yugoslavia produced numerous instances of mass killings and forced relocations in the name of "ethnic cleansing." Well-documented instances of rape camps, forced impregnation, mass graves, torture, shelling and sniping of civilians, and other forms of collective terror shocked a continent that had deluded itself that it was beyond such behavior. The destruction of mosques and other collective symbols of Islam by Serb militias brought the term "cultural genocide" into popular use. In Rwanda, the attempted genocide of Tutsis, led by extremist Hutu government officials, came close to succeeding. At the height of the genocide, in a blood bath that is difficult to conceive of, Hutu attackers killed more people per day than the efficiently organized Nazis managed at the height of the Holocaust. In Rwanda, this killing was done without the machinery of gas chambers and ovens. Most Tutsis were killed with machetes and other hand weapons.

In both of these late 20th-century events, the international community failed to respond to the crises in a timely matter. In fact, the international community even failed to use those resources available at the point of the attacks. United Nations troops in Rwanda, for example, withdrew as the killing began. In July 1995, the entire Muslim population of the UN-declared "safe haven" of Srebrenica, in Bosnia, was forcibly ejected, and in the worst slaughter of the war, 7,000 to 8,000 unarmed men and boys were killed. The ad hoc tribunals established by the UN after these events offer an after-the-fact attempt at justice and perhaps signal a new commitment to enforcing it.

As the 21st century begins, the ongoing work of the ad hoc UN tribunals and the establishment of a permanent ICC signal a renewed international commitment to addressing war atrocities at the same time that events signal a continuing need for that commitment. Ongoing internal conflicts in countries such as the Sudan include government-sanctioned starvation of civilians and enslavement. Israelis and Palestinians both continue to target noncombatants to push political agendas. America's "War on Terrorism" has already placed strains on long-cherished political and civil rights. Between 100,000,000 and 200,000,000 people were killed in the 20th century by the power of governments and other armed groups, and the potential to inflict enormous numbers of casualties only increases. Prevention and the search for justice for such large-scale offenders must remain an international priority.

THE PSYCHOLOGY OF ATROCITY

Studies of genocide and other wartime atrocities have converged to define a set of psychological constructs that make these acts possible. The key element is the dehumanization of the target group. This can occur through manipulation of existing prejudices or appeals based on aggravated racial, religious, or nationalist fanaticism. It is crucial to note that the level of perceived hatred in the period immediately prior to the atrocities does not have to be great. The intermarriage rate in urban areas of Bosnia, for example, far exceeded black and white intermarriage rates in the United States. Dehumanization is especially dangerous when it occurs in the context of economic and social instability and when a charismatic leader exploits the resulting fears and instabilities. If future atrocities are to be prevented, and not simply reacted to, instances of hate speech and other dehumanizing tactics must be monitored, identified, and countered as they occur.

The individual psychology of atrocity is less well understood. Why some people commit or tolerate the commission of atrocities while others resist, even at great personal risk, is not known. Much also remains to be learned about the effects of atrocities on their victims. The full range of emotional and psychological damage inflicted on victims and their survivors is only beginning to be recognized, and the proper treatment of victims of atrocities is an important emerging area of concern.

—L. Edward Day
and Margaret Vandiver

See also CRIMES OF OBEDIENCE; ETHNIC CLEANSING; GENOCIDE; HATE CRIMES; HISTORY OF VIOLENCE IN RELIGIONS; MASS VIOLENCE; MEDICAL VIOLENCE

Further Reading

Alvarez, A. (2001). *Governments, citizens, and genocide: A comparative and interdisciplinary approach.* Bloomington, IN: Indiana University Press.

Chalk, F., & Jonassohn, K. (1990). *The history and sociology of genocide: Analyses and case studies.* New Haven, CT: Yale University Press.

Gutman, R., & Rieff, D. (Eds.). (1999). *Crimes of war: What the public should know.* New York: Norton.

Neier, A. (1998). *War crimes: Brutality, genocide, terror, and the struggle for justice.* New York: Times Books.

Power, S. (2002). *A problem from Hell: America and the age of genocide.* New York: Basic Books.

Rummel, R. J. (1994). *Death by government: Genocide and mass murder in the twentieth century.* Rutgers, NJ: Transaction.

Weine, S. M. (1999). *When history is a nightmare: Lives and memories of ethnic cleansing in Bosnia-Herzegovina.* New Brunswick, NJ: Rutgers University Press.

For a list of on-line resources on international law and war crimes, see *Genocide: Resources for Teaching and Research.* Available on the World Wide Web: at http://www.people.memphis.edu/~genocide.

WAR ON DRUGS, *See* BLACK MARKET; DRUG CARTELS; DRUG TRADE

WEATHER UNDERGROUND, *See* BLACK GUERRILLA FAMILY

WEREWOLF KILLERS, *See* SERIAL MURDER: INTERNATIONAL INCIDENCE; VAMPIRES, WEREWOLVES, AND WITCHES

WHITE ARYAN RESISTANCE

The White Aryan Resistance (commonly known by the acronym WAR) was founded in 1983 by Tom Metzger, a television repairman from Fallbrook, California. He formed WAR to promote both his anti-Semitic, racist views and a philosophy he calls the "third force position," a form of labor-oriented national socialism based on the ideology of Otto and Gregor Strasser, two brothers who led a leftist wing of the German National Socialist movement in the 1920s.

Prior to the establishment of WAR, Metzger's background included membership in several right-wing extremist groups. During the 1960s, he was a member of the John Birch Society. In 1975, Metzger joined David Duke's Knights of the Ku Klux Klan (KKK) and became California's Grand Dragon. During this same time, he was ordained as a minister in the Christian Identity movement.

In the summer of 1980, Metzger broke away from Duke's Knights to form the California Knights of the KKK. In the fall of that same year, Metzger made an unsuccessful bid for Congress. Following his defeat, Metzger left the KKK and formed the White American Political Association (WAPA) to promote "pro-White" candidates for public office.

In 1983, Metzger abandoned his interest in mainstream politics, and his WAPA organization became WAR. It was at this time that Metzger synthesized his ideology to include issues such as racist separatism, left-wing National Socialism, right-wing religiosity, concern for the environment, and contempt for capitalism. One of the most important tenets of Metzger's activism is his support of the "lone wolf" or "leaderless resistance" model (i.e., individual or small-group underground activity versus membership in above-ground organizations), believing that this approach leaves the fewest clues for law enforcement officials, thereby decreasing the risk of being caught. Metzger urges activists never to answer questions posed by law enforcement authorities. His five-word recommended response to law enforcement questioning: "I have nothing to say."

Metzger has actively associated with and provided strategic guidance to and racist networks for the neo-Nazi skinhead movement since it first appeared in the United States in the mid-1980s. Contacts with the skinheads have been primarily made through Metzger's son, John, who has also worked to establish a network of White Student Unions on high school and college campuses to spread the message of WAR and recruit young members.

Metzger has mastered the use of the media to distribute WAR's racist message, including a monthly newsletter *(WAR—White Aryan Resistance)*, videos, books, a telephone hotline, a Web site, a weekly e-mail newsletter, a cable-access television show *(Race and Reason)*, and appearances on nationally syndicated talk shows.

By the late 1980s, because of its coherent, well-documented ideology and innovative use of the media, WAR had positioned itself as a leader among racialist organizations. However, at this same time, things took a negative turn for Metzger and his organization. In November 1988, three skinheads attacked and killed an Ethiopian immigrant, Mulugeta Seraw, on the streets of Portland, Oregon. Investigation into the murder revealed a close connection between WAR and the skinhead gang.

The skinheads who killed Seraw were arrested, tried, and convicted of murder. A civil suit was filed by the Southern Poverty Law Center, in conjunction with the Anti-Defamation League, seeking $7 million for the wrongful death of Seraw. Ultimately, the jury awarded $12.5 million in damages to the Seraw family, making it one of the largest civil verdicts in U.S. history (the judgment was upheld on appeal in 1993). Because of the Seraw civil suit and outcome, WAR's stronghold in the racist movement has weakened.

—Debbie Wray

See also HATE CRIMES; METZGER, TOM; NEO-NAZI
   SKINHEADS; VIGILANTISM; WHITE SUPREMACISTS

Further Reading

Anti-Defamation League (2001). *Tom Metzger/White Aryan Resistance.* Available on the World Wide Web at: http://www.adl.org/learn/Ext_US/Metzger.asp.

Kaplan, J. (Ed.). (2000). *The encyclopedia of white power: A sourcebook on the radical racist right.* Oxford: Alta Mira.

WHITE-COLLAR CRIME,
See AGGRESSION, BIOLOGICAL
AND SOCIOLOGICAL THEORIES

WHITE KNIGHTS

A *knight* is defined as a member of an order or society. "White Knights" are members of the Ku Klux

Klan (KKK), a white supremacist organization originally formed in the United States during the Reconstruction era following the Civil War. Since its inception in 1866 in Pulaski, Tennessee, the KKK has had varying levels of strength and membership, with membership highs reaching 5 million in the 1920s, down to approximately 5,000 members in 2001. The KKK has always been a fragmented organization, with various "realms" (branches) throughout the world. Their factions, however, have had the common goal of maintaining white supremacy over blacks and other minority groups (e.g., Jews, immigrants, homosexuals, non-Protestants, etc.) through intimidation and violence. Active KKK realms include, but are not limited to, the Alabama White Knights, Mississippi White Knights, North Georgia White Knights, Southern White Knights, American Knights, and Knights of the White Camelia.

—Debbie Wray

See also HATE CRIMES; METZGER, TOM; NEO-NAZI
   SKINHEADS; VIGILANTISM; WHITE SUPREMACISTS

WHITE SLAVERY

White slavery is the trafficking in women and girls by use of force, deception, or abuse of authority for purposes of engaging in sexual activity, including deviant sex, for the gratification of paying customers.

The term *white slavery* probably originated at a 1902 conference in Paris, France, on the subject of trafficking in persons. It was used as a means of differentiating between the enslavement of Africans (blacks) and the enslavement of white women and girls who were coerced into lives of prostitution and sexual slavery (indenture). This type of trafficking involves the use of force and deception, that is, the threat of violence, the abuse of authority, or the use of extortion, coercion, or deception, to exploit females sexually for commercial gain. It also involves the relocation and isolation of victims to facilitate the "seasoning" process that prepares the procured woman or girl for the life of a prostitute.

Some trafficked women and girls "service" migrant workers. Others have military personnel as their primary "clients," and others, particularly in countries like Thailand, Korea, and the Philippines, are subjected to the "sex tourism trade."

TRAFFICKING ACTIVITY

White slavery has existed for centuries throughout the world. According to United Nations estimates, white slavery is among the fastest-growing people-trafficking activity in the world today. Women and girls are systematically recruited or transported across boarders for the sex trade. The procurers of these individuals range from family members, to pimps, to organized syndicates. All share the characteristics of violence and coercion in the exploitation of their victims.

Trafficking in Children

The most pernicious form of sex trafficking, also included in the definition of white slavery, is something that has existed for centuries and seems to be proliferating in recent years. Millions of children, primarily girls, are being sexually exploited in the global sex trade. Sexual trafficking in children is difficult to quantify, but according to UNICEF (United Nations International Children's Emergency Fund), more than 1 million children are enslaved in the Asian sex tourism industry. There may be as many as 800,000 child prostitutes in Thailand alone, and 400,000 in India. The Philippines accounts for another 60,000.

A significant amount of exploitation of children is tied to international child pornography. In the United States, men have paid up to $800 for the opportunity to have sex with children as young as 8 years of age. The Internet has enabled pedophiles to have instant access to a "menu" of boys and girls from all over the world, available to satisfy their predilections.

In Japan, young virgin girls are sought out because it is deemed to enhance a man's virility to be the one to "take her virginity." The challenge in Japan is compounded by the social attitude toward prostitution, evidenced by many young girls who use intermittent prostitution to augment their incomes in an increasingly materialistic environment. In Thailand, many men seek out prepubescent girls because of a belief that young girls are less likely to be infected with sexually transmitted diseases, such as HIV.

Profiles of Trafficked Women and Traffickers

Runaways and Throwaways

One of the fastest-growing groups of exploited women and girls are runaways and "throwaways."

These are predominantly girls who have left or been pushed out of their homes. Most of these girls are between the ages of 13 and 16, are predominantly white, and come from both white-collar and blue-collar families. Significantly, research data shows that more than half of runaways have been victims of sexual or physical abuse. Thus, their departure from the home environment cannot actually be viewed as voluntary. In addition, when they end up on the streets, they are prime candidates for the "waiting arms" of predators, such as pimps and hustlers, who entice or coerce them into a life of prostitution.

The methodology used by predators, such as pimps, varies according to the way the predator "reads" a victim and the ease with which she may be "turned out" into a life of prostitution. Some procurers use the befriending or "love" approach; he convinces the victim that he is her friend or is the only one who loves her. This ploy works particularly well with naive, vulnerable, and needy teenage girls or young women who feel flattered at the attention being paid to them by this "man of the world" with the means to lavish gifts on them. Unfortunately, once the victim has been properly enticed, the "lover" pressures her to prove her love for him by "turning a trick" just one time to "help him out." Thereafter, he pressures or threatens her to continue in a life of prostitution. He may even sell her to participate in the sex trade in another state or country.

Pimps

Perhaps the most common perception of a sex procurer is the pimp: someone, usually a male, who is in the business of providing sexual services to a discrete male clientele. These men create a fantasy environment of support, warmth, and security for the individuals they victimize. As indicated above, pimps often lead naive, insecure girls to believe that they are the objects of the affections of someone who really cares for them. Once the victim has developed an attachment to the pimp, he then takes the victim through a process of seasoning to prepare her for life as a prostitute.

The seasoning process may be relatively painless or very violent. Whatever the approach, the pimp usually takes the victim through stages of conditioning, from sexual initiation, in which she is exposed to various sexual acts to desensitize her; to changing her name and her appearance, including, for example, tattooing; then, finally, to engaging in "turning tricks," perhaps at first to "prove how much she loves him." Particularly violent pimps may "break" the victim by repeated raping.

Foreign Models and Entertainers

Sometimes, phony dance companies and employment opportunities are used to entice young girls and women into the sex trade. Advertisements placed in newspapers offer the excitement of employment and opportunity in a foreign country, with no experience necessary. Job contracts and the necessary visa documents are secured. Once the victims arrive at the employment destinations, however, various tactics are used to coerce them into a life of prostitution. They may be told that the job for which they were hired is no longer available but that they still will have to pay off their transportation costs. They may then be offered jobs at bars, only to find that the duties involve more than just hostessing or serving drinks. Sometimes, the process is more direct, in that the victims are subjected to physical violence to ready them for a life of sexual slavery. Often, white women are enticed to apply for jobs in "exotic countries" in the Far East. Once they arrive, they are forced into prostitution to satisfy the sexual perceptions held by many males in the Asian sex market of European and American women.

Organized Syndicates

A significant amount of sex trafficking via the use of phony agencies is done by organizations in places such as Russia, Thailand, and Japan. These syndicates entice women with false advertising and then hold them in indenture to pay off the debt created by the "employment opportunity." This is particularly dangerous for girls who do not have the means to pay for travel or living expenses or the language skills to find jobs. According to the Global Survival Network, various means are used to control the victims. Often, "sex slaves" enter the foreign country on tourist visas and overstay to work off their debts. Passports are confiscated until the debts are worked off; then, most of the girls and young women are isolated from the local society and threatened with deportation because without their passports, they have no means of proving who they are. Thereafter, the cycle of coercion, brutality, and emotional abuse is used to keep the women entrapped in the sex trade.

Purchased Women and Children

A significant number of women and children in underdeveloped and developing countries are coerced into the sex trade after having been sold, either by family members or by procurers who kidnapped them. Agents from India, for example, recruit young girls from Nepal for use in the commercial sex trade in Bombay. Similarly, Burmese girls are brought to Thailand with the assistance of corrupt politicians and are exploited in the sex tourism trade. Indeed, a significant number of children are sold by their parents into the sex tourism trade in places like this.

Some families sell their children with full knowledge of the role they will be required to play; others hand over their daughters to agents who promise to find well-paying jobs for them so that they may help their families back in the rural villages. These agents often give the families sufficient funds as an "advance" to cover 6 months to a year of the anticipated income that the daughters will bring in. Once these girls leave the village and the protection of their families, they are turned over to the sex trade as slaves and required to "work off" the debt owed from the advance given to their parents. For family members who sell their children to agents, needed income is obtained, as well as the freedom from the responsibility of raising the child. For the child, however, what lies before them is a life of violent exploitation via pornography and the varied sexual deviations involved in the sex tourism industry.

International Sex Trafficking

Thailand and the Philippines

A primary beneficiary of "sex tourism" is that significant revenues are generated for Thailand by the promotion of young females to foreign businessmen. These girls are seen as exotic by their clientele and are presented by their procurers as being "ripe for the taking."

As early as the mid-19th century, Thailand provided women to satisfy the sexual appetites of Chinese migrant workers. By 1933, the League of Nations reported Thailand as being a receiving nation for the trafficking in foreign women. In the mid- to late 1960s, the sex trade increased in response to the presence of U.S. military personnel involved in the Vietnam War. Subsequently, the sex tourism industry and the increasing income it provides has driven local and international trafficking in women in Thailand.

As in Thailand, the exploitation of women and girls persists in the Philippines because of the income derived from the sex tourism industry. The presence of military personnel served as a contributing factor, as women and girls were solicited by personnel stationed at the bases.

In both Thailand and the Philippines, the traffic in women often includes not only girls from poverty-stricken areas but also European, Canadian, or American sex slaves who were either abducted, or conned into migrating for employment and forced into slavery to pay off their debts. Asian girls and women are promoted to the European and American clientele, and Europeans and Americans are promoted to the Asian clientele.

Russia

The breakup of the Soviet Union has facilitated an explosion in the exploitation of women from the former Soviet states. The Russian Mafia plays a large role in the deception and coercion of poverty-stricken women into prostitution and domestic servitude in the international sex trade.

Russian traffickers use fronts such as employment agencies, entertainment companies, and marriage agencies to entice women to become entangled in the worldwide sex trade. These women become involved with the traffickers thinking that they will be hired as foreign models or considered as potential mail order brides, only to find themselves beaten, raped, and forced into slavery in places such as Germany, Switzerland, Japan, and the United States.

CONCLUSION

White slavery, the trafficking in females for sex, has existed for centuries. It is now apparently on the increase, particularly in certain "markets" such as Asia. Many factors influence growth in the sex trade: the sex tourism industry in various countries; increasing demand for pornography and other sex industry markets fueled by the growth of the Internet; access to children and young women in third world countries, who are sold or enticed into the sex trade as a means of providing income for their families; and the demand for younger children to avoid the risks of HIV infection. Quite clearly, the worldwide growth in child sex slavery alone is cause for international concern. It is essential that countries cooperate in enacting and enforcing international laws against such practices.

—*Arthur V. N. Wint*

See also CYBERSTINGS; EXPLOITATION OF CHILDREN; PEDOPHILE ORGANIZATIONS; ORGANIZED CRIME; RAPE; SEXUAL OFFENSES

Further Reading

Barry, K. (1979). *Female sexual slavery.* Englewood Cliffs, NJ: Prentice Hall.

Campagna, D. S., & Poffenberger, D. L. (1988). *The sexual trafficking in children.* Dover, MA: Auburn.

Flowers, R. B. (1998). *The prostitution of women and girls.* Jefferson, NC: McFarland.

O'Callaghan, S. (1968). *The yellow slave trade.* London: Anthony Blond.

Skrobanek, S., Boonpakdee, N., & Jantateero, C. (1997). *The traffic in women: Human realities of the international sex trade.* London: Zed Books.

Williams, P. (Ed.). (1999). *Illegal immigration and commercial sex: The new slave trade.* Portland, OR: Frank Cass.

WHITE SUPREMACISTS

White supremacists follow a doctrine that believes in the superiority of the white race over races of color. This view moves beyond prejudice by claiming that the white race is "supreme" above all others and, as such, should have power over nonwhite groups. The bigotry of white supremacists has expanded over time, targeting groups for other reasons than race (e.g., homosexuals).

One of the earliest and most influential racist thinkers was Joseph Arthur comte de Gobineau, a 19th-century French writer and diplomat. His four-volume *Essay on the Inequality of Human Races* professed that the white race was superior over all others and that Aryans (i.e., the Germanic people) were at the pinnacle of it. Gobineau theorized that a civilization's fate is determined by its racial composition and that the white race would flourish only if it was not tainted by mixing with nonwhite races. Gobineau's theories influenced and inspired other scholars and political leaders in the 19th and 20th centuries, including Friedrich Nietzsche and Adolph Hitler.

The white supremacy movement gained momentum in the United States in the late 1860s with the organization of the Ku Klux Klan (KKK), one of the most recognized white supremacist groups. Originally formed as a social club, it soon transformed into a violent resistance group aimed at restoring white power after the Civil War and keeping basic civil rights (such as the right to vote) away from blacks. Over the years, the KKK has had fluctuations in both its strength and numbers. Today, it is a very fractured organization, with total membership estimated at around 5,000; however, its message of hate has expanded to include not only blacks, but Jews, homosexuals, immigrants, and non-Protestants.

Although the KKK is the most notorious of the white supremacist hate groups, there are other more powerful, globally linked groups and movements in existence that provide platforms for hate-filled rhetoric and a call to violent action. These include Christian Identity, the National Alliance, Aryan Nations, the National Socialist White People's Party, the World Church of the Creator (WCOTC), neo-Nazi skinheads, The Order, and the White Aryan Resistance (WAR). No two groups are the same, but their basic, common ideology, whether based in racism, politics and/or religion, is to create a society that is dominated by whites and denies the rights of nonwhites and other groups.

Violence is the hallmark of these white supremacist organizations. The anti-Semitic WCOTC, believing that the federal government, international banking, and media are under Jewish control, supports a racial holy war (or RAHOWA) to rid the world of "mud races." Courses in urban terrorism and guerrilla warfare are offered by the Aryan Nations at their various summer festivals. They also participate in prison outreach programs, corresponding with prisoners through newsletters and correspondence. This has led to an offshoot of their organization, the Aryan Brotherhood, a network of prison gang members.

One of the most violent factions of the white supremacist movement is the neo-Nazi skinheads. They have been linked to numerous murder and assault crimes against blacks, Hispanics, Asians, homosexuals, and even the homeless. The skinheads have become firmly established within the ranks of other white supremacist groups, such as the Aryan Nations and WAR.

White supremacists continue to recruit new members, spreading their gospel of hate and committing acts of violence to promote their cause.

—*Debbie Wray*

See also Gangs; Hate Crimes; History of Violence in Religions; Neo-Nazi Skinheads; Vigilantism; White Aryan Resistance

Further Reading

Ross, L. J. (1995). *White supremacy in the 1990s.* Available on the World Wide Web at: http://www.publiceye.org/eyes/whitsup.html.

WHITMAN, CHARLES, *See* Mass Murder; Spree Murders

WAYNE WILLIAMS

Between 1980 and 1981, the residents of Atlanta lived in growing fear and outrage as a serial killer methodically hunted their children. The body count reached 22 victims before the killer was apprehended. They ranged in age from 7 to 28, and most were young males. Some were shot or strangled; others were stabbed, bludgeoned, or suffocated. All the victims were black. The deaths of so many black young people gave rise to a variety of theories and accusations, including the belief in a plot by white supremacists to systematically kill all black children. Others began to think the children were being killed by Satan worshippers, blood cultists, or even copycat murderers. The Ku Klux Klan came under close scrutiny, but no link could be made between their members and any of the murders. Atlanta resembled a city under siege and inevitably attracted the attention of the entire country, including the resources of the federal government.

It appeared the murders would never stop, until one night, as police staked out a bridge over the Chattahoochee River, they heard a car on the bridge come to a stop, followed by the distinct splash of something being dropped into the river. They stopped Wayne B. Williams, 23, for questioning and finally arrested him as a suspect in the child murder cases. Williams was found to be a bright, young black man who lived with his retired parents and involved himself in photography. A media and police "groupie," Williams often listened on his shortwave radio and responded to ambulance, fire, and police emergency calls. He then sold his exclusive pictures to the local newspapers. At age 18, he was arrested for impersonating a police officer. He spent 1 year at Georgia State University but dropped out when he felt his "rising star" was moving too slowly.

Williams's freelance work as a cameraman was never steady, and he began to focus his energies on music. As a self-employed talent scout, he eventually lured his victims into his control. He was known to distribute leaflets offering "private and free" interviews to blacks between the ages of 11 and 21 who sought a career in music. At his trial, Williams was depicted as a man who hated his own race and wanted to eliminate future generations. He was described as a homosexual or a bisexual who paid young boys to have sex with him. A boy, 15, claimed he had been molested by Williams, and several witnesses testified they had seen him with some of the victims.

Williams denied everything, and the prosecution had only elaborate forensics on which to base their case against him. The forensic evidence suggested a distinct link between Williams and at least 10 of the homicides and indicated a pattern surrounding the murders. The judge ruled the evidence admissible, and Williams was found guilty of murdering two of his older victims, Nathaniel Cater, 27, and Ray Payne, 21. Because of the nature of the circumstantial evidence, the judge sentenced Williams to two consecutive life sentences. He was eventually named as being responsible for 24 of the Atlanta slayings, although some believe the child killings have not ended with Williams's arrest.

—*Eric W. Hickey*

Portions of this entry are drawn from *Serial Murderers and Their Victims*, 3rd edition (2002) by E. W. Hickey, published by Wadsworth: Belmont, CA.

See also FORENSIC SCIENCE; SERIAL MURDER

WILSON, JAMES, *See* MASS MURDER

WOMEN AND VIOLENCE

Although *violence against women* and *violence by women* are seemingly disparate topics, they are linked

not only by the obvious (gender) but in other ways as well. For example, women are victimized by intimates and friends at a high rate and are also more likely to victimize those with whom they are intimate. In many cases, women's victimizers and victims may be different people, but sometimes they are one and the same. In domestic violence, for example, women's violence is retaliation against the violence that has been perpetrated upon them. Both violence against women and violence by women can be linked by a theory of aggression that accounts for the interaction between both the individual and societal antecedents of violence.

VIOLENCE AGAINST WOMEN

Historically, violence against women had gone largely unnoticed and unspoken, but in recent years, it has become a topic of great concern. As then Senator Joseph Biden (1993) wrote:

If the leading newspapers were to announce tomorrow a new disease, that over the past year, had afflicted from 3 to 4 million citizens, few would fail to appreciate the seriousness of the illness. Yet, when it comes to the 3 to 4 million women who are victimized by violence each year, the alarms ring softly (p. 1059).

Throughout their lifetimes, women are at risk of becoming victims of every form of criminal violence. The APA Task Force on Male Violence Against Women conceptualized violence on a continuum ranging from coercive uses of power in a nonphysical sense (e.g., threatening one's job through sexual harassment) to abuses of power in a physical sense (e.g., incest, rape, domestic violence). Although females can be victimized in many ways and at any age, here, only physical forms of violence against adult women will be discussed.

In recent years, the violent victimization rates of men and women have converged. In 1973, women's likelihood of victimization was less than half that of men, but by 1994, women were approximately two thirds as likely as men to be victims of violent crimes (Craven, 1996). This was propelled by a decrease in violence against men and a stable or slightly increasing rate of violence against women. However, for both fatal and nonfatal violence, women were at higher risk from intimate others than were men. Only 23% of women indicated that the offenders who victimized them were strangers, compared with 49% the of men who indicated their victimizers were strangers (Craven, 1996).

Using data gathered from the National Crime Victim Survey (NCVS), Greenfeld (1997) reported that in most cases, sexual assault (by both intimates and non-intimates) is a crime committed against a female by a male; 99 of 100 rapists are male and 91% of the victims are female. One of the most striking characteristics of sexual assault is that although people of all ages are victimized, in a high percentage of cases, the victims are young women. In fact, the per capita rate of sexual assault is highest among those in the 16- to 19-year-old age range (Greenfeld, 1997). The number of sexual assaults has been decreasing in recent years; still, in 1995, there was one violent offense for every 625 residents. However, of the approximately 355,000 rapes and sexual assaults experienced in 1995, only 113,000 were reported to the authorities (Greenfeld, 1997). Many cases of sexual assault are also accompanied by other physical injuries. For example, about 40% of rape victims suffer some additional injury, and 5% suffer a major injury in addition to the rape (Greenfeld, 1997).

Public awareness of intimate partner violence has increased dramatically in recent years, in part due to an increase in research. However, research results have at times been contradictory because of different sampling procedures, different populations, and different methods of inquiry. Thus, statistics on the incidence and nature of intimate partner violence vary greatly, depending on the source of the information. As with data on all forms of sexual assault (i.e., by intimates and nonintimates), numbers based on official reports may be an underestimate. Unlike sexual assault, however, there is debate as to how many victims are male and how many are female, but there is widespread agreement that female victims of domestic violence are most likely to be injured. In fact, for every 75 men killed by their spouses or intimate others, 100 women are killed by the same (Greenfeld, 1997).

The National Violence Against Women Survey (NVAWS) indicates the pervasiveness of intimate partner violence in U.S. society and the higher likelihood of female victimization. This survey, which was administered in the context of personal safety rather than crime, indicates higher victimization rates than previous surveys. This may be because in earlier studies and surveys (NCVS, for example), violence was included only when the victims had labeled it as criminal and were willing to report it as such.

The NVAWS data indicates that 25% of the women surveyed and 7.6% of the men surveyed said they had been raped or sexually assaulted by a current or former spouse (Tjaden & Thoennes, 2000). The actual numbers are higher than these percentages suggest because many people are assaulted more than once, elevating the number of intimate partner rapes and sexual assaults against women to approximately 4.8 million annually. In contrast, the number of intimate partner rapes and sexual assaults against men is approximately 2.9 million annually (Tjaden & Thoennes, 2000). The perpetrators of the violence, however, are primarily men. Although more data is needed, survey results suggest that women living with women experience less intimate partner violence than do men, and men living with men experience almost twice the intimate violence reported by men who live with women (Tjaden & Thoennes, 2000).

Interestingly, intimate partner violence varies greatly by racial ethnic category (Tjaden & Thoennes, 2000). Native American women and Alaska native women report the highest rates of intimate partner violence, with 37.5% reporting victimization over the course of a lifetime. The groups with the lowest rate of victimization, Asian and Pacific Islanders, report a lifetime victimization of only 15%. Caucasian and African American women report a victimization rate between these two groups at 24.8% and 29.1%, respectively. The comparison between Hispanic and non-Hispanic women revealed little difference in overall rates of victimization by intimate others but were more likely to have reported rape by an intimate other. This is interesting in light of previous data that Hispanic women are less likely to report rape by a nonintimate.

Overall, statistics support the notion that intimate violence is more likely to be perpetrated by men against women and that it is more likely to result in injury than is violence by women against men. Violence against women is best described as part of a larger picture that begins with verbal abuse and seems to have its roots in a social structure that has historically encouraged males to be dominant and females to be submissive.

VIOLENT WOMEN

Historically, aggression by women was as ignored as was violence against women. Women were considered too weak in both a mental and physical sense to be dangerous. Moreover, social and cultural expectations limited them to roles in which they were expected to be submissive. Despite this, women engaged in violent behaviors then and continue to do so today. In recent years, however, increased attention has been directed toward understanding the nature of women's aggression. For example, we have learned that in the majority of cases, violence committed by women (particularly violence that is extreme in nature) is perpetrated against intimate others. We have also learned that the women who perpetrate such violence are unlike their male counterparts in many ways.

Crime Rates

The most recent Sourcebook of Criminal Justice Statistics (U.S. Department of Justice, 2000) indicates that in the year 2000, more than 72,000 women were arrested for violent crimes, including murder, nonnegligent manslaughter, forcible rape, robbery, and aggravated assault. Violent crime continues to occur at discomforting rates, but many do not recognize that rates of violent crime have actually been falling in recent years. In fact, the number of women arrested annually for violent crimes has actually decreased almost every year since 1995, when more than 92,000 females were arrested and charged with violent offenses.

Despite the recent decreases in arrests for violent crime, every year, offenses committed by women account for a larger percentage of all violent crimes committed. For example, females were arrested for slightly more than 13% of all violent crimes in 1993 but nearly 17.5% of violent crimes in 2000 (most recent statistics available; U.S. Department of Justice, 2000). Despite committing fewer violent crimes, women's contribution to the total percentage of violent crime arrests continues to rise. This is because the numbers of violent crimes committed by males is decreasing dramatically every year, at a greater rate than the decrease seen in violent crimes committed by women. Specifically, recent statistics from 1998 to 1999 reflect a 4.4% decrease in female arrests for violent crimes but a 6.6% decrease in male arrests for the same period (U.S. Department of Justice, 2000).

In sum, these statistics indicate that female criminality in general remains a problem, particularly as violent crimes committed by females have not shown the same decreases over time that have been seen with males.

Characteristics of Female Criminality

Recent attention to female criminality has led to increased study about the nature of women and violence. This research helps to shed light on the characteristics of the victims of crime, the perpetrators of crime, and the nature of the criminal offenses themselves.

The targets of women's violence are most often those with whom the offender has had interpersonal relationships (i.e., intimate, relative, acquaintance). Some literature indicates that the most common victim of a woman's violence is her significant other (i.e., sexual partner), with the next most frequent victim being her child/children. Reasons cited for the commission of violent behavior by women range from mental illness (in the case of child abuse) to self-defense (in the case of domestic abuse, often following repeated instances of being the target of violence herself).

The typical age at which the violent woman commits such acts differs, on average, depending on the lethality of the act. Women who commit nonfatal violent acts, such as simple assault and robbery, tend to be younger, whereas women committing fatal crimes tend to be older. Thus, nonlethal acts of violence were most likely to be committed by those less than 25 years of age, whereas the perpetrators of lethal acts of violence tended to be 25 years old or older. The likely exception to this trend, however, is in the case of neonaticide (i.e., the killing of an infant less than 24 hours old), in which a younger mother is generally responsible for such deadly violence. Also, violent women generally tend to have abbreviated criminal histories compared with other offenders (e.g., nonviolent offenders).

The Bureau of Justice Statistics (BJS; Greenfeld & Snell, 1999) indicated that slightly over half of all violent crimes reported between 1993 and 1997 occurred when the perpetrator was alone with the victim, with 40% of violent acts occurring in the presence of another female and 8% in the presence of a male. Females used weapons in the commission of approximately 15% of violent acts (Greenfeld & Snell, 1999). About half the acts of violence occurred near the victim's residence or educational institution (Greenfeld & Snell, 1999). Finally, less than half of the violent offenders (approximately 40%) were reported to have been under the influence of substances at the time of their crime (Greenfeld & Snell, 1999).

Some literature indicates that compared with women of other races, African American females tend to commit the majority of violent crimes (cf. Rumgay, 1999). Proposed reasons for this racial disparity in violent criminality include African Americans' disparate exposure to poverty and the stresses most commonly associated with this, including a history of violent victimization, exposure to violent models, and the availability of drugs. Although a higher percentage of African Americans than Caucasians are arrested for crimes when compared with their respective numbers in the general population, there is little evidence to suggest that African American offenders are committing the actual majority of crimes. Greenfeld and Snell (1999) recently published a report indicating that more than 50% of violent female offenders committing crimes between 1993 and 1997 were Caucasian, whereas only about 35% were African American. Moreover, although approximately equal numbers of Caucasian and African American females committed robbery and aggravated assaults between 1993 and 1997, African Americans in general committed only 30%, whereas Caucasians committed approximately 58%. Thus, the perception that African American females are indeed the primary perpetrators of violence is not supported by this data. However, there is one type of crime in which African Americans outnumber Caucasian females: homicide. Approximately 60% of female offenders committing homicide were African American (Greenfeld & Snell, 1999). Perhaps it is because African American women commit more of the most violent of crimes (i.e., murder) that a misperception of racial disparity in the commission of all violent crimes has arisen in literature.

Between 1993 and 2000, female-perpetrated homicide arrest rates declined annually. For example, women were responsible for more than 1,900 murders and cases of nonnegligent manslaughter in 1993 (9.4% of total homicides that year); 1,581 in 1995 (9.5% of total); 1,317 in 1997 (10.3% of total); and 926 in 2000 (10.6% of total; U.S. Department of Justice, 2000). However, it is evident from these statistics that although the number of annual arrests for homicide has been declining, the percentage of murder and manslaughter committed by females has continued to rise. Again, this reflects the fact that the number of homicides committed by males is decreasing at a greater rate than that of female-perpetrated homicides.

In addition to the difference in rates of murder, there is a clear difference in victim-offender relationships seen between males who kill and females who kill. According to the BJS (Greenfeld & Snell, 1999), whereas spousal murders accounted for 6.8% of all murders committed by men from 1976 to 1997, spousal murders accounted for 28.3% of all female homicides during that period. Likewise, girlfriends were the victims in 3.9% of male-perpetrated murders, whereas boyfriends were the victims in 14% of female-perpetrated murders. Similarly, in 2.2% of male homicides, the perpetrator's victim was a child or stepchild, whereas children and stepchildren accounted for 10.4% of female-perpetrated murders. However, when the murder victim is a stranger, male perpetrator rates (25.1%) drastically exceed female perpetrator rates (7.2%). Interestingly, nonfamilial acquaintances accounted for the largest percentage of victims of murder as committed by both males (54.6%) and females (31.9%), respectively, between 1976 and 1997. However, although women kill a higher percentage of intimate others, the absolute number of people killed by women (59,996) pales in comparison to the number of homicides attributed to men (395,446) in the same time period, 1976 to 1997 (Greenfeld & Snell, 1999).

In approximately 36,000 murders occurring over a period of 21 years, women targeted intimates or relatives. This number represents about 60% of the total number of homicides committed by women over that period of time (Greenfeld & Snell, 1999). In instances when women kill, they are likely to focus their violence toward a single victim, likely to commit such violence in the home, and are most likely to do so when there are no individuals other than the victim present in the home (Rumgay, 1999). In more than a few cases, the homicide victims are children.

The killing of a child is generally categorized as either neonaticide, the killing of an infant within 24 hours after birth, or filicide/infanticide, the killing of an infant who is at least 1 day old. In their study, Mendlowicz et al. (1998) found that mothers committing neonaticide were more likely to be younger, unmarried, and undereducated, with fewer prior pregnancies and greater nondesirability of the pregnancy, than were a comparison group of mothers who did not kill their infants within a day of delivery. Mothers committing neonaticide are generally in denial about their pregnancy and may attempt to conceal their pregnancies throughout term, leading to a greater likelihood that such births will occur outside a hospital setting.

Filicide, on the other hand, was generally committed by those mothers who were either mentally ill or who accidentally/impulsively killed their children, sometimes in the process of abusing them. Mental illness (e.g., severe depression or psychosis) leading to filicide might result in the killing of more than one child on a single occasion. When filicide was accidental and more impulsive in nature, the female perpetrator was likely to have been the sole provider of care for the child with little support of any kind (i.e., financial, parenting skills training) from family or the community, and the violence was likely to occur during particularly stressful times. From 1976 to 1997, mothers and stepmothers committed approximately 5,500 filicides, with slightly over half the victims (52%) being male (Greenfeld & Snell, 1999).

Overall, statistics support that although women commit less violent crimes than men do, they are still responsible for many and varied acts of aggression. Despite trends in the last decade that have seen annual decreases in both violent crime rates and homicide rates, the percentage of these crimes committed by women continues to rise yearly. In other words, female violent crime is not decreasing to the same degree that male-perpetrated crime is. In sum, female violence remains a problem in need of social attention.

THEORY

How can violence against women and violence by women be explained? Is there a single theory that accounts for both? The "algebra of aggression" (Megargee, 2002) may be able to explain these two disparate phenomena. The algebra of aggression describes behavior as a result of the complex interactions between personal and social factors and attempts to explain how the choice is made between aggressive and nonaggressive behavior. The five factors in the algebra of aggression are instigation to aggression, habit strength, inhibitions against aggression, situational factors, and reaction potential. Together, these constructs help to explain aggressive acts, and each will be examined in the context of violence committed against and by women, respectively.

In the case of violent behavior against women, a would-be male rapist will serve as an example of how Megargee's (2002) factors interact. The first variable, *instigation to aggression,* includes both intrinsic instigation to aggression (also described as anger or hostility) and extrinsic instigation to aggression.

Intrinsic aggression is personal in nature and may be the result of, among other things, a genetic predisposition or a psychological cause such as frustration or unreasonable expectations. Extrinsic instigation to aggression may include personal gain and satisfaction or achieving power. In the case of a rapist, he may exhibit both intrinsic (e.g., unreasonable expectations about his entitlements) and extrinsic (e.g., satisfaction from exerting power over another person) instigators.

The second factor, *habit strength,* acquired by reinforcement of an individual response or by the secondary reinforcement of observing violence in the media, can be easily understood in the case of rape. The rapist is directly reinforced by exerting power over a woman and indirectly reinforced by seeing depictions of violence against women in the media. The third factor, *inhibitions against aggression,* is difficult to assess, but includes concerns that the aggression will fail or that there will be negative consequences for the action. Thus, a rapist might be inhibited in a certain circumstance by the presence of witnesses who could lead to retribution. The fourth construct, *situational factors,* such as the availability of drugs and alcohol, the availability of a victim, and the presence of bystanders, are important determinants of aggression. For example, the rapist will be less likely to rape in the middle of the day in a crowded park. The final factor, *reaction potential* (i.e., response competition), explains that an aggressive act is possible when the aggressive act is the one that would satisfy the most needs at the least cost to the aggressor.

Violence by women can be explained in a similar way. In the case of a woman who murders her abusive spouse, the same factors can be considered. Although the victim of domestic abuse may have low intrinsic instigation to aggression, her extrinsic instigation may be high, in that she may engage in violence to protect herself from further abuse. Although habit strength would be low, this does not guarantee a lack of aggression, congruent with the concept of overcontrolled hostility. In their study of female offenders, Verona and Carbonell (2000) found that some women in prison demonstrated a pattern of onetime violence. These women had shorter criminal histories, scored higher on a measure of overcontrolled hostility, and were more likely to have committed an extremely violent crime than were nonviolent or repeat violent offenders. The overcontrolled hostility would be perhaps part of the intrinsic instigation. The situational factors may be of great importance here, as protecting one's life in the long run, protecting children, or perhaps an overcoming of the inhibitions against aggression. Once again, if aggression will satisfy the most needs with the least cost, it will become a possibility.

Thus, both violence against women and violence by women may be explained in the same way: by examining the interaction between social, cultural, and individual factors. The history of women as possessions, and thus their protection, may underlie their vulnerability to becoming victims of violence. This may also be the reason behind the higher probability of women engaging in intimate violence. As women's roles were primarily in the home, this may have lead to the high rates of female-perpetrated violent behavior occurring in the home. Given these common roots, the solutions to both violence against women and violence by women may be found in social and cultural change as well as personal interventions.

—Joyce L. Carbonell and Lorraine R. Reitzel

See also AGGRESSION; BATTERERS AND ABUSIVE PARTNERS; CHILD KILLERS; DOMESTIC VIOLENCE; FAMILY HOMICIDE; GENDER VIOLENCE; POISONERS; RAPE; VICTIMOLOGY; VIOLENT FEMALE JUVENILE OFFENDERS

Further Reading

Biden, J. Jr. (1993). Violence against women. *American Psychologist, 48,* 1059-1069.

Craven, D. (1996, December). *Female victims of violent crime* (Report No. NCJ-162602). Washington, DC: U.S. Department of Justice.

Goodman, L. A., Koss, M. P., Fitzgerald, L. F., Russo, N. F., & Keita, G. P. (1993). Male violence against women: Current research and future directions. *American Psychologist, 48,* 1054-1058.

Greenfeld, L. A. (1997, February). *Sex offenses and offenders: An analysis of data on rape and sexual assault* (Report No. NCJ-163392). Washington, DC: U.S. Department of Justice.

Greenfeld, L. A., & Snell, T. L. (1999, December). *Women offenders* (Report No. NCJ-175688). Washington, DC: U.S. Department of Justice.

Megargee, E. I. (2002). Assessing the risk of aggression and violence. In J. Butcher (Ed.), *Clinical assessment: Practical approaches* (2nd ed., pp. 435-451). New York: Oxford University Press.

Mendlowicz, M. V., Rapaport, M. H., Mecler, K., Golshan, S., & Moraes, T. M. (1998). A case-control study on the socio-demographic characteristics of 53 neonaticidal mothers. *International Journal of Law and Psychiatry, 21,* 209-219.

Rumgay, J. (1999). Violent women: Building knowledge-based intervention strategies. In H. Kemshall & J. Prichard (Eds.), *Good practice in working with violence* (pp. 106-127). Philadelphia: Jessica Kingsley Publishers.

Tjaden, R., & Thoennes, N. (2000, July). *Extent, nature and consequences of intimate partner violence: Findings from the National Violence Against Women Survey* (Report No. NCJ-181867). Washington, DC: U.S. Department of Justice.

U.S. Department of Justice. (2000). *Sourcebook of Criminal Justice Statistics* [CD-ROM] (Report No. NCJ-191914). Washington, DC: Author.

Verona, E., & Carbonell, J. L. (2000). Female violence and personality: Evidence for a pattern of overcontrolled hostility among onetime violent offenders. *Criminal Justice and Behavior, 27,* 176-195.

Warren, J. I., & Kovnick, J. (1999). Women who kill. In V. B. Van Hasselt & M. Hersen (Eds.), *Handbook of psychological approaches with violent offenders: Contemporary strategies and issues* (pp. 189-204). New York: Kluwer Academic/Plenum.

WOOD, CATHERINE, AND GWENDOLYN GRAHAM, *See* SIGNATURE KILLERS; TEAM KILLERS

WOODHAM, LUKE, *See* SCHOOL SHOOTINGS

WORKPLACE VIOLENCE AND HOMICIDE

Since the 1980s, workplace violence has become a growing concern for employees as well as their employers. The term "going postal" has been used to describe disgruntled employees who seek revenge on their employers, releasing their frustration on their coworkers and supervisors through acts of lethal rage. However, this type of workplace violence, which is sensationalized by the media, represents only a small percentage of violent incidents occurring in the workplace.

VIOLENT WORKPLACE INCIDENTS

United States

The Bureau of Labor and Statistics (BLS) Census of Fatal Occupational Injuries (CFOI) gathers and reports data on fatal incidents involving workplace violence in the United States. Since the 1980s, violence in the workplace has shown a considerable increase, with work-related homicide at the highest rate ever in 1994. However, over the past 6 years, the occurrence of fatal incidents involving workplace violence has seen a substantial decline. This is partly due to the increased awareness of the problem and the development of prevention programs. Employers and employees are more aware of the dangers and warning signs of potential violence, and preventative actions are taken more frequently.

In 2000, the preliminary data captured by BLS show that there were approximately 5,915 fatalities in the work environment per 100,000 workers. Of those, 10.1% were classified as homicides, which represents 599 homicides per 100,00 workers. This figure is up slightly from the previous year, recording 585 homicides, which represents 9.6% of the total fatalities. In 1999, there were 6,054 fatalities in the workplace per 100,000 workers. Figure 1 shows data from 1992 through 2000 on work-related homicide in the United States.

In addition to data collected on fatal incidents due to violence in the workplace, the BLS reported approximately 5,650,100 nonfatal injuries and illnesses occurring in the workplace in 2000. These

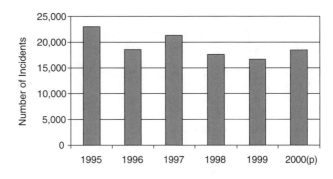

Figure 2   Nonfatal Injuries and Illnesses Related to Violent Incidents in the Workplace in the United States (1995-2000)

figures have shown a decrease over the past 5 years. Nonfatal injuries involving assaults and violent acts resulted in 18,418 reported incidents for 2000. This is up from the previous year of 16,644 reported incidents. Over the past 6 years, data show that assaults and violent acts appear to be decreasing. Because the numbers are sporadic from year to year, tracking of future data will determine whether a pattern is developing. Figure 2 shows data collected on nonfatal injuries and illnesses in the workplace involving assaults and violent acts from 1995 through 2000 in the United States.

Workplace violence encompasses not only single acts of homicides and mass murders in the work environment but has also been defined to include threats, assaults, bodily injury, rape, and harassment. A growing concern in the workplace is the potential of terrorist attacks, such as the attacks that took place on September 11, 2001. Four jetliners were hijacked by terrorists; two planes were flown into the twin towers of the World Trade Center in New York, killing thousands in the 100-plus story buildings, as well as the flight crew, and passengers. A third plane crashed into the Pentagon, in Washington, D.C., killing workers within the building and everyone on the plane. The fourth plane, which crashed in the Pennsylvania countryside, is believed to have been destined for the White House.

This event created unrest across the nation, as well as causing great fear for those who continued to carry on their work in environments vulnerable to such attacks. These terrorist acts will permanently change the way security is enforced in the work environment.

Another type of violence seen in the workplace is the attack and sabotage of computer files and

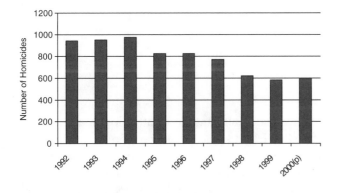

Figure 1   Work-Related Homicide in the United States (1992-2000).

programs. Although this is not associated with physical injury to a person, the infectious nature of a computer virus can delete vital records and cause major problems in the work environment and for an organization as a whole.

International Settings

Workplace violence is seen in other countries as well, referred to in Australia, the United Kingdom, and Canada as "bullying." Australia is experiencing such incidents as a backlash from corporate downsizing, government cutbacks, and increased poverty levels. Canada is experiencing similar conditions as in the United States. Several third world countries are experiencing workplace violence in the form of terrorist attacks. Suicide terrorists in the Middle East sacrifice themselves as human bombs, resulting in injuries and death to those near and around them in public places, such as restaurants, stores, and other businesses. This type of attack may not be the most common cause of homicides within the workplace, but the threat of it causes severe distress.

CHARACTERISTICS OF WORKPLACE VIOLENCE

Workplace violence is the second leading cause of occupational fatality (transportation accidents are the first). To understand the dynamics of this type of fatality, there must be an understanding of many factors and circumstances.

Victims in the Workplace

Individuals involved in high-risk jobs or who work in high-risk environments are at a greater risk of becoming victims. Taxi drivers run the highest risk of work-related homicide. Of the transportation fatalities reported by the BLS, cabdrivers represented 70% of the deaths caused by assaults and violent acts. Of the fatalities in retail stores, such as liquor stores and convenience stores, 47% of the homicides were workers. Of the law enforcement fatalities, 22% occurred as a result of violence in the workplace.

Men disproportionately represent 92% of all fatalities in the workplace overall, though half the modern workforce is made up of women. Workers between the ages of 24 and 54 are at a higher risk for workplace violence, and Asian American and African American employees are also at a disproportionately higher risk of becoming victims.

Occupational Settings and Circumstances

Workplace violence can occur in any business, but most tend to occur in a specific type of environment. Not only is the setting an important element in determining the risk for violence, the type of business conducted also contributes to the vulnerability of attacks and injuries. Businesses that engage in sales and cash transactions and maintain only limited staff on work shifts are at higher risk for violent attacks. More then two thirds of workplace violence occurs in the form of robbery. Convenience stores are particularly vulnerable because of accessibility, and proximity to major highways.

Twenty-one percent of violent incidents in the workplace take place between 8 p.m. and 12 a.m., yet time frames between 8 a.m. to 12 p.m.; 12 p.m. to 4 p.m.; and 4 p.m. to 8 p.m. represent almost equal percentages. In other words, it is difficult to distinguish what the most critical time frames are, and the timing probably has as much to do with the circumstances in establishments, as mentioned, such as gas stations and convenience stores, which are usually minimally staffed and conduct cash transactions.

As mentioned, taxi driving is the highest-ranking occupation among homicides associated with fatalities in the workplace. Cabdrivers are extremely vulnerable because they work alone, their transactions are frequently in cash, and their shifts can run late into the night, often driving to secluded and unsafe areas.

Law enforcement officers and detectives work in violent environments and are extremely vulnerable, facing dangerous and volatile situations that can turn deadly with little warning. Fortunately, many advances have been made in protecting officers from harm and fatal injuries.

Perpetrators

A considerable amount of attention is given to the offenders in workplace violence who are perceived to have exhausted all avenues of rationalization only to release their destructive and often fatal outbursts. In the 1980s, United States postal worker Patrick Sherill went on a rampage, killing 14 of his coworkers in a shooting spree at his workplace and wounding

6 others. Airline worker David Burke was fired from his job and later smuggled a firearm onto a plane, where he is believed to have fired off 6 rounds once the plane was in midair; all 43 passengers were killed in the crash. In Sunnyvale, California, a male worker shot and killed seven of his coworkers because he was upset that a female coworker had turned down his advances.

Fortunately, this type of violence by disgruntled employees represents a small percentage of fatalities in the workplace, though the media notoriously sensationalize such events all out of proportion. In 2000, the BLS reported that 10.1% of the fatalities in the workplace were the result of homicides, and the most predominant causes of these fatalities were robberies or other crimes. From 1992 to 1998, homicides at the hands of coworkers represented just 7% of the homicides in the workplace.

As in any crime, a perpetrator's characteristics comprise biological, sociological, and psychological components, which determine their threshold of frustration and ability to control their behavior. Violent attacks in the workplace demonstrate a lack of self-control as an individual feels pushed to the edge, where any behavior inhibitors are depleted and the frustration becomes uncontrollable.

Motivating Factors

The motivating factors that cause a person to commit lethal violence in the workplace are varied, but most incidents are related to criminal activities. The BLS reports that robberies were the most common circumstance for homicides, the motivating factor being financial gain such as monies or property. Other motivating factors in coworkers or past coworkers were rage and anger, representing 9% of the fatalities. Domestically related factors were responsible for 5% of the fatalities in the workplace, and dissatisfied customers represented 6% of the homicides.

PREVENTION MEASURES

The Occupational Safety and Health Administration (OSHA) has developed guidelines within the health care and social service organizations for policies and practices to be implemented concerning violence in the workplace. These guidelines can be carried over to different types work environments by adjusting them to the specific needs of the organization: (a) Have a workplace policy addressing the prevention of violence;

(b) identify contributing factors of potentially violent situations; (c) train staff how to defuse escalating incidents that have the potential to become volatile; (d) staff should be aware of cultural issues; and (e) written procedures should be in place as to the necessary actions in the case of a violent incident.

The employer's first step in taking action toward workplace violence is the initial screening of potential employees. Policy and procedures should be reviewed with potential employees, including the discipline policy, such as a probation period that could result in termination should the employee not be able to meet the agency's needs.

The second step is to create and implement a policy and procedure plan with "zero tolerance" toward violence in the workplace and see that the policy is strictly enforced. A comprehensive written plan should be developed detailing the agency's philosophy on violence and detailed actions to be taken in the event of such occurrence. Employees, including management and supervisors, should be thoroughly trained on the details of workplace violence and expectations. All staff should be thoroughly trained on how to assess and appropriately respond to potentially violent situations.

Preventative measures must also be addressed by changing patterns of behavior in the workplace, as well as the physical environment. To begin this task, risk factors must first be addressed. As mentioned, some work settings are more susceptible than others to violence.

Businesses handling cash transactions should seek ways to limit the amount of money carried by workers or in cash registers. Posting signs stating that the clerk carries limited monies may deter criminals, as the monetary gain may not outweigh the potential risk of arrest. Cashless transactions available to customers for direct payment of services or goods, such as ATM machines and credit card payment, can also reduce the potential for criminal acts.

Face-to-face contact with clients and customers increases the risk of potential attacks. Creating a barrier, such as a bulletproof glass window, can reduce physical attacks on employees. Agencies can develop policies on how clients are seen, such as setting up a reception area and conducting initial screenings of customers prior to contact. Having the presence of a security guard in a secured area where customers or clients come through can also assist in reducing and preventing potential violence.

The physical makeup of a workplace environment must also be considered. An assessment of the workplace surroundings should be conducted, paying careful attention to the parking areas and the lighting available, the location of dumpsters or trash receptacles that must be accessed by employees, and the number of entrances and exits, perhaps installing a card swipe or code pad system. Securing these areas will reduce the risk factor for potential attacks and injuries.

Protective equipment can be used to personally safeguard employees from attacks and injuries. Employees who spend a lot of time out in the field should carry radio or cellphone devices and have them readily available. Equipping a business with a "panic button" can alert law enforcement for an immediate response, possibly reducing potentially lethal outcomes. Closed-circuit cameras are used in many convenience stores and aid in deterring and apprehending criminals. Law enforcement has gone to great lengths to equip their officers with safety equipment, such as bulletproof vests. This has had a major effect on saving lives in otherwise deadly attacks.

Once the work environment has been thoroughly assessed, employees versed and trained in company policy and procedures, and safety features created and installed, the employer then needs to continually monitor the effectiveness of its policies and procedures. Changes in the organization's practice as well as adjustments to the work environment may evolve as the safety needs of the agency and its employees are further identified.

—*Donna Mobley-Lutz*

See also MASS MURDER; MEDIA, VIOLENCE IN THE; PREVENTION OF CRIME AND VIOLENT BEHAVIOR

Further Reading

Canadian Initiative on Workplace Violence. (2000). *Behaviour at its best.* Available on the World Wide Web at: http//www.workplaceviolence.ca.

Join Together Online. (1997, January). *Australia faces increase in workplace violence.* Available on the World Wide Web at:: http//www.jointogether.org/gv/news.

National Institute of Health and Safety. (1996, July). *Violence in the workplace.* Available on the World Wide Web at http//www.cdc.gov.niosh.

Southerland, M. D., Colins, P. A., & Scarborough, K. E. (1997). *Workplace violence: A continuum from threat to death.* Cincinnati, OH: Anderson.

Sygnatur, E. F., & Toscano, G. A. (2000, Spring). Work-related homicides: The facts. *Compensation and Working Conditions,* pp. 3-7.

Toscano, G., & Windau, J. (1996). *National census of fatal occupation injuries, 1995.* Available on the World Wide Web at: http://www.bls.gov\oshhome.htm.

U.S. Department of Labor, Bureau of Labor and Statistics. (2000). *Health and safety: Fatal and nonfatal occupational illnesses and injuries.* Available on the World Wide Web at: http//www.bls.gov.

WORLD TRADE CENTER BOMBINGS, *See* AERONAUTICAL MASS MURDER; BIN LADEN, OSAMA; MASS VIOLENCE; MEDIA, VIOLENCE IN THE; METHODS OF MURDER; MOTIVES FOR MURDER; TERRORISM; WORKPLACE VIOLENCE AND HOMICIDE

XYY SYNDROME

Based in Lombrosian theory that criminal behavior is rooted in heredity, some contemporary theorists have focused their research on genetic composition that may influence or even cause criminal conduct. The notion that criminal conduct may be biologically predisposed is certainly not new, nor is it without foundation. However, the research on genetic makeup, specifically the XYY chromosomal syndrome, has been very controversial. In 1965, Jacobs and associates reported that the presence of an extra Y chromosome in human males was correlated with mental retardation, tall stature, and excessive levels of aggressive conduct. This report spawned a number of researchers to hypothesize that the XYY chromosomal anomaly was related to violent crime by certain males.

Chromosomes are chains of genetic material known as *DNA,* which direct the growth of living cells in all living organisms. This includes eye color, height, temperament, and predisposition for all other human traits, such as depression. Each cell of a normal female has two X chromosomes, whereas normal males have an X and a Y chromosome in each cell. When combined, these cells constitute 23 pairs. In rare instances, two Y chromosomes in the male pair with a single X, leaving the person with 47 chromosomes rather than the normal 46. Such persons can demonstrate unusual height, acne, borderline intelligence, and bouts of extreme aggressiveness.

A few noted cases of murder have involved persons with the XYY syndrome, including Daniel Hugon in Paris in 1968. He was charged with the savage killing of an elderly woman. Another was Sean Farley, known as "Big Bad John," a giant of a man from New York City who murdered and mutilated a woman in 1969. In neither case did the XYY syndrome acquit the offender by reason of insanity.

Thus far, the research on XYY syndrome has failed to adequately substantiate linkage between possessing the extra chromosome and violent criminal conduct. Indeed, the possibility that in rare cases some persons possessing the XYY anomaly commit violent crimes is certainly feasible. But how does that explain the majority of cases of XYY syndrome that do not result in violent criminal behavior? Jarvik, in a global review of 26 studies that included over 5,000 criminals, found that in the general population, the presence of XYY is between .11% and .14%, in psychiatric patients between .13% and .20%, and in criminal populations significantly higher at 1.9%. The 1.9% is an extremely small part of the total prison population and does little to support the occurrence of violence in society. In fact, most of the crimes committed by persons with XYY syndrome were crimes against property, not people.

—*Eric W. Hickey*

See also AGGRESSION; VIOLENT BEHAVIOR

Further Reading

Bartol, C. R. (2002). *Criminal behavior, a psychosocial approach* (6th ed.). Upper Saddle River, NJ: Prentice Hall.

Borgaonkar, D. S. (1997). *Chromosomal variation in man: A catalog of chromosomal variants and anomalies* (8th ed.). New York: John Wiley.

Jacobs, P. A., Brunton, M., Melville, H. M., Brittian, R. P., & McClemont, W. F. (1965). Aggressive behavior, mental subnormality and the XYY male. *Nature, 208,* 1351-1352.

Jarvik, L., Klodin, V., & Matsuyama, S. (1973). Human aggression and the extra Y chromosome. *American Psychologist, 28,* 674-682.

Y

ANDREA YATES

On June 20, 2001, Andrea P. Yates, a wife and mother of five children under the age of 8, filled her bathtub with water and proceeded to drown each child. The eldest child, Noah, age 7, saw her drowning his 6-month-old sister and tried to flee. He was caught, carried back to the bathroom, and drowned. Yates then called her husband, Rusty, at work, and told him that he needed to come home because she had done something to the children. The mass murder in Houston, Texas, drew immediate national and international attention. Most mass murders are perpetrated by males and seldom involve as many young children. Also, not only was the killing done by a woman but the mode of death was even more shocking.

At her trial, Yates did not contest that she did the killings but claimed that she was insane at the time. Her defense documented a long history of mental illness brought on by postpartum depression. Each successive pregnancy increased her level of depression. When questioned about wanting Andrea to have more children even though it was clear that it contributed to her mental illness, Rusty explained that it was God's will that they bring children into the world even if it did affect her health. Her defense documented a long history of Andrea using antipsychotic medications and a suicide attempt.

About 80% of women who give birth experience minor mood swings often referred to as the "baby blues." Only 10% to 20% of women actually suffer postpartum depression; or about 1 in every 500 births in the United States produces short-term postpartum psychosis. Postpartum depression that results in psychosis is a difficult defense because the defendant has to prove that she did not know right from wrong at the time of her crime. It is recognized as a legal defense in at least 29 countries. These countries, such as Britain, Canada, Australia, and the United States all have infanticide laws. These laws allow for a woman who has killed a child under the age of 1 year to prove that the balance of her mind was disturbed as a result of giving birth. In such cases, the maximum charge is

Andrea Yates drowned each of her five children in the bathroom of their home on August 8, 2001, and then called her husband Rusty to give him the news. When women kill, the victims are usually family members, such as children or husbands. Although Yates had a long history of mental illness, she was found guilty of murder and sent to prison.

manslaughter. Andrea Yates killed children who were both under and over 1 year old. In the Yates case, there was hope that at least the insanity defense would mitigate a conviction and a reduction in sentence.

A finding of NGRI, or not guilty by reason of insanity, would have seen her committed to a psychiatric institution until she was restored to health and the presiding judge deemed her safe to return to society. She would not have been confined in the hospital any longer than if she were convicted and sent to prison. Yates, however, faced a capital murder case that could require the death penalty or life without the possibility of parole. Several women's groups criticized the prosecutor for seeking the death penalty.

Both the prosecution and defense agreed that Yates was mentally ill, but the prosecution was able to convince the jury that she knew at the time of the killings that what she was doing was wrong. Andrea Yates was found guilty of capital murder in the slayings of three of her five children. Because the Texas jury was also convinced that she was no longer a threat to society, in March 2002, Yates was spared the death penalty and given life in prison. She will be eligible for parole after she has served 40 years.

Rusty Yates had vowed to stand by his wife because he loved her. Within a year, he decided to divorce her so he could remarry and have more children.

—*Eric W. Hickey*

See also CHILD KILLERS; COURT-ORDERED PSYCHOLOGICAL ASSESSMENTS; FAMILY HOMICIDE; HOMICIDE, TYPES OF, AND DEGREES OF MURDER; MASS MURDER; METHODS OF MURDER; NOT GUILTY BY REASON OF INSANITY (NGRI); WOMEN AND VIOLENCE

Further Reading

Kleiman, K., & Raskin, V. D. (1994). *This isn't what I expected: Overcoming postpartum depression.* New York: Bantam Books.

Smith, D. (1996). *Beyond all reason: My life with Susan Smith.* Pinnacle.

Spencer, S. (2002). *Breaking point.* New York: St. Martin's.

YOUTH VIOLENCE, *See* GANGS; JUVENILE FIRESETTERS; JUVENILE KILLERS; JUVENILE OFFENDERS; VIOLENT FEMALE JUVENILE OFFENDERS

YORKSHIRE RIPPER, *See* RIPPERS

YOSEMITE PARK KILLER, *See* PROFILING

Z

THE ZEBRA KILLINGS

The "Zebra Killings" were classified as hate crimes: A group of African Americans known as "Death Angels" methodically stalked and killed Caucasian victims in San Francisco, California, from 1972 to 1974. The murders were dubbed "Zebra" because the police investigators used the radio channel "Z." Five men were implicated in the majority of the murders: Jesse Lee Cooks, J. C. Simon, Larry Green, Manuel Moore, and Anthony Harris. The Death Angels believed Caucasians to be an inferior race and that they were earning "points" toward going to heaven for killing them. They also believed that an insane African scientist had created Caucasians 3,000 years ago so that the African race would have others to rule over. Many of their victims were women or elderly men, because they posed the least threat of fighting back. Brutality and lack of remorse were key components in the execution of the murders.

The final death toll was suspected by law enforcement to be around 70 victims. Some of the offenders were associated with the Nation of Islam and other Black Muslim groups. The Nation of Islam provided legal representation for each of the killers, who are now all eligible for parole hearings. Since 1972, a memorial service has been held in October on the steps of the San Francisco City Hall to remember the victims of the Zebra killings.

—*Brianna Satterthwaite*

See also HATE CRIMES

Further Reading

Lubinskas, J. (2001, August 30). *Remembering the Zebra Killings.* Retrieved on June 4, 2002, from the World Wide Web at: http://www.frontpagemag.com/guestcolumnist/lubinskas08-30-01.htm.

THE ZODIAC MURDERS

The "Zodiac Killings" began in 1966 and ended in 1974, without the perpetrator being apprehended. The case was cloaked in mystery as investigators sifted through thousands of possible leads. To this day, many questions remain as to the identity and whereabouts of the killer. The actual number of victims is also undetermined, but most agree that the offender murdered between 6 and 49 victims. Following a letter sent to the San Francisco Police Department that read "Me-37—SFPD-0," many concluded that the Zodiac killer had murdered 37 people. During his reign of terror, 21 coded letters were sent to newspapers and police departments. Some of the letters have yet to be deciphered, and there is some question as to their authenticity. The killer earned the moniker of "Zodiac" from the letters he sent to the newspapers. He began each letter with the phrase "This is the Zodiac speaking." He was also known for leaving his signature mark of a crossed circle on or around his victims. In a few cases, he carved the sign into their bodies.

The first victims, a young couple, were shot with a .22 caliber while in a lakeside parking lot in Vallejo, California. Seven months later, another young Vallejo couple was attacked in a parked car; the woman was killed and the man critically wounded. The killer called the police department shortly after this attack to inform them of what he had done and that he was also responsible for the killings the year before. The Zodiac seemed to enjoy killing, and 3 months later, another young couple was attacked, with similar results: The female died, and her male companion was critically stabbed with a 10-inch knife. The final victim was a 29-year-old male cab driver in San Francisco, who was shot in the head.

The most famous suspect in the case was Arthur Leigh Allen, a convicted pedophile. Several pieces of evidence linked Allen to the crimes. Allen lived within minutes of the lakeside crime scene where four victims had been attacked. He was unable to produce solid alibis for the times most murders occurred but was never arrested for any of the Zodiac killings. The fact that Allen was a pedophile and preferred children raised serious doubts that he would have been the Zodiac. Arthur Leigh Allen died of natural causes in 1992 at the age of 58. The case remains open.

—Eric W. Hickey

See also SERIAL MURDER; SIGNATURE KILLERS

Further Readings

Anderson, W. R. (1999). Can personality disorders be used as predictors of serial killers? *Futurics, 23*(3&4), 34-43.

THE ZOOT SUIT RIOTS

For 10 days in June 1943, several thousand Anglo American servicemen and civilians fought in the streets of Los Angeles with young Mexican Americans who wore fingertipped coats and pegged, draped pants. Although rocks, sticks, fists, and some knives were used, no lives were lost, and only a few sustained serious injuries. Property damage was relatively minor. The riot was partly rooted in xenophobia fueled by World War II hysteria. Some thought the "zoot suiters'" darker skin resembled the enemy and feared that perhaps they were actually collaborating with the Japanese. Servicemen were frustrated and anxious about the war and needed to vent. When the media began focusing on the zoot suits, tensions soon became explosive.

The well-manicured and immaculately dressed Chicano youth embraced a fad that had already appeared in other parts of the United States and Europe. They were youth in the process of finding a collective identity in the barrios of Los Angeles, but their exclusivity alienated them not only from whites but from other Hispanics as well.

—Eric W. Hickey

See also HATE CRIMES; VIGILANTISM

Further Reading

Bankston, C. L. (1999). Politics and racial/ethnic relations in Canada: Zoot Suit Riots. In *Racial and ethnic relations in America, Vol. 3: Pol-Z.* Salem Press.

Mazon, M. (1984). *The Zoot Suit Riots.* Austin: University of Texas Press.

Appendix 1: Criminological Theorists

Theoretical approaches to the study of criminology are best studied by examining the prevailing thinking of individuals during a particular time period. The time periods most frequently referred to are the Demonic Era, prior to the 17th century; the Age of Enlightenment, in the 17th and 18th centuries; the Classical School, 18th century; biological and ecological theories, 19th and 20th centuries; and the psychological, subculture, social structure, social process, and social conflict theories, 20th century. With this in mind, each time period will be represented by basic information about the premier thinkers in the field of criminology at the time.

— Marlene Deal

Table 1   Theoretical Approaches to the Study of Criminology

Era	Criminologist	Time Period	Proposed Theory	Basic Tenets
Demonic		1600s		People who commit crimes are possessed by demons.
Age of Enlightenment	John Locke	1600s	Utopian society Felicific calculus	Accepted only that authority that could vindicate itself through reason. Government is instituted by a reciprocal agreement. The powers are limited, and they involve reciprocal agreement.
	Thomas Hobbes	1600s	First suggestion of law	Individuals must be willing to give up some freedom so that laws can be developed for the greater good of society.
Classical	Cesare Beccaria	1764	Free will	Criminals choose to commit crimes because of hedonistic reasons. Punishment should fit the crime.
	Jeremy Bentham	1789	Utilitarian hedonism Felicific calculus	The purpose of law is to support the complete happiness of the community. Punishment should prevent crime or convince the criminal to commit a lesser crime.
Neo-classical		1970s-present		

(Continued)

Table 1 (Continued)

Era	Criminologist	Time Period	Proposed Theory	Basic Tenets
	Jack Katz	1988	Seductions of crime theory	Treats all forms of criminality as reactive responses to humiliation.
	Lawrence Cohen and Marcus Felson		Routine activities	The occurrence of crime requires a motivated offender, a suitable target, and the lack of a guardian. Crime results from and changes according to routine activities in everyday life.
Biological		1880s-present		
	Franz Joseph Gall	1810	Scientific understanding of crime	Phrenology
	Cesare Lombroso	1836-1909	Born criminal Atavism	Criminals are people who are born with characteristics consistent with a lower form of human life.
	Richard Dugdale	1877	Jukes family	Criminality is inherited.
	Enrico Ferri	1878	Law of criminal saturation	All crime is involuntary behavior. Criminals are affected by their social environments as well as by biological and psychological factors.
	Raffaele Garofolo	1880		Suggested elimination of unfit offspring.
	Charles B. Goring	1901		Hereditary mental disease is the cause of crime.
	Henry Goddard	1912	Kallikak family	Criminality is inherited. Criminality is related to feeblemindedness.
	Ernst Kretschmer	1925	Somatotyping	Body type is related to criminality.
	Earnest Hooton	1939	Supported Lombroso	Environment plus Low-grade individual = Criminality.
	William Sheldon	1949	Somatotype theory	Three body types.
	Patricia Jacobs	1965	Genetic	XYY supermales are more prone to criminality.
	Edward O. Wilson	1975	Sociobiology	Altruism Territoriality Tribalism Survival of the gene pool
Personality theories		1950s-present		
	Samuel Yochelson and Stanton Samenow	1960s-present	Criminal personality theory	Some individuals are born criminals.
Psychological theories		1920s-present		

Era	Criminologist	Time Period	Proposed Theory	Basic Tenets
Modeling theories	Gabriel Tarde	1904	Laws of imitation	Society perpetuates behavior by imitation from one generation to another.
	Albert Bandura	1973	Modeling theory	Aggression is learned. Aggression is rewarded. Disengagement.
Psychoanalytic criminology	Sigmund Freud	1920s-1930s	Psychoanalysis	Id, ego, superego Sublimination
	John Dollard	1939	Frustration-aggression theory	Displacement, catharsis
	S. M. Halleck	1971		Alloplastic adaptation Autoplastic adaptation
	Arnold Linsky, Ronet Bachman, and Murray Straus	1995		Societal stress creates aggression.
Forensic psychology	Hans Eysenck	1964		Criminal personality Biopsychology
	B. F. Skinner	1950s-1970s	Behavioral theory	Operant conditioning Rewards/punishments Stimulus response
	John Bowlby	1950s	Attachment theory	Secure attachment Anxious resistant attachment Anxious avoidant attachment
	Michael Gottfredson and Travis Hirschi	1990	Self-control theory	Failure of self-control
	Harold Grasmick	1993		Self-control Gratification
Ecological theories/Social disorganization theories		1820s-present		
	Querry	1825		Used maps and crime statistics to analyze crime.
	Adolphe Quetelet	1842		Father of modern sociological and psychological statistics.
	Robert Park and Ernest Burgess	1952	Concentric zone theory	Cities are composed of five concentric zones. The zones are less socially organized in the center of the city and become more organized as they move out.
	Clifford Shaw and Henry Mckay	1942	Cultural deviance theory	Areas of low socioeconomic status in which delinquency rates are high are characterized by a wide diversity of norms. Children exposed to criminal values adopt

(Continued)

Table 1 (Continued)

Era	Criminologist	Time Period	Proposed Theory	Basic Tenets
				them as a means of succeeding.
Anomie theories		1880s–present		
	Emile Durkheim	1893	Anomie	Crime is necessary in society. It allows for social change by strengthening the collective consciousness and validates the majority of the population.
	Robert K. Merton	1938	Strain theory	There is an inevitable chronic disassociation between culturally proscribed goals and socially structured avenues to realizing these goals. Failure to achieve success in legal ways may cause individuals to choose illegal ways to achieve goals.
Subculture theories		1920s–present		
	Albert K. Cohen	1955	Middle-class measuring theory	Delinquency is a lower-class reaction to middle class values.
	Walter B. Miller	1958	Focal-concerns theory	Society is composed of different social groups, each with its own subculture characterized by focal concerns unique to the group.
	Frederick M. Thrasher	1927	Gang-formation theory	The gang is an interstitial group that is formed spontaneously and then integrated through conflict. It is characterized by certain behaviors and traditions.
	Richard A. Cloward and Lloyd E. Ohlin	1960	Differential-opportunity theory	Each individual occupies a position in both legitimate and illegitimate opportunity structures. People have different levels of access to legitimate means of achieving success and illegitimate means of achieving success.
	Marvin Wolfgang and Franco Ferracuti	1967	Subculture of violence	Refers to "culture within a culture" that exists mainly among ethnic and lower-class groups and demonstrates favorable attitudes toward the use of violence as a means of resolving interpersonal grievances.
Social process theories		1930s–present		

Era	Criminologist	Time Period	Proposed Theory	Basic Tenets
Social learning theories	Edwin Sutherland	1939	Differential association	Criminal behavior is learned in interaction with others, within intimate personal groups. Learning includes techniques of committing the crime and motives, drives, rationalizations, and attitudes about the criminal behavior.
	Robert L. Burgess and Ronald L. Akers	1966	Differential association-reinforcement theory	Respondent behavior is governed by the stimuli that elicit it. When a pleasing response accompanies a particular behavior, it increases the likelihood that the behavior will occur again in the future.
	Gresham Sykes and David Matza	1960s	Neutralization theory	Juveniles participating in criminal activities learn techniques that allow them to neutralize values and attitudes that contribute to lawful behavior.
Social control theories	Walter Reckless	1950s	Containment theory	Inner and outer containment
	Howard Kaplan	1970s		Self-derogation
	Travis Hirschi	1969	Social bond theory	The stronger the social bonds, the less likely a juvenile will become delinquent. Social bonds are attachment, commitment, belief, and involvement.
Labeling theories		1930s-present		Crime results from a social definition of unacceptable behavior developed through legislative morality.
	Frank Tannenbaum	1938	Dramatization of evil	Father of labeling theory. Process of creating a criminal includes tagging, defining, segregating, and creating acceptance of the label within the individual.
	Edwin Lemert	1951	Societal reaction theory	Primary deviance Secondary deviance
	Howard Becker	1963	Outsiders	Moral enterprise
Social conflict theories		1960s-present		Conflict theorists contend that the rule of law, formal agencies, and those that have power and wealth in society coerce the powerless into abiding by the established rules, which favor the rich and powerful.

(Continued)

Table 1 (Continued)

Era	Criminologist	Time Period	Proposed Theory	Basic Tenets
	Karl Marx	1848		Haves/have nots Proletariat Bourgeoisie Social Class
Radical criminology	Thorsten Sellin	1938	Cultural conflict	There is conflict between the cultural norms of two groups, which consists of primary conflicts between two different cultures and secondary conflicts between two segments of the same culture.
	George Vold	1958	Group conflict theory	Political conflict between groups. Conflict is normal.
	Ralph Dahrendorf	1959		Conflict is normal. Destructive change.
	Austin Turk	1969		Social orders = Pattern of conflict. Laws serve to control.
	William Chambliss	1970s		Power gaps. Crime reduces surplus labor.
	Richard Quinney	1974	Class, state, and crime	As the surplus population grows, so does the criminal justice system. Incarceration is a way of handling excess, unemployed people.
Feminist criminology	Freda Adler and Rita Simon	1975	Emancipation theory	Gender socialization
	Carol Smart	1977		Gender bias in criminology
	Kathleen Daly and Meda Chesney-Lind	1988		Androcentricity. Crime may not be normal.
	John Hagan	1989	Power control theory	There are different types of capital, and one type is *social capital.* The lack of social capital may contribute to poor life choices, including committing crimes.
Peacemaking criminology	Harold Pepinsky and Richard Quinney	1986		Making peace with crime.
Left-realist criminology	Jock Young and Walter Dekeseredy	1980-1990s		Social justice Reality of crime

Appendix 2: Serial Killers

The following tables include many of the more well-known solo, serial, and team serial killers in the United States and internationally, but by no means all individuals who could be classified as such.

— Marlene Deal

Table 1   Solo Killers

Name	Nickname	Type/Motive	Location	Dates	No. of Victims	Disposition
Akin, Joe Dewey		Nomadic/Personal cause	Alabama Georgia	1990-1991	18 suspected killed	Convicted on 1 count, 1992
Albanese, Charles		Territorial/Inheritance	Illinois	1980-1981	Poisoned 3 family members	Executed, 1995
Albright, Charles	Dallas Ripper	Territorial/Sexual sadism	Dallas, TX	1930s-1965	Shot 13+ people	Life sentence on 1 count
Allam, Ibrahim Hamza		Nomadic/Personal cause/Commercial gain	Germany Austria France	1977-1983	4-6 victims	20 years prison in Austria
Amos, Lowell		Territorial/Insurance	Detroit, MI	1979-1987	3 wives and mother	Life without parole, 1 count
Andrade, Marcel de		Territorial/Sexual sadism	Brazil	1991	14 boys	Life sentence to mental institution
Angelo, Richard		Stationary/Personal cause	New York	1987	Hero killings of 10+ hospital patients	50 years to life, 4 counts
Atkins, Benjamin		Territorial/Sex	Michigan	1991-1992	Strangled 11 prostitutes	Life imprisonment
Barbeault, Marcel	Killer From the Shadows	Territorial/Unknown	France	1969-1976	8 random shootings	Life imprisonment
Barbosa, Daniel Camargo		Nomadic/Sexual sadism	Colombia Ecuador	1974-1988	Pedophile ripper of 72 girls	16-year term in Equador
Barfield, Margie Velma		Territorial/Inheritance/Insurance	North Carolina	1969-1978	Poisoned 5 family members	Executed, 1984

(Continued)

Table 1 (Continued)

Name	Nickname	Type/Motive	Location	Dates	No. of Victims	Disposition
Bathory, Elizabeth		Stationary/Torture	Hungary	1575	300-650 children	Died in custody
Baumeister, Herbert Richard		Nomadic/Lust killer	Indiana Ohio	1980-1995	16 gay men	Suicide while a fugitive
Bell, Larry Eugene		Territorial/Lust killer	South Carolina	1985	3 girls	Executed, 1996
Bergamo, Marco	Monster of Bolzano	Territorial/Sex	Italy	1985-1992	Randomly stabbed 5 women	Life sentence
Berkowitz, David Richard	Son of Sam .44-Caliber Killer	Territorial/Random shooter	New York City	1976	15 shot, 7 killed	Life sentence
Besnard, Marie	Queen of Poisoners	Territorial/Inheritance	England	1927-1949	Poisoned 13 family members	Acquitted despite confessions
Biegenwald, Richard	The Thrill Killer	Nomadic/Robbery/ Rape	New York New Jersey	1958-1982	Shot 7	Life imprisonment
Bishop, Aurthur Gary		Territorial/Rape	Utah	1979-1983	5 children	Executed, 1988
Black, Robert	Smelly Bob	Nomadic/Sex	England	1969-1990	5-8 children	105-year sentence
Bladel, Rudy		Nomadic/Revenge	Indiana Michigan	1963-1978	7 railway workers	3 consecutive life sentences
Bolin, Oscar Ray		Nomadic/Rape	Nationwide, U.S.	1986	30+ women	Death sentence, 1992
Britt, Eugene		Territorial/Sexual sadism	Indiana	1995	Random slaying of 11 people	Life without parole
Brogsdale, Rickey Henry	Peeping Tom Killer	Territorial/Homicidal voyeur	Washington, D.C.	1987	Shot 11 women, killed 4	63 years to life on 4 counts
Brudos, Jerome Henry		Territorial/Paraphilic killer	Oregon	1968-1969	4 women	Life sentence
Bundy, Theodore Robert	Ted	Nomadic/Sexual sadism	Washington Utah Colorado Florida	1974-1978	Strangled 22+ women	Executed, 1989
Carpenter, David Joseph	Trailside Killer	Nomadic/Random attacks	California	1979-1980	10 hikers	Death sentence
Chase, Richard Trenton	Sacramento Vampire	Territorial/Vampirism	California	1977-1978	6 victims	Prison suicide, 1980
Chikatilo, Andrei Romanovich	Russian Ripper	Nomadic/Paraphilic/ Sexual sadism	Russia	1978-1990	55 children and women	Executed, 1994

Name	Nickname	Type/Motive	Location	Dates	No. of Victims	Disposition
Cline, Alfred		Territorial/Inheritance	Western U.S.	1930-1945	8 wives and 1 male friend	Died in prison, 1948
Corio, Pier Luigi	Monster of Leffe	Territorial/Personal	Italy	1987-1989	3+ people shot and buried in garden	Life term
Corona, Juan		Territorial/Monetary gain	California	1970s	25 men	25 life terms
Dahmer, Jeffrey Lionel		Territorial/Sexual sadism/Paraphilia	Wisconsin	1978	15 young men	Killed in prison
Diaz, Robert Rubane		Territorial/Unknown	California	1981	12-50 patients	Death sentence
De Bardeleben, James Mitchell		Nomadic/Commercial gain Sexual sadism	Nationwide	1965-1983	8+ victims	375 years in prison
DeSalvo, Albert Henry	Boston Strangler The Green Man Measuring Man	Nomadic/Sex/ Signature killer	Massachusetts	1962-1964	11 women	Life term for rape; killed in prison
Dillon, Thomas		Nomadic/Unknown	Ohio Indiana Michigan	1989-1990	5-11 hunters shot randomly	165-year sentence in Ohio
Dodd, Westley Allan		Territorial/Sexual sadism	Washington	1989	3 children	Hanged, 1993
Doss, Nanny Hazel	Giggling Granny	Territorial/Insurance Inheritance	Alabama	1945-1954	Poisoned 10 family members	Died of leukemia in prison
Falling, Christine Laverne		Territorial/Irritated with victims	Florida	1980-1982	Smothered 5 children and an elderly man	25 years to life
Fish, Albert Howard	The Cannibal Moon Maniac	Territorial/Paraphilic killer	New York	1910-1928	15 people, all ages and genders	Executed, 1936
Gacy, John Wayne	The Killer Clown	Territorial/Sexual sadism	Illinois	1972-1978	33 young males	Executed, 1994
Gein, Edward Theodore		Territorial/Sexual sadism/Paraphilic killer	Wisconsin	1954-1957	2+ victims	Died of respiratory failure in a mental institution
Gunness, Belle		Territorial/Insurance/ Inheritance	Illinois	1896-1908	49 victims	Escaped prosecution
Hansen, Robert C.		Nomadic/Sexual sadism	Alaska	1973-1983	17 women	Life plus 461 years
Harvey, Donald		Territorial/Personal reasons	Kentucky	1975-1985	52 hospital patients	4 life sentences

(Continued)

Table 1 (Continued)

Name	Nickname	Type/Motive	Location	Dates	No. of Victims	Disposition
Heidnik, Gary Michael		Territorial/Paraphilic killer/Sexual sadism	Pennsylvania	1985-1987	Killed 2 women; 4 more tortured	Executed, 1999
Hilley, Audrey Marie		Territorial/Insurance/ Personal reasons	Alabama	1975-1979	4 family members killed	Life term; escaped prison; died while at large
Hoyt, Waneta Ethyl		Territorial/Unknown	New York	1965-1971	Smothered 5 of her own children	75 years to life; died in prison
Kaczynski, Theodore John	Unabomber	Nomadic/Unknown	Nationwide	1978-1993	Killed 3; sent 17 bombs	Life term without parole
Jones, Genene Ann		Territorial/Munchausen's syndrome by proxy	Texas	1977-1983	2 deaths documented; many more infants injected with succinylcholine	99 years
Lopez, Pedro Alonso	Monster of the Andes	Nomadic	South America	1970s	300+ young girls	
Kallinger, Joseph Michael	The Shoemaker	Nomadic/Sexual sadism Robbery	Pennsylvania	1976	2 killed; many more assaulted	Choked to death in prison, 1996
Kemper, Edmund Emil III	Co-ed Killer	Nomadic/Paraphilia/ Sexual sadism	California	1963-1973	Killed grandparents, 6 co-eds, his mother, and her friend	Life term with no parole
Kraft, Randy Steven	Scorecard Killer	Nomadic/Sexual sadism	California	1980-1983	Killed 16 young men, suspected in 51 others	Death sentence
Moore, Blanche Taylor		Territorial/Black widow	North Carolina	1966	4 family members	Death sentence
Mudgett, Herman Webster		Nomadic/Criminal enterprise/Sex	New Hampshire Illinois	1869-1895	27 confirmed deaths, many more suspected	Hanged, 1896
Nilsen, Dennis Andrew		Nomadic/Necrophilia	England	1978-1983	15 young men	Life sentence
Olson, Clifford Robert	Beast of British Columbia	Nomadic/Sexual sadism	Canada	1980-1981	Killed 11 young men and women, claimed responsibility for 143 deaths	11 life terms; bargained with prosecution, $10,000/victim

Name	Nickname	Type/Motive	Location	Dates	No. of Victims	Disposition
Puente, Dorothea Helen		Stationary/Financial gain	California	1982-1988	Poisoned 9 elderly men	Life without parole on 3 counts
Ramirez, Richard Leyva	The Night Stalker	Nomadic/Sexual sadism/Satanism	California	1984	14 dead	Death sentence
Rifkin, Joel		Territorial/Sexual sadism	New York	1991-1992	18 women	Multiple life terms
Rolling, Danny Harold	Campus Killer Gainesville Ripper	Nomadic/Sexual sadism	Louisiana Florida	1989-1990	8 random victims	Death sentence
Shawcross, Arthur		Territorial/Sex	New York	1972/1988-1989	2 children, 11 prostitutes	250 years on 10 counts
Speck, Richard Franklin		Nomadic/Sex	Indiana Illinois	1966	12 suspected killed	Death sentence; commuted in 1972; died in prison
Stano, Gerald Eugene		Nomadic/Enjoyed killing	New Jersey Pennsylvania	1969-1980	27 dead, 14 more suspected	Executed, 1998
Sutcliffe, Peter William	Yorkshire Ripper	Nomadic/Personal cause	England	1975-1980	17 women dead, 7 nonfatal bludgeonings	Life sentence to mental institution
Swango, Dr. Michael		Nomadic/Unknown	U.S. Africa	1978-1997	Dozens suspected deaths of hospital patients	Plea bargained for 42-month sentence in 1998
Toppan, Jane		Stationary/Liked killing	Massachusetts	1880-1901	31 patients killed with morphine; suspected of 70-100	Life term in mental institution; died in 1938
Tinning, Marybeth		Territorial/Unknown	New York	1972-1985	Killed 8 of her own children	Convicted on 1 count of murder
Unterweger, Jack		Nomadic/Sexual sadism	Worldwide	1990	12+ women	Convicted; committed suicide in custody
Wilder, Christopher Bernard		Nomadic/Sexual sadism		1984	14+ young women	Killed by police during capture
Williams, Wayne	Atlanta Child Killer	Territorial/Sex	Georgia	1980s	28 young men	Life sentence
Woodfield, Randall Brent	I-5 Killer	Nomadic/Sex Commercial enterprise	Oregon Washington California	1961	12+ suspected dead	Life + 90 years; 35 years more in second trial
Wuornos, Aileen		Territorial/Self-defense?	Florida	1989-1990	7 men	Death sentences

Table 2   Team Killers

Name	Nickname	Type/Motive	Location	Dates	No. of Victims	Disposition
Beck, Martha Fernandez, Ray	Lonely Heart's Club Killers	Territorial/Monetary gain	New York	1940s	12 elderly women, more suspected	Death sentences for both
Bernardo, Paul Homolka, Karla		Territorial/Sexual sadism	Canada	1990s	3, including Karla's sister.	Karla: 12 years Paul: life term
Bianchi, Kenneth Buono, Albert	Hillside Stranglers	Nomadic/Sexual sadism	Los Angeles	1977-1979	10 women	Life terms without parole
Bittaker, Lawrence Norris, Roy		Nomadic/Sexual sadism/Thrill killers	California	1970s	5+ young women	Bittaker: death sentence Norris: 45 to life
Brady, Ian Hindley, Myra	Moors Murderers	Territorial/Sexual sadism/Pedophilia	England	1963-1965	5 known, 10 suspected	Life terms for both
Clark, Douglas D. Bundy, Carol A.	Sunset Slayers	Territorial/Torture/ Sexual sadism	Los Angeles	1980	7 women	Clark: death penalty Bundy: 27 years to life
Coleman, Alton Brown, Debra		Nomadic/Sexual sadism/Commercial gain	Illinois Indiana Ohio	1984	8 victims aged 7-77 years old	Death sentence for both
Corll, Dean Henley, Elmer Wayne		Territorial/Sexual sadism	Texas	1970-1973	27 boys and young men	Corll: killed by Henley Henley: life sentence
Gallego, Gerald Gallego, Charlene		Nomadic/Sexual sadism	California Nevada Oregon	1978-1980	10 young women and men	Gerald: death sentence Charlene: released in 1997
Lake, Leonard Ng, Charles		Territorial/Sexual sadism	California	1984-1985	25 men, women, and children	Lake: committed suicide before prosecution Ng: death sentence
Lucas, Henry Lee Toole, Ottis		Nomadic/Personal	Nationwide	1970s- 1980s	100 victims	Life term without parole
Neeley, Alvin and Judith		Nomadic/Sexual sadism	Tennessee Georgia	1982-1983	3 victims	Alvin: 2 life terms Judith: life term without parole
Sithole, Moses Selepe, David		Territorial/Sex	South Africa	1990s	40+ victims	Sithole: in prison Selepe: killed during capture
West, Fred and Rosemary		Stationary/Sexual sadism	England	1990s	12+ including daughter and stepdaughter	Fred: hanged himself in jail. Rosemary: currently in prison

Source: Serial murderers are often given monikers by investigators and the press that describe their victims, location selection preference, or modus operandi.

Table 3   Monikers Given to Male Serial Killers in the United States

Dates of Activity	Name	Moniker
1871-1874	Edward H. Rulloff	The Educated Murderer
1874-1909	James P. Miller	Deacon Jim
1879	Stephen Lee Richards	Nebraska Fiend
1890-1905	Johann Otto Hoch	Bluebeard
1892-1896	Harry Howard Holmes	The Torture Doctor
1895	William H. T. Durrant	Demon of the Belfry
1910-1934	Albert Fish	The Cannibal The Moon Maniac
1911-1919	Joseph Mumfre	New Orleans Axeman
1921-1931	Harry Powers	American Bluebeard a.k.a. Herman Drenth
1926-1927	Earle L. Nelson	The Gorilla Murderer
1933-1935	Major Raymond Lisemba	Rattlesnake Lisemba
1942-1947	Jake Bird	Tacoma Axe Killer
1945-1946	William George Heirens	The Lipstick Murderer
1949	Harvey Louis Carignan	The Want-Ad Killer
1957-1960	Melvin David Rees	Sex Beast
1958-1983	Richard F. Biegenwald	The Thrill Killer
1962-1964	Albert Henry DeSalvo	The Measuring Man The Green Man The Boston Strangler
1964-1965	Charles H. Schmid	Pied Piper of Tucson
1964-1973	Edmund Emil Kemper	The Co-ed Killer
1965	Posteal Laskey	Cincinnati Strangler
1967-1969	John N. Collins	Co-ed Murderer
1970	Richard Macek	The Mad Biter
1970-1987	Donald Harvey	Angel of Death
1972-1978	John Wayne Gacy	The Killer Clown
1974-1975	Vaughn Greenwood	Skid Row Slasher
1974-1978	Theodore Robert Bundy	Ted
1974-1994	Ricardo Caputo	The Lady Killer
1976-1977	David R. Berkowitz	Son of Sam .44-Caliber Killer
1977-1978	Carlton Gary	Stocking Strangler
1977-1980	Richard Cottingham	The Ripper Jekyll/Hyde
1978	Richard T. Chase	Vampire Killer

(Continued)

Table 3 (Continued)

Dates of Activity	Name	Moniker
1978-1979	Gerald Parker	Bedroom Basher
1978-1996	Theodore Kaczynski	The Unabomber
1979-1980	William Bonin	Freeway Killer
1980s	Roger Kibbe	I-15 Killer
1980s	Paul M. Stephanie	Weepy-Voiced Killer
1980s	Craig Price	Slasher of Warwick
1980s	Randy Kraft	Scorecard Killer
1980-1981	David Carpenter	Trailside Killer
1980-1982	Randall Woodfield	The I-5 Killer
1981	Masrion A Pruett	Mad Dog Killer
1981-1982	Coral Eugene Watts	Sunday Morning Slasher
1984	Cleo Green	Red Demon
1984-2000	John Edward Robinson	Slavemaster
1985	Richard Ramirez	Night Stalker
1987	Richard Angelo	Angel of Death
1989-1990	Danny Rolling	Campus Killer Gainesville Ripper
1990-1995	Keith Jesperson	Happy Face Killer
1990-1991	Cleophus Prince	Clairmont Killer
1992	David L. Wood	Desert Killer
1992	Thomas Huskey	Zoo Man
1993-1995	Glenn Rogers	Cross Country Killer
1994-1995	Roy Enrique Conde	Tamiami Strangler
1994-1996	Anthony Balaam	Trenton Strangler
1999	Angel Reyes Resendis	Railroad Killer

Appendix 3:
Organized Crime, Domestic

Table 1   Figures in Organized Crime in the United States

Name	Organization/Position	Period of Activity	Major Crimes	Disposition
Accardo, Anthony Joseph "Joe Batters"	Head of Chicago outfit	1922-1958	Racketeering Enforcer	Retired to Palm Springs, CA
Adonis, Joseph	New York Syndicate	1930-1956	Racketeer Political "Fixer"	Deported to Italy, 1956 Died 1972
Agron, Evsei	Russian "Godfather" "Little Odessa" New York City	1975-1984	Black market operator Fuel tax scams	Assassinated, 1985
Aiuppa, Joseph John "Joey Doves"	Chicago Outfit leader	1960s-1986	Gambling Racketeering	Serving sentence in prison
Alex, Gus	Chicago Outfit boss	1950s-1995	Racketeering Casino Skimming	Serving 15-year prison sentence since 1995
Anastasia, Albert "Lord High Executioner" "The Mad Hatter"	Don of the Mangano crime family	1921-1957	Executioner Extortion	Assassinated in 1957
Angiulo, Gennaro	Boston Mafia	1950-1986	Illegal Gambling Racketeer	Serving 45-year prison sentence since 1986
Annenberg, Moses "Moe"	New York City Atlantic City Mob	Early 1900s-1939	Illegal Gambling Newspaper Racketeer	Died 1942
Barnes, Leroy "Nicky" "Mr. Untouchable"	African American organized crime New York City	1950s-1978	Drug Trafficker Heroin Dealer	Sentenced to life in prison, 1978 Cooperated with authorities, in Witness Security Program
Battle, Jose Miguel "El Padrino" "El Gordo"	Battle Gang, Cuban American crime boss Florida, New Jersey, New York City	1950s-present	Illegal Gambling Racketeering Cocaine Smuggling	Lives in Dade County, Florida Sometimes in Lima, Peru
Binaggio, Charles	Kansas City, Missouri Political crime leader	1932-1950	Gambling Lord Bootlegging Political Crimes	Assassinated in Kansas City, Missouri, 1950

(Continued)

Table 1 (Continued)

Name	Organization/Position	Period of Activity	Major Crimes	Disposition
Bioff, Willie Morris	Hollywood Union Gangster	1930s-1955	Hollywood Union Extortionist Movie Racketeer	Assassinated in 1955 car explosion
Boiardo, Ruggerio "Richie the Boot"	Luchese crime family boss New Jersey	Early 1920s-1983	Bootlegging Gambling Racketeering	Died in 1984
Bonanno, Joseph "Don Peppino" "Joe Bananas"	Mafia crime boss Founder of La Cosa Nostra	Early 1920s-1983	Drug Dealing Pornography	Retired to Arizona, 1968 Wrote book titled *Man of Honor* Imprisoned in 1983 for obstruction of justice
Brooklier, Dominic "Jimmy Regace"	Mickey Cohen's gambling operations Los Angeles, CA	Late 1920s-1978	Racketeering Extortion Pornography	Died in prison, 1984
Bruno, Angelo "Docile Don"	La Cosa Nostra family don Philadelphia	Late 1920s-1980s	Gambling	Assassinated, 1980
Buchalter, Louis "Lepke"	Syndicate boss	1920s-1944	Union Scams Industrial Racketeering	Electrocuted in Prison, 1944
Buscetta, Tommaso "Don Massino"	Sicilian Mafia boss	1940s-1980s	Drug Trafficker	Defector, 1986 Witness Protection Program
Capone, Alphonse "Scarface" "Big Al"	Major crime leader Chicago	Early 1920s-1931	Bootlegging	Died in 1947 at home from a stroke
Casso, Anthony "Gaspipe"	Crime family boss Luchese crime family	1960s-1991	Loan-sharking Enforcer	Government Witness Security Program
Castellano, Paul "The Pope"	La Cosa Nostra crime family boss Gambino crime family	1930s-1985	Stock Fraud Extortion Legal and illegal business activities	Assassinated, 1985
Chan, Eddie	Tong Boss, Chinatown New York City	1970s-1983	Extortion	Fled the United States, 1983
Cohen, Mickey	Chicago Syndicate Los Angeles	1940s-1976	Loan-sharking Gambling Movie industry Racketeering	Died of stomach cancer, 1976
Colombo, Joseph	Head of Colombo crime family Promoted to head of Profaci crime family by Gambino and Luchese	1930s-1971	Gambling Loan-sharking	Shot in 1971 In a coma for 7 years, died 1978
Coppola, Mike "Trigger Mike"	Luciano crime family capo	1930s-1960s	Racketeering	Left prison, 1963, abandoned by La Cosa Nostra Location unknown

Name	Organization/Position	Period of Activity	Major Crimes	Disposition
Corallo, Anthony "Tony Ducks"	Luchese crime family boss	Late 1920s-1986	Illegal Union Activities Extortion	Serving 100-year sentence since 1986
Costello, Frank "King of the Slots"	La Cosa Nostra national organized crime syndicate	Late 1920s-1973	Bootlegging Illegal gambling	Retired, 1957 Died, 1973
Dellacroce, Aniello "O'Neill"	Gambino crime family powerful underboss	Late 1920s-1985	Fraud Extortion Racketeering	Died, 1985
Eng, Johnny	Leader of the Flying Dragons "Onionheads"	Early 1980s-1988	Drug trafficking Heroin	Serving 25-year sentence since 1993
Escobar, Pablo Emilio Gavoroa "The Godfather"	Founder of Medellin drug cartel	Late 1960s-1993	Cocaine Marijuana Drug trafficking	Killed in shootout with police, 1993
Fort, Jeff	Leader of Chicago African American criminal organization	Early 1960s-present	Prostitution Extortion Narcotics	Incarcerated
Franzese, Michael	Capo, Colombo crime family	1970s-1986	Tax Fraud Fuel taxes Insurance claims Auto Dealerships	Released from prison
Gallo, Joseph "Crazy Joe"	Mafia Rebel Innovator	1950s-1972	Hijacking Gambling Extortion Enforcer	Assassinated, 1972
Gambino, Carlo "Don Carlo"	Powerful La Cosa Nostra don, Gambino crime family	1920s-1976	Extortion Bootlegging Gambling	Assassinated, 1971
Genovese, Vito "Don Vito"	Major crime family don	Late 1920s-1969	Gambling Drug trafficking	Sentenced to prison, 1959 Died in prison, 1969
Giancana, Sam "Mooney"	Chicago Syndicate leader	Early 1920s-1975	Drug trafficking Gambling Extortion	Murdered before scheduled congressional hearings about CIA/Organized Crime connection, 1975
Gigante, Vincent "The Chin"	Head of the Genovese crime family, enforcer	1940s-1997	Drug trafficking Narcotics Extortion Bid rigging, construction industry	Incarcerated, 1997
Gotti, John "Dapper Don"	Gambino crime family don	1960-1991	Construction Racketeering Loan-sharking Gambling Extortion	Sentenced to life in federal prison Died in prison of cancer, 2002

(Continued)

Table 1 (Continued)

Name	Organization/Position	Period of Activity	Major Crimes	Disposition
Gravano, Salvatore "Sammy the Bull"	Underboss, Gambino crime family	1960s-1992	Construction racket Loan-sharking Gambling Extortion	Served 5 years in prison Witness Protection Program, had plastic surgery Whereabouts unknown
Herrera-Buitrago, Helmer "Pacho"	Colombia/U.S. Cali cocaine cartel	1970s-1995	Cocaine Trafficking	Incarcerated
Hoffa, Jimmy	Teamsters Union President	1930s-1975	Racketeering Extortion	Incarcerated, 1964 Abducted, presumed murdered in 1975 after release from prison
Ianniello, Matthew "Matty the Horse"	Genovese Caporegime Vice and sex industries	1940s-1972	Racketeering Extortion Pornography	Imprisoned, 1986 Currently serving time in federal correctional facility
Ivankov, Vyacheslav	Russian Criminal Boss	Arrived in U.S., 1993	Extortion	Arrested, 1995
Johnson, Ellsworth "Bumpy"	African American drug trafficker Enforcer for Genovese crime family	1920s-1968	Drug trafficking Racketeering Enforcer Gambling	Died in 1968 while free on bail
Lansky, Meyer	Major underworld figure	1920s-1973	International money laundering Gambling	Retired in 1973 in Miami, deceased
Lanza, Joseph "Socks"	Racket boss, New York Fulton Fish Market Inducted into Luciano crime family	1920s-1968	Extortion Racketeering	Imprisoned, 1943 and 1957 Died while out of prison in 1968
Lehder-Rivas, Carlos	Medellin drug cartel lord	1970s-1987	Drug trafficking Cocaine	Convicted of cocaine trafficking Incarcerated in federal facility, life without parole
Licavoli, James "Blackie"	Cleveland La Cosa Nostra Crime family boss	1920s-1985	Gambling Bootlegging Racketeering	Convicted under RICO charges Died in prison, 1985
Lombardozzi, Carmine "The Doctor" "The King of Wall Street"	Gambino crime family capo	1940s-1992	Securities fraud Loan-sharking	Died of heart attack, 1992
Louie, Nicky	Founder of Ghost Shadows Chinatown gang New York City	1970s-1985	Racketeering	Released from prison, 1994 Pursuing interests in film production

Name	Organization/Position	Period of Activity	Major Crimes	Disposition
Luchese, Gaetano "Three-Finger Brown"	La Cosa Nostra crime family boss	Early 1920s-1967	Drug Trafficking Gambling Loan-sharking Hijacking	Died of natural causes, 1967
Luciano, Charles "Charley Lucky" "Charles Ross"	La Cosa Nostra don major crime syndicate architect	Late 1920s-1962	Bootlegging Racketeering Prostitution	Died of a heart attack in 1962, Palermo, Sicily
Maranzano, Salvatore "Little Caesar"	Capo di Tutti Capi "Boss of Bosses"	Late 1920s-1931	Organized La Cosa Nostra	Assassinated, 1931
Marcello, Carlos	Boss of New Orleans La Cosa Nostra	1930s-1993	Gambling Tax Evasion Robbery Extortion Drug trafficking	Died of natural causes in 1993
Matthews, Frank "The Black Luciano"	African American drug trafficker	1960s-1973	Drug trafficking	Disappeared in 1973, presumed dead
Moran, George "Bugs"	Chicago North Side gang boss	Early 1900s-1957	Robbery Murder	Died in 1957 of lung cancer in Leavenworth Penitentiary
Ochoa, Jorge Luis Vasquez	Principal leader of the Medellin cocaine cartel	Early 1980s- Present	Drug trafficking Cocaine	Released from prison in Colombia in 1996
Ong, Benny "Uncle Seven"	Hip Sing Tong Boss Chinatown "Godfather"	?-1994	Extortion Loan-sharking Gambling	Died in 1994
Patriarca, Raymond	Organized crime figure Head of New England La Cosa Nostra	Late 1920s-1984	Bootlegging Labor Racketeering Loan-sharking Lotteries Drug Trafficking Marijuana and Cocaine	Died of natural causes in 1984
Persico, Carmine "The Snake"	Colombo crime family don	Early 1960s-present	Hijacking Racketeering	Incarcerated, sentenced to 100 years in prison
Profaci, Joseph "The Old Man"	Cosa Nostra crime family boss	Early 1920s-1963	Racketeering Extortion Murder	Died in 1963 of a heart attack
Provenzano, Anthony	Major racketeer in Teamsters Union	Late 1930s-1975	Embezzlement Racketeering Extortion	Vanished, 1975, presumed dead
Rastelli, Philip "Rusty"	Bonanno crime family don	1930s-1991	Loan-sharking Gambling Racketeering	Died, 1991
Reina, Gaetano "Tommy"	Masseria Mafia family boss New York City	1920s-1930	Vice rackets	Assassinated in 1930
Rodriquez Gacha, Jose Gonzalo	Medellin cocaine cartel leader	1960s-1989	Drug trafficking	Killed in a gun battle in 1989

(Continued)

Table 1 (Continued)

Name	Organization/Position	Period of Activity	Major Crimes	Disposition
Rodriguez-Orejuela, Gilberto "The Chess Player"	Founder and original member of the Cali cocaine cartel	1970s-present	Drug trafficking	Incarcerated, 1995
Rodriguez-Orejuela, Miguel Angel "Transportation Specialist"	Cali cocaine cartel leader	1980s-present	Drug trafficking	Incarcerated
Rothstein, Arnold "The Brain"	Criminal Mastermind Syndicate leader	Early 1900s-1928	Bootlegging Gambling Racketeering	Assassinated, 1928
Rubenstein, Jacob "Ruby, Jack"	Dallas Racketeer Assassin	Late 1920s-1967	Gambling Racketeering Assassin	Sentenced in 1964 for assassinating Lee Harvey Oswald (assassin of President John Kennedy) Died in prison, 1967
Salerno, Anthony "Fat Tony"	Genovese crime family don	1930s-1992	Extortion Gambling Tax Evasion Loan-sharking Racketeering	Sentenced to 100 years, 1986 Died in prison, 1991
Santacruz-Londono, Jose "Chepe"	Principal leader of the Cali cocaine cartel	1970s-1996	Drug trafficking Cocaine	Killed in confrontation with Colombian National Police, 1996
Scarfo, Nicky "Little Nicky"	La Cosa Nostra family boss Philadelphia/Atlantic City	1950s-present	Gambling Racketeering Murder	Incarcerated in 1988 in Marion Penitentiary
Schultz, Dutch "Harman, Charles" "The Dutchman"	Organized crime family capo International Longshoremen's Union	1950s-present	Labor Racketeering Loan-sharking	Incarcerated in 1979 Released in 1984
Shapiro, Jacob "Gurrah"	Garment industry organized crime	Late 1920s-1947	Labor Racketeering Extortionist	Died in Sing-Sing Prison, 1947
Siegel, Benjamin "Bugsy"	Organized crime Las Vegas and Los Angeles	Early 1930s-1947	Gambling Narcotics Union Racketeering	Assassinated in 1947
Tieri, Frank "Funzi"	Genovese crime family don	1920s-1981	Racketeering Loan-sharking Armed Robbery	Died, 1981, while in prison on RICO charges
Trafficante, Santos Jr.	Reputed Mafia boss Tampa, Florida	1930s-1987	Gambling Key figure in plot to assassinate Fidel Castro	Died, 1987
Zerilli, Joe	La Cosa Nostra don Detroit	1920s-1977	Loan-sharking Narcotics Labor Racketeering Extortion	Died, 1977

Name	Organization/Position	Period of Activity	Major Crimes	Disposition
Zwillman, Abner "Longy"	Leader in the East Coast Prohibition Syndicate Crime boss of New Jersey	Early 1920s-1959	Bootlegging Hijacking Gambling Extortion Racketeering	Died, 1959 Possible suicide or more likely by assassination

—Jana Price-Sharps

Further Reading

Kelly, R. J. (2000). *Encyclopedia of organized crime in the United States.* Westport, CT: Greenwood.

Sifakis, C. (1999). *The Mafia encyclopedia* (2nd ed.). New York: Checkmark Books.

Appendix 4:
Organized Crime, International

Table 1   Figures in International Organized Crime

Crime Figure	Country	Affiliation	Major Crimes	Time Period	Outcome
Vito Cascioferro	Italy	Sicilian Mafia	Crime boss, murder	1900s to 1945	Died of heart failure, 1945
Tu "Big-Eared Tu" Yueh-sheng	China	Green Gang	Crime boss, extortion, prostitution, heroin and opium trade	1900s to early 1950s	Died, 1951
Vic "The Egg" Cotroni	Canada	Montreal Mafia	Crime boss, owned gambling rings, drug trafficking, money laundering	1930s to early 1970s	Died of cancer, September 19, 1984
Guiseppe "Pep" Cotroni	Canada	Montreal Mafia	Lieutenant, drug trafficking	1930s to 1979	Died of natural causes, September 1979
Kot Siu Wong	China	14K	Crime boss	1940s	Unknown
Calogero Vizzini	Italy	Sicilian Mafia	Crime boss	1940s to 1954	Died, 1954
Luigi Greco	Canada	Montreal Mafia	Underboss, drug trafficking, active in gambling rings, loan-sharking, extortion	Late 1940s to 1972	Died in accidental fire, December 7, 1972
Kazuo Taoka	Japan	Yamaguchi-gumi	Godfather, exploitation of laborers, gambling, loan-sharking	1940s to 1981	Died of a heart attack, 1981
Yoshio Kodama	Japan	Yakuza	Godfather, perjury, bribery, violation of exchange laws	1940s to 1984	Died of a stroke, January 17, 1984
Hisayuki Machii	Korea	Tosei-kai/ "Voice of the East" Gang	Godfather, prostitution, racketeering, kidnapping	Late 1940s to present	Retired

(Continued)

Table 1 (Continued)

Crime Figure	Country	Affiliation	Major Crimes	Time Period	Outcome
Luciano Leggio	Italy	Corleone Mafia Family	Crime boss, murder, extortion, drug trafficking	1940s to present	Retired
Ng "Limpy Ho" Sik-ho	China	Crime boss	Crime boss, drug trafficking, gambling	1950s to 1991	Died of cancer, 1991
Ronnie "Colonel" Kray	United Kingdom	The Firm	Crime boss, extortion, fraud, blackmail, murder	1950s to 1995	Died of a heart attack in prison, March 17, 1995
Nicola "Cola" Di Iorio	Canada	Montreal Mafia	Lieutenant, gambling, prostitution	Late 1950s to 1997	Died, March 1997
Reggie Kray	United Kingdom	The Firm	Crime boss, extortion, fraud, blackmail, murder	1950s to 2000	Died of cancer October 1, 2000
Nicolo "Nick" Rizzuto	Canada	Adviser to the Montreal Mafia (1978 to present)	Adviser, cocaine trafficking, money laundering, murder	Late 1950s to present	Still active
Bernardo "The Tractor" Provenzo	Italy	Corleone Mafia family	Crime boss	Late 1950s to present	Currently a fugitive and still active
Chung "5% Man" Mon	China	14K	Crime boss	1960s to 1975	Shot to death, March 1975
Frank Peter "Dunie" Ryan	Canada	West End Gang	Crime boss, theft with violence, burglary, drug trafficking	1960s to 1984	Shot and killed November 13, 1984
Charlie Richardson	United Kingdom	Richardson Gang / "Torture Gang"	Crime boss, murder, extortion	1960s	Unknown if active or retired
Eddie Richardson	United Kingdom	Richardson Gang / "Torture Gang"	Crime boss, murder, extortion	1960s	Unknown if active or retired
Francesco "Frank" Cotroni	Canada	Montreal Mafia	Lieutenant, extortion, drug trafficking, manslaughter, conspiring to commit robbery	1960s to present	Arrested for violating parole, June 2002 Otherwise, still active
Jos Di Maulo	Canada	Montreal Mafia	Lieutenant, murder, bribery	1960s to present	Still active
Richard Matticks	Canada	West End Gang	Lieutenant, hijacking contraband, fencing, drug trafficking	1960s to present	Still active

Crime Figure	Country	Affiliation	Major Crimes	Time Period	Outcome
William "Billy" McAllister	Canada	West End Gang	Lieutenant, armed robbery, murder, drug trafficking	1960s to present	Currently in prison
Claude Dubois	Canada	Dubois Gang	Crime boss, loan-sharking, fencing, extortion, prostitution, murder	1960s to present	Unknown if active or retired
Yvon Belzil	Canada	Dubois Gang	Lieutenant, fencing, assault, drug trafficking, murder	1960s to present	Still active
Adrien Dubois	Canada	Dubois Gang	Lieutenant, prostitution, loan-sharking, drug trafficking, money laundering, murder	1960s to present	Still active
Jean-Guy Dubois	Canada	Dubois Gang	Lieutenant, loan-sharking, drug trafficking, murder	1960s to present	Still active
Jean-Paul Dubois	Canada	Dubois Gang	Lieutenant, loan-sharking, drug trafficking, extortion, murder	1960s to present	Still active
Paolo Violi	Canada	Montreal Mafia	Crime boss, extortion, counterfeiting, smuggled bootleg alcohol	Early 1970s to 1978	Shot and killed, January 22, 1978
George Jung	Colombia	Medellin drug cartel	Drug trafficking	Early 1970s to present	Currently in prison
Vincenzo "Jimmy" Di Maulo	Canada	Montreal Mafia	Lieutenant, murder, money laundering, drug trafficking	1970s to present	Currently in prison
Valentino "Val" Morielli	Canada	Montreal Mafia	Lieutenant, drug trafficking, money laundering, bribery	1970s to present	Still active
Khozh-Ahmed "Dzjigit" Noukhaev	Russia	Chechen Mafia	Godfather	1970s to present	Still active
Raymond Desfossés	Canada	West End Gang	Lieutenant, murder, drug trafficking	1970s to present	Still active

(Continued)

Table 1 (Continued)

Crime Figure	Country	Affiliation	Major Crimes	Time Period	Outcome
Gerald Matticks	Canada	Boss of the West End Gang (1997 to present)	Crime boss, hijacking contraband, fencing, drug trafficking	1970s to present	Currently in prison
Allan Strong	Canada	West End Gang	Lieutenant, drug trafficking, murder	1970s to present	Currently in prison
Normand "Billy" Labelle	Canada	President of the Hell's Angels South Chapter (1997 to present)	Crime boss, assault, murder	1970s to present	Still active
Yves "Le Boss" Buteau	Canada	President of the Hell's Angels Montreal Chapter (1977 to 1983)	Crime boss, murder, drug trafficking	1970s to 1983	Shot to death, September 8, 1983
Jose "The Mexican" Gonzalo Rodriguez Gacha	Colombia	Medellin drug cartel	Drug lord	1970s to 1989	Shot and killed December 15, 1989
Carlos Lehder	Colombia	Medellin drug cartel	Drug lord	1970s to early 1990s	Currently in prison
Pablo Escobar	Colombia	Medellin drug cartel	Drug lord, drug smuggling, theft, murder, bombing, bribery, kidnapping	1970s to 1993	Shot and killed, December 2, 1993
Juan David Ochoa	Colombia	Medellin drug cartel	Drug trafficking, bribery	Late 1970s to 1990s	Retired
Jorge Luis Ochoa	Colombia	Medellin drug cartel	Drug lord	Late 1970s to 1990s	Retired
Abdullah Catli	Turkey	Grey Wolves	Crime boss, murder, drug trafficking	Late 1970s to 1996	Died in car accident, 1996
Jose Santacruz-Londono	Colombia	Cali drug cartel	Drug lord, drug trafficking, money laundering, murder	1970s to 1996	Shot and killed by police, March 5, 1996
Griselda Blanco	Colombia	Medellin drug cartel	Crime boss, drug trafficking, murder	Late 1970s to present	Currently in prison
Fabio Ochoa	Colombia	Medellin drug cartel	Drug trafficking	Late 1970s to present	Still active
Gilberto "The Chess Player" Rodriguez-Orejuela	Colombia	Cali drug cartel	Drug lord, drug trafficking, money laundering, racketeering, bribery	1970s to present	Currently in prison but believed still active

Crime Figure	Country	Affiliation	Major Crimes	Time Period	Outcome
Miguel Rodriguez-Orejuela	Columbia	Cali drug cartel	Drug lord, drug trafficking, racketeering	1970s to present	Currently in prison but believed still active
Benedetto "Nitto" Santapaola	Italy	Catania Mafia	Crime boss, murder	1970s to present	Currently in prison
Vito Rizzuto	Canada	Montreal Mafia	Crime boss, enforcer, drug trafficking	1978 to present	Still active
Salvatore "Totò" "The Beast" Riina	Italy	Corleone Mafia family	Godfather, murder	1970s or 1980s to present	Currently in prison
Carlos Toro	Colombia	Medellin drug cartel	Drug trafficking, bribery, political payoffs, money laundering	Early 1980s to 1990s	Retired
Miguel Angel Felix Gallardo	Mexico/Baja California	Arellano-Felix Organization, a.k.a. the "Tijuana Cartel"	Drug lord, kidnapping, murder	1980s	Currently in prison
General Manuel Noriega	Panama	Medellin drug cartel	Drug trafficking, money laundering, racketeering	1980s to early 1990s	Currently in prison
Maurice "Mom" Boucher	Canada	President of the Hell's Angels Nomads Chapter (1995-present)	Enforcer, murder, drug trafficking	1980s to present	Currently in prison
Mery "La Senora" Valencia	Colombia	Cali Cartel/The Valencia Organization	Drug lord, drug trafficking, money laundering	Mid-1980s to present	Currently in prison
Alaattin Cakici	Turkey	Turkish Mafia	Crime boss, murder, extortion	1980s to present	Currently in prison
Claude Faber	Canada	West End Gang	Lieutenant, drug trafficking, murder	1980s to present	Still active
Daniel "The Arab" Serero	Canada	West End Gang	Lieutenant, drug trafficking, fraud	1980s to present	Still active
Yoshinori Watanabe	Japan	Yamaguchi-gumi	Godfather	1980s-?	Unknown if active or retired
Kazuo Nakanishi	Japan	Yamaguchi-gumi	Crime boss	1980s-?	Unknown if active or retired
Benjamin "El Min" Arellano-Felix	Mexico/Baja California	Arellano-Felix Organization, a.k.a. the "Tijuana Cartel"	Drug leader, drug trafficking, conspiracy, money laundering, kidnapping, murder	1980s to present	Currently a fugitive and still active

(Continued)

Table 1 (Continued)

Crime Figure	Country	Affiliation	Major Crimes	Time Period	Outcome
Ramon "El Comandante Mon" Eduardo Arellano-Felix	Mexico/Baja California	Arellano-Felix Organization, a.k.a. the "Tijuana Cartel"	Drug leader, money laundering, violence, bribery	1980s to present	Still active
Jesús "Chuy" Avilés	Mexico/Baja California	Arellano-Felix Organization, a.k.a. the "Tijuana Cartel"	Drug trafficking	1980s to present	Currently in prison
Ismael "El Mayel" Higuera Guerrero	Mexico/Baja California	Arellano-Felix Organization, a.k.a. the "Tijuana Cartel"	Lieutenant, murder, drug trafficking, kidnapping, money laundering	1980s to present	Currently in prison
Francisco "El Tigrillo" Javier Arellano-Felix	Mexico/Baja California	Arellano-Felix Organization, a.k.a. the "Tijuana Cartel"	Drug trafficking	1980s to present	Still active
Francisco Rafael Arellano-Felix	Mexico / Baja California	Arellano-Felix Organization, a.k.a. the "Tijuana Cartel"	Murder, drug trafficking	1980s to present	Currently in prison
Allan "The Weasel" Ross	Canada	West End Gang	Crime boss, drug trafficking, murder	1984 to 1997	Currently in prison
Georges "Bo-Boy" Beaulieu	Canada	President of the Hell's Angels Sherbrooke Chapter (1984 to present)	Crime boss, murder, drug trafficking	1980s to present	Still active
Vyatcheslav "Little Japanese" Ivankov	Russia	Red Mafia/ Solntsevskaya	Crime boss, extortion, drug trafficking, money laundering, embezzlement	1980s to present	Unknown, possibly in prison
Daniel "Johnny" Royer	Canada	President of the Hell's Angels Trois-Rivieres Chapter (1995 to present)	Crime boss, tax evasion, drug trafficking	1990s to present	Currently in prison
Amondo "Lord of the Skies" Carillo-Fuentes	Mexico	Juarez Cartel	Drug lord, drug trafficking, money laundering	Early 1990s to 1997	Died, July 1997
Francesco Schiavone	Italy	Camorra Family	Crime boss, murder, fraud, arms and drug trafficking, bombings, robbery	1990s to present	Currently in prison

Crime Figure	Country	Affiliation	Major Crimes	Time Period	Outcome
Juan Garcia-Abrego	Mexico	Gulf cartel	Drug lord, drug trafficking, money laundering	1990s to present	Currently in prison
Oscar Malherbe de Leon	Mexico	Gulf cartel	Drug lord, drug trafficking, murder	1990s to present	Still active
Maria Rosaria Buccarella	Italy	Sacra Corona Unita	Godmother	1990s to present	Currently in prison
Guiseppe Montanti	Italy	Stidda Mafia	Crime boss, murder	1990s to present	Still active
Maria Lucciardi	Italy	Naples Mafia	Crime boss, drug trafficking, murder	1990s to present	Currently in prison
Erminia "Celeste" Giuliano	Italy	Naples Mafia	Crime boss	1990s to present	Currently in prison
Concetta Scalisi	Italy	Sicilian Mafia	Godmother, murder	1990s to present	Still active but may currently be in prison
Ciro "The Prince" "The Engineer" Mazzarella	Italy	Camorra family	Crime boss, tobacco smuggling	1990s to present	Currently on trial
Giovani "The Pig" Brusca	Italy	Corleone Mafia family	Crime boss, murder, bombing, kidnapping	1990s to present	Currently in prison
Pietro "The Little Gentleman" Aglieri	Italy	Corleone Mafia family	Crime boss, murder	1990s to present	Currently in prison
Nikolay Suleimanov	Russia	Obshina	Crime boss, money laundering, robbery, theft, trafficking of humans, kidnapping	1990s to present	Still active
Vladimir Gavrilenkov	Russia	Tambov	Crime boss, extortion	Date unknown to present	Still active

—*Nileen Clark*

Glossary

Abduction

In criminal law, the taking away of a wife, child, or ward by persuasion, fraud, or open violence. To abduct an individual is to restrain that person with intent to prevent his or her liberation by holding him or her in an unlikely place, and/or through the threat of deadly force. Although statutes regarding abduction vary from state to state, most specify that the taking and carrying away, detention, and harboring of a woman under a certain age (16 to 18 years of age), with or without her consent, constitutes abduction. In the case of abduction, the consent of her husband is no defense, although the consent of parents is a defense to abduction under some statutes.

Actus Reus

Any overt act that accompanies the intent to commit a crime. Brandishing a knife at a bank teller while in the process of robbing the bank is an *actus reus* or overt act. Building a bomb while plotting to destroy another person's property is an overt act that promotes the criminal conspiracy.

Affray

The unpremeditated fighting of two or more persons in a public place that disturbs the public peace. In English common law, an affray was a misdemeanor offense punishable by a fine or imprisonment. An affray differs from a riot or a duel in that it is not premeditated or planned, and it differs from assault and battery, which happens in a private rather than public place. Although the idea that an affray must be public has been debated, most statutes adhere to the common law definition.

Aggravated Assault

The intentional, unlawful attack by one person on another for the explicit purpose of inflicting serious bodily injury.

Aggravating Circumstances

Special circumstances that increase either the severity or the punishment for the crime. To aggravate means to make worse or to exacerbate the situation. The given punishment may increase with the presence of aggravating circumstances, such as murder for hire; extreme cruelty or depravity; vulnerability of the victim due to age, mental capacity, or disability; or a prior criminal record. In criminal cases, aggravating circumstances have the opposite effect of mitigating or extenuating circumstances.

Aggression: Intergenerational Transmission

The *cycle of violence hypothesis* proposes that children who were raised in violent families become violent with their children as adults. Although some studies indicate that children raised in violent families have significantly higher rates of creating family violence as adults, other important factors also contribute to the cycle of violence hypothesis (e.g., alcohol and/or other substance abuse, environment, and socioeconomic status). Albert Bandura's social learning theory proposes that violence is learned through interactions with others, especially intimates. He believed that human personality is mainly learned within a social context, with the family being the primary social environment for children. The social learning theory emphasizes the importance of watching and modeling behaviors, attitudes, and emotional reactions of others.

Anarchism

A theory of social organization representing individualism in an extreme form, and advocating that equality and justice are to be sought through the abolition of government as a necessary precondition for a free and just society. The term *anarchism* comes from the Greek meaning "without a ruler." Anarchists believe that people are naturally good and self-ruling but are corrupted by the law and ruling body, described as the twin sources of all social evils. Zeno of Citium, founder of stoic philosophy, has been called the "father of anarchy."

Anthrpophagy

The consumption of a victim's flesh postmortem.

Armed Robbery

Taking or attempting to take anything of value from the possession, care, control, or custody of another person by force or intimidation using some form of weapon or threat of a weapon. Examples are robbing a storeowner at gunpoint or pretending to have a bomb in order to force the storeowner into compliance to gain possession of his property.

571

Arson: *See Pyromania*

Assassins: Professional Killers

Professional killers, commonly referred to assassins or "hit men," are popular subjects of fiction, but, although a few assassins do exist, professional assassination is becoming more and more rare. A professional killer is engaged in a learned profession or occupation requiring a high level of training and proficiency. Most crime executions appear to be assigned to members of organized crime families in addition to their ordinary tasks. Professional killers, as opposed to other categories of criminal behavior, tend to come from better economic backgrounds, begin their careers at a later age, approach crime in a businesslike manner, are highly identified with criminal activity, and are proud of their work. Some of the most famous professional killers were members of *Murder Inc.* James Clarke identified five types of assassins (a) political assassins, (b) egocentric assassins, (c) psychopathic assassins, (d) insane assassins, and (e) "atypical."

Assault

Using illegal force or violence to harm, injure, or frighten a person.

Assault and Battery

An assault carried out by inflicting some form of harm or violence to another person.

Attempted Murder

An overt act, beyond mere preparation, characterized by (1) the intent to commit the unlawful killing of a human being with premeditation and malice aforethought (murder), and (2) action taken toward the commission of murder but that ultimately fails to accomplish the criminal act. If a person fires a weapon toward another human being with the intent to kill but the bullet misses the intended target, the individual who fired the weapon is guilty of attempted murder. The question of how close a person must come to completing the act of murder to be found guilty of attempted murder has no direct answer, although the attempt must consist of more than mere preparation.

Autoerotic Asphyxia

The practice of inducing cerebral anoxia, usually by the means of self-applied ligatures or suffocating devices, including scarves, ropes, and plastic bags, to enhance sexual gratification while the individual masturbates to orgasm. Also called *scarfing* or *sexual hanging*, autoerotic asphyxia is practiced most commonly by adolescent and young male adults. Research suggests that several hundred deaths each year are the result of autoerotic asphyxiation.

Battery

The intentional or negligent application of physical force or unlawful touching of any part of the person of another, or of anything worn or carried by another or intimately associated with another, without his or her consent at that moment. Contact must be intended by the aggressor, and it must be reasonably considered offensive. Physical injury or violence need not be present for a battery to take place. Battery includes *mens rea,* meaning that the contact was intentional or resulted from wanton misconduct. Battery may also be considered a tort, or civil wrong, giving rise to a cause of action for civil damages.

Bestiality

Sexual relations between a person and an animal. The laws regarding bestiality or zoophilia vary from state to state, as does the penalty classification for violation of law(s) when an individual is found guilty. Moreover, some states have no known laws specifically relating to bestiality. There is no federal law that prohibits sex between humans and animals; however, a few federal laws list bestiality under laws relating to acts prohibited when involving children.

Bludgeon

A noncutting injury wherein enough force has been applied to a body to cause trauma. Instruments of bludgeoning cause abrasions, contusions, lacerations, and bone fractures/breaks. These instruments can be fists, clubs, tire irons, pipes, or anything else without a sharp edge or point that would lacerate. Bludgeoning is categorized as *blunt force truma* and is synonymous with the term "beaten to death."

Bride Burning

The murder of a woman by members of her own family because of late or an unpaid dowry or because of divorce, which may be perceived as bringing shame on the entire family. Sometimes called "dowry death," bride burning involves dowsing the woman in kerosene or gasoline and setting her on fire. These horrific acts, typically dismissed as "kitchen accidents" by husbands and in-laws of the victims, remain largely unpunished and have, according to some sources, reached epic proportions. India's National Crimes Bureau, Home Ministry, has reported more than 5,000 deaths from bride burnings each year and estimates another 20,000 women a year are disfigured but not killed over dowry disputes. Cultural interpretations fault the dowry system and what is perceived as family dishonor as the major motivators for the crime. When a culture views a woman's worth only in terms of her dowry, her family's honoring of dowry payments becomes critical to the woman's well-being. Without a dowry, she faces a hostile living environment within her matrimonial home, much social stigma, and more often than not, no possibility of returning to her family or father's house. Government shelters offer little protection, and some people claim that shelter conditions are so horrible, brides may prefer death at the hands of her husband and in-laws.

Brutalization Effect

The hypothesis claiming that increased exposure to acts of violence causes a desensitization in individuals, thereby increasing the probability of such acts escalating in frequency because their occurrence no longer "bothers" the exposed individuals. In other words, rather than having a cathartic effect on an individual, repeated exposure to certain situations is believed to have the opposite effect: An individual is more likely to commit violent acts because of previous and continued exposure to them. Studies on the deterrent effects of capital punishment have endeavored to illustrate the brutalization effect by showing a relationship between increased rates of homicide and the period of time surrounding an execution.

Cadaver

A dead body. Human cadavers may be used for dissection and/or transplant purposes. Andreas Vesalius was one of the first anatomists to conduct systematic examinations of human cadavers and published his findings in 1543. Yielding an abundance of medical information, cadavers have enabled practitioners to gather valuable information relating to human anatomy and physiology. Cadavers are also major sources of transplant tissues and organs.

Caffey's Syndrome

A familial autosomal dominant disease of unknown etiology, also known as *infantile cortical hyperostosis*. Characteristic signs and symptoms include fever, irritability, swelling of soft tissues, and cortical bone thickening typically seen in the jaw and forearm, but other osteological involvement is not uncommon. The onset of Caffey's syndrome usually appears in an infant by 5 months of age. An affected infant may experience marked periods of remission and exacerbation. To the untrained practitioner, Caffey's syndrome may be mistaken as child abuse. Radiographic and serum lab work tests offer confirmation in the presence of this syndrome.

Capital Offense

Any offense punishable by death. The United States and China lead in the frequency of imposition of capital punishment. Since the 1970s, almost all capital sentences imposed in the United States have been for homicide. Capital offense cases occur at substantial economic expenditures compared with other types of cases.

Capital Punishment

Punishment by death for a crime. Capital punishment is one of the most debated, researched, and studied public policy issues relating to criminal justice. Historically, capital punishment was widely applied in ancient times but began to decline within the 18th century. Writings of Montesquieu, Voltaire, Beccaria, Bentham, and other philosophical theorists ushered in the modern movement to abolish capital punishment in a number of countries. The United States is one of the few remaining Western nations to employ the death penalty.

The three main points of contention in the debate over capital punishment are the allocation of resources (cost), general deterrence, and retribution/revenge. The resources allocated to capital punishment cases are consistently shown to be at least twice the cost of housing a convicted murderer for life in a high-security correctional institution. Proponents of the death penalty state that these costs are part of the sacrifice paid to obtain the desired deterrent effects of capital punishment. Opponents claim that no matter the expenditure, scholarly research illustrates that there is no deterrent effect from the use of capital punishment. Retribution/revenge arguments assume the certainty of a guilty verdict. Opponents claim that the lack of certainty about a verdict cannot warrant such a severe and final sentencing of an individual. The taking of another's life carries other religious, moral, and ethical considerations. Retribution/revenge arguments lie in the realm of philosophy and religion and illustrate the volume of conflicting emotions, morals, ethics, and values surrounding the use of capital punishment.

Carjacking

The opportunistic theft of a motor vehicle by force. Although not a new crime, carjackings have recently been popularized by the media. With newer and more technologically advanced alarms and antitheft devices, more criminals are resorting to this type of car theft. Most carjackings occur after dark and in various locations, such as intersections, shopping centers, gas stations, and other places that provide easy access to a freeway and a quick getaway.

Conduct Disorder

According to diagnostic criteria from *DSM-IV (Diagnostic and Statistical Manual of Mental Disorders* (4th ed.), "The essential feature of conduct disorder is a repetitive and persistent pattern of behavior in which the basic rights of others or major age-appropriate social norms or rules are violated." The disorder is broken into four groups: aggressive conduct, nonaggressive conduct, deceitfulness or theft, and serious violations of rules. All forms of the disorder range from mild to severe. There are two periods of onset: childhood onset, which occurs before the age of 10, and adolescent onset, which is characterized by an absence of the disorder prior to the age of 10. In recent years, the prevalence and recognition of the disorder have increased dramatically, and it has become a frequent diagnosis for children.

Coroner

An elected official (as opposed to a medical examiner, who is appointed) concerned with the investigation of unnatural or suspicious deaths. Depending on the state, the position of coroner may require a medical degree from an accredited university. A coroner determines whether the cause of death was the result of a crime. The process begins by calling an inquest in which inquiries are made regarding the circumstances surrounding the death. These inquiries may come from testimony heard in a courtroom or from an autopsy conducted postmortem.

Corporal Punishment

Inflicting pain or physial confinement as a measure of punishment. Most commonly referenced in the field of education, where corporal punishment occurs when any educational personnel, teacher or otherwise, disciplines a student through the use of pain. In the United States, corporal punishment is sometimes deemed child abuse, but this is not the case in many other nations. In 1867, New Jersey became the first state to make corporal punishment illegal in its schools. As of 1997, only 27 states had banned corporal punishment on all levels in their schools. With each year, however, new laws are introduced that further restrict corporal punishment nationwide.

Crime Index

Eight offenses—murder or nonnegligent manslaughter, forcible rape, robbery, aggravated assault, burglary, auto theft, arson, and larceny/theft—thought to provide a fair representation of the crime picture as a whole; their total number make up a *crime index*.

Crime Rates

Two major sources are commonly used to measure crime rates in the United States: the Uniform Crime Reports (UCR) and the National Crime Victim Survey (NCVS). The UCR is calculated by the FBI and based on arrest statistics from local police departments. NCVS, considered to be the more accurate of the two methods, uses a telephone survey by the U.S. Census Bureau to measure whether anyone in the home has been the victim of seven specific crimes. Crime rates are composed of numbers that can be manipulated with statistics; they are not exact in measuring crime data.

Crime Scene Investigation:

See Coroner, Dying Declaration, Postmortem

Criminal Enterprise

An organized, continuing criminal activity operated as a business for profit. Traditional criminal enterprises such as La Costra Nostra are the archetypes of the organized crime entity; other organizations, however, especially large, multinational drug traffickers can also be considered criminal enterprises. Within the United States, there are two broad sets of federal statutes to such activity: (a) the continuing criminal enterprise (21 U.S.C. 848) statutes, which target long-term and complex drug trafficking organizations and (b) the antiracketeering statutes (18 U.S.C. 1951-1968), which include the Racketeer Influenced and Corrupt Organizations Act (RICO). Both are used against top managers of criminal enterprise.

Criminal Homicide

The act of purposely, knowingly, recklessly, or negligently causing the death of another human being. Criminal homicide is prohibited and punishable by law, but not all homicides are illegal. For example, a law enforcement officer who must use deadly force to kill an individual but who has acted in accordance with law has committed a justifiable homicide. If it is shown, however, that the officer used deadly force in a manner that is against the law, the officer may be guilty of criminal homicide.

Criminal Intent

The state of a defendant's mind that prosecutors must prove existed at the time of the crime. Also known as *mens rea* (guilty mind) and the *mental element*, proving criminal intent is necessary to secure a conviction. See *Mens Rea*.

Criminal Law

The body of law that defines criminal offenses; regulates how suspects are investigated, charged, and tried; and establishes punishments for convicted offenders. In the United States, there are a number of sources for criminal law, including common law, case law, and statutory law. Federal, state, and local governments have differing jurisdictions and definitions of criminal law violations. Some of these laws overlap, and some are the exclusive venue of a particular jurisdiction. The location in which a violation occurred may determine which jurisdiction and which set of laws (federal, state, or local) will be applied in criminal proceedings.

Criminalist

One who practices the science of crime detection, or criminalistics, which involves the subjection of physical evidence to ballistic analysis, bloodstain analysis, and other tests that are helpful in determining guilt or innocence. Criminalists also perform DNA analysis and forensic anthropology, which have proven to be highly effective. Criminalists increasingly use computers as investigative tools for data analysis, to create forensic animations of crime scenes, to enhance photographs, and for data distribution. Criminalists are normally trained in the physical or biological sciences and are increasingly in demand.

Criminologist

One who studies the phenomena of crime. Early criminologists include Beccaria and Bentham (Europe, 18th century), Edwin Sutherland, Robert Merton, Thorsten Sellin, Clifford Shaw, and Henry McKay.

Criminology

The scientific study of (a) the causes and prevention of crime, (b) law enforcement and the punishment and/or rehabilitation of offenders, and (c) victims and victimization. Criminology encompasses disciplines that include sociology, psychology, and anthropology. Although closely related to criminal justice studies, criminology focuses on investigating the social aspects of criminal phenomena, whereas the study of criminal justice predominantly addresses issues surrounding law enforcement. Four broad categories of criminological theories attempt to explain crime: (a) classical or choice theories emphasize individual decision making and free will, (b) biological or positivist theories stress biological causes for criminal behavior, (c) Marxist or conflict theories explain crime as a byproduct of class struggle, and (d) sociological explanations understand crime as being a result of an individual's relation with family, community, and society.

Early attempts at studying and explaining crime began in Europe with the classical theories of Beccaria and Bentham in the 18th century. Scientific exploration into crime started with the positivist contributions of Lombroso and Ferri in the mid-1800s; the social perspectives of Durkheim appeared later that century. In the United States, Parks and Burgess of the University of Chicago helped lay the groundwork during the early 20th century for criminology to evolve into a subdiscipline of sociology.

Cruel and Unusual Punishment

Punishment that is torturous, disproportionate to the crime in question, degrading, inhuman, or otherwise shocking to the moral sense of the community. The Eighth Amendment of the United States Constitution states that such punishment is a violation of an individual's civil rights. The status of the death penalty as either legal or cruel and unusual has been in flux over time, and the debate is ongoing. Currently, the death penalty is legal in the United States providing it is carried out in a fair and nondiscriminatory manner.

Culpability

The state of responsibility for an event or situation deserving of moral blame. In penal code usage, culpability is the state of mind of a person who commits a criminal act that makes the person liable for prosecution for that act.

Deadly Force

Violent action known to create a substantial risk of causing death or serious bodily harm. A person may use deadly force in self-defense only if retaliating against another's deadly force. Law enforcement officers generally may use deadly force in the course of their duties when their lives are in danger, another person's life is in danger, or a person presents a serious and grave threat to others. The use of force by police is governed by the general rule that the level of force used to control an individual must be proportional to the situation. Consequently, considering the circumstances, all other force options should have been considered before an officer resorts to using deadly force.

Death Penalty: *See Capital Offense, Capital Punishment, Death Warrant, Executive Clemancy, Lying in Wait*

Death Warrant

A document issued by a competent authority, usually a court body or official, which provides a warden or prison official with specific information about how and when (time and place) to carry out a death sentence.

Domestic Violence

Violence that results in injury to children, spouses, and/or others living in the home by someone presently or previously close to the victim. Domestic violence can be psychological, physical, or sexual in nature and includes a range of controlling and abusive behaviors, such as threatening to injure or kill, name-calling, hitting, torturing, and raping. Partner violence, spousal abuse, battering, and wife beating are all forms of domestic violence. See also *soul murder*.

Dying Declaration

A deathbed confession of personal knowledge of a crime. An exception to the hearsay rule, which declares that statements other than those made by witnesses testifying at a hearing are not admissible, a dying declaration is admissible in court as evidence.

Executive Clemency

The power entrusted to the president by means of the United States Constitution, and to state governors by most state constitutions, to pardon or commute a criminal sentence, including the death penalty, of a person who was previously convicted in a court within their jurisdiction. The act involves granting mercy or leniency to an offender. If pardoned, a person is often relieved of further punishment unless conditions are specified, as seen in the case of a conditional pardon.

Euthanasia or Mercy Killing

Ending a person's life, justified by the belief that such termination relieves the victim from the misery of a terminal illness. Euthanasia or mercy killing can be with or without the individual's consent. In addition, someone can assist another person to commit suicide by providing the means to do so without actively participating in the death itself by an action such as unplugging a life-sustaining machine or giving the individual a lethal dose of medicine. The Netherlands is the first and only country at this time to legalize euthanasia. In 1994, voters in the state of Oregon passed the Death with Dignity Act, by which terminally ill patients may obtain prescriptions for self-administered, lethal medications from their physicians, but this act specifically prohibits euthanasia, whereby a physician or other person participates in the act itself.

Execution

Carrying out a death sentence imposed on a person who has been convicted of a crime. The death penalty, or capital punishment, is most often imposed on a person who has been convicted of murder but may be imposed for other serious crimes such as armed robbery, kidnapping, rape, or treason. Capital punishment is state-imposed, and the laws vary from state to state, dictating specific circumstances under which a judge or jury may impose it.

An executioner carries out capital punishment on the state's behalf. This is done in a manner congruent with procedures and conditions specified in a death warrant. Throughout the United States, states that impose the death penalty may use more than one method of execution, including death by lethal injection, hanging, electrocution, a firing squad, or the gas chamber.

In the late 1990s, 38 states had laws that allowed the death penalty. The U.S. Supreme Court has heard cases challenging the constitutionality of the death penalty on the grounds that it constitutes "cruel and unusual punishment" in violation of the Eighth Amendment, made applicable to the states via the Fourteenth Amendment. In a 1972 U.S. Supreme Court decision, the court held that the death penalty itself was not cruel and unusual but that the indiscriminatory manner in which it was applied did qualify as such, in violation of the Eighth Amendment (see *Furman v. Georgia,* 408 U.S. 238, 1972). Reforms were made, and today the death penalty continues to be imposed for certain crimes and applied by execution according to clear standards as dictated by the law.

Expert Witness

A witness qualified by knowledge, skill, experience, training, or education to give testimony about a particular issue or piece of evidence presented in court. The expert witness, also called a *skilled witness,* may provide the court with scientific, technical, or other specialized information pertinent to the case at hand and may give *expert testimony* under oath or affirmation, by affidavit, or in person, or by oral or written deposition.

Family Slaying: *See Bride Burning*

Family Violence: *See Domestic Violence*

Felon

Someone who commits an offense of such a serious nature that he or she is punishable by significant fines and/or incarceration in a state or federal correctional facility for a period of one 1 year or longer. Similar terms include *serious criminal* and *dangerous offender.*

Felony

One of two designations used by the legal system to distinguish the seriousness of a crime and the appropriateness of punishment. *Felony offense* is the more serious classification, whereas a *misdemeanor* is considered a less serious offense. Conviction of a felony can result in lengthy and severe punishment compared with conviction for a misdemeanor. In the United States, each state and the federal government have the jurisdiction to determine which crimes constitute felonies. Common felony offenses include armed robbery, murder, rape, and aggravated assault. Using weapons or force during the commission of a crime often results in felony criminal charges. Punishments for felony offenses usually include incarceration, although this varies between states and within federal jurisdiction.

Felony Murder Rule

A doctrine that applies to cases in which an individual commits or attempts to commit a felony and a person is killed in the process. The felony murder rule holds that any death resulting from the commission or attempted commission of a felony is murder. Some states restrict this rule to inherently dangerous felonies such as rape, arson, robbery, or burglary; criteria may vary from state to state.

Feticide

The intentional killing of a fetus in vitro by means other than elective or therapeutic abortion. Currently, most states have case law or statutes that govern feticide. As an example, Oklahoma's *Hughes v. State,* 868 P.2nd 730 Okla. Cr. (1994) involved an intoxicated driver who collided with a car driven by a woman who was 9 months pregnant. The fetus died as a result of the collision but would have been viable given the number of weeks of gestation. The driver, Hughes, was convicted of feticide. One state, Minnesota, has a comprehensive feticide statute with graded severity that parallels the murder statute and provides for first-, second-, and third-degree convictions. *See also Filicide.*

Filicide

The murder of children by their parents. Several distinctions are made based on the age of the victim. *Neonaticide* is the murdering of a newborn within the first 24 hours of life. *Infanticide* is the murdering of a child between the period after the first 24 hours of life and up to 5 years of age. *Filicide* is the term used for the murder of one's own child over the age of 5 years. *Early filicide* is defined as the killing of one's child between the ages of 5 and 18 years; and *late filicide* is the term for killing one's adult child over the age of 18 years.

First-Degree Murder

Murder that is willful, deliberate, or premeditated, or murder committed during the course of another serious felony. Also called *murder of the first degree* or *murder one*. All murder that is perpetrated by poisoning or by lying in wait is also included in this classification.

Fratricide

Killing one's own brother or sister. *See also Filicide.*

Gerontophilia

Engaging in sexual activity with elderly people. The perpetrator often relies on fantasy as a key component in the commission of this behavior or sexual act.

Habitual Offender

A person convicted of two or more felonies, which, in turn, may qualify that person to be sentenced under the habitual offender statute. Habitual offender classification usually draws longer prison sentences. In many states, conviction of three or more serious felonies within a specific time frame can result in a mandatory life sentence. Each state has specific behaviors that qualify a person as a habitual offender. For example, California Penal Code defines an habitual offender as any person convicted of a felony in which the person inflicted great bodily injury or personally used force that was likely to produce great bodily injury or who has served two or more prior separate prison terms for the crime of murder, attempted murder, voluntary manslaughter, mayhem, rape by force, and many other acts of violence, intimidation, and duress toward others.

Homicide: *See Attempted Murder, Criminal Homicide, Criminal Intent, Culpability, Felon, Felony, Felony Murder Rule, Feticide, Filicide, First Degree Murder, Fratricide, Kinicide, Malum in se Crimes, Manslaughter, Mens Rea, Murder, Parricide, Siblicide, Sororicide, Thanatology*

Inchoate Offenses

Behaviors deemed criminal even though the conduct has not yet created the harm that the law seeks to prevent. These are considered preparatory to carrying out other crimes, for example, solicitation for sex or conspiracy to commit robbery.

Insanity

A defense for crimes that require intent. Insanity (mental illness, mental defect, or derangement) can mean that the offender is not responsible for his or her actions and can thus enter a "not guilty by reason of insanity" plea. In California, the test for insanity is whether the suspect is capable of knowing or understanding the nature and quality of his or her act and of distinguishing right from wrong at the time of the commission of the offense (California Penal Code Section 25).

Irresistible Impulse Rule

In homicide defense, establishes a provision for an impulse to commit an unlawful or criminal act that cannot be resisted or overcome because mental disease has destroyed the freedom of will, the power of self-control, and the choice of actions. The test of this rule is broader than the M'Naughten Rule: Persons may avoid criminal responsibility even though they are capable of distinguishing right from wrong and are fully aware of the nature and quality of the act, provided they establish that they were unable to refrain from committing the act.

Juvenile Delinquents

Youthful offenders who violate the law. Similar terms include *delinquent minors, delinquent children, juvenile delinquents, juvenile offenders, youthful offenders,* or *minors,* all of which usually describe a person who has not reached the age of 18 years of age, which is the point at which the criminal justice system treats the person as an adult. Minors found guilty of criminal behavior are punishable by special laws not pertaining to adults. In fact, *juvenile delinquent* was originally a legal term established so that young lawbreakers could avoid the disgrace of being classified in legal records as criminals.

Juvenile delinquency laws were designed to provide treatment rather than punishment. In the late 1800s, the juvenile court appeared in the court structure to effectively handle delinquent children who had committed a broad range of offenses, from murder to habitual truancy. Juvenile court proceedings, also referred to as juvenile hearings, are considered civil in nature, not criminal. The objectives of the juvenile court are to provide measures of guidance and rehabilitation for the child and protection to society. When going through the court proceedings, juvenile delinquents have certain constitutional guarantees. If, as a result of the hearing, the judge declares the child to be delinquent, he or she becomes a ward of the court, and the judge must then determine what action should be taken to benefit both the child and the public. The delinquent may be placed on probation, informal or formal, or may be required to serve a specified number of months or years in a juvenile facility.

Kidnapping: *See Abduction*

Kinicide

Murdering members of one's extended family: aunts, uncles, grandparents, cousins, and so on.

Lycanthropy

The folklore of a human being—man, woman, or child—either voluntarily or involuntarily changing or morphing into the form of a wolf, who then possesses all the characteristics, appetites, ferocity, strength, and swiftness of the animal. The word comes from the Greek legend of King Lycaon, who was changed into a wolf by Zeus after offending him. Jeffrey Dahmer has been exemplified as the contemporary "werewolf" because he killed, dismembered, and cannibalized his victims. One of the most famous werewolf-type killers was Jack the Ripper, who is believed to have butchered as many as 15 women in London's East End in the late 1800s.

Lying in Wait

Hiding, holding, or concealing oneself so as to watch for and wait for a victim for the purpose of committing a crime, making an unexpected attack, or murdering or inflicting bodily injury when the opportunity arises. In some jurisdictions in which there are several degrees of murder, it must be shown that lying in wait implied premeditated intent or malice aforethought necessary for a first-degree murder conviction.

Lynching

Killing a person, usually by hanging, via mob action without legal sanction or due process of law. In U.S. history, lynching has been most often associated with African Americans during the Civil Rights Movement of the 1960s being tortured, dismembered, hung, or burned at the stake.

Maim

To willfully inflict bodily injury upon a person, often resulting in the loss of a body part such as an organ or limb.

Malice

The intent to commit a wrongful act without acceptable or legitimate reason or having legal justification.

Malice Aforethought

The *mens rea* requirement for murder that includes the intention to kill while at the same time being fully aware that the right to kill does not exist.

Malum in Se Crimes

Illegal acts that are inherently wrong or intrinsically evil, such as arson, rape, or murder.

Manslaughter

The unintentional killing of another person.

Mass Murder: *See Multicide*

Mens Rea

The state of a defendant's mind that prosecutors must prove existed at the time of the crime. Also known as *guilty mind,*

the *mental element,* or *criminal intent.* For example, in the crime of receiving stolen goods, knowing that the goods were stolen; in the case of murder, premeditation; in the case of theft, a conscious intent to steal. Prosecutors may combine mens rea with *actus reus,* the guilty act, to establish that a particular individual committed a criminal act.

Misdemeanor

An offense less serious than a felony; any crime not a felony is considered a misdemeanor. Misdemeanor crimes are usually punishable by a fine and/or up to 1 year in a county jail. Individuals charged with misdemeanors may also receive probation, depending on their specific case. Examples of common misdemeanor offenses are resisting arrest, disorderly conduct, battery, prostitution, and petty theft. Most people charged with these types of crimes receive formal judgment in a mandatory court appearance. Repeated misdemeanors may likely be reclassified as felonies.

Modus Operandi

The *mode of operation* that a perpetrator uses to commit his or her crimes. By studying the modus operandi or *MO,* forensic analysts can learn important details about criminals as well as link their crimes. The MO includes type of victim, location of crime, and means of attack. In addition, crime scene investigators examine what was taken from the scene and what evidence was left behind. MO is learned behavior that is constantly changing. Offenders adapt their techniques based on past mistakes and successes to gain a more effective method of operation. The study of these methods allows investigators to make crucial decisions in solving crimes.

Multicide

Multiple homicides, usually committed by one individual. Perpetrators of multicide can be categorized into three groups according to the time frame in which the murders were committed. *Serial killers* murder multiple victims over a period of time and may kill numerous people within several days or years. *Mass murderers* kill their victims during the same time period, usually within hours of each other, although not all victims may have been murdered at the same location. *Spree killers* murder their victims within a short time period.

Murder

The taking of a human life intentionally or with malice aforethought. Most U.S. criminal codes distinguish between two degrees of murder, although as many as five degrees exist in some states. In general, murder in the first degree involves a deliberate, premeditated design to cause the death of the person. Murder in the second degree involves the intent to cause death, but without premeditation and deliberation. Most states classify a homicide that occurs during the commission of a felony as first-degree murder, even though the element of premeditated intent is absent. Some states classify the commission of an act that is imminently dangerous to others, such as throwing a bomb into a crowd and causing death, as first-degree murder.

Mysoped

A type of sadistic pedophile or child molester who hates children. After killing their victims, these extremely violent offenders often sexually mutilate and, in some cases, cannibalize them. They often travel significant distances to stalk their preferred victims and may plan an elaborate blitz attack or abduction ploy in efforts to sidetrack parents and authorities. Mysopeds sometimes lead rather transient existences but studies show them most likely to be of middle income and with white-collar jobs.

Necrophilia

Sexual relations with a victim postmortem.

Neglect

The omission, failure, or forbearance of proper attention to an action that can be done or is mandated to be done, or a disregard of duty resulting from carelessness, indifference, or unwillingness to perform one's duties. Neglect can be both physical and psychological. The notion of neglect includes *culpable neglect,* which occurs when a party is careless or folly, as well as *willful neglect,* which is the failure to provide (for one's family) out of idleness or recklessness, even when one has the ability to do so. *Child neglect* is a form of child abuse in which one fails to provide a child under one's care with the proper food, clothing, shelter, supervision, medical care, or emotional stability.

Paraphilia

A pattern of recurrent, intense, sexually arousing fantasies, sexual urges, or behaviors that involve arousal through deviant or bizarre images or activities.

Parricide

The murder of parents by their children. The two forms of parricide are *matricide,* or the killing of one's mother or stepmother, and *patricide,* or the killing of one's father or stepfather.

Pedophiles: *See Mysoped*

Postmortem

Actions done, occurring, or collected after death. Postmortem generally applies to an autopsy or examination of the body of a deceased person to determine the cause of death.

Predatory Crimes

Crimes committed by individuals who injure their victims by unjust and excessive means. As with predatory animals, perpetrators of predatory crimes kill or prey on the weakest, least desirable, or most easily victimized members of the population, including women, children, and mentally or physically disabled people. Predatory crimes include rape, child sexual abuse, pedophilia, and certain forms of stalking.

Proxy Murders

When people become murder victims simply because they represent or resemble someone hated by the offender. For example, serial killers often kill for real or imagined wrongdoings. Ed Kemper killed several college students at University of California at Santa Cruz because his mother, whom he both loathed and loved, worked there. According to Kemper, he had to kill his mother before he could stop killing students. Some killers murder because of the rejection or abandonment experienced at the hands of a parent. Donald Harvey killed more than 50 men, all hospital patients, because they reminded him of the men who had repeatedly raped and molested him as a child. Frequently, proxy murders represent tangible or intangible goals that cannot be obtained by the offender, such as love, beauty, power, or assertiveness. Proxy victims sometimes remind offenders of their own limitations. Others victims symbolize what proxy killers fear or loathe, including gays, the homeless, prostitutes, the elderly, and the infirm.

Pyromania

The intentional and uncontrollable impulse to set fires, repeatedly, by a person experiencing tension or affective arousal. Pyromania is a symptom of a severe emotional disorder and is much more common in men than in women. Offenders often express feelings of gratification or relief when watching fires in progress. Occasionally, pyromaniacs report sexual gratification in setting or watching fire scenes. For these *erotic pyromaniacs,* fire is seen as a destructive force symbolizing the intensity of a sexual urge. Pyromania develops in childhood or adolescence and may persist into adulthood and throughout one's life. In children, pyromania is explained as a conduct disorder in the *DSM-IV (Diagnostic and Statistical Manual of Mental Disorders,* 4th ed.). Fire setting in children may begin as a response to stressors in the family environment, possibly stemming from frustration, disappointment, or rejection. Pyromania in children should be differentiated from the occasional or accidental setting of a fire by a child, satisfying normal curiosity.

Recidivism

A relapse into criminal behavior or activity. A criminal recidivist is referred to as a *second offender* or a *habitual criminal.* Recidivists are often subject to extended terms of imprisonment under habitual offender statutes. A multitude of programs have been implemented to reduce the level of recidivism in the United States, including boot camps (highly regimented programs designed to instill discipline and accountability for first-time offenders in their later teens and early twenties), drug courts (as opposed to sending the criminals to prison or probation), and the ideology of punishment as a specific deterrent to criminal activity. None of these options, however, have substantially reduced the level of recidivism among criminals.

Siblicide

The murder of a sibling by a sibling.

Simple Assault

An illegal attack on another person that results in little or no physical harm or injury.

Soul Murder

The purposeful attempt to destroy the identity of another person through domestic violence or other abuse. Victims of soul murder feel trapped in a state of emotional bondage and have been brainwashed to suppress their feelings, leaving them unable to break away from their abusers. Sometimes, in order to cope with the abuse, the victims of soul murder *disassociate*, distancing themselves emotionally from the anger, depression, guilt, confusion, or other feelings associated with the abuse.

Sororicide

Murdering one's own sister.

Thanatology

The study of dying, death, and grief, including aging, AIDS, art, children's and parents' problems, euthanasia, funerals, history, hospices, life-threatening diseases, medical ethics, pain, poetry, pharmacology, stress, suicide, urban violence, widows and widowers, and gravestones.

Index